Bioethics

Principles, Issues, and Cases

Third Edition

Lewis Vaughn

New York   Oxford
OXFORD UNIVERSITY PRESS

Oxford University Press is a department of the University of Oxford.
It furthers the University's objective of excellence in research, scholarship,
and education by publishing worldwide. Oxford is a registered trade mark of
Oxford University Press in the UK and certain other countries.

Published in the United States of America by Oxford University Press
198 Madison Avenue, New York, NY 10016, United States of America.

For titles covered by Section 112 of the US Higher Education
Opportunity Act, please visit www.oup.com/us/he for the
latest information about pricing and alternate formats.

Library of Congress Cataloging-in-Publication Data

Names: Vaughn, Lewis, author.
Title: Bioethics : principles, issues, and cases / Lewis Vaughn.
Description: Third Edition. | New York : Oxford University Press, 2016. |
    Includes index. | Description based on print version record and CIP data
    provided by publisher; resource not viewed.
Identifiers: LCCN 2016019418 (print) | LCCN 2016018150 (ebook) | ISBN
    9780190250164 (Ebook) | ISBN 9780190250102 (pbk.)
Subjects: LCSH: Medical ethics. | Bioethics.
Classification: LCC R724 (print) | LCC R724 .V38 2016 (ebook) | DDC
    174.2—dc23
LC record available at https://lccn.loc.gov/2016019418

9 8 7 6 5 4 3

Printed by LSC Communications, United States of America

BRIEF CONTENTS

CONTENTS

Chapter 10

EUTHANASIA AND PHYSICIAN-ASSISTED SUICIDE 625

Part 4. Justice and Health Care

Chapter 11

DIVIDING UP HEALTH CARE RESOURCES 719

A revision of a new textbook is supposed to maintain the best of the old, judiciously enhance where possible, and prudently add where needed (without raising the price). This third edition of *Bioethics* does just that. Over the years, the text has been judged by numerous teachers to be exactly suitable to their teaching approach, and the aim of this new edition is to keep it that way.

Bioethics provides in-depth discussions of the philosophical, medical, scientific, social, and legal aspects of controversial bioethical issues and combines this material with a varied collection of thought-provoking readings. But on this foundation are laid elements that other texts sometimes forgo:

1. An extensive introduction to ethics, bioethics, moral principles, critical thinking, and moral reasoning
2. Full coverage of influential moral theories, including criteria and guidelines for evaluating them (the focus is on utilitarianism, Kantian ethics, natural law theory, Rawls' contract theory, virtue ethics, the ethics of care, and feminist ethics)
3. Detailed examinations of the classic cases that have helped shape debate in major issues
4. Collections of current, news-making cases for evaluation
5. Many pedagogical features to engage students and reinforce lessons in the main text
6. Writing that strives hard for clarity and concision to convey both the excitement and complexity of issues without sacrificing accuracy

TOPICS AND READINGS

Nine chapters cover many of the most controversial issues in bioethics, detailing the main arguments and filling out the discussions with background on the latest medical, legal, and social developments. The main issues include paternalism and patient autonomy, truth-telling, confidentiality, informed consent, research ethics, clinical trials, abortion, assisted reproduction, surrogacy, cloning, genetic testing, gene therapy, stem cells, euthanasia, physician-assisted suicide, and the just allocation of health care.

Every issues chapter contains seven to ten readings, with each selection prefaced by a brief summary. The articles—old standards as well as new ones—reflect the major arguments and latest thinking in each debate. They present a diversity of perspectives on each topic, with pro and con positions well represented. In most cases, the relevant court rulings are also included.

SPECIAL FEATURES

A two-chapter introduction to bioethics, moral reasoning, moral theories, and critical thinking. These chapters are designed not only to introduce the subject matter of bioethics but also to add coherence to subsequent chapter material and to provide the student with a framework for thinking critically about issues and cases. Chapter 1 is an introduction to basic ethical concepts, the field of bioethics, moral principles and judgments, moral reasoning and arguments, the challenges of relativism, and the relationship between ethics and both religion and the law. Chapter 2 explores moral theory, shows how theories relate to moral principles and judgments, examines influential theories (including virtue ethics, the ethics of care, and feminist ethics), and demonstrates how they can be applied to moral problems. It also explains how to evaluate moral theories using plausible criteria of adequacy.

Helpful chapter elements. Each issues chapter contains:

1. Analyses of the most important arguments offered by the various parties to the debate. They reinforce and illustrate the lessons on moral reasoning in Chapter 1.
2. A section called "Applying Major Theories" showing how the moral theories can be applied to the issues. It ties the discussions of moral theories in Chapter 2 to the moral problems and illustrates the theories' relevance.
3. A section labeled "Classic Case File" that examines in detail a famous bioethics case. The stories covered in these sections include those of Elizabeth Bouvia, Jerry Canterbury, Nancy Klein, Baby M, Nancy Cruzan, the Kingsburys, Christine deMeurers, and the UCLA Schizophrenia Study. These are in addition to many other controversial cases covered elsewhere in the book—for example, the Terri Schiavo controversy, the Tuskegee tragedy, the Willowbrook experiments, and the U.S. government's human radiation studies.
4. A bank of "Cases for Evaluation" at the end of each chapter. These are recent news stories followed by discussion questions. They give students the chance to test their moral reasoning on challenging new scenarios that range across a broad spectrum of current topics.

A diverse package of pedagogical aids. Each issues chapter contains a chapter summary, suggestions for further reading, and a variety of text boxes. The boxes are mainly of three types:

1. "In Depth"—additional information, illustrations, or analyses of matters touched on in the main text.
2. "Fact File"—statistics on the social, medical, and scientific aspects of the chapter's topic.
3. "Legal Brief"—summaries of important court rulings or updates on the status of legislation.

NEW TO THIS EDITION

Eleven new readings

- Shelly K. Schwartz, "Is It Ever OK to Lie to Patients?"
- Susan Wolf, "Moral Saints"
- "Patient Autonomy and Physician Responsibility," with commentaries by Patrick C. Beeman and Ryan C. VanWoerkom
- Rosalind Hursthouse, "Virtue Theory and Abortion"
- Margaret Olivia Little, "Abortion"
- Bonnie Steinbock, "Egg Donation and Commodification"
- Julian Savulescu, "Genetic Interventions and the Ethics of Enhancement of Human Beings"
- John Hardwig, "Dying at the Right Time: Reflections on (Un)Assisted Suicide"
- Jeff McMahan, "An Alternative to Brain Death"
- James F. Childress et al., "Public Health Ethics: Mapping the Terrain"
- D. Tarantola and S. Gruskin, "Human Rights Approach to Public Health Policy"

New Topics

- Physician autonomy
- Truth-telling and cultural diversity
- Decision-making capacity
- Public health and bioethics
- Surrogacy: The Sherri Shepherd case
- Fetal pain
- Casuistry

Clarifications and Further Discussions

Topics: Religion and ethics, autonomy and consent, moral principles, human rights and health, enhancement, cultural issues, direct-to-consumer genetic tests, and gene therapy

Updates

Updated further reading, opinion surveys, statistics, and legal developments

ANCILLARIES

The Oxford University Press Ancillary Resource Center (ARC) at www.oup-arc.com/vaughn-bioethics-3e houses an Instructor's Manual with Test Bank and PowerPoint Lecture Outlines for instructor use. Student resources are available on the companion website at www.oup.com/us/vaughn and include self-quizzes, flashcards, and helpful web links.

ACKNOWLEDGMENTS

This edition of the text is measurably better than the first thanks to the good people at Oxford University Press—especially my editor Robert Miller and assistant editor Alyssa Palazzo—and many reviewers:

Keith Abney, Polytechnic State University at San Luis Obispo

Kim Amer, DePaul University

Jami L. Anderson, University of Michigan

Carol Isaacson Barash, Boston University

Deb Bennett-Woods, Regis University

Don Berkich, Texas A&M University

Stephan Blatti, University of Memphis

William Bondeson, University of Missouri, Columbia

Lori Brown, Eastern Michigan University

David W. Concepción, Ball State University

Catherine Coverston, Brigham Young University

Russell DiSilvestro, Assistant Professor, California State University, Sacramento

John Doris, Washington University in St. Louis

Denise Dudzinski, University of Washington School of Medicine

Craig Duncan, Ithaca College

Anne Edwards, Austin Peay State University

John Elia, University of Georgia

Christy Flanagan-Feddon, Regis University

Jacqueline Fox, University of South Carolina School of Law

Leslie P. Francis, University of Utah

Devin Frank, University of Missouri–Columbia

Kathryn M. Ganske, Shenandoah University

Martin Gunderson, Macalester College

Helen Habermann, University of Arizona

Stephen Hanson, University of Louisville

Karey Harwood, North Carolina State University

Sheila R. Hollander, University of Memphis

Scott James, University of North Carolina, Wilmington

James Joiner, Northern Arizona University

William P. Kabasenche, Washington State University

Susan Levin, Smith College

Margaret Levvis, Central Connecticut State University

Burden S. Lundgren, Old Dominion University

Joan McGregor, Arizona State University

Tristram McPherson, Virginia Tech

Jonathan K. Miles, Bowling Green State University

James Lindemann Nelson, Michigan State University

Thomas Nenon, University of Memphis

Laura Newhart, Eastern Kentucky University

Steve Odmark, Century College

Assya Pascalev, Howard University

Viorel Pâslaru, University of Dayton

David J. Paul, Western Michigan University

Anthony Preus, Binghamton University

Susan M. Purviance, University of Toledo

Sara Schuman, Washtenaw Community College

David Schwan, Bowling Green State University

M. Josephine Snider, University of Florida

Anita Silvers, San Francisco State University

Gladys B. White, Georgetown University

Joseph Wellbank, Northeastern University

David Yount, Mesa Community College

Bioethics

Principles, Issues, and Cases

Principles and Theories

CHAPTER I

Moral Reasoning in Bioethics

Any serious and rewarding exploration of bioethics is bound to be a challenging journey. What makes the trip worthwhile? As you might expect, this entire text is a long answer to that question. You therefore may not fully appreciate the trek until you have already hiked far along the trail. The short answer comes in three parts.

First, bioethics—like ethics, its parent discipline—is about morality, and morality is about life. Morality is part of the unavoidable, bittersweet drama of being persons who think and feel and choose. **Morality** concerns beliefs regarding morally right and wrong actions and morally good and bad persons or character. Whether we like it or not, we seem confronted continually with the necessity to deliberate about right and wrong, to judge someone morally good or bad, to agree or disagree with the moral pronouncements of others, to accept or reject the moral outlook of our culture or community, and even to doubt or affirm the existence or nature of moral concepts themselves. Moral issues are thus inescapable—including (or especially) those that are the focus of bioethics. In the twenty-first century, few can remain entirely untouched by the pressing moral questions of fair distribution of health care resources, abortion and infanticide, euthanasia and assisted suicide, exploitative research on children and populations in developing countries, human cloning and genetic engineering, assisted reproduction and surrogate parenting, prevention and treatment of HIV/AIDS, the confidentiality and consent of patients, the refusal of medical treatment on religious grounds, experimentation on human embryos and fetuses, and the just allocation of scarce life-saving organs.

Second, it would be difficult to imagine moral issues more important—more closely gathered around the line between life and death, health and illness, pain and relief, hope and despair—than those addressed by bioethics. Whatever our view of these questions, there is little doubt that they matter immensely. Whatever answers we give will surely have weight, however they fall.

Third, as a systematic study of such questions, bioethics holds out the possibility of answers. The answers may or may not be to our liking; they may confirm or confute our preconceived notions; they may take us far or not far enough. But, as the following pages will show, the trail has more light than shadow—and thinking critically and carefully about the problems can help us see our way forward.

ETHICS AND BIOETHICS

Morality is about people's moral judgments, principles, rules, standards, and theories—all of which help direct conduct, mark out moral practices, and provide the yardsticks for measuring moral worth. We use *morality* to refer generally to these aspects of our lives (as in "Morality is essential") or more specifically to the beliefs or practices of particular groups or persons (as in "American morality" or "Kant's morality"). *Moral*, of course, pertains to morality as just defined, though it is also sometimes employed as a synonym for right or good, just as *immoral* is often meant to be equivalent to wrong or bad. *Ethics*, as used in this text, is not synonymous with *morality*. **Ethics** is the study of morality using the tools and methods of philosophy. Philosophy is a discipline that systematically examines life's big questions through critical reasoning, logical argument, and careful reflection. Thus ethics—also known as *moral philosophy*—is a reasoned way of delving into the meaning and import of moral concepts and issues and of evaluating the merits of moral judgments and standards. (As with *morality* and *moral*, we may use *ethics* to say such things as "Kant's ethics" or may use *ethical* or *unethical* to mean right or wrong, good or bad.) Ethics seeks to know whether an action is right or wrong, what moral standards should guide our conduct, whether moral principles can be justified, what moral virtues are worth cultivating and why, what ultimate ends people should pursue in life, whether there are good reasons for accepting a particular moral theory, and what the meaning is of such notions as *right*, *wrong*, *good*, and *bad*. Whenever we try to reason carefully about such things, we enter the realm of ethics: We *do* ethics.

Science offers another way to study morality, and we must carefully distinguish this approach from that of moral philosophy. **Descriptive ethics** is the study of morality using the methodology of science. Its purpose is to investigate the *empirical* facts of morality—the actual beliefs, behaviors, and practices that constitute people's moral experience. Those who carry out these inquiries (usually anthropologists, sociologists, historians, and psychologists) want to know, among other things, what moral beliefs a person or group has, what caused the subjects to have them, and how the beliefs influence behavior or social interaction. Very generally, the difference between ethics and descriptive ethics is this: In ethics we ask, as Socrates did, *How ought we to live?* In descriptive ethics we ask, *How do we in fact live?*

Ethics is a big subject, so we should not be surprised that it has three main branches, each dealing with more or less separate but related sets of ethical questions. **Normative ethics** is the search for, and justification of, moral standards, or norms. Most often the standards are moral principles, rules, virtues, and theories, and the lofty aim of this branch is to establish rationally some or all of these as proper guides for our actions and judgments. In normative ethics, we ask questions like these: What moral principles, if any, should inform our moral judgments? What role should virtues play in our lives? Is the principle of autonomy justified? Are there any exceptions to the moral principle of "do not kill"? How should we resolve conflicts between moral norms? Is contractarianism a good moral theory? Is utilitarianism a *better* theory?

A branch that deals with much deeper ethical issues is metaethics. **Metaethics** is the study of the meaning and justification of basic moral beliefs. In normative ethics we might ask whether an action is right or whether a person is good, but in metaethics we would more likely ask *what it means* for an action to be right or for a person to be good. For example, does *right* mean *has the best consequences*, or *produces the most happiness*, or *commanded by God*? It is the business of metaethics to explore these and other equally fundamental questions: What, if anything, is the difference between moral and nonmoral beliefs? Are there such things as moral facts? If so, what sort of things are they, and how can they be known? Can moral statements be true or false—or are they just expressions of emotions or attitudes without any truth value? Can moral norms be justified or proven?

The third main branch is **applied ethics**, the use of moral norms and concepts to resolve practical moral issues. Here, the usual challenge is to employ moral principles, theories, arguments, or analyses to try to answer moral questions that confront people every day. Many such questions relate to a particular professional field such as law, business, or journalism, so we have specialized subfields of applied ethics like legal ethics, business ethics, and journalistic ethics. Probably the largest and most energetic subfield is bioethics.

Bioethics is applied ethics focused on health care, medical science, and medical technology. (*Biomedical ethics* is often used as a synonym, and *medical ethics* is a related but narrower term used most often to refer to ethical problems in medical practice.) Ranging far and wide, bioethics seeks answers to a vast array of tough ethical questions: Is abortion ever morally permissible? Is a woman justified in having an abortion if prenatal genetic testing reveals that her fetus has a developmental defect? Should people be allowed to select embryos by the embryos' sex or other genetic characteristics? Should human embryos be used in medical research? Should human cloning be prohibited? Should physicians, nurses, physicians' assistants, and other health care professionals always be truthful with patients whatever the consequences? Should severely impaired newborns be given life-prolonging treatment or be allowed to die? Should people in persistent vegetative states be removed from life support? Should physicians help terminally ill patients commit suicide? Is it morally right to conduct medical research on patients without their consent if the research would save lives? Should human stem-cell research be banned? How should we decide who gets life-saving organ transplants when usable organs are scarce and many patients who do not get transplants will die? Should animals be used in biomedical research?

The ethical and technical scope of bioethics is wide. Bioethical questions and deliberations now fall to nonexpert and expert alike—to patients, families, and others as well as to philosophers, health care professionals, lawyers, judges, scientists, clergy, and public policy specialists. Though the heart of bioethics is moral philosophy, fully informed bioethics cannot be done without a good understanding of the relevant nonmoral facts and issues, especially the medical, scientific, technological, and legal ones.

ETHICS AND THE MORAL LIFE

Morality then is a normative, or evaluative, enterprise. It concerns moral norms or standards that help us decide the rightness of actions, judge the goodness of persons or character, and prescribe the form of moral conduct. There are, of course, other sorts of norms we apply in life—*nonmoral* norms. Aesthetic norms help us make value judgments

about art; norms of etiquette about polite social behavior; grammatical norms about correct use of language; prudential norms about what is in one's interests; and legal norms about lawful and unlawful acts. But moral norms differ from these nonmoral kinds. Some of the features they are thought to possess include the following.

Normative Dominance. In our moral practice, moral norms are presumed to dominate other kinds of norms, to take precedence over them. Philosophers call this characteristic of moral norms *overridingness* because moral considerations so often seem to override other factors. A maxim of prudence, for example, may suggest that you should steal if you can avoid getting caught, but a moral prohibition against stealing would overrule such a principle. An aesthetic (or pragmatic) norm implying that homeless people should be thrown in jail for blocking the view of a beautiful public mural would have to yield to moral principles demanding more humane treatment of the homeless. A law mandating brutal actions against a minority group would conflict with moral principles of justice and would therefore be deemed illegitimate. We usually think that immoral laws are defective, that they need to be changed, or that, in rare cases, they should be defied through acts of civil disobedience.

Universality. Moral norms (but not *exclusively* moral norms) have universality: Moral principles or judgments apply in all relevantly similar situations. If it is wrong for you to tell a lie in a particular circumstance, then it is wrong for everyone in relevantly similar circumstances to tell a lie. Logic demands this sort of consistency. It makes no sense to say that Maria's doing action A in circumstances C is morally wrong, but John's doing A in circumstances relevantly similar to C is morally right. Universality, however, is not unique to moral norms; it's a characteristic of all normative spheres.

Impartiality. Implicit in moral norms is the notion of impartiality—the idea that everyone should be considered equal, that everyone's interests should count the same. From the perspective of morality, no person is any better than any other. Everyone should be treated the same unless there is a morally relevant difference between persons. We probably would be completely baffled if someone seriously said something like "murder is wrong . . . except when committed by myself," when there was no morally relevant difference between that person and the rest of the world. If we took such a statement seriously at all, we would likely not only reject it but also would not even consider it a bona fide moral statement.

The requirement of moral impartiality prohibits discrimination against people merely because they are different—different in ways that are not morally relevant. Two people can be different in many ways: skin color, weight, gender, income, age, occupation, and so forth. But these are not differences relevant to the way they should be treated as persons. On the other hand, if there are morally relevant differences between people, then we may have good reasons to treat them differently, and this treatment would not be a violation of impartiality. This is how philosopher James Rachels explains the point:

> The requirement of impartiality, then, is at bottom nothing more than a proscription against arbitrariness in dealing with people. It is a rule that forbids us from treating one person differently from another *when there is no good reason to do so.* But if this explains what is wrong with racism, it also explains why, in some special kinds of cases, it is not racist to treat people differently. Suppose a film director was making a movie about the life of Martin Luther King, Jr. He would have a perfectly good reason for ruling out Tom Cruise for the starring role. Obviously, such casting would make no sense. Because there would be a good reason for it, the director's "discrimination" would not be arbitrary and so would not be open to criticism.[1]

Reasonableness. To participate in morality—to engage in the essential, unavoidable practices of the moral life—is to do moral reasoning. If our moral judgments are to have any weight at all, if they are to be anything more than mere personal taste or knee-jerk emotional response, they must be backed by the best of reasons. They must be the result of careful reflection in which we arrive at good reasons for accepting them, reasons that could be acknowledged as such by any other reasoning persons.

Both logic and our commonsense moral experience demand that the thorough sifting of reasons constitutes the main work of our moral deliberations—regardless of our particular moral outlook or theory. We would think it odd, perhaps even perverse, if someone asserted that physician-assisted suicide is always morally wrong—and then said she has no reasons at all for believing such a judgment but *just does.* Whatever our views on physician-assisted suicide, we would be justified in ignoring her judgment, for we would have no way to distinguish it from personal whim or wishful thinking. Likewise she herself (if she genuinely had no good reasons for her assertion) would be in the same boat, adrift with a firm opinion moored to nothing solid.

Our feelings, of course, are also part of our moral experience. When we ponder a moral issue we care about (abortion, for example), we may feel anger, sadness, disgust, fear, irritation, or sympathy. Such strong emotions are normal and often useful, helping us empathize with others, deepening our understanding of human suffering, and sharpening our insight into the consequences of our moral decisions. But our feelings can mislead us by reflecting not moral truth but our own psychological needs, our own personal or cultural biases, or our concern for personal advantage. Throughout history, some people's feelings led them to conclude that women should be burned for witchcraft, that whole races should be exterminated, that black men should be lynched, and that adherents of a different religion were evil. Critical reasoning can help restrain such terrible impulses. It can help us put our feelings in proper perspective and achieve a measure of impartiality. Most of

IN DEPTH
MORALITY AND THE LAW

Some people confuse morality with the law, or identify the one with the other, but the two are distinct though they may often coincide. Laws are norms enacted or enforced by the state to protect or promote the public good. They specify which actions are *legally* right or wrong. But these same actions can also be judged *morally* right or wrong, and these two kinds of judgments will not necessarily agree. Lying to a friend about a personal matter, deliberately trying to destroy yourself through reckless living, or failing to save a drowning child (when you easily could have) may be immoral—but not illegal. Racial bias, discrimination based on gender or sexual orientation, slavery, spousal rape, and unequal treatment of minority groups are immoral—but, depending on the society, they may not be illegal.

Much of the time, however, morality and the law overlap. Often what is immoral also turns out to be illegal. This is usually the case when immoral actions cause substantial harm to others, whether physical or economic. Thus murder and embezzlement are both immoral and illegal, backed by social disapproval and severe sanctions imposed by law. Controversy often arises when an action is not obviously or seriously harmful but is considered immoral by some who want the practice prohibited by law. The contentious notion at work is that something may be made illegal solely on the grounds that it is immoral, regardless of any physical or economic harm involved. This view of the law is known as *legal moralism*, and it sometimes underlies debates about the legalization of abortion, euthanasia, reproductive technology, contraception, and other practices.

Many issues in bioethics have both a moral and legal dimension, and it is important not to confuse the two. Sometimes the question at hand is a moral one (whether, for example, euthanasia is ever morally permissible); whether a practice should be legal or illegal then is beside the point. Sometimes the question is about legality. And sometimes the discussion concerns both. A person may consider physician-assisted suicide morally acceptable but argue that it should nevertheless be illegal because allowing the practice to become widespread would harm both patients and the medical profession.

---

all, it can guide us to moral judgments that are trustworthy because they are supported by the best of reasons.

The moral life, then, is about grappling with a distinctive class of norms marked by normative dominance, universality, impartiality, and reasonableness. As we saw earlier, these norms can include moral principles, rules, theories, and judgments. We should notice that we commonly apply these norms to two distinct spheres of our moral experience—to both moral *obligations* and moral *values*.

Moral obligations concern our duty, what we are obligated to do. That is, obligations are about conduct, how we ought or ought not to behave. In this sphere, we talk primarily about *actions*. We may look to moral principles or rules to guide our actions, or study a moral theory that purports to explain right actions, or make judgments about right or wrong actions.

Moral values, on the other hand, generally concern those things that we judge to be morally good, bad, praiseworthy, or blameworthy. Normally we use such words to describe persons (as in "He is a good person" or "She is to blame for hurting them"), their character ("He is virtuous"; "She is honest"), or their motives ("She did wrong but did not mean to"). Note that we also attribute *nonmoral* value to things. If we say that a book or bicycle or vacation is good, we mean good in a nonmoral sense. Such things in themselves cannot have *moral* value.

Strictly speaking, only actions are morally *right* or *wrong*, but persons are morally *good* or *bad* (or some degree of goodness or badness). With this distinction we can acknowledge a simple fact of the moral life: A good person can do something wrong, and a bad person can do something right. A Gandhi can tell a lie, and a Hitler can save a drowning man.

In addition, we may judge an action right or wrong depending on the motive behind it. If John knocks a stranger down in the street to prevent her from being hit by a car, we would deem his action right (and might judge him a good person). But if he knocks her down because he dislikes the color of her skin, we would believe his action wrong (and likely think him evil).

The general meaning of *right* and *wrong* seems clear to just about everyone. But we should be careful to differentiate degrees of meaning in these moral terms. *Right* can mean either "obligatory" or "permissible." An obligatory action is one that would be wrong *not* to perform. We are obligated or required to do it. A permissible action is one that is permitted. It is not wrong to perform it. *Wrong* means "prohibited." A prohibited action is one that would be wrong to perform. We are obligated or required *not* to do it. A *supererogatory* action is one that is "above and beyond" our duty. It is praiseworthy—a good thing to do—but not required. Giving all your possessions to the poor is generally considered a supererogatory act.

MORAL PRINCIPLES IN BIOETHICS

As noted earlier, the main work of bioethics is trying to solve bioethical problems using the potent resources and methods of moral philosophy, which include, at a minimum, critical reasoning, logical argument, and conceptual analysis. Many, perhaps most, moral philosophers would be quick to point out that beyond these tools of reason we also have the considerable help of moral principles. (The same could be said about moral theories, which we explore in the next chapter.) Certainly to be useful, moral principles must be interpreted, often filled out with specifics, and balanced with other moral concerns. But both in everyday life and in bioethics, moral principles are widely thought to be indispensable to moral decision-making.

We can see appeals to moral principles in countless cases. Confronted by a pain-racked, terminally ill patient who demands to have his life ended, his physician refuses to comply, relying on the principle that "it is wrong to intentionally take a life." Another physician makes a different choice in similar circumstances, insisting that the relevant principle is "ending the suffering of a hopelessly ill patient is morally permissible." An infant is born anencephalic (without a brain); it will never have a conscious life and will die in a few days. The parents decide to donate the infant's organs to other children so they might live, which involves taking the organs right away before they deteriorate. A critic of the parents' decision argues that "it is unethical to kill in order to save." But someone else appeals to the principle "save as many children as possible."[2] In such ways moral principles help guide our actions and inform our judgments about right and wrong, good and evil.

As discussed in Chapter 2, moral principles are often drawn from a moral theory, which is a moral standard on the most general level. The principles are derived from or supported by the theory. Many times we simply appeal directly to a plausible moral principle without thinking much about its theoretical underpinnings.

Philosophers make a distinction between absolute and prima facie principles (or duties). An *absolute* principle applies without exceptions. An absolute principle that we should not lie demands that we never lie regardless of the circumstances or the consequences. In contrast, a *prima facie* principle applies in all cases unless an exception is warranted. Exceptions are justified when the principle conflicts with other principles and is thereby overridden. W. D. Ross is given credit for drawing this distinction in his 1930 book *The Right and the Good*.[3] It is essential to his account of ethics, which has a core of several moral principles or duties, any of which might come into conflict.

Physicians have a prima facie duty to be truthful to their patients as well as a prima facie duty to promote their welfare. But if these duties come in conflict—if, for example, telling a patient the truth about his condition would somehow result in his death—a physician might decide that the duty of truthfulness should yield to the weightier duty to do good for the patient.

Moral principles are many and varied, but in bioethics the following have traditionally been extremely influential and particularly relevant to the kinds of moral issues that arise in health care, medical research, and biotechnology. In fact, many—perhaps most—of the thorniest issues in bioethics arise from conflicts among these basic principles. In one formulation or another, each one has been integral to major moral theories, providing evidence that the principles capture something essential in our moral experience. The principles are (1) autonomy, (2) nonmaleficence, (3) beneficence, (4) utility, and (5) justice.[4]

Autonomy

Autonomy refers to a person's rational capacity for self-governance or self-determination—the ability to direct one's own life and choose for oneself. The principle of autonomy insists on full respect for autonomy. One way to express the principle is: *Autonomous persons should be allowed to exercise their capacity for self-determination.* According to one major ethical tradition, autonomous persons have intrinsic worth precisely because they have the power to make rational decisions and moral choices. They therefore must be treated with respect, which means not violating their autonomy by ignoring or thwarting their ability to choose their own paths and make their own judgments.

The principle of respect for autonomy places severe restraints on what can be done to an autonomous person. There are exceptions, but in general we are not permitted to violate people's autonomy just because we disagree with their decisions, or because society might benefit, or because the violation is for their own good. We cannot legitimately impair someone's autonomy without strong justification for doing so. Conducting medical experiments on patients without

their consent, treating competent patients against their will, physically restraining or confining patients for no medical reason—such practices constitute obvious violations of personal autonomy.

Not all restrictions on autonomy, however, are of the physical kind. Autonomy involves the capacity to make personal choices, but choices cannot be considered entirely autonomous unless they are fully informed. When we make decisions in ignorance—without relevant information or blinded by misinformation—our autonomy is diminished just as surely as if someone physically manipulated us. If this is correct, then we have a plausible explanation of why lying is generally prohibited: Lying is wrong because it undermines personal autonomy. Enshrined in bioethics and in the law, then, is the precept of *informed consent*, which demands that patients be allowed to freely consent to or decline treatments and that they receive the information they need to make informed judgments about them.

In many ways, autonomy is a delicate thing, easily compromised and readily thwarted. Often a person's autonomy is severely undermined not by other people but by nature, nurture, or his or her own actions. Some drug addicts and alcoholics, people with serious psychiatric illness, and those with severe mental impairment are thought to have drastically diminished autonomy (or to be essentially nonautonomous). Bioethical questions then arise about what is permissible to do to them and who will represent their interests or make decisions regarding their care. Infants and children are also not fully autonomous, and the same sorts of questions are forced on parents, guardians, and health care workers.

Like all the other major principles discussed here, respect for autonomy is thought to be prima facie. It can sometimes be overridden by considerations that seem more important or compelling—considerations that philosophers and other thinkers have formulated as principles of autonomy restriction. The principles are articulated in various ways, are applied widely to all sorts of social and moral issues, and are themselves the subject of debate. Chief among these is the harm principle: a person's autonomy may be curtailed to prevent harm to others. To prevent people from being victimized by thieves and murderers, we have a justice system that prosecutes and imprisons the perpetrators. To discourage hospitals and health care workers from hurting patients through carelessness or fraud, laws and regulations limit what they can do to people in their care. To stop someone from spreading a deadly, contagious disease, health officials may quarantine him against his will.

Another principle of autonomy restriction is paternalism. **Paternalism** is the overriding of a person's actions or decision-making for her own good. Some cases of paternalism (sometimes called *weak paternalism*) seem permissible to many people—when, for example, seriously depressed or psychotic patients are temporarily restrained to prevent them from injuring or killing themselves. Other cases are more controversial. Researchers hoping to develop a life-saving treatment give an experimental drug to someone without his knowledge or consent. Or a physician tries to spare the feelings of a competent, terminally ill patient by telling her that she will eventually get better, even though she insists on being told the truth. The paternalism in such scenarios (known as *strong paternalism*) is usually thought to be morally objectionable. Many controversies in bioethics center on the morality of strong paternalism.

Nonmaleficence

The principle of *nonmaleficence* asks us not to intentionally or unintentionally inflict harm on others. In bioethics, nonmaleficence is the most widely recognized moral principle. Its aphoristic expression has been embraced by practitioners of medicine for centuries: "Above all, do no harm." A more precise formulation of the principle is: *We should not cause unnecessary injury or harm to those in our care.* In whatever form, nonmaleficence is the bedrock precept of countless codes of professional conduct, institutional regulations, and governmental rules and laws designed to protect the welfare of patients.

A health care professional violates this principle if he or she deliberately performs an action that harms or injures a patient. If a physician intentionally administers a drug that she knows will induce a heart attack in a patient, she obviously violates the principle—she clearly does something that is morally (and legally) wrong. But she also violates it if she injures a patient through recklessness, negligence, or inexcusable ignorance. She may not intend to hurt anyone, but she is guilty of the violation just the same.

Implicit in the principle of nonmaleficence is the notion that health professionals must exercise "due care." The possibility of causing some pain, suffering, or injury is inherent in the care and treatment of patients, so we cannot realistically expect health professionals never to harm anyone. But we do expect them to use due care—to act reasonably and responsibly to minimize the harm or the chances of causing harm. If a physician must cause patients some harm to effect a cure, we expect her to try to produce the least amount of harm possible to achieve the results. And even if her treatments cause no actual pain or injury in a particular instance, we expect her not to use treatments that have a higher chance of causing harm than necessary. By the lights of the nonmaleficence principle, subjecting patients to unnecessary risks is wrong even if no damage is done.

Beneficence

The principle of *beneficence* has seemed to many to constitute the very soul of morality—or very close to it. In its most general form, it says that *we should do good to others.* (*Benevolence* is different, referring more to an attitude of goodwill toward others than to a principle of right action.) *Beneficence* enjoins us to advance the welfare of others and prevent or remove harm to them.

Beneficence demands that we do more than just avoid inflicting pain and suffering. It says that *we should actively promote the well-being of others and prevent or remove harm to them.* In bioethics, there is little doubt that physicians, nurses, researchers, and other professionals have such a duty. After all, helping others, promoting their good, is a large part of what these professionals are obliged to do.

But not everyone thinks that *we all* have a duty of active beneficence. Some argue that though there is a general (applicable to all) duty not to harm others, there is no general duty to help others. They say we are not obligated to aid the poor, feed the hungry, or tend to the sick. Such acts are not required, but are supererogatory, beyond the call of duty. Others contend that though we do not have a general duty of active beneficence, we are at least sometimes obligated to look to the welfare of people we care about most—such as our parents, children, spouses, and friends. In any case, it is clear that in certain professions—particularly medicine, law, and nursing—benefiting others is often not just supererogatory but obligatory and basic.

Utility

The principle of *utility* says that *we should produce the most favorable balance of good over bad (or benefit over harm) for all concerned.* The principle acknowledges that in the real world, we cannot always *just* benefit others or *just* avoid harming them. Often we cannot do good for people without also bringing them some harm, or we cannot help everyone who needs to be helped, or we cannot help some without also hurting or neglecting others. In such situations, the principle says, we should do what yields the best overall outcome—the maximum good and minimum evil, everyone considered. The utility principle, then, is a supplement to, not a substitute for, the principles of autonomy, beneficence, and justice.

In ethics this maxim comes into play in several ways. Most famously it is the defining precept of the moral theory known as utilitarianism (discussed in Chapter 2). But it is also a stand-alone moral principle applied everywhere in bioethics to help resolve the kind of dilemmas just mentioned. A physician, for example, must decide whether a treatment is right for a patient, and that decision often hinges on whether the possible benefits of the treatment outweigh its risks by an acceptable margin. Suppose a man's clogged artery can be successfully treated with open-heart surgery, a procedure that carries a considerable risk of injury and death. But imagine that the artery can also be successfully opened with a regimen of cholesterol-lowering drugs and a low-fat diet, both of which have a much lower chance of serious complications. The principle of utility seems to suggest that the latter course is best and that the former is morally impermissible.

The principle also plays a major role in the creation and evaluation of the health policies of institutions and society. In these large arenas, most people aspire to fulfill the requirements of beneficence and maleficence, but they recognize that perfect beneficence or maleficence is impossible: Trade-offs and compromises must be made, scarce resources must be allotted, help and harm must be balanced, life and death must be weighed—tasks almost always informed by the principle of utility.

Suppose, for example, we want to mandate the immunization of all schoolchildren to prevent the spread of deadly communicable diseases. The cost in time and money will be great, but such a program could save many lives. There is a down side, however: A small number of children—perhaps as many as 2 for every 400,000 immunizations—will die because of a rare allergic reaction to the vaccine. It is impossible to predict who will have such a reaction (and impossible to prevent it), but it is almost certain to occur in a few cases. If our goal is social beneficence, what should we do? Children are likely to die whether we institute the program or not. Guided by the principle of utility (as well as other principles), we may decide to proceed with the program since many more lives would likely be saved by it than lost because of its implementation.

Again, suppose governmental health agencies have enough knowledge and resources to develop fully a cure for only one disease—either a rare heart disorder or a common form of skin cancer. Trying to split resources between these two is sure to prevent development of any cure at all. The heart disorder kills 200 adults each year; the cancer occurs in thousands of people, causing them great pain and distress, but is rarely fatal. How best to maximize the good? On which disease should the government spend its time and treasure? Answering this question (and others like it) requires trying to apply the utility principle—a job often involving complex calculations of costs and benefits and frequently generating controversy.

Justice

In its broadest sense, *justice* refers to people getting what is fair or what is their due. In practice, most of us seem to have a rough idea of what justice entails in many situations, even if we cannot articulate exactly what it is. We know, for example, that it is unjust for a bus driver to make a woman sit in the back of the bus because of her religious beliefs, or for a judicial system to arbitrarily treat one group of citizens more harshly than others, or for a doctor to care for some patients but refuse to treat others just because he dislikes them.

Questions of justice arise in different spheres of human endeavor. *Retributive justice*, for example, concerns the fair meting out of punishment for wrongdoing. On this matter, some argue that justice is served only when people are punished for past wrongs, when they get their just deserts. Others insist that justice demands that people be punished not because they deserve punishment, but because the punishment will deter further unacceptable behavior. *Distributive justice* concerns the fair distribution of society's advantages and disadvantages—for example, jobs, income, welfare aid, health care, rights, taxes, and public service. Distributive justice is a major issue in bioethics, where many of the most intensely debated questions are about who gets health care, what or how much they should get, and who should pay for it.

Distributive justice is a vast topic, and many theories have been proposed to identify and justify the properties, or traits, of just distributions. A basic precept of most of these theories is what may plausibly be regarded as the core of the principle of justice: *Equals should be treated equally.* (Recall that this is one of the defining elements of ethics itself, impartiality.) The idea is that people should be treated the same unless there is a morally relevant reason for treating them differently. We would think it unjust for a physician or nurse to treat his white diabetic patients more carefully than he does his black diabetic patients—and to do so without a sound medical reason. We would think it unfair to award the only available kidney to the transplant candidate who belongs to the "right" political party or has the best personal relationship with hospital administrators.

The principle of justice has been at the heart of debates about just distribution of benefits and burdens (including health care) for society as a whole. The disagreements have generally not been about the legitimacy of the principle, but about how it should be interpreted. Different theories of justice try to explain *in what respects* equals should be treated equally.

Libertarian theories emphasize personal freedoms and the right to pursue one's own social and economic well-being in a free market without interference from others. Ideally the role of government is limited to night-watchman functions—the protection of society and free economic systems from coercion and fraud. All other social or economic benefits are the responsibility of individuals. Government should not be in the business of helping the socially or economically disadvantaged, for that would require violating people's liberty by taking resources from the haves to give to the have-nots. So universal health care is out of the question. For the libertarian, then, people have equal intrinsic worth, but this does not entitle them to an equal distribution of economic advantages. Individuals are entitled only to what they can acquire through their own hard work and ingenuity.

Egalitarian theories maintain that a just distribution is an *equal* distribution. Ideally, social benefits—whether jobs, food, health care, or something else—should be allotted so that everyone has an equal share. Treating people equally means making sure everyone has equal access to certain minimal goods and services. To achieve this level of equality, individual liberties will have to be restricted, measures that libertarians would never countenance. In a pure egalitarian society, universal health care would be guaranteed.

Between strict libertarian and egalitarian views of justice lie some theories that try to achieve a plausible fusion of both perspectives. With a nod toward libertarianism, these theories may exhibit a healthy respect for individual liberty and limit governmental interference in economic enterprises. But leaning toward egalitarianism, they may also mandate that the basic needs of the least well-off citizens be met.

In bioethics, the principle of justice and the theories used to explain it are constantly being marshaled to support or reject health care policies of all kinds. They are frequently used—along with other moral principles—to evaluate, design, and challenge a wide range of health care programs and strategies. They are, in other words, far from being merely academic.

ETHICAL RELATIVISM

The commonsense view of morality and moral standards is this: There are moral norms or principles that are valid or true for everyone. This claim is known as **moral objectivism,** the idea that at least some moral standards are objective. Moral objectivism, however, is distinct from **moral absolutism,** the belief that objective moral principles allow no exceptions or must be applied the same way in all cases and cultures. A moral objectivist can be absolutist about moral principles, or she can avoid absolutism by accepting that moral principles are prima facie. In any case, most people probably assume some form of moral objectivism and would not take seriously any claim implying that valid moral norms can be whatever we want them to be.

But moral objectivism is directly challenged by a doctrine that some find extremely appealing and that, if true, would undermine ethics itself: **ethical relativism.** According to this view, moral standards are not objective but are relative to what individuals or cultures believe. There simply are no *objective* moral truths, only *relative* ones. An action is morally right if endorsed by a person or culture and morally wrong if condemned by a person or culture. So euthanasia is right for person A if he approves of it but wrong for person B if she disapproves of it, and the same would go for cultures with similarly diverging views on the subject. In this way, moral norms are not discovered but made; the individual or culture makes right and wrong. Ethical relativism pertaining to individuals is known as **subjective relativism,** more precisely stated as the view that right actions are those sanctioned by a person. Ethical relativism regarding cultures is called **cultural relativism,** the view that right actions are those sanctioned by one's culture.

In some ways, subjective relativism is a comforting position. It relieves individuals of the burden of serious critical reasoning about morality. After all, determining right and wrong is a matter of inventorying one's beliefs, and any sincerely held beliefs will do. Morality is essentially a matter of personal taste, which is an extremely easy thing to establish. Determining what one's moral views are may indeed involve deliberation and analysis—but neither of these is a necessary requirement for the job. Subjective relativism also helps people short-circuit the unpleasantness of moral debate. The subjective relativist's familiar refrain—"That may be *your* truth, but it's not *my* truth"—has a way of stopping conversations and putting an end to reasoned arguments.

The doctrine, however, is difficult to maintain consistently. On issues that the relativist cares little about (the moral rightness of gambling, say), she may be content to point out that moral norms are relative to each individual and that "to each his own." But on more momentous topics (such as genocide in Africa or the Middle

IN DEPTH
**ANTHROPOLOGY
AND MORAL DIVERSITY**

Many moral philosophers have been quick to point out that differences in moral judgments from culture to culture do not in themselves prove a difference in moral standards. Some anthropologists have made the same argument. Solomon Asch, for example, says,

> We consider it wrong to take food away from a hungry child, but not if he is overeating. We consider it right to fulfill a promise, but not if it

is a promise to commit a crime. . . . It has been customary to hold that diverse evaluations of the same act are automatic evidence for the presence of different principles of evaluation. The preceding examples point to an error in this interpretation. Indeed, an examination of the relational factors points to the operation of constant principles in situations that differ in concrete details. . . . Anthropological evidence does not furnish proof of relativism. We do not know of societies in which bravery is despised and cowardice held up to honor, in which generosity is considered a vice and ingratitude a virtue. It seems rather that the relations between valuation and meaning are invariant.[5]

East), she may slip back into objectivism and declare that genocide is morally wrong—not just wrong for her but wrong *period*.

Such inconsistencies hint that there may be something amiss with subjective relativism, and indeed there is: It seems to conflict violently with commonsense realities of the moral life. For one thing, the doctrine implies that each person is morally infallible. An action is morally right for someone if he approves of it—if he sincerely believes it to be right. His approval makes the action right, and—if his approval is genuine—he cannot be mistaken. His believing it to be right makes it right, and that's the end of it. If he endorses infanticide as a method of population control, then infanticide is morally permissible. His sincere approval settles the issue, and he cannot be in error. But our commonsense moral experience suggests that this relativist account is absurd. Our judgments about moral matters—actions, principles, and people—are often wide of the mark. We are morally fallible, and we are rightly suspicious of anyone who claims to be otherwise.

There is a more disturbing way to frame this point. Suppose former Iraqi leader Saddam Hussein approved of slaughtering thousands of Iraqis during his reign. Suppose Hitler approved of killing millions of Jews during World War II. Suppose American serial killer and cannibal Jeffrey Dahmer approved of his murdering 17 men and boys. Then by the lights of subjective relativism, all these mass killings were morally right because their perpetrators deemed them so. But we would find this conclusion almost impossible to swallow. We would think these actions morally wrong whether the killers approved of their own actions or not.

Subjective relativism also implies that another commonplace of the moral life is an illusion: moral disagreement. Consider: Hernando tells Sophia that allowing seriously impaired infants to die is morally right. Sophia replies that allowing seriously impaired infants to die is morally wrong. We may think that Hernando and Sophia are having a straightforward disagreement over an important moral issue. But according to subjective relativism, no such disagreement is happening or could ever happen. In stating his approval of the actions in question, Hernando is essentially expressing his personal taste on the issue, and Sophia is expressing her personal taste. He is saying he likes something; she says she does not like it—and they could both be correct. Subjective relativism implies that they are not uttering conflicting claims at all—they are discussing different subjects, their own personal feelings or preferences. But this strange dance is not at all what we think we are doing when we have a moral disagreement. Because subjective relativism conflicts with what we take to be a basic fact of the moral life, we have good reason to doubt it.

Cultural relativism seems to many to be a much more plausible doctrine. In fact, many people think it obviously true, supported as it is by a convincing argument and the common conviction that it is admirably consistent with social tolerance and understanding in a pluralistic world. The argument in its favor goes like this:

1. If people's moral judgments differ from culture to culture, moral norms are relative to culture (there are no objective moral standards).
2. People's moral judgments do differ from culture to culture.
3. Therefore, moral norms are relative to culture (there are no objective moral standards).

Is this a good argument? That is, does it provide us with good reason to accept the conclusion (statement 3)? For an argument to be good, its conclusion must follow logically from the premises, and the premises must be true. In this case, the conclusion does indeed follow logically from the premises (statements 1 and 2). The truth of the premises is another matter.

Let us look first at premise 2. All sorts of empirical evidence—including a trove of anthropological and sociological data—show that the premise is in fact true. Clearly, the moral beliefs of people from diverse cultures often do differ drastically on the same moral issue. Some societies condone infanticide; others condemn it. Some approve of the killing of wives and daughters to protect a family's honor; others think this tradition evil. Some bury their dead; others cremate them. Some judge the killing of one's elders to be a kindly act; others say it is cold-hearted murder. Some think polygamy morally permissible; others believe it deplorable. Some consider

it a solemn duty to surgically remove the clitorises of young girls; others say this is immoral and cruel. Some commend the killing of people who practice a different religion; others believe such intolerance is morally reprehensible. We are forced to conclude that diversity of moral judgments among cultures is a reality.

But what of premise 1—is it also true? It says that because cultures have different moral beliefs, they must also have different moral standards, which means morality is relative to cultures. If diverse moral standards arise from each culture, then morality cannot be objective, applying to all people everywhere. There is no objective morality, just *moralities*.

Premise 1, however, is false. First, from the fact that cultures have divergent moral beliefs on an issue, it does not logically follow that there is no objective moral truth to be sought, that there is no opinion that is objectively correct. People may disagree about the existence of biological life on Mars, but the disagreement does not demonstrate that there is no fact of the matter or that no statement on the subject could be objectively true. Disagreements on a moral question may simply indicate that there is an objective fact of the matter but that someone (or everyone) is wrong about it.

Second, a conflict between moral beliefs does not necessarily indicate a fundamental conflict between basic moral norms. Moral disagreements between cultures can arise not just because their basic moral principles clash, but because they have differing nonmoral beliefs that put those principles in a very different light. From the annals of anthropology, for example, we have the classic story of a culture that sanctions the killing of parents when they become elderly but not yet enfeebled. Our society would condemn such a practice, no doubt appealing to moral precepts urging respect for parents and for human life. But consider: This strange (to us) culture believes that people enter heaven when they die and spend eternity in the same physical condition they were in when they passed away. Those who kill their parents are doing so because they do not want their elders to spend eternity in a state of senility but rather in good health. This culture's way is not our way; we are unlikely to share these people's nonmoral beliefs. But it is probable that they embrace the same moral principles of respect for parents and life that we do. According to some anthropologists, diverse cultures often share basic moral standards while seeming to have little or nothing in common.

The argument we are considering, then, fails to support cultural relativism. Moreover, many considerations count strongly against the view. Specifically, the logical implications of the doctrine give us substantial reasons to doubt it.

Like subjective relativism, cultural relativism implies moral infallibility, a very hard implication to take seriously. As the doctrine would have it, if a culture genuinely approves of an action, then there can be no question about the action's moral rightness: It is right, and that's that. Cultures make moral rightness, so they cannot be mistaken about it. But is it at all plausible that cultures cannot be wrong about morality? Throughout history, cultures have approved of ethnic cleansing, slavery, racism, holocausts, massacres, mass rape, torture of innocents, burning of heretics, and much more. Is it reasonable to conclude that the cultures that approved of such deeds could not have been mistaken?

Related to the infallibility problem is this difficulty: Cultural relativism implies that we cannot legitimately criticize other cultures. If a culture approves of its actions, then those actions are morally right—and it does not matter one bit whether another culture disapproves of them. Remember, there is no objective moral code to appeal to. Each society is its own maker of the moral law. It makes no sense for society X to accuse society Y of immorality, for what society Y approves of *is* moral. Some may be willing to accept this consequence of cultural relativism, but look at what it would mean. What if the people of Germany approved of the extermination of millions of Jews, Gypsies, and others during World War II? Then the extermination was morally right. Suppose the people of Libya approved of the

terrorist bombing of Pan Am flight 103 over Lockerbie, Scotland, killing 270 people (a tragedy for which the Libyan government eventually took responsibility). Then the bombing was morally right, and those who placed the bomb on board did no wrong. But all this seems very much at odds with our moral experience. We think it makes perfect sense sometimes to condemn other cultures for morally wrong actions.

Now consider the notion of moral progress. We sometimes compare what people did in the past with what they do now, noting that current practices are morally better than they used to be. We no longer countenance such horrors as massacres of native peoples, slavery, and lynchings, and we think that these changes are signs of moral progress. But cultural relativism implies that there cannot be any such thing as moral progress. To claim legitimately that there has been moral progress, there must be an objective, transcultural standard for comparing cultures of the past and present. But according to cultural relativism, there are no objective moral standards, just norms relative to each culture. On the other hand, if there is moral progress as we think there is, then there must be objective moral standards.

Cultural relativism also has a difficult time explaining the moral status of social reformers. We tend to believe they are at least sometimes right and society is wrong. When we contemplate social reform, we think of such moral exemplars as Martin Luther King, Jr., Mahatma Gandhi, and Susan B. Anthony, all of whom agitated for justice and moral progress. But one of the consequences of cultural relativism is that social reformers could *never* be morally right. By definition, what society judges to be morally right is morally right, and since social reformers disagree with society, they could not be right—ever. But surely on occasion it's the reformers who are right and society is wrong.

There is also the serious difficulty of using cultural relativism to make moral decisions. Cultural relativism says that moral rightness is whatever a culture or society approves of, but determining which culture or society one truly belongs to seems almost impossible. The problem is that we each belong to many social groups, and there is no fact of the matter regarding which one is our "true" society. Suppose you are an African-American Catholic Republican living in an artists colony in Alabama and enjoying the advantages of membership in an extremely large extended family. What is your true society? If you cannot identify your proper society, you cannot tell which cultural norms apply to you.

Some people may be willing to overlook these problems of cultural relativism because they believe it promotes cultural tolerance, an attitude that seems both morally praiseworthy and increasingly necessary in a pluralistic world. After all, human history has been darkened repeatedly by the intolerance of one society toward another, engendering vast measures of bloodshed, pain, oppression, injustice, and ignorance. The thought is that because all cultures are morally equal, there is no objective reason for criticizing any of them. Tolerance is then the best policy.

Cultural relativism, however, does not necessarily lead to tolerance and certainly does not logically entail it. In fact, cultural relativism can easily justify either tolerance or intolerance. It says that if a society sanctions tolerance, then tolerance is morally right for that society. But if a society approves of intolerance, then *intolerance* is morally right for that society—and the society cannot be legitimately criticized for endorsing such an attitude. According to cultural relativism, intolerance can be morally permissible just as tolerance can. In addition, though moral relativists may want to advocate universal tolerance, they cannot consistently do so. To say that all cultures should be tolerant is to endorse an objective moral norm, but cultural relativists insist that there are no objective moral norms. To endorse universal tolerance is to abandon cultural relativism.

ETHICS AND RELIGION

How is ethics related to religion? One obvious connection is that historically religion has always had moral content—mostly in the form of moral precepts, codes, or commandments to guide the conduct of adherents. In Western civilization, this content has been so influential in moral (and legal) matters that many now take for granted that religion is the fundamental basis of morality. Secular or nontheistic systems of ethics (for example, the ethics of Stoicism, Confucianism, Buddhism, utilitarianism, and contractarianism) have also shaped how we think about morality. But for millions of people, religion is the fountainhead of the moral law.

Many religious people, however, do not embrace a moral theory related to a religious tradition. They are comfortable being guided by one of the nontheistic systems. Others prefer the very influential moral perspective known as *natural law theory* (discussed in Chapter 2)—a view that comes in both secular and religious versions but has been nurtured and adopted by the Roman Catholic Church. Still others accept the pervasive idea that morality itself comes from God.

An important query in ethics is whether this latter view of morality is correct: whether morality depends fundamentally on religion, whether—to state the question in its traditional form—the moral law is constituted by the will of God. The view that morality does have this kind of dependence is known as the **divine command theory.** It says that right actions are those commanded by God, and wrong actions are those forbidden by God. God is the author of the moral law, making right and wrong by his will.

But many people—both religious and non-religious—have found this doctrine troubling. Philosophers have generally rejected it, including some famous theistic thinkers such as Thomas Aquinas (1225–1274), Gottfried Leibniz (1646–1710), and Immanuel Kant (1724–1804).

The problem is that the theory presents us with a disconcerting dilemma first spelled out in Plato's *Euthyphro*. In this dialogue, Socrates asks a penetrating question that is often expressed like this: Are actions morally right because God commands them, or does God command them because they are morally right? In the first option, God creates the moral law (the divine command theory); in the second, the moral law is independent of God's will so that even God is subject to it. Critics of the divine command theory have argued that the first option implies the moral law is entirely arbitrary. The second option denies the theory.

The arbitrariness is thought to arise like this: If actions are morally right just because God commands them to be so, then it is possible that any actions whatsoever could be morally right. The murder and rape of innocents, the oppression of the weak, the abuse of the poor—these and many other awful deeds would be morally permissible if God so willed. There would be no independent standard to judge that these acts are wrong, no moral reasons apart from God's will to suggest that such deeds are evil. God would be free to establish arbitrarily any actions whatsoever as morally right.

Defenders of the divine command theory have replied to the arbitrariness charge by saying that God would never command something evil because God is all-good. But critics point out that if the theory is true, the assertion that God is all-good would be meaningless, and the traditional religious idea of the goodness of God would become an empty notion. If God makes the moral law, then the moral term *good* would mean "commanded by God." But then "God is good" would mean something like "God does what God commands" or even "God is what God is," which tells us nothing about the goodness of God. Likewise, "God's commands are good" would translate as "God's commands are God's commands." This attempt to escape the charge of arbitrariness seems to have intolerable implications.

Theists and nontheists alike find this horn of Socrates' dilemma—the idea of an arbitrary, divinely ordained morality—incredible. They therefore reject the divine command theory and embrace the other horn, the view that right and wrong are independent of God's will. Moral standards are external to God, binding on both God and mortals. If there are divine commands, they will conform to these independent moral norms. The religious may then claim that God is good—good because he abides perfectly by the moral law and guides the conduct of believers accordingly.

If moral standards are not grounded in the divine will, if they are logically independent of religion, then morality is a legitimate concern for the religious and nonreligious alike, and everyone has equal access to moral reflection and the moral life. The best evidence for the latter is ethics itself. The fact is that people *do ethics*. They use critical reasoning and experience to determine moral norms, explore ethical issues, test moral theories, and live a good life. The results of these explorations are moral outlooks and standards founded on good reasons and arguments and assented to by reflective people everywhere.

In bioethics, the informed opinions of religious people are as relevant as those of secularists. But all parties must be willing to submit their views to the tests and criteria of critical reasoning and evidence.

But even if ethics does not have this independent status, there are still good reasons for religious believers to know how to use the critical tools that ethics offers. First, like many secular moral rules, religious moral codes are often vague and difficult to apply to conflicts and issues, especially in complex fields such as bioethics. Getting around this problem requires interpreting the codes, and this task involves consideration of broader norms or theories, a typical job for ethics. Second, like everyone else, believers must deal with moral conflicts of all sorts—including clashes between the moral beliefs of religious adherents, religious leaders, and religious traditions. What is often needed is a neutral standard and critical analyses to arrive at a resolution—tools that ethics can easily provide. Third, public debate on ethical issues in a diverse society requires ground rules—chief among them being that positions must be explained and reasons must be given in their support. Unexplained assertions without supporting reasons or arguments are likely to be ignored. In this arena, ethics is essential.

MORAL ARGUMENTS

Critical reasoning is something we employ every time we carefully and systematically assess the truth of a statement or the merits of a logical argument. We ask: Are there good reasons for believing this statement? Is this a good argument—does it prove its case? These sorts of questions are asked in every academic field and in every serious human endeavor. Wherever there is a need to acquire knowledge, to separate truth from falsity, and to come to a reliable understanding of how the world works, these questions are asked and answers are sought. Ethics is no exception. Critical reasoning in ethics—called *moral reasoning*—employs the same general principles of logic and evidence that guide the search for truth in every other field. So we need not wonder whether we use critical reasoning in ethics but whether we use it well.

Argument Fundamentals

Most critical reasoning is concerned in one way or another with the construction or evaluation of arguments. As you may have guessed, here *argument* denotes not an altercation but a patterned set of assertions: at least one statement providing support for another statement. We have an argument when one or more statements give us reasons for believing another one. The supporting statements are *premises*, and the supported statement is the *conclusion*. In critical reasoning, the term *statement* also has a technical meaning. A statement (or claim) is an assertion that something is or is not the case and is therefore the kind of utterance that is either true or false.

You need to understand at the outset that *argument* in this sense is not synonymous with *persuasion*. An argument provides us with reasons for accepting a claim; it is an attempted "proof" for an assertion. But persuasion does not necessarily involve giving any reasons at all for accepting a claim. To persuade is to influence people's opinions, which can be accomplished by offering a good argument but also by misleading with logical fallacies, exploiting emotions and prejudices, dazzling with rhetorical gimmicks, hiding or distorting the facts, threatening or coercing people—the list is long. Good arguments prove something whether or not they persuade. Persuasive ploys can change minds but do not necessarily prove anything.

So we formulate an argument to try to show that a particular claim (the conclusion) should be believed, and we analyze an argument to see if it really does show what it purports to show. If the argument is good, we are entitled to believe its conclusion. If it is bad, we are not entitled to believe it.

Consider these two simple arguments:

ARGUMENT 1
Law enforcement in the city is a complete failure. Incidents of serious crime have doubled.

ARGUMENT 2
It's wrong to take the life of an innocent person. Abortion takes the life of an innocent person. So abortion is wrong.

In Argument 1, the conclusion is "Law enforcement in the city is a complete failure," which is supported by the premise "Incidents of serious crime have doubled." The conclusion of Argument 2 is "abortion is wrong," and it is backed by two premises: "It's wrong to take the life of an innocent person" and "Abortion takes the life of an innocent person." Despite the differences between these two passages (differences in content, the number of premises, and the order of their parts), they are both arguments because they exemplify basic argument structure: a conclusion supported by at least one premise.

Though the components of an argument seem clear enough, people often fail to distinguish between arguments and strong statements that contain no arguments at all. Suppose we change Argument 1 into this:

Law enforcement in the city is a complete failure. Nothing seems to work anymore. This situation is intolerable.

Now there is no argument, just an expression of annoyance or anger. There are no statements giving us reasons to believe a conclusion. What we have are some unsupported assertions that may merely *appear* to make a case. If we ignore the distinction between genuine arguments and nonargumentative material, critical reasoning is undone.

Assuming we can recognize an argument when we see it, how can we tell if it is a good one? Fortunately, the general criteria for judging the merits of an argument are simple and clear. A good argument—one that gives us good reasons for believing a claim—must have (1) solid logic and (2) true premises. Requirement (1) means that the conclusion should follow logically from the premises, that there must be a proper logical connection between supporting statements and the statement supported. Requirement (2) says that what the premises assert must in fact be the case. An argument that fails in either respect is a bad argument.

There are two basic kinds of arguments—deductive and inductive—and our two requirements hold for both of them, even though the logical connections in each type are distinct. **Deductive arguments** are intended to give *logically conclusive* support to their conclusions so that if the premises are true, the conclusion absolutely must be true. Argument 2 is a deductive argument and is therefore supposed to be constructed so that if the two premises are true, its conclusion cannot possibly be false. Here it is with its structure laid bare:

ARGUMENT 2
1. It's wrong to take the life of an innocent person.
2. Abortion takes the life of an innocent person.
3. Therefore, abortion is wrong.

Do you see that, given the form or structure of this argument, if the premises are true, then the conclusion *has to be true*? It would be very strange—illogical, in fact—to agree that the two premises are true but that the conclusion is false.

Now look at this one:

ARGUMENT 3
1. All dogs are mammals.
2. Rex is a dog.
3. Therefore, Rex is a mammal.

Again, there is no way for the premises to be true while the conclusion is false. The deductive form of the argument guarantees this.

So a deductive argument is intended to have this sort of airtight structure. If it actually does have this structure, it is said to be *valid*. Argument 2 is deductive because it is intended to provide logically conclusive support to its conclusion. It is valid because, as a matter of fact, it does offer this kind of support. A deductive argument that fails to provide conclusive support to its conclusion is said to be *invalid*. In such an argument, it is possible for the premises to be true and the conclusion false. Argument 3 is intended to have a deductive form, and because it actually does have this form, the argument is also valid.

An elementary fact about deductive arguments is that their validity (or lack thereof) is a separate issue from the truth of the premises. Validity is a structural matter, depending entirely on how an argument is put together. Truth concerns the nature of the claims made in the premises and conclusion. A deductive argument is supposed to be built so that *if* the premises are true, the conclusion must be true—but in a particular case, the premises might *not* be true. A valid argument can have true or false premises and a true or false conclusion. (By definition, of course, it cannot have true premises and a false conclusion.) In any case, being invalid or having false premises dooms a deductive argument.

Inductive arguments are supposed to give *probable* support to their conclusions. Unlike deductive arguments, they are not designed to support their conclusions decisively. They can establish only that, if their premises are true, their conclusions are probably true (more likely to be true than not). Argument 1 is an inductive argument meant to demonstrate the probable truth that "law enforcement in the city is a complete failure." Like all inductive arguments (and unlike deductive ones), it can have true premises and a false conclusion. So the sole premise—"incidents of serious crime have doubled"—can be true while the conclusion is false.

If inductive arguments succeed in lending probable support to their conclusions, they are said to be *strong*. Strong arguments are such that if their premises are true, their conclusions are probably true. If they fail to provide this probable support, they are termed *weak*. Argument 1 is a weak argument because its premise, even if true, does not show that more likely than not law enforcement in the city is a complete failure. After all, even if incidents of serious crime have doubled, law enforcement may be successful in other ways, or incidents of serious crime may be up for reasons unrelated to the effectiveness of law enforcement.

But consider this inductive argument:

ARGUMENT 4
1. Eighty-five percent of the students at this university are Republicans.
2. Sonia is a student at this university.
3. Therefore, Sonia is probably a Republican.

This argument is strong. If its premises are true, its conclusion is likely to be true. If eighty-five percent of the university's students are Republicans, and Sonia is a university student, she is more likely than not to be a Republican, too.

When a valid (deductive) argument has true premises, it is a good argument. A good deductive argument is said to be *sound*. Argument 2 is valid, but we cannot say whether it is sound until we determine the truth of the premises. Argument 3 is valid, and if its premises are true, it is sound. When a strong (inductive) argument has true premises, it is also a good argument. A good inductive argument is said to be *cogent*. Argument 1 is weak, so there is no way it can be cogent. Argument 4 is strong, and if its premises are true, it is cogent.

Checking the validity or strength of an argument is often a plain, commonsense undertaking.

Using our natural reasoning ability, we can examine how the premises are linked to the conclusion and can see quickly whether the conclusion follows from the premises. We are most likely to make an easy job of it when the arguments are simple. Many times, however, we need some help, and help is available in the form of methods and guidelines for evaluating arguments.

Having a familiarity with common argument patterns, or forms, is especially useful when assessing the validity of deductive arguments. We are likely to encounter these forms again and again in bioethics as well as in everyday life. Here is a prime example:

ARGUMENT 5
1. If the surgeon operates, then the patient will be cured.
2. The surgeon is operating.
3. Therefore, the patient will be cured.

This argument form contains a *conditional* premise—that is, a premise consisting of a conditional, or if-then, statement (actually a compound statement composed of two constituent statements). Premise 1 is a conditional statement. A conditional statement has two parts: the part beginning with *if* (called the *antecedent*) and the part beginning with *then* (known as the *consequent*). So the antecedent of premise 1 is "If the surgeon operates," and the consequent is "then the patient will be cured."

The best way to appreciate the structure of such an argument (or any deductive argument, for that matter) is to translate it into traditional argument symbols in which each statement is symbolized by a letter. Here is the symbolization for Argument 5:

1. If p, then q.
2. p.
3. Therefore, q.

We can see that p represents "the surgeon operates," and q represents "the patient will be cured." But notice that we can use this same symbolized argument form to represent countless other arguments—arguments with different statements but having the same basic structure.

It just so happens that the underlying argument form for Argument 5 is extremely common—common enough to have a name, *modus ponens* (or affirming the antecedent). The truly useful fact about *modus ponens* is that any argument having this form is valid. We can plug any statements we want into the formula and the result will be a valid argument, a circumstance in which if the premises are true, the conclusion must be true.

Another common argument form is *modus tollens* (or denying the consequent). For example:

ARGUMENT 6
1. If the dose is low, then the healing is slow.
2. The healing is not slow.
3. Therefore, the dose is not low.

1. If *p*, then *q*.
2. Not *q*.
3. Therefore, not *p*.

Modus tollens is also a valid form, and any argument using this form must also be valid.

There are also common argument forms that are *invalid*. Here are two of them:

AFFIRMING THE CONSEQUENT
ARGUMENT 7
1. If the patient is getting better, then drugs are unnecessary.
2. Drugs are unnecessary.
3. Therefore, the patient is getting better.

1. If *p*, then *q*.
2. *q*.
3. Therefore, *p*.

DENYING THE ANTECEDENT
ARGUMENT 8
1. If the rate of infection is increasing, then the patients will die.
2. The rate of infection is not increasing.
3. Therefore, the patients will not die.

1. If *p*, then *q*.
2. Not *p*.
3. Therefore, not *q*.

The advantage of being able to recognize these and other common argument forms is that you can use that skill to determine readily the validity of many deductive arguments. You know, for example, that any argument having the same form as *modus ponens* or *modus tollens* must be valid, and any argument in one of the common invalid forms must be invalid.

Patterns of Moral Arguments

All that you have learned about argument fundamentals thus far applies directly to that subspecies of argument we are most interested in: moral argument. A **moral argument** is an argument whose conclusion is a moral statement, an assertion that an action is right or wrong or that a person or motive is good or bad. We utter a moral statement when we say such things as "Physician-assisted suicide is wrong," or "Maria should not have had an abortion," or "Dr. Jones is a good person." We are constantly making moral statements and including them in our moral arguments, which we frequently devise and hold up for inspection and evaluation.

Recall Argument 2, a simple (and common) moral argument:

1. It's wrong to take the life of an innocent person.
2. Abortion takes the life of an innocent person.
3. Therefore, abortion is wrong.

Here, we can see all the standard features of a typical moral argument: (1) At least one premise (premise 1) is a moral statement asserting a general moral norm such as a moral principle; (2) at least one premise (premise 2) is a nonmoral statement describing an action or circumstance; and (3) the conclusion is a moral statement expressing a moral judgment about a specific action or circumstance.

REVIEW: Valid and Invalid Argument Forms

Valid Forms

Affirming the Antecedent (*Modus Ponens*)

If *p, then q.*
p.
Therefore, *q.*

Example:
If Spot barks, a burglar is in the house.
Spot is barking.
Therefore, a burglar is in the house.

Denying the Consequent (*Modus Tollens*)

If *p, then q.*
Not q.
Therefore, *not p.*

Example:
If it's raining, the park is closed.
The park is not closed.
Therefore, it's not raining.

Invalid Forms

Affirming the Consequent

If *p, then q.*
q.
Therefore, *p.*

Example:
If the cat is on the mat, she is asleep.
She is asleep.
Therefore, she is on the mat.

Denying the Antecedent

If *p, then q.*
Not p.
Therefore, *not q.*

Example:
If the cat is on the mat, she is asleep.
She is not on the mat.
Therefore, she is not asleep.

Notice how natural this pattern seems. If we want to argue that a particular action (or kind of action) is wrong, for example, we must provide a reason for this moral judgment. The natural (and logical) move is to reach for a general moral principle that supports the judgment. Why is performing surgery on Mrs. Johnson without her consent wrong? Because, we might say, treating people without their consent is a violation of their autonomy (a moral principle), and performing surgery on Mrs. Johnson without her consent would be an instance of such a violation (a nonmoral fact).

This natural way of proceeding reflects the logical realities of moral reasoning. In a moral argument, we *must* have at least one moral premise to draw a conclusion about the morality of a particular state of affairs. Without a moral premise, we cannot legitimately arrive at a moral conclusion. That is, from a nonmoral premise alone, a moral conclusion does not logically follow. For example, from the nonmoral fact that abortions are frequently performed, we cannot conclude that abortion is immoral. Nonmoral premises cannot support a conclusion expressing a moral judgment. Likewise, we cannot reason from a moral premise alone (one affirming a general moral principle) to a conclusion about the morality of a particular action. We need a nonmoral premise affirming that the particular action in question is an instance of the general class of actions referred to in the general moral premise. In Argument 2, the moral premise tells us it's wrong to take the life of an innocent person, but we need the nonmoral premise to assert that abortion is an instance of taking the life of an innocent

The world is full of bad arguments. Many of them occur again and again in different guises and contexts, being so common that they have been given names and are studied by those who wish to avoid such mistakes. These common, defective arguments are called *fallacies*. Here are a few that often crop up in moral reasoning.

STRAW MAN

The straw man fallacy is the misrepresentation of a person's views so they can be more easily attacked or dismissed. Suppose you argue that because an immunization program will save the lives of thousands of children and will likely cause the death of only 1 child out of every 500,000, we should fund the immunization program. But then your opponent replies that you think the life of a child isn't worth much. Thus your point has been distorted, made to look extreme or unsavory—and is now an easier target. The straw man fallacy, of course, proves nothing, though many people fall for it every day.

APPEAL TO THE PERSON

Closely related to the straw man fallacy is appeal to the person (also known as the *ad hominem* fallacy). Appeal to the person is the rejecting of a statement on the grounds that it comes from a particular person, not because the statement, or claim, itself is false or dubious. For example:

> You can safely discard anything that Susan has to say about abortion. She's a Catholic.

> Johnson argues that our current health care system is defective. But don't listen to him— he's a liberal.

These arguments are defective because they ask us to reject a claim because of a person's character, background, or circumstances—things that are generally irrelevant to the truth of claims. A statement must stand or fall on its own merits. The personal characteristics of the person espousing the view do not necessarily have a bearing on its truth. Only if we can show that someone's dubious traits somehow make the claim dubious are we justified in rejecting the claim because of a person's personal characteristics. Such a circumstance is rare.

APPEAL TO IGNORANCE

As its name implies, this fallacy tries to prove something by appealing to what we don't know. The appeal to ignorance is arguing either that (1) a claim is true because it has not been proven false or (2) a claim is false because it has not been proven true. For example:

> No one has proven that a fetus is not a person, so it is in fact a person.

> It is obviously false that a fetus is a person because science has not proven that it is a person.

The first argument tries to prove a claim by pointing out that it has not been proven false. The second argument tries to prove that a claim is false because it has not been proven true. Both kinds of arguments are bogus because they assume that a lack of evidence proves something. But a lack of evidence can prove nothing. Being ignorant of the facts does not enlighten us. Notice that if a lack of evidence could prove something, then you could prove just about anything you wanted. You could reason, for instance, that since no one can prove that horses cannot fly, horses must be able to fly.

BEGGING THE QUESTION

The fallacy of begging the question is trying to prove a conclusion by using that very same conclusion as support. It is arguing in a circle. This way of trying to prove something says, in effect, "X is true because X is true." Here is a classic example:

> The Bible says that God exists.

> The Bible is true because God wrote it.

> Therefore, God exists.

The conclusion here ("God exists") is supported by premises that assume that very conclusion.

Here's another one:

All citizens have the right to a fair trial because those whom the state is obliged to protect and give consideration are automatically due judicial criminal proceedings that are equitable by any reasonable standard.

This passage may at first seem like a good argument, but it isn't. It reduces to this unimpressive assertion: "All citizens have the right to a fair trial because all citizens have the right to a fair trial." The conclusion is "All citizens have the right to a fair trial," but that is more or less what the premise says. The premise—"those whom the state is obliged to protect and give consideration are automatically due judicial criminal proceedings that are equitable by any reasonable standard"—is equivalent to "All citizens have the right to a fair trial."

SLIPPERY SLOPE

The metaphor behind this fallacy suggests the danger of stepping on a dicey incline, losing your footing, and sliding to disaster. The fallacy of slippery slope, then, is arguing erroneously that a particular action should not be taken because it will lead inevitably to other actions resulting in some dire outcome. The key word here is *erroneously*. A slippery slope scenario becomes fallacious when there is no reason to believe that the chain of events predicted will ever happen. For example:

If dying patients are permitted to refuse treatment, then soon doctors will be refusing the treatment on their behalf. Then physician-assisted suicide will become rampant, and soon killing patients for almost any reason will become the norm.

This argument is fallacious because there are no reasons for believing that the first step will ultimately result in the chain of events described. If good reasons could be given, the argument might be salvaged.

person. After all, that a fetus is a person—the kind of entity that is deserving of full moral rights—is not obviously true and not assented to by everyone. We must spell out in a premise what we take to be the nonmoral fact of the matter.

This discussion underscores a previously mentioned fact about moral disagreements. When people disagree on a moral issue, they may or may not be disagreeing about moral principles. They may actually share the relevant moral principles but disagree about the nonmoral facts—or vice versa. So when people take contradictory stands on the conclusion of a moral argument, the source of the conflict could lie with the moral premises or the nonmoral premises or both.

Unfortunately, in everyday life moral arguments do not come with their premises clearly labeled, so we need to be able to identify the premises ourselves. This job is made more difficult by a simple fact of the moral life: Often premises (moral and nonmoral) are left unsaid and are merely implied. Sometimes premises are unstated because they are obvious assumptions that need not be mentioned. But if we are to perform a thorough evaluation of an argument, we must drag the implicit premises into the open so they can be fully assessed. Such careful scrutiny is especially important in moral arguments because the implicit premises are often questionable assumptions—the secret, weak links in the chain of reasoning. For example:

ARGUMENT 9
1. In vitro fertilization is an entirely unnatural process, as far from natural reproduction as one could imagine.
2. Therefore, in vitro fertilization should not be used.

As it stands, this is a bad argument; the conclusion does not follow from the premise. But there is an implied (moral) premise lurking here, and if we make it explicit, the argument will be valid:

1. In vitro fertilization is an entirely unnatural process, as far from natural reproduction as one could imagine.
2. Any process that is unnatural should not be used.
3. Therefore, in vitro fertilization should not be used.

Now the argument is complete, and we can see both the nonmoral premise (premise 1) and the moral premise (premise 2), which is a moral principle. But now that we have brought the moral premise into the light of day, we can see that it is false or at least debatable. We use many processes and products that are unnatural (for example, modern pharmaceuticals, intravenous feeding, surgery, CAT scans, artificial limbs, and contact lenses), but we generally do not regard them as morally impermissible.

Very often we can tell that an argument has an unstated premise because there is a logical leap between the stated premises and the conclusion. The inference from stated premises to conclusion does not work unless the missing premise is supplied. A good candidate for the implicit premise will make the argument valid or strong and will be plausible in the context of the argument. The most straightforward approach, however, is to treat the argument as deductive and look for a premise that will make the argument valid, as we did in Argument 9.

Evaluating Premises

As we have seen, good arguments have true premises. But how do we know if the premises are true? Fortunately, there are ways to test, or evaluate, the truth of premises. The tests differ, however, depending on whether the premises are nonmoral or moral.

Checking the truth of nonmoral premises can involve the exploration of either empirical or conceptual matters. An empirical belief, or claim, is one that can be confirmed by sense experience—that is, by observation or scientific investigation. Most nonmoral premises are empirical claims that we can check by examining our own experience or that of others or by consulting the relevant scientific findings. By these methods we can test (and support) a wide variety of empirical assertions, such as many of the nonmoral premises examined earlier: "Incidents of serious crime have doubled"; "Eighty-five percent of the students at this university are Republicans"; "If the patient is getting better, then drugs are unnecessary."

In bioethics, among the most controversial nonmoral premises are those affirming that a medical treatment or program will or will not have a particular effect on people. The issue is whether it will help or harm and to what degree. Sometimes reliable data are available to resolve the issue. Sometimes no clear evidence exists, leaving people to make educated guesses that are often in dispute.

In any case, critical reasoning in bioethics demands that we always seek the most reliable evidence available and try to assess its worth objectively. It requires that our empirical claims be supported by good empirical evidence and that we expect the same from others who make empirical assertions.

A conceptual matter has to do with the meaning of terms, something we need to pay attention to because disputes in bioethics sometimes hinge on the meaning of a concept. For example, in disagreements about the moral permissibility of abortion, the crux of the matter is often how the disputants define *person* (as in Argument 2), or *human life*, or *human being*. Similarly, whether someone supports or opposes euthanasia often hangs on how it is defined. Some, for example, define it in the narrow sense of taking direct action to kill someone for his sake (mercy killing), while others insist on a wider sense that encompasses both mercifully killing and allowing to die. Whether we are devising our own arguments or evaluating those of others, being clear on the meaning of terms is essential, and any proposed definition must be backed by good reasons.

Moral premises are like nonmoral ones in that they, too, should be supported by good reasons and be subjected to serious scrutiny. But just how are moral premises supported and scrutinized?

Support for a moral premise (a moral principle or standard) can come from at least three sources: other moral principles, moral theories, or our most reliable moral judgments. Probably the most common way to support a moral principle is to appeal to a higher-level principle (which often turns out to be one of the four major moral principles discussed earlier). Suppose the moral premise in question is "The patient's wishes about whether surgery is performed on him should not be ignored." Some would argue that this principle is derived from, or is based on, the higher principle that autonomous persons should be allowed to exercise their capacity for self-determination. Or let's say the premise is "Individuals in a persistent vegetative state should never have their feeding tubes removed so they can 'die with dignity.'" Many would base this assertion on the principle that human life is sacred and should be preserved at all costs. Frequently, the higher principle appealed to is plausible, seemingly universal, or accepted by all parties so that further support for the principle is not necessary. At other times, the higher principle itself may be controversial and in need of support.

Moral premises can also be supported by a moral theory, a general explanation of what makes an action right or a person or motive good. (In Chapter 2 we discuss moral theories in depth.) For example, traditional utilitarianism is a moral theory affirming that right actions are those that produce the greatest happiness for all concerned. Appealing to utilitarianism, then, someone might insist that a baby born with severe brain damage who will die within a few days should not be allowed to wither slowly away in pain but should be given a lethal injection. The justification for this policy is that it would produce the least amount of unhappiness (including pain and suffering) for all concerned, including baby, parents, and caregivers. Those who reject this policy would have to argue that

there was something wrong with utilitarianism or that other considerations (including alternative theories) outweigh utilitarian concerns.

Another possible source of support for moral premises is what philosophers call our *considered moral judgments*. These are moral judgments we deem plausible or credible after careful reflection that is as unbiased as possible. They may apply to both particular cases and more general moral statements. For example, after deliberation we might conclude that "inflicting undeserved and unnecessary pain on someone is wrong," or that "emergency care for accident victims should be provided regardless of their race or religion," or that "amputating a patient's leg for no good reason is never morally permissible." Like moral principles and theories, such judgments can vary in how much weight they carry in moral arguments and can be given more or less credibility (or undermined completely) by relevant reasons. (We examine more closely the relationships among theories, principles, and considered judgments in Chapter 2.)

Moral premises can be called into question by showing that they somehow conflict with credible principles, theories, or judgments. One way to do this is to cite *counterexamples*, instances in which the moral principle in question seems not to hold. Recall that a counterexample helps us see that the moral premise in Argument 9 is dubious. The premise says "Any process that is unnatural should not be used," but we often use unnatural products or processes (CAT scans and contact lenses, for instance) and do not think these actions morally wrong. In the same way, we can use counterexamples to evaluate the moral premise in Argument 2:

1. It's wrong to take the life of an innocent person.
2. Abortion takes the life of an innocent person.
3. Therefore, abortion is wrong.

Are there no exceptions to premise 1? Is it always wrong to kill an innocent person? We can imagine cases in which this premise seems either doubtful or at least not obviously true. What about situations in which many lives can be saved by taking the life of one person? What if all 50 people in a lifeboat at sea will drown unless one of them is cast overboard? What if the one unlucky person *agrees* to be cast overboard to save all the others? Or suppose a person is dying of cancer and is suffering unspeakable pain that cannot be relieved by any medical means—and she begs for a lethal injection of morphine. Some would argue that these scenarios raise serious questions about premise 1, suggesting that at least in its current form, it may not be true. In response to these counterexamples, some who wish to defend the premise might modify it to take the scenarios into account or even try to show that despite its implications premise 1 is justified.

Assessing Whole Arguments

Moral argument, like any other kind of arguments, usually come to us embedded in larger tracts of speech or writing. Often the premises and conclusion are embellished or obscured by other elements—by explanations, asides, reiterations, descriptions, examples, amplifications, or irrelevancies. So how do we evaluate such arguments in the rough?

Following this procedure will help:

Step 1. Study the text until you thoroughly understand it. You can't locate the conclusion or premises until you know what you're looking for—and that requires having a clear idea of what the author is driving at. Don't attempt to find the conclusion or premises until you "get it." This understanding entails having an overview of a great deal of text, a bird's-eye view of the whole work.

Step 2. Find the conclusion. When you evaluate arguments surrounded by a lot of other prose, *your first task is to find the conclusion.* There may be a single conclusion, or several main conclusions, or one primary conclusion with several subconclusions. Or the conclusion may be nowhere explicitly stated but embodied in metaphorical language or implied by large expanses

of prose. In any case, your job is to come up with a single conclusion statement for each conclusion—even if you have to paraphrase large sections of text to do it. When you identify the conclusion, the hunt for premises gets easier.

Step 3. Identify the premises. Like the search for a conclusion, unearthing the premises may involve condensing large sections of text into manageable form—namely, single premise statements. To do this, you need to disregard extraneous material and keep your eye on the "big picture." Remember that in moral arguments you are looking for both moral and nonmoral premises.

Let's see how this procedure works on the following passage:

[1] John and Nancy Jones had a two-year-old son who suffered from a serious but very curable bowel obstruction. [2] For religious reasons, the Joneses decide to treat their son with prayer instead of modern medicine. [3] They refused medical treatment even though they were told by several doctors that the child would die unless medically treated. [4] As it turned out, the boy did die. [5] The Joneses were arrested and charged with involuntary manslaughter. [6] Were the Joneses wrong to refuse treatment for their son?

[7] The answer is yes. [8] Regardless of what faith or religious dogma would have the Joneses do, they allowed their child to die. [9] According to just about any moral outlook, the care of a child by the parents is a fundamental obligation. [10] Above all other concerns, parents have a duty to ensure the health and safety of their children and to use whatever means are most likely to secure those benefits. [11] In other words, allowing a child to die when the death could easily have been prevented is morally reprehensible. [12] The Joneses were therefore guilty of a shockingly immoral act.

The first order of business is to find the conclusion, and in doing so we can see that the first paragraph is entirely background information. The conclusion is in sentence 12, and with this information, we can tell that sentence 7 is a short affirmation of the conclusion. We can also locate the premises. The nonmoral premise is in sentence 8: the nonmoral fact is that the Joneses permitted their child to die. The moral premise is stated most explicitly in sentence 11. Sentences 9 and 10 are equivalent to 11, although stated more generally.

The bare-bones arguments then is:

[8] Regardless of what faith or religious dogma would have the Joneses do, they allowed their child to die.
[11] In other words, allowing a child to die when the death could easily have been prevented is morally reprehensible.
[12] The Joneses were therefore guilty of a shockingly immoral act.

This argument is deductively valid, so the crucial question is whether the premises are true. Presumably the nonmoral premise 8 is an uncontested assertion. We can imagine that everyone knows that the Joneses let their child die. Premise 11, the moral statement, seems to be a plausible moral principle—some would say it's just common sense. Most people would find it difficult to think of a credible counterexample to it. But that is precisely what is at issue here: whether it's ever morally permissible to allow a child to die when the death can easily be prevented. To justify premise 11, those who accept it may appeal to a moral theory (utilitarianism or Kantian ethics, say) or to more general moral principles such as "always act to preserve life," "treat persons with respect," or "humans have a right to life." On the other hand, it's hard to see how the rejection of premise 11 could be based on anything other than a religious moral principle.

KEY TERMS
applied ethics
bioethics
cultural relativism
deductive argument
descriptive ethics
divine command theory
ethical relativism
ethics

inductive argument
metaethics
moral absolutism
moral argument
moral objectivism
morality
normative ethics
paternalism
subjective relativism

SUMMARY
Morality refers to beliefs about right and wrong actions and morally good and bad persons or character. Ethics is the study of morality using the tools and methods of philosophy. The study of morality using the methodology of science is known as descriptive ethics. Ethics has three main branches: (1) normative ethics, the search for, and justification of, moral standards, or norms; (2) metaethics, the study of the meaning and justification of basic moral beliefs; and (3) applied ethics, the use of moral norms and concepts to resolve practical moral issues. Bioethics is applied ethics focused on health care, medical science, and medical technology.

Moral norms differ from other kinds of norms because they are characterized by (1) normative dominance, (2) universality, (3) impartiality, and (4) reasonableness. We apply moral norms to two distinct spheres of our moral experience—obligations and values. Moral obligations concern our duty, what we are obligated to do or not do, and refer primarily to right and wrong actions. Moral values generally concern those things that we judge to be morally good, bad, praiseworthy, or blameworthy. A right action can be obligatory (one that would be wrong not to perform) or permissible (one that is not wrong to perform). A prohibited action would be one that would be wrong to perform. A supererogatory action is one that is "above and beyond" our duty.

In bioethics, five moral principles have been extremely influential and particularly relevant: (1) autonomy (autonomous persons should be allowed to exercise their capacity for self-determination); (2) nonmaleficence (we should not cause unnecessary harm to others); (3) beneficence (we should do good to others and prevent or remove harm); (4) utility (we should produce the most favorable balance of good over bad for all concerned); and (5) justice (we should treat equals equally).

According to ethical relativism, moral standards are not objective but are relative to what individuals or cultures believe. A familiar argument for cultural relativism is that if people's moral judgments differ from culture to culture, then moral norms are relative to culture, and people's moral judgments obviously do differ from culture to culture. But the first premise in the argument is false. In addition, cultural relativism seems implausible because it implies moral infallibility, immunity of all cultures from moral criticism from the outside, the automatic wrongness of the moral stance of social reformers, and the incoherence of the idea of moral progress. Moreover, cultural relativism does not necessarily lead to tolerance and does not logically entail it.

The divine command theory says that right actions are those commanded by God, and wrong actions are those forbidden by God. But many religious and nonreligious people have rejected the theory because it seems to imply that God's commands are arbitrary.

Most critical reasoning is concerned in one way or another with the construction or evaluation of arguments. All the skills required in dealing with arguments generally can be applied directly to handling moral arguments in particular. A moral argument is one whose conclusion is a moral statement, an assertion that an action is right or wrong or that a person or motive is good or bad.

ARGUMENT EXERCISES

(All answers appear in the Appendix.)

Exercise 1.1
In each of the following passages, add a moral premise to turn it into a valid moral argument.

1. Noah promised to drive Thelma to Los Angeles, so he should stop bellyaching and do it.
2. The refugees were shot at and lied to, and the authorities did nothing to stop any of this. The authorities should have intervened.
3. There was never any imminent threat from the Iraqi government, so the United States should not have invaded Iraq.
4. The Indian government posed an imminent threat to Pakistan and the world, so the Pakistanis were justified in attacking Indian troops.
5. Burton used a gun in the commission of a crime; therefore he should get a long prison term.
6. Ellen knew that a murder was going to take place. It was her duty to try to stop it.
7. Ahmed should never have allowed his daughter to receive in vitro fertilization. Such a procedure is unnatural.
8. The doctors performed the experiment on twenty patients without their consent. Obviously, that was wrong.
9. What you did was immoral. You hacked into a database containing personal information on thousands of people and invaded their privacy.
10. Ling spent all day weeding Mrs. Black's garden for no pay. The least Mrs. Black should do is let Ling borrow some gardening tools.

Exercise 1.2
For each of the following arguments, specify the conclusion and premises and indicate where possible whether it is cogent or sound.

1. Anyone who runs away from an automobile accident should be arrested. Janet ran away from an automobile accident. She should be arrested.
2. I write in response to the Nov. 4 *News* article, "Plans for group home, storage facility opposed." As the sister and

guardian of a profoundly retarded woman who lives in a group home, I can assure the gentlemen quoted that their fears are very much unfounded. The home in which my sister resides is large, lovely, brand new, well staffed and well maintained. It does nothing but enhance the community, bring neighbors together and create a wonderfully diverse neighborhood—Letter to the editor, *Buffalo News*

3. Scrawling "Rape all Asian bitches and dump them" on classroom walls is not a hate crime, and graffiti should be protected by the First Amendment, according to assistant professor of communication Laura Leets. This is outrageous. I hope Ms. Leets is simply arguing from a narrow legalistic interpretation and is merely insensitive to the tremendous hurt such graffiti can inflict, not to mention the additional damage caused when a professor on campus defends it. Words can be just as destructive as physical violence. Drawing a technical distinction between the two is at best insensitive, at worst evil—Letter to the editor, *Stanford Magazine*

4. Yolanda took the money from petty cash even though she had plenty of money in her pocket. People shouldn't steal unless they are destitute. She shouldn't have taken that money.

5. There is one principle we can never avoid: We should never do anything to disrespect human life. The artificial use of human cells—as scientists are now doing in stem-cell research—shows a complete disregard for human life. Stem-cell research is immoral.

Exercise 1.3
Evaluate the following arguments:

1. Any form of expression or speech that offends people of faith should not be tolerated. *Penthouse* magazine definitely offends people of faith. Ban it!

2. Anyone who disagrees with the basic moral dictums of the prevailing culture should be censored. Dr. Tilden's graduation speech clearly was inconsistent with the prevailing moral opinions on campus. She should be reprimanded.

Exercise 1.4
Identify the moral arguments in each of the following passages. Specify the premises and the conclusion, adding implicit premises where needed.

1. The movie *Lorenzo's Oil* is about a family's struggle to find a cure for their young son's fatal genetic disease, an illness that usually kills boys before they reach their eleventh birthday. The script is based on the true story of a family's attempt to save Lorenzo, their son, from this fatal genetic disease through the use of a medicinal oil. The movie is a tear-jerker, but it ends on a hopeful note that suggests that the oil will eventually cure Lorenzo and that the oil is an effective treatment for the genetic disease. The problem is, there is no cure for the disease and no good scientific evidence showing that the oil works. But the movie touts the oil anyway—and gives false hope to every family whose son suffers from this terrible illness. Worse, the movie overplays the worth of the oil, seriously misleading people about the medical facts. The movie, therefore, is immoral. It violates the ageless moral dictum to, above all else, "do no harm." *Lorenzo's Oil* may be just a movie, but it has done harm nonetheless.

2. I, like many of my fellow Muslims, was appalled by the latest bombing in Saudi Arabia ('Among the Saudis, Attack Has Soured Qaeda Supporters,' front page, Nov. 11). Yet I was disturbed to get the sense that Saudis were angered by this latest act of barbarity because the targets were mainly Arab and Muslim.

You quote one person as saying of the bombing in Riyadh in May, "At that time it was seen as justifiable because there was an invasion of a foreign country, there was frustration." Another says, "Jihad is not against your own people."

Regardless of whether the victims are Muslim or not, the vicious murder of innocent human beings is reprehensible and repugnant, an affront to everything Islam stands for. Any sympathy for Al Qaeda among the minority of Saudis should have evaporated after the May bombings in Riyadh, and it should have surprised no one in Saudi Arabia that Al Qaeda would attack a housing complex full of Arabs and Muslims.

That is what Al Qaeda is: a band of bloodthirsty murderers.—Letter to the editor, *New York Times*

FURTHER READING

Anita L. Allen, *New Ethics: A Guided Tour of the Twenty-First Century Moral Landscape* (New York: Miramax, 2004).

John Arras, "Theory and Bioethics," *The Stanford Encyclopedia of Philosophy* (Summer 2013), Edward N. Zalta (ed.), http://plato.stanford.edu/archives/sum2013/entries/theory-bioethics/ (15 October 2015).

Robert Audi, *Moral Knowledge and Ethical Character* (New York: Oxford University Press, 1997).

Tom L. Beauchamp and James F. Childress, *Principles of Biomedical Ethics*, 5th ed. (New York: Oxford University Press, 2001).

Bioethics.com, http://www.bioethics.com/ (15 October 2015).

Richard B. Brandt, *Ethical Theory* (Englewood Cliffs, NJ: Prentice-Hall, 1959).

Steven M. Cahn and Joram G. Haber, *Twentieth Century Ethical Theory* (Upper Saddle River, NJ: Prentice-Hall, 1995).

Jean Bethke Elshtain, "Judge Not?," *First Things* 46 (October 1994): 36–41.

Fred Feldman, *Introductory Ethics* (Englewood Cliffs, NJ: Prentice-Hall, 1978).

Richard M. Fox and Joseph P. DeMarco, *Moral Reasoning*, 2nd ed. (New York: Harcourt, 2001).

William K. Frankena, *Ethics*, 2nd ed. (Englewood Cliffs, NJ: Prentice-Hall, 1973).

Bernard Gert, *Morality: Its Nature and Justification* (New York: Oxford University Press, 1998).

John-Stewart Gordon, "Bioethics," *The Internet Encyclopedia of Philosophy*, http://www.iep.utm.edu/ (15 October 2015).

Chris Gowans, "Moral Relativism," in *The Stanford Encyclopedia of Philosophy* (Spring 2004), ed. Edward N. Zalta, http://plato.stanford.edu/archives/spr2004/entries/moral-relativism/.

C. E. Harris, *Applying Moral Theories* (Belmont, CA: Wadsworth, 1997).

The Hastings Center, http://www.thehastingscenter.org/ (15 October 2015).

Melville Herskovits, *Cultural Relativism: Perspectives in Cultural Pluralism* (New York: Vintage, 1972).

Albert R. Jonsen, *The Birth of Bioethics* (New York: Oxford University Press, 1998).

Kai Nielsen, *Ethics Without God* (Buffalo, NY: Prometheus, 1973).

Louis P. Pojman, *Ethics: Discovering Right and Wrong*, 4th ed. (Belmont, CA: Wadsworth, 2002).

Louis P. Pojman and Lewis Vaughn, eds., *The Moral Life*, 3rd ed. (New York: Oxford University Press, 2007).

James Rachels, *The Elements of Moral Philosophy*, 4th ed. (New York: McGraw-Hill, 2003).

Theodore Schick, Jr. and Lewis Vaughn, *Doing Philosophy*, 2nd ed. (New York: McGraw-Hill, 2002), chap. 5.

Russ Shafer-Landau, *Whatever Happened to Good and Evil?* (New York: Oxford University Press, 2004).

Peter Singer, ed., *A Companion to Ethics* (Cambridge, UK: Blackwell, 1993).

Walter T. Stace, "Ethical Relativism," in *The Concept of Morals* (New York: Macmillan, 1965), 8–58.

Bonnie Steinbock, ed., *The Oxford Handbook of Bioethics* (Oxford: Oxford University Press, 2007).

Paul Taylor, *Principles of Ethics* (Encino, CA: Dickenson, 1975).

Lewis Vaughn, *Doing Ethics: Moral Reasoning and Contemporary Issues* (New York: W.W. Norton, 2008).

Lewis Vaughn, *The Power of Critical Thinking*, 2nd ed. (New York: Oxford University Press, 2008).

Thomas F. Wall, *Thinking Critically About Moral Problems* (Belmont, CA: Wadsworth, 2003).

G. J. Warnock, *The Object of Morality* (London: Methuen & Co. 1971).

NOTES

1. James Rachels, *The Elements of Moral Philosophy,* 4th ed. (New York: McGraw-Hill, 2003), 14.

2. This example is derived from James Rachels' unique description of the case in "Ethical Theory and Bioethics," from *A Companion to Bioethics,* ed. Helga Kuhse and Peter Singer (Oxford: Blackwell, 2001), 16–17.

3. W. D. Ross, *The Right and the Good* (Oxford: Clarendon Press, 1930).

4. In their classic text *Principles of Biomedical Ethics* (New York: Oxford University Press, 2001), Tom L. Beauchamp and James F. Childress work out a comprehensive approach to biomedical ethics using a framework of four moral principles. They choose to treat beneficence and nonmaleficence separately and regard utility as part of beneficence.

5. Solomon Asch, *Social Psychology* (Englewood Cliffs, NJ: Prentice-Hall, 1952), 378–79.

CHAPTER 2

Bioethics and Moral Theories

As we have seen, the moral life is dynamic, complex, and inescapable. In it we wrestle with momentous questions of moral value and moral rightness. We assert, challenge, accept, and reject moral statements. We make moral judgments about the rightness of actions, the goodness of persons or their character, and the moral quality and worth of our lives. Through general moral norms or principles, we direct our actions and inform our choices. We formulate and critique moral arguments, thereby testing what we know or think we know about moral realities. We do all this and one thing more: We naturally and unavoidably venture into the realm of moral theory, trying to see the larger moral meaning behind particular situations and precepts. In this chapter, we explore this realm and try to discern how it fits into the moral life in general and into bioethics in particular.

THE NATURE OF MORAL THEORIES

In science, theories help us understand the empirical world by explaining the causes of events, why things are the way they are. The germ theory of disease explains how particular diseases arise and spread in a human population. The heliocentric (sun-centered) theory of planetary motion explains why the planets in our solar system behave the way they do. In ethics, moral theories have a similar explanatory role. A **moral theory** explains not why one event causes another but why an action is right or wrong or why a person or a person's character is good or bad. A moral theory tells us what it is about an action that *makes it right*, or what it is about a person that *makes him or her good*. The divine command

theory of morality, for example, says that right actions are those commanded or willed by God. Traditional utilitarianism says that right actions are those that produce the greatest happiness for all concerned. These and other moral theories are attempts to define rightness or goodness. In this way, they are both more general and more basic than moral principles or other general norms.

Moral theorizing—that is, making, using, or assessing moral theories or parts of theories—is normal and pervasive in the moral life, though it is often done without much recognition that theory is playing a part in the deliberations. Whenever we try to understand what a moral property such as rightness or goodness means, or justify a moral principle or other norm, or resolve a conflict between two credible principles, or explain why a particular action or practice is right or wrong, or evaluate the plausibility of specific moral intuitions or assumptions, we do moral theorizing. In fact, we *must* theorize if we are to make headway in such investigations. We must stand back from the situation at hand and try to grasp the larger pattern that only theory can reveal.

Moral theories that concentrate on right and wrong actions are known as theories of obligation (or duty) or simply as *theories of right action*. The divine command theory and utilitarianism are theories of right action. Philosophers often distinguish these from moral theories that focus on good and bad persons or character—so-called *virtue-based theories*. Virtue ethics (covered later in this chapter) is a prime example.

How do moral theories fit into our everyday moral reasoning? In answering that, let's focus on theories of right action, probably the most influential type in bioethics. First, moral theories can figure directly in our moral arguments. As we saw earlier, moral arguments contain both moral and nonmoral premises. A moral premise can consist of a moral principle, a moral rule (a less general norm derived from or based on a principle), or a claim expressing a central tenet of a moral theory. Using such a tenet, someone might argue, for example, that stem-cell research should be fully funded rather than halted altogether because such a step would eventually lead to a greater benefit for more people, and right actions (according to utilitarianism) are those that result in the greatest overall benefit for the greatest number. Thus the fundamental moral standard of utilitarianism becomes a premise in an argument for a specific action in a particular case.

Second, theories can have an indirect impact on moral arguments because principles appealed to are often supported in turn by a moral theory. The principles can be either derived from or supported by the theory's account of right and wrong action. Consider the prohibition against murder, the basic precept that it is wrong to take the life of an innocent person. This principle can be drawn from theories built around the fundamental notion of respect for persons. As one such theory would have it, murder is wrong because it treats people not as persons with inherent worth but as mere things to be used or dispensed with as one wishes.

Some people are tempted to deduce from all this that moral theories are the dominant force in moral reasoning as well as in the moral life. This view would be an oversimplification. By design, moral theories are certainly more general in scope than moral principles, rules, or judgments. But from this fact it does not follow that theories alone are the ultimate authority in moral deliberations. For one thing, to be truly useful, moral theories must be filled out with details about how to apply them in real life and the kinds of cases to which they are relevant. For another, there is more to morality than what can be captured in the general norms of a theory.

There is also the testimony of the particular, the evidence of individual moral judgments.

Our moral deliberations, then, involve both the general and the particular. Suppose we embrace a moral theory that seems to offer us a plausible explanation of what makes an action right or wrong. When we must decide which action is morally right in a particular situation, we look to our theory for general guidance. From our theory we may glean a set of moral principles that seem to apply to the case at hand. If the principles lead us to conflicting choices, we look again to the theory for insight in resolving the conflict. But we also must take into account our considered judgments about the case. (We may also formulate considered judgments about the relevant principles or rules.) If our considered judgments and the deliverances of our theory are consistent with one another, we have additional assurance that our decision in the case is correct. If our judgments clash with our theory or principles, we must decide which to revise or discard—for critical reasoning demands that our beliefs be coherent, that they do not harbor contradictions. If we believe our judgments to be more credible than the implications of our theory (or principles), we may modify the theory accordingly (or, rarely, regard the theory as irreparable and give it up). But if the theory seems more credible in this case, we may conclude that our judgment is untrustworthy and set it aside.

So a moral theory can show us what is important and reasonable in morality, guiding our judgments through overarching insights that may help us with specific cases and issues, sometimes correcting erring judgments along the way. Our considered judgments are fallible indicators of moral common sense and are checks against wayward theory or flawed principle. In bioethics, both of these moral resources are highly respected and widely used.

INFLUENTIAL MORAL THEORIES

Several moral theories have played major roles in bioethics, and they continue to influence how people think about bioethical issues. Theories of right action (in contrast to virtue-based theories) have dominated the field, each usually based on one of two broad views about the essential character of right actions. **Consequentialist** moral theories insist that the rightness of actions depends solely on their consequences or results. The key question is what or how much good the actions produce, however *good* is defined. **Deontological** (or **nonconsequentialist**) theories say that the rightness of actions is determined not solely by their consequences but partly or entirely by their intrinsic nature. For some or all actions, rightness depends on the kind of actions they are, not on how much good they produce. A consequentialist theory, then, may say that stealing is wrong because it causes more harm than good. But a deontological theory may contend that stealing is inherently wrong regardless of its consequences, good or bad.

Utilitarianism

The leading consequentialist theory is **utilitarianism**, the view that right actions are those that result in the most beneficial balance of good over bad consequences for everyone involved. It says we should maximize the nonmoral good (the *utility*) of everyone affected, regardless of the contrary urgings of moral rules or unbending moral principles. Various forms of utilitarianism differ in how they define utility, with some equating it with happiness or pleasure (the hedonistic view), others with satisfaction of preferences or desires or some other intrinsically valuable things or states such as knowledge or perfection.

In applying the utilitarian moral standard (the greatest good, everyone considered), some moral philosophers concentrate on specific acts and some on rules covering kinds of acts. The former approach is called **act-utilitarianism**, the idea that the rightness of actions depends solely on the relative good produced by *individual actions*. An act is right if in a particular situation it produces a greater balance of good over bad than any alternative acts; determining rightness is a matter of weighing the effects of each possible act. The latter approach, known as **rule-utilitarianism**,

avoids judging rightness by specific acts and focuses instead on *rules governing categories of acts*. It says a right action is one that conforms to a rule that, if followed consistently, would create for everyone involved the most beneficial balance of good over bad. We are to adhere to the rules because they maximize the good for everyone considered—even though a given act may produce bad effects in a particular situation.

The classic version of utilitarianism was devised by English philosopher Jeremy Bentham (1748–1832) and given more detail and plausibility by another English philosopher, John Stuart Mill (1806–1873). Classic utilitarianism is hedonistic in that the utility to be maximized is pleasure, broadly termed happiness, the only intrinsic good. A right action produces more net happiness (amounts of happiness minus unhappiness) than any alternative action, everyone considered. As Mill put it,

> [Actions] are right in proportion as they tend to promote happiness, wrong as they tend to produce the reverse of happiness. By "happiness" is intended pleasure, and the absence of pain; by "unhappiness," pain and the privation of pleasure.[1]

Bentham and Mill, however, had different ideas about what happiness entailed, as do many philosophers today. Bentham thinks that happiness is one-dimensional: It is pleasure, pure and simple, something that varies only in the amount that an agent can experience. On this scheme, it seems that the moral ideal would be to experience maximum amounts of pleasure, as does the glutton or the debauchee. But Mill thinks that pleasures can vary in quality as well as quantity. For him, there are lower and higher pleasures—the lower and inferior ones indulged in by the glutton and his ilk and the higher and more satisfying ones found in such experiences as the search for knowledge and the appreciation of art and music. Mill famously sums up this contrast by saying, "It is better to be a human being dissatisfied than a pig satisfied; better to be Socrates dissatisfied than a fool satisfied."[2]

Like all forms of utilitarianism, the classic formulation demands a strong sense of impartiality. When promoting happiness, we must not only take into account the happiness of everyone affected but also give everyone's needs or interests equal weight. Mill explains:

> [The] happiness which forms the utilitarian standard of what is right conduct, is not the agent's own happiness, but that of all concerned. As between his own happiness and that of others, utilitarianism requires him to be as strictly impartial as a disinterested and benevolent spectator.[3]

In classic utilitarianism, the emphasis is on maximizing the total quantity of net happiness, not ensuring that it is rationed in any particular amounts among the people involved. This means that an action resulting in 1,000 units of happiness for 10 people is better than an action yielding only 900 units of happiness for those same 10 people—regardless of how the units of happiness are distributed among them. Classic utilitarians do want to allocate the total amount of happiness among as many people as possible (thus their motto, "the greatest happiness for the greatest number"). But maximizing total happiness is the fundamental concern whether everyone gets an equal portion or one person gets the lion's share.

How might utilitarianism apply to a bioethical issue? Consider this scenario: Johnny is a 10-year-old boy with cerebral palsy, emaciated and bedridden, hooked to feeding tubes and monitors, his body twisted in pain that is almost impossible to control, his days measured out by one agonizing surgical operation after another, locked in the mental life of an infant and acknowledged by all the experts to be without hope. His anguished parents, wanting desperately to end his suffering, beg the physician to give Johnny a lethal injection. What should the physician do?

Suppose in this case there are only two options: indefinitely maintaining Johnny in his present condition or carrying out the parents' wishes. An act-utilitarian might reason like this. Allowing the current situation to continue would

cause enormous unhappiness—Johnny's own physical agony, the unimaginable misery of the distraught parents, the anxiety of other family members and friends, and the distress and frustration of the physician and nurses who can do little more than stand by as Johnny withers away. On the other hand, administering the lethal injection would immediately end Johnny's pain and prevent future suffering. The parents would grieve for Johnny but would at least find some relief—and perhaps peace—in knowing that his torture was over. The medical staff would probably also be relieved for the same reason. There would, of course, also be possible negative consequences to take into account. In administering the lethal injection, the physician would be risking both professional censure and criminal prosecution. If her actions were to become public, people might begin to mistrust physicians who treat severely impaired children, undermining the whole medical profession. Perhaps the physician's action would lead to a general devaluing of the lives of disabled or elderly people everywhere. These dire consequences, however, would probably not be very likely if the physician acted discreetly. On balance, the act-utilitarian might say, greater net happiness (the least unhappiness) would result from the mercy killing, which would therefore be the morally permissible course.

A rule-utilitarian might judge the situation differently. The key question would be which rule if consistently followed would produce the greatest net happiness. Let us say that there are only two rules to consider. One says "Do not kill seriously impaired children, regardless of their suffering or the wishes of their parents." The other one is "Killing seriously impaired children is permissible if they are suffering severely and improvement is hopeless." The rule-utilitarian might reason that consistently following the second rule would have terrible consequences. It would cause widespread suspicion about the actions and motives of physicians who treat seriously impaired and disabled children. People would come to distrust physicians, which in turn would damage the entire health care system.

Probably much to the dismay of his religious critics, John Stuart Mill defended his radical doctrine of utilitarianism by arguing that it was entirely consistent with a fundamental Christian teaching:

> In the golden rule of Jesus of Nazareth, we read the complete spirit of the ethics of utility. To do as one would be done by, and to love one's neighbour as oneself, constitute the ideal perfection of utilitarian morality. As the means of making the nearest approach to this ideal, utility would enjoin, first, that laws and social arrangements should place the happiness, or (as speaking practically it may be called) the interest, of every individual, as nearly as possible in harmony with the interest of the whole; and secondly, that education and opinion, which have so vast a power over human character, should so use that power as to establish in the mind of every individual an indissoluble association between his own happiness and the good of the whole; especially between his own happiness and the practice of such modes of conduct, negative and positive, as regard for the universal happiness prescribes: so that not only he may be unable to conceive the possibility of happiness to himself, consistently with conduct opposed to the general good, but also that a direct impulse to promote the general good may be in every individual one of the habitual motives of action, and the sentiments connected therewith may fill a large and prominent place in every human being's sentient existence.[4]

Society might begin to devalue the lives of disabled people generally as well as the elderly and other vulnerable populations. The rule would also appear to entail a blatant violation of the cardinal principle of medical practice—do no harm. Adhering to it might therefore cause an erosion of all ethical codes and professional standards in medicine. But following the first rule would have no such consequences. It would permit the suffering of some impaired children, but this consequence seems not to be as catastrophic as those produced by consistently conforming to the second rule. For the rule-utilitarian, then, the morally right action would be *not* to administer the lethal injection, despite the parents' pleas.

Kantian Ethics

From the great German philosopher Immanuel Kant (1724–1804) comes what is widely regarded as probably the most sophisticated and influential deontological theory ever devised. It is the very antithesis of utilitarianism, holding that right actions do not depend in the least on consequences, the maximization of utility, the production of happiness, or the desires and needs of human beings. For Kant, the core of morality consists of following a rational and universally applicable moral rule and doing so solely out of a sense of duty. An action is right only if it conforms to such a rule, and we are morally praiseworthy only if we perform it for duty's sake alone.

In Kant's system, all our moral duties are expressed in the form of *categorical imperatives*. An imperative is a command to do something; it is categorical if it applies without exception and without regard for particular needs or purposes. A categorical imperative says, "Do this—regardless." In contrast, a *hypothetical imperative* is a command to do something if we want to achieve particular aims, as in "If you want good pay, work hard." The moral law, then, rests on absolute directives that do not depend on the contingencies of desire or utility.

Kant says that through reason and reflection we can derive our duties from a single moral principle, what he calls *the* categorical imperative. He formulates it in different ways, the first one being "Act only on that maxim through which you can at the same time will that it should become a universal law."[5] For Kant, our actions have logical implications—they imply general rules, or maxims, of conduct. If you tell a lie for financial gain, you are in effect acting according to a maxim like "It's okay to lie to someone when doing so benefits you financially." The question is whether the maxim corresponding to an action is a legitimate moral law. To find out, we must ask if we could consistently will that the maxim become a universal law applicable to everyone—that is, if everyone could consistently act on the maxim and we would be willing to have them do so. If we could do this, then the action described by the maxim is morally permissible; if not, it is prohibited. Thus moral laws embody two characteristics thought to be essential to morality itself: universality and impartiality.

To show us how to apply this formulation of the categorical imperative to a specific situation, Kant uses the example of a lying promise. Suppose you need to borrow money from a friend, but you know you could never pay her back. So to get the loan, you decide to lie, falsely promising to repay the money. To find out if such a lying promise is morally permissible, Kant would have you ask if you could consistently will the maxim of your action to become a universal law, to ask, in effect, "What would happen if everyone did this?" The maxim is "Whenever you need to borrow money you cannot pay back, make a lying promise to repay." So what *would* happen if everyone in need of a loan acted in accordance with this maxim? People would make lying promises to obtain loans, but everyone would also know that such promises were worthless, and the custom of loaning money on promises would disappear. So willing the maxim to be a universal law involves a contradiction: If everyone made lying promises, promise-making itself would be no more; you cannot consistently will the maxim to become a universal law. Therefore, your duty is clear: Making a lying promise to borrow money is morally wrong.

Kant's first formulation of the categorical imperative yields several other duties, some of which are particularly relevant to bioethics. Notably he argues that there is an absolute moral prohibition against killing the innocent, lying, committing suicide, and failing to help others when feasible.

Perhaps the most renowned formulation of the categorical imperative is the principle of respect for persons (a formulation distinct from the first one, though Kant thought them equivalent). As he puts it, "Act in such a way that you always treat humanity, whether in your own person or in the person of any other, never simply as a means, but always at the same time as an end."[6] People must never be treated as if they were mere instruments for achieving some further end, for people are ends in themselves, possessors of ultimate inherent worth. People have ultimate value because they are the ultimate source of value for other things. They bestow value; they do not have it bestowed upon them. So we should treat both ourselves and other persons with the respect that all inherently valuable beings deserve.

According to Kant, the inherent worth of persons derives from their nature as free, rational beings capable of directing their own lives, determining their own ends, and decreeing their own rules by which to live. Thus, the inherent value of persons does not depend in any way on their social status, wealth, talent, race, or culture. Moreover, inherent value is something that all persons possess equally. Each person deserves the same measure of respect as any other.

Kant explains that we treat people merely as a means instead of an end-in-themselves if we disregard these characteristics of personhood—if we thwart people's freely chosen actions by coercing them, undermine their rational decision-making by lying to them, or discount their equality by discriminating against them. In bioethics, clear-cut cases of not respecting persons in Kant's sense would normally include experimenting on people without their knowledge and consent, lying to them about their medical condition and prognosis, and forcing patients to receive treatment against their will.

Notice that this formulation of the categorical imperative does not actually prohibit treating a person as a means but forbids treating a person *simply*, or *merely*, as a means—as nothing but a means. Kant recognizes that in daily life we often must use people to achieve our various ends. To buy milk, we use the cashier; to find books, we use the librarian; to get well, we use the doctor. But because their actions are freely chosen and we do not undermine their status as persons, we do not use them *solely* as instruments of our will. Medical researchers use their human subjects as a means to an end—but not merely as a means to an end if the subjects give their informed consent to participate in the research.

Natural Law Theory

From ancient times to the present day, many people have thought that the outlines of the moral law are plain to see because they are written large and true in nature itself. This basic notion has been developed over the centuries into what is known as **natural law theory**, the view that right actions are those that conform to moral standards discerned in nature through human reason. Undergirding this doctrine is the belief that all of nature (including humankind) is teleological, that it is somehow directed toward particular goals or ends, and that humans achieve their highest good when they follow their true, natural inclinations leading to these goals or ends. There is, in other words, a way things *are*—natural processes and functions that accord with the natural law—and how things are shows how things *should be*. The prime duty of humans, then, is to guide their lives toward these natural ends, acting in accordance with the requirements of natural law.

Implicit in all this is the element of rationality. According to natural law theory, humans are rational beings empowered by reason to perceive the workings of nature, determine the natural inclinations of humans, and recognize the implications therein for morally permissible actions. That is, reason enables human beings to ascertain the moral law implicit in nature and to apply that objective, universal standard to their lives.

Though natural law theory has both religious and nonreligious forms, the theistic formulation of theologian-philosopher Thomas Aquinas (1225–1274) has been the theory's dominant version. It is not only the official moral outlook of the Roman Catholic Church, but it has also been the intellectual starting point for many contemporary variations of the theory, secular and otherwise. For Aquinas, God is the author of the natural law who gave humans the gift of reason to discern the law for themselves and live accordingly. Aquinas argues that human beings naturally tend toward—and therefore have a duty of—preserving human life and health (and so must not kill the innocent), producing and raising children, seeking knowledge (including knowledge of God), and cultivating cooperative social relationships. In all this, Aquinas says, the overarching aim is to do and promote good and avoid evil.

Natural law theory does not provide a relevant moral rule covering every situation, but it does offer guidance through general moral principles, some of which are thought to apply universally and absolutely (admitting no exceptions). Among these principles are absolutist prohibitions against directly killing the innocent, lying, and using contraceptives. In his list of acts considered wrong no matter what, Aquinas includes adultery, blasphemy, and sodomy.

Of course, moral principles or rules often conflict, demanding that we fulfill two or more incompatible duties. We may be forced, for example, to either tell a lie and save people's lives or tell the truth and cause their death—but we cannot do both. Some moral theories address these problems by saying that all duties are prima facie: When duties conflict, we must decide which ones override the others. Theories that posit absolute duties—natural law theory being a prime example—often do not have this option. How does the natural law tradition resolve such dilemmas? Among other resources, it uses the **doctrine of double effect**.

This principle, a cornerstone of Roman Catholic ethics, affirms that performing a bad action to bring about a good effect is never morally acceptable but that performing a good action may sometimes be acceptable even if it produces a bad effect. More precisely, the principle says it is always wrong to intentionally perform a bad action to produce a good effect, but doing a good action that results in a bad effect may be permissible if the bad effect is not intended although foreseen. In the former case, a bad thing is said to be directly intended; in the latter, a bad thing is not directly intended.

These requirements have been detailed in four "tests" that an action must pass to be judged morally permissible. We can express a traditional version of these tests like this:

1. The action itself must be morally permissible.
2. Causing a bad effect must not be used to obtain a good effect (the end does not justify the means).
3. Whatever the outcome of an action, the intention must be to cause only a good effect (the bad effect can be foreseen but never intended).
4. The bad effect of an action must not be greater in importance than the good effect.

Consider the application of these tests to euthanasia. Suppose an 80-year-old hopelessly ill patient is in continuous, unbearable pain and begs to be put out of her misery. Is it morally permissible to grant her request (either by giving a lethal injection or ending all ordinary life-sustaining measures)? If we apply the doctrine of double effect as just outlined, we must conclude that the answer is *no*: Euthanasia—either active or passive—is not a morally permissible option here. (In the Roman Catholic view, all forms of euthanasia are wrong, although it is permissible not to treat a hopelessly ill person for whom ordinary life-sustaining treatments are useless.) Failing even one of the tests would render an action impermissible, but in this case let us run through all four as a natural law theorist might:

1. Taking steps to terminate someone's life is a clear violation of test 1. Whatever its effects, the action of taking a life is in itself immoral, a violation of the cardinal duty to preserve innocent life.
2. Ending the woman's life to save her from terrible suffering is an instance of causing a bad effect (the woman's death) as a means of achieving a good effect (cessation of pain)—a failure of test 2.
3. The death of the woman is intended; it is not merely a tragic side effect of the attempt solely to ease her pain. So the action fails test 3.
4. Causing the death of an innocent person is a great evil that cannot be counterbalanced by the good of pain relief. So the action does not pass test 4.

The verdict in such a case would be different, however, if the patient's death were not intentionally caused but unintentionally brought about. Suppose, for example, that the physician sees that the woman is in agony and so gives her a large injection of morphine to minimize her suffering—knowing full well that the dose will also probably speed her death. In this scenario, the act of easing the woman's pain is itself morally permissible (test 1). Her death is not a means to achieve some greater good; the goal is to ease her suffering (test 2). Her death is not intended; the intention is to alleviate her pain, though the unintended (but foreseen) side effect is her hastened death (test 3). Finally, the good effect of an easier death seems more or less equivalent in importance to the bad effect of a hastened death. Therefore, unintentionally but knowingly bringing about the woman's death in this way is morally permissible.

We get similar results if we apply the double-effect principle in the traditional way to abortion. We find that as the intentional destruction of an innocent human life (so-called direct), abortion is always immoral (test 1). Moreover, it is wrong even (or especially) if it is performed to bring about some good result, such as saving the mother's life or preventing serious harm to her (tests 2 and 3). On the other hand, actions leading unintentionally to the death of a fetus (so-called indirect abortion) may be permissible in rare cases. Say a pregnant woman has an infectious disease that will kill her unless she gets injections of a powerful drug. But the drug will abort the fetus. According to the doctrine of double effect, receiving the injections may be morally permissible if the action itself is morally permissible, which it is (test 1); if the death of the fetus is not used to rescue the woman (test 2); if the injections are given with the intention of curing the woman's disease, not of inducing an abortion (test 3); and if the death of the fetus is balanced by the life of the woman (test 4).

Rawls' Contract Theory

In its broadest sense, **contractarianism** refers to moral theories based on the idea of a social contract, or agreement, among individuals for mutual advantage. The most influential contemporary form of contractarianism is that of philosopher John Rawls (1921–2002), who uses the notion of a social contract to generate and defend moral principles governing how members of a society should treat one another. He asks, in effect, by what principles should a just society structure itself to ensure a fair distribution of rights, duties, and advantages of social cooperation?

His answer is that the required principles—essentially principles of justice—are those that people would agree to under hypothetical conditions that ensure fair and unbiased choices. He believes that if the starting point for the social contract is fair—if the initial conditions and bargaining process for producing the principles are fair—then the principles themselves will be just and will define the essential makeup of a just society. As Rawls says,

> [The] guiding idea is that the principles of justice
> for the basic structure of society are the object
> of the original agreement. They are the principles
> that free and rational persons concerned to
> further their own interests would accept in
> an initial position of equality as defining the
> fundamental terms of their association. These

principles are to regulate all further agreements; they specify the kinds of social cooperation that can be entered into and the forms of government that can be established.[7]

At the hypothetical starting point—what Rawls calls the "original position"—a group of normal, self-interested, rational individuals come together to choose the principles that will determine their basic rights and duties and their share of society's benefits and burdens. But to ensure that their decisions are as fair and impartial as possible, they must meet behind a metaphorical "veil of ignorance." Behind the veil, no one knows his own social or economic status, class, race, sex, abilities, talents, level of intelligence, or psychological makeup. Since the participants are rational and self-interested but ignorant of their situation in society, they will not agree to principles that will put any particular group at a disadvantage because they might very well be members of that group. They will choose principles that are unbiased and nondiscriminatory. The assumption is that since the negotiating conditions in the original position are fair, the agreements reached will also be fair—the principles will be just.

Rawls contends that given the original position, the participants would agree to arrange their social relationships according to these fundamental principles:

1. Each person is to have an equal right to the most extensive total system of equal basic liberties compatible with a similar system of liberty for all.
2. Social and economic inequalities are to be arranged so that they are both:
   (a) to the greatest benefit of the least advantaged . . . and
   (b) attached to offices and positions open to all under conditions of fair equality of opportunity.[8]

The first principle—the equal liberty principle—says that everyone is entitled to the most freedom possible in exercising basic rights and duties (for example, the right to vote and hold office and freedom of speech, assembly, and thought). Each person should get a maximum degree of basic liberties but no more than anyone else. This principle takes precedence over all other considerations (including the second principle) so that basic liberties cannot be reduced or canceled just to improve economic well-being.

The second principle concerns social and economic goods such as income, wealth, opportunities, and positions of authority. Part (b) says that everyone is entitled to an equal chance to try to acquire these basic goods. No one is guaranteed an equal share of them, but opportunities to obtain these benefits must be open to all, regardless of social standing.

Rawls knows that social and economic inequalities will naturally arise in society. But as he asserts in part (a), they are not unjust if they work to everyone's benefit, especially to the benefit of the least well off in society. "[There] is no injustice," he says, "in the greater benefits earned by a few provided that the situation of persons not so fortunate is thereby improved."[9] For Rawls, such a policy is far more just than one in which some people are made to suffer for the greater good of others: "[I]t is not just that some should have less in order that others may prosper."

In Rawls' scheme, the demands of the first principle must be satisfied before satisfying the second, and the requirements of part (b) must be met before those of part (a). In any just distribution of benefits and burdens, then, the first priority is to ensure equal basic liberties for all concerned, then equality of opportunity, then the arrangement of any inequalities to the benefit of the least advantaged.

As a theory of distributive justice, Rawls' contractarianism seems to have significant implications for the allocation of society's health care resources. For example, one prominent line of argument goes like this: As Rawls claims, everyone is entitled to fair equality of opportunity, and adequate (basic) health care enables fair equality of opportunity (by ensuring "normal species functioning"). Therefore, everyone is entitled to adequate health care, which includes all appropriate measures for eliminating or compensating for the disadvantages of disease and impairment.[10] In such a system, there would be universal access to a basic level of health care, while more elaborate or elective services would be available to anyone who could afford them.

Another implication: Suppose that to provide a basic level of health care to everyone (and meet the equality-of-opportunity requirement), society would have to spend 90 percent of its health care resources. But say that in the current system, 50 percent of the resources are being spent on acute care for the elderly—that is, expensive measures to extend the lives of people who have already lived a long time. According to Rawlsian principles, is the current system of health care unjust?

Virtue Ethics

Most moral theories—including all those just discussed—are theories of obligation. They emphasize the rightness of actions and the duties of moral agents. Their main concern is knowing and doing what's right, and their chief guide to these aims is moral principles or directives. **Virtue ethics**, however, is a radically different kind of moral theory: It focuses on the development of virtuous character. According to virtue ethics, character is the key to the moral life, for it is from a virtuous character that moral conduct and values naturally arise. Virtues are ingrained dispositions to act by standards of excellence, so having the proper virtues leads as a matter of course to right actions properly motivated. The central task in morality, then, is not knowing and applying principles but being and becoming a good person, someone possessing the virtues that define moral excellence. In virtue ethics, someone determines right action not by consulting rules but by asking what a truly virtuous person would do or whether an action would accord with the relevant virtues.

Aristotle (384–322 B.C.E.) is the primary inspiration for contemporary versions of virtue ethics. For him, as for many modern virtue ethicists, the highest goal of humanity is the good life, or "human flourishing" (what Aristotle calls *eudaimonia*, or happiness), and developing virtues is the way to achieve such a rich and satisfying life. Thus virtues are both the traits that make us good persons and the dispositions that enable us to live good lives. The good life is the virtuous life.

Unlike many theories of obligation, virtue ethics asks us to do more than just observe minimal moral rules—it insists that we *aspire to moral excellence*, that we cultivate the virtues that will make us better persons. In this sense, virtue ethics is goal-directed, not rule-guided. The moral virtues—benevolence, honesty, loyalty, compassion, fairness, and the like—are ideals that we must ever strive to attain. (There are also nonmoral virtues such as patience, prudence, and reasonableness, which need not concern us here.) By the lights of both Aristotle and modern virtue ethicists, character is not static. We can become more virtuous by reflecting on our lives and those of others, practicing virtuous behavior, or imitating moral exemplars such as Gandhi, Buddha, Jesus, Muhammad, and Socrates. We can—and should—be better than we are.

To the virtue ethicist, possessing the right virtues means having the proper motivations that naturally accompany those virtues. To act morally, we must act from virtue, and acting from virtue means acting with the appropriate motives. It is not enough to do right; we must do right for the right motivating reasons. If we save a drowning friend, we should do so out of genuine feelings of compassion, kindness, or loyalty—not because of the prodding of moral rules or social expectations. In contrast, some moral theories (notably Kant's) maintain that acting morally is solely a matter of acting for duty's sake—performing an action simply because duty requires it. Virtuous motives are irrelevant; we act morally if we do our duty regardless of our motivations. But this notion seems to many to offer a barren picture of the moral life. Surely, they say, motivations for acting are often relevant to our evaluations of

people's character and actions. The friend we saved from drowning would probably be appalled if we declared that we saved her out of duty even though we did not really care whether she lived or died. Many moral philosophers agree that motivations are indeed important considerations in moral judgments, and they have incorporated virtues into their theories of obligation.

Virtue ethics fits well with the emphasis on virtues that has always been part of the healing arts. Physicians and nurses are expected to possess particular virtues, including compassion, trustworthiness, justice, and honesty. They are expected to be more than just technically skilled and knowledgeable and to do more than merely follow the rules of conduct or procedure. They are obliged to do right by their patients, and this obligation is most likely met through the cultivation and possession of virtues.

The virtue ethics approach to bioethical issues is distinctive. On abortion, for example, the virtue ethicist might argue that a woman's decision to have an abortion should be judged by the virtues (or lack thereof) that she draws on in deciding what to do. If she decides to have an abortion just because she is afraid of the responsibilities of parenthood, she shows cowardice. If she wants to go through with an abortion merely because pregnancy would disrupt her vacation plans, she shows self-centeredness and callousness. In neither case is the virtue ethicist likely to call the woman's decision virtuous.[11]

The Ethics of Care

The ethics of care is a distinctive moral perspective that arose out of feminist concerns and grew to challenge core elements of most other moral theories. Generally those theories emphasize abstract principles, general duties, individual rights, impartial judgments, and deliberative reasoning. But the ethics of care shifts the focus to the unique demands of specific situations and to the virtues and feelings that are central to close personal relationships—empathy, compassion, love, sympathy, and fidelity. The heart of the moral life is feeling for and caring for those with

---

IN DEPTH
CAN VIRTUE BE TAUGHT?

Aristotle believes that moral virtues are not the sort of thing you can learn by merely studying them, as you would if you wanted to learn calculus. He insists that moral virtues can only be learned through practice, by *living* the virtues. As he says,

[M]oral virtue comes about as a result of habit. . . . From this it is also plain that none of the moral virtues arises in us by nature. . . . [B]ut the virtues we get by first exercising them, as also happens in the case of the arts as well. For the things we have to learn before we can do them, we learn by doing them, e.g., men become builders by building and lyreplayers by playing the lyre; so too we become just by doing just acts, temperate by doing temperate acts, brave by doing brave acts.[12]

---

whom you have a special, intimate connection—an approach that especially resonates with physicians and nurses.

Early on, the ethics of care drew inspiration from the notion that men and women have dramatically different styles of moral decision-making, with men seizing on principles, duties, and rights, and women homing in on personal relationships, caring, and empathy. This difference was highlighted in research done by psychologist Carol Gilligan and published in her 1982 book *In a Different Voice*.[13] Typically men recognize an ethic of justice and rights, she says, and women are guided by an ethic of compassion and care. In her view the latter is as legitimate as the former, and both have their place in ethics.

Other research has suggested that the differences between men and women in styles of moral thinking may not be as great as Gilligan suggests. But the credibility of the empirical claim does not affect the larger insight that the research seemed to some writers to suggest: Caring is an essential part of morality, and the most influential theories have not fully taken it into account.

These points get support along several lines. First, virtue ethics reminds us that virtues are part of the moral life. If caring is viewed as a virtue—in the form of compassion, empathy, or kindness—then caring too must be an element of morality. A moral theory then would be deficient if it made no room for care.

Moreover many argue that unlike the ethics of care, most moral theories push the principle of

impartiality too far. Recall that impartiality in morality requires us to consider everyone as equal, counting everyone's interests the same. The principle applies widely, especially in matters of public justice, but less so in personal relationships of love, family, friendship, and the like. We seem to have special obligations (partiality) to close friends, family members, and others we care for, duties that we do not have to strangers or to universal humanity. As some philosophers explain it,

> The care perspective is especially meaningful for roles such as parent, friend, physician, and nurse, in which contextual response, attentiveness to subtle clues, and deepening special relationships are likely to be more important morally than impartial treatment.[14]
>
> May I devote my time and resources to caring for my own friends and family, even if this means ignoring the needs of other people whom I could also help? From an impartial point of view, our duty is to promote the interests of everyone alike. But few of us accept that view. The ethics of care confirms the priority that we naturally give to our family and friends, and so it seems a more plausible moral conception.[15]

Most moral theories emphasize duties and downplay the role of emotions, attitudes, and motivations. Kant, for example, would have us do our duty for duty's sake, whatever our feelings. For him, to be a morally good parent, we need only act from duty. But taking care of our children as a matter of moral obligation alone seems an empty exercise. Surely being a morally good parent also involves having feelings of love and attitudes of caring. The ethics of care eagerly takes these emotional elements into account.

Many philosophers, including several writing from a feminist perspective, have lodged such criticisms against the most influential moral theories while suggesting that a mature morality should accommodate both an ethic of obligation and an ethic of care. Annette Baier, for example, has taken this approach:

> It is clear, I think, that the best moral theory has to be a cooperative product of women and men, has to harmonize justice and care. The morality it theorizes about is after all for all persons, for men and for women, and will need their combined insights. As Gilligan said, what we need now is a "marriage" of the old male and the newly articulated female insights.[16]

For many nurses, the ethics of care seems like a fitting, natural approach to morality in nursing practice. After all, caring has always been an essential part of what nurses do and how they think about their jobs. When the focus of concern is, say, a very sick patient and her family, traditional moral theories would have those involved attend to relevant moral principles, strive for an impartial stance, emphasize individual rights, and engage in impassive moral deliberations. But the ethics of care insists that medical care providers pay more attention to the specific needs of the patient and her family, be aware of the special relationships they have with each other, understand the attitudes and feelings at work among them, and act with compassion, sympathy, and respect.

Feminist Ethics

Feminist ethics is an approach to morality aimed at advancing women's interests and correcting injustices inflicted on women through social oppression and inequality. It is defined by a distinctive focus on these issues, rather than by a set of doctrines or common ideology among feminists, many of whom may disagree on the nature of feminist ethics or on particular moral issues. A variety of divergent perspectives have been identified as examples of feminist ethics, including the ethics of care.

Feminist ethics generally downplays the role of moral principles and traditional ethical concepts, insisting instead that moral reflection must take into account the social realities—the relevant social practices, relationships, institutions, and power arrangements. Many feminists think that the familiar principles of Western ethics—autonomy, utility, freedom, equality, and so forth—are too broad and abstract to help us make moral judgments about specific persons who are enmeshed in concrete social situations. It is not enough, for example, to respect a woman's decision to have an abortion if she is too poor to have one, or if her culture is so oppressive (or oppressed) as to make abortion impossible to obtain, or if social conditioning leads her to believe that she has no choice or that her views don't count. Theoretical autonomy does not mean much if it is so thoroughly undermined in reality.

Many theorists in feminist ethics also reject the traditional concept of the moral agent. Jan Crosthwaite says that the old notion is that of "abstract individuals as fundamentally autonomous agents, aware of their own preferences and values, and motivated by rational self-interest (though not necessarily selfish)."[17] But, she says, many feminists

> present a richer conception of persons as historically and culturally located, socially related and essentially embodied. Individuals are located in and formed by specific relationships (chosen and unchosen) and ties of affection and responsibility. . . . Such a conception of socially embedded selves refocuses thinking about autonomy, shifting the emphasis from independent self-determination towards ideals of integrity within relatedness. . . . Respecting autonomy becomes less a matter of protecting individuals from "coercive" influences than one of positive empowerment, recognizing people's interdependence and supporting individuals' development of their own understanding of their situation and options.[18]

Though all adherents of feminist ethics support liberation and equality for women, they disagree on how these values apply to specific moral issues. Most support unimpeded access to abortion, but some do not. As later chapters show, opinions among feminists also diverge on surrogacy and reproductive technologies such as in vitro fertilization.

Casuistry

Casuistry is a method of moral reasoning that emphasizes cases and analogy rather than universal principles and theories from which moral judgments are supposed to be deduced. Casuists say reasonable moral judgments are arrived at not by applying theories, rights, and rules, but by paying careful attention to specific cases and circumstances. In casuistry, judgments about new cases are made by analogy with similar or paradigm cases; as in law, casuistry operates by consulting precedent. Casuists point out that problems in moral reasoning are especially likely when theories or principles are strictly applied without regard to the relevant details of cases. They also note that we are often far more confident of specific moral judgments than we are of decisions based on general principles.

Moral philosophers, however, have voiced several concerns about the method. For one thing, it seems that casuistry is dependent on rules or principles just as moral theories are. Consider this criticism:

> Casuists sometimes write as if paradigm cases speak for themselves or inform moral judgment by their facts alone, an implausible thesis. For the casuist to move constructively from case to case, a recognized and morally relevant norm must connect the cases. The norm is not part of the facts or narrative of the cases involved; it is a way of interpreting, evaluating, and linking cases. All analogical reasoning in casuistry requires a connecting norm to indicate that one sequence of events is morally like or unlike another sequence in relevant respects.[19]

Some critics also question the ability of casuistry to justify a moral decision or the selection of a paradigm case. Casuists hold that justification comes from a society's traditions, values, or conventions. But it seems that a solid set of principles or standards would be necessary to counteract the bias, arbitrariness, or vagueness of these influences.

Casuistry has made valuable contributions to our understanding and use of moral reasoning. But in its purest form it seems problematic. More recent scholarship, however, has demonstrated ways that casuistry can take into account some moral principles or norms.

CRITERIA FOR JUDGING MORAL THEORIES

As you can see, as explanations of what makes actions right or character good, moral theories can differ dramatically in both content and quality. In their own fashion, they try to identify the true determinants of rightness or goodness, and they vary in how close they seem to get to the mark. Most moral philosophers would readily agree: Some moral theories are better than others, and a vital task in ethics is to try to tell which is which. Moral theories can be useful and valuable to us only if there are criteria for judging their worth—and fortunately there are such standards.

In several ways, moral theories are analogous to scientific theories. Scientists devise theories to explain the causes of events. The germ theory is offered to explain the cause and spread of infectious diseases. The Big Bang theory is used to explain the structure and expansion of the universe. The "greenhouse effect" is put forth to explain climate change. For each phenomenon to be explained, scientists usually have several possible theories to consider, and the challenge is to determine which one is best (and is therefore most likely to be correct). The superior theory is the one that fares best when judged by generally accepted yardsticks known as the *scientific criteria of adequacy*. One criterion often invoked is *fruitfulness*—whether the theory makes successful predictions of previously unknown phenomena. All things being equal, a theory that makes successful predictions of novel phenomena is more likely to be true than one that does not. Another important criterion is *conservatism*—how well a theory fits with established facts, with what scientists already know. All things being equal, a theory that conflicts with what scientists already have good reasons to believe is less likely to be true than a theory that has no such conflicts. Of course, an unconservative theory can turn out to be correct, and a conservative theory wrong, but the odds are against this outcome. Analogously, moral theories are meant to explain what makes an action right or a person good, and to try to determine which moral theory is most likely correct, we apply conceptual yardsticks—the *moral criteria of adequacy*. Any plausible moral theory must measure up to these critical standards.

An important criterion of adequacy for moral theories is *Criterion I: consistency with our considered moral judgments*. Any plausible scientific theory must be consistent with the data that the theory is supposed to explain; there should be no conflicts between the theory and the relevant facts. A theory put forth to explain planetary motion, for example, must account for the relevant data—scientific observations of the movements of the planets and related objects. Likewise, a moral theory must also be consistent with the data it is supposed to explain: our considered moral judgments, what some call our moral common sense. We arrive at these judgments after careful deliberation that is as free of bias, self-interest, and other distorting influences as possible. Moral philosophers grant these judgments considerable respect and try to take them into account in their moral theorizing. As we have seen, these judgments are fallible, and they are often revised under pressure from trustworthy principles or theories. But we are entitled to trust them unless we have good reason to doubt them. Therefore, any moral theory that is seriously inconsistent with our considered judgments must

be regarded as badly flawed, perhaps fatally so, and in need of radical revision. Our considered judgments, for example, tell us that slavery, murder, rape, and genocide are wrong. A moral theory that implies otherwise fails this criterion and is a candidate for rejection.

In applying this standard, we must keep in mind that in both science and ethics, there is tension between theory and data. A good theory explains the data, which in turn influence the shape of the theory. Particularly strong data can compel scientists to alter a theory to account for the information, but a good theory can also give scientists reasons to question or reject particular data. In the same way, there is a kind of give and take between a moral theory and the relevant data. Our considered moral judgments may give us good reasons for altering or even rejecting our moral theory. But if our moral theory is coherent and well supported, it may oblige us to rethink or reject our considered judgments. In both science and ethics, the goal is to ensure that the fit between theory and data is as tight as possible. The fit is acceptably close when no further changes in the theory or the data are necessary—when there is a kind of balance between the two that moral philosophers call "reflective equilibrium."

Another test of adequacy is *Criterion II: consistency with the facts of the moral life*. In science, good theories are consistent with scientific background knowledge, with what scientists already have good reasons to believe. They are, as mentioned earlier, conservative. This background knowledge includes other well-founded theories, highly reliable findings, and scientific (natural) laws. Moral theories should also be consistent with background knowledge—the *moral* background knowledge, the basic, inescapable experiences of the moral life. These experiences include making moral judgments, disagreeing with others on moral issues, being mistaken in our moral beliefs, and giving reasons for accepting moral beliefs. That we do in fact experience these things from time to time is a matter of moral common sense—seemingly

> ## REVIEW: Evaluating Moral Theories: Criteria of Adequacy
>
> Criterion I: consistency with our considered moral judgments
> Criterion II: consistency with the facts of the moral life
> Criterion III: resourcefulness in moral problem-solving

obvious facts of the moral life. Thus, any moral theory that is inconsistent with these aspects of the moral life is deeply problematic. It is possible that we are deluded about the moral life—that we, for example, merely think we are disagreeing with others on moral issues but are actually just venting our feelings. But our experience gives us good grounds for taking the commonsense view until we are given good reasons to believe otherwise.

Finally, we have *Criterion III: resourcefulness in moral problem-solving*. If a scientific theory helps scientists answer questions, solve problems, and control facets of the natural world, it demonstrates both its plausibility and usefulness. All things being equal, such a resourceful theory is better than one that has none of these advantages. Much the same is true for moral theories. A resourceful moral theory helps us solve moral problems. It can help us identify morally relevant aspects of conduct, judge the rightness of actions, resolve conflicts among moral principles and judgments, test and correct our moral intuitions, and understand the underlying point of morality itself. Any moral theory that lacks problem-solving resourcefulness is neither useful nor credible.

APPLYING THE CRITERIA

In this section, we apply the three moral criteria of adequacy to two theories we discussed earlier (one consequentialist, the other deontological). As we do, keep in mind that evaluating moral theories using these yardsticks is not a rote process. There is no standard procedure for applying the criteria to a theory and no set of instructions for assigning conceptual weight to each criterion

as we judge a theory's worth. But the criteria do help us make broad judgments on rational grounds about a theory's strengths and weaknesses. We must use them as guides, relying on our best judgment in applying them, just as scientists must use their own educated judgment in wielding their kind of criteria of adequacy. In neither case is there a neat algorithm for theory assessment, but nonetheless in both arenas the process is objective, reasonable, and essential.

We should also remember that no moral theory is perfect, and none is likely to get the highest marks on every test. But there is much to learn even from flawed theories. If we look closely, we can see that each of the most influential theories of past centuries, even with its faults apparent, seems to have grasped at least a modest, gleaming piece of the truth about the moral life.

Utilitarianism

For simplicity's sake, let us try to apply the criteria to classic act-utilitarianism, the view that right actions are those that result in the greatest overall happiness for everyone involved. First, note that the theory seems to pass the test suggested by Criterion II (consistency with the facts of the moral life). Utilitarianism assumes that we can indeed make moral judgments, have moral disagreements, be mistaken in our moral beliefs, and provide supporting reasons for our moral judgments.

The theory, however, has been accused of a lack of usefulness—failing Criterion III (resourcefulness in moral problem-solving). The usual charge is that utilitarianism is a poor guide to the moral life because the theory demands too much of us and blurs the distinction between obligatory and supererogatory actions. Utilitarianism says that we should always try to maximize happiness for everyone considered, to do our utmost to increase overall utility. But some say this requirement would lead us to extreme beneficence—to, for example, give away most of our possessions, spend most of our time in charity work, and deem mandatory many acts that we would normally consider above and beyond the call of duty. Some defenders of the theory have suggested that it can be modified easily to ease the demands that it places on us. A few utilitarians have insisted that, contrary to the popular view, the commonsense distinction between obligatory and supererogatory acts is mistaken and that morality does demand the kind of sacrifice that utilitarianism implies.

The most serious accusation against classic utilitarianism is that it flies in the face of our considered moral judgments (Criterion I), especially concerning issues of justice and rights. Consider the case of a medical researcher trying to develop a cure for Alzheimer's disease. To devise this cure that would save countless lives, she needs only to conduct a single, secret experiment in which she gives a lethal drug to 10 early-stage Alzheimer's patients (without their knowledge) and does a postmortem examination on their brains. By increasing the unhappiness of 10 people (and depriving them of all possible happiness in the future), she can maximize happiness for thousands. Should she conduct the experiment? According to classic utilitarianism, if her actions would go undetected and have no additional unhappy effects, the answer is yes. The experiment would be justified by the enormous amount of net happiness it would generate. But the utilitarian verdict seems to conflict strongly with our considered judgments about justice. Taking the lives of a few people to benefit many others appears unjust, regardless of the good consequences that would flow from the deed. Critics claim that cases like this show that utilitarianism is a seriously inadequate theory.

Now consider the case of a competent patient with a serious illness who refuses medical treatment on religious grounds. He knows that he would suffer much less pain and have a longer and happier life if he were treated, but he still objects. But his physician wants to maximize the happiness and well-being of all her patients, so she surreptitiously treats the patient anyway without his consent. (Let us assume that no additional legal, professional, or psychological consequences ensue.) Does the physician do right? The utilitarian seems obliged to say yes. But our commonsense judgment would likely be that the physician violated her patient's autonomy—specifically, his right of self-determination.

Some utilitarians have replied to such Criterion I criticisms by saying that scenarios like those just presented are unrealistic and misleading. In the real world, they say, actions that seem to conflict with our moral intuitions almost always produce such bad consequences that the actions cannot be justified even on utilitarian grounds. Once *all* the possible consequences are taken into account, it becomes clear that the proposed actions do not maximize happiness and that commonsense morality and utilitarianism coincide. In real life, for example, the deeds of the researcher and the physician would almost certainly be exposed, resulting in a great deal of unhappiness for all concerned. Critics respond to the utilitarian by admitting that many times the judgments of commonsense morality and utilitarianism do in fact coincide when all the facts are known—but not always. Even the utilitarian must admit that there could be cases in which actions that maximize utility do clash with our considered moral judgments, and this possibility raises doubts about the utilitarian standard.

Kant's Theory

Like utilitarianism, Kant's theory seems generally consistent with the basic facts of the moral life (Criterion II), but many philosophers argue that it is not consistent with moral common sense (Criterion I). A major cause of the problem, they say, is Kant's insistence that we have absolute (or "perfect") duties—obligations that must be honored without exception. Thus in Kantian ethics, we have an absolute duty not to lie or to break a promise or to kill the innocent, come what may. Imagine that a band of killers wants to murder an innocent man who has taken refuge in your house, and the killers come to your door and ask you point blank if he is in your house. To say no is to lie; to answer truthfully is to guarantee the man's death. What should you do? In a case like this, says Kant, you must *do your duty*—you must tell the truth though murder is the result and a lie would save a life. But in this case such devotion to moral absolutes seems completely askew, for saving an innocent life seems far more important morally than blindly obeying a rule. Our considered judgments suggest that sometimes the consequences of our actions do matter more than adherence to the letter of the law, even if the law is generally worthy of our respect and obedience.

Some have thought that Kant's theory can yield implausible results for another reason. Recall that the first formulation of the categorical imperative says that an action is permissible if persons could consistently act on the relevant maxim, and we would be willing to have them do so. This requirement seems to make sense if the maxim in question is something like "Do not kill the innocent" or "Treat equals equally." But what if the maxim is "Enslave all Christians" or "Kill all Ethiopians"? We could—without contradiction—will either one of these precepts to become a universal law. And if we were so inclined, we could be willing for everyone to act accordingly, even if we ourselves were Christians or Ethiopians. So by Kantian lights, these actions could very well be morally permissible, and their permissibility would depend on whether someone was willing to have them apply universally. Critics conclude that because the first formulation of the categorical imperative seems to sanction such obviously immoral acts, the theory is deeply flawed. Defenders of Kant's theory, on the other hand, view the problems as repairable and have proposed revisions.

This apparent arbitrariness in the first formulation can significantly lessen the theory's usefulness (Criterion III). The categorical imperative is supposed to help us discern moral directives that are rational, universal, and

objective. But if it is subjective in the way just described, its helpfulness as a guide for living morally is dubious. Defenders of Kant's theory, however, believe there are remedies for this difficulty. Some argue, for example, that the problem disappears if the second formulation is viewed as a supplement to the first, rather than as two independent principles.

KEY TERMS
act-utilitarianism
consequentialist theory
contractarianism
deontological (or nonconsequentialist) theory
doctrine of double effect
moral theory
natural law theory
rule-utilitarianism
utilitarianism
virtue ethics

SUMMARY
A moral theory explains why an action is right or wrong or why a person or a person's character is good or bad. Making, using, or assessing moral theories is a normal, pervasive feature of the moral life.

Consequentialist moral theories assume that the rightness of actions depends on their consequences or results. Deontological theories say that the rightness of actions is determined partly or wholly by their intrinsic nature. The leading consequentialist theory is utilitarianism, the view that right actions are those that result in the most beneficial balance of good over bad consequences for everyone involved. The theory comes in two main types. Act-utilitarianism is the idea that the rightness of actions depends on the relative good produced by individual actions. Rule-utilitarianism says a right action is one that conforms to a rule that, if followed consistently, would create for everyone involved the most beneficial balance of good over bad. Kantian ethics is opposed to consequentialist theories, holding that morality consists of following a rational and universally applicable moral rule and doing so solely out of a sense of duty. An action is right only if it conforms to such a rule, and we are morally praiseworthy only if we perform it for duty's sake alone. Natural law theory is a centuries-old view of ethics that maintains that right actions are those conforming to moral standards discerned in nature through human reason. Rawls' theory is a form of contractarianism, which means it is based on the idea of a social contract, or agreement, among individuals for mutual advantage. He argues for a set of moral principles that he believes would be arrived at through a fair, but hypothetical, bargaining process. Virtue ethics focuses on the development of virtuous character. The central task in morality is not knowing and applying principles but being and becoming a good person, someone possessing the virtues that define moral excellence. The ethics of care emphasizes the virtues and feelings that are central to close personal relationships.

The worth of moral theories can be assessed through the application of the moral criteria of adequacy. Criterion I is consistency with our considered moral judgments; Criterion II, consistency with the facts of the moral life; and Criterion III, resourcefulness in moral problem-solving.

FURTHER READING

Thomas Aquinas, *Summa Theologica*, in *Basic Writings of St. Thomas Aquinas*, trans. A. C. Pegis (New York: Random House, 1945), volume II, 3–46.

Jeremy Bentham, "Of the Principle of Utility," in *An Introduction to the Principles of Morals and Legislation* (Oxford: Clarendon Press, 1879), 1–7.

Baruch A. Brody, *Moral Theory and Moral Judgments in Medical Ethics* (Dordrecht: Kluwer, 1988).

Curtis Brown, "Ethical Theories Compared," http://www.trinity.edu/cbrown/intro/ethical_theories.html (19 October 2015).

Stephen Buckle, "Natural Law," in *A Companion to Ethics*, ed. Peter Singer (Cambridge, UK: Blackwell, 1993), 161–74.

Steven M. Cahn and Joram G. Haber, *Twentieth Century Ethical Theory* (Upper Saddle River, NJ: Prentice-Hall, 1995).

Robert Cavalier, *Online Guide to Ethics and Moral Philosophy*, http://caae.phil.cmu.edu/Cavalier/80130/part2/sect9.html (19 October 2015).

Fred Feldman, "Act Utilitarianism: Pro and Con," in *Introductory Ethics* (Englewood Cliffs, NJ: Prentice-Hall, 1978), 30–60.

John Finnis, *Natural Law and Natural Rights* (New York: Oxford University Press, 1980).

William K. Frankena, *Ethics*, 2nd ed. (Englewood Cliffs, NJ: Prentice-Hall, 1973).

C. E. Harris, *Applying Moral Theories* (Belmont, CA: Wadsworth, 1997).

Dale Jamieson, "Method and Moral Theory," in *A Companion to Ethics*, ed. Peter Singer (Cambridge, UK: Blackwell, 1993), 476–87.

Rob Lawlor, "Moral Theories in Teaching Applied Ethics," *Journal of Medical Ethics*, June 2007, vol. 33, no. 6, http://www.ncbi.nlm.nih.gov/pmc/articles/PMC2598269/ (19 October 2015).

Mark Murphy, "The Natural Law Tradition in Ethics," in *The Stanford Encyclopedia of Philosophy* (Winter 2002 ed.), ed. Edward N. Zalta, http://plato.stanford.edu/archives/win2002/entries/natural-law-ethics/.

Kai Nielsen, "A Defense of Utilitarianism," *Ethics* 82 (1972): 113–24.

Kai Nielsen, *Ethics Without God* (Buffalo, NY: Prometheus, 1973).

Robert Nozick, "The Experience Machine," in *Anarchy, State and Utopia* (New York: Basic Books, 1974).

Onora O'Neill, "Kantian Ethics," in *A Companion to Ethics*, ed. Peter Singer, (Cambridge, UK: Blackwell, 1993), 175–85.

Louis P. Pojman and Lewis Vaughn, eds., *The Moral Life*, 3rd ed. (New York: Oxford University Press, 2007).

James Rachels, *The Elements of Moral Philosophy*, 4th ed. (New York: McGraw-Hill, 2003).

James Rachels, ed., *Ethical Theory 2: Theories About How We Should Live* (Oxford: Oxford University Press, 1998).

John Rawls, "Some Remarks About Moral Theory," in *A Theory of Justice* (Cambridge, MA: Harvard University Press, 1999), 40–46.

J. J. C. Smart, "Extreme and Restricted Utilitarianism," in *Essays Metaphysical and Moral* (Oxford: Blackwell, 1987).

Bonnie Steinbock, ed., *The Oxford Handbook of Bioethics* (Oxford: Oxford University Press, 2007).

Paul Taylor, *Principles of Ethics* (Encino, CA: Dickenson, 1975).

Lewis Vaughn, *Doing Ethics: Moral Reasoning and Contemporary Issues* (New York: W.W. Norton, 2008).

Bernard Williams, "A Critique of Utilitarianism," in *Utilitarianism: For and Against*, ed. J. J. C. Smart and Bernard Williams (New York: Cambridge University Press, 1973), 82–117.

Scott D. Wilson, "Ethics," *The Internet Encyclopedia of Philosophy*, http://www.iep.utm.edu/ (19 October 2015).

NOTES

1. John Stuart Mill, "What Utilitarianism Is," in *Utilitarianism*, 7th ed. (London: Longmans, Green, and Co., 1879), chap. 2.
2. *Ibid.*
3. *Ibid.*
4. Mill, *Utilitarianism,* chap. II.
5. Immanuel Kant, *Groundwork of the Metaphysics of Morals,* trans. H. J. Paton (New York: Harper & Row, 1964), 88.
6. *Ibid.,* 96.
7. John Rawls, *A Theory of Justice,* rev. ed. (Cambridge, MA: Harvard University Press, 1999), 10.
8. *Ibid.,* 266.
9. *Ibid.,* 13.
10. Norman Daniels, *Just Health Care* (New York: Cambridge University Press, 1985), 34–58.
11. Examples from Rosalind Hursthouse, *Beginning Lives* (Oxford: Blackwell, 1987), cited in Justin Oakley, "A Virtue Ethics Approach," in *A Companion to Bioethics* (Oxford: Blackwell, 2001), 86–97.
12. Aristotle, *Nicomachean Ethics,* trans. W. D. Ross, revised by J. L. Ackrill and J. O. Urmson (Oxford: Oxford University Press, 1925, 1980), book II, chap. 1.
13. Carol Gilligan, *In a Different Voice: Psychological Theory and Women's Development* (Cambridge, MA: Harvard University Press, 1982).
14. Tom L. Beauchamp and James F. Childress, *Principles of Biomedical Ethics,* 5th ed. (New York: Oxford University Press, 2001), 372.
15. James Rachels, *The Elements of Moral Philosophy* (New York: McGraw-Hill, 2003), 168.
16. Annette C. Baier, "The Need for More Than Justice," *Canadian Journal of Philosophy,* suppl. vol. 13 (1988):56.
17. Jan Crosthwaite, "Gender and Bioethics," in *A Companion to Bioethics,* ed. Helga Kuhse and Peter Singer (Malden, MA: Blackwell, 2001), 32–40.
18. *Ibid.,* 37.
19. Tom L. Beauchamp and James F. Childress, *Principles of Biomedical Ethics* (New York: Oxford University Press, 2013), 401.

READINGS

Utilitarianism

JOHN STUART MILL

English philosopher John Stuart Mill argues for his view of ethics in *Utilitarianism* (1861), from which this excerpt is taken. He explains that utilitarians judge the morality of conduct by a single standard, the *principle of utility*: Right actions are those that result in greater overall well-being (or *utility*) for the people involved than any other possible actions. We are duty bound to maximize the utility of everyone affected, regardless of the contrary urgings of moral rules or unbending moral principles.

...The creed which accepts as the foundation of morals, Utility, or the Greatest Happiness Principle, holds that actions are right in proportion as they tend to promote happiness, wrong as they tend to produce the reverse of happiness. By happiness is intended pleasure, and the absence of pain; by unhappiness, pain, and the privation of pleasure. To give a clear view of the moral standard set up by the theory, much more requires to be said; in particular, what things it includes in the ideas of pain and pleasure; and to what extent this is left an open

From *Utilitarianism*, 7th ed. (London: Longmans, Green, and Co., 1879).

question. But these supplementary explanations do not affect the theory of life on which this theory of morality is grounded—namely, that pleasure, and freedom from pain, are the only things desirable as ends; and that all desirable things (which are as numerous in the utilitarian as in any other scheme) are desirable either for the pleasure inherent in themselves, or as means to the promotion of pleasure and the prevention of pain.

Now, such a theory of life excites in many minds, and among them in some of the most estimable in feeling and purpose, inveterate dislike. To suppose that life has (as they express it) no higher end than pleasure—no better and nobler object of desire and pursuit—they designate as utterly mean and groveling; as a doctrine worthy only of swine, to whom the followers of Epicurus were, at a very early period, contemptuously likened; and modern holders of the doctrine are occasionally made the subject of equally polite comparisons by its German, French, and English assailants.

When thus attacked, the Epicureans have always answered, that it is not they, but their accusers, who represent human nature in a degrading light; since the accusation supposes human beings to be capable of no pleasures except those of which swine are capable. If this supposition were true, the charge could not be gainsaid, but would then be no longer an imputation; for if the sources of pleasure were precisely the same to human beings and to swine, the rule of life which is good enough for the one would be good enough for the other. The comparison of the Epicurean life to that of beasts is felt as degrading, precisely because a beast's pleasures do not satisfy a human being's conceptions of happiness. Human beings have faculties more elevated than the animal appetites, and when once made conscious of them, do not regard anything as happiness which does not include their gratification. I do not, indeed, consider the Epicureans to have been by any means faultless in drawing out their scheme of consequences from the utilitarian principle. To do this in any sufficient manner, many Stoic, as well as Christian elements require to be included. But there is no known Epicurean theory of life which does not assign to the pleasures of the intellect; of the feelings and imagination, and of the moral sentiments, a much higher value as

pleasures than to those of mere sensation. It must be admitted, however, that utilitarian writers in general have placed the superiority of mental over bodily pleasures chiefly in the greater permanency, safety, uncostliness, &c., of the former—that is, in their circumstantial advantages rather than in their intrinsic nature. And on all these points utilitarians have fully proved their case; but they might have taken the other, and, as it may be called, higher ground, with entire consistency. It is quite compatible with the principle of utility to recognise the fact, that some *kinds* of pleasure are more desirable and more valuable than others. It would be absurd that while, in estimating all other things, quality is considered as well as quantity, the estimation of pleasures should be supposed to depend on quantity alone.

If I am asked, what I mean by difference of quality in pleasures, or what makes one pleasure more valuable that another, merely as a pleasure, except its being greater in amount, there is but one possible answer. Of two pleasures, if there be one to which all or almost all who have experience of both give a decided preference, irrespective of any feeling of moral obligation to prefer it, that is the more desirable pleasure. If one of the two is, by those who are competently acquainted with both, placed so far above the other that they prefer it, even though knowing it to be attended with a greater amount of discontent, and would not resign it for any quantity of the other pleasure which their nature is capable of, we are justified in ascribing to the preferred enjoyment a superiority in quality, so far outweighing quantity as to render it, in comparison, of small account.

Now it is an unquestionable fact that those who are equally acquainted with, and equally capable of appreciating and enjoying, both, do give a most marked preference to the manner of existence which employs their higher faculties. Few human creatures would consent to be changed into any of the lower animals, for a promise of the fullest allowance of a beast's pleasures; no intelligent human being would consent to be a fool, no instructed person would be an ignoramus, no person of feeling and conscience would be selfish and base, even though they should be persuaded that the fool, the dunce, or the rascal is better satisfied with his lot than they are with theirs. They would not resign what they possess more than he, for the most complete satisfaction of all the desires which they have in common with him. If they ever fancy they would, it is only in cases of unhappiness so extreme, that to escape from it they would exchange their lot for almost any other, however undesirable in their own eyes. A being of higher faculties requires more to make him happy, is capable probably of more acute suffering, and is certainly accessible to it at more points, than one of an inferior type; but in spite of these liabilities, he can never really wish to sink into what he feels to be a lower grade of existence. We may give what explanation we please of this unwillingness; we may attribute it to pride, a name which is given indiscriminately to some of the most and to some of the least estimable feelings of which mankind are capable; we may refer it to the love of liberty and personal independence, an appeal to which was with the Stoics one of the most effective means for the inculcation of it; to the love of power, or to the love of excitement, both of which do really enter into and contribute to it: but its most appropriate appellation is a sense of dignity, which all human beings possess in one form or other, and in some, though by no means in exact, proportion to their higher faculties, and which is so essential a part of the happiness of those in whom it is strong, that nothing which conflicts with it could be, otherwise than momentarily, an object of desire to them. Whoever supposes that this preference takes place at a sacrifice of happiness—that the superior being, in anything like equal circumstances, is not happier than the inferior—confounds the two very different ideas, of happiness, and content. It is indisputable that the being whose capacities of enjoyment are low, has the greatest chance of having them fully satisfied; and a highly-endowed being will always feel that any happiness which he can look for, as the world is constituted, is imperfect. But he can learn to bear its imperfections, if they are at all bearable; and they will not make him envy the being who is indeed unconscious of the imperfections, but only because he feels not at all the good which those imperfections qualify. It is better to be a human being dissatisfied than a pig satisfied; better to be Socrates dissatisfied than a fool satisfied. And if the fool, or

the pig, is of a different opinion, it is because they only know their own side of the question. The other party to the comparison knows both sides.

It may be objected, that many who are capable of the higher pleasures, occasionally, under the influence of temptation, postpone them to the lower. But this is quite compatible with a full appreciation of the intrinsic superiority of the higher. Men often, from infirmity of character, make their election for the nearer good, though they know it to be the less valuable; and this no less when the choice is between two bodily pleasures, than when it is between bodily and mental. They pursue sensual indulgences to the injury of health, though perfectly aware that health is the greater good. It may be further objected, that many who begin with youthful enthusiasm for everything noble, as they advance in years sink into indolence and selfishness. But I do not believe that those who undergo this very common change, voluntarily choose the lower description of pleasures in preference to the higher. I believe that before they devote themselves exclusively to the one, they have already become incapable of the other. Capacity for the nobler feelings is in most natures a very tender plant, easily killed, not only by hostile influences, but by mere want of sustenance; and in the majority of young persons it speedily dies away if the occupations to which their position in life has devoted them, and the society into which it has thrown them, are not favourable to keeping that higher capacity in exercise. Men lose their high aspirations as they lose their intellectual tastes, because they have not time or opportunity indulging them; and they addict themselves to inferior pleasures, not because they deliberately prefer them, but because they are either the only ones to which they have access, or the only ones which they are any longer capable of enjoying. It may be questioned whether any one who has remained equally susceptible to both classes of pleasures, ever knowingly and calmly preferred the lower; though many, in all ages, have broken down in an ineffectual attempt to combine both.

From this verdict of the only competent judges, I apprehend there can be no appeal. On a question which is the best worth having of two pleasures, or which of two modes of existence is the most grateful to the feelings, apart from its moral attributes and from its consequences, the judgment of those who are qualified by knowledge of both, or, if they differ, that of the majority among them, must be admitted as final. And there needs be the less hesitation to accept this judgment respecting the quality of pleasures, since there is no other tribunal to be referred to even on the question of quantity. What means are there of determining which is the acutest of two pains, or the intensest of two pleasurable sensations, except the general suffrage of those who are familiar with both? Neither pains nor pleasures are homogeneous, and pain is always heterogeneous with pleasure. What is there to decide whether a particular pleasure is worth purchasing at the cost of a particular pain, except the feelings and judgment of the experienced? When, therefore, those feelings and judgment declare the pleasures derived from the higher faculties to be preferable in *kind,* apart from the question of intensity, to those of which the animal nature, disjoined from the higher faculties, is susceptible, they are entitled on this subject to the same regard....

The Moral Law

IMMANUEL KANT

Kant argues that his moral theory is the very antithesis of utilitarianism, holding that right actions do not depend in the least on consequences, the production of happiness, or the desires and needs of human beings. For Kant, the core of morality consists of following a rational and universally applicable moral rule—the Categorical Imperative—and doing so solely out of a sense of duty. An action is right only if it conforms to such a rule, and we are morally praiseworthy only if we perform it for duty's sake alone.

Preface

As my concern here is with moral philosophy, I limit the question suggested to this: Whether it is not of the utmost necessity to construct a pure moral philosophy, perfectly cleared of everything which is only empirical, and which belongs to anthropology? for that such a philosophy must be possible is evident from the common idea of duty and of the moral laws. Everyone must admit that if a law is to have moral force, *i.e.,* to be the basis of an obligation, it must carry with it absolute necessity; that, for example, the precept, "Thou shall not lie," is not valid for men alone, as if other rational beings had no need to observe it; and so with all the other moral laws properly so called; that, therefore, the basis of obligation must not be sought in the nature of man, or in the circumstances in the world in which he is placed, but *a priori* simply in the conception of pure reason; and although any other precept which is founded on principles of mere experience may be in certain respects universal, yet in as far as it rests even in the least degree on an empirical basis, perhaps only as to motive, such a precept, while it may be a practical rule, can never be called a moral law....

The Good Will

Nothing can possibly be conceived in the world, or even out of it, which can be called good, without qualification, except a Good Will. Intelligence, wit, judgment, and the other *talents* of the mind, however they may be named, or courage, resolution, perseverance, as qualities of temperament, are undoubtedly good and desirable in many respects; but these gifts of nature may also become extremely bad and mischievous if the will which is to make use of them, and which, therefore, constitutes what is called *character,* is not good. It is the same with

Reprinted from The *Foundations of the Metaphysic of morals,* translated by T. K. Abbott (this translation first published in 1873).

the *gifts of fortune*. Power, riches, honour, even health, and the general well-being and contentment with one's conditions which is called *happiness*, inspire pride, and often presumption, if there is not a good will to correct the influence of these on the mind, and with this also to rectify the whole principle of acting, and adapt it to its end. The sight of a being who is not adorned with a single feature of a pure and good will, enjoying unbroken prosperity, can never give pleasure to an impartial rational spectator. Thus a good will appears to constitute the indispensable condition even of being worthy of happiness.

There are even some qualities which are of service to this good will itself, and may facilitate its action, yet which have no intrinsic unconditional value, but always presuppose a good will, and this qualifies the esteem that we justly have for them, and does not permit us to regard them as absolutely good. Moderation in the affections and passions, self-control, and calm deliberation are not only good in many respects, but even seem to constitute part of the intrinsic worth of the person but they are far from deserving to be called good without qualification, although they have been so unconditionally praised by the ancients. For without the principles of a good will, they may become extremely bad; and the coolness of a villain not only makes him far more dangerous, but also directly makes him more abominable in our eyes than he would have been without it.

A good will is good not because of what it performs or effects, not by its aptness for the attainment of some proposed end, but simply by virtue of the volition, that is, it is good in itself, and considered by itself to be esteemed much higher than all that can be brought about by it in favor of any inclination, nay, even of the sum-total of all inclinations. Even if it should happen that, owing to special disfavor of fortune, or the niggardly provision of a step-motherly nature, this will should wholly lack powder to accomplish its purpose, if with its greatest efforts it should yet achieve nothing, and there should remain only the good will (not, to be sure, a mere wish, but the summoning of all means in our power), then, like a jewel, it would still shine by its own light, as a thing which has its whole value in itself. Its usefulness or fruitlessness can neither add to nor take away anything from this value. It would be, as it were, only the setting to enable us to handle it the more conveniently in common commerce, or to attract to it the attention of those who are not yet connoisseurs, but not to recommend it to true connoisseurs, or to determine its value. . . .

The Supreme Principle of Morality: The Categorical Imperative

As I have deprived the will of every impulse which could arise to it from obedience to any law, there remains nothing but the universal conformity of its actions to law in general, which alone is to serve the will as principle, *i.e.*, I am never to act otherwise than so *that I could also will that my maxim should become a universal law.* Here, now, it is the simple conformity to law in general, without assuming any particular law applicable to certain actions, that serves the will as its principle, and must so serve it, if duty is not to be a vain delusion and a chimerical notion. The common reason of men in its practical judgments perfectly coincides with this, and always has in view the principle here suggested. Let the question be, for example: May I when in distress make a promise with the intention not to keep it? I readily distinguish here between the two significations which the question may have: Whether it is prudent, or whether it is right, to make a false promise? The former may undoubtedly often be the case. I see clearly indeed that it is not enough to extricate myself from a present difficulty by means of this subterfuge, but it must be well considered whether there may not hereafter spring from this lie much greater inconvenience than that from which I now free myself, and as, with all my supposed *cunning*, the consequences cannot be so easily foreseen but the credit once lost may be much more injurious to me than any mischief which I seek to avoid at present, it should be considered whether it would not be more *prudent* to act herein according to a universal maxim, and to make it a habit to promise nothing except with the intention of keeping it. But it is soon clear to me that such a maxim will still only be based on the fear of consequences. Now it is a wholly different thing to be truthful from duty, and to be so from apprehension of injurious consequences. In the first case, the very notion of the action already implies a law for me; in the second case, I must first look about elsewhere to see what results may be combined with it which would affect myself. For to deviate from the principle of duty is beyond all doubt wicked; but to be unfaithful to my maxim of prudence may often be very advantageous to me, although to abide by it is certainly safer. The shortest way, however, and an unerring one, to discover the answer to this question whether a lying promise is consistent with duty, is to ask myself, Should I be content that my maxim (to extricate myself from difficulty by a false promise) should hold good as a universal law, for myself as well as for others? And should I be able to say to myself, "Every one may make a deceitful promise when he finds himself in a difficulty from which he cannot otherwise extricate himself"? Then I presently become aware that while I can will the lie, I can by no means will that lying should be a universal law. For with such a law there would be no promises at all, since it would be in vain to allege my intention in regard to my future actions to those who would not believe this allegation, or if they over-hastily did so, would pay me back in my own coin. Hence my maxim, as soon as it should be made a universal law, would necessarily destroy itself.

I do not, therefore, need any far-reaching penetration to discern what I have to do in order that my will may be morally good. Inexperienced in the course of the world, incapable of being prepared for all its contingencies, I only ask myself: canst thou also will that thy maxim should be a universal law? If not, then it must be rejected, and that not because of a disadvantage accruing from myself or even to others, but because it cannot enter as a principle into a possible universal legislation, and reason extorts from me immediate respect for such legislation. I do not indeed as yet *discern* on what this respect is based (this the philosopher may inquire), but at least I understand this, that it is an estimation of the worth which far outweighs all worth of what is recommended by inclination, and that the necessity of acting from *pure* respect for the practical law is what constitutes duty, to which every other motive must give place, because it is the condition of a will being good in *itself,* and the worth of such a will is above everything.

Thus, then, without quitting the moral knowledge of common human reason, we have arrived at its principle. And although, no doubt, common men do not conceive it in such an abstract and universal form, yet they always have it really before their eyes, and use it as the standard of their decision....

Nor could anything be more fatal to morality than that we should wish to derive it from examples. For every example of it that is set before me must be first itself tested by principles of morality, whether it is worthy to serve as an original example, *i.e.,* as a pattern, but by no means can it authoritatively furnish the conception of morality. Even the Holy one of the Gospels must first be compared with our ideal of moral perfection before we can recognize Him as such; and so He says of Himself, "Why call ye Me [whom you see] good; none is good [the model of good] but God only [whom ye do not see]." But whence have we the conception of God as the supreme good? Simply from the *idea* of moral perfection, which reason frames a *priori,* and connects inseparably with the notion of a free will. Imitation finds no place at all in morality, and examples serve only for encouragement, *i.e.,* they put beyond doubt the feasibility of what the law commands, they make visible that which the practical rule expresses more generally, but they can never authorize us to set aside the true original which lies in reason, and to guide ourselves by examples.

From what has been said, it is clear that all moral conceptions have their seat and origin completely *a priori* in the reason, and that, moreover, in the commonest reason just as truly as in that which is in the highest degree speculative; that they cannot be obtained by abstraction from any empirical, and therefore merely contingent knowledge; that it is just this purity of their origin that makes them worthy to serve as our supreme practical principle, and that just in proportion as we add anything empirical, we detract from their genuine influence, and from the absolute value of actions; that it is not only of the greatest necessity, in a purely speculative point of view, but is also of the greatest practical importance, to derive these notions and laws from pure reason, to present them pure and unmixed, and even to determine the compass of this practical or pure rational knowledge, *i.e.* to determine the whole faculty of pure practical reason; and, in doing so, we must not make its principles dependent on the particular nature of human reason, though in speculative philosophy this may be permitted, or may even at times be necessary; but since moral laws ought to hold good for every rational creature, we must derive them from the general concept of a rational being. In this way, although for its *application* to man morality has need of anthropology, yet, in the first instance, we must treat it independently as pure philosophy, *i.e.,* as metaphysic, complete in itself (a thing which in such distinct branches of science is easily done); knowing well that unless we are in possession of this, it would not only be vain to determine the moral element of duty in right actions for purposes of speculative criticism, but it would be impossible to base morals on their genuine principles, even for common practical purposes, especially of moral instruction, so as to produce pure moral dispositions, and to engraft them on men's minds to the promotion of the greatest possible good in the world....

First Formulation of the Categorical Imperative: Universal Law

In this problem we will first inquire whether the mere conception of a categorical imperative may not perhaps supply us also with the formula of it, containing the proposition which alone can be a categorical imperative; for even if we know the tenor of such an absolute command, yet how it is possible will require further special and laborious study, which we postpone to the last section.

When I conceive a hypothetical imperative, in general I do not know beforehand what it will contain until I am given the condition. But when I conceive a categorical imperative, I know at once what it contains. For as the imperative contains besides the law only the necessity that the maxims shall conform to this law, while the law contains no conditions restricting it, there remains nothing but the general statement that the maxim of the action should conform to a universal law, and it is this conformity alone that the imperative properly represents as necessary.

There is therefore but one categorical imperative, namely, this: *Act only in that maxim whereby thou canst at the same time will that it should become a universal law.*

Now if all imperatives of duty can be deduced from this one imperative as from their principle, then, although it should remain undecided whether what is called duty is not merely a vain notion, yet at least we shall be able to show what we understand by it and what this notion means.

Since the universality of the law according to which effects are produced constitutes what is properly called *nature* in the most general sense (as to form), that is the existence of things so far as it is determined by general laws, the imperative of duty may be expressed thus: *Act as if the maxim of thy action were to become by thy will a universal law of nature.*

Four Illustrations

We will now enumerate a few duties, adopting the usual division of them into duties to ourselves and to others and into perfect and imperfect duties.

1. A man reduced to despair by a series of misfortunes feels wearied of life, but is still so far in possession of his reason that he can ask himself whether it would not be contrary to his duty to himself to take his own life. Now he inquires whether the maxim of his action could become a universal law of nature. His maxim is: From self-love I adopt it as a principle to shorten my life when its longer duration is likely to bring more evil than satisfaction. It is asked then simply whether this principle founded on self-love can become a universal law of nature. Now we see at once that a system of nature of which it should be a law to destroy life by means of the very feeling whose special nature it is to impel to the improvement of life would contradict itself, and therefore could not exist as a system of nature, and consequently would be wholly inconsistent with the supreme principle of all duty.

2. Another finds himself forced by necessity to borrow money. He knows that he will not be able to repay it, but sees also that nothing will be lent to him, unless he promises stoutly to repay it in a definite time. He desires to make this promise, but he has still so much conscience as to ask himself: Is it not unlawful and inconsistent with duty to get out of a

difficulty in this way? Suppose, however, that he resolves to do so, then the maxim of his action would be expressed thus: When I think myself in want of money, I will borrow money and promise to repay it, although I know that I never can do so. Now this principle of self-love or of one's own advantage may perhaps be consistent with my whole future welfare; but the question is, Is it right? I change then the suggestion of self-love into a universal law, and state the question thus: How would it be if my maxim were a universal law? Then I see at once that it could never hold as a universal law of nature, but would necessarily contradict itself. For supposing it to be a universal law that everyone when he thinks himself in a difficulty should be able to promise whatever he pleases, with the purpose of not keeping his promise, the promise itself would become impossible, as well as the end that one might have in view in it, since no one would consider that anything was promised to him, but would consider that anything was promised to him, but would ridicule all such statements as vain pretenses.

3. A third finds in himself a talent which with the help of some culture might make him a useful man in many respects. But he finds himself in comfortable circumstances, and prefers to indulge in pleasure rather than to take pains in enlarging and improving his happy natural capacities. He asks, however, whether his maxim of neglect of his natural gifts, besides agreeing with his inclination to indulgence, agrees also with what is called duty. He sees then that a system of nature could indeed subsist with such a universal law although men (like the South Sea islanders) should let their talents rest, and resolve to devote their lives merely to idleness, amusement, and propagation of their species— in a word, to enjoyment; but he cannot possibly *will* that this should be a universal law of nature, or be implanted in us as such by a natural instinct. For, as a rational being, he necessarily wills that his faculties be developed, since they serve him, and have been given him, for all sorts of possible purposes.

4. A fourth, who is in prosperity, while he sees that others have to contend with great wretchedness and that he could help them, thinks: What concern is it of mine? Let everyone be as happy as Heaven Pleases, or as he can make himself; I will take nothing from him nor even envy him, only I do not wish to contribute anything to his welfare or to his assistance in distress! Now no doubt if such a mode of thinking were a universal law, the human race might very well subsist, and doubtless even better than in a state in which everyone talks of sympathy and goodwill, or even takes care occasionally to put it into practice, but, on the other side, also cheats when he can, betrays the right of men, or otherwise violates them. But although it is possible that a universal law of nature might exist in accordance with that maxim, it is impossible to *will* that such a principle should have the universal validity of a law of nature. For a will which resolved this would contradict itself, inasmuch as many cases might occur in which one would have need of the love and sympathy of others, and in which, by such a law of nature, sprung from his own will, he would deprive himself of all hope of the aid he desires.

These are a few of the many actual duties, or at least what we regard as such, which obviously fall into two classes on the one principle that we have laid down. We must be *able to will* that a maxim of our action should be a universal law. This is the canon of the moral appreciation of the action generally. Some actions are of such a character that their maxim cannot without contradiction be even *conceived* as a universal law of nature, far from it being possible that we should *will* that it *should* be so. In others this intrinsic impossibility is not found, but still it is impossible to *will* that their maxim should be raised to the universality of a law of nature, since such a will would contradict itself. It is easily seen that the former violate strict or rigorous (inflexible) duty; the latter only laxer (meritorious) duty. Thus it has been completely shown by these examples how all duties depend as regards the nature of the obligation (not the object of the action) on the same principle.

Second Formulation of the Categorical Imperative: Humanity as an End in Itself

...Now I say: man and generally any rational being *exists* as an end in himself, *not merely as a means* to be arbitrarily used by this or that will, but in all his actions, whether they concern himself or other rational beings, must be always regarded at the same time as an end. All objects of the inclinations have only a conditional worth; for if the inclinations and the wants founded on them did not exist, then their object would be without value. But the inclinations themselves being sources of want are so far from having an absolute worth for which they should be desired, that on the contrary, it must be the universal wish of every rational being to be wholly free from them. Thus the worth of any object which is *to be acquired* by our action is always conditional. Beings whose existence depends not on our will but on nature's, have nevertheless, if they are nonrational beings, only a relative value as means, and are therefore called *things*; rational beings, on the contrary, are called *persons*, because their very nature points them out as ends in themselves, that is as something which must not be used merely as means, and so far therefore restricts freedom of action (and is an object of respect). These, therefore, are not merely subjective ends whose existence has a worth *for us* as an effect of our action, but *objective ends,* that is things whose existence is an end in itself: an end moreover for which no other can be substituted, which they should subserve *merely* as means, for otherwise nothing whatever would possess *absolute worth;* but if all worth were conditioned and therefore contingent, then there wouldbe no supreme practical principle of reason whatever.

If then there is a supreme practical principle or, in respect of the human will, categorical imperative, it must be one which, being drawn from the conception of that which is necessarily an end for everyone because it is *an end in itself,* constitutes an *objective* principle of will, and can therefore serve as a universal practical law. The foundation of this principle is: *rational nature exists as an end in itself.* Man necessarily conceives his own existence as being so; so far then this is a *subjective* principle of human actions. But every other rational being regards its existence similarly, just on the same rational principle that holds for me: so that it is at the same time an objective principle, from which as a supreme practical law all laws of the will must be capable of being deduced. Accordingly the practical imperative will be as follows. *So act as to treat humanity, whether in thine own person or in that of any other, in every case as an end withal, never as means only....*

...Looking back now on all previous attempts to discover the principle of morality, we need not wonder why they all failed. It was seen that man was bound to laws by duty, but it was not observed that the laws to which he is subject are *only those of his own giving,* though at the same time they are *universal,* and that he is only bound to act in conformity with his own will; a will, however, which is designed by nature to give universal laws. For when one has conceived man only as subject to a law (no matter what), then this law required some interest, either by way of attraction or constraint, since it did not originate as a law from *his own* will, but his will was according to a law obliged by *something else* to act in a certain manner. Now by this necessary consequence all the labour spent in finding a supreme principle of duty was irrevocably lost. For men never elicited *duty,* but only a necessity of acting from a certain interest. Whether this interest was private or otherwise, in any case the imperative must be conditional, and could not by any means be capable of being a moral command. I will therefore call this the principle of *Autonomy* of the will, in contrast with every other which I accordingly reckon as *Heteronomy.*

Virtue and the Moral Life

BERNARD MAYO

The British philosopher Bernard Mayo (1920–2000) is the author of *Ethics and the Moral Life*, from which this excerpt is taken. He contrasts moral theories based on right actions with those that emphasize moral character. He argues that saints and heroes demonstrate that moral examples are what is really important in morality, not rigid rules. We should strive not to regiment our lives according to moral tenets, but to be virtuous people.

The philosophy of moral principles, which is characteristic of Kant and the post-Kantian era, is something of which hardly a trace exists in Plato. . . . Plato says nothing about rules or principles or laws, except when he is talking politics. Instead he talks about virtues and vices, and about certain types of human character. The key word in Platonic ethics is Virtue; the key word in Kantian ethics is Duty. And modern ethics is a set of footnotes, not to Plato, but to Kant. . . .

Attention to the novelists can be a welcome correction to a tendency of philosophical ethics of the last generation or two to lose contact with the ordinary life of man which is just what the novelists, in their own way, are concerned with. Of course there are writers who can be called in to illustrate problems about Duty (Graham Greene is a good example). But there are more who perhaps never mention the words duty, obligation, or principle. Yet they are all concerned—Jane Austen, for instance, entirely and absolutely—with the moral qualities or defects of their heroes and heroines and other characters. This points to a radical one-sidedness in the philosophers' account of morality in terms of principles: it takes little or no account of qualities, of what people *are*. It is just here that the old-fashioned word Virtue used to have a place; and it is just here that the work of Plato and Aristotle can be instructive. Justice, for Plato, though it is closely connected with acting according to law, does not *mean* acting according to law: it is a quality of character, and a just action is one such as a just man would do. Telling the truth, for Aristotle, is not, as it was

for Kant, fulfilling an obligation; again it is a quality of character, or, rather, a whole range of qualities of character, some of which may actually be defects, such as tactlessness, boastfulness, and so on—a point which can be brought out, in terms of principles, only with the greatest complexity and artificiality, but quite simply and naturally in terms of character.

If we wish to enquire about Aristotle's moral views, it is no use looking for a set of principles. Of course we can find *some* principles to which he must have subscribed—for instance, that one ought not to commit adultery. But what we find much more prominently is a set of character-traits, a list of certain types of person—the courageous man, the niggardly man, the boaster, the lavish spender, and so on. The basic moral question, for Aristotle, is not. What shall I do? but, What shall I be?

These contrasts between doing and being, negative and positive, and modern as against Greek morality were noted by John Stuart Mill; I quote from the *Essay on Liberty*:

> Christian morality (so-called) has all the characters of a reaction; it is, in great part, a protest against Paganism. Its ideal is negative rather than positive, passive rather than active; Innocence rather than Nobleness; Abstinence from Evil, rather than energetic Pursuit of the Good; in its precepts (as has been well said) "Thou shalt not" predominates unduly over "Thou shalt . . ." Whatever exists of magnanimity, high-mindedness, personal dignity, even the sense of honour, is derived from the purely human, not the religious part of our education, and never could have grown out of a standard of ethics in which the only worth, professedly recognized, is that of obedience.

Of course, there are connections between being and doing. It is obvious that a man cannot just *be*; he can only be what he is by doing what he does; his moral qualities are ascribed to him because of his actions, which are said to manifest those qualities. But the point is that an ethics of Being must include this obvious fact, that Being involves Doing; whereas an ethics of Doing, such as I have been examining, may easily overlook it. As I have suggested, a morality of principles is concerned only with what people do or fail to do, since that is what rules are for. And as far as this sort of ethics goes, people might well have no moral qualities at all except the possession of principles and the will (and capacity) to act accordingly.

When we speak of a moral quality such as courage, and say that a certain action was courageous, we are not merely saying something about the action. We are referring, not so much to what is done, as to the kind of person by whom we take it to have been done. We connect, by means of imputed motives and intentions, with the character of the agent as courageous. This explains, incidentally, why both Kantians and Utilitarians encounter, in their different ways, such difficulties in dealing with motives, which their principles, on the face of it, have no room for. A Utilitarian, for example, can only praise a courageous action in some such way as this: the action is of a sort such as a person of courage is likely to perform, and courage is a quality of character the cultivation of which is likely to increase rather than diminish the sum total of human happiness. But Aristotelians have no need of such circumlocution. For them a courageous action just is one which proceeds from and manifests a certain type of character, and is praised because such a character trait is good, or better than others, or is a virtue. An evaluative criterion is sufficient: there is no need to look for an imperative criterion as well, or rather instead, according to which it is not the character which is good, but the cultivation of the character which is right....

No doubt the fundamental moral question is just "What ought I to do?" And according to the philosophy of moral principles, the answer (which must be an imperative "Do this") must be derived from a conjunction of premises consisting (in the simplest case) firstly of a rule, or universal imperative, enjoining

(or forbidding) all actions of a certain type in situations of a certain type, and, secondly, a statement to the effect that this is a situation of that type, falling under that rule. In practice the emphasis may be on supplying only one of these premises, the other being assumed or taken for granted: one may answer the question "What ought I to do?" either by quoting a rule which I am to adopt, or by showing that my case is legislated for by a rule which I do adopt.... [I]f I am in doubt whether to tell the truth about his condition to a dying man, my doubt may be resolved by showing that the case comes under a rule about the avoidance of unnecessary suffering, which I am assumed to accept. But if the case is without precedent in my moral career, my problem may be soluble only by adopting a new principle about what I am to do now and in the future about cases of this kind.

This second possibility offers a connection with moral ideas. Suppose my perplexity is not merely an unprecedented situation which I could cope with by adopting a new rule. Suppose the new rule is thoroughly inconsistent with my existing moral code. This may happen, for instance, if the moral code is one to which I only pay lip-service, if...its authority is not yet internalised, or if it has ceased to be so; it is ready for rejection, but its final rejection awaits a moral crisis such as we are assuming to occur. What I now need is not a rule for deciding how to act in this situation and others of its kind. I need a whole set of rules, a complete morality, new principles to live by.

Now, according to the philosophy of moral character, there is another way of answering the fundamental question "What ought I to do?" Instead of quoting a rule, we quote a quality of character, a virtue: we say "Be brave," or "Be patient" or "Be lenient." We may even say "Be a man": if I am in doubt, say, whether to take a risk, and someone says "Be a man," meaning a morally sound man, in this case a man of sufficient courage. (Compare the very different ideal invoked in "Be a gentleman." I shall not discuss whether this is a *moral* ideal.) Here, too, we have the extreme cases, where a man's moral perplexity extends not merely to a particular situation but to his whole way of living. And now the question "What ought I to do?" turns into the question "What ought I to be?"—as, indeed, it was treated in the first place. ("Be brave.") It is answered, not by quoting a rule or a set of rules, but by describing a quality of character or a type of person. And here the ethics of character gains a practical simplicity which offsets the greater logical simplicity of the ethics of principles. We do not have to give a list of characteristics or virtues, as we might list a set of principles. We can give a unity to our answer.

Of course we can in theory give a unity to our principles: this is implied by speaking of a *set* of principles. But if such a set is to be a system and not merely aggregate, the unity we are looking for is a logical one, namely the possibility that some principles are deductible from others, and ultimately from one. But the attempt to construct a deductive moral system is notoriously difficult, and in any case ill-founded. Why should we expect that all rules of conduct should be ultimately reducible to a few?

Saints and Heroes

But when we are asked "What shall I be?" we can readily give a unity to our answer, though not a logical unity. It is the unity of character. A person's character is not merely a list of dispositions; it has the organic unity of something that is more than the sum of its parts. And we can say, in answer to our morally perplexed questioner, not only "Be this" and "Be that," but also "Be like So-and-So"—where So-and-So is either an ideal type of character, or else an actual person taken as representative of the ideal, as exemplar. Examples of the first are Plato's "just man" in the Republic; Aristotle's man of practical wisdom, in the *Nicomachean Ethics*; Augustine's citizen of the City of God; the good Communist; the American way of life (which is a collective expression for a type of character). Examples of the second kind, the exemplar, are Socrates, Christ, Buddha, St. Francis, the heroes of epic writers and of novelists. Indeed the idea of the Hero, as well as the idea of the Saint, are very much the expression of this attitude to morality. Heroes and saints are not merely people who did things. They are people whom we are expected, and expect ourselves, to imitate. And imitating them means not merely doing what they did; it means being like them. Their status is not in the least like that of legislators whose laws we admire; for the character of a legislator is irrelevant to our judgment about his legislation. The heroes and saints did not merely give us principles to live by (though some of them did that as well): they gave us examples to follow.

Kant, as we should expect, emphatically rejects this attitude as "fatal to morality." According to him, examples serve only to render *visible* an instance of the moral principle, and thereby to demonstrate its practical feasibility. But every exemplar, such as Christ himself, must be judged by the independent criterion of the moral law, before we are entitled to recognize him as worthy of imitation. I am not suggesting that the subordination of exemplars to principles is incorrect, but that it is one-sided and fails to do justice to a large area of moral experience.

Imitation can be more or less successful. And this suggests another defect of the ethics of principles. It has no room for ideals, except the ideal of a perfect set of principles (which, as a matter of fact, is intelligible only in terms of an ideal character or way of life), and the ideal of perfect conscientiousness (which is itself a character-trait). This results, of course, from the "black-or-white" nature of moral verdicts based on rules. There are degrees by which we approach or recede from the attainment of a certain quality or virtue; if there were not, the word "ideal" would have no meaning. Heroes and saints are not people whom we try to be *just* like, since we know that is impossible. It is precisely because it is impossible for ordinary human beings to achieve the same qualities as the saints, and in the same degree, that we do set them apart from the rest of humanity. It is enough if we try to be a little like them....

The Ethics of Care

VIRGINIA HELD

Virginia Held has taught philosophy at Hunter College and The Graduate Center of the City University of New York. In this reading, she explores the ethics of care, identifying its central themes, showing how it relates to an "ethic of justice," and distinguishing it from virtue ethics.

The ethics of care is only a few decades old.[1] Some theorists do not like the term "care" to designate this approach to moral issues and have tried substituting "the ethic of love," or "relational ethics," but the discourse keeps returning to "care" as the so far more satisfactory of the terms considered, though dissatisfactions with it remain. The concept of care has the advantage of not losing sight of the work involved in caring for people and of not lending itself to the interpretation of morality as ideal but impractical to which advocates of the ethics of care often object. Care is both value and practice.

By now, the ethics of care has moved far beyond its original formulations, and any attempt to evaluate it should consider much more than the one or two early works so frequently cited. It has been developed as a moral theory relevant not only to the so-called private realms of family and friendship but to medical practice, law, political life, the organization of society, war, and international relations.

The ethics of care is sometimes seen as a potential moral theory to be substituted for such dominant moral theories as Kantian ethics, utilitarianism, or Aristotelian virtue ethics. It is sometimes seen as a form of virtue ethics. It is almost always developed as emphasizing neglected moral considerations of at least as much importance as the considerations central to moralities of justice and rights or of utility and preference satisfaction. And many who contribute to the understanding of the ethics of care seek to integrate the moral considerations, such as justice, which other moral theories have clarified, satisfactorily with those of care, though

they often see the need to reconceptualize these considerations.

Features of the Ethics of Care

Some advocates of the ethics of care resist generalizing this approach into something that can be fitted into the form of a moral theory. They see it as a mosaic of insights and value the way it is sensitive to contextual nuance and particular narratives rather than making the abstract and universal claims of more familiar moral theories.[2] Still, I think one can discern among various versions of the ethics of care a number of major features.

First, the central focus of the ethics of care is on the compelling moral salience of attending to and meeting the needs of the particular others for whom we take responsibility. Caring for one's child, for instance, may well and defensibly be at the forefront of a person's moral concerns. The ethics of care recognizes that human beings are dependent for many years of their lives, that the moral claim of those dependent on us for the care they need is pressing, and that there are highly important moral aspects in developing the relations of caring that enable human beings to live and progress. All persons need care for at least their early years. Prospects for human progress and flourishing hinge fundamentally on the care that those needing it receive, and the ethics of care stresses the moral force of the responsibility to respond to the needs of the dependent. Many persons will become ill and dependent for some periods of their later lives, including in frail old age, and some who are permanently disabled will need care the whole of their lives. Moralities built on the image of the independent, autonomous, rational individual largely overlook the reality of human dependence and the

From *The Ethics of Care: Personal, Political, and Global* by Virginia Held (2006). "The Ethics of Care as Moral Theory."

morality for which it calls. The ethics of care attends to this central concern of human life and delineates the moral values involved. It refuses to relegate care to a realm "outside morality." How caring for particular others should be reconciled with the claims of, for instance, universal justice is an issue that needs to be addressed. But the ethics of care starts with the moral claims of particular others, for instance, of one's child, whose claims can be compelling regardless of universal principles.

Second, in the epistemological process of trying to understand what morality would recommend and what it would be morally best for us to do and to be, the ethics of care values emotion rather than rejects it. Not all emotion is valued, of course, but in contrast with the dominant rationalist approaches, such emotions as sympathy, empathy, sensitivity, and responsiveness are seen as the kind of moral emotions that need to be cultivated not only to help in the implementation of the dictates of reason but to better ascertain what morality recommends.[3] Even anger may be a component of the moral indignation that should be felt when people are treated unjustly or inhumanely, and it may contribute to (rather than interfere with) an appropriate interpretation of the moral wrong. This is not to say that raw emotion can be a guide to morality; feelings need to be reflected on and educated. But from the care perspective, moral inquiries that rely entirely on reason and rationalistic deductions or calculations are seen as deficient.

The emotions that are typically considered and rejected in rationalistic moral theories are the egoistic feelings that undermine universal moral norms, the favoritism that interferes with impartiality, and the aggressive and vengeful impulses for which morality is to provide restraints. The ethics of care, in contrast, typically appreciates the emotions and relational capabilities that enable morally concerned persons in actual interpersonal contexts to understand what would be best. Since even the helpful emotions can often become misguided or worse—as when excessive empathy with others leads to a wrongful degree of self-denial or when benevolent concern crosses over into controlling domination—we need an *ethics* of care, not just care itself. The various aspects and expressions of care

and caring relations need to be subjected to moral scrutiny and *evaluated,* not just observed and described.

Third, the ethics of care rejects the view of the dominant moral theories that the more abstract the reasoning about a moral problem the better because the more likely to avoid bias and arbitrariness, the more nearly to achieve impartiality. The ethics of care respects rather than removes itself from the claims of particular others with whom we share actual relationships.[4] It calls into question the universalistic and abstract rules of the dominant theories. When the latter consider such actual relations as between a parent and child, if they say anything about them at all, they may see them as permitted and cultivating them a preference that a person may have. Or they may recognize a universal obligation for all parents to care for their children. But they do not permit actual relations ever to take priority over the requirements of impartiality. As Brian Barry expresses this view, there can be universal rules permitting people to favor their friends in certain contexts, such as deciding to whom to give holiday gifts, but the latter partiality is morally acceptable only because universal rules have already so judged it.[5] The ethics of care, in contrast, is skeptical of such abstraction and reliance on universal rules and questions the priority given to them. To most advocates of the ethics of care, the compelling moral claim of the particular other may be valid even when it conflicts with the requirement usually made by moral theories that moral judgments be universalizeable, and this is of fundamental moral importance.[6] Hence the potential conflict between care and justice, friendship and impartiality, loyalty and universality. To others, however, there need be no conflict if universal judgments come to incorporate appropriately the norms of care previously disregarded.

Annette Baier considers how a feminist approach to morality differs from a Kantian one and Kant's claim that women are incapable of being fully moral because of their reliance on emotion rather than reason. She writes, "Where Kant concludes 'so much the worse for women,' we can conclude 'so much the worse for the male fixation on the *special skill of drafting* legislation, for the bureaucratic mentality of rule worship, and for the male exaggeration of the importance of independence over mutual interdependence."[7]

Margaret Walker contrasts what she sees as feminist "moral understanding" with what has traditionally been thought of as moral "knowledge." She sees the moral understanding she advocates as involving "attention, contextual and narrative appreciation, and communication in the event of moral deliberation." This alternative moral epistemology holds that "the adequacy of moral understanding decreases as its form approaches generality through abstraction."[8]

The ethics of care may seek to limit the applicability of universal rules to certain domains where they are more appropriate, like the domain of law, and resist their extension to other domains. Such rules may simply be inappropriate in, for instance, the contexts of family and friendship, yet relations in these domains should certainly be *evaluated*, not merely described, hence morality should not be limited to abstract rules. We should be able to give moral guidance concerning actual relations that are trusting, considerate, and caring and concerning those that are not.

Dominant moral theories tend to interpret moral problems as if they were conflicts between egoistic individual interests on the one hand, and universal moral principles on the other. The extremes of "selfish individual" and "humanity" are recognized, but what lies between these is often overlooked. The ethics of care, in contrast, focuses especially on the area between these extremes. Those who conscientiously care for others are not seeking primarily to further their own *individual* interests; their interests are intertwined with the persons they care for. Neither are they acting for the sake of *all others* or *humanity in general*; they seek instead to preserve or promote an actual human relation between themselves and *particular others*. Persons in caring relations are acting for self-and-other together. Their characteristic stance is neither egoistic nor altruistic; these are the options in a conflictual situation, but the well-being of a caring relation involves the cooperative well-being of those in the relation and the well-being of the relation itself.

In trying to overcome the attitudes and problems of tribalism and religious intolerance, dominant moralities have tended to assimilate the domains of family and friendship to the tribal, or to a source of the unfair favoring of one's own. Or they have seen the attachments people have in these areas as among the nonmoral private preferences people are permitted to pursue if restrained by impartial moral norms. The ethics of care recognizes the *moral* value and importance of relations of family and friendship and the need for *moral* guidance in these domains to understand how existing relations should often be changed and new ones developed. Having grasped the value of caring relations in such contexts as these more personal ones, the ethics of care then often examines social and political arrangements in the light of these values. In its more developed forms, the ethics of care as a feminist ethic offers suggestions for the radical transformation of society. It demands not just equality for women in existing structures of society but equal consideration for the experience that reveals the values, importance, and moral significance, of caring.

A fourth characteristic of the ethics of care is that like much feminist thought in many areas, it re-conceptualizes traditional notions about the public and the private. The traditional view, built into the dominant moral theories, is that the household is a private sphere beyond politics into which government, based on consent, should not intrude. Feminists have shown how the greater social, political, economic, and cultural power of men has structured this "private" sphere to the disadvantage of women and children, rendering them vulnerable to domestic violence without outside interference, often leaving women economically dependent on men and subject to a highly inequitable division of labor in the family. The law has not hesitated to intervene into women's private decisions concerning reproduction but has been highly reluctant to intrude on men's exercise of coercive power within the "castles" of their homes.

Dominant moral theories have seen "public" life as relevant to morality while missing the moral significance of the "private" domains of family and friendship. Thus the dominant theories have assumed that morality should be sought for unrelated, independent, and mutually indifferent individuals assumed to be equal. They have posited an abstract, fully rational "agent as such" from which to construct morality,[9] while missing the moral issues that arise between interconnected persons in the contexts of family, friendship, and social groups. In the context of the family, it is typical for relations to be between persons with highly unequal power who did not choose the ties and obligations in which they find themselves enmeshed. For instance, no child can choose her parents yet she may well have obligations to care for them. Relations of this kind are standardly noncontractual, and conceptualizing them as contractual would often undermine or at least obscure the trust on which their worth depends. The ethics of care addresses rather than neglects moral issues arising in relations among the unequal and dependent, relations that are often laden with emotion and involuntary, and then notices how often these attributes apply not only in the household but in the wider society as well. For instance, persons do not choose which gender, racial, class, ethnic, religious, national, or cultural groups to be brought up in, yet these sorts of ties may be important aspects of who they are and how their experience can contribute to moral understanding.

A fifth characteristic of the ethics of care is the conception of persons with which it begins. This will be dealt with in the next section.

The Critique of Liberal Individualism

The ethics of care usually works with a conception of persons as relational, rather than as the self-sufficient independent individuals of the dominant moral theories. The dominant theories can be interpreted as importing into moral theory a concept of the person developed primarily for liberal political and economic theory, seeing the person as a rational, autonomous agent, or a self-interested individual. On this view, society is made up of "independent, autonomous units who cooperate only when the terms of cooperation are such as to make it further the ends of each of the parties," in Brian Barry's words.[10] Or, if they are Kantians, they refrain from actions that they could not will to be universal laws to which all fully rational and autonomous individual agents

could agree. What such views hold, in Michael Sandel's critique of them, is that "what separates us is in some important sense prior to what connects us—epistemologically prior as well as morally prior. We are distinct individuals first and *then* we form relationships."[11] In Martha Nussbaum's liberal feminist morality, "the flourishing of human beings taken one by one is both analytically and normatively prior to the flourishing" of any group.[12]

The ethics of care, in contrast, characteristically sees persons as relational and interdependent, morally and epistemologically. Every person starts out as a child dependent on those providing us care, and we remain interdependent with others in thoroughly fundamental ways throughout our lives. That we can think and act as if we were independent depends on a network of social relations making it possible for us to do so. And our relations are part of what constitute our identity. This is not to say that we cannot become autonomous; feminists have done much interesting work developing an alternative conception of autonomy in place of the liberal individualist one.[13] Feminists have much experience rejecting or reconstituting relational ties that are oppressive. But it means that from the perspective of an ethics of care, to construct morality *as if we were* Robinson Crusoes, or, to use Hobbes's image, mushrooms sprung from nowhere, is misleading.[14] As Eva Kittay writes, this conception fosters the illusion that society is composed of free, equal, and independent individuals who can choose to associate with one another or not. It obscures the very real facts of dependency for everyone when they are young, for most people at various periods in their lives when they are ill or old and infirm, for some who are disabled, and for all those engaged in unpaid "dependency work."[15] And it obscures the innumerable ways persons and groups are interdependent in the modern world.

Not only does the liberal individualist conception of the person foster a false picture of society and the persons in it, it is, from the perspective of the ethics of care, impoverished also as an ideal. The ethics of care values the ties we have with particular other persons and the actual relationships that partly constitute our identity. Although persons often may and should reshape their relations with others—distancing themselves from some persons and groups and developing or strengthening ties with others—the autonomy sought within the ethics of care is a capacity to reshape and cultivate new relations, not to ever more closely resemble the unencumbered abstract rational self of liberal political and moral theories. Those motivated by the ethics of care would seek to become more admirable relational persons in better caring relations.

Even if the liberal ideal is meant only to instruct us on what would be rational in the terms of its ideal model, thinking of persons as the model presents them has effects that should not be welcomed. As Annette Baier writes, "Liberal morality, if unsupplemented, may *unfit* people to be anything other than what its justifying theories suppose them to be, ones who have no interest in each other's interests."[16] There is strong empirical evidence of how adopting a theoretical model can lead to behavior that mirrors it. Various studies show that studying economics, with its "repeated and intensive exposure to a model whose unequivocal prediction" is that people will decide what to do on the basis of self-interest, leads economics students to be less cooperative and more inclined to free ride than other students.[17]

The conception of the person adopted by the dominant moral theories provides moralities at best suitable for legal, political, and economic interactions between relative strangers, once adequate trust exists for them to form a political entity.[18] The ethics of care is, instead, hospitable to the relatedness of persons. It sees many of our responsibilities as not freely entered into but presented to us by the accidents of our embeddedness in familial and social and historical contexts. It often calls on us to *take* responsibility, while liberal individualist morality focuses on how we should leave each other alone. The view of persons as embedded and encumbered seems fundamental to much feminist thinking about morality and especially to the ethics of care....

NOTES

1. I use the term "ethics" to suggest that there are multiple versions of this ethic, though they all have much in common, making it understandable that some prefer "the ethic of care." I use "the ethics of care" as a collective and singular noun. Some moral philosophers have tried to establish a definitional distinction between "ethics" and "morality"; I think such efforts fail, and I use the terms more or less interchangeably, though I certainly distinguish between the moral or ethical beliefs groups of people in fact have and moral or ethical recommendations that are justifiable or admirable.

2. See, for example, Annette C. Baier, *Moral Prejudices: Essays on Ethics* (Cambridge, Mass.: Harvard University Press, 1994), esp. chap. 1; Peta Bowden, *Caring: Gender Sensitive Ethics* (London: Routledge, 1997); and Margaret Urban Walker, "Feminism, Ethics, and the Question of Theory," *Hypatia: A Journal of Feminist Philosophy* 7 (1992): 23–38.

3. See, for example, Baier, *Moral Prejudices*, Virginia Held, *Feminist Morality: Transforming Culture, Society, and Politics* (Chicago: University of Chicago Press, 1993); Diana Tietjens Meyers, *Subjection and Subjectivity* (New York: Routledge, 1994); and Margaret Urban Walker, *Moral Understandings: A Feminist Study in Ethics* (New York: Routledge, 1998).

4. See, for example, Seyla Benhabib, *Situating the Self: Gender, Community, and Postmodernism in Contemporary Ethics* (New York: Routledge, 1992); Marilyn Friedman, *What Are Friends For? Feminist Perspectives on Personal Relationships* (Ithaca, N.Y.: Cornell University Press, 1993); Held, *Feminist Morality*; and Eva Feder Kittay, *Love's Labor: Essays on Women, Equality, and Dependency* (New York: Routledge, 1999).

5. See Brian Barry, *Justice as Impartiality* (Oxford: Oxford University Press, 1995); Diemut Bubeck, *Care, Gender, and Justice* (Oxford: Oxford University Press, 1995), pp. 239–40; and Susan Mendus, *Impartiality in Moral and Political Philosophy* (Oxford: Oxford University Press, 2002).

6. It is often asserted that to count as moral, a judgment must be universalizeable: If we hold that it would be right (or wrong) for one person to do something, then we are committed to holding that it would be right (or wrong) for anyone similar in similar circumstances to do it. The subject terms in moral judgments must thus be universally quantified variables and the predicates universal. "I ought to take care of Jane because she is my child" is not universal; "all parents ought to take care of their children" is. The former judgment could be universalizeable if it were derived from the latter, but if, as many advocates of the ethics of care think, it is taken as a *starting* moral commitment (rather than as dependent on universal moral judgments), it might not be universalizeable.

7. Baier, *Moral Prejudices*, p. 26.

8. Margaret Urban Walker, "Moral Understandings: Alternative 'Epistemology' for a Feminist Ethics," *Hypatia* 4 (summer 1989): 15–28, pp. 19–20.

9. Good examples are Stephen L. Darwall, *Impartial Reason* (Ithaca, N.Y.: Cornell University Press, 1983), and

David Gauthier, *Morals by Agreement* (Oxford: Oxford University Press, 1986).

10. Brian Barry, *The Liberal Theory of Justice* (London: Oxford University Press, 1973), p. 166.

11. Michael Sandel, *Liberalism and the Limits of Justice* (Cambridge, U.K.: Cambridge University Press, 1982), p. 133. Other examples of the communitarian critique that ran parallel to the feminist one are Alasdair MacIntyre, *After Virtue: A Study in Moral Theory* (Notre Dame, Ind.: University of Notre Dame Press, 1981), and *Whose Justice? Which Rationality?* (Notre Dame, Ind.: University of Notre Dame Press, 1988); Charles Taylor, *Hegel and Modern Society* (Cambridge , U.K.: Cambridge University Press, 1979); and Roberto Mangabeire Unger, *Knowledge and Politics* (New York: Free Press, 1975).

12. Martha Nussbaum, *Sex and Social Justice* (New York: Oxford University Press, 1999), p. 62.

13. See, for example, Diana T. Meyers, *Self, Society, and Personal Choice* (New York: Columbia University Press, 1989); Grace Clement, *Care, Autonomy, and Justice* (Boulder, Colo.: Westview Press, 1996); Diana T. Meyers, ed., *Feminists Rethink the Self* (Boulder, Colo.: Westview Press, 1997); and Catriona MacKenzie and Natalie Stoljar, eds.,

Relational Autonomy: Feminist Perspectives on Autonomy, Agency, and the Social Self (New York: Oxford University Press, 2000). See also Marina Oshana, "Personal Autonomy and Society," *Journal of Social Philosophy* 29(1) (spring 1998): 81–102.

14. This image is in Thomas Hobbes's *The Citizen: Philosophical Rudiments Concerning Government and Society*, ed. B. Gert (Garden City, N.Y.: Doubleday, 1972), p. 205. For a contrasting view, see Sibyl Schwarzenbach, "On Civic Friendship," *Ethics* 107(1) (1996): 97–128.

15. Kittay, *Love's Labor*.

16. Baier, *Moral Prejudices*, p. 29.

17. See Robert A. Frank, Thomas Gilovich, and Dennis T. Regan, "Does Studying Economics Inhibit Cooperation?" *Journal of Economic Perspectives* 7(2) (spring 1993): 159–71; and Gerald Marwell and Ruth Ames, "Economists Free Ride, Does Anyone Else?: Experiments on the Provision of Public Goods, IV," *Journal of Public Economics* 15(3) (June 1981): 295–310.

18. See Virginia Held, Rights and *Goods: Justifying Social Action* (Chicago: University of Chicago Press, 1989), chap. 5, "The Grounds for Social Trust."

MORAL SAINTS

SUSAN WOLF

Susan Wolf is a professor of philosophy at the University of North Carolina, Chapel Hill, working mostly in ethics and the related areas of philosophy of mind, philosophy of action, political philosophy, and aesthetics. In this selection, she examines the idea of moral saints, exploring the implications of moral sainthood for utilitarianism, Kantian ethics, and moral philosophy generally.

I don't know whether there are any moral saints. But if there are, I am glad that neither I nor those about whom I care most are among them. By *moral saint* I mean a person whose every action is as morally good as possible, a person, that is, who is as morally worthy as can be. Though I shall in a moment acknowledge the variety of types of person that might be thought to satisfy this description, it seems to me that none of these types serve as unequivocally compelling personal ideals. In other

words, I believe that moral perfection, in the sense of moral saintliness, does not constitute a model of personal well-being toward which it would be particularly rational or good or desirable for a human being to strive.

Outside the context of moral discussion, this will strike many as an obvious point. But, within that context, the point, if it be granted, will be granted with some discomfort. For within that context it is generally assumed that one ought to be as morally good as possible and that what limits there are to morality's hold on us are set by features of human nature of which we ought not to be proud. If, as I believe, the ideals that are derivable from

From Susan Wolf, "Moral Saints," *Journal of Philosophy*, vol. LXXIX, no. 8, 1982.

common sense and philosophically popular moral theories do not support these assumptions, then something has to change. Either we must change our moral theories in ways that will make them yield more palatable ideals, or, as I shall argue, we must change our conception of what is involved in affirming a moral theory.

In this paper, I wish to examine the notion of a moral saint, first, to understand what a moral saint would be like and why such a being would be unattractive, and, second, to raise some questions about the significance of this paradoxical figure for moral philosophy. I shall look first at the model(s) of moral sainthood that might be extrapolated from the morality or moralities of common sense. Then I shall consider what relations these have to conclusions that can be drawn from utilitarian and Kantian moral theories. Finally, I shall speculate on the implications of these considerations for moral philosophy.

Moral Saints and Common Sense

Consider first what, pretheoretically, would count for us—contemporary members of Western culture—as a moral saint. A necessary condition of moral sainthood would be that one's life be dominated by a commitment to improving the welfare of others or of society as a whole. As to what role this commitment must play in the individual's motivational system, two contrasting accounts suggest themselves to me which might equally be thought to qualify a person for moral sainthood.

First, a moral saint might be someone whose concern for others plays the role that is played in most of our lives by more selfish, or, at any rate, less morally worthy concerns. For the moral saint, the promotion of the welfare of others might play the role that is played for most of us by the enjoyment of material comforts, the opportunity to engage in the intellectual and physical activities of our choice, and the love, respect, and companionship of people whom we love, respect, and enjoy. The happiness of the moral saint, then, would truly lie in the happiness of others, and so he would devote himself to others gladly, and with a whole and open heart.

On the other hand, a moral saint might be someone for whom the basic ingredients of happiness are not unlike those of most of the rest of us. What

makes him a moral saint is rather that he pays little or no attention to his own happiness in light of the overriding importance he gives to the wider concerns of morality. In other words, this person sacrifices his own interests to the interests of others, and feels the sacrifice as such.

Roughly, these two models may be distinguished according to whether one thinks of the moral saint as being a saint out of love or one thinks of the moral saint as being a saint out of duty (or some other intellectual appreciation and recognition of moral principles). We may refer to the first model as the model of the Loving Saint; to the second, as the model of the Rational Saint.

The two models differ considerably with respect to the qualities of the motives of the individuals who conform to them. But this difference would have limited effect on the saints' respective public personalities. The shared content of what these individuals are motivated to be—namely, as morally good as possible—would play the dominant role in the determination of their characters. Of course, just as a variety of large-scale projects, from tending the sick to political campaigning, may be equally and maximally morally worthy, so a variety of characters are compatible with the ideal of moral sainthood. One moral saint may be more or less jovial, more or less garrulous, more or less athletic than another. But, above all, a moral saint must have and cultivate those qualities which are apt to allow him to treat others as justly and kindly as possible. He will have the standard moral virtues to a nonstandard degree. He will be patient, considerate, even-tempered, hospitable, charitable in thought as well as in deed. He will be very reluctant to make negative judgments of other people. He will be careful not to favor some people over others on the basis of properties they could not help but have.

Perhaps what I have already said is enough to make some people begin to regard the absence of moral saints in their lives as a blessing. For there comes a point in the listing of virtues that a moral saint is likely to have where one might naturally begin to wonder whether the moral saint isn't, after all, too good—if not too good for his own good, at least too good for his own well-being. For the moral virtues, given that they are, by hypothesis, *all* present in the same individual, and to an extreme degree, are apt to crowd out the nonmoral virtues, as well as many of the interests and personal characteristics that we generally think contribute to a healthy, well-rounded, richly developed character.

In other words, if the moral saint is devoting all his time to feeding the hungry or healing the sick or raising money for Oxfam, then necessarily he is not reading Victorian novels, playing the oboe, or improving his backhand. Although no one of the interests or tastes in the category containing these latter activities could be claimed to be a necessary element in a life well lived, a life in which *none* of these possible aspects of character are developed may seem to be a life strangely barren.

The reasons why a moral saint cannot, in general, encourage the discovery and development of significant nonmoral interests and skills are not logical but practical reasons. There are, in addition, a class of nonmoral characteristics that a moral saint cannot encourage in himself for reasons that are not just practical. There is a more substantial tension between having any of these qualities unashamedly and being a moral saint. These qualities might be described as going against the moral grain. For example, a cynical or sarcastic wit, or a sense of humor that appreciates this kind of wit in others, requires that one take an attitude of resignation and pessimism toward the flaws and vices to be found in the world. A moral saint, on the other hand, has reason to take an attitude in opposition to this—he should try to look for the best in people, give them the benefit of the doubt as long as possible, try to improve regrettable situations as long as there is any hope of success. This suggests that, although a moral saint might well enjoy a good episode of *Father Knows Best,* he may not in good conscience be able to laugh at a Marx Brothers movie or enjoy a play by George Bernard Shaw.

An interest in something like gourmet cooking will be, for different reasons, difficult for a moral saint to rest easy with. For it seems to me that no plausible argument can justify the use of human resources involved in producing a *paté de canard en croute* against possible alternative beneficent ends to which these resources might be put. If there is a justification for the institution of haute cuisine, it is

one which rests on the decision *not* to justify every activity against morally beneficial alternatives, and this is a decision a moral saint will never make. Presumably, an interest in high fashion or interior design will fare much the same, as will, very possibly, a cultivation of the finer arts as well.

A moral saint will have to be very, very nice. It is important that he not be offensive. The worry is that, as a result, he will have to be dull-witted or humorless or bland.

This worry is confirmed when we consider what sorts of characters, taken and refined both from life and from fiction, typically form our ideals. One would hope they would be figures who are morally good—and by this I mean more than just not morally bad—but one would hope, too, that they are not *just* morally good, but talented or accomplished or attractive in nonmoral ways as well. We may make ideals out of athletes, scholars, artists—more frivolously, out of cowboys, private eyes, and rock stars. We may strive for Katharine Hepburn's grace, Paul Newman's "cool"; we are attracted to the high-spirited passionate nature of Natasha Rostov; we admire the keen perceptiveness of Lambert Strether. Though there is certainly nothing immoral about the ideal characters or traits I have in mind, they cannot be superimposed upon the ideal of a moral saint. For although it is a part of many of these ideals that the characters set high, and not merely acceptable, moral standards for themselves, it is also essential to their power and attractiveness that the moral strengths go, so to speak, alongside of specific, independently admirable, nonmoral ground projects and dominant personal traits.

When one does finally turn one's eyes toward lives that are dominated by explicitly moral commitments, moreover, one finds oneself relieved at the discovery of idiosyncrasies or eccentricities not quite in line with the picture of moral perfection. One prefers the blunt, tactless, and opinionated Betsy Trotwood to the unfailingly kind and patient Agnes Copperfield; one prefers the mischievousness and the sense of irony in Chesterton's Father Brown to the innocence and undiscriminating love of St. Francis.

It seems that, as we look in our ideals for people who achieve nonmoral varieties of personal excellence in conjunction with or colored by some version of high moral tone, we look in our paragons of moral excellence for people whose moral achievements occur in conjunction with or colored by some interests or traits that have low moral tone. In other words, there seems to be a limit to how much morality we can stand. . . .

Moreover, there is something odd about the idea of morality itself, or moral goodness, serving as the object of a dominant passion in the way that a more concrete and specific vision of a goal (even a concrete *moral* goal) might be imagined to serve. Morality itself does not seem to be a suitable object of passion. Thus, when one reflects, for example, on the Loving Saint easily and gladly giving up his fishing trip or his stereo or his hot fudge sundae at the drop of the moral hat, one is apt to wonder not at how much he loves morality, but at how little he loves these other things. One thinks that, if he can give these up so easily, he does not know what it is to truly love them. There seems, in other words, to be a kind of joy which the Loving Saint, either by nature or by practice, is incapable of experiencing. The Rational Saint, on the other hand, might retain strong nonmoral and concrete desires—he simply denies himself the opportunity to act on them. But this is no less troubling. The Loving Saint one might suspect of missing a piece of perceptual machinery, of being blind to some of what the world has to offer. The Rational Saint, who sees it but foregoes it, one suspects of having a different problem—a pathological fear of damnation, perhaps, or an extreme form of self-hatred that interferes with his ability to enjoy the enjoyable in life.

In other words, the ideal of a life of moral sainthood disturbs not simply because it is an ideal of a life in which morality unduly dominates. The normal person's direct and specific desires for objects, activities, and events that conflict with the attainment of moral perfection are not simply sacrificed but removed, suppressed, or subsumed. The way in which morality, unlike other possible goals, is apt to dominate is particularly disturbing, for it seems to require either the lack or the denial of the existence of an identifiable, personal self. . . .

It must be remembered that from the fact that there is a tension between having any of these qualities and being a moral saint it does not follow that having any of these qualities is immoral. For it is not part of common-sense morality that one ought to be a moral saint. Still, if someone just happened to want to be a moral saint, he or she would not have or encourage these qualities, and, on the basis of our common-sense values, this counts as a reason *not* to want to be a moral saint. . . .

Moral Saints and Moral Theories

I have tried so far to paint a picture—or, rather, two pictures—of what a moral saint might be like, drawing on what I take to be the attitudes and beliefs about morality prevalent in contemporary, common-sense thought. To my suggestion that common-sense morality generates conceptions of moral saints that are unattractive or otherwise unacceptable, it is open to someone to reply, "so much the worse for common-sense morality." After all, it is often claimed that the goal of moral philosophy is to correct and improve upon common-sense morality, and I have as yet given no attention to the question of what conceptions of moral sainthood, if any, are generated from the leading moral theories of our time.

A quick, breezy reading of utilitarian and Kantian writings will suggest the images, respectively, of the Loving Saint and the Rational Saint. A utilitarian, with his emphasis on happiness, will certainly prefer the Loving Saint to the Rational one, since the Loving Saint will himself be a happier person than the Rational Saint. A Kantian, with his emphasis on reason, on the other hand, will find at least as much to praise in the latter as in the former. Still, both models, drawn as they are from common sense, appeal to an impure mixture of utilitarian and Kantian intuitions. A more careful examination of these moral theories raises questions about whether either model of moral sainthood would really be advocated by a believer in the explicit doctrines associated with either of these views.

Certainly, the utilitarian in no way denies the value of self-realization. He in no way disparages the development of interests, talents, and other personally attractive traits that I have claimed the moral saint would be without. Indeed, since just these features enhance the happiness both of the individuals who possess them and of those with whom they associate, the ability to promote these features both in oneself and in others will have considerable positive weight in utilitarian calculations.

This implies that the utilitarian would not support moral sainthood as a universal ideal. A world in which everyone, or even a large number of people, achieved moral sainthood—even a world in which they *strove* to achieve it—would probably contain less happiness than a world in which people realized a diversity of ideals involving a variety of personal and perfectionist values. More pragmatic considerations also suggest that, if the utilitarian wants to influence more people to achieve more good, then he would do better to encourage them to pursue happiness-producing goals that are more attractive and more within a normal person's reach.

These considerations still leave open, however, the question of what kind of an ideal the committed utilitarian should privately aspire to himself. Utilitarianism requires him to want to achieve the greatest general happiness, and this would seem to commit him to the ideal of the moral saint.

One might try to use the claims I made earlier as a basis for an argument that a utilitarian should choose to give up utilitarianism. If, as I have said, a moral saint would be a less happy person both to be and to be around than many other possible ideals, perhaps one could create more total happiness by not trying too hard to promote the total happiness. But this argument is simply unconvincing in light of the empirical circumstances of our world. The gain in happiness that would accrue to oneself and one's neighbors by a more well-rounded, richer life than that of the moral saint would be pathetically small in comparison to the amount by which one could increase the general happiness if one devoted oneself explicitly to the care of the sick, the downtrodden, the starving, and the homeless. Of course, there may be psychological limits to the extent to which a person can devote himself to such things without going crazy. But the utilitarian's individual limitations would not thereby become a positive feature of his personal ideals.

The unattractiveness of the moral saint, then, ought not rationally convince the utilitarian to abandon his utilitarianism. It may, however, convince him to take efforts not to wear his saintly moral aspirations on his sleeve. If it is not too difficult, the utilitarian will try not to make those around him uncomfortable. He will not want to appear "holier than thou"; he will not want to inhibit others' ability to enjoy themselves. In practice, this might make the perfect utilitarian a less nauseating companion than the moral saint I earlier portrayed. But insofar as this kind of reasoning produces a more bearable public personality, it is at the cost of giving him a personality that must be evaluated as hypocritical and condescending when his private thoughts and attitudes are taken into account.

Still, the criticisms I have raised against the saint of common-sense morality should make some difference to the utilitarian's conception of an ideal which neither requires him to abandon his utilitarian principles nor forces him to fake an interest he does not have or a judgment he does not make. For it may be that a limited and carefully monitored allotment of time and energy to be devoted to the pursuit of some nonmoral interests or to the development of some nonmoral talents would make a person a better contributor to the general welfare than he would be if he allowed himself no indulgences of this sort. The enjoyment of such activities in no way compromises a commitment to utilitarian principles as long as the involvement with these activities is conditioned by a willingness to give them up whenever it is recognized that they cease to be in the general interest.

This will go some way in mitigating the picture of the loving saint that an understanding of utilitarianism will on first impression suggest. But I think it will not go very far. For the limitations on time and energy will have to be rather severe, and the need to monitor will restrict not only the extent but also the quality of one's attachment to these interests and traits. They are only weak and somewhat peculiar sorts of passions to which one can consciously remain so conditionally committed. Moreover, the way in which the utilitarian can enjoy these "extracurricular" aspects of his life is simply not the way in which these aspects are to be enjoyed insofar as they figure into our less saintly ideals.

The problem is not exactly that the utilitarian values these aspects of his life only as a means to an end, for the enjoyment he and others get from these aspects are not a means to, but a part of, the general happiness. Nonetheless, he values these things only because of and insofar as they *are* a part of the general happiness. He values them, as it were, under the description "a contribution to the general happiness." This is to be contrasted with the various ways in which these aspects of life may be valued by nonutilitarians. A person might love literature because of the insights into human nature literature affords. Another might love the cultivation of roses because roses are things of great beauty and delicacy. It may be true that these features of the respective activities also explain why these activities are happiness-producing. But, to the nonutilitarian, this may not be to the point. For if one values these activities in these more direct ways, one may not be willing to exchange them for others that produce an equal, or even a greater amount of happiness. From that point of view, it is not because they produce happiness that these activities are valuable; it is because these activities are valuable in more direct and specific ways that they produce happiness. . . .

The Kantian believes that being morally worthy consists in always acting from maxims that one could will to be universal law, and doing this not out of any pathological desire but out of reverence for the moral law as such, Or, to take a different formulation of the categorical imperative, the Kantian believes that moral action consists in treating other persons always as ends and never as means only. Presumably, and according to Kant himself, the Kantian thereby commits himself to some degree of benevolence as well as to the rules of fair play. But we surely would not will that *every* person become a moral saint, and treating others as ends hardly requires bending over backwards to protect and promote their interests. On one interpretation of Kantian doctrine, then, moral perfection would be achieved simply by unerring obedience to a limited set of side-constraints. On this interpretation, Kantian theory simply does not yield an ideal conception of a person of any fullness comparable to that of the moral saints I have so far been portraying.

On the other hand, Kant does say explicitly that we have a duty of benevolence, a duty not only to allow others to pursue their ends, but to take up their ends as our own. In addition, we have positive

duties to ourselves, duties to increase our natural as well as our moral perfection. These duties are unlimited in the degree to which they *may* dominate a life. If action in accordance with and motivated by the thought of these duties is considered virtuous, it is natural to assume that the more one performs such actions, the more virtuous one is. Moreover, of virtue in general Kant says, "it is an ideal which is unattainable while yet our duty is constantly to approximate to it."[1] On this interpretation, then, the Kantian moral saint, like the other moral saints I have been considering, is dominated by the motivation to be moral.

Which of these interpretations of Kant one prefers will depend on the interpretation and the importance one gives to the role of the imperfect duties in Kant's over-all system. Rather than choose between them here, I shall consider each briefly in turn.

On the second interpretation of Kant, the Kantian moral saint is, not surprisingly, subject to many of the same objections I have been raising against other versions of moral sainthood. Though the Kantian saint may differ from the utilitarian saint as to *which* actions he is bound to perform and which he is bound to refrain from performing, I suspect that the range of activities acceptable to the Kantian saint will remain objectionably restrictive. Moreover, the manner in which the Kantian saint must think about and justify the activities he pursues and the character traits he develops will strike us, as it did with the utilitarian saint, as containing "one thought too many." As the utilitarian could value his activities and character traits only insofar as they fell under the description of "contributions to the general happiness," the Kantian would have to value his activities and character traits insofar as they were manifestations of respect for the moral law. If the development of our powers to achieve physical, intellectual, or artistic excellence, or the activities directed toward making others happy are to have any moral worth, they must arise from a reverence for the dignity that members of our species have as a result of being endowed with pure practical reason. This is a good and noble motivation, to be sure. But it is hardly what one expects to be dominantly behind a person's aspirations to dance as well as Fred Astaire, to paint as well as Picasso, or to solve some outstanding problem in abstract algebra, and it is hardly what one hopes to find lying dominantly behind a father's action on behalf of his son or a lover's on behalf of her beloved. . . .

Moral Saints and Moral Philosophy

In pointing out the regrettable features and the necessary absence of some desirable features in a moral saint, I have not meant to condemn the moral saint or the person who aspires to become one. Rather, I have meant to insist that the ideal of moral sainthood should not be held as a standard against which any other ideal must be judged or justified, and that the posture we take in response to the recognition that our lives are not as morally good as they might be need not be defensive.[2] It is misleading to insist that one is *permitted* to live a life in which the goals, relationships, activities, and interests that one pursues are not maximally morally good. For our lives are not so comprehensively subject to the requirement that we apply for permission, and our nonmoral reasons for the goals we set ourselves are not excuses, but may rather be positive, good reasons which do not exist *despite* any reasons that might threaten to outweigh them. In other words, a person may be *perfectly wonderful* without being *perfectly moral*.

Recognizing this requires a perspective which contemporary moral philosophy has generally ignored. This perspective yields judgments of a type that is neither moral nor egoistic. Like moral judgments, judgments about what it would be good for a person to be are made from a point of view outside the limits set by the values, interests, and desires that the person might actually have. And, like moral judgments, these judgments claim for themselves a kind of objectivity or a grounding in a perspective which any rational and perceptive being can take up. Unlike moral judgments, however, the good with which these judgments are concerned is not the good of anyone or any group other than the individual himself.

Nonetheless, it would be equally misleading to say that these judgments are made for the sake of the individual himself. For these judgments are not concerned with what kind of life it is in a person's interest to lead, but with what kind of interests it would be good for a person to have, and it need not be in a person's interest that he acquire or maintain objectively good interests. Indeed, the model of the Loving Saint, whose interests are identified with the interests of morality, is a model of a person for whom the dictates of rational self-interest and the dictates of morality coincide. Yet, I have urged that we have reason not to aspire to this ideal and that some of us would have reason to be sorry if our children aspired to and achieved it.

The moral point of view, we might say, is the point of view one takes up insofar as one takes the recognition of the fact that one is just one person among others equally real and deserving of the good things in life as a fact with practical consequences, a fact the recognition of which demands expression in one's actions and in the form of one's practical deliberations. Competing moral theories offer alternative answers to the question of what the most correct or the best way to express this fact is. In doing so, they offer alternative ways to evaluate and to compare the variety of actions, states of affairs, and so on that appear good and bad to agents from other, nonmoral points of view. But it seems that alternative interpretations of the moral point of view do not exhaust the ways in which our actions, characters, and their consequences can be comprehensively and objectively evaluated. Let us call the point of view from which we consider what kinds of lives are good lives, and what kinds of persons it would be good for ourselves and others to be, the *point of view of individual perfection.*

Since either point of view provides a way of comprehensively evaluating a person's life, each point of view takes account of, and, in a sense, subsumes the other. From the moral point of view, the perfection of an individual life will have some, but limited, value—for each individual remains, after all, just one person among others. From the perfectionist point of view, the moral worth of an individual's relation to his world will likewise have some, but limited, value—for, as I have argued, the (perfectionist) goodness of an individual's life does not vary proportionally with the degree to which it exemplifies moral goodness.

It may not be the case that the perfectionist point of view is like the moral point of view in being a point of view we are ever *obliged* to take up and express in our actions. Nonetheless, it provides us with reasons that are independent of moral reasons for wanting ourselves and others to develop our characters and live our lives in certain ways. When we take up this point of view and ask how much it would be good for an individual to act from the moral point of view, we do not find an obvious answer.[3]

The considerations of this paper suggest, at any rate, that the answer is not "as much as possible." This has implications both for the continued development of moral theories and for the development of metamoral views and for our conception of moral philosophy more generally. From the moral point of view, we have reasons to want people to live lives that seem good from outside that point of view. If, as I have argued, this means that we have reason to want people to live lives that are not morally perfect, then any plausible moral theory must make use of some conception of supererogation.[4]

If moral philosophers are to address themselves at the most basic level to the question of how people should live, however, they must do more than adjust the content of their moral theories in ways that leave room for the affirmation of nonmoral values. They must examine explicitly the range and nature of these nonmoral values, and, in light of this examination, they must ask how the acceptance of a moral theory is to be understood and acted upon. For the claims of this paper do not so much conflict with the content of any particular currently popular moral theory as they call into question a metamoral assumption that implicitly surrounds discussions of moral theory more generally. Specifically, they call into question the assumption that it is always better to be morally better.

The role morality plays in the development of our characters and the shape of our practical deliberations need be neither that of a universal medium into which all other values must be translated nor that of an ever-present filter through which all other values must pass. This is not to say that moral value should not be an important, even the most important, kind of value we attend to in evaluating and improving ourselves and our world. It is to say that

our values cannot be fully comprehended on the model of a hierarchical system with morality at the top.

The philosophical temperament will naturally incline, at this point, toward asking, "What, then, *is* at the top—or, if there is no top, how *are* we to decide when and how much to be moral?" In other words, there is a temptation to seek a metamoral—though not, in the standard sense, metaethical—theory that will give us principles, or, at least, informal directives on the basis of which we can develop and evaluate more comprehensive personal ideals. Perhaps a theory that distinguishes among the various roles a person is expected to play within a life—as professional, as citizen, as friend, and so on—might give us some rules that would offer us, if nothing else, a better framework in which to think about and discuss these questions. I am pessimistic, however, about the chances of such a theory to yield substantial and satisfying results. For I do not see how a metamoral theory could be constructed which would not be subject to considerations parallel to those which seem inherently to limit the appropriateness of regarding moral theories as ultimate comprehensive guides for action.

This suggests that, at some point, both in our philosophizing and in our lives, we must be willing to raise normative questions from a perspective that is unattached to a commitment to any particular well-ordered system of values. It must be admitted that, in doing so, we run the risk of finding normative answers that diverge from the answers given by whatever moral theory one accepts. This, I take it, is the grain of truth in G. E. Moore's "open question" argument. In the background of this paper, then, there lurks a commitment to what seems to me to be a healthy form of intuitionism. It is a form of intuitionism which is not intended to take the place of more rigorous, systematically developed, moral theories—rather, it is intended to put these more rigorous and systematic moral theories in their place.

NOTES

1. Immanuel Kant, *The Doctrine of Virtue*, Mary J. Gregor, trans. (New York: Harper & Row, 1964), p. 71.
2. George Orwell makes a similar point in "Reflections on Gandhi," in *A Collection of Essays by George Orwell*

(New York: Harcourt Brace Jovanovich, 1945), p. 176: "sainthood is . . . a thing that human beings must avoid . . . It is too readily assumed that . . . the ordinary man only rejects it because it is too difficult; in other words, that the average human being is a failed saint. It is doubtful whether this is true. Many people genuinely do not wish to be saints, and it is probable that some who achieve or aspire to sainthood have never felt much temptation to be human beings."

3. A similar view, which has strongly influenced mine, is expressed by Thomas Nagel in "The Fragmentation of Value," in *Mortal Questions* (New York: Cambridge, 1979), pp. 128–141. Nagel focuses on the difficulties such apparently incommensurable points of view create for specific, isolable practical decisions that must be made both by individuals and by societies. In focusing on the way in which these points of view figure into the development of individual personal ideals, the questions with which I am concerned are more likely to lurk in the background of any individual's life.

4. The variety of forms that a conception of supererogation might take, however, has not generally been noticed. Moral theories that make use of this notion typically do so by identifying some specific set of principles as universal moral requirements and supplement this list with a further set of directives which it is morally praiseworthy but not required for an agent to follow. [See, e.g., Charles Fried, *Right and Wrong* (Cambridge, Mass.: Harvard, 1979).] But it is possible that the ability to live a morally blameless life cannot be so easily or definitely secured as this type of theory would suggest. The fact that there are some situations in which an agent is morally required to do something and other situations in which it would be good but not required for an agent to do something does not imply that there are specific principles such that, in any situation, an agent is required to act in accordance with these principles and other specific principles such that, in any situation, it would be good but not required for an agent to act in accordance with those principles.

2

Medical Professional
and Patient

CHAPTER 3

Paternalism and Patient Autonomy

On its face, the relationship between patient and health care provider seems technically simple and morally clear. The provider—physician, nurse, physician's assistant, or other professional—has a duty of beneficence toward the patient, an obligation to use her medical expertise to do him good and to avoid doing him harm. The patient has a right to this skilled beneficence and to respect for his autonomous choices regarding what the provider does. But below the surface, complications simmer. The principles of beneficence and autonomy are frequently at odds. The values of providers and patients can diverge. The cultures of patients, physicians, and nurses can clash. And often the stakes for everyone involved are extraordinarily high.

In this chapter we explore several moral issues arising from these conflicts, focusing on questions of medical paternalism, refusing treatment, and "futile" treatment. Chapter 4 delves into other aspects of patient-provider relationships, notably truth-telling, deception, and confidentiality. Chapter 5 examines the patient-provider relationship further by studying the many sides of informed consent and patient competence.

SHADES OF AUTONOMY AND PATERNALISM

Autonomy is a person's rational capacity for self-governance or self-determination. It is an individual's power to deliberate about available options, to choose freely among those possibilities, and to act accordingly. We fully exercise our autonomy when our choices and actions are truly our own, free from the overriding pressure of people and factors that rob us of control. The requirement to respect autonomy runs through all of bioethics, expressed in the *autonomy principle,* which we can state as *autonomous persons should be allowed to exercise their capacity for self-determination.* In bioethics it is considered a fundamental standard that can be violated only for good reasons and with explicit justification. In the name of the autonomy principle, medicine has developed the doctrine of informed consent and has devised countless procedures and guidelines to ensure that the principle is honored in the details.

Limitations on a person's autonomy can be physical or psychological, obvious or subtle, justified or unjustified, and generally accepted or widely controversial. Physically restraining a patient violates his autonomy, and so does misinforming him about the seriousness of his illness. Forcing a healthy woman to have a hysterectomy is obvious coercion. Using false information to persuade her to have the operation is a subtler kind of compulsion. We tend to think that physicians are sometimes justified in confining and treating a mentally ill man who is a danger to himself and others. We would not think so if the man were perfectly healthy. Giving a 12-year-old girl a blood transfusion to save her life seems like normal medical practice. Withholding the transfusion because her parents say it is an affront to their religious faith is controversial.

Conflicts between respect for patients' autonomy and providers' duty of beneficence usually raise the issue of **paternalism**, which we can define as the overriding of a person's actions or decision-making for his own good. Early medical practice was strongly paternalistic, inspired by the Hippocratic tradition of devotion to the welfare of patients and fatherly insistence on deciding unilaterally what is best for them. The Hippocratic Oath and many later professional codes of medical practice had much to say about obligations to help and not to harm patients but little or nothing to declare about patients' rights to decide about their own medical care. But over the last few decades, this kind of heavy-handed paternalism has abated as society has placed more value on the rights of patients to know important facts about their medical care, to make choices regarding their medical treatment, and even to refuse treatment that physicians recommend.

We can distinguish between two kinds of paternalism. **Weak paternalism** refers to paternalism directed at persons who cannot act autonomously or whose autonomy is greatly diminished—who may be, for example, dangerously psychotic, severely retarded, extremely depressed, or acutely addicted. Weak paternalism is not usually considered an objectionable violation of autonomy because patients are already substantially nonautonomous to some degree. Generally it is thought to be morally acceptable because its purpose is to protect people from harm while they are nonautonomous, to determine if they are in fact nonautonomous, or to restore them to full autonomy. **Strong paternalism** is the overriding of a person's actions or choices even though he is substantially autonomous. Cases involving strong paternalism often provoke debate and sometimes legal wrangling. A man who normally behaves autonomously and rationally is involuntarily committed to a mental institution because he occasionally becomes confused and disoriented and doctors fear that he might someday become a threat to himself or others. A physician discovers that his patient has a malignant breast tumor, but because he knows she is terrified of the disease, he tells her that the tumor is benign and should be surgically removed just in case. A woman who needs a life-saving blood transfusion refuses it on religious grounds, but when she lapses into a coma, surgeons operate and give her the transfusion anyway. These and other scenarios play out more

often than we might think and prompt not only ethical disagreement but also personal and professional anguish.

Many people are staunchly anti-paternalistic, condoning (as most do) acts of weak paternalism but rejecting all forms of strong paternalism. They argue that strong paternalism is wrong because it violates the rights of persons to determine for themselves what is good and what is right. Persons are sovereigns over their own lives, and overriding their sovereignty is impermissible regardless of the benefits gained by violating it. Others are more willing to countenance some acts of paternalism (including strong paternalism) on the grounds that the persons involved *would* consent to the acts if circumstances were ideal (if, say, the persons were thinking more rationally). These thinkers, for example, might be willing to commit a substantially autonomous person to a mental institution involuntarily if he would have trouble living independently and might be a danger to himself. Still others argue that the only satisfactory justification for paternalism is not consent but beneficence— intervening simply to promote someone's welfare. On this view, the benefits of paternalistic actions must be balanced against the importance of respecting autonomy. Actions that minimally restrict autonomy but benefit the person greatly would be justified; actions that seriously violate autonomy while offering only minor benefits would not be acceptable. Far less important would be concerns about what the individual would or would not consent to under different circumstances.[1]

REFUSING TREATMENT

Patients want physicians to treat them; physicians want to treat patients. But often when patients (or their surrogates) refuse treatment, patient autonomy and physician beneficence collide, sparking personal frustration and moral perplexity all around. In such cases the most vexing bioethical questions include: Is it ever morally permissible for a physician to treat a patient against her will?

IN DEPTH
THE HIPPOCRATIC OATH

For centuries the Hippocratic Oath has been one of the great inspirations for Western medical ethics. It is one of several writings attributed to an ancient Greek school of medicine whose head was Hippocrates, born about 460 B.C.

I swear by Apollo Physician and Asclepius and Hygieia and Panaceia and all the gods and goddesses, making them my witness, that I will fulfill according to my ability and judgment this oath and this covenant:

To hold him who has taught me this art as equal to my parents and to live my life in partnership with him, and if he is in need of money to give him a share of mine, and to regard his offspring as equal to my brothers in male lineage and to teach them this art—if they desire to learn it—without fee and covenant; to give a share of precepts and oral instruction and all the other learning to my sons and to the sons of him who has instructed me and to pupils who have signed the covenant and have taken an oath according to the medical law, but to no one else.

I will apply dietetic measures for the benefit of the sick according to my ability and judgment; I will keep them from harm and injustice.

I will neither give a deadly drug to anybody if asked for it, nor will I make a suggestion to this effect. Similarly I will not give to a woman an abortive remedy. In purity and holiness I will guard my life and my art.

I will not use the knife, not even on sufferers from stone, but will withdraw in favor of such men as are engaged in this work.

Whatever houses I may visit, I will come for the benefit of the sick, remaining free of all intentional injustice, of all mischief and in particular of sexual relations with both female and male persons, be they free or slaves.

What I may see or hear in the course of the treatment or even outside of the treatment in regard to the life of men, which on no account one must spread abroad, I will keep to myself holding such things shameful to be spoken about.

If I fulfill this oath and do not violate it, may it be granted to me to enjoy life and art, being honored with fame among all men for all time to come; if I transgress it and swear falsely, may the opposite of all this be my lot.

From Ludwig Edelstein, *Ancient Medicine: Selected Papers of Ludwig Edelstein,* ed. Owsei Temkin and C. Lillian Temkin (Baltimore: Johns Hopkins University Press, 1967), 3–65.

If so, what justifies the action, and under what conditions is it acceptable?

Until the late 1980s, the right of competent patients to turn down treatments ordered by physicians was unsettled. (Very roughly, competent patients are autonomous persons able to make decisions about treatment options.) In some situations, patients were thought to have no right to decline recommended treatments. Physicians sometimes forced pregnant patients to have cesarean deliveries if failure to do so put the fetuses at extreme risk. The courts frequently overruled the right to refuse treatment if the patient had dependent children or if the patient was not terminally ill. But later court rulings reversed the trend and carved out the bedrock principle that a competent patient has a right to reject recommended treatments, even life-saving ones. The legal principle now parallels the prevailing view in bioethics, which shifts the weight to patient autonomy over physician and nurse beneficence.

The courts have also stretched this right of competent patients to situations in which they become incompetent, as when they lapse into coma. Through advance directives or other evidence of their preferences, they can refuse

Patient autonomy is not the only kind of autonomy debated these days. There is also concern about *physician autonomy*, the freedom of doctors to determine the conditions they work in and the care they give to patients. Many factors can adversely affect physician autonomy. Here's a brief inventory of some that doctors believe are most problematic:

> Both physicians and patients are inundated with arbitrary treatment regulations and financial punishments for "out-of-system treatments." Physicians have added pressures from pharmaceutical industry inducements that encourage the use of expensive treatments of marginal efficacy. They are penalized for low productivity, which threatens their willingness to discuss complex patient problems, even those that are most likely to affect the patient's health. Patterns of physician reimbursement encourage procedure-oriented interventions and minimize counseling, in spite of the greater benefit of brief counseling for patient health. . . .
>
> As a result of all these complex, sometimes contradictory, often covert and self-interested inducements from third parties, physicians often are confronted with resistance when they explain their treatment decisions to patients. The case of antibiotic treatment for viral infections is a prime example. Antibiotics have not been shown to improve medical outcomes for otherwise healthy patients with early symptoms of upper respiratory infections. In fact, patients incur the risk of side effects (allergic reactions, GI disturbance, and cost) without the potential for benefit. From the social justice point of view, prescribing antibiotics for URIs in otherwise healthy people wastes resources and could contribute to resistant bacteria in the population. Yet, patients frequently request, and sometimes demand, these antibiotics and interpret physicians' withholding them as undermining their autonomy. . . .
>
> In cases such as this, the value the patient places on having access to prescribed medication on demand appears to be in conflict with the physician's obligation to put patient welfare first and to consider social justice in allocation of medical resources. . . .

From Geoffrey C. Williams and Timothy E. Quill, "Physician Autonomy, Paternalism, and Professionalism: Finding Our Voice amid Conflicting Duties," *AMA Journal of Ethics*, vol. 6, no. 2 (February 2004).

---

life-sustaining treatment. This expression of prior intentions is now widely recognized as a legitimate exercise of autonomous choice.

The right to refuse treatment seems a relatively straightforward issue when the patient is a competent adult, but what if the patient is a child whose parents reject the recommended medical treatment on religious grounds? Consider the case of 11-year-old Ian Lundman of Minneapolis, Minnesota, who died on May 9, 1989, after slipping into a diabetic coma. His diabetes had remained medically untreated, his mother and stepfather forgoing insulin in favor of prayers from Christian Science practitioners.[2] (Christian Scientists believe that disease is a spiritual disorder requiring spiritual healing, not medical treatment.) Or consider this scenario, typical of such cases: A 6-year-old girl is seriously injured in a traffic accident, and the only way to save her life is to give her a blood transfusion—which her Jehovah's Witness parents reject because the procedure is explicitly forbidden by their faith. The physicians proceed with the transfusion and save the girl's life, and the parents sue the physicians and the hospital.

Parents who for religious reasons reject medical treatment for their children insist on the right to decide what's best for them and sincerely believe what's best is avoiding medical interventions. They demand the freedom to practice their religion as they see fit. But others have argued (including the courts) that though parents may decide many matters on the well-being of their children, they do not have the right to bring serious harm to them, especially since children cannot decide such issues for themselves. This view was summed up in a famous 1944 Supreme Court decision: "Parents may be free to become martyrs themselves. But it does not follow they are free . . . to make martyrs of their children."[3]

The situation takes on a different hue when children are considered competent to decide for themselves. States differ on whether an adolescent can be a "mature minor" to make health decisions, and the courts have waffled on the issue. Judges have ruled, for example, that a 15-year-old Jehovah's Witness girl dying of leukemia could refuse a blood transfusion that would save her life—but that a 16-year-old boy injured in a train accident could not decline a transfusion needed during surgery to save his arm. Nevertheless, many argue that if adolescents are not competent to decide such things, competent adults (including physicians and nurses) should step in to protect their welfare, even if intervening means defying religious doctrine.

FUTILE TREATMENT

The classic pattern of paternalism involves a physician who wants to treat a patient who prefers not to be treated. But sometimes things happen the other way around—when the patient or the patient's family wants a treatment that the physician, typically from beneficent motives, does not want to provide. The main moral conflict is between patient autonomy and the physician's view of what constitutes morally acceptable care.

The most dramatic (and heart-rending) of such cases center on whether to supply life-sustaining treatment to the patient. Consider the much discussed story of 85-year-old Helga Wanglie, who in 1990 suddenly had to be placed on a ventilator because of serious breathing problems. Over the following weeks, her condition worsened as she sank into unconsciousness and then into a persistent vegetative state (a deep coma that is usually irreversible). She received round-the-clock life-sustaining treatment consisting of ventilator, antibiotics, tube feedings, and other measures. But physicians told Helga's husband and two children that the treatment was not helping her and should be stopped. Her family, however, demanded that the treatment continue. They hoped for a miracle and asserted that Helga was not better off dead and that physicians should not play God. Her husband claimed that Helga had never expressed an opinion about life-sustaining treatment for herself. Later a second team of physicians confirmed the views of the first, calling the ventilator "nonbeneficial" because it could not ease Helga's suffering, repair her body, or help her experience life.

The struggle over whether to discontinue Helga's treatment eventually moved into court, but its decision did little to resolve the stalemate. Three days after the court ruling, Helga died.[4]

Such physician-patient conflicts are commonly described as confrontations about **medical futility**, the alleged pointlessness or ineffectiveness of administering particular treatments. Physicians may claim that a treatment is futile and therefore should not be used or continued. Patients or their surrogates may reject the label of futility and insist that everything be done that can be done. But physicians and patients often have different ideas about what constitutes futility. The former may judge a treatment futile if it cannot achieve a specified physiological benefit (cannot, for example, repair tissue, restore functioning, or ease suffering); the latter may think a treatment futile only if it cannot keep the body alive. For both, the issue of futility is a question of values— of what should be done in the circumstances.

In tugs of war over the acceptability of treatment, physicians appeal to a widely recognized principle: Physicians are not obligated to provide treatments that are inconsistent with reasonable standards of medical practice. They are not morally bound to comply, for example, when a patient

LEGAL BRIEF

Refusing Treatment for Children on Religious Grounds

Since the 1970s, several children have died after their parents refused medical treatment because of religious beliefs. The deaths have sparked fierce debates and legal conflicts, with some jurisdictions offering religious parents exemptions from child abuse and neglect laws while medical organizations such as the American Academy of Pediatrics (AAP) and the American Medical Association (AMA) have opposed the laws. In its policy statement on the issue, the AAP declares, "Constitutional guarantees of freedom of religion do not permit children to be harmed through religious practices, nor do they allow religion to be a valid defense when an individual harms or neglects a child." According to a recent tally of the religious exemptions:

- Thirty-eight states and the District of Columbia have religious exemptions in their civil codes on child abuse or neglect, largely because of a federal government policy from 1974 to 1983 requiring states to pass such exemptions in order to get federal funding for child protection work. The states are Alabama, Alaska, Arizona, Arkansas, California, Colorado, Connecticut, Delaware, Florida, Georgia, Idaho, Illinois, Indiana, Iowa, Kansas, Kentucky, Louisiana, Maine, Michigan, Minnesota, Mississippi, Missouri, Montana, Nevada, New Hampshire, New Jersey, New Mexico, North Dakota, Oklahoma, Pennsylvania, Rhode Island, South Carolina, Utah, Vermont, Virginia, Washington, Wisconsin, and Wyoming. Additionally, Tennessee exempts caretakers who withhold medical care from being adjudicated as negligent if they rely instead on non-medical "remedial treatment" that is "legally recognized or legally permitted."

- Sixteen states have religious defenses to felony crimes against children: Arkansas, Idaho, Indiana, Iowa, Louisiana, Minnesota, New Jersey, Ohio, Oklahoma, Tennessee, Texas, Utah, Virginia, Washington, West Virginia, and Wisconsin.

- Fifteen states have religious defenses to misdemeanors: Alabama, Alaska, California, Colorado, Delaware, Georgia, Kansas, Maine, Mississippi, Missouri, Nevada, New Hampshire, New York, South Carolina, and South Dakota.

- Florida has a religious exemption only in the civil code, but the Florida Supreme Court nevertheless held that it caused confusion about criminal liability and required overturning a felony conviction of Christian Scientists for letting their daughter die of untreated diabetes.

States with a religious defense to the most serious crimes against children include:

- Idaho, Iowa, and Ohio with religious defenses to manslaughter
- West Virginia with religious defenses to murder of a child and child neglect resulting in death
- Arkansas with a religious defense to capital murder

From childrenshealthcare.org (10 October 2015)

requests that his legs be amputated for no reason or demands injections of a worthless and dangerous cancer remedy. Not every patient request must be regarded as legitimate, and not every medical technology must be supplied.

Many times in futility cases, physicians and surrogates find resolution. They agree to an extension of the treatment for a specified period or to reasonable goals that the treatment can achieve, or the surrogates eventually view the treatment as useless, or the patient dies. But sometimes resolution eludes everyone. The sharpest clash of values is likely to occur between physicians and those who argue for the sanctity of

The medical procedure used to restart a person's heart and breathing is known as cardiopulmonary resuscitation, or *CPR*. It typically consists of mouth-to-mouth resuscitation and external chest compression but may involve more advanced procedures such as defibrillation (electric shock to restore normal heart rhythm). A do-not-resuscitate order, or *DNR*, is a directive telling the medical staff to forgo CPR on a patient if his heart or breathing stops. DNR orders are generally thought to be medically appropriate and morally permissible when the performing of CPR on seriously or terminally ill patients would be ineffective or futile and would only prolong dying or intensify the patient's pain and suffering. Patients can consent to DNR orders in person, in written instructions in an advance directive such as a living will, or through someone they designate as their representative, or proxy. The AMA declares, "The physician has an ethical obligation to honor the resuscitation preferences expressed by the patient. Physicians should not permit their personal value judgments about quality of life to obstruct the implementation of a patient's preferences regarding the use of CPR."

Critically important bioethical issues can arise for nurses from their relationships with patients, with physicians, and with the institutional ethic under which they serve.

As nurses interact with patients, they must come to terms with many of the same moral questions and principles that weigh so heavily on physicians: beneficence versus patient autonomy, patient-provider confidentiality, truth-telling, refusal of treatment, informed consent, and futile treatment.

The issues generated from physician–nurse interactions can be just as pressing. The traditional notion of a nurse is that of a caregiver subordinate to physicians and duty bound to carry out their directives for patient care and treatment. But for many nurses this model seems fraught with conflicts between the nurse's obligation to follow the doctor's orders and her duty of beneficence toward her patients. She may wonder whether she has this sort of duty to physicians even when their orders seem clearly to be in error, or likely to harm her patients, or obviously in violation of patients' autonomy, or evidently contrary to well-established standards of care.

Some writers have defended the traditional model of nursing, arguing that (at least in hospitals) physicians must always be the ultimate authority on treatment in urgent or serious cases. After all, only doctors have the requisite training and experience to deal with such situations, and for the sake of efficiency, their decisions should not be questioned. The nurse's proper role is therefore subservient.

But others reject the traditional model, arguing instead that the nurse's ultimate responsibility is to be an advocate for patients, that adopting a subservient role would likely harm patients, and that blindly following physicians' orders does not serve the patient well.

human life. On this view, the moral imperative is to keep the body alive at all costs. For someone who accepts this principle, the physicians' claim that the treatment does not benefit the patient will carry little weight. A common argument against the position is that it makes no sense to treat a body when the person whose body it is no longer exists.

Elizabeth Bouvia

The central issue in this famous case—both moral and legal—is whether a competent patient has the right to refuse life-sustaining medical treatment. In *Bouvia v. Superior Court*, the California Court of Appeal answered the question with an emphatic yes, and other courts soon followed with similar rulings.

In 1983 Elizabeth Bouvia was 25 years old, bright, articulate, and mentally competent. But she had cerebral palsy from birth and was quadriplegic, her whole body paralyzed except for her right hand and a few muscles allowing minor face and head movements. She also suffered from degenerative arthritis, which, despite her paralysis, caused constant pain that could not be relieved entirely even with doses of morphine. She needed continuous care, but her family would not oblige. She had no job, no income, no home, and no hope of getting help except through public assistance.

She finally got her father to drive her to a public hospital in Riverside County, California, where she asked to be given pain medicine and hygienic care while she slowly committed suicide by starving herself to death. The hospital admitted her but refused to be part of her plan for suicide. She then asked for legal help from the American Civil Liberties Union (ACLU), and her case went before a judge in Riverside County.

Her attending physician at the hospital declared at the first hearing that he would not allow her to die by starvation and that if necessary he would force-feed her. Bouvia asked the judge to disallow the force-feeding, but he ruled that it was permissible, saying that letting her starve to death would have a terrible effect on the hospital staff as well as on physically handicapped people generally. He asserted that she may have the right to commit suicide but not the right to compel others to help her do it. He said that society's interest in preserving life was more important than Elizabeth Bouvia's constitutional right to privacy, the right to be left alone.

So the force-feeding began. Liquid nourishment was pumped into her through a plastic tube snaked into her nose to her stomach, a procedure known as nasogastric feeding. Opinions among medical professionals about the practice were mixed, with some saying that it was necessary and others that it was horrible and coercive, amounting to battery.

Bouvia lost an appeal of the judge's decision, was later transferred to another hospital, and eventually ended up at High Desert Hospital, a public long-term care facility. At High Desert, her physicians ordered, against her will, that she be once again force-fed to head off possible starvation. They thought nasogastric feeding appropriate because her condition was life-threatening and because with adequate nutrition she could possibly live another 15 or 20 years.

She sued the hospital, asking the Superior Court of Los Angeles to order the force-feeding halted. But the court refused, saying that she clearly intended suicide and that the state could do whatever was necessary to preserve her life.

She appealed the decision to a higher court and, this time, won. In a 1986 ruling, the California Court of Appeal declared unequivocally that competent adults have a "constitutionally guaranteed right" to decide for themselves whether to submit to medical treatments:

> [S]uch a patient has the right to refuse *any* medical treatment, even that which may save or prolong her life. . . . The right to refuse medical treatment is basic and fundamental. It is recognized as a part of the right of privacy protected by both the state and federal constitutions. . . . Its exercise requires no one's approval. It is not merely one vote subject to being overridden by medical opinion. . . . A long line of cases, approved by the Supreme court in *Cobbs v. Grant* (1972) . . . have held that where a doctor performs treatment in the absence of informed consent, there is an actionable battery. The obvious corollary to this principle is that *"a competent patient has the legal right to refuse medical treatment."*[5]

The court also held that the previous judge had put too much importance on the *length* of Elizabeth Bouvia's life if treated (15 to 20 years) without considering the *quality* of that extended life:

> We do not believe it is the policy of this State that all and every life must be preserved against the will of the sufferer. It is incongruous, if not monstrous, for medical practitioners to assert their right to preserve a life that someone else must live, or, more accurately, endure, for "15 to 20 years." We cannot conceive it to be the policy of this State to inflict such an ordeal upon anyone. . . . It is, therefore, immaterial that the removal of the nasogastric tube will hasten or cause Bouvia's eventual death.[6]

Throughout Bouvia's long ordeal, physicians had noted that her obvious intention was to commit suicide and that they did not want to be accomplices in such an act. But the court maintained that her intentions were irrelevant and that she had a right to refuse treatment regardless of her intentions. Moreover, caregivers who honored refusals of treatment in such cases would not be subject to legal penalty.

Thus *Bouvia v. Superior Court* tilted the moral and legal scales from physician beneficence to patient autonomy. No other judicial ruling had so strongly and unequivocally asserted that competent patients have a right to reject treatments needed to keep them alive—and that this right supersedes the interests of doctors, hospitals, and the state.

APPLYING MAJOR THEORIES

The major moral theories imply diverse stands on paternalism. As a theory driven by the principle of beneficence, utilitarianism demands that we maximize the good for everyone involved—a requirement that may justify paternalistic actions. To promote the greatest good for patients—to minimize suffering and maximize well-being—a physician or nurse may think it sometimes legitimate to breach confidentiality or mislead patients about their condition or proposed treatment. She may believe it morally permissible to override a patient's refusal of treatment or to reject the use of requested treatments thought to be futile.

Act- and rule-utilitarians can disagree dramatically on such matters. (They may also differ in their estimates of the probabilities involved and ideas about the nature of the good to be maximized.) In act-utilitarianism, the rightness of actions depends on the relative good produced by individual actions; in rule-utilitarianism, rightness depends on the good maximized by rules governing categories of actions. On act-utilitarian

grounds, a physician may judge that it is morally permissible to lie to a patient about a beneficial treatment to overcome the patient's refusal to be treated. But based on rule-utilitarianism, a physician may believe that in the long run, lies do more harm than good because they erode public trust in the medical profession. Better to adhere to a rule barring deceit as a means of getting patients to accept a treatment.

Utilitarians who follow John Stuart Mill's lead, however, would reject such paternalism. Mill believes that the principle of utility implies a strong respect for individual self-determination and asserts that no one may interfere with a person's liberty except to prevent harm to others. As Mill says, "[A person] cannot rightfully be compelled to do or forbear because it will be better for him to do so, because it will make him happier, because, in the opinion of others, to do so would be wise, or even right."[7] On this view people should typically be permitted to decide what is to be done to their own bodies, to refuse treatments, and to give their informed consent.

Generally, Kantian ethics also rejects paternalism. The means-end form of the categorical imperative insists on respect for the rights and autonomy of persons—respect that must not be weakened by calculations of utility and paternalistic urges to act for the patient's own good. The principle would require physicians to honor a patient's decision to refuse treatment, even when they believe the treatment is life-saving. Informed consent of the patient for any treatment would be mandatory, and misleading the patient about treatment would be out of the question. To ignore any of these requirements would be to treat the patient merely as a means and not as an end.

In cases of medical futility, a Kantian could argue that if a physician believes a treatment is pointless and that giving it would be unethical or inappropriate, then the physician's withholding or withdrawing the treatment is morally permissible. Forcing the physician to do what she thinks is wrong would be a violation of her autonomy.

Natural law theory is more paternalistic than Kantian ethics, a characteristic we can see in cases involving euthanasia. A physician guided by the doctrine of double effect would deny a terminally ill patient's request to be given a lethal injection or to have ordinary life-sustaining measures stopped so she could die. The Roman Catholic corollary to this approach, however, is that a hopelessly ill patient has the right to refuse *extraordinary* life-sustaining treatments—measures that cause suffering or hardship but offer no medical benefit.

KEY TERMS
autonomy
medical futility
paternalism
strong paternalism
weak paternalism

SUMMARY
Autonomy is a person's rational capacity for self-governance or self-determination. The requirement to respect autonomy is expressed in the autonomy principle: Autonomous persons should be allowed to exercise their capacity for self-determination. In bioethics this principle is thought to be a fundamental standard that can be violated only for good reasons and with explicit justification.

Paternalism is the overriding of a person's actions or decision-making for his own good. Weak paternalism refers to paternalism directed at persons who cannot act autonomously or whose autonomy is greatly diminished. It is not usually considered an objectionable violation of autonomy because patients are already substantially nonautonomous and because the point is to protect people from harm while they are nonautonomous, to determine if they are in fact nonautonomous, or to restore them to full autonomy. Strong paternalism is the overriding of a person's actions or choices even though he or she is substantially autonomous.

Patient autonomy and physician or nurse beneficence often conflict when patients refuse treatment. The central question in such cases is whether it is ever permissible for a provider to treat a patient against her will. Both physicians and the courts now recognize the right of competent patients to refuse treatment. But controversy arises when the patient is a child whose parents refuse medical treatment on religious grounds.

Physician-patient conflicts also surface when patients demand treatments that the physician thinks are inappropriate. These clashes are about medical futility, the alleged pointlessness or ineffectiveness of administering particular treatments. Physicians often appeal to the principle that they are not obligated to provide treatments that are inconsistent with reasonable standards of medical practice. Patients may appeal to other principles such as the sanctity of life.

Utilitarianism demands that we maximize the good for everyone involved—a requirement that may justify paternalistic actions. But utilitarian opinions on paternalism can vary depending on whether they are based on act- or rule-utilitarian approaches. Kantian ethics generally rejects paternalism, insisting on the rights and autonomy of persons. Natural law theory is more paternalistic, denying through the doctrine of double effect a terminally ill patient's request to be given a lethal injection or to have ordinary life-sustaining measures stopped so she could die.

Cases for Evaluation

CASE 1

Faith-Healing Parents Arrested for Death of Second Child

A religious couple already on probation for choosing prayer over medicine in the death of their toddler son may be facing similar charges in the death of their newest child. "They lost their 8-month-old son, Brandon, last week after he suffered from diarrhea and breathing problems for at least a week, and stopped eating. Four years ago, another son died from bacterial pneumonia."

That boy, a two-year-old named Kent, died after the Schaibles refused to take him to the doctor when he became sick, relying instead on faith and prayer. The couple were convicted of involuntary manslaughter and sentenced to 10 years on probation.

In the latest tragedy, they told police that they prayed for God to heal Brandon instead of taking him to a doctor when he fell ill. Officials said that an autopsy will be performed on the child, and depending on those results the parents may be charged with a crime.

The couple attend, and have taught at, Philadelphia's First Century Gospel Church, which cites Biblical scripture favoring prayer and faith over modern medicine. Other religions, including Followers of Christ Church, Christian Scientists, and Scientology, have doctrines that prohibit or discourage modern medicine and therapeutic interventions.

This is not the first time that parents have gone on trial for child abuse or neglect for refusing their children medical attention. Though freedom of religion is guaranteed by the First Amendment to the U.S. Constitution, the practice of that religion does not give followers license to break the law—especially when the result is injury or death to a child.*

Do you agree with the court's sentence of ten years of probation? Should the sentence have been harsher? Why or why not? Do you think that parents should have the right to reject medical treatment for their children on the basis of religious beliefs? What moral principle would support your judgment? Should religious liberty be construed to allow parents to do anything *with their children as long as the actions are based on religious considerations? If not, what sorts of actions should and should not be allowed?*

*Discovery.com, 24 April 2013.

CASE 2

State Paternalism and Pregnant Women

(AP)—Public hospitals cannot test pregnant women for drugs and turn the results over to police without consent, the Supreme Court said Wednesday in a ruling that buttressed the Constitution's protection against unreasonable searches [Ferguson v. City of Charleston].

Some women who tested positive for drugs at a South Carolina public hospital were arrested from their beds shortly after giving birth.

The justices ruled 6-3 that such testing without patients' consent violates the Constitution even though the goal was to prevent women from harming their fetuses by using crack cocaine.

"It's a very, very important decision in protecting the right to privacy of all Americans," said Priscilla Smith, lawyer for the Center for Reproductive Law and Policy, who represented the South Carolina women. "It reaffirms that pregnant women have that same right to a confidential relationship with their doctors."

Justice John Paul Stevens wrote for the court that while the ultimate goal of the hospital's testing program may have been to get women into drug treatment, "the immediate objective of the searches was to generate evidence for law enforcement purposes in order to reach that goal."

When hospitals gather evidence "for the specific purpose of incriminating those patients, they have a special obligation to make sure that the patients are fully informed about their constitutional rights," Stevens said.

South Carolina Attorney General Charles Condon, who as a local prosecutor in Charleston began the testing program, issued a statement saying the program can continue if police get a search warrant or the patient's consent. "There is no right of a mother to jeopardize the health and safety of an unborn child through her own drug abuse," Condon wrote.

Condon developed the policy along with officials at the Medical University of South Carolina, a Charleston hospital that treats indigent patients. The women were arrested under the state's child-endangerment law, but their lawyers contended the policy was counterproductive and would deter women from seeking prenatal care. . . .

The decision reversed a federal appeals court ruling that said the South Carolina hospital's drug-testing policy was a valid effort to reduce crack cocaine use by pregnant women.

The hospital began the drug testing in 1989 during the crack cocaine epidemic. If a woman's urine test indicated cocaine use, she was arrested for distributing the drug to a minor. In 1990 the hospital gave drug-using maternity patients a choice between arrest or enrolling for drug treatment.

Ten women sued the hospital in 1993, saying the policy violated the Constitution. The hospital dropped the policy the following year, but by then police had arrested 30 women.[*]

Do you agree with the Supreme Court's decision? Why or why not? Should the state force pregnant women to behave in certain ways while carrying a fetus? If pregnant women can be legally punished for "fetal abuse," how should it be defined? Is a pregnant woman guilty of fetal abuse if she refuses to eat properly? Drinks any amount of alcohol? Forgoes prenatal care? Whose interests should be given greater weight—the woman's or the fetus'?

---

*Associated Press, "Court: Consent Needed to Drug-Test Pregnant Women," CNN.com., 21 March 2001.

CASE 3
Medical Futility

(*Washington Post*)—A 17-month-old deaf, blind and terminally ill child on life support is the latest focus in an emotional fight against a Texas law that allows hospitals to withdraw care when a patient's ongoing treatment is declared "medically futile."

Since Dec. 28, baby Emilio Gonzales has spent his days in a pediatric intensive care unit, mostly asleep from the powerful drugs he is administered, and breathing with the help of a respirator. Children's Hospital here declared his case hopeless last month and gave his mother 10 days, as legally required, to find another facility to take the baby. That deadline, extended once already, was due to expire Wednesday, at which time the hospital was to shut off Emilio's respirator. Without the machine, Emilio would die within minutes or hours, hospital officials have said.

But the child's mother, Catarina Gonzales, 23, and lawyers representing a coalition of state and national disability rights advocates and groups that favor prolonging life persuaded a Travis County judge Tuesday to force the hospital to maintain Emilio's care while the search for a facility to accept him continues. The group's attempt last week to persuade a federal judge to intervene in the case failed.

County Probate Judge Guy Herman appointed a guardian ad litem, or attorney, to represent Emilio's interests and issued a temporary restraining order prohibiting Children's Hospital from removing life-sustaining care from the child. He set an April 19 hearing on the mother's and lawyers' request for a temporary injunction against the hospital.

"I believe there is a hospital that is going to accept my son," said Gonzales following the brief hearing. "I just want to spend time with my son. . . . I want to let him die naturally without someone coming up and saying we're going to cut off on a certain day."

Michael Regier, senior vice president for legal affairs of the Seton Family of Hospitals, which includes Children's Hospital, said the child's condition continues to deteriorate although he has not met the criteria to be declared brain dead. He said the hospital has contacted 31 facilities "without any single indication of interest in taking the transfer."

Gonzales and her lawyers are seeking a transfer for the child, diagnosed with a terminal neuro-metabolic disorder called Leigh's disease, to a hospital that will perform a tracheotomy and insert a feeding tube so that he can live out his life in the facility or at home with his mother. But Children's Hospital doctors have declared that continuing treatment is potentially painful and is prolonging the child's suffering.

Emilio's case has drawn interest and support nationwide, including from the siblings of Terri Schiavo, the Florida woman who was in a persistent vegetative state and who died in 2005 after doctors, acting on a court order, removed her life-sustaining feeding tube.

Texas's six-year-old "futile-care" law is one of two in the country that allow a hospital's ethics committee to declare the care of a terminally ill patient to be of no benefit and to discontinue care within a certain time frame. The patient's family or guardian must be informed in advance of the ethics committee meeting and must be allowed to participate. The family must also be given 10 days to find a medical facility willing to accept their terminal relative. After that period, the hospital may withdraw life support. Virginia gives a family 14 days to transfer a patient once a futile-care decision is made.*

Do you agree with the hospital's reasons for wanting to withdraw care? Do you agree with the child's parents? Explain. Do you believe that life should be preserved at all costs (the sanctity of life view)? Why or why not? Do you believe that quality of life is more important than the preservation of life in cases like this? If so, how would you justify that view?

---

*Sylvia Moreno, "Case Puts Futile-Treatment Law Under a Microscope," *Washington Post*, 11 April 2007.

FURTHER READING

Tom L. Beauchamp and James F. Childress, *Principles of Biomedical Ethics*, 5th ed. (New York: Oxford University Press, 2001), 176–94, 283–336.

Dax Cowart and Robert Burt, "Confronting Death: Who Chooses, Who Controls? A Dialogue Between Dax Cowart and Robert Burt," *Hastings Center Report* 28.1 (1998): 14–17.

Harriet Hall, "Paternalism Revisited," *Science-Based Medicine*, December 16, 2008, https://www.sciencebasedmedicine.org/paternalism-revisited/ (20 October 2015).

Charles E. Gessert, "The Problem with Autonomy," *Minnesota Medicine*, http://www.minnesotamedicine.com/Past-Issues/Past-Issues-2008/April-2008/Commentary-April-2008 (20 October 2015).

Helga Kuhse and Peter Singer, *A Companion to Bioethics* (Oxford: Blackwell, 2001).

Ravi Parikh, "When Paternalism Doesn't Work for Patients," *Huffington Post*, May 29, 2015, http://www.huffingtonpost.com/ravi-parikh/doctor-patient-relationship_b_7447236.html (20 October 2015).

Edmund D. Pellegrino, "The Virtuous Physician and the Ethics of Medicine," in *Virtue and Medicine: Explorations in the Character of Medicine*, ed. Earl E. Shelp (Dordrecht: D. Reidel, 1985), 248–53.

Gregory E. Pence, *The Elements of Bioethics* (New York: McGraw-Hill, 2007).

Robert M. Veatch, "The Dying Cancer Patient," in *Case Studies in Medical Ethics* (Cambridge, MA: Harvard University Press, 1977), 141–47.

NOTES

1. This summary of positions takes its inspiration from Tom L. Beauchamp and James F. Childress, *Principles of Biomedical Ethics,* 5th ed. (New York: Oxford University Press, 2001), 182–87.
2. Linda Greenhouse, "Supreme Court Roundup: Christian Scientists Rebuffed in Ruling by Supreme Court," *New York Times,* 23 January 1996.
3. *Prince v. Commonwealth of Massachusetts,* 321 U.S. 1958 (1944).
4. Steven H. Miles, "Informed Consent for 'Non-Beneficial' Medical Treatment," *The New England Journal of Medicine* 325.7 (15 August 1991): 512–15; "Brain Damaged Woman at Center of Lawsuit over Life-Support Dies," *New York Times* (6 July 1991), 8.
5. John Stuart Mill, *On Liberty* (1859; rpt. Gateway ed., Chicago: Henry Regnery, 1955), 17–18.
6. *Bouvia v. Superior Court,* 179 Cal. 3d 1127, 1135–43, 225 Cal. Rptr. 297 (Ct. App. 1986).
7. *Ibid.*

READINGS

Paternalism

GERALD DWORKIN

Dworkin accepts the notion (famously articulated by John Stuart Mill) that society may sometimes justifiably restrict a person's liberty for purposes of self-protection or the prevention of harm to others. But he takes issue with Mill's related anti-paternalistic idea that a person "cannot rightfully be compelled to do or forbear because it will be better for him to do so." He argues that some limited forms of state paternalism can be justified, for "[u]nder certain conditions it is rational for an individual to agree that others should force him to act in ways which, at the time of action, the individual may not see as desirable." In a representative government, rational people could agree to restrict their liberty even when the interests of others are not affected. But in such cases the state bears a heavy burden of proof to show "the exact nature of the harmful effects (or beneficial consequences) to be avoided (or achieved) and the probability of their occurrence."

Neither one person, nor any number of persons, is warranted in saying to another human creature of ripe years, that he shall not do with his life for his own benefit what he chooses to do with it.

—MILL

l do not want to go along with a volunteer basis. I think a fellow should be compelled to become better and not let him use his discretion whether he wants to get smarter, more healthy or more honest.

—GENERAL HERSHEY

I take as my starting point the "one very simple principle" proclaimed by Mill in *On Liberty* . . . "That principle is, that the sole end for which mankind are warranted, individually or collectively, in interfering with the liberty of action of any of their number, is self-protection. That the only purpose for which power can be rightfully exercised over any member of a civilized community, against his will, is to prevent harm to others. He cannot rightfully be compelled to do or forbear because it will be better for him to do so, because it will make him happier,

From *The Moral Foundations of Professional Ethics* by Alan Goldman, Rowman & Littlefield, 1980. Reprinted with permission of the publisher. Notes omitted.

because, in the opinion of others, to do so would be wise, or even right."

This principle is neither "one" nor "very simple." It is at least two principles; one asserting that self-protection or the prevention of harm to others is sometimes a sufficient warrant and the other claiming that the individual's own good is *never* a sufficient warrant for the exercise of compulsion either by the society as a whole or by its individual members. I assume that no one with the possible exception of extreme pacifists or anarchists questions the correctness of the first half of the principle. This essay is an examination of the negative claim embodied in Mill's principle—the objection to paternalistic interferences with a man's liberty.

I

By paternalism I shall understand roughly the interference with a person's liberty of action justified by reasons referring exclusively to the welfare, good, happiness, needs, interests or values of the person being coerced. One is always well-advised to illustrate one's definitions by examples but it is not easy to find "pure" examples of paternalistic interferences. For almost any piece of legislation is justified by several different kinds of reasons and even if historically a piece of legislation can be shown to have been introduced for purely paternalistic motives, it may be that advocates of the legislation with an anti-paternalistic outlook can find sufficient reasons justifying the legislation without appealing to the reasons which were originally adduced to support it. Thus, for example, it may be the original legislation requiring motorcyclists to wear safety helmets was introduced for purely paternalistic reasons. But the Rhode Island Supreme Court recently upheld such legislation on the grounds that it was "not persuaded that the legislature is powerless to prohibit individuals from pursuing a course of conduct which could conceivably result in their becoming public charges," thus clearly introducing reasons of a quite different kind. Now I regard this decision as being based on reasoning of a very dubious nature but it illustrates the kind of problem one has in finding examples. The following is a list of the kinds of interferences I have in mind as being paternalistic.

II

1. Laws requiring motorcyclists to wear safety helmets when operating their machines.
2. Laws forbidding persons from swimming at a public beach when lifeguards are not on duty.
3. Laws making suicide a criminal offense.
4. Laws making it illegal for women and children to work at certain types of jobs.
5. Laws regulating certain kinds of sexual conduct, e.g. homosexuality among consenting adults in private.
6. Laws regulating the use of certain drugs which may have harmful consequences to the user but do not lead to anti-social conduct.
7. Laws requiring a license to engage in certain professions with those not receiving a license subject to fine or jail sentence if they do engage in the practice.
8. Laws compelling people to spend a specified fraction of their income on the purchase of retirement annuities. (Social Security)
9. Laws forbidding various forms of gambling (often justified on the grounds that the poor are more likely to throw away their money on such activities than the rich who can afford to).
10. Laws regulating the maximum rates of interest for loans.
11. Laws against duelling.

In addition to laws which attach criminal or civil penalties to certain kinds of action there are laws, rules, regulations, decrees, which make it either difficult or impossible for people to carry out their plans and which are also justified on paternalistic grounds. Examples of this are:

1. Laws regulating the types of contracts which will be upheld as valid by the courts, e.g. (an example of Mill's to which I shall return) no man may make a valid contract for perpetual involuntary servitude.
2. Not allowing as a defense to a charge of murder or assault the consent of the victim.
3. Requiring members of certain religious sects to have compulsory blood transfusions. This is made possible by not allowing the patient to have recourse to civil suits for assault and battery and by means of injunctions.
4. Civil commitment procedures when these are specifically justified on the basis of preventing the person being committed from harming himself. (The D. C. Hospitalization of the Mentally Ill Act provides for involuntary hospitalization of a person who "is mentally ill, and because of that illness, is likely to injure *himself* or others if allowed to remain at liberty." The term injure in this context applies to unintentional as well as intentional injuries.)
5. Putting fluorides in the community water supply.

All of my examples are of existing restrictions on the liberty of individuals. Obviously one can think of interferences which have not yet been imposed. Thus one might ban the sale of cigarettes, or require that people wear safety-belts in automobiles (as opposed to merely having them installed) enforcing this by not allowing motorists to sue for injuries even when caused by other drivers if the motorist was not wearing a seat-belt at the time of the accident. . . .

III

Bearing these examples in mind let me return to a characterization of paternalism. I said earlier that I meant by the term, roughly, interference with a person's liberty for his own good. But as some of the examples show the class of persons whose good is invoiced is not always identical with the class of persons whose freedom is restricted. Thus in the case of professional licensing it is the practitioner who is directly interfered with and it is the would-be patient whose interests are presumably being served. Not allowing the consent of the victim to be a defense to certain types of crime primarily affects the would-be aggressor but it is the interests of the willing victim that we are trying to protect. Sometimes a person may fall into both classes as would be the case if we banned the manufacture and sale of cigarettes and a given manufacturer happened to be a smoker as well.

Thus we may first divide paternalistic interferences into "pure" and "impure" cases. In "pure" paternalism the class of persons whose freedom is restricted is identical with the class of persons whose benefit is intended to be promoted by such restrictions. Examples: the making of suicide a crime, requiring passengers in automobiles to wear seat-belts, requiring a Christian Scientist to receive a blood transfusion. In the case of "impure" paternalism in trying to protect the welfare of a class of persons we find that the only way to do so will involve restricting the freedom of other persons besides those who are benefited. Now it might be thought that there are no cases of "impure" paternalism since any such case could always be justified on non-paternalistic grounds, i.e. in terms of preventing harm to others. Thus we might ban cigarette manufacturers from continuing to manufacture their product on the grounds that we are preventing them from causing illness to others in the same way that we prevent other manufacturers from releasing pollutants into the atmosphere, thereby causing danger to the members of the community. The difference is, however, that in the former but not the latter case the harm is of such a nature that it could be avoided by those individuals affected if they so chose. The incurring of the harm requires, so to speak, the active co-operation of the victim. It would be mistaken theoretically and hypocritical in practice to assert that our interference in such cases is just like our interference in standard cases of protecting others from harm. At the very least someone interfered with in this way can reply that no one is complaining about his activities. It may be that impure paternalism requires arguments or reasons of a stronger kind in order to be justified since there are persons who are losing a portion of their liberty and they do not even have the solace of having it be done "in their own interest." Of course in some sense, if paternalistic justifications are ever correct then we are protecting others, we are preventing some from injuring others, but it is important to see the differences between this and the standard case.

Paternalism then will always involve limitations on the liberty of some individuals in their own interest but it may also extend to interferences with the liberty of parties whose interests are not in question.

IV

Finally, by way of some more preliminary analysis, I want to distinguish paternalistic interferences with liberty from a related type with which it is often confused. Consider, for example, legislation which forbids employees to work more than, say, 40 hours per week. It is sometimes argued that such legislation is paternalistic for if employees desired such a restriction on their hours of work they could agree among themselves to impose it voluntarily. But because they do not the society imposes its own conception of their best interests upon them by the use of coercion. Hence this is paternalism.

Now it may be that some legislation of this nature is, in fact, paternalistically motivated. I am not denying that. All I want to point out is that there is another possible way of justifying such measures which is not paternalistic in nature. It is not paternalistic because as Mill puts it in a similar context such measures are "required not to overrule the judgment of individuals respecting their own interest, but to give effect to that judgment they being unable to give effect to it except by concert, which concert again cannot be effectual unless it receives validity and sanction from the law."

The line of reasoning here is a familiar one first found in Hobbes and developed with great sophistication by contemporary economists in the last decade or so. There are restrictions which are in the interests of a class of persons taken collectively but are such that the immediate interest of each individual is furthered by his violating the rule when others adhere to it. In such cases the individuals involved may need the use of compulsion to give effect to their collective judgment of their own interest by guaranteeing each individual compliance by the others. In these cases compulsion is not used to achieve some benefit which is not recognized to be a benefit by those concerned, but rather because it is the only feasible means of achieving some benefit which *is* recognized as such by all concerned. This way of viewing matters provides us with another characterization of paternalism in general. Paternalism might be thought of as the use of coercion to achieve a good which is not recognized as such by those persons for whom the good is intended. Again while this formulation captures the heart of the matter—it is surely what Mill is objecting to in *On Liberty*—the matter is not always quite like that. For example when we force motorcylists to wear helmets we are trying to promote a good—the protection of the person from injury—which is surely recognized by most of the individuals concerned. It is not that a cyclist doesn't value his bodily integrity; rather, as a supporter of such legislation would put it, he either places, perhaps irrationally, another value or good (freedom from wearing a helmet) above that of physical well-being or, perhaps, while recognizing the danger in the abstract, he either does not fully appreciate it or he underestimates the likelihood of its occurring. But now we are approaching the question of possible justifications of paternalistic measures and the rest of this essay will be devoted to that question.

V

I shall begin for dialectical purposes by discussing Mill's objections to paternalism and then go on to discuss more positive proposals. . . . The stucture of Mill's argument is as follows:

1. Since restraint is an evil the burden of proof is on those who propose such restraint.
2. Since the conduct which is being considered is purely self-regarding, the normal appeal to the protection of the interests of others is not available.

3. Therefore we have to consider whether reasons involving reference to the individual's own good, happiness, welfare, or interests are sufficient to overcome the burden of justification.
4. We either cannot advance the interests of the individual by compulsion, or the attempt to do so involves evil which outweighs the good done.
5. Hence the promotion of the individual's own interests does not provide a sufficient warrant for the use of compulsion.

Clearly the operative premise here is 4 and it is bolstered by claims about the status of the individual as judge and appraiser of his welfare, interests, needs, etc.

> With respect to his own feelings and circumstances, the most ordinary man or woman has means of knowledge immeasurably surpassing those that can be possessed by any one else.
> He is the man most interested in his own well-being: the interest which any other person, except in cases of strong personal attachment, can have in it, is trifling, compared to that which he himself has.

These claims are used to support the following generalizations concerning the utility of compulsion for paternalistic purposes.

> The interferences of society to overrule his judgment and purposes in what only regards himself must be grounded in general presumptions; which may be altogether wrong, and even if right, are as likely as not to be misapplied to individual cases.
> But the strongest of all the arguments against the interference of the public with purely personal conduct is that when it does interfere, the odds are that it interferes wrongly and in the wrong place.
> All errors which the individual is likely to commit against advice and warning are far outweighed by the evil of allowing others to constrain him to what they deem his good.

Performing the utilitarian calculation by balancing the advantages and disadvantages we find that:

> Mankind are greater gainers by suffering each other to live as seems good to themselves, than by compelling each other to live as seems good to the rest.

From which follows the operative premise 4.

This classical case of a utilitarian argument with all the premises spelled out is not the only line of reasoning present in Mill's discussion. There are asides, and more than asides, which look quite different and I shall deal with them later. But this is clearly the main channel of Mill's thought and it is one which has been subjected to vigorous attack from the moment it appeared—most often by fellow Utilitarians. The link that they have usually seized on is, as Fitzjames Stephen put it, the absence of proof that the "mass of adults are so well acquainted with their own interests and so much disposed to pursue them that no compulsion or restraint put upon them by any others for the purpose of promoting their interest can really promote them." . . .

Now it is interesting to note that Mill himself was aware of some of the limitations on the doctrine that the individual is the best judge of his own interests. In his discussion of government intervention in general (even where the intervention does not interfere with liberty but provides alternative institutions to those of the market) after making claims which are parallel to those just discussed, e.g.

> People understand their own business and their own interests better, and care for them more, than the government does, or can be expected to do.

He goes on to an intelligent discussion of the "very large and conspicuous exceptions" to the maxim that:

> Most persons take a juster and more intelligent view of their own interest, and of the means of promoting it than can either be prescribed to them by a general enactment of the legislature, or pointed out in the particular case by a public functionary.

Thus there are things

> of which the utility does not consist in ministering to inclinations, nor in serving the daily uses of life, and the want of which is least felt where the need is greatest. This is peculiarly true of those things which are chiefly useful as tending to raise the character of human beings. The uncultivated cannot be competent judges of cultivation. Those who most need to be made wiser and better, usually desire it least, and, if they desired it, would be incapable of finding the way to it by their own lights.
> . . . A second exception to the doctrine that individuals are the best judges of their own interest, is

when an individual attempts to decide irrevocably now what will be best for his interest at some future and distant time. The presumption in favor of individual judgment is only legitimate, where the judgment is grounded on actual, and especially on present, personal experience; not where it is formed antecedently to experience, and not suffered to be reversed even after experience has condemned it.

The upshot of these exceptions is that Mill does not declare that there should never be government interference with the economy but rather that

> . . . in every instance, the burden of making out a strong case should be thrown not on those who resist but on those who recommend government interference. Letting alone, in short, should be the general practice: every departure from it, unless required by some great good, is a certain evil.

In short, we get a presumption not an absolute prohibition. The question is why doesn't the argument against paternalism go the same way?

A consistent Utilitarian can only argue against paternalism on the grounds that it (as a matter of fact) does not maximize the good. It is always a contingent question that may be refuted by the evidence. But there is also a non-contingent argument which runs through *On Liberty*. When Mill states that "there is a part of the life of every person who has come to years of discretion, within which the individuality of that person ought to rein uncontrolled either by any other person or by the public collectively" he is saying something about what it means to be a person, an autonomous agent. It is because coercing a person for his own good denies this status as an independent entity that Mill objects to it so strongly and in such absolute terms. To be able to choose is a good that is independent of the wisdom of what is chosen. A man's "mode" of laying out his existence is the best, not because it is the best in itself, but because it is his own mode.

> It is the privilege and proper condition of a human being, arrived at the maturity of his faculties, to use and interpret experience in his own way.

As further evidence of this line of reasoning in Mill consider the one exception to his prohibition against paternalism.

In this and most civilised countries, for example, an engagement by which a person should sell himself, or allow himself to be sold, as a slave, would be null and void; neither enforced by law nor by opinion. The ground for thus limiting his power of voluntarily disposing of his own lot in life, is apparent, and is very clearly seen in this extreme case. The reason for not interfering, unless for the sake of others, with a person's voluntary acts, is consideration for his liberty. His voluntary choice is evidence that what he so chooses is desirable, or at least endurable, to him, and his good is on the whole best provided for by allowing him to take his own means of pursuing it. But by selling himself for a slave, he abdicates his liberty; he foregoes any further use of it beyond that single act.

He therefore defeats, in his own case, the very purpose which is the justification of allowing him to dispose of himself. He is no longer free; but is thenceforth in a position which has no longer the presumption in its favour, that would be afforded by his voluntarily remaining in it. The principle of freedom cannot require that he should be free not to be free. It is not freedom to be allowed to alienate his freedom.

Now leaving aside the fudging on the meaning of freedom in the last line it is clear that part of this argument is incorrect. While it is true that *future* choices of the slave are not reasons for thinking that what he chooses then is desirable for him, what is at issue is limiting his immediate choice; and since this choice is made freely, the individual may be correct in thinking that his interests are best provided for by entering such a contract. But the main consideration for not allowing such a contract is the need to preserve the liberty of the person to make future choices. This gives us a principle—a very narrow one, by which to justify some paternalistic interferences. Paternalism is justified only to preserve a wider range of freedom for the individual in question. How far this principle could be extended, whether it can justify all the cases in which we are inclined upon reflection to think paternalistic measures justified remains to be discussed. What I have tried to show so far is that there are two strains of argument in Mill— one a straightforward Utilitarian mode of reasoning and one which relies not on the goods which free choice leads to but on the absolute value of the choice itself. The first cannot establish any absolute prohibition but at most a presumption and indeed a fairly weak one given some fairly plausible assumptions about human psychology; the second while a stronger line of argument seems to me to allow on its own grounds a wider range of paternalism than might be suspected. I turn now to a consideration of these matters.

VI

We might begin looking for principles governing the acceptable use of paternalistic power in cases where it is generally agreed that it is legitimate. Even Mill intends his principles to be applicable only to mature individuals, not those in what he calls "non-age." What is it that justifies us in interfering with children? The fact that they lack some of the emotional and cognitive capacities required in order to make fully rational decisions. It is an empirical question to just what extent children have an adequate conception of their own present and future interests but there is not much doubt that there are many deficiencies. For example it is very difficult for a child to defer gratification for any considerable period of time. Given these deficiencies and given the very real and permanent dangers that may befall the child it becomes not only permissible but even a duty of the parent to restrict the child's freedom in various ways. There is however an important moral limitation on the exercise of such parental power which is provided by the notion of the child eventually coming to see the correctness of his parents' interventions. Parental paternalism may be thought of as a wager by the parent on the child's subsequent recognition of the wisdom of the restrictions. There is an emphasis on what could be called future-oriented consent—on what the child will come to welcome, rather than on what he does welcome.

The essence of this idea has been incorporated by idealist philosophers into various types of "real-will" theory as applied to fully adult persons. Extensions of paternalism are argued for by claiming that in various respects, chronologically mature individuals share the same deficiencies in knowledge, capacity to think rationally, and the ability to carry out decisions that children possess. Hence in interfering with such people we are in effect doing what they would do if they were fully rational. Hence we are not really opposing their will, hence we are not really interfering with their freedom. The dangers of this move have been sufficiently exposed by Berlin in his "Two Concepts of Liberty." I see no gain in theoretical clarity nor in practical advantage in trying to pass over the real nature of the interferences with liberty that we impose on others. Still the basic notion of consent is important and seems to me the only acceptable way of trying to delimit an area of justified paternalism.

Let me start by considering a case where the consent is not hypothetical in nature. Under certain conditions it is rational for an individual to agree that others should force him to act in ways which, at the time of action, the individual may not see as desirable. If, for example, a man knows that he is subject to breaking his resolves when temptation is present, he may ask a friend to refuse to entertain his request at some later stage.

A classical example is given in the Odyssey when Odysseus commands his men to tie him to the mast and refuse all future orders to be set free because he knows the power of the Sirens to enchant men with their songs. Here we are on relatively sound ground in later refusing Odysseus' request to be set free. He may even claim to have changed his mind but since it is just such changes that he wishes to guard against we are entitled to ignore them.

A process analogous to this may take place on a social rather than individual basis. An electorate may mandate its representatives to pass legislation which when it comes time to "pay the price" may be unpalatable. I may believe that a tax increase is necessary to halt inflation though I may resent the lower pay check each month. However in both this case and that of Odysseus the measure to be enforced is specifically requested by the party involved and at some point in time there is genuine consent and agreement on the part of those persons whose liberty is infringed. Such is not the case for the paternalistic measures we have been speaking about. What must be involved here is not consent to specific measures but rather consent to a system of

government, run by elected representatives, with an understanding that they may act to safeguard our interests in certain limited ways.

I suggest that since we are all aware of our irrational propensities, deficiencies in cognitive and emotional capacities and avoidable and unavoidable ignorance it is rational and prudent for us to in effect take out "social insurance policies." We may argue for and against proposed paternalistic measures in terms of what fully rational individuals would accept as forms of protection. Now, clearly since the initial agreement is not about specific measures we are dealing with a more-or-less blank check and therefore there have to be carefully defined limits. What I am looking for are certain kinds of conditions which make it plausible to suppose that rational men could reach agreement to limit their liberty even when other men's interests are not affected.

Of course as in any kind of agreement schema there are great difficulties in deciding what rational individuals would or would not accept. Particularly in sensitive areas of personal liberty, there is always a danger of the dispute over agreement and rationality being a disguised version of evaluative and normative disagreement.

Let me suggest types of situations in which it seems plausible to suppose that fully rational individuals would agree to having paternalistic restrictions imposed upon them. It is reasonable to suppose that there are "goods" such as health which any person would want to have in order to pursue his own good—no matter how that good is conceived. This is an argument that is used in connection with compulsory education for children but it seems to me that it can be extended to other goods which have this character. Then one could agree that the attainment of such goods should be promoted even when not recognized to be such, at the moment, by the individuals concerned.

An immediate difficulty that arises stems from the fact that men are always faced with competing goods and that there may be reasons why even a value such as health—or indeed life—may be overridden by competing values. Thus the problem with the Christian Scientist and blood transfusions. It may be more important for him to reject "impure substances" than to go on living. The difficult problem that must be faced is whether one can give sense to the notion of a person irrationally attaching weights to competing values.

Consider a person who knows the statistical data on the probability of being injured when not wearing seat-belts in an automobile and knows the types and gravity of the various injuries. He also insists that the inconvenience attached to fastening the belt every time he gets in and out of the car outweighs for him the possible risks to himself. I am inclined in this case to think that such a weighing is irrational. Given his life plans which we are assuming are those of the average person, his interests and commitments already undertaken, I think it is safe to predict that we can find inconsistencies in his calculations at some point. I am assuming that this is not a man who for some conscious or unconscious reasons is trying to injure himself nor is he a man who just likes to "live dangerously." I am assuming that he is like us in all the relevant respects but just puts an enormously high negative value on inconvenience—one which does not seem comprehensible or reasonable.

It is always possible, of course to assimilate this person to creatures like myself. I, also, neglect to fasten my seat-belt and I concede such behavior is not rational but not because I weigh the inconvenience differently from those who fasten the belts. It is just that having made (roughly) the same calculation as everybody else I ignore it in my actions. [Note: a much better case of weakness of the will than those usually given in ethics texts.] A plausible explanation for this deplorable habit is that athough I know in some intellectual sense what the probabilities and risks are I do not fully appreciate them in an emotionally genuine manner.

We have two distinct types of situation in which a man acts in a non-rational fashion. In one case he attaches incorrect weights to some of his values; in the other he neglects to act in accordance with his actual preferences and desires. Clearly there is a stronger and more persuasive argument for paternalism in the latter situation. Here we are really not—by assumption—imposing a good on another person. But why may we not extend our interference

to what we might call evaluative delusions? After all in the case of cognitive delusions we are prepared, often, to act against the expressed will of the person involved. If a man believes that when he jumps out the window he will float upwards—Robert Nozick's example—would not we detain him, forcibly if necessary? The reply will be that this man doesn't wish to be injured and if we could convince him that he is mistaken as to the consequences of his actions he would not wish to perform the action. But part of what is involved in claiming that a man who doesn't fasten his seat-belts is attaching an irrational weight to the inconvenience of fastening them is that if he were to be involved in an accident and severely injured he would look back and admit that the inconvenience wasn't as bad as all that. So there is a sense in which if I could convince him of the consequences of his actions he also would not wish to continue his present course of action. Now the notion of consequences being used here is covering a lot of ground. In one case it's being used to indicate what will or can happen as a result of a course of action and in the other it's making a prediction about the future evaluation of the consequences—in the first sense—of a course of action. And whatever the difference between facts and values—whether it be hard and fast or soft and slow—we are genuinely more reluctant to consent to interferences where evaluative differences are the issue. Let me now consider another factor which comes into play in some of these situations which may make an important difference in our willingness to consent to paternalistic restrictions.

Some of the decisions we make are of such a character that they produce changes which are in one or another way irreversible. Situations are created in which it is difficult or impossible to return to anything like the initial stage at which the decision was made. In particular some of these changes will make it impossible to continue to make reasoned choices in the future. I am thinking specifically of decisions which involve taking drugs that are physically or psychologically addictive and those which are destructive of one's mental and physical capacities.

I suggest we think of the imposition of paternalistic interferences in situations of this kind as being a kind of insurance policy which we take out against making decisions which are far-reaching, potentially dangerous and irreversible. . . .

A second class of cases concerns decisions which are made under extreme psychological and sociological pressure. I am not thinking here of the making of the decision as being something one is pressured into—e.g. a good reason for making duelling illegal is that unless this is done many people might have to manifest their courage and integrity in ways in which they would rather not do so—but rather of decisions such as that to commit suicide which are usually made at a point where the individual is not thinking clearly and calmly about the nature of his decision. In addition, of course, this comes under the previous heading of all-too-irrevocable decision. Now there are practical steps which a society could take if it wanted to decrease the possibility of suicide—for example not paying social security benefits to the survivors or as religious institutions do, not allowing such persons to be buried with the same status as natural deaths. I think we may count these as interferences with the liberty of persons to attempt suicide and the question is whether they are justifiable.

Using my argument schema the question is whether rational individuals would consent to such limitations. I see no reason for them to consent to an absolute prohibition but I do think it is reasonable for them to agree to some kind of enforced waiting period. Since we are all aware of the possibility of temporary states, such as great fear or depression, that are inimical to the making of well-informed and rational decisions, it would be prudent for all of us if there were some kind of institutional arrangement whereby we were restrained from making a decision which is (all too) irreversible. What this would be like in practice is difficult to envisage and it may be that if no practical arrangements were feasible then we would have to conclude that there should be no restriction at all on this kind of action. But we might have a "cooling off" period, in much the same way that we now require couples who file for divorce to go through a waiting period. Or, more far-fetched, we might imagine a Suicide Board

composed of a psychologist and another member picked by the applicant. The Board would be required to meet and talk with the person proposing to take his life, though its approval would not be required.

A third class of decisions—these classes are not supposed to be disjoint—involves dangers which are either not sufficiently understood or appreciated correctly by the persons involved. Let me illustrate, using the example of cigarette smoking, a number of possible cases.

1. A man may not know the facts—e.g. smoking between 1 and 2 packs a day shortens life expectancy 6.2 years, the cost and pain of the illness caused by smoking, etc.
2. A man may know the facts, wish to stop smoking, but not have the requisite willpower.
3. A man may know the facts but not have them play the correct role in his calculation because, say, he discounts the danger psychologically because it is remote in time and/or inflates the attractiveness of other consequences of his decision which he regards as beneficial.

In case 1 what is called for is education, the posting of warnings, etc. In case 2 there is no theoretical problem. We are not imposing a good on someone who rejects it. We are simply using coercion to enable people to carry out their own goals. (Note: There obviously is a difficulty in that only a subclass of the individuals affected wish to be prevented from doing what they are doing.) In case 3 there is a sense in which we are imposing a good on someone since given his current appraisal of the facts he doesn't wish to be restricted. But in another sense we are not imposing a good since what is being claimed—and what must be shown or at least argued for—is that an accurate accounting on his part would lead him to reject his current course of action. Now we all know that such cases exist, that we are prone to disregard dangers that are only possibilities, that immediate pleasures are often magnified and distorted.

If in addition the dangers are severe and far-reaching we could agree to allowing the state a certain degree of power to intervene in such situations. The difficulty is in specifying in advance, even vaguely, the class of cases in which intervention will be legitimate.

A related difficulty is that of drawing a line so that it is not the case that all ultra-hazardous activities are ruled out, e.g. mountain-climbing, bullfighting, sports-car racing, etc. There are some risks—even very great ones—which a person is entitled to take with his life.

A good deal depends on the nature of the deprivation—e.g. does it prevent the person from engaging in the activity completely or merely limit his participation—and how important to the nature of the activity is the absence of restriction when this is weighed against the role that the activity plays in the life of the person. In the case of automobile seatbelts, for example, the restriction is trivial in nature, interferes not at all with the use or enjoyment of the activity, and does, I am assuming, considerably reduce a high risk of serious injury. Whereas, for example, making mountain climbing illegal prevents completely a person engaging in an activity which may play an important role in his life and his conception of the person he is.

In general the easiest cases to handle are those which can be argued about in the terms which Mill thought to be so important—a concern not just for the happiness or welfare, in some broad sense, of the individual but rather a concern for the autonomy and freedom of the person. I suggest that we would be most likely to consent to paternalism in those instances in which it preserves and enhances for the individual his ability to rationally consider and carry out his own decisions.

I have suggested in this essay a number of types of situations in which it seems plausible that rational men would agree to granting the legislative powers of a society the right to impose restrictions on what Mill calls "self-regarding" conduct. However, rational men knowing something about the resources of ignorance, ill-will and stupidity available to the lawmakers of a society—a good case in point is the history of drug legislation in the United States—will be concerned to limit such intervention to minimum. I suggest in closing two principles designed to achieve this end.

In all cases of paternalistic legislation there must be a heavy and clear burden of proof placed on the authorities to demonstrate the exact nature of the harmful effects (or beneficial consequences) to be avoided (or achieved) and the probability of their occurrence. The burden of proof here is twofold—what lawyers distinguish as the burden of going forward and the burden of persuasion. That the authorities have the burden of going forward means that it is up to them to raise the question and bring forward evidence of the evils to be avoided. Unlike the case of new drugs where the manufacturer must produce some evidence that the drug has been tested and found not harmful, no citizen has to show with respect to self-regarding conduct that it is not harmful or promotes his best interests. In addition the nature and cogency of the evidence for the harmfulness of the course of action must be set at a high level. To paraphrase a formulation of the burden of proof for criminal proceedings—better 10 men ruin themselves than one man be unjustly deprived of liberty.

Finally I suggest a principle of the least restrictive alternative. If there is an alternative way of accomplishing the desired end without restricting liberty then although it may involve great expense, inconvenience, etc. the society must adopt it.

The Refutation of Medical Paternalism

ALAN GOLDMAN

Except in a few extraordinary cases, strong paternalism in medicine is unjustified, Goldman argues. Patients have a right of self-determination, a right of freedom to make their own choices. Decisions regarding their own futures should be left up to them because persons are the best judges of their own interests and because self-determination is valuable for its own sake regardless of its generally positive effects. This right implies "the right to be told the truth about one's condition, and the right to accept or refuse or withdraw from treatment on the basis of adequate information regarding alternatives, risks and uncertainties." The faulty premise in the argument for medical paternalism, says Goldman, is that health and prolonged life can be assumed to be the top priorities for patients (and so physicians may decide for patients accordingly). But very few people always prioritize these values in this way.

There are two ways to attack an argument in favor of paternalistic measures (while accepting our criteria for justified paternalism). One is to argue that honoring rather than overriding the right of the person will not in fact harm him. The other is to admit that the satisfaction of the person's right may harm in some way, but argue that the harm does not merit exception to the right, all things considered. The first is principally an empirical, the second a moral counterargument.

The latter is not a perfectly clear-cut distinction, either in general or in application to the question of paternalism. For one thing, the most inclusive notion of harm is relative to the values and preferences of the particular individual. (This point will be important in the argument to follow.) A person is harmed when a state of affairs below a certain level on his preference scale is realized rather than one higher up. Our notion of harm derives what objectivity it has from two sources, again one principally empirical and the other more purely moral. The first is the fact that certain states of affairs are such that the vast majority of us would wish to avoid them in almost all conceivable contexts: physical injury, hastened death, or depression itself for example. It is an empirical question whether these states of affairs result from certain courses of conduct, hence, when they are predicted results, principally an empirical question whether harm ensues. The second source of a concept of harm independent of individual differences in subjective preferences is ideal-regarding: when the development of an individual capable of freely and creatively formulating and acting to realize central life projects is blocked, that person is harmed, whether or not he realizes it, and whether or not any of his present desires are frustrated.

The first argument against paternalistic interference holds that allowing an individual free choice is not most likely to result in harm taken in its objective sense. The second argument is somewhat more complex. It admits likely harm in the objective sense—worsened health, depression, or even hastened death in the examples we are considering—but holds that even greater harm to the individual is likely to ensue from the interference, harm in the more inclusive sense that takes account of his whole range of value orderings and the independent value of his integrity as an individual. In this latter situation there is one sense in which the individual is likely to suffer harm no matter what others do, since a state of affairs will be realized that he would

From *The Moral Foundations of Professional Ethics* by Alan Goldman, Rowman & Littlefield, 1980. Reprinted with permission of the publisher. Notes omitted.

wish to avoid, other things being equal, a state of affairs well below the neutral level in his preference orderings. But from the point of view of others, they impose harm only by interfering, since only that action results in a state of affairs lower on his scale of preferences than would otherwise be realized. In this sense harm is a relative notion, first because it is relative to subjective value orderings, and second because it is imposed only when a situation *worse* that what would otherwise occur is caused. We appeal to this second more inclusive notion in the second type of argument against paternalism.

Empirical Arguments

Returning to the medical context, other philosophers have recently questioned the degree of truth in the empirical premise that patients are likely to be harmed when doctors fully inform them. Sissela Bok, for example, has noted that in general it appears to be false that patients do not really want bad news, cannot accept or understand it, or are harmed by it. Yet she does not deny that information can sometimes harm patients, can cause depression, prolong illness, or even hasten death; and she explicitly allows for concealment when this can be shown in terminal cases. Allen Buchanan questions the ability of the doctor to make a competent judgment on the probability of harm to the patient, a judgment that would require both psychiatric expertise and intimate knowledge of the patient himself. Doctors are not generally trained to judge long-term psychological reactions, and even if they were, they would require detailed psychological histories of patients in order to apply this expertise in particular cases. As medical practices tend to become more impersonal, certainly a trend in recent years, such intimate knowledge of patients, even on a nontheoretical level, will normally be lacking. Physicians would then have to rely upon loose generalizations, based on prior impressions of other patients and folklore from colleagues, in order to predict the effect of information on particular patients.

Buchanan appears to consider this point sufficient to refute the argument for paternalism, eschewing appeal to patients' rights. But unless we begin with a strong presumption of a right of the patient to the truth, I do not see why the difficulties for the doctor in judging the effect of information on the patient recommends a practice of disclosure. If the decision is to be based upon risk-benefit calculation (as it would be without consideration of rights), then, just as in other decisions regarding treatment, no matter how difficult to make, it seems that the doctor should act on his best estimate. The decision on what to say must be made by him one way or the other; and without a right-based presumption in favor of revealing the truth, its difficulty is no argument for one outcome rather than the other. In fact, the difficulty might count against revelation, since telling the truth is generally more irreversible than concealment or delay.

One could, it is true, attempt to make out a case for full disclosure on strict risk-benefit grounds, without appeal to rights. As we have seen in earlier chapters, utilitarians can go to great lengths to show that their calculations accord with the intuitive recognition of particular rights. In the case of lying or deceiving, they standardly appeal to certain systematic disutilities that might be projected, e.g. effects upon the agent's trustworthiness and upon the trust that other people are willing to accord him if his lies are discovered. In the doctor's case, he might fear losing patients or losing the faith of patients who continue to consult him, if he is caught in lies or deceptions. A utilitarian could argue further that, even in situations in which these disutilities appear not to figure, this appearance tends to be misleading, and that potential liars should therefore resist the temptation on this ground. One problem with this argument, as pointed out in the chapter on political ethics, is that it is empirically falsified in many situations. It is not always so difficult to foretell the utilitarian effects of deception, at least no more difficult than is any other future-looking moral calculation. In the case of terminally ill patients, for example, by the time they realize that their doctors have been deceiving them, they will be in no condition to communicate this fact to other patients or potential patients, even if such communication were otherwise commonplace. Thus the doctor has little to fear in the way of losing patients or patients' faith from his policy of disclosure or concealment from the terminally ill. He can safely calculate risks and benefits with little regard for such systematic disutilities. Again we have little reason to prefer honoring a right, in this case a right to be told the truth, without appealing to the right itself. The only conclusion that I would draw from the empirical points taken in themselves is that doctors should perhaps be better trained in psychology in order to be better able to judge the effects of disclosure upon patients, not that they should make a practice of full disclosure and of allowing patients full control over decisions on treatment. These conclusions we must reach by a different rights-based route.

I shall then criticize the argument for paternalistic strong role differentiation on the more fundamental moral ground. To do so I shall restrict attention to cases in which there is a definite risk or probability of eventual harm (in the objective sense) to the patient's health from revealing the truth about his condition to him, or from informing him of all risks of alternative treatments and allowing him a fully informed decision. These cases are those in which the high probability of harm can be supported or demonstrated, but in which the patient asks to know the truth. Such cases are not decided by the points of Bok or Buchanan, and they are the crucial ones for the question of strong role differentiation. The issue is whether such projected harm is sufficient to justify concealment. If the patient's normal right to self-determination prevails, then the doctor, in having to honor this right, is acting within the same moral framework as the rest of us. If the doctor acquires the authority to decide for the patient, a normally competent adult, or to withhold the truth about his own condition from him, then he has special professional license to override otherwise obtaining rights, and his position is strongly differentiated.

Before presenting the case against strong role differentiation on this basis, I want to dispense quickly with a possible conceptual objection. One might claim that the justification of medical paternalism would not in itself satisfy the criteria for strong role differentiation as defined. Since paternalism is justified as well in other contexts, the exceptions to the rights in question need not be seen to derive from a special principle unique to medical ethics, but can be held simply to instantiate a generally recognized ground for restricting rights or freedoms. If serious harm to a person himself generally can be counted as overriding evidence that the projected action is contrary to his own true preferences or values, and if this generally justifies paternalistic interference or delegation of authority for decisions to others, if, for example, legislators assume authority to apply coercive sanctions to behavior on these grounds, then the authority to be paternalistic would not uniquely differentiate doctors.

The above may be true in so far as paternalism is sometimes justified in other than medical contexts, but that does not alter the import of the argument for medical paternalism to our perception of the doctor's role. If the argument were sound, the medical profession might still be the only one, or one of only a few, paternalistic in this way. This would differentiate medical ethics sufficiently. I argued earlier that legislators must in fact honor normal moral rights. While paternalistic legislation is sometimes justified, as in the requirement that motorcycle riders wear helmets, such legislation is so relatively small a part of the legislator's concerns, and the amount of coercion justified itself so relatively light, that this does not alter our perception of the legislator's general moral framework. If the paternalist argument were sound in relation to doctors, on the other hand, this would substantially alter the nature of their practice and our perception of their authority over certain areas of our lives. We can therefore view the paternalist argument as expressing the underlying moral purposes that elevate the Hippocratic principle and augment the doctor's authority to ignore systematically rights that would obtain against all but those in the medical profession. The values expressed and elevated are viewed by doctors themselves as central to their role, which again distinguishes this argument from claims of justified paternalism in other contexts. Furthermore, viewing the argument in this way brings out the interesting relations between positions of doctors and those in other professions and social roles. It brings out that doctors tend to assume broader moral responsibility for decisions than laymen, while those in certain other professions tend to assume less. In any case, while I shall not in the end view the doctor's role as strongly differentiated, I do not want to rely upon this terminological point, but rather to refute the argument for overriding patients' rights to further the medical goal of optimal treatment.

The Moral Argument

In order to refute an argument, we of course need to refute only one of its premises. The argument for medical paternalism, stripped to its barest outline, was:

1. Disclosure of information to the patient will sometimes increase the likelihood of depression and physical deterioration, or result in choice of medically inoptimal treatment.

2. Disclosure of information is therefore sometimes likely to be detrimental to the patient's health, perhaps even to hasten his death.

3. Health and prolonged life can be assumed to have priority among preferences for patients who place themselves under physicians' care.

4. Worsening health or hastening death can therefore be assumed to be contrary to patients' own true value orderings.

5. Paternalism is therefore justified: doctors may sometimes override patients' prima facie rights to information about risks and treatments or about their own conditions in order to prevent harm to their health.

The Relativity of Values: Health and Life

The fundamentally faulty premise in the argument for paternalistic role differentiation for doctors is that which assumes that health or prolonged life must take absolute priority in the patient's value orderings. In order for paternalistic interference to be justified, a person must be acting irrationally or inconsistently with his own long-range preferences. The value ordering violated by the action to be prevented must either be known to be that of the person himself, as in the train example, or else be uncontroversially that of any rational person, as in the motorcycle helmet case. But can we assume that health and prolonged life have top priority in any rational ordering? *If* these values could be safely assumed to be always overriding for those who seek medical assistance, then medical expertise would become paramount in decisions regarding treatment,

and decisions on disclosure would become assimilated to those within the treatment context. But in fact very few of us act according to such an assumed value ordering. In designing social policy we do not devote all funds or efforts toward minimizing loss of life, on the highways or in hospitals for example.

If our primary goal were always to minimize risk to health and life, we should spend our entire federal budget in health-related areas. Certainly such a suggestion would be ludicrous. We do not in fact grant to individuals rights to minimal risk in their activities or to absolutely optimal health care. From another perspective, if life itself, rather than life of a certain quality with autonomy and dignity, were of ultimate value, then even defensive wars could never be justified. But when the quality of life and the autonomy of an entire nation is threatened from without, defensive war in which many lives are risked and lost is a rational posture. To paraphrase Camus, anything worth living for is worth dying for. To realize or preserve those values that give meaning to life is worth the risk of life itself. Such fundamental values (and autonomy for individuals is certainly among them), necessary within a framework in which life of a certain quality becomes possible, appear to take precedence over the value of mere biological existence.

In personal life too we often engage in risky activities for far less exalted reasons, in fact just for the pleasure or convenience. We work too hard, smoke, exercise too little or too much, eat what we know is bad for us, and continue to do all these things even when informed of their possibly fatal effects. To doctors in their roles as doctors all this may appear irrational, although they no more act always to preserve their own health than do the rest of us. If certain risks to life and health are irrational, others are not. Once more the quality and significance of one's life may take precedence over maximal longevity. Many people when they are sick think of nothing above getting better; but this is not true of all. A person with a heart condition may decide that important unfinished work or projects must take priority over increased risk to his health; and his priority is not uncontroversially irrational. Since people's lives derive meaning and fulfillment from their projects and accomplishments, a person's risking a shortened life for one more fulfilled might well justify actions detrimental to his health. . . .

To doctors in their roles as professionals whose ultimate concern is the health or continued lives of patients, it is natural to elevate these values to ultimate prominence. The death of a patient, inevitable as it is in many cases, may appear as an ultimate defeat to the medical art, as something to be fought by any means, even after life has lost all value and meaning for the patient himself. The argument in the previous section for assuming this value ordering was that health, and certainly life, seem to be necessary conditions for the realization of all other goods or values. But this point, even if true, leaves open the question of whether health and life are of ultimate, or indeed any, intrinsic value, or whether they are valuable *merely* as means. It is plausible to maintain that life itself is not of intrinsic value, since surviving in an irreversible coma seems no better than death. It therefore again appears that it is the quality of life that counts, not simply being alive. Although almost any quality might be preferable to none, it is not irrational to trade off quantity for quality, as in any other good.

Even life with physical health and consciousness may not be of intrinsic value. Consciousness and health may not be sufficient in themselves to make the life worth living, since some states of consciousness are intrinsically good and others bad. Furthermore, if a person has nothing before him but pain and depression, then the instrumental worth of being alive may be reversed. And if prolonging one's life can be accomplished only at the expense of incapacitation or ignorance, perhaps preventing lifelong projects from being completed, then the instrumental value of longer life again seems overbalanced. It is certainly true that normally life itself is of utmost value as necessary for all else of value, and that living longer usually enables one to complete more projects and plans, to satisfy more desires and derive more enjoyments. But this cannot be assumed in the extreme circumstances of severe or terminal illness. Ignorance of how long one has left may block realization of such values, as may treatment with the best chance for cure, if it also risks incapacitation or immediate death.

Nor is avoidance of depression the most important consideration in such circumstances, as a shallow hedonism might assume. Hedonistic theories of value, which seek only to produce pleasure or avoid pain and depression, are easily disproven by our abhorrence at the prospect of a "brave new world," or our unwillingness, were it possible, to be plugged indefinitely into a "pleasure machine." The latter prospect is abhorrent not only from an ideal-regarding viewpoint, but, less obviously, for want-regarding reasons (for most persons) as well. Most people would in fact be unwilling to trade important freedoms and accomplishments for sensuous pleasures, or even for the illusion of greater freedoms and accomplishments. As many philosophers have pointed out, while satisfaction of wants may bring pleasurable sensations, wants are not primarily *for* pleasurable sensations, or even for happiness more broadly construed, per se. Conversely, the avoidance of negative feelings or depression is not uppermost among primary motives. Many people are willing to endure frustration, suffering, and even depression in pursuit of accomplishment, or in order to complete projects once begun. Thus information relevant to such matters, such as medical information about one's own condition or possible adverse effects of various treatments, may well be worth having at the cost of psychological pain or depression.

The Value of Self-Determination

We have so far focused on the inability of the doctor to assume a particular value ordering for his patient in which health, the prolonging of life, or the avoidance of depression is uppermost. The likelihood of error in this regard makes it probable that the doctor will not know the true interests of his patient as well as the patient himself. He is therefore less likely than the patient himself to make choices in accord with that overall interest, and paternalistic assumption of authority to do so is therefore unjustified. There is in addition another decisive consideration mentioned earlier, namely the independent value of self-determination or freedom of choice. Personal autonomy over important decisions in one's life, the ability to attempt to realize one's own value ordering, is indeed so important that normally no amount of other goods, pleasures or avoidance of personal evils can take precedence. This is why it is wrong to contract oneself into slavery, and another reason why pleasure machines do not seem attractive. Regarding the latter, even if people were willing to forego other goods for a life of constant pleasure, the loss in variety of other values, and in the creativity that can generate new sources of value, would be morally regrettable. The value of self-determination explains also why there is such a strong burden of proof upon those who advocate paternalistic measures, why they must show that the person would otherwise act in a way inconsistent with his own value ordering, that is irrationally. A person's desires are not simply evidence of what is in his interest—they have extra weight.

Especially when decisions are important to the course of our lives, we are unwilling to relinquish them to others, even in exchange for a higher probability of happiness or less risk of suffering. Even if it could be proven, for example, that some scientific method of matching spouses greatly increased chances of compatibility and happiness, we would insist upon retaining our rights over marriage decisions. Given the present rate of success in marriages, it is probable that we could in fact find some better method of matching partners in terms of increasing that success rate. Yet we are willing to forego increased chances of success in order to make our own choices, choices that tend to make us miserable in the long run. The same might be true of career choices, choices of schools, and others central to the course of our lives. Our unwillingness to delegate these crucial decisions to experts or computers, who might stand a better chance of making them correctly (in terms of later satisfactions), is not to be explained simply in terms of our (sometimes mistaken) assumptions that we know best how to satisfy our own interests, or that we personally will choose correctly, even though most other people do not. If our retaining such authority for ourselves is not simply irrational, and I do not believe it is, this can only be because of the great independent value of self-determination. We value the exercise of free choice itself in personally important decisions, no matter what the effects of those decisions upon other satisfactions. The independent value of self-determination in decisions of great personal importance adds also to our reluctance to relinquish medical decisions with crucial effects on our lives to doctors, despite their medical expertise.

Autonomy or self-determination is independently valuable, as argued before, first of all because we value it in itself. But we may again add to this want-regarding or utilitarian reason a second ideal-regarding or perfectionist reason. What has value does so because it is valued by a rational and autonomous person. But autonomy itself is necessary to the development of such valuing individual persons or agents. It is therefore not to be sacrificed to other derivative values. To do so as a rule is to destroy the ground for the latter. Rights in general not only express and protect the central interests of individuals (the raison d'être usually emphasized in their exposition); they also express the dignity and inviolability of individuality itself. For this reason the most fundamental right is the right to control the course of one's life, to make decisions crucial to it, including decisions in life-or-death medical contexts. The other side of the independent value of self-determination from the point of view of the individual is the recognition of him by others, including doctors, as an individual with his own possibly unique set of values and priorities. His dignity demands a right to make personal decisions that express those values.

Why Doctors Should Intervene

TERRENCE F. ACKERMAN

Respect for patient autonomy is distorted when autonomy is understood as mere noninterference, says Ackerman. On this prevalent hands-off view, "[t]he doctor need be only an honest and good technician, providing relevant information and dispensing professionally competent care." But this approach fails to respect autonomy genuinely, he argues, for it does not recognize that many factors can compromise autonomy, including illness and a host of psychological, social, and cultural constraints. At times, true respect for autonomy may require the physician to intervene, to deviate from the patient's stated preferences. The goal of the physician-patient relationship should be "to resolve the underlying physical (or mental) defect, and to deal with cognitive, psychological, and social constraints in order to restore autonomous functioning."

Patient autonomy has become a watchword of the medical profession. According to the revised 1980 AMA Principles of Medical Ethics,[1] no longer is it permissible for a doctor to withhold information from a patient, even on grounds that it may be harmful. Instead the physician is expected to "deal honestly with patients" at all times. Physicians also have a duty to respect the confidentiality of the doctor-patient relationship. Even when disclosure to a third party may be in the patient's interests, the doctor is instructed to release information only when required by law. Respect for the autonomy of patients has given rise to many specific patient rights—among them the right to refuse treatment, the right to give informed consent, the right to privacy, and the right to competent medical care provided with "respect for human dignity."

While requirements of honesty, confidentiality, and patients' rights are all important, the underlying moral vision that places exclusive emphasis upon these factors is more troublesome. The profession's notion of respect for autonomy makes noninterference its essential feature. As the Belmont Report has described it, there is an obligation to "give weight to autonomous persons' considered opinions and choices while refraining from obstructing their

actions unless they are clearly detrimental to others."[2] Or, as Tom Beauchamp and James Childress have suggested, "To respect autonomous agents is to recognize with due appreciation their own considered value judgments and outlooks even when it is believed that their judgments are mistaken." They argue that people "are entitled to autonomous determination without limitation on their liberty being imposed by others."[3]

When respect for personal autonomy is understood as noninterference, the physician's role is dramatically simplified. The doctor need be only an honest and good technician, providing relevant information and dispensing professionally competent care. Does noninterference really respect patient autonomy? I maintain that it does not, because it fails to take account of the transforming effects of illness.

"Autonomy," typically defined as self-governance, has two key features. First, autonomous behavior is governed by plans of action that have been formulated through deliberation or reflection. This deliberative activity involves processes of both information gathering and priority setting. Second, autonomous behavior issues, intentionally and voluntarily, from choices people make based upon their own life plans.

But various kinds of constraints can impede autonomous behavior. There are physical constraints—confinement in prison is an example—where internal or external circumstances bodily prevent a person

From *Hastings Center Report*, vol. 12, no. 4 (August 1982), pp. 14–17. Reprinted by permission of the author and the publisher.

from deliberating adequately or acting on life plans. Cognitive constraints derive from either a lack of information or an inability to understand that information. A consumer's ignorance regarding the merits or defects of a particular product fits the description. Psychological constraints, such as anxiety or depression, also inhibit adequate deliberation. Finally, there are social constraints—such as institutionalized roles and expectations ("a woman's place is in the home," "the doctor knows best") that block considered choices.

Edmund Pellegrino suggests several ways in which autonomy is specifically compromised by illness:

> In illness, the body is interposed between us and reality—it impedes our choices and actions and is no longer fully responsive. . . . Illness forces a reappraisal and that poses a threat to the old image; it opens up all the old anxieties and imposes new ones—often including the real threat of death or drastic alterations in life-style. This ontological assault is aggravated by the loss of . . . freedoms we identify as peculiarly human. The patient . . . lacks the knowledge and skills necessary to cure himself or gain relief of pain and suffering. . . . The state of being ill is therefore a state of "wounded humanity," of a person compromised in his fundamental capacity to deal with his vulnerability.[4]

The most obvious impediment is that illness "interposes" the body or mind between the patient and reality, obstructing attempts to act upon cherished plans. An illness may not only temporarily obstruct long-range goals; it may necessitate permanent and drastic revision in the patient's major activities, such as working habits. Patients may also need to set limited goals regarding control of pain, alteration in diet and physical activity, and rehabilitation of functional impairments. They may face considerable difficulties in identifying realistic and productive aims.

The crisis is aggravated by a cognitive constraint—the lack of "knowledge and skills" to overcome their physical or mental impediment. Without adequate medical understanding, the patient cannot assess his or her condition accurately. Thus the choice of goals is seriously hampered and subsequent decisions by the patient are not well founded.

Pellegrino mentions the anxieties created by illness, but psychological constraints may also include denial, depression, guilt, and fear. I recently visited an eighteen-year-old boy who was dying of a cancer that had metastasized extensively throughout his abdomen. The doctor wanted to administer further chemotherapy that might extend the patient's life a few months. But the patient's nutritional status was poor, and he would need intravenous feedings prior to chemotherapy. Since the nutritional therapy might also encourage tumor growth, leading to a blockage of the gastrointestinal tract, the physician carefully explained the options and the risks and benefits several times, each time at greater length. But after each explanation the young man would say only that he wished to do whatever was necessary to get better. Denial prevented him from exploring the alternatives.

Similarly, depression can lead patients to make choices that are not in harmony with their life plans. Recently, a middle-aged woman with a history of ovarian cancer in remission returned to the hospital for the biopsy of a possible pulmonary metastasis. Complications ensued and she required the use of an artificial respirator for several days. She became severely depressed and soon refused further treatment. The behavior was entirely out of character with her previous full commitment to treatment. Fully supporting her overt wishes might have robbed her of many months of relatively comfortable life in the midst of a very supportive family around which her activities centered. The medical staff stalled for time. Fortunately, her condition improved.

Fear may also cripple the ability of patients to choose. Another patient, diagnosed as having a cerebral tumor that was probably malignant, refused lifesaving surgery because he feared the cosmetic effects of neurosurgery and the possibility of neurological damage. After he became comatose and new evidence suggested that the tumor might be benign, his family agreed to surgery and a benign tumor was removed. But he later died of complications related to the unfortunate delay in surgery. Although while competent he had agreed to chemotherapy, his fears (not uncommon among candidates for neurosurgery) prevented him from accepting the medical intervention that might have secured him the health he desired.

Social constraints may also prevent patients from acting upon their considered choices. A recent case involved a twelve-year-old boy whose rhabdomyosarcoma had metastasized extensively. Since all therapeutic interventions had failed, the only remaining option was to involve him in a phase 1 clinical trial. (A phase 1 clinical trial is the initial testing of a drug in human subjects. Its primary purpose is to identify toxicities rather than to evaluate therapeutic effectiveness.) The patient's course had been very stormy, and he privately expressed to the staff his desire to quit further therapy and return home. However, his parents denied the hopelessness of his condition, remaining steadfast in their belief that God would save their child. With deep regard for his parents' wishes, he refused to openly object to their desires and the therapy was administered. No antitumor effect occurred and the patient soon died.

Various social and cultural expectations also take their toll. According to Talcott Parsons, one feature of the sick role is that the ill person is obligated "... to seek *technically competent* help, namely, in the most usual case, that of a physician and to *cooperate* with him in the process of trying to get well."[5] Parsons does not describe in detail the elements of this cooperation. But clinical observation suggests that many patients relinquish their opportunity to deliberate and make choices regarding treatment in deference to the physician's superior educational achievement and social status ("Whatever you think, doctor!"). The physical and emotional demands of illness reinforce this behavior.

Moreover, this perception of the sick role has been socially taught from childhood—and it is not easily altered even by the physician who ardently tries to engage the patient in decision making. Indeed, when patients are initially asked to participate in the decision-making process, some exhibit considerable confusion and anxiety. Thus, for many persons, the institutional role of patient requires the physician to assume the responsibilities of making decisions.

Ethicists typically condemn paternalistic practices in the therapeutic relationship, but fail to investigate the features that incline physicians to be paternalistic. Such behavior may be one way to assist persons whose autonomous behavior has been impaired by illness. Of course, it is an open moral question whether the constraints imposed by illness ought to be addressed in such a way. But only by coming to grips with the psychological and social dimensions of illness can we discuss how physicians can best respect persons who are patients.

Returning Control to Patients

In the usual interpretation of respect for personal autonomy, noninterference is fundamental. In the medical setting, this means providing adequate information and competent care that accords with the patient's wishes. But if serious constraints upon autonomous behavior are intrinsic to the state of being ill, then noninterference is not the best course, since the patient's choices will be seriously limited. Under these conditions, real respect for autonomy entails a more inclusive understanding of the relationship between patients and physicians. Rather than restraining themselves so that patients can exercise whatever autonomy they retain in illness, physicians should actively seek to neutralize the impediments that interfere with patients' choices.

In *The Healer's Art*, Eric Cassell underscored the essential feature of illness that demands a revision in our understanding of respect for autonomy:

> If I had to pick the aspect of illness that is most destructive to the sick, I would choose the loss of control. Maintaining control over oneself is so vital to all of us that one might see all the other phenomena of illness as doing harm not only in their own right but doubly so as they reinforce the sick person's perception that he is no longer in control."[6]

Cassell maintains, "The doctor's job is to return control to his patient." But what is involved in "returning control" to patients? Pellegrino identifies two elements that are preeminent duties of the physician: to provide technically competent care and to fully inform the patient. The noninterference approach emphasizes these factors, and their importance is clear. Loss of control in illness is precipitated by a physical or mental defect. If technically competent therapy can fully restore previous health, then the patient will again be in control. Consider a patient who is treated with antibiotics for a routine throat infection of streptococcal origin. Similarly, loss of control is fueled by lack of knowledge—not knowing what is the matter, what it portends for life and limb, and how it might be dealt with. Providing information that will enable the patient to make decisions and adjust goals enhances personal control.

If physical and cognitive constraints were the only impediments to autonomous behavior, then Pellegrino's suggestions might be adequate. But providing information and technically competent care will not do much to alter psychological or social impediments. Pellegrino does not adequately portray the physician's role in ameliorating these.

How can the doctor offset the acute denial that prevented the adolescent patient from assessing the benefits and risk of intravenous feedings prior to his additional chemotherapy? How can he deal with the candidate for neurosurgery who clearly desired that attempts be made to restore his health, but feared cosmetic and functional impairments? Here strategies must go beyond the mere provision of information. Crucial information may have to be repeatedly shared with patients. Features of the situation that the patient has brushed over (as in denial) or falsely emphasized (as with acute anxiety) must be discussed in more detail or set in their proper perspective. And the physician may have to alter the tone of discussions with the patient, emphasizing a positive attitude with the overly depressed or anxious patient, or a more realistic, cautious attitude with the denying patient, in order to neutralize psychological constraints.

The physician may also need to influence the beliefs or attitudes of other people, such as family members, that limit their awareness of the patient's perspective. Such a strategy might have helped the parents of the dying child to conform with the patient's wishes. On the other hand, physicians may need to modify the patient's own understanding of the sick role. For example, they may need to convey that the choice of treatment depends not merely upon the physician's technical assessment, but on the quality of life and personal goals that the patient desires.

Once we admit that psychological and social constraints impair patient autonomy, it follows that physicians must carefully assess the psychological and social profiles and needs of patients. Thus,

Pedro Lain-Entralgo insists that adequate therapeutic interaction consists in a combination of "objectivity" and "cooperation." Cooperation "is shown by psychologically reproducing in the mind of the doctor, insofar as that is possible, the meaning the patient's illness has for him."[7] Without such knowledge, the physician cannot assist patients in restoring control over their lives. Ironically, some critics have insisted that physicians are not justified in acting for the well-being of patients because they possess no "expertise" in securing the requisite knowledge about the patient.[8] But knowledge of the patient's psychological and social situation is also necessary to help the patient to act as a fully autonomous person.

Beyond Legalism

Current notions of respect for autonomy are undergirded by a legal model of doctor-patient interaction. The relationship is viewed as a typical commodity exchange—the provision of technically competent medical care in return for financial compensation. Moreover, physicians and patients are presumed to have an equal ability to work out the details of therapy, *provided that* certain moral rights of patients are recognized. But the compromising effects of illness, the superior knowledge of physicians, and various institutional arrangements are also viewed as giving the physician an unfair power advantage. Since the values and interests of patients may conflict with those of the physician, the emphasis is placed upon noninterference.[9]

This legal framework is insufficient for medical ethics because it fails to recognize the impact of illness upon autonomous behavior. Even if the rights to receive adequate information and to provide consent are secured, affective and social constraints impair the ability of patients to engage in contractual therapeutic relationships. When people are sick, the focus upon equality is temporally misplaced. The goal of the therapeutic relationship is the "development" of the patient—helping to resolve the underlying physical (or mental) defect, and to deal with cognitive, psychological, and social constraints in order to restore autonomous functioning. In this sense, the doctor-patient interaction is not unlike the parent-child or teacher-student relationship.

The legal model also falls short because the therapeutic relationship is not a typical commodity exchange in which the parties use each other to accomplish mutually compatible goals, without taking a direct interest in each other. Rather, the status of patients as persons whose autonomy is compromised constitutes the very stuff of therapeutic art. The physician is attempting to alter the fundamental ability of patients to carry through their life plans. To accomplish this delicate task requires a personal knowledge about and interest in the patient. If we accept these points, then we must reject the narrow focus of medical ethics upon noninterference and emphasize patterns of interaction that free patients from constraints upon autonomy.

I hasten to add that I am criticizing the legal model only as a *complete* moral framework for therapeutic interaction. As case studies in medical ethics suggest, physicians and patients *are* potential adversaries. Moreover, the disability of the patient and various institutional controls provide physicians with a distinct "power advantage" that can be abused. Thus, a legitimate function of medical ethics is to formulate conditions that assure noninterference in patient decision making. But various positive interventions must also be emphasized, since the central task in the therapeutic process is assisting patients to reestablish control over their own lives.

In the last analysis, the crucial matter is how we view the patient who enters into the therapeutic relationship. Cassell points out that in the typical view ". . . the sick person is seen simply as a well person with a disease, rather than as qualitatively different, not only physically but also socially, emotionally, and even cognitively." In this view, ". . . the physician's role in the care of the sick is primarily the application of technology . . . and health can be seen as a commodity."[10] But if, as I believe, illness renders sick persons "qualitatively different," then respect for personal autonomy requires a therapeutic interaction considerably more complex than the noninterference strategy.

Thus the current "Principles of Medical Ethics" simply exhort physicians to be honest. But the crucial requirement is that physicians tell the truth in a way, at a time, and in whatever increments are necessary to allow patients to effectively use the information in adjusting their life plans.[11] Similarly, respecting a patient's refusal of treatment maximizes autonomy only if a balanced and thorough deliberation precedes the decision. Again, the "Principles" suggest that physicians observe strict confidentiality. But the more complex moral challenge is to use confidential information in a way that will help to give the patient more freedom. Thus, the doctor can keep a patient's report on family dynamics private, and still use it to modify attitudes or actions of family members that inhibit the patient's control.

At its root, illness is an evil primarily because it compromises our efforts to control our lives. Thus, we must preserve an understanding of the physician's art that transcends noninterference and addresses this fundamental reality.

REFERENCES

1. American Medical Association, *Current Opinions of the Judicial Council of the American Medical Association* (Chicago, Illinois: American Medical Association, 1981). p. ix. Also see Robert Veatch, "Professional Ethics: New Principles for Physicians?," *Hastings Center Report* 10 (June 1980), 16–19.

2. The National Commission for the Protection of Human Subjects of Biomedical and Behavioral Research. *The Belmont Report: Ethical Principles and Guidelines for the Protection of Human Subjects of Research* (Washington, D.C.: U.S. Government Printing Office, 1978), p. 58.

3. Tom Beauchamp and James Childress, *Principles of Biomedical Ethics* (New York: Oxford University Press, 1980), p. 59.

4. Edmund Pellegrino, "Toward a Reconstruction of Medical Morality: The Primacy of the Act of Profession and the Fact of Illness," *The Journal of Medicine and Philosophy* 4 (1979), 44–45.

5. Talcott Parsons, *The Social System* (Glencoe, Illinois: The Free Press, 1951), p. 437.

6. Eric Cassell, *The Healer's Art* (New York: Lippincott. 1976), p. 44. Although Cassell aptly describes the goal of the healer's art, it is unclear whether he considers it to be based upon the obligation to respect the patient's autonomy or the duty to enhance the well-being of the patient. Some parts of his discussion clearly suggest the latter.

7. Pedro Lain-Entralgo, *Doctor and Patient* (New York: McGraw-Hill, 1969), p. 155.

8. See Allen Buchanan, "Medical Paternalism," *Philosophy and Public Affairs* 7 (1978), 370–90.

9. My formulation of the components of the legal model differs from, but is highly indebted to, John Ladd's

stimulating analysis in "Legalism and Medical Ethics," in John Davis et al., editors, *Contemporary Issues in Biomedical Ethics* (Clifton, N.J.: The Humana Press, 1979), pp. 1–35. However, I would not endorse Ladd's position that the moral principles that define our duties in the therapeutic setting are of a different logical type from those that define our duties to strangers.

10. Eric Cassell, "Therapeutic Relationship: Contemporary Medical Perspective," in Warren Reich, editor, *Encyclopedia of Bioethics* (New York: Macmillan, 1978), p. 1675.
11. Cf. Norman Cousins, "A Layman Looks at Truth-telling," *Journal of the American Medical Association* 244 (1980), 1929–30. Also see Howard Brody, "Hope," *Journal of the American Medical Association* 246 (1981), pp. 1411–12.

Autonomy, Futility, and the Limits of Medicine

ROBERT L. SCHWARTZ

Does respecting the principle of autonomy require physicians to provide any treatment that an autonomous patient requests? Schwartz says that physicians are not obligated to give scientifically futile treatment (a worthless cancer therapy, for example). More importantly, neither are they morally required to provide treatment that is outside the scope of medical practice (such as surgical amputation of a limb for purely religious reasons). In many instances (including the famous Wanglie case), the central question was not whether the treatment requested by the patient was futile, but whether the treatment was beyond the proper limits of medicine. Schwartz contends that defining the scope of medicine should be left to physicians themselves.

SURGEON: I don't seem to understand; why, precisely, have you come to see me today?

PATIENT: I am here because I need to have my right arm amputated, and I have been told that you are one of the finest surgeons in town.

SURGEON: That is, of course, correct. Tell me, though—I do not see a referral here—what makes you think that you need your arm amputated?

PATIENT: It is the only way I can expiate my sins. I could describe those sins to you in detail, and I could tell you why this is the only way I can seek expiation, but that hardly seems appropriate or necessary. In any case, I am sure that the only way I can expiate them is by having my right arm amputated.

SURGEON: Do I understand this? You came to see me because you want a good surgeon to amputate your right arm so that you can expiate your sins.

PATIENT: Exactly; I knew you would understand. By the way, I am fully insured.

SURGEON: Are you crazy? You've come to a surgeon just because you want your arm lopped off?

PATIENT: I would be crazy if I went any place else. I mean, you wouldn't recommend a butcher or a chiropractor, would you?

SURGEON: I'm sorry; your request is simply unacceptable. My values do not permit me to provide the services you seek. I just don't think it would be right.

PATIENT: Wait just a minute. I am not hiring you for your ability to make moral judgments. I am hiring you because of your technical skill in removing limbs. We are talking about my arm, my life, and my values. I have decided I need the surgery and I ask you merely to respect my autonomy and to apply your medical skill so that my values can be served. If you want to expiate your sins in some other way, that's just fine with me. I don't want your religious and ethical peccadillos to interfere with a high-quality technical medical service that I am paying you to provide for me.

Most of us find the surgeon's surprise at this patient's request understandable, and it is hard to imagine any surgeon acceding to this patient's demand. On the other hand (the one left), the patient is right—the surgeon is denying his technical skill because his values are different from those of the patient, whose values the surgeon does not respect.[1] The autonomy of the patient is being limited by the values of the doctor whose own interests, other than his interest in practicing medicine according to his own ethical values, would remain unaffected by his decision to provide the service.

Autonomy and Patient Control of Medical Decision Making

Autonomy is the authority to make decisions in accord with one's own values, unrestrained by the values of others who do not suffer the consequences of the decision. Ordinarily, the principle of autonomy authorizes patients to make healthcare decisions unrestrained by the values of their physicians, others in the healthcare industry, or the rest of society. Despite this, even the strongest supporters of the primacy of the principle of autonomy in healthcare decision making—even those who believe that autonomy virtually always trumps beneficence—would be likely to support (or even require) the surgeon's decision *not* to offer surgery in this case. But why?

The principle of autonomy has never been understood to authorize patients to choose from among an unrestricted range of alternatives, As Fenella Rouse points out in the next note on the *Wanglie* case, autonomy has often been misconstrued and improperly applied by courts in cases involving medical decision making. In any case, there are at least three kinds of limitations on the exercise of autonomy by those making healthcare choices. First, patients may not require that they be treated by nonmedical means. Second, patients may not require that they be given scientifically futile treatment. Finally, and most significantly, patients may not require that they be treated in ways that are inconsistent with the ends of medicine, that is, in ways that are outside of the scope of medicine.

First, for example, a tense and depressed streetcar operator is not denied autonomy by our healthcare system if he is not given the option of choosing three weeks on the beach in Tahiti as a cure for his condition, even though it may well be effective. Three weeks on the beach in Tahiti is simply not a medical means of treatment—it is not among the medical alternatives for the treatment of that (or any other) condition.

Second, where the issue is one of scientific futility, i.e., whether a medical procedure will have the scientific consequences that are expected, the issue is left entirely to the medical profession. Physicians are not required to prescribe pasque-flower tea for the treatment of cancer, for example, because, as a scientific matter, there is simply no efficacy in treatment by pasque-flower tea. From a purely scientific perspective, the treatment of cancer by pasque-flower tea really is futile.

Unlike beach rest, amputation is within the therapeutic arsenal of the medical profession; it is a medical procedure. Unlike pasque-flower tea as a cure for cancer, surgical amputation is a proven effective way of removing a limb; thus, it is not futile in a scientific sense. Despite this, though, we would not allow the patient in the opening vignette to demand that his arm be amputated because patients are not permitted to demand surgery that is inconsistent with the definition of the scope of medical practice accepted by the surgeon.[2] In their exercise of autonomy, patients may choose only from among reasonable medical alternatives. The hard question is how doctors, patients, and others define which medically and scientifically proven procedures are among the reasonable medical alternatives.

The Wanglie Case

The limitations on a patient's autonomy to choose healthcare has come to the forefront of the bioethics debate over the past year. In December 1989, Helga Wanglie, an 87-year-old retired school teacher in

Minneapolis, tripped on a rug in her home and fractured her hip.[3] One month later, after surgery in one hospital, she was transferred to Hennepin County Medical Center, where her doctors determined she needed assistance in breathing and placed her on a ventilator. Three months later, in May 1990, she was transferred to yet another hospital to see if she could be weaned from her ventilator. While there, she suffered cardiac arrest and was resuscitated, but only after she suffered severe and irreversible brain damage that put her in a persistent vegetative state. She was moved back to Hennepin County Medical Center, where she was maintained on a ventilator and fed through a gastrostomy tube. Mrs. Wanglie remained in a persistent vegetative state for several months before her physicians determined that the continuation of high-tech medical intervention was inappropriate. In essence, the doctors determined that the care Mrs. Wanglie was receiving was no longer among the reasonable medical alternatives for a person in her condition—it was, to her doctors, morally analogous to amputating a limb to expiate sins.

Mrs. Wanglie's husband and her two children disagreed. As Mrs. Wanglie's husband pointed out, "Only He who gave life has the right to take life." He also pointed out, "I am a pro-lifer. I take the position that human life is sacred."[4] He and the children agreed that Mrs. Wanglie would want treatment continued, even if the doctors believed that there were no chance of recovery. This was, as the family pointed out, a determination based on the patient's values, and there was no reason to defer to the doctors' collective ethical judgment.

The physicians and the hospital searched in vain for some healthcare facility in Minnesota that would be willing to take Mrs. Wanglie and continue to provide her care. None came forward. Frustrated by what they considered the continued inappropriate use of medicine, the hospital sought a court order appointing a conservator to replace Mr. Wanglie to make healthcare decisions for Mrs. Wanglie. On 1 July 1991, the trial court judge refused to issue an order and effectively confirmed Mr. Wanglie's right to continue to make healthcare decisions for his wife of 53 years.[5] Three days after the order was issued, Mrs. Wanglie died "of natural causes."

Her hospitalization cost nearly 1 million dollars, which was paid by Medicare and her private medigap insurance carrier. Neither objected to the care for financial or cost-benefit reasons, and the cost properly did not enter into the judicial analysis of the case.

Asking the Wrong Question: Substitute Decision Makers and the Wanglie Court

Unfortunately, the litigation in this case obscured the real issue. The hospital's decision to seek a conservatorship did nothing more than raise the issue of whether Mr. Wanglie was the best decision maker for his wife. The lawsuit asked nothing more than whether Mr. Wanglie was the most able to apply his wife's values to the medical facts in this case.[6] Indeed, the hospital supplied no evidence that anyone else would be more likely to be able to determine and apply Mrs. Wanglie's values. To the extent that the litigation focused on how best to carry to fruition Mrs. Wanglie's autonomy, not on the limits of that autonomy, the hospital was left without a prayer of success.

The real question, however, should not have been what Mrs. Wanglie would have desired (or what was in her "best personal medical interest")—there was no reason to doubt her family on that point—but whether the continuation of ventilator support and gastrostomy feeding were among the reasonable medical alternatives that should have been available to Mrs. Wanglie or her surrogate decision maker, whoever that might be. The question, really, was whether the provision of this kind of treatment in this kind of case was outside the limits of medicine and, thus, beyond her power of choice.

Mrs. Wanglie's healthcare providers should have argued that medical practice simply did not include providing a ventilator and gastrostomy feeding under circumstances of this case, and that no surrogate decision maker—whether it be Mr. Wanglie or another substituted by the court—should be able to choose this option. If, for example, Mr. Wanglie requested that his wife be frozen and cryopreserved so that she could be brought back to life and "cured" when there were sufficient advances in the science of her underlying ailments, there is no doubt that this request would not have to be honored by Mrs. Wanglie's medical team. A request for cryopreservation, like a request for surgery that a patient believes will expiate his sins, may well reflect the true desires of the patient, but it is a request that asks something that is beyond the limits of medicine.[7] Why is the Wanglie family request in this case any different? The real question in the *Wanglie* case was whether the continuation of life-sustaining treatment for an 87-year-old woman in a persistent vegetative state with no hope of return to sentience constitutes treatment outside of the limits of medicine.

Although the question of the propriety of treatment for Mrs. Wanglie has been discussed as if it were a question of "futility," there is no doubt that the treatment was *not* futile in the purely scientific sense. The treatment was designed to keep Mrs. Wanglie alive, and it served this end effectively. Those who have viewed the *Wanglie* case as one dealing with futility in a scientific sense have brought the wrong perspective to the case. The question is not whether the treatment offered would successfully do what Mrs. Wanglie's family said she desired—keep her alive—but whether keeping her alive, under the circumstances, was beyond the proper scope of medicine. Like most questions in medicine, this is not purely a question of science or a question of values, but a hybrid question.

The Role of the Physician in Healthcare Decision Making

Even when the question is not a purely scientific one, even when it involves a determination of whether medical treatment justifies the quality of life that results, our society has generally left to physicians the determination of whether a particular treatment is among the reasonable medical alternatives. There are, of course, problems with this approach.[8] Why should physicians have the exclusive authority to define the extent of their own professional conduct? Does this lead to too much variation from doctor to doctor and from hospital to hospital? Could doctors decide that providing treatment to HIV-positive patients is beyond the limits of medicine? Leaving the question of what constitutes a reasonable medical alternative in the hands of Dr. Kevorkian yields a very different result than leaving that same question in the hands of the doctors who are

associated with the right-to-life movement. As the national debate over euthanasia has demonstrated, doctors disagree over the appropriate scope of medicine with as much vigor, and probably with more concern, than the rest of us.

In the end, though, that is exactly why these decisions should be left to physicians. If a patient who desires a particular course of treatment can find a healthcare provider—*any* healthcare provider—who believes that the proposed course of treatment is within the realm of reasonable medical alternatives, that patient will have access to that course of treatment. It is only when a patient desires treatment that not a single healthcare provider believes to be within the limits of medicine that the patient will be denied that course of treatment. If a patient seeks amputation for the expiation of sins, for example, it is unlikely that the patient will find any surgeon willing to perform the task. When there is universal agreement among healthcare providers that the patient's request seeks something beyond the limits of medicine, that should constitute very strong evidence that the request is inappropriate.

The Wanglie family could not find any healthcare provider in Minnesota who would offer the medical services the family thought appropriate. Although the technical services that were sought (the ventilator, for example) were clearly within the scope of medical practice, there was no healthcare provider in Minnesota who believed that the provision of those services in Mrs. Wanglie's circumstance was within the range of reasonable medical alternatives—at least, no one who was capable of providing the services was willing to do so. In effect, the court required Hennepin County Medical Center to provide a service that was, in the universal conclusion of Minnesota healthcare providers, inappropriate.

Asking the Right Question: The Courts and Ethics Committees

Courts focus only on the best way to serve the autonomy of patients; after all, the courts are largely responsible for making the principle of autonomy the guiding principle for medical decision-making. The *Wanglie* court was simply unable to get beyond the question of who could best identify the values and interests of the patient and move on to the question of whether the proposed treatment was within the limits of medicine. The court did not decide that continued use of the ventilator and the continued gastrostomy feedings were reasonable medical alternatives for Mrs. Wanglie; it did not address these questions at all. Similarly, in October 1991, an Atlanta judge finessed the same issue in just the same way when she determined in the *Jane Doe* case that a 13-year-old with a degenerative neurologic condition must be continued on a treatment dictated by her father, who believed in miracles, despite the testimony of her pediatric neurologist that it was "ethically and morally unconscionable" to do so.[9]

If the courts continue to miss the real issue in these cases, as they will, that issue will have to be addressed in some other forum where there is both the moral and medical sophistication to understand the limits of medicine and the sensitivity to understand (and help define) society's reasonable expectations of medicine. Within their roles as educators, as mediators, and as sources for discussion of exactly these questions, broadly interdisciplinary ethics committees seem particularly well suited to the task. When a court is forced to face a determination by such a committee that a particular treatment, in a particular case, is beyond the limits of medicine—even though this treatment is exactly what the patient desires, even though the treatment employs a clearly medical procedure, and even though the treatment is not scientifically futile—that court may be forced to take the real question seriously.

NOTES

1. One might argue that the surgeon's only real concern is over the competency of the patient, but there is no reason outside of this medical request itself to question that competency. Indeed, we accept the fact that competent people can make unusual requests—requests that the vast majority of us find strange—and still be competent. We are even more likely to find unusual behavior (such as various kinds of abstinence and abnegation) consistent with competence when the behavior is religious, or quasi-religious, as it is here. In any case, there is very little left to any meaningful notion of competence if we determine a patient's competence to choose a particular form of treatment solely by reference to the treatment choice he makes.

2. Analogously, the American Medical Association has found it unacceptable to have physicians administer lethal doses of drugs to execute condemned prisoners, even if the condemned prisoners request the administration of the drugs because the alternative methods of execution are more painful or degrading. Although the administration of the relevant drugs is appropriately limited to physicians, their use *for this purpose* is simply outside of the scope of medicine, whatever the prisoner-patient may desire.

3. A great deal has been written about the *Wanglie* case. Several relevant articles are found in the July–August 1991 issue of the *Hastings Center Report*, which includes a summary of the facts prepared by Ronald Cranford of the Department of Neurology at the hospital in which Mrs. Wanglie remained a patient at her death. The facts are fleshed out in various newspaper articles: Colen. Fight over life. *Newsday* (1991 Jan. 29): City p. 57; Belkin. As family protests, hospital seeks an end to woman's life support. *New York Times* (1991 Jan. 10): Sec. A, p. 1; Steinbrook Hospital or family: who decides right to die? *Los Angeles Times* (1991 Feb. 17): Part A, p. 1.

4. See note 3. Colen (1991): 57.

5. *Conservatorship of Wanglie*, No. PX-91-283 (Minn., Hennepin Co. Dist. Ct., July 1, 1991).

6. The hospital argued that Mr. Wanglie should be disqualified from making the decision for his wife because his decision was not in the "patient's best *personal medical interest*." Cranford. Helga Wanglie's ventilator. *Hastings Center Report* (1991; Jul.–Aug.): 23–4.

7. The courts have been unsympathetic to those who seek cryopreservation, as you might guess. For a description of the case of Thomas Donaldson, who did not convince a court to allow the removal and freezing of his head before his certain death from a brain tumor, see Corwin. Tumor victim loses bid to freeze head before death. *Los Angeles Times* (1990 Sept. 15): Sec. A, p. 28. As one might expect, the case was subsequently turned into an episode of *L.A. Law* (#7D08, copyright 1990).

8. To the extent these problems flow from the use of a "futility" exception to normal requirements of consent, they are cogently and thoughtfully expressed in Scofield. Is consent useful when resuscitation isn't. *Hastings Center Report* (1991; Nov.–Dec.): 28–6. As Scofield points out (in the context of CPR);

> In reality the futility exception is a dishonest solution to the tragic choice that decisions to limit treatment represent. It purports to represent, but in fact departs from the fundamental values consent is intended to serve. It will not generate the conversation we need if we are to attain consensus about limiting treatment; nor will it make physicians sensitive in their dealings with patients, especially dying patients. It promotes a model of consent that is antithetical to setting limits in a democratic, caring manner. (p. 30)

9. Colen. Judge bars letting girl in coma die. *Newsday* (1991 Oct. 18): News p. 4.1.

Patient Autonomy and Physician Responsibility

COMMENTARIES BY PATRICK C. BEEMAN AND RYAN C. VANWOERKOM

Two medical school students provide separate commentaries on balancing patient autonomy and physician duties in the case of an HIV-positive, hospitalized patient.

Mr. Smith, 50, was HIV positive. Having given informed consent, he underwent cardiac catheterization following a positive stress test. He was found to have mild-to-moderate single vessel coronary artery disease. Mr. Smith did well during and immediately after the procedure and was discharged.

After discharge, however, he had complications and severe pain. He returned to the hospital the day after the catheterization and was found to have massive groin and scrotal swelling, diagnosed as scrotal hematoma. A vascular surgeon was consulted and reported that there was no need for surgical evacuation. Accordingly, Mr. Smith's hematoma was managed conservatively by elevation of the scrotum, and he was given analgesia for his pain. On admission, his hemoglobin was 12.3g/dl and remained stable throughout his hospital stay. Mr. Smith also received occupational and physical therapy. His hematoma decreased in size only minimally over the course of his stay, and he continued to complain of pain.

By hospital day 5, the primary team decided that Mr. Smith was medically stable and could be discharged safely to the extended care facility (ECF). There, physical therapy and the conservative management of his hematoma would continue. Upon mention of the plan for his transfer, Mr. Smith became upset. He remarked that the complication was not his fault and that, since the hospital "did this to [him]," the least it could do was provide him a place to recuperate. "I will leave when I'm ready," he stated.

The attending cardiologist had apologized to Mr. Smith for the complication when he was readmitted to the hospital. Now the cardiologist politely

explained that, given his HIV status, an extended hospital stay was dangerous for him because of "the bad bugs that live here." This made matters worse. One of the medical students on the team later discovered that the patient had misinterpreted the cardiologist's statement to mean that his HIV status increased the risk of infection for others. All in all, Mr. Smith felt that he had not been treated well, stating he did not appreciate what he perceived to be the flippant way in which the attending cardiologist had announced his HIV status for others in the room, including the patient's roommate, to hear. Further, he said, one morning when he had not felt well enough for physical therapy and asked the therapist to return in the afternoon, a nurse had said to him, "You can lie around at an ECF just as easily as you can lie around here." Understandably, this offended Mr. Smith. He was discharged from the hospital after 14 days.

Commentary I

PATRICK C. BEEMAN

This case raises many ethical and professionalism issues: the importance of good communication in the patient-doctor relationship, the conflict between a patient's wishes and a doctor's clinical judgment, how one should manage the complications that inevitably occur, and others. But the chief ethical concern in this case is the classic conflict between autonomy and beneficence. What do we do when a patient's demands don't accord with the physician's judgment about what is in the patient's best interest—in this case, a short hospital stay?

Autonomy, the principle of patient self-determination, gained ascendance as a kind of uber-principle in medical ethics in the decades after 1970. Edmund Pellegrino, MD, chair of the President's Council on

From "Patient Autonomy and Physician Responsibility," *AMA Journal of Ethic*, vol. 11, no. 8 (August 2009), 598–602.

Bioethics and elder statesman of the discipline, has observed that, in our time, "the center of gravity of clinical decision making has shifted almost completely from the doctor to the patient" as a way to combat the "historical dominance of benign authoritarianism or paternalism in the traditional ethics of medicine" [1].

Pellegrino argues that the proper focus of autonomy, the reason it is owed respect, is the principle of beneficence. Paternalism is not synonymous with physician beneficence, nor is it compatible with either autonomy or beneficence. Beneficence means acting in the patient's quadripartite good, his or her biomedical, subjective, personal, and ultimate good [2, 3].

In this case, achieving the patient's *biomedical* good requires managing his hematoma and the complications related to it. By hospital day 5, it was apparent that this goal was well on its way to being met. The *personal* good of the patient, "what is good for humans as humans and members of the human community," includes maximizing his ability to decide for himself, to set his own course in life [3]. The achievement of this subtle and demanding aspect of the good lies in respecting a patient's autonomy, for instance, not coercing him into treatment with which he is uncomfortable, but enhancing his understanding so that agreement to decisions about his care spring from who he is as a rational, decision-making being. The *ultimate* good of the person—at once the most important and intrinsic of the four aspects of the good—involves respecting the religious, spiritual, and other all-important beliefs of patients. This case does not illustrate pursuit of that good, though certainly it was not openly or intentionally opposed. But it was principally the *subjective* good of the patient, the desires and wishes Mr. Smith identified for himself in relation to treatment, which posed the conflict in this case. Whatever the reason, Mr. Smith's subjective good included staying in the hospital on his own terms, not on those of his physician.

The miscommunications and recriminations that occurred at the outset of discharge planning complicated the case. What could have been done better? Knowing of the patient's dissatisfaction with his care (the attending physician had been forewarned by one of the students about the patient's allusions to having a "legal case"), the physician might have taken into account the precariousness of the situation before bringing up the idea of discharge to the patient.

Admittedly, Mr. Smith was what some would call "a difficult patient," but the attending cardiologist, to be fair, had apologized to Mr. Smith. Still, a further exploration of Mr. Smith's understanding of his situation and his goals and frustrations was warranted. After discerning these, the search for common ground may have begun by providing the patient with realistic discharge options and explaining to him the physician's concerns regarding increased risk of nosocomial infections in HIV-positive patients [4–7]. The doctor's actions unquestionably were motivated by solicitude for Mr. Smith's biomedical good. At the same time, Mr. Smith's frustrations were exacerbated by a perceived high-handed disregard for his subjective good.

The focus on autonomy that we have experienced in medical ethics has encouraged greater participation by patients in their own care. Of course, doctors are not obligated to do whatever patients ask of them, but providing options such as, "Would you like to leave tomorrow morning or Wednesday?" rather than marching into the room during rounds and announcing that the patient must leave would have allowed the patient a measure of self-determination in his care. Such an action may have prevented the conflict between the patient's subjective interest in a lengthened stay and the biomedical good of preventing nosocomial illness while simultaneously maximizing the patient's autonomy in the context of beneficence.

REFERENCES
1. Pellegrino ED. The four principles and the doctor-patient relationship: the need for a better linkage. In: Gillon R, Lloyd A. *Principles of Health Care Ethics*. New York, NY: John Wiley & Sons; 1994: 353–367.
2. Pellegrino ED. Moral choice, the good of the patient, and the patient's good. In: Moskop JC, Kopelman L. *Ethics and Critical Care Medicine*. Dordrecht, Netherlands: D. Reidel; 1985: 117–138.
3. Pellegrino, The four principles, 193.
4. Duse AG. Nosocomial infections in HIV-infected/AIDS patients. *J Hosp Infect*. 1999; 43: S191–201.

5. Laing RB. Nosocomial infections in patients with HIV disease. *J Hosp Infect.* 1999; 43(3): 179–185.
6. Petrosillo N, Pagani L, Ippolito G; Gruppo HIV e Infezioni Ospedaliere. Nosocomial infections in HIV-positive patients: an overview. *Infection.* 2003; 31: Suppl 2: 28–34.
7. Padoveze MC, Trabasso P, Branchini ML. Nosocomial infections among HIV-positive and HIV-negative patients in a Brazilian infectious diseases unit. *Am J Infect Control,* 2002; 30(6): 346–350.

Commentary 2

RYAN C. VANWOERKOM

The first commentator provides an illustrative account of ethical questions critical to a sound fiduciary physician-patient relationship. What is not adequately stated is that a thorough discussion of the risks and benefits of the cardiac catheterization as part of the informed consent process might have prevented some of Mr. Smith's anger or at least prepared him for the possibility of complications such as those he experienced.

In our relatively limited clinical experience, students pass through the majority of clinical inpatient rotations. Within this environment, time, priority management, urgency, and economics drive only the briefest of patient interactions. In less-pressing circumstances, offering better information organizes the patient's expectations for a workable treatment plan. This information would include a discussion of the patient's potential increased risk of adverse outcomes and modified subsequent recovery in context of his HIV status. If the patient chose the procedure after understanding the properly explained risks, he then would have stepped into the realm of autonomous decision making with a feeling of ownership of the adverse outcome. Moreover, a simple question, "I sense you are concerned about leaving the hospital; can you tell me about this?" would show empathy and might succeed in alleviating Mr. Smith's underlying apprehension.

Mr. Smith's HIV status should not only influence the management of his expectations but should serve as the source for another vital aspect and discussion point in this case and in ethics—patient confidentiality. Understandably, it is difficult in crowded hospitals to maintain the highest standards of confidentiality. Asking the nurse to take Mr. Smith's roommate for a walk, however, or asking the patient

if he felt up to joining you on the couch or bench in a corner of an isolated hall, or simply making an effort to speak more softly to conserve his confidentiality might have instilled confidence that you value preserving his privacy—perhaps more so in the offering than in the actual event. The Council of Judicial and Ethical Affairs at the American Medical Association states, "Such respect for patient privacy is a fundamental expression of patient autonomy and is a prerequisite to building the trust that is at the core of the patient-physician relationship. . . . Physicians should be aware of and respect the special concerns of their patients regarding privacy" [1].

The nurse's comment illustrates an important aspect of expectation management that is often overlooked. If the expectations of the entire team are not unified, discord can ensue. Rather than helping resolve Mr. Smith's concerns, the nurse fed into his perception that the staff wished to be free from him by passing on his care to an ECF. Perhaps this perception engendered a fear of abandonment, or it might have suggested to Mr. Smith that being discharged to the ECF was a punishment. In either case, the comment fueled Mr. Smith's sense that his autonomy was not being respected and that the physicians' purported beneficence was really paternalism.

The pendulum of autonomy may swing toward the patient in many contemporary circumstances. A physician who fully understands, accepts, and exercises the professional rights of his position will teach the patient about the risks and benefits of procedures as related to their own health. He or she will explain the finite nature of medical resources with their accompanying financial obligations as well as alternatives, in a cooperative and confidential environment in conjunction with health-care staff. If these guidelines, and those suggested by the first case commentator, are heeded, greater understanding may pervade the healing halls of hospitals and clinics.

REFERENCES
1. American Medical Association. Opinion 5.059. Privacy in the context of health care. *Code of Medical Ethics.* Chicago, IL: American Medical Association. 2007. http://www.ama-assn.org/ama/pub/physician-resources/medical-ethics/code-medical-ethics/opinion5059.shtml. Accessed July 17, 2009.

Bouvia v. Superior Court

CALIFORNIA COURT OF APPEAL

In this 1986 ruling, the court asserted that competent adults have a "constitutionally guaranteed right" to decide for themselves whether to submit to medical treatments, a right that outweighs the interests of physicians, hospitals, and the state. A competent patient may refuse treatments even if they are needed to keep her alive.

Petitioner. Elizabeth Bouvia, a patient in a public hospital, seeks the removal from her body of a nasogastric tube inserted and maintained against her will and without her consent by physicians who so placed it for the purpose of keeping her alive through involuntary forced feeding.

Petitioner has here filed a petition for writ of mandamus and other extraordinary relief after the trial court denied her a preliminary injunction requiring that the tube be removed and that the hospital and doctors be prohibited from using any other similar procedures. We issued an alternative writ. We have heard oral argument from the parties and now order issuance of a peremptory writ, granting petitioner, Elizabeth Bouvia, the relief for which she prayed. . . .

The trial court denied petitioner's request for the immediate relief she sought. It concluded that leaving the tube in place was necessary to prolong petitioner's life, and that it would, in fact, do so. With the tube in place petitioner probably will survive the time required to prepare for trial, a trial itself and an appeal, if one proved necessary. The real party-physicians also assert, and the trial court agreed, that physically petitioner tolerates the tube reasonably well and thus is not in great physical discomfort.

Real parties' counsel therefore argue that the normal course of trial and appeal provide a sufficient remedy. But petitioner's ability to tolerate physical discomfort does not diminish her right to immediate relief. Her mental and emotional feelings are equally entitled to respect. She has been subjected to the forced intrusion of an artificial mechanism

From California Court of Appeal, *Bouvia v. Superior Court*, 225 Cal. Rptr. 297 (Ctr. App. 1986).

into her body against her will. She has a right to refuse the increased dehumanizing aspects of her condition created by the insertion of a permanent tube through her nose and into her stomach.

To petitioner it is a dismal prospect to live with this hated and unwanted device attached to her, through perhaps years of the law's slow process. She has the right to have it removed immediately. This matter constitutes a perfect paradigm of the axiom: "Justice delayed is justice denied."

By refusing petitioner the relief which she sought, the trial court, with the most noble intentions, attempted to exercise its discretion by issuing a ruling which would uphold what it considered a lawful object, i.e., keeping Elizabeth Bouvia alive by a means which it considered ethical. Nonetheless, it erred for it had no discretion to exercise. Petitioner sought to enforce only a right which was exclusively hers and over which neither the medical profession nor the judiciary have any veto power. The trial court could but recognize and protect her exercise of that right.

In explanation of its ruling, the trial court stated that it considered petitioner's "motives" to be indicative of an attempt to commit suicide with the state's help rather than a bona fide exercise of her right to refuse medical treatment. No evidence supports this conclusion.

As previously noted, the legal remedies available to petitioner through the normal course of trial and appeal are wholly inadequate. Therefore, a prompt resolution, even though based upon a provisional ruling, is justified, particularly when it will probably completely resolve this tragic case.

Petitioner is a 28-year-old woman. Since birth she has been afflicted with and suffered from severe cerebral palsy. She is quadriplegic. She is now a patient at a public hospital maintained by one of the real parties in interest, the County of Los Angeles. Other parties are physicians, nurses and the medical and support staff employed by the County of Los Angeles. Petitioner's physical handicaps of palsy and quadriplegia have progressed to the point where she is completely bedridden. Except for a few fingers of one hand and some slight head and facial movements, she is immobile. She is physically helpless and wholly unable to care for herself. She is totally dependent upon others for all of her needs. These include feeding, washing, cleaning, toileting, turning, and helping her with elimination and other bodily functions. She cannot stand or sit upright in bed or in a wheelchair. She lies flat in bed and must do so the rest of her life. She suffers also from degenerative and severely crippling arthritis. She is in continual pain. Another tube permanently attached to her chest automatically injects her with periodic doses of morphine which relieves some, but not all of her physical pain and discomfort.

She is intelligent, very mentally competent. She earned a college degree. She was married but her husband has left her. She suffered a miscarriage. She lived with her parents until her father told her that they could no longer care for her. She has stayed intermittently with friends and at public facilities. A search for a permanent place to live where she might receive the constant care which she needs has been unsuccessful. She is without financial means to support herself and, therefore, must accept public assistance for medical and other care.

She has on several occasions expressed the desire to die. In 1983 she sought the right to be cared for in a public hospital in Riverside County while she intentionally "starved herself to death." A court in that county denied her judicial assistance to accomplish that goal. She later abandoned an appeal from that ruling. Thereafter, friends took her to several different facilities, both public and private, arriving finally at her present location. Efforts by the staff of real party in interest County of Los Angeles and its social workers to find her an apartment of her own with publicly paid live-in help or regular visiting nurses to care for her, or some other suitable facility, have proved fruitless.

Petitioner must be spoon fed in order to eat. Her present medical and dietary staff have determined that she is not consuming a sufficient amount of nutrients. Petitioner stops eating when she feels she cannot orally swallow more, without nausea and vomiting. As she cannot now retain solids, she is fed soft liquid-like food. Because of her previously announced resolve to starve herself, the medical staff feared her weight loss might reach a life-threatening level. Her weight since admission to real parties' facility seems to hover between 65 and 70 pounds. Accordingly, they inserted the subject tube against her will and contrary to her express written instructions.

Petitioner's counsel argue that her weight loss was not such as to be life threatening and therefore the tube is unnecessary. However, the trial court found to the contrary as a matter of fact, a finding which we must accept. Nonetheless, the point is immaterial, for, as we will explain, a patient has the right to refuse any medical treatment or medical service, even when such treatment is labeled "furnishing nourishment and hydration." This right exists even if its exercise creates a "life threatening condition." . . .

The right to refuse medical treatment is basic and fundamental. It is recognized as a part of the right of privacy protected by both the state and federal constitutions. Its exercise requires no one's approval. It is not merely one vote subject to being overridden by medical opinion. . . .

[A]ddressing one part of the problem, California passed the "Natural Death Act," Health and Safety Code section 7185 et seq. Although addressed to terminally ill patients, the significance of this legislation is its expression as state policy "that adult persons have the fundamental right to control the decisions relating to the rendering of their own medical care. . . ." Section 7188 provides the method whereby an adult person may execute a directive for the withholding or withdrawal of life-sustaining procedures. Recognition of the right of other persons who may not be terminally ill and may wish to give other forms of direction concerning their medical care is expressed in section 7193: "Nothing in this chapter shall impair or supersede any legal right or legal responsibility which any person may have to effect the withholding or withdrawal of life-sustaining procedures in any lawful manner. In such respect the provisions of this chapter are cumulative."

Moreover, as the Bartling decision holds, there is no practical or logical reason to limit the exercise of this right to "terminal" patients. The right to refuse treatment does not need the sanction or approval by any legislative act, directing how and when it shall be exercised. . . .

A recent Presidential Commission for the Study of Ethical Problems in Medicine and Biomedical and Behavioral Research concluded in part: "The voluntary choice of a competent and informed patient should determine whether or not life-sustaining therapy will be undertaken, just as such choices provide the basis for other decisions about medical treatment. Health care institutions and professionals should try to enhance patients' abilities to make decisions on their own behalf and to promote understanding of the available treatment options. . . . Health care professionals serve patients best by maintaining a presumption in favor of sustaining life, while recognizing that competent patients are entitled to choose to forego any treatments, including those that sustain life."

On December 11, 1985, the Los Angeles County Bar Association, and on January 6, 1986, the Los Angeles County Medical Association recognized as general principles for decision making the conclusions as expressly stated in the cases of Barber and Bartling and endorsed the conclusion of the Presidential Commission cited above.

The American Hospital Association (AHA) Policy and Statement of Patients' Choices of Treatment Options, approved by the American Hospital Association in February of 1985 discusses the value of a collaborative relationship between the patient and the physician and states in pertinent part: "Whenever possible, however, the authority to determine the course of treatment, if any, should rest with the patient" and "the right to choose treatment includes the right to refuse a specific treatment or all treatment. . . ."

Again, this statement reflects the fact that the controlling decision belongs to a competent, informed patient. It also contains a discussion of how that consent should be documented, and the desirability of a cooperative effort. Of course, none of the problems of incapacity due to age, unconsciousness, mental disease or disability mentioned in the policy statement affect the case before us.

Significant also is the statement adopted on March 15, 1986, by the Council on Ethical and Judicial Affairs of the American Medical Association. It is entitled "Withholding or Withdrawing Life Prolonging Medical Treatment." In pertinent part, it declares: "The social commitment of the physician is to sustain life and relieve suffering. Where the performance of one duty conflicts with the other, the choice of the patient, or his family or legal representative if the patient is incompetent to act in his own behalf, should prevail. Life prolonging medical treatment includes medication and artificially or technologically supplied respiration, nutrition or hydration. In treating a terminally ill or irreversibly comatose patient, the physician should determine whether the benefits of treatment outweigh its burdens. At all times, the dignity of the patient should be maintained."

We do not believe that all of the foregoing case law and statements of policy and statutory recognition are mere lip service to a fictitious right. As noted in Bartling "We do not doubt the sincerity of [the hospital and medical personnel's] moral and ethical beliefs, or their sincere belief in the position they have taken in this case. However, if the right of the patient to self-determination as to his own medical treatment is to have any meaning at all, it must be paramount to the interests of the patient's hospital and doctors. . . . The right of a competent adult patient to refuse medical treatment is a constitutionally guaranteed right which must not be abridged."

It is indisputable that petitioner is mentally competent. She is not comatose. She is quite intelligent, alert, and understands the risks involved. . . .

At bench the trial court concluded that with sufficient feeding petitioner could live an additional 15 to 20 years; therefore, the preservation of petitioner's life for that period outweighed her right to decide. In so holding the trial court mistakenly attached undue importance to the amount of time possibly available to petitioner, and failed to give equal weight and consideration for the quality of that life; an equal, if not more significant, consideration.

All decisions permitting cessation of medical treatment or life-support procedures to some degree hastened the arrival of death. In part, at least, this was permitted because the quality of life during the time remaining in those cases had been terribly diminished. In Elizabeth Bouvia's view, the quality of her life has been diminished to the point of hopelessness, uselessness, unenjoyability and frustration. She, as the patient, lying helplessly in bed, unable to care for herself, may consider her existence meaningless. She cannot be faulted for so concluding. If her right to choose may not be exercised because there remains to her, in the opinion of a court, a physician or some committee, a certain arbitrary number of years, months, or days, her right will have lost its value and meaning.

Who shall say what the minimum amount of available life must be? Does it matter if it be 15 to 20 years, 15 to 20 months, or 15 to 20 days, if such life has been physically destroyed and its quality, dignity and purpose gone? As in all matters lines must be drawn at some point, somewhere, but that decision must ultimately belong to the one whose life is in issue.

Here Elizabeth Bouvia's decision to forego medical treatment or life-support through a mechanical means belongs to her. It is not a medical decision for her physicians to make. Neither is it a legal question whose soundness is to be resolved by lawyers or judges. It is not a conditional right subject to approval by ethics committees or courts of law. It is a moral and philosophical decision that, being a competent adult, is hers alone.

Adapting the language of *Satz v. Perlmutter*, "It is all very convenient to insist on continuing [Elizabeth Bouvia's] life so that there can be no question of foul play, no resulting civil liability and no possible trespass on medical ethics. However, it is quite another matter to do so at the patient's sole expense and against [her] competent will, thus inflicting never ending physical torture on [her] body until the inevitable, but artificially suspended, moment of death. Such a course of conduct invades the patient's constitutional right of privacy, removes [her] freedom of choice and invades [her] right to self-determine."

Here, if force fed, petitioner faces 15 to 20 years of a painful existence, endurable only by the constant administration of morphine. Her condition is irreversible. There is no cure for her palsy or arthritis. Petitioner would have to be fed, cleaned, turned, bedded, toileted by others for 15 to 20 years. Although alert, bright, sensitive, perhaps even brave

and feisty, she must lie immobile, unable to exist except through physical acts of others. Her mind and spirit may be free to take great flights but she herself is imprisoned and must lie physically helpless subject to the ignominy, embarrassment, humiliation and dehumanizing aspects created by her helplessness. We do not believe it is the policy of this state that all and every life must be preserved against the will of the sufferer. It is incongruous, if not monstrous, for medical practitioners to assert their right to preserve a life that someone else must live, or, more accurately, endure, for "15 to 20 years." We cannot conceive it to be the policy of this state to inflict such an ordeal upon anyone.

It is, therefore, immaterial that the removal of the nasogastric tube will hasten or cause Bouvia's eventual death. Being competent she has the right to live out the remainder of her natural life in dignity and peace. It is precisely the aim and purpose of the many decisions upholding the withdrawal of life-support systems to accord and provide as large a measure of dignity, respect and comfort as possible to every patient for the remainder of his days, whatever be their number. This goal is not to hasten death, though its earlier arrival may be an expected and understood likelihood.

Real parties assert that what petitioner really wants is to "commit suicide" by starvation at their facility. The trial court in its statement of decision said: "It is fairly clear from the evidence and the court cannot close its eyes to the fact that [petitioner] during her stay in defendant hospital, and for some time prior thereto, has formed an intent to die. She has voiced this desire to a member of the staff of defendant hospital. She claims, however, she does not wish to commit suicide. On the evidence, this is but a semantic distinction. The reasonable inference to be drawn from the evidence is that [petitioner] in defendant facility has purposefully engaged in a selective rejection of medical treatment and nutritional intake to accomplish her objective and accept only treatment which gives her some degree of comfort pending her demise. Stated another way, [petitioner's] refusal of medical treatment and nutritional intake is motivated not by a bona fide exercise of her right of privacy but by a desire to terminate her life. . . . Here [petitioner] wishes to pursue her objective to die by the use of public facilities with staff standing by to furnish her medical treatment to which she consents and to refrain from that which she refuses."

Overlooking the fact that a desire to terminate one's life is probably the ultimate exercise of one's right to privacy, we find no substantial evidence to support the court's conclusion. Even if petitioner had the specific intent to commit suicide in 1983, while at Riverside, she did not carry out that plan. Then she apparently had the ability, without artificial aids, to consume sufficient nutrients to sustain herself; now she does not. That is to say, the trial court here made the following express finding, "Plaintiff, when she chooses, can orally ingest food by masticating 'finger food' though additional nutritional intake is required intravenously and by nasogastric tube. . . ." As a consequence of her changed condition, it is clear she has now merely resigned herself to accept an earlier death, if necessary, rather than live by feedings forced upon her by means of a nasogastric tube. Her decision to allow nature to take its course is not equivalent to an election to commit suicide with real parties aiding and abetting therein.

Moreover, the trial court seriously erred by basing its decision on the "motives" behind Elizabeth Bouvia's decision to exercise her rights. If a right exists, it matters not what "motivates" its exercise. We find nothing in the law to suggest the right to refuse medical treatment may be exercised only if the patient's motives meet someone else's approval. It certainly is not illegal or immoral to prefer a natural, albeit sooner, death than a drugged life attached to a mechanical device.

Fundamental Elements of the Patient-Physician Relationship

AMA COUNCIL ON ETHICAL AND JUDICIAL AFFAIRS

In this section of its medical code of ethics, the AMA declares that the patient-physician relationship is a collaborative alliance in which both parties have responsibilities. Physicians should serve as their patients' advocates and respect their rights, including the right to accept or refuse recommended treatment, to receive complete information about treatments and their alternatives, and to have their confidentiality protected.

From ancient times, physicians have recognized that the health and well-being of patients depends upon a collaborative effort between physician and patient. Patients share with physicians the responsibility for their own health care. The patient-physician relationship is of greatest benefit to patients when they bring medical problems to the attention of their physicians in a timely fashion, provide information about their medical condition to the best of their ability, and work with their physicians in a mutually respectful alliance. Physicians can best contribute to this alliance by serving as their patients' advocate and by fostering these rights:

1. The patient has the right to receive information from physicians and to discuss the benefits, risks, and costs of appropriate treatment alternatives. Patients should receive guidance from their physicians as to the optimal course of action. Patients are also entitled to obtain copies or summaries of their medical records, to have their questions answered, to be advised of potential conflicts of interest that their physicians might have, and to receive independent professional opinions.

2. The patient has the right to make decisions regarding the health care that is recommended by his or her physician. Accordingly, patients may accept or refuse any recommended medical treatment.

3. The patient has the right to courtesy, respect, dignity, responsiveness, and timely attention to his or her needs.

4. The patient has the right to confidentiality. The physician should not reveal confidential communications or information without the consent of the patient, unless provided for by law or by the need to protect the welfare of the individual or the public interest.

5. The patient has the right to continuity of health care. The physician has an obligation to cooperate in the coordination of medically indicated care with other health care providers treating the patient. The physician may not discontinue treatment of a patient as long as further treatment is medically indicated, without giving the patient reasonable assistance and sufficient opportunity to make alternative arrangements for care.

6. The patient has a basic right to have available adequate health care. Physicians, along with the rest of society, should continue to work toward this goal. Fulfillment of this right is dependent on society providing resources so that no patient is deprived of necessary care because of an inability to pay for the care. Physicians should continue their traditional assumption of a part of the responsibility for the medical care of those who cannot afford essential health care. Physicians should advocate for patients in dealing with third parties when appropriate.

In Defense of the Traditional Nurse

LISA H. NEWTON

In this essay Newton rejects the contemporary model of a nurse as an "autonomous professional" who can challenge physicians' authority and be a strong advocate for patients. She argues instead for the traditional notion of nurse as a caregiver *cum* surrogate mother who is subordinate to physicians. She insists that unambiguous lines of authority and clearly specified roles are essential to a well-run hospital and that in this setting physicians alone must be in charge when serious medical problems come up.

When a truth is accepted by everyone as so obvious that it blots out all its alternatives and leaves no respectable perspectives from which to examine it, it becomes the natural prey of philosophers, whose essential activity is to question accepted opinion. A case in point may be the ideal of the "autonomous professional" for nursing. The consensus that this ideal and image are appropriate for the profession is becoming monolithic and may profit from the

From Lisa H. Newton, "In Defense of the Traditional Nurse," *Nursing Outlook*, vol. 29 (June 1981). Reprinted with permission.

presence of a full-blooded alternative ideal to replace the cardboard stereotypes it routinely condemns. That alternative, I suggest, is the traditional ideal of the skilled and gentle caregiver, whose role in health care requires submission to authority as an essential component. We can see the faults of this traditional ideal very clearly now, but we may perhaps also be able to see virtues that went unnoticed in the battle to displace it. It is my contention that the image and ideal of the traditional nurse contain virtues that can be found nowhere else in the health care professions, that perhaps make an irreplaceable contribution to the care of patients, and that should not be lost in the transition to a new definition of the profession of nursing.

A word should be said about what this article is, and what it is not. It is an essay in philosophical analysis, starting from familiar ideas, beliefs, and concepts, examining their relationships and implications and reaching tentative conclusions about the logical defensibility of the structures discovered. It is not the product of research in the traditional sense. Its factual premises—for example, that the "traditional" nursing role has been criticized by those who prefer an "autonomous professional" role—are modest by any standard, and in any event may be taken as hypothetical by all who may be disposed to disagree with them. It is not a polemic against any writer or writers in particular, but a critique of lines of reasoning that are turning up with increasing frequency in diverse contexts. Its arguments derive no force whatsoever from any writings in which they may be found elsewhere.

Role Components

The first task of any philosophical inquiry is to determine its terminology and establish the meanings of its key terms for its own purposes. To take the first term: a *role* is a norm-governed pattern of action undertaken in accordance with social expectations. The term is originally derived from the drama, where it signifies a part played by an actor in a play. In current usage, any ordinary job or profession (physician, housewife, teacher, postal worker) will do as an example of a social role; the term's dramatic origin is nonetheless worth remembering, as a key to the limits of the concept.

Image and ideal are simply the descriptive and prescriptive aspects of a social role. The *image* of a social role is that role as it is understood to be in fact, both by the occupants of the role and by those with whom the occupant interacts. It describes the character the occupant plays, the acts, attitudes, and expectations normally associated with the role. The *ideal* of a role is a conception of what that role could or should be—that is, a conception of the norms that should govern its work. It is necessary to distinguish between the private and public aspects of image and ideal.

Since role occupants and general public need not agree either on the description of the present operations of the role or on the prescription for its future development, the private image, or self-image of the role occupant, is therefore distinct from the public image or general impression of the role maintained in the popular media and mind. The private ideal, or aspiration of the role occupant, is distinct from the public ideal or normative direction set for the role by the larger society. Thus, four role-components emerge, from the public and private, descriptive and prescriptive, aspects of a social role. They may be difficult to disentangle in some cases, but they are surely distinct in theory, and potentially in conflict in fact.

Transitional Roles

In these terms alone we have the materials for the problematic tensions within transitional social roles. Stable social roles should exhibit no significant disparities among images and ideals: what the public generally gets is about what it thinks it should get; what the job turns out to require is generally in accord with the role-occupant's aspirations; and public and role-occupant, beyond a certain base level of "they-don't-know-how-hard-we-work" grumbling, are in general agreement on what the role is all about. On the other hand, transitional roles tend to exhibit strong discrepancies among the four elements of the role during the transition; at least the components will make the transition at different times, and there may also be profound disagreement on the direction that the transition should take.

The move from a general discussion of roles in society to a specific discussion of the nursing profession is made difficult by the fact that correct English demands the use of a personal pronoun. How shall we refer to the nurse? It is claimed that consistent reference to a professional as "he" reinforces the stereotype of male monopoly in the professions, save for the profession of nursing, where consistent reference to the professional as "she" reinforces the stereotype of subservience. Though we ought never to reinforce sex and dominance stereotypes, the effort to write in gender-neutral terms involves the use of circumlocutions and "he/she" usages that quickly becomes wearisome to reader and writer alike. Referring to most other professions, I would simply use the universal pronouns "he" and "him", and ignore the ridiculous accusations of sexism. But against a background of a virtually all-female profession, whose literature until the last decade universally referred to its professionals as "she", the consistent use of "he" to refer to a nurse calls attention to itself and distracts attention from the argument.

A further problem with gender-neutral terminology in the discussion of this issue in particular is that it appears to render the issue irrelevant. The whole question of autonomy for the nurse in professional work arises because nurses have been, and are, by and large, women, and the place of the profession in the health care system is strongly influenced by the place of women in society. To talk about nurses as if they were, or might as well be, men, is to make the very existence of a problem a mystery. There are, therefore good reasons beyond custom to continue using the pronoun "she" to refer to the nurse. I doubt that such use will suggest to anyone who might read this essay that it is not appropriate for men to become nurses; presumably we are beyond making that at this time.

Barriers to Autonomy

The first contention of my argument is that the issue of autonomy in the nursing profession lends itself to misformulation. A common formulation of the issue, for example, locates it in a discrepancy between public image and private image. On this account, the public is asserted to believe that nurses are ill-educated, unintelligent, incapable of assuming responsibility, and hence properly excluded from professional status and responsibility. In fact they are now prepared to be truly autonomous professionals through an excellent education, including a thorough theoretical grounding in all aspects of their profession. Granted, the public image of the nurse has many favorable aspects—the nurse is credited with great manual skill, often saintly dedication to service to others, and, at least below the supervisory level, a warm heart and gentle manners. But the educational and intellectual deficiencies that the public mistakenly perceives outweigh the "positive" qualities when it comes to deciding how the nurse shall be treated, and are called upon to justify not only her traditionally inferior status and low wages, but also the refusal to allow nursing to fill genuine needs in the health care system by assuming tasks

that nurses are uniquely qualified to handle. For the sake of the quality of health care as well as for the sake of the interests of the nurse, the public must be educated through a massive educational campaign to the full capabilities of the contemporary nurse; the image must be brought into line with the facts. On this account, then, the issue of nurse autonomy is diagnosed as a public relations problem: the private ideal of nursing is asserted to be that of the autonomous professional and the private image is asserted to have undergone a transition from an older subservient role to a new professional one but the public image of the nurse ideal is significantly not mentioned in this analysis.

An alternative account of the issue of professional autonomy in nursing locates it in a discrepancy between private ideal and private image. Again, the private ideal is that of the autonomous professional. But the actual performance of the role is entirely slavish, because of the way the system works—with its tight budgets, insane schedules, workloads bordering on reckless endangerment for the seriously ill, bureaucratic red tape, confusion, and arrogance. Under these conditions, the nurse is permanently barred from fulfilling her professional ideal, from bringing the reality of the nurse's condition into line with the self-concept she brought to the job. On this account, then, the nurse really is not an autonomous professional, and total reform of the power structure of the health care industry will be necessary in order to allow her to become one.

A third formulation locates the issue of autonomy in a struggle between the private ideal and an altogether undesirable public ideal: on this account, the public does not want the nurse to be an autonomous professional, because her present subservient status serves the power needs of the physicians; because her unprofessional remuneration serves the monetary needs of the entrepreneurs and callous municipalities that run the hospitals; and because the low value accorded her opinions on patient care protects both physicians and bureaucrats from being forced to account to the patient for the treatment he receives. On this account, the nurse needs primarily to gather allies to defeat the powerful interest groups that impose the traditional ideal for their own unworthy purposes, and to replace that degrading and dangerous prescription with one more appropriate to the contemporary nurse.

These three accounts, logically independent, have crucial elements of content in common. Above all, they agree on the objectives to be pursued: full professional independence, responsibility, recognition, and remuneration for the professional nurse. And as corollary to these objectives, they agree on the necessity of banishing forever from the hospitals and from the public mind that inaccurate and demeaning stereotype of the nurse as the Lady with the Bedpan: an image of submissive service, comforting to have around and skillful enough at her little tasks, but too scatterbrained and emotional for responsibility.

In none of the interpretations above is any real weight given to a public ideal of nursing, to the nursing role as the public thinks it ought to be played. Where public prescription shows up at all, it is seen as a vicious and false demand imposed by power alone, thoroughly illegitimate and to be destroyed as quickly as possible. The possibility that there may be real value in the traditional role of the nurse, and that the public may have good reasons to want to retain it, simply does not receive any serious consideration on any account. It is precisely that possibility that I take up in the next section.

Defending the "Traditional Nurse"

As Aristotle taught us, the way to discover the peculiar virtues of any thing is to look to the work that it accomplishes in the larger context of its environment. The first task, then, is to isolate those factors of need or demand in the nursing environment that require the nurse's work if they are to be met. I shall concentrate, as above, on the hospital environment, since most nurses are employed in hospitals.

The work context of the hospital nurse actually spans two societal practices or institutions: the hospital as a bureaucracy and medicine as a field of scientific endeavor and service. Although there is enormous room for variation in both hospital bureaucracies and medicine, and they may therefore interact with an infinite number of possible results, the most general facts about both institutions allow us to sketch the major demands they make on those whose function lies within them.

To take the hospital bureaucracy first: its very nature demands that workers perform the tasks assigned to them, report properly to the proper superior, avoid initiative, and adhere to set procedures. These requirements are common to all bureaucracies, but dramatically increase in urgency when the tasks are supposed to be protective of life itself and where the subject matter is inherently unpredictable and emergency prone. Since there is often no time to re-examine the usefulness of a procedure in a particular case, and since the stakes are too high to permit a gamble, the institution's effectiveness, not to mention its legal position, may depend on unquestioning adherence to procedure.

Assuming that the sort of hospital under discussion is one in which the practice of medicine by qualified physicians is the focal activity, rather than, say, a convalescent hospital, further contextual requirements emerge. Among the prominent features of the practice of medicine are the following: it depends on esoteric knowledge which takes time to acquire and which is rapidly advancing; and, because each patient's illness is unique, it is uncertain. Thus, when a serious medical situation arises without warning, only physicians will know how to deal with it (if their licensure has any point), and they will not always be able to explain or justify their actions to nonphysicians, even those who are required to assist them in patient care.

If the two contexts of medicine and the hospital are superimposed, three common points can be seen. Both are devoted to the saving of life and health; the atmosphere in which that purpose is carried out is inevitably tense and urgent; and, if the purpose is to be accomplished in that atmosphere, all participating activities and agents must be completely subordinated to the medical judgments of the physicians. In short, those other than physicians, involved in medical procedures in a hospital context, have no right to insert their own needs, judgments, or personalities into the situation. The last thing we need at that point is another autonomous professional on the job, whether a nurse or anyone else.

Patient Needs: The Prime Concern

From the general characteristics of hospitals and medicine, that negative conclusion for nursing follows. But the institutions are not, after all, the focus of the endeavor. If there is any conflict between the needs of the patient and the needs of the institutions established to serve him, his needs take precedence and constitute the most important requirements of the nursing environment. What are these needs?

First, because the patient is sick and disabled, he needs specialized care that only qualified personnel can administer, beyond the time that the physician is with him. Second, and perhaps most obviously to the patient, he is likely to be unable to perform simple tasks such as walking unaided, dressing himself, and attending to his bodily functions. He will need assistance in these tasks, and is likely to find this need humiliating; his entire self-concept as an independent human being may be threatened. Thus, the patient has serious emotional needs brought on by the hospital situation itself, regardless of his disability. He is scared, depressed, disappointed, and possibly, in reaction to all of these, very angry. He needs reassurance, comfort, someone to talk to. The person he really needs, who would be capable of taking care of all these problems, is obviously his mother, and the first job of the nurse is to be a mother surrogate.

That conclusion, it should be noted, is inherent in the word "nurse" itself: it is derived ultimately from the Latin *nutrire*, "to nourish or suckle"; the first meaning of "nurse" as a noun is still, according to *Webster's New Twentieth Century Unabridged Dictionary* "one who suckles a child not her own." From the outset, then, the function of this nurse is identical with that of the mother, to be exercised when the mother is unavailable. And the meanings proceed in logical order from there: the second definitions given for both noun and verb involve caring for children, especially young children, and the third, caring for those who are childlike in their dependence—the sick, the injured, the very old, and the handicapped. For all those groups—infants, children, and helpless adults—it **is** appropriate to bring children's caretakers, surrogate mothers, nurses, into the situation to minister to them. It is especially appropriate to do so, for the sake of the psychological economies realized by the patient: the sense of self, at least for the Western adult, hangs on the self-perception of independence. Since disability requires the relinquishing of this self-perception, the patient

must either discover conditions excusing his dependence somewhere in his self-concept, or invent new ones, and the latter task is extremely difficult. Hence the usefulness of the maternal image association: it was, within the patient's understanding of himself "all right" to be tended by mother; if the nurse is (at some level) mother, it is "all right" to reassume that familiar role and to be tended by her.

Limits on the "Mother" Role

The nurse's assumption of the role of mother **is** therefore justified etymologically and historically but most importantly by reference to the psychological demands of and on the patient. Yet the maternal role cannot be imported into the hospital care situation without significant modification—specifically, with respect to the power and authority inherent in the role of mother. Such maternal authority, includes the right and duty to assume control over children's lives and make all decisions for them; but the hospital patient most definitely does not lose adult status even if he **is** sick enough to want to. The ethical legitimacy as well as the therapeutic success of his treatment depend on his voluntary and active cooperation in it and on his deferring to some forms of power and authority—the hospital rules and the physician's sapiential authority, for example. But these very partial, conditional, restraints are nowhere near the threat to patient autonomy that the real presence of mother would be; maternal authority, total, diffuse, and unlimited, would be incompatible with the retention of moral freedom. And it is just this sort of total authority that the patient is most tempted to attribute to the nurse, who already embodies the nurturant component of the maternal role. To prevent serious threats to patient autonomy, then, the role of nurse must be from the outset, as essentially as it is nurturant, unavailable for such attribution of authority. Not only must the role of nurse not include authority; it must be incompatible with authority: essentially, a subservient role.

The nurse role, as required by the patient's situation, is the nurturant component of the maternal role and excludes elements of power and authority. A further advantage of this combination of maternal nurturance and subordinate status is that, just as it permits the patient to be cared for like a baby without threatening his autonomy, it also permits him to unburden himself to a sympathetic listener of his doubts and resentments, about physicians and hospitals in general, and his in particular, without threatening the course of his treatment. His resentments are natural, but they lead to a situation of conflict, between the desire to rebel against treatment and bring it to a halt (to reassert control over his life), and the desire that the treatment should continue (to obtain its benefits). The nurse's function speaks well to this condition: like her maternal model, the nurse is available for the patient to talk to (the physician is too busy to talk), sympathetic, understanding, and supportive; but in her subordinate position, the nurse can do absolutely nothing to change his course of treatment. Since she has no more control over the environment than he has, he can let off steam in perfect safety, knowing that he cannot do himself any damage.

The norms for the nurse's role so far derived from the patient's perspective also tally, it might be noted, with the restrictions on the role that arise from the needs of hospitals and medicine. The patient does not need another autonomous professional at his bedside, any more than the physician can use one or the hospital bureaucracy contain one. The conclusion so far, then is that in the hospital environment, the traditional (nurturant and subordinate) role of the nurse seems more adapted to the nurse function than the new autonomous role.

Provider of Humanistic Care

So far, we have defined the hospital nurse's function in terms of the specific needs of the hospital, the physician, and the patient. Yet there is another level of function that needs to be addressed. If we consider the multifaceted demands that the patient's family, friends, and community make on the hospital once the patient is admitted, it becomes clear that this concerned group cannot be served exclusively by attending to the medical aspect of care, necessary though that is. Nor is it sufficient for the hospital-as-institution to keep accurate and careful records, maintain absolute cleanliness, and establish procedures that protect the patient's safety, even though this is important. Neither bureaucracy nor medical professional can handle the human needs of the human beings involved in the process.

The general public entering the hospital as patient or visitor encounters and reacts to that health care system as an indivisible whole, as if under a single heading of "what the hospital is like." It is at this level that we can make sense of the traditional claim that the nurse represents the "human" as opposed to "mechanical" or "coldly professional" aspect of health care, for there is clearly something terribly missing in the combined medical and bureaucratic approach to the "case": they fail to address the patient's fear for himself and the family's fear for him, their grief over the separation, even if temporary, their concern for the financial burden, and a host of other emotional components of hospitalization.

The same failing appears throughout the hospital experience, most poignantly obvious, perhaps, when the medical procedures are unavailing and the patient dies. When this occurs, the physician must determine the cause and time of death and the advisability of an autopsy, while the bureaucracy must record the death and remove the body; but surely this is not enough. The death of a human being is a rending of the fabric of human community, a sad and fearful time; it is appropriately a time of bitter regret, anger, and weeping. The patient's family, caught up in the institutional context of the hospital, cannot assume alone the burden of discovering and expressing the emotions appropriate to the occasion; such expression, essential for their own regeneration after their loss must originate somehow within the hospital context itself. The hospital system must, somehow, be able to share pain and grief as well as it makes medical judgments and keeps records.

The traditional nurse's role addresses itself directly to these human needs. Its derivation from the maternal role classifies it as feminine and permits ready assumption of all attributes culturally typed as "feminine": tenderness, warmth, sympathy, and a tendency to engage much more readily in the expression of feeling than in the rendering of judgment. Through the nurse, the hospital can be concerned, welcoming, caring, and grief-stricken; it can break through the cold barriers of efficiency essential to its other functions and share human feeling.

The nurse therefore provides the in-hospital health care system with human capabilities that would otherwise be unavailable to it and hence unavailable to the community in dealing with it. Such a conclusion is unattractive to the supporters of the autonomous role for the nurse, because the tasks of making objective judgments and of expressing emotion are inherently incompatible; and since the nurse shows grief and sympathy on behalf of the system, she is excluded from decision-making and defined as subordinate.

However unappealing such a conclusion may be, it is clear that without the nurse role in this function, the hospital becomes a moral monstrosity, coolly and mechanically dispensing and disposing of human life and death, with no acknowledgement at all of the individual life, value, projects, and relationships of the persons with whom it deals. Only the nurse makes the system morally tolerable. People in pain deserve sympathy, as the dead deserve to be grieved; it is unthinkable that the very societal institution to which we generally consign the suffering and the dying should be incapable of sustaining sympathy and grief. Yet its capability hangs on the presence of nurses willing to assume the affective functions of the traditional nursing role, and the current attempt to banish that role, to introduce instead an autonomous professional role for the nurse, threatens to send the last hope for a human presence in the hospital off at the same time.

The Feminist Perspective

From this conclusion it would seem to follow automatically that the role of the traditional nurse should be retained. It might be argued, however, that the value of autonomy is such that any non-autonomous role ought to be abolished, no matter what its value to the current institutional structure.

Those who aimed to abolish black slavery in the United States have provided a precedent for this argument. They never denied the slave's economic usefulness; they simply denied that it could be right to enslave any person and insisted that the nation find some other way to get the work done, no matter what the cost. On a totally different level, the feminists of our own generation have proposed that the traditional housewife and mother role for the woman, which confined women to domestic life and made them subordinate to men, has been very useful for everyone except the women trapped in it. All the feminists have claimed is that the profit of others is not a sufficient reason to retain a role that demeans its occupant. As they see it, the "traditional nurse" role is analogous to the roles of slave and housewife—it is derived directly, in fact, as we have seen, from the "mother" part of the latter role—exploitative of its occupants and hence immoral by its very nature and worthy of abolition.

But the analogy does not hold. A distinction must be made between an autonomous person—one who, over the course of adult life, is self-determining in all major choices and a significant number of minor ones, and hence can be said to have chosen, and to be responsible for, his own life—and an autonomous *role*—a role so structured that its occupant is self-determining in all major and most minor role-related choices. An autonomous person can certainly take on a subordinate role without losing his personal autonomy. For example, we can find examples of slaves (in ancient world at least) and housewives who have claimed to have, and shown every sign of having, complete personal integrity and autonomy with their freely chosen roles.

Furthermore, slave and housewife are a very special type of role, known as "life-roles." They are to be played 24 hours a day, for an indefinite period of time; there is no customary or foreseeable respite from them. Depending on circumstances, there may be de facto escapes from these roles, permitting their occupants to set up separate personal identities (some of the literature from the history of American slavery suggests this possibility), but the role-definitions do not contemplate part-time occupancy. Such life-roles are few in number; most roles are the part-time "occupational roles," the jobs that we do eight hours a day and have little to do with the structuring of the rest of the twenty-four. An autonomous person can, it would seem, easily take up a subordinate role of this type and play it well without threat to personal autonomy. And if there is excellent reason to choose such a role—if, for example, an enterprise of tremendous importance derives an essential component of its moral worth from that role—it would seem to be altogether rational and praiseworthy to do so.

The role of "traditional nurse" would certainly fall within this category.

But even if the traditional nurse role is not inherently demeaning, it might be argued further, it should be abolished as harmful to the society because it preserves the sex stereotypes that we are trying to overcome. "Nurse" is a purely feminine role, historically derived from "mother," embodying feminine attributes of emotionality, tenderness, and nurturance, and it is subordinate—thus reinforcing the link between femininity and subordinate status. The nurse role should be available to men, too, to help break down this unfavorable stereotype.

This objective to the traditional role embodies the very fallacy it aims to combat. The falsehood we know as sexism is not the belief that some roles are autonomous, calling for objectivity in judgment, suppression of emotion, and independent initiative in action, but discouraging independent judgment and action and requiring obedience to superiors; the falsehood is the assumption that only men are eligible for the first class and only women are eligible for the second class.

One of the most damaging mistakes of our cultural heritage is the assumption that warmth, gentleness, and loving care, such as are expected of the nurse, are simply impossible for the male of the species, and that men who show emotion, let alone those who are ever known to weep, are weaklings, "sissies," and a disgrace to the human race. I suspect that this assumption has done more harm to the culture than its more publicized partner, the assumption that women are {or should be) incapable of objective judgment or executive function. Women will survive without leadership roles, but it is not clear that a society can retain its humanity if all those eligible for leadership are forbidden, by virtue of that eligibility, to take account of the human side of human beings: their altruism, heroism, compassion, and grief, their fear and weakness, and their ability to love and care for others.

In the words of the current feminist movement, men must be liberated as surely as women. And one of the best avenues to such liberation would be the encouragement of male participation in the health care system, or other systems of the society, in roles

like the traditional nursing role, which permit, even require, the expressive side of the personality to develop, giving it a function in the enterprise and restoring it to recognition and respectability.

Conclusions

In conclusion, then, the traditional nurse role is crucial to health care in the hospital context; its subordinate status, required for its remaining features, is neither in itself demeaning nor a barrier to its assumption by men or women. It is probably not a role that everyone would enjoy. But there are certainly many who are suited to it, and should be willing to undertake the job.

One of the puzzling features of the recent controversy is the apparent unwillingness of some of the current crop of nursing school graduates to take on the assignment for which they have ostensibly been prepared, at least until such time as it shall be redefined to accord more closely with their notion of professional. These frustrated nurses who do not want the traditional nursing role, yet wish to employ their skills in the health care system in some way, will clearly have to do something else. The health care industry is presently in the process of very rapid expansion and diversification, and has created significant markets for those with a nurse's training and the capacity, and desire, for autonomous roles. Moreover, the nurse in a position which does not have the "nurse" label, does not need to combat the "traditional nurse" image and is ordinarily accorded greater freedom of action. For this reason alone it would appear that those nurses intent on occupying autonomous roles and tired of fighting stereotypes that they find degrading and unworthy of their abilities, should seek out occupational niches that do not bear the label, and the stigma, of "nurse."

I conclude, therefore: that much of the difficulty in obtaining public acceptance of the new "autonomous professional" image of the nurse may be due, not to public ignorance, but to the opposition of a vague but persistent public ideal of nursing; that the ideal is a worthy one, well-founded in the hospital context in which it evolved; and that the role of traditional nurse, for which that ideal sets the standard, should therefore be maintained and held open for any who would have the desire, and the personal and professional qualifications, to assume it. Perhaps the current crop of nursing school graduates do not desire it, but there is ample room in the health care system for the sort of "autonomous professional" they wish to be, apart from the hospital nursing role. Wherever we must go to fill this role, it is worth going there, for the traditional nurse is the major force remaining for humanity in a system that will turn into a mechanical monster without her.

Advocacy or Subservience for the Sake of Patients?

HELGA KUHSE

Kuhse asks whether nurses should be patient advocates ready when necessary to question physician authority, or be skilled and caring professionals who must always defer to physicians on important medical decisions. Contrary to Lisa Newton's view, she favors the former, arguing that the nurse's subservience to physicians is not necessary for managing serious medical problems and issues and that requiring nurses to be subservient would probably harm patients.

The view that doctors were gods whose commands must always be obeyed was beginning to be seriously questioned in the 1960s and 1970s. There had always been courageous nurses who had occasionally challenged orders, but it is almost as if nurses needed a new metaphor to capture their new understanding of their role before they could finally attempt to free themselves from the shackles of the past. This new focus was provided by the metaphor of the nurse as patient advocate. Whereas the old metaphors had focused attention on such virtues as submissiveness and unquestioning obedience and loyalty to those in command, the new metaphor of patient advocate highlighted the virtues of assertiveness and courage, and marked a revolutionary shift in the self-perception of nurses and their role. The nurse's first loyalty, the metaphor suggested, is owed not to the doctor but to the patient. In thus focusing on the nurse's responsibilities to patients, that is, on the *recipients* rather than the *providers* of medical care, the metaphor of the nurse as patient advocate made it possible for nurses to see themselves as *professionals*. No longer were they, as the old metaphors had suggested, the loyal handmaidens of medical men: they were professionals whose primary responsibility—like that of all professionals—was to their clients or patients....

Nursing—a Naturally Subservient Profession?

...Our first question must be this: *should* nurses reject their traditional largely subservient role and act as patient advocates?...

...I shall, without argument, assume that a profession such as medicine or nursing does not exist for the sole or even primary purpose of benefiting its members. This view is widely shared and is implicit in most if not all professional codes; it is also regarded as one of the necessary conditions for an organization to claim professional status. For the purposes of our discussion, then, I shall assume that both nursing and medicine are professions which are, or ought to be, aiming at the welfare of others, where those others are patients or clients.

This raises the question of the relationship between medicine and nursing, and between doctors and nurses. Might it not be the case that the subordinate role of nurses has its basis not in objectionable sexism but rather in a natural hierarchy between the professions, a hierarchy that serves patients best?

From *Caring: Nurses, Women and Ethics*, Helga Kuhse (New York: Wiley-Blackwell, 1997), 35–36, 41–53, 58–60.

Robert Baker is among those who have pointed out that we cannot simply assume that the nurse's subservient role has a sexist basis. He does not deny that sexism exists or that the subservient nursing role has traditionally been seen as a feminine one; but, he writes,

it is not at all clear whether the role of the nurse is seen as dependent because it is filled by females, who are held to be incapable of independent action by a male-dominated, sexist society... *or* whether females have been channelled into nursing because the profession, *by its very nature*, requires its members to play a dependent and subservient role (i.e., the traditional female role in a sexist society).

In other words, the facts that almost all nurses are women, that the traditional nurse's role has been a subservient one and that most societies were and are male-dominated and sexist, cannot lead us to the conclusion that the nurse's role necessarily rests on objectionable sexism. The nurse's role may, 'by its very nature', be a subservient one. But is nursing 'by its very nature' subservient to medicine—is it a naturally subservient profession?

There is clearly something odd about speaking of the 'natural subservience' of nursing to medicine, or for that matter of 'the natural subservience' of any profession in relation to another. To speak of 'natural subservience' suggests that the subservient or dominant character of the relevant profession is somehow naturally given and in that sense fixed and largely unchangeable. But is this view correct? As we have seen above, nursing has developed in a very particular social and historical context, in response to the then prevailing goals and purposes of medicine on the one hand and the social roles of women and men on the other. Would this not make it more appropriate to view the character of the two health-care professions, and the tasks and privileges that attach to them, as a historically contingent accident or social construct, rather than as a compelling natural necessity?

It seems to me the answer must be 'yes'. There are no natural professional hierarchies that exist independently of human societies, and we should reject the idea that professions have fixed natures and instead view them as changing and changeable social

institutions. When looking at professions in this way we may, of course, still want to think of them as having particular characteristics by which they can be defined ('social natures', if you like), but we would now view these characteristics as socially constructed, in much the same way as the institution itself is a social and historical construct.

How, then, might one go about capturing the 'social nature' or characteristics of a profession?. One might do this in one of two ways: either by focusing on the functions or roles performed by members of the profession or by focusing on the profession's philosophical presuppositions or goals.

Function or Role

What is the function or role of a nurse? What is a nurse? The clear and neat boundaries and distinctions presupposed by our everyday language and by the terms we use rarely accord with the real world. We often speak of 'the role' or 'the function' of the nurse, or of the 'the role' or 'the function' of the doctor. These terms are problematical because nurses and doctors working in different areas of health care perform very different functions and act in many different roles, and there is a considerable degree of overlap between the changeable and changing functions performed by members of the two professions.

The expansion of knowledge, of nursing education, and of medical science and technology has resulted in the redefinition and scope of nursing practice. Nurses now carry out a range of procedures that were formerly exclusively performed by doctors. Some nurses give injections, take blood samples, administer medication, perform diagnostic procedures, do physical examinations, respond to medical emergencies and so on.

Take diagnosis and medical treatment. The diagnosis and treatment of medical problems had always been regarded as the realm solely of doctors. But, as Tristram H. Engelhardt notes, if one looks closely at the diagnostic activities performed by nurses, it is difficult to see them as essentially different from medical diagnoses. Nursing diagnoses such as '"Airway clearance, ineffective"; "Bowel elimination, alteration in: Diarrhoea"; "Cardiac output, alteration in, decrease"; "Fluid volume deficit",' Engelhardt points out, all have their medical equivalents; and the diagnosis of psychological or psychiatric disturbances, such as ' "Coping, ineffective individual", or "Thought processes, alteration in" can be given analogues in the *Diagnostic and Statistical Manual of Mental Disorders* of the American Psychiatric Association.'

Nurses are not permitted by law to perform any 'medical acts', but in practice the line between medical and nursing acts has become rather blurred and is, in any case, the result of social and historical choice. Moreover, as nurses have become more assertive and conscious of their own knowledge and expertise, there has been a broadening of the definitions of nursing practice. In 1981 the American Nursing Association thus produced a model definition of nursing practice, which included 'diagnosis . . . in the promotion and maintenance of health'. By 1984, 23 US states had included [nursing] diagnoses, or similar terms, in their nursing practice acts.

To conclude, then, the fact that nurses work in very different areas of health care, where they perform very different functions, and the fact that there are considerable overlaps between contemporary nursing functions and the functions traditionally performed by doctors makes it difficult to see how it would be possible to define nursing in terms of a particular function or role performed by nurses. If we thus think of 'the nature' of nursing in terms of some specific function or role performed by all nurses, this suggests not only that nursing lacks a particular nature, but also makes it difficult to claim that nursing is 'naturally subservient' to medicine.

It is true, of course, that nurses frequently work under the direction of doctors, and that control over many of the functions performed by them is retained by the medical profession. It is also true that only doctors may, by law, perform operations, prescribe medical treatments and authorize access to certain drugs. This might lead one to the conclusion that nursing and medicine can be distinguished by the range of socially and legally sanctioned tasks and privileges that members of one but not of the other profession may lawfully engage in. Such a distinction would, of course, be possible. But it is not a distinction that allows one to

infer anything about the subservient or dominant 'nature' of either one of the two professions. The distribution of socially and legally sanctioned privileges and powers between medicine and nursing is itself a historically contingent fact, and there is nothing to suggest that the current distribution of powers and privileges is either natural or that it is the one that we should, upon reflection, adopt.

For example, why should it be the doctor who decides whether a patient should be resuscitated or not? Should it not be the patient? And if not the patient, why not the nurse?

Philosophical Commitment

Is it possible to distinguish the two professions by their philosophical commitment, that is, by the philosophical presuppositions that guide their respective health-care endeavours? It is, again, not easy to see how this might be done. Someone intent on rejecting the view that nursing is naturally subservient to medicine might point out that there is no essential difference between the philosophical commitment of the two professions that would allow one to speak of one of them as being subservient to the other. Both nursing and medicine are other-directed and committed to the welfare of clients or patients; members of both professions have a similar understanding of pain and of suffering, of well-being and of health, and both accept the same scientific presuppositions. If there are differences between individual doctors and nurses, these are no more pronounced than those found between individuals from the same professions. Hence, one might conclude, nursing does not have a nature which is different from that of medicine and can therefore not be said to be naturally subservient to medicine.

Another, diametrically opposed avenue is sometimes chosen by those writing in the field to prove wrong the claim that the nurse's role is a naturally subservient one. Rather than trying to show that the nurse's role is—either functionally or in terms of its philosophical commitment—*indistinguishable* from that of doctors, this second group of nurses claims that the nursing commitment is fundamentally *different* from that of medicine. In other words, those who take this approach start with the premise that medicine and nursing have different philosophical commitments or 'natures', and then go on to deny that this will necessarily lead to the conclusion that nursing ought to be playing a subservient role to medicine.

This is generally done in one of two ways. The first involves drawing a distinction in terms of a commitment to 'care' and to 'cure'. Whereas medicine is said to be directed at 'cure', the therapeutic commitment or moral end of nursing is identified as 'care'. Medicine and doctors, it is said, often focus on treating or curing the patient's medical condition; nursing, on the other hand, is based on holistic care, where patients are treated as complex wholes. As a number of Australian nurses put it in their submission to a 1987 inquiry into professional issues in nursing:

> Medical science and technology is concerned with disease diagnosis and cure. This reductionist model of care inevitably dissects, fragments and depersonalises human beings in the process of caring. The nurse's caring role demands the preservation and integrity of the wholeness of human beings.

The second way of attempting to draw a distinction between nursing and medicine involves an appeal to two different ethics. Whereas medicine is said to be based on principles and rules (a so-called [male] ethics of justice), nursing is said to be based on relational caring (a so-called [female] ethics of care). This means, very roughly, that doctors will put ethical principles or rules before the needs or wants of individual patients, whereas nurses regard the needs or wants of individual patients as more important than adherence to abstract principles or rules.

These two views do not deny that nursing is context-dependent or that nurses perform very different functions in different health-care settings; they also acknowledge that nurses and doctors sometimes perform very similar or identical functions and act in very similar roles. None the less, those who take this view assume that nursing is different from medicine because it has a different philosophical commitment or end—that of care. 'Care'—the nurture, the physical care, and the emotional support provided by nurses to preserve the 'human

face' of medicine and the dignity of the patient—cannot, the suggestion is, 'be absent if nursing is present'.

There are a number of reasons why I am pessimistic about the endeavour of distinguishing nursing from medicine and nurses from doctors in this way. We will discuss some of these at length in later chapters of this book. Here the following will suffice: it seems very difficult, in a straightforward and practical sense, to make philosophical commitments, such as the commitment to care, the defining characteristic of a profession. Such a definition would presumably include all nurses who have this commitment, but would exclude all those who do not. A registered nurse, who has all the relevant professional knowledge and expertise, who performs her nursing functions well, but—let us assume—subscribes to 'the scientific medical model' or to an 'ethics of justice' would now, presumably, no longer be a nurse. Would her philosophical commitment make her a doctor? And would a doctor, who subscribes to 'care' now more appropriately be described as a nurse?

The problem is raised particularly poignantly in settings, such as intensive care units (ICUs), where the emphasis is on survival and 'cure'. After Robert Zussman, a sociologist, had observed doctors and nurses in two American ICUs for some time, he reached the conclusion that ICU nurses were not 'gentle carers' but technicians. Zussman does not deny that other nurses may well be differently motivated, but in the ICU, he says, they are 'mini-interns'. 'They are not patient advocates. They are not "angels of mercy". Like physicians, they have become technicians.'

For all practical purposes, attempts to define a profession in terms of its philosophical commitment simply would not work. How would one test a potential nursing candidate for it? How could one ensure continued commitment—especially in a high-technology environment such as intensive care? And why should we assume that 'care' should always have priority over either principle or cure? Are there not times when proper care demands that we attempt to 'cure' or when ethical principle ought to trump care? If the answer is 'yes', as I think it should be, then we should abandon the attempt to draw a distinction between nursing and medicine in these ways.

There is, of course, another reason as well: Even if a sound distinction in the philosophical or ethical commitments of nursing and medicine could be drawn, this would not settle the question of whether nursing is or is not a naturally subservient profession. The fact (if it is a fact) that medicine has one philosophical commitment or nature and nursing another is quite independent of the further question of whether one of the professions is, or ought to be, subservient to the other. Further argument would be needed to show that, for nothing of substance follows from establishing that one thing, or one profession, is different from another.

Subservience for the Sake of Life or Limb?

What arguments could be provided to show that nurses and nursing ought to adopt a subservient role to doctors and medicine? In accordance with our assumption that nursing is an other-directed profession, a profession that primarily aims at the good of patients, such arguments would have to show that nurses' subservience would benefit patients more than nurses' autonomy....

[O]ur main focus will be hospital-based nurses. Most nurses work in hospitals, and it is part of their role to carry out the treatment plans of doctors. Here a powerful argument is sometimes put that, regardless of what is true for other nurses, it is essential that nurses who work in acute-care settings adopt a subservient role. Those who take this view do not necessarily deny that it may be quite appropriate for some nurses, in some contexts, to play an autonomous role; but, they insist, when we are talking about hospitals matters are different.

Hospitals are bureaucratic institutions and bureaucratic institutions, so a typical argument goes, rely for efficient functioning on vertical structures of command, on strict adherence to procedure and on avoidance of initiative by those who have been charged with certain tasks. While this is true of all bureaucratic institutions, strict adherence to rules and to chains of command becomes critically important when we are focusing on hospitals. In such a setting much is at stake. A patient's health, and even her life, will often depend on quick and reliable responses by members of the health-care team to the directions of the person in charge.

Let us accept that efficiency will often depend on some of the central criteria identified above. This does not, however, answer questions regarding the proper relationship between nurses and doctors. Take the notion of a bureaucratic hierarchy. A simple appeal to that notion does not tell us how the bureaucratic hierarchy should be arranged. Here it is generally assumed that it is appropriate for doctors to be in charge and appropriate for nurses to follow the doctors' orders. But why should this be so? Why is it so widely assumed that doctors should perform the role of 'captain of the ship' and nurses those of members of the crew?

The Argument from Expertise

The reason most commonly given for this type of arrangement is that doctors, but not nurses, have the relevant medical knowledge and expertise to deal with the varied and often unique medical conditions that afflict patients, and the different emergencies that might arise. Just as it would not do to put crew-members with only a limited knowledge of navigation in charge of a ship traversing unpredictable and potentially dangerous waters, so it would not do to put nurses with only a limited knowledge of medicine in charge of the treatment plans of patients. Many a ship and many a patient would be lost as a result of such an arrangement. Hence, if we want ships and patients to be in good hands, it follows that those with expertise—doctors and captains—must be in charge.

Such an argument is put by Lisa H. Newton, a vocal critic of nursing's quest for autonomy. If the purpose of saving life and health is to be accomplished in an atmosphere which is often tense and urgent, then, Newton argues,

> all participating activities and agents must be completely subordinated to the medical judgments of the physician. . . . [T]hose other than physicians, involved in medical procedures in a hospital context, have no right to insert their own needs, judgments, or personalities into the situation. The last thing we need at that point is another autonomous professional on the job, whether a nurse or anyone else.

There is something right and something wrong about the above kind of argument. To see this, the argument needs untangling.

Shared Goals, Urgency and Medical Authority

In her argument Newton implicitly assumes that the therapeutic goals of doctors are morally worthy ones, and that the ethical question of whether a doctor should, for example, prolong a patient's life or allow her to die is not in dispute. This assumption is inherent in her observation that the tasks at hand are, or ought to be 'protective of life itself'. While we know that this very question is frequently in dispute, let us, for the purpose of our initial discussion, accept and work with that assumption. We shall question it later.

There is no doubt that doctors have special medical expertise that is relevant to the achievement of various therapeutic goals, including the goal of saving or prolonging life. Extensive medical studies and registration or licensing procedures ensure that doctors are experts in medical diagnosis and medical therapy. Their education equips them well to act quickly and decisively in complicated and unforeseen medical circumstances. As a general rule (but only as a general rule—there could be exceptions to this rule) doctors would thus be better equipped than nurses to respond to a range of medical emergencies. In emergency situations, then, where urgent action is required, it is likely that the best outcome for patients as a whole will be achieved if doctors are in charge. Moreover, since the outcome of medical measures in such contexts often depends crucially on the practical assistance of nurses, it is important that nurses will, as a general rule, quickly and unquestioningly respond to the doctor's orders.

It seems that we should accept this type of argument. During emergency procedures it is more likely that the desired outcome will be achieved if there is not only a single decision-maker, but if this single decision-maker is also the most expert medical professional in the field. This will typically be the doctor.

In addition to those cases where urgent action by a medical expert is required to achieve the desired therapeutic goal, there are also some other specialized contexts, such as the operating room, where it is appropriate for doctors to exercise and for nurses to recognize medical authority....

There is a connection, then, between the possession of particular expertise and authority. Expertise can be crucial to the achievement of goals and, provided the goals are shared, it will frequently be appropriate for people who are authorities in a particular field to also be in authority.

If we accept this argument, it follows that doctors ought, other things being equal, to be in charge in medical emergencies and in other specialized contexts that are characterized by an element of urgency. They ought to be in charge because this arrangement best ensures that the therapeutic goal will be reached.

Acceptance of this view has, however, less farreaching consequences than might be assumed. First, even if particular therapeutic treatment goals are most likely to be achieved if a single medically trained person is in charge *during*, for example, operations or resuscitation procedures, this does not entail that the doctor should have overall authority as far as the patient's treatment is concerned. The authority to decide on an operation or on the desirability of implementing resuscitation procedures might, for example, rest with the patient or her relatives, and the nurse could conceivably be in charge of the overall treatment plan of the patient.

Second, it does not follow that nurses must, even during emergency procedures, *blindly* follow a doctor's order. Doctors, like the rest of us, are fallible human beings and sometimes make mistakes. This means that the nurse's obligation to follow a doctor's order, even in these specialized contexts, cannot be absolute and may at times be overridden by other considerations, such as the avoidance of harm to patients.

A study conducted in 1966, when nurses were probably more likely unquestioningly to follow a doctor's order than they are now, demonstrates that unquestioning obedience to doctors is likely to have some rather undesirable consequences for patients. In the 1966 study, nurses were asked by a doctor, by telephone, to prepare medication which was obviously excessive and to give it to a patient. Twenty-one out of 22 nurses followed the doctors' orders and were ready to give the medication to the patient when the researchers intervened....

Given, then, that doctors will occasionally make mistakes and that nurses frequently have the professional knowledge to detect them, it will be best if nurses do not understand their duty to follow a doctor's order as an absolute and exceptionless one. If the doctor's order is, in the nurse's professional judgment, clearly wrong, then the nurse must bring her 'professional intelligence' into play and question it....

Does a nurse who subscribes to the general proposition or rule that there are times when it will best serve the interests of patients that she accept the authority of doctors thereby necessarily adopt a subservient or non-autonomous role? Does she abrogate her autonomy? I think not. As long as a nurse does not *surrender* her autonomy or judgment, that is, does not blindly follow every order she is given, but rather *decides*, after reflection, to adopt a general rule that it will be best to accept and act on the doctor's authority under certain circumstances, then she is not a subservient tool in the doctor's hands. She is not, as was once proposed, simply 'an intelligent machine'. She is a moral agent who, in distinction from a mere machine, *chooses* to act in one way rather than another.

To sum up, then: the argument that nurses should—for the sake of achieving certain worthy therapeutic goals such as the saving of life—adopt a subservient role to doctors typically rests on at least two rather dubious assumptions. The first assumption is that all or most decision-making is characterized by great urgency. The second assumption is that the therapeutic goal is best achieved by nurses adopting an absolute rather than a prima facie rule to carry out the doctor's orders. But, as we have seen, both assumptions must be rejected, on the grounds outlined above....

Do Patients Need Subservient Mother Surrogates?

A different kind of argument is sometimes put to show that nurses should, for the sake of patients, adopt a subservient role to doctors. Only then, the argument asserts, will nurses be able to meet the emotional needs of patients. To examine that claim, we shall once again focus on an argument provided by Lisa H. Newton. In her defence of the traditional role

of the nurse, Newton appeals to an argument based on the patient's needs. Because a patient may not be able to take care of himself, Newton points out,

> his entire self-concept of an independent human being may be threatened. . . . He needs comfort, reassurance, someone to talk to. The person he really needs, who would be capable of taking care of all these problems, is obviously his mother, and the first job of the nurse is to be a mother surrogate.

But, Newton continues her argument, mothers are not only figures of considerable authority; it is also ordinarily part of the mother's role to take control of various aspects of her dependent children's lives, and to make important decisions for them. Patients are, however, not children. Their autonomy must be protected from the threatening authority of the mother surrogate. This requires, Newton asserts, that

> the role of the nurse must be from the outset, as essentially as it is nurturant, unavailable for such attribution of authority. Not only must the role of the nurse not include authority; it must be incompatible with authority: essentially, a subservient role.

This non-threatening caring function, performed by the nurse, would not only permit the patient 'to be cared for like a baby', but would also allow patients to unburden themselves and to express their doubts and resentments about doctors and the treatments prescribed by them. Patients, Newton notes, may sometimes be torn between the desire to discontinue treatment (to reassert control over their lives) and a desire to continue treatment (to reap its benefits). The nurse will be there as a sympathetic listener 'but in her subordinate position . . . can do absolutely nothing to change the course of treatment,' that is, both nurse and patient are subject to what she calls the 'sapiential authority' of the physician.

The traditional subordinate role of the nurse is thus justified by the needs of patients. Patients, Newton holds, need the emotional support of a mother surrogate but, to protect the patient's autonomy and to ensure compliance with the medical treatment plan, the nurse must completely surrender her autonomy.

Should we accept this type of argument? The first point to be noted is this: Newton's claims about humiliating treatment, about strong emotional needs and about the threatened loss of the patient's self-concept as an independent human being, while undoubtedly correct in some cases, do not apply to all patients and in all circumstances. Many patients enter hospital for relatively minor treatments or observations and do not feel that their self-concept is threatened in any way by their status of patient. They do not need or want a mother surrogate. Rather, their needs are much more likely to be met by a nurse who not only provides them with professional nursing care, but who also refuses to surrender her professional intelligence and autonomy to the doctor to protect the patient from potential harm.

Then there are the patients who are seriously ill and whose self-concept may indeed be threatened by the medical treatment they are receiving or by their incapacitated state. Many of these patients will undoubtedly benefit from the presence of a caring and sympathetic nurse, who will listen to them with warmth and understanding. But would they want the subservient nurse Newton holds in store for them? Would their emotional needs really be satisfied by talking to a self-effacing health-care professional who, afraid of either posing a threat to the patient's autonomy or the 'sapiential authority' of the doctor, would be making sympathetic clucking noises, but would not engage with the patient in any meaningful way? I doubt it very much. By refusing to engage with patients in a meaningful way, she would be signalling to them that she does not take their concerns seriously, no more seriously than a well-meaning mother would take the incoherent babbling of her sick baby. This would not only be extremely upsetting to many patients, but would also enforce their sense of powerlessness, the feeling that they have lost control over their lives—as indeed they may have....

As we noted above, Newton recognizes that a patient may wish to discontinue treatment so as to 'reassert control over his life'. Would supporting the patient in this desire—assuming that it is a reasonable one—really threaten his autonomy? And is not the nurse's refusal ever to take the patient's desire seriously tantamount to abandoning him to another authority—the authority of the doctor? While we should not ignore the possibility that a powerful mother figure might pose a threat to the patient's autonomy, why should we assume that a powerful father figure—that of the doctor—might not pose a similar or a greater threat?

Newton simply assumes that the therapeutic success of treatment presupposes that the patient defer to the 'physician's sapiential authority'. What she does not explain, however, is why the physician's ends or goals—therapeutic success or prolongation of life, for example—should count for more than, say, the judgment of the patient or the nurse. In other words, we are not told where the doctor's moral authority comes from or why we should regard his decisions as sound.

I doubt that a totally subservient nurse could even meet the basic emotional needs of patients, or that she could meet them any better than an autonomous nurse could; and a subservient and self-effacing nurse certainly could not meet the perhaps even stronger needs of patients who want to retain or regain control of their lives and make treatment decisions for themselves.

The adoption by nurses of a subservient role of the kind envisaged by Newton would most likely harm patients more than it would benefit them; it would also be an utterly demoralizing role for many contemporary nurses, even if it would be compatible with some understanding of autonomy. Nurses would be required to stand by, doing nothing, while doctors make the occasional mistake, or provide treatment to unwilling but disempowered patients. To conclude, then, I can see no good reason why nurses should adopt a subservient mother surrogate role for the sake of patients. On the contrary, there are a number of strong reasons why nurses should reject it.

CHAPTER 4

Truth-Telling and Confidentiality

A major moral issue in patient-provider relationships is how to handle the truth—specifically, whether doctors and nurses should always tell the truth to patients and whether doctors and nurses should ever reveal the truth about their patients to others. The former question is about the presumed duty of providers not to deceive patients or withhold relevant medical information from them. The latter is about confidentiality, a provider's obligation to protect a patient's privacy. In both, the issues raised are contentious and ongoing, reverberating among patients, families, and caregivers and often forcing shifts in the policies and culture of medical practice. Though the debates are complex, they usually come down to disagreements about the limits of paternalism and the proper balance between the principles of autonomy and beneficence.

PATERNALISM AND DECEPTION

From ancient times, the principle of nonmaleficence—the duty to do no harm—has been enshrined in codes of medical ethics. But not so with the duty of truthfulness. The Hippocratic Oath does not mention an obligation of truth-telling or disclosure, and until 1980 even the professional code of the American Medical Association did not say anything about dealing honestly with patients. Many physicians have viewed the truth as something to conceal or reveal for the therapeutic good of the patient. For them, the overriding principle was beneficence (or nonmaleficence), which was best honored by delicately managing what patients knew about their own cases. The truth could be harmful, unsettling, and depressing—so why inflict it on

vulnerable patients? In a famously blunt formulation of this view, an early-twentieth-century physician declared that to be compassionate and gracious, doctors "must frequently withhold the truth from their patients, which is tantamount to telling a lie. Moreover, the physician soon learns that the art of medicine consists largely in skillfully mixing falsehood and truth."[1]

Nowadays, in the age of patient autonomy and informed consent, such strong paternalistic sentiments are less common. Most physicians value truth-telling, and professional standards encourage it while counseling sensitivity in conveying vital information to patients. But the moral problem of truthfulness still presses both physicians and patients, prompting questions with which they still wrestle. Is it ever morally permissible for a physician to lie to a patient? Does a physician's duty of beneficence sometimes justify deception? Does respect for patient autonomy rule it out? If there are exceptions to a duty of truthfulness, what are they?

Consider how easily (and painfully) such questions can arise. Karen, a 30-year-old woman with two small children, is admitted to the hospital after experiencing headaches, vomiting, memory loss, and partial paralysis. Dr. Smith runs numerous tests and discovers that Karen has a malignant brain tumor. It is advanced and untreatable, leaving Karen with only weeks to live. Before the tests, she had told Dr. Smith that she was terrified of cancer because her husband died of lung cancer and her mother of breast cancer. And if she succumbed to cancer, what would happen to her children? Who would care for them?

Dr. Smith considers carefully whether to tell Karen of the dire prognosis. He thinks about the

- In 1961, a survey of physicians found that 90 percent of them would avoid telling patients of a diagnosis of cancer. But in a similar 1979 survey, 97 percent of physicians said that they would disclose a diagnosis of cancer.

- More recent research suggests that most physicians in Western cultures inform their cancer patients of their diagnosis, but fewer of them tell cancer patients about their prognosis.
- Several studies indicate that most cancer patients want to know the details of their disease, whether the news is good or bad.
- Surveys suggest that patients differ in the kinds of medical information they would like to have and how it is communicated to them.

From L. J. Fallowfield, V. A. Jenkins, and H. A. Beveridge, "Truth May Hurt but Deceit Hurts More: Communication in Palliative Care," *Palliative Medicine* 16 (2002), 297–303.

misery that full disclosure would cause her, the days spent in terror before the end, the dark depression that would likely spoil her remaining time with her children.

He decides to shield her from the terrible facts, shrouding them in vague statements and irrelevant details. He tells her that she has a brain disease requiring neither surgery nor radiation, and he assures her that he has many drugs at his disposal for treating her symptoms. Karen is relieved to hear the news and does not question Dr. Smith's explanation. Sensing that disturbing details might lie behind his murky pronouncements, she presses him no further and tries to rouse a sense of optimism. She is eager to go home so things can get back to normal.

The next day she does go home. But after two weeks of trying to resume her normal routine, after enduring more headaches and vomiting, she collapses and dies.[2]

Notice that in this scenario Dr. Smith does not actually lie to Karen (that is, intentionally give her false information), but he does deliberately mislead her by withholding crucial facts and avoiding definite statements. Either way, he handles her paternalistically. Notice also that this story is about protecting a patient from a dreadful prognosis, but such paternalism can also apply to the truth about diagnoses and treatments.

Some medical writers would agree with Dr. Smith's decision. They think there are good reasons for occasionally misleading or lying to patients. Their main argument is that truth-telling can be injurious, evoking in patients feelings of panic, hopelessness, fear, and depression—any of which can worsen the patient's condition, sap her will to live, or tempt her to suicide. Honest disclosure must be modulated to promote the patient's welfare. The physician's duty to do no harm must take precedence over the obligation of veracity.

Others reject this argument, contending that it exaggerates the harm done to patients by full disclosure (and underestimates the beneficial effects of truthfulness) and fails to recognize that misleading or lying to patients can also do damage. A common suggestion is that if patients knew the truth about their situation, they would likely live their lives very differently than if they remained ignorant. If so, not knowing the truth robs patients of informed life decisions. If they knew their prognosis was terminal, for example, they might try harder to make every remaining day meaningful, to put their financial and legal affairs in order, and to behave differently toward their family and friends.

Advocates of full disclosure (that is, honest communication of the essential facts) also insist that informed patients are better patients—that patients who know where they stand are more likely to comply with the requirements of their treatment.

Moreover, some argue that deception breeds distrust—and not just between patient and doctor:

> [T]he long-term effect of lies on the family and, perhaps most importantly, on society, is incalculable. If trust is gradually corroded, if the "wells are poisoned," progress is hard. Mistrust creates lack of communication and increased fear, and this generation has seen just such a fearful myth created around cancer.[3]

The impact of the truth on patients may also depend largely on how it's told. As one writer puts it, cases that seem to indicate that truth-telling is harmful to patients may instead

> argue, not for no telling, but for better telling, for sensitivity and care in determining how much the patient wants to know, explaining carefully in ways the patient can understand, and providing full support and "after-care" as in other treatments.[4]

Another argument against full disclosure is that patients do not want to know the truth, especially if the prognosis is grim. A common claim is that even when patients say they want all the facts, they actually do not. Many writers counter this view with data from surveys suggesting that most patients really do prefer to be told the truth about their diagnosis. In light of these findings, presuming that patients do not mean what they say seems questionable at best.

None of this implies that the truth should be forced upon patients who genuinely choose not to be informed about their medical condition. As one commentator notes, autonomy can be served by offering a patient "the opportunity to learn the truth, at whatever level of detail that patient desires."[5]

Many skeptics of full disclosure have argued that physicians have no duty to tell patients the truth because patients are incapable of understanding it anyway. The practice of medicine is technically complex—so complex that even when a physician tries to explain the relevant facts to patients, they cannot grasp them. Telling patients the whole truth, the skeptics say, is impossible.

Critics of this argument say that even if communicating the whole truth is impossible, physicians still have a duty of complete honesty—an obligation to try hard to convey to patients the essential and relevant information. What's more, some argue that conveying the "whole truth and nothing but the truth" is unnecessary:

> [T]he explanation of a complicated situation in ways a layperson can understand is not a challenge unique to physicians. The same problem is faced by lawyers, electricians, automobile mechanics, and computer help-line workers. In none of these fields, including medicine, is it necessary to provide the layperson with a complete explanation (the "complete truth") of a situation. All a patient requires is an understanding adequate to appreciate the nature and seriousness of his illness and the potential benefits and risks of the available therapies. A diabetic need not know the stages of oxidative phosphorylation to grasp the importance of insulin and the role of diet in maintaining her health.[6]

The main argument in favor of truth-telling rests on the principle of autonomy. The gist is that we must always respect people's autonomy—their rational capacity for self-determination. Autonomous persons must be allowed to freely exercise this capacity: to decide how to live their own lives and what can and cannot be done to their own bodies. To respect their autonomy is to respect their freedom to act by their own lights, as long as their actions accord with the freedom of others. When physicians deceive a patient, they fail to respect his autonomy by constraining his ability to make informed choices. They compel him to make important decisions in a fog of distorted or missing information.

Many who insist on truth-telling and respect for autonomy admit that deceiving a patient may sometimes be necessary, but they say that any deception requires strong justification and should be a last resort. Some contend that deceiving a patient is permissible only when the deception is small and the benefits to the patient are great (as when a minor lie will save the patient's life). Most who argue in this vein believe that cases of permissible deception are rare.

CONFIDENTIAL TRUTHS

Truth-telling, then, is about health professionals imparting relevant facts to patients. **Confidentiality** concerns patients imparting information to health professionals who promise, implicitly or explicitly, not to disclose that information to others. It is an obligation or pledge of physicians, nurses, and others to keep secret the personal health information of patients unless they consent to disclosure. Most people probably assume they have a right to confidentiality. Physicians also take seriously their duty to protect patient privacy, though they may differ on whether the duty is absolute or prima facie. Their respect for confidentiality goes back centuries, having been boldly expressed in a long line of medical codes from ancient Greece onward. The Hippocratic Oath has the physician swear that "whatever I see or hear, professionally or privately, which ought not to be divulged, I will keep secret and tell no one."

Arguments for confidentiality can take both consequentialist and nonconsequentialist forms. The consequentialist can argue that unless patients are able to rely on a physician to keep their secrets, they would be reluctant to reveal truthful information about themselves—information needed if the physician is to correctly diagnose their illnesses, devise effective treatments, and provide informed prognoses. Without respect for confidentiality, physicians would have a difficult time fulfilling their duty of beneficence. Worse, trust between physician and patient would break down, and trust is what makes the practice of medicine possible. But beyond issues of trust, the consequentialist can offer other dire consequences to consider. Disclosure of confidential medical information could expose patients to

discrimination from insurance companies and employers, disrupt their personal relationships, and subject them to shame or public ridicule.

The nonconsequentialist can argue from the principle of autonomy the idea that people should be allowed to exercise their capacity for self-determination. Autonomous persons, the argument goes, have a right to determine what may or may not be done to them—not just to their bodies and to their property, but to their private lives. They therefore have a right to control access to information about themselves and to limit intrusion into their personal affairs. They have, in other words, a **right to privacy**, the authority of persons to control who may possess and use information about themselves.

A related argument is that the physician-patient relationship is based in part on the physician's implicit promise to patients to preserve confidentiality and to respect their privacy. Patients' confidentiality must therefore be protected because the physician has promised to do so. Confidentiality arises from the physician's obligation to keep promises, what some call a duty of fidelity. Others see this line as another argument from autonomy because, as Kant would have it, to break a promise is to violate autonomy.

As hinted earlier, an important issue is whether the obligation to respect confidentiality is absolute (applying in all cases) or prima facie (allowing exceptions when other duties obtain). Some argue for absolute confidentiality, insisting that *any* breech of it undermines trust between physicians and patients and amounts to impermissible deception. But many believe that exceptions are sometimes justified when confidentiality must be weighed against other duties, such as the duty to prevent serious harm to the patient and others. The law reflects this prima facie view of confidentiality. It recognizes that communication between physicians and patients is "privileged" and should generally be safeguarded from invasion—yet requires physicians to breech confidentiality in some cases. State law, for example, may oblige physicians to reveal information about a patient if she has a serious contagious disease, suffers from

Confidentiality and a Duty to Warn

In the landmark 1976 case *Tarasoff v. Regents of the University of California*, the court held that duties of patient-psychotherapist confidentiality can be over-ridden when "a patient poses a serious danger of violence to others." In related cases:

- In 1983 people who were shot by John Hinckley as he tried to assassinate Ronald Reagan sued the psychiatrist who had been treating Hinckley. In *Brady v. Hopper*, a federal district court ruled that unless a patient makes a specific threat to a readily identifiable person, the patient's therapist cannot be held responsible for injuries inflicted on third parties by the patient.
- In *Bradley Center Inc. v. Wessner* (1982) and *Hedlund v. Superior Court of Orange County* (1983), the courts found that therapists are obligated to take reasonable steps to determine the degree of danger posed by a patient.
- In *Ewing v. Goldstein* (2004) and *Ewing v. Northridge Hospital Medical Center* (2004), the California Court of Appeal held that a therapist has a duty to warn third parties of a possible danger posed by a patient even if the threat is communicated not by the patient but by the patient's family.

gunshot wounds, or is the apparent victim of abuse or assault (whether she is a child or an adult). Thus physicians can find themselves pulled not only between clashing moral duties but also between moral duties and legal requirements.

These sorts of conflicts were drawn in high relief by the famous 1976 California Supreme Court case of *Tarasoff v. Regents of the University of California*. It concerned Prosenjit Poddar, a student at UC Berkeley who sought counseling from psychotherapists employed by the university hospital. He confided in them that he intended to kill another student, Tatiana Tarasoff, when she returned from a summer trip in Brazil. The psychotherapists told the police of Poddar's intentions but warned neither Tatiana nor her parents of the threat. Judging Poddar to be rational, the police soon released him. When Tatiana returned from Brazil, Poddar murdered her just as he said he would. Her parents sued the university for failing to warn them of the danger to Tatiana, and they won. The court recognized the importance of confidentiality but ruled that in this case the psychotherapists had a duty to breech it to warn a third party of a serious risk of harm. "We conclude," the majority opinion said, "that the public policy favoring protection of the confidential character of patient-psychotherapist communications must yield to the extent to which disclosure is essential to avert danger to others. The protective privilege ends where the public peril begins."

High-stakes collisions between the duties of confidentiality and preventing harm are more common than *Tarasoff* may suggest. Prime examples are cases involving patients who are HIV positive. Let's say a physician tells her patient that he has tested positive for HIV infection, that his wife could also become infected through sexual intercourse, and that he should inform her of the risk. But he says he will not disclose his condition to anyone and demands full physician-patient confidentiality. Or suppose this patient has no sexual partner but will be cared for at home by people who are unaware of his HIV status (and may be exposed to his body fluids). He refuses to inform them and asks his physician to tell no one. In both cases, if the physician maintains confidentiality, there is a high risk of serious harm to people, but revealing the patient's diagnosis to others destroys confidentiality. What should the physician do?

IN DEPTH
TRUTH-TELLING AND CULTURAL DIVERSITY

Several studies have shown that views toward truth-telling when people are seriously ill vary dramatically by culture. Here's a partial summary of the results of one of the more recent studies:

> This study of 800 elderly subjects showed that major differences exist in the way people of different ethnicities view the issue of truth-telling. One of the core differences, around which many of the themes circled, is the question of how the truth affects the terminally ill patient. On one hand, the truth can be seen as an essential tool that allows the patient to maintain a sense of personal agency and control. Seen in this light, telling the truth, however painful, is empowering. On the other hand, the truth can be seen as traumatic and demoralizing, sapping the patient of hope and the will to live. For those who hold this view, truth-telling is an act of cruelty.
>
> In fact, many, if not most, of our subjects held both views. They differed in the relative weight given to each view. In weighing the positive benefits of the truth versus its potential to harm, the deciding factor seems to be the way the self is understood. Are we mainly autonomous agents whose dignity and worth come from the individual choices we make with our lives, or is our most important characteristic the web of social relations in which we exist? If we hold the former view (as most of our African-American and European-American respondents did), then lack of access to the truth is almost dehumanizing since it strips us of our ability to make choices, without which we are something less than fully human. If, however, we tend to see ourselves not as individuals, but as a part of a larger social network (as was more common in the Mexican-American and Korean-American groups), then the notion of personal choice loses something of its force, and we may expect that those close to us will act on our behalf to protect and nurture us in our time of need.
>
> Beliefs commonly held in the European-American culture about individuality, self-determination, and the importance of maintaining control too often have been treated as if they were universal ethical principles. Only by allowing diverse voices to speak, and hearing the sometimes surprising things they have to say, can we ensure that we are addressing the real concerns of the communities we serve.

From *Journal of Urban Health: Bulletin of the New York Academy of Medicine*, vol. 78, no. 1 (March 2001), pp. 59–71.

Many physicians and ethicists say that violating confidentiality in such a case is morally permissible if there is no other way to avoid the harm to others. They assert that violations should be a last resort after exploring other alternatives, which include getting the patient to agree to notify those at risk or to cease behavior that produces the risk.

But even with such careful attention to protecting patient privacy, is complete confidentiality really feasible? According to some observers, despite the high value we put on confidentiality, it is not what it used to be. It has been eroded, they say—not by physicians and nurses, but by our computerized, bureaucratized health care systems. The number of people who need to know the intimate details of a patient's records—physicians, nurses, medical technicians, students, consultants, secretaries, financial officers, data managers, insurance auditors, administrators, and more—has grown beyond all expectation. And in a digitized, networked world, the opportunities for improper or unethical access to the records have multiplied at every step. Critics contend that the traditional ideal of complete confidentiality is no longer possible, if it ever was. So they suggest that we give up the traditional notion and try to salvage the features of confidentiality that matter to us most.

Carlos R.

For many who are HIV positive, their anguish only deepens if others know about their condition. They demand medical confidentiality, and physicians are obliged to comply—but the "duty to warn" others of the risk of infection haunts both physicians and patients. Typically those thought to need warning are sexual partners and spouses, but sometimes caregivers—whether professionals or family members—are the ones of concern. This case is of the latter kind. It recounts the events that lead up to the question at issue—whether the physician's weightier duty is confidentiality or warning—then provides the opposing views of two commentators.

Twenty-one-year-old Carlos R. entered the hospital for treatment of gunshot wounds received in gang violence. During his stay, he confided to the attending physician that he was HIV positive, and testing proved him correct. Eventually he recovered well enough to leave the hospital to have his wounds cared for at home. The attending physician advised Carlos to have daily visits from a nurse to tend to his wounds. But Carlos was uninsured, and Medicaid would not pay for the home nursing visits because his 22-year-old sister Consuela was willing and able to care for him. For 10 years since their mother died, Consuela had assumed the role of mother for both Carlos and their younger sister.

Carlos was willing to let Consuela be his nurse, but he was adamant that she not be told about his HIV status. She was unaware of his homosexual activity, and so too was his father. More than anything else he feared that his father would learn the truth. There was also the cultural factor. Among many Hispanics, homosexuality is a social stigma.

The choice for Carlos' physician, then, was between preserving confidentiality and breeching it to warn Consuela of the risks involved in caring for an HIV-positive patient.

One commentator on this case argues against violating confidentiality. He contends that for a physician to have a duty to warn, there must be (1) "an imminent threat of serious and irreversible harm," (2) no other way to avert that threat except by breeching confidentiality, and (3) a situation in which the harm done by the breech is on a par with the harm avoided by the breech. In his view, none of these conditions are fully met in this case. He does not believe that the risk of Consuela becoming infected with HIV is very great—and certainly not "imminent." He also thinks that there are alternatives to breeching confidentiality—the main one being instructing Consuela in safe wound care. Moreover, he insists that the risks to Consuela from not telling her about Carlos' HIV status are far outweighed by the awful disruption of family relations that breeching confidentiality would cause.

The second commentator argues for violating confidentiality to warn Consuela. She maintains that Consuela has a right to information whether or not there is an appreciable risk to her. One reason is that if Consuela is not being told the truth, she is being deceived. Most people in Consuela's situation would want to know the facts and would probably assume that Carlos was not HIV positive because no one said so. Furthermore, in getting Consuela to provide nursing care, "the health care system is using her to avoid providing a service it would otherwise be responsible for." If so, then the system has an obligation to give her the information she needs to decide whether to accept the responsibility.

In the end, the physician should require the patient to choose: "Carlos can decide to accept Consuela's generosity—in return for which he must tell her he is HIV-infected (or ask the doctor to tell her)—or he can decide not to tell her and do without her nursing care."[7]

APPLYING MAJOR THEORIES

In Kantian ethics, the morality of truth-telling and confidentiality seems unambiguous. Physicians who adopt the means-end formulation of the categorical imperative, for example, seem committed to an absolute duty of preserving both. In the Kantian view, treating people merely as a means to an end is impermissible, a violation of the principle of autonomy. Lying to patients and breeching confidentiality (by breaking a promise to respect privacy) are clear instances of such violations. For a strict Kantian, these prohibitions would have no exceptions; there would be no allowances made for extraordinary circumstances. Arguments that truth-telling could be injurious to patients and must therefore be done with an eye to medical consequences would carry no weight. Likewise, there would be no place for the notion that confidentiality may be set aside if there is a conflicting "duty to warn."

For an act-utilitarian, the morality of truth-telling and confidentiality must be judged case by case, the right action being the one that maximizes the good for all concerned. In each instance, physicians must decide carefully what to disclose to a patient, calculating the impact that any disclosure would have on the patient, her family, and everyone else involved. For each decision about confidentiality, physicians must weigh the effect of the choice on the patient, the physician-patient relationship, third parties who may be harmed by maintaining confidentiality, and themselves (who may have to contend with legal consequences).

Rule-utilitarianism tries to regulate actions by rules that, if generally followed, would result in the best consequences, everyone considered. A rule-utilitarian might argue that the greatest amount of good is produced by a rule stating that a physician should, with care and sensitivity, tell patients the truth about their condition. This rule would presumably not only be beneficial to patients, but also help foster trust in patients for their physicians and for medicine generally. A similar case could be made for a rule mandating strict adherence to the principle of confidentiality. But a rule-utilitarian could also reason that the best rules are those that require less than full disclosure to patients and less than absolute confidentiality—that is, rules with some exceptions built in. For example, the best confidentiality rule might demand full respect for a patient's privacy—except when maintaining confidentiality could put someone's life in danger.

Virtue ethics also has something to say about veracity and confidentiality. Many who favor this moral outlook might contend that if a physician cultivates the virtues of honesty and fidelity, he will be more likely to communicate truthfully with patients, to keep his promises to them, and to maintain their confidences. Moreover, if he possesses the virtue of compassion, he will be sensitive to the effect that blunt truthfulness could have on patients and will adapt his truth-telling accordingly. He will also be able to empathize with patients and understand why confidentiality matters so much to them.

KEY TERMS
confidentiality
right to privacy

SUMMARY
Some medical writers contend that there are good reasons for misleading or lying to patients, claiming that truth-telling can evoke in patients feelings of panic, hopelessness, and depression that can worsen the patient's condition or state of mind. Honest disclosure must be modulated to promote the patient's welfare. Others reject this argument, saying that it exaggerates the harm done to patients by full disclosure and does not recognize that misleading or lying to patients can also do damage. They maintain that informed patients are better patients and that deception breeds distrust. In these debates we often hear that patients do not want to know the truth, but scientific surveys suggest that most patients do want accurate information about their diagnosis. The main argument for truth-telling rests on the

principle of autonomy, the idea that people should be allowed to exercise freely their rational capacity for self-determination.

Confidentiality concerns patients imparting information to health professionals who promise, implicitly or explicitly, not to disclose that information to others. Consequentialist arguments for confidentiality say that without it, physicians would be hard pressed to obtain information from patients that could help in treatment, and trust between physician and patient would break down. Moreover, disclosure of confidential medical information could expose patients to discrimination, disrupt their personal relationships, and subject them to shame or public ridicule. Nonconsequentialist arguments appeal to the principle of autonomy, contending that autonomous persons have a right to determine what may or may not be done to their bodies as well as to their private lives. They have a right to privacy, the authority of persons to control who may possess and use information about themselves.

A major issue is whether the obligation to respect confidentiality is absolute or prima facie. Some argue for absolute confidentiality, insisting that any breach of it undermines trust between physicians and patients and amounts to impermissible deception. But many believe that exceptions are sometimes justified when confidentiality must be weighed against other duties, such as the duty to prevent serious harm to the patient and others.

Cases for Evaluation

CASE I
Disclosing Information about the Risk of Inherited Disease

Mrs. Durham was diagnosed with an invasive epithelial ovarian cancer and, in conjunction with conversations about her treatment, was offered genetic testing for the BRCA1 and BRCA2 mutations. It was revealed that she carried a harmful BRCA1 mutation that is known to increase the lifetime risk of breast and ovarian cancer significantly. Once the results came back, her oncologist brought up the option of a prophylactic mastectomy and advised her to inform her living relatives of the results of the test.

Mrs. Durham's primary care physician, Dr. Bartlett, expected she would do so, too. At her first appointment after the diagnosis, Dr. Bartlett asked Mrs. Durham how she was holding up and how her sister, Mrs. Weir—her only living family member and also one of Dr. Bartlett's patients—had taken the news.

"Oh. Well, I haven't told her."

"Are you going to?" asked Dr. Bartlett.

Mrs. Durham responded, "You know we haven't spoken in quite some time, and I can't imagine making this the topic of our first conversation."

"Yes, I know...but I think this is important information that may affect her health."

Mrs. Durham sighed. "We're estranged, for one thing, and for another, I want to keep my cancer private. I don't want people knowing I'm sick and pitying me."

Dr. Bartlett felt pulled in two directions—his obligation to respect Mrs. Durham's wishes and protect her privacy conflicted with his obligation to promote Mrs. Weir's health. BRCA1 mutations are not "reportable" illnesses like HIV and tuberculosis, so he was not compelled by law to break Mrs. Durham's confidentiality. Dr. Bartlett considered how he might be able to encourage Mrs. Durham's sister to be tested for the BRCA mutations while preserving Mrs. Durham's confidentiality.*

Does Mrs. Durham have a moral obligation to inform her sister of the results of the test? Why or why not? For Dr. Bartlett, what moral principles are in conflict? If Mrs. Durham refuses to inform her sister, should Dr. Bartlett tell her? What should Dr. Bartlett do if he can't subtly ask Mrs. Weir to be tested (that is, if he can't ask her without revealing the real reason for his request)?

*AMA Journal of Ethics, vol. 17, no. 9 (September 2015), pp. 819–825.

CASE 2

HIV and a Researcher's Duty to Warn

John, a licensed psychologist, is Principal Investigator for the "Assist" Project. His project is designed to identify behavioral trends among HIV+ adults in the New York City area. Participants were recruited from HIV/AIDS support groups, HIV/AIDS advocacy and service organizations, and through publicity in local bars, clinics and media outlets. John uses several measures to identify patterns among these individuals. He looks at help-seeking behaviors, physical and emotional symptoms, nutrition and diet habits, sexual behavior and knowledge of HIV/AIDS.

John uses an individual interview format as the method for the study. Each participant is asked to sign an informed consent form, which guarantees that all information revealed during the interviews will be kept confidential. The consent form describes the study and informs participants of the risks involved, which John identifies as minimal. Each participant is paid $50 for each interview. Participants in the study are also provided free psychological counseling and medical care. Participants are interviewed three times over a two-year period.

In accordance with the research protocol, John asks a participant during one of the initial interviews about her current sexual practices. The participant tells John that she is having unprotected sex with her boyfriend. She states that her boyfriend does not know about her HIV status and that she has no plans to reveal her condition. Later during the interview she mentions the name of her boyfriend. John notes the information and continues with the interview.

Upon going back to his office, John becomes anxious about what he was told by the participant. He ponders what he should do. John thinks about his moral responsibility from a relational perspective, assessing the ethical problem from the standpoint of his responsibility to preserve the scientific integrity of the project, the participants' confidentiality and the boyfriend's welfare.*

What moral principles seem to be in conflict in this scenario? How would you resolve the conflict? Suppose John's only options are either to maintain confidentiality or to violate it by revealing the subject's HIV status to her boyfriend (the subject refuses to notify him voluntarily). What should John do, and on what grounds could either action be justified? Suppose that state law prohibits researchers from revealing a subject's HIV status. Would this fact change your judgment? Should any such legal fact change your judgment?

*Brian Schrag, ed. (Association for Practical and Professional Ethics), "Graduate Research Ethics: Cases and Commentaries—Volume 3, 1999," Online Ethics Center for Engineering, 27 March 2006, www.onlineethics.org/CMS/research/rescases/gradres/gradresv3.aspx. (14 November 2007).

CASE 3

Emergency Department Dilemma

A 25-year-old young man is dropped off by a friend at the emergency department (ED) and states that he was in a motor vehicle accident 30 min before arriving. He says that his car was extensively damaged but that he was able to get out of the car and walk around at the scene. There was no loss of consciousness. He states that the police were at the scene investigating. He does not volunteer whether the police questioned him personally or why the police let him leave. Except for bumps and bruises, he is not significantly injured enough to justify a radiograph or computed tomography scan of his head. However, I detect the odor of ethanol on his breath, and so I order a blood ethanol to evaluate his capacity further. It is my opinion that if he is legally impaired, then he cannot leave the ED unless someone picks him up and assumes responsibility for him. He does not refuse the test and his blood ethanol level is 0.17 mg/dl, indicating that he is legally impaired.

Emergency physicians know that people who think they might be legally impaired have a strong incentive to leave the scene of accidents to avoid detection by investigating police. This patient's story about being involved in a multicar crash severe enough to cause significant property damage, and then the investigating police allowing him to leave the scene without checking him for potential ethanol intoxication does not ring true.*

Should the physician maintain doctor-patient confidentiality? Should he tell the police that his impaired patient probably broke the law and may have hurt others? What moral principles are relevant to deciding what to do? How much weight would you give to them? Should regard for public safety and the law ever outweigh doctor-patient confidentiality? Explain.

---

*"Ethics Roundtable Debate: Is a Physician-Patient Confidentiality Relationship Subservient to the Greater Good?" ccforum. com, 25 April 2005, http://ccforum.com/content/9/3/233 (15 November 2007).

FURTHER READING

Tom L. Beauchamp and James F. Childress, *Principles of Biomedical Ethics*, 6th ed. (New York: Oxford University Press, 2009), 288–98.

FindLaw, "Breaches of Doctor-Patient Confidentiality," http://injury.findlaw.com/medical-malpractice/breaches-of-doctor-patient-confidentiality.html, 2015 (21 October 2015).

Jessica Wilen Berg, "Patient Confidentiality: Privacy and Public Health," *The Doctor Will See You Now*, http://www.thedoctorwillseeyounow.com/content/bioethics/art3401.html, 17 August 2011 (21 October 2015).

Benjamin Freedman, "Offering Truth: One Ethical Approach to the Uninformed Cancer Patient," *Archives of Internal Medicine* 153 (8 March 1993), 572–76.

Raanan Gillon, "Telling the Truth, Confidentiality, Consent, and Respect for Autonomy," in *Bioethics* (Oxford: Oxford University Press, 2001), 507–28.

Roger Higgs, "On Telling Patients the Truth," in *Moral Dilemmas in Modern Medicine,* ed. Michael Lockwood (New York: Oxford University Press, 1985), 187–91, 193–202.

Charles C. Lund, "The Doctor, the Patient, and the Truth," *Annals of Internal Medicine* 24 (1946), 955–59.

Daniel K. Sokol, "Truth-Telling in the Doctor–Patient Relationship: A Case Analysis," *Medical Ethicist*, 2006, http://medicalethicist.net/documents/Case-analysistruthtelling.pdf (21 October 2015).

NOTES

1. Joseph Collins, "Should Doctors Tell the Truth?," *Harper's Monthly Magazine* 155 (1927), 320–26.

2. This scenario was inspired by one discussed in Susan Cullen and Margaret Klein, "Respect for Patients, Physicians, and the Truth," in Ronald Munson, *Intervention and Reflection* (Belmont, CA: Wadsworth/Thomson Learning, 2004), 157–58.

3. Roger Higgs, "On Telling Patients the Truth," in *Moral Dilemmas in Modern Medicine,* ed. Michael Lockwood (New York: Oxford University Press, 1985), 187–91, 193–202.

4. *Ibid.,* 201.

5. Benjamin Freedman, "Offering the Truth: One Ethical Approach to the Uninformed Cancer Patient," *Archives of Internal Medicine* 153 (8 March 1993), 572–76.

6. Cullen and Klein, "Respect for Patients," 161.

7. Leonard Fleck and Marcia Angell (commentators), "Please Don't Tell: A Case About HIV and Confidentiality," *Hastings Center Report* 21 (Nov.–Dec. 1991), 39–40.

READINGS

Telling the Truth to Patients: A Clinical Ethics Exploration

DAVID C. THOMASMA

According to Thomasma, truth-telling is important because it is "a right, a utility, and a kindness," but it can be trumped by more important values. "[T]ruth is a secondary good," he says. "Although important, other primary values take precedence over the truth. The most important of these values is survival of the individual and the community. A close second would be preservation of the relationship itself."

In this essay I will examine why the truth is so important to human communication in general, the types of truth, and why truth is only a relative value. After those introductory points, I will sketch the ways in which the truth is overridden or trumped by other concerns in the clinical setting. I will then discuss cases that fall into five distinct categories. The conclusion emphasizes the importance of truth telling and its primacy among secondary goods in the healthcare professional-patient relationship.

Reasons for Telling the Truth

...In all human relationships, the truth is told for a myriad of reasons. A summary of the prominent reasons are that it is a right, a utility, and a kindness.

It is a right to be told the truth because respect for the person demands it. As Kant argued, human society would soon collapse without truth telling, because it is the basis of interpersonal trust, covenants, contracts, and promises.

The truth is a utility as well, because persons need to make informed judgments about their actions. It is a mark of maturity that individuals advance and grow morally by becoming more and more self-aware of their needs, their motives, and their limitations. All these steps toward maturity require honest and forthright communication, first

From *Cambridge Quarterly of Healthcare Ethics*, vol. 3, no. 3 (1994), pp. 372–82. Copyright © 1994 Cambridge University Press. Reprinted with permission of Cambridge University Press.

from parents and later also from siblings, friends, lovers, spouses, children, colleagues, co-workers, and caregivers.[1]

Finally, it is a kindness to be told the truth, a kindness rooted in virtue precisely because persons to whom lies are told will of necessity withdraw from important, sometimes life-sustaining and life-saving relationships. Similarly, those who tell lies poison not only their relationships but themselves, rendering themselves incapable of virtue and moral growth.[2]...When we stop and think of it, there are times when, at least for the moment, protecting us from the truth can save our egos, our self-respect, and even our most cherished values. Not all of us act rationally and autonomously at all times. Sometimes we are under sufficient stress that others must act to protect us from harm. This is called necessary paternalism. Should we become seriously ill, others must step in and rescue us if we are incapable of doing it ourselves....

In General Relationships

In each of the three main reasons why the truth must be told, as a right, a utility, and a kindness, lurk values that may from time to time become more important than the truth. When this occurs, the rule of truth telling is trumped, that is, overridden by a temporarily more important principle. The ultimate value in all instances is the survival of the community and/or the well-being of the individual. Does this mean for paternalistic reasons, without the person's consent, the right to the truth, the utility, and the kindness, can be shunted aside? The answer is "yes." The truth in a relationship responds to a multivariate complexity of values, the context for which helps determine which values in that relationship should predominate.

Nothing I have said thus far suggests that the truth may be treated in a cavalier fashion or that it can be withheld from those who deserve it for frivolous reasons. The only values that can trump the truth are recipient survival, community survival, and the ability to absorb the full impact of the truth at a particular time. All these are only temporary trump cards in any event. They only can be played under certain limited conditions because respect for persons is a foundational value in all relationships.

In Healthcare Relationships

It is time to look more carefully at one particular form of human relationship, the relationship between the doctor and the patient or sometimes between other healthcare providers and the patient.

Early in the 1960s, studies were done that revealed the majority of physicians would not disclose a diagnosis of cancer to a patient. Reasons cited were mostly those that derived from nonmaleficence. Physicians were concerned that such a diagnosis might disturb the equanimity of a patient and might lead to desperate acts. Primarily physicians did not want to destroy their patients' hope. By the middle 1970s, however, repeat studies brought to light a radical shift in physician attitudes. Unlike earlier views, physicians now emphasized patient autonomy and informed consent over paternalism. In the doctor-patient relation, this meant the majority of physicians stressed the patient's right to full disclosure of diagnosis and prognosis.

One might be tempted to ascribe this shift of attitudes to the growing patients' rights and autonomy movements in the philosophy of medicine and in public affairs. No doubt some of the change can be attributed to this movement. But also treatment interventions for cancer led to greater optimism about modalities that could offer some hope to patients. Thus, to offer them full disclosure of their diagnosis no longer was equivalent to a death sentence. Former powerlessness of the healer was supplanted with technological and pharmaceutical potentialities.

A more philosophical analysis of the reasons for a shift comes from a consideration of the goal of medicine. The goal of all healthcare relations is to receive/provide help for an illness such that no further harm is done to the patient, especially in that patient's vulnerable state.[3] The vulnerability arises because of increased dependency. Presumably, the doctor will not take advantage of this vulnerable condition by adding to it through inappropriate use of power or the lack of compassion. Instead, the vulnerable person should be assisted back to a state of human equality, if possible, free from the prior dependency.[4]

First, the goal of the healthcare giver–patient relation is essentially to restore the patient's autonomy. Thus, respect for the right of the patient to the truth is measured against this goal. If nothing toward that goal can be gained by telling the truth at a particular time, still it must be told for other reasons. Yet, if the truth would impair the restoration of autonomy, then it may be withheld on grounds of potential harm. Thus the goal of the healing relationship enters into the calculus of values that are to be protected.

Second, most healthcare relationships of an interventionist character are temporary, whereas relationships involving primary care, prevention, and chronic or dying care are more permanent. These differences also have a bearing on truth telling. During a short encounter with healthcare strangers, patients and healthcare providers will of necessity require the truth more readily than during a long-term relation among near friends. In the short term, decisions, often dramatically important ones, need to be made in a compressed period. There is less opportunity to maneuver or delay for other reasons, even if there are concerns about the truth's impact on the person.

Over a longer period, the truth may be withheld for compassionate reasons more readily. Here, the patient and physician or nurse know one another. They are more likely to have shared some of their values. In this context, it is more justifiable to withhold the truth temporarily in favor of more important long-term values, which are known in the relationship.

Finally, the goal of healthcare relations is treatment of an illness. An illness is far broader than its subset, disease. Illness can be viewed as a disturbance in the life of an individual, perhaps due to many nonmedical factors. A disease, by contrast, is a medically caused event that may respond to more interventionist strategies.[5]

Helping one through an illness is a far greater personal task than doing so for a disease. A greater, more enduring bond is formed. The strength of this bond may justify withholding the truth as well, although in the end "the truth will always out."

Clinical Case Categories

The general principles about truth telling have been reviewed, as well as possible modifications formed from the particularities of the healthcare professional–patient relationship. Now I turn to some contemporary examples of how clinical ethics might analyze the hierarchy of values surrounding truth telling.

There are at least five clinical case categories in which truth telling becomes problematic: intervention cases, long-term care cases, cases of dying patients, prevention cases, and nonintervention cases.

Intervention Cases

Of all clinically difficult times to tell the truth, two typical cases stand out. The first usually involves a mother of advanced age with cancer. The family might beg the surgeon not to tell her what has been discovered for fear that "Mom might just go off the deep end." The movie *Dad*, starring Jack Lemmon, had as its centerpiece the notion that Dad could not tolerate the idea of cancer. Once told, he went into a psychotic shock that ruptured standard relationships with the doctors, the hospital, and the family. However, because this diagnosis requires patient participation for chemotherapeutic interventions and the time is short, the truth must be faced directly. Only if there is not to be intervention might one withhold the truth from the patient for a while, at the family's request, until the patient is able to cope with the reality. A contract about the time allowed before telling the truth might be a good idea.

The second case is that of ambiguous genitalia. A woman, 19 years old, comes for a checkup because she plans to get married and has not yet had a period. She is very mildly retarded. It turns out that she has no vagina, uterus, or ovaries but does have an undescended testicle in her abdomen.

She is actually a he. Should she be told this fundamental truth about herself? Those who argue for the truth do so on grounds that she will eventually find out, and more of her subsequent life will have been ruined by the lies and disingenuousness of others. Those who argue against the truth usually prevail. National standards exist in this regard. The young woman is told that she has something like a "gonadal mass" in her abdomen that might turn into cancer if not removed, and an operation is performed. She is assisted to remain a female.

More complicated still is a case of a young Hispanic woman, a trauma accident victim, who is gradually coming out of a coma. She responds only to commands such as "move your toes." Because she is now incompetent, her mother and father are making all care decisions in her case. Her boyfriend is a welcome addition to the large, extended family. However, the physicians discover that she is pregnant. The fetus is about 5 weeks old. Eventually, if she does not recover, her surrogate decision makers will have to be told about the pregnancy, because they will be involved in the terrible decisions about continuing the life of the fetus even if it is a risk to the mother's recovery from the coma. This revelation will almost certainly disrupt current family relationships and the role of the boyfriend. Further, if the mother is incompetent to decide, should not the boyfriend, as presumed father, have a say in the decision about his own child?

In this case, revelation of the truth must be carefully managed. The pregnancy should be revealed only on a "need to know" basis, that is, only when the survival of the young woman becomes critical. She is still progressing moderately towards a stable state.

Long-Term Cases

Rehabilitation medicine provides one problem of truth telling in this category. If a young man has been paralyzed by a football accident, his recovery to some level of function will depend upon holding out hope. As he struggles to strengthen himself, the motivation might be a hope that caregivers know to be false, that he may someday be able to walk again. Yet this falsehood is not corrected, lest he slip into despair. Hence, because this is a long-term relationship, the truth will be gradually discovered by the patient under the aegis of encouragement by his physical therapists, nurses, and physicians, who enter his life as near friends.

Cases of Dying Patients

Sometimes, during the dying process, the patient asks directly, "Doctor, am I dying?" Physicians are frequently reluctant to "play God" and tell the patient how many days or months or years they have left. This reluctance sometimes bleeds over into a less-than-forthright answer to the question just asked. A surgeon with whom I make rounds once answered this question posed by a terminally ill cancer patient by telling her that she did not have to worry about her insurance running out!

Yet in every case of dying patients, the truth can be gradually revealed such that the patient learns about dying even before the family or others who are resisting telling the truth. Sometimes, without directly saying "you are dying," we are able to use interpretative truth and comfort the patient. If a car driver who has been in an accident and is dying asks about other family members in the car who are already dead, there is no necessity to tell him the truth. Instead, he can be told that "they are being cared for" and that the important thing right now is that he be comfortable and not in pain. One avoids the awful truth because he may feel responsible and guilt ridden during his own dying hours if he knew that the rest of his family were already dead.

Prevention Cases

A good example of problems associated with truth telling in preventive medicine might come from screening. The high prevalence of prostate cancer among men over 50 years old may suggest the utility of cancer screening. An annual checkup for men over 40 years old is recommended. Latent and asymptomatic prostate cancer is often clinically unsuspected and is present in approximately 30% of men over 50 years of age. If screening were to take place, about 16.5 million men in the United States alone would be diagnosed with prostate cancer, or about 2.4 million men each year. As of now, only 120,000 cases are newly diagnosed each year. Thus, as Timothy Moon noted in a recent sketch of the disease, "a majority of patients with prostate cancer

that is not clinically diagnosed will experience a benign course throughout their lifetime."[6]

The high incidence of prostate cancer coupled with a very low malignant potential would entail a whole host of problems if subjected to screening. Detection would force patients and physicians to make very difficult and life-altering treatment decisions. Among them are removal of the gland (with impotence a possible outcome), radiation treatment, and most effective of all, surgical removal of the gonads (orchiectomy). But why consider these rather violent interventions if the probable outcome of neglect will overwhelmingly be benign? For this reason the U.S. Preventive Services Task Force does not recommend either for or against screening for prostate cancer. Quality-of-life issues would take precedence over the need to know.

Nonintervention Cases

This last example more closely approximates the kind of information one might receive as a result of gene mapping. This information could tell you of the likelihood or probability of encountering a number of diseases through genetic heritage, for example, adult onset or type II diabetes, but could not offer major interventions for most of them (unlike a probability for diabetes).

Some evidence exists from recent studies that the principle of truth telling now predominates in the doctor–patient relationship. Doctors were asked about revealing diagnosis for Huntington's disease and multiple sclerosis, neither of which is subject to a cure at present. An overwhelming majority would consider full disclosure. This means that, even in the face of diseases for which we have no cure, truth telling seems to take precedence over protecting the patient from imagined harms.

The question of full disclosure acquires greater poignancy in today's medicine, especially with respect to Alzheimer's disease and genetic disorders that may be diagnosed in utero. There are times when our own scientific endeavors lack a sufficient conceptual and cultural framework around which to assemble facts. The facts can overwhelm us without such conceptual frameworks. The future of genetics poses just such a problem. In consideration of the new genetics, this might be the time to stress values over the truth.

Conclusion

Truth in the clinical relationship is factored in with knowledge and values.

First, truth is contextual. Its revelation depends upon the nature of the relationship between the doctor and patient and the duration of that relationship.

Second, truth is a secondary good. Although important, other primary values take precedence over the truth. The most important of these values is survival of the individual and the community. A close second would be preservation of the relationship itself.

Third, truth is essential for healing an illness. It may not be as important for curing a disease. That is why, for example, we might withhold the truth from the woman with ambiguous genitalia, curing her disease (having a gonad) in favor of maintaining her health (being a woman).

Fourth, withholding the truth is only a temporary measure. *In vino, veritas* it is said. The truth will eventually come out, even if in a slip of the tongue.

Its revelation, if it is to be controlled, must always aim at the good of the patient for the moment.

At all times, the default mode should be that the truth is told. If, for some important reason, it is not to be immediately revealed in a particular case, a truth-management protocol should be instituted so that all caregivers on the team understand how the truth will eventually be revealed.

NOTES

1. Bok S. *Lying: Moral Choice in Public and Personal Life.* New York: Vintage Books, 1989.
2. Pellegrino E. D., Thomasma D. C. *The Virtues in Medical Practice.* New York: Oxford University Press, 1993.
3. Cassell E. The nature of suffering and the goals of medicine. *New England Journal of Medicine* 1982; 306(11):639–45.
4. See Nordenfelt L., issue editor. Concepts of health and their consequences for health care. *Theoretical Medicine* 1993; 14(4).
5. Moon T. D. Prostate cancer. *Journal of the American Geriatrics Society* 1992; 40:622–7 (quote from 626).
6. See note 5. Moon. 1992; 40:622–7.

On Telling Patients the Truth

MACK LIPKIN

Lipkin urges a decidedly paternalistic attitude toward truth-telling. He argues that because the stress of being sick can distort patients' thinking and because they lack understanding of medical concepts, it is usually impossible to convey to patients the full medical truth. Many times, telling the whole truth can do more harm than good. Moreover, many patients prefer not to know the full details about their condition. "Often enough," Lipkin says, "the ethics of the situation, the true moral responsibility, may demand that the naked facts not be revealed." The critical question is not whether deception occurs, but whether the deception is meant to benefit the patient or the physician.

Should a doctor always tell his patients the truth? In recent years there has been an extraordinary increase in public discussion of the ethical problems involved in this question. But little has been heard from physicians themselves. I believe that gaps in understanding the complex interactions between

From *Newsweek*, 4 June 1979, p. 13. Reprinted with permission.

doctors and patients have led many laymen astray in this debate.

It is easy to make an attractive case for always telling patients the truth. But as L. J. Henderson, the great Harvard physiologist-philosopher of decades ago, commented:

> To speak of telling the truth, the whole truth and nothing but the truth to a patient is absurd. Like absurdity in mathematics, it is absurd simply

because it is impossible.... The notion that the truth, the whole truth, and nothing but the truth can be conveyed to the patient is a good specimen of that class of fallacies called by Whitehead "the fallacy of misplaced concreteness." It results from neglecting factors that cannot be excluded from the concrete situation and that are of an order of magnitude and relevancy that make it imperative to consider them. Of course, another fallacy is also often involved, the belief that diagnosis and prognosis are more certain than they are. But that is another question.

Words, especially medical terms, inevitably carry different implications for different people. When these words are said in the presence of anxiety-laden illness, there is a strong tendency to hear selectively and with emphases not intended by the doctor. Thus, what the doctors means to convey is obscured.

Indeed, thoughtful physicians know that transmittal of accurate information to patients is often impossible. Patients rarely know how the body functions in health and disease, but instead have inaccurate ideas of what is going on; this hampers the attempts to "tell the truth."

Take cancer, for example. Patients seldom know that while some cancers are rapidly fatal, others never amount to much; some have a cure rate of 99 percent, others less than 1 percent; a cancer may grow rapidly for months and then stop growing for years; may remain localized for years or spread all over the body almost from the beginning; some can be arrested for long periods of time, others not. Thus, one patient thinks of cancer as curable, the next thinks it means certain death.

How many patients understand that "heart trouble" may refer to literally hundreds of different abnormalities ranging in severity from the trivial to the instantly fatal? How many know that the term "arthritis" may refer to dozens of different types of joint involvement? "Arthritis" may raise a vision of the appalling disease that made Aunt Eulalee a helpless invalid until her death years later; the next patient remembers Grandpa grumbling about the damned arthritis as he got up from his chair. Unfortunately but understandably, most people's ideas about the implications of medical terms are based on what they have heard about a few cases.

The news of serious illness drives some patients to irrational and destructive behavior; others handle it sensibly. A distinguished philosopher forestalled my telling him about his cancer by saying, "I want to know the truth. The only thing I couldn't take and wouldn't want to know about is cancer." For two years he had watched his mother die slowly of a painful form of cancer. Several of my physician patients have indicated they would not want to know if they had a fatal illness.

Most patients should be told "the truth" to the extent that they can comprehend it. Indeed, most doctors, like most other people, are uncomfortable with lies. Good physicians, aware that some may be badly damaged by being told more than they want or need to know, can usually ascertain the patient's preference and needs.

Discussions about lying often center about the use of placebos. In medical usage, a "placebo" is a treatment that has no specific physical or chemical action on the condition being treated, but is given to affect symptoms by a psychologic mechanism, rather than a purely physical one. Ethicists believe that placebos necessarily involve a partial or complete deception by the doctor, since the patient is allowed to believe that the treatment has a specific effect. They seem unaware that placebos, far from being inert (except in the rigid pharmacological sense), are among the most powerful agents known to medicine.

Placebos are a form of suggestion, which is a direct or indirect presentation of an idea, followed by an uncritical, i.e., not thought-out, acceptance. Those who have studied suggestion or looked at medical history know its almost unbelievable potency; it is involved to a greater or lesser extent in the treatment of every conscious patient. It can induce or remove almost any kind of feeling or thought. It can strengthen the weak or paralyze the strong; transform sleeping, feeding, or sexual patterns; remove or induce a vast array of symptoms; mimic or abolish the effect of very powerful drugs. It can alter the function of most organs. It can cause illness or a great sense of well-being. It can kill. In fact, doctors often add a measure of suggestion when they prescribe even potent medications for those who also need psychologic support. Like all potent agents, its proper use requires judgment based on experience and skill.

Communication between physician and the apprehensive and often confused patient is delicate and uncertain. Honesty should be evaluated not only in terms of a slavish devotion to language often misinterpreted by the patient, but also in terms of intent. *The crucial question is whether the deception was intended to benefit the patient or the doctor.*

Physicians, like most people, hope to see good results and are disappointed when patients do poorly. Their reputations and their livelihood depend on doing effective work; purely selfish reasons would dictate they do their best for their patients. Most important, all good physicians have a deep sense of responsibility toward those who have entrusted their welfare to them.

As I have explained, it is usually a practical impossibility to tell patients "the whole truth." Moreover, often enough, the ethics of the situation, the true moral responsibility, may demand that the naked facts not be revealed. The now popular complaint that doctors are too authoritarian is misguided more often than not. Some patients who insist on exercising their right to know may be doing themselves a disservice.

Judgment is often difficult and uncertain. Simplistic assertions about telling the truth may not be helpful to patients or physicians in times of trouble.

Is It Ever OK to Lie to Patients?

SHELLY K. SCHWARTZ

In this essay, Shelly Schwartz explores the issue of truth-telling as it relates to physicians' responsibilities, discussing legal, moral, and emotional aspects.

Here's What You Need to Know About the Legal and Ethical Ramifications of Withholding Information from Patients

If there's one thing sacred in the doctor-patient relationship, it's trust. Open and honest dialogue on both sides of the exam table is by all accounts critical to effective care. Patients have to be truthful to ensure diagnostic accuracy and an appropriate treatment plan, while doctors need to provide full disclosure about their patient's health—the good and the bad—to help patients make informed decisions. Indeed, patient autonomy is the cornerstone of modern medicine and patient-centered care.

That patients are entitled to the truth, then, is a given, but just how much doctors are obligated to reveal is in fact a matter of much debate—particularly as it relates to the sick and dying. Physicians are often

From Shelly K. Schwartz, *Physicians Practice*, October 21, 2010, 1–3 (October 28, 2015).

forced to balance compassion with the patient's right to know. There are patients, for example, who are too emotionally frail to be told about the progressive symptoms of their disease. There are accident victims who are alert enough to learn of a loved one's death—but whose relatives ask that the news be delivered later by a family member. There are elderly patients with dementia who would be mercilessly forced to relive the loss of a spouse on a daily basis. There are adult children who demand that you spare their elderly parent from a grim diagnosis. And there are patients whose cultural beliefs differ greatly on the topic of medical disclosure. Such scenarios beg the question: Is it ever appropriate to spin the truth or withhold information from a patient? Is it ever OK to lie?

"There are rarely cut and dry ethical issues because you've got competing interests," says Nancy Berlinger, a research scholar who specializes in end-of-life healthcare ethics at The Hastings Center, an independent bioethics research institute in Garrison, New York. "It's very complex. No one in medicine gets up in the morning and says, 'I'm going to lie to people today.' It's more about saying, 'How do I balance my obligation to be truthful with my desire to be compassionate and how does that work, really, in practice?'"

The Law

Informed consent wasn't always the mantra. Thirty years ago, cancer patients in the United States were frequently misled about the extent of their illness. "I remember being in medical school years ago and being distinctly told that when a person has lung cancer, never tell them they have lung cancer," says Peter Dixon, a former oncologist and current primary-care doctor with a geriatric group in Essex, Connecticut. "We were told to give them a dose of morphine and wash our hands of it. Things have certainly changed." Today, doctors are expected to treat patients as partners, delivering a complete picture of their prognosis and treatment options so patients can take an active role in their own healthcare.

Aside from the ethical mandate of truth telling in the modern age of medicine, physicians in most states are also legally obligated to disclose all relevant health information to patients. At least one exception, however, exists. Earlier this year, the Oklahoma legislature passed a law that prevents women who give birth to a disabled child from suing a doctor who misled them or outright lied about the health of their baby while they were pregnant—including cases where the fetus had a fatal anomaly that would not allow it to live outside the womb. Bill sponsors say the law is designed to prevent lawsuits by women who wish, later on, that their doctor had counseled them to abort. But opponents say it protects physicians who mislead pregnant women on purpose, to prevent them from having an abortion.

Sean F. X. Dugan, a medical malpractice defense trial lawyer and senior partner with Martin Clearwater & Bell LLP in New York, says he's also starting to see some "cracks in the citadel" over which parties physicians are obligated to be truthful to. "The law clearly indicates that the physician's fiduciary obligation runs to her patient—period," says Dugan, "But over my 30 years in practice, I've seen that iron-bound rule start to crack." In recent years, he notes, several lawsuits have been passed up through the courts in which a physician informed

the spouse of a patient who was diagnosed with a life-threatening sexually transmitted disease. "Once, that would have been summarily dismissed, but now we as a society are beginning to dip our toe in the water," says Dugan. "Some courts are now beginning to say that maybe, under those circumstances, the doctor should go beyond the physician-patient relationship, and that they have a duty to disclose information to another party if they know someone is in danger." Where to draw that line is the trick. Consider patients with a contagious and deadly disease who live with someone they are not married to, or with young kids.

A Case for Compassion?

While outright lying to patients is rare, many physicians (particularly oncologists) say that at some point in their career they have failed to answer questions directly, given incomplete information about the burden or benefit of treatment, and otherwise avoided "imminent death" discussions with patients suffering from an advanced disease, says Thomas J. Smith, professor of internal medicine, hematology/oncology at Virginia Commonwealth University and cofounder of the Thomas Palliative Care Unit at VCU Massey Cancer Center in Richmond, Virginia. Just 37 percent of terminally ill patients, he notes, have explicit conversations with their doctors about the fact that they are going to die from their disease.

The most common argument against obligatory truth telling is the impact it may have on a patient's physical or emotional state. Healthcare providers in other parts of the world, like central Asia and the former Soviet Union, still censor information from cancer patients on the grounds that it causes depression and an earlier death. "None of that is true," says Smith, whose study earlier this year found that giving honest information to patients with terminal cancer did not rob them of hope. "Most patients, certainly in the Western world, want to know what they have, what their options are, and what's going to happen to them."

Above all else, Smith notes, patients want assurances that their doctors and nurses won't abandon them when their treatment options run dry. "When there's nothing left to be done to make the cancer go away, there are still lots of things to be done to help that person adapt to their new reality and maximize the time they have left," he says, noting the benefits of knowing the gravity of their condition far outweigh [the benefits of] sparing patients from any anxiety. Disclosure enables patients to plan—to create a will and living will, make their wishes known to family members, pass along what they've learned to loved ones, name a durable power of medical attorney, decide where they want to spend the rest of their life, and make spiritual and family member amends. "You get the chance to do what some people call a life review," says Smith.

Indeed, most studies over the last decade found that patients who were told candidly they are going to die lived just as long, had better medical care, spent less time in the hospital, and had fewer "bad deaths"—those whose lives ended in the ICU, ER, or with CPR—than those who were not. A 2008 study of 332 terminally ill patients and their caregivers by researchers at the Dana-Farber Cancer Institute also found that patients who had end-of-life discussions were not more depressed, worried, or sad than those who did not. Instead they were far more likely to accept their illness and preferred comfort care over aggressive life-extending therapies, which often create upsetting side effects and hamper communication with loved ones. Interestingly, these results of full disclosure also had a "cascading effect" on the patients' loved one's ability to cope with their loss. Individuals whose loved ones died in an ICU were more likely to develop a major depressive disorder than those whose loved ones did not receive such intensive care.

What's Your Motive?

Another reason doctors give for creating a less painful truth is that a full discussion takes too much time, the same reason doctors cite for their reluctance to initiate DNR discussions, says Smith. "It does take more time to say, 'Let's talk about your illness and how you're coping with it,' than it does to say, 'Well, the next chemo we're going to try is XYZ,' because if you start talking about the fact that treatment has a marginal if any benefit and that person is going to die sooner rather than later it takes a lot longer," he says. "A good doctor will sit and listen to the answers and that takes time."

And then, of course, there's the simple fact that it's tough. "The real reason doctors avoid having these discussions is that it's just really hard to look another person in the eye and tell them that there's nothing more that can be done to make them live longer or give them a miraculous chance of a cure," says Smith. "Anyone who says, 'Oh, that's just part of your job,' probably hasn't done it very much."

It's All in the Delivery

Dixon says an important part of delivering difficult truths to your patients is learning how to read your patients' personalities. While all are entitled to the truth about their condition, some are satisfied with a broad picture of their illness and the options available. Some need a greater degree of detail and others need it all in small doses. Patients facing death also differ significantly in the type of medical care they wish to pursue. Some, particularly younger patients, will seek more aggressive treatment options, while others (primarily the elderly) just want your support with as little medical intervention as possible. "If you sense that you're going too fast, or that it seems too scary, you can say, 'Look, sometimes we talk awfully fast. Do you want to stop here and come back next week and talk more about this? We don't need to do it all right away.'"

Remember, too, that honesty and an emphasis on the positive are not mutually exclusive. "You need to focus on what's important about their condition, but there is an art to presenting things to people in different ways," says Dixon. "You can give bad news but put a positive spin on it. When patients come to me with a spot on their liver from an X-ray, their primary-care doctor has already told them they have cancer. When they see me, I can say, well, 98 percent of your liver looks great."

When faced with family members who wish to shield their aging parents or grandparents from a poor prognosis, Dixon says he simply levels with them. "I don't think that's fair to the person who is sick," he says. "I express my opinion, that I'm not comfortable with hiding things. You don't have to go into explicit detail [about their fragile state] and you can be more general, but I tell them to put themselves in the patient's shoes and think about what they would want."

Though doctors in private practice rarely encounter such scenarios, physicians who work in a hospital setting may also be asked by the friends or family of an [auto] accident victim to delay information about another passenger's death until a parent can break the news. In those cases, says Berlinger, it's a judgment call. "It would have to be clear how long we're talking about—an hour or four days, because if it was several days that might be tantamount to deception," she says, noting this is a case where a hospital ethics consult can assist. "It's about the information, but it's also about providing support to a person who is getting bad news. It's a very stressful situation and they need to feel continuity of care—that someone, like a nurse, their doctor, a chaplain, or a family member, is sticking with them and attending to their emotional needs."

Whatever your motivation for being less than truthful with patients, Berlinger says, there is really never good cause to keep patients in the dark. "If a doctor is considering withholding information, the first thing they have to ask themselves is why would I do this—given my obligation to disclose information to my patients and their right to information about their own health?" she says.

For most patients, full disclosure about their condition takes fear off the table. "One of the problems is that physicians don't level with people and discuss openly what happens next and what to expect—what you're going to feel like," says Dixon. "When people are prepared they're not afraid anymore."

In Summary

Treating patients is a complex business. Sometimes you have to have tough conversations with patients about their diagnoses. Is it ever appropriate to spin the truth or withhold information from a patient? Consider the following:

- In most states physicians are legally obligated to disclose all relevant health information to patients.
- Is it more compassionate to patients to withhold upsetting details about life-threatening diseases or to give them the comfort of knowing the truth and making their own decisions about the end of their lives?
- Physicians should examine their motive for withholding information: Is it compassion, fear of the time it takes to have more involved discussions, avoidance because it's hard to deliver such news, or something else?

Respect for Patients, Physicians, and the Truth

SUSAN CULLEN AND MARGARET KLEIN

Cullen and Klein argue that deception to benefit patients is wrong because it disrespects them by restricting their freedom to make choices about their own lives. But if a patient explicitly states that she does not want to know the facts about her condition, generally physicians should respect her wishes. Those who claim that it's not possible to tell patients the truth are confusing the "whole truth" with the "wholly true." Patients cannot and need not understand the whole truth—that is, all the medical details of a disease process. But they can understand enough to appreciate the nature and seriousness of the disease and the benefits and risks of treatments. Cullen and Klein concede that in rare cases, it is permissible for doctors to deceive a patient—but only if the deception is for a short while and if the potential gain from the deception is probable and significant. By this criterion, a brief deception to save the patient's life may be justified.

A long tradition in medicine holds that because medicine aims to promote the health of patients, it is permissible for a physician to deceive a patient if the deception would contribute to that end. "The crucial question," as one writer observes, "is whether the deception is intended to benefit the patient."[1]

Thus, according to this view, if Dr. Allison tells Mr. Barton he is making a good recovery from a kidney transplant, when in fact the transplanted kidney is not functioning well and his recovery is slower than expected, Dr. Allison's action is justified on the grounds that she is trying to keep up her patient's spirits and encouraging him to fight to regain his health. A sick person isn't made better by gloomy assessments.

This deception-to-benefit-the-patient (DBP) view has a prima facie appeal. At the least it is motivated by the physician's effort to do something to help the patient. Were a physician to tell a healthy patient he had a vitamin deficiency so she could sell him vitamin supplements or recommend unneeded surgery so she could collect a fee for performing it, we would condemn such actions outright. The physician is practicing deception in such cases to benefit herself, not the patient.

We all realize that a physician wouldn't be justified in engaging in just any form of action to benefit her patients. We reject as morally grotesque, for example, the notion that a surgeon should remove the vital organs from a healthy person and use them to save the lives of four others. Having the aim of benefiting a patient does not license using any means whatsoever. Rather, the physician must use means that are morally acceptable. While deceiving a patient for his own good is very different from killing an innocent person to provide the patient a benefit, we will argue that such deception is nonetheless wrong. In all but the rarest cases, deceiving a patient "for his own good" is an unacceptable way for a physician to try to help her patient.

Respect for Persons

While the DBP view seems unobjectionable at first sight, it is wrong for the same reason it is wrong for

From Ronald Munson, *Intervention and Reflection: Basic Issues in Medical Ethics*, 8th edition. Wadsworth Publishing Company: Belmont, CA, 2008. Used with permission.

a physician to tell a healthy patient he needs vitamins so she can benefit from selling them to him. Such behavior is wrong (in both cases), because it doesn't treat a human being with respect.

Humans are, at the very least, rational beings. We have the capacity to guide our actions on the basis of deliberation, rather than being moved only by instinct or psychological conditioning. Our ability to reason makes all of us worth more than a tree, a dog, or maybe anything else in the natural world.[2]

If we are each special because of our ability to make choices, then others should not destroy this ability or interfere with our exercise of it. All of us have an equal right to choose how to lead our lives, and others have a responsibility to respect that right. (Working out arrangements allowing each person maximum freedom while also guaranteeing the freedom of others is a major task of social and political philosophy.) Treating humans with respect means recognizing their autonomy by allowing them the freedom to make choices about their lives. By contrast, to disrespect people means taking away their freedom to live as they choose.

Disrespect and the Physician's Good

If Dr. Mires, a gynecological surgeon, tells Ms. Sligh she needs a hysterectomy, when in fact the medical indications are insufficient to justify the surgery and he is recommending it only for the money he will receive for the operation, Dr. Mires is treating Ms. Sligh with disrespect. By lying to Ms. Sligh, Dr. Mires is damaging her autonomy. She is put in the position of having to make a decision on the basis of the false information Dr. Mires provides to her. Hence, the option of deciding to do what is most likely to contribute to protecting and promoting her health is closed off to her. She can only *believe* she is making that decision, for Dr. Mires has forced her to deliberate on the basis of a false assumption.

When knowledge is power, ignorance is slavery. When Dr. Mires deliberately misinforms Ms. Sligh, he cripples her ability to carry out any plans she might have. It doesn't matter if she decides she doesn't want to have a hysterectomy and so avoids the risks, pain, and expense of surgery. Not only has she been made to worry needlessly and perhaps agonize over her decision, Dr. Mires' deception has put her in a false position with respect to making decisions about her life. Unknown to her, he has restricted her freedom to make meaningful choices. He has discounted her ability to reason and make decisions, and in this way, he has treated her with disrespect.

Disrespect and the Patient's Good

The most serious cases in which physicians have traditionally considered themselves justified (and perhaps even obligated) to deceive a patient are ones in which the patient is dying and the disease can no longer be treated effectively.[3] In the past, the question was most often one of whether to tell a patient he had cancer. Now that cancer treatments have become more effective, the question has usually become one of whether to tell a patient a treatment is not likely to be effective in extending his life. The central issue remains the same, because the physician must still decide whether to deceive the patient.

Consider the following case. Susan Cruz, a thirty-four-year-old single mother of a six-year-old boy, suffered for more than two months from excruciating headaches that were often accompanied by vomiting and dizziness. Yet it wasn't until after she lost control of the left side of her body and collapsed in the bathroom in what she thought of as a fit that she went to see her HMO doctor. He immediately referred her to Dr. Charles Lambert, a neurologist, who, after a detailed examination, ordered an MRI of her brain. Susan had two seizures in the hospital, right after the scan. She was admitted, and the MRI was followed by a brain biopsy performed by Dr. Clare Williams, a neurosurgeon.

The results of the tests showed Susan had an aggressive form of malignant brain cancer affecting the glial cells. The cancer was so extensive Dr. Williams advised Dr. Lambert that not only was a surgical cure out of the question, surgery to reduce the amount of cancerous tissue would not be worth the risk of additional brain damage. Radiation treatments might shrink some of the tumor, but Susan's disease was so far advanced they would have little effect on the outcome.

After reviewing all the information in Susan's case, Dr. Lambert concluded it was not likely that whatever was done would extend Susan's life to an appreciable extent. Most likely, she would be dead

within a few weeks, a month or two at the most. But should he tell her this? Wouldn't it be better to allow her to spend her last days free of the dread and anxiety that knowledge of the imminence of her death was sure to cause her? She and her son, Bryan, could share some time together free from the worst kind of worry. She could do nothing to prevent her death, so shouldn't he leave her feeling hopeful about the future? After all, he couldn't *know* she would die in a few weeks.

"You have a disease of the supporting cells in the brain," Dr. Lambert told Susan. "That's the reason for the headaches, dizziness, vomiting, muscular weakness, and seizures."

"Is there a treatment?" Susan asked. "Will I have to have brain surgery?"

"Not for your stage of the disease," Dr. Lambert said. To avoid explaining why, he quickly added, "Radiation therapy is the best treatment we can offer, because X-rays will help kill off the abnormal tissue putting pressure on your brain."

"Will that make the headaches and all the rest go away?"

"It will help," Dr. Lambert said. "But we have medications that will help also. I can give you steroids to reduce the brain swelling and an anticonvulsant to control your seizures. I can also treat the headaches with effective drugs."

"When do my treatments start?"

"I'll prescribe some drugs today and set you up with the therapeutic radiologists," Dr. Lambert said. "I imagine they can start your treatments in a day or so."

"Great," Susan said. "I've got to get well so I can take care of Bryan. He's staying with my mom, and she's got a heart problem. A six-year-old boy can be a real handful."

Susan followed the treatment plan outlined by Dr. Lambert. She took the drugs prescribed and, with the help of her friend Mandy, showed up at the hospital for her radiation treatments for four weeks. She missed the fifth treatment, because she began having uncontrollable seizures and was taken to the hospital. She died the day after her admission.

Dr. Lambert never told Susan she had brain cancer, nor that the reason surgery wasn't appropriate was that the disease was so far advanced it would be useless. He didn't tell her that, by his estimation, she had only a few weeks of life remaining. Dr. Lambert didn't lie to Susan, but he deceived her. What he told her about her medical condition was vague and limited. He didn't share with her information he possessed that was relevant to her condition. He chose his words so that she would believe she had a disease that might be either cured or controlled by the treatments he prescribed.

While Susan did not (we may suppose) press Dr. Lambert for more information than he provided or ask him questions about her illness, this does not mean Dr. Lambert was not engaged in deception.[4] Susan (like many people) may not have known enough about medicine or her own body to ask the right sort of questions, may have been so intimidated by doctors not to dare to ask questions, or may have been psychologically incapable of asking questions about her illness, preferring to leave everything in the hands of her physician. Dr. Lambert, at the least, should have found out from Susan how much she wanted to know. A willful ignorance is, after all, quite different from an enforced ignorance.

It was also disingenuous for Dr. Lambert to reason that because he cannot be *certain* Susan will die of her disease within a few weeks, he should withhold information from her. Uncertainty of that kind is an ineliminable part of medical practice, and Dr. Lambert has every reason to believe Susan has a relatively short time to live. Judges instructing juries in death penalty cases often distinguish between real doubt and philosophical doubt in explaining the meaning of "reasonable doubt." Dr. Lambert has no real doubt about Susan's fate, and she is entitled to his best medical judgment.

Dr. Lambert's deception of Susan Cruz, like Dr. Mires' deception of Ms. Sligh, is morally wrong. Dr. Lambert deceives Susan with the aim of doing something good for her, while Dr. Mires deceives Ms. Sligh with the aim of doing something good for himself. We might thus say that the deception practiced by Dr. Mires is morally worse than that practiced by Dr. Lambert. Even so, Dr. Lambert's deception of Susan Cruz is still wrong, because it treats her disrespectfully.

By failing to provide Susan with crucial information, Dr. Lambert violates Susan's right to shape what is left of her own life. He deceives her into believing that, with the treatments he prescribes, she can go back to living a normal life and might eventually become healthy again. Because this is not so, Susan is thus denied the opportunity to decide how to spend the final weeks of her life.

She is unable to do what she might prefer to do, if she knew she had a fatal disease and a relatively short time left to live. She might reestablish a connection with her ex-husband, complete the novel she was writing, or visit New York. Most important, she might arrange for someone to take care of her six-year-old son. Prevented by Dr. Lambert's deception from knowing she may soon die, Susan is barred from pursuing what she values most in the time she has remaining.

Respect for persons bars the deception of patients. When the deception is for the physician's benefit, the wrong is obvious. Yet even when the deception is intended to benefit the patient, the physician's good intention doesn't alter the fact that the deception violates the patient's autonomy.

Three Critical Questions

Three questions about physicians' telling the truth to their patients arise with sufficient frequency as to warrant their being addressed explicitly.

1. What if a Patient Doesn't Want to Know About His Disease or the State of His Health? Some writers have argued that many patients don't want to know what's wrong with them.[5] Although they may say they do, some don't mean it. Part of the physician's job is to assess how much information and what sort a patient can handle, then provide him with an appropriate amount and kind. Thus, a physician may decide that a man in his mid-thirties doesn't want to know he is showing the first symptoms of (say) Huntington's disease. Although the disease is invariably fatal and essentially untreatable, it is slow acting, and the patient may have another ten or fifteen years of more-or-less normal life before the worst symptoms of the disease manifest themselves. The physician may decide to spare the patient the anguish of living with the knowledge that he is eventually going to develop a fatal and particularly nasty disease. The patient, she judges, really wants her to protect him from the years of agony and uncertainty.

But with no more than her own assessment to guide her, in making judgments about what a patient wants to know, the physician is taking too much on herself. Huntington's disease is a genetic disorder that occurs when a parent passes on the HD gene to a child. Someone with one parent who has HD may already know he has a fifty-fifty chance of developing the disorder. He may want to know whether the problems he is experiencing are symptoms of the disease. If they are, he may choose to live his life in a way very different than he might if the problems are not symptoms. He might decide, for example, not to have a child and to avoid the risk of passing on the gene for the disease. Or if he and his partner decide to have a child, they might opt for artificial insemination and embryo screening to eliminate embryos carrying the HD gene. The physician is generally in no position to decide what information needs to be withheld from a patient. Full disclosure should be the default position for physicians.

The Patient Is Explicit. If a patient clearly and explicitly expresses the wish not to know the truth about his medical condition physicians should generally respect this desire. No disrespect is involved in not telling the truth (not providing information) to someone who decides he does not want to know it. The ignorance he imposes on himself may be necessary for him to go on with his life in the way he wishes.

Thus, someone may know himself well enough to realize that if he were diagnosed with inoperable cancer, he wouldn't be able to think about anything else, and the remainder of his life would be a misery of anxiety and fear. His physician should respect such a wish to remain ignorant, for it is as much an expression of autonomy as is the wish to be informed.

When a patient expresses the desire not to be informed about his medical condition, this does not justify his physician's *deceiving* him about his condition. The physician is warranted in withholding the truth from a patient who has asked to be kept ignorant, but the physician is not warranted in telling the patient nothing is wrong with him when there is or falsely assuring him he doesn't have metastatic prostate cancer.

Overriding Considerations? Cases in which patients do not wish to know about their medical condition may not be as rare as they once were. Some patients don't want to know if they are infected with HIV, for example, and request that they not be informed of test results that might show they are HIV-positive.

Such cases raise the question of whether the respect for persons that grounds the physician's obligation to allow a patient to make his own decisions requires the physician always to be bound by a patient's explicit wish not to be informed about his medical condition. We think not.

Where HIV or some other contagious disease is involved, the patient has a need to know, not necessarily for his own sake, but for the sake of others. Those who do not want to know they are HIV-positive lack information crucial to decisions concerning their own behavior with respect to others. The physician has an obligation to a particular patient, but she also has an obligation to prevent harm to others who may come into contact with that patient. Failing to tell a patient he is HIV-positive, even if he has requested not to know, makes her complicitous in the spread of the disease. She is not responsible for her patient's actions, but she is responsible for making sure he has information relevant to decisions affecting others. Violating his autonomy to the extent needed to inform him is justified by the possibility that it may save the lives of others. (If she discovered an airline pilot suffered from a seizure disorder, it would be morally wrong for her not to make sure the airline was informed.)

A question similar to that about infectious diseases arises about the "vertical transmission" of genetic diseases. Suppose a thirty-four-year-old man whose mother died of Huntington's doesn't want to be tested to find out whether he is carrying the gene (and so will develop the disease). He is bothered by some movement problems and episodes of mental confusion. He wants his physician to treat him for these but not tell him whether they are symptoms of the onset of Huntington's. The man is about to be married, and he has told his physician he and his wife intend to have children.

After examination and testing, the physician believes the patient's problems are symptoms of HD and are likely to get progressively worse. Moreover, the physician knows that offspring of the man have a fifty percent chance of inheriting the gene that causes the disease. Should the physician go against the patient's explicit request and inform him it is likely he has HD?

Once again, violating a patient's autonomy to the extent of telling him something he does not want to hear seems warranted. If the patient knows he may have HD, he might decide either not to have children or to employ embryo screening to avoid having a child that inherits the HD gene. In the absence of this knowledge, he may be more likely to have a child who will inherit the gene and eventually develop a painful, lingering, and fatal disease. Decreasing the likelihood of bringing a child into the world who will eventually develop such a disease justifies the physician's going against her patient's wishes. (Before reaching this stage, the physician might talk to the patient and attempt to get him to change his mind by telling him what might be at stake and making sure he understands his reproductive options.)

In summary, we hold that while a physician has a prima facie obligation to withhold the truth about a patient's condition from the patient at the patient's request, in some circumstances the physician may have a duty to ignore the request and provide the patient with information he doesn't want to hear.

Patients Who Don't Say. What about patients like Susan Cruz who express neither a desire to be fully informed nor a wish to be kept ignorant? Physicians are justified in presuming that patients want to know about the state of their health, diseases they may have, and the appropriate treatments for them. This presumption is no less than the recognition that patients are persons, that they are rational agents who may be assumed to want to make informed decisions about matters affecting their lives. Setting aside this prior presumption requires that a patient explicitly inform a physician that he or she wishes to remain in ignorance. Informing patients about their medical condition is, again, the default position for physicians.

Further, if a physician has doubts about whether a patient wants to be informed about her medical condition (as we discussed earlier in connection with Susan Cruz), he should make an effort to determine at the beginning of the relationship whether the patient wants to know about the nature and seriousness of her disease. "Don't ask, don't tell" is by no means an appropriate model for physician-patient communication, and because the physician holds the stronger position in the relationship, it is up to him to find out about how much his patient wants to know.

Studies indicate that a significant majority of patients do want to know about the state of their health. In most studies, over eighty percent of patients surveyed reported that they would want to be informed if they were diagnosed with cancer or some other serious disease.[6] Thus, telling a patient the truth can be regarded as the default position for the physician on grounds that are empirical as well as moral.

2. What if a Physician Is Unable to Tell a Patient the Truth?

Physicians cannot tell patients what they don't know themselves. Nothing is wrong with a physician's admitting that little is known about the patient's disease or that the patient's symptoms don't point to a clear diagnosis. Patients are aware that physicians aren't omniscient, and a physician who confesses to ignorance or puzzlement may be showing respect for the patient. A physician must recognize his own limitations, as distinct from the limitations of the state of medicine, and be prepared to refer a patient to someone more able to address the patient's problem.

Actual ignorance and the consequent impossibility of telling a patient the truth is not the issue that physicians and patients typically focus on in the conflict over truth-telling. The issue is usually about whether physicians, when they know the truth, are able to tell it to their patients.

A complaint often expressed by physicians about the need to get a patient's informed consent before carrying out a surgical procedure is that patients are unable to understand their explanations. The notion underlying this complaint is that, even when physicians try, it is impossible to inform patients about their medical condition.

This notion lies at the base of the argument that physicians, even when they do their best, cannot tell their patients the truth. Patients (the argument goes) lack the technical background and experience of physicians, so even intelligent and educated patients are not able to understand the medical terms and concepts physicians must use to describe a patient's condition. Physicians, if they are to communicate at all with the patient, must then switch to using terms and concepts that neither adequately nor accurately convey to the patient what is wrong with him. Thus, it is impossible for physicians to tell patients the truth.

Critics have pointed out that this argument that physicians are not able even in principle to tell patients "the truth" rests on a confusion between "whole truth" and "wholly true." Physicians, we can agree, cannot tell patients the "whole truth," meaning that no patient is going to be able to understand all the known details of a disease process as it affects him. Medicine is an information-rich enterprise, and even physicians are quickly out of their depth in areas beyond their expertise. How many of us really understand the pancreas?

Even so, the explanation of a complicated situation in ways a layperson can understand is not a challenge unique to physicians. The same problem is faced by lawyers, electricians, automobile mechanics, and computer help-line workers. In none of these fields, including medicine, is it necessary to provide the layperson with a complete explanation (the "complete truth") of a situation. All a patient requires is an understanding adequate to appreciate the nature and seriousness of his illness and the potential benefits and risks of the available therapies. A diabetic need not know the stages of oxidative phosphorylation to grasp the importance of insulin and role of diet in maintaining her health.

The argument also does not support the claim endorsed by some writers that, because a physician cannot tell their patients "the truth" (the "whole truth"), it's all right to tell them what is not "wholly true"—that is, to deceive them. Such deception may involve using vague language to explain a patient's medical condition. Thus, Dr. Lambert tells Susan Cruz, "You have a disease of the supporting cells in the brain," when he should have explained to her that she had a particular kind of brain cancer, one that was aggressive and that had advanced to an inoperable stage. The view that the impossibility of telling a patient "the whole truth" makes it all right to tell the patient something not wholly true is analogous to saying, "Because I can't pay you the money I owe you, it's okay for me to rob you." Not being able to tell "the truth" is not a license to deceive.

Respect for persons requires that physicians tell their patients the relevant facts about their medical condition in a comprehensible way. It doesn't require trying to tell patients all the facts. Telling the truth is no more an impossibility for physicians than it is for automobile mechanics.

3. Don't Physicians Sometimes Have a Duty to Lie to Their Patients?

Some writers have argued that respect for persons and their autonomy sometimes permits physicians to deliberately deceive their patients. Granting that a sick patient desires to regain his health, then if that desire can most likely be attained by his physician's deceiving him, the physician is justified in carrying out the deception.[7] Deceiving the patient in such a case assists him in securing his goal, so a respect for the patient's goal makes the deception permissible. The physician violates the patient's autonomy a little while the patient is sick so that he will regain his health.

This is not a view that can be dismissed as obviously flawed, but it is one we ought to be cautious about adopting without qualification.

First, it is easy to overestimate the extent to which lying to a patient will be useful in helping him regain his health. We certainly don't have any data that show the relative advantage of deceiving patients about their illnesses. The old notion that if a patient with a serious illness is protected from anxiety and worry about his condition, he will heal faster is no more than speculation. As such, it will not justify our infringing someone's autonomy for the sake of what is at best a hypothetical gain.

Second, it is easy to underestimate the benefits of informing patients about the character of disease and the aim of the treatment. Most treatments for serious diseases require the full cooperation of the patient. A woman diagnosed with metastatic breast cancer must go through a rigorous course of therapy, ranging from surgery through chemotherapy and radiation treatments. If she knows that her cancer has spread from the breast to other places in her body and knows her chances of survival, she is more likely to adhere to the treatment plan mapped out by her oncologist. Deceiving the patient about her medical problem is probably, in most cases, more likely to work against her goal of preserving her life and regaining her health. Thus, deception may not only violate her autonomy, it may contribute to the loss of her life.

Let us suppose, however, that in some cases we can know with reasonable certainty that if we deceive someone about her illness this will contribute to her recovery. Is it acceptable to use deception and violate autonomy in the short run, if the deception can be expected to promote autonomy in the longer run?

Recalling an example mentioned earlier should make us wary of answering this question in the affirmative. It would be wrong, we said, to kill one healthy person to obtain organs to save the lives of four people. Such examples suggest it is wrong to interfere with autonomy (that of the healthy person) for the sake of promoting autonomy (that of the four sick ones).

Yet we generally agree it is acceptable for the federal government to tax people with a certain income, then use part of the money to help feed starving foreigners. This suggests it is *not* wrong to interfere with autonomy (that of taxpayers) to promote autonomy (that of the starving). Are our responses in these two cases inconsistent, or is there a difference between the cases? We suggest there is a difference.

In both cases, the gain in autonomy is great (lives saved), but in the tax case, the infringement of autonomy needed to achieve a great gain is minor. Taxing us as citizens takes away some of our resources and thus counts as an infringement of our autonomy. Yet we still retain a substantial degree of control over the important parts of our lives.

The contrast between these two cases suggests the following principle: It does not show a disrespect for persons to violate their autonomy, if the violation is minor and the potential gain is both probable and significant. Thus, for example, if a physician is confident she can save a patient's life by deceiving him for a short while, it is not wrong for her to deceive him. Suppose Ms. Cohen has an irrational fear of taking antibiotics, yet if she is not treated for a bacterial lung infection, she will,

almost certainly die. Her physician, in such circumstances, would be justified in telling her something like, "The pills I'm giving you will help your body fight the infection."

Such cases are sure to be rare, however. In most cases, either the stakes will not be high enough (someone's life) to justify deception or deception will not be likely to help. Most often, the physician's only legitimate course is to respect her patient's status as an autonomous agent. This means not trying to deceive him and helping him make decisions by providing him with information relevant to his disease and the treatment options open to him.

Conclusion

We have argued that a principle of respect for persons requires that physicians not engage in deceiving patients. It is clearly wrong for physicians to tell patients they need surgery that they don't need. Such a lie is wrong, we have contended, because it prevents patients from making informed choices about their lives. This is also true of deception intended to benefit a patient. In all but the rarest cases, deceiving a patient "for his own good" is an unacceptable way for physicians to try to help their patients.

NOTES

1. Mark Lipkin, *Newsweek* (June 4, 1979), p. 13. See also Joseph Ellin, "Lying and Deception: The Solution to a Dilemma in Medical Ethics," *Westminster Institute Review* (May 1981), pp. 3–6, and Joseph Collins, "Should Doctors Tell the Truth?" in Samuel Gorovitz *et al.*, eds., *Moral Problems in Medicine,* 2nd ed (New York: Prentice-Hall, 1983), pp. 190–201.

2. Immanuel Kant was the first to articulate this idea. See his *Groundwork of the Metaphysic of Morals,* tr. H. Paton (New York: Harper Torchbooks, 1964), esp. p. 96.

3. Lipkin, *loc. cit.*

4. Sissela Bok, *Lying: Moral Choice in Public and Private Life* (New York: Pantheon Books, 1978), p. 229.

5. Lipkin, *loc. cit.* See also Lawrence Henderson, "Physician and Patient as a Social System," *New England Journal of Medicine* (1955), p. 212.

6. Bok, p. 227.

7. Jane Zembaty, "A Limited Defense of Paternalism in Medicine," *Proceedings of the 13th Conference on Value Inquiry: The Life Sciences and Human Values* (Geneseo, NY: State University of New York, 1979), pp. 145–158. See also Terence Ackerman, "Why Doctors Should Intervene," *Hastings Center Report* (August 1982), pp. 14–17.

Why Privacy Is Important

JAMES RACHELS

Why should we care so much about privacy? Rachels asks. He notes that we have a sense of privacy that cannot be explained fully by our fear of being embarrassed or our concerns about being disadvantaged in some material way. He argues that "privacy is necessary if we are to maintain the variety of social relationships with other people that we want to have, and that is why it is important to us." To manage the relationships that we have with people, we must have "control over who has access to us."

Privacy is one of those familiar values that seem unproblematic until we start thinking about them, and then puzzles appear at every turn. The first puzzle is why, exactly, privacy is important. According to Justice Brandeis, it is "the right most valued by civilized men."[1] But why should we care so much about it? At first it may appear that no unitary explanation is possible, because people have so many interests that may be harmed by invasions of their privacy:

1. Privacy is sometimes necessary to protect people's interests in competitive situations. For example, it obviously would be a disadvantage to Bobby Fischer if he could not analyze the adjourned position in a chess game in private, without his opponent learning his results.

2. In other cases someone may want to keep some aspect of his life or behavior private simply because it would be embarrassing for other people to know about it. There is a splendid example of this in John Barth's novel *End of the Road*. The narrator of the story, Jake Horner, is with Joe Morgan's wife, Rennie, and they are approaching the Morgan house where Joe is at home alone:

    "Want to eavesdrop? I whispered impulsively to Rennie. "Come on, it's great! See the animals in their natural habitat."

    Rennie looked shocked. "What for?"

    "You mean you never spy on people when they're alone? It's wonderful! Come on, be a sneak! It's the most unfair thing you can do to a person."

From *Philosophy & Public Affairs*, vol. 4, no. 4, 1975, pp. 323–33. Copyright © 1975. Reprinted with permission of Blackwell Publishing Ltd.

"You disgust me, Jake!" Rennie hissed. "He's just reading. You don't know Joe at all, do you?"

"What does that mean?"

"*Real* people aren't any different when they're alone. No masks. What you see of them is authentic."

…Quite reluctantly, she came over to the window and peeped in beside me.

It is indeed the grossest of injustices to observe a person who believes himself to be alone. Joe Morgan, back from his Boy Scout meeting, had evidently intended to do some reading, for there were books lying open on the writing table and on the floor beside the bookcase. But Joe wasn't reading. He was standing in the exact center of the bare room, fully dressed, smartly executing military commands. About *face! Right dress! 'Ten-shun! Parade rest!* He saluted briskly, his cheeks blown out and his tongue extended, and then proceeded to cavort about the room— spinning, pirouetting, bowing, leaping, kicking. I watched entranced by his performance, for I cannot say that in my strangest moments (and a bachelor has strange ones) I have surpassed him. Rennie trembled from head to foot.[2]

The scene continues even more embarrassingly.

3. There are several reasons medical records should be kept private, having to do with the consequences to individuals of facts about them becoming public knowledge. The president of the American Medical Association warned, "The average patient doesn't realize the importance of the confidentiality of medical records. Passing out information on venereal disease can wreck a marriage. Revealing a pattern of

alcoholism or drug abuse can result in a man's losing his job or make it impossible for him to obtain insurance protection."[3]

4. When people apply for credit (or for large amounts of insurance or for jobs of certain types), they are often investigated, and the result is a fat file of information about them. There is something to be said in favor of such investigations, for business people surely do have the right to know whether credit applicants are financially reliable. The trouble is that all sorts of other information can find its way into such files—information about the applicant's sex life, his political views, and so on. Clearly, it is unfair for one's application for credit to be influenced by such irrelevant matters.

These examples illustrate the variety of interests that may be protected by guaranteeing people's privacy, and it would be easy to give further examples of the same general sort. However, I do not think that examining such cases will provide a complete understanding of the importance of privacy, for two reasons.

First, these cases all involve relatively unusual sorts of situations, in which someone has something to hide or in which information about a person might provide someone with a reason for mistreating him in some way. Thus, reflection on these cases gives us little help in understanding the value that privacy has in *normal* or *ordinary* situations. By this I mean situations in which there is nothing embarrassing or shameful or unpopular in what we are doing and nothing ominous or threatening connected with its possible disclosure. For example, even married couples whose sex lives are normal (whatever that is), and so who have nothing to be ashamed of, by even the most conventional standards, and certainly nothing to be blackmailed about, do not want their bedrooms bugged. We need an account of the value that privacy has for us not only in the few special cases but in the many common and remarkable cases as well.

Second, even those invasions of privacy that do result in embarrassment or in some specific harm are objectionable on other grounds. A woman may rightly be upset if her credit rating is adversely affected by a report about her sexual behavior, because the use of such information is unfair; however, she may also object to the report simply because she feels—as most of us would—that her sex life is *nobody else's business*. This is an extremely important point. We have a sense of privacy that is violated in such affairs, and this sense of privacy cannot adequately be explained merely in terms of our fear of being embarrassed or disadvantaged in one of the obvious ways. An adequate account of privacy should help us to understand what makes something "someone's business" and why intrusions into things that are "none of your business" are, as such, offensive.

These considerations suggest that there is something important about privacy that we will miss if we confine our attention to examples such as (1)–(4). In what follows I will try to bring out what this something is.

Social Relationships and Appropriate Behavior

I will give an account of the value of privacy based on the idea that there is a close connection between our ability to control who has access to us and to information about us and our ability to create and maintain different sorts of social relationships with different people. According to this account, privacy is necessary if we are to maintain the variety of social relationships with other people that we want to have, and that is why it is important to us. By a "social relationship" I do not mean anything unusual or technical; I mean the sort of thing that we usually have in mind when we say of two people that they are friends or that they are husband and wife or that one is the other's employer.

We may begin by noticing that there are fairly definite *patterns of behavior* associated with these relationships. Our relationships with other people determine, in large part, how we act toward them and how they behave toward us. Moreover, there are different patterns of behavior associated with different sorts of relationships. Thus a man may be playful and affectionate with his children (although sometimes firm), businesslike with his employees, and respectful and polite with his mother-in-law. And to his close friends he may show a side of his personality that others never see—perhaps he is secretly a poet, and rather shy about it, and shows his verse only to his closest friends.

It is sometimes suggested that there is something deceitful or hypocritical about such variations in behavior. It is suggested that underneath all the role-playing there is the "real" person and that the various "masks" that we wear are some sort of phony disguise that we use to conceal our "true" selves. I take it that this is what is behind Rennie's remark, in the passage from Barth: "*Real* people aren't any different when they're alone. No masks. What you see of them is authentic." According to this way of looking at things, the fact that we observe different standards of conduct with different people is merely a sign of dishonesty. Thus the coldhearted businessman who reads poetry to his friends is "really" a gentle, poetic soul whose businesslike demeanor in front of his employees is only a false front; and the man who curses and swears when talking to his friends, but who would never use such language around his mother-in-law, is just putting on an act for her.

This is wrong. Of course the man who does not swear in front of his mother-in-law may be just putting on an act so that, for example, she will not disinherit him, when otherwise he would curse freely in front of her without caring what she thinks. But it may be that his conception of how he ought to behave with his mother-in-law is simply different from his conception of how he may behave with his friends. (Or it may not be appropriate for him to swear around *her* because "she is not that sort of person.") Similarly, the businessman may be putting up a false front for his employees, perhaps because he dislikes his work and has to make a continual, disagreeable effort to maintain the role. But on the other hand he may be, quite comfortably and naturally, a businessman with a certain conception of how it is appropriate for a businessman to behave; and this conception is compatible with his also being a husband, a father, and a friend, with different conceptions of how it is appropriate to behave with his wife, his children, and his friends. There need be nothing dishonest or hypocritical in any of this, and neither side of his personality need be the "real" him, any more than any of the others.

It is not merely accidental that we vary our behavior with different people according to the different social relationships that we have with them. Rather, the different patterns of behavior are (partly) what define the different relationships; they are an important part of what makes the different relationships what they are. The relation of friendship, for example, involves bonds of affection and special obligations, such as the duty of loyalty, that friends owe to one another; but it is also an important part of what it means to have a friend that I welcome her company, confide in her, tell her things about myself, and show her sides of my personality that I would not tell or show to just anyone.[4] Suppose I believe someone is my close friend, and then I discover that she is worried about her job and is afraid of being fired. But while she has discussed this situation with several other people, she has not mentioned it at all to me. And then I learn that she writes poetry and that this is an important part of her life; but while she has shown her poems to other people, she has not shown them to me. Moreover, I learn that she behaves with her other friends in a much more informal way than she behaves with me, that she makes a point of seeing them socially much more than she sees me, and so on. In the absence of some special explanation of her behavior, I would have to conclude that we are not as close as I had thought.

The same general point can be made about other sorts of human relationships: employer to employee, minister to congregant, doctor to patient, husband to wife, parent to child, and so on. In each case, the sort of relationship that people have to one another involves a conception of how it is appropriate for them to behave with each other and, what is more, a conception of the kind and degree of knowledge concerning one another that it is appropriate for them to have. Of course such relationships are not structured in exactly the same way for everyone. Some parents are casual and easygoing with their children, while others are more formal and reserved. Some doctors want to be friends with at least some of their patients; others are businesslike with all. Moreover, the requirements of social roles may vary from community to community—the role of wife may not require exactly the same sort of behavior in rural Alabama that it does in New York or New Guinea. And the requirements of social roles may change; the women's movement, for example, has made a tremendous impact on our understanding of the husband-wife relationship. The examples that I have been giving are drawn, loosely speaking, from contemporary American society, but this is mainly a matter of convenience. The important point is that however one conceives one's relations with other people, there is inseparable from that conception an idea of how it is appropriate to behave with and around them and what information about oneself it is appropriate for them to have.

Privacy and Personal Relationships

All of this has to do with the way that a crucial part of our lives—our relations with other people—is organized, and as such, its importance to us can hardly be exaggerated. Therefore, we have good reason to object to anything that interferes with these relationships and makes it difficult or impossible for us to maintain them in the way that we want. That is why the loss of privacy is so disturbing. Our ability to control who has access to us and to information about us allows us to maintain the variety of relationships with other people that we want to have.

Consider what happens when close friends are joined by a casual acquaintance. The character of the group changes; one of the changes is that conversation about intimate matters is now out of order. Suppose these friends could never be alone; suppose there were always third parties (let us say casual acquaintances or strangers) intruding. Then they could do either of two things. They could carry on as close friends do, sharing confidences, freely expressing their feelings about things, and so on. But this would mean violating their sense of how it is appropriate to behave around casual acquaintances or strangers. Or they could avoid doing or saying anything that they think inappropriate to do or say around the third party. But this would mean that they could no longer behave with one another in the way that friends do and, further, that, eventually, they would no longer *be* close friends.

Again, consider the differences between the way that a husband and wife behave when they are alone and the way they behave in the company of third parties. Alone, they may be affectionate, sexually intimate, have their fights and quarrels, and so on; but with others, a more "public" face is in order. If they

could never be alone together, they would either have to abandon the relationship that they would otherwise have as husband and wife or else behave in front of others in ways they now deem inappropriate.[5]

These considerations suggest that we need to separate our associations, at least to some extent, if we are to maintain a system of different relationships with different people. Separation allows us to behave with certain people in the way that is appropriate to the sort of relationship we have with them, without at the same time violating our sense of how it is appropriate to behave with, and in the presence of, others with whom we have different kinds of relationships. Thus if we are to be able to control the relationships that we have with other people, we must have control over who has access to us.

We now have an explanation of the value of privacy in ordinary situations in which we have nothing to hide. The explanation is that even in the most common and unremarkable circumstances, we regulate our behavior according to the kinds of relationships we have with the people around us. If we cannot control who has access to us, sometimes including and sometimes excluding various people, then we cannot control the patterns of behavior we need to adopt (this is one reason that privacy is an aspect of liberty) or the kinds of relations with other people that we will have.

What about our feeling that certain facts about us are "nobody else's business"? Here, too, it is useful to consider the nature of our relationships. If someone is our doctor, then it literally is her business to keep track of our health; if someone is our employer, then it literally is his business to know what salary we are paid; our financial dealings literally are the business of the people who extend us credit; and so on. In general, a fact about ourselves is someone's business if there is a specific relationship between us that entitles him to know. We are often free to choose whether or not to enter into such relationships, and those who want to maintain as much privacy as possible will enter them only reluctantly. What we cannot do is accept such a social role with respect to another person and then expect to retain the same degree of privacy relative to him or her that we had before. Thus, if we are asked how much money we have in the bank, we cannot say

"It's none of your business" to our banker, prospective creditors, or our spouses. But, at the risk of being boorish, we could say that to others with whom we have no such relationship.

Thomson's View

In an important essay,[6] Judith Jarvis Thomson suggests that the key to understanding the right to privacy is to realize that there is nothing special about it. She suggests, "as a simplifying hypothesis, that the right to privacy is itself a cluster of rights, and that it is not a distinct cluster of rights but itself intersects with the cluster of rights which the right over the person consists of, and also with the cluster of rights which owning property consists of." This is an appealing idea because these other rights seem less puzzling than the right to privacy. Therefore, if the simplifying hypothesis is correct, the right to privacy may be much easier to understand.

Thomson explains that "the right over the person" consists of such "un-grand" rights as the right not to have various parts of one's body looked at, the right not to have one's elbow painted green, and so on. She understands these rights as analogous to property rights. The idea is that our bodies are ours and so we have the same rights with respect to them that we have with respect to our other possessions.

Is this plausible? Is a woman's right to prevent a Peeping Tom from looking at her breasts no different from her right to control who drives her car or who uses her fountain pen? These seem importantly different because the kind of interest we have in controlling who looks at what parts of our bodies is different from the interest we have in our cars or pens. For most of us, physical intimacy is a part of special sorts of personal relationships. Exposing one's knee or one's face to someone does not count for us as physical intimacy, but exposing a breast, and allowing it to be seen and touched, does. Of course the details are to some extent a matter of social convention; it is easy to understand that for a Victorian woman an exposed knee could be a sign of intimacy. She would be right to be distressed at learning that she had left a knee uncovered and that someone was staring at it. By dissociating the body from ideas of physical intimacy and the complex of personal relationships of which such intimacies are

a part, we can make this "right over the body" seem to be an ungrand kind of property right; but that dissociation separates this right from the matters that make privacy important.

Thomson suggests the following case as a possible source of trouble for the simplifying hypothesis:

> Some acquaintances of yours indulge in some very personal gossip about you. Let us imagine that all of the information they share was arrived at without violation of any right of yours, and that none of the participants violates a confidence in telling what he tells. Do they violate a right of yours in sharing the information? If they do, there is trouble for the simplifying hypothesis, for it seems to me there is no right not identical with, or included in, the right to privacy cluster which they could be thought to violate.[7]

But, she adds, this case does not really cause trouble, because the gossips "don't violate any right of yours. It seems to me we simply do not have rights against others that they shall not gossip about us."

This is, as Thomson says, a debatable case, but if our account of why privacy is important is correct, we have at least some reason to think that your right to privacy can be violated in such a case. Let us fill in some details. Suppose you are recently divorced, and the reason your marriage failed is that you became impotent shortly after the wedding. You have shared your troubles with your closest friend, but this is not the sort of thing you want everyone to know. Not only would it be humiliating for everyone to know, it is none of their business. It is the sort of intimate fact about you that is not appropriate for strangers or casual acquaintances to know. But now the gossips have obtained the information. Perhaps one of them innocently overheard your conversation with a friend; it was not his fault, so he did not violate your privacy in the hearing, but then you did not know he was within earshot. And now the gossips are spreading it around to everyone who knows you and to some who do not. Are they violating your right to privacy? Surely they are. If so, it is not surprising, for the interest involved in this case is just the sort of interest that the right to privacy typically protects. Since the right that is violated in this case is not also a property right or a right over the person, the simplifying hypothesis fails. But this should not be surprising, either, for if the right to privacy has a different point than these other rights, we should not expect it always to overlap with them. And even if it did always overlap, we could still regard the right to privacy as a distinctive sort of right in virtue of the special kind of interest it protects.

NOTES

1. Olmstead v United States, 277 US 438,478 (1928).

2. John Barth, *End of the Road* (New York: Avon, 1960), 57–58.

3. Dr. Malcolm Todd, quoted in the *Miami Herald*, 26 October 1973, sec. A, p. 18.

4. This is similar to Charles Fried's view of the relation between friendship and privacy in his illuminating book *An Anatomy of Values* (Cambridge: Harvard University Press, 1970).

5. This is from a television program guide in the *Miami Herald*, 21 October 1973, p. 17:

"I think it was one of the most awkward scenes I've ever done," said actress Brenda Benet after doing a romantic

scene with her husband, Bill Bixby, in his new NBC-TV series, "The Magician."

"It was even hard to kiss him," she continued. "It's the same old mouth, but it was terrible. I was so abnormally shy; I guess because I don't think it's anybody's business. The scene would have been easier had I done it with a total stranger because that would be real acting. With Bill, it was like being on exhibition."

On the view presented here, it is not "abnormal shyness" or shyness of any type that is behind such feelings. Rather, it is a sense of what is appropriate with and around people with whom one has various sorts of personal relationships. Kissing *another actor* in front of the camera crew, the director, and so on, is one thing; but kissing *one's husband* in front of all these people is quite another thing. What made Ms. Benet's position confusing was that her husband was another actor, and the behavior that was permitted by one relationship was discouraged by the other.

6. Judith Jarvis Thomson, "The Right to Privacy," *Philosophy and Public Affairs* 4 (1975): 295–314.

7. Thomson, "Right to Privacy," 311–12.

Confidentiality in Medicine—A Decrepit Concept

MARK SIEGLER

Siegler points out that in this age of high-technology health care, the traditional ideal of patient-physician confidentiality does not exist in practice. Modern health care involves teams of specialists—medical, financial, governmental, social, and more—and they all require access to, and dissemination of, a great deal of confidential information about patients. These developments seem to be in response to people's demand for better and more comprehensive care. But they also are changing our traditional concept of medical confidentiality. Confidentiality is important because it shows respect for the patient's individuality and privacy and nurtures the bond of trust between patient and doctor.

Medical confidentiality, as it has traditionally been understood by patients and doctors, no longer exists. This ancient medical principle, which has been included in every physician's oath and code of ethics since Hippocratic times, has become old, worn-out, and useless; it is a decrepit concept. Efforts to preserve it appear doomed to failure and

From *The New England Journal of Medicine*, vol. 307, no. 24, pp. 1518–21. Copyright © 1982. Reprinted with permission of the Massachusetts Medical Society.

often give rise to more problems than solutions. Psychiatrists have tacitly acknowledged the impossibility of ensuring the confidentiality of medical records by choosing to establish a separate, more secret record. The following case illustrates how the confidentiality principle is compromised systematically in the course of routine medical care.

A patient of mine with mild chronic obstructive pulmonary disease was transferred from the surgical intensive-care unit to a surgical nursing floor two days after an elective cholecystectomy. On the day of transfer, the patient saw a respiratory therapist writing in his medical chart (the therapist was recording the results of an arterial blood gas analysis) and became concerned about the confidentiality of his hospital records. The patient threatened to leave the hospital prematurely unless I could guarantee that the confidentiality of his hospital record would be respected.

The patient's complaint prompted me to enumerate the number of persons who had both access to his hospital record and a reason to examine it. I was amazed to learn that at least 25 and possibly as many as 100 health professionals and administrative personnel at our university hospital had access to the patient's record and that all of them had a legitimate need, indeed a professional responsibility, to open and use that chart. These persons included 6 attending physicians (the primary physician, the surgeon, the pulmonary consultant, and others); 12 house officers (medical, surgical, intensive-care unit, and "covering" house staff); 20 nursing personnel (on three shifts); 6 respiratory therapists; 3 nutritionists; 2 clinical pharmacists; 15 students (from medicine, nursing, respiratory therapy, and clinical pharmacy); 4 unit secretaries; 4 hospital financial officers; and 4 chart reviewers (utilization review, quality assurance review, tissue review, and insurance auditor). It is of interest that this patient's problem was straightforward, and he therefore did not require many other technical and support services that the modern hospital provides. For example, he did not need multiple consultants and fellows, such specialized procedures as dialysis, or social workers, chaplains, physical therapists, occupational therapists, and the like.

Upon completing my survey I reported to the patient that I estimated that at least 75 health professionals and hospital personnel had access to his medical record. I suggested to the patient that these people were all involved in providing or supporting his health-care services. They were, I assured him, working for him. Despite my reassurances the patient was obviously distressed and retorted, "I always believed that medical confidentiality was part of a doctor's code of ethics. Perhaps you should tell me just what you people mean by 'confidentiality'!"

Two Aspects of Medical Confidentiality
Confidentiality and Third-Party Interests
Previous discussions of medical confidentiality usually have focused on the tension between a physician's responsibility to keep information divulged by patients secret and a physician's legal and moral duty, on occasion, to reveal such confidences to third parties, such as families, employers, public health authorities, or police authorities. In all these instances, the central question relates to the stringency of the physician's obligation to maintain patient confidentiality when the health, well-being, and safety of identifiable others or of society in general would be threatened by a failure to reveal information about the patient. The tension in such cases is between the good of the patient and the good of others.

Confidentiality and the Patient's Interest
As the example above illustrates, further challenges to confidentiality arise because the patient's personal interest in maintaining confidentiality comes into conflict with his personal interest in receiving the best possible health care. Modern high-technology health care is available principally in hospitals (often, teaching hospitals), requires many trained and specialized workers (a "health-care team"), and is very costly. The existence of such teams means that information that previously had been held in confidence by an individual physician will now necessarily be disseminated to many members of the team. Furthermore, since health-care teams are expensive and few patients can afford to pay such costs directly, it becomes essential to grant access to the patient's medical record to persons who are responsible for obtaining third-party payment. These persons include chart reviewers, financial officers, insurance auditors, and quality-of-care assessors. Finally, as medicine expands from a narrow, disease-based model to a model that encompasses psychological, social, and economic problems, not only will the size of the health-care team and medical costs increase, but more sensitive information (such as one's personal habits and financial condition) will now be included in the medical record and will no longer be confidential.

The point I wish to establish is that hospital medicine, the rise of health-care teams, the existence of third-party insurance programs, and the expanding limits of medicine all appear to be responses to the wishes of people for better and more comprehensive medical care. But each of these developments necessarily modifies our traditional understanding of medical confidentiality.

The Role of Confidentiality in Medicine

Confidentiality serves a dual purpose in medicine. In the first place, it acknowledges respect for the patient's sense of individuality and privacy. The patient's most personal physical and psychological secrets are kept confidential in order to decrease a sense of shame and vulnerability. Secondly, confidentiality is important in improving the patient's health care—a basic goal of medicine. The promise of confidentiality permits people to trust (i.e., have confidence) that information revealed to a physician in the course of a medical encounter will not be disseminated further. In this way patients are encouraged to communicate honestly and forthrightly with their doctors. This bond of trust between patient and doctor is vitally important both in the diagnostic process (which relies on an accurate history) and subsequently in the treatment phase, which often depends as much on the patient's trust in the physician as it does on medications and surgery. These two important functions of confidentiality are as important now as they were in the past. They will not be supplanted entirely either by improvements in medical technology or by recent changes in relations between some patients and doctors toward a rights-based, consumerist model.

Possible Solutions to the Confidentiality Problem

First of all, in all nonbureaucratic, noninstitutional medical encounters—that is, in the millions of doctor-patient encounters that take place in physicians' offices, where more privacy can be preserved—meticulous care should be taken to guarantee that patients' medical and personal information will be kept confidential.

Secondly, in such settings as hospitals or large-scale group practices, where many persons have opportunities to examine the medical record, we should aim to provide access only to those who have "a need

to know." This could be accomplished through such administrative changes as dividing the entire record into several sections—for example, a medical and financial section—and permitting only health professionals access to the medical information.

The approach favored by many psychiatrists—that of keeping a psychiatric record separate from the general medical record—is an understandable strategy but one that is not entirely satisfactory and that should not be generalized. The keeping of separate psychiatric records implies that psychiatry and medicine are different undertakings and thus drives deeper the wedge between them and between physical and psychological illness. Furthermore, it is often vitally important for internists or surgeons to know that a patient is being seen by a psychiatrist or is taking a particular medication. When separate records are kept, this information may not be available. Finally, if generalized, the practice of keeping a separate psychiatric record could lead to the unacceptable consequence of having a separate record for each type of medical problem.

Patients should be informed about what is meant by "medical confidentiality." We should establish the distinction between information about the patient that generally will be kept confidential regardless of the interest of third parties and information that will be exchanged among members of the health-care team in order to provide care for the patient. Patients should be made aware of the large number of persons in the modern hospital who require access to the medical record in order to serve the patient's medical and financial interests.

Finally, at some point most patients should have an opportunity to review their medical record and to make informed choices about whether their entire record is to be available to everyone or whether certain portions of the record are privileged and should be accessible only to their principal physician or to others designated explicitly by the patient. This approach would rely on traditional informed-consent procedural standards and might permit the patient to balance the personal value of medical confidentiality against the personal value of high-technology, team health care. There is no reason that the same procedure should not be used with psychiatric records instead of the arbitrary system now employed, in which every-thing related to psychiatry is kept secret.

Afterthought: Confidentiality and Indiscretion

There is one additional aspect of confidentiality that is rarely included in discussions of the subject. I am re-ferring here to the wanton, often inadvertent, but avoidable exchanges of confidential information that occur frequently in hospital rooms, elevators, cafete-rias, doctors' offices, and at cocktail parties. Of course, as more people have access to medical information about the patient the potential for this irresponsible abuse of confidentiality increases geometrically.

Such mundane breaches of confidentiality are probably of greater concern to most patients than the broader issue of whether their medical records may be entered into a computerized data bank or whether a respiratory therapist is reviewing the results of an arterial blood gas determination. Somehow, privacy is violated and a sense of shame is heightened when intimate secrets are revealed to people one knows or is close to—friends, neighbors, acquaintances, or hospital roommates—rather than when they are dis-closed to an anonymous bureaucrat sitting at a com-puter terminal in a distant city or to a health professional who is acting in an official capacity.

I suspect that the principles of medical confi-dentiality, particularly those reflected in most medical codes of ethics, were designed principally to prevent just this sort of embarrassing personal indiscretion rather than to maintain (for social, political, or economic reasons) the absolute se-crecy of doctor-patient communications. In this regard, it is worth noting that Percival's Code of Medical Ethics (1803) includes the following ad-monition: "Patients should be interrogated con-cerning their complaint in a tone of voice which cannot be overheard" [Leake, C. D., ed., *Percival's Medical Ethics*. Baltimore: Williams and Wilkins, 1927]. We in the medical profession frequently ne-glect these simple courtesies.

Conclusion

The principle of medical confidentiality described in medical codes of ethics and still believed in by patients no longer exists. In this respect, it is a de-crepit concept. Rather than perpetuate the myth of confidentiality and invest energy vainly to preserve it, the public and the profession would be better served if they devoted their attention to determin-ing which aspects of the original principle of confi-dentiality are worth retaining. Efforts could then be directed to salvaging those.

Ethical Relativism in a Multicultural Society

RUTH MACKLIN

Macklin investigates moral dilemmas brought on by clashes between the cultural background of physicians and that of patients. Tolerance is an important value in developed Western countries, but sometimes tolerance of the beliefs and practices of other cultures can lead physicians either to harm patients or to violate patient autonomy. Macklin concludes that Western physicians should respect non-Western cultural and religious beliefs as far as possible, but they need not embrace beliefs that can result in practices detrimental to patients or others.

Cultural pluralism poses a challenge to physicians and patients alike in the multicultural United States,

From Ruth Macklin, "Ethical Relativism in a Multicultural Society," *Kennedy Institute of Ethics Journal*, vol. 8, no. 1 (March 1998), 1–2, 4–15, 17–22.

where immigrants from many nations and diverse religious groups visit the same hospitals and doctors. Multiculturalism is defined as "a social-intellectual movement that promotes the value of diversity as a core principle and insists that all cultural groups be treated with respect and as equals" (Fowers and

Richardson 1996, p. 609). This sounds like a value that few enlightened people could fault, but it produces dilemmas and leads to results that are, at the least, problematic if not counterintuitive.

Critics of mainstream bioethics within the United States and abroad have complained about the narrow focus on autonomy and individual rights. Such critics argue that much—if not most—of the world embraces a value system that places the family, the community, or the society as a whole above that of the individual person. The prominent American sociologist Renée Fox is a prime example of such critics: "From the outset, the conceptual framework of bioethics has accorded paramount status to the value-complex of individualism, underscoring the principles of individual rights, autonomy, self-determination, and their legal expression in the jurisprudential notion of privacy" (Fox 1990, p. 206).

The emphasis on autonomy, at least in the early days of bioethics in the United States, was never intended to cut patients off from their families by focusing monistically on the patient. Instead, the intent was to counteract the predominant and long-standing paternalism on the part of the medical profession. In fact, there was little discussion of where the family entered in and no presumption that a family-centered approach to sick patients was somehow a violation of the patient's autonomy. Most patients want and need the support of their families, regardless of whether they seek to be autonomous agents regarding their own care. Respect for autonomy is perfectly consistent with recognition of the important role that families play when a loved one is ill. Autonomy has fallen into such disfavor among some bioethicists that the pendulum has begun to swing in the direction of families, with urgings to "take families seriously" (Nelson 1992) and even to consider the interests of family members equal to those of the competent patient (Hardwig 1990)....

Perspectives of Health Care Workers and Patients

A circumstance that arises frequently in multicultural urban settings is one that medical students bring to ethics teaching conferences. The patient and family are recent immigrants from a culture in which physicians normally inform the family rather than the patient of a diagnosis of cancer. The medical students wonder whether they are obligated to follow the family's wish, thereby respecting their cultural custom, or whether to abide by the ethical requirement at least to explore with patients their desire to receive information and to be a participant in their medical care. When medical students presented such a case in one of the conferences I co-direct with a physician, the dilemma was heightened by the demographic picture of the medical students themselves. Among the 14 students, 11 different countries of origin were represented. Those students either had come to the United States themselves to study or their parents had immigrated from countries in Asia, Latin America, Europe, and the Middle East.

The students began their comments with remarks like, "Where I come from, doctors never tell the patient a diagnosis of cancer" or "In my country, the doctor always asks the patient's family and abides by their wishes." The discussion centered on the question of whether the physician's obligation is to act in accordance with what contemporary medical ethics dictates in the United States or to respect the cultural difference of their patients and act according to the family's wishes. Not surprisingly, the medical students were divided on the answer to this question.

Medical students and residents are understandably confused about their obligation to disclose information to a patient when the patient comes from a culture in which telling a patient she has cancer is rare or unheard of. They ask: "Should I adhere to the American custom of disclosure or the Argentine custom of withholding the diagnosis?" That question is miscast, since there are some South Americans who want to know if they have cancer and some North Americans who do not. It is not, therefore, the cultural tradition that should determine whether disclosure to a patient is ethically appropriate, but rather the patient's wish to communicate directly with the physician, to leave communications to the family, or something in between. It would be a simplistic, if not unethical response on the part of doctors to reason that "This is the United States, we adhere to the tradition of patient autonomy, therefore I must disclose to this immigrant from the Dominican Republic that he has cancer."

Most patients in the United States do want to know their diagnosis and prognosis, and it has been amply demonstrated that they can emotionally and psychologically handle a diagnosis of cancer. The same may not be true, however, for recent immigrants from other countries, and it may be manifestly untrue in certain cultures. Although this, too, may change in time, several studies point to a cross-cultural difference in beliefs and practice regarding disclosure of diagnosis and informed consent to treatment.

One survey examined differences in the attitudes of elderly subjects from different ethnic groups toward disclosure of the diagnosis and prognosis of a terminal illness and regarding decision making at the end of life (Blackhall et al. 1995). This study found marked differences in attitudes between Korean Americans and Mexican Americans, on the one hand, and African Americans and Americans of European descent, on the other. The Korean Americans and Mexican Americans were less likely than the other two groups to believe that patients should be told of a prognosis of terminal illness and also less likely to believe that the patient should make decisions about the use of life-support technology. The Korean- and Mexican Americans surveyed were also more likely than the other groups to have a family-centered attitude toward these matters; they believed that the family and not the patient should be told the truth about the patient's diagnosis and prognosis. The authors of the study cite data from other countries that bear out a similar gap between the predominant "autonomy model" in the United States and the family-centered model prevalent in European countries as well as in Asia and Africa.

The study cited was conducted at 31 senior citizen centers in Los Angeles. In no ethnic group did 100 percent of its members favor disclosure or non-disclosure to the patient. Forty-seven percent of Korean Americans believed that a patient with metastatic cancer should be told the truth about the diagnosis, 65 percent of Mexican Americans held that belief, 87 percent of European Americans believed patients should be told the truth, and 89 percent of African Americans held that belief.

It is worth noting that the people surveyed were all 65-years-old or older. Not surprisingly, the Korean- and Mexican American senior citizens had values closer to the cultures of their origin than did the African Americans and European Americans who were born in the United States. Another finding was that among the Korean American and Mexican American groups, older subjects and those with lower socioeconomic status tended to be opposed to truth telling and patient decision making more strongly than the younger, wealthier, and more highly educated members of these same groups. The authors of the study draw the conclusion that physicians should ask patients if they want to receive information and make decisions regarding treatment or whether they prefer that their families handle such matters.

Far from being at odds with the "autonomy model," this conclusion supports it. To ask patients how much they wish to be involved in decision making does show respect for their autonomy: patients can then make the autonomous choice about who should be the recipient of information or the decision maker about their illness. What would fail to show respect for autonomy is for physicians to make these decisions without consulting the patient at all. If doctors spoke only to the families but not to the elderly Korean American or Mexican American patients without first approaching the patients to ascertain their wishes, they would be acting in the paternalistic manner of the past in America, and in accordance with the way many physicians continue to act in other parts of the world today. Furthermore, if physicians automatically withheld the diagnosis from Korean Americans because the majority of people in that ethnic group did not want to be told, they would be making an assumption that would result in a mistake almost 50 percent of the time.

Intolerance and Overtolerance

A medical resident in a New York hospital questioned a patient's ability to understand the medical treatment he had proposed and doubted whether the patient could grant truly informed consent. The patient, an immigrant from the Caribbean islands, believed in voodoo and sought to employ voodoo rituals in addition to the medical treatment she was receiving.

"How can anyone who believes in that stuff be competent to consent to the treatment we offer?" the resident mused. The medical resident was an observant Jew who did not work, drive a car, or handle money on the sabbath and adhered to Kosher dietary laws. Both the Caribbean patient and the Orthodox Jew were devout believers in their respective faiths and practiced the accepted rituals of their religions.

The patient's voodoo rituals were not harmful to herself or to others. If the resident had tried to bypass or override the patient's decision regarding treatment, the case would have posed an ethical problem requiring resolution. Intolerance of another's religious or traditional practices that pose no threat of harm is, at least, discourteous and at worst, a prejudicial attitude. And it does fail to show respect for persons and their diverse religious and cultural practices. But it does not (yet) involve a failure to respect persons at a more fundamental level, which would occur if the doctor were to deny the patient her right to exercise her autonomy in the consent procedures.

At times, however, it is the family that interferes with the patient's autonomous decisions. Two brothers of a Haitian immigrant were conducting a conventional Catholic prayer vigil for their dying brother at his hospital bedside. The patient, suffering from terminal cancer and in extreme pain, had initially been given the pain medication he requested. Sometime later a nurse came in and found the patient alert, awake, and in excruciating pain from being undermedicated. When questioned, another nurse who had been responsible for the patient's care said that she had not continued to administer the pain medication because the patient's brothers had forbidden her to do so. Under the influence of the heavy dose of pain medication, the patient had become delirious and mumbled incoherently. The brothers took this as an indication that evil spirits had entered the patient's body and, according to the voodoo religion of their native culture, unless the spirit was exorcised it would stay with the family forever, and the entire family would suffer bad consequences. The patient manifested the signs of delirium only when he was on the medication, so the brothers asked the nurse to withhold the pain medication, which they believed was responsible for the entry of the evil spirit. The nurse sincerely believed

that respect for the family's religion required her to comply with the patient's brothers' request, even if it contradicted the patient's own expressed wish. The person in charge of pain management called an ethics consultation, and the clinical ethicist said that the brothers' request, even if based on their traditional religious beliefs, could not override the patient's own request for pain medication that would relieve his suffering.

There are rarely good grounds for failing to respect the wishes of people based on their traditional religious or cultural beliefs. But when beliefs issue in actions that cause harm to others, attempts to prevent those harmful consequences are justifiable. An example that raises public health concerns is a ritual practiced among adherents of the religion known as Santería, practiced by people from Puerto Rico and other groups of Caribbean origin. The ritual involves scattering mercury around the household to ward off bad spirits. Mercury is a highly toxic substance that can harm adults and causes grave harm to children. Shops called "botánicas" sell mercury as well as herbs and other potions to Caribbean immigrants who use them in their healing rituals.

The public health rationale that justifies placing limitations on people's behavior in order to protect others from harm can justify prohibition of the sale of mercury and penalties for its domestic use for ritual purposes. Yet the Caribbean immigrants could object: "You are interfering with our religious practices, based on your form of scientific medicine. This is our form of religious healing and you have no right to interfere with our beliefs and practices." It would not convince this group if a doctor or public health official were to reply: "But ours is a well-confirmed, scientific practice while yours is but an ignorant, unscientific ritual." It may very well appear to the Caribbean group as an act of cultural imperialism: "These American doctors with their Anglo brand of medicine are trying to impose it on us." This raises the difficult question of how to implement public health measures when the rationale is sufficiently compelling to prohibit religious or cultural rituals. Efforts to eradicate mercury sprinkling should enlist members of the community who agree with the public health position but who are also respected members of the cultural or religious group.

Belief System of a Subculture

Some widely held ethical practices have been transformed into law, such as disclosure of risks during an informed consent discussion and offering to patients the opportunity to make advanced directives in the form of a living will or appointing a health care agent. Yet these can pose problems for adherents of traditional cultural beliefs. In the traditional culture of Navajo Native Americans, a deeply rooted cultural belief underlies a wish not to convey or receive negative information. A study conducted on a Navajo Indian reservation in Arizona demonstrated how Western biomedical and bioethical concepts and principles can come into conflict with traditional Navajo values and ways of thinking (Carrese and Rhodes 1995). In March 1992, the Indian Health Service adopted the requirements of the Patient Self-Determination Act, but the Indian Health Service policy also contains the following proviso: "Tribal customs and traditional beliefs that relate to death and dying will be respected to the extent possible when providing information to patients on these issues" (Carrese and Rhodes 1995, p. 828).

The relevant Navajo belief in this context is the notion that thought and language have the power to shape reality and to control events. The central concern posed by discussions about future contingencies is that traditional beliefs require people to "think and speak in a positive way." When doctors disclose risks of a treatment in an informed consent discussion, they speak "in a negative way," thereby violating the Navajo prohibition. The traditional Navajo belief is that health is maintained and restored through positive ritual language. This presumably militates against disclosing risks of treatment as well as avoiding mention of future illness or incapacitation in a discussion about advance care planning. Western-trained doctors working with the traditional Navajo population are thus caught in a dilemma. Should they adhere to the ethical and legal standards pertaining to informed consent now in force in the rest of the United States and risk harming their patients by "talking in a negative way"? Or should they adhere to the Navajo belief system with the aim of avoiding

harm to the patients but at the same time violating the ethical requirement of disclosure to patients of potential risks and future contingencies?

The authors of the published study draw several conclusions. One is that hospital policies complying with the Patient Self-Determination Act are ethically troublesome for the traditional Navajo patients. Since physicians who work with that population must decide how to act, this problem requires a solution. A second conclusion is that "the concepts and principles of Western bioethics are not universally held" (Carrese and Rhodes 1995, p. 829). This comes as no surprise. It is a straightforward statement of the thesis of descriptive ethical relativism, the evident truth that a wide variety of cultural beliefs about morality exist in the world. The question for normative ethics endures: What follows from these particular facts of cultural relativity? A third conclusion the authors draw, in light of their findings, is that health care providers and institutions caring for Navajo patients should reevaluate their policies and procedures regarding advance care planning.

This situation is not difficult to resolve, ethically or practically. The Patient Self-Determination Act does not mandate patients to actually make an advance directive; it requires only that health care institutions provide information to patients and give them the opportunity to make a living will or appoint a health care agent. A physician or nurse working for the Indian Health Service could easily fulfill this requirement by asking Navajo patients if they wish to discuss their future care or options, without introducing any of the negative thinking. This approach resolves one of the limitations of the published study. As the authors acknowledge, the findings reflect a more traditional perspective and the full range of Navajo views is not represented. So it is possible that some patients who use the Indian Health Service may be willing or even eager to have frank discussions about risks of treatment and future possibilities, even negative ones, if offered the opportunity.

It is more difficult, however, to justify withholding from patients the risks of proposed treatment in an informed consent discussion. The article about the Navajo beliefs recounts an episode told by a Navajo woman who is also a nurse. Her father was a candidate for bypass surgery. When the surgeon informed the patient of the risks of surgery, including the possibility that he might not wake up, the elderly Navajo man refused the surgery altogether. If the patient did indeed require the surgery and refused because he believed that telling him of the risk of not waking up would bring about that result, then it would be justifiable to withhold that risk of surgery. Should not that possibility be routinely withheld from all patients, then, since the prospect of not waking up could lead other people—Navajos and non-Navajos alike—to refuse the surgery? The answer is no, but it requires further analysis.

Respect for autonomy grants patients who have been properly informed the right to refuse a proposed medical treatment. An honest and appropriate disclosure of the purpose, procedures, risks, benefits, and available alternatives, provided in terms the patient can understand, puts the ultimate decision in the hands of the patient. This is the ethical standard according to Western bioethics. A clear exception exists in the case of patients who lack decisional capacity altogether, and debate continues regarding the ethics of paternalistically overriding the refusal of marginally competent patients. This picture relies on a key feature that is lacking in the Navajo case: a certain metaphysical account of the way the world works. Western doctors and their patients generally do not believe that talking about risks of harm will produce those harms (although there have been accounts that document the "dark side" of the placebo effect). It is not really the Navajo values that create the cross-cultural problem but rather, their metaphysical belief system holding that thought and language have the power to shape reality and control events. In fact, the Navajo values are quite the same as the standard Western ones: fear of death and avoidance of harmful side effects. To understand the relationship between cultural variation and ethical relativism, it is essential to distinguish between cultural relativity that stems from a difference in values and that which can be traced to an underlying metaphysics or epistemology.

Against this background, only two choices are apparent: insist on disclosing to Navajo patients the risks of treatment and thereby inflict unwanted negative thoughts on them; or withhold information about the risks and state only the anticipated benefits of the proposed treatment. Between those two choices, there is no contest. The second is clearly ethically preferable. It is true that withholding information about the risks of treatment or potential adverse events in the future radically changes what is required by the doctrine of informed consent. It essentially removes the "informed" aspect, while leaving in place the notion that the patient should decide. The physician will still provide some information to the Navajo patient, but only the type of information that is acceptable to the Navajos who adhere to this particular belief system. True, withholding certain information that would typically be disclosed to patients departs from the ethical ideal of informed consent, but it does so in order to achieve the ethically appropriate goal of beneficence in the care of patients.

The principle of beneficence supports the withholding of information about risks of treatment from Navajos who hold the traditional belief system. But so, too, does the principle of respect for autonomy. Navajos holding traditional beliefs can act autonomously only when they are not thinking in a negative way. If doctors tells them about bad contingencies, that will lead to negative thinking, which in their view will fail to maintain and restore health. The value of both doctor and patient is to maintain and restore health. A change in the procedures regarding the informed consent discussion is justifiable based on a distinctive background condition: the Navajo belief system about the causal efficacy of thinking and talking in a certain way. The less-than-ideal version of informed consent does constitute a "lower" standard than that which is usually appropriate in today's medical practice. But the use of a "lower" standard is justified by the background assumption that that is what the Navajo patient prefers.

What is relative and what is nonrelative in this situation? There is a clear divergence between the Navajo belief system and that of Western science. That divergence leads to a difference in what sort of discussion is appropriate for traditional Navajos in the medical setting and that which is standard in Western medical practice. According to one description, "always disclose the risks as well as the benefits of treatment to patients," the conclusion points to ethical relativism. But a more general description, one that heeds today's call for cultural awareness and sensitivity, would be: "Carry out an informed consent discussion in a manner appropriate to the patient's beliefs and understanding." That obligation is framed in a nonrelative way. A heart surgeon would describe the procedures, risks, and benefits of bypass surgery in one way to a patient who is another physician, in a different way to a mathematician ignorant of medical science, in yet another way to a skilled craftsman with an eighth grade education, and still differently to a traditional Navajo. The ethical principle is the same; the procedures differ.

Obligations of Physicians

The problem for physicians is how to respond when an immigrant to the United States acts according to the cultural values of her native country, values that differ widely from accepted practices in American medicine. Suppose an African immigrant asks an obstetrician to perform genital surgery on her baby girl. Or imagine that a Laotian immigrant from the Iu Mien culture brings her four-month-old baby to the pediatrician for a routine visit and the doctor discovers burns on the baby's stomach. The African mother seeks to comply with the tradition in her native country, Somalia, where the vast majority of women have had clitoridectomies. The Iu Mien woman admits that she has used a traditional folk remedy to treat what she suspected was her infant's case of a rare folk illness.

What is the obligation of physicians in the United States when they encounter patients in such situations? At one extreme is the reply that in the United States, physicians are obligated to follow the ethical and cultural practices accepted here and have no obligation to comply with patients' requests that embody entirely different cultural values. At the other extreme is the view that cultural sensitivity requires physicians to adhere to the traditional beliefs and practices of patients who have emigrated from other cultures.

A growing concern on the part of doctors and public health officials is the increasing number of requests for genital cutting and defense of the practice by immigrants to the United States and European countries. A Somalian immigrant living in Houston said he believed his Muslim faith required him to have

his daughters undergo the procedure; he also stated his belief that it would preserve their virginity. He was quoted as saying, "It's my responsibility. If I don't do it, I will have failed my children" (Dugger 1996, p. 1). Another African immigrant living in Houston sought a milder form of the cutting she had undergone for her daughter. The woman said she believed it was necessary so her daughter would not run off with boys and have babies before marriage. She was disappointed that Medicaid would not cover the procedure, and planned to go to Africa to have the procedure done there. A New York City physician was asked by a father for a referral to a doctor who would do the procedure on his three-year-old daughter. When the physician told him this was not done in America, the man accused the doctor of not understanding what he wanted (Dugger 1996, pp. 1, 9).

However, others in our multicultural society consider it a requirement of "cultural sensitivity" to accommodate in some way to such requests of African immigrants. Harborview Medical Center in Seattle sought just such a solution. A group of doctors agreed to consider making a ritual nick in the fold of skin that covers the clitoris, but without removing any tissue. However, the hospital later abandoned the plan after being flooded with letters, postcards, and telephone calls in protest (Dugger 1996).

A physician who conducted research with East African women living in Seattle held the same view as the doctors who sought a culturally sensitive solution. In a talk she gave to my medical school department, she argued that Western physicians must curb their tendency to judge cultural practices different from their own as "rational" or "irrational." Ritual genital cutting is an "inalienable" part of some cultures, and it does a disservice to people from those cultures to view it as a human rights violation. She pointed out that in the countries where female genital mutilation (FGM) is practiced, circumcised women are "normal." Like some anthropologists who argue for a "softer" linguistic approach (Lane and Rubinstein 1996), this researcher preferred the terminology of "circumcision" to that of "female genital mutilation."

One can understand and even have some sympathy for the women who believe they must adhere to a cultural ritual even when they no longer live in the society where it is widely practiced. But it does not follow that the ritual is an "inalienable" part of that culture, since every culture undergoes changes over time. Furthermore, to contend that in the countries where FGM is practiced, circumcised women are "normal" is like saying that malaria or malnutrition is "normal" in parts of Africa. That a human condition is statistically normal implies nothing whatever about whether an obligation exists to seek to alter the statistical norm for the betterment of those who are affected.

Some Africans living in the United States have said they are offended that Congress passed a law prohibiting female genital mutilation that appears to be directed specifically at Africans. France has also passed legislation, but its law relies on general statutes that prohibit violence against children (Dugger 1996). In a recent landmark case, a French court sent a Gambian woman to jail for having had the genitals of her two baby daughters mutilated by a midwife. French doctors report an increasing number of cases of infants who are brought to clinics hemorrhaging or with severe infections.

Views on what constitutes the appropriate response to requests to health professionals for advice or referrals regarding the genital mutilation of their daughters vary considerably. Three commentators gave their opinions on a case vignette in which several African families living in a U.S. city planned to have the ritual performed on their daughters. If the procedure could not be done in the U.S., the families planned to have it done in Africa. One of the parents sought advice from health professionals.

One commentator, a child psychiatrist, commented that professional ethical practice requires her to respect and try to understand the cultural and religious practices of the group making the request (Brant 1995). She then cited another ethical requirement of clinical practice: her need to promote the physical and psychological well-being of the child and refusal to condone parenting practices that constitute child abuse according to the social values and laws of her city and country. Most of what this child psychiatrist would do with the mother who comes to her involves discussion, mutual understanding, education, and the warning that in this location performing the genital cutting ritual would probably be considered child abuse.

The psychiatrist would remain available for a continuing dialogue with the woman and others in her community, but would stop short of making a child-abuse report since the woman was apparently only considering carrying out the ritual. However, the psychiatrist would make the report if she had knowledge that the mother was actually planning to carry out the ritual or if it had already been performed. She would make the child-abuse report reluctantly, however, and only if she believed the child to be at risk and if there were no other option. She concluded by observing that the mother is attempting to act in the best interest of her child and does not intend to harm her. The psychiatrist's analysis demonstrates the possible ambiguities of the concept of child abuse. Is abuse determined solely by the intention of the adult? Should child abuse be judged by the harmful consequences to the child, regardless of the adult's intention? Of course, if a law defines the performance of female genital mutilation as child abuse, then it is child abuse, from a legal point of view, and physicians are obligated to report any case for which there is a reasonable suspicion. Legal definitions aside, intentions are relevant for judging the moral worth of people, but not for the actions they perform. This means that the good intentions of parents could exonerate them from blame if their actions cause harm to their children, but the harmful actions nevertheless remain morally wrong.

The second commentator, a clinical psychologist and licensed sex therapist, would do many of the same things as the child psychiatrist, but would go a bit further in finding others from the woman's community and possibly another support network (Wyatt 1995). Like most other commentators on female genital mutilation, this discussant remarked that "agents of change must come from within a culture" (Wyatt 1995, p. 289).

The third commentator on this case vignette was the most reluctant to be critical. A British historian and barrister, he began with the observation that "a people's culture demands the highest respect" (Martin 1995). On the one hand, he noted that custom, tradition and religion are not easily uprooted. But on the other hand, he pointed out that no human practice is beyond questioning. He contended that the debate over the nature and impact of female circumcision is a "genuine debate," and the ritual probably had practical utility when it was introduced into the societies that still engage in it. Of the three commentators, he voiced the strongest opposition to invoking the child abuse laws because it "would be an unwarranted criminalization of parents grappling in good faith with a practice that is legal and customary in their home country" (Martin 1995, p. 291). In the end, this discussant would approach the parents "much as a lawyer would address a jury," leaving the parents (like a jury) to deliberate and come to an informed decision. He would also involve the girls in this process, since they are adolescents, and should have input into the deliberations.

It is tempting to wonder whether the involvement of adolescent girls in deliberations of their parents would, in traditional Gambian culture, be even remotely considered, much less accepted. The "lawyer-jury-adolescent involvement" solution looks to be very Western. If these families living in the United States still wish to adhere to their cultural tradition of genital mutilation, is it likely that they will appreciate the reasoned, deliberative approach this last commentator proposed?

Exactly where to draw the line in such cases is a difficult matter. Presumably, one could go farther than any of these commentators and inform the African families that since U.S. law prohibits female genital mutilation, which has been likened to child abuse, a health professional would be obligated to inform relevant authorities of an intention to commit child abuse.

Another case vignette describes a Laotian woman from the Mien culture who immigrated to the United States and married a Mien man. When she visited her child's pediatrician for a routine four-month immunization, the doctor was horrified to see five red and blistered quarter-inch round markings on the child's abdomen (Case Study: Culture, Healing, and Professional Obligations 1993). The mother explained that she used a traditional Mien "cure" for pain, since she thought the infant was experiencing a rare folk illness among Mien babies characterized by incessant crying and loss of appetite, in addition to other symptoms. The "cure" involves dipping a reed in pork fat, lighting the reed, and passing the burning substance over the skin, raising a blister that "pops like popcorn."

The popping indicates that the illness is not related to spiritual causes; if no blisters appear, then a shaman may have to be summoned to conduct a spiritual ritual for a cure. As many as 11 burns might be needed before the end of the "treatment." The burns are then covered with a mentholated cream.

The Mien woman told the pediatrician that infection is rare and the burns heal in a week or so. Scars sometimes remain but are not considered disfiguring. She also told the doctor that the procedure must be done by someone skilled in burning, since if a burn is placed too near the line between the baby's mouth and navel, the baby could become mute or even retarded. The mother considered the cure to have been successful in the case of her baby, since the child had stopped crying and regained her appetite. Strangely enough, the pediatrician did not say anything to the mother about her practice of burning the baby, no doubt from the need to show "cultural sensitivity." She did, however, wonder later whether she should have said something since she thought the practice was dangerous and also cruel to babies.

One commentator who wrote about this case proposed using "an ethnographic approach" to ethics in the cross-cultural setting (Carrese 1993). This approach need not result in a strict ethical relativism, however, since one can be respectful of cultural differences and at the same time acknowledge that there are limits. What is critical is the perceived degree of harm; some cultural practices may constitute atrocities and violations of fundamental human rights. The commentator argued that the pediatrician must first seek to understand the Mien woman in the context of her world before trying to educate her in the ways of Western medicine. The commentator stopped short of providing a solution, but noted that many possible resolutions can be found for cross-cultural ethical conflicts. Be that as it may, we still need to determine which of the pediatrician's obligations should take precedence: to seek to protect her infant patient (and possibly also the Mien woman's other children) from harmful rituals or to exhibit cultural sensitivity and refrain from attempts at reeducation or critical admonitions.

A second pair of commentators assumed a nonjudgmental stance. These commentators urged respect for cultural diversity and defended the Mien woman's belief system as entirely rational: "It is well grounded in her culture; it is practiced widely; the reasons for it are widely understood among the Iu Mien; the procedure, from a Mien point of view, works" (Brown and Jameton 1993, p. 17). This is a culturally relative view of rationality. The same argument could just as well be used to justify female genital mutilation. Nevertheless, the commentators rejected what they said was the worst choice: simply to tolerate the practice as a primitive cultural artifact and do nothing more. They also rejected the opposite extreme: a referral of child abuse to the appropriate authorities. The mother's actions did not constitute intentional abuse, since she actually believed she was helping the child by providing a traditional remedy. Here I think the commentators are correct in rejecting a referral to the child-abuse authorities, since a charge of child abuse can have serious consequences that may ultimately run counter to the best interests of the child.

What did these commentators recommend? Not to try to prohibit the practice directly, which could alienate the parent. Instead, the pediatrician could discuss the risk of infection and suggest safer pain remedies. The doctor should also learn more about the rationale for and technique of the traditional burning "cure." The most she should do, according to these commentators, is consider sharing her concerns with the local Mien community, but not with the mother alone.

There is in these commentaries a great reluctance to criticize, scold, or take legal action against parents from other cultures who employ painful and potentially harmful rituals that have no scientific basis. This attitude of tolerance is appropriate against the background knowledge that the parents do not intend to harm the child and are simply using a folk remedy widely accepted in their own culture. But tolerance of these circumstances must be distinguished from a judgment that the actions harmful to children should be permitted to continue. What puzzles me is the notion that "cultural sensitivity" must extend so far as to refrain from providing a solid education to these parents about the potential harms and the infliction of gratuitous pain. In a variety of other contexts, we accept the role of physicians as educator of patients. Doctors

are supposed to tell their patients not to smoke, to lose weight, to have appropriate preventive medical checkups such as pap smears, mammograms, and proctoscopic examinations.

Pediatricians are thought to have an even more significant obligation to educate the parents of their vulnerable patients: inform them of steps that minimize the risks of sudden infant death syndrome, tell them what is appropriate for an infant's or child's diet, and give them a wide array of other social and psychological information designed to keep a child healthy and flourishing. Are these educational obligations of pediatricians only appropriate for patients whose background culture is that of the United States or Western Europe? Should a pediatrician not attempt to educate parents who, in their practice of the Santería religion, sprinkle mercury around the house? The obligation of pediatricians to educate and even to urge parents to adopt practices likely to contribute to the good health and well being of their children, and to avoid practices that will definitely or probably cause harm and suffering, should know no cultural boundaries.

My position is consistent with the realization that Western medicine does not have all the answers. This position also recognizes that some traditional healing practices are not only not harmful but may be as beneficial as those of Western medicine. The injunction to "respect cultural diversity" could rest on the premise that Western medicine sometimes causes harm without compensating benefits (which is true) or on the equally true premise that traditional practices such as acupuncture and herbal remedies, once scorned by mainstream Western medicine, have come to be accepted side-by-side with the precepts of scientific medicine. Typically, however, respect for multicultural diversity goes well beyond these reasonable views and requires toleration of manifestly painful or harmful procedures such as the burning remedy employed in the Mien culture. We ought to be able to respect cultural diversity without having to accept every single feature embedded in traditional beliefs and rituals.

The reluctance to impose modern medicine on immigrants from a fear that it constitutes yet another instance of "cultural imperialism" is misplaced. Is it not possible to accept non-Western cultural practices side by side with Western ones, yet condemn those that are manifestly harmful and have no compensating benefit except for the cultural belief that they are beneficial? The commentators who urged respect for the Mien woman's burning treatment on the grounds that it is practiced widely, the reasons for it are widely understood among the Mien, and the procedure works, from a Mien point of view, seemed to be placing that practice on a par with practices that "work" from the point of view of Western medicine. Recall that if the skin does not blister, the Mien belief holds that the illness may be related to spiritual causes and a shaman might have to be called. Should the pediatrician stand by and do nothing, if the child has a fever of 104° and the parent calls a shaman because the skin did not blister? Recall also that the Mien woman told the pediatrician that if the burns are not done in the right place, the baby could become mute or even retarded. Must we reject the beliefs of Western medicine regarding causality and grant equal status to the Mien beliefs? To refrain from seeking to educate such parents and to not exhort them to alter their traditional practices is unjust, as it exposes the immigrant children to health risks that are not borne by children from the majority culture.

It is heresy in today's postmodern climate of respect for the belief systems of all cultures to entertain the notion that some beliefs are demonstrably false and others, whether true or false, lead to manifestly harmful actions. We are not supposed to talk about the evolution of scientific ideas or about progress in the Western world, since that is a colonialist way of thinking. If it is simply "the white man's burden, medicalized" (Morsy 1991) to urge African families living in the United States not to genitally mutilate their daughters, or to attempt to educate Mien mothers about the harms of burning their babies, then we are doomed to permit ethical relativism to overwhelm common sense.

Multiculturalism, as defined at the beginning of this paper, appears to embrace ethical relativism and yet is logically inconsistent with relativism. The second half of the definition states that multiculturalism "insists that all cultural groups be treated with respect and as equals." What does this imply with regard to cultural groups that oppress or fail to respect other cultural groups? Must the cultural groups that violate the mandate to treat all cultural groups with respect and as equals be respected themselves? It is impossible to insist that all such groups be treated with respect and as equals, and at the same time accept any particular group's attitude toward and treatment of another group as inferior. Every cultural group contains subgroups within the culture: old and young, women and men, people with and people without disabilities. Are the cultural groups that discriminate against women or people with disabilities to be respected equally with those that do not?

What multiculturalism does not say is whether all of the beliefs and practices of all cultural groups must be equally respected. It is one thing to require that cultural, religious, and ethnic groups be treated as equals; that conforms to the principle of justice as equality. It is quite another thing to say that any cultural practice whatever of any group is to be tolerated and respected equally. This latter view is a statement of extreme ethical relativism. If multiculturalists endorse the principle of justice as equality, however, they must recognize that normative ethical relativism entails the illogical consequence of toleration and acceptance of numerous forms of injustice in those cultures that oppress women and religious and ethnic minorities.

Tarasoff v. Regents of the University of California

SUPREME COURT OF CALIFORNIA

In this 1976 case, the court held that the professional duties of confidentiality can be overridden when a patient poses a serious danger to others. It concluded that "the public policy favoring protection of the confidential character of patient-psychother-apist communications must yield to the extent to which disclosure is essential to avert danger to others. The protective privilege ends where the public peril begins."

On October 27, 1969, Prosenjit Poddar killed Tatiana Tarasoff. Plaintiffs, Tatiana's parents, allege that two months earlier Poddar confided his intention to kill Tatiana to Dr. Lawrence Moore, a psychologist employed by the Cowell Memorial Hospital at the University of California at Berkeley. They allege that on Moore's request, the campus police briefly detained Poddar, but released him when he appeared rational. They further claim that Dr. Harvey Powelson, Moore's superior, then directed that no further action be taken to detain Poddar. No one warned plaintiffs of Tatiana's peril....

Plaintiffs' complaints predicate liability on two grounds: defendants' failure to warn plaintiffs of the impending danger and their failure to bring about Poddar's confinement pursuant to the Lanterman-Petris-Short Act. Defendants, in turn, assert that they owed no duty of reasonable care to Tatiana and that they are immune from suit under the California Tort Claims Act of 1963.

We shall explain that defendant therapists cannot escape liability merely because Tatiana herself was not their patient. When a therapist determines, or pursuant to the standards of his profession should determine, that his patient presents a serious danger of violence to another, he incurs an obligation to use reasonable care to protect the intended victim against such danger. The discharge of this duty may require the therapist to take one or more of various steps, depending upon the nature of the case. Thus it may call for him to warn the intended victim or others likely to apprise the victim of the danger, to notify the police, or to take whatever other steps are reasonably necessary under the circumstances....

Supreme Court of California, 17 Cal.3d 423, July 1, 1976.

Plaintiffs' Complaints

Plaintiffs, Tatiana's mother and father, filed separate but virtually identical second amended complaints. The issue before us on this appeal is whether those complaints now state, or can be amended to state, causes of action against defendants. We therefore begin by setting forth the pertinent allegations of the complaints.

...Plaintiffs' first cause of action, entitled "Failure to Detain a Dangerous Patient," alleges that on August 20, 1969, Poddar was a voluntary outpatient receiving therapy at Cowell Memorial Hospital. Poddar informed Moore, his therapist, that he was going to kill an unnamed girl, readily identifiable as Tatiana, when she returned home from spending the summer in Brazil. Moore, with the concurrence of Dr. Gold, who had initially examined Poddar, and Dr. Yandell, assistant to the director of the department of psychiatry, decided that Poddar should be committed for observation in a mental hospital. Moore orally notified Officers Atkinson and Teel of the campus police that he would request commitment. He then sent a letter to Police Chief William Beall requesting the assistance of the police department in securing Poddar's confinement.

Officers Atkinson, Brownrigg, and Halleran took Poddar into custody, but, satisfied that Poddar was rational, released him on his promise to stay away from Tatiana. Powelson, director of the department of psychiatry at Cowell Memorial Hospital, then asked the police to return Moore's letter, directed that all copies of the letter and notes that Moore had taken as therapist be destroyed, and "ordered no action to place Prosenjit Poddar in 72-hour treatment and evaluation facility."

Plaintiffs' second cause of action, entitled "Failure to Warn on a Dangerous Patient," incorporates the allegations of the first cause of action, but adds the assertion that defendants negligently permitted Poddar to be released from police custody without "notifying the parents of Tatiana Tarasoff that their daughter was in grave danger from Prosenjit Poddar." Poddar persuaded Tatiana's brother to share an apartment with him near Tatiana's residence; shortly after her return from Brazil, Poddar went to her residence and killed her.

Plaintiffs' third cause of action, entitled "Abandonment of a Dangerous Patient," seeks $10,000 punitive damages against defendant Powelson. Incorporating the crucial allegations of the first cause of action, plaintiffs charge that Powelson "did the things herein alleged with intent to abandon a dangerous patient, and said acts were done maliciously and oppressively."

Plaintiffs' fourth cause of action, for "Breach of Primary Duty to Patient and the Public," states essentially the same allegations as the first cause of action, but seeks to characterize defendants' conduct as a breach of duty to safeguard their patient and the public. Since such conclusory labels add nothing to the factual allegations of the complaint, the first and fourth causes of action are legally indistinguishable....

...We direct our, attention...to the issue of whether Plaintiffs' second cause of action can be amended to state a basis for recovery.

Plaintiffs Can State a Cause of Action Against Defendant Therapists for Negligent Failure to Protect Tatiana

The second cause of action can be amended to allege that Tatiana's death proximately resulted from defendants' negligent failure to warn Tatiana or others likely to apprise her of her danger. Plaintiffs contend that as amended, such allegations of negligence and proximate causation, with resulting damages, establish a cause of action. Defendants, however, contend that in the circumstances of the present case they owed no duty of care to Tatiana or her parents and that, in the absence of such duty, they were free to act in careless disregard of Tatiana's life and safety.

In analyzing this issue, we bear in mind that legal duties are not discoverable facts of nature, but merely conclusory expressions that, in cases of a particular type, liability should be imposed for damage done. "The assertion that liability must...be denied because defendant bears no 'duty' to plaintiff 'begs the essential question—whether the plaintiff's interests are entitled to legal protection against the defendant's conduct.... [Duty] is not sacrosanct in itself, but only an expression of the sum total of those considerations of policy which lead the law to say that the particular plaintiff is entitled to protection.'"

In the landmark case of *Rowland v. Christian* (1968), Justice Peters recognized that liability should be imposed "for an injury occasioned to another by his want of ordinary care or skill" as expressed in section 1714 of the Civil Code. Thus, Justice Peters, quoting from *Heaven v. Pender* (1883) stated: "Whenever one person is by circumstances placed in such a position with regard to another...that if he did not use ordinary care and skill in his own conduct...he would cause danger of injury to the person or property of the other, a duty arises to use ordinary care and skill to avoid such danger.'"

We depart from "this fundamental principle" only upon the "balancing of a number of considerations"; major ones "are the foreseeability of harm to the plaintiff, the degree of certainty that the plaintiff suffered injury, the closeness of the connection between the defendant's conduct and the injury suffered, the moral blame attached to the defendant's conduct, the policy of preventing future harm, the extent of the burden to the defendant and consequences to the community of imposing a duty to exercise care with resulting liability for breach, and the availability, cost and prevalence of insurance for the risk involved."

The most important of these considerations in establishing duty is foreseeability. As a general principle, a "defendant owes a duty of care to all persons who are foreseeably endangered by his conduct, with respect to all risks which make the conduct unreasonably dangerous." As we shall explain, however, when the avoidance of foreseeable harm requires a defendant to control the conduct of another person, or to warn of such conduct, the common law has traditionally imposed liability only if the defendant bears some special relationship to the dangerous person or to the potential victim. Since the relationship between a therapist and his patient satisfies this requirement, we need not here decide whether foreseeability alone is sufficient to create a duty to exercise reasonable care to protect a potential victim of another's conduct.

Although, as we have stated above, under the common law, as a general rule, one person owed no duty to control the conduct of another nor to warn those endangered by such conduct, the courts have carved out an exception to this rule in cases in which the defendant stands in some special relationship to either the person whose conduct needs to be controlled or in a relationship to the foreseeable victim of that conduct. Applying this exception to the present case, we note that a relationship of defendant therapists to either Tatiana or Poddar will suffice to establish a duty of care; as explained in section 315 of the Restatement Second of Torts, a duty of care may arise from either "(a) a special relation...between the actor and the third person which imposes a duty upon the actor to control the third person's conduct, or (b) a special relation...between the actor and the other which gives to the other a right of protection."

Although Plaintiffs' pleadings assert no special relation between Tatiana and defendant therapists, they establish as between Poddar and defendant therapists the special relation that arises between a patient and his doctor or psychotherapist. Such a relationship may support affirmative duties for the benefit of third persons. Thus, for example, a hospital must exercise reasonable care to control the behavior of a patient which may endanger other persons. A doctor must also warn a patient if the patient's condition or medication renders certain conduct, such as driving a car, dangerous to others.

Although the California decisions that recognize this duty have involved cases in which the defendant stood in a special relationship *both* to the victim and to the person whose conduct created the danger, we do not think that the duty should logically be constricted to such situations. Decisions of other jurisdictions hold that the single relationship of a doctor to his patient is sufficient to support the duty to exercise reasonable care to protect others against dangers emanating from the patient's illness. The courts hold that a doctor is liable to persons infected by his patient if he negligently fails to diagnose a

contagious disease, or having diagnosed the illness, fails to warn members of the patient's family.

Since it involved a dangerous mental patient, the decision in *Merchants Nat. Bank & Trust Co. of Fargo v. United States* (1967) comes closer to the issue. The Veterans Administration arranged for the patient to work on a local farm, but did not inform the farmer of the man's background. The farmer consequently permitted the patient to come and go freely during non-working hours; the patient borrowed a car, drove to his wife's residence and killed her. Notwithstanding the lack of any "special relationship" between the Veterans Administration and the wife, the court found the Veterans Administration liable for the wrongful death of the wife.

In their summary of the relevant rulings Fleming and Maximov conclude that the "case law should dispel any notion that to impose on the therapists a duty to take precautions for the safety of persons threatened by a patient, where due care so requires, is in any way opposed to contemporary ground rules on the duty relationship. On the contrary, there now seems to be sufficient authority to support the conclusion that by entering into a doctor-patient relationship the therapist becomes sufficiently involved to assume some responsibility for the safety, not only of the patient himself, but also of any third person whom the doctor knows to be threatened by the patient." [Fleming & Maximov, *The Patient or His Victim: The Therapist's Dilemma* (1974) 62 Cal. L. Rev. 1025, 1030.]

Defendants contend, however, that imposition of a duty to exercise reasonable care to protect third persons is unworkable because therapists cannot accurately predict whether or not a patient will resort to violence. In support of this argument amicus representing the American Psychiatric Association and other professional societies cites numerous articles which indicate that therapists, in the present state of the art, are unable reliably to predict violent acts; their forecasts, amicus claims, tend consistently to overpredict violence, and indeed are more often wrong than right. Since predictions of violence are often erroneous, amicus concludes, the courts should not render rulings that predicate the liability of therapists upon the validity of such predictions.

The role of the psychiatrist, who is indeed a practitioner of medicine, and that of the psychologist who performs an allied function, are like that of the physician who must conform to the standards of the profession and who must often make diagnoses and predictions based upon such evaluations. Thus the judgment of the therapist in diagnosing emotional disorders and in predicting whether a patient presents a serious danger of violence is comparable to the judgment which doctors and professionals must regularly render under accepted rules of responsibility.

We recognize the difficulty that a therapist encounters in attempting to forecast whether a patient presents a serious danger of violence. Obviously we do not require that the therapist, in making the determination, render a perfect performance; the therapist need only exercise "that reasonable degree of skill, knowledge, and care ordinarily possessed and exercised by members of [that professional specialty] under similar circumstances." Within the broad range of reasonable practice and treatment in which professional opinion and judgment may differ, the therapist is free to exercise his or her own best judgment without liability; proof, aided by hindsight, that he or she judged wrongly is insufficient to establish negligence.

In the instant case, however, the pleadings do not raise any question as to failure of defendant therapists to predict that Poddar presented a serious danger of violence. On the contrary, the present complaints allege that defendant therapists did in fact predict that Poddar would kill, but were negligent in failing to warn.

Amicus contends, however, that even when a therapist does in fact predict that a patient poses a serious danger of violence to others, the therapist should be absolved of any responsibility for failing to act to protect the potential victim. In our view, however, once a therapist does in fact determine, or under applicable professional standards reasonably should have determined, that a patient poses a serious danger of violence to others, he bears a duty to exercise reasonable care to protect the foreseeable victim of that danger. While the discharge of this duty of due care will necessarily vary with the facts of each case, in each instance the adequacy of the therapist's conduct must be measured against the traditional negligence standard of the rendition of reasonable care under the circumstances. As

explained in Fleming and Maximov, *The Patient or His Victim: The Therapist's Dilemma* (1974), "...the ultimate question of resolving the tension between the conflicting interests of patient and potential victim is one of social policy, not professional expertise....In sum, the therapist owes a legal duty not only to his patient, but also to his patient's would-be victim and is subject in both respects to scrutiny by judge and jury...."

The risk that unnecessary warnings may be given is a reasonable price to pay for the lives of possible victims that may be saved. We would hesitate to hold that the therapist who is aware that his patient expects to attempt to assassinate the President of the United States would not be obligated to warn the authorities because the therapist cannot predict with accuracy that his patient will commit the crime.

Defendants further argue that free and open communication is essential to psychotherapy; that "unless a patient...is assured that...information [revealed by him] can and will be held in utmost confidence, he will be reluctant to make the full disclosure upon which diagnosis and treatment...depends." The giving of a warning, defendants contend, constitutes a breach of trust which entails the revelation of confidential communications.

We recognize the public interest in supporting effective treatment of mental illness and in protecting the rights of patients to privacy and the consequent public importance of safeguarding the confidential character of psychotherapeutic communication. Against this interest, however, we must weigh the public interest in safety from violent assault. The Legislature has undertaken the difficult task of balancing the countervailing concerns. In Evidence Code section 1014, it established a broad rule of privilege to protect confidential communications between patient and psychotherapist. In Evidence Code section 1024, the Legislature created a specific and limited exception to the psychotherapist-patient privilege: "There is no privilege...if the psychotherapist has reasonable cause to believe that the patient is in such mental or emotional condition as to be dangerous to himself or to the person or property of another and that disclosure of the communication is necessary to prevent the threatened danger."

We realize that the open and confidential character of psychotherapeutic dialogue encourages patients to express threats of violence, few of which are ever executed. Certainly a therapist should not be encouraged routinely to reveal such threats; such disclosures could seriously disrupt the patient's relationship with his therapist and with the persons threatened. To the contrary, the therapist's obligations to his patient require that he not disclose a confidence unless such disclosure is necessary to avert danger to others, and even then that he do so discreetly, and in a fashion that would preserve the privacy of his patient to the fullest extent compatible with the prevention of the threatened danger.

The revelation of a communication under the above circumstances is not a breach of trust or a violation of professional ethics; as stated in the Principles of Medical Ethics of the American Medical Association (1957), section 9: "A physician may not reveal the confidence entrusted to him in the course of medical attendance...*unless he is required to do so by law or unless it becomes necessary in order to protect the welfare of the individual or of the community.*" (Emphasis added.) We conclude that the public policy favoring protection of the confidential character of patient-psychotherapist communications must yield to the extent to which disclosure is essential to avert danger to others. The protective privilege ends where the public peril begins.

Our current crowded and computerized society compels the interdependence of its members. In this risk-infested society we can hardly tolerate the further exposure to danger that would result from a concealed knowledge of the therapist that his patient was lethal. If the exercise of reasonable care to protect the threatened victim requires the therapist to warn the endangered party or those who can reasonably be expected to notify him, we see no sufficient societal interest that would protect and justify concealment. The containment of such risks lies in the public interest. For the foregoing reasons, we find that Plaintiffs' complaints can be amended to state a cause of action against defendants Moore, Powelson, Gold, and Yandell and against the Regents as their employer, for breach of a duty to exercise reasonable care to protect Tatiana....

CHAPTER 5

Informed Consent

Most who have thought carefully about the issue believe that there is more to the ethics of provider-patient relationships than just a regard for truthfulness and confidentiality. A larger, more complex notion often guides such interactions: **informed consent**. At the simplest level, the term refers to the action of an autonomous, informed person agreeing to submit to medical treatment or experimentation. The idea arises from the intuition that patients, as autonomous persons, should have the ultimate say in what is done to their bodies, that they ought not to be treated without their voluntary, informed agreement. Informed consent, then, is thought to be an ethical ideal in which physicians are obligated to tell patients about possible medical interventions and to respect their choices regarding them. It is also a legal requirement, compelling health care providers to disclose information about interventions to patients and obtain their permission before proceeding. (Requirements of informed consent also apply to researchers and research subjects, as discussed in Chapter 6.) The ethical ideal has often proved difficult to define precisely, to apply in real-life cases, and to embody effectively in laws and policies. But among most health care professionals and many of the patients they serve, there is little doubt about its importance and influence.

AUTONOMY AND CONSENT

Philosophers and other thinkers have justified informed consent through appeals to the principles of autonomy and beneficence. The principle of autonomy tells us that we should respect people's capacity for self-determination.

To accept this standard is to reject strong medical paternalism, in which physicians or nurses decide unilaterally what is best for patients. Honoring the principle means letting patients voluntarily choose—even when their choices conflict with medical advice. The principle of beneficence urges physicians and nurses to promote patient welfare, and this goal is thought to be consistent with respecting patient autonomy. Thus bioethicists argue that informed consent promotes the good for patients because knowledgeable, autonomous patients who choose for themselves will advance their own best interests as they themselves conceive them. They will likely avoid unacceptable risks, protect themselves from abuses, and comply with the demands of their chosen treatment.

The ethical underpinnings of informed consent may be old and revered, but the concept as we know it today is young. Throughout most of medical history, devoted physicians practiced the healing arts while paying little attention to notions of patient self-determination and full disclosure. Beginning in the early twentieth century, judicial rulings began to challenge that approach bit by bit. The 1914 case *Schloendorff v. Society of New York Hospital* made it clear that "every human being of adult years and sound mind has a right to determine what shall be done with his own body," but there was no suggestion that any consent had to be informed.[1] Simple consent was sufficient. Not until 1957 in the California court case *Salgo v. Leland Stanford Junior University Board of Trustees* was the physician's disclosure of information firmly tied to the patient's consent. In a ruling that concocted the term "informed consent," the court held that "a physician violates his duty to his patient and subjects himself to liability if he withholds any facts which are necessary to form the basis of an intelligent consent by the patient to the proposed treatment."[2] In the 1960s other cases went further by identifying the basic features of informed consent: the patient's voluntary consent informed by physicians who have a duty to disclose information about the patient's illness, the proposed treatment, its risks and benefits, and treatment alternatives (including no treatment at all).

These rulings still left many unanswered questions about the legal doctrine, most conspicuous among them being how to judge the adequacy of the physician's disclosure. The prevailing view in the early rulings was that disclosure is adequate if it meets the customary standards of medical practice. Information given to patients is sufficient if the medical profession considers it sufficient. But in the 1970s, courts began to insist that the adequacy of disclosure should be judged by what patients themselves find relevant to their situation. The most influential ruling of this kind came in 1972 in the U.S. Court of Appeals case *Canterbury v. Spence*. "The scope of the physician's communication to the patient, then," says Judge Robinson, "must be measured by the patient's need, and that need is the information material to the decision."[3]

Despite such judicial clarifications (and the enactment of countless statutes and institutional policies), much about informed consent remains unsettled—and unsettling. For one thing, many critics see huge discrepancies between the ethical ideal of informed consent and the laws or rules meant to implement it. They know, for example, that too often a patient can sign a form disclosing treatment risks and thereby, according to local law and institutional policy, grant her informed consent. But she may be neither informed nor autonomous and may not intend to consent to anything. Laws and policies may require physicians merely to warn patients of the risks of treatment, a thin imitation of bona fide informed consent. Some observers also decry the gap between theory and everyday medical practice, contending that

physicians view informed consent as a bureaucratic or legalistic burden instead of a way to promote patient self-determination and well-being. As one critic put it, "The idea of physicians making decisions *for*, rather than *with*, patients, is still deeply embedded in the ideology of medical professionalism."[4]

CONDITIONS OF INFORMED CONSENT

Theorists break down informed consent into components believed to be necessary to the concept. Typically, they maintain that an informed consent exists if and only if (1) the patient is *competent* to decide, (2) she gets an adequate *disclosure* of information, (3) she *understands* the information, (4) she decides about the treatment *voluntarily*, and (5) she *consents* to the treatment.[5] This analysis seems straightforward enough, but complications (and controversy) ensue when we try to specify precisely what these conditions entail and to apply them to real-life cases.

As it pertains to informed consent, **competence** is very roughly the ability to render decisions about medical interventions. Individuals who are incompetent in this sense cannot give their informed consent, in which case the burden of decision-making falls to a surrogate (often a court-appointed guardian or a proxy selected through the patient's advance directive). Most of the time, however, people are presumed to be competent unless there are good reasons to think otherwise. Patients are often judged incompetent in cases of mental retardation, dementia, psychosis, alcoholism, and minority (being underage). But they may also be thought incompetent in less clear-cut situations—when they are overwhelmed by fear or pain, for instance. In addition, they are sometimes considered incompetent because they lack only one or two particular mental capacities—for example, the ability to communicate a decision, to understand the implications of a choice, to provide reasons, to explain decision-making, or to understand disclosed information. Still, incompetence is not necessarily total, or global; it may be specific to particular aspects of life. A woman who has been legally declared incompetent to handle her personal finances may be fully competent to give her informed consent. A man who has been involuntarily institutionalized for mental illness may still be able to make decisions regarding his medical treatment.

Sometimes a court will formally determine someone to be incompetent. But in most cases, the judicial system never gets involved, and the task of making informal determinations of incompetence goes to physicians (often in consultation with the patient's family).

To give their informed consent, competent patients must receive an adequate disclosure of information from physicians—but what is an adequate disclosure? What kind and amount of information are sufficient? The ethical doctrine of informed consent says that disclosure is adequate if it allows patients to weigh intelligently the risks and benefits of available choices. But how to achieve this ideal in practice is not obvious. Early court decisions suggested that physicians should be the arbiters of adequate disclosure (the physician-based standard); later rulings insisted that adequate disclosure is whatever satisfies the information needs of a hypothetically reasonable person (the patient-based standard); and others called for a subjective standard in which disclosure is supposed to be based on the information needs of a particular patient. But a purely physician-based standard for disclosure would ignore the patient's needs for information relevant to her own personal decisions. The kind of disclosure suitable for a hypothetically reasonable person would probably be very difficult to determine—and might, like the physician-based standard, impose disclosure criteria that have little to do with the information requirements of a particular patient. And an entirely subjective standard naively assumes that patients can always decide for themselves what facts they do and do not need to evaluate treatment options. Some courts have combined these standards, but no

configuration of requirements has been entirely true to the spirit of informed consent.

Despite these difficulties, courts and legislatures have generally mandated the disclosure of several pieces of important information:

1. The nature of the procedure (for example, whether it is a test or treatment, whether it is invasive, and how long it will take to perform)
2. The risks of the procedure (what kind of risks are involved, their seriousness, their probability of occurring, and when they might happen)
3. The alternatives to the proposed procedure—including the option of no treatment (includes information on the options' nature, risks, and benefits)
4. The expected benefits of the proposed treatment—including their extent and their likelihood of being achieved

Physicians are not obligated to provide disclosure in all situations; the duty of physicians to obtain informed consent has exceptions. Disclosure is often dispensed with in emergencies when stopping to obtain consent could seriously harm the patient. As suggested earlier, informed consent is not required when a patient is incompetent. Neither is it obligatory in cases of **waiver**, the patient's voluntary and deliberate giving up of the right to informed consent. It is an exercise in autonomous choice—the choice not to choose or decide. Authority to decide medical issues is turned over to the physician or surrogates. A much more controversial exception is **therapeutic privilege**, the withholding of relevant information from a patient when the physician believes disclosure would likely do harm. The idea behind it is that some patients are so distraught, depressed, or weak that disclosure could make their condition worse. Laws regarding therapeutic privilege vary on when invoking it is justified, with some allowing it only when disclosure would be extremely dangerous for the patient or when it would seriously diminish the patient's autonomy. Others permit physicians far

IN DEPTH
DECISION-MAKING CAPACITY

How can you tell if a patient is competent to make important decisions about her health? This question is not as easy to answer as you might think, and it is often controversial among medical providers. Here is one example of some carefully crafted guidelines.

Assessing for "decision-making capacity" involves determining whether or not a patient or subject is psychologically or legally capable of adequate decision-making. Illness or medications may impair the ability of patients to make decisions about their health—they may be unable to make decisions at all or may make choices that are not in their best interests and may result in serious harm. It is important to remember that this capacity relates to the specific medical decision at hand and does not imply a global ability to make any or all decisions about health care or other matters. Only a court can deem a patient incapable of making global health care decisions. If that is the case, the patient is deemed to lack "competence" and a surrogate is appointed for the patient. Rarely do we need to involve the court or deem someone to lack competence. Instead, we more commonly refer to decision-making capacity as it relates to individual medical decisions.

HOW IS DECISION-MAKING CAPACITY RELEVANT TO MEDICINE?

In order for a patient to make autonomous decisions or to give informed consent to medical treatments or research participation, an individual must have decision-making capacity. The principle of autonomy requires that a physician respect the authority of a patient to make decisions, even when the decisions appear to be unwise. However, beneficence requires that a physician act in the patient's best interest . . . . [S]ometimes tension exists between the principles of autonomy and beneficence, and it can be difficult to determine the best course of action. However, it is important to recognize that autonomy is only possible when the patient possesses the ability to make relevant health decisions. If individuals lack decision-making capability, they may make decisions that are contrary to their best interests and thus need to be protected from harm. If decision-making capacity is intact, the physician generally should respect the patient's choices. If it is impaired, other arrangements can be made for making health decisions on behalf of the patient.

WHAT ARE THE STANDARDS FOR ASSESSING DECISION-MAKING CAPACITY?

The standards for assessing decision-making capacity are somewhat subjective. However, the patient can generally be considered to possess decision-making capacity if:

- The patient makes and communicates a choice regarding medical treatment/course of action.
- The patient appreciates the following information regarding medical care:
  - medical diagnosis and prognosis
  - nature of the recommended care
  - alternative courses of care
  - risks, benefits, and consequences of each alternative.
- The patient makes decisions that are consistent with his/her values and goals.
- The decision is not the result of delusions.
- The patient uses logical reasoning to make a decision.

WHO DECIDES WHETHER A PATIENT HAS DECISION-MAKING CAPACITY?

In medicine, the attending physician is often the one who determines whether a patient is able make decisions regarding his/her medical care. Sometimes the courts may be involved, but usually this is too time-consuming and unnecessary. Psychiatrists may be consulted, as they have extensive training in dealing with mentally impaired patients and in talking with patients; however, the attending physician is ultimately responsible for determining whether the patient has decision-making capacity.

(continued)

HOW DO YOU DETERMINE WHETHER A PATIENT HAS DECISION-MAKING CAPACITY?

- *Does the patient understand disclosed information?*
  - "Tell me what you believe is wrong with your health now."
  - "What will the angiography do for you?"
- *Does the patient appreciate the consequences of his/her choices?*
  - "What do you believe will happen if you do not have the angiography?"
  - "I've described the probable benefits and risks. How do you think your daily activities would be affected if these benefits and risks were to occur?"
- *Does the patient use reasoning to make a choice?*
  - "Tell me how you reached your decision."
  - "Help me understand how you decided to refuse the angiogram."
  - "Tell me what makes angiography seem worse than the alternatives."
- *Talk to patient's family and friends.*
  - This will help to determine whether the patient's choices are consistent with the patient's values and beliefs. These individuals can also help clarify whether the patient's mental status has changed over time.
- *Mental status examinations.*
  - These tests may be used to evaluate whether the patient is oriented to person, place, and time, attention span, memory function, ability to perform simple calculations, and language skills. However, it is important to remember that these tests do not specifically assess the patient's understanding of the proposed interventions. Individuals with abnormal mental status may be competent to make decisions regarding their health care.
- *Enhance the ability of the patient to make decisions.*
  - Treating underlying medical or psychiatric illnesses may improve the patient's

decision-making capacity. Presenting information slowly, in simple language, more than once, and in digestible bits may help patients comprehend the details of their medical conditions and proposed interventions. Having family members present during presentation of information may reduce patient anxiety, help to focus on important points, and correct misunderstandings.

SPECIAL SITUATIONS

- *Mental illness*: Some psychiatric disorders, particularly schizophrenia and depression, can affect a patient's ability to appreciate the relevance of information to his/her situation or to have a rational perspective on treatments. Patients may be involuntarily committed if they pose a danger to self or others. . . . However, involuntary commitment does not give physicians the right to administer treatments without the patient's consent.
- *Religious beliefs*: Patients may make medical decisions on the basis of religious beliefs; this is commonly accepted as a valid reason for refusal of medical treatment. However, it is important to establish that the patient held the same religious beliefs before the treatment and that he/she is not experiencing delusions. In addition, physicians may seek court orders to override parents' refusal of treatment for their children on religious grounds.

HOW ARE DECISIONS MADE FOR PATIENTS WHO LACK DECISION-MAKING CAPACITY?

Once a physician determines that a patient lacks decision-making capacity, the medical community looks to *advance directives* and *surrogate decision-making* to help make medical decisions for the patient.

From Steven Pantilat, "Decision-Making Capacity," *Missing Link*, http://missinglink.ucsf.edu/lm/ethics/index.htm, the Regents, University of California, 2008 (Accessed October 30, 2015).

IN DEPTH
TWO VIEWS OF INFORMED CONSENT

While agreeing on the value of informed consent, theorists have differed on its core meaning. For example, some define informed consent as "autonomous authorization," and others seem to equate it with "shared decision-making." Consider these contrasting views:

> [The President's] Commission . . . believes that "shared decisionmaking" is the appropriate ideal for patient-professional relationships that a sound doctrine of informed consent should support. . . . [The doctor-patient interaction] should, at a minimum, provide the patient with a basis for effective participation in sound decisionmaking. . . . It will usually consist of discussions between professional and patient that bring the knowledge, concerns, and perspective of each to the process of seeking agreement on a course of treatment. Simply put, this means that the physician or other health professional invites the patient to participate in a dialogue in which the professional seeks to help the patient understand the medical situation and available courses of action, and the patient conveys his or her concerns and wishes. This does not involve a mechanical recitation of abstruse medical information, but should include disclosures that give the patient an understanding of his or her condition and an appreciation of its consequences.[6]

> The idea of informed consent suggests that a patient or subject does more than express agreement with, acquiesce in, yield to, or comply with an arrangement or a proposal. He or she actively *authorizes* the proposal in the act of consent. John may *assent* to a treatment plan without authorizing it. The assent may be a mere submission to the doctor's authoritative order, in which case John does not call on his *own* authority in order to give permission, and thus does not authorize the plan. Instead, he acts like a child who submits, yields, or assents to the school principal's spanking and in no way gives permission for or authorizes the spanking. . . . There is of course an historical relationship in clinical medicine between medical decisionmaking and informed consent. The emergence of the legal doctrine of informed consent was instrumental in drawing attention to issues of decisionmaking as well as authority in the doctor-patient relationship. Nevertheless, it is a confusion to treat informed consent and shared decisionmaking as anything like *synonymous*.[7]

more leeway in deciding when to claim the privilege.

Critics worry that too many physicians use therapeutic privilege when they should in fact tell patients the facts and that overuse of it can undo informed consent. In any case, informed consent seems to imply that physicians should not use therapeutic privilege merely to avoid giving patients unpleasant news or to prevent them from rejecting a treatment.

It seems obvious that there can be no informed consent unless patients understand the information disclosed to them (although the law is equivocal on this point). But it is less clear what such understanding amounts to. At a minimum, informed consent seems to require that patients be able to take in the relevant information and assess it well enough to appreciate the consequences of their choices. They need not completely fathom all the information given, but they should comprehend what is most relevant to their decision. And their refusal to submit to a recommended treatment should not be taken as evidence of a lack of understanding.

Of course, impediments to sufficient understanding abound. It can be deficient if physicians

LEGAL BRIEF

Important Informed Consent Cases

- *Schloendorff v. Society of New York Hospital* (1914)—Justice Cardozo underscored the value of patient self-determination and voluntary consent, declaring that "every human being of adult years and sound mind has a right to determine what shall be done with his body."
- *Salgo v. Leland Stanford Jr. University Board of Trustees* (1957)—The California Supreme Court found that physicians "have the duty to disclose any facts which are necessary to form the basis of an intelligent consent by the patient to proposed treatment."
- *Natanson v. Kline* (1960) and *Mitchell v. Robinson* (1960)—These decisions further specified the information to be conveyed to patients, insisting that the risks involved in a medical procedure should be disclosed.
- *Cobb v. Grant* (1972)—The California Supreme Court held that disclosure must consist of "all information relevant to a meaningful decisional process."
- *Canterbury v. Spence* (1972)—The U.S. Court of Appeals ruled that the adequacy of disclosure by a physician should not be judged by what the medical profession thinks is appropriate but by what information the patient finds relevant to his or her decision.
- *Catalano v. Moreland* (2002)—The Supreme Court of New York held that the adequacy of informed consent cannot be ascertained by merely applying a hospital's bylaws. The court declared, "Thus . . . the reasonableness of defendant's conduct will be measured, not against the Hospital bylaws, but rather against what would have been disclosed by a reasonable medical practitioner."

---

overload the patient with information or frame it in misleading ways (by playing up minimal benefits while playing down significant risks, for instance). The patient's ability to process or appreciate information can be shattered by fear, denial, wishful thinking, magical thinking, and false beliefs. But these problems do not show that acquiring an understanding sufficient for informed consent is impossible—only that it can be difficult and that physicians cannot assume that mere disclosure is enough.

The consent of an informed, competent, understanding patient cannot be legitimate unless it is given voluntarily—that is, freely, without undue (autonomy-robbing) pressure from others. Coercion and manipulation are the most obvious examples of such pressure. Some philosophers have plausibly defined coercion as the intentional use of "a credible and severe threat of harm or force to control another."[8] We might therefore judge a patient to be coerced if her doctor threatens to abandon her unless she submits to treatment, or if he plays on her fear of disability to get her to be more cooperative. Manipulation refers to many noncoercive ways of controlling someone's actions—for example, giving false or misleading information or withholding relevant facts. The use of therapeutic privilege to control a patient's decisions is, of course, manipulative—and corrosive to informed consent. But note that these forms of undue pressure can come not just from health care providers, but also from the patient's family and friends.

Everyday life is filled with social influences on our actions, beliefs, and reasoning. But these pressures are typically not so powerful that they overwhelm our autonomy. Likewise, physicians can influence patients through reasoning, emotional appeals, and authority—yet these pressures are not necessarily undue. In any given case, the line may be difficult to draw between pressures that render consent involuntary and those that do not.

In the ethical ideal, consent is more than assent—more than the patient's giving into the physician's wishes or doing what is expected. As several theorists have insisted, it is a kind of authorization to proceed with a course of action. When a patient authorizes her physician to treat her, she does not merely say yes, but autonomously, knowledgeably decides and *assumes responsibility* for the decision.[9] Actual practice, however, usually falls far short of the ideal, with form-signing and acquiescence substituting for free, informed authorization.

APPLYING MAJOR THEORIES

In what light would the major moral theories have us view informed consent? To ask a more precise question, would they require physicians to obtain informed consent before treating patients? Utilitarianism wants us to judge actions involving informed consent by the overall good they would produce, everyone considered. For an act-utilitarian, this standard must be applied to each individual case, and whether a physician should try to obtain informed consent depends on the benefits generated for all concerned (patient, medical providers, family, and others). There is both good and bad to weigh. Providing relevant information to the patient and seeking her authorization for treatment might reduce her anxiety and depression, increase her compliance and cooperation, enhance her satisfaction with treatment, or encourage her to be actively involved in her own care. But the process might also frighten or confuse her, force her to make decisions that she would rather leave to the physician, prompt her to choose a treatment judged by her physician not to be in her best interests, or take up too much of the physician's time. Forgoing the process altogether might also exact a toll in patient confusion, anxiety, and depression, and there would be the possibility of an erosion of trust between doctor and patient and, in the worst scenarios of mistrust, lawsuits.

So by act-utilitarian lights, in some instances a physician may be obliged to obtain informed consent, but in others she may be justified in ignoring it, even invoking therapeutic privilege. On this view, though informed consent may be frequently used, it is not a moral requirement.

A rule-utilitarian might conclude that the best overall consequences would be achieved if physicians consistently followed a rule requiring informed consent (except in a few extraordinary circumstances). In some cases, adhering to the rule might have worse results than ignoring it, but overall it would produce the greatest good for patients, physicians, nurses, and the medical profession.

The requirement of informed consent can be derived directly from Kantian ethics. As autonomous beings, people are entitled to respect, to be treated as ends in themselves, never merely as a means to an end. They therefore cannot be subjected to medical treatment just because physicians believe it is in their best interests. They must voluntarily consent to be treated, and for the choice to be fully autonomous, they must be informed truthfully about what is involved. To lie to them, withhold relevant information from them, coerce them, or manipulate them is to treat them merely as a means.

From a strictly Kantian viewpoint, therapeutic privilege is never permissible, but waiver is allowed because it represents an autonomous choice not to choose. Some theorists make an exception to these restrictions if the therapeutic privilege or other manipulative tactic is used to help restore or enhance a person's autonomy.

Rawls' contract theory calls for equal liberties for all, a demand that seems to support the doctrine of informed consent. Treating people without their informed authorization would be a violation of such liberties, and manipulation and coercion to obtain consent would be impermissible. This would be the case even if treating a few patients without informed consent would somehow benefit all of society.

Jerry Canterbury

How much are physicians obligated to disclose to patients, and by what standard should the adequacy of the disclosure be judged? In 1972 some answers came in the turning-point case *Canterbury v. Spence.*

Nineteen-year-old Jerry Canterbury entered the hospital for tests to determine the cause of the excruciating pain he felt between his shoulder blades. He had been in pain for months, and the prescription medications he had been taking weren't helping. Dr. William Spence ordered a myelogram, an x-ray of the spinal column taken after the column is injected with a traceable dye. After seeing the test results, Dr. Spence told Canterbury that the problem was probably a ruptured disk, and he recommended surgery on the spinal column to correct the problem. Canterbury consented to the procedure.

After the operation, he seemed to be recovering normally, but then he fell in the hospital and became paralyzed from the waist down. He learned later that paralysis was a possible risk of the kind of surgery he had undergone, but Dr. Spence had not mentioned it. Eventually he regained some muscle control but, even years later, needed crutches to walk and suffered from paralysis of the bowels and urinary incontinence.

Canterbury sued Dr. Spence for failure to tell him before the surgery of the risk of paralysis, and the court found in his favor, marking out some tenets of informed consent along the way. The court strongly affirmed the doctrine and the rationale upon which it rests:

> True consent to what happens to one's self is the informed exercise of a choice, and that entails an opportunity to evaluate knowledgeably the options available and the risks attendant upon each. The average patient has little or no understanding of the medical arts, and ordinarily has only his physician to whom he can look for enlightenment with which to reach an intelligent decision. From these almost axiomatic considerations springs

the need, and in turn the requirement, of a reasonable divulgence by physician to patient to make such a decision possible. . . . And it is evident that it is normally impossible to obtain a consent worthy of the name unless the physician first elucidates the options and the perils for the patient's edification.[10]

In a departure from most other rulings on informed consent, the court declared that the standard for judging whether a physician's disclosure is acceptable should not be the customary practices of physicians but the patient's requirements for pertinent information. In many situations, the court said, no relevant customary practice may exist, and—more importantly—to let the professional customs of physicians decide is to undermine the patient's right of self-determination. The rights and needs of patients set the bar:

> In our view, the patient's right of self-decision shapes the boundaries of the duty to reveal. That right can be effectively exercised only if the patient possesses enough information to enable an intelligent choice. The scope of the physician's communications to the patient, then, must be measured by the patient's need, and that need is the information material to the decision. Thus the test for determining whether a particular peril must be divulged is its materiality to the patient's decision: all risks potentially affecting the decision must be unmasked.[11]

The court characterized the test as what a reasonable person would likely need to know to make an informed decision about a proposed treatment.

Nevertheless, the judges recognized that the physician's invoking of therapeutic privilege (withholding information) is sometimes reasonable and proper. But they rejected "the paternalistic notion that the physician may remain silent simply because divulgence might prompt the patient to forgo therapy the physician feels the patient really needs."[12] Dr. Spence had cited this very notion in his defense.

Some have accused the court of being unclear on the issues of therapeutic privilege and the customary-practice standard of disclosure. But whether or not that's true, *Canterbury v. Spence* helped delineate essential features of the doctrine of informed consent that are now widely accepted. After *Canterbury*, there seemed no going back to the old ideas about disclosure.

KEY TERMS
competence
informed consent
therapeutic privilege
waiver

SUMMARY
Informed consent refers to the action of an autonomous, informed person agreeing to submit to medical treatment or experimentation. It is a powerful notion that thinkers have justified by appealing to the principles of autonomy and beneficence. Court decisions have helped to establish the doctrine in law and society, most notably the case of *Canterbury v. Spence*, which asserted that the adequacy of disclosure by physicians should be judged by what patients think is relevant to their situations.

Theorists maintain that an informed consent exists if and only if (1) the patient is competent to decide, (2) she gets an adequate disclosure of information, (3) she understands the information, (4) she decides about the treatment voluntarily, and (5) she consents to the treatment. Competence is the ability to render decisions about medical interventions. Incompetent patients cannot give their informed consent and must rely on surrogates. What constitutes an adequate disclosure of information to patients is controversial, but the courts have generally ruled that disclosure must include information about the nature of the procedure, its risks, its alternatives (including no treatment), and its expected benefits.

Informed consent is not obligatory in cases of waiver, the patient's voluntary and deliberate giving up of the right to informed consent. It is an exercise in autonomous choice; authority to decide medical issues is turned over to the physician or surrogates. A controversial exception to informed consent is therapeutic privilege, the withholding of relevant information from a patient when the physician believes disclosure would likely do harm. Laws regarding therapeutic privilege vary on when invoking it is justified, with some allowing it only when disclosure would be extremely dangerous for the patient or when it would seriously diminish the patient's autonomy. Others permit physicians far more leeway in deciding when to claim the privilege.

An act-utilitarian would judge whether a physician should try to obtain informed consent according to the benefits generated for all concerned. A rule-utilitarian might conclude that the best overall consequences would be achieved if physicians consistently followed a rule requiring informed consent. In Kantian ethics, informed consent is an absolute requirement, and therapeutic privilege is never permissible. Rawls' contract theory seems to support the doctrine of informed consent. Treating people without their informed authorization would be a violation of basic liberties.

Cases for Evaluation

CASE I

Informed Consent or Not?

A 64-year-old woman with multiple sclerosis (MS) is hospitalized. The team feels she may need to be placed on a feeding tube soon to assure adequate nourishment. They ask the patient about this in the morning and she agrees. However, in the evening (before the tube has been placed), the patient becomes disoriented and seems confused about her decision to have the feeding tube placed. She tells the team she doesn't want it in. They revisit the question in the morning, when the patient is again lucid. Unable to recall her state of mind from the previous evening, the patient again agrees to the procedure.*

Explain your answers: Has the woman given her informed consent? Should she be judged competent? Should her final agreement to the procedure be sufficient to establish informed consent, or should her earlier waffling and confusion also be taken into account?

*"Informed Consent," *Ethics in Medicine* (University of Washington School of Medicine), http://depts.washington. edu/bioethx/topics/consent.html (17 November 2007).

CASE 2

Informed Consent and Organ Transplants

(AP)—A woman in her 30s who is one of the four organ transplant patients [who became] infected with HIV and hepatitis [because of the transplant] was not told that the infected donor was high risk, and had previously rejected another donor "because of his lifestyle," her attorney said.

Attorney Thomas Demetrio filed a petition Thursday in Cook County Circuit Court on behalf of the woman, asking officials to keep a hospital and an organ procurement center from destroying or altering any records involving the donation.

"She's really a mess right now," Demetrio said of the Chicago-area woman. "She's still in shock."

The patient, identified in court documents as Jane Doe, received a kidney transplant at the University of Chicago Medical Center on Jan. 9, Demetrio said.

Gift of Hope Organ & Tissue Donor Network in Elmhurst and the University of Chicago both knew the kidney donor was high-risk and did not inform the patient, Demetrio said.

University of Chicago spokesman John Easton responded in an e-mail: "We believe we follow guidelines, and of course with the patient's consent we will provide necessary records and documents, as is consistent with our open process."

Gift of Hope did not immediately respond to requests for comment.

The woman had been told the donor was a healthy young man, her attorney said. But on Tuesday, hospital officials disclosed to the woman that he was actually high-risk, a 38-year-old gay man, Demetrio said. CDC guidelines say that gay men who are sexually active should not be used as organ donors unless the patient is in imminent danger of death.

The woman was told she had HIV and hepatitis on Nov. 1, he said.

"The (organ) procurement group knew, the hospital knew, but the most important person did not know," he said. "The people that dedicate their lives to these transplant surgeries, they're just great people, but they need to bring the patient into the mix and let them make an informed decision."

U.S. Centers for Disease Control and Prevention guidelines were violated twice, the attorney said. One violation was not informing the woman about the donor's status and then not testing her afterward for HIV until just recently, after HIV and hepatitis were found during tests on another patient who was being evaluated for a second transplant. . . .

She's been started on an HIV drug regimen "and unfortunately one of the side effects is it's not good for the kidneys," Demetrio said. She's not hospitalized.

Dr. Dan Berger, medical director of a large HIV-AIDS clinic in Chicago, said U.S. doctors have had several years of experience treating HIV-infected patients who went on to get transplant organs. Such patients need an HIV specialist and a transplant specialist to monitor their medications, which include anti-rejection drugs for the transplant and antiretrovirals for HIV, he said.

The four patients infected by the high-risk donor's organs have extra medical concerns, Berger said.

"When a patient first becomes infected with HIV there's a huge spike in viral load and (at the same time) severe immune compromise," he said. "The fact that they also are on immune-suppressive medications (after transplant) may put them at extreme risk for opportunistic infection."*

If Jane Doe had not become infected with HIV and hepatitis after her transplant, would the failure of the donor network and the university to fully inform her about the donor have been morally wrong? If so, why? Would her consenting to the transplant have been permissible if she had known that the donor was high risk? Should a patient have the right to consent to and undergo risky treatments? Explain.

---

*The Associated Press, "Atty: Woman Wasn't Told Donor Was a Risk," 16 November 2007.

CASE 3
Adolescent Informed Consent

In mid-summer, a 14-year-old youth was brought to the pediatric emergency department by his mother for evaluation for altered mental status. The mother returned from work to find her son acting strangely. She had last seen him the previous evening, and there were no problems or complaints at that time. Earlier in the week the child had sustained several mosquito bites. The child was now at times lethargic and at other times agitated. There were two episodes of vomiting. There was no history of fever trauma, medications, or known ingestions. The medical history was negative. The social history was significant for a high-achieving honor student who came from a very financially successful household. Physical examination revealed a drowsy and disoriented athletic male. The vital signs were temperature of 37.8° Celsius, heart rate of 107 beats per minute, respiratory rate of 20 per minute, and blood pressure of 123/87 mm Hg. The general physical examination was unremarkable. The neurologic examination revealed a disoriented teenager with ataxia, brisk reflexes throughout, reactive pupils, and intact cranial nerves II through XII. A bedside glucose test and pulse oximetry were both normal. Given the ongoing epidemic of West Nile virus at the time of presentation, the mother was convinced that the child had contracted the insect-borne disease because of the combination of mosquito bites and altered mental status. The mother was absolutely insistent that a spinal tap (lumbar puncture) be performed immediately, to evaluate for the possibility of West Nile virus.

The patient's pediatrician was also concerned and requested a full and thorough evaluation. An intravenous line was started and routine blood evaluations were ordered. The patient seemed at times to be more lucid, but at other times was again disoriented. When interviewed alone, he denied having West Nile virus, but he agreed to tell the physician why he believed this to be the case, but only if his parents were not told. The physician explained that all information given by the patient would be kept in strict confidence. Because of the assurance of confidentiality, the patient disclosed that he had bought a large amount of dextromethorphan on the Internet and had taken it with his friends after school.

Dextromethorphan ingestion, even in large quantities, generally does not require anything but supportive care. The mother, not knowing about the ingestion of this drug, continued to be insistent that further tests be performed, including a spinal tap.*

Who, if anyone, in this scenario should be allowed to give informed consent to treatment (or no treatment)? Why? Should the physician regard the 14-year-old as a mature minor? What actions should the physician take if she regarded him as a mature minor? What actions would the physician likely take if she decided to set aside the issue of informed consent and act only in the patient's best interests?

---

*Reza Keshavarz, "Adolescents, Informed Consent and Confidentiality: A Case Study," *The Mount Sinai Journal of Medicine* 72.4 (4 July 2005), 232–35.

FURTHER READING

American Cancer Society, "Informed Consent," http://www.cancer.org/treatment/ (22 October, 2015).

Jessica W. Berg et al., *Informed Consent: Legal Theory and Clinical Practice* (New York: Oxford University Press, 2001).

Tom L. Beauchamp and James F. Childress, "The Meaning and Justification of Informed Consent," in *Principles of Biomedical Ethics*, 5th ed. (New York: Oxford University Press, 2001), 77–98.

FindLaw, "Understanding Informed Consent: A Primer," http://healthcare.findlaw.com/patient-rights/understanding-informed-consent-a-primer.html (22 October 2015).

President's Commission for the Study of Ethical Problems in Medicine and Biomedical and Behavioral Research, *Making Health Care Decisions*, vol. 1: *Report* (Washington, DC: Government Printing Office, 1982), 2–6, 41–46.

Robert Young, "Informed Consent and Patient Autonomy," in *A Companion to Bioethics*, ed. Helga Kuhse and Peter Singer (Oxford: Blackwell, 2001), 441–51.

U. S. Department of Health and Human Services, "Informed Consent," http://www.hhs.gov/ohrp/policy/consent/ (22 October 2015).

NOTES

1. *Schloendorff v. Society of New York Hospitals,* 105 N.E. 92 (N.Y. 1914).

2. *Salgo v. Leland Stanford Jr. Univ. Bd. of Trustees,* 317 P.2d 170 (Cal. Ct. App. 1957).

3. *Canterbury v. Spence,* 464F.2d 772 (D.C. Cir. 1972).

4. Jay Katz, "Informed Consent to Medical Entrepreneurialism," in *Conflicts of Interest in Clinical Practice and Research,* ed. R. G. Speece et al. (New York: Oxford University Press, 1996).

5. Tom L. Beauchamp and James F. Childress, *Principles of Biomedical Ethics,* 5th ed. (New York: Oxford University Press, 2001), 79–80.

6. President's Commission for the Study of Ethical Problems in Medicine and Biomedical and Behavioral Research, *Making Health Care Decisions,* vol. 1: *Report* (Washington, DC: Government Printing Office, 1982), 38.

7. Ruth R. Faden and Tom L. Beauchamp, "The Concept of Informed Consent," in *A History and Theory of Informed Consent* (New York: Oxford University Press, 1986), 235–73.

8. Beauchamp and Childress, *Principles,* 94.

9. *Ibid.,* 77–79; Jessica W. Berg et al., *Informed Consent: Legal Theory and Clinical Practice* (New York: Oxford University Press, 2001), 15–17.

10. *Canterbury v. Spence.*

11. *Canterbury v. Spence.*

12. *Canterbury v. Spence.*

READINGS

The Concept of Informed Consent

RUTH R. FADEN AND TOM L. BEAUCHAMP

Faden and Beauchamp distinguish two common views of informed consent and argue that only one of them reflects the true meaning of the concept. Real informed consent involves more than a patient's merely agreeing to, or acquiescing in, some suggested course of action. An informed consent is a patient's autonomous action that *authorizes* a course of action. The other common meaning of the term is defined legally or institutionally and does not refer to autonomous authorization. Faden and Beauchamp also believe that the tendency to equate informed consent with shared decision-making is confused. Decision-making, which has been linked historically to informed consent, is not enough.

What is an informed consent? Answering this question is complicated because there are two common, entrenched, and starkly different meanings of "informed consent." That is, the term is analyzable in two profoundly different ways—not because of mere subtle differences of connotation that appear in different contexts, but because two different *conceptions* of informed consent have emerged from its history and are still at work, however unnoticed, in literature on the subject.

In one sense, which we label *sense₁*, "informed consent" is analyzable as a particular kind of action by individual patients and subjects: an autonomous authorization. In the second sense, *sense₂*, informed consent is analyzable in terms of the web of cultural and policy rules and requirements of consent that collectively form the social practice of informed consent in institutional contexts where *groups* of patients and subjects must be treated in accordance with rules, policies, and standard practices. Here, informed consents are not always *autonomous* acts, nor are they always in any meaningful respect *authorizations*.

Sense₁: Informed Consent as Autonomous Authorization

The idea of an informed consent suggests that a patient or subject does more than express agreement with, acquiesce in, yield to, or comply with an arrangement or a proposal. He or she actively *authorizes* the proposal in the act of consent. John may *assent* to a treatment plan without authorizing it. The assent may be a mere submission to the doctor's authoritative order, in which case John does not call on his own authority in order to give permission, and thus does not authorize the plan. Instead, he acts like a child who submits, yields, or assents to the school principal's spanking and in no way gives permission for or authorizes the spanking. Just as the child merely submits to an authority in a system where the lines of authority are quite clear, so often do patients.

Accordingly, an informed consent in sense₁ should be defined as follows: An informed consent

is an autonomous action by a subject or a patient that authorizes a professional either to involve the subject in research or to initiate a medical plan for the patient (or both). We can whittle down this definition by saying that an informed consent in sense₁ is given if a patient or subject with (1) substantial understanding and (2) in substantial absence of control by others (3) intentionally (4) authorizes a professional (to do intervention I).

All substantially autonomous acts satisfy conditions 1–3; but it does not follow from that analysis alone that all such acts satisfy 4. The fourth condition is what distinguishes informed consent as one *kind* of autonomous action. (Note also that the definition restricts the kinds of authorization to medical and research contexts.) A person whose act satisfies conditions 1–3 but who refuses an intervention gives an *informed refusal*.

The Problem of Shared Decisionmaking

This analysis of informed consent in sense₁ is deliberately silent on the question of how the authorizer and agent(s) being authorized *arrive at an agreement* about the performance of "I." Recent commentators on informed consent in clinical medicine, notably Jay Katz and the President's Commission, have tended to equate the idea of informed consent with a model of "shared decisionmaking" between doctor and patient. The President's Commission titles the first chapter of its report on informed consent in the patient-practitioner relationship "Informed Consent as Active, Shared Decision Making," while in Katz's work "the idea of informed consent" and "mutual decisionmaking" are treated as virtually synonymous terms.[1]

There is of course an historical relationship in clinical medicine between medical decisionmaking and informed consent. The emergence of the legal doctrine of informed consent was instrumental in drawing attention to issues of decisionmaking as well as authority in the doctor-patient relationship. Nevertheless, it is a confusion to treat informed consent and shared decisionmaking as anything like *synonymous*. For one thing, informed consent is not restricted to clinical medicine. It is a term that applies equally to biomedical and behavioral research contexts where a model of shared decisionmaking is frequently inappropriate. Even in clinical contexts, the social and psychological dynamics involved in selecting medical interventions should be distinguished from the patient's *authorization*.

We endorse Katz's view that effective communication between professional and patient or subject is often instrumental in obtaining informed consents (sense$_1$), but we resist his conviction that the idea of informed consent entails that the patient and physician "share decisionmaking," or "reason together," or reach a consensus about what is in the patient's best interest. This is a manipulation of the concept from a too singular and defined moral perspective on the practice of medicine that is in effect a moral program for changing the practice. Although the patient and physician *may* reach a decision together, they need not. It is the essence of informed consent in sense$_1$ only that the patient or subject *authorizes autonomously*; it is a matter of indifference where or how the proposal being authorized originates.

For example, one might advocate a model of shared decisionmaking for the doctor-patient relationship without simultaneously advocating that every medical procedure requires the consent of patients. Even relationships characterized by an ample slice of shared decisionmaking, mutual trust, and respect would and should permit many decisions about routine and low-risk aspects of the patient's medical treatment to remain the exclusive province of the physician, and thus some decisions are likely always to remain subject exclusively to the physician's authorization. Moreover, in the uncommon situation, a patient could autonomously authorize the physician to make *all* decisions about medical treatment, thus giving his or her informed consent to an arrangement that scarcely resembles the sharing of decisionmaking between doctor and patient.

Authorization

In authorizing, one both assumes responsibility for what one has authorized and transfers to another one's authority to implement it. There is no informed consent unless one *understands* these features of the act and *intends* to perform that act. That is, one must understand that one is assuming responsibility and warranting another to proceed.

To say that one assumes responsibility does not quite locate the essence of the matter, however, because a *transfer* of responsibility as well as of authority also occurs. The crucial element in an authorization is that the person who authorizes uses whatever right, power, or control he or she possesses in the situation to endow another with the right to act. In so doing, the authorizer assumes some responsibility for the actions taken by the other person. Here one could either authorize *broadly* so that a person can act in accordance with general guidelines, or *narrowly* so as to authorize only a particular, carefully circumscribed procedure.

Sense$_2$: Informed-Consent as Effective Consent

By contrast to sense$_1$, sense$_2$, or *effective* consent, is a policy-oriented sense whose conditions are not derivable solely from analyses of autonomy and authorization, or even from broad notions of respect for autonomy. "Informed consent" in this second sense does not refer to *autonomous* authorization, but to a legally or institutionally *effective* (sometimes misleadingly called *valid*) authorization from a patient or a subject. Such an authorization is "effective" because it has been obtained through procedures that satisfy the rules and requirements defining a specific institutional practice in health care or in research.

The social and legal practice of requiring professionals to obtain informed consent emerged in institutional contexts, where conformity to operative rules was and still is the sole necessary and sufficient condition of informed consent. Any consent is an informed consent in sense$_2$ if it satisfies whatever operative rules apply to the practice of informed consent. Sense$_2$ requirements for informed consent typically do not focus on the autonomy of the act of giving consent (as sense$_1$ does), but rather on regulating the behavior of the *consent-seeker* and on establishing *procedures and rules* for the context of consent. Such requirements of professional behavior and procedure are obviously more readily monitored and enforced by institutions.

However, because formal institutional rules such as federal regulations and hospital policies govern whether an act of authorizing is effective, a patient or subject can autonomously authorize an intervention, and so give an informed consent in sense$_1$, and yet *not effectively authorize* that intervention in sense$_2$.

Consider the following example. Carol and Martie are nineteen-year-old, identical twins attending the same university. Martie was born with multiple birth defects, and has only one kidney. When both sisters are involved in an automobile accident, Carol is not badly hurt, but her sister is seriously injured. It is quickly determined that Martie desperately needs a kidney transplant. After detailed discussions with the transplant team and with friends, Carol consents to be the donor. There is no question that Carol's authorization of the transplant surgery is substantially autonomous. She is well informed and has long anticipated being in just such a circumstance. She has had ample opportunity over the years to consider what she would do were she faced with such a decision. Unfortunately, Carol's parents, who were in Nepal at the time of the accident, do not approve of her decision. Furious that they were not consulted, they decide to sue the transplant team and the hospital for having performed an unauthorized surgery on their minor daughter. (In this state the legal age to consent to surgical procedures is twenty-one.)

According to our analysis, Carol gave her informed consent in sense$_1$ to the surgery, but she did not give her informed consent in sense$_2$. That is, she autonomously authorized the transplant and thereby gave an informed consent in sense$_1$ but did not give a consent that was effective under the operative legal and institutional policy, which in this case required that the person consenting be a legally authorized agent. Examples of other policies that can define sense$_2$ informed consent (but not sense$_1$) include rules that consent be witnessed by an auditor or that there be a one-day waiting period between solicitation of consent and implementation of the intervention in order for the person's authorization to be effective. Such rules can and do vary, both within the United States by jurisdiction and institution, and across the countries of the world.

Medical and research codes, as well as case law and federal regulations, have developed models of informed consent that are delineated entirely in a sense$_2$ format, although they have sometimes attempted to justify the rules by appeal to something like sense$_1$. For example, disclosure conditions for informed consent are central to the history of "informed consent" in sense$_2$, because disclosure has traditionally been a *necessary* condition of effective informed consent (and sometimes a *sufficient* condition!). The legal doctrine of informed consent is primarily a law of disclosure; satisfaction of disclosure rules virtually consumes "informed consent" in law. This should come as no surprise, because the legal system needs a generally applicable informed consent mechanism by which injury and responsibility can be readily and fairly assessed in court. These disclosure requirements in the legal and regulatory contexts are not conditions of "informed consent" in sense$_1$; indeed disclosure may be entirely irrelevant to giving an informed consent in sense$_1$. If a person has an adequate *understanding* of relevant information without benefit of a disclosure, then it makes no difference whether someone *discloses* that information.

Other sense$_2$ rules besides those of disclosure have been enforced. These include rules requiring evidence of adequate comprehension of information and the aforementioned rules requiring the presence of auditor witnesses and mandatory waiting periods. Sense$_2$ informed consent requirements generally take the form of rules focusing on disclosure, comprehension, the minimization of potentially controlling influences, and competence. These requirements express the present-day mainstream conception in the federal government of the United States. They are also typical of international documents and state regulations, which all reflect a sense$_2$ orientation.

The Relationship Between Sense$_1$ and Sense$_2$

A sense$_1$ "informed consent" can fail to be an informed consent in sense$_2$ by a lack of conformity to applicable rules and requirements. Similarly, an informed consent in sense$_2$ may not be an informed consent in sense$_1$. The rules and requirements that determine sense$_2$ consents need not result in autonomous authorizations at all in order to qualify as informed consents.

Such peculiarities in informed consent law have led Jay Katz to argue that the legal doctrine of "informed consent" bears a "name" that "promises much more than its construction in case law has delivered."

He has argued insightfully that the courts have, in effect, imposed a mere duty to warn on physicians, an obligation confined to risk disclosures and statements of proposed interventions. He maintains that "This judicially imposed obligation must be distinguished from the *idea* of informed consent, namely, that patients have a decisive role to play in the medical decisionmaking process. The idea of informed consent, though alluded to also in case law, cannot be implemented, as courts have attempted, by only expanding the disclosure requirements." By their actions and declarations, Katz believes, the courts have made informed consent a "cruel hoax" and have allowed "the idea of informed consent . . . to wither on the vine."[2]

The most plausible interpretation of Katz's contentions is through the $sense_1$/$sense_2$ distinction. If a physician obtains a consent under the courts' criteria, then an informed consent ($sense_2$) has been obtained. But it does not follow that the courts are using the *right* standards, or *sufficiently rigorous* standards in light of a stricter autonomy-based model—or "idea" as Katz puts it—of informed consent ($sense_1$).[3] If Katz is correct that the courts have made a mockery of informed consent and of its moral justification in respect for autonomy, then of course his criticisms are thoroughly justified. At the same time, it should be recognized that people can proffer legally or institutionally effective authorizations under prevailing rules even if they fall far short of the standards implicit in $sense_1$.

Despite the differences between $sense_1$ and $sense_2$, a definition of informed consent need not fall into one or the other class of definitions. It may conform to both. Many definitions of informed consent in policy contexts reflect at least a strong and definite reliance on informed consent in $sense_1$. Although the conditions of $sense_1$ are not logically necessary conditions for $sense_2$, we take it as morally axiomatic that they *ought* to serve—and in fact have served—as the benchmark or model against which the moral adequacy of a definition framed for $sense_2$ purposes is to be evaluated. This position is, roughly speaking, Katz's position.

A defense of the moral viewpoint that policies governing informed consent in $sense_2$ *should* be formulated to conform to the standards of informed consent in $sense_1$ is not hard to express. The goal of informed consent in medical care and in research—that is, the purpose behind the obligation to obtain informed consent—is to enable potential subjects and patients to make autonomous decisions about whether to grant or refuse authorization for medical and research interventions. Accordingly, embedded in the reason for having the social institution of informed consent is the idea that institutional requirements for informed consent in $sense_2$ *should* be intended to maximize the likelihood that the conditions of informed consent in $sense_1$ will be satisfied.

A major problem at the policy level, where rules and requirements must be developed and applied in the aggregate, is the following: The obligations imposed to enable patients and subjects to make authorization decisions must be evaluated not only in terms of the demands of a set of abstract conditions of "true" or $sense_1$ informed consent, but also in terms of the impact of imposing such obligations or requirements on various institutions with their concrete concerns and priorities. One must take account of what is fair and reasonable to require of health care professionals and researchers, the effect of alternative consent requirements on efficiency and effectiveness in the delivery of health care and the advancement of science, and—particularly in medical care—the effect of requirements on the welfare of patients. Also relevant are considerations peculiar to the particular social context, such as proof, precedent, or liability theory in case law, or regulatory authority and due process in the development of federal regulations and IRB consent policies.

Moreover, at the $sense_2$ level, one must resolve not only which requirements will define effective consent; one must also settle on the rules stipulating the conditions under which effective consents must be obtained. In some cases, hard decisions must be made about whether requirements of informed consent (in $sense_2$) should be imposed at all, even though informed consent (in $sense_1$) *could* realistically and meaningfully be obtained in the circumstances and could serve as a model for institutional rules. For example, should there be any consent requirements in the cases of minimal risk medical procedures and research activities?

This need to balance is not a problem for informed consent in $sense_1$, which is not policy oriented. Thus, it is possible to have a *morally acceptable* set of requirements for informed consent in sense$_2$ that deviates considerably from the conditions of informed consent in sense$_1$. However, the burden of moral proof rests with those who defend such deviations since the primary moral justification of the obligation to obtain informed consent is respect for autonomous action.

NOTES

1. President's Commission, *Making Health Care Decisions*, Vol. 1, 15 and Jay Katz, *The Silent World of Doctor and Patient* (New York: The Free Press, 1984),

87 and "The Regulation of Human Research—Reflections and Proposals," *Clinical Research* 21 (1973): 758–91. Katz does not provide a sustained analysis of joint or shared decisionmaking, and it is unclear precisely how he would relate this notion to informed consent.

2. Jay Katz, "Disclosure and Consent," in A. Milunsky and G. Annas, eds., *Genetics and the Law II* (New York: Plenum Press, 1980), 122, 128.

3. We have already noted that Katz's "idea" of informed consent—as the active involvement of patients in the medical decisionmaking process—is different from our sense$_1$.

Informed Consent—Must It Remain a Fairy Tale?

JAY KATZ

The ideal of informed consent with its presumptions of autonomy and joint decision-making is yet to be fully realized in practice, says Katz. The concept has been legally recognized, but genuine patient self-determination is still not the norm. Physicians acknowledge it but are likely to see it as a perfunctory fulfillment of legal requirements or as an enumeration of risks. The goal of joint decision-making between physicians and patients is still unfulfilled. Physicians must come to see that they have a "duty to respect patients as persons so that care will encompass allowing patients to live their lives in their own self-willed ways."

I. The Pre-History of Informed Consent in Medicine

The idea that, prior to any medical intervention, physicians must seek their patients' informed consent was introduced into American law in a brief paragraph in a 1957 state court decision,[1] and then elaborated on in a lengthier opinion in 1960.[2] The emerging legal idea that physicians were from now on obligated to share decisionmaking authority with their patients shocked the medical community, for it constituted a radical break with the silence that had been the hallmark of physician-patient interactions throughout the ages. Thirty-five years are perhaps not long enough for either law or medicine to resolve the tension between legal theory and medical practice, particularly since judges were reluctant to face up to implications of their novel

doctrine, preferring instead to remain quite deferential to the practices of the medical profession.

Viewed from the perspective of medical history, the doctrine of informed consent, if taken seriously, constitutes a revolutionary break with customary practice. Thus, I must review, albeit all too briefly, the history of doctor-patient communication. Only then can one appreciate how unprepared the medical profession was to heed these new legal commands. But there is more: Physicians could not easily reject what law had begun to impose on them, because they recognized intuitively that the radical transformation of medicine since the age of medical science made it possible, indeed imperative, for a doctrine of informed consent to emerge. Yet, bowing to the doctrine did not mean accepting it. Indeed, physicians could not accept it because, for reasons I shall soon explore, the nature of informed consent has remained in the words of Churchill, "an enigma wrapped in a mystery."

Originally published in the *Journal of Contemporary Health Law and Policy*, vol. 10, Spring 1994. Used with permission.

Throughout the ages physicians believed that they should make treatment decisions for their patients. This conviction inheres in the Hippocratic Oath: "I swear by Apollo and Aesculepius [that] I will follow that system of regimen which according to *my* ability and judgment *I* consider for the benefit of *my* patients . . . ."[3] The patient is not mentioned as a person whose ability and judgment deserve consideration. Indeed, in one of the few references to disclosure in the Hippocratic Corpus, physicians are admonished "to [conceal] most things from the patient while attending to him; [to] give necessary orders with cheerfulness and serenity, . . . revealing nothing of the patient's future or present condition."[4] When twenty-five centuries later, in 1847, the American Medical Association promulgated its first Code of Ethics, it equally admonished patients that their "obedience . . . to the prescriptions of [their] physician should be prompt and implicit. [They] should never permit [their] own crude opinions . . . to influence [their] attention to [their physicians]."[5]

The gulf separating doctors from patients seemed unbridgeable both medically and socially. Thus, whenever the Code did not refer to physicians and patients as such, the former were addressed as "gentlemen" and the latter as "fellow creatures." To be sure, caring for patients' medical needs and "abstain[ing] from whatever is deleterious and mischievous"[6] was deeply imbedded in the ethos of Hippocratic medicine. The idea that patients were also "autonomous" human beings, entitled to being partners in decision-making, was, until recently, rarely given recognition in the lexicon of medical ethics. The notion that human beings possess individual human rights, deserving of respect, of course, is of recent origin. Yet it antedates the twentieth century and therefore could have had an impact on the nature and quality of the physician-patient relationship.

It did not. Instead, the conviction that physicians should decide what is best for their patients, and, therefore, that the authority and power to do so should remain vested in them, continued to have a deep hold on the practices of the medical profession. For example, in the early 1950s the influential Harvard sociologist Talcott Parsons, who echoed physicians' views, stated that the physician is a technically competent person whose competence and specific judgments and measures cannot be competently judged by the layman and that the latter must take doctors' judgments and measures on 'authority.'[7] The necessity for such authority was supported by three claims:

First, *physicians' esoteric knowledge, acquired in the course of arduous training and practical experience, cannot be comprehended by patients.* While it is true that this knowledge, in its totality, is difficult to learn, understand and master, it does not necessarily follow that physicians cannot translate their esoteric knowledge into language that comports with patients' experiences and life goals (i.e., into language that speaks to quality of future life, expressed in words of risks, benefits, alternatives and uncertainties). Perhaps patients can understand this, but physicians have had too little training and experience with, or even more importantly, a commitment to, communicating their "esoteric knowledge" to patients in plain language to permit a conclusive answer as to what patients may comprehend.

Second, *patients, because of their anxieties over being ill and consequent regression to childlike thinking, are incapable of making decisions on their own behalf.* We do not know whether the childlike behavior often displayed by patients is triggered by pain, fear, and illness, or by physicians' authoritarian insistence that good patients comply with doctors' orders, or by doctors' unwillingness to share information with patients. Without providing such information, patients are groping in the dark and their stumbling attempts to ask questions, if made at all, makes them appear more incapable of understanding than they truly are.

We know all too little about the relative contributions which being ill, being kept ignorant, or being considered incompetent make to these regressive manifestations. Thus, physicians' unexamined convictions easily become self-fulfilling prophesies. For example, Eric Cassell has consistently argued that illness robs patients of autonomy and that only subsequent to the act of healing is autonomy restored.[8] While there is some truth to these contentions, they overlook the extent to which doctors can restore autonomy prior to the act of healing by not treating patients as children but as adults whose capacity for remaining authors of their own fate can be sustained and nourished. Cassell's views are reminiscent of Dostoyevsky's Grand Inquisitor who proclaimed that "at the most fearful moments of life," mankind is in need of "miracle, mystery and authority."[9] While, in this modern age, a person's capacity and right to take responsibility for his or her conduct has been given greater recognition than the Grand Inquisitor was inclined to grant, it still does not extend to patients. In the context of illness, physicians are apt to join the Grand Inquisitor at least to the extent of asserting that, while patients, they can only be comforted through subjugation to miracle, mystery and authority.

Third, *physicians' commitment to altruism is a sufficient safeguard for preventing abuses of their professional authority.* While altruism, as a general professional commitment, has served patients well in their encounters with physicians, the kind of protection it does and does not provide has not been examined in any depth. I shall have more to say about this later on. For now, let me only mention one problem: Altruism can only promise that doctors will try to place their patients' medical needs over their own personal needs. Altruism cannot promise that physicians will know, without inquiry, patients' needs. Put another way, patients and doctors do not necessarily have an identity of interest about matters of health and illness. Of course, both seek restoration of health and cure, and whenever such ends are readily attainable by only one route, their interests indeed may coincide.

In many physician-patient encounters, however, cure has many faces and the means selected affect the nature of cure in decisive ways. Thus, since quality of life is shaped decisively by available treatment options (including no treatment), the objectives of health and cure can be pursued in a variety of ways. Consider, for example, differences in value preferences between doctors and patients about longevity versus quality of remaining life. Without inquiry, one cannot presume identity of interest. As the surgeon Nuland cogently observed: "A doctor's altruism notwithstanding, his agenda and value system are not the same as those of the patient. That is the fallacy in the concept of beneficence so cherished by many physicians."[10]

II. The Age of Medical Science and Informed Consent

During the millennia of medical history, and until the beginning of the twentieth century, physicians could not explain to their patients, or—from the perspective of hindsight—to themselves, which of their treatment recommendations were curative and which were not. To be sure, doctors, by careful bedside observation, tried their level best "to abstain from what is deleterious and mischievous," to help if they could, and to be available for comfort during the hours, days or months of suffering. Doing more curatively, however, only became possible with the advent of the age of medical science. The introduction of scientific reasoning into medicine, aided by the results of carefully conducted research, permitted doctors for the first time to discriminate more aptly between knowledge, ignorance and conjecture in their recommendations for or against treatment. Moreover, the spectacular technological advances in the diagnosis and treatment of disease, spawned by medical science, provided patients and doctors with ever-increasing therapeutic options, each having its own particular benefits and risks.

Thus, for the first time in medical history it is possible, even medically and morally imperative, to give patients a voice in medical decisionmaking. It is possible because knowledge and ignorance can be better specified; it is medically imperative because a variety of treatments are available, each of which can bestow great benefits or inflict grievous harm; it is morally imperative because patients, depending on the lifestyle they wish to lead during and after treatment, must be given a choice.

All this seems self-evident. Yet, the physician-patient relationship—the conversations between the two parties—was not altered with the transformation of medical practice during the twentieth century. Indeed, the silence only deepened once laboratory data were inscribed in charts and not in patients' minds, once machines allowed physicians' eyes to gaze not at patients' faces but at the numbers they displayed, once x-rays and electrocardiograms began to speak for patients' suffering rather than their suffering voices.

What captured the medical imagination and found expression in the education of future physicians, was the promise that before too long the diagnosis of patients' diseases would yield objective, scientific data to the point of becoming algorithms. *Treatment*, however, required subjective data from patients and would be influenced by doctors' subjective judgments. This fact was overlooked in the quest for objectivity. Also overlooked was the possibility that greater scientific understanding of the nature of disease and its treatment facilitated better communication with patients. In that respect contemporary Hippocratic practices remained rooted in the past.

III. The Impact of Law

The impetus for change in traditional patterns of communication between doctors and patients came not from medicine but from law. In a 1957 California case,[11] and a 1960 Kansas case,[12] judges were astounded and troubled by these undisputed facts: That without any disclosure of risks, new technologies had been employed which promised great benefits but also exposed patients to formidable and uncontrollable harm. In the California case, a patient suffered a permanent paralysis of his lower extremities subsequent to the injection of a dye, sodium urokan, to locate a block in the abdominal aorta. In the Kansas case, a patient suffered severe injuries from cobalt radiation, administered, instead of conventional x-ray treatment, subsequent to a mastectomy for breast cancer. In the latter case, Justice Schroeder attempted to give greater specifications to the informed consent doctrine, first promulgated in the California decision: "To disclose and explain to the patient, in language as simple as necessary, the nature of the ailment, the nature of the proposed treatment, the probability of success or of alternatives, and perhaps the risks of unfortunate results and unforeseen conditions within the body."[13]

From the perspective of improved doctor-patient communication, or better, shared decisionmaking, the fault lines inherent in this American legal doctrine are many:

One: The common law judges who promulgated the doctrine restricted their task to articulating new and more stringent standards of liability whenever physicians withheld material information that patients should know, particularly in light of the harm that the spectacular advances in medical technology could inflict. Thus, the doctrine was limited in scope, designed to specify those minimal disclosure obligations that physicians must fulfill to escape *legal* liability for alleged non-disclosures. Moreover, it was shaped and confined by legal assumptions about the objectives of the laws of evidence and negligence, and by economic philosophies as to who should assume the financial burdens for medical injuries sustained by patients.

Even though the judges based the doctrine on "Anglo-American law['s] . . . premise of thoroughgoing self-determination,"[14] the Kansas court put it, or on "the root premise . . . fundamental in American jurisprudence that 'every human being of adult years and sound mind has a right to determine what shall be done with his own body,'"[15] as the Circuit Court for the District of Columbia put it in a subsequent opinion, the doctrine was grounded not in battery law (trespass); but in negligence law. The reasons are many. I shall only mention a compelling one: Battery law, based on unauthorized trespass, gives doctors only one defense—that they have made adequate disclosure. Negligence law, on the other hand, permits doctors to invoke many defenses, including "the therapeutic privilege" not to disclose when in their judgment, disclosure may prove harmful to patients' welfare.

Two recent opinions illustrate the problems identified here. First, in a rare opinion, the Supreme Court of Pennsylvania reconfirmed its adherence to the minority view among American jurisdictions that battery, not negligence, is the appropriate cause of action whenever lack of informed consent is alleged. The court held that whenever "the patient . . . demonstrated, and the jury found, that he was not advised of . . . material facts, risks, complications and alternatives to surgery which a reasonable man would have considered significant in deciding whether to have the operation . . . the causation inquiry ends. The sole issue remaining [is] a determination of damages."[16] Earlier in its opinion, the court quoted, with approval, a prior Pennsylvania decision:

> [W]here a patient is mentally and physically able to consult about his condition, in the absence of an

emergency, the consent of the patient is "a prerequisite to a surgical operation by his physician, and an operation without the patient's consent is a *technical assault*."[17]

Second, the Court of Appeals of California, in a ground-breaking opinion, significantly reduced the scope of the therapeutic privilege by requiring that in instances of hopeless prognosis (the most common situation in which the privilege has generally been invoked) the patient be provided with such information by asking, "If not the physician's duty to disclose a terminal illness, then whose?"[18] The duty to disclose prognosis had never before been identified specifically as one of the disclosure obligations in an informed consent opinion.

Thus, the appellate court's ruling constituted an important advance. It established that patients have a right to make decisions not only about the fate of their bodies but about the fate of their lives as well. The California Supreme Court, however, reversed. In doing so, the court made too much of an issue raised by the plaintiffs that led the appellate court to hold that doctors must disclose "statistical life expectancy information."[19] To be sure, disclosure of statistical information is a complex problem, but in focusing on that issue, the supreme court's attention was diverted from a more important new disclosure obligation promulgated by the appellate court: the duty to inform patients of their dire prognosis. The supreme court did not comment on that obligation. Indeed, it seemed to reverse the appellate court on this crucial issue by reinforcing the considerable leeway granted physicians to invoke the therapeutic privilege exception to full disclosure: "We decline to intrude further, either on the subtleties of the physician-patient relationship or in the resolution of claims that the physician's duty of disclosure was breached, by requiring the disclosure of information that may or may not be indicated in a given treatment context."[20]

Two: The doctrine of informed consent was not designed to serve as a *medical* blueprint for interactions between physicians and patients. The medical profession still faces the task of fashioning a "doctrine" that comports with its own vision of doctor-patient communication and that is responsive both to the realities of medical practices in an age of science and to the commands of law. As I said years ago,

> [T]ranslating the ingredients of [the informed consent] process into legal and useful medical prescriptions that respect patients' wishes to maintain and surrender autonomy, as well as physicians' unending struggles with omnipotence and impotence in the light of medical uncertainty, is a difficult task [which the medical profession] has not pursued . . . in any depth.[21]

Thus, disclosure practices only changed to the extent of physicians disclosing more about the risks of a proposed intervention in order to escape legal liability.

Three: Underlying the legal doctrine there lurks a broader assumption which has neither been given full recognition by judges nor embraced by physicians. The underlying idea is this: That from now on patients and physicians must make decisions jointly, with patients ultimately deciding whether to accede to doctors' recommendations. In *The Cancer Ward*, Solzhenitsyn captured, as only a novelist can, the fears that such an idea engenders. When doctor Ludmilla Afanasyevna was challenged by her patient, Oleg Kostoglotov, about physicians' rights to make unilateral decisions on behalf of patients, Afanasyevna gave a troubled, though unequivocal, answer: "But doctors *are* entitled to the right—doctors above all. Without that right, there'd be no such thing as medicine."[22]

If Afanasyevna is correct, then patients must continue to trust doctors silently. Conversation, to comport with the idea of informed consent, ultimately requires that both parties make decisions jointly and that their views and preferences be treated with respect. Trust, based on blind faith—on passive surrender to oneself or to another—must be distinguished from trust that is earned after having first acknowledged to oneself and then shared with the other what one knows and does not know about the decision to be made. If all of that had been considered by physicians, they would have appreciated that a new model of doctor-patient communication, that takes informed consent seriously required a radical break with current medical disclosure practice.

Four: The idea of joint decisionmaking is one thing, and its application in practice another. To translate theory into practice cannot be accomplished, as the Judicial Council of the American Medical Association attempted to do in one short paragraph. The Judicial Council stated that "[t]he patient should make his own determination on treatment. Informed consent is a basic *social* policy . . . ."[23] To translate social policy into *medical* policy is an inordinately difficult task. It requires a reassessment of the limits of medical knowledge in the light of medical uncertainty, a reassessment of professional authority to make decisions for patients in light of the consequences of such conduct for the well-being of patients, and a reassessment of the limits of patients' capacities to assume responsibility for choice in the light of their ignorance about medical matters and their anxieties when ill. Turning now to these problems, I wish to highlight that, in the absence of such reassessments, informed consent will remain a charade, and joint decisionmaking will elude us.

IV. Barriers to Joint Decisionmaking
A. Medical Uncertainty
The longer I reflect about doctor-patient decisionmaking, the more convinced I am that in this modern age of medical science, which for the first time permits sharing with patients the uncertainties of diagnosis, treatment, and prognosis, the problem of uncertainty poses the most formidable obstacle to disclosure and consent. By medical uncertainty I mean to convey what the physician Lewis Thomas observed so eloquently, albeit disturbingly:

> The only valid piece of scientific truth about which I feel totally confident is that we are profoundly ignorant about nature. . . . It is this sudden confrontation with the depth and scope of ignorance that represents the most significant contribution of twentieth-century science to the human intellect. *We are, at last facing up to it*. In earlier times, we either pretended to understand . . . or ignored the problem, or simply made up stories to fill the gap.[24]

Alvan Feinstein put this in more concrete language: "Clinicians are still uncertain about the best means of treatment for even such routine problems as . . . a fractured hip, a peptic ulcer, a stroke, a myocardial infarction. . . . At a time of potent drugs and formidable surgery, the exact effects of many therapeutic procedures are dubious or shrouded in dissension."[25]

Medical uncertainty constitutes a formidable obstacle to joint decisionmaking for a number of reasons: Sharing uncertainties requires physicians to be more aware of them than they commonly are. They must learn how to communicate them to patients and they must shed their embarrassment over acknowledging the true state of their own and of medicine's art and science. Thus, sharing uncertainties requires a willingness to admit ignorance about benefits and risks; to acknowledge the existence of alternatives, each with its own known and unknown consequences; to eschew one single authoritative recommendation; to consider carefully how to present uncertainty so that patients will not be overwhelmed by the information they will receive; and to explore the crucial question of how much uncertainty physicians themselves can tolerate without compromising their effectiveness as healers.

To so conduct oneself is most difficult. For, once doctors, on the basis of their clinical experience and knowledge, conclude which treatment is best, they tend to disregard, if not reject, the view of other colleagues who treat the same condition differently. Consider the current controversy over the management of localized prostate cancer: surgery, radiation or watchful waiting.[26] Some of the physicians involved in the debate are not even willing to accept that uncertainty exists, or at least they minimize its relevance to choice of treatment. Most who advocate treatment strongly prefer one type over another based on professional specialization (radiologists tend to recommend radiation; surgeons surgery).

Moreover, acknowledgment of uncertainty is undermined by the threat that it will undermine doctors' authority and sense of superiority. As Nuland put it, to feel superior to those dependent persons who are the sick, is after all a motivating factor that often influences their choice of medicine as a profession.[27] All of this suggests that implementation of the idea of informed consent is, to begin with, not a patient problem but a physician problem.

B. Patient Incompetence

Earlier, I touched on physicians' convictions that illness and medicine's esoteric knowledge rob patients of the capacity to participate in decisionmaking. Yet we do not know whether this is true. The evidence is compromised by the groping, half-hearted, and misleading attempts to inform patients about uncertainty and other matters which can make doctors' communications so confusing and incomprehensible. If patients then appear stupid and ignorant this should come as no surprise; nor should patients' resigned surrender to this dilemma: "You are the doctor, you decide."

It is equally debatable, as Thomas Duffy has contended, that "[p]aternalism exists in medicine . . . to fulfill a need created by illness."[28] It led him to argue, echoing Cassell, that "obviously autonomy cannot function as the cornerstone of the doctor-patient relationship [since] the impact of disease on personal integrity results in the patient's loss of autonomy. . . . In the doctor-patient relationship, the medical profession should always err on the side of beneficence."[29] If Duffy is correct, however, then informed consent is *ab initio* fatally compromised.

C. Patient Autonomy

Duffy's invocation of beneficence as the guiding principle is deeply rooted in the history of Hippocratic medicine. It finds expression in the ancient maxim: *primum non nocere*, above all do no harm, with "harm" remaining undefined but in practice being defined only as physical harm. Before presenting my views on the controversy over the primacy of autonomy or beneficence, let me briefly define their meaning.

In their authoritative book *Principles of Biomedical Ethics*, Thomas Beauchamp and James Childress defined these principles:

> Autonomy is a form of personal liberty of action where the individual determines his or her own course of action in accordance with a plan chosen by himself or herself. [Respect for individuals as autonomous agents entitles them] to such autonomous determinations without limitation on their liberty being imposed by others.[30]

Beneficence, on the other hand,

> [r]equires not only that we treat persons autonomously and that we refrain from harming them,

but also that we contribute to their welfare including their health. [Thus the principle asserts] the duty to help others further their important and legitimate interests . . . to *confer* benefits and actively to prevent and remove harms . . . [and] to *balance* possible goods against the possible harms of an action.[31]

Beauchamp and Childress' unequivocal and strong postulate on autonomy contrasts with the ambiguities contained in their postulate on beneficence. What do they mean by "benefits" and "harms" that allow invocation of beneficence? Do they mean only benefits and harms to patients' physical integrity, or to their dignitary integrity as choice-making individuals as well? Furthermore, what degree of discretion and license is permissible in the duty "to balance?" I have problems with balancing unless it is resorted to only as a *rare* exception to respect for autonomy. While human life is, and human interactions are, too complex to make any principle rule absolute, any exceptions must be rigorously justified.

I appreciate that mine is a radical proposal and constitutes a sharp break with Hippocratic practices. If informed consent, however, is ever to be based on the postulate of joint decisionmaking, the obligation "to respect the autonomous choices and actions of others,"[32] as Childress has put it, must be honored. Otherwise, informed consent is reduced to doctors providing more information but leaving decisionmaking itself to the authority of physicians.

As one physician once told me, echoing only an all too prevalent belief (and he was a physician allegedly deeply committed to informed consent), "I must first make the judgment which treatment alternative is best for patients, and only after I have exercised that professional judgment, will I discuss the risks and benefits of *the* recommended treatment." This story illustrates the emphasis doctors place on risk disclosures rather than alternatives. The latter, however, is more crucial to joint decisionmaking than the former. Such a view, however, again encounters the issue of disclosure of medical uncertainty inherent in any forthright discussion of treatment alternatives. Physicians remain most reluctant to acknowledge uncertainty to themselves, and even more to their patients.

V. Respect for Autonomy

It should be evident by now that physicians must embark on a prolonged period of self-examination about how to interact with patients in new ways in an age of medical science and informed consent. Physicians must cease to complain about lawyers forcing them "to do silly things." Whenever doctors do so, they often observe that they can easily present their disclosures in ways that lead patients to agree with what they had thought to be the best alternative in the first place. This contention is a correct assessment of what transpires in customary practices that continue to eschew joint decision-making. Therefore, as I have already suggested, informed consent in today's world, is largely a charade which misleads patients into thinking that they are making decisions when indeed they are not.

Any meaningful change in Hippocratic decision-making practices first requires a new and revolutionary commitment to one principle: that physicians must respect patients as autonomous persons. The most crucial reason for my placing such high value on autonomy and self-determination is because doing so safeguards, as nothing else can, the recognition by the other that the person before him or her is as much a person as he or she is. Beneficence can readily reduce persons to non-persons by "taking care of them" in all of the many not only caring, but also, non-caring meanings of this phrase.

VI. The Current State of Physician-Patient Decisionmaking

In his recent book, entitled *How We Die*, Sherwin Nuland, a distinguished surgeon, reflects with profundity and insight on his lifelong interactions with patients. In a chapter on cancer and its treatment he speaks movingly about "death belong[ing] to the dying and to those who love them."[33] Yet, that privilege is often wrested from them when,

> [d]ecisions about continuation of treatment are influenced by the enthusiasm of the doctors who propose them. Commonly, the most accomplished of the specialists are also the most convinced and unyielding believers in biomedicine's ability to over-come the challenge presented by a pathological process. . . . [W]hat is offered as objective clinical reality is often the subjectivity of a devout

disciple of the philosophy that death is an implacable enemy. To such warriors, even a temporary victory justifies the laying waste of the fields in which a dying man has cultivated his life.[34]

Looking back at his work, he concludes that "more than a few of my victories have been Pyrrhic. The suffering was sometimes not worth the success. . . . [H]ad I been able to project myself into the place of the family and the patient, I would have been less often certain that the desperate struggle should be undertaken."[35]

In his view, a surgeon,

> [t]hough he be kind and considerate of the patient he treats . . . allows himself to push his kindness aside because the seduction of The Riddle [the quest for diagnosis and cure] is so strong and the failure to solve it renders him so weak. [Thus, at times he convinces] patients to undergo diagnostic or therapeutic measures at a point in illness so far beyond reason that The Riddle might better have remained unsolved.[36]

Speaking then about the kind of doctor he will seek out when afflicted with a major illness, Nuland does not expect him to "understand my values, my expectations for myself . . . my philosophy of life. *That is not what he is trained for and that is not what he will be good at.*[37] Doctors can impart information, but "[i]t behooves every patient to study his or her own disease and learn enough about it. [Patients] should no longer expect from so many of our doctors what they cannot give."[38]

Nuland's views, supported by a great many poignant clinical vignettes, sensitively and forthrightly describe the current state of physician-patient decisionmaking, so dominated by physicians' judgments as to what is best. He presents many reasons for this state of affairs. One is based on doctors' "fear of failure":

> A need to control that exceeds in magnitude what most people would find reasonable. When control is lost, he who requires it is also a bit lost and so deals badly with the consequences of his impotence. In an attempt to maintain control, a doctor, usually without being aware of it, convinces himself that he knows better than the patient what course is proper. He dispenses only as much information as he deems fit, thereby influencing a

patient's decision-making in ways he does not recognize as self-serving.[39]

I have presented Nuland's observations at some length because they illustrate and support my contentions that joint decisionmaking between doctors and patients still eludes us. My critics had claimed earlier that work on informed consent was dated because informed consent had become an integral aspect of the practice of medicine. In the paperback edition of *The Silent World of Doctor and Patient*, I argued that they have dismissed too lightly my central arguments:

> [T]hat meaningful collaboration between physicians and patients cannot become a reality until physicians have learned (1) how to treat their patients not as children but as the adults they are; (2) how to distinguish between their ideas of the best treatment and their patients' ideas of what is best; (3) how to acknowledge to their patients (and often to themselves as well) their ignorance and uncertainties about diagnosis, treatment, and prognosis; [and to all this, I now want to add, (4) how to explain to patients the uncertainties inherent in the state of the art and science of medicine which otherwise permits doctors on the basis of their clinical experience to leave unacknowledged that their colleagues on the basis of their clinical experience have different beliefs as to which treatment is best].[40]

Nuland pleads for the resurrection of the family doctor[41] because he believes that the specialist is inadequate to the task of shouldering the burdens of decision with his patients. About this I differ with him. I believe that physicians (and surgeons as well) *can*, and *must*, learn to converse with patients in the spirit of joint decisionmaking. Physicians can and must learn to appreciate better than they do now that the principle of respect for person speaks to the caring commitment of physicians in old and new ways: *Old* in that it highlights the ancient and venerable medical duty not to abandon patients, and *new* by requiring doctors to communicate with them and remain at their sides, not only while their bodies are racked with pain and suffering but also while their minds are beset by fear, confusion, doubt and suffering over decisions to be made; also *new* in that implementation of the principle of psychological autonomy imposes the obligations on physicians both to invite, and respond to, questions about the decisions to be

made, and to do so by respecting patients' ultimate choices, a new aspect of the duty to care.

The moral authority of physicians will not be undermined by this caring view of interacting with patients. Doctors' authority resides in the medical knowledge they possess, in their capacity to diagnose and treat, in their ability to evaluate what can be diagnosed and what cannot, what is treatable and what is not, and what treatment alternatives to recommend, each with its own risks and benefits and each with its own prognostic implications as to cure, control, morbidity, exacerbation or even death.

The moral authority of physicians resides in knowing better than others the certainties and the uncertainties that accompany diagnosis, treatment, prognosis, health and disease, as well as the extent and the limits of their *scientific* knowledge and *scientific* ignorance. Physicians must learn to face up to and acknowledge the tragic limitations of their own professional knowledge, their inability to impart all their insights to all patients, and their own personal incapacities—at times more pronounced than others—to devote themselves fully to the needs of their patients. They must learn not to be unduly embarrassed by their personal and professional ignorance and to trust their patients to react appropriately to such acknowledgment. From all this it follows that ultimately the moral authority of physicians resides in their capacity to sort out *with* patients the choices to be made.

It is in this spirit that duty and caring become interwoven. Bringing these strands together imposes upon physicians the duty to respect patients as persons so that care will encompass allowing patients to live their lives in their own self-willed ways. To let patients follow their own lights is not an abandonment of them. It is a professional duty that, however painful, doctors must obey.

Without fidelity to these new professional duties, true caring will elude physicians. There is much new to be learned about caring that in decades to come will constitute the kind of caring that doctors in the past have wished for but have been unable to dispense, and that patients may have always yearned for.

I do not know whether my vision of a new physician-patient relationship defies medical reality. Thus, I may be wrong and I am willing to entertain this possibility as long as my critics are willing to admit that they too may be wrong. *As a profession we have never examined and tested in a committed manner what I have proposed.* It is this fact which, in conclusion, I want to highlight. For, I believe that in this age of medical science and informed consent the category of patient is in need of a radical reconceptualization. Throughout medical history, patients have been viewed as passive, ignorant persons whose welfare was best protected by their following doctors' orders, and physicians and patients were socialized to interact with one another on that basis. Throughout this essay, I have argued that such a view of the physician-patient relationship was dictated by doctors' inability to explain to themselves what was therapeutic and what was not in the practice of medicine. The advent of the age of medical science has changed all that and for the first time in medical history doctors now can distinguish better between knowledge, ignorance and conjecture. In turn, this permits physicians to take patients into their confidence.

Finally, my purpose in writing this essay is twofold: (1) To argue, notwithstanding any theories of tort law and cost containment to the contrary,[42] that patients must ultimately be given the deciding vote in matters that effect their lives; and (2) to suggest that informed consent will remain a fairy tale as long as the idea of joint decisionmaking, based on a commitment to patient autonomy and self-determination, does not become an integral aspect of the ethos of medicine and the law of informed consent. Until then, physicians, patients and judges can only deceive themselves or be deceived about patients having a vital voice in the medical decisionmaking process. Of course, there are alternatives to joint decisionmaking. One that I have briefly explored elsewhere suggested that we need a number of informed (and uninformed) consent doctrines depending on the nature of the decisions to be made, with the implication that only in certain medical contexts must informed consent rise to the rigor advanced in this essay.[43] Another alternative is to fashion an informed consent doctrine for law and medicine that is *not* based on "[t]he root premise . . . fundamental in American jurisprudence, that '[e]very human being of adult years and sound mind has a right to

determine what shall be done with his own body.'"[44] It is not a road on which I would like to travel and thus, I leave that task to others. It is important that those who disagree with me set forth their premises about who decides what; otherwise physicians and patients are condemned to interact with one another, under the rubric of what is now called "informed consent," by deception of both self and the other.

NOTES

1. Salgo v. Leland Stanford Jr. Univ. Bd. of Trustees, 317 P.2d 170, 181 (Cal. Dist. Ct. App. 1957).
2. Natanson v. Kline, 350 P.2d 1093 (Kan. 1960).
3. Hippocrates, *Oath of Hippocrates, in* 1 Hippocrates 299–301 (W.H.S. Jones trans., 1962).
4. 2 Hippocrates 297 (W.H.S. Jones trans., 1962).
5. American Medical Association: Code of Ethics (1847), reprinted in Jay Katz, The Silent World of Doctor and Patient 2 (1984), at 232.
6. Hippocrates, *supra* note 3, at 301.
7. Talcott Parsons, The Social System 464–65 (1951).
8. Eric Cassell, *The Function of Medicine*, Hastings Center Rep., Dec. 1977, at 16, 18.
9. Fyodor Dostoyevsky, The Brothers Karamazov 307 (A.P. MacAndrew trans., 1970).
10. Interview with Sherwin Nuland (1993).
11. Salgo v. Leland Stanford Jr. Univ. Bd. of Trustees, 317 P.2d 170 (Cal. Dist. Ct. App. 1957).
12. Natanson v. Kline, 350 P.2d 1093 (Kan. 1960).
13. *Id.* at 1106.
14. *Id.* at 1104.
15. Canterbury v. Spence, 464 F.2d 772, 780 (D.C. Cir. 1972).
16. Gouse v. Cassel, 615 A.2d 331, 335 (Pa. 1992).
17. *Id.* at 333–34 (emphasis added) (quoting Moscicki v. Shor, 163 A. 341, 342 (Pa. Super. Ct. 1932)).
18. Arato v. Avedon, 11 Cal. Rptr. 2d 169, 181 n.19 (Cal. Ct. App. 1992), *vacated*, 858 P.2d 598 (Cal. 1993).
19. *Arato*, 11 Cal. Rptr. 2d at 177.
20. *Arato*, 858 P.2d at 607.
21. Katz, *supra* note 5, at 84.
22. Alexander Solzhenitsyn, The Cancer Ward 77 (N. Bethell & D. Burg trans., 1969).
23. Judicial Council of the Am. Medical Ass'n., Current Opinions of the Judicial Council of the American Medical Association 25 (1981) (*emphasis added*).
24. Lewis Thomas, The Medusa and the Snail 73–74 (1979).
25. Alvan R. Feinstein, Clinical Judgment 23–24 (1967). Even though written 27 years ago, he has not changed his views. Interview with Alvan R. Feinstein (1994).
26. Gerald W. Chodak et al., *Results of Conservative Management of Clinically Localized Prostate Cancer*, 330 New Eng. J. Med. 242 (1994).
27. Interview with Sherwin B. Nuland (1994).

28. Thomas P. Duffy, *Agamemnon's Fate and the Medical Profession*, 9 W. New Eng. L. Rev. 21, 27 (1987).

29. *Id.* at 30.

30. Thomas L. Beauchamp & James F. Childress, Principles of Biomedical Ethics 56, 58 (1st ed. 1979).

31. Thomas L. Beauchamp & James F. Childress, Principles of Biomedical Ethics 148–49 (2d ed. 1983).

32. James F. Childress, *The Place of Autonomy in Bioethics*, Hastings Center Rep., Jan.–Feb. 1990, at 12, 12–13.

33. Sherwin B. Nuland, How We Die 265 (1994).

34. *Id.*

35. *Id.* at 266.

36. *Id.* at 249.

37. *Id.* at 266 (emphasis added).

38. *Id.* at 260.

39. *Id.* at 258.

40. Jay Katz, The Silent World of Doctor and Patient xi (1986).

41. Nuland, *supra* note 33, at 266.

42. *See, e.g.*, Peter H. Schuck, *Rethinking Informed Consent*, 103 Yale L.J. 899 (1994).

43. Jay Katz, *Physician-Patient Encounters "On a Darkling Plain,"* 9 W. New Eng. L. Rev. 207, 221–22 (1987).

44. Canterbury v. Spence, 464 F.2d 772, 780 (D.C. Cir. 1972).

Transparency: Informed Consent in Primary Care

HOWARD BRODY

Brody observes that the theory and the practice of informed consent are far apart and that accepted legal standards send physicians the wrong message about what they are supposed to do. He thinks that a conversation standard of informed consent does send the right message but is probably legally unworkable. He proposes instead a "transparency standard," which says that "disclosure is adequate when the physician's basic thinking has been rendered transparent to the patient."

While the patient's right to give informed consent to medical treatment is now well-established both in U.S. law and in biomedical ethics, evidence continues to suggest that the concept has been poorly integrated into American medical practice, and that in many instances the needs and desires of patients are not being well met by current policies.[1] It appears that the theory and the practice of informed consent are out of joint in some crucial ways. This is particularly true for primary care settings, a context typically ignored by medical ethics literature, but where the majority of doctor-patient encounters occur. Indeed, some have suggested that the concept of informed consent is virtually foreign to primary care medicine where benign paternalism appropriately reigns and where respect for patient autonomy is almost completely absent.[2]

It is worth asking whether current legal standards for informed consent tend to resolve the problem or

to exacerbate it. I will maintain that accepted legal standards, at least in the form commonly employed by courts, send physicians the wrong message about what is expected of them. An alternative standard that would send physicians the correct message, a conversation standard, is probably unworkable legally. As an alternative, I will propose a transparency standard as a compromise that gives physicians a doable task and allows courts to review appropriately. I must begin, however, by briefly identifying some assumptions crucial to the development of this position even though space precludes complete argumentation and documentation.

Crucial Assumptions

Informed consent is a meaningful ethical concept only to the extent that it can be realized and promoted within the ongoing practice of good medicine. This need not imply diminished respect for patient autonomy, for there are excellent reasons to regard respect for patient autonomy as a central feature of good medical care. Informed consent, properly understood, must be considered an essential ingredient of good patient care, and a physician who lacks the skills to inform patients appropriately and obtain proper consent should be viewed as lacking essential medical skills necessary for practice. It is not enough to see informed consent as a nonmedical, legalistic exercise designed to promote patient autonomy, one that interrupts the process of medical care.

However, available empirical evidence strongly suggests that this is precisely how physicians currently view informed consent practices. Informed consent is still seen as bureaucratic legalism rather than as part of patient care. Physicians often deny the existence of realistic treatment alternatives, thereby attenuating the perceived need to inform the patient of meaningful options. While patients may be informed, efforts are seldom made to assess accurately the patient's actual need or desire for information, or what the patient then proceeds to do with the information provided. Physicians typically underestimate patients' desire to be informed and overestimate their desire to be involved in decision-making. Physicians may also view informed consent as an empty charade, since they are confident in their abilities to manipulate consent by how they discuss or divulge information.[3]

A third assumption is that there are important differences between the practice of primary care medicine and the tertiary care settings that have been most frequently discussed in the literature on informed consent. The models of informed consent discussed below typically take as the paradigm case something like surgery for breast cancer or the performance of an invasive and risky radiologic procedure. It is assumed that the risks to the patient are significant, and the values placed on alternative forms of treatment are quite weighty. Moreover, it is assumed that the specialist physician performing the procedure probably does a fairly limited number of procedures and thus could be expected to know exhaustively the precise risks, benefits, and alternatives for each.

Primary care medicine, however, fails to fit this model. The primary care physician, instead of performing five or six complicated and risky procedures frequently, may engage in several hundred treatment modalities during an average week of practice. In many cases, risks to the patient are negligible and conflicts over patient values and the goals of treatment or non-treatment are of little consequence. Moreover, in contrast to the tertiary care patient, the typical ambulatory patient is much better able to exercise freedom of choice and somewhat less likely to be intimidated by either the severity of the disease or the expertise of the physician; the opportunities for changing one's mind once treatment has begun are also much greater. Indeed, in primary care, it is much more likely for the full process of informed consent to treatment (such as the beginning and the dose adjustment of an antihypertensive medication) to occur over several office visits rather than at one single point in time.

It might be argued that for all these reasons, the stakes are so low in primary care that it is fully appropriate for informed consent to be interpreted only with regard to the specialized or tertiary care setting. I believe that this is quite incorrect for three reasons. First, good primary care medicine ought to embrace respect for patient autonomy, and if patient autonomy is operationalized in informed consent, properly understood, then it ought to be part and parcel of good primary care. Second, the claim that the primary care physician cannot be expected to obtain the patient's informed consent seems to undermine the idea that informed consent could or ought to be part of the daily practice of medicine. Third, primary care encounters are statistically more common than the highly specialized encounters previously used as models for the concept of informed consent.[4]

Accepted Legal Standards

Most of the literature on legal approaches to informed consent addresses the tension between the community practice standard, and the reasonable patient standard, with the latter seen as the more satisfactory, emerging legal standard.[5] However, neither standard sends the proper message to the physician about what is expected of her to promote patient autonomy effectively and to serve the informational needs of patients in daily practice.

The community practice standard sends the wrong message because it leaves the door open too wide for physician paternalism. The physician is instructed to behave as other physicians in that specialty behave, regardless of how well or how poorly that behavior serves patients' needs. Certainly, behaving the way other physicians behave is a task we might expect physicians to readily accomplish; unfortunately, the standard fails to inform them of the end toward which the task is aimed.

The reasonable patient standard does a much better job of indicating the centrality of respect for patient autonomy and the desired outcome of the informed consent process, which is revealing the information that a reasonable person would need to make an informed and rational decision. This standard is particularly valuable when modified to include the specific informational and decisional needs of a particular patient.

If certain things were true about the relationship between medicine and law in today's society, the reasonable patient standard would provide acceptable guidance to physicians. One feature would be that physicians esteem the law as a positive force in guiding their practice, rather than as a threat to their well-being that must be handled defensively. Another element would be a prospective consideration by the law of what the physician could reasonably have been expected to do in practice, rather than a retrospective review armed with the foreknowledge that some significant patient harm has already occurred.

Unfortunately, given the present legal climate, the physician is much more likely to get a mixed or an undesirable message from the reasonable patient standard. The message the physician hears from the reasonable patient standard is that one must exhaustively lay out all possible risks as well as benefits and alternatives of the proposed procedure. If one remembers to discuss fifty possible risks, and the patient in a particular case suffers the fifty-first, the physician might subsequently be found liable for incomplete disclosure. Since lawsuits are triggered when patients suffer harm, disclosure of risk becomes relatively more important than disclosure of benefits. Moreover, disclosure of information becomes much more critical than effective patient participation in decisionmaking. Physicians consider it more important to document what they said to the patient than to document how the patient used or thought about that information subsequently.

In specialty practice, many of these concerns can be nicely met by detailed written or videotaped consent documents, which can provide the depth of information required while still putting the benefits and alternatives in proper context. This is workable when one engages in a limited number of procedures and can have a complete document or videotape for each.[6] However, this approach is not feasible for primary care, when the number of procedures may be much more numerous and the time available with each patient may be considerably less. Moreover, it is simply not realistic to expect even the best educated of primary care physicians to rattle off at a moment's notice a detailed list of significant risks attached to any of the many drugs and therapeutic modalities they recommend.

This sets informed consent apart from all other aspects of medical practice in a way that I believe is widely perceived by nonpaternalistic primary care physicians, but which is almost never commented upon in the medical ethics literature. To the physician obtaining informed consent, *you never know when you are finished*. When a primary care physician is told to treat a patient for strep throat or to counsel a person suffering a normal grief reaction from the recent death of a relative, the physician has a good sense of what it means to complete the task at hand. When a physician is told to obtain the patient's informed consent for a medical intervention, the impression is quite different. A list of as many possible risks as can be thought of may still omit some significant ones. A list of all the risks that actually have occurred may still not have dealt with the patient's need to know risks in relation to benefits and alternatives. A description of all benefits, risks, and alternatives may not establish whether the patient has understood the information. If the patient says he understands, the physician has to wonder whether he really understands or whether he is simply saying this to be accommodating. As the law currently *appears* to operate (in the perception of the defensively minded physician), there never comes a point at which you can be certain that you have adequately completed your legal as well as your ethical task.

The point is not simply that physicians are paranoid about the law; more fundamentally, physicians are getting a message that informed consent is very different from any other task they are asked to perform in medicine. If physicians conclude that informed consent is therefore not properly part of medicine at all, but is rather a legalistic and bureaucratic hurdle they must overcome at their own peril, blame cannot be attributed to paternalistic attitudes or lack of respect for patient autonomy.

The Conversation Model

A metaphor employed by Jay Katz, informed consent as conversation, provides an approach to respect for patient autonomy that can be readily integrated within primary care practice.[7] Just as the specific needs of an individual patient for information, or the meaning that patient will attach to the information as it is presented, cannot be known in advance, one cannot always tell in advance how a conversation is going to turn out. One must follow the process along and take one's cues from the unfolding conversation itself. Despite the absence of any formal rules for carrying out or completing a conversation on a specific subject, most people have a good intuitive grasp of what it means for a conversation to be finished, what it means to change the subject in the middle of a conversation, and what it means to later reopen a conversation one had thought was completed when something new has just arisen. Thus, the metaphor suggests that informed consent consists not in a formal process carried out strictly by protocol but in a conversation designed to encourage patient participation in all medical decisions to the extent that the patient wishes to be included. The idea of informed consent as physician-patient conversation could, when properly developed, be a useful analytic tool for ethical issues in informed consent, and could also be a powerful educational tool for highlighting the skills and attitudes that a physician needs to successfully integrate this process within patient care.

If primary care physicians understand informed consent as this sort of conversation process, the idea that exact rules cannot be given for its successful management could cease to be a mystery. Physicians would instead be guided to rely on their own intuitions and communication skills, with careful attention to information received from the patient, to determine when an adequate job had been done

in the informed consent process. Moreover, physicians would be encouraged to see informed consent as a genuinely mutual and participatory process, instead of being reduced to the one-way disclosure of information. In effect, informed consent could be demystified, and located within the context of the everyday relationships between physician and patient, albeit with a renewed emphasis on patient participation.[8]

Unfortunately, the conversation metaphor does not lend itself to ready translation into a legal standard for determining whether or not the physician has satisfied her basic responsibilities to the patient. There seems to be an inherently subjective element to conversation that makes it ill-suited as a legal standard for review of controversial cases. A conversation in which one participates is by its nature a very different thing from the same conversation described to an outsider. It is hard to imagine how a jury could be instructed to determine in retrospect whether or not a particular conversation was adequate for its purposes. However, without the possibility for legal review, the message that patient autonomy is an important value and that patients have important rights within primary care would seem to be severely undermined. The question then is whether some of the important strengths of the conversation model can be retained in another model that does allow better guidance.

The Transparency Standard

I propose the transparency standard as a means to operationalize the best features of the conversation model in medical practice. According to this standard, adequate informed consent is obtained when a reasonably informed patient is allowed to participate in the medical decision to the extent that patient wishes. In turn, "reasonably informed" consists of two features: (1) the physician discloses the basis on which the proposed treatment, or alternative possible treatments, have been chosen; and (2) the patient is allowed to ask questions suggested by the disclosure of the physician's reasoning, and those questions are answered to the patient's satisfaction.

According to the transparency model, the key to reasonable disclosure is not adherence to existing standards of other practitioners, nor is it adherence to a list of risks that a hypothetical reasonable patient would want to know. Instead, disclosure is adequate when the physician's basic thinking has been rendered transparent to the patient. If the physician arrives at a recommended therapeutic or diagnostic intervention only after carefully examining a list of risks and benefits, then rendering the physician's thinking transparent requires that those risks and benefits be detailed for the patient. If the physician's thinking has not followed that route but has reached its conclusion by other considerations, then what needs to be disclosed to the patient is accordingly different. Essentially, the transparency standard requires the physician to engage in the typical patient-management thought process, only to *do it out loud in language understandable to the patient.*[9]

To see how this might work in practice, consider the following as possible general decision-making strategies that might be used by a primary physician:

1. The intervention, in addition to being presumably low-risk, is also routine and automatic. The physician, faced with a case like that presented by the patient, almost always chooses this treatment.
2. The decision is not routine but seems to offer clear benefit with minimal risk.
3. The proposed procedure offers substantial chances for benefit, but also very substantial risks.
4. The proposed intervention offers substantial risks and extremely questionable benefits. Unfortunately, possible alternative courses of action also have high risk and uncertain benefit.

The exact risks entailed by treatment loom much larger in the physician's own thinking in cases 3 and 4 than in cases 1 and 2. The transparency standard would require that physicians at least mention the various risks to patients in scenarios 3 and 4, but would not necessarily require physicians exhaustively to describe risks, unless the patient asked, in scenarios 1 and 2.

The transparency standard seems to offer some considerable advantages for informing physicians what can legitimately be expected of them in the promotion of patient autonomy while carrying out

the activities of primary care medicine. We would hope that the well-trained primary care physician generally thinks before acting. On that assumption, the physician can be told exactly when she is finished obtaining informed consent—first, she has to share her thinking with the patient; secondly, she has to encourage and answer questions; and third, she has to discover how participatory he wishes to be and facilitate that level of participation. This seems a much more reasonable task within primary care than an exhaustive listing of often irrelevant risk factors.

There are also considerable advantages for the patient in this approach. The patient retains the right to ask for an exhaustive recital of risks and alternatives. However, the vast majority of patients, in a primary care setting particularly, would wish to supplement a standardized recital of risks and benefits of treatment with some questions like, "Yes, doctor, but what does this really mean for me? What meaning am I supposed to attach to the information that you've just given?" For example, in scenarios 1 and 2, the precise and specific risk probabilities and possibilities are very small considerations in the thinking of the physician, and reciting an exhaustive list of risks would seriously misstate just what the physician was thinking. If the physician did detail a laundry list of risk factors, the patient might very well ask, "Well, doctor, just what should I think about what you have just told me?" and the thoughtful and concerned physician might well reply, "There's certainly a small possibility that one of these bad things will happen to you; but I think the chance is extremely remote and in my own practice I have never seen anything like that occur." The patient is very likely to give much more weight to that statement, putting the risks in perspective, than he is to the listing of risks. And that emphasis corresponds with an understanding of how the physician herself has reached the decision.

The transparency standard should further facilitate and encourage useful questions from patients. If a patient is given a routine list of risks and benefits and then is asked "Do you have any questions?" the response may well be perfunctory and automatic. If the patient is told precisely the grounds on which the physician has made her recommendation, and then asked the same question, the response is much more likely to be individualized and meaningful.

There certainly would be problems in applying the transparency standard in the courtroom, but these do not appear to be materially more difficult than those encountered in applying other standards; moreover, this standard could call attention to more important features in the ethical relationship between physician and patient. Consider the fairly typical case, in which a patient suffers harm from the occurrence of a rare but predictable complication of a procedure, and then claims that he would not have consented had he known about that risk. Under the present "enlightened" court standards, the jury would examine whether a reasonable patient would have needed to know about that risk factor prior to making a decision on the proposed intervention. Under the transparency standard, the question would instead be whether the physician thought about that risk factor as a relevant consideration prior to recommending the course of action to the patient. If the physician did seriously consider that risk factor, but failed to reveal that to the patient, he was in effect making up the patient's mind in advance about what risks were worth accepting. In that situation, the physician could easily be held liable. If, on the other hand, that risk was considered too insignificant to play a role in determining which intervention ought to be performed, the physician may still have rendered his thinking completely transparent to the patient even though that specific risk factor was not mentioned. In this circumstance, the physician would be held to have done an adequate job of disclosing information.[10] A question would still exist as to whether a competent physician ought to have known about that risk factor and ought to have considered it more carefully prior to doing the procedure. But that question raises the issue of negligence, which is where such considerations properly belong, and removes the problem from the context of informed consent. Obviously, the standard of informed consent is misapplied if it is intended by itself to prevent the practice of negligent medicine.

Transparency in Medical Practice

Will adopting a legal standard like transparency change medical practice for the better? Ultimately only empirical research will answer this question. We know almost nothing about the sorts of conversations primary care physicians now have with their patients, or what would happen if these physicians routinely tried harder to share their basic thinking about therapeutic choices. In this setting it is possible to argue that the transparency standard will have deleterious effects. Perhaps the physician's basic thinking will fail to include risk issues that patients, from their perspective, would regard as substantial. Perhaps how physicians think about therapeutic choice will prove to be too idiosyncratic and variable to serve as any sort of standard. Perhaps disclosing basic thinking processes will impede rather than promote optimal patient participation in decisions.

But the transparency standard must be judged, not only against ideal medical practice, but also against the present-day standard and the message it sends to practitioners. I have argued that that message is, "You can protect yourself legally only by guessing all bad outcomes that might occur and warning each patient explicitly that he might suffer any of them." The transparency standard is an attempt to send the message, "You can protect yourself legally by conversing with your patients in a way that promotes their participation in medical decisions, and more specifically by making sure that they see the basic reasoning you used to arrive at the recommended treatment." It seems at least plausible to me that the attempt is worth making.

The reasonable person standard may still be the best way to view informed consent in highly specialized settings where a relatively small number of discrete and potentially risky procedures are the daily order of business. In primary care settings, the best ethical advice we can give physicians is to view informed consent as an ongoing process of conversation designed to maximize patient participation after adequately revealing the key facts. Because the conversation metaphor does not by itself suggest measures for later judicial review, a transparency standard, or something like it, may be a reasonable way to operationalize that concept in primary care practice. Some positive side-effects of this might be more focus on good diagnostic and therapeutic decisionmaking on the physician's part, since it will be understood that the patient will be made aware of what the physician's reasoning process has been like, and better documentation of management decisions in the patient record. If these occur, then it will be clearer that the standard of informed consent has promoted rather than impeded high quality patient care.

REFERENCE

1. Charles W. Lidz *et al.*, "Barriers to Informed Consent," *Annals of Internal Medicine* 99:4 (1983), 539–43.

2. Tom L. Beauchamp and Laurence McCullough, *Medical Ethics: The Moral Responsibilities of Physicians* (Englewood Cliffs, NJ: Prentice-Hall, 1984).

3. For a concise overview of empirical data about contemporary informed consent practices, see Ruth R. Faden and Tom L. Beauchamp, *A History and Theory of Informed Consent* (New York: Oxford University Press, 1986), 98–99 and associated footnotes.

4. For efforts to address ethical aspects of primary care practice, see Ronald J. Christie and Barry Hoffmaster, *Ethical Issues in Family Medicine* (New York: Oxford University Press, 1986); and Harmon L. Smith and Larry R. Churchill, *Professional Ethics and Primary Care Medicine* (Durham, NC: Duke University Press, 1986).

5. Faden and Beauchamp, *A History and Theory of Informed Consent*, 23–49 and 114–50. I have also greatly benefited from an unpublished paper by Margaret Wallace.

6. For a specialty opinion to the contrary, see W. H. Coles *et al.*, "Teaching Informed Consent," in *Further Developments in Assessing Clinical Competence*, Ian R. Hart and Ronald M. Harden, eds. (Montreal: Can-Heal Publications, 1987), 241–70. This paper is interesting in applying to specialty care a model very much like the one I propose for primary care.

7. Jay Katz, *The Silent World of Doctor and Patient* (New York: Free Press, 1984).

8. Howard Brody, *Stories of Sickness* (New Haven: Yale University Press, 1987), 171–81.

9. For an interesting study of physicians' practices on this point, see William C. Wu and Robert A Pearlman, "Consent in Medical Decisionmaking: The Role of Communication," *Journal of General Internal Medicine* 3:1 (1988), 9–14.

10. A court case that might point the way toward this line of reasoning is *Precourt v. Frederick*, 395 Mass. 689 (1985). See William J. Curran, "Informed Consent in Malpractice Cases: A Turn Toward Reality," *New England Journal of Medicine* 314:7 (1986), 429–31.

Informed Consent: Some Challenges to the Universal Validity of the Western Model

ROBERT J. LEVINE

Levine says that since different countries and cultures may have vastly different perspectives on the nature of persons, and since the point of informed consent is to show respect for persons, it is not possible to provide a definition of informed consent that is universally applicable. The rules of the Western model of informed consent are not appropriate for many cultures. The ethical principle of respect for persons is universally applicable, but applying it to specific cultures with varying notions of *person* can be problematic. Levine suggests that instead of insisting on sticking to the rules, we use practical procedures to deal with the cultural differences when they arise.

Informed Consent

Informed consent holds a central place in the ethical justification of research involving human subjects. This position is signaled by the fact that it is

From *Law, Medicine, and Health Care*, vol. 19, no. 3–4 (1991), pp. 207–13. Reprinted with permission of the American Society of Law, Medicine & Ethics.

the first-stated and, by far, the longest principle of the Nuremberg Code.[1]

> I. The voluntary consent of the human subject is absolutely essential. This means that the person involved should have the legal capacity to give consent; should be so situated as to be able to exercise free power of choice, without the intervention of any element of force, fraud, deceit, duress, overreaching, or other ulterior form of constraint or

coercion; and should have sufficient knowledge and comprehension of the elements of the subject matter involved as to enable him to make an understanding and enlightened decision. This latter element requires that before the acceptance of an affirmative decision by the experimental subject there should be made known to him the nature, duration, and purpose of the experiment; the method and means by which it is to be conducted; all inconveniences and hazards reasonably to be expected; and the effects upon his health or person which may possibly come from his participation in the experiment. . . .

The Nuremberg Code identifies four attributes of consent without which consent cannot be considered valid: consent must be "voluntary," "legally competent," "informed," and "comprehending." These four attributes stand essentially unchanged to this day. . . .

The National Commission grounded the requirement for informed consent in the ethical principle of respect for persons which it defined as follows:

> Respect for persons incorporates at least two basic ethical convictions: First, that individuals should be treated as autonomous agents, and second, that persons with diminished autonomy and thus in need of protection are entitled to such protections.

The National Commission defined an "autonomous person" as ". . . an individual capable of deliberation about personal goals and of acting under the direction of such deliberation." To show respect for autonomous persons requires that we leave them alone, even to the point of allowing them to choose activities that might be harmful, unless they agree or consent that we may do otherwise. We are not to touch them or to encroach upon their private spaces unless such touching or encroachment is in accord with their wishes. Our actions should be designed to affirm their authority and enhance their capacity to be self-determining; we are not to obstruct their actions unless they are clearly detrimental to others. We show disrespect for autonomous persons when we either repudiate their considered judgments or deny them the freedom to act on those judgments in the absence of compelling reasons to do so.

The National Commission's discussion of an autonomous person is consistent with the prevailing perception of the nature of the "moral agent" in Western civilization. A moral agent is an individual who is capable of forming a rational plan of life, capable of rational deliberation about alternative plans of action with the aim of making choices that are compatible with his or her life plan and who assumes responsibility for the consequences of his or her choices.

Although the National Commission did not cite either of the following sources as authoritative in developing its definition of respect for persons, it is clear to this observer that they found them influential: The first is the statement of the principle of respect for persons as articulated by the German philosopher, Immanuel Kant: "So act as to treat humanity, whether in thine own person or in that of any other, in every case as an end withal, never as a means only." A second influential statement is that of the American judge, Benjamin Cardozo: "Every human being of adult years and sound mind has the right to determine what will be done with his own body. . . ."

[S]ince the late 1950s the idea of "informed consent" has been used in place of the original idea of "voluntary consent" as presented in the Nuremberg Code. In the actual process of negotiating informed consent and in the reviews of plans for informed consent conducted by Institutional Review Boards (IRBs), there is a tendency to concentrate on the information to be presented to the prospective subject. Among the IRB's principal concerns are the following questions: Is there a full statement of each of the elements of informed consent? Is the information presented in a style of language that one could expect the prospective subject to understand? Implicit in this is a vision of informed consent as a two step process. First, information is presented to the subject by the investigator. Secondly, the subject satisfies himself or herself that he or she understands, and based upon this understanding either agrees or refuses to participate in the research project. . . .

In the paper I presented at an earlier CIOMS conference[2] I concluded:

> This brief survey of descriptions of relationships between health professionals and patients in three disparate cultures leads me to conclude that the informed consent standards of the Declaration of Helsinki are not universally valid. Imposition of

these standards as they are now written will not accomplish their purposes; i.e., they will not guide physicians in their efforts to show respect for persons because they do not reflect adequately the views held in these cultures of the nature of the person in his or her relationship to society.

This conclusion was based on a review of observations of the doctor–patient relationship, subject–investigator relationship and perspectives on the nature of disease in three cultures: Western Africa, China, and a Central American Mayan Indian culture.

The concept of personhood as it exists in various cultures has been addressed in an excellent paper by Willy De Craemer.[3] De Craemer is a cross-cultural sociologist with extensive experience in the field in, among other places, Central Africa and Japan.

In this paper he makes it clear that the Western vision of the person is a minority viewpoint in the world. The majority viewpoint manifest in most other societies, both technologically developing (e.g., Central Africa) and technologically developed (e.g., Japan), does not reflect the American perspective of radical individualism. . . .

> The special status that the Japanese accord to human relationships, with its emphasis on the empathic and solidary interdependence of many individuals, rather than on the autonomous independence of the individual person, includes within it several other core attributes. To begin with, the kind of reciprocity (*on*) that underlies human relationships means that both concretely and symbolically what anthropologist Marcel Mauss . . . termed "the theme of the gift" is one of its dominant motifs. A continuous, gift-exchange-structured flow of material and nonmaterial "goods" and "services" takes place between the members of the enclosed human nexus to which each individual belongs. Through a never-ending process of mutual giving, receiving, and repaying . . . a web of relations develops that binds donor and recipients together in diffuse, deeply personal, and overlapping creditor-debtor ways. Generalized benevolence is involved, but so is generalized obligation, both of which take into account another crucial parameter of Japanese culture: the importance attached to status, rank, and hierarchical order in interpersonal relationships, and to . . . "proper-place occupancy" within them. The

> triple obligation to give, receive, and repay are tightly regulated by this status-formalism and sense of propriety. . . .

It is not difficult to imagine how a research ethics committee in the Western world—particularly in the United States—would evaluate the custom of exchange of gifts—both material and immaterial—in a system that recognized the legitimacy of "status, rank, and hierarchical order." Attention would soon be focused on the problems of "conflicts of interest." Questions would be raised as to whether consent would be invalidated by "undue inducement," or what the Nuremberg Code calls "other ulterior form(s) of constraint or coercion." In my views, it is impossible to evaluate the meaning of cash payments, provision of free services, and other "inducements" without a full appreciation of the cultural significance of such matters.

It is against this backdrop that I have been asked by the CIOMS Conference Programme Committee to "provide a definition [of informed consent] which is widely applicable to different countries and cultures." Given that the purpose of informed consent is to show respect for persons, in recognition of the vastly different perspectives of the nature of "person," I cannot do this. Since I cannot provide a substantive definition of informed consent, I shall suggest a procedural approach to dealing with the problem.

As an American I am firmly committed to the Western vision of the person and deeply influenced by my experience with the American variant of this vision. . . .

Thus, it would not be prudent to trust an American to provide a universally applicable definition of informed consent. I suggest further, that it would not be prudent to rely on any person situated in any culture to provide a universally applicable definition of informed consent.

Before proceeding, I wish to comment on the continuing controversy on the topic of ethical justification of research that crosses national boundaries. There are those who contend that all research, wherever it is conducted, should be justified according to universally applicable standards; I refer to them as "universalists." Those opposed to the universalist position, whom I call "pluralists," accept some standards as universal, but argue that other standards must be adapted to accommodate the mores of particular cultures. Pluralists commonly refer to the universalist position as "ethical imperialism," while universalists often call that of their opponents, "ethical relativism."

Universalists correctly point out that most therapeutic innovations are developed in industrialized nations. Investigators from these countries may go to technologically developing countries to test their innovations for various reasons; some of these reasons are good and some of them are not (e.g., to save money and to take advantage of the less complex and sophisticated regulatory systems typical to technologically developing countries). Moreover, universalists observe that, once the innovations have been proved safe and effective, economic factors often limit their availability to citizens of the country in which they were tested. Requiring investigators to conform to the ethical standards of their own country when conducting research abroad is one way to restrain exploitation of this type. Universalists also point to the Declaration of Helsinki as a widely accepted universal standard for biomedical research that has been endorsed by most countries, including those labeled "technologically developing." This gives weight to their claim that research must be conducted according to universal principles. Furthermore, the complex regulations characteristic of technologically developed countries are, in general, patterned after the Declaration of Helsinki.

Marcia Angell, in a particularly incisive exposition of the universalists' position, suggests this analogy:[4]

> Does apartheid offend universal standards of justice, or does it instead simply represent the South African custom that should be seen as morally neutral? If the latter view is accepted, then ethical principles are not much more than a description of the mores of a society. I believe they must have more meaning than that. There must be a core of human rights that we would wish to see honored universally, despite local variations in their superficial aspects. . . . The force of local custom or law cannot justify abuses of certain fundamental rights, and the right of self-determination, on which the doctrine of informed consent is based, is one of them.

Pluralists join with universalists in condemning economic exploitation of technologically developing

countries and their citizens.[5] Unlike the universalists, however, they see the imposition of ethical standards for the conduct of research by a powerful country on a developing country as another form of exploitation. In their view, it is tantamount to saying, "No, you may not participate in this development of technology, no matter how much you desire it, unless you permit us to replace your ethical standards with our own." Pluralists call attention to the fact that the Declaration of Helsinki, although widely endorsed by the nations of the world, reflects a uniquely Western view of the nature of the person; as such it does not adequately guide investigators in ways to show respect for all persons in the world.

An example of pluralism may be found in the diversity of national policies regarding blind HIV-seroprevalence studies. The United States Centers for Disease Control are now conducting anonymous tests of leftover blood drawn for other purposes without notification in studies designed to "determine the level of HIV-seroprevalence in a nationwide sample of hospital patients and clients at family planning, sexually transmitted disease, tuberculosis, and drug treatment clinics. . . ." No personal identifiers are kept.[6] Although there seems to be widespread agreement among U.S. commentators that such anonymous testing without notification is ethically justified, different judgments have been reached in other countries, most notably in the United Kingdom and in the Netherlands.[7] Who is to say which of these nations has the correct ethical perspective that should be made part of the "universal standard"?

The legitimacy of the pluralists' position is recognized implicitly in U.S. policy on whether research subjects are required to be informed of the results of HIV antibody testing.[8] In general, this policy requires that all individuals "whose test results are associated with personal identifiers must be informed of their own test results . . . individuals may not be given the option 'not to know' the result. . . ." This policy permits several narrowly defined exceptions. One of these provides that research "conducted at foreign sites should be carefully evaluated to account for cultural norms, the health resource capability and official health policies of the host country." Then "the reviewing IRB must consider if any modification to the policy is significantly justified by the risk/benefit evaluation of the research."

WHO/CIOMS Proposed International Guidelines provide specific guidance for the conduct of research in which an investigator or an institution in a technologically developed country serves as the "external sponsor" of research conducted in a technologically developing "host country."[9] In my judgment these guidelines strike a sensitive balance between the universalist and pluralist perspectives. They require that "the research protocol should be submitted to ethical review by the initiating agency. The ethical standards applied should be no less exacting than they would be for research carried out within the initiating country" (Article 28). They also provide for accommodation to the mores of the culture within the "host country." For example:

> Where individual members of a community do not have the necessary awareness of the implications of participation in an experiment to give adequately informed consent directly to the investigators, it is desirable that the decision whether or not to participate should be elicited through the intermediary of a trusted community leader. (Article 15)

The conduct of research involving human subjects must not violate any universally applicable ethical standards. Although I endorse certain forms of cultural relativism, there are limits to how much cultural relativism ought to be tolerated. Certain behaviors ought to be condemned by the world community even though they are sponsored by a nation's leaders and seem to have wide support of its citizens. For example, the Nuremberg tribunal appealed to universally valid principles in order to determine the guilt of the physicians (war criminals) who had conducted research according to standards approved by their nation's leaders.

I suggest that the principle of respect for persons is one of the universally applicable ethical standards. It is universally applicable when stated at the level of formality employed by Immanuel Kant: "So act as to treat humanity, whether in thine own person or in that of any other, in every case as an end withal, never as a means only." The key concept is that persons are never to be treated only or merely as means to another's ends. When one goes beyond

this level of formality or abstraction, the principle begins to lose its universality. When one restates the principle of respect for persons in a form that reflects a peculiarly Western view of the person, it begins to lose its relevance to some people in Central Africa, Japan, Central America, and so on.

The Conference Programme Committee asked me to address the problem "of obtaining consent in cultures where non-dominant persons traditionally do not give consent, such as a wife." Having subscribed to the Western vision of the meaning of person, I believe that all persons should be treated as autonomous agents, wives included. Thus, I believe that we should show respect for wives in the context of research by soliciting their informed consent. But, if this is not permitted within a particular culture, would I exclude wives from participation in research?

Not necessarily. If there is a strong possibility either that the wife could benefit from participation in the research or that the class of women of which she is a representative could benefit (and there is a reasonable balance of risks and potential benefits), I would offer her an opportunity to participate. To do otherwise would not accomplish anything of value (e.g., her entitlement to self-determination); it would merely deprive her of a chance to secure the benefits of participation in the research. I would, of course, offer her an opportunity to decline participation, understanding that in some cultures she would consider such refusal "unthinkable."

. . . Lack of education in and of itself presents no problems that are unfamiliar to those experienced with negotiating informed consent with prospective subjects. These are barriers to comprehension which are not generally insurmountable. Greater problems are presented by those who hold beliefs about health and illness that are inconsistent with the concepts of Western medicine. It may, for example, be difficult to explain the purpose of vaccination to a person who believes that disease is caused by forces that Western civilization dismisses as supernatural or magical.[10] The meaning of such familiar (in the Western world) procedures as blood-letting may be vastly different and very disturbing in some societies.[11] Problems with such explanations can, I believe, be dealt with best by local ethical review committees.

Illiteracy, in and of itself, presents no problems to the process of informed consent which, when conducted properly, entails talking rather than reading. Rather, it presents problems with the documentation of informed consent. The process of informed consent, designed to show respect for persons, fosters their interests by empowering them to pursue and protect their own interests. The consent form, by contrast, is an instrument designed to protect the interests of investigators and their institutions and to defend them against civil or criminal liability. If it is necessary to have such protection of investigators, subjects may be asked to make their mark on a consent document and a witness may be required to countersign and attest to the fact that the subject received the information.

A Procedural Resolution

In "Proposal Guidelines for International Testing of Vaccines and Drugs Against HIV Infection and AIDS" (hereafter referred to as "Proposed HIV Guidelines"), reference is made to an ethical review system.[12] This system is based on that set forth in the WHO/CIOMS Proposed International Guidelines for Biomedical Research Involving Human Subjects. In the Proposed HIV Guidelines, there are suggestions for divisions of responsibility for ethical review. Here I shall elaborate how responsibilities should be divided for determining the adequacy of informed consent procedures.

This proposal presupposes the existence of an international standard for informed consent. I suggest that the standards for informed consent as set forth in the WHO/CIOMS Proposed International Guidelines and as elaborated in the Proposed HIV Guidelines, be recognized as the international standard for informed consent.

1. All plans to conduct research involving human subjects should be reviewed and approved by a research ethics committee (REC). Ideally the REC should be based in the community in which the research is to be conducted. However, as noted in CIOMS/WHO Proposed International Guidelines, under some circumstances regional or national committees may be adequate for these purposes. In such cases it is essential that regional or national committees have as members or consultants individuals who are highly familiar with the customs of the community in which the research is to be done.

The authority of the REC to approve research should be limited to proposals in which the plans for informed consent conform either to the international standard or to a modification of the international standard that has been authorized by a national ethical review body.

2. Proposals to employ consent procedures that do not conform to the international standard should be justified by the researcher and submitted for review and approval by a national ethical review body. Earlier in this paper I identified some conditions or circumstances that could justify such omissions or modifications.

The role of the national ethical review body is to authorize consent procedures that deviate from the international standard. The responsibility for review and approval of the entire protocol (with the modified consent procedure) remains with the REC. Specific details of consent procedures that conform to the international standard or to a modified version of the international standard approved by the national ethical review body should be reviewed and approved by the local ethical review committee.

3. There should be established an international ethical review body to provide advice, consultation and guidance to national ethical review bodies when such is requested by the latter.

4. In the case of externally sponsored research: Ethical review should be conducted in the initiating country. Although it may and should provide advice to the host country, its approval should be based on its finding that plans for informed consent are consistent with the international standard. If there has been a modification of consent procedures approved by the national ethical review body in the host country, the initiating country may either endorse the modification or seek consultation with the international review body.

NOTES

1. Reprinted in R. J. Levine: *Ethics and Regulation of Clinical Research.* Urban & Schwarzenberg, Baltimore & Munich, Second Edition, 1986.

2. R. J. Levine, "Validity of Consent Procedures in Technologically Developing Countries." In: *Human*

Experimentation and Medical Ethics. Ed. by Z. Bankowski and N. Howard-Jones, Council for International Organizations of Medical Sciences, Geneva, 1982, pp. 16–30.

3. W. De Craemer, "A Cross-Cultural Perspective on Personhood." *Milbank Memorial Fund Quarterly* 61:19–34, Winter 1983.

4. M. Angell, "Ethical Imperialism? Ethics in International Collaborative Clinical Research." *New England Journal of Medicine* 319:1081–1083, 1988.

5. M. Barry, "Ethical Considerations of Human Investigation in Developing Countries: The AIDS Dilemma." *New England Journal of Medicine* 319:1083–1086, 1988; N. A. Christakis, "Responding to a Pandemic: International Interests in AIDS Control." *Daedalus* 118 (No. 2):113–114, 1989; and N. A. Christakis, "Ethical Design of an AIDS Vaccine Trial in Africa." *Hastings Center Report* 18 (No. 3):31–37, June/July, 1988.

6. M. Pappaioanou et al., "The Family of HIV Seroprevalence Studies: Objectives, Methods and Uses of Sentinel Surveillance in the United States." *Public Health Reports* 105(2):113–119, 1990.

7. R. Bayer, L. H. Lumey, and L. Wan, "The American, British and Dutch Responses to Unlinked Anonymous HIV Seroprevalence Studies: An International Comparison." *AIDS* 4:283–290, 1990, reprinted in this issue of *Laws, Medicine and Health Care*, 19:3–4.

8. R. E. Windom, Assistant Secretary for Health, policy on informing those tested about HIV serostatus, letter to PHS agency heads, Washington, DC, May 9, 1988.

9. Proposed International Guidelines for Biomedical Research Involving Human Subjects, A Joint Project of the World Health Organization and the Council for International Organizations of Medical Sciences, CIOMS. Geneva, 1982.

10. See De Craemer, *supra* note 3 and Levine, *supra* note 2.

11. A. J. Hall, "Public Health Trials in West Africa: Logistics and Ethics." *IRB: A Review of Human Subjects Research* 11 (No. 5):8–10, Sept./Oct. 1989. See also Christakis, *supra* note 5.

12. R. J. Levine, and W. K. Mariner, "Proposed Guidelines for International Testing of Vaccines and Drugs Against HIV Infection and AIDS," prepared at the request of WHO, Global Programme on AIDS and submitted January 5, 1990.

Canterbury v. Spence

UNITED STATES COURT OF APPEALS

This 1972 case helped settle the question of what standard should be used to judge the adequacy of disclosure by a physician. The court ruled that adequacy should not be judged by what the medical profession thinks is appropriate but by what information the patient finds relevant to his decision. The scope of the communication to the patient "must be measured by the patient's need, and that need is the information material to the decision."

Suits charging failure by a physician adequately to disclose the risks and alternatives of proposed treatment are not innovations in American law. They date back a good half-century, and in the last decade they have multiplied rapidly. There is, nonetheless, disagreement among the courts and the commentators on many major questions, and there is no precedent of our own directly in point. For the tools enabling resolution of the issues on this appeal, we are forced to begin at first principles.

The root premise is the concept, fundamental in American jurisprudence, that "[e]very human being of adult years and sound mind has a right to determine what shall be done with his own body. . . ." True consent to what happens to one's self is the informed exercise of a choice, and that entails an opportunity to evaluate knowledgeably the options available and the risks attendant upon each. The average patient has little or no understanding of the medical arts, and ordinarily has only his physician to whom he can look for enlightenment with which to reach an intelligent decision. From these almost axiomatic considerations springs the need, and in turn the requirement, of a reasonable

From U. S. Court of Appeals, District of Columbia Circuit, *Canterbury v. Spence*, 464 F.2d 772 (D.C. Cir. 1972).

divulgence by physician to patient to make such a decision possible.

A physician is under a duty to treat his patient skillfully, but proficiency in diagnosis and therapy is not the full measure of his responsibility. The cases demonstrate that the physician is under an obligation to communicate specific information to the patient when the exigencies of reasonable care call for it. Due care may require a physician perceiving symptoms of bodily abnormality to alert the patient to the condition. It may call upon the physician confronting an ailment which does not respond to his ministrations to inform the patient thereof. It may command the physician to instruct the patient as to any limitations to be presently observed for his own welfare, and as to any precautionary therapy he should seek in the future. It may oblige the physician to advise the patient of the need for or desirability of any alternative treatment promising greater benefit than that being pursued. Just as plainly, due care normally demands that the physician warn the patient of any risks to his well-being which contemplated therapy may involve.

The context in which the duty of risk-disclosure arises is invariably the occasion for a decision as to whether a particular treatment procedure is to be undertaken. To the physician, whose training enables a self-satisfying evaluation, the answer may seem clear, but it is the prerogative of the patient, not the physician, to determine for himself the direction in which his interests seem to lie. To enable the patient to chart his course understandably, some familiarity with the therapeutic alternatives and their hazards becomes essential.

A reasonable revelation in these respects is not only a necessity but, as we see it, is as much a matter of the physician's duty. It is a duty to warn of the dangers lurking in the proposed treatment, and that is surely a facet of due care. It is, too, a duty to impart information which the patient has every right to expect. The patient's reliance upon the physician is a trust of the kind which traditionally has exacted obligations beyond those associated with arms-length transactions. His dependence upon the physician for information affecting his well-being, in terms of contemplated treatment, is well-nigh abject. As earlier noted, long before the instant litigation arose, courts had recognized that the physician had the responsibility of satisfying the vital informational needs of the patient. More recently, we ourselves have found "in the fiducial qualities of [the physician-patient] relationship the physician's duty to reveal to the patient that which in his best interests it is important that he should know." We now find, as a part of the physician's overall obligation to the patient, a similar duty of reasonable disclosure of the choices with respect to proposed therapy and the dangers inherently and potentially involved. . . .

Once the circumstances give rise to a duty on the physician's part to inform his patient, the next inquiry is the scope of the disclosure the physician is legally obliged to make. The courts have frequently confronted this problem but no uniform standard defining the adequacy of the divulgence emerges from the decisions. Some have said "full" disclosure, a norm we are unwilling to adopt literally. It seems obviously prohibitive and unrealistic to except physicians to discuss with their patients every risk of proposed treatment—no matter how small or remote—and generally unnecessary from the patient's viewpoint as well. Indeed, the cases speaking in terms of "full" disclosure appear to envision something less than total disclosure, leaving unanswered the question of just how much.

The larger number of courts, as might be expected, have applied tests framed with reference to prevailing fashion within the medical profession. Some have measured the disclosure by "good medical practice," others by what a reasonable practitioner would have bared under the circumstances, and still others by what medical custom in the community would demand. We have explored this rather considerable body of law but are unprepared to follow it. The duty to disclose, we have reasoned, arises from phenomena apart from medical custom and practice. The latter, we think, should no more establish the scope of the duty than its existence. Any definition of scope in terms purely of a professional standard is at odds with the patient's prerogative to decide on projected therapy himself. That prerogative, we have said, is at the very foundation of the duty to disclose, and both the patient's right to know and the physician's correlative obligation to tell him are diluted to the extent that its compass is dictated by the medical profession.

In our view, the patient's right of self-decision shapes the boundaries of the duty to reveal. That right can be effectively exercised only if the patient possesses enough information to enable an intelligent choice. The scope of the physician's communications to the patient, then, must be measured by the patient's need, and that need is the information material to the decision. Thus the test for determining whether a particular peril must be divulged is its materiality to the patient's decision: all risks potentially affecting the decision must be unmasked. And to safeguard the patient's interest in achieving his own determination on treatment, the law must itself set the standard for adequate disclosure.

Optimally for the patient, exposure of a risk would be mandatory whenever the patient would deem it significant to his decision, either singly or in combination with other risks. Such a requirement, however, would summon the physician to second-guess the patient, whose ideas on materiality could hardly be known to the physician. That would make an undue demand upon medical practitioners, whose conduct, like that of others, is to be measured in terms of reasonableness. Consonantly with orthodox negligence doctrine, the physician's liability for nondisclosure is to be determined on the basis of foresight, not hindsight; no less than any other aspect of negligence, the issue on nondisclosure must be approached from the viewpoint of the reasonableness of the physician's divulgence in terms of what he knows or should know to be the patient's informational needs. If, but only if, the fact-finder can say that the physician's communication was unreasonably inadequate is an imposition of liability legally or morally justified.

Of necessity, the content of the disclosure rests in the first instance with the physician. Ordinarily it is only he who is in position to identify particular dangers; always he must make a judgment, in terms of materiality, as to whether and to what extent revelation to the patient is called for. He cannot know with complete exactitude what the patient would consider important to his decision, but on the basis of his medical training and experience he can sense how the average, reasonable patient expectably

would react. Indeed, with knowledge of, or ability to learn, his patient's background and current condition, he is in a position superior to that of most others—attorneys, for example—who are called upon to make judgments on pain of liability in damages for unreasonable miscalculation.

From these considerations we derive the breadth of the disclosure of risks legally to be required. The scope of the standard is not subjective as to either the physician or the patient; it remains objective with due regard for the patient's informational needs and with suitable leeway for the physician's situation. In broad outline, we agree that "[a] risk is thus material when a reasonable person, in what the physician knows or should know to be the patient's position, would be likely to attach significance to the risk or cluster of risks in deciding whether or not to forgo the proposed therapy."

The topics importantly demanding a communication of information are the inherent and potential hazards of the proposed treatment, the alternatives to that treatment, if any, and the results likely if the patient remains untreated. The factors contributing significance to the dangerousness of a medical technique are, of course, the incidence of injury and the degree of the harm threatened. A very small chance of death or serious disablement may well be significant; a potential disability which dramatically outweighs the potential benefit of the therapy or the detriments of the existing malady may summon discussion with the patient.

There is no bright line separating the significant from the insignificant; the answer in any case must abide a rule of reason. Some dangers—infection, for example—are inherent in any operation; there is no obligation to communicate those of which persons of average sophistication are aware. Even more clearly, the physician bears no responsibility for discussion of hazards the patient has already discovered, or those having no apparent materiality to patients' decision on therapy. The disclosure doctrine, like others marking lines between permissible and impermissible behavior in medical practice, is in essence a requirement of conduct prudent under the circumstances. Whenever nondisclosure of particular risk information is open to debate by reasonable-minded men, the issue is for the finder of the facts.

Two exceptions to the general rule of disclosure have been noted by the courts. Each is in the nature of a physician's privilege not to disclose, and the reasoning underlying them is appealing. Each, indeed, is but a recognition that, as important as is the patient's right to know, it is greatly outweighed by the magnitudinous circumstances giving rise to the privilege. The first comes into play when the patient is unconscious or otherwise incapable of consenting, and harm from a failure to treat is imminent and outweighs any harm threatened by the proposed treatment. When a genuine emergency of that sort arises, it is settled that the impracticality of conferring with the patient dispenses with need for it. Even in situations of that character the physician should, as current law requires, attempt to secure a relative's consent if possible. But if time is too short to accommodate discussion, obviously the physician should proceed with the treatment.

The second exception obtains when risk-disclosure poses such a threat of detriment to the patient as to become unfeasible or contraindicated from a medical point of view. It is recognized that patients occasionally become so ill or emotionally distraught on disclosure as to foreclose a rational decision, or complicate or hinder the treatment, or perhaps even pose psychological damage to the patient. Where that is so, the cases have generally held that the physician is armed with a privilege to keep the information from the patient, and we think it clear that portents of that type may justify the physician in action he deems medically warranted. The critical inquiry is whether the physician responded to a sound medical judgment that communication of the risk information would present a threat to the patient's well-being.

The physician's privilege to withhold information for therapeutic reasons must be carefully circumscribed, however, for otherwise it might devour the disclosure rule itself. The privilege does not accept the paternalistic notion that the physician may remain silent simply because divulgence might prompt the patient to forgo therapy the physician feels the patient really needs. That attitude presumes instability or perversity for even the normal patient, and runs counter to the foundation principle that the patient should and ordinarily can make the choice for himself. Nor does the privilege contemplate operation save where the patient's reaction to risk information, as reasonably foreseen by the physician, is menacing. And even in a situation of that kind, disclosure to a close relative with a view to securing consent to the proposed treatment may be the only alternative open to the physician. . . .

No more than breach of any other legal duty does nonfulfillment of the physician's obligation to disclose alone establish liability to the patient. An unrevealed risk that should have been made known must materialize, for otherwise the omission however unpardonable, is legally without consequence. Occurrence of the risk must be harmful to the patient, for negligence unrelated to injury is nonactionable. And, as in malpractice actions generally, there must be a causal relationship between the physician's failure to adequately divulge and damage to the patient.

CHAPTER 6

Human Research

Two noble values help shape the vast, extraordinary enterprise known as medical science: knowledge and beneficence—the unceasing quest to know, to find out, and the aspiration to act for people's good. When humans are the subjects of the research, these values assume their greatest importance, the stakes are at their highest, and the resulting ethical problems take on their sharpest edge. The chief difficulty is that these dual purposes do not fit together easily. Consequently, in its short history (dating from the early 1700s), systematized human research has engendered both great good and disturbing instances of evil. It has transformed our understanding of health and disease, magnified our power to treat and cure, saved millions of lives—and brought forth some astonishing moral outrages.

To medical science we owe the development of vaccines against polio, smallpox, measles, rubella, yellow fever, and hepatitis; treatments for heart disease, diabetes, cancer, and AIDS; strategies to prevent heart attacks, deadly infections, and birth defects; and diagnostic technology ranging from stethoscopes to MRIs to genetic tests. But the search for knowledge through medical research has also led down some dark paths:

• During World War II, Nazi physicians performed horrifying experiments on prisoners of war and civilians, killing and maiming many. At their 1947 trial in Nuremberg, Germany, the doctors were convicted of "murders, tortures, and other atrocities committed in the name of medical science."[1] Their unwilling victims were infected with cholera, smallpox, typhus, malaria, and other diseases; given poisons to evaluate the

deadly results; shot to simulate battle wounds; frozen to death; starved to death; sterilized; and mutilated. The infamous Nazi doctor Josef Mengele liked to study twins:

> He had collected children from the camps, measured their physical features, performed cross-transfusions, transplanted genitals, and other organs, and even created artificial Siamese twins. He also used his twin collection for comparative studies, infecting one child and then killing both for autopsy.[2]

• In 1932 the U.S. Public Health Service began a 40-year experiment to study the damaging effects of untreated syphilis in human beings. The research, known as the Tuskegee Study, involved around 600 poor black men, about 400 of whom had syphilis when they entered the experiment. The men were deceived about the nature of the study, were never told they had syphilis, and were never treated for it even when an effective treatment (penicillin) became readily available to the researchers. Several of the men died because of their untreated disease.

• From 1944 to 1974, the U.S. government sponsored secret experiments to determine the effects of radiation on thousands of human subjects, including children. Some of the subjects were exposed to dangerously high doses of radiation, and many never consented to the research and were not told of the potential harm.

• In 1956 researchers began a study of the natural course of hepatitis in institutionalized children, hoping to understand the disease better and to test a vaccine. Their experimental subjects were several hundred children housed at

Willowbrook State Hospital in New York, the state's largest facility for retarded persons. In those days, conditions were such that most children admitted to Willowbrook eventually got hepatitis, which provoked flulike symptoms and immunity to future infections. For purposes of the experiment, the researchers infected the children with hepatitis when first admitted and monitored their bodies' responses. They were later condemned for using children—especially retarded children—in their study and for the methods they used to obtain consent from the children's parents.

Such stories shocked both the public and the medical world and provoked a sustained wave of soul-searching among policymakers and scientists about the ethics of human research. Out of the trial of Nazi doctors came the Nuremberg Code (one of the readings in this chapter), a set of minimal ethical principles meant to govern all scientific experiments involving humans. Later came other professional codes and government guidelines that reiterated and added to the principles. These included the Declaration of Helsinki, embraced by the World Medical Association (WMA) in 1964 (also a chapter reading); the 1979 Belmont Report (another selection), formulated by the congressionally established National Commission for the Protection of Human Subjects of Biomedical and Behavioral Research; and the 1993 international guidelines for biomedical human research, created by the World Health Organization (WHO) and the Council for International Organizations of Medical Sciences (CIOMS).

Obviously the moral dilemmas inherent in human research can be intense and difficult. But in this age of ambitious scientific inquiry, they cannot be safely ignored.

THE SCIENCE OF CLINICAL TRIALS

A scientific study designed to test a medical intervention in humans is known as a **clinical trial**. Normally the intervention is a drug or surgical procedure, and the point of the study is to determine the treatment's effects in the human body—specifically, whether it is safe and effective. Properly conducted, clinical trials provide the strongest and most trustworthy evidence of a treatment's impact on human health. Neither animal studies nor a physician's informal observations are as reliable and convincing.

Clinical trials can derive reliable answers because they are carefully configured to maximize objectivity, minimize bias, and avoid errors—all the problems that plague unscientific inquiries. A typical clinical trial devised to test the effectiveness of a treatment will consist of two groups of subjects: (1) an experimental group that gets the treatment to be evaluated and (2) a control group that closely resembles the experimental group but does not get the treatment. To learn anything useful about the treatment, researchers must study the relevant differences that arise between the two groups. Simply giving the treatment to the experimental group and observing what happens will not provide any useful answers. Usually, without a control group, the researchers cannot tell whether the subjects would have gotten better (or worse) without treatment, or if a factor other than the treatment was what most affected the subjects' condition (such as changes in their diet or behavior), or if the subjects' condition improved because of the placebo effect. (The placebo effect is a common phenomenon in which patients sometimes feel better after receiving treatment even when the treatment is inactive or fake.) With a control group, researchers can be more confident that relevant effects in the experimental group were brought about by the treatment and not by some extraneous element.

The control groups in clinical trials that investigate efficacy are of two kinds. In a placebo control group, subjects receive a **placebo**, an inactive or sham treatment—a "sugar pill," for example, or an inert pill that looks and tastes like the real drug. By using a placebo control group, researchers can take the placebo effect into account in assessing the worth of a treatment. For a treatment to be judged genuinely effective, subjects in the treatment group must

IN DEPTH
THE TUSKEGEE TRAGEDY

The shocking revelations about the Tuskegee Study came decades after the research had been conducted. When finally told, the story provoked outrage, moral debate, and an apology from President Bill Clinton. Here is one of many recent news accounts:

July 25, 2002—Thirty years ago today, the *Washington Evening Star* newspaper ran this headline on its front page: "Syphilis Patients Died Untreated." With those words, one of America's most notorious medical studies, the Tuskegee Syphilis Study, became public.

"For 40 years, the U.S. Public Health Service has conducted a study in which human guinea pigs, not given proper treatment, have died of syphilis and its side effects," Associated Press reporter Jean Heller wrote on July 25, 1972. "The study was conducted to determine from autopsies what the disease does to the human body."

The next morning, every major U.S. newspaper was running Heller's story. . . .

The Public Health Service, working with the Tuskegee Institute, began the study in 1932. Nearly 400 poor black men with syphilis from Macon County, Ala., were enrolled in the study. They were never told they had syphilis, nor were they ever treated for it. According to the Centers for Disease Control, the men were told they were being treated for "bad blood," a local term used to describe several illnesses, including syphilis, anemia and fatigue.

For participating in the study, the men were given free medical exams, free meals and free burial insurance.

At the start of the study, there was no proven treatment for syphilis. But even after penicillin became a standard cure for the disease in 1947, the medicine was withheld from the men. The Tuskegee scientists wanted to continue to study how the disease spreads and kills. The experiment lasted four decades, until public health workers leaked the story to the media.

By then, dozens of the men had died, and many wives and children had been infected. In 1973, the National Association for the Advancement of Colored People (NAACP) filed a class-action lawsuit. A $9 million settlement was divided among the study's participants. Free health care was given to the men who were still living, and to infected wives, widows and children.

But it wasn't until 1997 that the government formally apologized for the unethical study. President Clinton delivered the apology, saying what the government had done was deeply, profoundly and morally wrong:

"To the survivors, to the wives and family members, the children and the grandchildren, I say what you know: No power on Earth can give you back the lives lost, the pain suffered, the years of internal torment and anguish.

"What was done cannot be undone. But we can end the silence. We can stop turning our heads away. We can look at you in the eye and finally say, on behalf of the American people: what the United States government did was shameful.

"And I am sorry."

National Public Radio, "Remembering Tuskegee," *NPR*, 25 July 2002, http://www.npr.org/programs/morning/features/2002/jul/tuskegee/ (1 March 2008).

show significantly greater improvement than those in the placebo group. Studies using placebos in this way are called placebo-controlled trials. In an active control group, subjects get the standard treatment, one already proven to work. The results in the treatment group can then be compared to those in the active control group to see if the new treatment outperforms the old. Studies that use this type of control group are known as active-controlled trials.

In general, placebo-controlled trials are more trustworthy than other types of clinical trials, but sometimes active-controlled trials can also yield reliable results, especially when they are used to find out which treatment is superior (rather than merely equivalent).

Another indispensable feature of most clinical trials is **blinding**, a procedure for ensuring that subjects and researchers don't know which interventions the subjects receive (standard treatment, new treatment, or placebo). If subjects know they have received a placebo, their assessment of how they feel may be skewed or they may change their health habits, try to obtain an active treatment, or even drop out of the study. If they know they have received an active treatment, they may experience improvement regardless of whether the treatment works. Knowledge of who receives what intervention can also affect researchers, moving them to unconscious bias in evaluating study results. Thus good clinical trials testing for treatment efficacy are blinded—preferably *double-blinded* (when both subjects and researchers are unaware of what treatments the subjects get), or at least *single-blinded* (in which only the subjects are unaware).

If clinical trials are to generate reliable data about a treatment's value, they must be not only blinded but also randomized. **Randomization** is the assigning of subjects randomly to both experimental and control groups. To draw reliable conclusions about the effects of a treatment, the control and experimental groups have to be comparable in relevant characteristics—and assigning subjects randomly helps ensure this. Randomization also minimizes the bias that can creep into a study when researchers unconsciously assign preferred subjects to a particular group. A new treatment can appear to be highly effective if healthier subjects are assigned to the experimental group and less healthy subjects to the control group.

Rarely, if ever, can a single clinical trial establish the safety and effectiveness of a treatment. Usually many studies must be conducted before scientists can be confident of such a conclusion. This hard fact is illustrated most clearly in drug research. By law and professional assent, research to establish the safety and effectiveness of new drugs must involve several clinical trials conducted in three stages, known formally as Phases I, II, and III. Before a drug is recognized as a proven treatment, it must pass muster in each phase. Usually before the human studies can even begin, the treatment must be studied in animals.

A Phase I trial tests the drug in a few people for safety and adverse reactions and ascertains safe and unsafe doses. Researchers do not try to evaluate the drug's efficacy. This kind of trial is said to be *nontherapeutic* because it is not expected to provide a therapeutic benefit to the subjects. In Phase II trials, investigators give the drug to larger groups of subjects to get a preliminary indication of its effectiveness and to do more assessments of safety. In Phase III trials, researchers hope finally to establish whether the drug is effective, determine how it compares in efficacy with other proven treatments, and learn how to employ it in the safest way. These trials are larger still, frequently having thousands of subjects, and are capable of providing definitive answers about a treatment's worth. Unlike Phase I trials, they are generally considered *therapeutic* if they are expected to provide a therapeutic benefit to at least some of the subjects. If a drug does well in Phase III trials, it can be approved for widespread use by patients. Sometimes further studies—Phase IV trials—are done after the approved drug is marketed. Their purpose is to assess the effectiveness and side effects of taking it for a long time.

BENEFICENCE, SCIENCE, AND PLACEBOS

Many of the key features of clinical trials have provoked moral debate, yet among the host of official codes issued on human research is a solid consensus on such trials' ethical requirements.[3] For a clinical trial to be morally permissible:

- Subjects must give their informed voluntary consent to participate.

- The study must be designed to minimize risks to subjects and offer an acceptable balance of risks and benefits. (Even if subjects give their informed consent, risks to them should not be unnecessary or excessive, and the risks must be offset by potential benefits derived from the research.)
- Subjects must be selected fairly to avoid exploiting or unjustly excluding them.
- The subjects' privacy should be protected, and the confidentiality of research data must be preserved.
- Before the research is conducted, it must be reviewed and approved by an independent panel (often an institutional review board, or IRB).

There is also substantial agreement in bioethics on the general moral principles that should apply to human research, standards from which the more specific requirements are derived: (1) autonomy, or respect for persons as autonomous agents; (2) beneficence, doing good for and avoiding harm to persons; and (3) justice, treating equals equally. When disagreements occur, they usually turn on how best to interpret, employ, or extend the requirements in specific kinds of cases.

The principle of beneficence is at the heart of many of the disputes because, as we have seen, the obligation to help or not harm subjects often seems to conflict with the aim of doing science. Physicians (or physician-researchers) have a duty of beneficence toward patients (or patient-subjects), but it is not obvious that clinical trials are always consistent with this duty. As we have seen, a widely accepted answer to this dilemma has been supplied in the official codes: Risks to subjects should be kept as low as possible, and the potential benefits of the research should be greater than the risks. These tenets have been joined with the further stipulations that no subject should be exposed to extreme risks even if the expected benefits are substantial; a subject's informed consent cannot justify research that is too risky; and potential benefits to both the subjects and society

should be considered, although the subjects' welfare must predominate. From this perspective, therapeutic trials—assuming the subjects' informed consent and acceptable risks and benefits—can be justified by the potential good to the subjects and future patients, or society. Nontherapeutic trials—assuming informed consent and minimal risks to the subjects—can be justified by significant potential good to society.

The use of control groups touches on most of these issues of beneficence. A clinical trial is conducted to find out which of two treatments is better for patients or whether a particular treatment has any worth, but of course this process entails that patients in the control group will often get less than the best available treatment or no genuine treatment at all (a placebo). Some argue that the permissibility of enrolling patients in such a study is questionable since by doing so they are being treated merely as a means to the end of scientific knowledge. But many reject this worry. For example:

[I]f there is uncertainty about the efficacy of any given treatment, a randomized trial is the best way to yield objectively valid results. It will tell the doctor which treatment is better for the patient. So, recruiting a patient to be a subject in a randomized clinical trial does not by itself compromise the researcher's duty as a doctor to care for the patient. The better treatment will be determined by the results of the trial. In fact, patients can benefit more from a research setting than from standard clinical care because they receive more attention with the resources available to the research team. By entering a patient in a randomized controlled clinical trial, a doctor is treating the patient as a means for the sake of generating scientific knowledge. But the doctor is also treating the patient as an end by obtaining consent to participate in the trial and by ensuring that the potential risks are commensurate with the potential benefits. The physician is at once fulfilling the primary duty of a doctor to the patient and the secondary duty of a researcher to the research subject.[4]

Frequently the issue is framed around the doctor's duty given what she knows about the treatments to be tested. As a physician, she has an obligation to act in the best interests of her patients, which requires that she offer to them only those treatments she judges to be the best. But in clinical trials, patients are randomized into experimental and control groups where they may not receive the treatment that the physician believes is best. Some bioethicists have concluded from this that randomized clinical trials are morally problematic because they "ask physicians to sacrifice the interests of their particular patients for the sake of the study and that of the information that it will make available for the benefit of society."[5]

But defenders of randomized studies contend that doctors breach no duty to their patients if the efficacy of the treatments being tested is unknown—that is, if there is no good evidence for preferring that patients be assigned to one group rather than another (control or experimental). Being in doubt about the relative merits of the treatments, physicians are said to be in *equipoise*, rationally balanced between the alternatives. They therefore cannot be guilty of offering treatments known to be less than the best available.

Still, critics insist that a physician owes patients her best judgment about available treatments, and if she believes (even on the basis of a hunch or suspicion) that one treatment is better or worse than another, then letting a randomized clinical trial choose the patients' treatment is wrong—a violation of trust. A physician with a preference is not in a state of equipoise.

Others argue that this view misunderstands the notion of equipoise. They contend that true equipoise does not depend on uncertainty in the mind of a physician, but on genuine disagreement about treatment efficacy in the medical and scientific community. The disagreement arises because of a lack of the kind of evidence generated by randomized clinical trials. As long as this form of equipoise exists, including patients in randomized studies is permissible.

Those who take this view also point out that a clinical trial may show that the physician's educated guess about a treatment is incorrect, making better care of the patient possible. As one philosopher explains,

> Properly carried out, with informed consent, clinical equipoise, and a design adequate to answer the question posed, randomized clinical trials protect physicians and their patients from therapies that are ineffective or toxic. Physicians and their patients must be clear about the vast gulf separating promising and proved therapies. The only reliable way to make this distinction in the face of incomplete information about pathophysiology and treatment mechanism is to experiment, and this will increasingly involve randomized trials. The alternative—a retreat to older methods—is unacceptable.[6]

Whatever the value of the scientific approach, many see no conflict between (1) physicians revealing to patients their honest preferences regarding treatments and (2) giving those patients the chance to enter a clinical trial. The key element here is full disclosure and informed consent:

> The physician has a strict therapeutic obligation to offer his or her best professional judgment, but also to obtain the patient's informed consent prior to initiating treatment. The latter obligation entails explaining the risks and benefits of all reasonable alternatives, including enrollment in an appropriate [randomized controlled trial] to test one treatment against another.[7]

Moral concern about control groups takes on added seriousness when their "treatment" is a placebo. Again the moral friction occurs at the point where beneficence and science collide. Recall that placebo-controlled trials are often the most scientifically reliable way to determine the effectiveness of a treatment. But in such studies, the placebo group receives no genuine treatment, while the experimental group gets one that is at least possibly, and perhaps probably, effective. Can this deliberate nontreatment of patients be justified?

For many bioethicists and policy-making bodies, the answer is yes—but only in a restricted range of circumstances. The most widely accepted proviso is that the use of placebos is unethical when effective treatments are already available. In its 2004 version of the Declaration of Helsinki, the WMA asserts that in general a placebo-controlled trial "should only be used in the absence of existing proven therapy."[8] Testing a new, unproven treatment against a placebo is permissible, but usually only if no treatment has already been shown to work. If there is an established therapy, the new treatment must be pitted against it in an active-controlled trial.

This general rule has its greatest force in cases where the risks to subjects are large—when going without effective treatment can cause serious harm and threaten life. Some have argued that when the disease in question is potentially fatal, using placebo controls may be wrong even if there is no established treatment, just an unproven but promising one. A classic case seems to suggest this view. This is how bioethicists Tom Beauchamp and James Childress describe it:

> Promising laboratory tests led to a trial (phase I) to determine the safety of AZT among patients with AIDS. Several patients showed clinical improvement during this trial. Because AIDS was considered invariably fatal, many people argued that compassion dictated making it immediately available to all patients with AIDS. . . . However . . . as required by federal regulations, [the company] used a placebo-controlled trial of AZT to determine its effectiveness for certain groups of patients with AIDS. A computer randomly assigned some patients to AZT and others to a placebo. For several months, no major differences emerged in effectiveness, but then patients receiving the placebo began to die at a significantly higher rate. Of the 137 patients on the placebo, 16 died. Of the 145 patients on AZT, only one died. In view of these results, a data and safety monitoring board advised terminating the trial.

Subjects who had received the placebo in the trial were, as promised, the first to receive the drug.[9]

Many authorities recognize that the "no existing proven therapy" rule for placebo studies cannot be absolute. The WMA is among them, declaring in the Helsinki code that placebo-controlled trials may be permissible even when proven treatments exist, provided that the medical condition involved is minor. The WMA also implicitly acknowledges (as most authorities do) that sometimes the only way to identify the best therapies (and thereby ease the suffering of countless future patients) is to conduct a placebo-controlled trial, which may be a scientific necessity whether proven therapies exist or not. Bioethicists who accept this fact also typically believe that this research must be subject to at least two ethical restraints: Patients should never be exposed to undue risks (regardless of the potential benefits to society), and no research should be done without the patients' informed consent (which in itself cannot justify unsafe research).

SCIENCE AND INFORMED CONSENT

As discussed in the previous chapter, informed consent is the action of an autonomous, informed person agreeing to submit to medical treatment or experimentation. It is universally considered a moral prerequisite for medical treatment, and equally so for medical research. The first article of the Nuremberg Code asserts, "The voluntary consent of the human subject is absolutely essential"—an ethical requirement blatantly violated by the Nazi doctors. The underlying notion is that autonomous agents have the right to decide for themselves whether to expose their persons to the rigors and risks of clinical investigations. For bona fide informed consent, the person's decision must be informed by accurate information about the research, based on an adequate understanding of it, made voluntarily, and generated without coercion.

IN DEPTH
WOMEN IN CLINICAL TRIALS

Medical science has been accused of being unjust to women by frequently excluding them as subjects from studies of treatments that could help them. Too often in the past only men were included in studies of diseases that affected both men and women, and the treatments found to be effective in males would not necessarily have the same impact on females. The Institute of Medicine published a collection of papers on the ethical and legal problems arising from such research practices, including a critique by Susan Sherwin. She asserts that

> [W]e can identify several specific areas of feminist concern, including: (1) some or all women may be unjustly excluded from some studies and suffer as a result; (2) women may be unjustly enrolled in studies that expose them to risk without offering appropriate benefits; (3) the research agenda may be unresponsive to the interests of oppressed groups; and (4) most generally, the process by which research decisions are made and carried out may maintain and promote oppressive practices. . . .
>
> . . . The exclusion of women from important clinical studies is the best known of the problems of injustice identified as falling within the scope of the topic of women's role in clinical studies. Historically, many studies of diseases that are common to both sexes have systematically excluded women from participation, so the necessary data for guiding treatment decisions

for women are unavailable. Women's health care must often be based on untested inferences from data collected about men, but because there are important physiological differences between women and men, such inferences cannot always be presumed to be reliable; and, even when some data are collected about women's responses to the treatment in question, we may lack information about how a proposed treatment will affect specific groups of women (e.g., those who are disabled, elderly, or poor). Even according to traditional distributive conceptions of justice, it is clear that this sort of discrimination is unjust and bound to result in less effective health care for (some) women than for comparable men because the knowledge base which guides health care practices is unfairly skewed; if we accept the view that well-designed clinical studies are beneficial for a population, then the systematic exclusion of women from such studies must be seen as disadvantaging them unfairly. A social justice approach that is sensitive to matters of oppression helps us to recognize that this disadvantage is not random or accidental, but is a result and further dimension of women's generally oppressed status in society. According to the distributive models of justice, women ought to be represented proportionately to their health risk in any clinical studies likely to be of benefit to subject populations.

Susan Sherwin, "Women in Clinical Studies: A Feminist View," in *Women and Health Research: Ethical and Legal Issues of Including Women in Clinical Studies* (Washington, DC: National Academy Press, 1999), 11–17, http://www.nap.edu (16 June 2008).

The checklist of relevant information that researchers are expected to give subjects has become fairly standard. According to one international panel, it includes:

- That each individual is invited to participate as a subject in research and the aims and methods of the research

- The expected duration of the subject's participation
- The benefits that might reasonably be expected to result to the subjects or to others as an outcome of the research
- Any foreseeable risks or discomfort to the subject associated with participation in the research

- Any alternative procedures or courses of treatment that might be as advantageous to the subject as the procedure or treatment being tested
- The extent to which confidentiality of records in which the subject is identified will be maintained
- The extent of the investigator's responsibility, if any, to provide medical services to the subject
- That therapy will be provided free of charge for specified types of research-related injury
- Whether the subject or the subject's family or dependents will be compensated for disability or death resulting from such injury
- That the individual is free to refuse to participate and will be free to withdraw from the research at any time without penalty or loss of benefits to which he would otherwise be entitled[10]

Few doubt the reasonableness of such a list, but many have wondered whether the information can be conveyed to potential subjects so their consent is truly informed and voluntary. Probably the least plausible concern is an old paternalistic claim. Just as some physicians believe that patients are incapable of grasping the complexities of medical information, some researchers have argued that research subjects cannot fathom the alien language and arcane methods of science—so informed consent in clinical trials is impossible. Many bioethicists think this worry exaggerated (not to mention contemptuous of patient autonomy). They point out that subjects need not understand everything about a clinical study to give their informed consent; they need only comprehend enough to appreciate the most important implications, risks, and benefits of the research. Achieving this much understanding is possible although admittedly, in many situations and for many patients, extremely difficult.

Other concerns about informed consent relate to the unique circumstances that confront research volunteers. If patients are seriously ill and no proven treatment is available or none has helped

them, they may consent to the research out of desperation, fear, wishful thinking, or hope. Against their own best interests, they may pay little attention to the information provided, ignore all the possible risks, expect to be cured, believe that a benefit is highly probable when it is only possible, even come to believe that a nontherapeutic trial will likely help them despite written disclosures to the contrary. Their consent therefore may not be fully voluntary and informed.

Another issue concerns payments to research subjects. It is generally agreed that, in the words of one international body, "Subjects may be paid for inconvenience and time spent, and should be reimbursed for expenses incurred, in connection with their participation in research; they may also receive free medical services."[11] But additional payments (especially large ones) to entice patients into entering a trial might get them to consent though they ordinarily would refuse. Some think the payment could be so tempting as to be coercive (to constitute, in legal terms, "undue inducement") and thus may undermine informed consent. Several policies and regulations try to restrict the use of these inducements, but some think these edicts go too far. "All of these rules seem to be excessively paternalistic," says Baruch Brody,

> If the independent review panel has already concluded that the risk-benefit ratio of the research is acceptable (otherwise, the research could not be approved), how can the large payment harm the subject? And in what way are large payments for acceptable research coercive or exploitative?[12]

RESEARCH ON THE VULNERABLE

Many moral issues arise from clinical research on people thought to be easily exploited or mistreated—the most vulnerable in society. These subjects include children, the mentally disabled, prisoners, minorities, and people in developing countries. The essential moral conflict is between (1) the duty to shield the vulnerable from abuse and (2) the aspiration to benefit them or society through needed research. Serious study

The National Cancer Institute sponsors many clinical trials and maintains the most extensive database of cancer trials in the nation. It publicizes them for cancer patients, saying, "Whenever you need treatment for your cancer, clinical trials may be an option for you." It acknowledges that there are benefits and risks to taking part in such research and describes them like this:

POSSIBLE BENEFITS

- Clinical trials offer high-quality cancer care. If you are in a randomized study and do not receive the new treatment being tested, you will receive the best known standard treatment. This may be as good as, or better than, the new approach.
- If a new treatment is proven to work and you are taking it, you may be among the first to benefit.
- By looking at the pros and cons of clinical trials and your other treatment choices, you are taking an active role in a decision that affects your life.

- You have the chance to help others and improve cancer treatment.

POSSIBLE DRAWBACKS

- New treatments under study are not always better than, or even as good as, standard care.
- If you receive standard care instead of the new treatment being tested, it may not be as effective as the new approach.
- New treatments may have side effects that doctors do not expect or that are worse than those of standard treatment.
- Even if a new treatment has benefits, it may not work for you. Even standard treatments, proven effective for many people, do not help everyone.
- Health insurance and managed care providers do not always cover all patient care costs in a study. What they cover varies by plan and by study. To find out in advance what costs are likely to be paid in your case, check with your insurance company and talk to a doctor, nurse or social worker from the study.

National Cancer Institute, "Taking Part in Cancer Research Studies," *National Cancer Institute,* 17 July 2007, http://www .cancer.gov/clinicaltrials/Taking-Part-in-Cancer-Treatment-Research-Studies/page1 (29 February 2008).

---

of this clash of values has been goaded by a sad, historical fact: Many notorious cases in the ethics of clinical science involved research using vulnerable populations—among them the poor black men of Tuskegee, the children of Willowbrook, and the prisoners of the Nazi doctors.

The question of research on children acquires its edge partly because often the only way to devise treatments for children's diseases is to conduct clinical trials on these subjects. The physiology and pathology of children are so different from those of adults that trying to draw useful conclusions about the former from studies of the latter is frequently difficult, impossible, or dangerous. Many effective therapies now used to treat children could only have been developed

through clinical trials using children. Given the scientific necessity of this kind of research, important ethical questions exert their pressure: Is research on children ever permissible? How is informed consent to be handled? Can children give consent? What balance of risks and benefits for child subjects can justify experimentation on them? Can nontherapeutic trials ever be morally permissible? Are there limits to the risks that children should be allowed to bear?

Most official policies assert or assume that properly designed research in children is morally acceptable if it is conducted for their sake, if it is done to generate the therapies they need. The policies also agree on the necessity for consent before any research is begun and on the importance of a proper balance of risks and benefits for the research subjects. Disagreement comes in specifying the details of these requirements.

It is generally understood that consent to do research on children must in most cases be given by parents or guardians, who are supposed to decide in the children's best interests. Sometimes children may be allowed to give consent for themselves, provided they have reached the age of consent or maturity, but authorities disagree over when this point is reached. Existing policies require that in some circumstances child subjects must give their assent to the research (they must at least agree to it), even when parents or guardians have provided proxy informed consent. A few even claim that in some cases children may veto their participation in a trial. As one code phrases it, "The child's refusal to participate in research must always be respected unless according to the research protocol the child would receive therapy for which there is no medically-acceptable alternative."[13]

The prevailing view is that properly consented-to research involving children is permissible if it offers them benefits equaling or outweighing the risks and if the risks are limited. That is, therapeutic research is generally acceptable. Nontherapeutic research is another matter. Some oppose all such research, whether or not parents consent to it, on the grounds that it puts children at risk without hope of benefits for them in return. This position would rule out a great deal of science that could yield effective treatments for childhood diseases. Most official guidelines are less strict, allowing nontherapeutic research when the risk to the child subjects is minimal or close to it. The U.S. Department of Health and Human Services, for example, permits research that involves:

- No more than minimal risk to children, provided adequate steps are taken to solicit assent from the children and consent of the parents or guardians
- More than minimal risk to children and the prospect of direct benefits for them, provided (a) the benefits justify the risks, (b) no better alternative approaches exist,

and (c) adequate steps are taken to solicit assent from the children and consent of the parents or guardians
- More than minimal risk to children and no prospect of direct benefits for them, provided (a) the risk is only slightly greater than minimal risk, (b) the intervention involves experiences that are comparable to those that the subjects normally experience, (c) the intervention is likely to yield knowledge that is vitally important for understanding or treating the subjects' condition, and (d) adequate steps are taken to solicit assent from the children and consent of the parents or guardians[14]

Most of the pressing questions about research on children also apply to studies on the mentally impaired, and many of the answers are the same. This class of potential subjects includes adults who are severely retarded or suffer from psychiatric illness, in either situation being incompetent (at least much of the time) to make autonomous choices. As in the case of children, clinical research is scientifically necessary to develop therapies that could help these patients. There is widespread agreement that the research is justified if it is judged to be in their best interests and that appropriate surrogates must usually be the ones to make this judgment.

As might be expected, nontherapeutic research involving the mentally impaired is more contentious. Only if it entails minimal risk to the subjects, some argue, is this research legitimate. Others prefer a more relaxed policy. The National Institutes of Health, for example, permits studies on mentally impaired subjects if an appropriate consent process is used and if the research involves either (1) minimal risk, (2) greater than minimal risk but with the prospect of direct benefit to subjects, or (3) greater than minimal risk with no prospect of direct benefit to subjects but with the likelihood of gaining important knowledge about the subjects' illness.

An added complication in research on these vulnerable subjects is that their being in an institution can undermine attempts to obtain their voluntary consent. (Consent remains an issue with some mentally impaired patients because they may be competent though impaired, competent to decide some aspects of their care, or intermittently competent.) Institutionalized patients are especially susceptible to many forms of coercion or undue influence that can undermine the voluntariness of their decisions. They may feel intense pressure to submit to research because they have been conditioned to defer to people in authority, because they fear punishment or less consideration from caretakers for refusing to participate, or because the slightest advantages of being in a clinical trial (special attention or a change in routine, for example) can carry tremendous weight.

Official responses to these worries have emphasized close scrutiny of the research by independent review committees (and possibly other oversight panels) to identify sources of undue pressure on the subjects. Many contend that the alternative to continued (but closely monitored) research on the mentally impaired is no research at all, which is unacceptable.

A different set of ethical questions confronts us in research on vulnerable subjects in Third World countries. As the scientific testing of therapies in developing nations has increased, ethical controversy surrounding the research has also intensified. The main points of moral conflict were dramatically illustrated a decade ago in clinical trials of HIV-infected pregnant women in several African countries and Thailand. Research had previously demonstrated that the drug AZT (zidovudine) could substantially reduce the transmission of HIV from pregnant women to their fetuses (known as vertical transmission). But the dose of AZT used in the research was expensive—too expensive for widespread use in poor countries with large numbers of people with HIV. So scientists were eager to find out if a lower, cheaper dose of AZT would work. They reasoned that the best way to discover which AZT regimens were most effective at halting vertical transmission was to test them on women in the developing countries using placebo-controlled trials.

They ran the trials, and the results showed that a less expensive AZT treatment could indeed significantly reduce vertical transmission. Nevertheless, many observers charge on various grounds that the research was unethical. Probably the chief argument against the studies is that in using a placebo (no-treatment) group, some of the subjects were deprived of an effective treatment that could have prevented many babies from being infected with HIV. Thus the researchers violated the widely accepted moral tenet that the welfare of the human subjects should outweigh the concerns of science and society. Marcia Angell, the executive editor of the *New England Journal of Medicine*, compares the trials to the Tuskegee Study in which African-American men with syphilis were studied but never treated even after an effective treatment for syphilis was in wide use. "Only when there is no known effective treatment is it ethical to compare a potential new treatment with a placebo," she says. "When effective treatment exists, a placebo may not be used."[15] Yet before the AZT trials began, an effective treatment was already available. Thus the women in the studies were treated merely as a means to the end of scientific inquiry.

Other commentators defend the use of placebo control groups in the trials and reject the idea that it was morally problematic. They argue that those in the placebo groups were not deprived of treatment that they would have received under normal circumstances. Nothing was taken from them that they already had, and so no injustice was done. Baruch Brody takes this line and argues that an injustice is committed only if the study participants are "denied any treatment *that should otherwise be available to him or her in light of the practical realities of health care resources available in the country in question.*"[16] Judged by this standard, he says, "the trials in question were probably not unjust." Some defenders of the trials add the further point that if the research had not been done, many women would never have received any AZT at all.

Some critics of such trials allege a pattern of exploitation of people in developing countries. They say that researchers use impoverished or desperate subjects to determine the best therapies, and then that information is used to help people in rich countries, not the developing ones. Reflecting this concern about exploitation, international policies insist that any therapies developed through research should be shared with the community or country where the research was done. Brody thinks that these policies miss the mark. To avoid exploitation, we need not ensure that the benefits of research go to the larger community, but only to the subjects themselves:

> [W]e need to ask who needs to be protected from being exploited by the trials in question. It would seem that it is the participants. Are they getting a fair share of the benefits from the trial if it proves successful? This is a particularly troubling question when we consider those in the control group, whose major benefit from participation may have been an unrealized possibility of getting treated. If we judge that the participants have not received enough, then it is they who must receive more.[17]

APPLYING MAJOR THEORIES

Utilitarianism says that right actions are those that result in the most beneficial balance of good over bad consequences, everyone considered (see Chapter 2). What are the implications of this stance for human research? First, utilitarianism can provide an unequivocal justification for it. Through medical research, the causes of disease are unmasked, disease preventives are devised, treatments are developed, and the true worth of common but untested therapies is determined. Thus human well-being is advanced, and an important moral principle—beneficence—is satisfied.

On the utilitarian view, the moral justification for conducting any particular clinical trial depends on its offering a net benefit to all concerned. The maximization of benefit, in turn, hangs on the quality and aims of the research—on how well and why it is done. The utilitarian would agree then with the common ethical requirements that "the experiment should be such as to yield fruitful results for the good of society, unprocurable by other methods or means of study, and not random and unnecessary in nature. . . . The experiment should be so conducted as to avoid all unnecessary physical and mental suffering and injury."[18]

Ethical codes insist that people must not be included in clinical trials without their informed consent, but whether utilitarianism is consistent with this requirement is debatable. Some argue that there really is no inconsistency because informed consent is just another way to maximize utility. Others doubt that this tack is coherent.

In medical research, the utilitarian perspective often leads to the same conclusions about the permissibility of actions that other theories do. But frequently the judgments clash dramatically, as they did in disputes over the placebo-controlled AZT trials in developing countries. The utilitarians argued that the cheapest, fastest way to find out which treatment was best and to use it on the people who needed it most was to use a placebo group. But many rejected this view, arguing in Kantian fashion that subjects in the placebo (no-treatment) group were treated as a mere means to the end of scientific rigor, and many babies would become HIV-infected as a result.

The AZT episode was one of many in clinical research that illustrated the distinctive implications of a Kantian approach. Its means-ends requirement—the prohibition against using persons as if they were mere things—was implicit in the strong condemnations of the Nazi medical experiments, the Cold War radiation research, the Tuskegee Study, and many others. It proscribes the coercing of research subjects, deceiving them, deliberately harming them, and diminishing or destroying their autonomy. Kant's notion of the equal moral value of persons yields the imperative to treat equals equally, which seems to imply that even in research, some subjects should not be treated better (or worse) than others for no morally relevant reason. For some bioethicists, this means that research subjects in poor countries should receive the same treatments in clinical trials that they would get if they lived in rich countries.

Kant would insist that these limits on what can be done to subjects can never be weakened or ignored for the sake of utility. The categorical imperative must not be breached—even to find cures for humanity's ills.

The heart of the modern doctrine of informed consent is Kantian. Because persons are autonomous, rational agents, they must be allowed the freedom to make choices and to have them respected. They may give or withhold their consent to medical treatment or research, consent that is valid only if informed, competent, and voluntary. Within limits, informed consent can legitimize the indignities of clinical trials by ensuring that even though subjects are treated as a means to an end, they are not treated *solely* as a means to an end. But if a person refuses to give her informed consent, or if it is impeded by misinformation (or no information), coercion, or undue influence, using her in research would be wrong. Respect for persons also implies that obtaining their informed consent cannot justify subjecting them to substantial risk of reduced autonomy or death.

For Rawls, social and economic inequalities are not unjust if they work to everyone's benefit, especially to the benefit of the least well off in society. This implies that (1) research efforts should be aimed primarily at helping the neediest and (2) it is impermissible to conduct research on the neediest to provide therapeutic benefits only to those who are better off. Clinical trials, then, using poor, desperate, or mentally impaired subjects to develop treatments for the rest of society could not be condoned. Applied internationally, Rawls' principles would lead us to condemn research in developing countries to benefit only people in developed ones.

KEY TERMS
blinding
clinical trial
placebo
randomization

SUMMARY

Clinical trials are scientific studies designed to test medical interventions in humans. They can derive reliable answers because they maximize the objectivity of observations, minimize bias, and avoid errors. The main requirements for a scientifically adequate clinical trial are a control group (using either a placebo or an active treatment), blinding, and randomization.

Official ethical codes on human research agree that (1) subjects must give their informed voluntary consent to participate, (2) the study must be designed to minimize risks to subjects and offer an acceptable balance of risks and benefits, (3) subjects must be selected fairly to avoid exploiting or unjustly excluding them, (4) the subjects' privacy should be protected and the confidentiality of research data must be preserved, and (5) before the research is conducted, it must be reviewed and approved by an independent committee. There is also substantial agreement on the general moral principles that apply to human research—autonomy, beneficence, and justice.

The use of control groups has raised ethical concerns, with some critics arguing that controlled trials treat subjects merely as a means to the end of scientific knowledge. But many believe that physicians do no wrong to their patients who enter a clinical trial if the physicians are in equipoise, rationally balanced between the alternative treatments. Debate about using control groups intensifies in placebo-controlled trials. The most widely accepted view is that the use of placebos is unethical when effective treatments are already available.

Most agree that the informed consent of subjects is essential for morally acceptable research. But there is often concern about whether truly

The UCLA Schizophrenia Study

Studies in which researchers do not offer real treatment to subjects suffering from a serious illness or condition often raise troubling ethical questions. In 1994 one such study got the attention of the media, the federal government, Congress, the legal system, and clinical researchers.

In the early 1980s, scientists at the University of California at Los Angeles (UCLA) Medical School began a study to determine how well schizophrenic patients could function without their antipsychotic medication, prolixin decanoate. This knowledge would have been very valuable in treating schizophrenic patients because the drug is both boon and bane. In most patients the medication can ease (but not entirely banish) psychotic symptoms, including acute psychotic episodes. But it can also cause awful side effects, most notably tardive dyskinesia, a condition of involuntary muscle movements varying from mild to disabling and possibly becoming permanent.

People with schizophrenia are afflicted with delusions, hallucinations, depression, bizarre behavior, hostility, and—in a few cases—suicide. For many patients, taking prolixin decanoate and enduring the side effects are preferable to experiencing the symptoms of schizophrenia left untreated. But the UCLA researchers wanted to find a way around these problems. They knew that some patients who are taken off their medication can function adequately for a long time before full-blown symptoms return. Identifying these patients early would enable a physician to withdraw their medication so they could benefit

from it while avoiding its drawbacks. So the ultimate aim of the study was to uncover these identifying characteristics, and that required discontinuing the medication of the schizophrenic subjects to observe the recurrence of symptoms (relapse).

In this double-blind study, subjects were randomly assigned to either a placebo control group or a group receiving doses of prolixin decanoate. For 12 weeks the groups received their respective doses (placebo or active drug). Then the groups switched treatments and continued that way for another 12 weeks. At the end of the 24 weeks, subjects whose symptoms were still under control were taken off the drug (or allowed to continue untreated) and monitored for up to one year until they experienced full relapse or severe symptoms. Shortly after the no-drug phase began, one subject had an extreme psychotic breakdown, and after the phase ended, another subject committed suicide.

Complaints were lodged against the UCLA researchers, alleging, among other things, that the informed consent process was invalid and that the study design was too risky because it made relapses very likely. In 1994 an office in the National Institutes of Health released a report concerning the matter. It charged that the informed consent process failed to adequately explain to subjects the distinction between regular medical care and the treatment that might be provided in the study. Other observers faulted the consent process for obscuring some vital information—the probability and severity of relapse.

---

informed and voluntary consent can be obtained from certain kinds of patients, chief among them children, the very ill, the mentally disabled, prisoners, minorities, and people in developing countries.

Regarding all these groups there is often disagreement about the proper balance of risk and benefits in clinical trials. Research involving subjects in Third World countries raises issues of justice, especially whether these subjects are entitled to the same level of care that subjects in developed countries get.

Cases for Evaluation

CASE 1

Giving Placebos to Children

(*New York Times*)—Researchers give a 6-year-old girl who suffers from asthma attacks a promising new drug in addition to her old medicine, then withdraw it to see how she will do without it. A depressed teenager enrolls in a study for an antidepressant, but does not know if he will get a sugar pill or the real thing. The parents of an epileptic youngster enroll her in a test of a new drug that has worked well in adults. But no one knows whether she will get the new medication, or the one that has worked only moderately well for her in the past.

These quandaries, all based on actual experiences, are likely to be faced by an increasing number of parents, children, and medical researchers around the country as the federal government steps up its efforts to test drugs on children.

Over the last three years, largely because of financial incentives that Congress has given pharmaceutical companies, pediatric studies of new drugs have boomed. In December, the Food and Drug Administration will begin mandating that such tests be done on certain drugs, and the agency wants to make sure researchers protect child participants.

"What level of discomfort or risk should a child in a study be exposed to?" asked Dr. Steven Hirschfeld, a medical officer at the F.D.A.'s Center for Drug Research and Evaluation. "If a child gets an asthma attack and starts to wheeze, are people willing to tolerate that to get complete information about a potentially helpful drug for children?"

Today, an F.D.A. advisory panel met in Bethesda, Md., to begin discussions aimed at setting the first guidelines for researchers on the controversial use of placebos in drug trials for children. Placebos are sugar pills, injections, or other treatments that resemble the drug that is being tested without having any of the same effects.

Dr. Hirschfeld said that the particular vulnerability of children often makes placebo controls necessary. "Children are not only very susceptible to their own expectations," he said in an interview. "They are very susceptible to their parents' expectations."

But a panelist, Dr. Charles Weijer, a bioethicist and an assistant professor of medicine at Dalhousie University in Halifax, Nova Scotia, said it was wrong to submit children to risks while providing them no immediate benefit.

"An investigator's chief concern ought to be the health and well-being of her patients," Dr. Weijer said at the hearing. . . .

The panel of 27 researchers that met today included several researchers from Europe who are working on international standards for clinical trials in children.

"What you people decide will affect directly not only children in the U.S., but children in Europe and the world at large," said Francis Crawley, chairman of a group working to set standards in Europe.

Dianne Murphy, the associate director for pediatrics at the F.D.A.'s Center for Drug Evaluation and Research, said that use of placebos can reduce the number of children needed in a study and can ensure the most conclusive outcome. "If you need a placebo trial to get an answer, and you don't do it, then you've wasted that child's blood, time and possible chance, in a trial that won't give them an answer," she said. . . .

But experts disagree on the ethics of withholding effective treatment from children when studying nonfatal conditions such as allergies or skin rashes. And there is no consensus for how to treat children with other serious ailments, such as depression, where the best treatment is unknown.*

Is giving children placebos in clinical trials ever morally permissible? If so, under what conditions should placebos be used? What if in a clinical trial some children suffer asthma attacks because effective treatment is withheld from them—is that acceptable? What if no effective treatments for some childhood diseases could be developed without using children in placebo-controlled trials. Would that fact outweigh any objections to such trials? Give reasons for your answers.

---

*Alexis Jetter, "Efforts to Test Drugs on Children Hasten Drive for Research Guidelines," *New York Times,* 12 September 2000, http://www.nytimes.com/2000/09/12/science/12ETHI.html (6 March 2008).

CASE 2

Research and Medicine Collide in Haiti

(*New York Times*)—The impoverished patients who step from the dirt sidewalk into the modern AIDS research clinic run by Cornell Medical College in Port-au-Prince, Haiti, are offered a seemingly simple arrangement.

"We would like to test your blood because you live in an area where AIDS may be common," the English version of the clinic's consent form reads. "We will provide you with medicine if you fall sick and cannot afford such care."

But the transaction is not as straightforward as it sounds. Many Haitians who visit the clinic are at once patients and subjects of United States–financed medical research, and circumstances that are bad for their health are sometimes best for research results.

That conflict is especially true in Cornell's most tantalizing research in Haiti, a study of sex partners, only one of whom is infected with the AIDS virus. Researchers, seeking clues to developing a vaccine, study the blood of both partners, particularly the uninfected ones who continue to be exposed to the virus through unprotected sex. They are trying to find out whether some people have natural protections against infection with the AIDS virus that could be replicated in a vaccine.

The Haitians are ideal research subjects, largely because they are not receiving the kind of care now standard in the world's developed countries. Condom use is low in Haiti, for cultural and other reasons. Anti-retroviral drugs that are successful at suppressing the virus are unavailable except to the very wealthy, and are not included in Cornell's promise to provide medicine.

Nearly 20 years after Cornell opened the clinic, it provides some of the best AIDS treatment available in a country devastated by the epidemic, fighting the myriad illnesses that result from AIDS. But that is a lower standard of care than patients receive routinely at American institutions, including the hospital affiliated with Cornell in New York City.

If the research were done in the United States, experts agree, the physicians would be obligated to prescribe the anti-retrovirals and deliver the most effective possible counseling against unprotected sex.

The ethical questions posed by Cornell's work among Haiti's poor are at the heart of a global debate about AIDS research that is roiling international health organizations from Geneva to Thailand, challenging ethics formulations established decades ago.

"It's really like a Faustian bargain," said Marc Fleisher, a member of the committee at Cornell that reviews research on humans. "It's like, since we're making this a better place, we're going to exploit it in a way we could never get away with in the United States," said Mr. Fleisher, the outside member on a board made up mostly of university employees who are doctors.

Cornell doctors defended the couples study as vitally important and stressed that its subjects receive the same counseling about the dangers of AIDS and the same care as other patients at the Haitian clinic.

United States standards for research on humans were strongly influenced by outrage over the Tuskegee syphilis study earlier this century, which misled impoverished black subjects for years while tracking their disease, and withheld treatment even after penicillin was discovered.

Today's subjects are not to be pressured to participate in research, according to Federal regulations. They are to be fully informed about the research's purposes and risks. They must receive the best available therapy for their illnesses and be told about any findings relevant to their health.

In theory, the same rules apply to federally financed studies overseas. But an examination of

15 years of records related to the Haiti couples research shows that it has received scant scrutiny from Government officials in Washington.

And the Government's rules barely address the moral ambiguities of AIDS research in indigent countries. . . .

Dr. Warren D. Johnson, the chief of international medicine and infectious diseases at Cornell, called the couples study "a very high priority," though he said it had been temporarily suspended while the university concentrated on other research in Haiti. "This is the critical group in the world—couples—that's where the war is to be fought," he said.

At least 97 couples have been enrolled in the blood study since 1991, records show, but Dr. Johnson said only 30 couples are still being followed. The study will be expanded to new couples early next year, he said, and coordinated with AIDS vaccine trials, which are expected to start in Haiti this fall using similar couples as subjects.

Cornell's clinic in Haiti offers strong inducements to subjects. It is the only center in the country providing free screening and treatment for H.I.V., venereal disease, and tuberculosis, a common complication of AIDS. The thousands who flock to it are too poor to buy food, let alone the simple medicines and vitamins that serve as "a powerful incentive for study participation," in the words of one Cornell grant report.

The head of the clinic, Dr. Jean William Pape, is a Haiti native and Cornell professor who has studied AIDS in Haiti for two decades. Dr. Pape, who trained at Cornell, defended the treatment of research subjects in the couples study, saying they benefited from the same counseling and free condoms available to everyone who visits the clinic.

Dr. Pape said that offering the life-saving drugs to the handful of research subjects would be an unethical lure to participate. Treating all H.I.V.-infected citizens, he said, would cost 10 times Haiti's health budget.

If the research on couples succeeds, he said, it could help lead to a vaccine against AIDS. "You have to take into account people who mean well for their country and not impose on them things that you feel are good for Western ideas," he said. . . .

The Haitians were valuable for another reason. Unlike AIDS patients in the United States and Europe, they were not receiving the anti-retroviral drugs that proved effective in halting the disease's progress.

The lack of those drugs "may allow identification of novel findings not easily studied in the U.S.A.," Dr. John L. Ho, a Cornell immunologist, wrote in an application for Federal funds. In 1995, the Federal Government awarded Cornell an extra $60,000 to expand this part of the Haitian couples study. . . .

Ethical standards for Federally financed studies require that patients be told why researchers want to study them. But the written consent form approved at Cornell and read aloud in Creole to each potential subject does not mention that the study focuses on couples in which one sexual partner has tested positive for H.I.V.

The form tells subjects their blood is being tested because "you live in an area where AIDS may be common." It promises all patients that H.I.V. test results will be kept confidential. . . .

After reviewing clinic materials, Marie Saint Cyr, a native of Haiti who now directs an AIDS program for women in Harlem, said there was a "clear conflict of interest" between the desire to collect information from research subjects and the obligation to effectively warn patients at risk.

"If you know somebody is positive and is having sex with a partner who is negative, you have a life and death situation in front of you," she said. "You have to do individualized counseling to really tap into what those people value in life, to confront them with the reality of H.I.V. and AIDS. This in no way addresses those serious things."*

Is the Cornell research ethical? Should subjects in the study get the same AIDS treatment available to people in the United States? Should the researchers provide stronger warnings to subjects about the dangers of not using condoms? Is the informed consent process morally acceptable? Explain your answers.

---

*Nina Bernstein, "Strings Attached: For Subjects in Haiti Study, Free AIDS Care Has a Price," *New York Times*, 6 June 1999, http://www.nytimes.com/pages/health (6 March 2008).

CASE 3

To Stop or Not to Stop a Clinical Trial

(*New York Times*)—Recently, scientists made the startling decision to halt a large multinational clinical trial that was testing a new drug regimen for breast cancer. The five-year trial was stopped after just two and a half years when results showed that the study drug cut the yearly rate of breast cancer recurrence by nearly half.

The decision has already provoked controversy: breast cancer recurrence is not necessarily the same as death, the critics say, so it is not clear whether the new drug actually saves lives.

The National Breast Cancer Coalition, a patient advocacy group, argued that researchers should have continued the study to see if the new drug prolonged lives.

The issue gets to the core of biomedical research. What is ideal for researchers may not always be ideal for subjects or for the demands of public health.

In this study, the researchers were looking to see if letrozole, which blocks estrogen synthesis, was more effective than a placebo in preventing the recurrence of breast cancer in women who had already taken the estrogen-blocking drug tamoxifen.

Because the advantage of letrozole on disease-free survival was apparent early on, the researchers had to halt the study.

Dr. James N. Ingle of the Mayo Clinic and a principal investigator in the study said he was surprised by the criticism over ending the study. "Preventing disease recurrence is a valid endpoint," he said. "If you sit down with patients, they will tell you that they don't want their cancer to come back. That's their first concern.

"In fact, I can't think of a study of breast cancer where actual survival is the primary endpoint. Disease-free survival is a well-accepted outcome with strong precedence in cancer research."

But to some researchers, the study stopped short of answering important questions. Does letrozole promote actual survival? What are its long-term adverse effects? How long should women continue to take it?

The results, for example, suggest a slight increase in osteoporosis in women taking letrozole compared with a placebo. So, other side effects may emerge over time.

The pursuit of perfect data may be the researcher's dream, but the perspective of a woman with breast cancer is vastly different. If you were privy to the interim analysis, you would most likely choose the new drug over the placebo.

Imagine the outcry if investigators had withheld the early evidence of the drug's benefit and finished the study, hoping for better data. Millions of women with breast cancer could then have correctly claimed they were denied a new treatment.

"A woman with breast cancer who wakes up the next morning without a recurrence of her disease is a survivor," said Dr. Paul Goss of Princess Margaret Hospital and lead author of the study. "What most people and even doctors don't understand about the course of breast cancer is that it is a chronic relapsing disease over many years."

Proving that letrozole saves lives will require a study lasting many years, Dr. Goss said. "We've done the first step, which is to show that letrozole works in preventing breast cancer recurrence," he said. "The next step is to do an extended trial to find out the optimal duration of treatment and long-term side effects."

When people enroll in research studies they sign informed consent agreements explaining the potential risks and benefits. In this case, the form promised subjects that they would be told if new information about their disease was discovered in the study. This virtually mandated early disclosure.

And although subjects are explicitly told in a consent form that they themselves may receive no direct benefit, many continue to hope for it. At the very least, they reasonably expect to be kept from all foreseeable harm.

But avoiding harm is not the same thing as getting benefit. In fact, in many clinical trials subjects are randomly assigned to take the drug or a placebo.

This has prompted some researchers to question whether the use of placebos is even ethical because some very sick people will essentially get no active treatment and may get worse.

What about using placebos in studies of serious illnesses like depression? Treatments for it are known to be effective, though imperfect. There is little doubt that the most powerful way to show a drug's efficacy and safety is to assign patients at random to the drug or a placebo. But depressed patients who get a placebo may not improve; they may get worse and even become suicidal.

Sure, scientists could compare an experimental drug with a proven standard drug, but this would require a much larger sample and would expose more people to risks of the new drug. That's because research results differ more widely between the use of placebos and active drugs, than between two active treatments.*

Were the researchers right to halt the breast cancer study early? Suppose by extending the trial the scientists could gain valuable knowledge that would help save many women's lives in the future. Would halting the trial early then be wrong? Suppose extending the trial would save lives in the future but also result in the deaths of some women in the study. Would the extension then be permissible? Was the use of placebos ethical? Explain your answers.

---

*Richard Friedman, "Cases: Long-Term Questions Linger in Halted Breast Cancer Trial," *New York Times*, 21 October 2003, http://www.nytimes.com/pages/health (6 March 2008).

FURTHER READING

Lizbeth A. Adams and Timothy Callahan, University of Washington School of Medicine, "Research Ethics," 2014, https://depts.washington.edu/bioethx/topics/resrch.html (23 October 2015).

American Psychological Association, "Human Research Protections," 2015, http://www.apa.org/research/responsible/human/ (23 October 2015).

Jessica W. Berg, Paul S. Appelbaum, et al., *Informed Consent: Legal Theory and Clinical Practice*, 2nd ed. (New York: Oxford University Press, 2001).

Baruch A. Brody, *The Ethics of Biomedical Research: An International Perspective* (New York: Oxford University Press, 1998).

A. M. Capron, "Human Experimentation," in *Medical Ethics*, ed. Robert M. Veatch (Sudbury, MA: Jones and Bartlett, 1997), 135–84.

Steven S. Coughlin and Tom L. Beauchamp, eds., *Ethics and Epidemiology* (New York: Oxford University Press, 1996).

Council for International Organizations of Medical Sciences in Collaboration with the World Health Organization, *International Ethical Guidelines for Biomedical Research Involving Human Subjects* (Geneva: CIOMS, 1993), 1–45.

Leonardo D. DeCastro, "Ethical Issues in Human Experimentation," in *A Companion to Bioethics*, ed. Helga Kuhse and Peter Singer (Oxford: Blackwell, 2001), 379–96.

Ezekiel Emanuel, Emily Abdoler, and Leanne Stunkel, National Institutes of Health, *Research Ethics*, http://bioethics.nih.gov/education/FNIH_BioethicsBrochure_WEB.PDF (23 October 2015).

John H. Fennick, *Studies Show: A Popular Guide to Understanding Scientific Studies* (Amherst, NY: Prometheus Books, 1997).

Walter Glannon, *Biomedical Ethics* (New York: Oxford University Press, 2005), chap. 6, 47–70.

Jay Katz, ed., *Experimentation with Human Beings* (New York: Russell Sage Foundation, 1972).

Alex John London, "Clinical Equipoise: Foundational Requirement or Fundamental Error?" in *The Oxford Handbook of Bioethics*, ed. Bonnie Steinbock (Oxford: Oxford University Press, 2007), 572–96.

National Bioethics Advisory Commission, "Protecting Research Participants—A Time for Change," in *Ethical and Policy Issues in Research Involving Human Participants: Summary* (Bethesda, MD: NBAC, 2001), i–ix.

Paul Ramsey, *The Patient as Person* (New Haven, CT: Yale University Press, 1970).

Adil E. Shamoo and David B. Resnik, *Responsible Conduct of Research* (New York: Oxford University Press, 2003).

Lewis Vaughn, *The Power of Critical Thinking* (New York: Oxford University Press, 2008), chap. 10, 382–441.

NOTES

1. Quoted in Albert R. Jonson, *The Birth of Bioethics* (New York: Oxford University Press, 1998), 135.

2. *Ibid.*

3. Baruch A. Brody, *The Ethics of Biomedical Research: An International Perspective* (New York: Oxford University Press, 1998), 31–54.

4. Walter Glannon, *Biomedical Ethics* (New York: Oxford University Press, 2005), 52–53.

5. Samuel Hellman and Deborah S. Hellman, "Of Mice but Not Men: Problems of the Randomized Clinical Trial," *New England Journal of Medicine* 324.22 (1991), 1585–89.

6. Eugene Passamani, "Clinical Trials: Are They Ethical?," *New England Journal of Medicine* 324.22 (1991), 1589–91.

7. Tom L. Beauchamp and James F. Childress, *Principles of Biomedical Ethics,* 5th ed. (New York: Oxford University Press, 2001), 324.

8. World Medical Association, *Declaration of Helsinki* (2004), http:www.wma.net/e/policy/b3.html (17 October 2008).

9. Beauchamp and Childress, *Principles,* 324.

10. The Council for International Organizations of Medical Sciences (CIOMS) in Collaboration with the World Health Organization (WHO), *International Ethical Guidelines for Biomedical Research Involving Human Subjects* (Geneva: CIOMS, 1993).

11. *Ibid.*

12. Brody, *Ethics of Biomedical Research,* 44.

13. CIOMS in Collaboration with the WHO, *International Ethical Guidelines,* guideline 5.

14. Department of Health and Human Services, *Regulations for the Protection of Human Subjects* (1991), 46.401–46.406.

15. Marcia Angell, "The Ethics of Clinical Research in the Third World," *New England Journal of Medicine* 337.12 (1997), 847–49.

16. Baruch Brody, "Ethical Issues in Clinical Trials in Developing Countries," *Statistics in Medicine* 21 (2002), 2853–58.

17. Brody, "Ethical Issues."

18. The Nuremberg Code.

READINGS

The Nuremberg Code

1. The voluntary consent of the human subject is absolutely essential.

This means that the person involved should have legal capacity to give consent; should be so situated as to be able to exercise free power of choice, without the intervention of any element of force, fraud, deceit, duress, overreaching, or other ulterior form of constraint or coercion; and should have sufficient knowledge and comprehension of the elements of the subject matter involved as to enable him to make an understanding and enlightened decision. This latter element requires that before the acceptance of an affirmative decision by the experimental subject there should be made known to him the nature, duration, and purpose of the experiment; the method and means by which it is to be conducted; all inconveniences and hazards reasonably to be expected; and the effects upon his health or person which may possibly come from his participation in the experiment.

From *Trials of War Criminals Before the Nuremberg Military Tribunals under Control Council Law No. 10,* vol. 2 (Washington, D.C.: U.S. Government Printing Office, 1949), 181–182.

The duty and responsibility for ascertaining the quality of the consent rests upon each individual who initiates, directs or engages in the experiment. It is a personal duty and responsibility which may not be delegated to another with impunity.

2. The experiment should be such as to yield fruitful results for the good of society, unprocurable by other methods or means of study, and not random and unnecessary in nature.

3. The experiment should be so designed and based on the results of animal experimentation and a knowledge of the natural history of the disease or other problem under study that the anticipated results will justify the performance of the experiment.

4. The experiment should be so conducted as to avoid all unnecessary physical and mental suffering and injury.

5. No experiment should be conducted where there is an *a priori* reason to believe that death or disabling injury will occur; except, perhaps, in those experiments where the experimental physicians also serve as subjects.

6. The degree of risk to be taken should never exceed that determined by the humanitarian importance of the problem to be solved by the experiment.

7. Proper preparations should be made and adequate facilities provided to protect the experimental subject against even remote possibilities of injury, disability, or death.

8. The experiment should be conducted only by scientifically qualified persons. The highest degree of skill and care should be required through all stages of the experiment of those who conduct or engage in the experiment.

9. During the course of the experiment the human subject should be at liberty to bring the experiment to an end if he has reached the physical or mental state where continuation of the experiment seems to him to be impossible.

10. During the course of the experiment the scientist in charge must be prepared to terminate the experiment at any stage, if he has probable cause to believe, in the exercise of the good faith, superior skill and careful judgment required of him that a continuation of the experiment is likely to result in injury, disability, or death to the experimental subject.

Declaration of Helsinki: Ethical Principles for Medical Research Involving Human Subjects

WORLD MEDICAL ASSOCIATION

This international ethical code echoes principles in the Nuremberg Code and breaks some new ground as well. In addition to affirming the importance of informed consent, it provides guidelines for conducting research on subjects who cannot give their informed consent, insists on the review of research protocols by "independent committees," discusses the use of placebo controls, and declares that "considerations related to the well-being of the human subject should take precedence over the interests of science and society."

A. Introduction

1. The World Medical Association has developed the Declaration of Helsinki as a statement of ethical principles to provide guidance to physicians and other participants in medical research involving human subjects. Medical research involving human subjects includes research on identifiable human material or identifiable data.

2. It is the duty of the physician to promote and safeguard the health of the people. The physician's knowledge and conscience are dedicated to the fulfillment of this duty.

3. The Declaration of Geneva of the World Medical Association binds the physician with the words, "The health of my patient will be my first consideration," and the International Code of Medical Ethics declares that, "A physician shall act only in the patient's interest when providing medical care which might have the effect of weakening the physical and mental condition of the patient."

4. Medical progress is based on research which ultimately must rest in part on experimentation involving human subjects.

5. In medical research on human subjects, considerations related to the well-being of the human subject should take precedence over the interests of science and society.

6. The primary purpose of medical research involving human subjects is to improve prophylactic, diagnostic and therapeutic procedures and the understanding of the aetiology and pathogenesis of disease. Even the best proven prophylactic, diagnostic, and therapeutic methods must continuously be challenged through research for their effectiveness, efficiency, accessibility, and quality.

7. In current medical practice and in medical research, most prophylactic, diagnostic, and therapeutic procedures involve risks and burdens.

Reprinted with permission of the World Medical Association.

8. Medical research is subject to ethical standards that promote respect for all human beings and protect their health and rights. Some research populations are vulnerable and need special protection. The particular needs of the economically and medically disadvantaged must be recognized. Special attention is also required for those who cannot give or refuse consent for themselves, for those who may be subject to giving consent under duress, for those who will not benefit personally from the research and for those for whom the research is combined with care.

9. Research Investigators should be aware of the ethical, legal and regulatory requirements for research on human subjects in their own countries as well as applicable international requirements. No national ethical, legal or regulatory requirement should be allowed to reduce or eliminate any of the protections for human subjects set forth in this Declaration.

B. Basic Principles for All Medical Research

10. It is the duty of the physician in medical research to protect the life, health, privacy, and dignity of the human subject.

11. Medical research involving human subjects must conform to generally accepted scientific principles, be based on a thorough knowledge of the scientific literature, other relevant sources of information, and on adequate laboratory and, where appropriate, animal experimentation.

12. Appropriate caution must be exercised in the conduct of research which may affect the environment, and the welfare of animals used for research must be respected.

13. The design and performance of each experimental procedure involving human subjects should be clearly formulated in an experimental protocol. This protocol should be submitted for consideration, comment, guidance, and where appropriate, approval to a specially appointed ethical review committee, which must be independent of the investigator, the sponsor or any other kind of undue influence. This independent committee should be in conformity with the laws and regulations of the country in which the research experiment is performed. The committee has the right to monitor ongoing trials. The researcher has the obligation to provide monitoring information to the committee, especially any serious adverse events. The researcher should also submit to the committee, for review, information regarding funding, sponsors, institutional affiliations, other potential conflicts of interest and incentives for subjects.

14. The research protocol should always contain a statement of the ethical considerations involved and should indicate that there is compliance with the principles enunciated in this Declaration.

15. Medical research involving human subjects should be conducted only by scientifically qualified persons and under the supervision of a clinically competent medical person. The responsibility for the human subject must always rest with a medically qualified person and never rest on the subject of the research, even though the subject has given consent.

16. Every medical research project involving human subjects should be preceded by careful assessment of predictable risks and burdens in comparison with foreseeable benefits to the subject or to others. This does not preclude the participation of healthy volunteers in medical research. The design of all studies should be publicly available.

17. Physicians should abstain from engaging in research projects involving human subjects unless they are confident that the risks involved have been adequately assessed and can be satisfactorily managed. Physicians should cease any investigation if the risks are found to outweigh the potential benefits or if there is conclusive proof of positive and beneficial results.

18. Medical research involving human subjects should only be conducted if the importance of the objective outweighs the inherent risks and burdens to the subject. This is especially important when the human subjects are healthy volunteers.

19. Medical research is only justified if there is a reasonable likelihood that the populations in which the research is carried out stand to benefit from the results of the research.

20. The subjects must be volunteers and informed participants in the research project.

21. The right of research subjects to safeguard their integrity must always be respected. Every precaution should be taken to respect the privacy of the subject, the confidentiality of the patient's information and to minimize the impact of the study on the subject's physical and mental integrity and on the personality of the subject.

22. In any research on human beings, each potential subject must be adequately informed of the aims, methods, sources of funding, any possible conflicts of interest, institutional affiliations of the researcher, the anticipated benefits and potential risks of the study, and the discomfort it may entail. The subject should be informed of the right to abstain from participation in the study or to withdraw consent to participate at any time without reprisal. After ensuring that the subject has understood the information, the physician should then obtain the subject's freely given informed consent, preferably in writing. If the consent cannot be obtained in writing, the non-written consent must be formally documented and witnessed.

23. When obtaining informed consent for the research project the physician should be particularly cautious if the subject is in a dependent relationship with the physician or may consent under duress. In that case the informed consent should be obtained by a well-informed physician who is not engaged in the investigation and who is completely independent of this relationship.

24. For a research subject who is legally incompetent, physically or mentally incapable of giving consent or is a legally incompetent minor, the investigator must obtain informed consent from the legally authorized representative in accordance with applicable law. These groups should not be included in research unless the research is necessary to promote the health of the population represented and this research cannot instead be performed on legally competent persons.

25. When a subject deemed legally incompetent, such as a minor child, is able to give assent to decisions about participation in research, the investigator must obtain that assent in addition to the consent of the legally authorized representative.

26. Research on individuals from whom it is not possible to obtain consent, including proxy or advance consent, should be done only if the physical/mental condition that prevents obtaining informed consent is a necessary characteristic of the research population. The specific reasons for involving research subjects with a condition that renders them unable to give informed consent should be stated in the experimental protocol for consideration and approval of the review committee. The protocol should state that consent to remain in the research should be obtained as soon as possible from the individual or a legally authorized surrogate.

27. Both authors and publishers have ethical obligations. In publication of the results of research, the investigators are obliged to preserve the accuracy of the results. Negative as well as positive results should be published or otherwise publicly available. Sources of funding, institutional affiliations, and any possible conflicts of interest should be declared in the publication. Reports of experimentation not in accordance with the principles laid down in this Declaration should not be accepted for publication.

C. Additional Principles for Medical Research Combined with Medical Care

28. The physician may combine medical research with medical care, only to the extent that the research is justified by its potential prophylactic, diagnostic, or therapeutic value. When medical research is combined with medical care, additional standards apply to protect the patients who are research subjects.

29. The benefits, risks, burdens, and effectiveness of a new method should be tested against those of the best current prophylactic, diagnostic, and therapeutic methods. This does not exclude the use of placebo, or no treatment, in studies where no proven prophylactic, diagnostic, or therapeutic method exists.[1]

30. At the conclusion of the study, every patient entered into the study should be assured of access to the best proven prophylactic, diagnostic, and therapeutic methods identified by the study.[2]

31. The physician should fully inform the patient which aspects of the care are related to the research. The refusal of a patient to participate in a study must never interfere with the patient-physician relationship.

32. In the treatment of a patient, where proven prophylactic, diagnostic, and therapeutic methods do not exist or have been ineffective, the physician, with informed consent from the patient, must be free to use unproven or new prophylactic, diagnostic, and therapeutic measures, if in the physician's judgement it offers hope of saving life, reestablishing health or alleviating suffering. Where possible, these measures should be made the object of research, designed to evaluate their safety and efficacy. In all

cases, new information should be recorded and, where appropriate, published. The other relevant guidelines of this Declaration should be followed.

NOTES

1. Note of clarification on paragraph 29 of the WMA Declaration of Helsinki:

   The WMA hereby reaffirms its position that extreme care must be taken in making use of a placebo-controlled trial and that in general this methodology should only be used in the absence of existing proven therapy. However, a placebo-controlled trial may be ethically acceptable, even if proven therapy is available, under the following circumstances:

   • Where for compelling and scientifically sound methodological reasons its use is necessary to determine the efficacy or safety of a prophylactic, diagnostic, or therapeutic method; or

   • Where a prophylactic, diagnostic, or therapeutic method is being investigated for a minor condition and the patients who receive placebo will not be subject to any additional risk of serious or irreversible harm.

   All other provisions of the Declaration of Helsinki must be adhered to, especially the need for appropriate ethical and scientific review.

2. Note of clarification on paragraph 30 of the WMA Declaration of Helsinki:

   The WMA hereby reaffirms its position that it is necessary during the study planning process to identify post-trial access by study participants to prophylactic, diagnostic, and therapeutic procedures identified as beneficial in the study or access to other appropriate care. Post-trial access arrangements or other care must be described in the study protocol so the ethical review committee may consider such arrangements during its review.

The Belmont Report

THE NATIONAL COMMISSION FOR THE PROTECTION OF HUMAN SUBJECTS OF BIOMEDICAL AND BEHAVIORAL RESEARCH

In 1974 Congress created the commission to provide guidance on the ethical issues that arise in research on human subjects. The result of the commission's work is this report, which lays out a general approach to thinking about research ethics and elucidates the three most relevant moral principles—respect for persons, beneficence, and justice.

Ethical Principles and Guidelines for Research Involving Human Subjects

A. Boundaries Between Practice and Research

It is important to distinguish between biomedical and behavioral research, on the one hand, and the practice of accepted therapy on the other, in order to know what activities ought to undergo review for the protection of human subjects of research. The distinction between research and practice is blurred

partly because both often occur together (as in research designed to evaluate a therapy) and partly because notable departures from standard practice are often called "experimental" when the terms "experimental" and "research" are not carefully defined.

For the most part, the term "practice" refers to interventions that are designed solely to enhance the well-being of an individual patient or client and that have a reasonable expectation of success. The purpose of medical or behavioral practice is to provide diagnosis, preventive treatment or therapy to particular individuals. By contrast, the term "research" designates an activity designed to test an hypothesis, permit conclusions to be drawn, and thereby to develop or contribute to generalizable knowledge (expressed, for example, in theories,

From *The Belmont Report: Ethical Principles and Guidelines for the Protection of Human Subjects of Research* (April 18, 1979), The National Commission for the Protection of Human Subjects of Biomedical and Behavioral Research, http://ohsr.od.nih.gov/guidelines/belmont.html.

principles, and statements of relationships). Research is usually described in a formal protocol that sets forth an objective and a set of procedures designed to reach that objective.

When a clinician departs in a significant way from standard or accepted practice, the innovation does not, in and of itself, constitute research. The fact that a procedure is "experimental," in the sense of new, untested or different, does not automatically place it in the category of research. Radically new procedures of this description should, however, be made the object of formal research at an early stage in order to determine whether they are safe and effective. Thus, it is the responsibility of medical practice committees, for example, to insist that a major innovation be incorporated into a formal research project.

Research and practice may be carried on together when research is designed to evaluate the safety and efficacy of a therapy. This need not cause any confusion regarding whether or not the activity requires review; the general rule is that if there is any element of research in an activity, that activity should undergo review for the protection of human subjects.

B. Basic Ethical Principles

The expression "basic ethical principles" refers to those general judgments that serve as a basic justification for the many particular ethical prescriptions and evaluations of human actions. Three basic principles, among those generally accepted in our cultural tradition, are particularly relevant to the ethics of research involving human subjects: the principles of respect of persons, beneficence and justice.

1. Respect for Persons. Respect for persons incorporates at least two ethical convictions: first, that individuals should be treated as autonomous agents, and second, that persons with diminished autonomy are entitled to protection. The principle of respect for persons thus divides into two separate moral requirements: the requirement to acknowledge autonomy and the requirement to protect those with diminished autonomy.

An autonomous person is an individual capable of deliberation about personal goals and of acting under the direction of such deliberation. To respect autonomy is to give weight to autonomous persons' considered opinions and choices while refraining from obstructing their actions unless they are clearly detrimental to others. To show lack of respect for an autonomous agent is to repudiate that person's considered judgments, to deny an individual the freedom to act on those considered judgments, or to withhold information necessary to make a considered judgment, when there are no compelling reasons to do so.

However, not every human being is capable of self-determination. The capacity for self-determination matures during an individual's life, and some individuals lose this capacity wholly or in part because of illness, mental disability, or circumstances that severely restrict liberty. Respect for the immature and the incapacitated may require protecting them as they mature or while they are incapacitated.

Some persons are in need of extensive protection, even to the point of excluding them from activities which may harm them; other persons require little protection beyond making sure they undertake activities freely and with awareness of possible adverse consequence. The extent of protection afforded should depend upon the risk of harm and the likelihood of benefit. The judgment that any individual lacks autonomy should be periodically reevaluated and will vary in different situations.

In most cases of research involving human subjects, respect for persons demands that subjects enter into the research voluntarily and with adequate information. In some situations, however, application of the principle is not obvious. The involvement of prisoners as subjects of research provides an instructive example. On the one hand, it would seem that the principle of respect for persons requires that prisoners not be deprived of the opportunity to volunteer for research. On the other hand, under prison conditions they may be subtly coerced or unduly influenced to engage in research activities for which they would not otherwise volunteer. Respect for persons would then dictate that prisoners be protected. Whether to allow prisoners to "volunteer" or to "protect" them presents a dilemma. Respecting persons, in most hard cases, is often a matter of balancing competing claims urged by the principle of respect itself.

2. *Beneficence.* Persons are treated in an ethical manner not only by respecting their decisions and protecting them from harm, but also by making efforts to secure their well-being. Such treatment falls under the principle of beneficence. The term "beneficence" is often understood to cover acts of kindness or charity that go beyond strict obligation. In this document, beneficence is understood in a stronger sense, as an obligation. Two general rules have been formulated as complementary expressions of beneficent actions in this sense: (1) do not harm and (2) maximize possible benefits and minimize possible harms.

The Hippocratic maxim "do no harm" has long been a fundamental principle of medical ethics. Claude Bernard extended it to the realm of research, saying that one should not injure one person regardless of the benefits that might come to others. However, even avoiding harm requires learning what is harmful; and, in the process of obtaining this information, persons may be exposed to risk of harm. Further, the Hippocratic Oath requires physicians to benefit their patients "according to their best judgment." Learning what will in fact benefit may require exposing persons to risk. The problem posed by these imperatives is to decide when it is justifiable to seek certain benefits despite the risks involved, and when the benefits should be foregone because of the risks.

The obligations of beneficence affect both individual investigators and society at large, because they extend both to particular research projects and to the entire enterprise of research. In the case of particular projects, investigators and members of their institutions are obliged to give forethought to the maximization of benefits and the reduction of risk that might occur from the research investigation. In the case of scientific research in general, members of the larger society are obliged to recognize the longer term benefits and risks that may result from the improvement of knowledge and from the development of novel medical, psychotherapeutic, and social procedures.

The principle of beneficence often occupies a well-defined justifying role in many areas of research involving human subjects. An example is found in research involving children. Effective ways of treating childhood diseases and fostering healthy development

are benefits that serve to justify research involving children—even when individual research subjects are not direct beneficiaries. Research also makes it possible to avoid the harm that may result from the application of previously accepted routine practices that on closer investigation turn out to be dangerous. But the role of the principle of beneficence is not always so unambiguous. A difficult ethical problem remains, for example, about research that presents more than minimal risk without immediate prospect of direct benefit to the children involved. Some have argued that such research is inadmissible, while others have pointed out that this limit would rule out much research promising great benefit to children in the future. Here again, as with all hard cases, the different claims covered by the principle of beneficence may come into conflict and force difficult choices.

3. *Justice.* Who ought to receive the benefits of research and bear its burdens? This is a question of justice, in the sense of "fairness in distribution" or "what is deserved." An injustice occurs when some benefit to which a person is entitled is denied without good reason or when some burden is imposed unduly. Another way of conceiving the principle of justice is that equals ought to be treated equally. However, this statement requires explication. Who is equal and who is unequal? What considerations justify departure from equal distribution? Almost all commentators allow that distinctions based on experience, age, deprivation, competence, merit and position do sometimes constitute criteria justifying differential treatment for certain purposes. It is necessary, then, to explain in what respects people should be treated equally There are several widely accepted formulations of just ways to distribute burdens and benefits. Each formulation mentions some relevant property on the basis of which burdens and benefits should be distributed. These formulations are (1) to each person an equal share, (2) to each person according to individual need, (3) to each person according to individual effort, (4) to each person according to societal contribution, and (5) to each person according to merit.

Questions of justice have long been associated with social practice such as punishment, taxation and political representation. Until recently these questions have not generally been associated with scientific research. However, they are foreshadowed even in the earliest reflections on the ethics of research involving human subjects. For example, during the 19th and early 20th centuries the burdens of serving as research subjects fell largely upon poor ward patients, while the benefits of improved medical care flowed primarily to private patients. Subsequently, the exploitation of unwilling prisoners as research subjects in Nazi concentration camps was condemned as a particularly flagrant injustice. In this country, in the 1940's, the Tuskegee syphilis study used disadvantaged, rural black men to study the untreated course of a disease that is by no means confined to that population. These subjects were deprived of demonstrably effective treatment in order not to interrupt the project, long after such treatment became generally available.

Against this historical background, it can be seen how conceptions of justice are relevant to research involving human subjects. For example, the selection of research subjects needs to be scrutinized in order to determine whether some classes (e.g., welfare patients, particular racial and ethnic minorities, or persons confined to institutions) are being systematically selected simply because of their easy availability, their compromised position, or their manipulability, rather than for reasons directly related to the problem being studied. Finally, whenever research supported by public funds leads to the development of therapeutic devices and procedures, justice demands both that these not provide advantages only to those who can afford them and that such research should not unduly involve persons from groups unlikely to be among the beneficiaries of subsequent applications of the research.

Final Report: Human Radiation Experiments

ADVISORY COMMITTEE ON HUMAN RADIATION EXPERIMENTS

This official report details the government-sponsored radiation experiments conducted on thousands of human subjects from 1944 to 1974. Subjects were exposed to harmful levels of radiation, often without their consent and without being told of the potential dangers. The report also reviews the safety of contemporary human research using radiation and recommends apologies and compensation to the victimized subjects or their next of kin.

The Creation of the Advisory Committee

On January 15, 1994, President Clinton appointed the Advisory Committee on Human Radiation Experiments. The President created the Committee to investigate reports of possibly unethical experiments funded by the government decades ago.

The members of the Advisory Committee were fourteen private citizens from around the country: a representative of the general public and thirteen

From Advisory Committee on Human Radiation Experiments, Department of Energy, *Final Report: Executive Summary*, 1995, http://www.hss.energy.gov/healthsafety/ohre/roadmap/achre/report.html.

experts in bioethics, radiation oncology and biology, nuclear medicine, epidemiology and biostatistics, public health, history of science and medicine, and law.

President Clinton asked us to deliver our recommendations to a Cabinet-level group, the Human Radiation Interagency Working Group, whose members are the Secretaries of Defense, Energy, Health and Human Services, and Veterans Affairs; the Attorney General; the Administrator of the National Aeronautics and Space Administration; the Director of Central Intelligence; and the Director of the Office of Management and Budget. Some of the experiments the Committee was asked to investigate, and particularly a series that included the injection of plutonium into unsuspecting hospital patients, were of special concern to Secretary of Energy Hazel O'Leary. Her department had its origins in the federal agencies that had sponsored the plutonium experiments. These agencies were responsible for the development of nuclear weapons and during the Cold War their activities had been shrouded in secrecy. But now the Cold War was over.

The controversy surrounding the plutonium experiments and others like them brought basic questions to the fore: How many experiments were conducted or sponsored by the government, and why? How many were secret? Was anyone harmed? What was disclosed to those subjected to risk, and what opportunity did they have for consent? By what rules should the past be judged? What remedies are due those who were wronged or harmed by the government in the past? How well do federal rules that today govern human experimentation work? What lessons can be learned for application to the future? Our Final Report provides the details of the Committee's answers to these questions. This Executive Summary presents an overview of the work done by the Committee, our findings and recommendations, and the contents of the Final Report.

The President's Charge

The President directed the Advisory Committee to uncover the history of human radiation experiments during the period 1944 through 1974. It was in 1944 that the first known human radiation experiment of interest was planned, and in 1974 that the Department of Health, Education and Welfare adopted regulations governing the conduct of human research, a watershed event in the history of federal protections for human subjects.

In addition to asking us to investigate human radiation experiments, the President directed us to examine cases in which the government had intentionally released radiation into the environment for research purposes. He further charged us with identifying the ethical and scientific standards for evaluating these events, and with making recommendations to ensure that whatever wrongdoing may have occurred in the past cannot be repeated.

We were asked to address human experiments and intentional releases that involved radiation. The ethical issues we addressed and the moral framework we developed are, however, applicable to all research involving human subjects.

The breadth of the Committee's charge was remarkable. We were called on to review government programs that spanned administrations from Franklin Roosevelt to Gerald Ford. As an independent advisory committee, we were free to pursue our charge as we saw fit. The decisions we reached regarding the course of our inquiry and the nature of our findings and recommendations were entirely our own.

The Committee's Approach

At our first meeting, we immediately realized that we were embarking on an intense and challenging investigation of an important aspect of our nation's past and present, a task that required new insights and difficult judgments about ethical questions that persist even today.

Between April 1994 and July 1995, the Advisory Committee held sixteen public meetings, most in Washington, D.C. In addition, subsets of Committee members presided over public forums in cities throughout the country. The Committee heard from more than 200 witnesses and interviewed dozens of professionals who were familiar with experiments involving radiation. A special effort, called the Ethics Oral History Project, was undertaken to learn from eminent physicians about how research with human subjects was conducted in the 1940s and 1950s.

We were granted unprecedented access to government documents. The President directed all the federal agencies involved to make available to the Committee any documents that might further our inquiry, wherever they might be located and whether or not they were still secret.

As we began our search into the past, we quickly discovered that it was going to be extremely difficult to piece together a coherent picture. Many critical documents had long since been forgotten and were stored in obscure locations throughout the country. Often they were buried in collections that bore no obvious connection to human radiation experiments. There was no easy way to identify how many experiments had been conducted, where they took place, and which government agencies had sponsored them. Nor was there a quick way to learn what rules applied to these experiments for the period prior to the mid-1960s. With the assistance of hundreds of federal officials and agency staff, the Committee retrieved and reviewed hundreds of thousands of government documents. Some of the most important documents were secret and were declassified at our request. Even after this extraordinary effort, the historical record remains incomplete. Some potentially important collections could not be located and were evidently lost or destroyed years ago.

Nevertheless, the documents that were recovered enabled us to identify nearly 4,000 human radiation experiments sponsored by the federal government between 1944 and 1974. In the great majority of cases, only fragmentary data was locatable; the identity of subjects and the specific radiation exposures involved were typically unavailable.

Given the constraints of information, even more so than time, it was impossible for the Committee to review all these experiments, nor could we evaluate the experiences of countless individual subjects. We thus decided to focus our investigation on representative case studies reflecting eight different categories of experiments that together addressed our charge and priorities. These case studies included:

- Experiments with plutonium and other atomic bomb materials
- The Atomic Energy Commission's program of radioisotope distribution
- Nontherapeutic research on children
- Total body irradiation
- Research on prisoners
- Human experimentation in connection with nuclear weapons testing
- Intentional environmental releases of radiation
- Observational research involving uranium miners and residents of the Marshall Islands

In addition to assessing the ethics of human radiation experiments conducted decades ago, it was also important to explore the current conduct of human radiation research. Insofar as wrongdoing may have occurred in the past, we needed to examine the

likelihood that such things could happen today. We therefore undertook three projects:

- A review of how each agency of the federal government that currently conducts or funds research involving human subjects regulates this activity and oversees it.
- An examination of the documents and consent forms of research projects that are today sponsored by the federal government in order to develop insight into the current status of protections for the rights and interests of human subjects.
- Interviews of nearly 1,900 patients receiving outpatient medical care in private hospitals and federal facilities throughout the country. We asked them whether they were currently, or had been, subjects of research, and why they had agreed to participate in research or had refused.

The Historical Context

Since its discovery 100 years ago, radioactivity has been a basic tool of medical research and diagnosis. In addition to the many uses of the x-ray, it was soon discovered that radiation could be used to treat cancer and that the introduction of "tracer" amounts of radioisotopes into the human body could help to diagnose disease and understand bodily processes. At the same time, the perils of overexposure to radiation were becoming apparent.

During World War II the new field of radiation science was at the center of one of the most ambitious and secret research efforts the world has known—the Manhattan Project. Human radiation experiments were undertaken in secret to help understand radiation risks to workers engaged in the development of the atomic bomb.

Following the war, the new Atomic Energy Commission used facilities built to make the atomic bomb to produce radioisotopes for medical research and other peacetime uses. This highly publicized program provided the radioisotopes that were used in thousands of human experiments conducted in research facilities throughout the country and the world. This research, in turn, was part of a larger postwar transformation of biomedical research through the infusion of substantial government monies and technical support.

The intersection of government and biomedical research brought with it new roles and new ethical questions for medical researchers. Many of these researchers were also physicians who operated within a tradition of medical ethics that enjoined them to put the interests of their patients first. When the doctor also was a researcher, however, the potential for conflict emerged between the advancement of science and the advancement of the patient's well-being.

Other ethical issues were posed as medical researchers were called on by government officials to play new roles in the development and testing of nuclear weapons. For example, as advisers they were asked to provide human research data that could reassure officials about the effects of radiation, but as scientists they were not always convinced that human research could provide scientifically useful data. Similarly, as scientists, they came from a tradition in which research results were freely debated. In their capacity as advisers to and officials of the government, however, these researchers found that the openness of science now needed to be constrained.

None of these tensions were unique to radiation research. Radiation represents just one of several examples of the exploration of the weapons potential of new scientific discoveries during and after World War II. Similarly, the tensions between clinical research and the treatment of patients were emerging throughout medical science, and were not found only in research involving radiation. Not only were these issues not unique to radiation, but they were not unique to the 1940s and 1950s. Today society still struggles with conflicts between the openness of science and the preservation of national security, as well as with conflicts between the advancement of medical science and the rights and interests of patients.

Key Findings
Human Radiation Experiments

- Between 1944 and 1974 the federal government sponsored several thousand human radiation experiments. In the great majority of cases, the experiments were conducted to advance biomedical science; some experiments were conducted to advance national interests in defense or space exploration; and some experiments served both biomedical and defense or space exploration purposes. As noted, in the great majority of cases only fragmentary data are available.

- The majority of human radiation experiments identified by the Advisory Committee involved radioactive tracers administered in amounts that are likely to be similar to those used in research today. Most of these tracer studies involved adult subjects and are unlikely to have caused physical harm. However, in some nontherapeutic tracer studies involving children, radioisotope exposures were associated with increases in the potential lifetime risk for developing thyroid cancer that would be considered unacceptable today. The Advisory Committee also identified several studies in which patients died soon after receiving external radiation or radioisotope doses in the therapeutic range that were associated with acute radiation effects.

- Although the AEC, the Defense Department and the National Institutes of Health recognized at an early date that research should proceed only with the consent of the human subject, there is little evidence of rules or practices of consent except in research with healthy subjects. It was commonplace during the 1940s and 1950s for physicians to use patients as subjects of research without their awareness or consent. By contrast, the government and its researchers focused with substantial success on the minimization of risk in the conduct of experiments, particularly with respect to research involving radioisotopes. But little attention was paid during this period to issues of fairness in the selection of subjects.

- Government officials and investigators are blameworthy for not having had policies and practices in place to protect the rights and interests of human subjects who were used in research from which the subjects could not possibly derive direct medical benefit. To the extent that there was reason to believe that research might provide a direct medical benefit to subjects, government officials and biomedical professionals are less blameworthy for not having had such protections and practices in place.

Intentional Releases

- During the 1944–1974 period, the government conducted several hundred intentional releases of radiation into the environment for research purposes. Generally, these releases were not conducted for the purpose of studying the effects of radiation on humans. Instead they were usually conducted to test the operation of weapons, the safety of equipment, or the dispersal of radiation into the environment.
- For those intentional releases where dose reconstructions have been undertaken, it is unlikely that members of the public were directly harmed solely as a consequence of these tests. However, these releases were conducted in secret and despite continued requests from the public that stretch back well over a decade, some information about them was made public only during the life of the Advisory Committee.

Uranium Miners

- As a consequence of exposure to radon and its daughter products in underground uranium mines, at least several hundred miners died of lung cancer and surviving miners remain at elevated risk. These men, who were the subject of government study as they mined uranium for use in weapons manufacturing, were subject to radon exposures well in excess of levels known to be hazardous. The government failed to act to require the reduction of the hazard by ventilating the mines, and it failed to adequately warn the miners of the hazard to which they were being exposed.

Secrecy and the Public Trust

- The greatest harm from past experiments and intentional releases may be the legacy of distrust they created. Hundreds of intentional releases took place in secret, and remained secret for decades. Important discussion of the policies to govern human experimentation also took place in secret. Information about human experiments was kept secret out of concern for embarrassment to the government, potential legal liability, and worry that public misunderstanding would jeopardize government programs.
- In a few instances, people used as experimental subjects and their families were denied the opportunity to pursue redress for possible wrongdoing because of actions taken by the government to keep the truth from them. Where programs were legitimately kept secret for national security reasons, the government often did not create or maintain adequate records, thereby preventing the public, and those most at risk, from learning the facts in a timely and complete fashion.

Contemporary Human Subjects Research

- Human research involving radioisotopes is currently subjected to more safeguards and levels of review than most other areas of research involving human subjects. There are no apparent differences between the treatment of human subjects of radiation research and human subjects of other biomedical research.
- Based on the Advisory Committee's review, it appears that much of human subjects research poses only minimal risk of harm to subjects. In our review of research documents that bear on human subjects issues, we found no problems or only minor problems in most of the minimal-risk studies we examined.
- Our review of documents identified examples of complicated, higher-risk studies in which human subjects issues were carefully and adequately addressed and that included excellent consent forms. In our interview project, there was little evidence that patient-subjects felt coerced or pressured by investigators to participate in research. We interviewed patients who had declined offers to become research subjects, reinforcing the impression that there are often contexts in which potential research subjects have a genuine choice.

- At the same time, however, we also found evidence suggesting serious deficiencies in aspects of the current system for the protection of the rights and interests of human subjects. For example, consent forms do not always provide adequate information and may be misleading about the impact of research participation on people's lives. Some patients with serious illnesses appear to have unrealistic expectations about the benefits of being subjects in research.

Current Regulations on Secrecy in Human Research and Environmental Releases

- Human research can still be conducted in secret today, and under some conditions informed consent in secret research can be waived.
- Events that raise the same concerns as the intentional releases in the Committee's charter could take place in secret today under current environmental laws. . . .

Key Recommendations
Apologies and Compensation

The government should deliver a personal, individualized apology and provide financial compensation to those subjects of human radiation experiments, or their next of kin, in cases where:

- Efforts were made by the government to keep information secret from these individuals or their families, or the public, for the purpose of avoiding embarrassment or potential legal liability, and where this secrecy had the effect of denying individuals the opportunity to pursue potential grievances.
- There was no prospect of direct medical benefit to the subjects, or interventions considered controversial at the time were presented as standard practice, and physical injury attributable to the experiment resulted.

Uranium Miners

- The Interagency Working Group, together with Congress, should give serious consideration to amending the provisions of the Radiation Exposure Compensation Act of 1990 relating to uranium miners in order to provide compensation to *all* miners who develop lung cancer after some minimal duration of employment underground (such as one year), without requiring a specific level of exposure. The act should also be reviewed to determine whether the documentation standards for compensation should be liberalized.

Improved Protection for Human Subjects

- The Committee found no differences between human radiation research and other areas of research with respect to human subjects issues, either in the past or the present. In comparison to the practices and policies of the 1940s and 1950s, there have been significant advances in the federal government's system for the protection of the rights and interests of human subjects. But deficiencies remain. Efforts should be undertaken on a national scale to ensure the centrality of ethics in the conduct of scientists whose research involves human subjects.
- One problem in need of immediate attention by the government and the biomedical research community is unrealistic expectations among some patients with serious illnesses about the prospect of direct medical benefit from participating in research. Also, among the consent forms we reviewed, some appear to be overly optimistic in portraying the likely benefits of research, to inadequately explain the impact of research procedures on quality of life and personal finances, and to be incomprehensible to lay people.
- A mechanism should be established to provide for continuing interpretation and application in an open and public forum of ethics rules and principles for the conduct of human subjects research. Three examples of policy issues in need of public resolution that the Advisory Committee confronted in our work are: (1) Clarification of the meaning of minimal risk in research with healthy children; (2) regulations to cover the conduct of research with institutionalized children;

and (3) guidelines for research with adults of questionable competence, particularly for research in which subjects are placed at more than minimal risk but are offered no prospect of direct medical benefit.

Secrecy: Balancing National Security and the Public Trust

Current policies do not adequately safeguard against the recurrence of the kinds of events we studied that fostered distrust. The Advisory Committee concludes that there may be special circumstances in which it may be necessary to conduct human research or intentional releases in secret. However, to the extent that the government conducts such activities with elements of secrecy, special protections of the rights and interests of individuals and the public are needed.

Research Involving Human Subjects. The Advisory Committee recommends the adoption of federal policies requiring:

- The informed consent of all human subjects of classified research. This requirement should not be subject to exemption or waiver.

- That classified research involving human subjects be permitted only after the review and approval of an independent panel of appropriate nongovernmental experts and citizen representatives, all with the necessary security clearances.

Environmental Releases. There must be independent review to assure that the action is needed, that risk is minimized, and that records will be kept to assure a proper accounting to the public at the earliest date consistent with legitimate national security concerns. Specifically, the Committee recommends that:

- Secret environmental releases of hazardous substances should be permitted only after the review and approval of an independent panel. This panel should consist of appropriate, nongovernmental experts and citizen representatives, all with the necessary security clearances.
- An appropriate government agency, such as the Environmental Protection Agency, should maintain a program directed at the oversight of classified programs, with suitably cleared personnel. . . .

Of Mice but Not Men: Problems of the Randomized Clinical Trial

SAMUEL HELLMAN AND DEBORAH S. HELLMAN

The Hellmans contend that randomized clinical trials place physician-scientists (physicians who simultaneously act as scientists) in a terrible ethical bind. As physicians, they have a duty to look out for the best interests of their patients; as scientists, they have an obligation to ensure the integrity of the research. But often they cannot do both, the Hellmans say. Before or during a trial, if a physician-scientist believes that a new treatment is better (or worse) than the alternative treatment, she has a physician's duty to communicate this judgment to her patient-subjects and ensure that they get the best treatment. But if she does so, the validity of the research will be compromised. Thus randomized trials often pit the good of patients against the good of society. The authors "urge that such situations be avoided and that other techniques of acquiring clinical information be adopted."

As medicine has become increasingly scientific and less accepting of unsupported opinion or proof by anecdote, the randomized controlled clinical trial has become the standard technique for changing diagnostic or therapeutic methods. The use of this technique creates an ethical dilemma.[1,2] Researchers participating in such studies are required to modify their ethical commitments to individual patients and do serious damage to the concept of the physician as a practicing, empathetic professional who is primarily concerned with each patient as an individual. Researchers using a randomized clinical trial can be described as physician-scientists, a term that expresses the tension between the two roles. The physician, by entering into a relationship with an individual patient, assumes certain obligations, including the commitment always to act in the patient's best interests. As Leon Kass has rightly maintained, "the physician must produce unswervingly the virtues of loyalty and fidelity to his patient."[3] Though the ethical requirements of this relationship have been modified by legal obligations to report wounds of a suspicious nature and certain infectious diseases, these obligations in no way conflict with the central ethical obligation to act in the best interests of the patient medically. Instead, certain nonmedical interests of the patient are preempted by other social concerns.

The role of the scientist is quite different. The clinical scientist is concerned with answering questions—i.e., determining the validity of formally constructed hypotheses. Such scientific information, it is presumed, will benefit humanity in general. The clinical scientist's role has been well described by Dr. Anthony Fauci, director of the National Institute of Allergy and Infectious Diseases, who states the goals of the randomized clinical trial in these words: "It's not to deliver therapy. It's to answer a scientific question so that the drug can be available for everybody once you've established safety and efficacy."[4] The demands of such a study can conflict in a number of ways with the physician's duty to minister to patients. The study may create a false dichotomy in the physician's opinions; according to the premise of the randomized clinical trial, the physician may only know or not know whether a proposed course of treatment represents an improvement; no middle position is permitted. What the physician thinks, suspects, believes, or has a hunch about is assigned to the "not knowing" category, because knowing is defined on the basis of an arbitrary but accepted statistical test performed in a randomized clinical trial. Thus, little credence is given to information gained beforehand in other ways or to information accrued during the trial but without the required statistical degree of assurance that a difference is not due to chance. The randomized clinical trial also prevents the treatment technique from being modified on the basis of the growing knowledge of the physicians during their participation in the trial. Moreover, it limits access to the data as they are collected until specific milestones are achieved. This prevents physicians from profiting not only from their individual experience, but also from the collective experience of the other participants.

The randomized clinical trial requires doctors to act simultaneously as physicians and as scientists. This puts them in a difficult and sometimes untenable ethical position. The conflicting moral demands arising from the use of the randomized clinical trial reflect the classic conflict between rights-based moral theories and utilitarian ones. The first of these, which depend on the moral theory of Immanuel Kant (and seen more recently in neo-Kantian philosophers, such as John Rawls[5]), asserts that human beings, by virtue of their unique capacity for rational thought, are bearers of dignity. As such, they ought not to be treated merely as means to an end; rather, they must always be treated as ends in themselves. Utilitarianism, by contrast, defines what is right as the greatest good for the greatest number—that is, as social utility. This view, articulated by Jeremy Bentham and John Stuart Mill, requires that pleasures (understood broadly, to include such pleasures as health and well-being) and pains be added together. The morally correct act is the act that produces the most pleasure and the least pain overall.

A classic objection to the utilitarian position is that according to that theory, the distribution of pleasures and pains is of no moral consequence. This element of the theory severely restricts physicians from being utilitarians, or at least from following the theory's dictates. Physicians must care very deeply about the distribution of pain and pleasure, for they have entered into a relationship with one or a number of individual patients. They cannot be indifferent to whether it is these patients or others that suffer for the general benefit of society. Even though society might gain from the suffering of a few, and even though the doctor might believe that such a benefit is worth a given patient's suffering (i.e., that utilitarianism is right in the particular case), the ethical obligation created by the covenant between doctor and patient requires the doctor to see the interests of the individual patient as primary and compelling. In essence, the doctor-patient relationship requires doctors to see their patients as bearers of rights who cannot be merely used for the greater good of humanity.

As Fauci has suggested,[4] the randomized clinical trial routinely asks physicians to sacrifice the interests of their particular patients for the sake of the study and that of the information that it will make available for the benefit of society. This practice is ethically problematic. Consider first the initial formulation of a trial. In particular, consider the case of a disease for which there is no satisfactory therapy—for example, advanced cancer or the acquired immunodeficiency syndrome (AIDS). A new agent that promises more effectiveness is the subject of the study. The control group must be given either an unsatisfactory treatment or a placebo. Even though the therapeutic value of the new agent is unproved, if physicians think that it has promise, are they acting in the best interests of their patients in allowing them to be randomly assigned to the control group? Is persisting in such an assignment consistent with the specific commitments taken on in the doctor-patient relationship? As a result of interactions with patients with AIDS and their advocates, Merigan[6] recently suggested modifications in the design of clinical trials that attempt to deal with the unsatisfactory treatment given to the control group. The view of such activists has been expressed by Rebecca Pringle Smith of Community Research Initiative in New York: "Even if you have a supply of compliant martyrs, trials must have some ethical validity."[4]

If the physician has no opinion about whether the new treatment is acceptable, then random assignment is ethically acceptable, but such lack of enthusiasm for the new treatment does not augur well for either the patient or the study. Alternatively, the treatment may show promise of beneficial results but also present a risk of undesirable complications. When the physician believes that the severity and likelihood of harm and good are evenly balanced, randomization may be ethically acceptable. If the physician has no preference for either treatment (is in a state of equipoise[7,8]), then randomization is acceptable. If, however, he or she believes that the new treatment may be either more or less successful or more or less toxic, the use of randomization is not consistent with fidelity to the patient.

The argument usually used to justify randomization is that it provides, in essence, a critique of the usefulness of the physician's beliefs and opinions, those that have not yet been validated by a randomized clinical trial. As the argument goes, these not-yet-validated beliefs are as likely to be wrong as right. Although physicians are ethically required to provide their patients with the best available treatment, there simply is no best treatment yet known.

The reply to this argument takes two forms. First, and most important, even if this view of the reliability of a physician's opinions is accurate, the ethical constraints of an individual doctor's relationship with a particular patient require the doctor to provide individual care. Although physicians must take pains to make clear the speculative nature of their views, they cannot withhold these views from the patient. The patient asks from the doctor both knowledge and judgment. The relationship established between them rightfully allows patients to ask for the judgment of their particular physicians, not merely that of the medical profession in general. Second, it may not be true, in fact, that the not-yet-validated beliefs of physicians are as likely to be wrong as right. The greater certainty obtained with a randomized clinical trial is beneficial, but that does not mean that a lesser degree of certainty is without value. Physicians can acquire knowledge through methods other than the randomized clinical trial. Such knowledge, acquired over time and less formally than is required in a randomized clinical trial, may be of great value to a patient.

Even if it is ethically acceptable to begin a study, one often forms an opinion during its course—especially in studies that are impossible to conduct in a truly double-blinded fashion—that makes it ethically problematic to continue. The inability to remain blinded usually occurs in studies of cancer or AIDS, for example, because the therapy is associated by nature with serious side effects. Trials attempt to restrict the physician's access to the data in order to prevent such unblinding. Such restrictions should make physicians eschew the trial, since their ability to act in the patient's best interests will be limited. Even supporters of randomized clinical trials, such as Merigan, agree that interim findings should be presented to patients to ensure that no one receives what seems an inferior treatment.[6] Once physicians have formed a view about the new treatment, can they continue randomization? If random assignment is stopped, the study may be lost and the participation of the previous patients wasted. However, if physicians continue the randomization when they have a definite opinion about the efficacy of the experimental drug, they are not acting in accordance with the requirements of the doctor-patient relationship. Furthermore, as their opinion becomes more firm, stopping the randomization may not be enough. Physicians may be ethically required to treat the patients formerly placed in the control group with the therapy that now seems probably effective. To do so would be faithful to the obligations created by the doctor-patient relationship, but it would destroy the study.

To resolve this dilemma, one might suggest that the patient has abrogated the rights implicit in a doctor-patient relationship by signing an informed-consent form. We argue that such rights cannot be waived or abrogated. They are inalienable. The right to be treated as an individual deserving the physician's best judgment and care, rather than to be used as a means to determine the best treatment for others, is inherent in every person. This right, based on the concept of dignity, cannot be waived. What of

altruism, then? Is it not the patient's right to make a sacrifice for the general good? This question must be considered from both positions—that of the patient and that of the physician. Although patients may decide to waive this right, it is not consistent with the role of a physician to ask that they do so. In asking, the doctor acts as a scientist instead. The physician's role here is to propose what he or she believes is best medically for the specific patient, not to suggest participation in a study from which the patient cannot gain. Because the opportunity to help future patients is of potential value to a patient, some would say physicians should not deny it. Although this point has merit, it offers so many opportunities for abuse that we are extremely uncomfortable about accepting it. The responsibilities of physicians are much clearer; they are to minister to the current patient.

Moreover, even if patients could waive this right, it is questionable whether those with terminal illness would be truly able to give voluntary informed consent. Such patients are extremely dependent on both their physicians and the health care system. Aware of this dependence, physicians must not ask for consent, for in such cases the very asking breaches the doctor-patient relationship. Anxious to please their physicians, patients may have difficulty refusing to participate in the trial the physicians describe. The patients may perceive their refusal as damaging to the relationship, whether or not it is so. Such perceptions of coercion affect the decision. Informed-consent forms are difficult to understand, especially for patients under the stress of serious illness for which there is no satisfactory treatment. The forms are usually lengthy, somewhat legalistic, complicated, and confusing, and they hardly bespeak the compassion expected of the medical profession. It is important to remember that those who have studied the doctor-patient relationship have emphasized its empathetic nature.

> [The] relationship between doctor and patient partakes of a peculiar intimacy. It presupposes on the part of the physician not only knowledge of his fellow men but sympathy. . . . This aspect of the practice of medicine has been designated as the art; yet I wonder whether it should not, most properly, be called the essence.[9]

How is such a view of the relationship consonant with random assignment and informed consent? The Physician's Oath of the World Medical Association affirms the primacy of the deontologic view of patients' rights: "Concern for the interests of the subject must always prevail over the interests of science and society."[10]

Furthermore, a single study is often not considered sufficient. Before a new form of therapy is generally accepted, confirmatory trials must be conducted. How can one conduct such trials ethically unless one is convinced that the first trial was in error? The ethical problems we have discussed are only exacerbated when a completed randomized clinical trial indicates that a given treatment is preferable. Even if the physician believes the initial trial was in error, the physician must indicate to the patient the full results of that trial.

The most common reply to the ethical arguments has been that the alternative is to return to the physician's intuition, to anecdotes, or to both as the basis of medical opinion. We all accept the dangers of such a practice. The argument states that we must therefore accept randomized, controlled clinical trials regardless of their ethical problems because of the great social benefit they make possible, and we salve our conscience with the knowledge that informed consent has been given. This returns us to the conflict between patients' rights and social utility. Some would argue that this tension can be resolved by placing a relative value on each. If the patient's right that is being compromised is not a fundamental right and the social gain is very great, then the study might be justified. When the right is fundamental, however, no amount of social gain, or almost none, will justify its sacrifice. Consider, for example, the experiments on humans done by physicians under the Nazi regime. All would agree that these are unacceptable regardless of the value of the scientific information gained. Some people go so far as to say that no use should be made of the results of those experiments because of the clearly unethical manner in which the data were collected. This extreme example may not seem relevant, but we believe that in its hyperbole it clarifies the fallacy of a utilitarian approach to the physician's relationship with the patient. To consider the utilitarian gain is

consistent neither with the physician's role nor with the patient's rights.

It is fallacious to suggest that only the randomized clinical trial can provide valid information or that all information acquired by this technique is valid. Such experimental methods are intended to reduce error and bias and therefore reduce the uncertainty of the result. Uncertainty cannot be eliminated, however. The scientific method is based on increasing probabilities and increasingly refined approximations of truth.[11] Although the randomized clinical trial contributes to these ends, it is neither unique nor perfect. Other techniques may also be useful.[12]

Randomized trials often place physicians in the ethically intolerable position of choosing between the good of the patient and that of society. We urge that such situations be avoided and that other techniques of acquiring clinical information be adopted. For example, concerning trials of treatments for AIDS, Byar et al.[13] have said that "some traditional approaches to the clinical-trials process may be unnecessarily rigid and unsuitable for this disease." In this case, AIDS is not what is so different; rather, the difference is in the presence of AIDS activists, articulate spokespersons for the ethical problems created by the application of the randomized clinical trial to terminal illnesses. Such arguments are equally applicable to advanced cancer and other serious illnesses. Byar et al. agree that there are even circumstances in which uncontrolled clinical trials may be justified: when there is no effective treatment to use as a control, when the prognosis is uniformly poor, and when there is a reasonable expectation of benefit without excessive toxicity These conditions are usually found in clinical trials of advanced cancer.

The purpose of the randomized clinical trial is to avoid the problems of observer bias and patient selection. It seems to us that techniques might be developed to deal with these issues in other ways. Randomized clinical trials deal with them in a cumbersome and heavy-handed manner, by requiring large numbers of patients in the hope that random assignment will balance the heterogeneous distribution of patients into the different groups. By observing known characteristics of patients, such as age and sex, and distributing them equally between groups, it is thought that unknown factors important in determining outcomes will also be distributed equally. Surely, other techniques can be developed to deal with both observer bias and patient selection. Prospective studies without randomization, but with the evaluation of patients by uninvolved third parties, should remove observer bias. Similar methods have been suggested by Royall.[12] Prospective matched-pair analysis, in which patients are treated in a manner consistent with their physicians' views, ought to help ensure equivalence between the groups and thus mitigate the effect of patient selection, at least with regard to known covariates. With regard to unknown covariates, the security would rest, as in randomized trials, in the enrollment of large numbers of patients and in confirmatory studies. This method would not pose ethical difficulties, since patients would receive the treatment recommended by their physician. They would be included in the study by independent observers matching patients with respect to known characteristics, a process that would not affect patient care and that could be performed independently any number of times.

This brief discussion of alternatives to randomized clinical trials is sketchy and incomplete. We wish only to point out that there may be satisfactory alternatives, not to describe and evaluate them completely. Even if randomized clinical trials were much better than any alternative, however, the ethical dilemmas they present may put their use at variance with the primary obligations of the physician. In this regard, Angell cautions, "If this commitment to the patient is attenuated, even for so good a cause as benefits to future patients, the implicit assumptions of the doctor-patient relationship are violated."[14] The risk of such attenuation by the randomized trial is great. The AIDS activists have brought this dramatically to the attention of the academic medical community. Techniques appropriate to the laboratory may not be applicable to humans. We must develop and use alternative methods for acquiring clinical knowledge.

NOTES

1. Hellman S. Randomized clinical trials and the doctor-patient relationship: an ethical dilemma. *Cancer Clin Trials* 1979; 2:189–93.
2. *Idem.* A doctor's dilemma: the doctor-patient relationship in clinical investigation. In: Proceedings of the Fourth National Conference on Human Values and Cancer, New York, March 15–17, 1984. New York: American Cancer Society, 1984:144–6.
3. Kass LR. *Toward a more natural science: biology and human affairs.* New York: Free Press, 1985:196.
4. Palca J. AIDS drug trials enter new age. *Science* 1989; 246:19–21.
5. Rawls J. *A theory of justice.* Cambridge, Mass.: Belknap Press of Harvard University Press, 1971:183–92, 446–52.
6. Merigan TC. You *can* teach an old dog new tricks—how AIDS trials are pioneering new strategies. *N Engl J Med* 1990; 323:1341–3.
7. Freedman B. Equipoise and the ethics of clinical research *N Engl J Med* 1987; 317:141–5.
8. Singer PA, Lantos JD, Whitington PF, Broelsch CE, Siegler M. Equipoise and the ethics of segmental liver transplantation. *Clin Res* 1988; 36:539–45.
9. Longcope WT. Methods and medicine. *Bull Johns Hopkins Hosp* 1932; 50:4–20.
10. Report on medical ethics. *World Med Assoc Bull* 1949; 1:109, 111.
11. Popper K. The problem of induction. In: Miller D, ed., *Popper selections.* Princeton, N.J.: Princeton University Press, 1985:101–17.
12. Royall RM. Ethics and statistics in randomized clinical trials. *Stat Sci* 1991; 6(1):52–62.
13. Byar DP, Schoenfeld DA, Green SB, et al. Design considerations for AIDS trials. *N Engl J Med* 1990; 323:1343–8.
14. Angell M. Patients' preferences in randomized clinical trials *N Engl J Med* 1984; 310:1385–7.

A Response to a Purported Ethical Difficulty with Randomized Clinical Trials Involving Cancer Patients

BENJAMIN FREEDMAN

Defenders of randomized clinical trials claim that physician-scientists do not violate a duty of fidelity to patients if the effectiveness of the treatments being tested is unknown and if the physicians are therefore in doubt (in a state of equipoise) about the treatments' merits. But critics say that if a physician suspects even for flimsy reasons that one treatment is better or worse than another, he cannot be in equipoise. Freedman thinks this view of equipoise is mistaken. He argues that true equipoise does not depend on uncertainty in the physician but on genuine disagreement in the medical community about a treatment's value because of a lack of good evidence gleaned from randomized clinical trials. When this kind of doubt exists, randomized clinical studies are permissible.

In recent years, for a variety of reasons, the mainstay of clinical investigation—the randomized controlled clinical trial (RCT)—has increasingly come under attack. Since Charles Fried's influential monograph,[1] the opponents of controlled trials have claimed the moral high ground. They claim to perceive a conflict between the medical and scientific duties of the physician-investigator, and between the conduct of the trial and a patient's rights. Samuel and Deborah Hellman write, for example, that "the randomized clinical trial routinely asks physicians to sacrifice the interests of their particular patients for the sake of the study and that of the information that it will make available for the benefit of society."[2] Maurie Markman's attraction to this point of view is clear when he writes that "the individual physician's principal ethical responsibility is to the *individual patient* that he or she is treating, and *not* to future patients [emphases in original]." In the interests of returning Markman to the fold, I will concentrate on resolving this central challenge to the ethics of RCTs.

It is unfortunately true that the most common responses from pro-trialists, by revealing fundamental misunderstandings of basic ethical concepts,

do not inspire confidence in the ethics of human research as it is currently conducted. Proponents of clinical trials will commonly begin their apologia by citing benefits derived from trials—by validating the safety and efficacy of new treatments, and, at least as important, by discrediting accepted forms of treatment. So far so good. But they often go on to argue that there is a need to balance the rights of subjects against the needs of society. By this tactic, the proponents of clinical trials have implicitly morally surrendered, for to admit that something is a right is to admit that it represents a domain of action protected from the claims or interests of other individuals or of society itself. A liberal society has rightly learned to look askance at claims that rights of individuals need to yield to the demands of the collective. Patients' claims, then, because of their nature as rights, supersede the requirements of the collectivity.

Sometimes, indeed, the surrender is explicit. At the conclusion of a symposium on the ethics of research on human subjects, Sir Colin Dollery, a major figure in clinical trials, complained to the speaker: "You assume a dominant role for ethics—I think to the point of arrogance. Ethical judgments will be of little value unless the scientific innovations about which they are made . . . are useful."[3] But it is the nature of ethical judgments that they are, indeed, "dominant" as normative or accepted guides

From *The Journal of Clinical Ethics*, vol. 3, no. 3, pp. 231–34.

to action. One may say, "I know that X is the ethical thing to do, but I won't X." That expresses no logical contradiction, but simply weakness of will. But it is, by contrast, plainly contradictory to admit that X is ethical, yet to deny or doubt that one ought to X.

Closer examination and finer distinctions reveal, however, that the conflict between patients' rights and social interests is not at all at issue in controlled clinical trials. There is no need for proponents of clinical trials to concede the moral high ground.

What is the patient right that is compromised by clinical trials? The fear most common to patients who are hesitant about enrolling is that they would not receive the best care, that their right to treatment would be sacrificed in the interests of science. This presumes, of course, that the patient has a right to treatment. Such a right must in reason be grounded in patient need (a patient who is not ill has no right to treatment) and in medical knowledge and capability (a patient with an incurable illness has rights to be cared for, but no right to be cured).

That granted, we need to specify the kind of treatment to which a patient might reasonably claim a right. It was in this connection that I introduced the concept of *clinical equipoise* as critical to understanding the ethics of clinical trials.[4] Clinical equipoise is a situation in which there exists (or is pending) an honest disagreement in the expert clinical community regarding the comparative merits of two or more forms of treatment for a given condition. To be ethical, a controlled clinical trial must begin and be conducted in a continuing state of clinical equipoise—as between the arms of the study—and must, moreover, offer some reasonable hope that the successful conclusion of the trial will disturb equipoise (that is, resolve the controversy in the expert clinical community).

This theory presumes that a right to a specific medical treatment must be grounded in a professional judgment, which is concretized in the term *clinical equipoise*. A patient who has rights to medical treatment has rights restricted to, though not necessarily exhaustive of, those treatments that are understood by the medical community to be appropriate for his condition. A patient may eccentrically claim some good from a physician that is not recognized by the medical community as appropriate

treatment. A physician may even grant this claim; but in so doing, he must realize that he has not provided medical treatment itself. Contrariwise, by failing to fulfill this request, the physician has not failed to satisfy the patient's right to medical treatment.

Provided that a comparative trial is ethical, therefore, it begins in a state of clinical equipoise. For that reason, by definition, nobody enrolling in the trial is denied his or her right to medical treatment, for no medical consensus for or against the treatment assignment exists.

(The modern climate requires that I introduce two simple caveats. First, I am ignoring economic and political factors that go into the grounding of a right to treatment. This is easy enough for one in Canada to write, but may be difficult for someone in the United States to read. Second, when speaking of treatment that is recognized to be condition-appropriate by the medical community, I mean to include only those judgments grounded in medical knowledge rather than social judgments. I would hope to avoid the current bioethical muddle over "medical futility," but if my claims need to be translated into terms appropriate to that controversy, "physiological futility" is close but not identical to what I mean by "inappropriate." For simplicity's sake, the best model to have in mind is the common patient demand for antibiotic treatment of an illness diagnosed as viral.)

Two errors are commonly committed in connection with the concept of clinical equipoise. The first mistake is in thinking that clinical equipoise (or its disturbance) relates to a single endpoint of a trial—commonly, efficacy. As a function of expert clinical judgment, clinical equipoise must incorporate all of the many factors that go into favoring one regimen over its competitors. Treatment *A* may be favored over *B* because it is more effective; or, because it is almost as effective but considerably less toxic; or, because it is easier to administer, allowing, for example, treatment on an outpatient basis; or, because patients are more compliant with it; and so forth.

Just as equipoise may be based upon any one or a combination of these or other factors, it may be disturbed in the same way. Markman's second example, which discusses the efficacy of a multidrug combination chemotherapy regimen, seems vulnerable to this objection. Even were the results of the Mayo trial convincing with regard to the efficacy of this approach, it has not disturbed clinical equipoise in its favor unless other issues, such as toxicity, have been resolved as well. It is well worth pointing out that the endpoints of trials, particularly in cancer treatment, are far too narrow to disturb clinical equipoise in and of themselves, but they are necessary steps along a seriatim path. For that matter, in ignoring the compendious judgment involved in ascertaining equipoise, some studies spuriously claim that all of their arms are in equipoise on the basis of one variable (such as five-year survival rates), when they are clearly out of equipoise because of other factors (such as differences in pain and disfigurement).

The second mistake occurs in identifying clinical equipoise with an individual physician's point of indifference between two treatments. Citing the article in which I developed the concept and another article applying it, for example, the Hellmans write, "If the physician has no preference for either treatment (is in a state of equipoise), then randomization is acceptable."[5] But an individual physician is not the arbiter of appropriate or acceptable medical practice.

There are numerous occasions outside of clinical trials where outsiders need to determine whether the treatment provided was appropriate to the patient's condition. Regulators, as well as third-party payers—private or governmental—need to answer the question, as do health planners and administrators of health-care facilities. Disciplinary bodies of professional associations, and, most tellingly, courts judging allegations of malpractice, have to ascertain this as well. It is never the case that the judgment of an individual physician concerning whether a treatment is condition-appropriate (that is, whether it belongs within the therapeutic armamentarium) is sufficient. In all of these instances, however varied might be their rules of investigation and procedure, the ultimate question is: Does the expert professional community accept this treatment as appropriate for this condition? Since clinical equipoise and its disturbance applies to putative medical treatments for given conditions, this is a

matter that is determined legally, morally, and reasonably by that medical community with the recognized relevant expertise.

Markman may have fallen into this error, writing repeatedly of the judgment of the treating or enrolling physician (and, in the first page, of the responsibility of "the individual physician") with respect to the clinical trial. There is, however, another way of looking at this. Whereas the status of a putative treatment within the medical armamentarium must be settled by the medical *community*, the application of that judgment *vis-à-vis* a given patient is, of course, the judgment (and the responsibility) of the *individual physician*. This individual clinical judgment must be exercised when enrolling a subject, rather than subjugated to the judgment of those who constructed the trial. Indeed, many studies will list this as a criterion of exclusion: "Those subjects who, in the judgment of the accruing physician, would be put at undue risk by participating."

Another point: the Hellmans write of a physician's duty in treating a patient to employ what he "thinks, suspects, believes, or has a hunch about."[6] This is clearly overstated as a duty: why not add to the list the physician's hopes, fantasies, fond but dotty beliefs, and illusions? Yet patients do choose physicians, in part, because of trust in their tacit knowledge and inchoate judgment, and not merely their sapient grasp of the current medical consensus. It would be a disservice to patients for a physician to see his or her role simply as a vehicle for transmitting the wisdom received from the expert medical community in all cases (though when a departure is made, this is done at the legal peril of the doctor!).

But what follows from this inalienable duty of the treating physician? Not as much as the opponents of trials would have us believe. A physician certainly has the right to refuse to participate in a trial that he believes places some participants at a medical disadvantage. Moreover, if he or she is convinced of that, he or she has a *duty* to abstain from participating. But that only speaks to the physician, and does not necessarily affect the patient. What opponents of trials forget is that the patient—the subject—is the ultimate decision maker—in fact, in law, and in ethics. In at least some cases, the fact that there is an open trial for which a patient meets the eligibility criteria needs to be disclosed as one medical alternative, to satisfy ethical norms of informed consent. A physician with convictions that the trial will put subjects at undue risk should inform the prospective subject of that conviction and the reasons for it, and may well recommend to the subject to decline participation. It will then be up to the patient whether to seek enrollment via another physician.

Most commonly at issue, though, is a physician's preference rather than conviction. In such cases, it is perfectly ethical—and becomingly modest—for a physician to participate in a trial, setting aside private misgivings based upon anecdote as overbalanced by the medical literature.

Finally, something should be said about the underlying philosophical buttress on which anti-trialists rely. Following Kant, the Hellmans argue that the underlying issue is that persons "ought not to be treated merely as means to an end; rather, they must always be treated as ends in themselves."[7] Clinical trials, however, are designed to yield reliable data and to ground scientifically valid inferences. In that sense, the treatments and examinations that a subject of a clinical trial undergoes are means to a scientific end, rather than interventions done solely for the subject's own benefit.

But the Kantian formulation is notoriously rigoristic, and implausible in the form cited. We treat others as means all the time, in order to achieve ends the others do not share, and are so treated in return. When buying a carton of milk or leaving a message, I am treating the cashier or secretary as means to an end they do not share. Were this unvarnished principle to hold, all but purely altruistic transactions would be ethically deficient. Clinical trials would be in very good (and, indeed, very bad) company. Those who follow the Kantian view are not concerned about treating another as a means, but rather about treating someone in a way that contradicts the other's personhood itself—that is, in a way that denies the fact that the person is not simply a means but is also an end.

A paradigm case is when I treat someone in a way that serves my ends but, at the same time, is contrary to the other's best interests. It is time that a subject's participation in a clinical trial serves scientific ends, but what has not been shown is that it is contrary to the best interests of the subject. In cases where the two equipoise conditions are satisfied, this cannot be shown.

However, in some cases we are uncertain about whether an intervention will serve the best interests of the other, and so we ask that person. That is one reason for requiring informed consent to studies. There is another. By obtaining the consent of the other party to treat him as an end to one's own means, in effect, an identity of ends between both parties has been created. Applying this amended Kantian dictum, then, we should ask: Is there anything about clinical trials that necessarily implies that subjects are treated contrary to their personhood? And the answer is, of course, no—provided a proper consent has been obtained.

There remain many hard questions to ask about the ethics of controlled clinical studies. Many talents will be needed to address those questions and to reform current practice. Since those questions will only be asked by those who understand that such studies rest upon a sound ethical foundation, I am hopeful that Markman and others will reconsider their misgivings.

NOTES

1. Fried, *Medical Experimentation: Personal Integrity and Social Policy* (New York: Elsevier, 1974).
2. S. Hellman and D.S. Hellman, "Of Mice but Not Men," *New England Journal of Medicine* 324 (1991):1585–89, at 1586.
3. Comment by Sir Colin Dollery in discussion following H.-M. Sass, "Ethics of Drug Research and Drug Development," *Arzneimittel Forschung/Drug Research* 39 (II), Number 8a (1989):1041–48, at 1048.
4. B. Freedman, "Equipoise and the Ethics of Clinical Research," *New England Journal of Medicine* 317 (1987):141–45.
5. Hellman and Hellman, "Of Mice," 1586.
6. *Ibid.*
7. *Ibid.*

How to Resolve an Ethical Dilemma Concerning Randomized Clinical Trials

DON MARQUIS

Marquis addresses the well-known ethical dilemma of randomized clinical trials: A physician has a duty to see that her patients get a treatment that she judges best, but if she enters them in a clinical trial, they may not receive the treatment she prefers. He argues that a solution to the problem lies in the use of informed consent. By taking informed consent seriously, "a physician can both recommend a treatment and ask whether the patient is willing to enroll in the randomized clinical trial."

An apparent ethical dilemma arises when physicians consider enrolling their patients in randomized clinical trials. Suppose that a randomized clinical trial comparing two treatments is in progress, and a physician has an opinion about which treatment is better. The physician has a duty to promote the patient's best medical interests and therefore seems to be obliged to advise the patient to receive the treatment that the physician prefers. This duty creates a barrier to the enrollment of patients in randomized clinical trials.[1-10] Two strategies are often used to resolve the dilemma in favor of enrolling patients in clinical trials.

The "Either You Know Which Is Better or You Don't" Strategy

According to one strategy, physicians should not recommend one treatment over another if they do not really know which one is better, and they do not really know which treatment is better in the absence of data from randomized clinical trials.[11] Data from uncontrolled studies are often influenced by the desire on both the investigator's part and the patient's part to obtain positive results.[12] Journal editors are more likely to publish reports of studies with positive results than reports of studies with negative results.[13] A treatment recommendation based on weaker evidence than that obtained from a randomized clinical trial is like a recommendation based on a mere hunch or an idiosyncratic

preference.[14] Thus, according to this argument, in the absence of data from a randomized clinical trial, evidence that provides an adequate basis for recommending a treatment rarely exists, and the enrollment dilemma is based on a mistake.

This strategy for resolving the dilemma is simplistic. It assumes that evidence available to physicians can be only one of two kinds: gold standard evidence or worthless prejudice. But clinical judgments may be based on evidence of intermediate quality, including physicians' experience with their own patients, their conversations with colleagues concerning their colleagues' experience, their evaluation of the results of nonrandomized studies reported in the literature, their judgment about the mechanism of action of one or both treatments, or their view of the natural history of a given disease. Evidence need not be conclusive to be valuable; it need not be definitive to be suggestive. Because all good physicians allow evidence of intermediate quality to influence their professional judgment when a relevant randomized clinical trial is not being conducted, it is unreasonable to claim that such evidence has no worth when a relevant randomized clinical trial is being conducted. Therefore, the "either you know which is better or you don't" strategy for dealing with the enrollment dilemma is not persuasive.

Adopting a Less Strict Therapeutic Obligation

The dilemma about enrolling patients in randomized clinical trials is generated by the claim that a physician has a strict therapeutic obligation to inform the patients of the physician's treatment

From *The New England Journal of Medicine*, vol. 341, no. 9, pp. 691–93. Copyright © 1999 Massachusetts Medical Society. Reprinted with permission of the publisher.

preference, even when the preference is based on evidence that is not of the highest quality. The dilemma could be resolved if the physician's therapeutic obligation were less strict. This strategy was developed by Freedman.[14,15] He argued that the standard for determining whether a physician has engaged in medical malpractice or committed some other violation punishable by a professional disciplinary body is the standard of good practice as determined by a consensus of the medical community. There is no consensus about which of two treatments being compared in a randomized clinical trial is superior. (Otherwise, why conduct the trial?) Therefore, enrolling a patient in the trial does not violate the physician's therapeutic obligation to the patient, regardless of the physician's treatment preference. In addition, a patient who consults a physician with a preference for treatment A could have consulted a physician who preferred treatment B. Therefore, enrolling a patient in a randomized clinical trial in order to be randomly assigned (perhaps) to treatment B does not make such a patient worse off than he or she would otherwise have been.

Despite these points, compelling arguments for the stricter interpretation of therapeutic obligation remain. In the first place, consider what physicians expect when they seek professional advice from their malpractice attorneys, their tax advisors, or for that matter, their own physicians. Surely they expect—and believe they have a right to expect—not merely minimally competent advice, but the best professional judgments of the professionals they have chosen to consult. In the second place, patients choose physicians in order to obtain medical advice that is, in the judgment of those physicians, the best available. If physicians do not provide such advice, then they tacitly deceive the patients, unless they disclose to their patients that they are not bound by this strict therapeutic obligation. Physicians should adopt the strict therapeutic obligation.

A Resolution

The clash between a strict therapeutic obligation and a less strict one is only apparent. On the one hand, the less strict therapeutic obligation is supported by the argument that it is morally permissible to offer to enroll a patient in a randomized clinical trial. On the other hand, the strict therapeutic obligation is

supported by the arguments concerning treatment recommendations. Recommending is different from offering to enroll. A recognition of this difference provides the basis for a solution to the dilemma.

Suppose that a randomized clinical trial is being conducted to compare treatments A and B and that a physician prefers A and informs the patient of this preference. All physicians have an obligation to obtain their patients' informed consent to treatment. A physician has respected this right only if he or she explains to the patient the risks and benefits of reasonable alternatives to the recommended treatment and offers the patient an opportunity to choose an alternative, if that is feasible. Either treatment B or enrollment in the trial comparing A and B is a reasonable alternative to treatment A, because presumably, A is not known to be superior to B: Indeed, there is some evidence that enrollment in a randomized clinical trial is a superior therapeutic alternative when a trial is available.[16] Respect for a patient's values is a central purpose of informed consent. A particular patient may place a greater value on participation in a study that will contribute to medical progress and to the well-being of patients in the future than on the unproved advantages of following the physician's recommendation. Therefore, a physician can both recommend a treatment and ask whether the patient is willing to enroll in the randomized clinical trial.

This resolution is based on the recognition that there can be evidence of the superiority of a treatment that falls short of the gold standard for evidence but is better than worthless. It also takes into account the good arguments for the view that physicians have a strict obligation to recommend the best treatment on the basis of their professional judgment, even when the recommendation is based on evidence that falls short of the gold standard. Nevertheless, because all physicians have an obligation to take informed consent seriously, because respect for informed consent entails offering a patient the reasonable alternatives to the recommended treatment, and because enrollment in an appropriate randomized clinical trial is often a reasonable therapeutic option, one could argue that offering a patient the opportunity to be enrolled in a clinical trial is not only morally permissible but, in many cases, also morally obligatory, if a relevant trial is being conducted and if enrollment in it is feasible. Taking informed consent seriously resolves the dilemma about whether to enroll patients in randomized clinical trials.

Is this analysis clinically realistic? Some may argue that if clinicians inform their patients that they prefer treatment A, then few of their patients will consent to participate in a trial comparing A with B. Furthermore, many clinicians may be unwilling to invest the time necessary to explain the option of enrollment in a trial, particularly if it seems unlikely that a patient, knowing the physician's preference for one of the treatments, will choose to participate in the trial.

On the other hand, in recent years the public has been exposed to a barrage of medical information and misinformation. Explaining to patients the difference between solid scientific evidence of the merits of a treatment and weaker evidence of its merits is worthwhile, whether or not a relevant randomized clinical trial is being conducted. When a relevant trial is being conducted, offering the patient enrollment in the trial should not impose on the physician a large, additional burden of explanation. Physicians can promote enrollment by explaining that their preference is based only on limited evidence, which may or may not be reliable. They can also explain that data from randomized clinical trials have often shown that the initial studies of new treatments were overly optimistic.[17]

In addition, using this informed-consent strategy to resolve the enrollment dilemma may not be morally optional. My analysis is based on two important obligations of physicians. The first is the strict obligation to recommend the treatment that is, in the physician's professional judgment, the best choice for the patient. The second is the obligation to obtain the patient's informed consent to the recommended treatment. The duty of obtaining informed consent implies that the physician is obligated to offer the patient the opportunity to enroll in a clinical trial when one is available, even if the physician has a treatment preference. The physician owes this duty to the individual patient, not simply to future patients who may benefit from advances in medical knowledge. Thus, the informed-consent strategy for resolving the dilemma about enrolling patients in randomized clinical trials leads to the conclusion that physicians have a greater duty to offer their patients enrollment in trials than has previously been realized. A strict, thoroughly defensible, therapeutic obligation need not interfere with the conduct of randomized clinical trials.

REFERENCES

I am indebted to Erin Fitz-Gerald, Nina Ainslie, Stephen Williamson, Sarah Taylor, Jerry Menikoff, Don Hatton, and Ron Stephens for their criticisms.

1. Chalmers T. C. The ethics of randomization as a decision-making technique and the problem of informed consent. Report of the 14th conference of cardiovascular training grant program directors, June 3–4, 1967. Bethesda, Md.: National Heart Institute, 1967:87–93.

2. Shaw L. W., Chalmers T. C. Ethics in cooperative clinical trials. Ann NY Acad Sci 1970; 169:487–95.

3. Kolata G. B. Clinical trials: methods and ethics are debated. Science 1977; 198:1127–31.

4. Walker D. Ethical considerations in randomized clinical trials. Semin Oncol 1981; 8:437–41.

5. Schafer A. The ethics of the randomized clinical trial. N Engl J Med 1982; 307:719–24.

6. Marquis D. Leaving therapy to chance. Hastings Cent Rep 1983; 13: 40–7.

7. Gifford R. The conflict between randomized clinical trials and the therapeutic obligation. J Med Philos 1986; 11:347–66.

8. Hellman S., Hellman D. S. Of mice but not men: problems of the randomized clinical trial. N Engl J Med 1991; 324:1585–9.

9. Gifford R. Community equipoise and the ethics of randomized clinical trials. Bioethics 1995; 9:127–48.

10. Markman M. Ethical difficulties with randomized clinical trials involving cancer patients: examples from the field of gynecologic oncology. J Clin Ethics 1992; 3:193–5.

11. Spodick D. H. Ethics of the randomized clinical trial. N Engl J Med 1983; 308:343.

12. Passamani E. Clinical trials—are they ethical? N Engl J Med 1991; 324:1589–92.

13. Altman L. Negative results: a positive viewpoint. New York Times, April 29, 1986:B6.

14. Freedman B. Equipoise and the ethics of clinical research. N Engl J Med 1987; 317:141–5.

15. *Idem.* A response to a purported ethical difficulty with randomized clinical trials involving cancer patients. J Clin Ethics 1992; 3:231–4.

16. Davis S., Wright P. W., Schulman S. F., et al. Participants in prospective, randomized clinical trials for resected non-small cell lung cancer have improved survival compared with nonparticipants in such trials. Cancer 1985; 56:1710–8.

17. Sacks H., Chalmers T. C., Smith H. Jr. Randomized versus historical controls for clinical trials. Am J Med 1982; 72:233–40.

Racism and Research: The Case of the Tuskegee Syphilis Study

ALLAN M. BRANDT

Brandt recounts in detail the abuses of human rights and the deliberate harm perpetrated in the infamous Tuskegee Syphilis Study, probably the most egregious example of unethical research in American history. Brandt declares that "the Tuskegee study revealed more about the pathology of racism than it did about the pathology of syphilis."

In 1932 the U.S. Public Health Service (USPHS) initiated an experiment in Macon County, Alabama, to determine the natural course of untreated, latent syphilis in black males. The test comprised 400 syphilitic men, as well as 200 uninfected men who served as controls. The first published report of the study appeared in 1936 with subsequent papers issued every four to six years, through the 1960s. When penicillin became widely available by the early 1950s as the preferred treatment for syphilis, the men did not receive therapy. In fact on several occasions, the USPHS actually sought to prevent treatment. Moreover, a committee at the federally operated Center for Disease Control decided in 1969 that the study should be continued. Only in 1972, when accounts of the study first appeared in the national press, did the Department of Health, Education and Welfare halt the experiment. At that time seventy-four of the test subjects were still alive; at least twenty-eight, but perhaps more than 100, had died directly from advanced syphilitic lesions.[1] In August 1972, HEW appointed an investigatory panel which issued a report the following year. The panel found the study to have been "ethically unjustified," and argued that penicillin should have been provided to the men.[2]

This article attempts to place the Tuskegee Study in a historical context and to assess its ethical implications. Despite the media attention which the study received, the HEW *Final Report,* and the criticism expressed by several professional organizations, the

From Allan M. Brandt, "Racism and Research: The Case of the Tuskegee Syphilis Study," *Hastings Center Report,* Report 8, no. 6 (Dec. 1978): 21–29.

experiment has been largely misunderstood. The most basic questions of *how* the study was undertaken in the first place and *why* it continued for forty years were never addressed by the HEW investigation. Moreover, the panel misconstrued the nature of the experiment, failing to consult important documents available at the National Archives which bear significantly on its ethical assessment. Only by examining the specific ways in which values are engaged in scientific research can the study be understood.

Racism and Medical Opinion

A brief review of the prevailing scientific thought regarding race and heredity in the early twentieth century is fundamental for an understanding of the Tuskegee Study. By the turn of the century, Darwinism had provided a new rationale for American racism.[3] Essentially primitive peoples, it was argued, could not be assimilated into a complex, white civilization. Scientists speculated that in the struggle for survival the Negro in America was doomed. Particularly prone to disease, vice, and crime, black Americans could not be helped by education or philanthropy. Social Darwinists analyzed census data to predict the virtual extinction of the Negro in the twentieth century, for they believed the Negro race in America was in the throes of a degenerative evolutionary process.[4]

The medical profession supported these findings of late nineteenth- and early twentieth-century anthropologists, ethnologists, and biologists. Physicians studying the effects of emancipation on health concluded almost universally that freedom had caused the mental, moral, and physical deterioration of the black population.[5] They substantiated this argument by citing examples in the comparative anatomy of the black and white races. As Dr. W. T. English wrote: "A careful inspection reveals the body of the negro a mass of minor defects and imperfections from the crown of the head to the soles of the feet...."[6] Cranial structures, wide nasal apertures, receding chins, projecting jaws, all typed the Negro as the lowest species in the Darwinian hierarchy.[7]

Interest in racial differences centered on the sexual nature of blacks. The Negro, doctors explained, possessed an excessive sexual desire, which threatened the very foundations of white society. As one physician noted in the *Journal of the American Medical Association,* "The negro springs from a southern race, and as such his sexual appetite is strong; all of his environments stimulate this appetite, and as a general rule his emotional type of religion certainly does not decrease it."[8] Doctors reported a complete lack of morality on the part of blacks:

> Virtue in the negro race is like angels' visits—few and far between. In a practice of sixteen years I have never examined a virgin negro over fourteen years of age.[9]

A particularly ominous feature of this overzealous sexuality, doctors argued, was the black males' desire for white women. "A perversion from which most races are exempt," wrote Dr. English, "prompts the negro's inclination towards white women, whereas other races incline towards females of their own."[10] Though English estimated the "gray matter of the negro brain" to be at least a thousand years behind that of the white races, his genital organs were overdeveloped. As Dr. William Lee Howard noted:

> The attacks on defenseless white women are evidences of racial instincts that are about as amenable to ethical culture as is the inherent odor of the race.... When education will reduce the size of the negro's penis as well as bring about the sensitiveness of the terminal fibers which exist in the Caucasian, then will it also be able to prevent the African's birthright to sexual madness and excess.[11]

One southern medical journal proposed "Castration Instead of Lynching," as retribution for black sexual crimes. "An impressive trial by a ghost-like kuklux klan [sic] and a 'ghost' physician or surgeon to perform the operation would make it an event the 'patient' would never forget," noted the editorial.[12]

According to these physicians, lust and immorality, unstable families, and reversion to barbaric tendencies made blacks especially prone to venereal diseases. One doctor estimated that over 50 percent of all Negroes over the age of twenty-five were syphilitic.[13] Virtually free of disease as slaves, they were now overwhelmed by it, according to informed medical opinion. Moreover, doctors believed that treatment for venereal disease among blacks was impossible, particularly because in its latent stage the symptoms of syphilis become quiescent. As Dr. Thomas W. Murrell wrote:

> They come for treatment at the beginning and at the end. When there are visible manifestations or when harried by pain, they readily come, for as a race they are not averse to physic; but tell them not, though they look well and feel well, that they are still diseased. Here ignorance rates science a fool....[14]

Even the best educated black, according to Murrell, could not be convinced to seek treatment for syphilis.[15] Venereal disease, according to some doctors, threatened the future of the race. The medical profession attributed the low birth rate among blacks to the high prevalence of venereal disease which caused stillbirths and miscarriages. Moreover, the high rates of syphilis were thought to lead to increased insanity and crime. One doctor writing at the turn of the century estimated that the number of insane Negroes had increased thirteen-fold since the end of the Civil War.[16] Dr. Murrell's conclusion echoed the most informed anthropological and ethnological data:

> So the scourge sweeps among them. Those that are treated are only half cured, and the effort to assimilate a complex civilization driving their diseased minds until the results are criminal records. Perhaps here, in conjunction with tuberculosis, will be the end of the negro problem. Disease will accomplish what man cannot do.[17]

This particular configuration of ideas formed the core of medical opinion concerning blacks, sex, and disease in the early twentieth century. Doctors generally discounted socioeconomic explanations of the state of black health, arguing that better medical care could not alter the evolutionary scheme.[18] These assumptions provide the backdrop for examining the Tuskegee Syphilis Study.

The Origins of the Experiment

In 1929, under a grant from the Julius Rosenwald Fund, the USPHS conducted studies in the rural South to determine the prevalence of syphilis among blacks and explore the possibilities for mass treatment. The USPHS found Macon County, Alabama, in which the town of Tuskegee is located, to have the highest syphilis rate of the six counties surveyed. The Rosenwald Study concluded that mass treatment could be successfully implemented among rural blacks.[19] Although it is doubtful that the necessary funds would have been allocated even in the best economic conditions, after the economy collapsed in 1929, the findings were ignored. It is, however, ironic that the Tuskegee Study came to be based on findings of the Rosenwald Study that demonstrated the possibilities of mass treatment.

Three years later, in 1932, Dr. Taliaferro Clark, Chief of the USPHS Venereal Disease Division and author of the Rosenwald Study report, decided that conditions in Macon County merited renewed attention. Clark believed the high prevalence of syphilis offered an "unusual opportunity" for observation. From its inception, the USPHS regarded the Tuskegee Study as a classic "study in nature,"* rather than an experiment.[20] As long as syphilis was so prevalent in Macon and most of the blacks went untreated throughout life, it seemed only natural to Clark that it would be valuable to observe the

---

*In 1865, Claude Bernard, the famous French physiologist, outlined the distinction between a "study in nature" and experimentation. A study in nature required simple observation, an essentially passive act, while experimentation demanded intervention which altered the original condition. The Tuskegee Study was thus clearly not a study in nature. The very act of diagnosis altered the original conditions. "It is on this very possibility of acting or not acting on a body," wrote Bernard, "that the distinction will exclusively rest between sciences called sciences of observation and sciences called experimental."

consequences. He described it as a "ready-made situation."[21] Surgeon General H. S. Cumming wrote to R. R. Moton, Director of the Tuskegee Institute:

> The recent syphilis control demonstration carried out in Macon County, with the financial assistance of the Julius Rosenwald Fund, revealed the presence of an unusually high rate in this county and, what is more remarkable, the fact that 99 per cent of this group was entirely without previous treatment. This combination, together with the expected cooperation of your hospital, offers an unparalleled opportunity for carrying on this piece of scientific research which probably cannot be duplicated anywhere else in the world.[22]

Although no formal protocol appears to have been written, several letters of Clark and Cumming suggest what the USPHS hoped to find. Clark indicated that it would be important to see how disease affected the daily lives of the men:

> The results of these studies of case records suggest the desirability of making a further study of the effect of untreated syphilis on the human economy among people now living and engaged in their daily pursuits.[23]

It also seems that the USPHS believed the experiment might demonstrate that antisyphilitic treatment was unnecessary. As Cumming noted: "It is expected the results of this study may have a marked bearing on the treatment, or conversely the non-necessity of treatment, of cases of latent syphilis."[24]

The immediate source of Cumming's hypothesis appears to have been the famous Oslo Study of untreated syphilis. Between 1890 and 1910, Professor C. Boeck, the chief of the Oslo Venereal Clinic, withheld treatment from almost two thousand patients infected with syphilis. He was convinced that therapies then available, primarily mercurial ointment, were of no value. When arsenic therapy became widely available by 1910, after Paul Ehrlich's historic discovery of "606," the study was abandoned. E. Bruusgaard, Boeck's successor, conducted a follow-up study of 473 of the untreated patients from 1925 to 1927. He found that 27.9 percent of these patients had undergone a "spontaneous cure," and now manifested no symptoms of the disease. Moreover, he estimated that as many as 70 percent of all syphilitics went through life without inconvenience from the disease.[25] His study, however, clearly acknowledged the dangers of untreated syphilis for the remaining 30 percent.

Thus every major textbook of syphilis at the time of the Tuskegee Study's inception strongly advocated treating syphilis even in its latent stages, which follow the initial inflammatory reaction. In discussing the Oslo Study, Dr. J. E. Moore, one of the nation's leading venereologists wrote, "This summary of Bruusgaard's study is by no means intended to suggest that syphilis be allowed to pass untreated."[26] If a complete cure could not be effected, at least the most devastating effects of the disease could be avoided. Although the standard therapies of the time, arsenical compounds and bismuth injection, involved certain dangers because of their toxicity, the alternatives were much worse. As the Oslo Study had shown, untreated syphilis could lead to cardiovascular disease, insanity, and premature death.[27] Moore wrote in his 1933 textbook:

> Though it imposes a slight though measurable risk of its own, treatment markedly diminishes the risk from syphilis. In latent syphilis, as I shall show, the probability of progression, relapse, or death is reduced from a probable 25–30 percent without treatment to about 5 percent with it; and the gravity of the relapse if it occurs, is markedly diminished.[28]

"Another compelling reason for treatment," noted Moore, "exists in the fact that every patient with latent syphilis may be, and perhaps is, infectious for others."[29] In 1932, the year in which the Tuskegee Study began, the USPHS sponsored and published a paper by Moore and six other syphilis experts that strongly argued for treating latent syphilis.[30]

The Oslo Study, therefore, could not have provided justification for the USPHS to undertake a study that did not entail treatment. Rather, the suppositions that conditions in Tuskegee existed "naturally" and that the men would not be treated anyway provided the experiment's rationale. In turn, these two assumptions rested on the prevailing medical attitudes concerning blacks, sex, and disease. For example, Clark explained the prevalence of venereal disease in Macon County by emphasizing promiscuity among blacks:

> This state of affairs is due to the paucity of doctors, rather low intelligence of the Negro population in this section, depressed economic conditions, and the very common promiscuous sex relations of this population group which not only contribute to the spread of syphilis but also contribute to the prevailing indifference with regard to treatment.[31]

In fact, Moore, who had written so persuasively in favor of treating latent syphilis, suggested that existing knowledge did not apply to Negroes. Although he had called the Oslo Study "a never-to-be-repeated human experiment,"[32] he served as an expert consultant to the Tuskegee Study:

> I think that such a study as you have contemplated would be of immense value. It will be necessary of course in the consideration of the results to evaluate the special factors introduced by a selection of the material from negro males. Syphilis in the negro is in many respects almost a different disease from syphilis in the white.[33]

Dr. O. C. Wenger, chief of the federally operated venereal disease clinic at Hot Springs, Arkansas, praised Moore's judgment, adding, "This study will emphasize those differences."[34] On another occasion he advised Clark, "We must remember we are dealing with a group of people who are illiterate, have no conception of time, and whose personal history is always indefinite."[35]

The doctors who devised and directed the Tuskegee Study accepted the mainstream assumptions regarding blacks and venereal disease. The premise that blacks, promiscuous and lustful, would not seek or continue treatment, shaped the study. A test of untreated syphilis seemed "natural" because the USPHS presumed the men would never be treated; the Tuskegee Study made that a self-fulfilling prophecy.

Selecting the Subjects

Clark sent Dr. Raymond Vonderlehr to Tuskegee in September 1932 to assemble a sample of men with latent syphilis for the experiment. The basic design of the study called for the selection of syphilitic black males between the ages of twenty-five and sixty, a thorough physical examination including x-rays, and finally, a spinal tap to determine the incidence of neuro-syphilis.[36] They had no intention of providing any treatment for the infected men.[37] The USPHS originally scheduled the whole experiment to last six months; it seemed to be both a simple and inexpensive project.

The task of collecting the sample, however, proved to be more difficult than the USPHS had supposed. Vonderlehr canvassed the largely illiterate, poverty-stricken population of sharecroppers and tenant farmers in search of test subjects. If his circulars requested only men over twenty-five to attend his clinics, none would appear, suspecting he was conducting draft physicals. Therefore, he was forced to test large numbers of women and men who did not fit the experiment's specifications. This involved considerable expense since the USPHS had promised the Macon County Board of Health that it would treat those who were infected, but not included in the study.[38] Clark wrote to Vonderlehr about the situation: "It never once occured to me that we would be called upon to treat a large part of the county as return for the privilege of making this study....I am anxious to keep the expenditures for treatment down to the lowest possible point because it is the one item of expenditure in connection with the study most difficult to defend despite our knowledge of the need therefor."[39] Vonderlehr responded: "If we could find from 100 to 200 cases … we would not have to do another Wassermann on useless individuals...."[40]

Significantly, the attempt to develop the sample contradicted the prediction the USPHS had made initially regarding the prevalence of the disease in Macon County. Overall rates of syphilis fell well below expectations; as opposed to the USPHS projection of 35 percent, 20 percent of those tested were actually diseased.[41] Moreover, those who had sought and received previous treatment far exceeded the expectations of the USPHS. Clark noted in a letter to Vonderlehr:

> I find your report of March 6th quite interesting but regret the necessity for Wassermanning [sic]...such a large number of individuals in order to uncover this relatively limited number of untreated cases.[42]

Further difficulties arose in enlisting the subjects to participate in the experiment, to be "Wassermanned," and to return for a subsequent series of examinations. Vonderlehr found that only the offer of treatment elicited the cooperation of the men. They were told they were ill and were promised free care. Offered therapy, they became willing subjects.[43] The USPHS did not tell the men that they were participants in an experiment; on the contrary, the subjects believed they were being treated for "bad blood"—the rural South's colloquialism for syphilis. They thought they were participating in a public health demonstration similar to the one that had been conducted by the Julius Rosenwald Fund in Tuskegee several years earlier. In the end, the men were so eager for medical care that the number of defaulters in the experiment proved to be insignificant.[44]

To preserve the subjects' interest, Vonderlehr gave most of the men mercurial ointment, a non-effective drug, while some of the younger men apparently received inadequate dosages of neoarsphenamine.[45] This required Vonderlehr to write frequently to Clark requesting supplies. He feared the experiment would fail if the men were not offered treatment.

> It is desirable and essential if the study is to be a success to maintain the interest of each of the cases examined by me through to the time when the spinal puncture can be completed. Expenditure of several hundred dollars for drugs for these men would be well worth while if their interest and cooperation would be maintained in so doing....
> It is my desire to keep the main purpose of the work from the negroes in the county and continue their interest in treatment. That is what the vast majority wants and the examination seems relatively unimportant to them in comparison. It would probably cause the entire experiment to collapse if the clinics were stopped before the work is completed.[46]

On another occasion he explained:

> Dozens of patients have been sent away without treatment during the past two weeks and it would have been impossible to continue without the free distribution of drugs because of the unfavorable impression made on the negro.[47]

The readiness of the test subjects to participate of course contradicted the notion that blacks would not seek or continue therapy.

The final procedure of the experiment was to be a spinal tap to test for evidence of neuro-syphilis. The USPHS presented this purely diagnostic exam, which often entails considerable pain and complications, to the men as a "special treatment." Clark explained to Moore:

> We have not yet commenced the spinal punctures. This operation will be deferred to the last in order not to unduly disturb our field work by any adverse reports by the patients subjected to spinal puncture because of some disagreeable sensations following this procedure. These negroes are very ignorant and easily influenced by things that would be of minor significance in a more intelligent group.[48]

The letter to the subjects announcing the spinal tap read:

> Some time ago you were given a thorough examination and since that time we hope you have gotten a great deal of treatment for bad blood. You will now be given your last chance to get a second examination. This examination is a very special one and after it is finished you will be given a special treatment if it is believed you are in a condition to stand it....
> REMEMBER THIS IS YOUR LAST CHANCE FOR SPECIAL FREE TREATMENT. BE SURE TO MEET THE NURSE.[49]

The HEW investigation did not uncover this crucial fact: the men participated in the study under the guise of treatment.

Despite the fact that their assumption regarding prevalence and black attitudes toward treatment had proved wrong, the USPHS decided in the summer of 1933 to continue the study. Once again, it seemed only "natural" to pursue the research since the sample already existed, and with a depressed economy, the cost of treatment appeared prohibitive—although there is no indication it was ever considered. Vonderlehr first suggested extending the study in letters to Clark and Wenger:

> At the end of this project we shall have a considerable number of cases presenting various complications of syphilis, who have received only mercury and may still be considered untreated in the modern sense of therapy. Should these cases be followed over a period of from five to ten years many interesting facts could be learned regarding the course and complications of untreated syphilis.[50]

"As I see it," responded Wenger, "we have no further interest in these patients *until they die.*"[51] Apparently, the physicians engaged in the experiment believed that only autopsies could scientifically confirm the findings of the study. Surgeon General Cumming explained this in a letter to R. R. Moton, requesting the continued cooperation of the Tuskegee Institute Hospital:

> This study which was predominantly clinical in character points to the frequent occurrence of severe complications involving the various vital organs of the body and indicates that syphilis as a disease does a great deal of damage. Since clinical observations are not considered final in the medical world, it is our desire to continue observation on the cases selected for the recent study and if possible to bring a percentage of these cases to autopsy so that pathological confirmation may be made of the disease processes.[52]

Bringing the men to autopsy required the USPHS to devise a further series of deceptions and inducements. Wenger warned Vonderlehr that the men must not realize that they would be autopsied:

> There is one danger in the latter plan and that is if the colored population become aware that accepting free hospital care means a post-mortem, every darkey will leave Macon County and it will hurt [Dr. Eugene] Dibble's hospital.[53]

"Naturally," responded Vonderlehr, "it is not my intention to let it be generally known that the main object of the present activities is the bringing of the men to necropsy."[54] The subjects' trust in the USPHS made the plan viable. The USPHS gave Dr. Dibble, the Director of the Tuskegee Institute Hospital, an interim appointment to the Public Health Service. As Wenger noted:

> One thing is certain. The only way we are going to get post-mortems is to have the demise take place in Dibble's hospital and when these colored folks are told that Doctor Dibble is now a Government doctor too they will have more confidence.[55]*

After the USPHS approved the continuation of the experiment in 1933, Vonderlehr decided that it would be necessary to select a group of healthy, uninfected men to serve as controls. Vonderlehr, who had succeeded Clark as Chief of the Venereal

Disease Division, sent Dr. J. R. Heller to Tuskegee to gather the control group. Heller distributed drugs (noneffective) to these men, which suggests that they also believed they were undergoing treatment.[56] Control subjects who became syphilitic were simply transferred to the test group—a strikingly inept violation of standard research procedure.[57]

The USPHS offered several inducements to maintain contact and to procure the continued cooperation of the men. Eunice Rivers, a black nurse, was hired to follow their health and to secure approval for autopsies. She gave the men noneffective medicines—"spring tonic" and aspirin—as well as transportation and hot meals on the days of their examinations.[58] More important, Nurse Rivers provided continuity to the project over the entire forty-year period. By supplying "medicinals," the USPHS was able to continue to deceive the participants, who believed that they were receiving therapy from the government doctors. Deceit was integral to the study. When the test subjects complained about spinal taps one doctor wrote:

> They simply do not like spinal punctures. A few of those who were tapped are enthusiastic over the

results but to most, the suggestion causes violent shaking of the head; others claim they were robbed of their procreative powers (regardless of the fact that I claim it stimulates them).[59]

Letters to the subjects announcing an impending USPHS visit to Tuskegee explained: "[The doctor] wants to make a special examination to find out how you have been feeling and whether the treatment has improved your health."[60] In fact, after the first six months of the study, the USPHS had furnished no treatment whatsoever.

Finally, because it proved difficult to persuade the men to come to the hospital when they became severely ill, the USPHS promised to cover their burial expenses. The Milbank Memorial Fund provided approximately $50 per man for this purpose beginning in 1935. This was a particularly strong inducement as funeral rites constituted an important component of the cultural life of rural blacks.[61] One report of the study concluded, "Without this suasion it would, we believe, have been impossible to secure the cooperation of the group and their families."[62]

Reports of the study's findings, which appeared regularly in the medical press beginning in 1936, consistently cited the ravages of untreated syphilis. The first paper, read at the 1936 American Medical Association annual meeting, found "that syphilis in this period [latency] tends to greatly increase the frequency of manifestations of cardiovascular disease."[63] Only 16 percent of the subjects gave no sign of morbidity as opposed to 61 percent of the controls. Ten years later, a report noted coldly, "The fact that nearly twice as large a proportion of the syphilitic individuals as of the control group has died is a very striking one." Life expectancy, concluded the doctors, is reduced by about 20 percent.[64]

A 1955 article found that slightly more than 30 percent of the test group autopsied had died *directly* from advanced syphilitic lesions of either the cardiovascular or the central nervous system.[65] Another published account stated, "Review of those still living reveals that an appreciable number have late complications of syphilis which probably will result, for some at least, in contributing materially to the ultimate cause of death."[66] In 1950, Dr. Wenger had concluded, "We now know, where we could

---

*The degree of black cooperation in conducting the study remains unclear and would be impossible to properly assess in an article of this length. It seems certain that some members of the Tuskegee Institute staff such as R. R. Moton and Eugene Dibble understood the nature of the experiment and gave their support to it. There is, however, evidence that some blacks who assisted the USPHS physicians were not aware of the deceptive nature of the experiment. Dr. Joshua Williams, an intern at the John A. Andrew Memorial Hospital (Tuskegee Institute) in 1932, assisted Vonderlehr in taking blood samples of the test subjects. In 1973 he told the HEW panel: "I know we thought it was merely a service group organized to help the people in the area. We didn't know it was a research project at all at the time." (See, "Transcript of Proceedings," Tuskegee Syphilis Study Ad Hoc Advisory Panel, February 23, 1973, unpublished typescript. National Library of Medicine, Bethesda, Maryland.) It is also apparent that Eunice Rivers, the black nurse who had primary responsibility for maintaining contact with the men over the forty years, did not fully understand the dangers of the experiment. In any event, black involvement in the study in no way mitigates the racial assumptions of the experiment, but rather, demonstrates their power.

only surmise before, that we have contributed to their ailments and shortened their lives."[67] As black physician Vernal Cave, a member of the HEW panel, later wrote, "They proved a point, then proved a point, then proved a point."[68]

During the forty years of the experiment the USPHS had sought on several occasions to ensure that the subjects did not receive treatment from other sources. To this end, Vonderlehr met with groups of local black doctors in 1934, to ask their cooperation in not treating the men. Lists of subjects were distributed to Macon County physicians along with letters requesting them to refer these men back to the USPHS if they sought care.[69] The USPHS warned the Alabama Health Department not to treat the test subjects when they took a mobile VD unit into Tuskegee in the early 1940s.[70] In 1941, the Army drafted several subjects and told them to begin antisyphilitic treatment immediately. The USPHS supplied the draft board with a list of 256 names they desired to have excluded from treatment, and the board complied.[71]

In spite of these efforts, by the early 1950s many of the men had secured some treatment on their own. By 1952, almost 30 percent of the test subjects had received some penicillin, although only 7.5 percent had received what could be considered adequate doses.[72] Vonderlehr wrote to one of the participating physicians, "I hope that the availability of antibiotics has not interfered too much with this project."[73] A report published in 1955 considered whether the treatment that some of the men had obtained had "defeated" the study. The article attempted to explain the relatively low exposure to penicillin in an age of antibiotics, suggesting as a reason: "the stoicism of these men as a group; they still regard hospitals and medicines with suspicion and prefer an occasional dose of time-honored herbs or tonics to modern drugs."[74] The authors failed to note that the men believed they already were under the care of the government doctors and thus saw no need to seek treatment elsewhere. Any treatment which the men might have received, concluded the report, had been insufficient to compromise the experiment.

When the USPHS evaluated the status of the study in the 1960s they continued to rationalize the racial aspects of the experiment. For example, the minutes of a 1965 meeting at the Center for Disease Control recorded:

> Racial issue was mentioned briefly. Will not affect the study. Any questions can be handled by saying these people were at the point that therapy would no longer help them. They are getting better medical care than they would under any other circumstances.[75]

A group of physicians met again at the CDC in 1969 to decide whether or not to terminate the study. Although one doctor argued that the study should be stopped and the men treated, the consensus was to continue. Dr. J. Lawton Smith remarked, "You will never have another study like this; take advantage of it."[76] A memo prepared by Dr. James B. Lucas, Assistant Chief of the Venereal Disease Branch, stated: "Nothing learned will prevent, find, or cure a single case of infectious syphilis or bring us closer to our basic mission of controlling venereal disease in the United States."[77] He concluded, however, that the study should be continued "along its present lines." When the first accounts of the experiment appeared in the national press in July 1972, data were still being collected and autopsies performed.[78]

The HEW Final Report

HEW finally formed the Tuskegee Syphilis Study Ad Hoc Advisory Panel on August 28, 1972, in response to criticism that the press descriptions of the experiment had triggered. The panel, composed of nine members, five of them black, concentrated on two issues. First, was the study justified in 1932 and had the men given their informed consent? Second, should penicillin have been provided when it became available in the early 1950s? The panel was also charged with determining if the study should be terminated and assessing current policies regarding experimentation with human subjects.[79] The group issued their report in June 1973.

By focusing on the issues of penicillin therapy and informed consent, the *Final Report* and the investigation betrayed a basic misunderstanding of the experiment's purposes and design. The HEW report implied that the failure to provide penicillin constituted the study's major ethical misjudgment;

implicit was the assumption that no adequate therapy existed prior to penicillin. Nonetheless medical authorities firmly believed in the efficacy of arsenotherapy for treating syphilis at the time of the experiment's inception in 1932. The panel further failed to recognize that the entire study had been predicated on nontreatment. Provision of effective medication would have violated the rationale of the experiment—to study the natural course of the disease until death. On several occasions, in fact, the USPHS had prevented the men from receiving proper treatment. Indeed, there is no evidence that the USPHS ever considered providing penicillin.

The other focus of the *Final Report*—informed consent—also served to obscure the historical facts of the experiment. In light of the deceptions and exploitations which the experiment perpetrated, it is an understatement to declare, as the *Report* did, that the experiment was "ethically unjustified," because it failed to obtain informed consent from the subjects. The *Final Report's* statement, "Submitting voluntarily is not informed consent," indicated that the panel believed that the men had volunteered *for the experiment*.[80] The records in the National Archives make clear that the men did not submit voluntarily to an experiment; they were told and they believed that they were getting free treatment from expert government doctors for a serious disease. The failure of the HEW *Final Report* to expose this critical fact—that the USPHS lied to the subjects—calls into question the thoroughness and credibility of their investigation.

Failure to place the study in a historical context also made it impossible for the investigation to deal with the essentially racist nature of the experiment. The panel treated the study as an aberration, well-intentioned but misguided.[81] Moreover, concern that the *Final Report* might be viewed as a critique of human experimentation in general seems to have severely limited the scope of the inquiry. The *Final Report* is quick to remind the reader on two occasions: "The position of the Panel must not be construed to be a general repudiation of scientific research with human subjects."[82] The *Report* assures us that a better designed experiment could have been justified:

> It is possible that a scientific study in 1932 of untreated syphilis, properly conceived with a clear protocol and conducted with suitable subjects who fully understood the implications of their involvement, might have been justified in the pre-penicillin era. This is especially true when one considers the uncertain nature of the results of treatment of late latent syphilis and the highly toxic nature of therapeutic agents then available.[83]

This statement is questionable in view of the proven dangers of untreated syphilis known in 1932.

Since the publication of the HEW *Final Report*, a defense of the Tuskegee Study has emerged. These arguments, most clearly articulated by Dr. R. H. Kampmeier in the *Southern Medical Journal*, center on the limited knowledge of effective therapy for latent syphilis when the experiment began. Kampmeier argues that by 1950, penicillin would have been of no value for these men.[84] Others have suggested that the men were fortunate to have been spared the highly toxic treatments of the earlier period.[85] Moreover, even these contemporary defenses assume that the men never would have been treated anyway. As Dr. Charles Barnett of Stanford University wrote in 1974, "The lack of treatment was not contrived by the USPHS but was an established fact of which they proposed to take advantage."[86] Several doctors who participated in the study continued to justify the experiment. Dr. J. R. Heller, who on one occasion had referred to the test subjects as the "Ethiopian population," told reporters in 1972:

> I don't see why they should be shocked or horrified. There was no racial side to this. It just happened to be in a black community. I feel this was a perfectly straightforward study, perfectly ethical, with controls. Part of our mission as physicians is to find out what happens to individuals with disease and without disease.[87]

These apologies, as well as the HEW *Final Report*, ignore many of the essential ethical issues which the study poses. The Tuskegee Study reveals the persistence of beliefs within the medical profession about the nature of blacks, sex, and disease—beliefs that had tragic repercussions long after their alleged "scientific" bases were known to be incorrect. Most strikingly, the entire health of a community was jeopardized by leaving a communicable disease untreated.[88] There can be little doubt that the Tuskegee researchers regarded their subjects as less than human.[89] As a result, the ethical canons of experimenting on human subjects were completely disregarded.

The study also raises significant questions about professional self-regulation and scientific bureaucracy. Once the USPHS decided to extend the experiment in the summer of 1933, it was unlikely that the test would be halted short of the men's deaths. The experiment was widely reported for forty years without evoking any significant protest within the medical community. Nor did any bureaucratic mechanism exist within the government for the periodic reassessment of the Tuskegee experiment's ethics and scientific value. The USPHS sent physicians to Tuskegee every several years to check on the study's progress, but never subjected the morality or usefulness of the experiment to serious scrutiny. Only the press accounts of 1972 finally punctured the continued rationalizations of the USPHS and brought the study to an end. Even the HEW investigation was compromised by fear that it would be considered a threat to future human experimentation.

In retrospect the Tuskegee Study revealed more about the pathology of racism than it did about the pathology of syphilis; more about the nature of scientific inquiry than the nature of the disease process. The injustice committed by the experiment went well beyond the facts outlined in the press and the HEW *Final Report*. The degree of deception and damages have been seriously underestimated. As this history of the study suggests, the notion that science is a value-free discipline must be rejected. The need for greater vigilance in assessing the specific ways in which social values and attitudes affect professional behavior is clearly indicated.

REFERENCES

1. The best general accounts of the study are "The 40-Year Death Watch," *Medical World News* (August 18, 1972), pp. 15–17; and Dolores Katz, "Why 430 Blacks with Syphilis Went Uncured for 40 Years," Detroit *Free Press* (November 5, 1972). The mortality figure is based on a published report of the study which appeared in 1955. See Jesse J. Peters, James H. Peers, Sidney Olansky, John C. Cutler, and Geraldine Gleeson, "Untreated Syphilis in the Male Negro: Pathologic Findings in Syphilitic and Nonsyphilitic Patients," *Journal of Chronic Diseases* 1 (February 1955), 127–48. The article estimated that 30.4 percent of the untreated men would die from syphilitic lesions.

2. *Final Report* of the Tuskegee Syphilis Study Ad Hoc Advisory Panel, Department of Health, Education, and Welfare (Washington. D.C.: GPO, 1973). (Hereafter, HEW *Final Report*.)

3. See George M. Frederickson, *The Black Image in the White Mind* (New York: Harper and Row, 1971), pp. 228–55. Also, John H. Haller, *Outcasts From Evolution* (Urbana, Ill.: University of Illinois Press, 1971), pp. 40–68.

4. Frederickson, pp. 247–49.

5. "Deterioration of the American Negro," *Atlanta Journal-Record of Medicine* 5 (July 1903), 287–88. See also J. A. Rodgers, "The Effect of Freedom upon the Psychological Development of the Negro," *Proceedings of the American Medico-Psychological Association* 7 (1900), 88–99. "From the most healthy race in the country forty years ago," concluded Dr. Henry McHatton, "he is today the most diseased." "The Sexual Status of the Negro—Past and Present," *American Journal of Dermatology and Genito-Urinary Diseases* 10 (January 1906), 7–9.

6. W. T. English, "The Negro Problem from the Physician's Point of View," *Atlanta Journal-Record of Medicine* 5 (October 1903), 461. See also, "Racial Anatomical Peculiarities," *New York Medical Journal* 63 (April 1896), 500–01.

7. "Racial Anatomical Peculiarities," p. 501. Also, Charles S. Bacon, "The Race Problem," *Medicine* (Detroit) 9 (May 1903), 338–43.

8. H. H. Hazen, "Syphilis in the American Negro," *Journal of the American Medical Association* 63 (August 8, 1914), 463. For deeper background into the historical relationship of racism and sexuality see Winthrop D. Jordan, *White Over Black* (Chapel Hill: University of North Carolina Press, 1968; Pelican Books, 1969), pp. 32–40.

9. "Daniel David Quillian, "Racial Peculiarities: A Cause of the Prevalence of Syphilis in Negroes," *American Journal of Dermatology and Genito-Urinary Diseases* 10 (July 1906), p. 277.

10. English, p. 463.

11. William Lee Howard, "The Negro as a Distinct Ethnic Factor in Civilization," *Medicine* (Detroit) 9 (June 1903), 424. See also, Thomas W. Murrell, "Syphilis in the American Negro," *Journal of the American Medical Association* 54 (March 12, 1910), 848.

12. "Castration Instead of Lynching," *Atlanta Journal-Record of Medicine* 8 (October 1906), 457. The editorial added: "The badge of disgrace and emasculation might be branded upon the face or forehead, as a warning, in the form of an 'R,' emblematic of the crime for which this punishment was and will be inflicted."

13. Searle Harris, "The Future of the Negro from the Standpoint of the Southern Physician," *Alabama Medical Journal* 14 (January 1902), 62. Other articles on the prevalence of venereal disease among blacks are: H. L. McNeil, "Syphilis in the Southern Negro," *Journal of the American Medical Association* 67 (September 30, 1916), 1001–04; Ernest Philip Boas, "The Relative Prevalence of Syphilis Among Negroes and Whites," *Social Hygiene* 1 (September 1915), 610–16. Doctors went to considerable trouble to distinguish the morbidity and mortality of various diseases among blacks and whites. See, for example, Marion M. Torchia, "Tuberculosis Among American Negroes: Medical Research on a Racial Disease, 1830–1950," *Journal of the History of Medicine and Allied Sciences* 32 (July 1977), 252–79.

14. Thomas W. Murrell, "Syphilis in the Negro: Its Bearing on the Race Problem," *American Journal of Dermatology and Genito-Urinary Diseases* 10 (August 1906), 307.

15. "Even among the educated, only a very few will carry out the most elementary instructions as to personal hygiene. One thing you cannot do, and that is to convince the negro that he has a disease that he cannot see or feel. This is due to lack of concentration rather than lack of faith; even if he does believe, he does not care; a child of fancy, the sensations of the passing hour are his only guides to the future." Murrell, "Syphilis in the American Negro," p. 847.

16. "Deterioration of the American Negro," *Atlanta Journal-Record of Medicine* 5 (July 1903), 288.

17. "Murrell, "Syphilis in the Negro; Its Bearing on the Race Problem," p. 307.

18. "The anatomical and physiological conditions of the African must be understood, his place in the anthropological scale realized, and his biological basis accepted as being unchangeable by man, before we shall be able to govern his natural uncontrollable sexual passions." See, "As Ye Sow That Shall Ye Also Reap," *Atlanta Journal-Record of Medicine* 1 (June 1899), 266.

19. Taliaferro Clark, *The Control of Syphilis in Southern Rural Areas* (Chicago: Julius Rosenwald Fund, 1932), 53–58. Approximately 35 percent of the inhabitants of Macon County who were examined were found to be syphilitic.

20. See Claude Bernard, *An Introduction to the Study of Experimental Medicine* (New York: Dover, 1865, 1957), pp. 5–26.

21. Taliaferro Clark to M. M. Davis, October 29, 1932. Records of the USPHS Venereal Disease Division, Record Group 90, Box 239, National Archives, Washington National Record Center, Suitland, Maryland. (Hereafter, NA-WNRC.) Materials in this collection which relate to the early history of the study were apparently never consulted by the HEW investigation. Included are letters, reports, and memoranda written by the physicians engaged in the study.

22. H. S. Cumming to R. R. Moton, September 20, 1932, NA-WNRC.

23. Clark to Davis, October 29, 1932, NA-WNRC.

24. Cumming to Moton, September 20, 1932, NA-WNRC.

25. Bruusgaard was able to locate 309 living patients, as well as records from 164 who were diseased. His findings were published as *"Ueber das Schicksal der nicht specifizch behandelten Luetiken," Archives of Dermatology and Syphilis* 157 (1929), 309–32. The best discussion of the Boeck-Bruusgaard data is E. Gurney Clark and Niels Danbolt, "The Oslo Study of the Natural History of Untreated Syphilis," *Journal of Chronic Diseases* 2 (September 1955), 311–44.

26. Joseph Earle Moore, *The Modern Treatment of Syphilis* (Baltimore: Charles C. Thomas, 1933), p. 24.

27. Moore, pp. 231–47; see also John H. Stokes, *Modern Clinical Syphilology* (Philadelphia: W. B. Saunders, 1928), pp. 231–39.

28. Moore, p. 237.

29. Moore, p. 236.

30. J. E. Moore, H. N. Cole, P. A. O'Leary, J. H. Stokes, U. J. Wile, T. Clark, T. Parran, J. H. Usilton, "Cooperative Clinical Studies in the Treatment of Syphilis: Latent Syphilis," *Venereal Disease Information* 13 (September 20, 1932), 351. The authors also concluded that the latently syphilitic were potential carriers of the disease, thus meriting treatment.

31. Clark to Paul A. O'Leary, September 27, 1932, NA-WNRC. O'Leary, of the Mayo Clinic, misunderstood the design of the study, replying: "The investigation which you are planning in Alabama is indeed an intriguing one, particularly because of the opportunity it affords of observing treatment in a previously untreated group. I assure you such a study is of interest to me, and I shall look forward to its report in the future." O'Leary to Clark, October 3, 1932, NA-WNRC.

32. Joseph Earle Moore, "Latent Syphilis," unpublished typescript (n.d.), p. 7. American Social Hygiene Association Papers, Social Welfare History Archives Center, University of Minnesota, Minneapolis, Minnesota.

33. Moore to Clark, September 28, 1932, NA-WNRC. Moore had written in his textbook, "In late syphilis the negro is particularly prone to the development of bone or cardiovascular lesions." See Moore, *The Modern Treatment of Syphilis*, p. 35.

34. O. C. Wenger to Clark, October 3, 1932, NA-WNRC.

35. Wenger to Clark, September 29, 1932, NA-WNRC.

36. Clark Memorandum, September 26, 1932, NA-WNRC. See also, Clark to Davis, October 29, 1932, NA-WNRC.

37. As Clark wrote: "You will observe that our plan has nothing to do with treatment. It is purely a diagnostic procedure carried out to determine what has happened to the syphilitic Negro who has had no treatment." Clark to Paul A. O'Leary, September 27, 1932, NA-WNRC.

38. D. G. Gill to O. C. Wenger, October 10, 1932, NA-WNRC.

39. Clark to Vonderlehr, January 25, 1933, NA-WNRC.

40. Vonderlehr to Clark, February 28, 1933, NA-WNRC.

41. Vonderlehr to Clark, November 2, 1932, NA-WNRC. Also, Vonderlehr to Clark, February 6, 1933, NA-WNRC.

42. Clark to Vonderlehr, March 9, 1933, NA-WNRC.

43. Vonderlehr later explained: "The reason treatment was given to many of these men was twofold: First, when the study was started in the fall of 1932, no plans had been made for its continuation and a few of the patients were treated before we fully realized the need for continuing the project on a permanent basis. Second it was difficult to hold the interest of the group of Negroes in Macon County unless some treatment was given." Vonderlehr to Austin V. Diebert, December 5, 1938, Tuskegee Syphilis Study Ad Hoc Advisory Panel Papers, Box 1, National Library of Medicine, Bethesda, Maryland. (Hereafter, TSS-NLM.) This collection contains the materials assembled by the HEW investigation in 1972.

44. Vonderlehr to Clark, February 6, 1933, NA-WNRC.

45. H. S. Cumming to J. N. Baker, August 5, 1933, NA-WNRC.

46. January 22, 1933; January 12, 1933, NA-WNRC.

47. Vonderlehr to Clark, January 28, 1933, NA-WNRC.

48. Clark to Moore, March 25, 1933, NA-WNRC.

49. Macon County Health Department, "Letter to Subjects," n.d., NA-WNRC.

50. Vonderlehr to Clark, April 8, 1933, NA-WNRC. See also, Vonderlehr to Wenger, July 18, 1933, NA-WNRC.

51. Wenger to Vonderlehr, July 21, 1933, NA-WNRC. The italics are Wenger's.

52. Cumming to Moton, July 27, 1933, NA-WNRC.

53. Wenger to Vonderlehr, July 21, 1933, NA-WNRC.

54. Vonderlehr to Murray Smith, July 27, 1933, NA-WNRC.

55. Wenger to Vonderlehr, August 5, 1933, NA-WNRC.

56. Vonderlehr to Wenger, October 24, 1933, NA-WNRC. Controls were given salicylates.

57. Austin V. Diebert and Martha C. Bruyere, "Untreated Syphilis in the Male Negro, III," *Venereal Disease Information* 27 (December 1946), 301–14.

58. Eunice Rivers, Stanley Schuman, Lloyd Simpson, Sidney Olansky, "Twenty-Years of Followup Experience in a Long-Range Medical Study," *Public Health Reports* 68 (April 1953), 391–95. In this article Nurse Rivers explains her role in the experiment. She wrote: "Because of the low educational status of the majority of the patients, it was impossible to appeal to them from a purely scientific approach. Therefore, various methods were used to maintain their interest. Free medicines, burial assistance or insurance (the project being referred to as 'Miss Rivers' Lodge'), free hot meals on the days of examination, transportation to and from the hospital, and an opportunity to stop in town on the return trip to shop or visit with their friends on the streets all helped. In spite of these attractions, there were some who refused their examinations because they were not sick and did not see that they were being benefitted" (p. 393).

59. Austin V. Diebert to Raymond Vonderlehr, March 20, 1939, TSS-NLM, Box 1.

60. Murray Smith to Subjects, (1938), TSS-NLM, Box 1. See also, Sidney Olansky to John C. Cutler, November 6, 1951, TSS-NLM, Box 2.

61. The USPHS originally requested that the Julius Rosenwald Fund meet this expense. See Cumming to Davis, October 4, 1934, NA-WNRC. This money was usually divided between the undertaker, pathologist, and hospital. Lloyd Isaacs to Raymond Vonderlehr, April 23, 1940, TSS-NLM, Box 1.

62. Stanley H. Schuman, Sidney Olansky, Eunice Rivers, C. A. Smith, Dorothy S. Rambo, "Untreated Syphilis in the Male Negro: Background and Current Status of Patients in the Tuskegee Study," *Journal of Chronic Diseases* 2 (November 1955), 555.

63. R. A. Vonderlehr and Taliaferro Clark, "Untreated Syphilis in the Male Negro," *Venereal Disease Information* 17 (September 1936), 262.

64. J. R. Heller and P. T. Bruyere, "Untreated Syphilis in the Male Negro: II. Mortality During 12 Years of Observation," *Venereal Disease Information* 27 (February 1946), 34–38.

65. Jesse J. Peters, James H. Peers, Sidney Olansky, John C. Cutler, and Geraldine Gleeson, "Untreated Syphilis in the Male Negro: Pathologic Findings in Syphilitic and Non-Syphilitic Patients," *Journal of Chronic Diseases* 1 (February 1955), 127–48.

66. Sidney Olansky, Stanley H. Schuman, Jesse J. Peters, C. A. Smith, and Dorothy S. Rambo, "Untreated Syphilis in the Male Negro, X. Twenty Years of Clinical Observation of Untreated Syphilitic and Presumably Nonsyphilitic Groups," *Journal of Chronic Diseases* 4 (August 1956), 184.

67. O. C. Wenger, "Untreated Syphilis in Male Negro," unpublished typescript, 1950, p. 3. Tuskegee Files, Center for Disease Control, Atlanta, Georgia. (Hereafter TF-CDC.)

68. Vernal G. Cave, "Proper Uses and Abuses of the Health Care Delivery System for Minorities with Special Reference to the Tuskegee Syphilis Study," *Journal of the National Medical Association* 67 (January 1975), 83.

69. See for example, Vonderlehr to B. W. Booth, April 18, 1934; Vonderlehr to E. R. Lett, November 20, 1933, NA-WNRC.

70. "Transcript of Proceedings—Tuskegee Syphilis Ad Hoc Advisory Panel," February 23, 1973, unpublished typescript, TSS-NLM, Box 1.

71. Raymond Vonderlehr to Murray Smith, April 30, 1942; and Smith to Vonderlehr, June 8, 1942, TSS-NLM, Box 1.

72. Stanley H. Schuman, Sidney Olansky, Eunice Rivers, C. A. Smith, and Dorothy S. Rambo, "Untreated Syphilis in the Male Negro: Background and Current Status of Patients in the Tuskegee Study," *Journal of Chronic Diseases* 2 (November 1955), 550–53.

73. Raymond Vonderlehr to Stanley H. Schuman, February 5, 1952. TSS-NLM, Box 2.

74. Schuman et al., p. 550.

75. "Minutes, April 5, 1965" unpublished typescript, TSS-NLM, Box 1.

76. "Tuskegee Ad Hoc Committee Meeting—Minutes, February 6, 1969," TF-CDC.

77. James B. Lucas to William J. Brown, September 10, 1970, TF-CDC.

78. Elizabeth M. Kennebrew to Arnold C. Schroeter, February 24, 1971, TSS-NLM, Box 1.

79. See *Medical Tribune* (September 13, 1972), pp. 1, 20; and "Report on HEW's Tuskegee Report," *Medical World News* (September 14, 1973), pp. 57–58.

80. HEW *Final Report*, p. 7.

81. The notable exception is Jay Kate's eloquent "Reservations About the Panel Report on Charge 1," HEW *Final Report*, pp. 14–15.

82. HEW *Final Report*, pp. 8, 12.

83. HEW *Final Report*, pp. 8, 12.

84. See R. H. Kampmeier, "The Tuskegee Study of Untreated Syphilis," *Southern Medical Journal* 65 (October 1972), 1247–51; and "Final Report on the Tuskegee Syphilis Study,'" *Southern Medical Journal* 67 (November 1974), 1349–53.

85. Leonard J. Goldwater, "The Tuskegee Study in Historical Perspective," unpublished typescript, TSS-NLM; see also "Treponemes and Tuskegee," *Lancet* (June 23, 1973), p. 1438;

and Louis Lasagna, *The VD Epidemic* (Philadelphia: Temple University Press, 1975), pp. 64–66.

86. Quoted in "Debate Revives on the PHS Study," *Medical World News* (April 19, 1974), p. 37.

87. Heller to Vonderlehr, November 28, 1933, NA-WNRC; quoted in *Medical Tribune* (August 23, 1972), p. 14.

88. Although it is now known that syphilis is rarely infectious after its early phase, at the time of the study's inception latent syphilis was thought to be communicable. The fact that members of the control group were placed in the test group when they became syphilitic proves that at least some infectious men were denied treatment.

89. When the subjects are drawn from minority groups, especially those with which the researcher cannot identify, basic human rights may be compromised. Hans Jonas has clearly explicated the problem in his "Philosophical Reflections on Experimentation," *Daedalus* 98 (Spring 1969), 234–37. As Jonas writes: "If the properties we adduced as the particular qualifications of the members of the scientific fraternity itself are taken as general criteria of selection, then one should look for additional subjects where a maximum of identification, understanding, and spontaneity can be expected—that is, among the most highly motivated, the most highly educated, and the least 'captive' members of the community."

The Ethics of Clinical Research in the Third World

MARCIA ANGELL

Angell maintains that randomized clinical trials comparing two treatments are morally permissible only when investigators are in a state of equipoise—that is, when there is "no good reason for thinking one [treatment] is better than another." So studies comparing a potential new treatment with a placebo are unethical if an effective treatment exists. If there is an effective treatment, subjects in the control group must receive the best known treatment. By this standard, some ongoing trials in the Third World must be judged impermissible—namely, the trials testing regimens to prevent the mother-infant transmission of HIV infection. The studies use placebo control groups even though a proven preventive exists. Angell concludes that the research community needs to bolster its commitment to the highest ethical standards "no matter where the research is conducted."

An essential ethical condition for a randomized clinical trial comparing two treatments for a disease is that there be no good reason for thinking one is better than the other.[1,2] Usually, investigators hope and even expect that the new treatment will be better, but there should not be solid evidence one way or the other. If there is, not only would the trial be scientifically redundant, but the investigators would be guilty of knowingly giving inferior treatment to some participants in the trial. The necessity for investigators to be in this state of equipoise,[2] applies to placebo-controlled trials, as well. Only when there is no known effective treatment is it ethical to compare a potential new treatment with a placebo. When effective treatment exists, a placebo may not be used. Instead, subjects in the control group of the study must receive the best known treatment. Investigators are responsible for all subjects enrolled in a trial, not just some of them, and the goals of the research are always secondary to the well-being of the participants. Those requirements are made clear in the Declaration of Helsinki of the World Health Organization (WHO), which is widely regarded as providing the fundamental guiding principles of research involving human subjects.[3] It states, "In research on man [sic], the interest of science and society should never take precedence over considerations related to the well-being of the subject," and "In any medical study, every patient—including those of a control group, if any—should be assured of the best proven diagnostic and therapeutic method."

One reason ethical codes are unequivocal about investigators' primary obligation to care for the human subjects of their research is the strong temptation to subordinate the subjects' welfare to the objectives of the study. That is particularly likely when the research question is extremely important and the answer would probably improve the care of future patients substantially. In those circumstances, it is sometimes argued explicitly that obtaining a rapid, unambiguous answer to the research question is the primary ethical obligation. With the most altruistic of motives, then, researchers may find themselves slipping across a line that prohibits treating human subjects as means to an end. When that line is crossed, there is very little left to protect patients from a callous disregard of their welfare for the sake of research goals. Even informed consent, important though it is, is not protection enough, because of the asymmetry in knowledge and authority between researchers and their subjects. And approval by an institutional review board, though also important, is highly variable in its responsiveness to patients' interests when they conflict with the interests of researchers.

A textbook example of unethical research is the Tuskegee Study of Untreated Syphilis.[4] In that study, which was sponsored by the U.S. Public Health Service and lasted from 1932 to 1972, 412 poor African-American men with untreated syphilis were followed and compared with 204 men free of the disease to determine the natural history of syphilis. Although there was no very good treatment available at the time the study began (heavy metals were the standard treatment), the research continued even after penicillin became widely available and was known to be highly effective against syphilis. The study was not terminated until it came to the attention of a reporter and the outrage provoked by front-page stories in the *Washington Star* and *New York Times* embarrassed the Nixon administration into calling a halt to it.[5] The ethical violations were multiple: Subjects did not provide informed consent (indeed, they were deliberately deceived); they were denied the best known treatment; and the study was continued even after highly effective treatment became available. And what were the arguments in favor of the Tuskegee study? That these poor African-American men probably would not have been treated anyway, so the investigators were merely observing what would have happened if there were no study; and that the study was important (a "never-to-be-repeated opportunity," said one physician after penicillin became available).[6] Ethical concern was even stood on its head when it was suggested that not only was the information valuable, but it was especially so for people like the subjects—an impoverished rural population with a very high rate of untreated syphilis. The only lament seemed to be that many of the subjects inadvertently received treatment by other doctors.

Some of these issues are raised by Lurie and Wolfe elsewhere. They discuss the ethics of ongoing trials in the Third World of regimens to prevent the vertical transmission of human immunodeficiency virus (HIV) infection.[7] All except one of the trials employ placebo-treated control groups, despite the fact that zidovudine has already been clearly shown to cut the rate of vertical transmission greatly and is now recommended in the United States for all HIV-infected pregnant women. The justifications are reminiscent of those for the Tuskegee study: Women in the Third World would not receive antiretroviral treatment anyway, so the investigators are simply observing what would happen to the subjects' infants if there were no study. And a placebo-controlled study is the fastest, most efficient way to obtain unambiguous information that will be of greatest value in the Third World. Thus, in response to protests from Wolfe and others to the secretary of Health and Human Services, the directors of the National Institutes of Health (NIH) and the Centers for Disease Control and Prevention (CDC)—the organizations sponsoring the studies—argued, "It is an unfortunate fact that the current standard of perinatal care for the HIV-infected pregnant women in the sites of the studies does not include any HIV prophylactic intervention at all," and the inclusion of placebo controls "will result in the most rapid, accurate, and reliable answer to the question of the value of the intervention being studied compared to the local standard of care."[8]

Whalen et al. report the results of a clinical trial in Uganda of various regimens of prophylaxis against tuberculosis in HIV-infected adults, most of whom had positive tuberculin skin tests.[9] This study, too, employed a placebo-treated control group, and in some ways it is analogous to the studies criticized by Lurie and Wolfe. In the United States it would probably be impossible to carry out such a study, because of long-standing official recommendations that HIV-infected persons with positive tuberculin skin tests receive prophylaxis against tuberculosis. The first was issued in 1990 by the CDC's Advisory Committee for Elimination of Tuberculosis.[10] It stated that tuberculin-test-positive persons with HIV infection "should be considered candidates for preventive therapy." Three years later, the recommendation was reiterated more strongly in a joint statement by the American Thoracic Society and the CDC, in collaboration with the Infectious Diseases Society of America and the American Academy of Pediatrics.[11] According to this statement, ". . . the identification of persons with dual infection and the administration of preventive therapy to these persons is of great importance." However, some believe that these recommendations were premature, since they were based largely on the success of prophylaxis in HIV-negative persons.[12]

Whether the study by Whalen et al. was ethical depends, in my view, entirely on the strength of the preexisting evidence. Only if there was genuine doubt about the benefits of prophylaxis would a placebo group be ethically justified. This is not the place to review the scientific evidence, some of which is discussed in the editorial of Msamanga and Fawzi.[13] Suffice it to say that the case is debatable. Msamanga and Fawzi conclude that "future studies should not include a placebo group, since preventive therapy should be considered the standard of care." I agree. The difficult question is whether there should have been a placebo group in the first place.

Although I believe an argument can be made that a placebo-controlled trial was ethically justifiable because it was still uncertain whether prophylaxis would work, it should not be argued that it was ethical because no prophylaxis is the "local standard of care" in sub-Saharan Africa. For reasons discussed by Lurie and Wolfe, that reasoning is badly flawed.[7] As mentioned earlier, the Declaration of Helsinki requires control groups to receive the "best" current treatment, not the local one. The shift in wording between "best" and "local" may be slight, but the implications are profound. Acceptance of this ethical relativism could result in widespread exploitation of vulnerable Third World populations for research programs that could not be carried out in the sponsoring country.[14] Furthermore, it directly contradicts the Department of Health and Human Services' own regulations governing U.S.-sponsored research in foreign countries,[15] as well as joint guidelines for research in the Third World issued by WHO and the Council for International Organizations of Medical Sciences,[16] which require that human subjects receive protection at least equivalent to that in the sponsoring country. The fact that Whalen et al. offered isoniazid to the placebo group when it was found superior to placebo indicates that they were aware of their responsibility to all the subjects in the trial.

The *Journal* has taken the position that it will not publish reports of unethical research, regardless of their scientific merit.[14, 17] After deliberating at length about the study by Whalen at al., the editors concluded that publication was ethically justified, although there remain differences among us. The fact that the subjects gave informed consent and the study was approved by the institutional review board at the University Hospitals of Cleveland and Case Western Reserve University and by the Ugandan National AIDS Research Subcommittee certainly supported our decision but did not allay all our misgivings. It is still important to determine whether clinical studies are consistent with preexisting, widely accepted ethical guidelines, such as the Declaration of Helsinki, and with federal regulations, since they cannot be influenced by pressures specific to a particular study.

Quite apart from the merits of the study by Whalen et al., there is a larger issue. There appears to be a general retreat from the clear principles enunciated in the Nuremberg Code and the Declaration of Helsinki as applied to research in the Third World. Why is that? Is it because the "local standard of care" is different? I don't think so. In my view, that is merely a self-serving justification after the fact. Is it because diseases and their treatments are very different in the Third World, so that information gained in the industrialized world has no relevance and we have to start from scratch? That, too, seems an unlikely explanation, although here again it is often offered as a justification. Sometimes there may be relevant differences between populations, but that cannot be assumed. Unless there are specific indications to the contrary, the safest and most reasonable position is that people everywhere are likely to respond similarly to the same treatment.

I think we have to look elsewhere for the real reasons. One of them may be a slavish adherence to the tenets of clinical trials. According to these, all trials should be randomized, double-blind, and placebo-controlled, if at all possible. That rigidity may explain the NIH's pressure on Marc Lallemant to include a placebo group in his study, as described by Lurie and Wolfe.[7] Sometimes journals are blamed for the problem, because they are thought to demand strict conformity to the standard methods. That is not true, at least not at this journal. We do not want a scientifically neat study if it is ethically flawed, but like Lurie and Wolfe we believe that in many cases it is possible, with a little ingenuity, to have both scientific and ethical rigor.

The retreat from ethical principles may also be explained by some of the exigencies of doing clinical research in an increasingly regulated and competitive environment. Research in the Third World looks relatively attractive as it becomes better funded and regulations at home become more restrictive. Despite the existence of codes requiring that human subjects receive at least the same protection abroad as at home, they are still honored partly in the breach. The fact remains that many studies are done in the Third World that simply could not be done in the countries sponsoring the work. Clinical trials have become a big business, with many of the same imperatives. To survive, it is necessary to get the work done as quickly as possible, with a minimum of obstacles. When these considerations prevail, it seems as if we have not come very far from Tuskegee after all. Those of us in the research community need to redouble our commitment to the highest ethical standards, no matter where the research is conducted, and sponsoring agencies need to enforce those standards, not undercut them.

NOTES

1. Angell, M. "Patients' preferences in randomized clinical trials." *N Engl J Med* 1984; 310:1385–7.
2. Freedman, B. "Equipoise and the ethics of clinical research." *N Engl J Med* 1987;317:141–5.
3. Declaration of Helsinki IV, 41st World Medical Assembly, Hong Kong, September 1989. In: Annas G.J., Grodin M.A., eds. The Nazi doctors and the Nuremberg Code: human rights in human experimentation. New York: Oxford University Press, 1992: 339–42.
4. "Twenty years after: the legacy of the Tuskegee syphilis study." *Hastings Cent Rep* 1992;22(6):29–40.
5. Caplan, A.L. "When evil intrudes." *Hastings Cent Rep* 1992; 22(6):29–32.
6. "The development of consent requirements in research ethics." In: Faden, R.R., Beauchamp, T.L. *A History and Theory of Informed Consent.* New York: Oxford University Press, 1986: 151–99.
7. Lurie, P., Wolfe, S.M. "Unethical trials of interventions to reduce perinatal transmission of the human immuno-deficiency virus in developing countries." *N Engl J Med* 1997; 337:853–6.
8. The conduct of clinical trials of maternal-infant transmission of HIV supported by the United States Department of Health and Human Services in developing countries.

Washington, D.C.: Department of Health and Human Services, July 1997.

9. Whalen, C.C., Johnson, J.L., Okwera, A., et al. "A trial of three regimens to prevent tuberculosis in Ugandan adults infected with the human immunodeficiency virus." *N Engl J Med* 1997; 337:801–8.

10. "The use of preventive therapy for tuberculosis infection in the United States: recommendations of the Advisory Committee for Elimination of Tuberculosis." *MMWR Morb Mortal Wkly Rep* 1990; 39(RR-8):9–12.

11. Bass, J.B. Jr., Farer, L.S., Hopewell, P.C., et al. "Treatment of tuberculosis and tuberculosis infection in adults and children." *Am J Respir Crit Care Med* 1994; 149:1359–74.

12. De Cock, K.M., Grant, A., Porter, J.D. "Preventive therapy for tuberculosis in HIV-infected persons:

international recommendations, research, and practice." *Lancet* 1995; 345:833–6.

13. Msamanga, G.I., Fawzi, W.W., "The double burden of HIV infection and tuberculosis in sub-Saharan Africa." *N Engl J Med* 1997; 337:849–51.

14. Angell, M. "Ethical imperialism? Ethics in international collaborative clinical research." *N Engl J Med* 1988; 319:1081–3.

15. "Protection of human subjects," 45 CFR 46 (1996).

16. International ethical guidelines for biomedical research involving human subjects. Geneva: Council for International Organizations of Medical Sciences, 1993.

17. Angell, M. "The Nazi hypothermia experiments and unethical research today." *N Engl J Med* 1990; 322:1462–4.

Ethical Issues in Clinical Trials in Developing Countries

BARUCH BRODY

Brody responds to major doubts raised about the ethics of some Third World clinical trials conducted to evaluate a regimen to prevent mother-to-infant transmission of HIV. He argues that the use of placebo control groups was ethical because no subjects were denied "any treatment that should otherwise be available to him or her in light of the practical realities of health care resources available in the country in question." According to a reasonable understanding of coercion, he says, no subjects were coerced into participating in the trials. Finally, some have claimed that the trials exploit developing countries "because the interventions in question, even if proven successful, will not be available in these countries." But such trials will not be exploitative, Brody says, if after the studies the subjects themselves are given access to any treatment proven effective.

Since the publication of the results of AIDS Clinical Trials Group (ACTG) 076, it has been known that an extensive regimen of Zidovudine provided to the mother and to the newborn can drastically reduce (25.5 to 8.3%) the vertical transmission of HIV.[1] Unfortunately, the regimen in question is quite expensive and beyond the means of most developing countries, some of which are the countries most in

From *Statistics in Medicine*, vol. 21, no. 19 (2002), pp. 2853–58. Copyright © and reprinted with premission of John Wiley & Sons Ltd.

need of effective techniques for reducing vertical transmission. This realization led to a series of important clinical trials designed to test the effectiveness of less extensive and less expensive regimens of antiretroviral drugs. These trials were conducted by researchers from developed countries in the developing countries which were in need of these less expensive regimens.

These new trials have been very successful. The Thai CDC trial showed a 50% reduction (18.9 to 9.4%) in transmission from a much shorter antepartum regimen of Zidovudine combined with a more modest intrapartum regimen.[2] The PETRA trial showed that Zidovudine and Lamivudine provided in modest intrapartum and postpartum regimens also significantly reduced transmission, whether or not they were provided antepartum.[3] There was a trend to more reduction of transmission if they were provided in a short antepartum regimen (16.5 to 7.8%) than if they were not (16.5 to 10.8%). Most crucially, there was no reduction (16.5 to 15.7%) if they were not provided postpartum. Finally, a single dose of nevirapine provided intrapartum and postpartum was shown in HIVNET 012 to significantly reduce transmission (21.3 to 11.9%).[4] In all cases except HIVNET 012, the control group received only a placebo. In HIVNET 012, the control group received a modest regimen of intrapartum and postpartum Zidovudine.

As a result of these trials, developing countries with some financial capabilities have the opportunity to drastically reduce vertical transmission by proven less expensive regimens. This constitutes an important contribution of these trials. Unfortunately, the poorest developing countries (including some in which these trials have been run) may not be able to afford even these shorter regimens unless the drugs in question are priced far less expensively for those countries. Efforts have begun to make that possible.[5]

There have been many critics of these trials who have argued that they were unethical. Some have gone on to attempt to explain how the information might have been obtained in other more ethical trials while others have not. My focus in this paper is not on that question. Instead, *I want to focus on the arguments offered in support of the claim that these trials were unethical.* I see the critics as advancing three very different criticisms, although the critics often do not carefully distinguish them. We will do so to enable each criticism to be analyzed. The *first criticism* is that an *injustice was done to the control group* in each of these trials (with perhaps the exception of HIVNET 012) since they were denied proven effective therapy as they only received a placebo. The *second criticism* is that the *participants in the trial were coerced* into participating, and did not give voluntary consent, because they had no real choice about participating since antiretroviral therapy was otherwise unavailable to them. The *third criticism* is that the *countries in question were exploited*

by the investigators from the developed countries since they were testing the effectiveness of regimens that would not be available after the trial to the citizens of the countries in which the trials were conducted.

The Justice of the Use of the Placebo Control Group

The scientific importance of the use of concurrent placebo control groups is well illustrated by the PETRA trial. If there had been no such control group, and the various regimens had been compared to the historical control group in ACTG 076, then the intrapartum only arm would have been judged a success, since its transmission rate was only 15.7% as compared to the 25.5% transmission rate in the control group in ACTG 076. But it actually was no better than the placebo control group in PETRA (16.5%). When the rate of transmission varies from one setting to another, you really cannot use historical control groups. Despite this scientific value, the critics have argued that it was wrong to use a placebo control arm because the patients in that arm were being denied a proven therapy (the 076 regimen) and were being offered nothing in its place.[6] The critics claim that this did not meet the standard found in *earlier versions* of the Declaration at Helsinki: "In any medical study, every patient, including those of a control group, if any, should be assured of the best proven diagnostic and therapeutic method."[7]

Defenders of these trials quite properly note that none of the participants in these trials would otherwise have received any antiretroviral therapy, so nothing was being denied to them that they would otherwise have received. How then, ask the defenders, can the members of the control group have been treated unjustly? This led to a proposed, very controversial and eventually rejected, revision of the Declaration of Helsinki which read: "In any biomedical research protocol every patient-subject, including those of a control group, if any, should be assured that he or she will not be denied access to the best proven diagnostic, prophylactic, or therapeutic method that would otherwise be available to him or her."[8] The point is then that the justice or injustice of what is done to the control group depends on what the members of that group *would* have received if the trial had not been conducted.

While the reality of what the members of the control group would have received is obviously relevant, I am not satisfied that this proposed revision would have properly taken that into account. Would it be just, for example, to use such a placebo control group in a trial in a developed country where the antiretroviral therapy is widely available except to members of some persecuted minority, from whom the control group is drawn? They *would* not have received the treatment if the trial had not been conducted, although they *should* have been given the resources available in the developed country. Their use in a placebo control group is not therefore justified. The proposed revision made too much reference to what would have occurred and not enough to what should have occurred.

A recent workshop proposed instead that "study participants should be assured the highest standard of care practically attainable in the country in which the trial is being carried out."[9] This seems better, although it may suggest too much. Suppose that the treatment is practically attainable but only by inappropriately cutting corners on other forms of health care which may have a higher priority. I would suggest therefore that the normative nature of the standard be made explicit. It would then read that all participants in the study, including those in the control group, should not be denied any treatment *that should otherwise be available to him or her in light of the practical realities of health care resources available in the country in question*. The question for IRBs reviewing proposals for such research is then precisely the question of justice.

On that standard, the trials in question were probably not unjust, although there is some debate about the Thai CDC trial in light of donated resources that became available in Thailand between its being planned and its being implemented.[10] Such trials will be harder to justify in the future given the current availability of proven much less expensive therapies which should be available even in some of the poorest countries. It is of interest to note that HIVNET 012 was not a placebo-controlled trial, but it was a superiority trial, and active controlled trials are less problematic scientifically when they are superiority trials. That may well be the way future transmission trials will be run.

Coercive Offers

It has been suggested by other critics that the participants in these trials were coerced into participating because of their desperation. "The very desperation of women with no alternatives to protect their children from HIV infection can be extremely coercive," argue one set of critics.[11] One of the requirements of an ethical trial is that the participants voluntarily agree to participate, and how can their agreement to participate be voluntary if it was coerced?

This line of thinking is analogous to the qualms that many have about paying research subjects substantial sums of money for their participation in research. Such inducements are often rejected on the grounds that they are coercive, because they are too good to refuse. The ICH [International Conference on Harmonization] Guidelines for Good Clinical Practice is one of many standards which incorporate this approach when it stipulates that the "IRB/IEC should review both the amount and method of payment to subjects to assure that neither present problems of coercion or undue influences on the research subject."[12]

Normally, coercion involves a threat to put someone below their baseline unless they cooperate with the demands of the person issuing the threat.[13] As the researchers were not going to do anything to those who chose not to participate, they were clearly not threatening them. Further evidence of this comes from the reflection that threats are unwelcome to the parties being threatened, and there is no reason to suppose that the potential subjects saw the request to participate as something unwelcome. Even the critics recognize this. The potential subjects were being offered an opportunity that might improve their situation. This was an offer "too good to refuse," not a threat.

Should we expand the concept of coercion to include these very favorable offers? There are several reasons for thinking that we should not. First, it is widely believed that offering people valuable new opportunities is desirable. Moreover, the individuals in question want to receive these offers, and denying them the opportunity to receive them seems paternalistic or moralistic.[14] It is important that participants understand that what they are being offered is a chance to receive a treatment that may reduce transmission (since this is a randomized placebo-controlled trial of a new regimen), and ensuring that is essential for the consent to be informed. As long as care is taken to ensure that this information is conveyed in a culturally sensitive fashion, and is understood, then there seems to be little reason to be concerned about coercion simply because a good opportunity is being offered to those with few opportunities.

A colleague and I are currently working on one residual concern in this area. It has to do with studies in which there is a potential for long-term harms to subjects which they inappropriately discount because the very substantial short-term benefits cloud their judgment. This may be a ground for concern in some cases, but it is difficult to see how it would apply to the vertical transmission trials. For those trials, it is appropriate to conclude that concerns about coercion were unfounded.

Exploitation of Subjects

The final criticism of the trials is that they are exploitative of developing countries and their citizens because the interventions in question, even if proven successful, will not be available in these countries. To quote one of the critics: "To use a population as research subjects because of its poverty and its inability to obtain care, and then to not use that knowledge for the direct benefit of that population, is the very definition of exploitation. This exploitation is made worse by the fact that richer nations will unquestionably benefit from this research . . . [they] will begin to use these lower doses, thereby receiving economic benefit.[15]

There are really two claims being advanced in that quotation. The second, that the developed countries ran these trials to discover cheaper ways of treating their own citizens, is very implausible since pregnant women in developed countries are receiving even more expensive cocktails of drugs both to treat the woman and to reduce transmission. The crucial issue is whether the trials are exploitative of the developing countries.

There seems to be a growing consensus that they are exploitative unless certain conditions about future availability in the country in question are met. The Council for International Organizations of Medical Sciences (CIOMS) is the source of this movement, as it declared in its 1992 guidelines that "as a general rule, the initiating agency should insure that, at the completion of successful testing, any products developed will be made reasonably available to residents of the host community or country."[16] A slightly weaker version of this requirement was adopted by a recent workshop which concluded that "studies are only appropriate if there is a reasonable likelihood that the populations in which they are carried out stand to benefit from successful results."[17]

This growing consensus is part of what lies behind the effort to secure these benefits by negotiating more favorable prices for the use of the tested drugs in developing countries. It seems highly desirable that this goal be achieved. But I want to suggest that it should be viewed as an aspiration, rather than a requirement, and that a different, more modest requirement must be met to avoid charges of exploitation.

A good analysis of exploitation is that it is a wrong done to individuals who do not receive a fair share of the benefits produced by an activity in which they take part, even if they receive some benefit.[18] This is why a mutually beneficial activity, one from which both parties will be better off, can still be exploitative if one of the parties uses their greater bargaining power to harvest most of the benefits and the other party agrees because they need whatever modest benefit is being left for them.

As we apply this concept to the trials in question, we need to ask who needs to be protected from being exploited by the trials in question. It would seem that it is the participants. Are they getting a fair share of the benefits from the trial if it proves successful? This is a particularly troubling question when we consider those in the control group, whose major benefit from participation may have been an unrealized possibility of getting treated. If we judge that the participants have not received enough, then it is they who must receive more. An obvious suggestion is that they be guaranteed access to any regimen proved efficacious in any future pregnancies (or perhaps even that they be granted access to antiretroviral therapy for their own benefit). This would be analogous to familiar concepts of subjects receiving continued access to treatment after their participation in a trial is completed.

I certainly support every reasonable effort to increase access to treatments which will reduce vertical transmission. But imposing the types of community-wide requirements that have been suggested, but not necessarily justified if the above analysis is correct, may prevent important trials from being run because of the potential expense. Such proposals should be treated as moral aspirations, and exploitation should be avoided by focusing on what is owed to the subjects who have participated in the trials. It is they, after all, who are primarily at risk for being exploited.

These observations are about research in developing countries in general, and not just about research on vertical transmission. Three lessons have emerged. The standard for when a placebo control group is justified is a normative standard (what they should have received if they were not in the trial) rather than a descriptive standard (what they would have received it they were not in the trial). Coercion is not a serious concern in trials simply because attractive offers are made to the subjects. Legitimate concerns about exploiting subjects should be addressed by ensuring their future treatment, rather than by asking what will happen in their community at large.

NOTES

1. E. M. Connor, R. S. Sperling, R. Gelber, et al., "Reduction of Maternal-Infant Transmission of Human Immunodeficiency Virus Type I with Zidovudine Treatment," *New England Journal of Medicine*, 331 (1984):1173–80.

2. N. Shaffer, R. Chuachoowong, P. A. Mock, et al., "Short-Course Zidovudine for Perinatal HIV Transmission in Bangkok, Thailand: A Randomised Controlled Trial," *Lancet*, 353 (1999): 773–80.

3. Conference data cited in K. DeCock, M. Fowler, E. Mercier, et al., "Prevention of Mother-to-Child HIV Transmission in Resource Poor Countries," *JAMA,* 283 (2000): 1175–82.

4. L. A. Guay, P. Musoke, T. Fleming, et al., "Intrapartum and Neonatal Single-Dose Nevirapine Compared with Zidovudine for Prevention of Mother-to-Child Transmission of HIV-1 in Kampala, Uganda," *Lancet,* 354 (2000): 795–802.

5. P. Brown, "Cheaper AIDS Drugs Due for Third World," *Nature,* 405 (2000): 263.

6. P. Lurie and S. M. Wolfe, "Unethical Trials of Interventions to Reduce Perinatal Transmission of the Human Immunodeficiency Virus in Developing Countries," *New England Journal of Medicine,* 337 (1997): 853–56.

7. World Medical Association, Declaration of Helsinki, Principle 11.3.

8. "Proposed Revision of the Declaration of Helsinki," *Bulletin of Medical Ethics,* 18–21 (1999).

9. Perinatal HIV Intervention Research in Developing Countries Workshop Participants, "Science Ethics and the Future of Research into Maternal Infant Transmission of HIV-1," *Lancet,* 353 (1999): 832–35.

10. P. Phanuphak, "Ethical Issues in Studies in Thailand of the Vertical Transmission of HIV," *New England Journal of Medicine,* 338 (1998): 834–35.

11. E. Tafesse and T. Murphy, Letter, *New England Journal of Medicine,* 338 (1998): 838.

12. ICH. *Guideline for Good Clinical Practice* (Geneva: IFPMA, 1996), guideline 3.1.8.

13. R. Nozick, "Coercion." In Morgenbesser S., ed. *Philosophy, Science, and Method* (New York: St Martin's, 1969).

14. M. Wilkinson and A. Moore, "Inducement in Research," *Bioethics,* 11 (1997): 373–89.

15. I. Glantz and M. Grodin, Letter, *New England Journal of Medicine,* 338 (1998): 839.

16. CIOMS, *International Ethical Guidelines for Biomedical Research Involving Subjects* (Geneva: CIOMS, 1992), 68.

17. Perinatal HIV Intervention Research in Developing Countries Workshop Participants, "Science Ethics and the Future of Research into Maternal Infant Transmission of HIV-1," *Lancet,* 353 (1999): 832–35.

18. A. Wertheimer, *Exploitation* (Princeton, N.J.: Princeton University Press, 1996).

3

Life and Death

CHAPTER 7

Abortion

Abortion is among the most contentious and complex issues in bioethics. It has divided the public, exercised politicians, occupied the courts, busied the media, and engendered violence. Much of the public debate has been bitter and irrational, driven by partisans bent on racking up political points and by popular media obsessed with keeping score. But away from the scuffle and out of earshot of the quarrelers, a more useful debate has been going on—the philosophical give and take among thinkers who test claims about the morality of abortion through reasoned argument and careful reflection. They have achieved no grand consensus on the issue, but they have plumbed it, clarified it, and wrung from it some thoughtful answers worth considering. They have, in other words, done bioethics. Let us see, then, what this work can tell us.

STARTING POINT: THE BASICS

Views on abortion—whether held by church, state, or citizenry—have varied dramatically through time and across cultures. Abortions in the ancient world were common, and there was no shortage of methods for effecting them. Some writers of the time condemned the practice, and some recommended it. "Let there be a law that no deformed child shall live," says Aristotle, "and if couples have children in excess, let abortion be procured before life and sense have begun."[1] The Hippocratic Oath proscribed the use of abortifacients (substances or devices for inducing abortions), a prohibition respected by many physicians but ignored by others.

The Hebrew and Christian scriptures do not denounce abortion and do not suggest that the fetus is a person. A passage in Exodus Chapter 21 touches on the topic and implies that the unborn entity is not a full human being. The passage comes after the emphatic "You shall not murder" of the Ten Commandments and after a warning that the penalty for murder is death. But Exodus 21:22 says that if a man causes a woman to have a miscarriage "but [she] is not harmed in any other way," the penalty is just a fine. Causing the death of a fetus was not considered murder.

Christians have generally condemned abortion, though their ideas about the personhood of the fetus have changed through the centuries. Many contemporary Christians, especially Roman Catholics, assume that the unborn is a full human being from the moment of conception. But in the twelfth century, the church came to the view that an embryo cannot have a soul until several weeks after conception. The rationale, inspired by Aristotle, was that the unborn cannot have a soul until it is "formed"—that is, until it has a human shape, a stage that is reached long after conception. Thomas Aquinas accepted this view and maintained that male embryos are formed (and thus given a soul, or "ensouled") 40 days after conception; female embryos, 90 days. Thus, killing a fetus, though always sinful, is not murder until after it is formed. In 1312, this doctrine became the church's official position. Only in the late nineteenth century did the church decide that ensoulment happens at conception and that any abortion after that point is the killing of a human person.

In English common law, abortion was considered a crime only if performed after **quickening** (when the mother first detects fetal

Fact File **U. S. Abortions**

- Half of all pregnancies are unintended.
- 21 percent of unintended pregnancies (not including miscarriages) end in abortions.
- In 2011, 1.06 million abortions were performed (compared to 1.23 million in 2008).
- Each year, 1.7 percent of women aged 15–44 have an abortion.
- 37 percent of women having abortions say they are Protestant; 28 percent, Catholic.
- 51 percent of women who have abortions had used contraception during the month they became pregnant.
- The risk of death associated with abortion is one death per million abortions performed at eight weeks or earlier; one death in 29,000 abortions performed at 16–20 weeks; and one death per 11,000 performed at 21 weeks or later.
- Less than 0.5 percent of women having first-trimester abortions suffer major complications requiring hospitalization.
- Women in their twenties are responsible for over 50 percent of all abortions. Women who have one or more children account for 61 percent of abortions.

L. B. Finer and M. R. Zolna, "Shifts in Intended and Unintended Pregnancies in the United States, 2001–2008," *American Journal of Public Health* 23, no. 3 (2014), pp. e1–e9; R. K. Jones, L. B. Finer, and S. Singh, *Characteristics of U.S. Abortion Patients, 2008* (New York: Guttmacher Institute, 2010); S. K. Henshaw, "Unintended Pregnancy in the United States," *Family Planning Perspectives* 30, no. 1 (1998), pp. 24–29, 46; R. K. Jones and M. L. Kavanaugh, "Changes in Abortion Rates Between 2000 and 2008 and Lifetime Incidence of Abortion," *Obstetrics & Gynecology* 117, no. 6 (2011), pp. 1358–1366; L. A. Bartlett et al., "Risk Factors for Legal Induced Abortion-Related Mortality in the United States," *Obstetrics & Gynecology* 103 (2004), pp. 729–737; R. K. Jones, L. Frohwirth, and A. M. Moore, "More than Poverty: Disruptive Events Among Women Having Abortions in the USA," *Journal of Family Planning and Reproductive Health Care* 39, no. 1 (2012), pp. 36–43.

movement). From its beginnings through the nineteenth century, American law mostly reflected this tradition. Accordingly, in the early 1800s, several states passed statutes outlawing abortion after quickening except to save the life of the mother. But in the next 100 years, abortion laws gradually became stricter, dropping the quickening cutoff point and banning all abortions but those thought to preserve the life (or, rarely, the health) of the mother. The medical profession generally supported the tougher laws, and the views of physicians on abortion carried great weight.

In the 1950s, a trend toward liberalized laws began, and by 1970 the American Medical Association (AMA) and the American College of Obstetricians and Gynecologists were officially advocating less severe abortion policies. The latter declared, "It is recognized that abortion may be performed at a patient's request, or upon a physician's recommendation."[2] By that time, 12 states had amended their abortion statutes to make them less restrictive, and the public had warmed considerably to the idea of legalized abortion. The culmination of all these changes was the 1973 Supreme Court case of *Roe v. Wade*, which made abortions before viability legal.

The abortion policies of previous eras were handicapped by poor understanding of human development. But in modern times the facts are clear: *Fertilization*, or conception, happens when a sperm cell penetrates an egg, or ovum, forming a single cell known as a *zygote*, or conceptus. This meeting of sperm and egg usually takes place in one of the two fallopian tubes, the narrow tunnels linking the egg-producing ovaries with the uterus. For three to five days, the zygote moves down the fallopian tube to the uterus, dividing continually and thus getting larger along the way. In the fluid-filled uterus, it divides further, becoming a hollow sphere of cells known as a *blastocyst*. Within about five days, the blastocyst lodges firmly in the lining of the uterus (a feat called implantation) and is then known as an *embryo*.

The embryonic stage lasts until eight weeks after fertilization. During this time most of the embryo's internal organs form, the brain and spinal cord start to generate, and external features such as limbs and ears begin to appear. At eight weeks, though it is only about the size of a raspberry, the embryo has a rudimentary human shape.

From the end of the eighth week until birth, the unborn is technically known as a *fetus*. (In this text, however, we use the term to refer to the unborn at any stage from conception to birth.) At about 14 weeks of pregnancy, doctors can determine the fetus' sex. Around 16 to 20 weeks, the mother can feel the fetus moving inside her. Quickening was once thought to be a threshold event in pregnancy, signaling ensoulment or the presence of a human being. But it is of doubtful importance (except to the mother) since the fetus moves undetected before quickening, and the mother's sensing fetal movement is not associated with any significant change in development. A more meaningful benchmark is **viability**, the development stage at approximately 23 to 24 weeks of pregnancy when the fetus may survive outside the uterus. Babies born at this point, however, are at high risk of severe disabilities (mental retardation and blindness, among others) and death.

Development from fertilization to birth (called gestation) is nine months long, or about 40 weeks. This span of pregnancy is calculated from the first day of the woman's last menstrual period and is traditionally divided into three 3-month intervals—first trimester (0–12 weeks), second trimester (13–24 weeks), and third trimester (25 weeks to delivery). Babies delivered in the third trimester but before 37 weeks are considered premature.

Abortion is the ending of a pregnancy. Abortion due to natural causes—birth defect or injury, for example—is known as **spontaneous abortion** or **miscarriage**. The intentional termination of pregnancy through drugs or surgery is called **induced abortion** or, more commonly, simply abortion. Abortion in this sense is the issue over which most of the ideological and judicial struggles are waged. Such is generally not the case for **therapeutic abortion**—abortion performed to preserve the life or health of the mother. Most people believe therapeutic abortion to be morally permissible.

Several methods are used to perform abortions, some of them surgical and some pharmaceutical. The method used depends on, among other things, the woman's health and the length of her pregnancy. The most common technique is known as *suction curettage* (also, *vacuum aspiration*), which is used in the first 12 weeks of pregnancy (when nearly 90 percent of abortions are performed). A doctor inserts a thin, bendable tube through the opening of the cervix into the uterus and, using a vacuum syringe or a machine or hand pump, suctions the contents of the uterus out through the tube. The method used most often after the first 12 weeks is *dilation and evacuation*. It involves widening the cervix and employing both suction and forceps to extract the fetus and placenta.

Abortions can be induced with drugs (often referred to as "medical abortions") but only in the first seven to nine weeks of pregnancy. The most common regimen uses two medications: mifepristone (RU-486, the so-called abortion pill) and misoprostol, a prostaglandin (hormonelike substance). Mifepristone interferes with the hormone progesterone, thinning the lining of the

IN DEPTH
ABORTION AND PUBLIC OPINION

Do you think abortions should be legal under any circumstances, legal only under certain circumstances, or illegal in all circumstances?

Always Legal	Sometimes Legal	Always Illegal
29%	51%	19%

With respect to the abortion issue, would you consider yourself to be pro-choice or pro-life?

Pro-Choice	Pro-Life
50%	44%

Regardless of whether or not you think abortion should be illegal, do you personally believe that in general abortion is morally acceptable or morally wrong?

Morally Wrong	Morally Acceptable
45%	45%

Party identification

	Republicans	Independents	Democrats
Pro-choice	31%	50%	68%

Gallup poll results based on Gallup's May 6–10, 2015, Values and Beliefs poll, http://www.gallup.com/poll/183434/americans-choose-pro-choice-first-time-seven-years.aspx?g_source=abortion&g_medium=search&g_campaign=tiles.

uterus and preventing implantation of the embryo. Misoprostol prompts the uterus to contract, forcing the embryo out. A woman sees her physician to take mifepristone, then up to three days later takes misoprostol (either at home or in the physician's office). This two-step procedure causes abortion about 95 percent of the time.

The risk of complications (such as serious bleeding or internal injury) from abortion is low and varies directly with the length of pregnancy—the earlier an abortion is performed, the lower the risk. Less than 1 percent of women having early abortions experience complications; less than 2 percent of those having later abortions do. Death is a risk in any surgical procedure; the risk of death for suction curettage is less than 1 in 100,000 women. The risk for medical abortion is virtually the same.

The chances of a woman dying in childbirth are at least 10 times higher.[3]

Over half of women having abortions are under 25 years old, and almost one-fifth of these are teenagers. Fifty-seven percent of abortions are performed on women who have never married; 17 percent, on married women; and 16 percent, on women who are separated, divorced, or widowed.

Their reasons for terminating a pregnancy are varied. According to a recent survey of women who had abortions, the reasons include:

- Having a baby would change my life (interfere with education, employment, etc.).—74 percent
- I can't afford a baby now (I'm unmarried, unemployed, destitute, etc.).—73 percent

- I don't want to be a single mother, or I'm having relationship problems.—48 percent
- My relationship or marriage may break up soon.—11 percent
- I've already completed my childbearing.—38 percent
- My husband or partner wants me to have an abortion.—14 percent
- There are possible problems affecting the health of the fetus.—13 percent
- There are physical problems with my health.—12 percent
- I was a victim of rape.—1 percent
- I became pregnant as a result of incest.—less than 0.5 percent[4]

Polls gauging the attitudes of the American public toward abortion have revealed many divisions but also remarkable agreement on some points. Only a small minority of people (5–22 percent) think that abortion should be illegal or unavailable in all circumstances. Most reject a total ban but differ on the existence or extent of restrictions placed on abortion. Roughly half consider themselves to be "pro-life" and half "pro-choice." A sizable majority would not like to see *Roe v. Wade* completely overturned.

THE LEGAL STRUGGLE

As we have seen, abortion is both a moral and legal issue, and these two lines of debate must not be confused. But we cannot ignore how the legal conflict has influenced the ethical arguments, and vice versa. The former seized the attention of the nation when *Roe v. Wade* was handed down. Roe was "Jane Roe," a.k.a. Norma McCorvey, who had sought a nontherapeutic abortion in Texas where she lived. But Texas law forbade all abortions except those necessary to save the mother's life. So Roe sued the state of Texas in federal court, which ruled that the law was unconstitutional. Texas appealed the decision to the U.S. Supreme Court, and the Court sided with the federal court, declaring in *Roe v. Wade*

that no state can ban abortions performed before viability.

The Court saw in the Constitution (most notably the Fourteenth Amendment, which grants due process and equal protection under the law) a guaranteed right of personal privacy that limits interference by the state in people's private lives, and the majority believed that the right encompassed a woman's decision to terminate her pregnancy. But, the Court noted, "this right is not unqualified and must be considered against important state interests in regulation." So it balanced the woman's right and state interests according to trimester of pregnancy. In the first trimester, the woman's right to end her pregnancy cannot be curtailed by the state. Her decision must be respected, and "its effectuation must be left to the medical judgment of the pregnant woman's attending physician." In the second trimester, the state may limit—but not entirely prohibit—the woman's right by regulating abortion for the sake of her health. After viability, the state may regulate and even ban abortion except when it is necessary to preserve her life or health. The Court affirmed that its ruling "leaves the State free to place increasing restrictions on abortion as the period of pregnancy lengthens, so long as those restrictions are tailored to the recognized state interests."

The Court noted that the Constitution does not define "person" and that "the word 'person,' as used in the Fourteenth Amendment, does not include the unborn." In fact, the law has never maintained that the unborn are persons "in the whole sense."

After this historic case, the Supreme Court handed down numerous other decisions that circumscribed, but did not invalidate, the right to abortion defined in *Roe*. In these rulings, the Court held that (1) a woman can be required to give her written informed consent to abortion, (2) the government is not obliged to use taxpayer money to fund abortion services, (3) parental consent or a judge's authorization can be demanded of minors under age 18 who seek abortions, (4) a state can forbid the use of public facilities to

IN DEPTH
LATE-TERM ABORTION

Abortions performed late in pregnancy using a controversial surgical procedure have been the flashpoint for intense debate, legislative action, and court rulings. The procedure is known technically as *intact dilation and extraction* (D&X) and disparagingly as *partial-birth abortion*. Physicians use the first term; abortion opponents tend to use the latter. Late-term abortions are performed after the twentieth week of gestation and are uncommon, comprising around 1 percent of all abortions. Some women have them to protect their life or health and some to avoid having a severely impaired infant. Others have late abortions because they would not or could

not have them earlier (these include teenagers, the poor, drug addicts, and women who were unaware of their pregnancy).

In the principal form of D&X, the woman's cervix is dilated, the fetus' torso is drawn manually or with medical instruments through the birth canal, and the brain is suctioned out and the skull collapsed so the head can also be withdrawn. Depending on the length of gestation and many other variables, some of the fetuses aborted in this way may be viable, and many are not.

In 2003 President Bush signed the Partial-Birth Abortion Ban Act, which outlawed a type of late-term abortion. But several federal courts declared the law unconstitutional because it lacks a "health exception" for women whose health is threatened. In 2007 the U.S. Supreme Court upheld the law, effectively banning D&X abortions (and arguably some other late-term procedures).

---

perform abortions (except to save the woman's life), (5) a woman who consents to an abortion can be required to wait 24 hours before the procedure is performed, and (6) a state can mandate that a woman be given abortion information. Eventually the court came to a key doctrine concerning such limitations: Before viability, abortion can be restricted in many ways as long as the constraints do not amount to an "undue burden" on a woman trying to get an abortion. A state regulation constitutes an undue burden if it "has the purpose or effect of placing a substantial obstacle in the path of a woman seeking an abortion of a nonviable fetus."

PERSONS AND RIGHTS

People generally take one of three positions on the moral permissibility of abortion. The conservative view is that abortion is never morally acceptable (except possibly to preserve the mother's life), for the unborn is a human being in the full sense. The liberal view is that abortion is acceptable whenever the woman wants it, for the unborn is not a human being in the full

sense. The moderate stance falls between these two stands, rejecting both the conservative's zero-tolerance for abortion and the liberal's idea of abortion on request. For the moderate, some—but not all—abortions may be morally justified. (These labels are common but sometimes misleading; being a conservative or liberal on the abortion issue does not necessarily mean you are a conservative or liberal in the broader political sense.)

Despite appearances, between the conservatives and the liberals there is at least a patch of common ground. Both sides agree on some basic moral principles—for example, that murder is wrong, that persons have a right to life, and that personal freedom should not be curtailed except for very important reasons. Conflicts arise not over such fundamentals but over the nonmoral facts (such as the nature of the fetus) and over the meaning and application of moral standards.

The main conservative argument against abortion is straightforward and based on a widely shared intuition about the wrongness of killing innocents. One popular formulation says that

(1) the killing of an innocent human being is wrong; (2) the unborn is an innocent human being; (3) therefore, it is wrong to kill the unborn (abortion is immoral). At first glance, this argument may seem sound, but critics point out that the term *human being* improperly switches meanings in mid-argument, invalidating the inference (and thus committing what is known as the fallacy of equivocation). The problem is that in premise 2, *human being* means an entity that is biologically human, a member of the genetically distinct human species. But in premise 1, *human being* refers to an entity having all the psychological attributes and capacities that we normally associate with the possession of full moral rights (including a right to life)—what philosophers call a *person*. If *human being* referred to the same thing throughout the argument, the argument would be valid. But the argument equivocates on the term and is therefore invalid.

The conservative, however, avoids these difficulties by offering an improved version of the argument: (1) The killing of an innocent person is wrong; (2) the unborn is an innocent person from the moment of conception; (3) therefore, it is wrong to kill the unborn (abortion is immoral). This argument is valid, and premise 1 is obviously true. The crux of the matter is premise 2, which the conservative asserts and the liberal denies. What arguments can the conservative offer to support it?

One option is to start with this observation: In the continuous process of development from zygote to adult human, there seems to be no precise point at which the entity becomes unmistakably a bona fide human being (with a right to life). No clear line between nonperson and person can be found. Any point we select to indicate the nonperson/person boundary would be arbitrary and unsupportable. The conservative argues that the most plausible view then would be that personhood (and the right to life) begins at conception. It is at conception that, for example, a full complement of genetic information is present to propel development of a completely formed, mature human. As one philosopher puts it,

The positive argument for conception as the decision moment of humanization is that at conception the new being receives the genetic code. It is this genetic information which determines his characteristics, which is the biological carrier of the possibility of human wisdom, which makes him a self-evolving being. A being with a human genetic code is man.[5]

Critics respond in various ways to this view. They point out, for example, that just because no nonperson/person line can be drawn doesn't mean there is no difference to be observed between the two phenomena. We may not be able to specify the precise moment when a tadpole turns into a frog, but we know there is a real difference between the two states. The failure to pinpoint a distinct moment when the unborn becomes a person does not show that it must be a person from the moment of conception.

Some philosophers argue on empirical grounds that the zygote cannot be an individual human being:

[T]he very early conceptus cannot be identified with the embryo that may develop from it. This is because, for about the first two weeks of existence, it consists of a set of undifferentiated cells, any one of which could give rise to an embryo under certain circumstances. This "pre-embryo" may spontaneously divide, resulting in twins or triplets; alternatively, it may combine with another pre-embryo, giving rise to a single fetus.[6]

Some conservatives avoid such complications by arguing not that the fetus is a person, but that it is a *potential* person and thus has the same right to life as any existing person. The unborn may not be a person now, but its status as a possible future person puts it in the same moral category as any normal adult human being. One ethicist expresses the point like this:

What makes the difference between human beings and other life is the capacity human beings enjoy for a specially rich kind of life. The life already enjoyed by a human being cannot be taken away from him, only the prospect of such life in the future. But this prospect is pos-sessed as much by an infant or fetus as by a full-grown adult.[7]

A common response to this potentiality ar-gument is that there is a world of difference be-tween (1) possessing a particular trait that gives you a right and (2) *having the potential* to de-velop a trait that gives you a right. "[T]he right to vote in political elections may be granted to citi-zens who have reached the age of 18," says Mary Anne Warren, "but not to pre-adolescents—even though most of them clearly have the po-tential to reach the age of 18." From the fact that someone has the potential to become a Supreme Court justice does not follow that we should treat her as if she were a justice now.

Michael Tooley provides a more striking exam-ple. Suppose there existed a special chemical that could be injected into a kitten's brain to cause the kitten to gradually become a cat with a mind that was indistinguishable from the kind possessed by adult humans. The cat could think, talk, and feel just as humans do, acquiring all the proper traits that give it a right to life. Now consider:

> [C]ompare a member of *Homo sapiens* that has
> not developed far enough to have those proper-
> ties that in themselves give something a right to
> life, but which later will come to have them, with
> a kitten that has been injected with the special
> chemical but which has not yet had the chance to
> develop the relevant properties. It is clear that it
> cannot be any more seriously wrong to kill the
> human than to kill the kitten. The potentialities
> are the same in both cases.[8]

Some critics also think that the potentiality argument undermines itself because it seems to have bizarre implications. They argue, for ex-ample, that if a zygote is a potential person (and thus has the same right to life as an adult human), then other entities must also be poten-tial persons with a right to life—human ovum and spermatozoa for starters but also countless other cells in the human body. There is no dif-ference between a single-cell zygote and any

other single diploid cell that, through cloning, could also become a human being.

The liberal says that the unborn is not a person, not a full human being, and therefore does not have a right to life. If the unborn is a person, then killing it would be murder, and its right to life would be at least as weighty as the mother's. How can the liberal show that fetuses are not persons?

To start, the liberal will insist that merely being a *Homo sapiens*—a creature with human DNA—is not sufficient for personhood. To think so is to be guilty of a kind of prejudice called *speciesism*. The liberal argues that since whatever properties make us persons (and thus grant us a right to life) could conceivably be manifested by a nonhuman species, merely being a member of the human species cannot be sufficient for per-sonhood status. If we assume that an entity is a person just because it happens to belong to our favored biological classification, we stand con-victed of speciesism, close cousin to racism. There are properties that do qualify an entity as a person, but simply being human is not one of them.

The liberal tack is to identify these traits and point out that a fetus does not possess them. Ac-cording to Louis Pojman,

> These properties are intrinsically valuable traits
> that allow us to view ourselves as selves with
> plans and projects over time, properties like self-
> consciousness and rationality. . . . Although it is
> difficult to specify exactly what are the necessary
> and sufficient conditions for personhood, and lib-
> erals have described these conditions differently—
> some emphasizing desires and interests, others
> emphasizing agency or the ability to project into
> the future, others emphasizing the capacity for a
> notion of the self—they all point to a cluster of
> characteristics which distinguish children and
> adults from fetuses, infants, and most animals.[9]

Mary Anne Warren famously identifies five traits that are "most central" to personhood: (1) consciousness and the capacity to feel pain, (2) reasoning, (3) self-motivated activity, (4) the capacity to communicate, and (5) "the pres-ence of self-concepts, and self-awareness, either

IN DEPTH
DOES A FETUS FEEL PAIN?

In recent years this question has been hotly debated, with the pro-life side insisting that fetuses can experience pain as early as 20 weeks after conception (22 weeks after last menstrual period), and the pro-choice side asserting that fetuses cannot perceive pain until much later, no earlier than 24 weeks. Fetal pain has become controversial because it is now being used in an anti-abortion argument that abortions causing fetal pain are obviously immoral and therefore should be stopped. So several states have enacted laws banning abortions after 20 weeks, and in 2015 the U.S. House of Representatives passed a bill that would ban them after 22 weeks. (Such laws would pertain to relatively few abortions, since 99 percent of abortions occur before 21 weeks.)

Most scientists involved in this issue think fetal pain is probably not possible until after the time when most abortions take place. In 2005, a multidisciplinary analysis published in the *Journal of the American Medical Association* concluded that fetal perception of pain is unlikely before the third trimester, which begins at 27 weeks. In 2010, the British Royal College of Obstetricians and Gynaecologists said that fetuses cannot experience pain before 24 weeks. In 2012, the American Congress of Obstetricians and Gynecologists largely agreed with their British counterparts.

These reports, however, are hardly the last word on the subject. Abortion opponents cite research they say suggests that fetuses are conscious of pain at 20 weeks. Some experts point to the complexity of the pain response and how little science understands about it. They say it's best to assume that fetal pain can occur early and adjust our actions and attitudes accordingly.

individual or racial or both." To be considered a person, she says, a being need not possess all these traits, but surely "any being which satisfies *none* of (1)–(5) is certainly not a person." A fetus in fact satisfies none and is therefore not yet a person and "cannot coherently be said to have full moral rights."[10]

The conservative will counter that the liberal's standards for personhood are set too high, for they imply that cognitively impaired individuals—victims of serious dementia, retardation, or schizophrenia, for instance—are not persons and therefore do not have a right to life. The liberal view seems to condone the killing of these unfortunates, a repugnant implication. The liberal response is that even if cognitively impaired individuals do not qualify as persons, we may still have good reasons for not killing them—for example, because people value them or because a policy allowing them to be killed would be harmful to society (perhaps encouraging unnecessary killings or causing a general devaluing of life). In addition, the liberal points

out that the personhood status of many (or most) cognitively impaired individuals is unclear, so a policy of regarding them as less than persons would be risky.

The biggest challenge to the liberal notion of personhood is the charge that it sanctions infanticide. The argument is that if killing a fetus is morally permissible because it is not a person, then killing an infant must be acceptable as well, for it is not a person either. According to the liberal's personhood criteria mentioned earlier, neither a fetus nor an infant is a person. Moreover, there is a glaring problem with the common liberal assumption that birth is the point at which a fetus becomes a person: The fetus just before birth and the infant just after are biologically almost indistinguishable. Saying that the former has no right to life but the latter does seems hard to justify.

Liberals contend that even if infants are not persons, infanticide is rarely permissible (possible exceptions include cases of horrendous birth defects and terminal illness). Some (including

Warren) say that this is so because infants, though not persons, do have some moral standing. For example:

> In this country, and in this period of history, the deliberate killing of viable newborns is virtually never justified. This is in part because neonates are so very *close* to being persons that to kill them requires a very strong moral justification—as does the killing of dolphins, whales, chimpanzees, and other highly personlike creatures. It is certainly wrong to kill such beings just for the sake of convenience, or financial profit, or "sport."[11]

Others say that infanticide is to be condemned for reasons of social utility. As Joel Feinberg explains,

> The moral rule that condemns these killings [infanticide] and the legal rule that renders them punishable are both supported by "utilitarian reasons," that is, considerations of what is called "social utility," "the common good," "the public interest," and the like. Nature has apparently implanted in us an instructive tenderness toward infants that has proven extremely useful to the species, not only because it leads us to protect our young from death, and thus keep our population up, but also because infants usually grow into adults, and in Benn's words, "if as infants *they* are not treated with some minimal degree of tenderness and consideration, they will suffer for it later, as persons." One might add that when they are adults, others will suffer for it, too, at their hands. Spontaneous warmth and sympathy toward babies then clearly has a great deal of social utility, and insofar as infanticide would tend to weaken that socially valuable response, it is, on utilitarian grounds, morally wrong.[12]

Moderate views on abortion can be sketched out in a variety of ways. Many moderates claim the middle ground by arguing that the fetus achieves personhood at a point somewhere *between* conception and birth—at viability, at the time when fetal brain waves occur, or at some other notable point. Other moderates reject the notion of a distinct developmental line separating persons from nonpersons. They argue instead that the moral standing or right to life of the fetus increases gradually as it develops (expanding from minimal rights to almost full rights, for example) or that there is an indistinct threshold stage (when sentience emerges, say) beyond which the fetus has significantly increased moral standing. Departing dramatically from these strategies, some moderates stake out their position without appealing to fetal personhood.

The most famous example of the latter comes from Judith Jarvis Thomson. She argues that even if the conservative view is correct that the unborn is a person from the moment of conception, abortion may still be morally justified. A fetus may have a right to life, but this right "does not guarantee having either a right to be given the use of or a right to be allowed continued use of another person's body—even if one needs it for life itself."[13] The unborn's right to life is not absolute. It implies not that killing a fetus is always wrong, but that killing it unjustly is always wrong. Thomson argues her point with this striking analogy:

> You wake up in the morning and find yourself back to back in bed with an unconscious violinist. A famous unconscious violinist. He has been found to have a fatal kidney ailment, and the Society of Music Lovers has canvassed all the available medical records and found that you alone have the right blood type to help. They have therefore kidnapped you, and last night the violinist's circulatory system was plugged into yours, so that your kidneys can be used to extract poisons from his blood as well as your own. The director of the hospital now tells you, "Look, we're sorry the Society of Music Lovers did this to you—we would never have permitted it if we had known. But still, they did it, and the violinist now is plugged into you. To unplug you would be to kill him. But never mind, it's only for nine months. By then he will have recovered from his ailment, and can safely be unplugged from you."[14]

Thomson believes that our intuitions would tell us that this arrangement is outrageous, that the violinist's right to life would not give him the right to exploit someone's body against her will. Analogously, a fetus' right to life would not guarantee it unauthorized use of the mother's body; the mother has a right of self-defense. Abortion, therefore, is justified when the fetus takes up residence without the woman's consent, as when pregnancy is due to rape or failed contraception.

Some reject Thomson's argument by contending that it holds only if the woman bears no responsibility for her predicament, if the attached violinist or fetus takes up residence through no fault of her own. She may not be responsible for the fetus if she becomes pregnant through rape; she does not, after all, consent to be raped. But she can be held responsible if she voluntarily engages in sexual intercourse; she therefore is obligated to carry the fetus to term. Others maintain that the woman is obliged to sustain the life of the unborn because she has a filial obligation to it. The unborn has a natural claim to the woman's body.

APPLYING MAJOR THEORIES

A utilitarian can argue that abortion is morally permissible because without this option, women (and society) would suffer terrible consequences:

> Throughout history women have paid a terrible price for the absence of safe and legal contraception and abortion. Forced to bear many children, at excessively short intervals, they were often physically debilitated and died young—a common fate in most pre-twentieth-century societies and much of the Third World today. Involuntary childbearing aggravates poverty, increases infant and child death rates, and places severe strains upon the resources of families and states.[15]

To these calamities, a utilitarian might add the woman's physical and emotional distress caused by pregnancy; the risk of complications or death in childbirth; disruption of her employment, education, or other life plans; and unhappiness caused by a loss of personal control and freedom.

Utilitarian arguments for abortion can also appeal to the quality of life of the infant or child. By this reasoning, abortion may be acceptable if the fetus is likely to be born with severe defects—anencephalic (essentially without a brain), terminally ill, severely retarded, or seriously disabled. Abortion would be a way to avoid great suffering.

Utilitarians who take Mill's view of individual liberty might argue for abortion by claiming that a woman must be allowed the freedom to decide what happens to her own body, which includes the attached fetus. This position follows from Mill's liberty (or harm) principle: We may not interfere with a person's capacity for self-determination except to prevent harm to others.

Those opposed to abortion can appeal to consequences, too: Having an abortion can cause the woman tremendous emotional pain, and the child can bring much happiness to the family and to the world. Besides, as an alternative to abortion, there is always adoption.

A common response to utilitarian arguments for abortion is this: If the fetus is a person, the utilitarian considerations don't matter much, if at all. If fetuses have a right to life (the same as any normal adult human), then it does not matter that their presence will cause others grief or that their quality of life will be marginal. If it is not permissible to kill a normal adult human (a person) on such grounds, then it cannot be permissible to kill a fetus-person for the same reasons.

In Kantian ethics, much depends on whether the unborn is to be considered a person. If it is a person, it has inherent worth and therefore cannot be treated as merely a means to an end. It cannot be killed just for the convenience of the mother or of society. But if the unborn is not a person, then abortion would seem to be more easily justified. Since the woman is a person, she has a right to exercise her autonomy and sovereignty over her own body—which may include ending her pregnancy.

On Kantian grounds, some can claim justification for abortion even if the fetus is a person. According to Kant, persons have a right of self-defense, a right to preserve their own lives against those who would take them. This right includes killing another if necessary for self-protection. If so, perhaps a woman whose pregnancy threatens her life can kill the unborn person in self-defense—a therapeutic abortion. In addition, Kant's view can be plausibly construed as sanctioning abortion as a way of respecting a fetus' personhood. If the fetus is defective and faces a demeaning, miserable existence, we can show ultimate respect for its status by averting such indignities through abortion.

The natural law position on abortion as articulated in Roman Catholicism is clear and unequivocal. The fetus is an innocent person from conception (with a right to life equal to that of the mother), and directly killing any innocent person is wrong. Thus directly killing the unborn even for the purpose of saving the mother's life is impermissible, for "evil is never to be done that good may come of it." The doctrine of double effect, however, permits the *indirect* killing of the unborn—specifically, abortions done to save the mother's life while having the unintended yet foreseen effect of killing the fetus. Traditionally the only abortions thought to fit these requirements have involved ectopic pregnancies and uterine cancer.

KEY TERMS
abortion
induced abortion
quickening
spontaneous abortion (miscarriage)
therapeutic abortion
viability

SUMMARY
Abortion is the ending of a pregnancy. Abortion due to natural causes is known as spontaneous abortion, or miscarriage; intentional termination of pregnancy is called induced abortion; and abortion performed to preserve the life or health of the mother is referred to as therapeutic abortion. Over half of women having abortions are under 25 years old; one-fifth of these are teenagers. Women give varying reasons for having abortions, including that having a baby would interfere with their life, cause financial or social difficulties, or put their health or life at risk. They also cite possible problems affecting the health of the fetus.

Since 1973 the legal status of abortion in the United States has been dominated by the Supreme Court's ruling in *Roe v. Wade*. The justices held that in the first trimester, the woman's right to end her pregnancy cannot be curtailed by the state; in the second trimester, the state may limit—but not entirely prohibit—the woman's right by regulating abortion for the sake of her health; and after viability, the state may regulate and even ban abortion except when it's necessary to preserve her life or health. The Court affirmed that its ruling "leaves the State free to place increasing restrictions on abortion as the period of pregnancy lengthens, so long as those restrictions are tailored to the recognized state interests." In several cases after *Roe*, the Court circumscribed the right of abortion by, among other things, holding that a woman can be required to give her written informed consent to abortion, that the government is not obliged to use taxpayer money to fund abortion services, and that parental consent or a judge's authorization can be demanded of minors under age 18 who seek abortions. In 2007 the Court upheld the Partial-Birth Abortion Ban Act, which outlawed a type of late-term abortion (referred to rhetorically as "partial-birth abortion") even when a woman's health might be threatened.

There are three main positions on the moral permissibility of abortion. The conservative view is that abortion is never morally acceptable (except possibly to preserve the mother's life), for the unborn is a human being in the full sense. The liberal view is that abortion is acceptable whenever the woman wants it, for the unborn is not a human being in the full sense.

Nancy Klein

The most contentious—and usually the most agonizing—abortion cases are those involving what people take to be clashes between fetal and maternal rights or interests. Such conflicts have played out in many closely watched stories, including this one that grabbed headlines in 1989 and outraged people on all sides of the issue.

On December 13, 1988, 32-year-old Nancy Klein, wife and mother of a young daughter, was in an auto accident that damaged her brain and put her in a coma. At the time, she was 10 weeks pregnant. After six weeks she was still in the coma and still pregnant, and her doctors doubted that she would ever recover. But they did believe that her chances of coming out of the coma might improve if she had an abortion and that she could then be treated with medications that could not be safely given in pregnancy. So her husband, Martin, asked a New York State court to designate him as her guardian empowered to grant permission for the abortion.

But abortion opponents went to court to try to block the abortion. One of them petitioned to be named Nancy Klein's guardian, while another asked to become guardian for the fetus. "These people are ruining our family," Martin Klein declared. But one of the anti-abortion petitioners said, "I don't see this as interfering in the family's business. What we're trying to do is protect and support Nancy Klein and her child."

For two weeks, the legal battles raged, but ultimately Martin Klein won, and the requests of the abortion opponents were turned down by three state courts as well as by U.S. Supreme Court Justices Marshall and Scalia. Referring to the two anti-abortion petitioners, one court asserted, "The record confirms that these absolute strangers to the Klein family, whatever their motivation, have no place in the midst of this family tragedy."

Finally, at 18 weeks of pregnancy, the abortion was performed. Martin Klein and his wife's parents were relieved and said they expected that after the abortion Nancy would recover from her coma. Several weeks later, she did.

For the next two years, she struggled in rehabilitation hospitals to regain her memory and her ability to speak and walk. She eventually recovered much of what she had lost, though her speech and walking remained impaired. She condemned the actions of the abortion opponents: "I feel very strongly that it was my problem, not theirs, and that they had no right to interfere."

The moderate stance falls between these two stands, rejecting both the conservative's zero-tolerance for abortion and the liberal's idea of abortion on request. All sides tend to accept that murder is wrong, that persons have a right to life, and that personal freedom should not be curtailed except for very important reasons. Conservatives try to establish that the unborn should be recognized as an innocent person from the moment of conception by appealing to the lack of a precise cutoff point between zygote and adult human and by arguing that the fetus is a potential person. Liberals contend that merely being biologically human is not sufficient to establish personhood and that a fetus does not possess the properties that qualify an entity as a person. Taking a moderate position, Judith Jarvis Thomson argues that even if the conservative view is correct that the unborn is a person from the moment of conception, abortion may still be morally justified in some cases. The unborn's right to life is not absolute; it implies not that killing a fetus is always wrong, but that killing it unjustly is always wrong.

A utilitarian position can be staked out either for abortion or against it, depending on how the overall consequences of abortion are calculated. Kantian ethics can also yield pro- or anti-abortion positions depending on whether the unborn is considered a person. The natural law position on abortion as articulated in Roman Catholicism is that the fetus is an innocent person from conception, and directly killing any innocent person is wrong. Thus directly killing the unborn even for the purpose of saving the mother's life is impermissible. The doctrine of double effect, however, permits the indirect killing of the unborn—specifically, abortions done to save the mother's life while having the unintended yet foreseen effect of killing the fetus.

Cases for Evaluation

CASE 1
Abortions for Minor Disabilities

(London Times)—More than 50 babies with club feet were aborted in just one area of England in a three-year period, according to new statistics.

Thirty-seven babies with cleft lips or palates and 26 with extra or webbed fingers or toes were also aborted.

The data have raised concerns about abortions being carried out for minor disabilities that could be cured by surgery.

Abortions are allowed up to birth in Britain in cases of serious handicap, but the law does not define what conditions should be considered grave enough to allow a termination late in the pregnancy. That is left to the discretion of doctors.

The Commons science and technology committee is carrying out an inquiry into whether the law should be made more specific.

Some parents, doctors and campaign groups are worried by what they see as a tendency to stretch the definition of serious handicap.

In 2003 Joanna Jepson, a Church of England curate, instigated a legal challenge against West Mercia police for failing to prosecute doctors who carried out an abortion on a baby with a cleft palate at 28 weeks' gestation. The challenge failed but

raised public concerns over terminations for minor disabilities.

However, the latest figures—released by the South West Congenital Register—show that dozens of abortions are still carried out after the condition is discovered.

Jepson, now vicar of St Peter's church in Fulham, west London, said: "These figures raise grave questions about how the law is being implemented for babies diagnosed with a disability. I have strong doubts that the law is being used to protect the unborn."

Julia Millington, political director of the ProLife Alliance, added: "It is incomprehensible that a baby would be rejected for what amounts to little more than a cosmetic imperfection. Equality for the disabled cannot be achieved until we remove this discriminatory provision in the law."*

Do you think it is ever morally permissible to perform an abortion on a defective fetus? What about a fetus that is so deformed that it will certainly die within a few days after birth? Or a fetus with deformities that will guarantee it a lifetime of pain and serious disability and years of emotional and financial trauma for its family? Can abortions performed on fetuses with minor disabilities such as a cleft lip ever be justified? Give reasons for your answers.

---

*Sarah-Kate Templeton, "Babies Aborted for Minor Disabilities," TimesOnline, 21 October 2007, http://www.timesonline .co.uk/tol/news/uk/health/article2689787.ece (24 November 2007).

CASE 2
Sex-Selection Abortions

More than 10 [million] female births in India may have been lost to abortion and sex selection in the past 20 years, research published in the Lancet has claimed.

Researchers in India and Canada said prenatal selection and selective abortion was causing the loss of 500,000 girls a year. Their research was based on a national survey of 1.1 [million] households in 1998.

The research, by Prabhat Jha of St. Michael's Hospital at the University of Toronto, Canada, and Rajesh Kumar of the Postgraduate Institute of Medical Research in Chandigarh, India, found that there was an increasing tendency to select boys when previous children had been girls. In cases where the preceding child was a girl, the ratio of girls to boys in the next birth was 759 to 1,000. This fell even further when the two preceding children were both girls. Then the ratio for the third child born was just 719 girls to 1,000 boys. However, for a child following the birth of a male child, the gender ratio was roughly equal.

Prabhat Jha said conservative estimates in the research suggested half a million girls were being lost each year. "If this practice has been common for most of the past two decades since access to ultrasound became widespread, then a figure of 10 [million] missing female births would not be unreasonable." In 1994, India banned the use of technology to determine the sex of unborn children and the termination of pregnancies on the basis of gender. Leading campaigners say many of India's fertility clinics continue to offer a seemingly legitimate facade for a multi-billion-pound racket and that gender determination is still big business in India.

However, a top Indian doctors' association disputed the report. The Indian Medical Association said pre-birth gender checks had waned since a Supreme Court crackdown in 2001. A spokesman acknowledged that prenatal selections used to take place, but said they were not as widespread as before and that the *Lancet* report was exaggerated. "This has not been happening for the past four or five years after strict laws were put in place," the spokesman, Dr. Narendra Saini, said. Other experts say it is impossible that India could have lost 10 [million] females. "If there were half a million feticides a year, the sex ratio would have been very skewed indeed," said Prof. S.C. Gulati of Delhi's Institute of Economic Growth.

Are sex-selection abortions ever justified? Is the practice of "female foeticide" a form of discrimination against females? If so, can it ever be morally permissible? Explain your answers.

---

* "India: Dispute over Sex Ratio," http://www.reproductivereview.org/ (14 January 2016).

CASE 3

Abortions and Prenatal Testing

(*New York Times*) Sarah Itoh, a self-described "almost-eleven-and-a-half," betrayed no trace of nervousness as she told a roomful of genetic counselors and obstetricians about herself one recent afternoon.

She likes to read, she said. Math used to be hard, but it is getting easier. She plays clarinet in her school band. She is a junior girl scout and an aunt, and she likes to organize, so her room is very clean. Last year, she won three medals in the Special Olympics.

"I am so lucky I get to do so many things," she concluded. "I just want you to know, even though I have Down syndrome, it is O.K."

Sarah's appearance at Henry Ford Hospital here is part of an unusual campaign being undertaken by parents of children with Down syndrome who worry about their future in the face of broader prenatal testing that could sharply reduce the number of those born with the genetic condition.

Until this year, only pregnant women 35 and older were routinely tested to see if their fetuses had the extra chromosome that causes Down syndrome. As a result many couples were given the diagnosis only at birth. But under a new recommendation from the American College of Obstetricians and Gynecologists, doctors have begun to offer a new, safer screening procedure to all pregnant women, regardless of age.

About 90 percent of pregnant women who are given a Down syndrome diagnosis have chosen to have an abortion.

Convinced that more couples would choose to continue their pregnancies if they better appreciated what it meant to raise a child with Down syndrome, a growing group of parents is seeking to insert their own positive perspectives into a decision often dominated by daunting medical statistics and doctors who feel obligated to describe the difficulties of life with a disabled child.

They are pressing obstetricians to send them couples who have been given a prenatal diagnosis and inviting prospective parents into their homes to meet their children. In Massachusetts, for example, volunteers in a "first call" network linking veteran parents to new ones are now offering support to couples deciding whether to continue a pregnancy.

The parent evangelists are driven by a deep-seated fear for their children's well-being in a world where there are fewer people like them. But as prenatal tests become available for a range of other perceived genetic imperfections, they may also be heralding a broader cultural skirmish over where to draw the line between preventing disability and accepting human diversity.

"We want people who make this decision to know our kids," said Lucy Talbot, the president of a support group here who prevailed on the hospital to give Sarah and two teenage friends an audience. "We want them to talk to us."

The focus on the unborn is new for most parent advocates, who have traditionally directed their energy toward support for the born. But after broader testing was recommended in January, the subject began to hijack agendas at local support group meetings.

A dwindling Down syndrome population, which now stands at about 350,000, could mean less institutional support and reduced funds for medical research. It could also mean a lonelier world for those who remain.

"The impact of these changes on the Down syndrome community is going to be huge," said Dani Archer, a mother in Omaha who has set aside other Down syndrome volunteer work to strategize about how to reach prospective parents.

The 5,500 children born with Down syndrome each year in the United States suffer from mild to moderate mental retardation, are at high risk for congenital heart defects and a variety of other medical problems, and have an average life expectancy of 49. As adults, some hold jobs, but many have difficulty living independently.

"There are many couples who do not want to have a baby with Down syndrome," said Deborah A. Driscoll, chief of the obstetrics department at the University of Pennsylvania and a lead author of the new recommendation from the obstetricians' group. "They don't have the resources, don't have the emotional stamina, don't have the family support. We are recommending this testing be offered so that parents have a choice."*

Is it right for parents to have abortions to avoid giving birth to a Down syndrome baby? Should society encourage such abortions to prevent disabilities or discourage them to promote a respect for human diversity? Should the quality of a Down syndrome baby's future life be a factor in deciding whether to have the abortion? Explain your answers.

---

*Amy Harmon, "Prenatal Test Puts Down Syndrome in Hard Focus," *New York Times*, 9 May 2007, http://www.nytimes.com/2007/05/09/us/09down.html (24 November 2007).

FURTHER READING

Sidney Callahan, "A Case for Pro-Life Feminism," *Commonweal* 25 (April 1986), 232–38.

Philip Devine, *The Ethics of Homicide* (Ithaca, NY: Cornell University Press, 1978).

Joel Feinberg, "Abortion," in *Matters of Life and Death*, 3rd ed., ed. Tom Regan (New York: McGraw-Hill, 1993), 183–217.

Jonathan Glover, "The Sanctity of Life," in *Bioethics: An Anthology*, ed. Helga Kuhse and Peter Singer (Oxford: Blackwell, 1999), 193–202.

John Harris and Søren Holm, "Abortion," in *The Oxford Handbook of Practical Ethics*, ed. Hugh LaFollette (Oxford: Oxford University Press, 2003), 112–35.

Don Marquis, "Abortion Revisited," in *The Oxford Handbook of Bioethics*, ed. Bonnie Steinbock (Oxford: Oxford University Press, 2007), 395–415.

Jeff McMahan, *The Ethics of Killing: Problems at the Margins of Life* (New York: Oxford University Press, 2002).

Mark Murphy, "The Natural Law Tradition in Ethics," *Stanford Encyclopedia of Philosophy*, 11 March 2008, http://plato.stanford.edu/entries/natural-law-ethics (9 June 2008).

NARAL Pro-Choice America, http://www.prochoiceamerica.org/about-us/contact.html (27 October 2015).

National Right to Life, http://www.nrlc.org/ (27 October 2015).

Louis P. Pojman, *Life and Death: Grappling with the Moral Dilemmas of Our Time* (Boston: Jones and Bartlett, 1992).

Louis P. Pojman and Francis J. Beckwith, eds., *The Abortion Controversy: 25 Years After Roe v. Wade: A Reader*, 2nd ed. (Belmont, CA: Wadsworth, 1998).

ProCon.org, "Abortion," http://abortion.procon.org/ (27 October 2015).

James Rachels, "Killing, Letting Die, and the Value of Life," in *Can Ethics Provide Answers?* (Lanham, MD: Rowman & Littlefield, 1997), 69–79.

Stephen Schwarz, *The Moral Question of Abortion* (Chicago: Loyola University Press, 1990).

Susan Sherwin, *No Longer Patient: Feminist Ethics and Health Care* (Philadelphia: Temple University Press, 1992), 108–14.

L. W. Sumner, *Abortion and Moral Theory* (Princeton, NJ: Princeton University Press, 1981).

Michael Tooley, *Abortion and Infanticide* (New York: Oxford University Press, 1983).

NOTES

1. Aristotle, *Politics* VII, 16, 1335b.

2. American College of Obstetricians and Gynecologists, *Standards for Obstetric-Gynecological Hospital Services* (Washington, DC: ACOG, August 1970), 53; American College of Obstetrics and Gynecologists, *Statement of Policy: Abortion* (Washington, DC: ACOG, August 1970). Quoted in Albert R. Jonsen, *The Birth of Bioethics* (New York: Oxford University Press), 290.

3. Figures from the American College of Obstetricians and Gynecologists, *Induced Abortion*, June 2007, www.acog.org (20 June 2007).

4. Lawrence B. Finer et al., "Reasons U.S. Women Have Abortions: Quantitative and Qualitative Perspectives," *Perspectives on Sexual and Reproductive Health* 37.3 (2005), 110–18.

5. John T. Noonan, Jr., "An Almost Absolute Value in History," in *The Morality of Abortion: Legal and Historical Perspectives*, ed. John T. Noonan, Jr. (Cambridge, MA: Harvard University Press, 1970), 51–59.

6. Mary Anne Warren, "Abortion," in *A Companion to Bioethics*, ed. Helga Kuhse and Peter Singer (Oxford: Blackwell, 2001), 130.

7. Philip Devine, "The Scope of the Prohibition Against Killing," in *The Ethics of Homicide* (Ithaca, NY: Cornell University Press, 1978), 57.

8. Michael Tooley, "In Defense of Abortion and Infanticide," in *The Abortion Controversy*, ed. Louis P. Pojman and Francis J. Beckwith (Belmont, CA: Wadsworth, 1998), 209–33.

9. Louis P. Pojman, "Abortion: A Defense of the Personhood Argument," in *The Abortion Controversy*, ed. Pojman and Beckwith, 281.

10. Mary Anne Warren, "On the Moral and Legal Status of Abortion," *The Monist* 57.1 (1973), 43–61.

11. Mary Anne Warren, "Postscript on Infanticide," in *The Problem of Abortion*, 2nd ed., ed. Joel Feinberg (Belmont, CA: Wadsworth, 1984), 71–74.

12. Joel Feinberg, "Abortion," in *Matters of Life and Death: New Introductory Essays in Moral Philosophy*, ed. Tom Regan (New York: Random House, 1980); quoted in *The Abortion Controversy*, ed. Pojman and Beckwith, 287.

13. Judith Jarvis Thomson, "A Defense of Abortion," *Philosophy and Public Affairs* 1.1 (1971), 47–50, 54–66.

14. *Ibid.*

15. Mary Anne Warren, "Abortion," in *A Companion to Ethics*, ed. Peter Singer (Oxford: Blackwell, 1993), 303.

A Defense of Abortion

JUDITH JARVIS THOMSON

In this classic essay, Thomson argues that even if a fetus is a person at conception, at least some abortions could still be morally permissible. A fetus may have a right to life, but this right "does not guarantee having either a right to be given the use of or a right to be allowed continued use of another person's body—even if one needs it for life itself." A woman has a right not to have her body used by someone else against her will, which is essentially the case when she is pregnant due to no fault of her own (as a result of rape, for instance). The correct lesson about the unborn's right to life is not that killing a fetus is always wrong, but that killing it unjustly is always wrong.

Most opposition to abortion relies on the premise that the fetus is a human being, a person, from the moment of conception. The premise is argued for, but, as I think, not well. Take, for example, the most common argument. We are asked to notice that the development of a human being from conception through birth into childhood is continuous; then it is said that to draw a line, to choose a point in this development and say "before this point the thing is not a person, after this point it is a person" is to make an arbitrary choice, a choice for which in the nature of things no good reason can be given. It is concluded that the fetus is, or anyway that we had better say it is, a person from the moment of conception. But this conclusion does not follow. Similar things might be said about the development of an acorn into an oak tree, and it does not follow that acorns are oak trees, or that we had better say they are. Arguments of this form are sometimes called "slippery slope arguments"—the phrase is perhaps self-explanatory—and it is dismaying that opponents of abortion rely on them so heavily and uncritically.

I am inclined to agree, however, that the prospects for "drawing a line" in the development of the fetus look dim. I am inclined to think also that we shall probably have to agree that the fetus has already become a human person well before birth. Indeed, it comes as a surprise when one first learns how early in its life it begins to acquire human characteristics. By the tenth week, for example, it already has a face, arms and legs, fingers and toes; it has internal organs, and brain activity is detectable.[1] On the other hand, I think that the premise is false, that the fetus is not a person from the moment of conception. A newly fertilized ovum, a newly implanted clump of cells, is no more a person than an acorn is an oak tree. But I shall not discuss any of this. For it seems to me to be of great interest to ask what happens if, for the sake of argument, we allow the premise. How, precisely, are we supposed to get from there to the conclusion that abortion is morally impermissible? Opponents of abortion commonly spend most of their time establishing that the fetus is a person, and hardly any time explaining the step from there to the impermissibility of abortion. Perhaps they think the step too simple and obvious to require much comment. Or perhaps instead they are simply being economical in argument. Many of those who defend abortion rely on the premise that the fetus is not a person, but only a bit of tissue that will become a person at birth; and why pay out more arguments than you have to? Whatever the explanation, I suggest that the step they take is neither easy nor obvious, that it calls for closer examination than it is commonly given, and that when we do give it this closer examination we shall feel inclined to reject it.

From "A Defense of Abortion," *Philosophy & Public Affairs*, vol. 1, no. 1 (Fall 1971). Copyright © 1971. Reprinted with permission of Blackwell Publishing. (Notes edited.)

I propose, then, that we grant that the fetus is a person from the moment of conception. How does the argument go from here? Something like this, I take it. Every person has a right to life. So the fetus has a right to life. No doubt the mother has a right to decide what shall happen in and to her body; everyone would grant that. But surely a person's right to life is stronger and more stringent than the mother's right to decide what happens in and to her body, and so outweighs it. So the fetus may not be killed; an abortion may not be performed.

It sounds plausible. But now let me ask you to imagine this. You wake up in the morning and find yourself back to back in bed with an unconscious violinist. A famous unconscious violinist. He has been found to have a fatal kidney ailment, and the Society of Music Lovers has canvassed all the available medical records and found that you alone have the right blood type to help. They have therefore kidnapped you, and last night the violinist's circulatory system was plugged into yours, so that your kidneys can be used to extract poisons from his blood as well as your own. The director of the hospital now tells you, "Look, we're sorry the Society of Music Lovers did this to you—we would never have permitted it if we had known. But still, they did it, and the violinist now is plugged into you. To unplug you would be to kill him. But never mind, it's only for nine months. By then he will have recovered from his ailment, and can safely be unplugged from you." Is it morally incumbent on you to accede to this situation? No doubt it would be very nice of you if you did, a great kindness. But do you *have* to accede to it? What if it were not nine months, but nine years? Or longer still? What if the director of the hospital says, "Tough luck, I agree, but you've now got to stay in bed, with the violinist plugged into you, for the rest of your life. Because remember this. All persons have a right to life, and violinists are persons. Granted you have a right to decide what happens in and to your body, but a person's right to life outweighs your right to decide what happens in and to your body. So you cannot ever be unplugged from him." I imagine you would regard this as outrageous, which suggests that something really is wrong with that plausible-sounding argument I mentioned a moment ago.

In this case, of course, you were kidnapped; you didn't volunteer for the operation that plugged the violinist into your kidneys. Can those who oppose abortion on the ground I mentioned make an exception for a pregnancy due to rape? Certainly. They can say that persons have a right to life only if they didn't come into existence because of rape; or they can say that all persons have a right to life, but that some have less of a right to life than others, in particular, that those who came into existence because of rape have less. But these statements have a rather unpleasant sound. Surely the question of whether you have a right to life at all, or how much of it you have, shouldn't turn on the question of whether or not you are the product of a rape. And in fact the people who oppose abortion on the ground I mentioned do not make this distinction, and hence do not make an exception in case of rape.

Nor do they make an exception for a case in which the mother has to spend the nine months of her pregnancy in bed. They would agree that would be a great pity, and hard on the mother; but all the same, all persons have a right to life, the fetus is a person, and so on. I suspect, in fact, that they would not make an exception for a case in which, miraculously enough, the pregnancy went on for nine years, or even the rest of the mother's life.

Some won't even make an exception for a case in which continuation of the pregnancy is likely to shorten the mother's life; they regard abortion as impermissible even to save the mother's life. Such cases are nowadays very rare, and many opponents of abortion do not accept this extreme view. All the same, it is a good place to begin: a number of points of interest come out in respect to it.

1. Let us call the view that abortion is impermissible even to save the mother's life "the extreme view." I want to suggest first that it does not issue from the argument I mentioned earlier without the addition of some fairly powerful premises. Suppose a woman has *become pregnant,* and now learns that she has a cardiac condition such that she will die if she carries the baby to term. What may be done for her? The fetus, being a person, has a right to life, but as the mother is a person too, so has she a right to life. Presumably they have an equal right to life.

How is it supposed to come out that an abortion may not be performed? If mother and child have an equal right to life, shouldn't we perhaps flip a coin? Or should we add to the mother's right to life her right to decide what happens in and to her body, which everybody seems to be ready to grant—the sum of her rights now outweighing the fetus' right to life?

The most familiar argument here is the following. We are told that performing the abortion would be directly killing[2] the child, whereas doing nothing would not be killing the mother, but only letting her die. Moreover, in killing the child, one would be killing an innocent person, for the child has committed no crime, and is not aiming at his mother's death. And then there are a variety of ways in which this might be continued. (1) But as directly killing an innocent person is always and absolutely impermissible, an abortion may not be performed. Or, (2) as directly killing an innocent person is murder, and murder is always and absolutely impermissible, an abortion may not be performed.[3] Or, (3) as one's duty to refrain from directly killing an innocent person is more stringent than one's duty to keep a person from dying, an abortion may not be performed. Or, (4) if one's only options are directly killing an innocent person or letting a person die, one must prefer letting the person die, and thus an abortion may not be performed.[4]

Some people seem to have thought that these are not further premises which must be added if the conclusion is to be reached, but that they follow from the very fact that an innocent person has a right to life.[5] But this seems to me to be a mistake, and perhaps the simplest way to show this is to bring out that while we must certainly grant that innocent persons have a right to life, the theses in (1) through (4) are all false. Take (2), for example. If directly killing an innocent person is murder, and thus is impermissible, then the mother's directly killing the innocent person inside her is murder, and thus is impermissible. But it cannot seriously be thought to be murder if the mother performs an abortion on herself to save her life. It cannot seriously be said that she *must* refrain, that she *must* sit passively by and wait for her death. Let us look again at the case of you and the violinist. There you are, in bed with the violinist, and the director of the hospital says to you, "It's all most distressing, and I deeply sympathize, but you see this is putting an additional strain on your kidneys, and you'll be dead within the month. But you *have* to stay where you are all the same. Because unplugging you would be directly killing an innocent violinist, and that's murder, and that's impermissible." If anything in the world is true, it is that you do not commit murder, you do not do what is impermissible, if you reach around to your back and unplug yourself from that violinist to save your life.

The main focus of attention in writings on abortion has been on what a third party may or may not do in answer to a request from a woman for an abortion. This is in a way understandable. Things being as they are, there isn't much a woman can safely do to abort herself. So the question asked is what a third party may do, and what the mother may do, if it is mentioned at all, is deduced, almost as an after-thought, from what it is concluded that third parties may do. But it seems to me that to treat the matter in this way is to refuse to grant to the mother that very status of person which is so firmly insisted on for the fetus. For we cannot simply read off what a person may do from what a third party may do. Suppose you find yourself trapped in a tiny house with a growing child. I mean a very tiny house, and a rapidly growing child—you are already up against the wall of the house and in a few minutes you'll be crushed to death. The child on the other hand won't be crushed to death; if nothing is done to stop him from growing he'll be hurt, but in the end he'll simply burst open the house and walk out a free man. Now I could well understand it if a bystander were to say, "There's nothing we can do for you. We cannot choose between your life and his, we cannot be the ones to decide who is to live, we cannot intervene." But it cannot be concluded that you too can do nothing, that you cannot attack it to save your life. However innocent the child may be, you do not have to wait passively while it crushes you to death. Perhaps a pregnant woman is vaguely felt to have the status of house, to which we don't allow the right of self-defense. But if the woman houses the child, it should be remembered that she is a person who houses it.

I should perhaps stop to say explicitly that I am not claiming that people have a right to do anything whatever to save their lives. I think, rather, that there are drastic limits to the right of self-defense. If someone threatens you with death unless you torture someone else to death, I think you have not the right, even to save your life, to do so. But the case under consideration here is very different. In our case there are only two people involved, one whose life is threatened, and one who threatens it. Both are innocent: the one who is threatened is not threatened because of any fault, the one who threatens does not threaten because of any fault. For this reason we may feel that we bystanders cannot intervene. But the person threatened can.

In sum, a woman surely can defend her life against the threat to it posed by the unborn child, even if doing so involves its death. And this shows not merely that the theses in (1) through (4) are false; it shows also that the extreme view of abortion is false, and so we need not canvass any other possible ways of arriving at it from the argument I mentioned at the outset.

2. The extreme view could of course be weakened to say that while abortion is permissible to save the mother's life, it may not be performed by a third party, but only by the mother herself. But this cannot be right either. For what we have to keep in mind is that the mother and the unborn child are not like two tenants in a small house which has, by an unfortunate mistake, been rented to both: the mother *owns* the house. The fact that she does adds to the offensiveness of deducing that the mother can do nothing from the supposition that third parties can do nothing. But it does more than this: it casts a bright light on the supposition that third parties can do nothing. Certainly it lets us see that a third party who says "I cannot choose between you" is fooling himself if he thinks this is impartiality. If Jones has found and fastened on a certain coat, which he needs to keep him from freezing, but which Smith also needs to keep him from freezing, then it is not impartiality that says "I cannot choose between you" when Smith owns the coat. Women have said again and again "This body is *my* body!" and they have reason to feel angry, reason to feel that it has been like shouting into the wind. Smith,

after all, is hardly likely to bless us if we say to him, "Of course it's your coat, anybody would grant that it is. But no one may choose between you and Jones who is to have it."

We should really ask what it is that says "no one may choose" in the face of the fact that the body that houses the child is the mother's body. It may be simply a failure to appreciate this fact. But it may be something more interesting, namely the sense that one has a right to refuse to lay hands on people, even where it would be just and fair to do so, even where justice seems to require that somebody do so. Thus justice might call for somebody to get Smith's coat back from Jones, and yet you have a right to refuse to be the one to lay hands on Jones, a right to refuse to do physical violence to him. This, I think, must be granted. But then what should be said is not "no one may choose," but only "*I* cannot choose," and indeed not even this, but "*I* will not *act*," leaving it open that somebody else can or should, and in particular that anyone in a position of authority, with the job of securing people's rights, both can and should. So this is no difficulty. I have not been arguing that any given third party must accede to the mother's request that he perform an abortion to save her life, but only that he may.

I suppose that in some views of human life the mother's body is only on loan to her, the loan not being one which gives her any prior claim to it. One who held this view might well think it impartiality to say "I cannot choose." But I shall simply ignore this possibility. My own view is that if a human being has any just, prior claim to anything at all, he has a just, prior claim to his own body. And perhaps this needn't be argued for here anyway, since, as I mentioned, the arguments against abortion we are looking at do grant that the woman has a right to decide what happens in and to her body.

But although they do grant it, I have tried to show that they do not take seriously what is done in granting it. I suggest the same thing will reappear even more clearly when we turn away from cases in which the mother's life is at stake, and attend, as I propose we now do, to the vastly more common cases in which a woman wants an abortion for some less weighty reason than preserving her own life.

3. Where the mother's life is not at stake, the argument I mentioned at the outset seems to have a

much stronger pull. "Everyone has a right to life, so the unborn person has a right to life." And isn't the child's right to life weightier than anything other than the mother's own right to life, which she might put forward as ground for an abortion?

This argument treats the right to life as if it were unproblematic. It is not, and this seems to me to be precisely the source of the mistake.

For we should now, at long last, ask what it comes to, to have a right to life. In some views having a right to life includes having a right to be given at least the bare minimum one needs for continued life. But suppose that what in fact *is* the bare minimum a man needs for continued life is something he has no right at all to be given? If I am sick unto death, and the only thing that will save my life is the touch of Henry Fonda's cool hand on my fevered brow, then all the same, I have no right to be given the touch of Henry Fonda's cool hand on my fevered brow. It would be frightfully nice of him to fly in from the West Coast to provide it. It would be less nice, though no doubt well meant, if my friends flew out to the West Coast and carried Henry Fonda back with them. But I have no right at all against anybody that he should do this for me. Or again, to return to the story I told earlier, the fact that for continued life that violinist needs the continued use of your kidneys does not establish that he has a right to be given the continued use of your kidneys. He certainly has no right against you that *you* should give him continued use of your kidneys. For nobody has any right to use your kidneys unless you give him such a right; and nobody has the right against you that you shall give him this right—if you do allow him to go on using your kidneys, this is a kindness on your part, and not something he can claim from you as his due. Nor has he any right against anybody else that *they* should give him continued use of your kidneys. Certainly he had no right against the Society of Music Lovers that they should plug him into you in the first place. And if you now start to unplug yourself, having learned that you will otherwise have to spend nine years in bed with him, there is nobody in the world who must try to prevent you, in order to see to it that he is given something he has a right to be given.

Some people are rather stricter about the right to life. In their view, it does not include the right to be given anything, but amounts to, and only to, the right not to be killed by anybody. But here a related difficulty arises. If everybody is to refrain from killing that violinist, then everybody must refrain from doing a great many different sorts of things. Everybody must refrain from slitting his throat, everybody must refrain from shooting him—and everybody must refrain from unplugging you from him. But does he have a right against everybody that they shall refrain from unplugging you from him? To refrain from doing this is to allow him to continue to use your kidneys. It could be argued that he has a right against us that *we* should allow him to continue to use your kidneys. That is, while he had no right against us that we should give him the use of your kidneys, it might be argued that he anyway has a right against us that we shall not now intervene and deprive him of the use of your kidneys. I shall come back to third-party interventions later. But certainly the violinist has no right against you that *you* shall allow him to continue to use your kidneys. As I said, if you do allow him to use them, it is a kindness on your part, and not something you owe him.

The difficulty I point to here is not peculiar to the right to life. It reappears in connection with all the other natural rights; and it is something which an adequate account of rights must deal with. For present purposes it is enough just to draw attention to it. But I would stress that I am not arguing that people do not have a right to life—quite to the contrary, it seems to me that the primary control we must place on the acceptability of an account of rights is that it should turn out in that account to be a truth that all persons have a right to life. I am arguing only that having a right to life does not guarantee having either a right to be given the use of or a right to be allowed continued use of another person's body—even if one needs it for life itself. So the right to life will not serve the opponents of abortion in the very simple and clear way in which they seem to have thought it would.

4. There is another way to bring out the difficulty. In the most ordinary sort of case, to deprive someone of what he has a right to is to treat him

unjustly. Suppose a boy and his small brother are jointly given a box of chocolates for Christmas. If the older boy takes the box and refuses to give his brother any of the chocolates, he is unjust to him, for the brother has been given a right to half of them. But suppose that, having learned that otherwise it means nine years in bed with that violinist, you unplug yourself from him. You surely are not being unjust to him, for you gave him no right to use your kidneys, and no one else can have given him any such right. But we have to notice that in unplugging yourself, you are killing him; and violinists, like everybody else, have a right to life, and thus in the view we were considering just now, the right not to be killed. So here you do what he supposedly has a right you shall not do, but you do not act unjustly to him in doing it.

The emendation which may be made at this point is this: the right to life consists not in the right not to be killed, but rather in the right not to be killed unjustly. This runs a risk of circularity, but never mind: it would enable us to square the fact that the violinist has a right to life with the fact that you do not act unjustly toward him in unplugging yourself, thereby killing him. For if you do not kill him unjustly, you do not violate his right to life, and so it is no wonder you do him no injustice.

But if this emendation is accepted, the gap in the argument against abortion stares us plainly in the face: it is by no means enough to show that the fetus is a person, and to remind us that all persons have a right to life—we need to be shown also that killing the fetus violates its right to life, i.e., that abortion is unjust killing. And is it?

I suppose we may take it as a datum that in a case of pregnancy due to rape the mother has not given the unborn person a right to the use of her body for food and shelter. Indeed, in what pregnancy could it be supposed that the mother has given the unborn person such a right? It is not as if there were unborn persons drifting about the world, to whom a woman who wants a child says "I invite you in."

But it might be argued that there are other ways one can have acquired a right to the use of another person's body than by having been invited to use it by that person. Suppose a woman voluntarily indulges in intercourse, knowing of the chance it will issue in pregnancy, and then she does become pregnant; is she not in part responsible for the presence, in fact the very existence, of the unborn person inside her? No doubt she did not invite it in. But doesn't her partial responsibility for its being there itself give it a right to the use of her body?[6] If so, then her aborting it would be more like the boy's taking away the chocolates, and less like your unplugging yourself from the violinist—doing so would be depriving it of what it does have a right to, and thus would be doing it an injustice.

And then, too, it might be asked whether or not she can kill it even to save her own life: If she voluntarily called it into existence, how can she now kill it, even in self-defense?

The first thing to be said about this is that it is something new. Opponents of abortion have been so concerned to make out the independence of the fetus, in order to establish that it has a right to life, just as its mother does, that they have tended to overlook the possible support they might gain from making out that the fetus is *dependent* on the mother, in order to establish that she has a special kind of responsibility for it, a responsibility that gives it rights against her which are not possessed by any independent person—such as an ailing violinist who is a stranger to her.

On the other hand, this argument would give the unborn person a right to its mother's body only if her pregnancy resulted from a voluntary act, undertaken in full knowledge of the chance a pregnancy might result from it. It would leave out entirely the unborn person whose existence is due to rape. Pending the availability of some further argument, then, we would be left with the conclusion that unborn persons whose existence is due to rape have no right to the use of their mothers' bodies, and thus that aborting them is not depriving them of anything they have a right to and hence is not unjust killing.

And we should also notice that it is not at all plain that this argument really does go even as far as it purports to. For there are cases and cases, and the details make a difference. If the room is stuffy, and I therefore open a window to air it, and a burglar climbs in, it would be absurd to say, "Ah, now he can stay, she's given him a right to the use of her house—for she is partially responsible for his presence there, having voluntarily done what enabled him to get in, in full knowledge that there are such things as burglars, and that burglars burgle." It would be still more absurd to say this if I had had bars installed outside my windows, precisely to prevent burglars from getting in, and a burglar got in only because of a defect in the bars. It remains equally absurd if we imagine it is not a burglar who climbs in, but an innocent person who blunders or falls in. Again, suppose it were like this: people-seeds drift about in the air like pollen, and if you open your windows, one may drift in and take root in your carpets or upholstery. You don't want children, so you fix up your windows with fine mesh screens, the very best you can buy. As can happen, however, and on very, very rare occasions does happen, one of the screens is defective; and a seed drifts in and takes root. Does the person-plant who now develops have a right to the use of your house? Surely not—despite the fact that you voluntarily opened your windows, you knowingly kept carpets and upholstered furniture, and you knew that screens were sometimes defective. Someone may argue that you are responsible for its rooting, that it does have a right to your house, because after all you *could* have lived out your life with bare floors and furniture, or with sealed windows and doors. But this won't do—for by the same token anyone can avoid a pregnancy due to rape by having a hysterectomy, or anyway by never leaving home without a (reliable!) army.

It seems to me that the argument we are looking at can establish at most that there are *some* cases in which the unborn person has a right to the use of its mother's body, and therefore *some* cases in which abortion is unjust killing. There is room for much discussion and argument as to precisely which, if any. But I think we should sidestep this issue and leave it open, for at any rate the argument certainly does not establish that all abortion is unjust killing.

5. There is room for yet another argument here, however. We surely must all grant that there may be cases in which it would be morally indecent to detach a person from your body at the cost of his life. Suppose you learn that what the violinist needs

is not nine years of your life, but only one hour: all you need do to save his life is to spend one hour in that bed with him. Suppose also that letting him use your kidneys for that one hour would not affect your health in the slightest. Admittedly you were kidnapped. Admittedly you did not give anyone permission to plug him into you. Nevertheless it seems to me plain you *ought* to allow him to use your kidneys for that hour—it would be indecent to refuse.

Again, suppose pregnancy lasted only an hour, and constituted no threat to life or health. And suppose that a woman becomes pregnant as a result of rape. Admittedly she did not voluntarily do anything to bring about the existence of a child. Admittedly she did nothing at all which would give the unborn person a right to the use of her body. All the same it might well be said, as in the newly emended violinist story, that she *ought* to allow it to remain for that hour—that it would be indecent in her to refuse.

Now some people are inclined to use the term "right" in such a way that it follows from the fact that you ought to allow a person to use your body for the hour he needs, that he has a right to use your body for the hour he needs, even though he has not been given that right by any person or act. They may say that it follows also that if you refuse, you act unjustly toward him. This use of the term is perhaps so common that it cannot be called wrong; nevertheless it seems to me to be an unfortunate loosening of what we would do better to keep a tight rein on. Suppose that box of chocolates I mentioned earlier had not been given to both boys jointly, but was given only to the older boy. There he sits, stolidly eating his way through the box, his small brother watching enviously. Here we are likely to say "You ought not to be so mean. You ought to give your brother some of those chocolates." My own view is that it just does not follow from the truth of this that the brother has any right to any of the chocolates. If the boy refuses to give his brother any, he is greedy, stingy, callous—but not unjust. I suppose that the people I have in mind will say it does follow that the brother has a right to some of the chocolates, and thus that the boy does act unjustly if he refuses to give his brother any. But the effect of saying this is to obscure what we should keep distinct, namely the difference between the boy's refusal in this case and the boy's refusal in the earlier case, in which the box was given to both boys jointly, and in which the small brother thus had what was from any point of view clear title to half.

A further objection to so using the term "right" that from the fact that A ought to do a thing for B, it follows that B has a right against A that A do it for him, is that it is going to make the question of whether or not a man has a right to a thing turn on how easy it is to provide him with it; and this seems not merely unfortunate, but morally unacceptable. Take the case of Henry Fonda again. I said earlier that I had no right to the touch of his cool hand on my fevered brow, even though I needed it to save my life. I said it would be frightfully nice of him to fly in from the West Coast to provide me with it, but that I had no right against him that he should do so. But suppose he isn't on the West Coast. Suppose he has only to walk across the room, place a hand briefly on my brow—and lo, my life is saved. Then surely he ought to do it, it would be indecent to refuse. Is it to be said "Ah, well, it follows that in this case she has a right to the touch of his hand on her brow, and so it would be an injustice in him to refuse"? So that I have a right to it when it is easy for him to provide it, though no right when it's hard? It's rather a shocking idea that anyone's rights should fade away and disappear as it gets harder and harder to accord them to him.

So my own view is that even though you ought to let the violinist use your kidneys for the one hour he needs, we should not conclude that he has a right to do so—we should say that if you refuse, you are, like the boy who owns all the chocolates and will give none away, self-centered and callous, indecent in fact, but not unjust. And similarly, that even supposing a case in which a woman pregnant due to rape ought to allow the unborn person to use her body for the hour he needs, we should not conclude that he has a right to do so; we should conclude that she is self-centered, callous, indecent, but not unjust, if she refuses. The complaints are no less grave; they are just different. However, there is no need to insist on this point. If anyone does wish to deduce "he has a right" from "you ought," then all the same he must surely grant that there are cases in which it is not morally required of you that you allow that violinist to use your kidneys, and in which he does not have a right to use them, and in which you do not do him an injustice if you refuse. And so also for mother and unborn child. Except in such cases as the unborn person has a right to demand it—and we were leaving open the possibility that there may be such cases—nobody is morally *required* to make large sacrifices, of health, of all other interests and concerns, of all other duties and commitments, for nine years, or even for nine months, in order to keep another person alive.

6. We have in fact to distinguish between two kinds of Samaritan: the Good Samaritan and what we might call the Minimally Decent Samaritan. The story of the Good Samaritan, you will remember, goes like this:

> A certain man went down from Jerusalem to Jericho, and fell among thieves, which stripped him of his raiment, and wounded him, and departed, leaving him half dead.
>
> And by chance there came down a certain priest that way; and when he saw him, he passed by on the other side.
>
> And likewise a Levite, when he was at the place, came and looked on him, and passed by on the other side.
>
> But a certain Samaritan, as he journeyed, came where he was; and when he saw him he had compassion on him.
>
> And went to him, and bound up his wounds, pouring in oil and wine, and set him on his own beast, and brought him to an inn, and took care of him.
>
> And on the morrow, when he departed, he took out two pence, and gave them to the host, and said unto him, "Take care of him; and whatsoever thou spendest more, when I come again, I will repay thee." (Luke 10:30–35)

The Good Samaritan went out of his way, at some cost to himself, to help one in need of it. We are not told what the options were, that is, whether or not the priest and the Levite could have helped by doing less than the Good Samaritan did, but assuming they could have, then the fact they did nothing at all shows they were not even Minimally Decent Samaritans, not because they were not Samaritans, but because they were not even minimally decent.

These things are a matter of degree, of course, but there is a difference, and it comes out perhaps most clearly in the story of Kitty Genovese, who, as you will remember, was murdered while thirty-eight people watched or listened, and did nothing at all to help her. A Good Samaritan would have rushed out to give direct assistance against the murderer. Or perhaps we had better allow that it would have been a Splendid Samaritan who did this, on the ground that it would have involved a risk of death for himself. But the thirty-eight not only did not do this, they did not even trouble to pick up a phone to call the police. Minimally Decent Samaritanism would call for doing at least that, and their not having done it was monstrous.

After telling the story of the Good Samaritan, Jesus said "Go, and do thou likewise." Perhaps he meant that we are morally required to act as the Good Samaritan did. Perhaps he was urging people to do more than is morally required of them. At all events it seems plain that it was not morally required of any of the thirty-eight that he rush out to give direct assistance at the risk of his own life, and that it is not morally required of anyone that he give long stretches of his life—nine years or nine months—to sustaining the life of a person who has no special right (we were leaving open the possibility of this) to demand it.

Indeed, with one rather striking class of exceptions, no one in any country in the world is *legally* required to do anywhere near as much as this for anyone else. The class of exceptions is obvious. My main concern here is not the state of the law in respect to abortion, but it is worth drawing attention to the fact that in no state in this country is any man compelled by law to be even a Minimally Decent Samaritan to any person; there is no law under which charges could be brought against the thirty-eight who stood by while Kitty Genovese died. By contrast, in most states in this country women are compelled by law to be not merely Minimally Decent Samaritans, but Good Samaritans to unborn persons inside them. This doesn't by itself settle anything one way or the other, because it may well be argued that there should be laws in this country—as there are in many European countries—compelling at least Minimally Decent Samaritanism.[7] But it does show that there is a gross injustice in the existing state of the law. And it shows also that the groups currently working against liberalization of abortion laws, in fact working toward having it declared unconstitutional for a state to permit abortion, had better start working for the adoption of Good Samaritan laws generally, or earn the charge that they are acting in bad faith.

I should think, myself, that Minimally Decent Samaritan laws would be one thing, Good Samaritan laws quite another, and in fact highly improper. But we are not here concerned with the law. What we should ask is not whether anybody should be compelled by law to be a Good Samaritan, but whether we must accede to a situation in which somebody is being compelled—by nature, perhaps—to be a Good Samaritan. We have, in other words, to look now at third-party interventions. I have been arguing that no person is morally required to make large sacrifices to sustain the life of another who has no right to demand them, and this even where the sacrifices do not include life itself; we are not morally required to be Good Samaritans or anyway Very Good Samaritans to one another. But what if a man cannot extricate himself from such a situation? What if he appeals to us to extricate him? It seems to me plain that there are cases in which we can, cases in which a Good Samaritan would extricate him. There you are, you were kidnapped, and nine years in bed with that violinist lie ahead of you. You have your own life to lead. You are sorry, but you simply cannot see giving up so much of your life to the sustaining of his. You cannot extricate yourself, and ask us to do so. I should have thought that—in light of his having no right to the use of your body—it was obvious that we do not have to accede to your being forced to give up so much. We can do what you ask. There is no injustice to the violinist in our doing so.

7. Following the lead of the opponents of abortion, I have throughout been speaking of the fetus merely as a person, and what I have been asking is whether or not the argument we began with, which proceeds only from the fetus' being a person, really does establish its conclusion. I have argued that it does not.

But of course there are arguments and arguments, and it may be said that I have simply fastened on the wrong one. It may be said that what is important is not merely the fact that the fetus is a person, but that it is a person for whom the woman has a special kind of responsibility issuing from the fact that she is its mother. And it might be argued that all my analogies are therefore irrelevant—for you do not have that special kind of responsibility for that violinist, Henry Fonda does not have that special kind of responsibility for me. And our attention might be drawn to the fact that men and women both *are* compelled by law to provide support for their children.

I have in effect dealt (briefly) with this argument in section 4; but a (still briefer) recapitulation now may be in order. Surely we do not have any such "special responsibility" for a person unless we have assumed it, explicitly or implicitly. If a set of parents do not try to prevent pregnancy, do not obtain an abortion, and then at the time of birth of the child do not put it out for adoption, but rather take it home with them, then they have assumed responsibility for it, they have given it rights, and they cannot *now* withdraw support from it at the cost of its life because they now find it difficult to go on providing for it. But if they have taken all reasonable precautions against having a child, they do not simply by virtue of their biological relationship to the child who comes into existence have a special responsibility for it. They may wish to assume responsibility for it, or they may not wish to. And I am suggesting that if assuming responsibility for it would require large sacrifices, then they may refuse. A Good Samaritan would not refuse—or anyway, a Splendid Samaritan, if the sacrifices that had to be made were enormous. But then so would a Good Samaritan assume responsibility for that violinist; so would Henry Fonda, if he is a Good Samaritan, fly in from the West Coast and assume responsibility for me.

8. My argument will be found unsatisfactory on two counts by many of those who want to regard abortion as morally permissible. First, while I do argue that abortion is not impermissible, I do not argue that it is always permissible. There may well be cases in which carrying the child to term requires only Minimally Decent Samaritanism of the mother, and this is a standard we must not fall below. I am inclined to think it a merit of my account precisely that it does *not* give a general yes or a general no. It allows for and supports our sense that, for example, a sick and desperately frightened fourteen-year-old schoolgirl, pregnant due to rape, may *of course* choose abortion, and that any law which rules this out is an insane law. And it also allows for and supports our sense that in other cases resort to abortion is even positively indecent. It would be indecent in the woman to request an abortion, and indecent in a doctor to perform it, if she is in her seventh month, and wants the abortion just to avoid the nuisance of postponing a trip abroad, The very fact that the arguments I have been drawing attention to treat all cases of abortion, or even all cases of abortion in which the mother's life is not at stake, as morally on a par ought to have made them suspect at the outset.

Secondly, while I am arguing for the permissibility of abortion in some cases, I am not arguing for the right to secure the death of the unborn child. It is easy to confuse these two things in that up to a certain point in the life of the fetus it is not able to survive outside the mother's body; hence removing it from her body guarantees its death. But they are importantly different. I have argued that you are not morally required to spend nine months in bed, sustaining the life of that violinist; but to say this is by no means to say that if, when you unplug yourself, there is a miracle and he survives, you then have a right to turn round and slit his throat. You may detach yourself even if this costs him his life; you have no right to be guaranteed his death, by some other means, if unplugging yourself does not kill him. There are some people who will feel dissatisfied by this feature of my argument. A woman may be utterly devastated by the thought of a child, a bit of herself, put out for adoption and never seen or heard of again. She may therefore want not merely that the child be detached from her, but more, that it die. Some opponents of abortion are inclined to regard this as beneath contempt—thereby showing insensitivity to what is surely a powerful source of despair. All the same, I agree that the desire for the child's death is not one which anybody may gratify, should it turn out to be possible to detach the child alive.

At this place, however, it should be remembered that we have only been pretending throughout that the fetus is a human being from the moment of conception. A very early abortion is surely not the killing of a person, and so is not dealt with by anything I have said here.

NOTES

I am very much indebted to James Thomson for discussion, criticism, and many helpful suggestions.

1. Daniel Callahan, *Abortion: Law, Choice and Morality* (New York, 1970), p. 373. This book gives a fascinating survey of the available information on abortion. The Jewish tradition is surveyed in David M. Feldman, *Birth Control in Jewish Law* (New York, 1968), Part 5, the Catholic tradition in John T. Noonan, Jr., "An Almost Absolute Value in History," in *The Morality of Abortion*, ed. John T. Noonan, Jr. (Cambridge, Mass., 1970).

2. The term "direct" in the arguments I refer to is a technical one. Roughly, what is meant by "direct killing" is either killing as an end in itself, or killing as a means to some end, for example, the end of saving someone else's life. See note 5 for an example of its use.

3. Cf. *Encyclical Letter of Pope Pius XI on Christian Marriage,* St. Paul Editions (Boston, n.d.), p. 32: "however much we may pity the mother whose health and even life is gravely imperiled in the performance of the duty allotted to her by nature, nevertheless what could ever be a sufficient reason for excusing in any way the direct murder of the innocent? This is precisely what we are dealing with here." Noonan (*The Morality of Abortion*, p. 43) reads this as follows: "What cause can ever avail to excuse in any way the direct killing of the innocent? For it is a question of that."

4. The thesis in (4) is in an interesting way weaker than those in (1), (2), and (3): they rule out abortion even in cases in which both mother *and* child will die if the abortion is not performed. By contrast, one who held the view expressed in (4) could consistently say that one needn't prefer letting two persons die to killing one.

5. Cf. the following passage from Pius XII, *Address to the Italian Catholic Society of Midwives:* "The baby in the maternal breast has the right to life immediately from God.— Hence there is no man, no human authority, no science, no medical, eugenic, social, economic or moral 'indication' which can establish or grant a valid juridical ground for a direct deliberate position of an innocent human life, that is a disposition which looks to its destruction either as an end or as a means to another end perhaps in itself not illicit.— The baby, still not born, is a man in the same degree and for the same reason as the mother" (quoted in Noonan, *The Morality of Abortion*, p. 45).

6. The need for a discussion of this argument was brought home to me by members of the Society for Ethical and Legal Philosophy, to whom this paper was originally presented.

7. For a discussion of the difficulties involved, and a survey of the European experience with such laws, see *The Good Samaritan and the Law,* ed. James M. Ratcliffe (New York, 1966).

Why Abortion Is Immoral

DON MARQUIS

Marquis first identifies what it is that makes murder wrong, then applies this understanding to the case of abortion. He argues that murdering someone is wrong because it robs him or her of a future—a loss of all possible "experiences, activities, projects, and enjoyments." Likewise, abortion is almost always wrong because it deprives the fetus of all prospects of such future experiencing and being.

The view that abortion is, with rare exceptions, seriously immoral has received little support in the recent philosophical literature. No doubt most philosophers affiliated with secular institutions of higher education believe that the anti-abortion position is either a symptom of irrational religious dogma or a conclusion generated by seriously confused philosophical argument. The purpose of this essay is to undermine this general belief. This essay sets out an argument that purports to show, as well as any argument in ethics can show, that abortion is, except possibly in rare cases, seriously immoral,

From *Journal of Philosophy*, LXXXVI, 4 (April 1989), pp. 183–202. Reprinted with permission of the Journal of Philosophy, Inc. and the author.

that it is in the same moral category as killing an innocent adult human being.

The argument is based on a major assumption. Many of the most insightful and careful writers on the ethics of abortion—such as Joel Feinberg, Michael Tooley, Mary Anne Warren, H. Tristram Engelhardt, Jr, L. W. Sumner, John T. Noonan, Jr, and Philip Devine[1]—believe that whether or not abortion is morally permissible stands or falls on whether or not a fetus is the sort of being whose life it is seriously wrong to end. The argument of this essay will assume, but not argue, that they are correct.

Also, this essay will neglect issues of great importance to a complete ethics of abortion. Some anti-abortionists will allow that certain abortions, such as abortion before implantation or abortion when the life of a woman is threatened by a pregnancy or abortion after rape, may be morally permissible. This essay will not explore the casuistry of these hard cases. The purpose of this essay is to develop a general argument for the claim that the overwhelming majority of deliberate abortions are seriously immoral.

I

A sketch of standard anti-abortion and pro-choice arguments exhibits how those arguments possess certain symmetries that explain why partisans of those positions are so convinced of the correctness of their own positions, why they are not successful in convincing their opponents, and why, to others, this issue seems to be unresolvable. An analysis of the nature of this standoff suggests a strategy for surmounting it.

Consider the way a typical anti-abortionist argues. She will argue or assert that life is present from the moment of conception or that fetuses look like babies or that fetuses possess a characteristic such as a genetic code that is both necessary and sufficient for being human. Anti-abortionists seem to believe that (1) the truth of all of these claims is quite obvious, and (2) establishing any of these claims is sufficient to show that abortion is morally akin to murder.

A standard pro-choice strategy exhibits similarities. The pro-choicer will argue or assert that fetuses are not persons or that fetuses are not rational agents or that fetuses are not social beings. Pro-choicers seem to believe that (1) the truth of any of these claims is quite obvious, and (2) establishing any of these claims is sufficient to show that an abortion is not a wrongful killing.

In fact, both the pro-choice and the anti-abortion claims do seem to be true, although the "it looks like a baby" claim is more difficult to establish the earlier the pregnancy. We seem to have a standoff. How can it be resolved?

As everyone who has taken a bit of logic knows, if any of these arguments concerning abortion is a good argument, it requires not only some claim characterizing fetuses, but also some general moral principle that ties a characteristic of fetuses to having or not having the right to life or to some other moral characteristic that will generate the obligation or the lack of obligation not to end the life of a fetus. Accordingly, the arguments of the anti-abortionist and the pro-choicer need a bit of filling in to be regarded as adequate.

Note what each partisan will say. The anti-abortionist will claim that her position is supported by such generally accepted moral principles as "It is always prima facie seriously wrong to take a human life" or "It is always prima facie seriously wrong to end the life of a baby." Since these are generally accepted moral principles, her position is certainly not obviously wrong. The pro-choicer will claim that her position is supported by such plausible moral principles as "Being a person is what gives an individual intrinsic moral worth" or "It is only seriously prima facie wrong to take the life of a member of the human community." Since these are generally accepted moral principles, the pro-choice position is certainly not obviously wrong. Unfortunately, we have again arrived at a standoff.

Now, how might one deal with this standoff? The standard approach is to try to show how the moral principles of one's opponent lose their plausibility under analysis. It is easy to see how this is possible. On the one hand, the anti-abortionist will defend a moral principle concerning the wrongness of killing which tends to be broad in scope in order that even fetuses at an early stage of pregnancy will fall under it. The problem with broad principles is that they often embrace too much. In this particular instance, the principle "It is always prima facie wrong to take a human life" seems to entail that it is wrong to end the existence of a living human cancer-cell culture, on the grounds that the culture is both living and human. Therefore, it seems that the anti-abortionist's favored principle is too broad.

On the other hand, the pro-choicer wants to find a moral principle concerning the wrongness of killing which tends to be narrow in scope in order that fetuses will *not* fall under it. The problem with narrow principles is that they often do not embrace enough. Hence, the needed principles such as "It is prima facie seriously wrong to kill only persons" or "It is prima facie wrong to kill only rational agents" do not explain why it is wrong to kill infants or young children or the severely retarded or even perhaps the severely mentally ill. Therefore, we seem again to have a standoff. The anti-abortionist charges, not unreasonably, that pro-choice principles concerning killing are too narrow to be acceptable; the pro-choicer charges, not unreasonably, that anti-abortionist principles concerning killing are too broad to be acceptable.

Attempts by both sides to patch up the difficulties in their positions run into further difficulties. The anti-abortionist will try to remove the problem in her position by reformulating her principle concerning killing in terms of human beings. Now we end up with: "It is always prima facie seriously wrong to end the life of a human being." This principle has the advantage of avoiding the problem of the human cancer-cell culture counterexample. But this advantage is purchased at a high price. For although it is clear that a fetus is both human and alive, it is not at all clear that a fetus is a human *being*. There is at least something to be said for the view that something becomes a human being only after a process of development, and that therefore first trimester fetuses and perhaps all fetuses are not yet human beings. Hence, the anti-abortionist, by this move, has merely exchanged one problem for another.[2]

The pro-choicer fares no better. She may attempt to find reasons why killing infants, young children, and the severely retarded is wrong which are independent of her major principle that is supposed to explain the wrongness of taking human life, but which will not also make abortion immoral. This is no easy task. Appeals to social utility will seem satisfactory only to those who resolve not to think of the enormous difficulties with a utilitarian account of the wrongness of killing and the significant social costs of preserving the lives of the unproductive.[3] A pro-choice strategy that extends the definition of "person" to infants or even to young children seems just as arbitrary as an anti-abortion strategy that extends the definition of "human being" to fetuses. Again, we find symmetries in the two positions and we arrive at a standoff.

There are even further problems that reflect symmetries in the two positions. In addition to counterexample problems, or the arbitrary application problems that can be exchanged for them, the standard anti-abortionist principle "It is prima facie seriously wrong to kill a human being," or one of its variants, can be objected to on the grounds of ambiguity. If "human being" is taken to be a *biological* category, then the anti-abortionist is left with the problem of explaining why a merely biological category should make a moral difference. Why, it is asked, is it any more reasonable to base a moral conclusion on the number of chromosomes in one's cells than on the color of one's skin?[4] If "human being," on the other hand, is taken to be a *moral* category, then the claim that a fetus is a human being cannot be taken to be a premise in the anti-abortion argument, for it is precisely what needs to be established. Hence, either the anti-abortionist's main category is a morally irrelevant, merely biological category, or it is of no use to the anti-abortionist in establishing (noncircularly, of course) that abortion is wrong.

Although this problem with the anti-abortionist position is often noticed, it is less often noticed that the pro-choice position suffers from an analogous problem. The principle "Only persons have the right to life" also suffers from an ambiguity. The term "person" is typically defined in terms of psychological characteristics, although there will certainly be disagreement concerning which characteristics are most important. Supposing that this matter can be settled, the pro-choicer is left with the problem of explaining why *psychological* characteristics should make a *moral* difference. If the pro-choicer should attempt to deal with this problem by claiming that an explanation is not necessary, that in fact we do treat such a cluster of psychological properties as having moral significance, the sharp-witted anti-abortionist should have a ready response. We do treat being both living and human as having moral significance. If it is legitimate for the pro-choicer to demand that the anti-abortionist provide an explanation of the connection between the biological character of being a human being and the wrongness of being killed (even though people accept this connection), then it is legitimate for the anti-abortionist to demand that the pro-choicer provide an explanation of the connection between psychological criteria for being a person and the wrongness of being killed (even though that connection is accepted).[5]

Feinberg has attempted to meet this objection (he calls psychological personhood "commonsense personhood"):

> The characteristics that confer commonsense personhood are not arbitrary bases for rights and duties, such as race, sex or species membership; rather they are traits that make sense out of rights and duties and without which those moral attributes would have no point or function. It is because people are conscious; have a sense of their personal identities; have plans, goals, and projects; experience emotions; are liable to pains, anxieties, and frustrations; can reason and bargain, and so on—it is because of these attributes that people have values and interests, desires and expectations of their own, including a stake in their own futures, and a personal well-being of a sort we cannot ascribe to unconscious or nonrational beings. Because of their developed capacities they can assume duties and responsibilities and can have and make claims on one another. Only because of their sense of self, their life plans, their value hierarchies, and their stakes in their own futures can they be ascribed fundamental rights. There is nothing arbitrary about these linkages. ("Abortion," p. 270)

The plausible aspects of this attempt should not be taken to obscure its implausible features. There is a great deal to be said for the view that being a psychological person under some description is a necessary condition for having duties. One cannot

have a duty unless one is capable of behaving morally, and a being's capability of behaving morally will require having a certain psychology. It is far from obvious, however, that having rights entails consciousness or rationality, as Feinberg suggests. We speak of the rights of the severely retarded or the severely mentally ill, yet some of these persons are not rational. We speak of the rights of the temporarily unconscious. The New Jersey Supreme Court based their decision in the Quinlan case on Karen Ann Quinlan's right to privacy, and she was known to be permanently unconscious at that time. Hence, Feinberg's claim that having rights entails being conscious is, on its face, obviously false.

Of course, it might not make sense to attribute rights to a being that would never in its natural history have certain psychological traits. This modest connection between psychological personhood and moral personhood will create a place for Karen Ann Quinlan and the temporarily unconscious. But then it makes a place for fetuses also. Hence, it does not serve Feinberg's pro-choice purposes. Accordingly, it seems that the pro-choicer will have as much difficulty bridging the gap between psychological personhood and personhood in the moral sense as the anti-abortionist has bridging the gap between being a biological human being and being a human being in the moral sense.

Furthermore, the pro-choicer cannot any more escape her problem by making person a purely moral category than the anti-abortionist could escape by the analogous move. For if person is a moral category, then the pro-choicer is left without the resources for establishing (noncircularly, of course) the claim that a fetus is not a person, which is an essential premise in her argument. Again, we have both a symmetry and a standoff between pro-choice and anti-abortion views.

Passions in the abortion debate run high. There are both plausibilities and difficulties with the standard positions. Accordingly, it is hardly surprising that partisans of either side embrace with fervor the moral generalizations that support the conclusions they preanalytically favor, and reject with disdain the moral generalizations of their opponents as being subject to inescapable difficulties. It is easy to believe that the counterexamples to one's own moral principles are merely temporary difficulties that will dissolve in the wake of further philosophical research, and that the counterexamples to the principles of one's opponents are as straightforward as the contradiction between *A* and *O* propositions in traditional logic. This might suggest to an impartial observer (if there are any) that the abortion issue is unresolvable.

There is a way out of this apparent dialectical quandary. The moral generalizations of both sides are not quite correct. The generalizations hold for the most part, for the usual cases. This suggests that they are all *accidental* generalizations, that the moral claims made by those on both sides of the dispute do not touch on the *essence* of the matter.

This use of the distinction between essence and accident is not meant to invoke obscure metaphysical categories. Rather, it is intended to reflect the rather atheoretical nature of the abortion discussion. If the generalization a partisan in the abortion dispute adopts were derived from the reason why ending the life of a human being is wrong, then there could not be exceptions to that generalization unless some special case obtains in which there are even more powerful countervailing reasons. Such generalizations would not be merely accidental generalizations; they would point to, or be based upon, the essence of the wrongness of killing, what it is that makes killing wrong. All this suggests that a necessary condition of resolving the abortion controversy is a more theoretical account of the wrongness of killing. After all, if we merely believe, but do not understand, why killing adult human beings such as ourselves is wrong, how could we conceivably show that abortion is either immoral or permissible?

II

In order to develop such an account, we can start from the following unproblematic assumption concerning our own case: it is wrong to kill *us*. Why is it wrong? Some answers can be easily eliminated. It might be said that what makes killing us wrong is that a killing brutalizes the one who kills. But the brutalization consists of being inured to the performance of an act that is hideously immoral; hence, the brutalization does not explain the immorality.

It might be said that what makes killing us wrong is the great loss others would experience due to our absence. Although such hubris is understandable, such an explanation does not account for the wrongness of killing hermits, or those whose lives are relatively independent and whose friends find it easy to make new friends.

A more obvious answer is better. What primarily makes killing wrong is neither its effect on the murderer nor its effect on the victim's friends and relatives, but its effect on the victim. The loss of one's life is one of the greatest losses one can suffer. The loss of one's life deprives one of all the experiences, activities, projects, and enjoyments that would otherwise have constituted one's future. Therefore, killing someone is wrong, primarily because the killing inflicts (one of) the greatest possible losses on the victim. To describe this as the loss of life can be misleading, however. The change in my biological state does not by itself make killing me wrong. The effect of the loss of my biological life is the loss to me of all those activities, projects, experiences, and enjoyments which would otherwise have constituted my future personal life. These activities, projects, experiences, and enjoyments are either valuable for their own sakes or are means to something else that is valuable for its own sake. Some parts of my future are not valued by me now, but will come to be valued by me as I grow older and as my values and capacities change. When I am killed, I am deprived both of what I now value which would have been part of my future personal life, but also what I would come to value. Therefore, when I die, I am deprived of all of the value of my future. Inflicting this loss on me is ultimately what makes killing me wrong. This being the case, it would seem that what makes killing *any* adult human being prima facie seriously wrong is the loss of his or her future.[6]

How should this rudimentary theory of the wrongness of killing be evaluated? It cannot be faulted for deriving an "ought" from an "is," for it does not. The analysis assumes that killing me (or you, reader) is prima facie seriously wrong. The point of the analysis is to establish which natural property ultimately explains the wrongness of the killing, given that it is wrong. A natural property will ultimately explain the wrongness of killing, only if (1) the explanation fits with our intuitions about the matter and (2) there is no other natural property that provides the basis for a better explanation of the wrongness of killing. This analysis rests on the intuition that what makes killing a particular human or animal wrong is what it does to that particular human or animal. What makes killing wrong is some natural effect or other of the killing. Some would deny this. For instance, a divine-command theorist in ethics would deny it. Surely this denial is, however, one of those features of divine-command theory which renders it so implausible.

The claim that what makes killing wrong is the loss of the victim's future is directly supported by two considerations. In the first place, this theory explains why we regard killing as one of the worst of crimes. Killing is especially wrong, because it deprives the victim of more than perhaps any other crime. In the second place, people with AIDS or cancer who know they are dying believe, of course, that dying is a very bad thing for them. They believe that the loss of a future to them that they would otherwise have experienced is what makes their premature death a very bad thing for them. A better theory of the wrongness of killing would require a different natural property associated with killing which better fits with the attitudes of the dying. What could it be?

The view that what makes killing wrong is the loss to the victim of the value of the victim's future gains additional support when some of its implications are examined. In the first place, it is incompatible with the view that it is wrong to kill only beings who are biologically human. It is possible that there exists a different species from another planet whose members have a future like ours. Since having a future like that is what makes killing someone wrong, this theory entails that it would be wrong to kill members of such a species. Hence, this theory is opposed to the claim that only life that is biologically human has great moral worth, a claim which many anti-abortionists have seemed to adopt. This opposition, which this theory has in common with personhood theories, seems to be a merit of the theory.

In the second place, the claim that the loss of one's future is the wrong-making feature of one's being killed entails the possibility that the futures of some actual nonhuman mammals on our own planet are sufficiently like ours that it is seriously wrong to kill them also. Whether some animals do have the same right to life as human beings depends on adding to the account of the wrongness of killing some additional account of just what it is about my future or the futures of other adult human beings which makes it wrong to kill us. No such additional account will be offered in this essay. Undoubtedly, the provision of such an account would be a very difficult matter. Undoubtedly, any such account would be quite controversial. Hence, it surely should not reflect badly on this sketch of an elementary theory of the wrongness of killing that it is indeterminate with respect to some very difficult issues regarding animal rights.

In the third place, the claim that the loss of one's future is the wrong-making feature of one's being killed does not entail, as sanctity of human life theories do, that active euthanasia is wrong. Persons who are severely and incurably ill, who face a future of pain and despair, and who wish to die will not have suffered a loss if they are killed. It is, strictly speaking, the value of a human's future which makes killing wrong in this theory. This being so, killing does not necessarily wrong some persons who are sick and dying. Of course, there may be other reasons for a prohibition of active euthanasia, but that is another matter. Sanctity-of-human-life theories seem to hold that active euthanasia is seriously wrong even in an individual case where there seems to be good reason for it independently of public policy considerations. This consequence is most implausible, and it is a plus for the claim that the loss of a future of value is what makes killing wrong that it does not share this consequence.

In the fourth place, the account of the wrongness of killing defended in this essay does straightforwardly entail that it is prima facie seriously wrong to kill children and infants, for we do presume that they have futures of value. Since we do believe that it is wrong to kill defenseless little babies, it is important that a theory of the wrongness of killing easily account for this. Personhood theories of the wrongness of killing, on the other hand, cannot straightforwardly account for the wrongness of killing infants and young children.[7] Hence, such theories must add special ad hoc accounts of the wrongness of killing the young. The plausibility of such ad hoc theories seems to be a function of how desperately one wants such theories to work. The claim that the primary wrong-making feature of a killing is the loss to the victim of the value of its future accounts for the wrongness of killing young children and infants directly; it makes the wrongness of such acts as obvious as we actually think it is. This is a further merit of this theory. Accordingly, it seems that this value of a future-like-ours theory of the wrongness of killing shares strengths of both sanctity-of-life and personhood accounts while avoiding weaknesses of both. In addition, it meshes with a central intuition concerning what makes killing wrong.

The claim that the primary wrong-making feature of a killing is the loss to the victim of the value of its future has obvious consequences for the ethics of abortion. The future of a standard fetus includes a set of experiences, projects, activities, and such which are identical with the futures of adult human beings and are identical with the futures of young children. Since the reason that is sufficient to explain why it is wrong to kill human beings after the time of birth is a reason that also applies to fetuses, it follows that abortion is prima facie seriously morally wrong.

This argument does not rely on the invalid inference that, since it is wrong to kill persons, it is wrong to kill potential persons also. The category that is morally central to this analysis is the category of having a valuable future like ours; it is not the category of personhood. The argument to the conclusion that abortion is prima facie seriously morally wrong proceeded independently of the notion of person or potential person or any equivalent. Someone may wish to start with this analysis in terms of the value of a human future, conclude that abortion is, except perhaps in rare circumstances, seriously morally wrong, infer that fetuses have the right to life, and then call fetuses "persons" as a result of their having the right to life. Clearly, in this case, the category of person is being used to state the *conclusion* of the analysis

rather than to generate the *argument* of the analysis.

The structure of this anti-abortion argument can be both illuminated and defended by comparing it to what appears to be the best argument for the wrongness of the wanton infliction of pain on animals. This latter argument is based on the assumption that it is prima facie wrong to inflict pain on me (or you, reader). What is the natural property associated with the infliction of pain which makes such infliction wrong? The obvious answer seems to be that the infliction of pain causes suffering and that suffering is a misfortune. The suffering caused by the infliction of pain is what makes the wanton infliction of pain on me wrong. The wanton infliction of pain on other adult humans causes suffering. The wanton infliction of pain on animals causes suffering. Since causing suffering is what makes the wanton infliction of pain wrong and since the wanton infliction of pain on animals causes suffering, it follows that the wanton infliction of pain on animals is wrong.

This argument for the wrongness of the wanton infliction of pain on animals shares a number of structural features with the argument for the serious prima facie wrongness of abortion. Both arguments start with an obvious assumption concerning what it is wrong to do to me (or you, reader). Both then look for the characteristic or the consequence of the wrong action which makes the action wrong. Both recognize that the wrong-making feature of these immoral actions is a property of actions sometimes directed at individuals other than postnatal human beings. If the structure of the argument for the wrongness of the wanton infliction of pain on animals is sound, then the structure of the argument for the prima facie serious wrongness of abortion is also sound, for the structure of the two arguments is the same. The structure common to both is the key to the explanation of how the wrongness of abortion can be demonstrated without recourse to the category of person. In neither argument is that category crucial.

This defense of an argument for the wrongness of abortion in terms of a structurally similar argument for the wrongness of the wanton infliction of pain on animals succeeds only if the account regarding animals is the correct account. Is it? In the first place, it seems plausible. In the second place, its major competition is Kant's account. Kant believed that we do not have direct duties to animals at all, because they are not persons. Hence, Kant had to explain and justify the wrongness of inflicting pain on animals on the grounds that "he who is hard in his dealings with animals becomes hard also in his dealing with men."[8] The problem with Kant's account is that there seems to be no reason for accepting this latter claim unless Kant's account is rejected. If the alternative to Kant's account is accepted, then it is easy to understand why someone who is indifferent to inflicting pain on animals is also indifferent to inflicting pain on humans, for one is indifferent to what makes inflicting pain wrong in both cases. But, if Kant's account is accepted, there is no intelligible reason why one who is hard in his dealings with animals (or crabgrass or stones) should also be hard in his dealings with men. After all, men are persons: animals are no more persons than crabgrass or stones. Persons are Kant's crucial moral category. Why, in short, should a Kantian accept the basic claim in Kant's argument?

Hence, Kant's argument for the wrongness of inflicting pain on animals rests on a claim that, in a world of Kantian moral agents, is demonstrably false. Therefore, the alternative analysis, being more plausible anyway, should be accepted. Since this alternative analysis has the same structure as the anti-abortion argument being defended here, we have further support for the argument for the immorality of abortion being defended in this essay.

Of course, this value of a future-like-ours argument, if sound, shows only that abortion is prima facie wrong, not that it is wrong in any and all circumstances. Since the loss of the future to a standard fetus, if killed, is, however, at least as great a loss as the loss of the future to a standard adult human being who is killed, abortion, like ordinary killing, could be justified only by the most compelling reasons. The loss of one's life is almost the greatest misfortune that can happen to one. Presumably abortion could be justified in some circumstances, only if the loss consequent on failing to abort would be at least as great. Accordingly, morally permissible abortions will be rare indeed unless, perhaps, they occur so early in pregnancy that a fetus is not yet definitely an individual. Hence, this argument should be taken as showing that abortion is presumptively very seriously wrong, where the presumption is very strong—as strong as the presumption that killing another adult human being is wrong.

III

How complete an account of the wrongness of killing does the value of a future-like-ours account have to be in order that the wrongness of abortion is a consequence? This account does not have to be an account of the necessary conditions for the wrongness of killing. Some persons in nursing homes may lack valuable human futures, yet it may be wrong to kill them for other reasons. Furthermore, this account does not obviously have to be the sole reason killing is wrong where the victim did have a valuable future. This analysis claims only that, for any killing where the victim did have a valuable future like ours, having that future by itself is sufficient to create the strong presumption that the killing is seriously wrong.

One way to overturn the value of a future-like-ours argument would be to find some account of the wrongness of killing which is at least as intelligible and which has different implications for the ethics of abortion. Two rival accounts possess at least some degree of plausibility. One account is based on the obvious fact that people value the experience of living and wish for that valuable experience to continue. Therefore, it might be said, what makes killing wrong is the discontinuation of that experience for the victim. Let us call this the *discontinuation account*.[9] Another rival account is based upon the obvious fact that people strongly desire to continue to live. This suggests that what makes killing us so wrong is that it interferes with the fulfillment of a strong and fundamental desire, the fulfillment of which is necessary for the fulfillment of any other desires we might have. Let us call this the *desire account*.[10]

Consider first the desire account as a rival account of the ethics of killing which would provide the basis for rejecting the anti-abortion position. Such an account will have to be stronger than the value of a future-like-ours account of the wrongness of abortion if it is to do the job expected of it.

To entail the wrongness of abortion, the value of a future-like-ours account has only to provide a sufficient, but not a necessary, condition for the wrongness of killing. The desire account, on the other hand, must provide us also with a necessary condition for the wrongness of killing in order to generate a pro-choice conclusion on abortion. The reason for this is that presumably the argument from the desire account moves from the claim that what makes killing wrong is interference with a very strong desire to the claim that abortion is not wrong because the fetus lacks a strong desire to live. Obviously, this inference fails if someone's having the desire to live is not a necessary condition of its being wrong to kill that individual.

One problem with the desire account is that we do regard it as seriously wrong to kill persons who have little desire to live or who have no desire to live or, indeed, have a desire not to live. We believe it is seriously wrong to kill the unconscious, the sleeping, those who are tired of life, and those who are suicidal. The value-of-a-human-future account renders standard morality intelligible in these cases; these cases appear to be incompatible with the desire account.

The desire account is subject to a deeper difficulty. We desire life, because we value the goods of this life. The goodness of life is not secondary to our desire for it. If this were not so, the pain of one's own premature death could be done away with merely by an appropriate alteration in the configuration of one's desires. This is absurd. Hence, it would seem that it is the loss of the goods of one's future, not the interference with the fulfillment of a strong desire to live, which accounts ultimately for the wrongness of killing.

It is worth noting that, if the desire account is modified so that it does not provide a necessary, but only a sufficient, condition for the wrongness of killing, the desire account is compatible with the value of a future-like-ours account. The combined accounts will yield an anti-abortion ethic. This suggests that one can retain what is intuitively plausible about the desire account without a challenge to the basic argument of this paper.

It is also worth noting that, if future desires have moral force in a modified desire account of the wrongness of killing, one can find support for an anti-abortion ethic even in the absence of a value of a future-like-ours account. If one decides that a morally relevant property, the possession of which is sufficient to make it wrong to kill some individual, is the desire at some future time to live—one might decide to justify one's refusal to kill suicidal teenagers on these grounds, for example—then, since typical fetuses will have the desire in the future to live, it is wrong to kill typical fetuses. Accordingly, it does not seem that a desire account of the wrongness of killing can provide a justification of a pro-choice ethic of abortion which is nearly as adequate as the value of a human-future justification of an anti-abortion ethic.

The discontinuation account looks more promising as an account of the wrongness of killing. It seems just as intelligible as the value of a future-like-ours account, but it does not justify an anti-abortion position. Obviously, if it is the continuation of one's activities, experiences, and projects, the loss of which makes killing wrong, then it is not wrong to kill fetuses for that reason, for fetuses do not have experiences, activities, and projects to be continued or discontinued. Accordingly, the discontinuation account does not have the anti-abortion consequences that the value of a future-like-ours account has. Yet, it seems as intelligible as the value of a future-like-ours account, for when we think of what would be wrong with our being killed, it does seem as if it is the discontinuation of what makes our lives worthwhile which makes killing us wrong.

Is the discontinuation account just as good an account as the value of a future-like-ours account? The discontinuation account will not be adequate at all, if it does not refer to the *value* of the experience that may be discontinued. One does not want the discontinuation account to make it wrong to kill a patient who begs for death and who is in severe pain that cannot be relieved short of killing. (I leave open the question of whether it is wrong for other reasons.) Accordingly, the discontinuation account must be more than a bare discontinuation account. It must make some reference to the positive value of the patient's experiences. But, by the same token, the value of a future-like-ours account cannot be a bare future account either. Just having a future surely does not itself rule out killing the above patient. This account must make some reference to the value of the patient's future experiences and projects also. Hence, both accounts involve the value of experiences, projects, and activities. So far we still have symmetry between the accounts.

The symmetry fades, however, when we focus on the time period of the value of the experiences, etc., which has moral consequences. Although both accounts leave open the possibility that the patient in our example may be killed, this possibility is left open only in virtue of the utterly bleak future for the patient. It makes no difference whether the patient's immediate past contains intolerable pain, or consists in being in a coma (which we can imagine is a situation of indifference), or consists in a life of value. If the patient's future is a future of value, we want our account to make it wrong to kill the patient. If the patient's future is intolerable, whatever his or her immediate past, we want our account to allow killing the patient. Obviously, then, it is the value of that patient's future which is doing the work in rendering the morality of killing the patient intelligible.

This being the case, it seems clear that whether one has immediate past experiences or not does no work in the explanation of what makes killing wrong. The addition the discontinuation account makes to the value of a human future account is otiose. Its addition to the value-of-a-future account plays no role at all in rendering intelligible the wrongness of killing. Therefore, it can be discarded with the discontinuation account of which it is a part.

IV

The analysis of the previous section suggests that alternative general accounts of the wrongness of killing are either inadequate or unsuccessful in getting around the anti-abortion consequences of the value of a future-like-ours argument. A different strategy for avoiding these anti-abortion consequences involves limiting the scope of the value of a future argument. More precisely, the strategy involves arguing that fetuses lack a property that is essential for the value-of-a-future argument (or for any anti-abortion argument) to apply to them.

One move of this sort is based upon the claim that a necessary condition of one's future being valuable is that one values it. Value implies a valuer. Given this one might argue that, since fetuses cannot value their futures, their futures are not valuable to them. Hence, it does not seriously wrong them deliberately to end their lives.

This move fails, however, because of some ambiguities. Let us assume that something cannot be of value unless it is valued by someone. This does not entail that my life is of no value unless it is valued by me. I may think, in a period of despair, that my future is of no worth whatsoever, but I may be wrong because others rightly see value—even great value—in it. Furthermore, my future can be valuable to me even if I do not value it. This is the case when a young person attempts suicide, but is rescued and goes on to significant human achievements. Such young people's futures are ultimately valuable to them, even though such futures do not seem to be valuable to them at the moment of attempted suicide. A fetus's future can be valuable to it in the same way. Accordingly, this attempt to limit the anti-abortion argument fails.

Another similar attempt to reject the anti-abortion position is based on Tooley's claim that an entity cannot possess the right to life unless it has the capacity to desire its continued existence. It follows that, since fetuses lack the conceptual capacity to desire to continue to live, they lack the right to life. Accordingly, Tooley concludes that abortion cannot be seriously prima facie wrong.

What could be the evidence for Tooley's basic claim? Tooley once argued that individuals have a prima facie right to what they desire and that the lack of the capacity to desire something undercuts the basis of one's right to it. This argument plainly will not succeed in the context of the analysis of this essay, however, since the point here is to establish the fetus's right to life on other grounds. Tooley's argument assumes that the right to life cannot be established in general on some basis other than the desire for life. This position was considered and rejected in the preceding section of this paper.

One might attempt to defend Tooley's basic claim on the grounds that, because a fetus cannot apprehend continued life as a benefit, its continued life cannot be a benefit or cannot be something it has a right to or cannot be something that is in its interest. This might be defended in terms of the general proposition that, if an individual is literally incapable of caring about or taking an interest in some X, then one does not have a right to X or X is not a benefit or X is not something that is in one's interest.[11]

Each member of this family of claims seems to be open to objections. As John C. Stevens[12] has pointed out, one may have a right to be treated with a certain medical procedure (because of a health insurance policy one has purchased), even though one cannot conceive of the nature of the procedure. And, as Tooley himself has pointed out, persons who have been indoctrinated, or drugged, or rendered temporarily unconscious may be literally incapable of caring about or taking an interest in something that is in their interest or is something to which they have a right, or is something that benefits them. Hence, the Tooley claim that would restrict the scope of the value of a future-like-ours argument is undermined by counterexamples.[13]

Finally, Paul Bassen[14] has argued that, even though the prospects of an embryo might seem to be a basis for the wrongness of abortion, an embryo cannot be a victim and therefore cannot be wronged. An embryo cannot be a victim, he says, because it lacks sentience. His central argument for this seems to be that, even though plants and the permanently unconscious are alive, they clearly cannot be victims. What is the explanation of this? Bassen claims that the explanation is that their lives consist of mere metabolism and mere metabolism is not enough to ground victimizability. Mentation is required.

The problem with this attempt to establish the absence of victimizability is that both plants and the permanently unconscious clearly lack what Bassen calls "prospects" or what I have called "a future life like ours." Hence, it is surely open to one to argue that the real reason we believe plants and the permanently unconscious cannot be victims is that kill-ing them cannot deprive them of a future life like ours; the real reason is not their absence of present mentation.

Bassen recognizes that his view is subject to this difficulty, and he recognizes that the case of children seems to support this difficulty, for "much of what we do for children is based on prospects." He argues, however, that, in the case of children and in other such cases, "potentiality comes into play only where victimizability has been secured on other grounds" (p. 333).

Bassen's defense of his view is patently question-begging, since what is adequate to secure victimizability is exactly what is at issue. His examples do not support his own view against the thesis of this essay. Of course, embryos can be victims: when their lives are deliberately terminated, they are deprived of their futures of value, their prospects. This makes them victims, for it directly wrongs them.

The seeming plausibility of Bassen's view stems from the fact that paradigmatic cases of imagining someone as a victim involve empathy, and empathy requires mentation of the victim. The victims of flood, famine, rape, or child abuse are all persons with whom we can empathize. That empathy seems to be part of seeing them as victims.[15]

In spite of the strength of these examples, the attractive intuition that a situation in which there is victimization requires the possibility of empathy is subject to counterexamples. Consider a case that Bassen himself offers: "Posthumous obliteration of an author's work constitutes a misfortune for him only if he had wished his work to endure" (p. 318). The conditions Bassen wishes to impose upon the possibility of being victimized here seem far too strong. Perhaps this author, due to his unrealistic standards of excellence and his low self-esteem, regarded his work as unworthy of survival, even though it possessed genuine literary merit. Destruction of such work would surely victimize its author. In such a case, empathy with the victim concerning the loss is clearly impossible.

Of course, Bassen does not make the possibility of empathy a necessary condition of victimizability; he requires only mentation. Hence, on Bassen's actual view, this author, as I have described him, can be a victim. The problem is that the basic intuition that renders Bassen's view plausible is missing in the author's case. In order to attempt to avoid counterexamples, Bassen has made his thesis too weak to be supported by the intuitions that suggested it.

Even so, the mentation requirement on victimiz-ability is still subject to counterexamples. Suppose a severe accident renders me totally unconscious for a month, after which I recover. Surely killing me while I am unconscious victimizes me, even though I am incapable of mentation during that time. It follows that Bassen's thesis fails. Apparently, attempts to restrict the value of a future-like-ours argument so that fetuses do not fall within its scope do not succeed.

V

In this essay, it has been argued that the correct ethic of the wrongness of killing can be extended to fetal life and used to show that there is a strong presumption that any abortion is morally impermissible. If the ethic of killing adopted here entails, however, that contraception is also seriously immoral, then there would appear to be a difficulty with the analysis of this essay.

But this analysis does not entail that contraception is wrong. Of course, contraception prevents the actualization of a possible future of value. Hence, it follows from the claim that if futures of value should be maximized that contraception is prima facie immoral. This obligation to maximize does not exist, however; furthermore, nothing in the ethics of killing in this paper entails that it does. The ethics of killing in this essay would entail that contraception is wrong only if something were denied a human future of value by contraception. Nothing at all is denied such a future by contraception, however.

Candidates for a subject of harm by contraception fall into four categories: (1) some sperm or other, (2) some ovum or other, (3) a sperm and an ovum separately, and (4) a sperm and an ovum together. Assigning the harm to some sperm is utterly arbitrary, for no reason can be given for making a sperm the subject of harm rather than an ovum. Assigning the harm to some ovum is utterly arbitrary, for no reason can be given for making an ovum the subject of harm rather than a sperm. One might attempt to avoid these problems by insisting that contraception deprives both the sperm and the ovum separately of a valuable future like ours. On this alternative, too many futures are lost.

Contraception was supposed to be wrong, because it deprived us of one future of value, not two. One might attempt to avoid this problem by holding that contraception deprives the combination of sperm and ovum of a valuable future like ours. But here the definite article misleads. At the time of contraception, there are hundreds of millions of sperm, one (released) ovum and millions of possible combinations of all of these. There is no actual combination at all. Is the subject of the loss to be a merely possible combination? Which one? This alternative does not yield an actual subject of harm either. Accordingly, the immorality of contraception is not entailed by the loss of a future-like-ours argument simply because there is no nonarbitrarily identifiable subject of the loss in the case of contraception.

VI

The purpose of this essay has been to set out an argument for the serious presumptive wrongness of abortion subject to the assumption that the moral permissibility of abortion stands or falls on the moral status of the fetus. Since a fetus possesses a property, the possession of which in adult human beings is sufficient to make killing an adult human being wrong, abortion is wrong. This way of dealing with the problem of abortion seems superior to other approaches to the ethics of abortion, because it rests on an ethics of killing which is close to self-evident, because the crucial morally relevant property clearly applies to fetuses, and because the argument avoids the usual equivocations on "human life," "human being," or "person." The argument rests neither on religious claims nor on Papal dogma. It is not subject to the objection of "speciesism." Its soundness is compatible with the moral permissibility of euthanasia and contraception. It deals with our intuitions concerning young children.

Finally, this analysis can be viewed as resolving a standard problem—indeed, *the* standard problem—concerning the ethics of abortion. Clearly, it is wrong to kill adult human beings. Clearly, it is not wrong to end the life of some arbitrarily chosen single human cell. Fetuses seem to be like arbitrarily chosen human cells in some respects and like adult humans in other respects. The problem of the ethics of abortion is the problem of determining the fetal property that settles this moral controversy. The thesis of this essay is that the problem of the ethics of abortion, so understood, is solvable.

NOTES

1. Feinberg, "Abortion," in *Matters of Life and Death: New Introductory Essays in Moral Philosophy*, Tom Regan, ed. (New York: Random House, 1986), pp. 256–93; Tooley, "Abortion and Infanticide," *Philosophy and Public Affairs*, II, 1 (1972): 37–65, Tooley, *Abortion and Infanticide* (New York: Oxford, 1984); Warren, "On the Moral and Legal Status of Abortion," *The Monist*, 1. VII, 1 (1973): 43–61; Engelhardt, "The Ontology of Abortion," *Ethics*, I. XXXIV, 3 (1974): 217–34; Sumner, *Abortion and Moral Theory* (Princeton: University Press, 1981); Noonan, "An Almost Absolute Value in History," in *The Morality of Abortion: Legal and Historical Perspectives*, Noonan, ed. (Cambridge: Harvard, 1970); and Devine, *The Ethics of Homicide* (Ithaca: Cornell, 1978).

2. For interesting discussions of this issue, see Warren Quinn, "Abortion: Identity and Loss," *Philosophy and Public Affairs*, XIII, 1 (1984): 24–54; and Lawrence C. Becker, "Human Being: The Boundaries of the Concept," *Philosophy and Public Affairs*, IV, 4 (1975): 334–59.

3. For example, see my "Ethics and the Elderly: Some Problems," in Stuart Spicker, Kathleen Woodward, and David Van Tassel, eds., *Aging and the Elderly: Humanistic Perspectives in Gerontology* (Atlantic Highlands, NJ: Humanities, 1978), pp. 341–55.

4. See Warren, "On the Moral and Legal Status of Abortion," and Tooley, "Abortion and Infanticide."

5. This seems to be the fatal flaw in Warren's treatment of this issue.

6. I have been most influenced on this matter by Jonathan Glover, *Causing Death and Saving Lives* (New York: Penguin, 1977), ch. 3; and Robert Young, "What Is So Wrong with Killing People?" *Philosophy*, LIV, 210 (1979): 515–28.

7. Feinberg, Tooley, Warren, and Engelhardt have all dealt with this problem.

8. Kant "Duties to Animals and Spirits," in *Lectures on Ethics*, trans. Louis Infeld (New York: Harper, 1963), p. 239.

9. I am indebted to Jack Bricke for raising this objection.

10. Presumably a preference utilitarian would press such an objection. Tooley once suggested that his account has such a theoretical underpinning. See his "Abortion and Infanticide," pp. 44–5.

11. Donald VanDeVeer seems to think this is self-evident. See his "Whither Baby Doe?" in *Matters of Life and Death*, p. 233.

12. "Must the Bearer of a Right Have the Concept of That to Which He Has a Right?" *Ethics*, XCV, 1 (1984): 68–74.

13. See Tooley again in "Abortion and Infanticide," pp. 47–9.

14. "Present Sakes and Future Prospects: The Status of Early Abortion," *Philosophy and Public Affairs*, XI, 4 (1982): 322–6.

15. Note carefully the reasons he gives on the bottom of p. 316.

An Almost Absolute Value in History

JOHN T. NOONAN, JR.

Noonan asserts that a human entity becomes a person at fertilization. He points to problems with the notion that personhood arises at some other point in human development (at viability, the point of fetal experience, or social visibility). He argues that the most plausible view is that personhood (and the right to life) begins at conception, for it is at conception that the "new being receives the genetic code. It is this genetic information which determines his characteristics, which is the biological carrier of the possibility of human wisdom, which makes him a self-evolving being. A being with a human genetic code is man."

The most fundamental question involved in the long history of thought on abortion is: How do you determine the humanity of a being? To phrase the question that way is to put in comprehensive humanistic terms what the theologians either dealt with as an explicitly theological question under the heading of "ensoulment" or dealt with implicitly in their treatment of abortion. The Christian position as it originated did not depend on a narrow theological or philosophical concept. It had no relation to theories of infant baptism. It appealed to no special theory of instantaneous ensoulment. It took the world's view on ensoulment as that view changed from Aristotle to Zacchia. There was, indeed, theological influence affecting the theory of ensoulment finally adopted, and, of course, ensoulment itself was a theological concept, so that the position was always explained in theological terms. But the theological notion of ensoulment could easily be translated into humanistic language by substituting "human" for "rational soul"; the problem of knowing when a man is a man is common to theology and humanism.

If one steps outside the specific categories used by the theologians, the answer they gave can be analyzed as a refusal to discriminate among human beings on the basis of their varying potentialities. Once conceived, the being was recognized as man because he had man's potential. The criterion for humanity, thus, was simple and all-embracing: If you are conceived by human parents, you are human.

The strength of this position may be tested by a review of some of the other distinctions offered in the contemporary controversy over legalizing abortion. Perhaps the most popular distinction is in terms of viability. Before an age of so many months, the fetus is not viable, that is, it cannot be removed from the mother's womb and live apart from her. To that extent, the life of the fetus is absolutely dependent on the life of the mother. This dependence is made the basis of denying recognition to its humanity.

There are difficulties with this distinction. One is that the perfection of artificial incubation may make the fetus viable at any time: It may be removed and artificially sustained. Experiments with animals already show that such a procedure is possible. This hypothetical extreme case relates to an actual difficulty; there is considerable elasticity to the idea of viability. Mere length of life is not an exact measure. The viability of the fetus depends on the extent of its anatomical and functional development. The weight and length of the fetus are better guides to the state of its

development than age, but weight and length vary. Moreover, different racial groups have different ages at which their fetuses are viable. Some evidence, for example, suggests that Negro fetuses mature more quickly than white fetuses. If viability is the norm, the standard would vary with race and with many individual circumstances.

The most important objection to this approach is that dependence is not ended by viability. The fetus is still absolutely dependent on someone's care in order to continue existence; indeed a child of one or three or even five years of age is absolutely dependent on another's care for existence; uncared for, the older fetus or the younger child will die as surely as the early fetus detached from the mother. The unsubstantial lessening in dependence at viability does not seem to signify any special acquisition of humanity.

A second distinction has been attempted in terms of experience. A being who has had experience, has lived and suffered, who possesses memories, is more human than one who has not. Humanity depends on formation by experience. The fetus is thus "unformed" in the most basic human sense.

This distinction is not serviceable for the embryo which is already experiencing and reacting. The embryo is responsive to touch after eight weeks and at least at that point is experiencing. At an earlier stage the zygote is certainly alive and responding to its environment. The distinction may also be challenged by the rare case where aphasia has erased adult memory: has it erased humanity? More fundamentally, this distinction leaves even the older fetus or the younger child to be treated as an unformed inhuman thing. Finally, it is not clear why experience as such confers humanity. It could be argued that certain central experiences such as loving or learning are necessary to make a man human. But then human beings who have failed to love or to learn might be excluded from the class called man.

A third distinction is made by appeal to the sentiments of adults. If a fetus dies, the grief of the parents is not the grief they would have for a living child. The fetus is an unnamed "it" till birth, and is not perceived as personality until at least the fourth month of existence when movements in the womb manifest a vigorous presence demanding joyful recognition by the parents.

Yet feeling is notoriously an unsure guide to the humanity of others. Many groups of humans have had difficulty in feeling that persons of another tongue, color, religion, sex are as human as they. Apart from reactions to alien groups, we mourn the loss of a ten-year-old boy more than the loss of his one-day-old brother or his 90-year-old grandfather. The difference felt and the grief expressed vary with the potentialities extinguished, or the experience wiped out; they do not seem to point to any substantial difference in the humanity of baby, boy, or grandfather.

Distinctions are also made in terms of sensation by the parents. The embryo is felt within the womb only after about the fourth month. The embryo is seen only at birth. What can be neither seen nor felt is different from what is tangible. If the fetus cannot be seen or touched at all, it cannot be perceived as man.

Yet experience shows that sight is even more untrustworthy than feeling in determining humanity. By sight, color became an appropriate index for saying who was a man, and the evil of racial discrimination was given foundation. Nor can touch provide the test; a being confined by sickness, "out of touch" with others, does not thereby seem to lose his humanity. To the extent that touch still has appeal as a criterion, it appears to be a survival of the old English idea of "quickening"—a possible mistranslation of the Latin *animatus* used in the canon law. To that extent touch as a criterion seems to be dependent on the Aristotelian notion of ensoulment, and to fall when this notion is discarded.

Finally, a distinction is sought in social visibility. The fetus is not socially perceived as human. It cannot communicate with others. Thus, both subjectively and objectively, it is not a member of society. As moral rules are rules for the behavior of members of society to each other, they cannot be made for behavior toward what is not yet a member. Excluded from the society of men, the fetus is excluded from the humanity of men.

By force of the argument from the consequences, this distinction is to be rejected. It is more subtle than that founded on an appeal to physical sensation, but it is equally dangerous in its implications.

If humanity depends on social recognition, individuals or whole groups may be dehumanized by being denied any status in their society. Such a fate is fictionally portrayed in *1984* and has actually been the lot of many men in many societies. In the Roman empire, for example, condemnation to slavery meant the practical denial of most human rights; in the Chinese Communist world, landlords have been classified as enemies of the people and so treated as nonpersons by the state. Humanity does not depend on social recognition, though often the failure of society to recognize the prisoner, the alien, the heterodox as human has led to the destruction of human beings. Anyone conceived by a man and a woman is human. Recognition of this condition by society follows a real event in the objective order, however imperfect and halting the recognition. Any attempt to limit humanity to exclude some group runs the risk of furnishing authority and precedent for excluding other groups in the name of the consciousness or perception of the controlling group in society.

A philosopher may reject the appeal to the humanity of the fetus because he views "humanity" as a secular view of the soul and because he doubts the existence of anything real and objective which can be identified as humanity. One answer to such a philosopher is to ask how he reasons about moral questions without supposing that there is a sense in which he and the others of whom he speaks are human. Whatever group is taken as the society which determines who may be killed is thereby taken as human. A second answer is to ask if he does not believe that there is a right and wrong way of deciding moral questions. If there is such a difference, experience may be appealed to: to decide who is human on the basis of the sentiment of a given society has led to consequences which rational men would characterize as monstrous.

The rejection of the attempted distinctions based on viability and visibility, experience and feeling, may be buttressed by the following considerations: Moral judgments often rest on distinctions, but if the distinctions are not to appear arbitrary *fiat*, they should relate to some real difference in probabilities. There is a kind of continuity in all life, but the earlier stages of the elements of human life possess tiny probabilities of development. Consider for example, the spermatozoa in any normal ejaculate: There are about 200,000,000 in any single ejaculate, of which one has a chance of developing into a zygote. Consider the oocytes which may become ova: there are 100,000 to 1,000,00 oocytes in a female infant, of which a maximum of 390 are ovulated. But once spermatozoa and ovum meet and the conceptus is formed, such studies as have been made show that roughly in only 20 percent of the cases will spontaneous abortion occur. In other words, the chances are about 4 out of 5 that this new being will develop. At this stage in the life of the being there is a sharp shift in probabilities, an immense jump in potentialities. To make a distinction between the rights of spermatozoa and the rights of the fertilized ovum is to respond to an enormous shift in possibilities. For about twenty days after conception the egg may split to form twins or combine with another egg to form a chimera, but the probability of either event happening is very small.

It may be asked, What does a change in biological probabilities have to do with establishing humanity? The argument from probabilities is not aimed at establishing humanity but at establishing an objective discontinuity which may be taken into account in moral discourse. As life itself is a matter of probabilities, as most moral reasoning is an estimate of probabilities, so it seems in accord with the structure of reality and the nature of moral thought to found a moral judgment on the change in probabilities at conception. The appeal to probabilities is the most commonsensical of arguments, to a greater or smaller degree all of us based our actions on probabilities, and in morals, as in law, prudence and negligence are often measured by the account one has taken of the probabilities. If the chance is 200,000,000 to 1 that the movement in the bushes into which you shoot is a man's, I doubt if many persons would hold you careless in shooting; but if the chances are 4 out of 5 that the movement is a human being's, few would acquit you of blame. Would the argument be different if only one out of ten children conceived came to term? Of course this argument would be different. This argument is an appeal to probabilities that actually exist, not to any and all states of affairs which may be imagined.

The probabilities as they do exist do not show the humanity of the embryo in the sense of a demonstration in logic any more than the probabilities of the movement in the bush being a man demonstrate beyond all doubt that the being is a man. The appeal is a "buttressing" consideration, showing the plausibility of the standard adopted. The argument focuses on the decisional factor in any moral judgment and assumes that part of the business of a moralist is drawing lines. One evidence of the nonarbitrary character of the line drawn is the difference of probabilities on either side of it. If a spermatozoon is destroyed, one destroys a being which had a chance of far less than 1 in 200 million of developing into a reasoning being, possessed of the genetic code, a heart and other organs, and capable of pain. If a fetus is destroyed, one destroys a being already possessed of the genetic code, organs, and sensitivity to pain, and one which had an 80 percent chance of developing further into a baby outside the womb who, in time, would reason.

The positive argument for conception as the decisive moment of humanization is that at conception the new being receives the genetic code. It is this genetic information which determines his characteristics, which is the biological carrier of the possibility of human wisdom, which makes him a self-evolving being. A being with a human genetic code is man.

This review of current controversy over the humanity of the fetus emphasizes what a fundamental question the theologians resolved in asserting the inviolability of the fetus. To regard the fetus as possessed of equal rights with other humans was not, however, to decide every case where abortion might be employed. It did decide the case where the argument was that the fetus should be aborted for its own good. To say a being was human was to say it had a destiny to decide for itself which could not be taken from it by another man's decision. But human beings with equal rights often come in conflict with each other, and some decision must be made as to whose claims are to prevail. Cases of conflict involving the fetus are different only in two respects: the total inability of the fetus to speak for itself and the fact that the right of the fetus regularly at stake is the right to life itself.

The approach taken by the theologians to these conflicts was articulated in terms of "direct" and "indirect." Again, to look at what they were doing from outside their categories, they may be said to have been drawing lines or "balancing values." "Direct" and "indirect" are spatial metaphors; "line-drawing" is another. "To weigh" or "to balance" values is a metaphor of a more complicated mathematical sort hinting at the process which goes on in moral judgments. All the metaphors suggest that, in the moral judgments made, comparisons were necessary, that no value completely controlled. The principle of double effect was no doctrine fallen from heaven, but a method of analysis appropriate where two relative values were being compared. In Catholic moral theology, as it developed, life even of the innocent was not taken as an absolute. Judgments of acts affecting life issued from a process of weighing. In the weighing, the fetus was always given a value greater than zero, always a value separate and independent from its parents. This valuation was crucial and fundamental in all Christian thought on the subject and marked it off from any approach which considered that only the parents' interests needed to be considered.

Even with the fetus weighed as human, one interest could be weighed as equal or superior: that of the mother in her own life. The casuists between 1450 and 1895 were willing to weigh this interest as superior. Since 1895, that interest was given decisive weight only in the two special cases of the cancerous uterus and the ectopic pregnancy. In both of these cases the fetus itself had little chance of survival even if abortion were not performed. As the balance was once struck in favor of the mother whenever her life was endangered, it could be so struck again. The balance reached between 1895 and 1930 attempted prudentially and pastorally to forestall a multitude of exceptions for interests less than life.

The perception of the humanity of the fetus and the weighing of fetal rights against other human rights constituted the work of the moral analysts. But what spirit animated abstract judgments? For the Christian community it was the injunction of Scripture to love your neighbor as yourself. The fetus as human was a neighbor; his life had parity with one's own. The commandment gave life to what otherwise would have been only rational calculation.

The commandment could be put in humanistic as well as theological terms: do not injure your fellow man without reasons. In these terms, once the humanity of the fetus is perceived, abortion is never right except in self-defense. When life must be taken to save life, reason alone cannot say that a mother must prefer a child's life to her own. With this exception, now of great rarity, abortion violates the rational humanist tenet of the equality of human lives.

For Christians the commandment to love had received a special imprint in that the exemplar proposed of love was the love of the Lord for his disciples. In the light given by this example, self-sacrifice carried to the point of death seemed in the extreme situations not without meaning. In the less extreme cases, preference for one's own interests to the life of another seemed to express cruelty or selfishness irreconcilable with the demands of love.

On the Moral and Legal Status of Abortion

MARY ANNE WARREN

In this famous essay, Warren defends the view that abortion is always morally permissible. It is permissible, she says, because the unborn is not a person. Merely being human—a creature with human DNA—is not sufficient for personhood.

From *The Monist*, vol. 57, no. 1, 1973, 43–61. Copyright © 1973 *The Monist*, La Salle, IL 61301. Reprinted by permission.

To qualify as a person, an entity must possess certain intrinsically valuable traits. She identifies several traits that seem "most central" to personhood: (1) consciousness and the capacity to feel pain, (2) reasoning, (3) self-motivated activity, (4) the capacity to communicate, and (5) "the presence of self-concepts, and self-awareness, either individual or racial or both." Warren argues that any being that has none of these traits is surely not a person; a fetus has none of them and is therefore not yet a person and "cannot coherently be said to have full moral rights."

We will be concerned with both the moral status of abortion, which for our purposes we may define as the act which a woman performs in voluntarily terminating, or allowing another person to terminate, her pregnancy, and the legal status which is appropriate for this act. I will argue that, while it is not possible to produce a satisfactory defense of a woman's right to obtain an abortion without showing that a fetus is not a human being, in the morally relevant sense of that term, we ought not to conclude that the difficulties involved in determining whether or not a fetus is human make it impossible to produce any satisfactory solution to the problem of the moral status of abortion. For it is possible to show that, on the basis of intuitions which we may expect even the opponents of abortion to share, a fetus is not a person, and hence not the sort of entity to which it is proper to ascribe full moral rights.

Of course, while some philosophers would deny the possibility of any such proof,[1] others will deny that there is any need for it, since the moral permissibility of abortion appears to them to be too obvious to require proof. But the inadequacy of this attitude should be evident from the fact that both the friends and the foes of abortion consider their position to be morally self-evident. Because pro-abortionists have never adequately come to grips with the conceptual issues surrounding abortion, most if not all, of the arguments which they advance in opposition to laws restricting access to abortion fail to refute or even weaken the traditional antiabortion argument, i.e., that a fetus is a human being, and therefore abortion is murder.

These arguments are typically of one of two sorts. Either they point to the terrible side effects of the restrictive laws, e.g., the deaths due to illegal abortions, and the fact that it is poor women who suffer the most as a result of these laws, or else they state that to deny a woman access to abortion is to deprive her of her right to control her own body. Unfortunately, however, the fact that restricting access to abortion has tragic side effects does not, in itself, show that the restrictions are unjustified, since murder is wrong regardless of the consequences of prohibiting it; and the appeal to the right to control one's body, which is generally construed as a property right, is at best a rather feeble argument for the permissibility of abortion. Mere ownership does not give me the right to kill innocent people whom I find on my property, and indeed I am apt to be held responsible if such people injure themselves while on my property. It is equally unclear that I have any moral right to expel an innocent person from my property when I know that doing so will result in his or her death.

Furthermore, it is probably inappropriate to describe a woman's body as her property, since it seems natural to hold that a person is something distinct from her property, but not from her body. Even those who would object to the identification of a person with her body, or with the conjunction of her body and her mind, must admit that it would be very odd to describe, say, breaking a leg, as damaging one's property, and much more appropriate to describe it as injuring one*self*. Thus it is probably a mistake to argue that the right to obtain an abortion is in any way derived from the right to own and regulate property.

But however we wish to construe the right to abortion, we cannot hope to convince those who consider abortion a form of murder of the existence of any such right unless we are able to produce a clear and convincing refutation of the traditional antiabortion argument, and this has not, to my knowledge, been done. With respect to the two most vital issues which that argument involves, i.e., the humanity of the fetus and its implication for the moral status of abortion, confusion has prevailed on both sides of the dispute. Thus, both proabortionists and antiabortionists have tended to abstract the question of whether abortion is wrong to that of whether it is wrong to destroy a fetus, just as though the rights of another person were not necessarily involved. This mistaken abstraction has led to the almost universal assumption that if a fetus is a human being, with a right to life, then it follows immediately that abortion is wrong (except perhaps when necessary to save the woman's life), and that it ought to be prohibited. It has also been generally assumed that unless the question about the status of the fetus is answered, the moral status of abortion cannot possibly be determined.

Two recent papers, one by B. A. Brody,[2] and one by Judith Thomson,[3] have attempted to settle the question of whether abortion ought to be prohibited apart from the question of whether or not the fetus is human. Brody examines the possibility that the following two statements are compatible: (1) that abortion is the taking of innocent human life, and therefore wrong; and (2) that nevertheless it ought not to be prohibited by law, at least under the present circumstances.[4] Not surprisingly, Brody finds it impossible to reconcile these two statements, since, as he rightly argues, none of the unfortunate side effects of the prohibition of abortion is bad enough to justify legalizing the *wrongful* taking of human life. He is mistaken, however, in concluding that the incompatibility of (1) and (2), in itself, shows that "the legal problem about abortion cannot be resolved independently of the status of the fetus problem" (p. 369).

What Brody fails to realize is that (1) embodies the questionable assumption that if a fetus is a human being, then of course abortion is morally wrong, and that an attack on *this* assumption is more promising, as a way of reconciling the humanity of the fetus with the claim that laws prohibiting abortion are unjustified, than is an attack on the assumption that if abortion is the wrongful killing of innocent human beings then it ought to be prohibited. He thus overlooks the possibility that a fetus may have a right to life and abortion still be morally permissible, in that the right of a

woman to terminate an unwanted pregnancy might override the right of the fetus to be kept alive. The immorality of abortion is no more demonstrated by the humanity of the fetus, in itself, than the immorality of killing in self-defense is demonstrated by the fact that the assailant is a human being. Neither is it demonstrated by the *innocence* of the fetus, since there may be situations in which the killing of innocent human beings is justified.

It is perhaps not surprising that Brody fails to spot this assumption, since it has been accepted with little or no argument by nearly everyone who has written on the morality of abortion. John Noonan is correct in saying that "the fundamental question in the long history of abortion is, How do you determine the humanity of a being?"[5] He summarizes his own antiabortion argument, which is a version of the official position of the Catholic Church, as follows:

> . . . it is wrong to kill humans, however poor, weak, defenseless, and lacking in opportunity to develop their potential they may be. It is therefore morally wrong to kill Biafrans. Similarly, it is morally wrong to kill embryos.[6]

Noonan bases his claim that fetuses are human upon what he calls the theologians' criterion of humanity: that whoever is conceived of human beings is human. But although he argues at length for the appropriateness of this criterion, he never questions the assumption that if a fetus is human then abortion is wrong for exactly the same reason that murder is wrong.

Judith Thomson is, in fact, the only writer I am aware of who has seriously questioned this assumption; she has argued that, even if we grant the antiabortionist his claim that a fetus is a human being, with the same right to life as any other human being, we can still demonstrate that, in at least some and perhaps most cases, a woman is under no moral obligation to complete an unwanted pregnancy.[7] Her argument is worth examining, since if it holds up it may enable us to establish the moral permissibility of abortion without becoming involved in problems about what entitles an entity to be considered human, and accorded full moral rights. To be able to do this would be a great gain in the power and simplicity of the proabortion position, since, although I will argue that these problems can be solved at least as decisively as can any other moral problem, we should certainly be pleased to be able to avoid having to solve them as part of the justification of abortion.

On the other hand, even if Thomson's argument does not hold up, her insight, i.e., that it requires *argument* to show that if fetuses are human then abortion is properly classified as murder, is an extremely valuable one. The assumption she attacks is particularly invidious, for it amounts to the decision that it is appropriate, in deciding the moral status of abortion, to leave the rights of the pregnant woman out of consideration entirely, except possibly when her life is threatened. Obviously, this will not do; determining what moral rights, if any, a fetus possesses is only the first step in determining the moral status of abortion. Step two, which is at least equally essential, is finding a just solution to the conflict between whatever rights the fetus may have, and the rights of the woman who is unwillingly pregnant. While the historical error has been to pay far too little attention to the second step, Ms. Thomson's suggestion is that if we look at the second step first we may find that a woman has a right to obtain an abortion *regardless* of what rights the fetus has.

Our own inquiry will also have two stages. In Section I, we will consider whether or not it is possible to establish that abortion is morally permissible even on the assumption that a fetus is an entity with a full-fledged right to life. I will argue that in fact this cannot be established, at least not with the conclusiveness which is essential to our hopes of convincing those who are skeptical about the morality of abortion, and that we therefore cannot avoid dealing with the question of whether or not a fetus really does have the same right to life as a (more fully developed) human being.

In Section II, I will propose an answer to this question, namely, that a fetus cannot be considered a member of the moral community, the set of beings with full and equal moral rights, for the simple reason that it is not a person, and that it is personhood, and not genetic humanity, i.e., humanity as defined by Noonan, which is the basis for membership in this community. I will argue that a fetus, whatever its stage of development, satisfies none of the basic criteria of personhood, and is not even enough *like* a person to be accorded even some of the same rights on the basis of this resemblance. Nor, as we will see, is a fetus's *potential* personhood a threat to the morality of abortion, since, whatever the rights of potential people may be, they are invariably overridden in any conflict with the moral rights of actual people.

I

We turn now to Professor Thomson's case for the claim that even if a fetus has full moral rights, abortion is still morally permissible, at least sometimes, and for some reasons other than to save the woman's life. Her argument is based upon a clever, but I think faulty, analogy. She asks us to picture ourselves waking up one day, in bed with a famous violinist. Imagine that you have been kidnapped, and your bloodstream hooked up to that of the violinist, who happens to have an ailment which will certainly kill him unless he is permitted to share your kidneys for a period of nine months. No one else can save him, since you alone have the right type of blood. He will be unconscious all that time, and you will have to stay in bed with him, but after the nine months are over he may be unplugged, completely cured, that is provided that you have cooperated.

Now then, she continues, what are your obligations in this situation? The antiabortionist, if he is consistent, will have to say that you are obligated to stay in bed with the violinist: for all people have a right to life, and violinists are people, and therefore it would be murder for you to disconnect yourself from him and let him die. But this is outrageous, and so there must be something wrong with the same argument when it is applied to abortion. It would certainly be commendable of you to agree to save the violinist, but it is absurd to suggest that your refusal to do so would be murder. His right to life does not obligate you to do whatever is required to keep him alive; nor does it justify anyone else in forcing you to do so. A law which required you to stay in bed with the violinist would clearly be an unjust law, since it is no proper function of the law to force unwilling people to make huge sacrifices for the sake of other people toward whom they have no such prior obligation.

Thomson concludes that, if this analogy be an apt one, then we can grant the antiabortionist his claim that a fetus is a human being, and still hold that it is at least sometimes the case that a pregnant woman has the right to refuse to be a Good Samaritan towards the fetus, i.e., to obtain an abortion. For there is a great gap between the claim that x has a right to life, and the claim that y is obligated to do whatever is necessary to keep x alive, let alone that she ought to be forced to do so. It is y's duty to keep x alive only if she has somehow contracted a *special* obligation to do so; and a woman who is unwillingly pregnant, e.g., who was raped, has done nothing which obligates her to make the enormous sacrifice which is necessary to preserve the conceptus.

This argument is initially quite plausible, and in the extreme case of pregnancy due to rape it is probably conclusive. Difficulties arise, however, when we try to specify more exactly the range of cases in which abortion is clearly justifiable even on the assumption that the fetus is human. Professor Thomson considers it a virtue of her argument that it does not enable us to conclude that abortion is *always* permissible. It would, she says, be "indecent" for a woman in her seventh month to obtain an abortion just to avoid having to postpone a trip to Europe. On the other hand, her argument enables us to see that "a sick and desperately frightened schoolgirl pregnant due to rape may *of course* choose abortion, and that any law which rules this out is an insane law." So far, so good; but what are we to say about the woman who becomes pregnant not through rape but as a result of her own carelessness, or because of contraceptive failure, or who gets pregnant intentionally and then changes her mind about wanting a child? With respect to such cases, the violinist analogy is of much less use to the defender of the woman's right to obtain an abortion.

Indeed, the choice of a pregnancy due to rape, as an example of a case in which abortion is permissible even if a fetus is considered a human being, is extremely significant; for it is only in the case of pregnancy due to rape that the woman's situation is adequately analogous to the violinist case for our intuitions about the latter to transfer convincingly.

The crucial difference between a pregnancy due to rape and the normal case of an unwanted pregnancy is that in the *normal* case we cannot claim that the woman is in no way responsible for her predicament; she could have remained chaste, or taken her pills more faithfully, or abstained on dangerous days, and so on. If, on the other hand, you are kidnapped by strangers, and hooked up to a strange violinist, then you are free of any shred of responsibility for the situation, on the basis of which it could be argued that you are obligated to keep the violinist alive. Only when her pregnancy is due to rape is a woman clearly just as nonresponsible.[8]

Consequently, there is room for the antiabortionist to argue that in the normal case of unwanted pregnancy a woman has, by her own actions, assumed responsibility for the fetus. For if x behaves in a way which she could have avoided, and which she knows involves, let us say, a 1 percent chance of bringing into existence a human being, with a right to life, and does so knowing that if this should happen then that human being will perish unless x does certain things to keep it alive, then it is by no means clear that when it does happen x is free of any obligation to what she knew in advance would be required to keep that human being alive.

The plausibility of such an argument is enough to show that the Thomson analogy can provide a clear and persuasive defense of a woman's right to obtain an abortion only with respect to those cases in which the woman is in no way responsible for her pregnancy, e.g., where it is due to rape. In all other cases, we would almost certainly conclude that it was necessary to look carefully at the particular circumstances in order to determine the extent of the woman's responsibility, and hence the extent of her obligation. This is an extremely unsatisfactory outcome, from the viewpoint of the opponents of restrictive abortion laws, most of whom are convinced that a woman has a right to obtain an abortion regardless of how and why she got pregnant.

Of course a supporter of the violinist analogy might point out that it is absurd to suggest that forgetting her pill one day might be sufficient to obligate a woman to complete an unwanted pregnancy. And indeed it *is* absurd to suggest this. As we will see, the moral right to obtain an abortion is not in the least dependent upon the extent to which the woman is responsible for her pregnancy. But unfortunately, once we allow the assumption that a fetus has full moral rights, we cannot avoid taking this absurd suggestion seriously. Perhaps we can make this point more clear by altering the violinist story just enough to make it more analogous to a normal unwanted pregnancy and less to a pregnancy due to rape, and then seeing whether it is still obvious that you are not obligated to stay in bed with the fellow.

Suppose, then, that violinists are peculiarly prone to the sort of illness the only cure for which is the use of someone else's bloodstream for nine months, and that because of this there has been formed a society of music lovers who agree that whenever a violinist is stricken they will draw lots and the loser will, by some means, be made the one and only person capable of saving him or her. Now then, would you be obligated to cooperate in curing the violinist if you had voluntarily joined this society, knowing the possible consequences, and then your name had been drawn and you had been kidnapped? Admittedly, you did not promise ahead of time that you would, but you did deliberately place yourself in a position in which it might happen that a human life would be lost if you did not. Surely this is at least a prima facie reason for supposing that you have an obligation to stay in bed with the violinist. Suppose that you had gotten your name drawn deliberately; surely that would be quite a strong reason for thinking that you have such an obligation.

It might be suggested that there is one important disanalogy between the modified violinist case and the case of an unwanted pregnancy, which makes the woman's responsibility significantly less, namely, the fact that the fetus *comes into existence* as the result of the woman's actions. This fact might give her a right to refuse to keep it alive, whereas she would not have had this right had it existed previously, independently, and then as a result of her actions become dependent upon her for its survival.

My own intuition, however, is that x has no more right to bring into existence, either deliberately or as a foreseeable result of actions she could have avoided, a being with full moral rights (y), and then refuse to do what she knew beforehand would be required to

keep that being alive, than she has to enter into an agreement with an existing person, whereby she may be called upon to save that person's life, and then refuse to do so when so called upon. Thus, x's responsibility for y's existence does not seem to lessen her obligation to keep y alive, if she is also responsible for y's being in a situation in which only she can save him or her.

Whether or not this intuition is entirely correct, it brings us back once again to the conclusion that once we allow the assumption that a fetus has full moral rights it becomes an extremely complex and difficult question whether and when abortion is justifiable. Thus the Thomson analogy cannot help us produce a clear and persuasive proof of the moral permissibility of abortion. Nor will the opponents of the restrictive laws thank us for anything less; for their conviction (for the most part) is that abortion is obviously *not* a morally serious and extremely unfortunate, even though sometimes justified act, comparable to killing in self-defense or to letting the violinist die, but rather is closer to being a morally neutral act, like cutting one's hair.

The basis of this conviction, I believe, is the realization that a fetus is not a person, and thus does not have a full-fledged right to life. Perhaps the reason why this claim has been so inadequately defended is that it seems self-evident to those who accept it. And so it is, insofar as it follows from what I take to be perfectly obvious claims about the nature of personhood, and about the proper grounds for ascribing moral rights, claims which ought, indeed, to be obvious to both the friends and foes of abortion. Nevertheless, it is worth examining these claims, and showing how they demonstrate the moral innocuousness of abortion, since this apparently has not been adequately done before.

II

The question which we must answer in order to produce a satisfactory solution to the problem of the moral status of abortion is this: How are we to define the moral community, the set of beings with full and equal moral rights, such that we can decide whether a human fetus is a member of this community or not? What sort of entity, exactly, has the inalienable rights to life, liberty, and the pursuit of happiness? Jefferson attributed these rights to all *men*, and it may or may not be fair to suggest that he intended to attribute them *only* to men. Perhaps he ought to have attributed them to all human beings. If so, then we arrive, first, at Noonan's problem of defining what makes a being human, and, second, at the equally vital question which Noonan does not consider, namely, What reason is there for identifying the moral community with the set of all human beings, in whatever way we have chosen to define that term?

1. On the Definition of "Human"

One reason why this vital second question is so frequently overlooked in the debate over the moral status of abortion is that the term "human" has two distinct, but not often distinguished, senses. This fact results in a slide of meaning, which serves to conceal the fallaciousness of the traditional argument that since (1) it is wrong to kill innocent human beings, and (2) fetuses are innocent human beings, then (3) it is wrong to kill fetuses. For if "human" is used in the same sense in both (1) and (2) then, whichever of the two senses is meant, one of these premises is question-begging. And if it is used in two different senses then of course the conclusion doesn't follow.

Thus, (1) is a self-evident moral truth,[9] and avoids begging the question about abortion, only if "human being" is used to mean something like "a full-fledged member of the moral community." (It may or may not also be meant to refer exclusively to members of the species *Homo sapiens*.) We may call this the *moral* sense of "human." It is not to be confused with what we will call the *genetic* sense, i.e., the sense in which *any* member of the species is a human being, and no member of any other species could be. If (1) is acceptable only if the moral sense is intended, (2) is non-question-begging only if what is intended is the genetic sense.

In "Deciding Who Is Human," Noonan argues for the classification of fetuses with human beings by pointing to the presence of the full genetic code, and the potential capacity for rational thought (p. 35). It is clear that what he needs to show, for his version of the traditional argument to be valid, is that fetuses are human in the moral sense, the sense in which it is analytically true that all human beings have full moral rights. But, in the absence of any argument showing that whatever is genetically human is also morally human, and he gives none, nothing more than genetic humanity can be demonstrated by the presence of the human genetic code. And, as we will see, the *potential* capacity for rational thought can at most show that an entity has the potential for *becoming* human in the moral sense.

2. Defining the Moral Community

Can it be established that genetic humanity is sufficient for moral humanity? I think that there are very good reasons for not defining the moral community in this way. I would like to suggest an alternative way of defining the moral community, which I will argue for only to the extent of explaining why it is, or should be, self-evident. The suggestion is simply that the moral community consists of all and only *people*, rather than all and only human beings;[10] and probably the best way of demonstrating its self-evidence is by considering the concept of personhood, to see what sorts of entities are and are not persons, and what the decision that a being is or is not a person implies about its moral rights.

What characteristics entitle an entity to be considered a person? This is obviously not the place to attempt a complete analysis of the concept of personhood, but we do not need such a fully adequate analysis just to determine whether and why a fetus is or isn't a person. All we need is a rough and approximate list of the most basic criteria of personhood, and some idea of which, or how many, of these an entity must satisfy in order to properly be considered a person.

In searching for such criteria, it is useful to look beyond the set of people with whom we are acquainted, and ask how we would decide whether a totally alien being was a person or not. (For we have no right to assume that genetic humanity is necessary for personhood.) Imagine a space traveler who lands on an unknown planet and encounters a race of beings utterly unlike any she has ever seen or heard of. If she wants to be sure of behaving morally toward these beings, she has to somehow decide whether they are people, and hence have full moral rights, or whether they are the sort of thing which she need not feel guilty about treating as, for example, a source of food.

How should she go about making this decision? If she has some anthropological background, she might look for such things as religion, art, and the manufacturing of tools, weapons, or shelters, since these factors have been used to distinguish our human from our prehuman ancestors, in what seems to be closer to the moral than the genetic sense of "human." And no doubt she would be right to consider the presence of such factors as good evidence that the alien beings were people, and morally human. It would, however, be overly anthropocentric of her to take the absence of these things as adequate evidence that they were not, since we can imagine people who have progressed beyond, or evolved without ever developing, these cultural characteristics.

I suggest that the traits which are most central to the concept of personhood, or humanity in the moral sense, are, very roughly, the following:

1. Consciousness (of objects and events external and/or internal to the being), and in particular the capacity to feel pain;
2. Reasoning (the *developed* capacity to solve new and relatively complex problems);
3. Self-motivated activity (activity which is relatively independent of either genetic or direct external control);
4. The capacity to communicate, by whatever means, messages of an indefinite variety of types, that is, not just with an indefinite number of possible contents, but on indefinitely many possible topics;
5. The presence of self-concepts, and self-awareness, either individual or racial, or both.

Admittedly, there are apt to be a great many problems involved in formulating precise definitions of these criteria, let alone in developing universally valid behavior criteria for deciding when they apply. But I will assume that both we and our explorer know approximately what (1)–(5) mean, and that she is also able to determine whether or not they apply. How, then, should she use her

findings to decide whether or not the alien beings are people? We needn't suppose that an entity must have *all* of these attributes to be properly considered a person; (1) and (2) alone may well be sufficient for personhood, and quite probably (1)–(3) are sufficient. Neither do we need to insist that any one of these criteria is *necessary* for personhood, although once again (1) and (2) look like fairly good candidates for necessary conditions, as does (3), if "activity" is construed so as to include the activity of reasoning.

All we need to claim, to demonstrate that a fetus is not a person, is that any being which satisfies *none* of (1)–(5) is certainly not a person. I consider this claim to be so obvious that I think anyone who denied it, and claimed that a being which satisfied none of (1)–(5) was a person all the same, would thereby demonstrate that she had no notion at all of what a person is—perhaps because she had confused the concept of a person with that of genetic humanity. If the opponents of abortion were to deny the appropriateness of these five criteria, I do not know what further arguments would convince them. We would probably have to admit that our conceptual schemes were indeed irreconcilably different, and that our dispute could not be settled objectively.

I do not expect this to happen, however, since I think that the concept of a person is one which is very nearly universal (to people), and that it is common to both proabortionists and antiabortionists, even though neither group has fully realized the relevance of this concept to the resolution of their dispute. Furthermore, I think that on reflection even the antiabortionists ought to agree not only that (1)–(5) are central to the concept of personhood, but also that it is a part of this concept that all and only people have full moral rights. The concept of a person is in part a moral concept; once we have admitted that *x* is a person we have recognized, even if we have not agreed to respect, *x*'s right to be treated as a member of the moral community. It is true that the claim that *x* is a *human being* is more commonly voiced as part of an appeal to treat *x* decently than is the claim that *x* is a person, but this is either because "human being" is here used in the sense which implies personhood, or because the genetic and moral senses of "human" have been confused.

Now if (1)–(5) are indeed the primary criteria of personhood, then it is clear that genetic humanity is neither necessary nor sufficient for establishing that an entity is a person. Some human beings are not people, and there may well be people who are not human beings. A man or woman whose consciousness has been permanently obliterated but who remains alive is a human being which is no longer a person; defective human beings, with no appreciable mental capacity, are not and presumably never will be people; and a fetus is a human being which is not yet a person, and which therefore cannot coherently be said to have full moral rights. Citizens of the next century should be prepared to recognize highly advanced, self-aware robots or computers, should such be developed, and intelligent inhabitants of other worlds, should such be found, as people in the fullest sense, and to respect their moral rights. But to ascribe full moral rights to an entity which is not a person is as absurd as to ascribe moral obligations and responsibilities to such an entity.

3. Fetal Development and the Right to Life

Two problems arise in the application of these suggestions for the definition of the moral community to the determination of the precise moral status of a human fetus. Given that the paradigm example of a person is a normal adult human being, then (1) How like this paradigm, in particular how far advanced since conception, does a human being need to be before it begins to have a right to life by virtue, not of being fully a person as of yet, but of being *like* a person? and (2) To what extent, if any, does the fact that a fetus has the *potential* for becoming a person endow it with some of the same rights? Each of these questions requires some comment.

In answering the first question, we need not attempt a detailed consideration of the moral rights of organisms which are not developed enough, aware enough, intelligent enough, etc., to be considered people, but which resemble people in some respects. It does seem reasonable to suggest that the more like a person, in the relevant respects, a being is, the stronger is the case for regarding it as having

a right to life, and indeed the stronger its right to life is. Thus we ought to take seriously the suggestion that, insofar as "the human individual develops biologically in a continuous fashion . . . the rights of a human person might develop in the same way."[11] But we must keep in mind that the attributes which are relevant in determining whether or not an entity is enough like a person to be regarded as having some moral rights are no different from those which are relevant to determining whether or not it is fully a person—i.e., are no different from (1)–(5)—and that being genetically human, or having recognizably human facial and other physical features, or detectable brain activity, or the capacity to survive outside the uterus, are simply not among these relevant attributes.

Thus it is clear that even though a seven- or eight-month fetus has features which make it apt to arouse in us almost the same powerful protective instinct as is commonly aroused by a small infant, nevertheless it is not significantly more personlike than is a very small embryo. It is *somewhat* more personlike; it can apparently feel and respond to pain, and it may even have a rudimentary form of consciousness, insofar as its brain is quite active. Nevertheless, it seems safe to say that it is not fully conscious, in the way that an infant of a few months is, and that it cannot reason, or communicate messages of indefinitely many sorts, does not engage in self-motivated activity, and has no self-awareness. Thus, in the *relevant* respects, a fetus, even a fully developed one, is considerably less personlike than is the average mature mammal, indeed the average fish. And I think that a rational person must conclude that if the right to life of a fetus is to be based upon its resemblance to a person, then it cannot be said to have any more right to life than, let us say, a newborn guppy (which also seems to be capable of feeling pain), and that a right of that magnitude could never override a woman's right to obtain an abortion, at any stage of her pregnancy.

There may, of course, be other arguments in favor of placing legal limits upon the stage of pregnancy in which an abortion may be performed. Given the relative safety of the new techniques of artificially inducing labor during the third trimester, the danger to the woman's life or health is no longer such an argument. Neither is the fact that people tend to respond to the thought of abortion in the later stages of pregnancy with emotional repulsion, since mere emotional responses cannot take the place of moral reasoning in determining what ought to be permitted. Nor, finally, is the frequently heard argument that legalizing abortion, especially late in the pregnancy, may erode the level of respect for human life, leading, perhaps, to an increase in unjustified euthanasia and other crimes. For this threat, if it is a threat, can be better met by educating people to the kinds of moral distinctions which we are making here than by limiting access to abortion (which limitation may, in its disregard for the rights of women, be just as damaging to the level of respect for human rights).

Thus, since the fact that even a fully developed fetus is not personlike enough to have any significant right to life on the basis of its personlikeness shows that no legal restrictions upon the stage of pregnancy in which an abortion may be performed can be justified on the grounds that we should protect the rights of the older fetus; and since there is no other apparent justification for such restrictions, we may conclude that they are entirely unjustified. Whether or not it would be *indecent* (whatever that means) for a woman in her seventh month to obtain an abortion just to avoid having to postpone a trip to Europe, it would not, in itself, be *immoral*, and therefore it ought to be permitted.

4. Potential Personhood and the Right to Life

We have seen that a fetus does not resemble a person in any way which can support the claim that it has even some of the same rights. But what about its *potential*, the fact that if nurtured and allowed to develop naturally it will very probably become a person? Doesn't that alone give it at least some right to life? It is hard to deny that the fact that an entity is a potential person is a strong prima facie reason for not destroying it; but we need not conclude from this that a potential person has a right to life, by virtue of that potential. It may be that our feeling that it is better, other things being equal, not to destroy a potential person is better explained by the fact that potential people are still (felt to be) an invaluable resource, not to be lightly squandered.

Surely, if every speck of dust were a potential person, we would be much less apt to conclude that every potential person has a right to become actual.

Still, we do not need to insist that a potential person has no right to life whatever. There may well be something immoral, and not just imprudent, about wantonly destroying potential people, when doing so isn't necessary to protect anyone's rights. But even if a potential person does have some prima facie right to life, such a right could not possibly outweigh the right of a woman to obtain an abortion, since the rights of any actual person invariably outweigh those of any potential person, whenever the two conflict. Since this may not be immediately obvious in the case of a human fetus, let us look at another case.

Suppose that our space explorer falls into the hands of an alien culture, whose scientists decide to create a few hundred thousand or more human beings, by breaking her body into its component cells, and using these to create fully developed human beings, with, of course, her genetic code. We may imagine that each of these newly created individuals will have all of the original individual's abilities, skills, knowledge, and so on, and also have an individual self-concept, in short that each of them will be a bona fide (though hardly unique) person. Imagine that the whole project will take only seconds, and that its chances of success are extremely high, and that our explorer knows all of this, and also knows that these people will be treated fairly. I maintain that in such a situation she would have every right to escape if she could, and thus to deprive all of these potential people of their potential lives; for her right to life outweighs all of theirs together, in spite of the fact that they are all genetically human, all innocent, and all have a very high probability of becoming people very soon, if only she refrains from acting.

Indeed, I think she would have a right to escape even if it were not her life which the alien scientists planned to take, but only a year of her freedom, or, indeed, only a day. Nor would she be obligated to stay if she had gotten captured (thus bringing all these people-potentials into existence) because of her own carelessness, or even if she had done so deliberately, knowing the consequences. Regardless of how she got captured, she is not morally obligated to remain in captivity for *any* period of time for the sake of permitting any number of potential people to come into actuality, so great is the margin by which one actual person's right to liberty outweighs whatever right to life even a hundred thousand potential people have. And it seems reasonable to conclude that the rights of a woman will outweigh by a similar margin whatever right to life a fetus may have by virtue of its potential personhood.

Thus, neither a fetus's resemblance to a person, nor its potential for becoming a person provides any basis whatever for the claim that it has any significant right to life. Consequently, a woman's right to protect her health, happiness, freedom, and even her life,[12] by terminating an unwanted pregnancy, will always override whatever right to life it may be appropriate to ascribe to a fetus, even a fully developed one. And thus, in the absence of any overwhelming social need for every possible child, the laws which restrict the right to obtain an abortion, or limit the period of pregnancy during which an abortion may be performed, are a wholly unjustified violation of a woman's most basic moral and constitutional rights.[13]

Postscript on Infanticide

Since the publication of this article, many people have written to point out that my argument appears to justify not only abortion, but infanticide as well. For a new-born infant is not significantly more personlike than an advanced fetus, and consequently it would seem that if the destruction of the latter is permissible so too must be that of the former. Inasmuch as most people, regardless of how they feel about the morality of abortion, consider infanticide a form of murder, this might appear to represent a serious flaw in my argument.

Now, if I am right in holding that it is only people who have a full-fledged right to life, and who can be murdered, and if the criteria of personhood are as I have described them, then it obviously follows that killing a new-born infant isn't murder. It does *not* follow, however, that infanticide is permissible, for two reasons. In the first place, it would be wrong, at least in this country and in this period of history, and other things being equal, to kill a new-born infant, because even if its parents do not want it and would not suffer from its destruction, there are other people

who would like to have it, and would, in all probability, be deprived of a great deal of pleasure by its destruction. Thus, infanticide is wrong for reasons analogous to those which make it wrong to wantonly destroy natural resources, or great works of art.

Secondly, most people, at least in this country, value infants and would much prefer that they be preserved, even if foster parents are not immediately available. Most of us would rather be taxed to support orphanages than allow unwanted infants to be destroyed. So long as there are people who want an infant preserved, and who are willing and able to provide the means of caring for it, under reasonably humane conditions, it is, *ceteris paribus*, wrong to destroy it.

But, it might be replied, if this argument shows that infanticide is wrong, at least at this time and in this country, doesn't it also show that abortion is wrong? After all, many people value fetuses, and are disturbed by their destruction, and would much prefer that they be preserved, even at some cost to themselves. Furthermore, as a potential source of pleasure to some foster family, a fetus is just as valuable as an infant. There is, however, a crucial difference between the two cases: so long as the fetus is unborn, its preservation, contrary to the wishes of the pregnant woman, violates her rights to freedom, happiness, and self-determination. Her rights override the rights of those who would like the fetus preserved, just as if someone's life or limb is threatened by a wild animal, his right to protect himself by destroying the animal overrides the rights of those who would prefer that the animal not be harmed.

The minute the infant is born, however, its preservation no longer violates any of its mother's rights, even if she wants it destroyed, because she is free to put it up for adoption. Consequently, while the moment of birth does not mark any sharp discontinuity in the degree to which an infant possesses the right to life, it does mark the end of its mother's right to determine its fate. Indeed, if abortion could be performed without killing the fetus, she would never possess the right to have the fetus destroyed, for the same reasons that she has no right to have an infant destroyed.

On the other hand, it follows from my argument that when an unwanted or defective infant is born into a society which cannot afford and/or is not willing to care for it, then its destruction is permissible. This conclusion will, no doubt, strike many people as heartless and immoral; but remember that the very existence of people who feel this way, and who are willing and able to provide care for unwanted infants, is reason enough to conclude that they should be preserved.

NOTES

1. For example, Roger Wertheimer, who in "Understanding the Abortion Argument" (*Philosophy and Public Affairs*, 1, No. 1 [Fall, 1971], 67–95), argues that the problem of the moral status of abortion is insoluble, in that the dispute over the status of the fetus is not a question of fact at all, but only a question of how one responds to the facts.

2. B. A. Brody, "Abortion and the Law," *The Journal of Philosophy*, 68, No. 12 (June 17, 1971), 357–369.

3. Judith Thomson, "A Defense of Abortion," *Philosophy and Public Affairs*, 1, No. 1 (Fall, 1971), 47–66.

4. I have abbreviated these standards somewhat, but not in a way which affects the argument.

5. John Noonan, "Abortion and the Catholic Church: A Summary History," *Natural Law Forum*, 12 (1967), 125.

6. John Noonan, "Deciding Who Is Human," *Natural Law Forum*, 13 (1968), 134.

7. "A Defense of Abortion."

8. We may safely ignore the fact that she might have avoided getting raped, e.g., by carrying a gun, since by similar means you might likewise have avoided getting kidnapped, and in neither case does the victim's failure to take all possible precautions against a highly unlikely event (as opposed to reasonable precautions against a rather likely event) mean that she is morally responsible for what happens.

9. Of course, the principle that it is (always) wrong to kill innocent human beings is in need of many other modifications, e.g., that it may be permissible to do so to save a greater number of other innocent human beings, but we may safely ignore these complications here.

10. From here on, we will use "human" to mean genetically human, since the moral sense seems closely connected to, and perhaps derived from, the assumption that genetic humanity is sufficient for membership in the moral community.

11. Thomas L. Hayes, "A Biological View," *Commonwealth* 85 (March 17, 1967), 677–78; quoted by Daniel Callahan, in *Abortion, Law, Choice, and Morality* (London: Macmillan & Co., 1970).

12. That is, insofar as the death rate, for the woman, is higher for childbirth than for early abortion.

13. My thanks to the following people, who were kind enough to read and criticize an earlier version of this paper: Herbert Gold, Gene Glass, Anne Lauterbach, Judith Thomson, Mary Mothersill, and Timothy Binkley.

Virtue Theory and Abortion

ROSALIND HURSTHOUSE

Rosalind Hursthouse is a professor of philosophy at the University of Auckland. In this selection she reviews and rebuts major criticisms of virtue theory, a moral outlook whose lineage goes back to Aristotle and that offers an alternative to moral theories based on rules or principles. In applying virtue theory to the issue of abortion, she emphasizes the importance of the moral attitudes of the mother over the demands of rights.

The sort of ethical theory derived from Aristotle, variously described as virtue ethics, virtue-based ethics, or neo-Aristotelianism, is becoming better

From Rosalind Hursthouse, "Virtue Theory and Abortion," *The Stanford Encyclopedia of Philosophy* (Fall 2003), http://plato.stanford.edu/entries/ethics-virtue/ (10 September 2012).

known, and is now quite widely recognized as at least a possible rival to deontological and utilitarian theories. With recognition has come criticism, of varying quality. In this article I shall discuss nine separate criticisms that I have frequently encountered, most of which seem to me to betray an inadequate grasp either of the structure of virtue theory or of what would be involved in thinking about a real moral issue in its terms. In the first half I aim particularly to secure an understanding that will reveal that many of these criticisms are simply misplaced, and to articulate what I take to be the major criticism of virtue theory. I reject this criticism, but do not claim that it is necessarily misplaced. In the second half I aim to deepen that understanding and highlight the issues raised by the criticisms by illustrating what the theory looks like when it is applied to a particular issue, in this case, abortion.

VIRTUE THEORY

Virtue theory can be laid out in a framework that reveals clearly some of the essential similarities and differences between it and some versions of deontological and utilitarian theories. I begin with a rough sketch of familiar versions of the latter two sorts of theory, not, of course, with the intention of suggesting that they exhaust the field, but on the assumption that their very familiarity will provide a helpful contrast with virtue theory. Suppose a deontological theory has basically the following framework. We begin with a premise providing a specification of right action:

P.1. An action is right iff it is in accordance with a moral rule or principle.

This is a purely formal specification, forging a link between the concepts of *right action* and *moral rule,* and gives one no guidance until one knows what a moral rule is. So the next thing the theory needs is a premise about that:

P.2. A moral rule is one that . . .

Historically, an acceptable completion of P.2 would have been

(i) is laid on us by God

or

(ii) is required by natural law.

In secular versions (not, of course, unconnected to God's being pure reason, and the universality of natural law) we get such completions as

(iii) is laid on us by reason

or

(iv) is required by rationality

or

(v) would command universal rational acceptance

or

(vi) would be the object of choice of all rational beings

and so on. Such a specification forges a second conceptual link, between the concepts of *moral rule* and *rationality.*

We have here the skeleton of a familiar version of a deontological theory, a skeleton that reveals that what is essential to any such version is the links between *right action, moral rule,* and *rationality.* That these form the basic structure can be seen particularly vividly if we lay out the familiar act-utilitarianism in such a way as to bring out the contrasts.

Act-utilitarianism begins with a premise that provides a specification of right action:

P.1. An action is right iff it promotes the best consequences.

It thereby forges the link between the concepts of *right action* and *consequences.* It goes on to specify what the best consequences are in its second premise:

P.2. The best consequences are those in which happiness is maximized.

It thereby forges the link between *consequences* and *happiness.*

Now let us consider what a skeletal virtue theory looks like. It begins with a specification of right action:

P.1. An action is right iff it is what a virtuous agent would do in the circumstances.[1]

This, like the first premises of the other two sorts of theory, is a purely formal principle, giving one no guidance as to what to do, that forges the conceptual link between *right action* and *virtuous agent.* Like the other theories, it must, of course, go on to specify what the latter is. The first step toward this may appear quite trivial, but is needed to correct a prevailing tendency among many critics to define the virtuous agent as one who is disposed to act in accordance with a deontologist's moral rules.

> P.1a. A virtuous agent is one who acts virtuously, that is, one who has and exercises the virtues.

This subsidiary premise lays bare the fact that virtue theory aims to provide a nontrivial specification of the virtuous agent *via* a nontrivial specification of the virtues, which is given in its second premise:

> P.2. A virtue is a character trait a human being needs to flourish or live well.

This premise forges a conceptual link between *virtue* and *flourishing* (or *living well* or *eudaimonia*). And, just as déontology, in theory, then goes on to argue that each favored rule meets its specification, so virtue ethics, in theory, goes on to argue that each favored character trait meets its.

These are the bare bones of virtue theory. Following are five brief comments directed to some misconceived criticisms that should be cleared out of the way.

First, the theory does not have a peculiar weakness or problem in virtue of the fact that it involves the concept of *eudaimonia* (a standard criticism being that this concept is hopelessly obscure). Now no virtue theorist will pretend that the concept of human flourishing is an easy one to grasp. I will not even claim here (though I would elsewhere) that it is no more obscure than the concepts of *rationality* and *happiness,* since, if our vocabulary were more limited, we might, *faute de mieux,* call it (human) *rational happiness,* and thereby reveal that it has at least some of the difficulties of both. But virtue theory has never, so far as I know, been dismissed on the grounds of the *comparative* obscurity of this central concept; rather, the popular view is that it has a problem with this which deontology and utilitarianism in no way share. This, I think, is clearly false. Both *rationality* and *happiness,* as they figure in their respective theories, are rich and difficult concepts—hence all the disputes about the various tests for a rule's being an object of rational choice,

and the disputes, dating back to Mill's introduction of the higher and lower pleasures, about what constitutes happiness.

Second, the theory is not trivially circular; it does not specify right action in terms of the virtuous agent and then immediately specify the virtuous agent in terms of right action. Rather, it specifies her in terms of the virtues, and then specifies these, not merely as dispositions to right action, but as the character traits (which are dispositions to feel and react as well as act in certain ways) required for *eudaimonia.*[2]

Third, it does answer the question "What should I do?" as well as the question "What sort of person should I be?" (That is, it is not, as one of the catchphrases has it, concerned only with Being and not with Doing.)

Fourth, the theory does, to a certain extent, answer this question by coming up with rules or principles (contrary to the common claim that it does not come up with any rules or principles). Every virtue generates a positive instruction (act justly, kindly, courageously, honestly, etc.) and every vice a prohibition (do not act unjustly, cruelly, like a coward, dishonestly, etc.). So trying to decide what to do within the framework of virtue theory is not, as some people seem to imagine, necessarily a matter of taking one's favored candidate for a virtuous person and asking oneself, "What would they do in these circumstances?" (as if the raped fifteen-year-old girl might be supposed to say to herself, "Now would Socrates have an abortion if he were in my circumstances?" and as if someone who had never known or heard of anyone very virtuous were going to be left, according to the theory, with no way to decide what to do at all). The agent may instead ask herself, "If I were to do such and such now, would I be acting justly or unjustly (or neither), kindly or unkindly [and so on]?" I shall consider below the problem created by cases in which such a question apparently does not yield an answer to "What should I do?" (because, say, the alternatives are being unkind or being unjust); here my claim is only that it sometimes does—the agent may employ her concepts of the virtues and vices directly, rather than imagining what some hypothetical exemplar would do.

Fifth (a point that is implicit but should be made explicit), virtue theory is not committed to any sort of reductionism involving defining all of our moral concepts in terms of the virtuous agent. On the contrary, it relies on a lot of very significant moral concepts. Charity or benevolence, for instance, is the virtue whose concern is the *good* of others; that concept of *good* is related to the concept of *evil* or *harm,* and they are both related to the concepts of the *worthwhile,* the *advantageous,* and the *pleasant.* If I have the wrong conception of what is worthwhile and advantageous and pleasant, then I shall have the wrong conception of what is good for, and harmful to, myself and others, and, even with the best will in the world, will lack the virtue of charity, which involves getting all this right. (This point will be illustrated at some length in the second half of this article; I mention it here only in support of the fact that no virtue theorist who takes her inspiration from Aristotle would even contemplate aiming at reductionism.)[3]

Let me now, with equal brevity, run through two more standard criticisms of virtue theory (the sixth and seventh of my nine) to show that, though not entirely misplaced, they do not highlight problems peculiar to that theory but, rather, problems that are shared by familiar versions of deontology.

One common criticism is that we do not know which character traits are the virtues, or that this is open to much dispute, or particularly subject to the threat of moral skepticism or "pluralism"[4] or cultural relativism. But the parallel roles played by the second premises of both deontological and virtue theories reveal the way in which both sorts of theory share this problem. It is at the stage at which one tries to get the right conclusions to drop out of the bottom of one's theory that, *theoretically,* all the work has to be done. Rule deontologists know that they want to get "don't kill," "keep promises," "cherish your children," and so on as the rules that meet their specification, whatever it may be. They also know that any of these can be disputed, that some philosopher may claim, of any one of them, that it is reasonable to reject it, and that at least people claim that there has been, for each rule, some culture that rejected it. Similarly, the virtue theorists know that they want to get justice, charity, fidelity, courage,

and so on as the character traits needed for *eudaimonia*; and they also know that any of these can be disputed, that some philosopher will say of any one of them that it is reasonable to reject it as a virtue, and that there is said to be, for each character trait, some culture that has thus rejected it.

This is a problem for both theories, and the virtue theorist certainly does not find it any harder to argue against moral skepticism, "pluralism," or cultural relativism than the deontologist. Each theory has to stick out its neck and say, in some cases, "This person/these people/other cultures are (or would be) in error," and find some grounds for saying this.

Another criticism (the seventh) often made is that virtue ethics has unresolvable conflict built into it. "It is common knowledge," it is said, "that the requirements of the virtues can conflict; charity may prompt me to end the frightful suffering of the person in my care by killing him, but justice bids me to stay my hand. To tell my brother that his wife is being unfaithful to him would be honest and loyal, but it would be kinder to keep quiet about it. So which should I do? In such cases, virtue ethics has nothing helpful to say." (This is one version of the problem, mentioned above, that considering whether a proposed action falls under a virtue or vice term does not always yield an answer to "What should I do?")

The obvious reply to this criticism is that rule deontology notoriously suffers from the same problem, arising not only from the fact that its rules can apparently conflict, but also from the fact that, at first blush, it appears that one and the same rule (e.g., preserve life) can yield contrary instructions in a particular case.[5] As before, I agree that this is a problem for virtue theory, but deny that it is a problem peculiar to it.

Finally, I want to articulate, and reject, what I take to be the major criticism of virtue theory. Perhaps because it is *the* major criticism, the reflection of a very general sort of disquiet about the theory, it is hard to state clearly—especially for someone who does not accept it—but it goes something like this.[6] My interlocutor says:

Virtue theory can't *get* us anywhere in real moral issues because it's bound to be all assertion and no argument. You admit that the best it can come up with in the way of action-guiding rules are the ones that rely on the virtue and vice concepts, such as "act charitably," "don't act cruelly," and so on; and, as if that weren't bad enough, you admit that these virtue concepts, such as charity, presuppose concepts such as the *good,* and the *worthwhile,* and so on. But that means that any virtue theorist who writes about real moral issues must rely on her audience's agreeing with her application of all these concepts, and hence accepting all the premises in which those applications are enshrined. But some other virtue theorist might take different premises about these matters, and come up with very different conclusions, and, within the terms of the theory, there is no way to distinguish between the two. While there is agreement, virtue theory can repeat conventional wisdom, preserve the status quo, but it can't get us anywhere in the way that a normative ethical theory is supposed to, namely, by providing rational grounds for acceptance of its practical conclusions.

My strategy will be to split this criticism into two: one (the eighth) addressed to the virtue theorist's employment of the virtue and vice concepts enshrined in her rules—act charitably, honestly, and so on—and the other (the ninth) addressed to her employment of concepts such as that of the *worthwhile.* Each objection, I shall maintain, implicitly appeals to a certain *condition of adequacy* on a normative moral theory, and in each case, I shall claim, the condition of adequacy, once made explicit, is utterly implausible.

It is true that when she discusses real moral issues, the virtue theorist has to assert that certain actions are honest, dishonest, or neither; charitable, uncharitable, or neither. And it is true that this is often a very difficult matter to decide; her rules are not always easy to apply. But this counts as a criticism of the theory only if we assume, as a condition of adequacy, that any adequate action-guiding theory must make the difficult business of knowing what to do if one is to act well easy, that it must provide clear guidance about what ought and ought not to be done which any reasonably clever adolescent could follow if she chose. But such a condition of adequacy is implausible. Acting rightly *is* difficult, and *does* call for much moral wisdom, and the relevant

condition of adequacy, which virtue theory meets, is that it should have built into it an explanation of a truth expressed by Aristotle,[7] namely, that moral knowledge—unlike mathematical knowledge—cannot be acquired merely by attending lectures and is not characteristically to be found in people too young to have had much experience of life. There are youthful mathematical geniuses, but rarely, if ever, youthful moral geniuses, and this tells us something significant about the sort of knowledge that moral knowledge is. Virtue ethics builds this in straight off precisely by couching its rules in terms whose application may indeed call for the most delicate and sensitive judgment.

Here we may discern a slightly different version of the problem that there are cases in which applying the virtue and vice terms does not yield an answer to "What should I do?" Suppose someone "youthful in character," as Aristotle puts it, having applied the relevant terms, finds herself landed with what is, unbeknownst to her, a case not of real but of apparent conflict, arising from a misapplication of those terms. Then she will not be able to decide what to do unless she knows of a virtuous agent to look to for guidance. But her quandary is *(ex hypothesi)* the result of her lack of wisdom, and just what virtue theory expects. Someone hesitating over whether to reveal a hurtful truth, for example, thinking it would be kind but dishonest or unjust to lie, may need to realize, with respect to these particular circumstances, not that kindness is more (or less) important than honesty or justice, and not that honesty or justice sometimes requires one to act unkindly or cruelly, but that one does people no kindness by concealing this sort of truth from them, hurtful as it may be. This is the *type* of thing (I use it only as an example) that people with moral wisdom know about, involving the correct application of *kind,* and that people without such wisdom find difficult.

What about the virtue theorist's reliance on concepts such as that of the *worthwhile?* If such reliance is to count as a fault in the theory, what condition of adequacy is implicitly in play? It must be that any good normative theory should provide answers to questions about real moral issues whose truth is in no way determined by truths about what is worthwhile, or what really matters in human life. Now although people are initially inclined to reject out of hand the claim that the practical conclusions of a normative moral theory have to be based on premises about what is truly worthwhile, the alternative, once it is made explicit, may look even more unacceptable. Consider what the condition of adequacy entails. If truths about what is worthwhile (or truly good, or serious, or about what matters in human life) do *not* have to be appealed to in order to answer questions about real moral issues, then I might sensibly seek guidance about what I ought to do from someone who had declared in advance that she knew nothing about such matters, or from someone who said that, although she had opinions about them, these were quite likely to be wrong but that this did not matter, because they would play no determining role in the advice she gave me.

I should emphasize that we are talking about real moral issues and real guidance; I want to know whether I should have an abortion, take my mother off the life-support machine, leave academic life and become a doctor in the Third World, give up my job with the firm that is using animals in its experiments, tell my father he has cancer. Would I go to someone who says she has *no* views about what is worthwhile in life? Or to someone who says that, as a matter of fact, she tends to think that the only thing that matters is having a good time, but has a normative theory that is consistent both with this view and with my own rather more puritanical one, which will yield the guidance I need?

I take it as a premise that this is absurd. The relevant condition of adequacy should be that the practical conclusions of a good normative theory *must* be in part determined by premises about what is worthwhile, important, and so on. Thus I reject this "major criticism" of virtue theory, that it cannot get us anywhere in the way that a normative moral theory is supposed to. According to my response, a normative theory that any clever adolescent can apply, or that reaches practical conclusions that are in no way determined by premises about what is truly worthwhile, serious, and so on, is guaranteed to be an inadequate theory.

Although I reject this criticism, I have not argued that it is misplaced and that it necessarily manifests a failure to understand what virtue theory is. My rejection is based on premises about what an adequate normative theory must be like—what sorts of concepts it must contain, and what sort of account it must give of moral knowledge—and thereby claims, implicitly, that the "major criticism" manifests a failure to understand what an *adequate normative theory* is. But, as a matter of fact, I think the criticism is often made by people who have no idea of what virtue theory looks like when applied to a real moral issue; they drastically underestimate the variety of ways in which the virtue and vice concepts, and the others, such as that of the *worthwhile*, figure in such discussion.

As promised, I now turn to an illustration of such discussion, applying virtue theory to abortion. Before I embark on this tendentious business, I should remind the reader of the aim of this discussion. I am not, in this article, trying to solve the problem of abortion; I am illustrating how virtue theory directs one to think about it. It might indeed be said that thinking about the problem in this way "solves" it by *dis*solving it, insofar as it leads one to the conclusion that there is no single right answer, but a variety of particular answers, and in what follows I am certainly trying to make that conclusion seem plausible. But, that granted, it should still be said that I am not trying to "solve the problems" in the practical sense of telling people that they should, or should not, do this or that if they are pregnant and contemplating abortion in these or those particular circumstances.

I do not assume, or expect, that all of my readers will agree with everything I am about to say. On the contrary, given the plausible assumption that some are morally wiser than I am, and some less so, the theory has built into it that we are bound to disagree on some points. For instance, we may well disagree about the particular application of some of the virtue and vice terms; and we may disagree about what is worthwhile or serious, worthless or trivial. But my aim is to make clear how these concepts figure in a discussion conducted in terms of virtue theory. What is at issue is whether these concepts are indeed the ones that should come in, that is, whether virtue theory should be criticized for employing them. The problem of abortion highlights this issue dramatically since virtue theory quite transforms the discussion of it.

ABORTION

As everyone knows, the morality of abortion is commonly discussed in relation to just two considerations: first, and predominantly, the status of the fetus and whether or not it is the sort of thing that may or may not be innocuously or justifiably killed; and second, and less predominantly (when, that is, the discussion concerns the *morality* of abortion rather than the question of permissible legislation in a just society), women's rights. If one thinks within this familiar framework, one may well be puzzled about what virtue theory, as such, could contribute. Some people assume the discussion will be conducted solely in terms of what the virtuous agent would or would not do (cf. the third, fourth, and fifth criticisms above). Others assume that only justice, or at most justice and charity,[8] will be applied to the issue, generating a discussion very similar to Judith Jarvis Thomson's.[9]

Now if this is the way the virtue theorist's discussion of abortion is imagined to be, no wonder people think little of it. It seems obvious in advance that in any such discussion there must be either a great deal of extremely tendentious application of the virtue terms *just, charitable,* and so on or a lot of rhetorical appeal to "this is what only the virtuous agent knows." But these are caricatures; they fail to appreciate the way in which virtue theory quite transforms the discussion of abortion by dismissing the two familiar dominating considerations as, in a way, fundamentally irrelevant. In what way or ways, I hope to make both clear and plausible.

Let us first consider women's rights. Let me emphasize again that we are discussing the *morality* of abortion, not the rights and wrongs of laws prohibiting or permitting it. If we suppose that women do have a moral right to do as they choose with their own bodies, or, more particularly, to terminate their pregnancies, then it may well follow that a *law* forbidding abortion would be unjust. Indeed, even if they have no such right, such a law might be, as things stand at the moment, unjust, or impractical, or inhumane: on this issue I have nothing to

say in this article. But, putting all questions about the justice or injustice of laws to one side, and supposing only that women have such a moral right, *nothing* follows from this supposition about the morality of abortion, according to virtue theory, once it is noted (quite generally, not with particular reference to abortion) that in exercising a moral right I can do something cruel, or callous, or selfish, light-minded, self-righteous, stupid, inconsiderate, disloyal, dishonest—that is, act viciously.[10] Love and friendship do not survive their parties' constantly insisting on their rights, nor do people live well when they think that getting what they have a right to is of preeminent importance; they harm others, and they harm themselves. So whether women have a moral right to terminate their pregnancies is irrelevant within virtue theory, for it is irrelevant to the question "In having an abortion in these circumstances, would the agent be acting virtuously or viciously or neither?"

What about the consideration of the status of the fetus—what can virtue theory say about that? One might say that this issue is not in the province of *any* moral theory; it is a metaphysical question, and an extremely difficult one at that. Must virtue theory then wait upon metaphysics to come up with the answer?

At first sight it might seem so. For virtue is said to involve knowledge, and part of this knowledge consists in having the *right* attitude to things. "Right" here does not just mean "morally right" or "proper" or "nice" in the modern sense; it means "accurate, true." One cannot have the right or correct attitude to something if the attitude is based on or involves false beliefs. And this suggests that if the status of the fetus is relevant to the rightness or wrongness of abortion, its status must be known, as a truth, to the fully wise and virtuous person.

But the sort of wisdom that the fully virtuous person has is not supposed to be recondite; it does not call for fancy philosophical sophistication, and it does not depend upon, let alone wait upon, the discoveries of academic philosophers.[11] And this entails the following, rather startling, conclusion: that the status of the fetus—that issue over which so much ink has been spilt—is, according to virtue theory, simply not relevant to the rightness or wrongness of abortion (within, that is, a secular morality).

Or rather, since that is clearly too radical a conclusion, it is in a sense relevant, but only in the sense that the familiar biological facts are relevant. By "the familiar biological facts" I mean the facts that most human societies are and have been familiar with—that, standardly (but not invariably), pregnancy occurs as the result of sexual intercourse, that it lasts about nine months, during which time the fetus grows and develops, that standardly it terminates in the birth of a living baby, and that this is how we all come to be.

It might be thought that this distinction—between the familiar biological facts and the status of the fetus—is a distinction without a difference. But this is not so. To attach relevance to the status of the fetus, in the sense in which virtue theory claims it is not relevant, is to be gripped by the conviction that we must go beyond the familiar biological facts, deriving some sort of conclusion from them, such as that the fetus has rights, or is not a person, or something similar. It is also to believe that this exhausts the relevance of the familiar biological facts, that all they are relevant to is the status of the fetus and whether or not it is the sort of thing that may or may not be killed.

These convictions, I suspect, are rooted in the desire to solve the problem of abortion by getting it to fall under some general rule such as "You ought not to kill anything with the right to life but may kill anything else." But they have resulted in what should surely strike any nonphilosopher as a most bizarre aspect of nearly all the current philosophical literature on abortion, namely, that, far from treating abortion as a unique moral problem, markedly unlike any other, nearly everything written on the status of the fetus and its bearing on the abortion issue would be consistent with the human reproductive facts' (to say nothing of family life) being totally different from what they are. Imagine that you are an alien extraterrestrial anthropologist who does not know that the human race is roughly 50 percent female and 50 percent male, or that our only (natural) form of reproduction involves heterosexual intercourse, viviparous birth, and the female's (and only the female's) being pregnant for nine months, or that females are capable of childbearing from late childhood to late middle age, or that childbearing is painful, dangerous, and emotionally charged—do you think you would pick up these facts from the hundreds of articles written on the status of the fetus? I am quite sure you would not. And that, I think, shows that the current philosophical literature on abortion has got badly out of touch with reality.

Now if we are using virtue theory, our first question is not "What do the familiar biological facts show—what can be derived from them about the status of the fetus?" but "How do these facts figure in the practical reasoning, actions and passions, thoughts and reactions, of the virtuous and the nonvirtuous? What is the mark of having the right attitude to these facts and what manifests having the wrong attitude to them?" This immediately makes essentially relevant not only all the facts about human reproduction I mentioned above, but a whole range of facts about our emotions in relation to them as well. I mean such facts as that human parents, both male and female, tend to care passionately about their offspring, and that family relationships are among the deepest and strongest in our lives—and, significantly, among the longest-lasting.

These facts make it obvious that pregnancy is not just one among many other physical conditions; and hence that anyone who genuinely believes that an abortion is comparable to a haircut or an appendectomy is mistaken.[12] The fact that the premature termination of a pregnancy is, in some sense, the cutting off of a new human life, and thereby, like the procreation of a new human life, connects with all our thoughts about human life and death, parenthood, and family relationships, must make it a serious matter. To disregard this fact about it, to think of abortion as nothing but the killing of something that does not matter, or as nothing but the exercise of some right or rights one has, or as the incidental means to some desirable state of affairs, is to do something callous and light-minded, the sort of thing that no virtuous and wise person would do. It is to have the wrong attitude not only to fetuses, but more generally to human life and death, parenthood, and family relationships.

Although I say that the facts make this obvious, I know that this is one of my tendentious points. In partial support of it I note that even the most dedicated proponents of the view that deliberate abortion is just like an appendectomy or haircut rarely hold the same view of spontaneous abortion, that is, miscarriage. It is not so tendentious of me to claim that to react to people's grief over miscarriage by saying, or even thinking, "What a fuss about nothing!" would be callous and light-minded, whereas to try to laugh someone out of grief over an appendectomy scar or a botched haircut would not be. It is hard to give this point due prominence within act-centered theories, for the inconsistency is an inconsistency in attitude about the seriousness of loss of life, not in beliefs about which acts are right or wrong. Moreover, an act-centered theorist may say, "Well, there is nothing wrong with *thinking* 'What a fuss about nothing!' as long as you do not say it and hurt the person who is grieving. And besides, we cannot be held responsible for our thoughts, only for the intentional actions they give rise to." But the character traits that virtue theory emphasizes are not simply dispositions to intentional actions, but a seamless disposition to certain actions and passions, thoughts and reactions.

To say that the cutting off of a human life is always a matter of some seriousness, at any stage, is not to deny the relevance of gradual fetal development. Notwithstanding the well-worn point that clear boundary lines cannot be drawn, our emotions and attitudes regarding the fetus do change as it develops, and again when it is born, and indeed further as the baby grows. Abortion for shallow reasons in the later stages is much more shocking than abortion for the same reasons in the early stages in a way that matches the fact that deep grief over miscarriage in the later stages is more appropriate than it is over miscarriage in the earlier stages (when, that is, the grief is solely about the loss of *this* child, not about, as might be the case, the loss of one's only hope of having a child or of having one's husband's child). Imagine (or recall) a woman who already has children; she had not intended to have more, but finds herself unexpectedly expectedly pregnant. Though contrary to her plans, the pregnancy, once established as a fact, is welcomed—and then she

loses the embryo almost immediately. If this were bemoaned as a tragedy, it would, I think, be a misapplication of the concept of what is tragic. But it may still properly be mourned as a loss. The grief is expressed in such terms as "I shall always wonder how she or he would have turned out" or "When I look at the others, I shall think, 'How different their lives would have been if this other one had been part of them.'" It would, I take it, be callous and light-minded to say, or think, "Well, she has already *got* four children; what's the problem?"; it would be neither, nor arrogantly intrusive in the case of a close friend, to try to correct prolonged mourning by saying, "I know it's sad, but it's not a tragedy; rejoice in the ones you have." The application of *tragic* becomes more appropriate as the fetus grows, for the mere fact that one has lived with it for longer, conscious of its existence, makes a difference. To shrug off an early abortion is understandable just because it is very hard to be fully conscious of the fetus's existence in the early stages and hence hard to appreciate that an early abortion is the destruction of life. It is particularly hard for the young and inexperienced to appreciate this, because appreciation of it usually comes only with experience.

I do not mean "with the experience of having an abortion" (though that may be part of it) but, quite generally, "with the experience of life." Many women who have borne children contrast their later pregnancies with their first successful one, saying that in the later ones they were conscious of a new life growing in them from very early on. And, more generally, as one reaches the age at which the next generation is coming up close behind one, the counterfactuals "If I, or she, had had an abortion, Alice, or Bob, would not have been born" acquire a significant application, which casts a new light on the conditionals "If I or Alice have an abortion then some Caroline or Bill will not be born."

The fact that pregnancy is not just one among many physical conditions does not mean that one can never regard it in that light without manifesting a vice. When women are in very poor physical health, or worn out from childbearing, or forced to do very physically demanding jobs, then they cannot be described as self-indulgent, callous, irresponsible, or light-minded if they seek abortions mainly with a view to avoiding pregnancy as the physical condition that it is. To go through with a pregnancy when one is utterly exhausted, or when one's job consists of crawling along tunnels hauling coal, as many women in the nineteenth century were obliged to do, is perhaps heroic, but people who do not achieve heroism are not necessarily vicious. That they can view the pregnancy only as eight months of misery, followed by hours if not days of agony and exhaustion, and abortion only as the blessed escape from this prospect, is entirely understandable and does not manifest any lack of serious respect for human life or a shallow attitude to motherhood. What it does show is that something is terribly amiss in the conditions of their lives, which make it so hard to recognize pregnancy and childbearing as the good that they can be.

In relation to this last point I should draw attention to the way in which virtue theory has a sort of built-in indexicality. Philosophers arguing against anything remotely resembling a belief in the sanctity of life (which the above claims clearly embody) frequently appeal to the existence of other communities in which abortion and infanticide are practiced. We should not automatically assume that it is impossible that some other communities could be morally inferior to our own; maybe some are, or have been, precisely insofar as their members are, typically, callous or light-minded or unjust. But in communities in which life is a great deal tougher for everyone than it is in ours, having the right attitude to human life and death, parenthood, and family relationships might well manifest itself in ways that are unlike ours. When it is essential to survival that most members of the community fend for themselves at a very young age or work during most of their waking hours, selective abortion or infanticide might be practiced either as a form of genuine euthanasia or for the sake of the community and not, I think, be thought callous or light-minded. But this does not make everything all right; as before, it shows that there is something amiss with the conditions of their lives, which are making it impossible for them to live really well.[13]

The foregoing discussion, insofar as it emphasizes the right attitude to human life and death, parallels to a certain extent those standard discussions of abortion that concentrate on it solely as an issue of killing. But it does not, as those discussions do, gloss over the fact, emphasized by those who discuss the morality of abortion in terms of women's rights, that abortion, wildly unlike any other form of killing, is the termination of a pregnancy, which is a condition of a woman's body and results in *her* having a child if it is not aborted. This fact is given due recognition not by appeal to women's rights but by emphasizing the relevance of the familiar biological and psychological facts and their connection with having the right attitude to parenthood and family relationships. But it may well be thought that failing to bring in women's rights still leaves some important aspects of the problem of abortion untouched.

Speaking in terms of women's rights, people sometimes say things like, "Well, it's her life you're talking about too, you know; she's got a right to her own life, her own happiness." And the discussion stops there. But in the context of virtue theory, given that we are particularly concerned with what constitutes a good human life, with what true happiness or *eudaimonia* is, this is no place to stop. We go on to ask, "And is this life of hers a good one? Is she living well?"

If we are to go on to talk about good human lives, in the context of abortion, we have to bring in our thoughts about the value of love and family life, and our proper emotional development through a natural life cycle. The familiar facts support the view that parenthood in general, and motherhood and childbearing in particular, are intrinsically worthwhile, are among the things that can be correctly thought to be partially constitutive of a flourishing human life.[14] If this is right, then a woman who opts for not being a mother (at all, or again, or now) by opting for abortion may thereby be manifesting a flawed grasp of what her life should be, and be about—a grasp that is childish, or grossly materialistic, or shortsighted, or shallow.

I said *"may* thereby": this *need* not be so. Consider, for instance, a woman who has already had several children and fears that to have another will seriously affect her capacity to be a good mother to the ones she has—she does not show a lack of appreciation of the intrinsic value of being a parent by opting for abortion. Nor does a woman who has been a good mother and is approaching the age at which she may be looking forward to being a good grandmother. Nor does a woman who discovers that her pregnancy may well kill her, and opts for abortion and adoption. Nor, necessarily, does a woman who has decided to lead a life centered around some other worthwhile activity or activities with which motherhood would compete.

People who are childless by choice are sometimes described as "irresponsible," or "selfish," or "refusing to grow up," or "not knowing what life is about." But one can hold that having children is intrinsically worthwhile without endorsing this, for we are, after all, in the happy position of there being more worthwhile things to do than can be fitted into one lifetime. Parenthood, and motherhood in particular, even if granted to be intrinsically worthwhile, undoubtedly take up a lot of one's adult life, leaving no room for some other worthwhile pursuits. But some women who choose abortion rather than have their first child, and some men who encourage their partners to choose abortion, are not avoiding parenthood for the sake of other worthwhile pursuits, but for the worthless one of "having a good time," or for the pursuit of some false vision of the ideals of freedom or self-realization. And some others who say "I am not ready for parenthood yet" are making some sort of mistake about the extent to which one can manipulate the circumstances of one's life so as to make it fulfill some dream that one has. Perhaps one's dream is to have two perfect children, a girl and a boy, within a perfect marriage, in financially secure circumstances, with an interesting job of one's own. But to care too much about that dream, to demand of life that it give it to one and act accordingly, may be both greedy and foolish, and is to run the risk of missing out on happiness entirely. Not only may fate make the dream impossible, or destroy it, but one's own attachment to it may make it impossible. Good marriages, and the most promising children, can be destroyed by just one adult's excessive demand for perfection.

Once again, this is not to deny that girls may quite properly say "I am not ready for motherhood yet," especially in our society, and, far from

manifesting irresponsibility or light-mindedness, show an appropriate modesty or humility, or a fearfulness that does not amount to cowardice. However, even when the decision to have an abortion is the right decision—one that does not itself fall under a vice-related term and thereby one that the perfectly virtuous could recommend—it does not follow that there is no sense in which having the abortion is wrong, or guilt inappropriate. For, by virtue of the fact that a human life has been cut short, some evil has probably been brought about,[15] and that circumstances make the decision to bring about some evil the right decision will be a ground for guilt if getting into those circumstances in the first place itself manifested a flaw in character.

What "gets one into those circumstances" in the case of abortion is, except in the case of rape, one's sexual activity and one's choices, or the lack of them, about one's sexual partner and about contraception. The virtuous woman (which here of course does not mean simply "chaste woman" but "woman with the virtues") has such character traits as strength, independence, resoluteness, decisiveness, self-confidence, responsibility, serious-mindedness, and self-determination—and no one, I think, could deny that many women become pregnant in circumstances in which they cannot welcome or cannot face the thought of having *this* child precisely because they lack one or some of these character traits. So even in the cases where the decision to have an abortion is the right one, it can still be the reflection of a moral failing—not because the decision itself is weak or cowardly or irresolute or irresponsible or light-minded, but because lack of the requisite opposite of these failings landed one in the circumstances in the first place. Hence the common universalized claim that guilt and remorse are never appropriate emotions about an abortion is denied. They may be appropriate, and appropriately inculcated, even when the decision was the right one.

Another motivation for bringing women's rights into the discussion may be to attempt to correct the implication, carried by the killing-centered approach, that insofar as abortion is wrong, it is a wrong that only women do, or at least (given the preponderance of male doctors) that only women instigate. I do not myself believe that we can thus escape the fact that nature bears harder on women than it does on men,[16] but virtue theory can certainly correct many of the injustices that the emphasis on women's rights is rightly concerned about. With very little amendment, everything that has been said above applies to boys and men too. Although the abortion decision is, in a natural sense, the woman's decision, proper to her, boys and men are often party to it, for well or ill, and even when they are not, they are bound to have been party to the circumstances that brought it up. No less than girls and women, boys and men can, in their actions, manifest self-centeredness, callousness, and light-mindedness about life and parenthood in relation to abortion. They can be self-centered or courageous about the possibility of disability in their offspring; they need to reflect on their sexual activity and their choices, or the lack of them, about their sexual partner and contraception; they need to grow up and take responsibility for their own actions and life in relation to fatherhood. If it is true, as I maintain, that insofar as motherhood is intrinsically worthwhile, being a mother is an important purpose in women's lives, being a father (rather than a mere generator) is an important purpose in men's lives as well, and it is adolescent of men to turn a blind eye to this and pretend that they have many more important things to do.

CONCLUSION

Much more might be said, but I shall end the actual discussion of the problem of abortion here, and conclude by highlighting what I take to be its significant features. These hark back to many of the criticisms of virtue theory discussed earlier.

The discussion does not proceed simply by our trying to answer the question "Would a perfectly virtuous agent ever have an abortion and, if so, when?"; virtue theory is not limited to considering "Would Socrates have had an abortion if he were a raped, pregnant fifteen-year-old?" nor automatically stumped when we are considering circumstances into which no virtuous agent would have got herself. Instead, much of the discussion

proceeds in the virtue- and vice-related terms whose application, in several cases, yields practical conclusions (cf. the third and fourth criticisms above). These terms are difficult to apply correctly, and anyone might challenge my application of any one of them. So, for example, I have claimed that some abortions, done for certain reasons, would be callous or light-minded; that others might indicate an appropriate modesty or humility; that others would reflect a greedy and foolish attitude to what one could expect out of life. Any of these examples may be disputed, but what is at issue is, should these difficult terms be there, or should the discussion be couched in terms that all clever adolescents can apply correctly? (Cf. the first half of the "major objection" above.)

Proceeding as it does in the virtue- and vice-related terms, the discussion thereby, inevitably, also contains claims about what is worthwhile, serious and important, good and evil, in our lives. So, for example, I claimed that parenthood is intrinsically worthwhile, and that having a good time was a worthless end (in life, not on individual occasions); that losing a fetus is always a serious matter (albeit not a tragedy in itself in the first trimester) whereas acquiring an appendectomy scar is a trivial one; that (human) death is an evil. Once again, these are difficult matters, and anyone might challenge any one of my claims. But what is at issue is, as before, should those difficult claims be there or can one reach practical conclusions about real moral issues that are in no way determined by premises about such matters? (Cf. the fifth criticism, and the second half of the "major criticism.")

The discussion also thereby, inevitably, contains claims about what life is like (e.g., my claim that love and friendship do not survive their parties' constantly insisting on their rights; or the claim that to demand perfection of life is to run the risk of missing out on happiness entirely). What is at issue is, should those disputable claims be there, or is our knowledge (or are our false opinions) about what life is like irrelevant to our understanding of real moral issues? (Cf. both halves of the "major criticism.")

Naturally, my own view is that all these concepts should be there in any discussion of real moral issues and that virtue theory, which uses all of them, is the right theory to apply to them. I do not pretend to have shown this. I realize that proponents of rival theories may say that, now that they have understood how virtue theory uses the range of concepts it draws on, they are more convinced than ever that such concepts should not figure in an adequate normative theory, because they are sectarian, or vague, or too particular, or improperly anthropocentric, and reinstate what I called the "major criticism." Or, finding many of the details of the discussion appropriate, they may agree that many, perhaps even all, of the concepts should figure, but argue that virtue theory gives an inaccurate account of the way the concepts fit together (and indeed of the concepts themselves) and that another theory provides a better account; that would be interesting to see. Moreover, I admitted that there were at least two problems for virtue theory: that it has to argue against moral skepticism, "pluralism," and cultural relativism, and that it has to find something to say about conflicting requirements of different virtues. Proponents of rival theories might argue that their favored theory provides better solutions to these problems than virtue theory can. Indeed, they might criticize virtue theory for finding problems here at all. Anyone who argued for at least one of moral skepticism, "pluralism," or cultural relativism could presumably do so (provided their favored theory does not find a similar problem); and a utilitarian might say that benevolence is the only virtue and hence that virtue theory errs when it discusses even apparent conflicts between the requirements of benevolence and some other character trait such as honesty.

Defending virtue theory against all possible, or even likely, criticisms of it would be a lifelong task. As I said at the outset, in this article I aimed to defend the theory against some criticisms which I thought arose from an inadequate understanding of it, and to improve that understanding. If I have succeeded, we may hope for more comprehending criticisms of virtue theory than have appeared hitherto.

NOTES

Versions of this article have been read to philosophy societies at University College, London, Rutgers University, and the Universities of Dundee, Edinburgh, Oxford, Swansea, and California–San Diego; at a conference of the Polish and British Academies in Cracow in 1988 on "Life, Death and the Law," and as a symposium paper at the Pacific Division of the American Philosophical Association in 1989. I am grateful to the many people who contributed to the discussions of it on these occasions, and particularly to Philippa Foot and Anne Jaap Jacobson for private discussion.

1. It should be noted that this premise intentionally allows for the possibility that two virtuous agents, faced with the same choice in the same circumstances, may act differently. For example, one might opt for taking her father off the life-support machine and the other for leaving her father on it. The theory requires that neither agent thinks that what the other does is wrong (see note 4), but it explicitly allows that no action is uniquely right in such a case—both are right. It also intentionally allows for the possibility that in some circumstances—those into which no virtuous agent could have got herself—no action is right. I explore this premise at greater length in "Applying Virtue Ethics," forthcoming in a *festschrift* for Philippa Foot.

2. There is, of course, the further question of whether the theory eventually describes a larger circle and winds up relying on the concept of right action in its interpretation of *eudaimonia*. In denying that the theory is trivially circular, I do not pretend to answer this intricate question. It is certainly true that virtue theory does not claim that the correct conception of *eudaimonia* can be got from "an independent 'value-free' investigation of human nature" (John McDowell, "The Role of *Eudaimonia* in Aristotle's Ethics," in *Essays on Aristotle's Ethics,* ed. Amelie Rorty [Berkeley and Los Angeles: University of California Press, 1980]). The sort of training that is required for acquiring the correct conception no doubt involves being taught from early on such things as "Decent people do this sort of thing, not that" and "To do such and such is the mark of a depraved character" (cf. *Nicomachean Ethics* 1110a22). But whether this counts as relying on the concept of right (or wrong) action seems to me very unclear and requiring much discussion.

3. Cf. Bernard Williams' point in *Ethics and the Limits of Philosophy* (London: William Collins, 1985) that we need an enriched ethical vocabulary, not a cut-down one.

4. I put *pluralism* in scare quotes to serve as a warning that virtue theory is not incompatible with all forms of it. It allows for "competing conceptions" of *eudaimonia* and the worthwhile, for instance, in the sense that it allows for a plurality of flourishing lives—the theory need not follow Aristotle in specifying the life of contemplation as the only one that truly constitutes *eudaimonia* (if he does). But the

conceptions "compete" only in the sense that, within a single flourishing life, not everything worthwhile can be fitted in; the theory does not allow that two people with a correct conception of *eudaimonia* can disagree over whether the way the other is living constitutes flourishing. Moreover, the theory is committed to the strong thesis that the same set of character traits is needed for *any* flourishing life; it will not allow that, for instance, soldiers need courage but wives and mothers do not, or that judges need justice but can live well despite lacking kindness. (This obviously is related to the point made in note 1 above.) For an interesting discussion of pluralism (different interpretations thereof) and virtue theory, see Douglas B. Rasmussen, "Liberalism and Natural End Ethics," *American Philosophical Quarterly* 27 (1990): 153–61.

5. E.g., in Williams' Jim and Pedro case in J.J.C. Smart and Bernard Williams, *Utilitarianism: For and Against* (London: Cambridge University Press, 1973).

6. Intimations of this criticism constantly come up in discussion; the clearest statement of it I have found is by Onora O'Neill, in her review of Stephen Clark's "The Moral Status of Animals," in *Journal of Philosophy* 77 (1980): 440–46. For a response I am much in sympathy with, see Cora Diamond, "Anything But Argument?" in *Philosophical Investigations* 5 (1982): 23–41.

7. Aristotle, *Nicomachean Ethics* 1142a12–16.

8. It seems likely that some people have been misled by Foot's discussion of euthanasia (through no fault of hers) into thinking that a virtue theorist's discussion of terminating human life will be conducted exclusively in terms of justice and charity (and the corresponding vice terms) (Philippa Foot, "Euthanasia," *Philosophy & Public Affairs* 6, no. 2 [Winter 1977]: 85–112). But the act-category *euthanasia* is a very special one, at least as defined in her article, since such an act must be done "for the sake of the one who is to die." Building a virtuous motivation into the specification of the act in this way immediately rules out the application of many other vice terms.

9. Judith Jarvis Thomson, "A Defense of Abortion," *Philosophy & Public Affairs* 1, no. 1 (Fall 1971): 47–66. One could indeed regard this article as proto–virtue theory (no doubt to the surprise of the author) if the concepts of callousness and kindness were allowed more weight.

10. One possible qualification: if one ties the concept of justice very closely to rights, then if women do have a moral right to terminate their pregnancies it *may* follow that in doing so they do not act unjustly. (Cf. Thomson, "A Defense of Abortion.") But it is debatable whether even that much follows.

11. This is an assumption of virtue theory, and I do not attempt to defend it here. An adequate discussion of it would require a separate article, since, although most moral philosophers would be chary of claiming that intellectual sophistication is a necessary condition of moral wisdom or virtue, most of us, from Plato onward, tend to write as if this were so. Sorting out which claims about moral knowledge are committed to this kind of elitism and which can, albeit with difficulty, be reconciled with the idea that moral knowledge can be acquired by anyone who really wants it would be a major task.

12. Mary Anne Warren, in "On the Moral and Legal Status of Abortion," *Monist* 57 (1973), sec. 1, says of the opponents of restrictive laws governing abortion that "their conviction (for the most part) is that abortion is not a *morally* serious and extremely unfortunate, even though sometimes justified, act, comparable to killing in self-defense or to letting the violinist die, but rather is closer to being a *morally neutral* act, like cutting one's hair" (italics mine). I would like to think that no one *genuinely* believes this. But certainly in discussion, particularly when arguing against restrictive laws or the suggestion that remorse over abortion might be appropriate, I have found that some people *say* they believe it (and often cite Warren's article, albeit inaccurately, despite its age). Those who allow that it is morally serious, and far from morally neutral, have to argue against restrictive laws, or the appropriateness of remorse, on a very different ground from that laid down by the premise "The fetus is just part of the woman's body (and she has a right to determine what happens to her body and should not feel guilt about anything she does to it)."

13. For another example of the way in which "tough conditions" can make a difference to what is involved in having the right attitude to human life and death and family relationships, see the concluding sentences of Foot's "Euthanasia."

14. I take this as a premise here, but argue for it in some detail in my *Beginning Lives* (Oxford: Basil Blackwell, 1987). In this connection I also discuss adoption and the sense in which it may be regarded as "second best," and the difficult question of whether the good of parenthood may properly be sought, or indeed bought, by surrogacy.

15. I say "some evil has probably been brought about" on the ground that (human) life is (usually) a good and hence (human) death usually an evil. The exceptions would be (*a*) where death is actually a good or a benefit, because the baby that would come to be if the life were not cut short would be better off dead than alive, and (*b*) where death, though not a good, is not an evil either, because the life that would be led (e.g., in a state of permanent coma) would not be a good. (See Foot, "Euthanasia.")

16. I discuss this point at greater length in *Beginning Lives*.

Abortion and the Concept of a Person

JANE ENGLISH

English stakes out some middle ground in the abortion debate. Echoing points made by Judith Jarvis Thomson, she argues that whether or not a fetus is a person, a woman may be justified in some instances (most notably in early pregnancy) in having an abortion as a form of self-defense. But an abortion is not always permissible, for even if a fetus is not a person, it still has at least partial moral status—a status that increases the more the fetus resembles a person. So in the late months of pregnancy, abortion seems wrong except to spare a woman from great injury or death.

The abortion debate rages on. Yet the two most popular positions seem to be clearly mistaken. Conservatives maintain that a human life begins at conception and that therefore abortion must be wrong because it is murder. But not all killings of humans are murders. Most notably, self defense may justify even the killing of an innocent person.

Liberals, on the other hand, are just as mistaken in their argument that since a fetus does not become a person until birth, a woman may do whatever she pleases in and to her own body. First, you cannot do as you please with your own body if it affects other people adversely.[1] Second, if a fetus is not a person, that does not imply that you can do to it anything you wish. Animals, for example, are not persons, yet to kill or torture them for no reason at all is wrong.

At the center of the storm has been the issue of just when it is between ovulation and adulthood that a person appears on the scene. Conservatives draw the line at conception, liberals at birth. In this paper I first examine our concept of a person and conclude that no single criterion can capture the concept of a person and no sharp line can be drawn. Next I argue that if a fetus is a person, abortion is still justifiable in many cases; and if a fetus is not a person, killing it is still wrong in many cases. To a large extent, these two solutions are in agreement.

From *Canadian Journal of Philosophy*, vol. 5, no. 2 (Oct. 1975), pp. 233–43. Copyright © 1975. Reprinted with permission of the University of Calgary Press.

I conclude that our concept of a person cannot and need not bear the weight that the abortion controversy has thrust upon it.

I

The several factions in the abortion argument have drawn battle lines around various proposed criteria for determining what is and what is not a person. For example, Mary Anne Warren[2] lists five features (capacities for reasoning, self-awareness, complex communication, etc.) as her criteria for personhood and argues for the permissibility of abortion because a fetus falls outside this concept. Baruch Brody[3] uses brain waves. Michael Tooley[4] picks having-a-concept-of-self as his criterion and concludes that infanticide and abortion are justifiable, while the killing of adult animals is not. On the other side, Paul Ramsey[5] claims a certain gene structure is the defining characteristic. John Noonan[6] prefers conceived-of-humans and presents counterexamples to various other candidate criteria. For instance, he argues against viability as the criterion because the newborn and infirm would then be non-persons, since they cannot live without the aid of others. He rejects any criterion that calls upon the sorts of sentiments a being can evoke in adults on the grounds that this would allow us to exclude other races as non-persons if we could just view them sufficiently unsentimentally.

These approaches are typical: foes of abortion propose sufficient conditions for personhood which fetuses satisfy, while friends of abortion counter with necessary conditions for personhood which fetuses lack. But these both presuppose that the concept of a person can be captured in a strait jacket of necessary and/or sufficient conditions.[7] Rather, "person" is a cluster of features, of which rationality, having a self concept and being conceived of humans are only part.

What is typical of persons? Within our concept of a person we include, first, certain biological factors: descended from humans, having a certain genetic make-up, having a head, hands, arms, eyes, capable of locomotion, breathing, eating, sleeping. There are psychological factors: sentience, perception, having a concept of self and of one's own interests and desires, the ability to use tools, the ability to use language or symbol systems, the ability to joke, to be angry, to doubt. There are rationality factors: the ability to reason and draw conclusions, the ability to generalize and to learn from past experience, the ability to sacrifice present interests for greater gains in the future. There are social factors: the ability to work in groups and respond to peer pressures, the ability to recognize and consider as valuable the interests of others, seeing oneself as one among "other minds," the ability to sympathize, encourage, love, the ability to evoke from others the responses of sympathy, encouragement, love, the ability to work with others for mutual advantage. Then there are legal factors: being subject to the law and protected by it, having the ability to sue and enter contracts, being counted in the census, having a name and citizenship, the ability to own property, inherit, and so forth.

Now the point is not that this list is incomplete, or that you can find counterinstances to each of its points. People typically exhibit rationality, for instance, but someone who was irrational would not thereby fail to qualify as a person. On the other hand, something could exhibit the majority of these features and still fail to be a person, as an advanced robot might. There is no single core of necessary and sufficient features which we can draw upon with the assurance that they constitute what really makes a person; there are only features that are more or less typical.

This is not to say that no necessary or sufficient conditions can be given. Being alive is a necessary condition for being a person, and being a U.S. Senator is sufficient. But rather than falling inside a sufficient condition or outside a necessary one, a fetus lies in the penumbra region where our concept of a person is not so simple. For this reason I think a conclusive answer to the question whether a fetus is a person is unattainable.

Here we might note a family of simple fallacies that proceed by stating a necessary condition for personhood and showing that a fetus has that characteristic. This is a form of the fallacy of affirming the consequent. For example, some have mistakenly reasoned from the premise that a fetus is human (after all, it is a human fetus rather than, say, a canine fetus), to the conclusion that it is a human. Adding an equivocation on "being," we get the fallacious argument that since a fetus is something both living and human, it is a human being.

Nonetheless, it does seem clear that a fetus has very few of the above family of characteristics, whereas a newborn baby exhibits a much larger proportion of them—and a two-year-old has even more. Note that one traditional anti-abortion argument has centered on pointing out the many ways in which a fetus resembles a baby. They emphasize its development ("It already has ten fingers...") without mentioning its dissimilarities to adults (it still has gills and a tail). They also try to evoke the sort of sympathy on our part that we only feel toward other persons ("Never to laugh... or feel the sunshine?"). This all seems to be a relevant way to argue, since its purpose is to persuade us that a fetus satisfies so many of the important features on the list that it ought so be treated as a person. Also note that a fetus near the time of birth satisfies many more of these factors than a fetus in the early months of development. This could provide reason for making distinctions among the different stages of pregnancy, as the U.S. Supreme Court has done.[8]

Historically, the time at which a person has been said to come into existence has varied widely. Muslims date personhood from fourteen days after conception. Some medievals followed Aristotle in placing ensoulment at forty days after conception for a male fetus and eighty days for a female fetus.[9] In European common law since the Seventeenth Century, abortion was considered the killing of a person only after quickening, the time when a pregnant woman first feels the fetus move on its own. Nor is this variety of opinions surprising. Biologically, a human being develops gradually. We shouldn't expect there to be any specific time or sharp dividing point when a person appears on the scene.

For these reasons I believe our concept of a person is not sharp or decisive enough to bear the weight of a solution to the abortion controversy. To use it to solve that problem is to clarify *obscurum per obscurius*.

II

Next let us consider what follows if a fetus is a person after all. Judith Jarvis Thomson's landmark article, "A Defense of Abortion,"[10] correctly points out that some additional argumentation is needed at this point in the conservative argument to bridge the gap between the premise that a fetus is an innocent person and the conclusion that killing it is always wrong. To arrive at this conclusion, we would need the additional premise that killing an innocent person is always wrong. But killing an innocent person is sometimes permissible, most notably in self defense. Some examples may help draw out our intuitions or ordinary judgments about self defense.

Suppose a mad scientist, for instance, hypnotized innocent people to jump out of the bushes and attack innocent passers-by with knives. If you are so attacked, we agree you have a right to kill the attacker in self defense, if killing him is the only way to protect your life or to save yourself from serious injury. It does not seem to matter here that the attacker is not malicious but himself an innocent pawn, for your killing of him is not done in a spirit of retribution but only in self defense.

How severe an injury may you inflict in self defense? In part this depends upon the severity of the injury to be avoided: you may not shoot someone merely to avoid having your clothes torn. This might lead one to the mistaken conclusion that the defense may only equal the threatened injury in severity; that to avoid death you may kill, but to avoid a black eye you may only inflict a black eye or the equivalent. Rather, our laws and customs seem to say that you may create an injury somewhat, but not

enormously, greater than the injury to be avoided. To fend off an attack whose outcome would be as serious as rape, a severe beating or the loss of a finger, you may shoot; to avoid having your clothes torn, you may blacken an eye.

Aside from this, the injury you may inflict should only be the minimum necessary to deter or incapacitate the attacker. Even if you know he intends to kill you, you are not justified in shooting him if you could equally well save yourself by the simple expedient of running away. Self defense is for the purpose of avoiding harms rather than equalizing harms.

Some cases of pregnancy present a parallel situation. Though the fetus is itself innocent, it may pose a threat to the pregnant woman's well-being, life prospects or health, mental or physical. If the pregnancy presents a slight threat to her interests, it seems self defense cannot justify abortion. But if the threat is on a par with a serious beating or the loss of a finger, she may kill the fetus that poses such a threat, even if it is an innocent person. If a lesser harm to the fetus could have the same defensive effect, killing it would not be justified. It is unfortunate that the only way to free the woman from the pregnancy entails the death of the fetus (except in very late stages of pregnancy). Thus a self defense model supports Thomson's point that the woman has a right only to be freed from the fetus, not a right to demand its death.[11]

The self defense model is most helpful when we take the pregnant woman's point of view. In the pre-Thomson literature, abortion is often framed as a question for a third party: do you, a doctor, have a right to choose between the life of the woman and that of the fetus? Some have claimed that if you were a passer-by who witnessed a struggle between the innocent hypnotized attacker and his equally innocent victim, you would have no reason to kill either in defense of the other. They have concluded that the self defense model implies that a woman may attempt to abort herself, but that a doctor should not assist her. I think the position of the third party is somewhat more complex. We do feel some inclination to intervene on behalf of the victim rather than the attacker, other things equal. But if both parties are innocent, other factors come into consideration.

You would rush to the aid of your husband whether he was attacker or attackee. If a hypnotized famous violinist were attacking a skid row bum, we would try to save the individual who is of more value to society. These considerations would tend to support abortion in some cases.

But suppose you are a frail senior citizen who wishes to avoid being knifed by one of these innocent hypnotics, so you have hired a bodyguard to accompany you. If you are attacked, it is clear we believe that the bodyguard, acting as your agent, has a right to kill the attacker to save you from a serious beating. Your rights of self defense are transferred to your agent. I suggest that we should similarly view the doctor as the pregnant woman's agent in carrying out a defense she is physically incapable of accomplishing herself.

Thanks to modern technology, the cases are rare in which a pregnancy poses as clear a threat to a woman's bodily health as an attacker brandishing a switchblade. How does self defense fare when more subtle, complex and long-range harms are involved?

To consider a somewhat fanciful example, suppose you are a highly trained surgeon when you are kidnapped by the hypnotic attacker. He says he does not intend to harm you but to take you back to the mad scientist who, it turns out, plans to hypnotize you to have a permanent mental block against all your knowledge of medicine. This would automatically destroy your career which would in turn have a serious adverse impact on your family, your personal relationships and your happiness. It seems to me that if the only way you can avoid this outcome is to shoot the innocent attacker, you are justified in so doing. You are defending yourself from a drastic injury to your life prospects. I think it is no exaggeration to claim that unwanted pregnancies (most obviously among teenagers) often have such adverse lifelong consequences as the surgeon's loss of livelihood.

Several parallels arise between various views on abortion and the self defense model. Let's suppose further that these hypnotized attackers only operate at night, so that it is well known that they can be avoided completely by the considerable inconvenience of never leaving your house after dark. One view is that since you could stay home at night, therefore if you go out and are selected by one of these hypnotized people, you have no right to defend yourself. This parallels the view that abstinence is the only acceptable way to avoid pregnancy. Others might hold that you ought to take along some defense such as Mace which will deter the hypnotized person without killing him, but that if this defense fails, you are obliged to submit to the resulting injury, no matter how severe it is. This parallels the view that contraception is all right but abortion is always wrong, even in cases of contraceptive failure.

A third view is that you may kill the hypnotized person only if he will actually kill you, but not if he will only injure you. This is like the position that abortion is permissible only if it is required to save a woman's life. Finally we have the view that it is all right to kill the attacker, even if only to avoid a very slight inconvenience to yourself and even if you knowingly walked down the very street where all these incidents have been taking place without taking along any Mace or protective escort. If we assume that a fetus is a person, this is the analogue of the view that abortion is always justifiable, "on demand."

The self defense model allows us to see an important difference that exists between abortion and infanticide, even if a fetus is a person from conception. Many have argued that the only way to justify abortion without justifying infanticide would be to find some characteristic of personhood that is acquired at birth. Michael Tooley, for one, claims infanticide is justifiable because the really significant characteristics of person are acquired some time after birth. But all such approaches look to characteristics of the developing human and ignore the relation between the fetus and the woman. What if, after birth, the presence of an infant or the need to support it posed a grave threat to the woman's sanity or life prospects? She could escape this threat by the simple expedient of running away. So a solution that does not entail the death of the infant is available. Before birth, such solutions are not available because of the biological dependence of the fetus on the woman. Birth is the crucial point not because of any characteristics the fetus gains, but because after birth the woman can defend herself by a means less drastic than killing the infant. Hence self defense can be used to justify abortion without necessarily thereby justifying infanticide.

III

On the other hand, supposing a fetus is not after all a person, would abortion always be morally permissible? Some opponents of abortion seem worried that if a fetus is not a full-fledged person, then we are justified in treating it in any way at all. However, this does not follow. Non-persons do get some consideration in our moral code, though of course they do not have the same rights as persons have (and in general they do not have moral responsibilities), and though their interests may be overridden by the interests of persons. Still, we cannot just treat them in any way at all.

Treatment of animals is a case in point. It is wrong to torture dogs for fun or to kill wild birds for no reason at all. It is wrong Period, even though dogs and birds do not have the same rights persons do. However, few people think it is wrong to use dogs as experimental animals, causing them considerable suffering in some cases, provided that the resulting research will probably bring discoveries of great benefit to people. And most of us think it all right to kill birds for food or to protect our crops. People's rights are different from the consideration we give to animals, then, for it is wrong to experiment on people, even if others might later benefit a great deal as a result of their suffering. You might volunteer to be a subject, but this would be supererogatory; you certainly have a right to refuse to be a medical guinea pig.

But how do we decide what you may or may not do to non-persons? This is a difficult problem, one for which I believe no adequate account exists. You do not want to say, for instance, that torturing dogs is all right whenever the sum of its effects on people is good—when it doesn't warp the sensibilities of the torturer so much that he mistreats people. If that were the case, it would be all right to torture dogs if you did it in private, or if the torturer lived on a desert island or died soon afterward, so that his actions had no effect on people. This is an inadequate account, because whatever moral consideration animals get, it has to be indefeasible, too. It

will have to be a general proscription of certain actions, not merely a weighing of the impact on people on a case-by-case basis.

Rather, we need to distinguish two levels on which consequences of actions can be taken into account in moral reasoning. The traditional objections to Utilitarianism focus on the fact that it operates solely on the first level, taking all the consequences into account in particular cases only. Thus Utilitarianism is open to "desert island" and "lifeboat" counterexamples because these cases are rigged to make the consequences of actions severely limited.

Rawls' theory could be described as a teleological sort of theory, but with teleology operating on a higher level.[12] In choosing the principles to regulate society from the original position, his hypothetical choosers make their decision on the basis of the total consequences of various systems. Furthermore, they are constrained to choose a general set of rules which people can readily learn and apply. An ethical theory must operate by generating a set of sympathies and attitudes toward others which reinforces the functioning of that set of moral principles. Our prohibition against killing people operates by means of certain moral sentiments including sympathy, compassion and guilt. But if these attitudes are to form a coherent set, they carry us further: we tend to perform supererogatory actions, and we tend to feel similar compassion toward person-like non-persons.

It is crucial that psychological facts play a role here. Our psychological constitution makes it the case that for our ethical theory to work, it must prohibit certain treatment of non-persons which are significantly person-like. If our moral rules allowed people to treat some person-like non-persons in ways we do not want people to be treated, this would undermine the system of sympathies and attitudes that makes the ethical system work. For this reason, we would choose in the original position to make mistreatment of some sorts of animals wrong in general (not just wrong in the cases with public impact), even though animals are not themselves parties in the original position. Thus it makes sense that it is those animals whose appearance and behavior are most like those of people that get the most consideration in our moral scheme.

It is because of "coherence of attitudes," I think, that the similarity of a fetus to a baby is very significant. A fetus one week before birth is so much like a newborn baby in our psychological space that we cannot allow any cavalier treatment of the former while expecting full sympathy and nurturative support for the latter. Thus, I think that anti-abortion forces are indeed giving their strongest arguments when they point to the similarities between a fetus and a baby, and when they try to evoke our emotional attachment to and sympathy for the fetus. An early horror story from New York about nurses who were expected to alternate between caring for six-week premature infants and disposing of viable 24-week aborted fetuses is just that—a horror story. These beings are so much alike that no one can be asked to draw a distinction and treat them so very differently.

Remember, however, that in the early weeks after conception, a fetus is not very much unlike a person. It is hard to develop these feelings for a set of genes which doesn't yet have a head, hands, beating heart, response to touch or the ability to move by itself. Thus it seems to me that the alleged "slippery slope" between conception and birth is not so very slippery. In the early stages of pregnancy, abortion can hardly be compared to murder for psychological reasons, but in the latest stages it is psychologically akin to murder.

Another source of similarity is the bodily continuity between fetus and adult. Bodies play a surprisingly central role in our attitudes toward persons. One has only to think of the philosophical literature on how far physical identity suffices for personal identity or Wittgenstein's remark that the best picture of the human soul is the human body. Even after death, when all agree the body is no longer a person, we still observe elaborate customs of respect for the human body; like people who torture dogs, necrophiliacs are not to be trusted with people.[13] So it is appropriate that we show respect to a fetus as the body continuous with the body of a person. This is a degree of resemblance to persons that animals cannot rival.

Michael Tooley also utilizes a parallel with animals. He claims that it is always permissible to drown newborn kittens and draws conclusions about infanticide.[14] But it is only permissible to drown kittens when their survival would cause some hardship. Perhaps it would be a burden to feed and house six more cats or to find other homes for them. The alternative of letting them starve produces even more suffering than the drowning. Since the kittens get their rights secondhand, so to speak, *via* the need for coherence in our attitudes, their interests are often overriden by the interests of full-fledged persons. But if their survival would be no inconvenience of people at all, then it is wrong to drown them, *contra* Tooley.

Tooley's conclusions about abortion are wrong for the same reason. Even if a fetus is not a person, abortion is not always permissible, because of the resemblance of a fetus to a person. I agree with Thomson that it would be wrong for a woman who is seven months pregnant to have an abortion just to avoid having to postpone a trip to Europe. In the early months of pregnancy when the fetus hardly resembles a baby at all, then, abortion is permissible whenever it is in the interests of the pregnant woman or her family. The reasons would only need to outweigh the pain and inconvenience of the abortion itself. In the middle months, when the fetus comes to resemble a person, abortion would be justifiable only when the continuation of the pregnancy or the birth of the child would cause harms—physical, psychological, economic or social—to the woman. In the late months of pregnancy, even on our current assumption that a fetus is not a person, abortion seems to be wrong except to save a woman from significant injury or death.

The Supreme Court has recognized similar gradations in the alleged slippery slope stretching between conception and birth. To this point, the present paper has been a discussion of the moral status of abortion only, not its legal status. In view of the great physical, financial and sometimes psychological costs of abortion, perhaps the legal arrangement most compatible with the proposed moral solution would be the absence of restrictions, that is, so-called abortion "on demand."

So I conclude, first, that application of our concept of a person will not suffice to settle the abortion issue. After all, the biological development of a human being is gradual. Second, whether a fetus is a person or not, abortion is justifiable early in pregnancy to avoid modest harms and seldom justifiable late in pregnancy except to avoid significant injury or death.[15]

NOTES

1. We also have paternalistic laws which keep us from harming our own bodies even when no one else is affected. Ironically, anti-abortion laws were originally designed to protect pregnant women from a dangerous but tempting procedure.

2. Mary Anne Warren, "On the Moral and Legal Status of Abortion," *Monist* 57 (1973), p. 55.

3. Baruch Brody, "Fetal Humanity and the Theory of Essentialism," in Robert Baker and Frederick Elliston (eds.), *Philosophy and Sex* (Buffalo, N.Y., 1975).

4. Michael Tooley, "Abortion and Infanticide," *Philosophy and Public Affairs* 2 (1971).

5. Paul Ramsey, "The Morality of Abortion," in James Rachels, ed., *Moral Problems* (New York, 1971).

6. John Noonan, "Abortion and the Catholic Church: A Summary History," *Natural Law Forum* 12 (1967), pp. 125–131.

7. Wittgenstein has argued against the possibility of fifty capturing the concept of a game, *Philosophical Investigations* (New York, 1958), §66–71.

8. Not because the fetus is partly a person and so has some of the rights of persons, but rather because of the rights of person-like non-persons.

9. Aristotle himself was concerned, however, with the different question of when the soul takes form. For historical data, see Jimmye Kimmey, "How the Abortion Laws Happened," *Ms.* 1 (April, 1973), pp. 48ff and John Noonan, *loc. cit.*

10. J. J. Thomson, "A Defense of Abortion," *Philosophy and Public Affairs* 1 (1971).

11. *Ibid.*, p. 52.

12. John Rawls, *A Theory of Justice* (Cambridge, Mass., 1971), §§ 3–4.

13. On the other hand, if they can be trusted with people, then our moral customs are mistaken. It all depends on the facts of psychology.

14. *Op. cit.*, pp. 40, 60–61.

15. I am deeply indebted to Larry Crocker and Arthur Kuflik for their constructive comments.

Abortion

MARGARET OLIVIA LITTLE

Margaret Olivia Little is director of the Kennedy Institute of Ethics, and a professor of philosophy at Georgetown University. She offers an analysis of the issue of abortion that is more nuanced than assessments based only on questions of whether a fetus is a person. She explores values that women often wrestle with when deciding whether to end a pregnancy. These include the responsibilities of motherhood, respect for creation, the sanctity of developing human life, and the demands of kinship. Based on how they weigh these ideals, women might ultimately choose to continue a pregnancy or to end it.

. . . Just as we cannot assume that abortion is monstrous if fetuses are persons, so too we cannot assume that abortion is empty of moral import if they are not. Given all the ink that has been spilt on arbitrating the question of fetal personhood, one might be forgiven for having thought so: on some accounts, decisions about whether to continue or end a

From Margaret Olivia Little, "Abortion," in R. G. Frey and Christopher Health Wellmor, eds., *A Companion to Applied Ethics* (Oxford: Blackwell, 2003), 319–324.

pregnancy really are, from a moral point of view, just like decisions about whether to cut one's hair.

But as Ronald Dworkin (1993) has urged, to think abortion morally weighty does not require supposition that the fetus is a person, or even a creature with interests in continued life. Destruction of a Da Vinci painting, he points out, is not bad *for the painting*—the painting has no interests. Instead, it is regrettable because of the deep value it has. So, too, one of the reasons we might regard abortion as morally weighty does not have to do with its being bad *for the fetus*—a setback to its interests—for it may not satisfy the criteria of having interests. Abortion may be weighty, instead, because there is something precious and significant about germinating human life that deserves our deep respect. This, as Dworkin puts it, locates issues of abortion in a different neighborhood of our moral commitments: namely, the accommodation we owe to things of value. That an organism is a potential person may not make it a claims-bearer, but it does mean it has a kind of stature that is worthy of respect.

This intuition, dismissed by some as mere sentimentality, is, I think, both important and broadly held. Very few people regard abortion as the moral equivalent of contraception. Most think a society better morally—not just by public health measures—if it regards abortion as a back-up to failed contraception rather than as routine birth control. Reasons adequate for contraception do not translate transparently as reasons adequate for abortion. Indeed, there is a telling shift in presumption: for most people, it takes no reason at all to justify contracepting; it takes *some* reason to justify ending a pregnancy. That a human life has now begun matters morally.

Burgeoning human life, we might put it, is *respect-worthy*. This is why we care not just whether, but how, abortion is done—while crass jokes are made or with solemnity—and why we care how the fetal remains are treated. It is why the thought of someone aborting for genuinely trivial reasons—to fit into a favorite party dress, say—makes us morally queasy. Perhaps, most basically, it is why the thought of someone aborting with casual indifference fills us with misgiving. Abortion involves loss. Not just loss of the hope that various parties might have invested, but loss of something valuable in its own right. To respect something is to appreciate fully the value it has and the claims it presents to us; someone who aborts but never gives it a second thought has not exhibited genuine appreciation of the value and moral status of that which is now gone.

But if many share the intuition that early human life has a value deserving of respect, there is considerable disagreement about what that respect looks like. There is considerable conflict, that is, over what accommodation we owe to burgeoning human life. In part, of course, this is due to disagreement

over the *degree* of value such life should be accorded: those for whom it is thoroughly modest will have very different views on issues, from abortion to stem-cell research, from those for whom it is transcendent. But this is only part of the story. Obscured by analogies to Da Vinci paintings, some of the most important sources of conflict, especially for the vast middle rank of moderates, ride atop rough agreement on "degree" of fetal value. If we listen to women's own struggles about when it is morally decent to end pregnancy, what we hear are themes about *motherhood* and *respect for creation*. These themes are enormously complex, I want to argue, for they enter stories on both sides of the ledger: for some women, as reasons to continue pregnancy, and, for others, as reasons to end it. Let me start with motherhood.

For many women who contemplate abortion, the desire to end pregnancy is not, or not centrally, a desire to avoid the nine months of pregnancy; it is to avoid what lies on the far side of those months—namely, motherhood. If gestation were simply a matter of rendering, say, somewhat risky assistance to help a burgeoning human life they have come across—if they could somehow render that assistance without thereby adding a member to their family—the decision faced would be a far different one. But gestation does not just allow cells to become a person; it turns one into a mother.

One of the most common reasons women give for wanting to abort is that they do not want to become a mother—now, ever, again, with this partner, or no reliable partner, with these few resources, or these many that are now, after so many years of mothering, slated finally to another cause (Hursthouse, 1987: ch. 8.4). Nor does adoption represent a universal solution. To give up a child would be for some a life-long trauma; others occupy fortunate circumstances that would, by their own lights, make it unjustified to give over a child for others to rear. Or again—and most frequently—she does not *want* to raise a child just now but knows that if she *does* carry the pregnancy to term, she will not *want* to give up the child for adoption. Gestation, she knows, is likely to reshape her heart and soul, transforming her into a mother emotionally, not just officially; and it is precisely that transformation she does not want to undergo. It is because continuing pregnancy brings with it this new identity and, likely, relationship, then, that many feel it legitimate to decline.

But pregnancy's connection to motherhood also enters the phenomenology of abortion in just the opposite direction. For some women, that it would be her child is precisely why she feels she must continue the pregnancy, even if motherhood is not what she desired. To be pregnant is to have one's potential child knocking at one's door; to abort is to turn one's back on it, a decision, many women say, that would haunt them forever. On this view, the desire to avoid motherhood, so compelling as a reason to use contraception, is uneasy grounds to abort: for once an embryo is on the scene, it is not about rejecting motherhood, it is about rejecting one's *child*. Not literally, of course, since there is no child yet extant to stand as the object of rejection. But the stance one should take to pregnancy, sought or not, is one of *acceptance*: when a potential family member is knocking at the door, one should move over, make room, and welcome her in.

These two intuitive stances represent just profoundly different ways of *gestalting* the situation of ending pregnancy. On the first view, abortion is closer to contraception: hardly equivalent, because it means the demise of something of value. But the desire to avoid the enterprise and identity of motherhood is an understandable and honorable basis for deciding to end a pregnancy. Given that there is no child yet on the scene, one does not owe special openness to the relationship that stands at the end of pregnancy's trajectory. On the second view, abortion is closer to exiting a parental relationship: hardly equivalent, for one of the key relata is not yet fully present. But one's decision about whether to continue the pregnancy already feels specially constrained; that one would be related to the resulting person exerts now some moral force. It would take especially grave reasons to refuse assistance here, for the norms of parenthood already have toehold. Assessing the moral status of abortion, it turns out, then, is not just about assessing the contours of generic respect owed to burgeoning human life, it is about assessing the salience of *impending relationship*. And this is an issue that functions in different

ways for different women—and, sometimes, in one and the same woman.

In my own view, until the fetus is a person, we should recognize a moral prerogative to decline parenthood and end the pregnancy. Not because motherhood is necessarily a burden (though it can be), but because it so thoroughly changes what we might call one's fundamental *practical identity*. The enterprise of mothering restructures the self—changing the shape of one's heart, the primary commitments by which one lives one's life, the terms by which one judges one's life a success or a failure. If the enterprise is eschewed and one decides to give the child over to another, the identity of mother still changes the normative facts that are true of one, as there is now someone by whom one does well or poorly (see Ross, 1982). And either way—whether one rears the child or lets it go—to continue a pregnancy means that a piece of one's heart, as the saying goes, will forever walk outside one's body. As profound as the respect we should have for burgeoning human life, we should acknowledge moral prerogatives over identity-constituting commitments and enterprises as profound as motherhood.

Whether one agrees with this view or not, there is at any rate another layer of the moral story here. If women find themselves with different ways of *gestalting* the prospective relationship involved in pregnancy, it is in part because they have different identities, commitments, and ideals that such a prospect intersects with, commitments which, while permissibly idiosyncratic, are morally authoritative for *them*. If one woman feels already duty-bound by the norms of parenthood to nurture this creature, for example, it may be for the very good reason that, in an important personal sense, she already *is* its mother. She finds herself (perhaps to her surprise) with a maternal commitment to this creature. But taking on the identity of mother toward something just *is* to take on certain imperatives about its well-being as categorical. Her job is thus clear: it is to help this creature reach its fullest potential. For another woman, on the other hand, the identity of mother is yet to be taken on; it is tried on, perhaps accepted, but perhaps declined—in which case respect is owed, but love is saved, or confirmed, for others—other relationships, other projects, other passions.

And, again, if one woman feels she owes a stance of welcome to burgeoning human life that comes her way, it may be, not because she thinks such a stance authoritative for all, but because of the virtues around which her practical identity is now oriented: receptivity to life's agenda, for instance, or responsiveness to that which is most vulnerable. For another woman, the virtues to be exercised may tug in just the other direction: loyalty to treasured life plans, a commitment that it be she, not the chances of biology, that should determine her life's course, bolstering self-direction after a life too long ruled by serendipity and fate.

Deciding when it is morally decent to end a pregnancy, it turns out, is an admixture of settling impersonally or universally authoritative moral requirements, and of discovering and arbitrating— sometimes after agonizing deliberation, sometimes in a decision no less deep for its immediacy—one's own commitments, identity, and defining virtues.

A similarly complex story appears when we turn to the second theme. Another thread that appears in many women's stories in the face of unsought pregnancy is respect for the weighty responsibility involved in creating human life. Once again, it is a theme that pulls and tugs in different directions.

In its most familiar direction, it shows up in many stories of why an unsought pregnancy is continued. Many people believe that one's responsibility to nurture new life is importantly amplified if one is responsible for bringing about its existence in the first place. Just what it takes to count as responsible here is a point on which individuals diverge (whether voluntary intercourse with contraception is different from intercourse without use of birth control, and again from intentionally deciding to become pregnant at the IVF clinic). But triggering the relevant standard of responsibility for creation, it is felt, brings with it a heightened responsibility to nurture: it is disrespectful to create human life only to allow it to wither. Put more rigorously, one who is responsible for bringing about a creature that has intrinsic value in virtue of its potential to become a person has a special responsibility to enable it to reach that end state.

But the idea of respect for creation is also, if less frequently acknowledged, sometimes the reason why women are moved to *end* pregnancies. As Barbara Katz Rothman (1989) puts it, decisions to abort often represent, not a decision to destroy, but a refusal to create. Many people have deeply felt convictions about the circumstances under which they feel it right for them to bring a child into the world. Can it be brought into a decent world, an intact family, a society that can minimally respect its agency? These considerations may persist even after conception has taken place; for while the *embryo* has already been created, a person has not. Some women decide to abort, that is, not because they do not *want* the resulting child—indeed, they may yearn for nothing more, and desperately wish that their circumstances were otherwise—but because they do not think bringing a child into the world the right thing for them to do.

These are abortions marked by moral language. A woman wants to abort because she knows she could not give up a child for adoption but feels she could not give the child the sort of life, or be the sort of parent, she thinks a child *deserves*; a woman who would have to give up the child thinks it would be *unfair* to bring a child into existence already burdened by rejection, however well grounded its reasons; a woman living in a country marked by poverty and gender apartheid wants to abort because she decides it would be *wrong* for her to bear a daughter whose life, like hers, would be filled with so much injustice and hardship.

Some have thought that such decisions betray a simple fallacy: unless the child's life were literally going to be worse than non-existence, how can one abort out of concern for the future child? But the worry here is not that one would be imposing a *harm* on the child by bringing it into existence (as though children who are in the situations mentioned have lives that are not worth living). The claim is that bringing about a person's life in these circumstances would do violence to her ideals of creating and parenthood. She does not want to bring into existence a daughter she cannot love and care for, she does not want to bring into existence a person whose life will be marked by disrespect or rejection.

Nor does the claim imply judgment on women who *do* continue pregnancies in similar circumstances—as though there were here an obligation to abort. For the norms in question, once again, need not be impersonally authoritative moral claims. Like ideals of good parenting, they mark out considerations all should be sensitive to, perhaps, but equally reasonable people may adhere to different variations and weightings. Still, they are normative for those who do have them; far from expressing mere matters of taste, the ideals one does accept carry an important kind of categoricity, issuing imperatives whose authority is not reducible to mere desire. These are, at root, issues about *integrity,* and the importance of maintaining integrity over one's participation in this enterprise precisely because it is so normatively weighty.

What is usually emphasized in the morality of abortion is the ethics of destruction, but there is a balancing ethics of creation. And for many people, conflict about abortion is a conflict *within* that ethics. On the one hand, we now have on hand an entity that has a measure of sanctity: that it has begun is reason to help it continue, perhaps especially if one has had a role in its procreation, which is why even early abortion is not normatively equivalent to contraception. On the other hand, not to end a pregnancy *is* to do something else, namely, to continue creating a person, and, for some women, pregnancy strikes in circumstances in which they cannot countenance that enterprise. For some, the sanctity of developing human life will be strong enough to tip the balance toward continuing the pregnancy; for others, their norms of respectful creation will hold sway. For those who believe that the norms governing creation of a person are mild relative to the normative telos of embryonic life, being a responsible creator means continuing to gestate, and doing the best one can to bring about the conditions under which that creation will be more respectful. For others, though, the normativity of fetal telos is mild and their standards of respectful creation high, and the lesson goes in just the other direction: it is a sign of respect not to continue creating when certain background conditions, such as a loving family or adequate resources, are not in place.

However one thinks these issues settle out, they will not be resolved by austere contemplation of the value of human life. They require wrestling with the rich meanings of creation, responsibility, and kinship. And these issues, I have suggested, are just as much issues about one's integrity as they are about what is impersonally obligatory. On many treatments of abortion, considerations about whether or not to continue a pregnancy are exhausted by preferences, on the one hand, and universally authoritative moral demands, on the other; but some of the most important terrain lies in between.

REFERENCES

Bolton, M. B. (1979) Responsible women and abortion decisions. In O. O'Neil and W. Ruddick (eds), *Having Children.* New York: Oxford University Press.

Brody, B. (1975) *Abortion and the Sanctity of Life.* Cambridge, MA: MIT Press.

Dworkin, R. (1993) *Life's Dominion: An Argument about Abortion, Euthanasia, and Individual Freedom.* New York: Alfred A. Knopf.

Feinberg J. (1992) Abortion. In *Freedom and Fulfillment: Philosophical Essays.* Princeton, NJ: Princeton University Press.

Hursthouse, R. (1987) *Beginning Lives.* Oxford: Open University Press.

Kamm, F. M. (1992) *Creation and Abortion: A Study in Moral and Legal Philosophy.* New York: Oxford University Press.

MacKinnon, C. A. (1991) Reflections on sex equality under law. *The Yale Law Journal,* 100 (5): 1281–328.

Marquis, D. (1989) Why abortion is immoral. *The Journal of Philosophy,* 76: 183–202.

Quinn, W. (1993) Abortion: identity and loss. In *Morality and Action.* New York: Cambridge University Press.

Ross, S. L. (1982) Abortion and the death of the fetus. *Philosophy and Public Affairs,* 11: 232–45.

Rothman, B. K. (1989) *Recreating Motherhood: Ideology and Technology in a Patriarchal Society.* New York: Norton.

Silverstein, H. S. (1987) On a woman's "responsibility" for the fetus. *Social Theory and Practice,* 13: 103–19.

Steinbock, B. (1922) *Life before Birth: The Moral and Legal Status of Embryos and Fetuses.* New York: Oxford University Press.

Thomson, J. J. (1971) A defense of abortion. *Philosophy and Public Affairs,* 1: 47–66.

West, R. (1993) Jurisprudence and gender. In D. Kelly Weisberg (ed.)., *Feminist Legal Theory: Foundations,* pp. 75–98. Philadelphia: Temple University Press.

Abortion Through a Feminist Ethics Lens

SUSAN SHERWIN

Sherwin says that a central moral feature of pregnancy is that it takes place in women's bodies and has a tremendous impact on women's lives. Policies about abortion affect women uniquely. So we must evaluate how proposed abortion policies "fit into general patterns of oppression for women," and a decision to have or not to have an abortion must be left to the individual woman, the one who best understands the circumstances of the decision. A fetus has moral significance, but its moral standing depends on its relationship to the pregnant woman. Feminist views, says Sherwin, stress "the importance of protecting women's right to continue as well as to terminate pregnancies as each sees fit."

Abortion has long been a central issue in the arena of applied ethics, but, the distinctive analysis of feminist ethics is generally overlooked in most philosophic discussions. Authors and readers commonly presume a familiarity with the feminist position and equate it with liberal defences of women's right to choose abortion, but, in fact, feminist ethics yields a different analysis of the moral questions surrounding abortion than that usually offered by the more familiar liberal defenders of abortion rights. Most feminists can agree with some of the conclusions that arise from certain non-feminist arguments on abortion, but they often disagree about the way the issues are formulated and the sorts of reasons that are invoked in the mainstream literature.

Among the many differences found between feminist and non-feminist arguments about abortion, is the fact that most non-feminist discussions of abortion consider the questions of the moral or legal permissibility of abortion in isolation from other questions, ignoring (and thereby obscuring) relevant connections to other social practices that oppress women. They are generally grounded in masculinist conceptions of freedom (e.g., privacy, individual choice, individuals' property rights in their own bodies) that do not meet the needs, interests, and intuitions of many of the women concerned. In contrast, feminists seek to couch their arguments in

moral concepts that support their general campaign of overcoming injustice in all its dimensions, including those inherent in moral theory itself.[1] There is even disagreement about how best to understand the moral question at issue: non-feminist arguments focus exclusively on the morality and/or legality of performing abortions, whereas feminists insist that other questions, including ones about accessibility and delivery of abortion services must also be addressed.

Although feminists welcome the support of non-feminists in pursuing policies that will grant women control over abortion decisions, they generally envision very different sorts of policies for this purpose than those considered by non-feminist sympathizers. For example, Kathleen McDonnell (1984) urges feminists to develop an explicitly "'feminist morality' of abortion. . . . At its root it would be characterized by the deep appreciations of time complexities of life, the refusal to polarize and adopt simplistic formulas" (p. 52). Here, I propose one conception of the shape such an analysis should take.

Women and Abortion

The most obvious difference between feminist and non-feminist approaches to abortion can be seen in the relative attention each gives to the interests and experiences of women in its analysis. Feminists consider it self-evident that the pregnant woman is a subject of principal concern in abortion decisions. In most non-feminist accounts, however, not only is she not perceived as central, she is rendered

From *Dialogue: Canadian Philosophical Review*, vol. XXX, no. 1–2 (1991), pp. 327–342. Copyright © the Canadian Philosophical Association.

virtually invisible. Non-feminist theorists, whether they support or oppose women's right to choose abortion, focus almost all their attention on the moral status of the developing embryo or the fetus.

In pursuing a distinctively feminist ethics, it is appropriate to begin with a look at the role of abortion in women's lives. Clearly, the need for abortion can be very intense; women have pursued abortions under appalling and dangerous conditions, across widely diverse cultures and historical periods. No one denies that if abortion is not made legal, safe, and accessible, women will seek out illegal and life-threatening abortions to terminate pregnancies they cannot accept. Anti-abortion activists seem willing to accept this price, but feminists judge the inevitable loss of women's lives associated with restrictive abortion policies to be a matter of fundamental concern.

Although anti-abortion campaigners imagine that women often make frivolous and irresponsible decisions about abortion, feminists recognize that women have abortions for a wide variety of reasons. Some women, for instance, find themselves seriously ill and incapacitated throughout pregnancy; they cannot continue in their jobs and may face enormous difficulties in fulfilling their responsibilities at home. Many employers and schools will not tolerate pregnancy in their employees or students, and not every woman is able to put her job, career, or studies on hold. Women of limited means may be unable to take adequate care of children they have already borne and they may know that another mouth to feed will reduce their ability to provide for their existing children. Women who suffer from chronic disease, or who feel too young, or too old, or who are unable to maintain lasting relationships may recognize that they will not be able to care properly for a child at this time. Some who are homeless, or addicted to drugs, or who are diagnosed as carrying the AIDS virus may be unwilling to allow a child to enter the world under such circumstances. If the pregnancy is a result of rape or incest, the psychological pain of carrying it to term may be unbearable, and the woman may recognize that her attitude to the child after birth will always be tinged with bitterness. Some women have learned that the fetuses they carry have serious chromosomal anomalies and consider it best to prevent them from being born with a

condition bound to cause suffering. Others, knowing the fathers to be brutal and violent, may be unwilling to subject a child to the beatings or incestuous attacks they anticipate; some may have no other realistic way to remove the child (or themselves) from the relationship.

Or a woman may simply believe that bearing a child is incompatible with her life plans at this time, since continuing a pregnancy is likely to have profound repercussions throughout a woman's entire life. If the woman is young, a pregnancy will very likely reduce her chances of education and hence limit her career and life opportunities: "The earlier a woman has a baby, it seems, the more likely she is to drop out of school; the less education she gets, the more likely she is to remain poorly paid, peripheral to the labour market, or unemployed, and the more children she will have—between one and three more than her working childless counterpart" (Petchesky 1984, p. 150). In many circumstances, having a child will exacerbate the social and economic forces already stacked against her by virtue of her sex (and her race, class, age, sexual orientation, or the effects of some disability, etc.). Access to abortion is a necessary option for many women if they are to escape the oppressive conditions of poverty.

Whatever the reason, most feminists believe that a pregnant woman is in the best position to judge whether abortion is the appropriate response to her circumstances. Since she is usually the only one able to weigh all the relevant factors, most feminists reject attempts to offer any general abstract rules for determining when abortion is morally justified. Women's personal deliberations about abortion include contextually defined considerations reflecting their commitment to the needs and interests of everyone concerned—including herself, the fetus she carries, other members of her household, etc. Because there is no single formula available for balancing these complex factors through all possible cases, it is vital that feminists insist on protecting each woman's right to come to her own conclusions. Abortion decisions are, by their very nature, dependent on specific features of each woman's experience; theoretically dispassionate philosophers and other moralists should not expect to set the agenda for these considerations in any universal way. Women must be acknowledged as full moral agents with the responsibility for making moral decisions about their own pregnancies.[2] Although I think that it is possible for a woman to make a mistake in her moral judgment on this matter (i.e., it is possible that a woman may come to believe that she was wrong about her decision to continue or terminate a pregnancy), the intimate nature of this sort of decision makes it unlikely that anyone else is in a position to arrive at a more reliable conclusion; it is, therefore, improper to grant others the authority to interfere in women's decisions to seek abortions.

Feminist analysis regards the effects of unwanted pregnancies on the lives of women individually and collectively as a central element in the moral evaluation of abortion. Even without patriarchy, bearing a child would be a very important event in a woman's life. It involves significant physical, emotional, social, and (usually) economic changes for her. The ability to exert control over the incidence, timing, and frequency of child-bearing is often tied to her ability to control most other things she values. Since we live in a patriarchal society, it is especially important to ensure that women have the authority to control their own reproduction.[3] Despite the diversity of opinion among feminists on most other matters, virtually all feminists seem to agree that women must gain full control over their own reproductive lives if they are to free themselves from male dominance.[4] Many perceive the commitment of the political right wing to opposing abortion as part of a general strategy to reassert patriarchal control over women in the face of significant feminist influence (Petchesky 1980, p. 112).

Women's freedom to choose abortion is also linked with their ability to control their own sexuality. Women's subordinate status often prevents them from refusing men sexual access to their bodies. If women cannot end the unwanted pregnancies that result from male sexual dominance, their sexual vulnerability to particular men can increase, because caring for an(other) infant involves greater financial needs and reduced economic opportunities for women.[5] As a result, pregnancy often forces women to become dependent on men. Since a woman's dependence on a man is assumed to entail that she will remain sexually loyal to him, restriction of abortion serves to channel women's sexuality and further perpetuates the cycle of oppression.

In contrast to most non-feminist accounts, feminist analyses of abortion direct attention to the question of how women get pregnant. Those who reject abortion seem to believe that women can avoid unwanted pregnancies by avoiding sexual intercourse. Such views show little appreciation for the power of sexual politics in a culture that oppresses women. Existing patterns of sexual dominance mean that women often have little control over their sexual lives. They may be subject to rape by strangers, or by their husbands, boyfriends, colleagues, employers, customers, fathers, brothers, uncles, and dates. Often, the sexual coercion is not even recognized as such by the participants, but is the price of continued "good will"—popularity, economic survival, peace, or simple acceptance. Few women have not found themselves in circumstances where they do not feel free to refuse a man's demands for intercourse, either because he is holding a gun to her head or because he threatens to be emotionally hurt if she refuses (or both). Women are socialized to be compliant and accommodating, sensitive to the feelings of others, and frightened of physical power; men are socialized to take advantage of every opportunity to engage in sexual intercourse and to use sex to express dominance and power. Under such circumstances, it is difficult to argue that women could simply "choose" to avoid heterosexual activity if they wish to avoid pregnancy. Catherine MacKinnon neatly sums it up: "the logic by which women are supposed to consent to sex [is]: preclude the alternatives, then call the remaining option 'her choice'" (MacKinnon 1989, p. 192).

Nor can women rely on birth control alone to avoid pregnancy. There simply is no form of reversible contraception available that is fully safe and reliable. The pill and the IUD are the most effective means offered, but both involve significant health hazards to women and are quite dangerous for some. No woman should spend the 30 to 40 years of her reproductive life on either form of birth control. Further, both have been associated with subsequent problems of involuntary infertility, so they are far from optimum for women who seek to control the timing of their pregnancies.

The safest form of birth control involves the use of barrier methods (condoms or diaphragms) in combination with spermicidal foams or jelly. But these methods also pose difficulties for women. They may be socially awkward to use: young women are discouraged from preparing for sexual activity that might never happen and are offered instead romantic models of spontaneous passion. (Few films or novels interrupt scenes of seduction for the fetching of contraceptives.) Many women find their male partners unwilling to use barrier methods of contraception and they do not have the power to insist. Further, cost is a limiting factor for many women. Condoms and spermicides are expensive and are not covered under most health care plans. There is only one contraceptive option which offers women safe and fully effective birth control: barrier methods with the back-up option of abortion.[6]

From a feminist perspective, a central moral feature of pregnancy is that it takes place in *women's bodies* and has profound effects on *women's* lives. Gender-neutral accounts of pregnancy are not available; pregnancy is explicitly a condition associated with the female body.[7] Because the need for abortion is experienced only by women, policies about abortion affect women uniquely. Thus, it is important to consider how proposed policies on abortion fit into general patterns of oppression for women. Unlike non-feminist accounts, feminist ethics demands that the effects on the oppression of women be a principal consideration when evaluating abortion policies.

The Fetus

In contrast, most non-feminist analysts believe that the moral acceptability of abortion turns on the question of the moral status of the fetus. Even those who support women's right to choose abortion tend to accept the central premise of the anti-abortion proponents that abortion can only be tolerated if it can be proved that the fetus is lacking some criterion of full personhood.[8] Opponents of abortion have structured the debate so that it is necessary to define the status of the fetus as either valued the same as other humans (and hence entitled not to be killed) or as lacking in all value. Rather than challenging the logic of this formulation, many defenders of abortion have concentrated on showing that the fetus is indeed without significant value (Tooley

1972, Warren 1973); others, such as Wayne Sumner (1981), offer a more subtle account that reflects the gradual development of fetuses whereby there is some specific criterion that determines the degree of protection to be afforded them which is lacking in the early stages of pregnancy but present in the later stages. Thus, the debate often rages between abortion opponents who describe the fetus as an "innocent," vulnerable, morally important, separate being whose life is threatened and who must be protected at all costs, and abortion supporters who try to establish some sort of deficiency inherent to fetuses which removes them from the scope of the moral community.

The woman on whom the fetus depends for survival is considered as secondary (if she is considered at all) in these debates. The actual experiences and responsibilities of real women are not perceived as morally relevant (unless they, too, can be proved innocent by establishing that their pregnancies are a result of rape or incest). It is a common assumption of both defenders and opponents of women's right to choose abortion that many women will be irresponsible in their choices. The important question, though, is whether fetuses have the sort of status that justifies interfering in women's choices at all. In some contexts, women's role in gestation is literally reduced to that of "fetal containers"; the individual women disappear or are perceived simply as mechanical life-support systems.[9]

The current rhetoric against abortion stresses the fact that the genetic make-up of the fetus is determined at conception and the genetic code is incontestably human. Lest there be any doubt about the humanity of the fetus, we are assailed with photographs of fetuses at various stages of development demonstrating the early appearance of recognizably human characteristics, e.g., eyes, fingers, and toes. The fact that the fetus in its early stages is microscopic, virtually indistinguishable from other primate fetuses to the untrained eye, and lacking in the capacities that make human life meaningful and valuable is not deemed relevant by the self-appointed defenders of fetuses. The anti-abortion campaign is directed at evoking sympathetic attitudes towards this tiny, helpless being whose life is threatened by its own mother; it urges us to see the fetus as entangled in an adversarial relationship with the (presumably irresponsible) woman who carries it. We are encouraged to identify with the "unborn child" and not with the (selfish) woman whose life is also at issue.

Within the non-feminist literature, both defenders and opponents of women's right to choose abortion agree that the difference between a late term fetus and a newborn infant is "merely geographical" and cannot be considered morally significant. But a fetus inhabits a woman's body and is wholly dependent on her unique contribution to its maintenance while a newborn is physically separate though still in need of a lot of care. One can only view the distinction between being in or out of a woman's womb as morally irrelevant if one discounts the perspective of the pregnant woman; feminists seem to be alone in recognizing her perspective as morally important.[10]

Within anti-abortion arguments, fetuses are identified as individuals; in our culture which views the (abstract) individual as sacred, fetuses *qua* individuals should be honoured and preserved. Extraordinary claims are made to try to establish the individuality and moral agency of fetuses. At the same time, the women who carry these fetal individuals are viewed as passive hosts whose only significant role is to refrain from aborting or harming their fetuses. Since it is widely believed that the woman does not actually have to *do* anything to protect the life of the fetus, pregnancy is often considered (abstractly) to be a tolerable burden to protect the life of an individual so like us.[11]

Medicine has played its part in supporting these sorts of attitudes. Fetal medicine is a rapidly expanding specialty, and it is commonplace in professional medical journals to find references to pregnant women as "fetal environments." Fetal surgeons now have at their disposal a repertory of sophisticated technology that can save the lives of dangerously ill fetuses; in light of such heroic successes, it is perhaps understandable that women have disappeared from their view. These specialists see fetuses as their patients, not the women who nurture them. Doctors perceive themselves as the *active* agents in saving fetal lives and, hence, believe that they are the ones in direct relationship with the fetuses they treat.

Perhaps even more distressing than the tendency to ignore the woman's agency altogether and view her as a purely passive participant in the medically controlled events of pregnancy and childbirth is the growing practice of viewing women as genuine threats to the well-being of the fetus. Increasingly, women are viewed as irresponsible or hostile towards their fetuses, and the relationship between them is characterized as adversarial (Overall 1987, p. 60). Concern for the well-being of the fetus is taken as licence for doctors to intervene to ensure that women comply with medical "advice." Courts are called upon to enforce the doctors' orders when moral pressure alone proves inadequate, and women are being coerced into undergoing unwanted Caesarean deliveries and technologically monitored hospital births. Some states have begun to imprison women for endangering their fetuses through drug abuse and other socially unacceptable behaviours. An Australian state recently introduced a bill that makes women liable to criminal prosecution "if they are found to have smoked during pregnancy, eaten unhealthful foods, or taken any other action which can be shown to have adversely affected the development of the fetus" (Warren 1989, p. 60).

In other words, physicians have joined with anti-abortionist activists in fostering a cultural acceptance of the view that fetuses are distinct individuals, who are physically, ontologically, and socially separate from the women whose bodies they inhabit, and who have their own distinct interests. In this picture, pregnant women are either ignored altogether or are viewed as deficient in some crucial respect and hence subject to coercion for the sake of their fetuses. In the former case, the interests of the women concerned are assumed to be identical with those of the fetus; in the latter, the women's interests are irrelevant because they are perceived as immoral, unimportant, or unnatural. Focus on the fetus as an independent entity has led to presumptions which deny pregnant women their roles as active, independent, moral agents with a primary interest in what becomes of the fetuses they carry. Emphasis on the fetus's status has led to an assumed licence to interfere with women's reproductive freedom.

A Feminist View of the Fetus

Because the public debate has been set up as a competition between the rights of women and those of fetuses, feminists have often felt pushed to reject claims of fetal value in order to protect women's claims. Yet, as Addelson (1987) has argued, viewing abortion in this way "tears [it] out of the context of women's lives" (p. 107). There are other accounts of fetal value that are more plausible and less oppressive to women.

On a feminist account, fetal development is examined in the context in which it occurs, within women's bodies rather than in the imagined isolation implicit in many theoretical accounts. Fetuses develop in specific pregnancies which occur in the lives of particular women. They are not individuals housed in generic female wombs, nor are they full persons at risk only because they are small and subject to the whims of women. Their very existence is relational, developing as they do within particular women's bodies, and their principal relationship is to the women who carry them.

On this view, fetuses are morally significant, but their status is relational rather than absolute. Unlike other human beings, fetuses do not have any independent existence; their existence is uniquely tied to the support of a specific other. Most non-feminist commentators have ignored the relational dimension of fetal development and have presumed that the moral status of fetuses could be resolved solely in terms of abstract metaphysical criteria of personhood. They imagine that there is some set of properties (such as genetic heritage, moral agency, self-consciousness, language use, or self-determination) which will entitle all who possess them to be granted the moral status of persons (Warren 1973, Tooley 1972). They seek some particular feature by which we can neatly divide the world into the dichotomy of moral persons (who are to be valued and protected) and others (who are not entitled to the same group privileges); it follows that it is a merely empirical question whether or not fetuses possess the relevant properties.

But this vision misinterprets what is involved in personhood and what it is that is especially valued about persons. Personhood is a social category, not an isolated state. Persons are members of a community; they develop as concrete, discrete, and specific individuals. To be a morally significant category, personhood must involve personality as well as biological integrity.[12] It is not sufficient to consider persons simply as Kantian atoms of rationality; persons are all embodied, conscious beings with particular social histories. Annette Baier (1985) has developed a concept of persons as "second persons" which helps explain the sort of social dimension that seems fundamental to any moral notion of personhood:

> A person, perhaps, is best seen as one who was long enough dependent upon other persons to acquire the essential arts of personhood. Persons essentially are *second* persons, who grow up with other persons. . . . The fact that a person has a life *history*, and that a people collectively have a history depends upon the humbler fact that each person has a childhood in which a cultural heritage is transmitted, ready for adolescent rejection and adult discriminating selection and contribution. Persons come after and before other persons. (P. 84–85; her emphasis.)

Persons, in other words, are members of a social community which shapes and values them, and personhood is a relational concept that must be defined in terms of interactions and relationships with others.

A fetus is a unique sort of being in that it cannot form relationships freely with others, nor can others readily form relationships with it. A fetus has a primary and particularly intimate relationship with the woman in whose womb it develops; any other relationship it may have is indirect, and must be mediated through the pregnant woman. The relationship that exists between a woman and her fetus is clearly asymmetrical, since she is the only party to the relationship who is capable of making a decision about whether the interaction should continue and since the fetus is wholly dependent on the woman who sustains it while she is quite capable of surviving without it.

However much some might prefer it to be otherwise, no one else can do anything to support or harm a fetus without doing something to the woman who nurtures it. Because of this inexorable biological reality, she bears a unique responsibility and privilege in determining her fetus's place in the social scheme of things. Clearly, many pregnancies occur to women who place very high value on the lives of the particular fetuses they carry, and choose to see their pregnancies through to term despite the possible risks and costs involved; hence, it would be wrong of anyone to force such a woman to terminate her pregnancy under these circumstances. Other women, or some of these same women at other times, value other things more highly (e.g., their freedom, their health, or previous responsibilities which conflict with those generated by the pregnancies), and choose not to continue their pregnancies. The value that women ascribe to individual fetuses varies dramatically from case to case, and may well change over the course of any particular pregnancy. There is no absolute value that attaches to fetuses apart from their relational status determined in the context of their particular development.

Since human beings are fundamentally relational beings, it is important to remember that fetuses are characteristically limited in the relationships in which they can participate; within those relationships, they can make only the most restricted "contributions."[13] After birth, human beings are capable of a much wider range of roles in relationships with an infinite variety of partners; it is that very diversity of possibility and experience that leads us to focus on the abstraction of the individual as a constant through all her/his relationships. But until birth, no such variety is possible, and the fetus is defined as an entity within a woman who will almost certainly be principally responsible for it for many years to come.

No human, and especially no fetus, can exist apart from relationships; feminist views of what is valuable about persons must reflect the social nature of their existence. Fetal lives can neither be sustained nor destroyed without affecting the women who support them. Because of a fetus's unique physical status—*within* and dependent on a particular woman—the responsibility and privilege of determining its specific social status and value must rest with the woman carrying it. Fetuses are not persons because they have not developed sufficiently in social relationships to be persons in any morally significant sense (i.e., they are not yet second persons). Newborns, although just beginning

their development into persons, are immediately subject to social relationships, for they are capable of communication and response in interaction with a variety of other persons. Thus, feminist accounts of abortion stress the importance of protecting women's right to continue as well as to terminate pregnancies as each sees fit.

Feminist Politics and Abortion

. . . Feminists support abortion on demand because they know that women must have control over their reproduction. For the same reason, they actively oppose forced abortion and coerced sterilization, practices that are sometimes inflicted on the most powerless women, especially those in the Third World. Feminist ethics demands that access to voluntary, safe, effective birth control be part of any abortion discussion, so that women have access to other means of avoiding pregnancy.[14]

Feminist analysis addresses the context as well as the practice of abortion decisions. Thus, feminists also object to the conditions which lead women to abort wanted fetuses because there are not adequate financial and social supports available to care for a child. Because feminist accounts value fetuses that are wanted by the women who carry them, they oppose practices which force women to abort because of poverty or intimidation. Yet, the sorts of social changes necessary if we are to free women from having abortions out of economic necessity are vast; they include changes not only in legal and health-care policy, but also in housing, child care, employment, etc. (Petchesky 1980, p. 112). Nonetheless, feminist ethics defines reproductive freedom as the condition under which women are able to make truly voluntary choices about their reproductive lives, and these many dimensions are implicit in the ideal.

Clearly, feminists are not "pro-abortion," for they are concerned to ensure the safety of each pregnancy to the greatest degree possible; wanted fetuses should not be harmed or lost. Therefore, adequate pre- and post-natal care and nutrition are also important elements of any feminist position on reproductive freedom. Where anti-abortionists direct their energies to trying to prevent women from obtaining abortions, feminists seek to protect the health of wanted fetuses. They recognize that far more could be done to protect and care for fetuses if the state directed its resources at supporting women who continue their pregnancies, rather than draining away resources in order to police women who find that they must interrupt their pregnancies. Caring for the women who carry fetuses is not only a more legitimate policy than is regulating them; it is probably also more effective at ensuring the health and well-being of more fetuses.

Feminist ethics also explores how abortion policies fit within the politics of sexual domination. Most feminists are sensitive to the fact that many men support women's right to abortion out of the belief that women will be more willing sexual partners if they believe that they can readily terminate an unwanted pregnancy. Some men coerce their partners into obtaining abortions the women may not want.[15] Feminists understand that many women oppose abortion for this very reason, being unwilling to support a practice that increases women's sexual vulnerability (Luker 1984, pp. 209–15). Thus, it is important that feminists develop a coherent analysis of reproductive freedom that includes sexual freedom (as women choose to define it). That requires an analysis of sexual freedom that includes women's right to refuse sex; such a right can only be assured if women have equal power to men and are not subject to domination by virtue of their sex.[16]

In sum, then, feminist ethics demands that moral discussions of abortion be more broadly defined than they have been in most philosophic discussions. Only by reflecting on the meaning of ethical pronouncements on actual women's lives and the connections between judgments on abortion and the conditions of domination and subordination can we come to an adequate understanding of the moral status of abortion in our society. As Rosalind Petchesky (1980) argues, feminist discussion of abortion "must be moved beyond the framework of a 'woman's right to choose' and connected to a much broader revolutionary movement that addresses all of the conditions of women's liberation" (p. 113).

NOTES

Earlier versions of this paper were read to the Department of Philosophy, Dalhousie University and to the Canadian Society for Women in Philosophy in Kingston. I am very grateful for the comments received from colleagues in both forums: particular thanks go to Lorraine Code, David Braybrooke, Richmond Campbell, Sandra Taylor, Terry Tomkow and Kadri Vihvelin for their patience and advice.

1. For some idea of the ways in which traditional moral theory oppresses women, see Morgan (1987) and Hoagland (1988).

2. Critics continue to want to structure the debate around the *possibility* of women making frivolous abortion decisions and hence want feminists to agree to setting boundaries on acceptable grounds for choosing abortion. Feminists ought to resist this injunction, though. There is no practical way of drawing a line fairly in the abstract; cases that may appear "frivolous" at a distance, often turn out to be substantive when the details are revealed, i.e., frivolity is in the eyes of the beholder. There is no evidence to suggest that women actually make the sorts of choices worried critics hypothesize about: e.g., a woman eight months pregnant who chooses to abort because she wants to take a trip or gets in "a tiff" with her partner. These sorts of fantasies, on which demands to distinguish between legitimate and illegitimate personal reasons for choosing abortion chiefly rest, reflect an offensive conception of women as irresponsible; they ought not to be perpetuated. Women, seeking moral guidance in their own deliberations about choosing abortion, do not find such hypothetical discussions of much use.

3. In her monumental historical analysis of the early roots of Western patriarchy, Gerda Lerner (1986) determined that patriarchy began in the period from 3100 to 600 B.C. when men appropriated women's sexual and reproductive capacity; the earliest states entrenched patriarchy by institutionalizing the sexual and procreative subordination of women to men.

4. There are some women who claim to be feminists against choice in abortion. See, for instance, Callahan (1987), though few spell out their full feminist program. For reasons I develop in this paper, I do not think this is a consistent position.

5. There is a lot the state could do to ameliorate this condition. If it provided women with adequate financial support, removed the inequities in the labour market, and provided affordable and reliable childcare, pregnancy need not so often lead to a woman's dependence on a particular man. The fact that it does not do so is evidence of the state's complicity in maintaining women's subordinate position with respect to men.

6. See Petchesky (1984), especially Chapter 5, "Considering the Alternatives: The Problems of Contraception," where she documents the risks and discomforts associated with pill use and IUD's and the increasing rate at which women are choosing the option of diaphragm or condom with the option of early legal abortions as backup.

7. See Zillah Eisenstein (1988) for a comprehensive theory of the role of the pregnant body as the central element in the cultural subordination of women.

8. Thomson (1971) is a notable exception to this trend.

9. This seems reminiscent of Aristotle's view of women as "flower pots" where men implant the seed with all the important genetic information and the movement necessary for development and women's job is that of passive gestation, like the flower pot. For exploration of the flower pot picture of pregnancy, see Whitbeck (1973) and Lange (1983).

10. Contrast Warren (1989) with Tooley (1972).

11. The definition of pregnancy as a purely passive activity reaches its ghoulish conclusion in the increasing acceptability of sustaining brain-dead women on life support systems to continue their functions as incubators until the fetus can be safely delivered. For a discussion of this new trend, see Murphy (1989).

12. This apt phrasing is taken from Petchesky (1986), p. 342.

13. Fetuses are almost wholly individuated by the women who bear them. The fetal "contributions" to the relationship are defined by the projections and interpretations of the pregnant woman in the latter stages of pregnancy if she chooses to perceive fetal movements in purposeful ways (e.g., it likes classical music, wine, exercise").

14. Therefore, the Soviet model, where women have access to multiple abortions but where there is no other birth control available, must also be opposed.

15. See CARAL/Halifax (1990), p. 20–21, for examples of this sort of abuse.

16. It also requires that discussions of reproductive and sexual freedom not be confined to "the language of control and sexuality characteristic of a technology of sex" (Diamond and Quinby 1988, p. 197), for such language is alienating and constrains women's experiences of their own sexuality.

REFERENCES

Addelson, Kathryn Pyne, 1987. "Moral Passages." In *Women and Moral Theory.* Edited by Eva Feder Kittay and Diana T. Meyers. Totowa, NJ: Rowman & Littlefield.

Baier, Annette, 1985. *Postures of the Mind: Essays on Mind and Morals.* Minneapolis: University of Minnesota Press.

Callahan, Sidney, 1987. "A Pro-life Feminist Makes Her Case." *Utne Reader* (March/April): 104–14.

CARAL/Halifax, 1990. *Telling Our Stories: Abortion Stories from Nova Scotia.* Halifax: CARAL/Halifax (Canadian Abortion Rights Action League).

Daly, Mary, 1973. *Beyond God the Father: Toward a Philosophy of Women's Liberation.* Boston: Beacon Press.

Diamond, Irene, and Lee Quinby, 1988. "American Feminism and the Language of Control." In *Feminism and Foucault: Reflections on Resistance.* Edited by Irene Diamond and Lee Quinby. Boston: Northeastern University Press.

Eisenstein, Zillah R., 1988. *The Female Body and the Law.* Berkeley: University of California Press.

Hoagland, Sara Lucia, 1988. *Lesbian Ethics: Toward New Value.* Palo Alto, CA: Institute of Lesbian Studies.

Lange, Lynda, 1983. "Woman Is Not a Rational Animal: On Aristotle's Biology of Reproduction." In *Discovering Reality: Feminist Perspectives on Epistemology, Metaphysics, Methodology, and Philosophy of Science.* Edited by Sandra Harding and Merill B. Hintickka. Dordrecht, Holland: D. Reidel.

Lerner, Gerda, 1986. *The Creation of Patriarchy.* New York: Oxford.

Luker, Kristin, 1984. *Abortion and the Politics of Motherhood.* Berkeley: University of California Press.

MacKinnon, Catherine, 1989. *Toward a Feminist Theory of the State.* Cambridge, MA: Harvard University Press.

McDonnell, Kathleen, 1984. *Not an Easy Choice: A Feminist Re-examines Abortion.* Toronto: The Women's Press.

McLaren, Angus, and Arlene Tigar McLaren, 1986. *The Bedroom and the State: The Changing Practices and Politics of Contraception and Abortion in Canada, 1880–1980.* Toronto: McClelland and Stewart.

Morgan, Kathryn Pauly, 1987. "Women and Moral Madness." In *Science, Morality and Feminist Theory.* Edited by Marsha Hanen and Kai Nielsen. *Canadian Journal of Philosophy,* Supplementary Volume 13: 201–26.

Murphy, Julien S., 1989. "Should Pregnancies Be Sustained in Brain-dead Women?: A Philosophical Discussion of Postmortem Pregnancy." In *Healing Technology: Feminist Perspectives.* Edited by Kathryn Srother Ratcliff et al. Ann Arbor: University of Michigan Press.

Overall, Christine, 1987. *Ethics and Human Reproduction: A Feminist Analysis.* Winchester, MA: Allen & Unwin.

Petchesky, Rosalind Pollack, 1980. "Reproductive Freedom: Beyond 'A Woman's Right to Choose.'" In *Women: Sex and Sexuality.* Edited by Catharine R. Stimpson and Ethel Spector Person. Chicago: University of Chicago Press.

———,1984. *Abortion and Woman's Choice: The State, Sexuality, and Reproductive Freedom.* Boston: Northeastern University Press.

Sumner, L. W., 1981. *Abortion and Moral Theory.* Princeton: Princeton University Press.

Thomson, Judith Jarvis, 1971. "A Defense of Abortion." *Philosophy and Public Affairs,* 1: 47–66.

Tooley, Michael, 1972. "Abortion and Infanticide." *Philosophy and Public Affairs,* 2, 1 (Fall): 37–65.

Van Wagner, Vicki, and Bob Lee, 1989. "'Principles into Practice: An Activist Vision of Feminist Reproductive Health Care." In *The Future of Human Reproduction.* Edited by Christine Overall. Toronto: The Women's Press.

Warren, Mary Anne, 1973. "On the Moral and Legal Status of Abortion." *The Monist,* 57: 43–61.

———,1989. "The Moral Significance of Birth." *Hypatia,* 4, 2 (Summer): 46–65.

Whitbeck. Carolyn, 1973. "Theories of Sex Difference." *The Philosophical Forum,* 5, 1–2 (Fall/Winter 1973–74): 54–80.

Roe v. Wade

UNITED STATES SUPREME COURT

In this decision, the Court ruled that no state can ban abortions performed before viability. The Court thought that the Constitution implied a guaranteed right of personal privacy that limits interference by the state in people's private lives and that the right encompassed a woman's decision to have an abortion. But the woman's right is not absolute and must be balanced against important state interests. Thus the Court held that in the first trimester, the woman's right to an abortion cannot be restrained by the state. In the second trimester, the state may limit—but not entirely prohibit—the woman's right by regulating abortion for the sake of her health. After viability, the state may regulate and even ban abortion except when necessary to preserve her life or health.

Majority Opinion (Delivered by Justice Blackmun)

Three reasons have been advanced to explain historically the enactment of criminal abortion laws in the 19th century and to justify their continued existence.

It has been argued occasionally that these laws were the product of a Victorian social concern to discourage illicit sexual conduct. Texas, however, does not advance this justification in the present case, and it appears that no court or commentator has taken the argument seriously. The appellants and *amici* contend, moreover, that this is not a proper state purpose at all and suggest that, if it were, the Texas statutes are overbroad in protecting it since the law fails to distinguish between married and unwed mothers.

A second reason is concerned with abortion as a medical procedure. When most criminal abortion laws were first enacted, the procedure was a hazardous one for the woman. This was particularly true prior to the development of antisepsis. Antiseptic techniques, of course, were based on discoveries by Lister, Pasteur, and others first announced in 1867, but were not generally accepted and employed until about the turn of the century. Abortion mortality was high. Even after 1900, and perhaps until as late as the development of antibiotics in the 1940s,

United States Supreme Court, 410 U.S. 113, 93 S. Ct. 705. January 22, 1973.

standard modern techniques such as dilation and curettage were not nearly so safe as they are today. Thus, it has been argued that a state's real concern in enacting a criminal abortion law was to protect the pregnant woman, that is, to restrain her from submitting to a procedure that placed her life in serious jeopardy.

Modern medical techniques have altered this situation. Appellants and various *amici* refer to medical data indicating that abortion in early pregnancy, that is, prior to the end of the first trimester, although not without its risk, is now relatively safe. Mortality rates for women undergoing early abortions, where the procedure is legal, appear to be as low as or lower than the rates for normal childbirth. Consequently, any interest of the state in protecting the woman from an inherently hazardous procedure except when it would be equally dangerous for her to forgo it, has largely disappeared. Of course, important state interests in the areas of health and medical standards do remain. The state has a legitimate interest in seeing to it that abortion, like any other medical procedure, is performed under circumstances that insure maximum safety for the patient. This interest obviously extends at least to the performing physician and his staff, to the facilities involved, to the availability of after-care, and to adequate provision for any complication or emergency that might arise. The prevalence of high mortality rates at illegal "abortion mills" strengthens, rather than weakens, the state's interest in regulating the conditions under which abortions are performed. Moreover, the risk to the woman increases as her pregnancy continues. Thus, the state retains a definite interest in protecting the woman's own health and safety when an abortion is proposed at a late stage of pregnancy.

The third reason is the state's interest—some phrase it in terms of duty—in protecting prenatal life. Some of the argument for this justification rests on the theory that a new human life is present from the moment of conception. The state's interest and general obligation to protect life then extends, it is argued, to prenatal life. Only when the life of the pregnant mother herself is at stake, balanced against the life she carries within her, should the interest of the embryo or fetus not prevail. Logically, of course, a legitimate state interest in this area need not stand or fall on acceptance of the belief that life begins at conception or at some other point prior to live birth. In assessing the state's interest, recognition may be given to the less rigid claim that as long as at least potential life is involved, the state may assert interests beyond the protection of the pregnant woman alone.

Parties challenging state abortion laws have sharply disputed in some courts the contention that a purpose of these laws, when enacted, was to protect prenatal life. Pointing to the absence of legislative history to support the contention, they claim that most state laws were designed solely to protect the woman. Because medical advances have lessened this concern, at least with respect to abortion in early pregnancy, they argue that with respect to such abortions the laws can no longer be justified by any state interest. There is some scholarly support for this view of original purpose. The few state courts called upon to interpret their laws in the late 19th and early 20th centuries did focus on the state's interest in protecting the woman's health rather than in preserving the embryo and fetus. Proponents of this view point out that in many states, including Texas, by statute or judicial interpretation, the pregnant woman herself could not be prosecuted for self-abortion or for cooperating in an abortion performed upon her by another. They claim that adoption of the "quickening" distinction through received common law and state statutes

tacitly recognizes the greater health hazards inherent in late abortion and impliedly repudiates the theory that life begins at conception.

It is with these interests, and the weight to be attached to them, that this case is concerned.

The Constitution does not explicitly mention any right of privacy. In a line of decisions, however, going back perhaps as far as *Union Pacific R. Co. v. Botsford,* 141 U.S. 250, 251 (1891), the court has recognized that a right of personal privacy, or a guarantee of certain areas or zones of privacy, does exist under the Constitution. In varying contexts, the court or individual justices have, indeed, found at least the roots of that right in the first amendment, in the fourth and fifth amendments, in the penumbras of the Bill of Rights, in the ninth amendment, or in the concept of liberty guaranteed by the first section of the fourteenth amendment. These decisions make it clear that only personal rights that can be deemed "fundamental" or "implicit" in the concept of ordered liberty are included in this guarantee of personal privacy. They also make it clear that the right has some extension to activities relating to marriage, procreation, contraception, family relationships, and child rearing and education.

This right of privacy, whether it be founded in the fourteenth amendment's concept of personal liberty and restrictions upon state action, as we feel it is, or, as the district court determined, in the ninth amendment's reservation of rights to the people, is broad enough to encompass a woman's decision whether or not to terminate her pregnancy. The detriment that the state would impose upon the pregnant woman by denying this choice altogether is apparent. Specific and direct harm medically diagnosable even in early pregnancy may be involved. Maternity, or additional offspring, may force upon the woman a distressful life and future. Psychological harm may be imminent. Mental and physical health may be taxed by child care. There is also the distress, for all concerned, associated with the unwanted child, and there is the problem of bringing a child into a family already unable, psychologically and otherwise, to care for it. In other cases, as in this one, the additional difficulties and continuing stigma factors the woman and her responsible physician necessarily will consider in consultation.

On the basis of elements such as these, appellant and some *amici* argue that the woman's right is absolute and that she is entitled to terminate her pregnancy at whatever time, in whatever way, and for whatever reason she alone chooses. With this we do not agree. Appellant's arguments that Texas either has no valid interest strong enough to support any limitation upon the woman's sole determination are unpersuasive. The court's decisions recognizing a right of privacy also acknowledge that some state regulation in areas protected by that right is appropriate. As noted above, a state may properly assert important interests in safeguarding health, in maintaining medical standards, and in protecting potential life. At some point in pregnancy, to sustain regulation of the factors that govern the abortion decision. The privacy right involved, therefore, cannot be said to be absolute. In fact, it is not clear to us that the claim asserted by some *amici* that one has an unlimited right to do with one's body as one pleases bears a close relationship to the right of privacy previously articulated in the court's decisions. The court has refused to recognize an unlimited right of this kind in the past.

We, therefore, conclude that the right of personal privacy includes the abortion decision, but that this right is not unqualified and must be considered against important state interests in regulation.

We note that those federal and state courts that have recently considered abortion law challenges have reached the same conclusion. A majority, in addition to the district court in the present case, have held state laws unconstitutional, at least in part, because of vagueness or because of overbreadth and abridgment of rights.

Although the results are divided, most of these courts have agreed that the right of privacy, however based, is broad enough to cover the abortion decision; that the right, nonetheless, is not absolute and is subject to some limitations; and that at some point the state interests as to protection of health, medical standards, and prenatal life, become dominant. We agree with this approach.

Where certain "fundamental rights" are involved, the court has held that regulation limiting these rights may be justified only by a "compelling state interest," and that legislative enactments must be narrowly drawn to express only the legitimate state interests at stake.

In the recent abortion cases, cited above, courts have recognized these principles. Those striking down state laws have generally scrutinized the state's interests in protecting health and potential life, and have concluded that neither interest justified broad limitations on the reasons for which a physician and his pregnant patient might decide that she should have an abortion in the early stages of pregnancy. Courts sustaining state laws have held that the state's determinations to protect health or prenatal life are dominant and constitutionally justifiable.

The district court held that the appellee failed to meet his burden of demonstrating that the Texas statute's infringement upon Roe's rights was necessary to support a compelling state interest, and that, although the appellee presented "several compelling justifications for state presence in the area of abortions," the statutes outstripped these justifications and swept "far beyond any areas of compelling state interest." Appellant and appellee both contest that holding. Appellant, as has been indicated, claims an absolute right that bars any state imposition of criminal penalties in the area. Appellee argues that the state's determination to recognize and protect prenatal life from and after conception constitutes a compelling state interest. As noted above, we do not agree fully with either formulation.

A. The appellee and certain *amici* argue that the fetus is a "person" within the language and meaning of the fourteenth amendment. In support of this, they outline at length and in detail the well-known facts of fetal development. If this suggestion of personhood is established, the appellant's case, of course, collapses, for the fetus' right to life would then be guaranteed specifically by the amendment. The appellant conceded as much on reargument. On the other hand, the appellee conceded on reargument that no case could be cited that holds that a fetus is a person within the meaning of the fourteenth amendment.

The Constitution does not define "person" in so many words. Section 1 of the fourteenth amendment contains three references to "person ..." but in nearly all these instances, the use of the word is such that it has application only postnatally. None indicates, with any assurance, that it has any possible prenatal application.

All this, together with our observation, supra, that throughout the major portion of the 19th century prevailing legal abortion practices were far freer than they are today, persuades us that the word "person," as used in the fourteenth amendment, does not include the unborn. . . .

B. The pregnant woman cannot be isolated in her privacy. She carries an embryo and, later, a fetus, if one accepts the medical definitions of the developing young in the human uterus. See Dorland's *Illustrated Medical Dictionary* 478–479, 547 (7th ed. 1965). The situation therefore is inherently different from marital intimacy, or bedroom possession of obscene material, or marriage, or procreation, or education, with which *Eisenstadt, Griswold, Stanley, Loving, Skinner, Pierce*, and *Meyer* were respectively concerned. As we have intimated above, it is reasonable and appropriate for a state to decide that at some point in time another interest, that of health of the mother or that of potential human life, becomes significantly involved. The woman's privacy is no longer sole and any right of privacy she possesses must be measured accordingly.

Texas urges that, apart from the fourteenth amendment, life begins at conception and is present throughout pregnancy, and that, therefore, the state has a compelling interest in protecting that life from and after conception. We need not resolve the difficult question of when life begins. When those trained in the respective disciplines of medicine, philosophy, and theology are unable to arrive at any consensus, the judiciary, at this point in the development of man's knowledge, is not in a position to speculate as to the answer.

It should be sufficient to note briefly the wide divergence of thinking on this most sensitive and difficult question. There has always been strong support for the view that life does not begin until live birth. This was the belief of the Stoics. It appears to be the predominant, though not the unanimous, attitude of the Jewish faith. It may be taken to represent also the position of a large segment of the Protestant community, insofar as that can be

ascertained; organized groups that have taken a formal position on the abortion issue have generally regarded abortion as a matter for the conscience of the individual and her family. As we have noted, the common law found greater significance in quickening. Physicians and their scientific colleagues have regarded that event with less interest and have tended to focus either upon conception, upon live birth, or upon the interim point at which the fetus becomes "viable," that is, potentially able to live outside the mother's womb, albeit with artificial aid. Viability is usually placed at about seven months (28 weeks) but may occur earlier, even at 24 weeks. The Aristotelian theory of "mediate animation," that held sway throughout the Middle Ages and the Renaissance in Europe, continued to be official Roman Catholic dogma until the 19th century, despite opposition to this "ensoulment" theory from those in the church who would recognize the existence of life from the moment of conception. The latter is now, of course, the official belief of the Catholic church. As one brief *amicus* discloses, this is a view strongly held by many non-Catholics as well, and by many physicians. Substantial problems for precise definition of this view are posed, however, by new embryological data that purport to indicate that conception is a "process" over time, rather than an event, and by new medical techniques: implantation of embryos, artificial insemination, and even artificial wombs.

In areas other than criminal abortion, the law has been reluctant to endorse any theory that life, as we recognize it, begins before live birth or to accord legal rights to the unborn except in narrowly defined situations and except when the rights are contingent upon live birth. For example, the traditional rule of tort law denied recovery for prenatal injuries even though the child was born alive. That rule has been changed in almost every jurisdiction. In most states, recovery is said to be permitted only if the fetus was viable, or at least quick, when the injuries were sustained, though few courts have squarely so held. In a recent development, generally opposed by the commentators, some states permit the parents of a stillborn child to maintain an action for wrongful death because of prenatal injuries. Such an action, however, would appear to be one to vindicate the parents' interest and is thus consistent with the view that the fetus, at most, represents only the potentiality of life. Similarly, unborn children have been recognized as acquiring rights or interests by way of inheritance or other devolution of property, and have been represented by guardians ad litem. Perfection of the interests involved, again, has generally been contingent upon live birth. In short, the unborn have never been recognized in the law as persons in the whole sense.

In view of all this, we do not agree that, by adopting one theory of life, Texas may override the rights of the pregnant woman that are at stake. We repeat, however, that the state does have an important and legitimate interest in preserving and protecting the health of the pregnant woman, whether she be a resident of the state or a nonresident who seeks medical consultation and treatment there, and that it has still another important and legitimate interest in protecting the potentiality of human life. These interests are separate and distinct. Each grows in substantiality as the woman approaches term and, at a point during pregnancy, each becomes "compelling."

With respect to the state's important and legitimate interest in the health of the mother, the "compelling" point, in the light of present medical knowledge, is at approximately the end of the first trimester. This is so because of the now-established medical fact, referred to above at 149, that until the end of the first trimester mortality in abortion may be less than mortality in normal childbirth. It follows that, from and after this point, a state may regulate the abortion procedure to the extent that the regulation reasonably relates to the preservation and protection of maternal health. Examples of permissible state regulation in this area are requirements as to the qualifications of the person who is to perform the abortion; as to the licensure of that person; as to the facility in which the procedure is to be performed, that is, whether it must be a hospital or may be a clinic or some other place of less-than-hospital status; as to the licensing of the facility; and the like.

This means, on the other hand, that, for the period of pregnancy prior to this "compelling" point, the attending physician, in consultation with his patient, is free to determine, without regulation by the state, that, in his medical judgment, the patient's pregnancy should be terminated. If that decision is reached, the judgment may be effectuated by an abortion free of interference by the state.

With respect to the state's important and legitimate interest in potential life, the "compelling" point is at viability. This is so because the fetus then presumably has the capability of meaningful life outside the mother's womb. State regulation protective of fetal life after viability thus has both logical and biological justifications. If the state is interested in protecting fetal life after viability, it may go so far as to proscribe abortion during that period, except when it is necessary to preserve the life or health of the mother.

Measured against these standards, art. 1196 of the Texas penal code, in restricting legal abortions to those "procured or attempted by medical advice for the purpose of saving the life of the mother," sweeps too broadly. The statute makes no distinction between abortions performed early in pregnancy and those performed later, and it limits to a single reason, "saving" the mother's life, the legal justification for the procedure. The statute, therefore, cannot survive the constitutional attack made upon it here. . . .

To summarize and to repeat:

1. A state criminal abortion statute of the current Texas type, that excepts from criminality only a life-saving procedure on behalf of the mother, without regard to pregnancy stage and without recognition of the other interests involved, is violative of the due process clause of the fourteenth amendment.

a. For the stage prior to approximately the end of the first trimester, the abortion decision and its effectuation must be left to the medical judgment of the pregnant woman's attending physician.

b. For the stage subsequent to approximately the end of the first trimester, the state, in promoting its interest in the health of the mother, may, if it chooses, regulate the abortion procedure in ways that are reasonably related to maternal health.

c. For the stage subsequent to viability, the state in promoting its interest in the potentiality of human life may, if it chooses, regulate, and even proscribe, abortion except where it is necessary, in appropriate medical judgment, for the preservation of the life or health of the mother.

2. The state may define the term "physician," as it has been employed in the preceding paragraphs of this part XI of this opinion, to mean only a physician currently licensed by the state, and may proscribe any abortion by a person who is not a physician as so defined. . . .

This holding, we feel, is consistent with the relative weights of the respective interests involved, with the lessons and examples of medical and legal history, with the lenity of the common law, and with the demands of the profound problems of the present day. The decision leaves the state free to place increasing restrictions on abortion as the period of pregnancy lengthens, so long as those restrictions are tailored to the recognized state interests. The decision vindicates the right of the physician to administer medical treatment according to his professional judgment up to the points where important state interests provide compelling justifications for intervention. Up to those points, the abortion decision in all its aspects is inherently, and primarily, a medical decision, and basic responsibility for it must rest with the physician. If an individual practitioner abuses the privilege of exercising proper medical judgment, the usual remedies, judicial and intra-professional, are available. . . .

Planned Parenthood of Southeastern Pennsylvania v. Casey

UNITED STATES SUPREME COURT

In this 1992 ruling, the Court found that "the essential holding of *Roe v. Wade* should be retained and once again reaffirmed." But it rejected *Roe's* trimester framework and established an "undue burden" test for assessing the restrictions that states put on abortion. Before viability, abortion can be restricted in many ways as long as the constraints do not amount to an undue burden on a woman wishing to obtain an abortion. The Court held that several restrictions do not impose such burdens, including the requirement that a woman give her written informed consent to abortion and that minors under age 18 who seek abortions obtain parental consent or a judge's authorization. But a spousal notification provision does constitute an undue burden.

I

Liberty finds no refuge in a jurisprudence of doubt. Yet, 19 years after our holding that the Constitution protects a woman's right to terminate her pregnancy in its early stages, *Roe v. Wade* (1973), that definition of liberty is still questioned. Joining the respondents as amicus curiae, the United States, as it has done in five other cases in the last decade, again asks us to overrule *Roe*.

At issue . . . are five provisions of the Pennsylvania Abortion Control Act of 1982, as amended in 1988

United States Supreme Court, 505 U.S. 833, 112 S. Ct. 2791, June 29, 1992.

and 1989. . . . The Act requires that a woman seeking an abortion give her informed consent prior to the abortion procedure, and specifies that she be provided with certain information at least 24 hours before the abortion is performed. Section 3205. For a minor to obtain an abortion, the Act requires the informed consent of one of her parents, but provides for a judicial bypass option if the minor does not wish to or cannot obtain a parent's consent. Section 3206. Another provision of the Act requires that, unless certain exceptions apply, a married woman seeking an abortion must sign a statement indicating that she has notified her husband of her intended abortion. Section 3209. The Act exempts compliance with these three requirements in the event of a "medical emergency," which is defined in Section 3 of the Act. See Section 3205(a), Section 3206(a), Section 3209(c). In addition to the above provisions regulating the performance of abortions, the Act imposes certain reporting requirements on facilities that provide abortion services.

Before any of these provisions took effect, the petitioners, who are five abortion clinics and one physician representing himself as well as a class of physicians who provide abortion services, brought this suit seeking declaratory and injunctive relief. Each provision was challenged as unconstitutional on its face. The District Court entered a preliminary injunction against the enforcement of the regulations, and, after a 3-day bench trial, held all the provisions at issue here unconstitutional, entering a permanent injunction against Pennsylvania's enforcement of them. The Court of Appeals for the Third Circuit affirmed in part and reversed in part, upholding all of the regulations except for the husband notification requirement. . . . [W]e find it imperative to review once more the principles that define the rights of the woman and the legitimate authority of the State respecting the termination of pregnancies by abortion procedures.

After considering the fundamental constitutional questions resolved by *Roe*, principles of institutional integrity, and the rule of stare decisis, we are led to conclude this: the essential holding of *Roe v. Wade* should be retained and once again reaffirmed.

It must be stated at the outset and with clarity that *Roe*'s essential holding, the holding we reaffirm, has three parts. First is a recognition of the right of the woman to choose to have an abortion before viability and to obtain it without undue interference from the State. Before viability, the State's interests are not strong enough to support a prohibition of abortion or the imposition of a substantial obstacle to the woman's effective right to elect the procedure. Second is a confirmation of the State's power to restrict abortions after fetal viability if the law contains exceptions for pregnancies which endanger the woman's life or health. And third is the principle that the State has legitimate interests from the outset of the pregnancy in protecting the health of the woman and the life of the fetus that may become a child. These principles do not contradict one another; and we adhere to each.

II

Constitutional protection of the woman's decision to terminate her pregnancy derives from the Due Process Clause of the Fourteenth Amendment. It declares that no State shall "deprive any person of life, liberty, or property, without due process of law." The controlling word in the cases before us is "liberty."

. . . It is a promise of the Constitution that there is a realm of personal liberty which the government may not enter. We have vindicated this principle before. Marriage is mentioned nowhere in the Bill of Rights, and interracial marriage was illegal in most States in the 19th century, but the Court was no doubt correct in finding it to be an aspect of liberty protected against state interference by the substantive component of the Due Process Clause. . . .

Neither the Bill of Rights nor the specific practices of States at the time of the adoption of the Fourteenth Amendment marks the outer limits of the substantive sphere of liberty which the Fourteenth Amendment protects. . . . It is settled now, as it was when the Court heard arguments in *Roe v. Wade*, that the Constitution places limits on a State's right to interfere with a person's most basic decisions about family and parenthood, as well as bodily integrity.

The inescapable fact is that adjudication of substantive due process claims may call upon the Court in interpreting the Constitution to exercise that same capacity which, by tradition, courts always have exercised: reasoned judgment. Its boundaries are not susceptible of expression as a simple rule. That does not mean we are free to invalidate state policy choices with which we disagree; yet neither does it permit us to shrink from the duties of our office. . . .

III

. . . No evolution of legal principle has left *Roe*'s doctrinal footings weaker than they were in 1973. No development of constitutional law since the case was decided has implicitly or explicitly left *Roe* behind as a mere survivor of obsolete constitutional thinking. . . .

We have seen how time has overtaken some of *Roe*'s factual assumptions: advances in maternal health care allow for abortions safe to the mother later in pregnancy than was true in 1973, and advances in neonatal care have advanced viability to a point somewhat earlier. But these facts go only to the scheme of time limits on the realization of competing interests, and the divergences from the factual premises of 1973 have no bearing on the validity of *Roe*'s central holding, that viability marks the earliest point at which the State's interest in fetal life is constitutionally adequate to justify a legislative ban on nontherapeutic abortions. The soundness or unsoundness of that constitutional judgment in no sense turns on whether viability occurs at approximately 28 weeks, as was usual at the time of *Roe*, at 23 to 24 weeks, as it sometimes does today, or at some moment even slightly earlier in pregnancy, as it may if fetal respiratory capacity can somehow be enhanced in the future. Whenever it may occur, the attainment of viability may continue to serve as the critical fact, just as it has done since *Roe* was decided; which is to say that no change in *Roe*'s factual underpinning has left its central holding obsolete, and none supports an argument for overruling it.

The sum of the precedential enquiry to this point shows *Roe*'s underpinnings unweakened in any way affecting its central holding. While it has engendered disapproval, it has not been unworkable. . . .

The Court's duty in the present case is clear. In 1973, it confronted the already-divisive issue of governmental power to limit personal choice to undergo abortion, for which it provided a new resolution based on the due process guaranteed by the Fourteenth Amendment. Whether or not a new social consensus is developing on that issue, its divisiveness is no less today than in 1973, and pressure to overrule the decision, like pressure to retain it, has grown only more intense. A decision to overrule *Roe*'s essential holding under the existing circumstances would address error, if error there was, at the cost of both profound and unnecessary damage to the Court's legitimacy, and to the Nation's commitment to the rule of law. It is therefore imperative to adhere to the essence of *Roe*'s original decision, and we do so today.

IV

From what we have said so far, it follows that it is a constitutional liberty of the woman to have some freedom to terminate her pregnancy. We conclude that the basic decision in *Roe* was based on a constitutional analysis which we cannot now repudiate. The woman's liberty is not so unlimited, however,

that from the outset the State cannot show its concern for the life of the unborn, and at a later point in fetal development the State's interest in life has sufficient force so that the right of the woman to terminate the pregnancy can be restricted. . . .

We conclude the line should be drawn at viability, so that, before that time, the woman has a right to choose to terminate her pregnancy. We adhere to this principle for two reasons. First, as we have said, is the doctrine of stare decisis. Any judicial act of line-drawing may seem somewhat arbitrary, but *Roe* was a reasoned statement, elaborated with great care. We have twice reaffirmed it in the face of great opposition. . . .

The second reason is that the concept of viability, as we noted in *Roe*, is the time at which there is a realistic possibility of maintaining and nourishing a life outside the womb, so that the independent existence of the second life can, in reason and all fairness, be the object of state protection that now overrides the rights of the woman. . . . We must justify the lines we draw. And there is no line other than viability which is more workable. To be sure, as we have said, there may be some medical developments that affect the precise point of viability, see supra, but this is an imprecision within tolerable limits, given that the medical community and all those who must apply its discoveries will continue to explore the matter. The viability line also has, as a practical matter, an element of fairness. In some broad sense, it might be said that a woman who fails to act before viability has consented to the State's intervention on behalf of the developing child.

The woman's right to terminate her pregnancy before viability is the most central principle of *Roe v. Wade*. It is a rule of law and a component of liberty we cannot renounce. . . .

Yet it must be remembered that *Roe v. Wade* speaks with clarity in establishing not only the woman's liberty but also the State's "important and legitimate interest in potential life." That portion of the decision in *Roe* has been given too little acknowledgment and implementation by the Court in its subsequent cases. . . .

Roe established a trimester framework to govern abortion regulations. Under this elaborate but rigid construct, almost no regulation at all is permitted during the first trimester of pregnancy; regulations designed to protect the woman's health, but not to further the State's interest in potential life, are permitted during the second trimester; and, during the third trimester, when the fetus is viable, prohibitions are permitted provided the life or health of the mother is not at stake. Most of our cases since *Roe* have involved the application of rules derived from the trimester framework.

The trimester framework no doubt was erected to ensure that the woman's right to choose not become so subordinate to the State's interest in promoting fetal life that her choice exists in theory, but not in fact. We do not agree, however, that the trimester approach is necessary to accomplish this objective. A framework of this rigidity was unnecessary, and, in its later interpretation, sometimes contradicted the State's permissible exercise of its powers.

Though the woman has a right to choose to terminate or continue her pregnancy before viability, it does not at all follow that the State is prohibited from taking steps to ensure that this choice is thoughtful and informed. Even in the earliest stages of pregnancy, the State may enact rules and regulations designed to encourage her to know that there are philosophic and social arguments of great weight that can be brought to bear in favor of continuing the pregnancy to full term, and that there are procedures and institutions to allow adoption of unwanted children as well as a certain degree of state assistance if the mother chooses to raise the child herself. . . . It follows that the States are free to enact laws to provide a reasonable framework for a woman to make a decision that has such profound and lasting meaning. This, too, we find consistent with *Roe*'s central premises, and indeed the inevitable consequence of our holding that the State has an interest in protecting the life of the unborn. . . .

Numerous forms of state regulation might have the incidental effect of increasing the cost or decreasing the availability of medical care, whether for abortion or any other medical procedure. The fact that a law which serves a valid purpose, one not designed to strike at the right itself, has the incidental effect of making it more difficult or more expensive to procure an abortion cannot be enough to invalidate it. Only where state regulation imposes an undue

burden on a woman's ability to make this decision does the power of the State reach into the heart of the liberty protected by the Due Process Clause. . . .

. . . Before viability, *Roe* and subsequent cases treat all governmental attempts to influence a woman's decision on behalf of the potential life within her as unwarranted. This treatment is, in our judgment, incompatible with the recognition that there is a substantial state interest in potential life throughout pregnancy.

The very notion that the State has a substantial interest in potential life leads to the conclusion that not all regulations must be deemed unwarranted. Not all burdens on the right to decide whether to terminate a pregnancy will be undue. In our view, the undue burden standard is the appropriate means of reconciling the State's interest with the woman's constitutionally protected liberty. . . .

. . . We give this summary:

a. To protect the central right recognized by *Roe v. Wade* while at the same time accommodating the State's profound interest in potential life, we will employ the undue burden analysis as explained in this opinion. An undue burden exists, and therefore a provision of law is invalid, if its purpose or effect is to place a substantial obstacle in the path of a woman seeking an abortion before the fetus attains viability.

b. We reject the rigid trimester framework of *Roe v. Wade*. To promote the State's profound interest in potential life, throughout pregnancy, the State may take measures to ensure that the woman's choice is informed, and measures designed to advance this interest will not be invalidated as long as their purpose is to persuade the woman to choose childbirth over abortion. These measures must not be an undue burden on the right.

c. As with any medical procedure, the State may enact regulations to further the health or safety of a woman seeking an abortion. Unnecessary health regulations that have the purpose or effect of presenting a substantial obstacle to a woman seeking an abortion impose an undue burden on the right.

d. Our adoption of the undue burden analysis does not disturb the central holding of *Roe v. Wade*, and we reaffirm that holding. Regardless of whether exceptions are made for particular circumstances, a State may not prohibit any woman from making the ultimate decision to terminate her pregnancy before viability.

e. We also reaffirm *Roe*'s holding that, "subsequent to viability, the State, in promoting its interest in the potentiality of human life, may, if it chooses, regulate, and even proscribe, abortion except where it is necessary, in appropriate medical judgment, for the preservation of the life or health of the mother."

These principles control our assessment of the Pennsylvania statute, and we now turn to the issue of the validity of its challenged provisions.

V

The Court of Appeals applied what it believed to be the undue burden standard, and upheld each of the provisions except for the husband notification requirement. We agree generally with this conclusion, but refine the undue burden analysis in accordance with the principles articulated above. We now consider the separate statutory sections at issue.

(B)

We next consider the informed consent requirement. Section 3205. Except in a medical emergency, the statute requires that at least 24 hours before performing an abortion a physician inform the woman of the nature of the procedure, the health risks of the abortion and of childbirth, and the "probable gestational age of the unborn child." The physician or a qualified nonphysician must inform the woman of the availability of printed materials published by the State describing the fetus and providing information about medical assistance for childbirth, information about child support from the father, and a list of agencies which provide adoption and other services as alternatives to abortion. An abortion may not be performed unless the woman certifies in writing that she has been informed of the availability of

these printed materials and has been provided them if she chooses to view them.

Our prior decisions establish that, as with any medical procedure, the State may require a woman to give her written informed consent to an abortion. . . .

In *Akron v. Akron Center for Reproductive Health, Inc.* (1983) (*Akron I*) we invalidated an ordinance which required that a woman seeking an abortion be provided by her physician with specific information "designed to influence the woman's informed choice between abortion or childbirth." As we later described the *Akron I* holding in *Thornburgh v. American College of Obstetricians and Gynecologists*, there were two purported flaws in the Akron ordinance: the information was designed to dissuade the woman from having an abortion, and the ordinance imposed "a rigid requirement that a specific body of information be given in all cases, irrespective of the particular needs of the patient." . . .

. . . It cannot be questioned that psychological wellbeing is a facet of health. Nor can it be doubted that most women considering an abortion would deem the impact on the fetus relevant, if not dispositive, to the decision. In attempting to ensure that a woman apprehend the full consequences of her decision, the State furthers the legitimate purpose of reducing the risk that a woman may elect an abortion, only to discover later, with devastating psychological consequences, that her decision was not fully informed. If the information the State requires to be made available to the woman is truthful and not misleading, the requirement may be permissible.

We also see no reason why the State may not require doctors to inform a woman seeking an abortion of the availability of materials relating to the consequences to the fetus, even when those consequences have no direct relation to her health. An example illustrates the point. We would think it constitutional for the State to require that, in order for there to be informed consent to a kidney transplant operation, the recipient must be supplied with information about risks to the donor as well as risks to himself or herself. A requirement that the physician make available information similar to that mandated by the statute here was described in *Thornburgh* as an outright attempt to wedge the

Commonwealth's message discouraging abortion into the privacy of the informed consent dialogue between the woman and her physician. We conclude, however, that informed choice need not be defined in such narrow terms that all considerations of the effect on the fetus are made irrelevant. As we have made clear, we depart from the holdings of *Akron I* and *Thornburgh* to the extent that we permit a State to further its legitimate goal of protecting the life of the unborn by enacting legislation aimed at ensuring a decision that is mature and informed, even when, in so doing, the State expresses a preference for childbirth over abortion. In short, requiring that the woman be informed of the availability of information relating to fetal development and the assistance available should she decide to carry the pregnancy to full term is a reasonable measure to ensure an informed choice, one which might cause the woman to choose childbirth over abortion. This requirement cannot be considered a substantial obstacle to obtaining an abortion, and, it follows, there is no undue burden. . . .

The Pennsylvania statute also requires us to reconsider the holding in *Akron I* that the State may not require that a physician, as opposed to a qualified assistant, provide information relevant to a woman's informed consent. Since there is no evidence on this record that requiring a doctor to give the information as provided by the statute would amount, in practical terms, to a substantial obstacle to a woman seeking an abortion, we conclude that it is not an undue burden. Our cases reflect the fact that the Constitution gives the States broad latitude to decide that particular functions may be performed only by licensed professionals, even if an objective assessment might suggest that those same tasks could be performed by others. Thus, we uphold the provision as a reasonable means to ensure that the woman's consent is informed.

Our analysis of Pennsylvania's 24-hour waiting period between the provision of the information deemed necessary to informed consent and the performance of an abortion under the undue burden standard requires us to reconsider the premise behind the decision in *Akron I* invalidating a parallel requirement. In *Akron I* we said: Nor are we convinced that the State's legitimate concern that the

woman's decision be informed is reasonably served by requiring a 24-hour delay as a matter of course. We consider that conclusion to be wrong. The idea that important decisions will be more informed and deliberate if they follow some period of reflection does not strike us as unreasonable, particularly where the statute directs that important information become part of the background of the decision. The statute, as construed by the Court of Appeals, permits avoidance of the waiting period in the event of a medical emergency, and the record evidence shows that, in the vast majority of cases, a 24-hour delay does not create any appreciable health risk. In theory, at least, the waiting period is a reasonable measure to implement the State's interest in protecting the life of the unborn, a measure that does not amount to an undue burden.

Whether the mandatory 24-hour waiting period is nonetheless invalid because, in practice, it is a substantial obstacle to a woman's choice to terminate her pregnancy is a closer question. The findings of fact by the District Court indicate that, because of the distances many women must travel to reach an abortion provider, the practical effect will often be a delay of much more than a day because the waiting period requires that a woman seeking an abortion make at least two visits to the doctor. The District Court also found that, in many instances, this will increase the exposure of women seeking abortions to "the harassment and hostility of anti-abortion protestors demonstrating outside a clinic." As a result, the District Court found that, for those women who have the fewest financial resources, those who must travel long distances, and those who have difficulty explaining their whereabouts to husbands, employers, or others, the 24-hour waiting period will be "particularly burdensome."

These findings are troubling in some respects, but they do not demonstrate that the waiting period constitutes an undue burden. . . .

(C)

Section 3209 of Pennsylvania's abortion law provides, except in cases of medical emergency, that no physician shall perform an abortion on a married woman without receiving a signed statement from the woman that she has notified her spouse that she is about to undergo an abortion. The woman has the option of providing an alternative signed statement certifying that her husband is not the man who impregnated her; that her husband could not be located; that the pregnancy is the result of spousal sexual assault which she has reported; or that the woman believes that notifying her husband will cause him or someone else to inflict bodily injury upon her. A physician who performs an abortion on a married woman without receiving the appropriate signed statement will have his or her license revoked, and is liable to the husband for damages. . . .

. . . In well-functioning marriages, spouses discuss important intimate decisions such as whether to bear a child. But there are millions of women in this country who are the victims of regular physical and psychological abuse at the hands of their husbands. Should these women become pregnant, they may have very good reasons for not wishing to inform their husbands of their decision to obtain an abortion. Many may have justifiable fears of physical abuse, but may be no less fearful of the consequences of reporting prior abuse to the Commonwealth of Pennsylvania. Many may have a reasonable fear that notifying their husbands will provoke further instances of child abuse; these women are not exempt from Section 3209's notification requirement. Many may fear devastating forms of psychological abuse from their husbands, including verbal harassment, threats of future violence, the destruction of possessions, physical confinement to the home, the withdrawal of financial support, or the disclosure of the abortion to family and friends. These methods of psychological abuse may act as even more of a deterrent to notification than the possibility of physical violence, but women who are the victims of the abuse are not exempt from Section 3209's notification requirement. And many women who are pregnant as a result of sexual assaults by their husbands will be unable to avail themselves of the exception for spousal sexual assault, because the exception requires that the woman have notified law enforcement authorities within 90 days of the assault, and her husband

will be notified of her report once an investigation begins. If anything in this field is certain, it is that victims of spousal sexual assault are extremely reluctant to report the abuse to the government; hence, a great many spousal rape victims will not be exempt from the notification requirement imposed by Section 3209. . . .

(D)

We next consider the parental consent provision. Except in a medical emergency, an unemancipated young woman under 18 may not obtain an abortion unless she and one of her parents (or guardian) provides informed consent as defined above. If neither a parent nor a guardian provides consent, a court may authorize the performance of an abortion upon a determination that the young woman is mature and capable of giving informed consent and has, in fact, given her informed consent, or that an abortion would be in her best interests.

We have been over most of this ground before. Our cases establish, and we reaffirm today, that a State may require a minor seeking an abortion to obtain the consent of a parent or guardian, provided that there is an adequate judicial bypass procedure. Under these precedents, in our view, the one-parent consent requirement and judicial bypass procedure are constitutional.

The only argument made by petitioners respecting this provision and to which our prior decisions do not speak is the contention that the parental consent requirement is invalid because it requires informed parental consent. For the most part, petitioners' argument is a reprise of their argument with respect to the informed consent requirement in general, and we reject it for the reasons given above. Indeed, some of the provisions regarding informed consent have particular force with respect to minors: the waiting period, for example, may provide the parent or parents of a pregnant young woman the opportunity to consult with her in private, and to discuss the consequences of her decision in the context of the values and moral or religious principles of their family.

Reproductive Technology

For most of human history, there was only one way to conceive a child (through sexual intercourse), one way to gestate it (in the womb of the woman who conceived it), and—according to common practice—one way to raise it (under the control of those contributing the egg and sperm).

Not anymore. The revered, time-tested order of procreation and parenthood has changed, thanks to an explosion of innovation in what is known as assisted reproductive technology (ART). Through ART procedures, doctors can fertilize a woman's egg in a laboratory dish to produce an embryo that can be implanted in any normal uterus; test ART embryos for genetic abnormalities before implantation (and cull defective ones); mechanically bring together selected sperm and eggs in fallopian tubes for fertilization; freeze embryos, eggs, and sperm for later use (and possible destruction); create embryos from donor eggs and sperm to offer up for adoption; and, in a sterile laboratory container, fertilize an egg by injecting into it a single sperm cell. The technology has also made possible the novel role of reproductive surrogate, a woman who contracts to gestate a baby for others who may or may not be genetically related to it. And behind these new realities lurks the theoretical possibility of what some believe will be the ultimate ART, both intriguing and disturbing: human reproductive cloning.

Assisted reproductive technologies are meant to address the agonizing problem of infertility and the powerful desire that many people have for children of their own, especially children with whom they have a biological link. The point of these advances is widely understood, but their uses are controversial. At every turn, they generate ethical questions and serious debate about the nature and meaning of the family, the welfare of children, the treatment of women, the moral status of embryos, the value of human life, the sanctity of natural procreation, and the legitimacy of reproductive rights.

But despite the complexity and seriousness of these issues, it's possible to make at least modest progress in sorting them out. Historically the field of bioethics cut its teeth on the moral problems arising from reproductive technology and has much to offer those who want to try to make sense of them.

IN VITRO FERTILIZATION

In normal (unassisted) reproduction, sperm inches through the woman's uterus and into one of the fallopian tubes, where a single sperm cell penetrates and thus fertilizes the egg released that month from an ovary. The resulting embryo (technically a zygote) backtracks through the fallopian tube, returning to the uterus where it implants itself in the uterine lining. At successful implantation, pregnancy begins. **Infertility** (usually defined as the inability to get pregnant after one year of unprotected sex) can befall a couple if there is a problem with any one of these processes. That is, a couple can become infertile if ovulation does not happen, either sperm or egg is of low quality, the fallopian tubes are blocked (often because of malformation or injury), the embryo is abnormal, or implantation is unsuccessful. In up to 90 percent of cases, physicians can treat such problems with conventional methods—drugs and surgery. But increasingly they turn to some form of ART, which usually means in vitro fertilization.

Fact File **Assisted Reproduction**

- In 2011–2013, about 11 percent of the 61 million women of reproductive age (ages 15 to 44) had received fertility services at some time in their lives.
- In 2011–2013, about 6 percent of married women of reproductive age were infertile (unable to get pregnant after trying for 12 consecutive months to conceive).
- In 2013, of the 93,787 fresh nondonor ART cycles started, 33,425 (36 percent) led to a pregnancy, and only 27,406 (29 percent) resulted in a live birth. That is, almost 20 percent of ART pregnancies did not result in a live birth.
- There were 190,773 ART cycles performed at 467 reporting clinics in the United States in 2013, resulting in 54,323 live births (deliveries of one or more living infants) and 67,996 live-born infants.
- About 1.5 percent of all infants born in the United States are conceived using ART.
- In 2012, the average percentage of fresh, nondonor ART cycles that led to a live birth was 40 percent in women younger than 35 years; 31 percent in women 35 to 37 years; 12 percent in women 41 to 42 years; 2 percent in women 44 years and older.
- The average cost of a single IVF cycle is $12,400.

From *2015 Assisted Reproductive Technology: Fertility Clinic Success Rates Report*, Centers for Disease Control and Prevention (CDC), Society for Assisted Reproductive Technology, and the American Society of Reproductive Medicine, UNSW Embryology, National Infertility Association.

In vitro fertilization (IVF) is the uniting of sperm and egg in a laboratory dish, instead of inside a woman's body. (*In vitro* means "in glass" and refers to such outside-the-body containers; the term contrasts with *in utero*, or "in the uterus.") The idea is to create embryos that can be transferred to the woman's uterus, where they can develop to term. (In the much older technique known as artificial insemination, sperm is mechanically inserted into the uterus without sexual intercourse in hopes of achieving fertilization in the woman's body.) The process of IVF and embryo transfer is technically complex, typically consisting of five main steps:

1. **Ovarian stimulation (superovulation).** The woman takes ovulation stimulants (fertility drugs) to prompt her ovaries to produce several eggs at once instead of the usual one per month. Standard IVF procedure calls for multiple eggs because often some of them will be defective, and not every embryo may implant or develop properly once transferred to the uterus.

2. **Egg retrieval.** When the eggs are ready, they are extracted from the egg sacs, or follicles, of the ovaries—usually a 30-minute outpatient surgery. In a typical egg retrieval, an ultrasound-guided needle is inserted into the vagina, through the vaginal wall, and into the ovaries to the egg-bearing follicles. One by one, the eggs are suctioned out through the needle.

3. **Insemination/fertilization.** The retrieved eggs are inspected, and the ones judged to be of highest quality are mixed with sperm (a step called insemination), which results within a few hours in sperm cells penetrating the eggs (fertilization). Typically some eggs will not fertilize,

and occasionally none will. Sometimes the chances of fertilization are greatly increased by a technique known as intra-cytoplasmic sperm injection (ICSI), in which an egg is pierced and a single sperm cell is injected into it.

4. **Embryo culture**. After fertilization, the embryos are left to grow in a culture medium. Within 48 hours, each one consists of 2 to 4 cells; in three days, 6 to 10 cells. Around the third day, fertility experts can screen the embryos for genetic diseases using a technique known as pre-implantation genetic diagnosis (PGD). Only embryos found to be free of defective genes are selected to be transferred to the uterus.

5. **Embryo transfer**. Delivery of embryos to the uterus is generally painless and is performed in the doctor's office up to six days after egg retrieval. To increase the chances of pregnancy, two or more embryos are usually transferred at once. The embryos, along with the fluid surrounding them, are placed in a long, strawlike tube called a transfer catheter. Then the catheter is eased into the vagina and through the cervix, and the embryos are pushed from the tube into the uterus. If all goes well, an embryo implants in the uterine lining.

Fertility experts have developed numerous variations on these steps. One is gamete intrafal-lopian transfer (GIFT). In this process, ovarian stimulation and egg retrieval proceed as they do in IVF, but then the eggs and sperm (gametes) are transferred together to a fallopian tube to fertilize. GIFT is rarely used (less than 1 percent of ART procedures performed are GIFTs), but it is an option for some who prefer that fertiliza-tion take place inside the body. Another variant of IVF is zygote intrafallopian transfer (ZIFT). Like IVF, this procedure depends on fertiliza-tion occurring in vitro, but an embryo (zygote) is transferred not to the uterus but to a fallopian tube. Some people believe that ZIFT offers an in-creased chance of implantation, but it too consti-tutes less than 1 percent of attempts at assisted reproduction.

Couples are generally not limited to using their own sperm and eggs in IVF and its variations. They can also rely on donors, either anonymous or known, primarily to avoid the transmission of a genetic disorder or to substitute donor sperm or eggs for their own abnormal or absent gametes. Sperm donors are screened for sexually transmit-ted diseases and other health problems, and donor sperm is collected, frozen, analyzed, stored (in sperm banks), and used when needed. Egg donors are screened in the same way that sperm donors are, and donor eggs are acquired through standard ovarian stimulation and egg retrieval. The eggs are checked for maturity and, usually soon after retrieval, fertilized with donor sperm or sperm from the partner of the woman trying to become pregnant. (Increasingly eggs are also being frozen and stored for later use in achieving pregnancy.)

As with all forms of reproductive technology, in vitro fertilization (plus embryo transfer) brings with it a long list of risks and benefits—most of which have provoked or underscored a raft of thorny ethical questions. On the plus side is IVF's indisputable power to help many people overcome infertility, to enable desperate couples to do what they otherwise could not: have healthy, biologically related children. The need is great; at last count, in the United States there were over 2 million infertile couples. But since 1981, when the technology was introduced in America, the country has seen the birth of hun-dreds of thousands of IVF babies.

The other side of the ledger includes two dis-concerting facts: IVF is expensive, and its success rates are much lower than most people think. The average cost of a single attempt to overcome infertility using IVF is $12,400. (An attempt, called a cycle, typically includes the steps from retrieval to transfer, a sequence lasting about two weeks.) Some couples end up paying tens of thousands of dollars. On average, a live birth is the outcome in only about 30 percent of IVF cycles in which the woman's own eggs are used. This rate varies with age: The older the woman, the lower the chances of a live birth. In most cases, then, more than one (expensive) cycle is required to achieve a live birth, and many health insurance plans will not cover the cost.

IVF cycles pose health risks for both woman and child. For the woman, the physical demands of the IVF process—the surgery, the monitoring, the waiting—can be uncomfortable, inconvenient, and stressful. The surgery itself comes with a risk, however low, of side effects such as bleeding, infection, and damaged tissue. There is also a chance of complications from taking the fertility drugs that instigate superovulation, including abdominal pain, memory loss, mood swings, and headaches. The most worrisome among these is a rare but potentially dangerous condition known as ovarian hyperstimulation syndrome, characterized by swollen and painful ovaries. Multiple pregnancies—caused mainly by transferring several embryos at once—increase the chances of high blood pressure, anemia, gestational diabetes, and uterine rupture. For the child, there are concerns that ART techniques may lead to birth defects, low birth weight, and diseases such as cancer. Some research has suggested a link between ART and a higher incidence of such problems than occurs in non-ART children, although the disorders are still rare. Researchers are generally not sure, however, if the link is causal, and they have been unable so far to rule out the possibility that these problems are related not to ART but to the infertility itself.

Multiple pregnancies—a common result of IVF cycles—dramatically raise the risks to children's life and health. The chances of prenatal and postnatal death are higher than for single pregnancies, and premature birth is much more likely. Prematurity increases the risk of cerebral palsy, blindness, heart defects, serious infection, respiratory distress syndrome, and other grave maladies. Even aside from prematurity, babies born after a multiple pregnancy have an elevated risk of birth defects and low birth weight,

the latter being a separate risk factor for many diseases. One way that practitioners try to lower the risks of multiple pregnancy is to use fetal reduction (also known as selective abortion) to eliminate some of the fetuses in utero. But the procedure itself carries with it a risk of miscarriage.

Several issues—technological and ethical—arise from the handling of the unused embryos that inevitably result from IVF. The common practice is to freeze, or cryopreserve, the extra embryos for possible transfer in the future. Fertility clinics freeze thousands of embryos every year, and hundreds of thousands of them are now in cryostorage. Freezing a woman's leftover embryos gives her the option of using them in future IVF cycles rather than going through another arduous (and expensive) round of ovarian stimulation and egg retrieval. By having her embryos frozen, she can also select the timing of embryo transfer to avoid causing or aggravating any health problems in pregnancy. A significant drawback to the process is that cryopreserved embryos are less likely to result in live births than unfrozen embryos are. Another is that many embryos do not live through freezing and thawing.

Frozen embryos can remain in cryostorage for years—because the couple divorces, because one or both of them die, because they disagree about what to do with the embryos (for example, if one wants to donate them but the other does not), or because they have changed their minds about getting pregnant. The moral and legal implications of these possibilities are being debated now. One alternative is to donate the unused embryos to an infertile couple, which means that the prospective parents will have no genetic connection to the child born to them. Such an arrangement seems unproblematic to some people but is morally or legally questionable to others. Without legal guidance and ethical consensus, fertility clinics must decide what to do with frozen embryos that are unused, unclaimed, or undonated. Often they either donate the embryos for research or destroy them. To those who believe that embryos have a right to life, both of these options are morally impermissible. But even people who don't believe that embryos are persons may think that embryonic life should not be treated as if it has no moral worth at all.

Many of the moral arguments about IVF have involved objections only to a particular step or outcome of the technology, but much of the debate has been about the moral acceptability of IVF itself—about whether it should be used at all. A host of arguments against IVF have been based on alleged harm to children, harm to families or the natural order of procreation, and harm to women. The strongest arguments for IVF have appealed to individual autonomy or reproductive rights.

Some have objected to IVF because of its potential for causing birth defects and disease in children. As we have seen, research supports this worry, though the exact degree of risk is unknown. One commentator argues that

> it would be wrong to use reproductive technologies to create children if this bore a significant chance of producing serious disease and impairments in these very children. Questions are being raised about whether in vitro fertilization (IVF) and other reproductive technologies do, in fact, create serious illness and deficits in a small but significant proportion of children who are born of them. If these technologies were found to do so, it would be wrong to forge ahead with their use.[1]

For many, much depends on the magnitude of the risk. A low level of risk may be acceptable since even normal methods of conception carry a small risk of birth defects and other problems. To insist that IVF and its variants be safer than the usual way of bringing children into the world (or even risk free) seems unreasonable.

Several writers argue that it would not be wrong to use reproductive technology to bring forth severely damaged children because if the technology had not been used, the children would not be alive—and being alive is better than not being alive. That is, compared to not existing at all, being brought into the world—even to suffer horribly—is a net gain. As one proponent of this view says,

> [A] higher incidence of birth defects in such offspring would not justify banning the [reproductive] technique in order to protect the offspring, because without these techniques these children would not have been born at all. Unless their lives are so full of suffering as to be worse than no life at all, a very unlikely supposition, the defective children of such a union have not been harmed if they would not have been born healthy.[2]

Others believe this view is confused. One critic says that it is based on the false assumption that nonexistence before birth is bad while existence is good and that the two can be meaningfully compared. The view assumes, she says,

> that children with an interest in existing are waiting in a spectral world of nonexistence where their situation is less desirable than it would be were they released into this world. . . . Their admission into this realm is thwarted by the failure to use available new reproductive technologies. This failure negates their interest in existing and thereby harms them.[3]

On the contrary, she says, nonexistence before birth is neither good nor bad. Moreover, the notion that children cannot really be harmed by ART "justifies allowing the new technologies to create almost any harm to children conceived as a result of their use—as long as this is not devastating harm in which death is preferable to life with it."[4]

Some people claim that the use of ART undermines the value we place on offspring. They argue that children are supposed to be regarded as inherently valuable but that reproductive technology tempts us to view them as manufactured products and as commodities acquired in the marketplace for a price. But others see no reason to assume that a couple who creates a child through ART would not love and care for it as they would a child produced through the usual means. They also maintain that the mere involvement of money does not necessarily entail the treatment of children as commodities—otherwise adoption, which involves prices and payments, would also have to be considered morally unacceptable.

IVF has been condemned by some religious groups because it breaks the natural connection between procreation and sexual intercourse in marriage. The only morally permissible way to conceive a child, they say, is through sexual union between husband and wife. According to the Vatican, IVF and other forms of assisted reproduction are "contrary to the unity of marriage, to the dignity of the spouses, to the vocation proper to parents, and to the child's right to be conceived and brought into the world in marriage and from marriage."[5] Some critics, however, think this view has little credibility outside the particular religious tradition espousing it. According to Peter Singer,

> Few infertile couples will take seriously the view that their marital relationship will be damaged if they use the technique [IVF] which offers them the best chance of having their own child. It is in any case extraordinarily paternalistic for anyone else to tell a couple that they should not use IVF because it will harm their marriage. That, surely, is for them to decide.[6]

Whether or not IVF harms marriages, it surely changes family relationships, and that is a pressing concern for many. Through ART, a child can have many parents—genetic (those who contribute egg or sperm), gestational (the woman who carries the baby to term), and social (the people who raise the child). With all these possibilities, the family can take forms that were unthinkable a few decades ago. These changes have prompted some to argue that by weakening the *biological* connections between parents and children, reproductive technology will also loosen the *social* bonds between them—the values, commitments, and feelings that have characterized families in the past. A common reply is that such a claim requires empirical support, for it is not at all obvious that new family structures will be bad for all concerned. Research is scarce on the harm and benefits of new parental arrangements, and to assume the worst is unreasonable.

Many people insist that IVF is a boon to women because it enhances their freedom by multiplying their reproductive choices. But some feminists have repudiated this view. They argue that the pressure from patriarchal society for women to establish their worth by becoming mothers is so powerful that their choices regarding reproduction are not truly free but coerced. If so, then the existence of IVF and other reproductive technologies does not bring more freedom—it just reinforces social stereotypes.

Mary Anne Warren disagrees. She acknowledges that IVF comes with substantial risks and burdens but denies that women are too constrained or coerced by society to decide about the technology for themselves:

> Neither the patriarchal power structure nor pronatalist [pro-childbearing] ideology makes women incapable of reasoned choice about childbearing. Rather, the social pressures upon some women to have children—and the pressures upon others not to have children—are circumstances which we must take into account in our deliberations. . . . In deliberating about either "natural" motherhood or the use of IVF, we may sometimes be wrong about what is in our own interests, and perhaps some of us are excessively influenced by pronatalist ideology. But it does not follow that we would benefit from additional paternalistic restraints. Autonomy necessarily implies the right to make our own mistakes.[7]

To defend the use of IVF, many commentators appeal to autonomy or individual rights. John Robertson, for example, argues for what he calls "procreative liberty"—the freedom to reproduce or not to reproduce. This amounts to a right to make a reproductive choice without interference from others, including a choice about use of reproductive technologies. He contends that only very weighty considerations can override a person's procreative liberty:

> If procreative liberty is taken seriously, a strong presumption in favor of using technologies that centrally implicate reproductive interests should

be recognized. Although procreative rights are not absolute, those who would limit procreative choice should have the burden of establishing substantial harm. . . . This will give persons directly involved the final say about use of a particular technology, unless tangible harm to the interests of others can be shown.[8]

As we have seen, many would argue that such substantial harms are inherent in reproductive technologies—most notably, harms to children, women, and families. Others would insist that at least some moral or religious rules (those concerning the treatment of embryos or the role of reproduction in marriage, for example) can always trump autonomy.

SURROGACY

A **surrogate** is a woman who gestates a fetus for others, usually for a couple or another woman. She contracts with them to carry the pregnancy to term, to relinquish the baby at birth, and to let them legally adopt it. The surrogacy can take two different forms. In what has been called *traditional surrogacy*, sperm from either the couple's male partner or a donor is used to artificially inseminate the surrogate (the "surrogate mother"). Since the egg fertilized is the surrogate's, the baby produced from this arrangement is genetically related only to the surrogate and to whoever supplies the sperm. In *gestational surrogacy*, the surrogate receives a transferred embryo created through IVF using the sperm and egg of others (the contracting couple or donors). Because the gestational surrogate (also called the gestational carrier) does not contribute her own egg, she has no genetic connection to the baby.

In surrogacy relationships, we can distinguish between genetic (or biological), gestational, and social (or rearing) parents. Thus we can say that a traditional surrogate is the genetic mother because she contributes her egg to conception. She is also the gestational mother because she carries the pregnancy. But she is not meant to be the social mother who raises the child; the contractual, or intended, parents plan to do that. The man who contributes the sperm (typically the intended father) is the genetic father. In gestational surrogacy, the surrogate is the gestational mother while the prospective mother and father are usually the genetic parents, who are also likely to be the social parents. In moral and legal disputes over surrogacy arrangements, these distinctions come up again and again and are often used to parse questions about who the "real" parents are.

A woman may opt for gestational surrogacy because she has an abnormal uterus or no uterus (because of hysterectomy or congenital defect) or because she suffers from health problems that make pregnancy dangerous, such as cystic fibrosis and serious forms of diabetes and heart disease. A couple may turn to a traditional surrogate for many of the same reasons. In both kinds of surrogacy, the intended parents generally want more than just a child—they want a biologically related child. For them, then, adoption may be less attractive. (Couples may also decide against adoption for other reasons, including its expense and the scarcity of adoptable children.)

Surrogate arrangements are generally complex and legally unsettled. Surrogacy contracts may specify all of the surrogate's prenatal duties (including those regarding her alcohol consumption, smoking, prenatal testing, medical treatment, and sexual intercourse), the involvement of the intended parents in the pregnancy (for example, their presence or absence at the birth), the permissibility of abortion in case of fetal abnormalities, the arrangements for adoption of the child, and the money to be paid to the surrogate (including prorated compensation if there is a miscarriage). Whatever the financial arrangements, they cannot be construed as transactions involving the buying or selling of children, which is illegal. (Some states forbid surrogacy agreements allowing any kind of payment.) So money paid to surrogates—now probably in the range of $10,000 to $30,000—is supposed to be regarded as compensation for such things as her time and effort or her diminished job opportunities. (A few women agree to become surrogates for altruistic reasons and do not expect payment.)

IN DEPTH
IVF AND CHILDREN'S FUTURE CHILDREN

IVF and the technology for freezing embryos have opened up an array of possibilities for treating infertility that until recently were unthinkable. Here is one example, one of many stunning reports from this new frontier:

> (BBC News)—Israeli scientists say that they have extracted and matured eggs from girls as young as five to freeze for possible fertility treatment in the future.
>
> The team said that the technique could give child cancer sufferers left infertile by chemotherapy treatment a shot at parenthood later in life.
>
> The team took eggs from a group of girls between the ages of five and 10 who had cancer.
>
> They artificially matured the eggs to make them viable and froze them.
>
> Experts had previously thought the eggs of pre-pubescent girls could not be used in this way.
>
> Dr. Ariel Revel, from Hadassah University Hospital in Jerusalem, is to present the team's findings at a fertility conference in Lyon, France, this week.
>
> "No eggs have yet been thawed, so we do not know whether pregnancies will result," he said in a statement.
>
> "But we are encouraged by our results so far, particularly the young ages of the patients from whom we have been able to collect eggs."
>
> Childhood cancers have a good cure rate—between 70% and 90%—but often require aggressive chemotherapy which can mean the child will be sterile in later life.
>
> Geoff Thaxter, of the children's cancer charity CLIC Sargent, said: "This report represents interesting initial research into potential fertility treatments for children being treated for cancer, and could help to make sure that childhood cancer does not have a lifelong impact."
>
> But Josephine Quintavalle, of Comment on Reproductive Ethics, expressed concern that if the eggs were donated to a woman of child-bearing age, a resulting child could have a biological mother who was only a few years older.[9]

Complicating the picture further is the hodge-podge of surrogacy laws from state to state and the absence of national laws. Some states have outlawed surrogacy, some allow it with varying restrictions, some allow it but declare that the contracts are unenforceable, and some have no relevant legislation.

The kinds of questions and conflicts that surrogacy can engender have been accentuated in numerous cases, the most famous one being that of "Baby M." Over 20 years ago Mary Beth Whitehead agreed to become a surrogate mother for William and Elizabeth Stern. For $10,000 she consented to be artificially inseminated with Mr. Stern's sperm, to carry the child to term, and to relinquish it to the Sterns after birth. The baby—named Melissa by the Sterns but known to the world as Baby M—was born on March 27, 1986. But then Whitehead had a change of heart. After declaring that she could not give the infant up, she left the state with her. The case eventually ended up in a New Jersey court, where the judge ruled that the surrogate agreement was binding and that Whitehead had to turn over Baby M to the Sterns. Whitehead appealed the ruling to the New Jersey Supreme Court and won a reversal. The court ruled that the surrogacy contract was actually invalid and that Whitehead was the legal mother. Citing the best interests of the child, however, the court also held that Baby M should live with the Sterns and that Whitehead should have visitation rights.

Many of the arguments about surrogacy mirror those about IVF, clustering around reproductive autonomy and alleged harm to children, families, and women. But probably the most pervasive argument—and perhaps the strongest on the anti-surrogacy side—is that surrogacy arrangements amount to baby-selling, a blatant affront to human dignity. (The charge is usually made against commercial surrogacy, in which money changes hands, not against altruistic surrogacy, in which women volunteer their surrogate services.) As one surrogacy critic says,

> Commercial surrogacy substitutes market norms for some of the norms of parental love. Most importantly, it requires us to understand parental rights no longer as trusts but as things more like property rights—that is, rights of use and disposal over the things owned. For in this practice the natural mother deliberately conceives a child with the intention of giving it up for material advantage. . . . By engaging in the transfer of children by sale, all of the parties to the surrogate contract express a set of attitudes toward children which undermine the norms of parental love.[10]

Defenders of surrogacy deny that it constitutes baby-selling, claiming instead that a surrogate is simply relinquishing her right as a parent to have a relationship with the child. She is not selling an existing close relationship with someone; she is selling, or forfeiting, the right to enjoy a future parent-child relationship—and it is not obvious that doing so is wrong.

Moreover, says the surrogacy advocate, the practice is not that different from adoption, in which biological parents give away their children (as well as the hope of any relationship with them). On the contrary, says Elizabeth Anderson, adoption and surrogacy differ substantially:

> The purpose of adoption is to provide a means for placing children in families when their parents cannot or will not discharge their parental responsibilities. It is not a sphere for the existence of a supposed parental right to dispose of one's children for profit.[11]

Laura Purdy, however, reminds us that surrogacy provides a socially valuable service and asks,

Why then must it be motivated by altruistic considerations? We do not frown upon those who provide other socially valuable services even when they do not have the "right" motives. Nor do we require them to be unpaid. For instance, no one expects physicians, no matter what their motivation, to work for beans. They provide an important service; their motivation is important only to the extent that it affects quality.[12]

Bonnie Steinbock thinks that surrogacy arrangements have sometimes involved baby-selling, and she points to the Baby M case as an example. But she argues that this unsavory element can be eliminated if we view surrogacy as prenatal adoption:

> The question, then, is whether we can reconcile paying the surrogate, beyond her medical expenses, with the idea of surrogacy as prenatal adoption. We can do this by separating the terms of the agreement, which include surrendering the infant at birth to the biological father, from the justification for payment. The payment should be seen as justification for the risks, sacrifice, and discomfort the surrogate undergoes during pregnancy. This means that if, through no fault on the part of the surrogate, the baby is stillborn, she should still be paid in full, since she has kept her part of the bargain. . . . If, on the other hand, the surrogate changes her mind and decides to keep the child, she would break the agreement, and would not be entitled to any fee, or compensation for expenses incurred during pregnancy.[13]

CLONING

Clones, in the sense used by biologists, are genetically identical entities, whether cells, DNA molecules, plants, animals, or humans. **Cloning** is the asexual production of a genetically identical entity from an existing one. In animals and humans, since the genetic blueprint for an individual is in each of its cells (mostly in the nucleus), all the cells of a clone contain the same blueprint as all the cells of the clone's progenitor.

An animal or human clone is not a perfect copy of an individual—not like a photocopy of an original document—but a living thing that shares a set of genetic instructions with another.

In agriculture, cloning to propagate plant strains is commonplace, and for years scientists have been cloning human and animal cells for research purposes. Molecular biologists often clone fragments of DNA for study. Among animals and humans, clones appear naturally in the form of identical twins, individuals with identical sets of DNA. Scientists have managed to duplicate this process in a form of cloning known as *twinning*. Through in vitro fertilization they produce an embryo (zygote), and when it consists of two to four identical cells, they separate them and let them grow into discrete but genetically identical organisms.

The cloning that has provoked the most public consternation and media attention is the creation of a genetic duplicate of an adult animal or human, what has often been called **reproductive cloning**. The aim of this work is the live birth of an individual. (Cloning for other purposes is called **therapeutic**, or **research, cloning**, a topic we discuss further in Chapter 9.) This kind of cloning suddenly became front-page news in 1997 when scientists announced that they had managed to clone an adult sheep, resulting in the birth of an apparently healthy clone called Dolly. She was the genetic twin of her adult "parent" and the first mammal so cloned. After her, scientists cloned additional animals in similar fashion—cattle, goats, pigs, cats, rabbits, mice, and more—and are working on others.

The primary cloning method for producing live-birth mammals, and the one most likely to be considered for human cloning, is known as somatic cell nuclear transfer (SCNT). The usual steps are:

1. Extract the DNA-packed nucleus from an egg cell (creating an enucleated egg).
2. Replace the egg's nucleus with the donor nucleus of an ordinary body (somatic) cell from the adult individual to be cloned.

(It's also possible to use cells from existing embryos.)
3. Stimulate the reconfigured cell with chemicals or electricity to start cell division and growth to the embryo stage.
4. Transfer the cloned embryo to a host uterus for development and birth.

The egg and somatic nucleus can come from two different individuals or the same individual. If from two different ones, the largest portion of the clone's DNA will be from the nucleus donor since almost all DNA resides in the nucleus, with only a tiny amount located outside the nucleus in the cell's mitochondria. If from the same individual, the clone will get its entire complement of DNA from the nucleus and mitochondria of the same individual.

To date, no human has been successfully cloned, and for technical and moral reasons none is likely to be cloned any time soon. At this stage of the technology, both scientists and policymakers have serious concerns about the safety and ethics of human reproductive cloning.

A typical response to the prospect of human cloning is moral outrage—which too often is based on misunderstandings. Chief among these is the notion that a human clone would be identical to an existing person, the clone's "parent." This idea has led to a host of silly fantasies played out in movies, literature, and the popular mind: an army of Hitler clones spawned from one of the Führer's cells, a laboratory of Albert Einsteins discovering the secrets of the universe, the perfect team of Hank Aaron or Michael Jordan clones, a houseful of identical children who are exact copies of a rich, eccentric egotist. The underlying fallacy is that genes make the person, that genetics ordains all of an individual's characteristics. This view is known as genetic determinism, and it is a myth. The National Academy of Sciences makes the point this way:

> Even if clones are genetically identical with one another, they will not be identical in physical or behavioral characteristics, because DNA is not the only determinant of these characteristics.

A pair of clones will experience different environments and nutritional inputs while in the uterus, and they would be expected to be subject to different inputs from their parents, society, and life experience as they grow up. If clones derived from identical nuclear donors and identical mitochondrial donors are born at different times, as is the case when an adult is the donor of the somatic cell nucleus, the environmental and nutritional differences would be expected to be more pronounced than for monozygotic (identical) twins. And even monozygotic twins are not fully identical genetically or epigenetically because mutations, stochastic [random] developmental variations, and varied imprinting effects (parent-specific chemical marks on the DNA) make different contributions to each twin.[14]

Einstein's clone would have Einstein's genes but would not and could not be Einstein. The clone would be unique and probably not much like his famous progenitor at all.

At this stage of scientific knowledge, human cloning seems likely to result in high rates of serious birth defects.[15] Under these circumstances, most commentators agree that cloning should not be attempted. (A few question this conclusion, noting that even now parents who are certain to conceive and bear children with terrible genetic disorders are permitted to do so.) Nevertheless, since 1997 the dispute over the moral permissibility of cloning has raged on, fueled by the thought that, given the usual pace of scientific progress, the problem of congenital malformations will be solved and the efficient cloning of human beings will soon be technologically feasible.

As we would expect, many of those who favor the use of cloning rest their case on its likely benefits. For some people, their only hope of having a child with whom they are genetically related would be through cloning. Some men have no sperm; some women, no eggs; cloning could get around the problem. For couples who value this genetic connection and who also want to avoid passing on a genetic disease or health risk to their child, cloning would be an attractive option—perhaps the only option. Parents whose only child dies could have her cloned from a cell harvested from her body, ensuring that some part of her would live on. A boy who needs an organ transplant to live could be cloned so his clone could provide the needed organ, perfectly matched to avoid transplant rejection.

As in the case of IVF, many claim a moral right to use cloning, arguing that people have a basic right of reproductive liberty and that cloning is covered by that right. They deny that this right to cloning is absolute (overriding all other considerations) but believe that it carries great weight nonetheless. As one writer puts it:

> [I]t is reasonable to hold that the freedom of infertile couples to use cloning is a form of procreative freedom. Procreative freedom is worthy of respect in part because freedom in general is worthy of respect. But more than this, procreative freedom is an especially important freedom because of the significance that procreative decisions can have for persons' lives. For these reasons, the freedom of infertile couples to use cloning is worthy of respect.[16]

Some critics of cloning have charged that it violates the rights of the resulting clone—specifically, the right to a unique identity. A clone by definition is not genetically unique; his genome is iterated in his "parent." Aside from doubts about whether such a right exists, the strongest reply to this worry is that genetic uniqueness is neither necessary nor sufficient for personal uniqueness:

> What is the sense of identity that might plausibly be each person has a right to have uniquely, which constitutes the special uniqueness of each individual? Even with the same genes, two individuals, for example homozygous twins, are numerically distinct and not identical, so what is intended must be the various properties and characteristics that make each individual qualitatively unique and different than others. Does having the same genome as another person

IN DEPTH
CLONING TIME LINE

1970 British developmental biologist John Gurdon clones a frog.

1978 Louise Brown is born, the first baby conceived through IVF.

1980 The U.S. Supreme Court holds that a genetically engineered life form—a bacterium—can be patented.

1996 Through the work of Ian Wilmut and his colleagues, the first animal cloned from adult cells—a sheep named Dolly—is born.

1997 President Bill Clinton declares a five-year moratorium on federal funding for research into human cloning.

1997 Wilmut and his colleagues create Polly, a sheep with a human gene in each of its cells.

1998 From a single cow, eight calves are cloned.

2001 Scientists in Massachusetts clone the first human embryo.

2002 The President's Council on Bioethics recommends a ban on reproductive cloning.

2003 Dolly, now 6 years old, is euthanized when she is found to have progressive lung disease.

2003 Italian scientists claim they have produced the first cloned horse.

2004 A company called Genetics Savings and Clone says it will clone people's cats for them for $50,000 per cat.

2005 The creator of Dolly is licensed to clone human embryos for medical research.

2011 In South Korea, seven Labrador retriever clones are used to sniff out contraband luggage; they are genetically identical to a dog that was for a while the top dog in drug detection.

2013 Researchers at Oregon Health and Science University say in the journal *Cell* they have used cloning to produce embryonic stem cells. They first created human embryos with skin cells, then used those embryos to produce the stem cells.

2014 Cloning is used to produce stem cells that are genetically matched to the genome of adult patients.

---

undermine that unique qualitative identity? Only in the crudest genetic determinism. . . . But there is no reason whatever to believe in that kind of genetic determinism, and I do not think that anyone does.[17]

A similar rights argument says that cloning would be wrong because it violates what has been called a "right to ignorance" or a "right to an open future." Consider a situation in which a clone begins his life many years after his older twin does. The younger twin lives in the shadow of the older one, thinking—correctly or incorrectly—that his genetically identical sibling has already lived the life that he (the younger twin) has barely started. He believes that his future is already set. His sense of personal freedom and of a future of possibilities is diminished. In this way, the argument goes, his right to an open-ended life story has been flouted.

But some think this argument is built on flimsy assumptions:

[A]ll of these concerns are not only quite speculative, but are directly related to certain specific cultural values. Someone created through the use of somatic cell nuclear transfer techniques may or may not believe that their future is relatively constrained. Indeed, they may believe the opposite. In addition, quite normal parenting usually involves many constraints on a child's behavior that children may resent.[18]

Would the younger twin's right to ignorance or to an open future be violated just because she *believes* her future is fated, although her belief is false? Dan W. Brock insists that the answer is no:

> I believe that if the twin's future in reality remains open and his to freely choose, then someone acting in a way that unintentionally leads him to believe that his future is closed and determined has not violated his right to ignorance or to an open future. . . . If we know that the twin will believe that his open future has been taken from him as a result of being cloned, even though in reality it has not, then we know that cloning will cause him psychological distress, but not that it will violate his right.[19]

Many oppose the use of cloning technology (and any other ART) because it is unnatural, a deviant way of bringing children into the world. But this view is criticized as narrowly dogmatic, for some natural processes are bad (such as bacterial infection), and some unnatural ones are good (such as medical treatment). A few believe that naturalness should be defined according to a thing's function. They reason that since each part of the human body has a natural function, we should not subvert that part by giving it an additional function. Cloning, then, would be unnatural and wrong. But this take on naturalness has many detractors. For example:

> Although there are certainly unhealthy or unwise uses of our body parts, there's no reason for us to always adhere to an organ's primary function. The bridge of a nose has the primary function of allowing us to exhale and inhale air, but do we sin if we use it to support our spectacles? . . . . Bypass surgery improves our cardiovascular systems. Kidney dialysis allows people with kidney failure to survive. Transplants replace increasing numbers of our organs. All of these are human artificial interventions in nature. They seem morally justified, if anything does. So why not extend this reasoning to genetic engineering? Why not use genetics to produce a healthy child rather than a sickly one?[20]

A kindred objection to cloning and other reproductive technologies holds that they replace natural procreation with the artificial *manufacture* of children as products—a demeaning process that erodes our respect for human beings. Cloning is thus profoundly dehumanizing. "Human nature," says Leon Kass, "becomes merely the last part of nature to succumb to the technological project, which turns all of nature into raw material at human disposal."[21]

But why assume cloning is dehumanizing? Dan Brock says that we should not:

> It would be a mistake, however, to conclude that a human being created by human cloning is of less value or is less worthy of respect than one created by sexual reproduction. It is the nature of a being, not how it is created, that is the source of its value and makes it worthy of respect.[22]

APPLYING MAJOR THEORIES

We have the power to control human reproduction as never before. The question is: Should we? In the name of reproductive freedom and control, is it morally permissible to employ ART, surrogacy, even cloning?

The utilitarian will answer yes if the benefits of the technology outweigh its harms, no if they do not. Based on current knowledge of the good and bad effects, most utilitarians would probably see a net gain in the use of IVF and surrogacy arrangements, and they would likely endorse cloning if its risks to children could be decreased to an acceptable level. They presumably would calculate that IVF's real but low risk of birth defects and maternal complications is outweighed by the happiness brought to infertile couples, and the loss of embryos in the process would not be a major factor. They would likely make a similar calculation regarding surrogacy, assuming that surrogacy arrangements are properly regulated. But some utilitarians may embrace a different calculus. They may reason that cloning and IVF are impermissible because the considerable money spent on them could yield far more happiness

IN DEPTH
SHERRI SHEPHERD: HOW SURROGACY CAN GO WRONG

When people involved in surrogacy arrangements change their minds about the surrogacy agreements, they find themselves in new legal, social, and emotional territory. Here's a report on a recent case that has lit up the news media and the social networks.

Last week, a Pennsylvania judge issued a ruling in a surrogacy case involving the actress Sherri Shepherd. It's a sad and complicated scenario: Shepherd and her ex-husband, Lamar Sally, conceived a baby using Sally's sperm, a donor's egg, and a surrogate's womb. Shepherd and Sally split in the middle of the pregnancy, and Shepherd subsequently claimed that she was tricked into signing the surrogacy documents so that Sally might get more money from her in the form of child support. Shepherd disavowed the child, who was born in August. The Pennsylvania judge ruled that Shepherd's name must go on the birth certificate as the child's legal mother. Before the ruling, the surrogate's name was on the certificate, and she, not Shepherd, was held responsible for child support in California.

To complicate matters further, this decision is just from one of three court cases pending in Shepherd and Sally's split, all of which are in different states. In addition to the Pennsylvania parentage case, which has been decided, there's a divorce action pending in New Jersey and a child support case pending in California. The surrogate resides in Pennsylvania, where the baby was born; Shepherd filed for divorce in New Jersey, and Sally filed in California.

This type of dispute is rare, says Raegen N. Rasnic, an attorney at the Seattle law firm Skellenger Bender who focuses on assisted reproduction. Andrew W. Vorzimer, a surrogacy lawyer, told the New York Times in 2014 that there have been 81 cases where intended parents changed their minds about a surrogacy agreement, and 35 in which the surrogate wanted to keep the baby (24 of those involved surrogates whose eggs were also used)....

Despite the fact that Shepherd now claims she was tricked into the surrogacy agreement, her past statements to the press tell a different story. In June 2013, she spoke frankly and jokingly about finding a surrogate to Essence.com. "We're starting the process of making sure the uterus that we picked is not crazy," she said back then. And she did sign the papers, even if she now says it was under duress.

So what does it mean that Shepherd has been declared the parent of this baby? It means she's responsible for child support until the child is 18—or longer, if college support comes into play, says Rasnic. Shepherd can also seek custody or visitation, and the child could be entitled to certain benefits, like Social Security, upon Shepherd's death. The Pennsylvania ruling does not cover these specifics, though; the specifics will be determined by the other cases pending in Shepherd and Sally's divorce proceedings.

From Jessica Grose, "The Sherri Shepherd Surrogacy Case Is in a Mess. Prepare for More Like It," *Slate/blog: XXfactor*, 28 April 2015, http://www.slate.com/blogs/xx_factor/2015/04/28 (6 November 2015).

---

if spent on, say, food for the hungry people of the world.

On the other hand, if the widespread use of reproductive technologies would harm society—if, for example, surrogacy or cloning would result in a general disregard for human life and welfare, as some critics argue—a rule-utilitarian might oppose these innovations. She could, with logical consistency, acknowledge that the technologies often increase net happiness in particular cases but oppose a public policy that allowed their use.

From a Kantian perspective, it is possible to either oppose or defend reproductive technologies. Someone could argue, for example, that IVF, surrogacy, and cloning are impermissible because they treat children merely as a means, instead of an end in themselves. Children are "manufactured" and sold as commodities to serve the ends of others. But a Kantian could refuse to take this view, arguing instead that couples who create children do so precisely because they wish to respect and love their offspring as persons. What matters is not how children are brought into the world, but how they are treated after they arrive.

According to the Roman Catholic interpretation of natural law theory, reproductive technologies must be rejected across the board. IVF is wrong because it defies the natural link between procreation and sexual union. It also involves the destruction of human embryos, each of which has a right to life. Surrogacy is immoral because it too is procreation outside of marriage and an affront to the integrity of the family. Human cloning is to be repudiated because it unnaturally separates procreation from sex and is a violation of the rights of the child.

KEY TERMS
cloning
cloning, reproductive
cloning, therapeutic or research
cycle (in assisted reproductive technology)
infertility
in vitro fertilization
surrogate

SUMMARY
Assisted reproductive technology (ART) is designed to address the problem of infertility, which affects millions of couples in the United States and worldwide. In vitro fertilization (IVF) is one such technology, consisting of the uniting of sperm and egg in a laboratory dish, instead of inside a woman's body. There are numerous variations on basic IVF, including gamete intrafallopian transfer (GIFT) and zygote intrafallopian transfer (ZIFT). IVF can help many couples overcome infertility, but it is expensive, and IVF cycles pose health risks to both woman and child. Paramount among the risks are multiple pregnancies, a frequent result of IVF cycles. Problems also arise from the practice of cryopreserving extra embryos often left over after IVF, a key question being what ultimately should be done with them.

Critics contend that IVF should not be used because it leads to birth defects and disease in children, undermines the value we place on children, breaks the natural connection between procreation and sexual intercourse in marriage, and dramatically changes common family relationships. Others argue that IVF enhances women's freedom by multiplying their reproductive choices or that IVF should be allowed in the name of procreative liberty.

A surrogate is a woman who gestates a fetus for others, usually for a couple or another woman. She contracts with them to carry the pregnancy to term, to relinquish the baby at birth, and to let them legally adopt it. Thus, in surrogacy relationships, we can distinguish between genetic (or biological), gestational, and social (or rearing) parents. Probably the most pervasive argument against surrogacy is that surrogacy arrangements amount to baby-selling, a blatant affront to human dignity. Defenders of surrogacy deny that it constitutes baby-selling, claiming instead that a surrogate is simply relinquishing her right as a parent to have a relationship with the child. The surrogacy advocate says that the practice is not that different from adoption, in which biological parents give away their children (as well as the hope of any relationship with them).

Cloning is the asexual production of a genetically identical entity from an existing one. All the cells of a clone contain the same blueprint as all the cells of the clone's progenitor. The cloning that has provoked the most debate

Baby M

In recent years, no issue in assisted reproduction has generated more controversy than surrogate pregnancy. The kinds of questions and conflicts that surrogacy can engender have been accentuated in numerous cases, the most famous one being that of "Baby M."

In 1985 Mary Beth Whitehead agreed to become a surrogate mother for William and Elizabeth Stern. For $10,000 she consented to be artificially inseminated with William Stern's sperm, to carry the child to term, to relinquish all rights to it, and to surrender it to the Sterns at birth. At the time, she was married and had two school-age children. She said that she had no desire for more children to raise and that her aim was to give a child to a couple who could not have any children of their own. The Sterns said that they decided on surrogacy because Mrs. Stern had a medical condition that made pregnancy risky for her.

The baby—named Melissa by the Sterns but known to the world as Baby M—was born on March 27, 1986. Whitehead turned over the baby to the Sterns as agreed, but then she had a change of heart. The next day she went to the Sterns and pleaded with them to allow her to take the baby home with her for a while. The Sterns quoted her as saying, "I just want her for a week and I'll be out of your lives forever." She was distraught and persistent, and the Sterns thought she was suicidal. "Something took over," Whitehead would say later. "I think it was just being a mother." Reluctantly the Sterns agreed to let Whitehead keep the baby for a few days.

Two weeks later Mary Beth Whitehead let the Sterns know that she was not going to give the baby back. With a court order granting them custody of the child and backed by several police officers, the Sterns went to Whitehead's home to take custody. But the Whiteheads took the baby and fled to Florida, where they eluded the authorities for weeks. On July 31, however, a private detective located the baby, and authorities turned her over to the Sterns.

Whitehead tried to regain legal custody, and the case eventually ended up in a New Jersey court, where the judge ruled that the surrogate agreement was binding and that Whitehead had to turn over Baby M to the Sterns. After the judge's ruling, he signed papers allowing Elizabeth Stern to adopt her.

Whitehead appealed the ruling to the New Jersey Supreme Court and, on February 3, 1988, won an almost total reversal of the earlier decision. The court held in a unanimous ruling that the surrogacy contract was actually invalid, that it violated the state's adoption laws against selling babies, and that Whitehead was to have parental rights. "We thus restore the surrogate as the mother of the child," declared the court. "She is not only the natural mother, but also the legal mother, and is not to be penalized one iota because of the surrogate contract." Citing the best interests of the child, however, the court also held that Baby M should live with the Sterns and that Whitehead should have visitation rights. The ruling made it clear that, in New Jersey at least, surrogacy was permitted as long as the surrogate was not paid and she had the right to change her mind about giving up the baby.

The decision made history as the first one from a state's top court on the rights of surrogate mothers.

---

and media attention is human reproductive cloning, the creation of a genetic duplicate of an adult human. So far, no human has been successfully cloned and is not likely to be any time soon. Nevertheless, fear or outrage regarding human cloning is widespread, much of it based on incorrect information. A common myth is genetic determinism, the view that genes make the person, that genetics ordains all of an individual's characteristics.

Many in favor of human cloning appeal to reproductive liberty and to cloning's possible benefits, such as enabling infertile couples to have a child that is genetically related to them. Critics charge that cloning is unnatural, that it violates the right of the resulting clone to a unique identity or future, and that it will result in the demeaning artificial manufacture of children as products.

Cases for Evaluation

CASE 1
The Fate of Frozen Embryos

Abstract

BACKGROUND. The moral status of the human embryo is particularly controversial in the United States, where one debate has centered on embryos created in excess at in vitro fertilization (IVF) clinics. Little has been known about the disposal of these embryos.

METHODS. We mailed anonymous, self-administered questionnaires to directors of 341 American IVF clinics.

RESULTS. 217 of 341 clinics (64 percent) responded. Nearly all (97 percent) were willing to create and cryopreserve extra embryos. Fewer, but still a majority (59 percent), were explicitly willing to avoid creating extras. When embryos did remain in excess, clinics offered various options: continual cryopreservation for a charge (96 percent) or for no charge (4 percent), donation for reproductive use by other couples (76 percent), disposal prior to (60 percent) or following (54 percent) cryopreservation, and donation for research (60 percent) or embryologist training (19 percent). Qualifications varied widely among those personnel responsible for securing couples' consent for disposal and for conducting disposal itself. Some clinics performed a religious or quasi-religious disposal ceremony. Some clinics required a couple's participation in disposal; some allowed but did not require it; some others discouraged or disallowed it.

CONCLUSIONS. The disposal of human embryos created in excess at American IVF clinics varies in ways suggesting both moral sensitivity and ethical divergence.*

One study estimates that as many as 400,000 embryos remain frozen in fertility clinics in the United States; this survey tried to document what happens to them. If you were faced with trying to decide what to do with frozen embryos, which of the options described here would you choose? Why? Do you believe that parents should have a say in what happens to their embryos? Do you think embryos have a right to exist regardless of the parents' wishes? Explain. Given that a frozen embryo is minute (comprising only two to four cells), do you think it merits a disposal ceremony? Why or why not?

---

*Andrea D. Gurmankin, Dominic Sisti, and Arthur L. Caplan, "Embryo Disposal Practices in IVF Clinics in the United States," *Politics and Life Sciences* 22.2 (August 2004), 3–8.

CASE 2
Surrogate Versus Father

(MSNBC)—Despite a court ruling against them, a Florida couple vows to continue their legal battle to gain custody of a child born by the woman they hired as a surrogate, but who then decided to keep the baby.

The issue, Tom and Gwyn Lamitina say, is not about Florida surrogacy law, which clearly gives the woman the right to the child. They are fighting for Tom Lamitina's rights as the father of the child.

"We filed an appeal," Scott Alan Salomon, the attorney for the couple, told TODAY co-host Meredith Vieira when all three appeared on the program Tuesday. "The trial judge overstepped his bounds. He had no right whatsoever to terminate parental rights in a paternity action."

Gwyn Lamitina, 46, said the couple wants custody of the child they think is rightfully theirs.

"We would ultimately like to have primary custody," she said. "If the judge deems that [the surrogate] has visitation, we would be up for that."

The child, Emma Grace, was born five months ago to Stephanie Eckard, whom the Lamitinas had met through an online site on which women who want to be surrogates advertise their availability.

Eckard, 30, is a teacher and a single mother of two other children of her own. According to Salomon, she had delivered three surrogate children for other couples before meeting the Lamitinas. Eckard lives in Jacksonville, in the northeast corner of the state, while the Lamitinas live in the Central Florida town of Oviedo. Eckard has declined all requests to be interviewed.

But a month after Eckard became pregnant, she and the Lamitinas had a confrontation over Eckard's smoking. Eckard broke off contact and decided to keep the child as her own. The Lamitinas had paid her $1,500 to carry the child.

The Lamitinas have never seen the girl. "I haven't known anything about her," Gwyn Lamitina told Vieira. "I had to find out she was born through the press."

Because Emma Grace was conceived with Eckard's egg and not Gwyn Lamitina's, Florida law gives Eckard the absolute right to decide to keep the child up until 48 hours after the birth. The trial court upheld that law on Oct. 11.

For that reason, Florida surrogacy lawyer Charlotte Danciu told NBC News in a recorded interview, "Couples should never let a surrogate use her own egg." . . .

As Danciu said, the law in Florida is very clear: A surrogate pregnancy with the surrogate's own egg is treated as an adoption and the birth mother can decide to keep the child, even if there is a signed contract. Tom Lamitina is the father of the child, but the law treats him as a sperm donor with no parental rights.

"That is absolutely incorrect," said Salomon. "A sperm donor is one that signs a contract that says 'I am waiving my parental rights.' Tom voluntarily paid money to give a woman his sperm. He is not a sperm donor. He was doing this with the sole intent to become a father. That's the biggest joke of this whole case."

He said the Lamitinas' case is rightly a paternity case in which Tom Lamitina is seeking custody of his own daughter.

"Half of this child's DNA is Tom's," Salomon said. "The judge unilaterally said, 'We don't care about that. You have no rights.'"

Vieira asked if there is a legal precedent for that claim, to which Salomon replied, "There will be one now."*

Should the father have any rights to the child in this case? Is Florida law correct in giving the surrogate the right to decide to keep the child up until 48 hours after the birth, even if she had signed a surrogacy contract? In determining the custody of a child, should who gestates it carry more weight than genetic links to it (that is, where the egg and sperm come from)? Should genetic or gestational links carry more weight than the ability to properly care for the child? Explain your answers.

---

*Mike Celizic, "Couple Vows to Fight Surrogate Who Kept Baby," *MSNBC.com*, 23 October 2007, http://www.msnbc.msn.com/id/21435600/ (29 November 2007).

CASE 3

Cloning to Bring Back a Child

(MSNBC)—Katherine Gordon of Great Falls, Mont., whose 17-year-old daughter, Emily, was killed by a drunk driver five years ago, says she became obsessed with bringing a part of her daughter back in some way. Spurred on by the news of [the birth of the cloned sheep Dolly], she had her daughter's cells frozen and stored for possible future cloning. "I started to spend all day researching on the Internet and contacting biologists," she recalls. "I really went off the deep end."

Now she's resigned herself to the fact that the technology probably won't be available in time to help her bear Emily's clone, as she's now 42. But she says that if it were possible in the next couple of years, she would do it.

"I know it wouldn't be Emily—it would be her twin sister," she says. "Emily was perfect—she was beautiful and smart, too, and most of that is genetic. Her predisposition was real kind. Even if the clone had some of her negative qualities that would be fine, too. I don't know what the new person would be like, but she would have a good start in life." . . .

Dr. William Hurlbut, a bioethicist at Stanford University and member of President Bush's Council on Bioethics, urges parents to look at cloning from the perspective of the child. "I don't think anyone should have to live their life in the footsteps of someone else," he says. "The baby may be held up in comparison with some idealized image of the lost child. It seems morbid and insensitive to the love of the child."

But Gregory Pence, a pro-cloning bioethicist at the University of Alabama, Birmingham, and author of "Who's Afraid of Human Cloning?" defends that choice. "People have replacement children all the time. It's as good a reason as any to have a child sexually. Why are people creating children anyway? To create a sense of family, someone to take care of them when they're older. There are many self-centered reasons people have kids, parents just normally don't have to [spell] out these reasons."*

If Katharine Gordon could give birth to a clone of her deceased daughter, should she? Is grief over the loss of a child a morally legitimate reason for wanting to clone him or her? Is there a morally relevant difference between sexually producing a child to replace a lost one and producing a child through cloning for the same reason? Explain your answers.

---

*Julia Sommerfeld, "Coveting a Clone," MSNBC.com, undated, 2006, http://www.msnbc.msn.com/id/3076918/ (29 November 2007).

FURTHER READING

Kenneth D. Alpern, ed., *The Ethics of Reproductive Technology* (New York: Oxford University Press, 1992).

American Society for Reproductive Medicine, "Reproductive Facts," 2015, https://www.asrm.org/ (29 October 2015).

Elizabeth Anderson, "Is Women's Labor a Commodity?" *Philosophy and Public Affairs* 19 (Winter 1990), 71–92.

Dan W. Brock, "An Assessment of the Ethical Issues Pro and Con," in *Cloning Human Beings: Report and Recommendations of the National Bioethics Advisory Commission,* vol. II, sect. E (Rockville, MD: NBAC, June 1997), 1–23.

Justine Burley, ed., *The Genetic Revolution and Human Rights* (Oxford: Oxford University Press, 1999).

Centers for Disease Control and Prevention, "Assisted Reproductive Technology (ART)," 27 October, 2015, http://www.cdc.gov/art/patientresources/index.html (29 October 2015).

Walter Glannon, "Reproductive Rights and Technologies," in *Biomedical Ethics* (New York: Oxford University Press, 2005), 71–94.

Jonathan Glover, *Choosing Children: The Ethical Dilemmas of Genetic Intervention* (Oxford: Oxford University Press, 2006).

John Harris and Søren Holm, eds., *The Future of Human Reproduction: Ethics, Choice, and Regulation* (Oxford: Oxford University Press, 1998).

Mark Murphy, "The Natural Law Tradition in Ethics," in *Stanford Encyclopedia of Philosophy*, 11 March 2008, http://plato.stanford.edu/entries/natural-law-ethics (9 June 2008).

National Bioethics Advisory Commission, *Cloning Human Beings,* June 1997, http://bioethics.georgetown.edu (14 July 2007).

New York State Task Force on Life and the Law, *Assisted Reproductive Technologies: Analysis and Recommendations for Public Policy* (Albany: New York State Department of Health, April 1998).

President's Council on Bioethics, "Assisted Reproduction," in *Reproduction & Responsibility: The Regulation of New Biotechnologies* (Washington, DC: Government Printing Office, 2004).

President's Council on Bioethics, *Human Cloning and Human Dignity: An Ethical Inquiry,* undated, 2002, www.bioethics.gov (14 July 2007).

Laura Purdy, "Genetics and Reproductive Risk: Can Having Children Be Immoral?" in *Genetics Now*, ed. John L. Buckley (Washington, DC: University Press of America, 1978).

John Robertson, *Children of Choice: Freedom and the New Reproductive Technologies* (Princeton, NJ: Princeton University Press, 1994).

Susan Sherwin, "Feminist Ethics and In Vitro Fertilization," in *Science, Morality and Feminist Theory*, ed. Marsha Hanen and Kai Nielsen (Calgary, Alberta: University of Calgary Press, 1987), 265–84.

Society for Assisted Reproductive Technology, "SART," 2015, http://www.sart.org/NCOART/ (29 October 2015).

Bonnie Steinbock, "Surrogate Motherhood as Prenatal Adoption," *Law, Medicine, & Health Care* 16 (Spring/Summer 1988), 4050.

Margaret Tighe, Nicholas Tonti-Filippini, Robyn Rowland, and Peter Singer, "IVF: A Debate," in *Bioethics: An Anthology*, ed. Helga Kuhse and Peter Singer (Oxford: Blackwell, 1999), 91–102.

Robert Wachbroit and David Wasserman, "Reproductive Technology," in *The Oxford Handbook of Practical Ethics*, ed. Hugh LaFollette (Oxford: Oxford University Press, 2003), 136–60.

NOTES

1. Cynthia B. Cohen, "'Give Me Children or I Shall Die!' New Reproductive Technologies and Harm to Children," *Hastings Center Report* 26.2 (1996), 19–27.

2. John A. Robertson, "Procreative Liberty and the Control of Conception, Pregnancy, and Childbirth," *University of Virginia Law Review* 69 (1983), 434.

3. Cohen, "'Give Me Children,'" 21.

4. *Ibid.*, 22.

5. Vatican Congregation for the Doctrine of the Faith, "Instruction on Respect for Human Life in Its Origin and on the Dignity of Procreation," *Origins* 16.40 (19 March 1987).

6. Peter Singer, "IVF: The Simple Case," in *Ethical Issues at the Outset of Life*, ed. William B. Weil, Jr., and Martin Benjamin (Boston: Blackwell Scientific Publications, 1989), 44–49.

7. Mary Anne Warren, "IVF and Women's Interests: An Analysis of Feminist Concerns," *Bioethics* 2.1 (1988), 37–57.

8. John Robertson, "The Presumptive Primacy of Procreative Liberty," in *Children of Choice: Freedom and the New Reproductive Technologies* (Princeton, NJ: Princeton University Press, 1994), 22–42.

9. Michelle Roberts, "IVF Hope for Child Cancer Cases," BBC News, 2 July 2007, http://news.bbc.co.uk/2/hi/health/6259864.stm (27 November 2007).

10. Elizabeth S. Anderson, "Is Women's Labor a Commodity?" *Philosophy and Public Affairs* 19 (Winter 1990), 71–92.

11. *Ibid.*

12. Laura M. Purdy, "Surrogate Mothering: Exploitation or Empowerment?" *Bioethics* 3 (January 1989), 18–34.

13. Bonnie Steinbock, "Surrogate Motherhood as Prenatal Adoption," *Law, Medicine & Health Care* 16 (Spring/Summer 1988), 40–50.

14. National Academy of Sciences, Committee on Science, Engineering, and Public Policy, *Scientific and Medical Aspects of Human Reproductive Cloning* (Washington, DC: National Academy Press, 2002), 26.

15. Human Genome Project Information, "Cloning Fact Sheet," Genomics.Energy.Gov, 29 August 2006, www.ornl.gov/sci/techsources/Human_Genome/elsi/cloning.shtml (15 June 2008).

16. Carson Strong, "The Ethics of Human Reproductive Cloning," *Ethics, Law and Moral Philosophy of Reproductive Biomedicine* 1.1 (March 2005), 45–49.

17. Dan W. Brock, "Cloning Human Beings: An Assessment of the Ethical Issues Pro and Con," paper prepared for the National Bioethics Advisory Commission, 1997.

18. National Bioethics Advisory Commission, *Cloning Human Beings: Report and Recommendations* (Rockville, MD: NBAC, June 1997), 67.

19. Brock, "Cloning Human Beings."

20. Louis P. Pojman, "Cloning," in *Life and Death: Grappling with the Moral Dilemmas of Our Time* (Belmont, CA: Wadsworth, 2000), 124.

21. Leon R. Kass, "The Wisdom of Repugnance," *The New Republic*, 2 June 1997, 17–26.

22. Brock, "Cloning Human Beings."

READINGS

IVF: The Simple Case

PETER SINGER

Singer addresses seven moral objections that have been lodged against in vitro fertilization (IVF), focusing on its use in the "simple case" ("a married, infertile couple use an egg taken from the wife and sperm taken from the husband, and all embryos created are inserted into the womb of the wife"). The objections include the charges that IVF is unnatural, that it is risky for the offspring, and that it separates the procreative and conjugal aspects of marriage and so damages the marital relationship. He concludes that all the objections are weak and that "[t]hey should not count against going ahead with IVF when it is the best way of overcoming infertility" and when the infertile couple decides against adoption.

The so-called simple case of IVF is that in which a married, infertile couple use an egg taken from the wife and sperm taken from the husband, and all embryos created are inserted into the womb of the wife. This case allows us to consider the ethics of IVF in itself, without the complications of the many other issues that can arise in different circumstances. Then we can go on to look at these complications separately.

The Technique

The technique itself is now well known and is fast becoming a routine part of infertility treatment in many countries. The infertile woman is given a hormone treatment to induce her ovaries to produce more than one egg in her next cycle. Her hormone levels are carefully monitored to detect the precise moment at which the eggs are ripening. At this time the eggs are removed. This is usually done by laparoscopy, a minor operation in which a fine tube is inserted into the woman's abdomen and the egg is sucked out up the tube. A laparoscope, a kind of

From *Ethical Issues at the Outset of Life* (1987), edited by William B. Weil, Jr., and Martin Benjamin, pp. 44–49. Based on work done with Deane Wells and previously published in *Making Babies* (revised edition, 1985). Published by Scribner, an imprint of Simon & Schuster Adult Publishing Group. Copyright © 1984, 1985 by Peter Singer and Deane Wells.

periscope illuminated by fiber optics, is also inserted into the abdomen so that the surgeon can locate the place where the ripe egg is to be found. Instead of laparoscopy, some IVF teams are now using ultrasound techniques, which eliminate the need for a general anesthetic.

Once the eggs have been collected they are placed in culture in small glass dishes known as Petri dishes, not in test tubes despite the popular label of "test-tube babies." Sperm is then obtained from the male partner by means of masturbation and placed with the egg. Fertilization follows, in at least 80 percent of the ripe eggs. The resulting embryos are allowed to cleave once or twice and are usually transferred to the woman some 48 to 72 hours after fertilization. The actual transfer is done via the vagina and is a simple procedure.

It is after the transfer, when the embryo is back in the uterus and beyond the scrutiny of medical science, that things are most likely to go wrong. Even with the most experienced IVF teams, the majority of embryos transferred fail to implant in the uterus. One pregnancy for every five transfers is currently considered to be a good working average for a competent IVF team. Many of the newer teams fail to achieve anything like this rate. Nevertheless, there are so many units around the world now practicing IVF that thousands of babies have been produced as a result of the technique.

IVF has ceased to be experimental and is now a routine, if still "last resort" method of treating some forms of infertility.

Objections to the Simple Case

There is some opposition to IVF even in the simple case. The most frequently heard objections are as follows:

1. IVF is unnatural.
2. IVF is risky for the offspring.
3. IVF separates the procreative and the conjugal aspects of marriage and so damages the marital relationship.
4. IVF is illicit because it involves masturbation.
5. Adoption is a better solution to the problem of childlessness.
6. IVF is an expensive luxury and the resources would be better spent elsewhere.
7. IVF allows increased male control over reproduction and hence threatens the status of women in the community.

We can deal swiftly with the first four of these objections. If we were to reject medical advances on the grounds that they are "unnatural" we would be rejecting modern medicine as a whole, for the very purpose of the medical enterprise is to resist the ravages of nature which would otherwise shorten our lives and make them much less pleasant. If anything is in accordance with the nature of our species, it is the application of our intelligence to overcome adverse situations in which we find ourselves. The application of IVF to infertile couples is a classic example of this application of human intelligence.

The claim that IVF is risky for the offspring is one that was argued with great force before IVF became a widely used technique. It is sufficient to note that the results of IVF so far have happily refuted these fears. The most recent Australian figures, for example, based on 934 births, indicate that the rate of abnormality was 2.7%, which is very close to the national average of 1.5%. When we take into account the greater average age of women seeking IVF, as compared with the childbearing population as a whole, it does not seem that the *in vitro* technique itself adds to the risk of an abnormal offspring. This view is reinforced by the fact that the

abnormalities were all ones that arise with the ordinary method of reproduction; there have been no new "monsters" produced by IVF.[1] Perhaps we still cannot claim with statistical certainty that the risk of defect is no higher with IVF than with the more common method of conception; but if the risk is higher at all, it would appear to be only very slightly higher, and still within limits which may be considered acceptable.

The third and fourth objections have been urged by spokesmen for certain religious groups, but they are difficult to defend outside the confines of particular religions. Few infertile couples will take seriously the view that their marital relationship will be damaged if they use the technique which offers them the best chance of having their own child. It is in any case extraordinarily paternalistic for anyone else to tell a couple that they should not use IVF because it will harm their marriage. That, surely, is for them to decide.

The objection to masturbation comes from a similar source and can be even more swiftly dismissed. Religious prohibitions on masturbation are taboos from past times which even religious spokesmen are beginning to consider outdated. Moreover, even if one could defend a prohibition on masturbation for sexual pleasure—perhaps on the (very tenuous) ground that sexual activity is wrong unless it is directed either toward procreation or toward the strengthening of the bond between marriage partners—it would be absurd to extend a prohibition with that kind of rationale to a case in which masturbation is being used in the context of a marriage and precisely in order to make reproduction possible. (The fact that some religions do persist in regarding masturbation as wrong, even in these circumstances, is indicative of the folly of an ethical system based on absolute rules, irrespective of the circumstances in which those rules are being applied, or the consequences of their application.)

Overpopulation and the Allocation of Resources

The next two objections, however, deserve more careful consideration. In an overpopulated world in which there are so many children who cannot be properly fed and cared for, there is something incongruous about using all the ingenuity of modern medicine to create more children. And similarly, when there are so many deaths caused by preventable diseases, is there not something wrong with the priorities which lead us to develop expensive techniques for overcoming the relatively less serious problem of infertility?

These objections are sound to the following extent: in an ideal world we would find loving families for unwanted children before we created additional children; and in an ideal world we would clear up all the preventable ill-health and malnutrition-related diseases before we went on to tackle the problem of infertility. But is it appropriate to ask, of IVF alone, whether it can stand the test of measurement against what we would do in an ideal world? In an ideal world, none of us would consume more than our fair share of resources. We would not drive expensive cars while others die for the lack of drugs costing a few cents. We would not eat a diet rich in wastefully produced animal products while others cannot get enough to nourish their bodies. We cannot demand more of infertile couples than we are ready to demand of ourselves. If fertile couples are free to have large families of their own, rather than adopt destitute children from overseas, infertile couples must also be free to do what they can to have their own families. In both cases, overseas adoption, or perhaps the adoption of local children who are unwanted because of some impairment, should be considered; but if we are not going to make this compulsory in the former case, it should not be made compulsory in the latter.

There is a further question: to what extent do infertile couples have a right to assistance from community medical resources? Again, however, we must not single out IVF for harsher treatment than we give to other medical techniques. If tubal surgery is available and covered by one's health insurance, or is offered as part of a national health scheme, then why should IVF be treated any differently? And if infertile couples can get free or subsidized psychiatry to help them overcome the psychological problems of infertility, there is something absurd about denying them free or subsidized treatment which could overcome the root of the problem, rather than the symptoms. By today's standards,

after all, IVF is not an inordinately expensive medical technique; and there is no country, as far as I know, which limits its provision of free or subsidized health care to those cases in which the patient's life is in danger. Once we extend medical care to cover cases of injury, incapacity, and psychological distress, IVF has a strong claim to be included among the range of free or subsidized treatments available.

The Effect on Women

The final objection is one that has come from some feminists. In a recently published collection of essays by women titled *Test-Tube Women: What Future for Motherhood?*, several contributors are suspicious of the new reproductive technology. None is more hostile than Robyn Rowland, an Australian sociologist, who writes:

> Ultimately the new technology will be used for the benefit of men and to the detriment of women. Although technology itself is not always a negative development, the real question has always been— who controls it? Biological technology is in the hands of men.[2]

And Rowland concludes with a warning as dire as any uttered by the most conservative opponents of IVF:

> What may be happening is the last battle in the long war of men against women. Women's position is most precarious . . . we may find ourselves without a product of any kind with which to bargain. For the history of "mankind" women have been seen in terms of their value as childbearers. We have to ask, if that last power is taken and controlled by men, what role is envisaged for women in the new world? Will women become obsolete? Will we be fighting to retain or reclaim the right to bear children—has patriarchy conned us once again? I urge you sisters to be vigilant.

I can see little basis for such claims. For a start, women have figured quite prominently in the leading IVF teams in Britain, Australia, and the United States: Jean Purdy was an early colleague of Edwards and Steptoe in the research that led to the birth of Louise Brown; Linda Mohr has directed the development of embryo freezing at the Queen Victoria Medical Centre in Melbourne; and in the United States

Georgeanna Jones and Joyce Vargyas have played leading roles in the groundbreaking clinics in Norfolk, Virginia, and at the University of Southern California, respectively. It seems odd for a feminist to neglect the contributions these women have made.

Even if one were to grant, however, that the technology remains predominantly in male hands, it has to be remembered that it was developed in response to the needs of infertile couples. From interviews I have conducted and meetings I have attended, my impression is that while both partners are often very concerned about their childlessness, in those cases in which one partner is more distressed than the other by this situation, that partner is usually the woman. Feminists usually accept that this is so, attributing it to the power or social conditioning in a patriarchal society; but the origin of the strong female desire for children is not really what is in question here. The question is: in what sense is the new technology an instrument of male domination over women? If it is true that the technology was developed at least as much in response to the needs of women as in response to the needs of men, then it is hard to see why a feminist should condemn it.

It might be objected that whatever the origins of IVF and no matter how benign it may be when used to help infertile couples, the further development of techniques such as ectogenesis—the growth of the embryo from conception totally outside the body, in an artificial womb—will reduce the status of women. Again, it is not easy to see why this should be so. Ectogenesis will, if it is ever successful, provide a choice for women. Shulamith Firestone argued several years ago in her influential feminist work *The Dialectic of Sex*[3] that this choice will remove the fundamental biological barrier to complete equality. Hence Firestone welcomed the prospect of ectogenesis and condemned the low priority given by our male-dominated society to research in this area.

Firestone's view is surely more in line with the drive to sexual equality than the position taken by Rowland. If we argue that to break the link between women and childbearing would be to undermine the status of women in our society, what are we saying about the ability of women to obtain true equality in other spheres of life? I am not so pessimistic about the abilities of women to achieve equality with men across the broad range of human endeavor. For that reason I think women will be helped, rather than harmed, by the development of a technology which makes it possible for them to have children without being pregnant. As Nancy Breeze, a very differently inclined contributor to the same collection of essays, puts it:

> Two thousand years of morning sickness and stretch marks have not resulted in liberation for women or children. If you should run into a Petri dish, it could turn out to be your best friend. So rock it; don't knock it![4]

So to sum up this discussion of the ethics of the simple case of IVF: the ethical objections urged against IVF under these conditions are not strong. They should not count against going ahead with IVF when it is the best way of overcoming infertility and when the infertile couple are not prepared to consider adoption as a means of overcoming their problems. There is, admittedly, a serious question about how much of the national health budget should be allocated to this area. But then, there are serious questions about the allocation of resources in other areas of medicine as well.

REFERENCES

1. Abstract. *Proceedings of the Fifth Scientific Meeting of the Fertility Society of Australia*, Adelaide, Dec 2–6, 1986.
2. Rowland R. Reproductive technologies: The final solution to the woman question? In: Arditti R., Klein R. D., Minden, S., eds., *Test-tube Women: What Future for Motherhood?* London: Pandora, 1984.
3. Firestone S. *The Dialectic of Sex*. New York: Bantam, 1971.
4. Breeze N. Who is going to rock the petri dish? In: Arditti R., Klein R. D., Minden S., eds, *Test-tube Women: What Future for Motherhood?* London: Pandora, 1984.

IVF and Women's Interests:
An Analysis of Feminist Concerns

MARY ANNE WARREN

In this essay, Warren examines some feminist objections to IVF and other new
reproductive technologies. Because of the risks and costs to women from IVF,
she says, it is not at all clear that it provides a net benefit to them. But if the
disadvantages do not clearly outweigh the possible benefits, "then the matter is
properly left to individual choice," and it would be wrong to conclude that women's
interests demand an end to research in IVF and related technologies. She finds
no merit in the argument by some feminists that because of the pressure from
patriarchal society for women to have children (the "pronatalist" attitude), women
cannot give genuine voluntary consent to IVF treatments even if well informed.
On the contrary, "Neither the patriarchal power structure nor pronatalist ideology
makes women incapable of reasoned choice about childrearing."

Thus far, little of the public and professional debate about the ethics of *in vitro* fertilization (IVF) and other new reproductive technologies (NRTs) has focused upon the possible negative effects of these technologies on women. There is endless discussion of the moral status of the fertilized ovum or pre-embryo, and its possible moral rights.[1] Theologians and nonreligious critics debate the propriety of conceiving human beings "artificially," that is, without heterosexual intercourse.[2] Concern is also voiced—and appropriately so—about the possible physical or mental effects of technologically assisted reproduction upon the resulting children. But with the exception of a small group of feminist critics, few have paid much attention to the dangers to the women who serve as experimental subjects in reproductive research and, indirectly, to all women.

In what follows, I will examine some of the feminist objections to IVF and other NRTs. I will argue that, although the NRTs pose some significant dangers for women, it would be wrong to conclude that women's interests demand an end to IVF and other reproductive research. But if we are to understand the ethics of IVF, we must ask not only whether it is

From *Bioethics* 2, no. 1, 1988, 37–57. Reprinted by
permission of Blackwell Publishing Ltd.

in itself morally objectionable, but also whether it is (part of) an adequate societal response to the problem of involuntary infertility among women. IVF is at best a small part of a solution to that problem; it can help only a small minority of infertile women, and does nothing to address the underlying social causes which contribute to the problem. Moreover, the publicity surrounding IVF and other NRTs may deflect attention and resources from the potentially more important tasks of understanding and counteracting the preventable causes of infertility.

I. Feminist Criticisms: The Microlevel

Feminist critiques of the NRTs operate in part on the microlevel, that is, the level of individual behavior, individual rights and wrongs; and in part on the macrolevel, the level of historical context and social implications. I will begin with the microlevel criticisms.

At the microlevel, the primary issue is whether IVF is sufficiently beneficial to IVF patients to justify the commercial marketing of the procedure, or even continued research and development. IVF is usually depicted as an astonishing success story: infertile women are enabled to have beautiful, healthy children. We hear far less about the associated dangers. We do not yet know the long-term side effects of the use of drugs and hormones to induce superovulation. The collection of ova through ab-dominal surgery, usually under general anaesthesia, carries a significant risk of mortality or morbidity.[3] The replacement of the fertilized ovum in the uterus may cause infection, physical damage, or ectopic pregnancy. An abnormally high percentage of IVF pregnancies end in spontaneous abortion or still-birth. There are additional risks to mother and infant, associated not with the IVF procedure itself but with the ways in which IVF pregnancies are generally monitored (e.g., through ultrasound, am-niocentesis, and endometrial biopsy), and with the exceptionally high rate of cesarean section which is typical of IVF births.[4]

In addition to these physical risks, women who undergo IVF bear personal and psychological bur-dens. These include the emotional ups and downs inherent in the cycle of hope and disappointment; the disruption of work and, often, personal rela-tionships; and the humiliation and depersonaliza-tion that may result from the submission to painful and embarrassing invasions of their bodies. When these costs are considered in conjunction with the fact that only a small minority of women who un-dergo IVF treatments will give birth to a viable infant,[5] it is far from clear that IVF provides a net benefit to participating patients.

2. IVF and Informed Consent

Whether or not the benefits of IVF treatment will outweigh its costs and risks to female patients de-pends in part upon just how severe these costs and risks turn out to be, and in part upon whether suc-cess rates can be improved in existing programs and high standards maintained in new ones. It also de-pends upon just how great a boon motherhood is to those women for whom IVF leads to a successful preg-nancy. Those who regard motherhood as the greatest pleasure or achievement of which (some) women are capable will be prepared to tolerate greater risks and uncertainties than those who see motherhood—or, rather, the way it is institutionalized—as a signi-ficant burden.

In spite of these uncertainties—indeed, precisely because of them—it may be argued that women have the right to undertake the risks associated with IVF if *they* judge those risks to be worth taking.

If women's right to reproductive autonomy means anything, it must mean that we are entitled to take some risks with our physical and psychological health, in the attempt to either have or not have children. Neither abortion nor many forms of con-traception are entirely safe, but women sometimes reasonably judge that the alternatives are even less desirable. Having a wanted child can be as impor-tant a goal as avoiding an unwanted birth. If the costs and dangers of IVF to individual women and children were so great that no informed and re-sponsible person would attempt that route to par-enthood, then perhaps the paternalistic protection of women through the prohibition of IVF would be appropriate. But if these costs and dangers are not, so far as we can now determine, so great as to *clearly* outweigh the possible benefits, then the matter is properly left to individual choice.

Of course, the right to the voluntary use of contraception, abortion, or the newer reproductive technologies is meaningless unless the requirements are met for informed and voluntary consent. In-formed consent requires, among other things, an understanding of the medical and psychological risks, and the probability of success. There are troubling questions about whether all of the women who have been patients and experimental subjects in IVF programs have fully understood the risks to which they were being exposed and the often slight chances that they themselves would benefit from the research done.[6] Debate continues about the adequacy of the counselling and infor-mation received by women in current IVF pro-grams.[7] However, many of these women are very well-informed, not only through counselling but through their own reading and investigation. For them, at least, participation in an IVF program would seem to be an exercise of the right to repro-ductive autonomy.

Some of the feminist critics of IVF accept this argument for reproductive autonomy, arguing only for the kinds of legal regulation and ethical super-vision necessary to ensure that women's consent to IVF treatments is adequately informed and volun-tary, and that necessary precautions are taken to make the procedure as safe as possible.[8] Others, however, reject this argument as superficial. In their view, women cannot give truly voluntary consent to IVF treatments, regardless of how well-informed they may be about the risks, costs, and odds of success. They argue that women's reproductive "choices" are conditioned by the patriarchal power structure and the pronatalist ideology with which it is associated. Having children is still commonly regarded as a duty or a prerequisite for adult status, especially for women. This pronatalist ideology makes it difficult for women to make genuinely free choices about reproduction in general, or IVF in particular. Gena Corea says,

> The propaganda . . . that women are nothing unless they bear children, that if they are infertile, they lose their most basic identity as women . . . has a coercive power. It conditions a woman's choices as well as her *motivations* to choose. Her most heartfelt desire, the pregnancy for which she so desperately yearns, has been—to varying degrees— conditioned.[9]

There is surely some truth in this response. The "desperation of women who cannot meet the cultural definition of womanhood by becoming mothers"[10] is, to some extent, a cultural artifact. We hear far less about the plight of infertile men. There are, in all probability, infertile men who are equally "desperate" to have children; some even undergo painful surgical procedures (e.g., vasectomy reversal) in the pursuit of that goal. But we do not often see photographs in the newspaper of smiling fathers, proudly displaying infants that they have conceived with the help of such surgery.

It is true that female infertility is, in some respects, a more severe problem for a heterosexual couple than male infertility. Male infertility, though no easier to cure, is more easily circumvented: it is much easier for the couple to use AID (artificial insemination with donated sperm) than to obtain a donor egg or to "rent" another woman's womb, if the infertility is on the female side—and much less legally and morally problematic. Nevertheless, the apparently greater desperation of many infertile women, and the attention paid to that supposed desperation,[11] probably also reflect the degree to which the perception of women's social worth is still tied to their function as childbearers.

The question is whether or not these points demonstrate that the opportunity to make their own choices about IVF and other NRTs is of no value to women. I think that they do not. Freedom is not an all-or-nothing affair. We can rarely be completely free of unjust or inappropriate social and economic pressures, but we can sometimes make sound and appropriate decisions, in the light of our own circumstances.

Neither the patriarchal power structure nor pronatalist ideology makes women incapable of reasoned choice about childbearing. Rather, the social pressures upon some women to have children—and the pressures upon others not to have children—are circumstances which we must take into account in our deliberations. Either having children or not having them can be socially (and financially) expensive. Motherhood is apt to interfere with other life goals to a degree that fatherhood usually does not. This is not so much because of female biology as because of the social expectation that mothers will also be the primary childrearers, and the shortage of adequate childcare facilities and flexible working arrangements which would enable women to combine parenting and paid working without heroic effort. Yet childlessness, especially when it is involuntary, can be a great and lasting grief. This is particularly true in a society like our own, in which most people who are not parents have little opportunity to have long-term nurturing relationships with children.

Women are not unaware of these social realities. In deliberating about either "natural" motherhood or the use of IVF, we may sometimes be wrong about what is in our own interests, and perhaps some of us are excessively influenced by pronatalist ideology. But it does not follow that we would benefit from additional paternalistic constraints. Autonomy necessarily implies the right to make our own mistakes.

Unfortunately, not all infertile women have the opportunity to make use of IVF. Some causes of infertility (e.g., some anatomical or hormonal abnormalities) cannot be circumvented by external fertilization. Worse, IVF—like AID—is often restricted, either by law or by medical practice, to married heterosexual women. It is often argued that this discrimination is pragmatically necessary, since making IVF available to all infertile women who can afford it might provoke so much conservative opposition that IVF programs would be eliminated altogether. It is nevertheless an injustice. Such discrimination could be justified only if there were some evidence that women who are single or lesbian are more likely to be inadequate parents than are married and heterosexual women; and there is no such evidence. It is also arguably unjust—and certainly unfortunate—that the high cost of IVF treatments effectively excludes many women. But denying IVF to all women, for paternalistic reasons, would also be an injustice. To be subject to inappropriate social pressures is not necessarily to be deprived of either judgment or will. We need to be suspicious of analyses which "deny our power and our ability to make choices, even within the constraints of patriarchy."[12]

Of course, the right of individuals to make their own choices must sometimes be constrained for the sake of the general welfare. If the advent of IVF and other NRTs can be proved detrimental to women or to society as a whole, then we shall have to regard women who serve as researchers or clinicians, patients or experimental subjects in IVF programs, as unwittingly working against women's larger interests. Their choices may be individually rational, but collectively harmful. Arguments to this effect are what I call macrolevel arguments.

3. The Macrolevel Critique

Some feminist critics have sought to place the NRTs in their social and historical context, by looking at the history of iatrogenic harms to women caused by male-dominated medicine, and at the possible future abuses of reproductive technologies. Mary O'Brien and others have argued that men suffer from an envy of the larger role that women play in human procreation, and from their own natural inability to know with certainty which children are genetically their own.[13] On this view, men have long sought to control women and women's reproductive processes, in order to assure themselves biological as well as social heirs. Patriarchal marriage, the sexual double standard, the confinement and legal disenfranchisement of women, the massacre of women healers and wise women during the witch-craze era, and the subsequent ascendancy of male-dominated obstetrics and gynecology, are all seen as part of this male project of control.[14]

It would be difficult to deny that women have suffered from the male domination of medicine, not only in the loss of control over their own reproductive processes, but in iatrogenic illness and death. The entry of male physicians into obstetric practice in the seventeenth century led to a centuries-long plague of puerperal fever.[15] Male physicians in the nineteenth century campaigned successfully for the prohibition of abortion and contraception, and castrated thousands of women for supposed psychological problems. In this century, the DES, thalidomide, and Dalkon Shield disasters, the overuse of hysterectomy and other gynecological surgery,[16] and the over-technologization of birth,[17] all illustrate the same tendency to intervene in women's reproductive processes without good evidence of the safety and/or necessity of the intervention. Needless to say, modern obstetrics and gynecology have also produced some benefits for women. Many of the physical problems associated with pregnancy and birth can be more effectively treated than in the past. But we cannot know how much greater these benefits might have been had the medical profession not excluded women for many generations.

Given this history of iatrogenic harm to women, it is not surprising that many women regard the advent of IVF and other NRTs with suspicion. They fear that the new reproductive technologies will not only intensify male control of female reproductive processes, but may eventually remove women from the process of reproduction altogether. Irene Elia warns that,

> If men ever controlled parthenogenesis, using sperm nuclei placed in thawed or simulated egg cytoplasm and gestated in artificial or non-human wombs, they could enjoy total domination. With their gametes, they could produce either males or females—motherless all![18]

(There does, however, seem to be a biological problem here which Elia has overlooked: parthenogenesis using a sperm with a Y nucleus would produce a nonviable YY embryo; while the use of an X sperm would produce an XX—or female—offspring.)

Another cause for concern, not only among feminists, is that the NRTs are providing a means for the possible implementation of repressive eugenics programs. Many fear that the new methods for controlling the quality of our offspring, e.g., by embryo screening, prenatal diagnosis and selective abortion, or the use of donor gametes, will eventually become socially and/or legally mandatory. Corea asks, "Will those searching for perfect babies begin first by socially outlawing major . . . birth defects . . . and then . . . move on to ever lesser defects like asthma?"[19] Perhaps in the future women who try to reproduce with-out such eugenic interventions will be accused of child abuse, as are women today who give birth at home with the help of a midwife, rather than in a hospital setting.

4. The Shape of the Future

The dangers of male control of women's reproductive processes, and of the implementation of repressive eugenics programs, are real. There are, however, ways of resisting those dangers without calling for the termination of IVF and other reproductive research. None are simple, but all are morally essential for independent reasons.

Perhaps the most essential need is for more equal participation by women in all areas of medicine and biomedical research. It is difficult for any male-dominated profession either to understand women's needs or to serve them effectively. The new reproductive technologies should not be primarily in the hands of male physicians and researchers, but neither should any other form of medical treatment. It is equally essential that women (and men) from the various racial and ethnic groups and socioeconomic classes have a voice in determining the kinds of reproductive technologies that are developed and the ways in which they are used; for each of these groups may also be especially vulnerable to possible misuses of these technologies.

Many members of the medical professions would deny that the lesser participation of women in these fields is due to any remaining discrimination. The legal barriers to women's entry to medical studies and practice have been largely removed, and more or less nondiscriminatory criteria are increasingly used in the selection of medical students. But this is not enough. It would not even be enough if 50 percent of all medical *students* were women; for there are still powerful social and structural barriers to women's entry and success in such medical and scientific specialities as gynecology, obstetrics, embryology, neonatology, and endocrinology. These barriers include simple prejudice, as well as the excessively long hours required during the years of training and apprenticeship, and the difficulty of resuming that training after an extended break. All medical specializations need to be made more compatible with the needs of many women (and many men as well) for flexible working hours and interruptible career schedules. Otherwise, women in medicine will continue to be forced either to curtail their professional aspirations, or to forgo childbearing, or postpone it beyond the biologically optimal years.

Opening the medical and research professions to greater participation by women and other underrepresented groups is a long-term goal. In the meantime, it is essential that every government body with responsibility for the regulation of the NRTs, every ethical oversight committee, and every public agency which funds reproductive research be at least 50 percent composed of women. Among these, there should be some who have been on the receiving end of the new reproductive technologies—and some who have chosen not to be. An effort should also be made to include (proportionate numbers of) individuals from diverse racial, ethnic, and socioeconomic groups. This is probably the best immediate way of improving the likelihood that the interests of the consumers of reproductive technologies will be fairly represented in making of policy decisions.

But will this be enough to prevent the NRTs from being used coercively? Will women in the future be *required* to submit to IVF treatments, in order that their embryos may be screened for imperfections, genetically engineered, or replaced with embryos derived from "superior" individuals? This could happen only if our most basic civil liberties were lost. However, basic civil liberties, especially those affecting reproductive rights, are still far from adequate, and could easily be lost. In Australia, the legal status of abortion is still somewhat ambiguous.[20] And in the United States, the right to legal abortion may stand or fall upon the confirmation or rejection by the Senate of a single Supreme Court nominee.

This fact provides reason for continued feminist struggle; but it does not provide support for the suppression of all reproductive technologies that can be used coercively. Women's reproductive autonomy cannot be secured through such suppression. The history of coercive population control programs, e.g., in India and China, amply demonstrates that even the older—but still most important—reproductive technologies of contraception and abortion can be coercively used. Yet it is also clear that the *suppression* of contraception and abortion could virtually ensure the reproductive enslavement of women, as it has in the past. Nor do coercive eugenics programs require new reproductive technologies. The Nazi genocides of World War II, which are often cited as grounds for rejecting new technologies that could be used to implement immoral eugenics programs, clearly demonstrate that innovative biotechnology is not essential for the commission of atrocities in the name of eugenics. For these reasons, the defense of basic civil rights seems to be a more promising way of preventing the implementation of immoral eugenics programs than the suppression of reproductive technologies.

More to be feared, perhaps, is the covertly coercive force of social expectation. New technologies often have a momentum of their own; once they exist, they are likely to be seen as pragmatically and morally superior to any less highly technological option, even when the reverse may be the case. Some feminists argue that the very existence of IVF as a treatment for female infertility increases the pressures on infertile women to keep on trying until they have exhausted every possible treatment for their infertility.[21] The prevailing pronatalist ideology may thereby be strengthened, and the social stigma and suffering of all infertile women increased.

This is a realistic concern. The possibility of an IVF baby, however slight, may make it harder for infertile women to accept their condition and get on with their lives, or to defend the childlessness they may prefer. So too, the new methods for the prenatal diagnosis and selective abortion of defective fetuses may be eroding women's freedom *not*

to try to control the quality of their children, but simply to accept them as they are.[22] But this subtle erosion of freedom is not inevitable. Women can learn to exercise the legal right to refuse medical interventions that they do not need or want. We shall also have to work to retain that legal right, and to extend it in some areas.[23] These are difficult tasks, but they are tasks that would be no less essential if there were no *new* reproductive technologies.

5. The Final Solution?

Perhaps the most alarming scenario suggested by some critics of the NRTs is that women may be altogether eliminated from the reproductive process.[24] Once ectogenesis is perfected, natural pregnancy may come to be seen as dangerous and irresponsible; it may even be outlawed. Some speculate further, that once men have ectogenesis they will see no reason for women to exist at all, and consequently will create an all-male world.

But neither of these scenarios is likely to come about. Even if there were a realistic prospect for the achievement of total (i.e., conception-to-birth) ectogenesis in the nonremote future—which there is not—there would be little danger that ectogenesis will replace uterine gestation as the usual way of making babies. It will almost certainly be economically impossible to replace natural wombs with artificial ones. Extrauterine gestation, should it become possible, could hardly be much less expensive than contemporary neonatal intensive care. Thus, it would be beyond the reach of all but the very wealthy. This is an excellent reason for not devoting massive public resources to the attempt to develop methods of total ectogenesis. But it also shows that even if ectogenesis were perfected tomorrow, the elimination of natural pregnancy would remain a remote possibility.

It is still less likely that artificial gestation would threaten women's continued existence. Robyn Rowland asks, as man gets closer to reproducing himself, what forces can possibly stop him? . . . Will this last act of power make women obsolete; permanently unemployed; disposable?[25] Ectogenesis would likely lead to women's perceived obsolescence only if women were valued exclusively or primarily for our reproductive function. But that is clearly false, even in the most highly patriarchal societies. There are, no doubt, many men who agree in principle with Thomas Aquinas's dictum that women were created to help men in the work of reproduction, and *only* in that work "since [a] man can be more efficiently helped by another man in other works."[26] There is, and perhaps has always been, a strong current of misogyny in much male culture. Yet most men still regard heterosexual practices as preferable to the alternatives—and not just because of the reproductive function of these practices. More importantly, perhaps, women's paid and unpaid labor is essential to the functioning of virtually every social and economic institution throughout the world. Few men are willing to undertake the tasks of homemaking and childrearing without female assistance. If there has been a central patriarchal project, it has been to control women and channel their energies into the service of male needs—not to eliminate women, which would be self-defeating.[27]

6. The Mystique of Motherhood

There is a deeper reason why some women are angered and alarmed by the NRTs. Some have argued the increased control of the female reproductive process which the NRTs give (certain) men will be detrimental to women's social status and sense of personal agency. These feminist critics maintain that women's procreativity has long been a source of social power, but that the NRTs are progressively robbing us of that power. Corea deplores the way that, "Woman, once deified as the life-creating Goddess, is now lying on a table with her mouth taped shut, having the eggs sucked out of her body."[28] Rowland says,

> How powerful we have always seemed; we who can bleed regularly and not die; we who can grow another human being inside our own bodies. Dubious though it has been in real terms, this has since "primitive" times been a source of mythical power for women when all else was kept from them. For many women it is the only experience of power they will ever have.[29]

Despite these eloquent pleas, I doubt that the NRTs are depriving women of any important source of social power which we now enjoy, or once enjoyed. The contrast between the hypothetical days when women were worshipped as the sole givers of life, and the new age in which some women need medical assistance in order to conceive, is probably less great than is sometimes supposed. Women may have sought supernatural or "professional" help in conceiving since prehistoric times. Neolithic images of fecund women predate the written word by tens of thousands of years. These images seem to express an awe of female procreativity; but they may have also had a practical use, e.g., as fertility charms. There is little reason to believe that early fertility magic was entirely in the hands of women—though it may have been. In any case, the essential role of the male in conception has been known in most societies for at least several millennia. Thus, if the resort to male assistance inevitably undermines the awe of female fertility, then women in earlier times may have derived less social power from this source than is sometimes assumed.

There are other reasons for doubting the practical value of whatever mystical power may be ascribed to the female role in procreation. The power that supposedly flows from motherhood is often cited by apologists for patriarchy, as a reason why women have no need for other forms of power or even for personal autonomy. These apologists would have us believe that the hand that rocks the cradle rules the world—even if the hand's owner is deprived of the most basic civil liberties. But such "power" is a poor substitute for social, economic, and political equality. It may even make life worse for women. The suspicion of mystical or supernatural power, especially when associated with women, inspires not just respect, but fear and hostility. The women who were burned as witches at the dawn of the so-called age of reason had good reason to wish that they had not been credited with supernatural agency.

What feminists want, or should want, for women is not the largely symbolic power that comes from the awe of female procreativity, but respect for women as persons. Persons are due respect, not primarily because of the mystical powers that may act in or through them, but because of their capacity to think, feel, and act. The power to act effectively is achieved through the use of "our intellects, our imaginations, and our capacity for collective action."[30] The mystification of motherhood can do little to enhance that power. On the contrary, it would seem more apt to encourage the notion that women's "natural task . . . [is] accomplished by being rather than doing."[31] It may also reinforce the tendency to view women less as persons than as parts of "alien Nature," vessels of a force that is awesome but not entirely human.[32] If the new reproductive technologies, by subjecting some female reproductive processes to apparently greater control, serve to undermine that mystification, then the appropriate feminist reaction may be, "So much the better."

7. The Social Causes of Female Infertility

I have saved for last what may be the most important feminist objection to IVF. It is an objection not to the continuation of IVF programs at some level of funding, but rather to the relative neglect of potentially more effective ways of approaching the problem.

Involuntary infertility has always been a problem for some women, and (though this was less often recognized) some men. Whether it currently affects a larger proportion of women than in previous generations is unclear, though many believe that it does. The causes of human infertility are not well understood, but neither are they entirely mysterious. A study of 708 couples attending fertility clinics in one part of England found that in 28 percent of cases the cause of the failure to conceive could not be identified, while in 26 percent, the problem was on the male side.[33] The most common cause of female infertility was ovulatory failure, which apparently responded very well to treatment; the pregnancy rate after two years was approximately 96 percent. The next most common cause was infective damage to the fallopian tubes; here, the outlook was much poorer, with only about 19 percent conceiving after two years, despite surgery and other treatments. IVF was originally developed primarily for the treatment of this kind of female infertility, though it is now also used in some cases where the cause of the woman's infertility is unclear, or where the problem is due to some defect in the male's sperm.

For some infertile women or couples, for whom other treatments have failed, IVF probably offers the best remaining hope of biological parenthood—though it is often a rather slim hope. But it would obviously be better to prevent infertility in the first place, if this were possible. Much female infertility is socially caused, and probably could have been prevented. Prevention and cure are obviously not mutually exclusive approaches. But feminist critics have argued that the primary focus of the medical profession and the society as a whole has been too much on the treatment of infertility and too little on its prevention, and that the publicity given to IVF is symptomatic of this imbalance. In Heather Dietrich's words,

> IVF is valenced towards a medical, high-tech solution rather than the prevention of infertility. . . . It will emphasize and extend the isolation and analysis of fertility, as a discrete process, rather than [contributing to] a holistic approach to fertility within a woman's body and life.[34]

A more holistic approach to the problem of infertility would include an investigation of the social, as well as the physiological, causes of involuntary infertility. One group of social causes comprises a large range of sexual and contraceptive practices. As noted above, much female infertility is caused by infective damage to the fallopian tubes. Such infections are, in the majority of cases, sexually transmitted; and sexual practices and modes of contraception can affect the likelihood of contracting such sexually transmitted diseases (STDs).

Other things being equal, the more sexual partners a woman has, and the more partners each of them has had, the greater her risk of contracting an infection which will eventually damage her fertility. Thus, some might be tempted simply to blame the apparent increase in this form of female infertility on the so-called sexual revolution, which has meant that more women have become sexually active earlier, and have had, on the average, more sexual partners. But this would be a mistake. The sexual revolution need not have led to an increase in the incidence of STDs, or in consequent infertility. If it has, this is due in part to the kinds of contraceptives and prophylactics that have—or have not—been used. Some contraceptives are known to increase the danger of pelvic inflammatory disease (PID).

IUDs, for instance, can cause acute or chronic inflammation, and are associated with a 600 percent increase in PID.[35] Hormone-based contraceptives also appear, at least in some cases, to increase susceptibility to PID. In contrast, barrier methods, particularly condoms, and particularly when used in combination with spermicides, provide a fair degree of protection against most STDs—although they also tend to be somewhat less effective in preventing pregnancy. For maximum protection against both unwanted pregnancy and the transmission of infection, heterosexual couples who have not practiced long-term monogamy probably should use both condoms and some female contraceptive. But, for a variety of reasons, most do not.

The particular sexual activities in which people commonly engage may also increase the risk of infertility. Heterosexual intercourse, of the kind usually described as "normal" or "ordinary" is much more likely to transmit infection than either oral sex or masturbation (mutual or solitary). If the orientation of the majority of adults towards such "normal" sexual practice is an inalterable result of human biology, as most assume, then social mores can make little difference to this particular cause of infertility. But if, as some have argued, heterosexuality and the ways in which it is commonly expressed are social institutions rather than strictly natural phenomena,[36] then some of these institutions must be included among the social causes of infertility.

There are many other social causes of infertility. Exposure to toxic substances, in the workplace and the general environment, is certainly involved in some cases. Among the poor, inadequate nutrition, generally poor health, and limited access to health care are often contributing factors. Where abortion is illegal or beyond the reach of many women, improperly performed abortions are a common cause of infertility—and often death. Poor women are sometimes surgically sterilized against their will, or without an understanding of the permanence of the procedure. Because their other options are likely to be more limited, poor women are also more likely to choose surgical sterilization, and some of them may later regret that decision. Unnecessary hysterectomies and other surgical procedures are another cause of involuntary infertility. In parts of Africa and the Middle East, the complications of genital mutilation ("female circumcision") undoubtedly cause much infertility.[37]

While this is not a complete list of the social causes of female infertility, it is enough to show that they are many and varied. Some, such as involuntary sterilization and unnecessary surgery, are clear abuses. Few would dispute the need to prevent such abuses, though there is much debate about just how commonly they occur. Some, such as the lack of legal, safe, and affordable abortion in much of the world, could readily be remedied through changes in the law, but there is bitter controversy about the morality of such changes. And some, such as the relative frequency of "ordinary" heterosexual intercourse, would probably be extremely resistant to change, even if we could agree that such change would be desirable.

Thus, there can be no simple solution to the problem of socially caused involuntary infertility. Yet there is room for a wider societal response to that problem. That response should include a more concerted effort to develop safer new contraceptives and to improve the older barrier methods. Often, it will need to include a more equitable distribution of medical resources, and better access to contraception and abortion—and to some of the NRTs. But the first step should be the better dissemination of information about ways of protecting oneself and others from the more common and preventable causes of infertility.

The international AIDS epidemic has led to a widespread recognition of a distinction between "safe" and "unsafe" sex. Although AIDS can be transmitted in many ways besides sexual contact, that mode of transmission is common, and some sexual practices are evidently more dangerous than others in this regard. Thus, in many parts of the world, public information campaigns and school sex education programs are being created or supplemented to teach basic facts about AIDS, how it is transmitted, and how the danger of transmission can be minimized.

A skeptical feminist might wonder whether it is coincidental that this public concern with safer sexual practices has arisen only when—perhaps for the first time ever—more men than women are suffering some of the most lethal consequences of unsafe sexual practices.[38] On the other hand, gay rights advocates may be correct in their suspicion that more might have been done to help the victims of AIDS and to stop the spread of the illness, had not so many of these victims been homosexual males. Yet, however belated or inadequate, the new openness to the dissemination of information about relatively safe and unsafe sexual practices, prophylactics, and the like, is surely a positive development. This new openness may facilitate the prevention of other STDs as well, including those that—though not usually fatal—can lead to infertility.

But the idea that making sex safer is a legitimate public goal meets strong opposition from sexual and religious conservatives. Right-wing groups have long opposed attempts to ameliorate the harmful consequences of sexual activity, e.g., through the legalization of contraception and abortion, sex education in schools, or the public advertising of condoms and other contraceptives. They believe that women who do not want to have children should either avoid heterosexual intercourse altogether, or "accept the consequences," and that anyone who wants to avoid contracting a sexually transmitted disease should either remain celibate or practice lifelong monogamy with a partner who does likewise.

These attitudes have had a considerable influence, particularly in societies strongly influenced by Christianity. In effect, both "Pregnancy and disease have been pervasively and systematically used to inhibit sexual activity."[39] This punitive attitude is often based upon the distinctively—though not universally—Christian idea that all sexual activity is inherently sinful, except that which is apt for the production of children within a monogamous marriage. (This exception is only partial, since some Christian authorities have held that even procreative marital sexual intercourse can be sinful, if it is motivated by lust.) From this perspective, it can seem entirely appropriate, a kind of natural justice, that those who engage in nonmonogamous or nonprocreative sexual activities should be penalized by unwanted pregnancies, sexually transmitted diseases, and perhaps infertility. Attempts to prevent these

harmful consequences of unsafe sex will therefore be seen as encouraging immoral sexual behavior.

Far from receding into the past, this punitive attitude towards much human sexual activity may currently be gaining strength, at least in some parts of the world. In this social context, it is doubly unrealistic to approach involuntary female infertility as though it were basically a medical problem. Improving IVF and other medical treatments for infertility would remain an important goal even if all of the social causes of infertility were eliminated, since not all infertility is socially caused. But there is some danger that the enormous publicity attendant upon the development of IVF and other NRTs will foster the illusion that the problem of involuntary infertility is being largely solved, when it is not.

8. Conclusion

Taken together, these objections are sufficient to cast some doubt upon the net value of IVF to women. They do not, however, support the conclusion that a just concern for women's interests demands the elimination of IVF and other NRTs. The costs and risks of IVF treatments to the female patient are substantial, but they are not known to be so great as to clearly outweigh the potential benefits in every case. Pronatalist ideology may put undue pressure upon infertile women to submit to IVF, but so long as potential IVF patients are adequately informed about the costs, risks, and odds of success, such covert social pressures need not make valid consent impossible.

Feminists are rightly concerned that if the NRTs continue to be developed and delivered by largely male teams, women's interests will not be as well served as they ought to be. The interests of women and men will be affected in different ways by the development of these technologies. Insofar as it is women who more often undergo invasive and/or potentially dangerous medical procedures associated with the NRTs, their interests are somewhat more centrally affected. Women should, therefore, be at least equally represented in the development of these technologies. Members of various racial, ethnic, or socioeconomic groups may also have special needs, or be especially vulnerable to harmful uses or abuses of the NRTs, and they too should be represented.

There is a need for more participation by women in all aspects of the practice, funding, and supervision of such biomedical research, as well as in the provision of medical care. Some of the ways in which the medical and research professions have been structured have served, perhaps inadvertently, as barriers to women, and other "minority" groups in these professions. The members of those professions have an obligation to remove those barriers—not by lowering standards, but by altering institutions and practices that discriminate needlessly against some competent individuals.

Even with greater participation by women in the development of the NRTs, there will remain some danger that the NRTs will contribute to the subtle erosion of women's reproductive autonomy. The use of new reproductive technologies might in time become legally or socially mandatory even for (some) fertile women, e.g., as a way of implementing eugenic goals. But this danger can better be counteracted by protecting individual civil rights than by seeking to eliminate the new reproductive technologies.

If these conclusions are correct, then IVF is probably a justifiable means of attempting to overcome infertility. But IVF can help only a small proportion of infertile women and men, and it inflicts heavy costs and risks on all who undergo it. It can, therefore, be only a small part of an adequate societal response to the problem of involuntary infertility.

One major element of a more adequate societal response to that problem is the better dissemination of knowledge about the preventable causes of infertility, e.g., those associated with particular sexual practices and contraceptive methods. A more concerted effort should also be made to develop safer (and cheaper) contraceptives and prophylactics, especially of the kinds that protect against both pregnancy and the transmission of STDs. Contraceptives, safe abortion, and other kinds of medical care need to be available to all women, including those who are underage or unable to pay. These are practical goals, which need not be prohibitively expensive, and which have already been at least partially achieved in some places.

If more is done to counteract the social causes of infertility, there may eventually be less need for IVF. Yet IVF may remain the best (medical) approach to the treatment of some forms of infertility. Thus, it is too soon to conclude that this new reproductive technology will not serve women's interests. If women and other underrepresented groups can gain a larger presence in the medical and research professions, and if suitable modes of regulation can be implemented, then the NRTs may provide more benefits than dangers. If not, then feminists may be right to remain somewhat skeptical about the long-term value of these new technologies for women.

NOTES

1. See, for instance, G. R. Dunstan, 'The Ethical Debate,' in *In Vitro Fertilisation: Past, Present, Future*, edited by S. Fishel and E. M. Symonds (Oxford, Washington, D.C: IRL Press, 1986): and Brian Johnstone, Helga Kuhse and Peter Singer, 'The Moral Status of the Embryo: Two Viewpoints,' in *Test-Tube Babies: A Guide to the Moral Questions, Present Techniques, and Future Possibilities*, edited by William Walters and Peter Singer (Melbourne: Oxford University Press, 1982), pp. 49–64.

2. See Paul Ramsey, *Fabricated Man: The Ethics of Genetic Control* (New Haven and London, Yale University Press, 1974), and Leon Kass, 'New Beginnings in Life,' in *The New Genetics and the Future of Man* (Grand Rapids, Michigan: Eerdman's Publishing, 1972), pp. 53–54.

3. In some IVF programmes, e.g., that at the Monash Medical Centre in Victoria, the collection of ova through laparoscopy is being superceded by the use of ultrasound to guide the aspiration needle. This procedure can be performed without surgery, and usually with only local anaesthesia. However, laparoscopy remains the method in use in many other IVF programmes. (See H. Wickland, L. Hamberger and L. Enk, 'Ultrasound for Oocyte Recovery,' in *In Vitro Fertilisation*, edited by S. Fishel and E. M. Symonds (Oxford and Washington D.C: IRL Press, 1986), pp. 69–76.)

4. For a more extensive discussion of the medical risks of IVF treatment see Gena Corea, *The Mother Machine: Reproductive Technologies from Artificial Insemination to Artificial Wombs* (New York: Harper and Row, 1985), pp. 149–59.

5. Estimates of the success rate of IVF treatment range from 4% to 25%. Not surprisingly, the critics of IVF tend to favour the lower estimates, while the proponents favour the higher.

6. Corea, pp. 167–9.

7. See Janet Winfield, 'Reproduction, Technology and the Search for Reproduction Control and Freedom—A Question of Choice,' a paper presented at the National Conference on Reproductive Technologies, sponsored by the National

Feminist Network on Reproductive Technology, Canberra, May 1986 (hereafter referred to as the "Canberra conference").

8. See Lori B. Andrews, 'Remaking Conception and Pregnancy: How the Laws Influence Reproductive Technology,' *Frontiers* 9:1 (1986), pp. 36–40, and Amadeo F. D'Adamo Jr. and Elaine Hoffman Baruch, 'Whither the Womb? Myths, Machines, and Mothers,' *op, cit*, pp. 72–79.

9. Corea, p. 170. See also Robyn Rowland, 'Choice or Control? Women and Our Relationship to the New Reproductive Technologies,' (Canberra conference, 1986).

10. Rebecca Albury, 'Who Owns the Embryo?' in *Test-Tube Women: What Future for Motherhood?*, edited by Rita Arditti, Renate Duelli Klein and Shelly Minden (London: Pandora Press, 1984), p. 57.

11. See, for instance, Lois Leiderman Davitz, *Baby Hunger: Every Woman's Longing for a Baby* (Minneapolis: Winston Press, 1984).

12. Lynne M. Foltrow, review of *Test-Tube Women, Women's Rights Law Reporter* 8:4 (1985), p. 307.

13. Mary O'Brien, *The Politics of Reproduction* (London and Boston: Routledge and Kegan Paul, 1981).

14. See Mary Daly, *Gynaecology: The Metaethics of Radical Feminism* (Boston: Beacon Press, 1978), p. 224. The history of the suppression of female healers and midwives is well documented in Barbara Ehrenreich and Deirdre English, *Witches, Midwives and Nurses: A History of Women Healers* (Old Westbury, New York: The Feminist Press, 1973).

15. The primary reason for the higher incidence of often-fatal puerperal fever among women attended by male physicians in the seventeenth through nineteenth centuries appears to be that male physicians, unlike traditional midwives, not only attended women in labour, but also treated persons with infectious diseases. Consequently, although they may not have washed their hands any less frequently than the midwives did, they spread far more infection. See Daly, pp. 236–7, and Adrienne Rich, *Of Woman Born: Motherhood as Experience and Institution* (London: Virago, 1977), p. 151.

16. See, for instance, Robert H. Keyser, *Women Under the Knife* (New York: Warner Books, Inc., 1984).

17. Obstetrics continues to impose upon birthing women a great many interventions, the therapeutic value of which has never satisfactorily been demonstrated. These include the routine induction and augmentation of labour; routine use of ultrasound; electronic fetal monitoring; artificial rupture of membranes; enemas and perineal shaves; routine episiotomy; the use of forceps and vacuum extraction; routine use of analgesic drugs and epidurals; and the current high rates of Caesarian section. (See Belinda Court and Carolyn Noble Spruel, 'Report on Discussion in Workshop on Politics of Homebirth,' (Canberra conference, 1986).

18. Irene Elia, *The Female Animal* (Oxford, New York, Tokyo: Oxford University Press, 1985), p. 280.

19. Corea, p. 93.

20. In all Australian states there are sections of various acts that make it a crime to *unlawfully* perform or procure an abortion. In most states, these statutes—which were once used to prohibit all or almost all abortions—remain in force, but case law has progressively expanded the class of abortions that are not considered unlawful. In South Australia, the statute dealing with abortion states specific exceptions to the general prohibition, e.g., abortions that are necessary to preserve the woman's life, or her physical or mental health, or when there is a substantial risk of fetal malformation. Such exceptions can be interpreted as including most actual abortions. However, because the exceptions cannot entirely negate the rule, there is necessarily in each state some class of abortions which remain illegal. The definition of that class is highly ambiguous, since each exception can be interpreted more or less liberally. Thus, although abortion is readily available in most of (the urban areas) of Australia, those who perform or procure abortions do so in the face of some uncertainty about the legality of their actions.

21. See, for example, Marion Brown, 'Female Infertility—Causes, Options, Priorites and IVF' (Canberra conference, 1986), p. 3.

22. Barbara Katz Rothman, *The Tentative Pregnancy: Prenatal Diagnosis and the Future of Motherhood* (New York: Viking Press, 1986), p. 11.

23. The legal right of competent adults to refuse medical treatment is not absolute. In the United States, a number of women have been forced by court order to undergo Caesarean sections against their will. A San Diego woman, whose son was born with brain damage and consequently died, was charged with negligent child abuse for not following physician's instructions during her pregnancy (she was, however, acquitted).

24. See Robyn Rowland, 'Reproductive Technologies: The Final Solution to the Woman Question?' in *Test-Tube Women*, pp. 356–369.

25. Rowland, 'Reproductive Technologies,' p. 365.

26. Thomas Aquinas, *Summa Theologica*, Vol. 1, Part 1, Question 92, Article I (New York: Benziger Brothers, 1947, p. 466).

27. This claim might appear to be contradicted by the widespread practice of female infanticide; generally speaking, the poorer a society, and the more severely patriarchal, the fewer female infants are likely to be raised. But female infanticide shows only that families are reluctant to raise female children, not that adult women are not in demand; where female infanticide creates a shortage of adult women, men often wage war to capture women from other groups.

28. Corea, p. 176.

29. Rowland, 'Reproductive Technologies,' p. 363.

30. Poltrow, p. 304.

31. John Stuart Mill, *Early Essays on Marriage and Divorce*, in *Essays on Sex Equality*, edited by Alice Rossi (Chicago and London: University of Chicago Press, 1979), p. 77.

32. See Simone de Beauvoir, *The Second Sex* (New York, London, Tornot: Bantam Books, 1961), p. 63.

33. M. G. R. Hill, 'Infertility: Nature and Extent of the Problem,' In *Human Embryo Research: Yes or No?* (London and New York: Tavistock Publications, 1986), pp. 25–34.

34. Heather Dietrich, 'IVF: What Can We Do?' (Canberra conference), p. 8.

35. Population Information Programme, Johns Hopkins University, 'Infertility and Sexually Transmitted Disease: A Public Health Challenge,' *Population Reports*, Series L(4), July 1983; cited by Adele Clark, 'Subtle Forms of Sterilisation Abuse: A Reproductive Rights Analysis', in *Test-Tube Women*, p. 199.

36. See for instance, Adrienne Rich, 'Compulsory Heterosexuality and Lesbian Existence,' *Signs: Journal of Women in Culture and Society* 5:4 (Summer 1980), pp. 631–60.

37. See Fran P. Hosken, *The Hosken Report: Genital and Sexual Mutilation of Females* (Lexington, Massachusetts: Women's International Network News, 1979), and Asma El Daree, *Woman Why Do You Weep? Circumcision and Its Consequences* (London: Zed Press, 1982).

38. While in much of the world, the great majority of AIDS victims are men, in some parts of Africa the disease seems to affect women and children just about as often.

39. Cindy Patton, *Sex and Germs: The Politics of AIDS* (Boston: South End Press, 1985), p. 10.

"Give Me Children or I Shall Die!" New Reproductive Technologies and Harm to Children

CYNTHIA B. COHEN

Cohen points out that some evidence indicates that reproductive technologies cause serious illness and defects in a small percentage of children. She argues that if these technologies do in fact cause such harm, it would be wrong to use them. Some who disagree put forth the "Interest in Existing Argument," which says that even if the new technologies caused children to be born with serious disorders, the harm done would be morally permissible (except in rare cases) because "it is better to be alive—even with serious disease and deficits—than not." Cohen sees several problems in this argument. For one thing, she says, it is based on the false assumption that "children with an interest in existing are waiting in a spectral world of nonexistence where their situation is less desirable than it would be were they released into this world."

"Be fruitful and multiply," God urged newly created humans. Those who take this command to heart cherish the opportunity to procreate and nurture children, to pass on their individual traits and family heritage to their offspring. Having children, for many, is a deeply significant experience that offers overall meaning for their lives. Not all who wish to do so, however, can fulfill the biblical injunction to multiply. Those who cannot often experience a terrible sense of loss. Rachel, in Genesis, felt such despair over her failure to conceive that she cried out to Jacob, "Give me children, or I shall die!" Some who echo her cry today turn to the new reproductive technologies.

There are ethical limits, however, to what may be done to obtain long-sought offspring. Having a deep desire and even a need for something does not justify doing anything whatsoever to obtain it. If the means used to bring children into the world were to create substantial harm to others or to these very children, this would provide strong moral reason not to employ them. It would be wrong, for instance, for infertile couples to place women at risk of substantial harm by enticing those who are not in peak physical condition to "donate" eggs with handsome sums of money. By the same token, it would be wrong to use reproductive technologies to create children if this bore a significant chance of producing serious disease and impairments in these very children. Questions are being raised about whether in vitro fertilization (IVF) and other reproductive technologies do, in fact, create serious illness and deficits in a small but significant proportion of children who are born of them. If these technologies were found to do so, it would be wrong to forge ahead with their use.

Yet advocates of procreative liberty reject this seemingly inescapable conclusion. They contend that even if children were born with serious disorders traceable to their origin in the new reproductive technologies, this would not, except in rare cases, provide moral reason to refrain from using them. Those who conclude otherwise, they maintain, do not understand the peculiar sort of substantial harm to which children born of these novel reproductive means are susceptible. Surely, John Robertson and like-minded thinkers claim, it is better to be alive—even with serious disease and deficits—than not. And these children would not be alive, but for the use of the new reproductive techniques. Therefore, they argue, these children cannot be substantially harmed by the use of these means to bring them into the world. Only if they are caused by these technologies to suffer devastating illness that makes life worse than nonexistence can they be said to be substantially harmed by them.

This startling claim raises intriguing questions. What do we mean by substantial harm—particularly when children who might experience it have not yet been conceived? What degree of disease and suffering that a child would experience as a result of the application of these novel means of conception would make it wrong to use them? Would it be wrong if the child's life would be so terrible that nonexistence would be better? Few conditions would be excluded by this standard. Would it be wrong if the child's life would not be awful, but would include major physical impairments, severe mental disability and/or considerable pain and suffering?

In responding to such questions, we must consider the possibility that different standards of substantial harm may apply to children at the time when we consider conceiving them and after conception and birth. If so, we must develop a standard of substantial harm that applies to children who might be conceived that is distinct from one that applies to those already born—and must explain how children who are not born can be harmed. We must also address the concern that decisions not to conceive children because they would have serious deficits devalue the lives of those already living who were born with such deficits. Finally, we must grapple with the question of what parents and infertility specialists ought to do in the current state of inadequate knowledge about the effects of the new reproductive technologies on the children who result from their use.

The Harm to Children Argument

To ask what it means to attribute substantial harm to children who result from the new reproductive technologies is not just to pose an interesting abstract question. Studies indicate this may be a very practical, real question, as they raise the possibility that these technologies may create serious deficits in some proportion of the children born of them. To get a sense of the harms at issue, let us consider the claims of critics of the use of these technologies about their effect on the children born of them.

A primary harm that they attribute to the use of the new reproductive technologies is physical damage. Few long-term studies have been undertaken of the kinds and rates of physical diseases and abnormalities incurred by children born of the new reproductive technologies. Moreover, the evidence these investigations provide is conflicting. Australia is the only country that has kept statistics on the condition at birth *and* subsequent progress of children born of IVF since the inception of this technique in the late 1970s. Data from that country indicate that these children are two or three times more likely to suffer such serious diseases as spina bifida and transposition of the great vessels (a heart abnormality). Australian data also suggest that some drugs used to stimulate women's ovaries to produce multiple oocytes in preparation for IVF increase the risk of serious birth impairments in the resulting children. Other investigations and commentators support this finding.[1] Still other reports, however, suggest that there is no increase in disorders at birth among children resulting from the use of the new reproductive technologies.[2] One small American follow-up study of the health status of children born of IVF and gamete intrafallopian transfer (GIFT) could find no significant differences in the rate of physical or neurological abnormalities in children born of techniques of assisted conception.[3] No controlled study to date, however, has incorporated an adequate sample size or sufficiently long follow-up monitoring period to determine accurately the risk of physical disorders associated with children born of IVF.

And little is known about the physiological impact on children who result from such other procedures as embryo freezing, gamete donation, zona drilling, and intracytoplasmic sperm injection.

It is well known that the higher rate of multiple births in IVF due to the implantation of several embryos in the uterus at a time contributes to an increased rate of preterm and low birth-weight babies. This, in turn, is associated with a higher incidence of perinatal, neonatal, and infant mortality in children conceived by IVF than those conceived coitally.[4] In France, for instance, the rates of prematurity and intrauterine growth retardation among IVF births in a two-year period were 16 percent and 14 percent respectively, whereas the expected rates for the general population were 7 percent and 3 percent.[5] An analysis of IVF outcome data from France between 1986 and 1990 indicated that perinatal mortality among IVF births also was higher than that in the general population, even when data were stratified according to gestational number. French neonatologists who had worked to prevent low birth weight, congenital anomalies, and genetic disorders among newborns observed that "[n]ow, we suddenly find our NICU filled with high-risk newborns . . . [as a result of the expansion of IVF services]."

Critics also express concern that the new reproductive technologies may jeopardize the psychological and social welfare of the children who result from them, particularly when they involve third parties in donor or surrogacy arrangements and depend on secrecy.[6] These children, they hypothesize, will view themselves as manufactured products, rather than distinctive individuals born of love between a man and a woman.[7] They will be denied the stable sense of identity that comes from knowing their biological heritage and family lineage should their rearing parents differ from their genetic parents.[8] Moreover, the social stigma these children will experience when others learn that they were conceived by these novel means will increase their difficulties, opponents contend. Little research is available on the effect of the use of assisted reproduction on the psychosocial development of the resulting children. In the first controlled study of family relationships and the psychological development of children created by the new reproductive technologies, no group differences in the emotions, behavior, or relationships with parents between children born of assisted reproduction and children conceived naturally or adopted could be found.[9]

One commentator summarizes the issues of harm raised by the use of the new reproductive technologies as follows:

> The technology for both IVF and GIFT as well as adjunct technologies such as zona drilling, embryo freezing, and gamete donation have not been accompanied by careful scrutiny and analysis of the risks involved. Indeed, even when risks are clearly established (as with multiple pregnancy), there has been no discernible attempt to reduce these risks by altering procedures and protocols. There also has been an appalling lack of follow-up studies to determine the long-term health, psychological, and social consequence of these procedures.[10]

In view of the current lack of systematic knowledge about difficulties these methods may create in children born of them, opponents of the new reproductive technologies maintain it is wrong to use them. Those who resort to these techniques, they claim, bear the burden of proof of their safety. They have an obligation to establish whether these ever-increasing methods of assisted reproduction do, in fact, harm a small but significant proportion of children before they are used. For ease of reference, we will call their claims the Harm to Children Argument against the use of the new reproductive technologies.

The Interest in Existing Argument

The basic response to the Harm to Children Argument by several proponents of the use of the new reproductive technologies,[11] of whom John Robertson is a respected spokesperson, is that even if children born of the new reproductive technologies were to suffer serious impairments as a result of their origin, this would not necessarily render it wrong to use these techniques. We might call this response the Interest in Existing Argument: since it is, in almost all cases, better to be alive than not, and these children would not be alive but for the employment of these techniques, using them to bring these children into the world is justified. Robertson writes:

> [A] higher incidence of birth defects in such offspring would not justify banning the technique in order to protect the offspring, because without these techniques these children would not have been born at all. Unless their lives are so full of suffering as to be worse than no life at all, a very unlikely supposition, the defective children of such a union have not been harmed if they would not have been born healthy.[12]

Only where "from the perspective of the child, viewed solely in light of his interests as he is then situated, any life at all with the conditions of his birth would be so harmful to him that from his perspective he would prefer not to live,"[13] could it be said to be a substantial harm to have been brought into existence by means of the new reproductive technologies.

Robertson here implicitly distinguishes between *devastating harm*—harm that brings such suffering into a person's life that this life is worse than no life at all—[and] *serious harm*—harm that does not render life worse than death, but that includes such detriments as major physical impairments, severe mental disability, and/or considerable pain and suffering. He labels only the former *substantial harm*. Indeed, at certain points, Robertson maintains that children damaged by their origin in the new reproductive technologies cannot be said to suffer harm at all, since their birth is an overriding benefit.

The Harm to Children Argument is logically flawed, Robertson and like-minded thinkers maintain, because the benefit of life that children born of these techniques receive outweighs almost any detriment they might experience as a result of their origins. Robertson notes:

> Preventing harm would mean preventing the birth of the child whose interests one is trying to protect. Yet a child's interests are hardly protected by preventing the child's existence. If the child has no way to be born or raised free of that harm, a person is not injuring the child by enabling her to be born in the circumstances of concern.[14]

It is not open to children damaged by the use of the new reproductive technologies to live free of impairment, since they could not have existed without the use of these technologies. The alternative for them would have been not to live at all, a state which is not in their interests. Consequently, according to the Interest in Existing Argument, it is, in almost all instances, in the interests of children who might be born of the new reproductive technologies to be brought into the world by these means, even if this would risk serious harm to them.

This argument applies only to children who suffer harm that is a necessary result of the use of these techniques. Thus, if it were claimed that contract surrogacy creates psychological harm for a child because the biological mother and rearing parents would be in a constant state of conflict with each other, the Interest in Existing Argument could not be used in response. This is because the warring trio could behave in a different manner less likely to cause this sort of harm to the child. According to advocates of the Interest in Existing Argument it was not a necessary condition of the child's very existence that the conflict among these various parents occur.

The Harm of Not Existing

The Interest in Existing Argument assumes that children with an interest in existing are waiting in a spectral world of nonexistence where their situation is less desirable than it would be were they released into this world. This presupposition is revealed by such observations as "a child's interests are hardly protected by preventing the child's existence" and that it is a disadvantage to such children that they "have no way of being born." In the Interest in Existing Argument children who might be conceived are pictured as pale preexisting entities with an interest in moving into the more full-blooded reality of this world. Their admission into this realm is thwarted by the failure to use available new reproductive technologies. This failure negates their interest in existing and thereby harms them.

Before a person exists, however, he or she does not reside in some other domain. Prior to conception, there is *no one who waits to be brought into this world.* Joel Feinberg argues, "Since it is necessary to *be* if one is to *be better off,* it is a logical contradiction to say that someone could be better off though not in existence."[15] To say that it was good for someone already in existence to have been born does not imply that his existence in this world is better than his life in some other realm. Nor does it imply that if he had not been caused to exist, this would have been bad for him.[16] Although a wealth of possible children can be conceived, their interests cannot be diminished if they are not. Therefore, it cannot be coherently argued that it is "better" for children to be created by means of the new reproductive technologies, even when this would result in serious disorders to them, since there is no alternative state in which their lot could be worse.

Part of the confusion at the heart of the Interest in Existing Argument stems from an incoherence found in tort actions for "wrongful life," to which this argument has an acknowledged debt. In these suits, children born with impairments claim that their current condition is worse than the state of nonexistence they would have had were it not for negligence on the part of physicians, hospitals, or testing laboratories. The wrong done to them, they contend, is not that their impaired condition was negligently caused, but that their very existence was negligently caused. This, they maintain, is a serious injury, since they would have been better off not being born at all. They ask for compensation for the injury of being brought into this world.

In an early wrongful life case, *Gleitman v. Cosgrove,* a child born with impairments whose mother had been told erroneously that her exposure to German measles during pregnancy would not harm the fetus,

brought suit for damages for the injury of being born.[17] The traditional method of measuring damages in tort is to compare the condition of the plaintiff before and after an injury and to compensate for the difference. When the putative wrong done to the plaintiff is to have been brought into existence in an impaired state, the court must measure the difference between nonexistence and existence with impairments. In *Gleitman,* the court found it "logically impossible" to "weigh the value of life with impairments against the nonexistence of life itself." We cannot, according to the court, conceptualize a world in which the plaintiff did not exist and ask what benefits and burdens he experienced in that world in order to compare it with his situation in this world.

Even so, the *Gleitman* court concluded that the value of life, no matter how burdened, outweighs the disvalue of not existing, and that damages therefore could not be awarded to the child for "wrongful life." In drawing this conclusion, the court implicitly compared the world of existence with that of nonexistence and declared the former always preferable to the latter. Yet this is precisely the step the court had said it could not take. Similarly, in another leading case, *Berman v. Allan,* the court ruled against recognition of a "wrongful life" claim on grounds that "life—whether experienced with or without a major physical handicap—is more precious than non-life."[18] These courts were concerned that awarding damages for being alive would diminish the high value that the law places on human life. This public policy concern, however, caused them to lapse into incoherence. They claimed that the world of existence cannot be measured against that of nonexistence. However, if existence is better than nonexistence, as they also declared, nonexistence must be conceptually accessible in some sense so that an intelligible comparison can be made between it and existence.

Proponents of the Interest in Existing Argument adopt the two-world view underlying the logically impossible thesis of the early wrongful life cases when they claim that children are harmed if they are not brought out of the world of nonexistence into the world of existence. This leaves them with two problems: (1) explaining how to conceptualize and comprehend nonexistence and (2) justifying the claim that it is better to exist than not. Moreover, their dependence on the wrongful life decisions causes them to overlook an essential feature of their opponents' argument. The Harm to Children Argument is a *before-the-fact* one that applies to the time when a decision must be made about whether to employ the new reproductive technologies. *At this time, unlike the wrongful life cases, no child exists who could be harmed.* The Harm to Children Argument holds that at this preconception time, the morally right decision is not to use such technologies until further research establishes the degree of harm this might do to children who result. The Interest in Existing Argument, however, is an after-the-fact argument meant to apply at a time when children are already born. It must be used as a response to those who object to having already brought children into the world. Since the harm posited by the critics has not yet occurred when the decision is made whether to employ them, it is not an adequate response to say that without these technologies the resulting children would not have been born.[19] That is precisely what is at issue—*whether these children ought to have been conceived and born.*

A further difficulty is that the Interest in Existing Argument justifies allowing the new reproductive technologies to create almost any harm to children conceived as a result of their use—as long as this is not devastating harm in which death is preferable to life with it. As Bonnie Steinbock and Ron McClamrock observe, "Very few lives meet the stringent conditions imposed by the wrongful life analysis. . . . Even the most dismal sorts of circumstances of opportunity (including, for example . . . an extremely high chance of facing an agonizing death from starvation in the early years of life, severe retardation plus quadriplegia) fail to be covered"[20] by the standard of devastating harm. Yet it would strike many as ethically objectionable to proceed with reproductive techniques should such serious, but not devastating harms result from them in a significant proportion of cases.

The "Wrongful Life" Standard of Substantial Harm

Those who present the Interest in Existing Argument, adopting the standard applied in wrongful life cases, describe substantial harm as that which, in Robertson's words, puts one in a condition that renders life so "horrible"[21] and so "full of unavoidable suffering" (p. 169) that it is worse than "no life at all."[22] Robertson does not give a more precise definition of substantial harm, nor does he present specific examples of conditions which fall under that rubric in his discussion of harm to children and the new reproductive technologies. Feinberg expands on the "wrongful life" standard of substantial harm:

> Surely in most cases of suffering and impairment we think of death as even worse. This is shown by the widespread human tendency to "cling to life at all costs." And even for severe genetic handicaps and inherited maladies, most competent persons who suffer from them will not express regret that they were born in the first place. . . . In the most extreme cases, however, I think it is rational to prefer not to have come into existence at all, and while I cannot prove this judgment, I am confident that most people will agree that it is at least plausible. I have in mind some of the more severely victimized sufferers from brain malformation, spina bifida, Tay-Sachs disease, polycystic kidney disease, Lesch-Nyhan syndrome, and those who, from whatever cause, are born blind and deaf, permanently incontinent, severely retarded, and in chronic pain or near-total paralysis, with life-expectancies of only a few years.[23]

To talk about death, both Feinberg and Robertson assume, is the same as to talk about "not coming into existence at all." They assimilate nonexistence before life and nonexistence after having lived. This is a mistake. *Nonexistence before coming into being* and *nonexistence after having lived* are two distinct concepts.

Lucretius observed that we do not express concern about nonexistence before creation, but we do fear our nonexistence after death. Why is this? The reason we perceive death as bad, Thomas Nagel proposes, is that it causes us to have fewer goods of this life than we would have had if we had continued to live.[24] Frances Kamm further observes that it is not only the absence of future goods in this life that leads us to fear death, but that death "takes away what already was and would have continued to be."[25] Preconception nonexistence, however, does not deprive us of what was ours already. In it there is no particular individual whose life ends and who thereby loses out on life's goods. Consequently, non-existence before conception and birth does not seem as bad as death. We are indifferent to it.

Several other features of death that are also not characteristic of preconception nonexistence contribute to our assessment of it as bad. Death, for instance, happens to a person, whereas preconception nonexistence does not include an event in which nonexistence happens to a person. Death reveals our vulnerability in that through it a person is destroyed and deprived of life's goods. If a person does not exist, in contrast, this does not reflect negatively on "his" or "her" capacities.[26] Because of significant differences between them, preconception and posthumous nonexistence are qualitatively distinct concepts that are not interchangeable. Death has characteristics that lead us to evaluate it as bad, whereas preconception nonexistence strikes us as neither good nor bad.

Do we, too, fall into the trap of positing a shadowy world of nonexistence by distinguishing between preconception and posthumous nonexistence? We do not claim that either of these forms of nonexistence is a metaphysical locale. Instead, we view both as logical constructs built out of what we know about being alive. For both Nagel and Kamm, the meaning of death is derived from what we know about our existence in this world. The same is true of preconception nonexistence. Although the multitude of children whom it is possible for us to bring into the world do not exist, we can conceptualize certain things about them and what their lives would be like were we to conceive and bear them. We can also comprehend certain things about the negation of their existence were they to be born. That is, we can understand what they would lose if we decided not to conceive them and bring them into the world. Thus, we can meaningfully compare preconception nonexistence with life. We can consider children who might be brought into existence and ask whether we ought to conceive them without having to postulate a separate sphere of nonexistence in which they wait as we ponder the question.

While we can make sense of the notion of preconception nonexistence, can we also intelligibly claim that children who have not yet been conceived can have interests? It might be argued that those who do not exist cannot have interests and that therefore possible children can have no interest in not being conceived and brought into the world with serious disorders. Yet possible children can have interests, if these are taken in the sense of what contributes to their good, rather than as psychological states. We can conceive of what would promote their welfare were they to be brought into the world. To deny them such interests is mistakenly to reason by analogy with the dead. It has been supposed that the dead can have no interests because we cannot perform any actions that will affect the condition of their lives.[27] We cannot causally impinge on them for better or worse, it has been argued, for their lives have been completed. But this is not the case with possible children. We can affect them causally for better or worse by our present actions. Thus, we can ascribe to possible children certain interests that can be thwarted or fulfilled by actions that we take.

The interests of children who might be born of the new reproductive technologies are not adequately captured by the "wrongful life" standard. The comparison that parents and physicians must make when they assess whether use of these technologies would negatively affect the good of children who might result is not between *death* and the condition of these children were they to be born with certain deficits. The appropriate comparison is between *preconception nonexistence* and their condition were they to be born with certain deficits. If preconception nonexistence, unlike death, is neither good nor bad, then any life that will be worse than it *will not have to be as bad as the life of devastating deficits set out in the wrongful life standard*. A life with serious, but not devastating, deficits could be bad and therefore worse than preconception nonexistence, which is neither good nor bad. Therefore, we must modify the wrongful life standard of substantial harm to indicate that if new reproductive technologies were shown to cause a significant proportion of children born of them to suffer either devastating *or* serious deficits, they would cause substantial harm to these children and consequently ought not be used.

The Inadequate Opportunity for Health Standard of Substantial Harm

How are we to identify the serious deficits that—along with devastating deficits—would constitute substantial harm to these children? The boundary between moderate, serious, and devastating deficits is sufficiently blurred that reasonable people can disagree about where it lies in particular cases. Many would disagree with Feinberg that children knowingly conceived with such disorders as spina bifida, blindness, deafness, severe retardation, or permanent incontinence should be considered to be suffering from devastating deficits that make their lives worse than death. However, they might well view these disorders as amounting to serious deficits that make their lives worse than preconception non-existence. What is needed is a conceptual framework that marks off those deficits that have such a negative impact on children that reasonable people would agree that knowingly to conceive children with these disorders would be to impose substantial harm on them in the vast majority of cases.

Laura Purdy suggests that we cause substantial harm to future children and therefore ought not knowingly conceive them "when there is a high risk of transmitting a serious disease or defect [of a sort that would deny them] a normal opportunity for health."[28] At points in Purdy's discussion, as when she states that "every parent should try to ensure normal health for his child," she can be taken to mean that having an abnormal state of health would constitute a disorder sufficiently serious to warrant not conceiving a child who would have it. On this approach, children with a particular biological, chemical, or mental state different from the norm would be said to lack "normal health" and therefore to suffer from a "serious disease or defect" that would justify not conceiving them. Yet it would not strike us as wrong knowingly to conceive children who are not "normal" because they have myopia or albinism. Normality does not appear to provide an adequate standard for deciding that a disorder is a serious deficit that substantially harms a child knowingly conceived with it.

At other points, however, Purdy seems to suggest that the focus for defining a serious deficit that falls under the substantial harm rubric should be on the failure to provide an adequate opportunity for a healthy life, as this is defined within a culture. Here she seems on the right track, for notions of health and disease—for better and for worse—are embedded within a society. What constitutes health and what represents a serious falling away from it varies from culture to culture and changes from time to time. As the notion of health and of an adequate opportunity for health vary according to the cultural context and conditions, so, too, does the meaning of a serious disease or deficit. Moreover, access to health services and the resulting opportunity for health—or lack of it—also affect what is meant by health, serious disorder, and substantial harm.

In our society, children who are color-blind are considered to have only a mild deficit and no diminution of their opportunity for health. However, in certain African cultures in which the capacity to distinguish a great variety of shades of green is needed to function at a minimal level for survival, color blindness is a serious deficit. Children born with this condition in such cultures do not have an adequate opportunity for health because their condition cannot be remedied. Thus, cultural values affect the meanings of health and of serious disorders. Stanley Hauerwas observes that "disease descriptions and remedies are relative to a society's values and needs. Thus 'retardation' might not 'exist' in a society which values cooperation more than competition and ambition."[29] Further, medical practices in different cultures reflect different views of what constitutes health and serious diseases. In Germany children with blood pressure that differs from the norm for their age on both the high and low end are suspected to be at risk of serious disease, whereas in America only high blood pressure is considered an indicator of serious disease.

What makes a disorder serious, however, is not only a matter of cultural needs, expectations, constructions, and practices. Some children are born with remediable conditions that are transformed into serious deficits when they are not ameliorated due to circumstances of injustice and neglect within a culture. The child born with spina bifida to poor parents in the hills of Appalachia has a minimal opportunity for health and a more serious disorder than the child born with this same condition to professional parents in Los Angeles. It might not be unfair to a child knowingly to conceive him or her with paralysis of the lower limbs if that child, once born, would have access to support structures giving him or her adequate mobility.[30] Nor would we have grounds for considering it wrong for parents knowingly to conceive a blind child if that child would receive compensatory education and ameliorative instruments enabling him or her to have an adequate opportunity for health within a society.

This relativity of the notion of health and of an adequate opportunity for health means that no definition of serious disease or disorder amounting to substantial harm that would apply across all cultures, times, and places can be given. Instead, the assessment of serious disease amounting to substantial harm must be made under specific circumstances within particular cultures. It must be defined not only in terms of a given physical or mental condition that damages a child's ability to function within a culture, but also in terms of the failure or inability of a culture to provide a child with access to ameliorative resources.

Sidney Callahan maintains that a principle of proportionality should be applied when making decisions concerning reproduction.[31] This would mean that the lower the risk and gravity of impairment to the child and the more would-be parents, family, and the institutional structures of a society are able and willing to ameliorate the impairment, the less the likelihood that a child would suffer a serious deficit and the more ethically justifiable it would be to conceive him or her. Should the probability and gravity of impairment be great, however, and the would-be parents, family, and social structure unwilling or unable to provide ameliorative measures for the child with such impairment, the higher the likelihood the child would suffer a serious deficit and the less ethically justifiable it would be to conceive that child. We do not end up with a black letter definition of a deficit serious enough to be termed substantial harm on this approach, but one that requires us to consider the nature of the disorder from which the child would suffer, the circumstances into which the child would be brought, and the ameliorative resources available for that child. Under current circumstances in our culture

in which children born with disabling disorders have inadequate support, it would be morally questionable, at least, knowingly to conceive a child suffering from some of the deficits listed by Feinberg above.

Obligations to Actual and Possible Children

Although we consider it ethically necessary to provide treatment to keep children alive who have serious illnesses, we do not consider it ethically necessary knowingly to conceive children with those same disorders. Why is this? Why do we assume that our obligations to children who already exist differ from our obligations to children whom we might conceive?

The difference between an actual and possible child and between our evaluations of preconception nonexistence and death help to explain this distinction. Since we view death as an evil in relation to being alive, we tend to maintain that once children are born, only if they suffer devastating harms that make life worse than death would we be justified in not doing what we can to prevent their death. Being alive is better than being dead, except in rare circumstances. However, we do not believe that we have an obligation to do everything we can to conceive and bring into the world possible children who would suffer serious or devastating illness as a result. This is because no one exists who is wronged by not being conceived and also because preconception nonexistence does not strike us as being either bad or good. To fail to actualize a possible child, therefore, does not put that child in a worse situation or wrong that child.

Furthermore, we have no obligation to conceive children if this would detrimentally affect the good of the family or culture into which they would be born. We have no obligation, for instance, to conceive a sixth child if we believe our family can only function adequately with five. And we need not bring children into the world when this would contribute to a problem of overpopulation or of limited resources. It is morally acceptable, indeed, some would say, morally required, that *before* we bring children into the world, we consider not only their well-being were they to be born, but the good of those who would be affected by their birth. *After* birth, however, the interest in existing of the living child comes into play and morally outweighs remnants of a parental or societal interest in not having had that child.

These conclusions may appear to intimate that the lives of children born with serious or even devastating disorders are not valued or valuable. This conclusion does not follow from the preceding argument. Should parents, after receiving convincing evidence that use of the new reproductive technologies would harm the resulting children, decide against employing them, this could say one of two things to living children with serious or devastating disorders. It could suggest that it would have been better for their families if a different child had been born without these disorders and she was not. Or it could imply that it would have been better for this child to have been born without these disorders.[32] The first implication suggests that it would be better for others if children with these disorders were not born, whereas the second maintains that it would be better for the children themselves if they had not been born with them. The first implies that it is regrettable that these children are alive instead of "normal" children. The second implies that it is regrettable that these children have these disorders. The second implication is the one on which we tend to act. This is exhibited by efforts we make to avoid serious or devastating disorders in children during pregnancy and to treat and care for children with such disorders after they are born. All of this suggests that it is not the children we disvalue, but the disorders that they have sustained. Consequently, it is not necessarily a reproach to disabled children who are already born if decisions are made against knowingly conceiving children who would have the same disabilities.

It is, however, a reproach to us and to our social institutions that once children with serious and devastating disorders are born, we provide woefully insufficient services and resources to them and their families. Does this contradict the claim that we value living children with disabilities and have their interests at heart? Hauerwas provides one perceptive explanation of our ambivalent and complex attitude toward those who live with serious disabilities in the course of discussing those who are developmentally delayed. He observes:

After all, what we finally seek is not simply to help the retarded better negotiate their disability but to be like us: not retarded. Our inability to accomplish that frustrates and angers us, and sometimes the retarded themselves become the object of our anger. We do not like to be reminded of the limits of our power, and we do not like those who remind us.[33]

We wish to remedy the disabilities with which children may be born, but find it difficult to cope with the recognition of our own vulnerability that they inadvertently call forth. Therefore, we relegate them to a separate domain within the world of existence where we believe unknown others will assist them to meet the special challenges they face. This is uncharitable and unjust. We have a responsibility to overcome our misplaced frustration about being unable to render those who have serious or devastating disorders more like those who do not. We have a responsibility to assist them to make their own way in the world unhampered by our irrational fears.

Taking Harms Seriously

The biblical injunction to multiply does not exhort us to do anything whatsoever to have children. It would be wrong to have children if it were known before conception that the means used to bring this about could inflict serious or devastating deficits on those very children. Yet the logic of the Interest in Existing Argument leads its proponents to brush aside the question whether these technologies might create such serious impairments. The thrust of this argument is that use of the new reproductive technologies provides its own justification—it produces children. This claim disregards the welfare of these children. Moreover, it creates a barrier to more extensive and detailed investigations of the effect of the new reproductive technologies on children born of them.

On the approach presented here, if it were known ahead of time that children conceived with the assistance of the new reproductive technologies would not have an adequate opportunity for health, it would be wrong to use them. Assessment of when and whether this could be the case would be carried out in light of the personal, familial, and social circumstances into which these children would be born.

This means that would-be parents who consider resorting to the new reproductive technologies must be informed about the risks these techniques would present to the children born as a result of their use, the means available for ameliorating deficits these children might experience, and what social support would be available should they lack the resources to address such deficits on their own. Only then can they decide whether they ought to proceed with these techniques. To implement this recommendation, evidence for and against the contention that the new reproductive technologies cause serious or devastating physical, psychological, or social harm to the resulting children should be investigated more thoroughly than at present. Because of limited knowledge of the possible effects of these measures on their children, those who repeat Rachel's cry today face an agonizingly difficult decision when they consider whether to use the new reproductive technologies.

REFERENCES

1. National Perinatal Statistics Unit, Fertility Society of Australia, *In Vitro Fertilization Pregnancies. Australia and New Zealand* 1979–1985, Sydney, Australia, 1987; Paul L. Lancaster, "Congenital Malformations after In-Vitro Fertilisation," [letter] *Lancet* 2 (1987): 1392–93; see also AIHW National Perinatal Statistics Unit, Fertility Society of Australia, *Assisted Conception in Australia and New Zealand 1990* (Sydney: AIHW National Perinatal Statistics Unit, 1992); Gail Vines, "Shots in the Dark for Infertility," *New Scientist* 140 (1993): 13–15; Lene Koch, "Physiological and Psychosocial Risks of the New Reproductive Technologies," in *Tough Choices: In Vitro Fertilization and the Reproductive Technologies*, ed. Patricia Stephenson and Marsden G. Wagner (Philadelphia: Temple University Press, 1993), pp. 122–34.

2. U. B. Wennerholm et al., "Pregnancy Complications and Short-Term Follow-Up of Infants Born after In Vitro Fertilization and Embryo Transfer," *Acta Obstetrica et Gynecologicia Scandinavica* 70 (1991): 565–73; B. Rizk et al., "Perinatal Outcome and Congenital Malformations in In-Vitro Fertilization Babies from the Bourn-Hallam Group," *Human Reproduction* 6 (1991): 1259–64; S. Friedler, S. Mashiach, and N. Laufer, "Births in Israel Resulting from In-Vitro Fertilization/Embryo Transfer, 1982–1989: National Registry of the Israeli Association for Fertility Research," *Human Reproduction* 7 (1992): 1159–63; Society for Assisted Reproductive Technology, American Society for Reproductive Medicine, Assisted Reproductive Technology in the United States and Canada, "1993 Results Generated from the American Society for Reproductive Medicine/Society for Assisted Reproductive Technology Registry," *Fertility and Sterility* 64(1995): 13–21.

3. Norma C. Morin et al., "Congenital Malformations and Psychosocial Development in Children Conceived by In Vitro Fertilization," *Journal of Pediatrics* 115 (1989): 222–27.

4. V. Beral et al., "Outcome of Pregnancies Resulting from Assisted Conception," *British Medical Bulletin* 46, no. 3 (1990): 753–68; I. Craft and T. al-Shawaf, "Outcome and Complications of Assisted Reproduction," *Current Opinion in Obstetrics and Gynecology* 3 (1991): 668–73; Rizk et al., "Perinatal Outcome and Congenital Malformations in In-Vitro Fertilization Babies from the Bourn-Hallam Group"; P. Doyle, V. Beral, and N. Maconochie, "Preterm Delivery, Low Birthweight and Small-for-Gestational-Age in Liveborn Singleton Babies Resulting from In-Vitro Fertilization," *Human Reproduction* 7 (1992): 425–28; Friedler et al., "Births in Israel," pp. 1160–63.

5. Jean-Pierre Relier, Michele Couchard, and Catherine Huon, "The Neonatologist's Experience of In Vitro Fertilization Risks," *Tough Choices*, pp. 135–143; see also P. Rufat et al., "Task Force Report on the Outcome of Pregnancies and Children Conceived by In Vitro Fertilization (France: 1987 to 1989)," *Fertility and Sterility* 61 (1994): 324–30; FIVNAT (French In Vitro National), "Pregnancies and Births Resulting from In Vitro Fertilization: French National Registry, Analysis of Data 1986 to 1990," *Fertility and Sterility* 64 (1995): 746–56.

6. Cynthia B. Cohen, "Reproductive Technologies: Ethical Issues," in *Encyclopedia of Bioethics*, ed. Warren Thomas Reich (New York: Simon and Schuster Macmillan, 1995), vol. 4, pp. 2233–41; A. Baran and R. Pannor, *Lethal Secrets: The Shocking Consequences and Unsolved Problems of Artificial Insemination* (New York: Warner Books, 1989); D. N. Mushin, J. Spensley, and M. Barreda-Hanson, "In Vitro Fertilization Children: Early Psychosocial Development," *Journal of In Vitro Fertilization and Embryo Transfer* 4 (1986): 247–52.

7. Margaret Radin, "Market-Inalienability," *Harvard Law Review* 100 (1987): 1921–36; Sidney Callahan, "The Ethical Challenges of the New Reproductive Technologies," in *Medical Ethics: A Guide for Health Professionals*, ed. J. Monagle and David Thomas (Rockville, Md.: Aspen, 1988), pp. 26–37.

8. Leon Kass, *Toward a More Natural Science: Biology and Human Affairs* (New York: Free Press, 1985), p. 113; Lisa Sowle Cahill, "The Ethics of Surrogate Motherhood: Biology, Freedom, and Moral Obligation," *Law, Medicine and Health Care* 16, nos. 1–2 (1988): 65–71, at 69; Cynthia B. Cohen, "Parents Anonymous," in *New Ways of Making Babies: The Case of Egg Donation*, ed. Cynthia B. Cohen (Bloomington: Indiana University Press, 1996).

9. Susan Golombok et al., "Parents and Their Children Happy with Assisted Conception," [letter] *British Medical Journal* 307 (1994): 1032.

10. Lene Koch, "Physiological and Psychosocial Risks of the New Reproductive Technologies," p. 128.

11. Ruth F. Chadwick, "Cloning," *Philosophy* 57 (1982): 201–9; John A. Robertson, "Procreative Liberty and the Control of Conception, Pregnancy, and Childbirth," *University of Virginia Law Review* 69 (1983): 405–462, at 434; John A. Robertson, "Embryos, Families, and Procreative Liberty: The Legal Structure of the New Reproduction," *Southern California Law Review* 59 (1986): 942–1041, at 958, 988; John A. Robertson, "Procreative Liberty, Embryos, and Collaborative Reproduction: A Legal Perspective," in *Embryos, Ethics, and Women's Rights: Exploring the New Reproductive Technologies*, ed. E. F. Baruch, A. F. Adamo, Jr., and J. Seager (New York: Howarth Press, 1988), pp. 179–94; John A. Robertson, "The Question of Human Cloning," *Hastings Center Report* 24, no. 3 (1994): 6–14; John A. Robertson, *Children of Choice: Freedom and the New Reproductive Technologies* (Princeton, N.J.: Princeton University Press, 1994), pp. 75–76, 110–11, 122–23, 152, 169–70; Ruth Macklin, "Splitting Embryos on the Slippery Slope," *Kennedy Institute of Ethics Journal* 4 (1994): 209–25, at 219–20.

12. Robertson, "Procreative Liberty and the Control of Conception, Pregnancy, and Childbirth," p. 434.

13. Robertson, *Children of Choice*, pp. 75–76.

14. Robertson, *Children of Choice*, pp. 75–76.

15. Joel Feinberg, "Wrongful Life and the Counterfactual Element in Harming," *Social Philosophy and Policy* 4 (1988):145–78, at 158.

16. Derek Parfit, *Reasons and Persons* (Oxford: Oxford University Press, 1985), p. 487.

17. *Gleitman v. Cosgrove*, 49 N.J. 22, 227A. 2d 689 (1967).

18. *Berman v. Allan*, 80 N.J. 421, 404 A. 2d 8 (1979).

19. Robertson, *Children of Choice*, pp. 75, 117; "Embryos, Families, and Procreative Liberty," pp. 958, 988.

20. Bonnie Steinbock and Ron McClamrock, "When Is Birth Unfair to the Child?" *Hastings Center Report* 24, no. 6 (1994): 16–22, at 17.

21. Robertson, *Children of Choice*, pp. 82, 85.

22. Robertson, "Procreative Liberty and the Control of Conception, Pregnancy, and Childbirth," p. 434.

23. Feinberg, "Wrongful Life," p. 159.

24. Thomas Nagel, "Death," in *Mortal Questions* (Cambridge: Cambridge University Press: 1979), pp. 1–10.

25. Frances M. Kamm, *Morality, Mortality, Volume I. Death and Whom to Save from It* (New York: Oxford University Press, 1993), p. 40.

26. Kamm, *Morality, Mortality*, pp. 40–41.

27. Joan Callahan, "On Harming the Dead," *Ethics* 97 (1987): 341–52; Ernest Partridge, "Posthumous Interests and Posthumous Respect," *Ethics*, 91 (1981): 243–64.

28. Laura Purdy, "Genetic Diseases: Can Having Children Be Immoral?" in *Genetics Now: Ethical Issues in Genetic Research*, ed. John Buckly, Jr. (Washington, D.C.: University Press of America, 1978), pp. 25–39, at 25.

29. Stanley Hauerwas, "Suffering the Retarded: Should We Prevent Retardation?" in *Suffering Presence: Theological Reflections on Medicine, the Mentally Handicapped, and the Church*, ed. Stanley Hauerwas (Notre Dame: University of Notre Dame Press, 1986), pp. 159–81.

30. Steinbock and McClamrock, "When Is Birth Unfair to the Child?" and Sidney Callahan, "An Ethical Analysis of Responsible Parenthood," in *Genetic Counseling: Facts, Values, and Norms*, ed. Alexander M. Capron, Marc Lappé, and Robert F. Murray (New York: Alan R. Liss, 1979), pp. 217–38.

31. Callahan, "An Ethical Analysis of Responsible Parenthood."

32. Mary Warnock, "Ethical Challenges in Embryo Manipulation," *British Medical Journal* 304 (1992): 1045–49, at 1047.

33. Hauerwas, "Suffering the Retarded," p. 176.

Instruction on Respect for Human Life in Its Origin and on the Dignity of Procreation

CONGREGATION FOR THE DOCTRINE OF THE FAITH

This document articulates the official position of the Roman Catholic Church, declaring that many kinds of reproductive technology or practices are morally impermissible. Among other affirmations, it asserts that (1) nontherapeutic

From Congregation for the Doctrine of the Faith, *Instruction on Respect for Human Life in Its Origin and on the Dignity of Procreation*, February 22, 1987. © Libreria Editrice Vaticana.

experimentation on embryos is illicit, (2) "it is immoral to produce embryos destined to be exploited as disposable 'biological material,'" (3) nontherapeutic genetic manipulations are contrary to human dignity, (4) artificial fertilization involving sperm and egg from unmarried individuals is illicit, and (5) in vitro fertilization is not morally legitimate.

Biomedical Research and the Teaching of the Church

The gift of life which God the Creator and Father has entrusted to man calls him to appreciate the inestimable value of what he has been given and to take responsibility for it: This fundamental principle must be placed at the center of one's reflection in order to clarify and solve the moral problems raised by artificial interventions on life as it originates and on the processes of procreation.

Thanks to the progress of the biological and medical sciences, man has at his disposal ever more effective therapeutic resources; but he can also acquire new powers, with unforeseeable consequences, over human life at its very beginning and in its first stages. Various procedures now make it possible to intervene not only in order to assist, but also to dominate the processes of procreation. These techniques can enable man to "take in hand his own destiny," but they also expose him "to the temptation to go beyond the limits of a reasonable dominion over nature." (1) They might constitute progress in the service of man, but they also involve serious risks. Many people are therefore expressing an urgent appeal that in interventions on procreation the values and rights of the human person be safeguarded. Requests for clarification and guidance are coming not only from the faithful, but also from those who recognize the church as "an expert in humanity" (2) with a mission to serve the "civilization of love" (3) and of life.

The church's magisterium does not intervene on the basis of a particular competence in the area of the experimental sciences; but having taken account of the data of research and technology, it intends to put forward, by virtue of its evangelical mission and apostolic duty, the moral teaching corresponding to the dignity of the person and to his or her integral vocation. It intends to do so by expounding the criteria of moral judgment as regards the applications of scientific research and technology, especially in relation to human life and its beginnings. These criteria are the respect, defence and promotion of man, his "primary and fundamental right" to life, (4) his dignity as a person who is endowed with a spiritual soul and with moral responsibility (5) and who is called to beatific communion with God. . . .

Anthropology and Procedures in the Biomedical Field

Which moral criteria must be applied in order to clarify the problems posed today in the field of biomedicine? The answer to this question presupposes a proper idea of the nature of the human person in his bodily dimension.

For it is only in keeping with his true nature that the human person can achieve self-realization as a "unified totality"; and this nature is at the same time corporal and spiritual. By virtue of its substantial union with a spiritual soul, the human body cannot be considered as a mere complex of tissues, organs and functions, nor can it be evaluated in the same way as the body of animals; rather, it is a constitutive part of the person who manifests and expresses himself through it.

The natural moral law expresses and lays down the purposes, rights and duties which are based upon the bodily and spiritual nature of the human person. Therefore this law cannot be thought of as simply a set of norms on the biological level; rather, it must be defined as the rational order whereby man is called by the Creator to direct and regulate his life and actions and in particular to make use of his own body.

A first consequence can be deduced from these principles: An intervention on the human body affects not only the tissues, the organs and their functions, but also involves the person himself on different levels. It involves, therefore, perhaps in an implicit but nonetheless real way, a moral significance and responsibility. . . .

Applied biology and medicine work together for the integral good of human life when they come to the aid of a person stricken by illness and infirmity and when they respect his or her dignity as a creature of God. No biologist or doctor can reasonably claim, by virtue of his scientific competence, to be able to decide on people's origin and destiny. This norm must be applied in a particular way in the field of sexuality and procreation, in which man and woman actualize the fundamental values of love and life.

God, who is love and life, has inscribed in man and woman the vocation to share in a special way in his mystery of personal communion and in his work as Creator and Father. For this reason marriage possesses specific goods and values in its union and in procreation which cannot be likened to those existing in lower forms of life. Such values and meanings are of the personal order and determine from the moral point of view the meaning and limits of artificial interventions on procreation and on the origin of human life. These interventions are not to be rejected on the grounds that they are artificial. As such, they bear witness to the possibilities of the art of medicine. But they must be given a moral evaluation in reference to the dignity of the human person, who is called to realize his vocation from God to the gift of love and the gift of life.

Fundamental Criteria for a Moral Judgment

The fundamental values connected with the techniques of artificial human procreation are two: the life of the human being called into existence and the special nature of the transmission of human life in marriage. The moral judgment on such methods of artificial procreation must therefore be formulated in reference to these values.

Physical life, with which the course of human life in the world begins, certainly does not itself contain the whole of a person's value, nor does it represent the supreme good of man, who is called to eternal life. However it does constitute in a certain way the "fundamental" value of life precisely because upon this physical life all the other values of the person are based and developed. The inviolability of the innocent human being's right to life "from the moment of conception until death" is a sign and requirement of the very inviolability of the person to whom the Creator has given the gift of life.

By comparison with the transmission of other forms of life in the universe, the transmission of human life has a special character of its own, which derives from the special nature of the human person. "The transmission of human life is entrusted by nature to a personal and conscious act and as such is subject to the all-holy laws of God: immutable and inviolable laws which must be recognized and observed. For this reason one cannot use means and follow methods which could be licit in the transmission of the life of plants and animals."

Advances in technology have now made it possible to procreate apart from sexual relations through the meeting *in vitro* of the germ cells previously taken from the man and the woman. But what is technically possible is not for that very reason morally admissible. Rational reflection on the fundamental values of life and of human procreation is therefore indispensable for formulating a moral evaluation of such technological interventions on a human being from the first stages of his development. . . .

I. Respect for Human Embryos

What respect is due to the human embryo, taking into account his nature and identity?
The human being must be respected—as a person— from the very first instant of his existence. . . .

This congregation is aware of the current debates concerning the beginning of human life, concerning the individuality of the human being and concerning the identity of the human person. The congregation recalls the teachings found in the Declaration on Procured Abortion:

"From the time that the ovum is fertilized, a new life is begun which is neither that of the father nor of the mother; it is rather the life of a new human being with his own growth. It would never be made human if it were not human already.

To this perpetual evidence . . . modern genetic science brings valuable confirmation. It has demonstrated that, from the first instant, the program is fixed as to what this living being will be: a man, this individual man with his characteristic aspects already well determined. Right from fertilization is begun the adventure of a human life, and each of its great capacities requires time . . . to find its place and to be in a position to act."

This teaching remains valid and is further confirmed, if confirmation were needed, by recent findings of human biological science which recognize that in the zygote (the cell produced when the nuclei of the two gametes have fused) resulting from fertilization the biological identity of a new human individual is already constituted.

Certainly no experimental datum can be in itself sufficient to bring us to the recognition of a spiritual soul; nevertheless, the conclusions of science regarding the human embryo provide a valuable indication for discerning by the use of reason a personal presence at the moment of this first appearance of a human life: How could a human individual not be a human person? The magisterium has not expressly committed itself to an affirmation of a philosophical nature, but it constantly reaffirms the moral condemnation of any kind of procured abortion. This teaching has not been changed and is unchangeable.

Thus the fruit of human generation from the first moment of its existence, that is to say, from the moment the zygote has formed, demands the unconditional respect that is morally due to the human being in his bodily and spiritual totality. The human being is to be respected and treated as a person from the moment of conception and therefore from that same moment his rights as a person must be recognized, among which in the first place is the inviolable right of every innocent human being to life. This doctrinal reminder provides the fundamental criterion for the solution of the various problems posed by the development of the biomedical sciences in this field: Since the embryo must be treated as a person, it must also be defended in its integrity, tended and cared for, to the extent possible, in the same way as any other human being as far as medical assistance is concerned. . . .

How is one to evaluate morally research and experimentation on human embryos and fetuses?
Medical research must refrain from operations on live embryos, unless there is a moral certainty or not causing harm to the life or integrity of the unborn child and the mother, and on condition that the parents have given their free and informed consent to the procedure. It follows that all research, even when limited to the simple observation of the embryo, would become illicit were it to involve risk to the embryo's physical integrity or life by reason of the methods used or the effects induced. As regards experimentation, and presupposing the general distinction between experimentation for purposes which are not directly therapeutic and experimentation which is clearly therapeutic for the subject himself, in the case in point one must also distinguish between experimentation carried out on embryos which are still alive and experimentation carried out on embryos which are dead. *If the embryos are living, whether viable or not, they must be respected just like any other human person; experimentation on embryos which is not directly therapeutic is illicit.* No objective, even though noble in itself such as a foreseeable advantage to science, to other human beings or to society, can in any way justify experimentation on living human embryos or fetuses, whether viable or not, either inside or outside the mother's womb. The informed consent ordinarily required for clinical experimentation on adults cannot be granted by the parents, who may not freely dispose of the physical integrity or life of the unborn child. Moreover, experimentation on embryos and fetuses always involves risk, and indeed in most cases it involves the certain expectation of harm to their physical integrity or even their death. To use human embryos or fetuses as the object or instrument of experimentation constitutes a crime against their dignity as human beings having a right to the same respect that is due to the child already born and to every human person. . . .

. . . The practice of keeping alive human embryos *in vivo* or *in vitro* for experimental or commercial purposes is totally opposed to human dignity. In the case of experimentation that is clearly therapeutic, namely, when it is a matter of experimental forms of therapy used for the benefit of the embryo itself in a final attempt to save its life and in the absence of other reliable forms of therapy, recourse to drugs or procedures not yet fully tested can be licit.

The corpses of human embryos and fetuses, whether they have been deliberately aborted or not, must be respected just as the remains of other human beings. In particular, they cannot be subjected to mutilation or to autopsies if their death has not yet been verified and without the consent of the parents or of the mother. Furthermore, the moral requirements must be safeguarded that there be no complicity in deliberate abortion and that the risk of scandal be avoided. Also, in the case of dead fetuses, as for the corpses of adult persons, all commercial trafficking must be considered illicit and should be prohibited. . . .

How is one to evaluate morally the use for research purposes of embryos obtained by fertilization "in vitro"? Human embryos obtained *in vitro* are human beings and subjects with rights: Their dignity and right to life must be respected from the first moment of their existence. *It is immoral to produce human embryos destined to be exploited as disposable "biological material."*

In the usual practice of *in vitro* fertilization, not all of the embryos are transferred to the woman's body; some are destroyed. Just as the church condemns induced abortion, so she also forbids acts against the life of these human beings. *It is a duty to condemn the particular gravity of the voluntary destruction of human embryos obtained "in vitro" for the sole purpose of research, either by means of artificial insemination or by means of "twin fission." By acting in this way the researcher usurps the place of God; and even though he may be unaware of this, he sets himself up as the master of the destiny of others inasmuch as he arbitrarily chooses whom he will allow to live and whom he will send to death and kills defenseless human beings.*

Methods of observation or experimentation which damage or impose grave and disproportionate risks upon embryos obtained *in vitro* are morally illicit for the same reasons. Every human being is to be respected for himself and cannot be reduced in worth to a pure and simple instrument for the advantage of others. *It is therefore not in conformity with the moral law deliberately to expose to death human embryos obtained "in vitro."* In consequence of the fact that they have been produced *in vitro*, those embryos which are not transferred into the body of the mother and are called "spare" are exposed to an absurd fate, with no possibility of their being offered safe means of survival which can be licitly pursued.

What judgment should be made on other procedures of manipulating embryos connected with the "techniques of human reproduction?" Techniques of fertilization *in vitro* can open the way to other forms of biological and genetic manipulation of human embryos, such as attempts or plans for fertilization between human and animal gametes and the gestation of human embryos in the uterus of animals, or the hypothesis or project of constructing artificial uteruses for the human embryo. *These procedures are contrary to the human dignity proper to the embryo, and at the same time they are contrary to the right of every person to be conceived and to be born within marriage and from marriage. Also, attempts or hypotheses for obtaining a human being without any connection with sexuality through "twin fission," cloning or parthenogenesis are to be considered contrary to the moral law, since they are in opposition to the dignity both of human procreation and of the conjugal union.*

The freezing of embryos, even when carried out in order to preserve the life of an embryo— cryopreservation—*constitutes an offense against the respect due to human beings* by exposing them to grave risks of death or harm to their physical integrity and depriving them, at least temporarily, of maternal shelter and gestation, thus placing them in a situation in which further offenses and manipulation are possible.

Certain attempts to influence chromosomic or genetic inheritance are not therapeutic, but are aimed at producing human beings selected according to sex or other predetermined qualities. These manipulations are contrary to the personal dignity of the human being and his or her integrity and identity. . . .

II. Interventions upon Human Procreation

. . . A preliminary point for the moral evaluation of [*in vitro* fertilization and artificial insemination] is constituted by the consideration of the circumstances and consequences which those procedures involve in relation to the respect due the human embryo. Development of the practice of *in vitro* fertilization has required innumerable fertilizations and destructions of human embryos. Even today, the usual practice presupposes a hyperovulation on the part of the woman: A number of ova are withdrawn, fertilized and then cultivated *in vitro* for some days. Usually not all are transferred into the genital tracts of the woman; some embryos, generally called "spare," are destroyed or frozen. On occasion, some of the implanted embryos are sacrificed for various eugenic, economic or psychological reasons. Such deliberate destruction of human beings or their utilization for different purposes to the detriment of their integrity and life is contrary to the doctrine on procured abortion already recalled. The connection between *in vitro* fertilization and the voluntary destruction of human embryos occurs too often. This is significant: Through these procedures, with apparently contrary purposes, life and death are subjected to the decision of man, who thus sets himself up as the giver of life and death by decree. This dynamic of violence and domination may remain unnoticed by those very individuals who, in wishing to utilize this procedure, become subject to it themselves. The facts recorded and the cold logic which links them must be taken into consideration for a moral judgment on *in vitro* fertilization and embryo transfer: The abortion mentality which has made this procedure possible thus leads, whether one wants it or not, to man's domination over the life and death of his fellow human beings and can lead to a system of radical eugenics. . . .

A. Heterologous[†] Artificial Fertilization

Why must human procreation take place in marriage?
Every human being is always to be accepted as a gift and blessing of God. However, from the moral point of view a truly responsible procreation vis-à-vis the unborn child must be the fruit of marriage.

For human procreation has specific characteristics by virtue of the personal dignity of the parents

---

†[Heterologous: using gametes coming from at least one donor other than the spouses who are married to each other.]

and of the children: The procreation of a new person, whereby the man and the woman collaborate with the power of the Creator, must be the fruit and the sign of the mutual self-giving of the spouses, of their love and of their fidelity. *The fidelity of the spouses in the unity of marriage involves reciprocal respect of their right to become a father and a mother only through each other.* The child has the right to be conceived, carried in the womb, brought into the world and brought up within marriage: It is through the secure and recognized relationship to his own parents that the child can discover his own identity and achieve his own proper human development. The parents find in their child a confirmation and completion of their reciprocal self-giving: The child is the living image of their love, the permanent sign of their conjugal union, the living and indissoluble concrete expression of their paternity and maternity. By reason of the vocation and social responsibilities of the person, the good of the children and of the parents contributes to the good of civil society; the vitality and stability of society require that children come into the world within a family and that the family be firmly based on marriage. The tradition of the church and anthropological reflection recognize in marriage and in its indissoluble unity the only setting worthy of truly responsible procreation.

Does heterologous artificial fertilization conform to the dignity of the couple and to the truth of marriage?
Through *in vitro* fertilization and embryo transfer and heterologous artificial insemination, human conception is achieved through the fusion of gametes of at least one donor other than the spouses who are united in marriage. *Heterologous artificial fertilization is contrary to the unity of marriage, to the dignity of the spouses, to the vocation proper to parents, and to the child's right to be conceived and brought into the world in marriage and from marriage.* Respect for the unity of marriage and for conjugal fidelity demands that the child be conceived in marriage; the bond existing between husband and wife accords the spouses, in an objective and inalienable manner, the exclusive right to become father and mother solely through each other. Recourse to the gametes of a third person in order to have sperm or ovum available constitutes a violation of the reciprocal commitment of the spouses and a grave lack in regard to that

essential property of marriage which is its unity. Heterologous artificial fertilization violates the rights of the child: it deprives him of his filial relationship with his parental origins and can hinder the maturing of his personal identity. Furthermore, it offends the common vocation of the spouses who are called to fatherhood and motherhood: It objectively deprives conjugal fruitfulness of its unity and integrity; it brings about and manifests a rupture between genetic parenthood, gestational parenthood and responsibility for upbringing. Such damage to the personal relationships within the family has repercussions on civil society: What threatens the unity and stability of the family is a source of dissension, disorder and injustice in the whole of social life.

These reasons lead to a negative moral judgment concerning heterologous artificial fertilization: Consequently, fertilization of a married woman with the sperm of a donor different from her husband and fertilization with the husband's sperm of an ovum not coming from his wife are morally illicit. Furthermore, the artificial fertilization of a woman who is unmarried or a widow, whoever the donor may be, cannot be morally justified.

The desire to have a child and the love between spouses who long to obviate sterility which cannot be overcome in any other way constitute understandable motivations; but subjectively good intentions do not render heterologous artificial fertilization conformable to the objective and inalienable properties of marriage or respectful of the rights of the child and of the spouses.

Is "surrogate" motherhood morally licit?
No, for the same reasons which lead one to reject heterologous artificial fertilization: For it is contrary to the unity of marriage and to the dignity of the procreation of the human person. . . .

B. Homologous† Artificial Fertilization
Since heterologous artificial fertilization has been declared unacceptable, the question arises of how to evaluate morally the process of homologous

---

†[Homologous: using gametes of two spouses joined in marriage.]

artificial fertilization: *in vitro* fertilization and embryo transfer and artificial insemination between husband and wife. First a question of principle must be clarified.

What connection is required from the moral point of view between procreation and the conjugal act?

1. The church's teaching on marriage and human procreation affirms the "inseparable connection, willed by God and unable to be broken by man on his own initiative, between the two meanings of the conjugal act: the unitive meaning and the procreative meaning. Indeed, by its intimate structure the conjugal act, while most closely uniting husband and wife, capacitates them for the generation of new lives according to laws inscribed in the very being of man and of woman." . . . "By safeguarding both these essential aspects, the unitive and the procreative, the conjugal act preserves in its fullness the sense of true mutual love and its ordination toward man's exalted vocation to parenthood." The same doctrine concerning the link between the meanings of the conjugal act and between the goods of marriage throws light on the moral problem of homologous artificial fertilization, since "it is never permitted to separate these different aspects to such a degree as positively to exclude either the procreative intention or the conjugal relation." Contraception deliberately deprives the conjugal act of its openness to procreation and in this way brings about a voluntary dissociation of the ends of marriage. Homologous artificial fertilization, in seeking a procreation which is not the fruit of a specific act of conjugal union, objectively effects an analogous separation between the goods and the meanings of marriage. Thus, *fertilization is licitly sought when it is the result of a "conjugal act which is per se suitable for the generation of children to which marriage is ordered by its nature and by which the spouses become one flesh." But from the moral point of view procreation is deprived of its proper perfection when it is not desired as the fruit of the conjugal act, that is to say of the specific act of the spouses' union.*

2. The moral value of the intimate link between the goods of marriage and between the meanings of the conjugal act is based upon the unity of the

human being, a unity involving body and spiritual soul. Spouses mutually express their personal love in the "language of the body," which clearly involves both "spousal meanings" and parental ones. The conjugal act by which the couple mutually express their self-gift at the same time expresses openness to the gift of life. It is an act that is inseparably corporal and spiritual. It is in their bodies and through their bodies that the spouses consummate their marriage and are able to become father and mother. In order to respect the language of their bodies and their natural generosity, the conjugal union must take place with respect for its openness to procreation; and the procreation of a person must be the fruit and the result of married love. The origin of the human being thus follows from a procreation that is "linked to the union, not only biological but also spiritual, of the parents, made one by the bond of marriage." Fertilization achieved outside the bodies of the couple remains by this very fact deprived of the meanings and the values which are expressed in the language of the body and in the union of human persons.

3. Only respect for the link between the meanings of the conjugal act and respect for the unity of the human being make possible procreation in conformity with the dignity of the person. In his unique and irrepeatable origin, the child must be respected and recognized as equal in personal dignity to those who give him life. The human person must be accepted in his parents' act of union and love; the generation of a child must therefore be the fruit of that mutual giving which is realized in the conjugal act wherein the spouses cooperate as servants and not as masters in the work of the Creator, who is love.

In reality, the origin of a human person is the result of an act of giving. The one conceived must be the fruit of his parents' love. He cannot be desired or conceived as the product of an intervention of medical or biological techniques; that would be equivalent to reducing him to an object of scientific technology. No one may subject the coming of a child into the world to conditions of technical efficiency which are to be evaluated according to standards of control and dominion. *The moral relevance of the link between the meanings of the conjugal act*

and between the goods of marriage, as well as the unity of the human being and the dignity of his origin, demand that the procreation of a human person be brought about as the fruit of the conjugal act specific to the love between spouses. . . .

Is homologous "in vitro" fertilization morally licit?
The answer to this question is strictly dependent on the principles just mentioned. Certainly one cannot ignore the legitimate aspirations of sterile couples. For some, recourse to homologous *in vitro* fertilization and embryo transfer appears to be the only way of fulfilling their sincere desire for a child. The question is asked whether the totality of conjugal life in such situations is not sufficient to ensure the dignity proper to human procreation. It is acknowledged that *in vitro* fertilization and embryo transfer certainly cannot supply for the absence of sexual relations and cannot be preferred to the specific acts of conjugal union, given the risks involved for the child and the difficulties of the procedure. But it is asked whether, when there is no other way of overcoming the sterility which is a source of suffering, homologous *in vitro* fertilization may not constitute an aid, if not a form of therapy, whereby its moral licitness could be admitted. The desire for a child—or at least an openness to the transmission of life—is a necessary prerequisite from the moral point of view for responsible human procreation. But this good intention is not sufficient for making a positive moral evaluation of *in vitro* fertilization between spouses. The process of *in vitro* fertilization and embryo transfer must be judged in itself and cannot borrow its definitive moral quality from the totality of conjugal life of which it becomes part nor from the conjugal acts which may precede or follow it. . . .

It has already been recalled that, in the circumstances in which it is regularly practised, IVF and ET involves the destruction of human beings, which is something contrary to the doctrine on the illicitness of abortion previously mentioned. But even in a situation in which every precaution were taken to avoid the death of human embryos, homologous *in vitro* fertilization and embryo transfer dissociates from the conjugal act the actions which are directed to human fertilization. For this reason the very nature of homologous *in vitro* fertilization and embryo transfer also must be taken into account, even abstracting from the link with procured abortion. Homologous *in vitro* fertilization and embryo transfer is brought about outside the bodies of the couple through actions of third parties whose competence and technical activity determine the success of the procedure. Such fertilization entrusts the life and identity of the embryo into the power of doctors and biologists and establishes the domination of technology over the origin and destiny of the human person. Such a relationship of domination is in itself contrary to the dignity and equality that must be common to parents and children.

Conception *in vitro* is the result of the technical action which presides over fertilization. *Such fertilization is neither in fact achieved nor positively willed as the expression and fruit of a specific act of the conjugal union. In homologous "in vitro" fertilization and embryo transfer, therefore, even if it is considered in the context of de facto existing sexual relations, the generation of the human person is objectively deprived of its proper perfection: namely, that of being the result and fruit of a conjugal act* in which spouses can become "cooperators with God for giving life to a new person." . . . Although the manner in which human conception is achieved with *in vitro* fertilization and embryo transfer cannot be approved, every child which comes into the world must in any case be accepted as a living gift of the divine Goodness and must be brought up with love.

How is homologous artificial insemination to be evaluated from the moral point of view?

Homologous artificial insemination within marriage cannot be admitted except for those cases in which the technical means is not a substitute for the conjugal act but serves to facilitate and to help so that the act attains its natural purpose. . . .

"In its natural structure, the conjugal act is a personal action, a simultaneous and immediate cooperation on the part of the husband and wife, which by the very nature of the agents and the proper nature of the act is the expression of the mutual gift which, according to the words of Scripture, brings about union 'in one flesh.'" Thus moral conscience

"does not necessarily proscribe the use of certain artificial means destined solely either to the facilitating of the natural act or to ensuring that the natural act normally performed achieves its proper end." If the technical means facilitates the conjugal act or helps it to reach its natural objectives, it can be morally acceptable. If, on the other hand, the procedure were to replace the conjugal act, it is morally illicit.

Artificial insemination as a substitute for the conjugal act is prohibited by reason of the voluntarily achieved dissociation of the two meanings of the conjugal act. Masturbation, through which the sperm is normally obtained, is another sign of this dissociation: Even when it is done for the purpose of procreation the act remains deprived of its unitive meaning: "It lacks the sexual relationship called for by the moral order, namely the relationship which realizes 'the full sense of mutual self-giving and human procreation in the context of true love.'" . . .

What moral criterion can be proposed with regard to medical intervention in human procreation?

The medical act must be evaluated not only with reference to its technical dimension, but also and above all in relation to its goal, which is the good of persons and their bodily and psychological health. The moral criteria for medical intervention in procreation are deduced from the dignity of human persons, of their sexuality and of their origin.

Medicine which seeks to be ordered to the integral good of the person must respect the specifically human values of sexuality. The doctor is at the service of persons and of human procreation. He does not have the authority to dispose of them or to decide their fate. A medical intervention respects the dignity of persons when it seeks to assist the conjugal act either in order to facilitate its performance or in order to enable it to achieve its objective once it has been normally performed.

On the other hand, it sometimes happens that a medical procedure technologically replaces the conjugal act in order to obtain a procreation which is neither its result nor its fruit. In this case the medical act is not, as it should be, at the service of conjugal union, but rather appropriates to itself the procreative function and thus contradicts the dignity and the inalienable rights of the spouses and of the child to be born.

The humanization of medicine, which is insisted upon today by everyone, requires respect for the integral dignity of the human person first of all in the act and at the moment in which the spouses transmit life to a new person. It is only logical therefore to address an urgent appeal to Catholic doctors and scientists that they bear exemplary witness to the respect due to the human embryo and to the dignity of procreation. The medical and nursing staff of Catholic hospitals and clinics are in a special way urged to do justice to the moral obligations which they have assumed, frequently also, as part of their contract. Those who are in charge of Catholic hospitals and clinics and who are often religious will take special care to safeguard and promote a diligent observance of the moral norms recalled in the present instruction.

The suffering caused by infertility in marriage.
The suffering of spouses who cannot have children or who are afraid of bringing a handicapped child into the world is a suffering that everyone must understand and properly evalutate.

On the part of the spouses, the desire for a child is natural: It expresses the vocation to fatherhood and motherhood inscribed in conjugal love. This desire can be even stronger if the couple is affected by sterility which appears incurable. Nevertheless, marriage does not confer upon the spouses the right to have a child, but only the right to perform those natural acts which are per se ordered to procreation.

A true and proper right to a child would be contrary to the child's dignity and nature. The child is not an object to which one has a right nor can he be considered as an object of ownership: Rather, a child is a gift, "the supreme gift" and the most gratuitous gift of marriage, and is a living testimony of the mutual giving of his parents. For this reason, the child has the right as already mentioned, to be the fruit of the specific act of the conjugal love of his parents; and he also has the right to be respected as a person from the moment of his conception.

Nevertheless, whatever its cause or prognosis, sterility is certainly a difficult trial. The community of believers is called to shed light upon and support the suffering of those who are unable to fulfill their legitimate aspiration to motherhood and fatherhood. Spouses who find themselves in this sad situation are called to find in it an opportunity for sharing in a particular way in the Lord's cross, the source of spiritual fruitfulness. Sterile couples must not forget that "even when procreation is not possible, conjugal life does not for this reason lose its value. Physical sterility in fact can be for spouses the occasion for other important services to the life of the human person, for example, adoption, various forms of educational work and assistance to other families and to poor or handicapped children." Many researchers are engaged in the fight against sterility. While fully safeguarding the dignity of human procreation, some have achieved results which previously seemed unattainable. Scientists therefore are to be encouraged to continue their research with the aim of preventing the causes of sterility and of being able to remedy them so that sterile couples will be able to procreate in full respect for their own personal dignity and that of the child to be born.

The Presumptive Primacy of Procreative Liberty

JOHN A. ROBERTSON

Robertson argues for the fundamental freedom to reproduce or not to reproduce. This "procreative liberty," he says, equates to the right to make a reproductive choice without interference from others. The right not to procreate includes the freedom to use various methods to avoid begetting or bearing offspring, including abortion. The right to procreate includes the right to use "noncoital technologies" such as IVF. Robertson contends that procreative liberty can be overridden—but only by very weighty considerations.

Procreative liberty has wide appeal but its scope has never been fully elaborated and often is contested. The concept has several meanings that must be clarified if it is to serve as a reliable guide for moral debate and public policy regarding new reproductive technologies.

What Is Procreative Liberty?

At the most general level, procreative liberty is the freedom either to have children or to avoid having them. Although often expressed or realized in the context of a couple, it is first and foremost an individual interest. It is to be distinguished from freedom in the ancillary aspects of reproduction, such as liberty in the conduct of pregnancy or choice of place or mode of childbirth.

The concept of reproduction, however, has a certain ambiguity contained within it. In a strict sense, reproduction is always genetic. It occurs by provision of one's gametes to a new person, and thus includes having or producing offspring. While female reproduction has traditionally included gestation, in vitro fertilization (IVF) now allows female genetic and gestational reproduction to be separated. Thus a woman who has provided the egg that is carried by another has reproduced, even if she has not gestated and does not rear resulting offspring. Because of the close link between gestation and female reproduction, a woman who gestates the embryo of another may also reasonably be viewed as having a reproductive experience, even though she does not reproduce genetically.

In any case, reproduction in the genetic or gestational sense is to be distinguished from child rearing. Although reproduction is highly valued in part because it usually leads to child rearing, one can produce offspring without rearing them and rear children without reproduction. One who rears an adopted child has not reproduced, while one who has genetic progeny but does not rear them has.

In this [excerpt] the terms "procreative liberty" and "reproductive freedom" will mean the freedom to reproduce or not to reproduce in the genetic sense, which may also include rearing or not, as intended by the parties. Those terms will also include female gestation whether or not there is a genetic connection to the resulting child.

Often the reproduction at issue will be important because it is intended to lead to child rearing. In cases where rearing is not intended, the value to be assigned to reproduction *tout court* will have to be determined. Similarly, when there is rearing without genetic or gestational involvement, the value of nonreproductive child rearing will also have to be assessed. In both cases the value assigned may depend on the proximity to reproduction where rearing is intended.

Two further qualifications on the meaning of procreative liberty should be noted. One is that "liberty" as used in procreative liberty is a negative right. It means that a person violates no moral duty in making a procreative choice, and that other persons have a

From John A. Robertson, "The Presumptive Primacy of Procreative Liberty," *Children of Choice: Freedom and the New Reproductive Liberties* (Princeton Univ. Press, 1994). Notes deleted.

duty not to interfere with that choice. However, the negative right to procreate or not does not imply the duty of others to provide the resources or services necessary to exercise one's procreative liberty despite plausible moral arguments for governmental assistance.

As a matter of constitutional law, procreative liberty is a negative right against state interference with choices to procreate or to avoid procreation. It is not a right against private interference, though other laws might provide that protection. Nor is it a positive right to have the state or particular persons provide the means or resources necessary to have or avoid having children. The exercise of procreative liberty may be severely constrained by social and economic circumstances. Access to medical care, child care, employment, housing, and other services may significantly affect whether one is able to exercise procreative liberty. However, the state presently has no constitutional obligation to provide those services. Whether the state should alleviate those conditions is a separate issue of social justice.

The second qualification is that not everything that occurs in and around procreation falls within liberty interests that are distinctively procreative. Thus whether the father may be present during childbirth, whether midwives may assist birth, or whether childbirth may occur at home rather than in a hospital may be important for the parties involved, but they do not implicate the freedom to reproduce (unless one could show that the place or mode of birth would determine whether birth occurs at all). Similarly, questions about a pregnant woman's drug use or other conduct during pregnancy..., implicates liberty in the course of reproduction but not procreative liberty in the basic sense....

Procreative liberty should enjoy presumptive primacy when conflicts about its exercise arise because control over whether one reproduces or not is central to personal identity, to dignity, and to the meaning of one's life. For example, deprivation of the ability to avoid reproduction determines one's self-definition in the most basic sense. It affects women's bodies in a direct and substantial way. It also centrally affects one's psychological and social identity and one's social and moral responsibilities. The resulting burdens are especially onerous for women, but they affect men in significant ways as well.

On the other hand, being deprived of the ability to reproduce prevents one from an experience that is central to individual identity and meaning in life. Although the desire to reproduce is in part socially constructed, at the most basic level transmission of one's genes through reproduction is an animal or species urge closely linked to the sex drive. In connecting us with nature and future generations, reproduction gives solace in the face of death. As Shakespeare noted, "nothing 'gainst Time's scythe can make defense/save breed." For many people "breed"—reproduction and the parenting that usually accompanies it—is a central part of their life plan, and the most satisfying and meaningful experience they have. It also has primary importance as an expression of a couple's love or unity. For many persons, reproduction also has religious significance and is experienced as a "gift from God." Its denial—through infertility or governmental restriction—is experienced as a great loss, even if one has already had children or will have little or no rearing role with them.

Decisions to have or to avoid having children are thus personal decisions of great import that determine the shape and meaning of one's life. The person directly involved is best situated to determine whether that meaning should or should not occur. An ethic of personal autonomy as well as ethics of community or family should then recognize a presumption in favour of most personal reproductive choices. Such a presumption does not mean that reproductive choices are without consequence to others, nor that they should never be limited. Rather, it means that those who would limit procreative choice have the burden of showing that the reproductive actions at issue would create such substantial harm that they could justifiably be limited. Of course, what counts as the "substantial harm" that justifies interference with procreative choice may often be contested, as the discussion of reproductive technologies in this book will show.

A closely related reason for protecting reproductive choice is to avoid the highly intrusive measures that governmental control of reproduction usually entails. State interference with reproductive choice may extend beyond exhortation and penalties to gestapo and police state tactics. Margaret Atwood's powerful futuristic novel *The Handmaid's Tale* expresses this danger by creating a world where fertile women are forcibly impregnated by the ruling powers and their pregnancies monitored to replenish a decimated population....

Two Types of Procreative Liberty

To see how values of procreative liberty affect the ethical and public policy evaluation of new reproductive technologies, we must determine whether the interests that underlie the high value accorded procreative liberty are implicated in their use. This is not a simple task because procreative liberty is not unitary, but consists of strands of varying interests in the conception and gestation of offspring. The different strands implicate different interests, have different legal and constitutional status, and are differently affected by technology.

An essential distinction is between the freedom to avoid reproduction and the freedom to reproduce. When people talk of reproductive rights, they usually have one or the other aspect in mind. Because different interests and justifications underlie each and countervailing interests for limiting each aspect vary, recognition of one aspect does not necessarily mean that the other will also be respected; nor does limitation of one mean that the other can also be denied.

However, there is a mirroring or reciprocal relationship here. Denial of one type of reproductive liberty necessarily implicates the other. If a woman is not able to avoid reproduction through contraception or abortion, she may end up reproducing, with all the burdens that unwanted reproduction entails. Similarly, if one is denied the liberty to reproduce through forcible sterilization, one is forced to avoid reproduction, thus experiencing the loss that absence of progeny brings. By extending reproductive options, new reproductive technologies present challenges to both aspects of procreative choice.

Avoiding Reproduction: The Liberty Not to Reproduce

One sense in which people commonly understand procreative liberty is as the freedom to avoid reproduction—to avoid begetting or bearing offspring and the rearing demands they make. Procreative liberty in this sense could involve several different choices, because decisions to avoid procreation arise at several different stages. A decision not to procreate could occur prior to conception through sexual abstinence, contraceptive use, or refusal to seek treatment for infertility. At this stage, the main issues concern freedom to refrain from sexual intercourse, the freedom to use contraceptives, and the freedom to withhold gametes for use in noncoital conception. Countervailing interests concern societal interests in increasing population, a partner's interest in sexual intimacy and progeny, and moral views about the unity of sex and reproduction.

Once pregnancy has occurred, reproduction can be avoided only by termination of pregnancy. Procreative freedom here would involve the freedom to abort the pregnancy. Competing interests are protection of embryos and fetuses and respect for human life generally, the most heated issue of reproductive rights. They may also include moral or social beliefs about the connectedness of sex and reproduction, or views about a woman's reproductive and work roles.

Once a child is born, procreation has occurred, and the procreators ordinarily have parenting obligations. Freeing oneself from rearing obligations is not strictly speaking a matter of procreative liberty, though it is an important personal interest. Even if parents relinquish the child for adoption, the psychological reality that one has reproduced remains. Opposing interests at this stage involve the need to provide parenting, nurturing, and financial support to offspring. The right to be free of those obligations, as well as the right to assume them after birth occurs, is not directly addressed in this book except to the extent that those rights affect reproductive decisions....

The Freedom to Procreate

In addition to freedom to avoid procreation, procreative liberty also includes the freedom to procreate—the freedom to beget and bear children if one chooses. As with avoiding reproduction, the right to reproduce is a negative right against public or private interference, not a positive right to the services or the resources needed to reproduce. It is an important freedom that is widely accepted as a basic, human right. But its various components and dimensions have never been fully analyzed, as technologies of conception and selection now force us to do.

As with avoiding reproduction, the freedom to procreate involves the freedom to engage in a series of actions that eventuate in reproduction and usually in child rearing. One must be free to marry or find a willing partner, engage in sexual intercourse, achieve conception and pregnancy, carry a pregnancy to term, and rear offspring. Social and natural barriers to reproduction would involve the unavailability of willing or suitable partners, impotence or infertility, and lack of medical and child-care resources. State barriers to marriage, to sexual intercourse, to conception, to infertility treatment, to carrying pregnancies to term, and to certain child-rearing arrangements would also limit the freedom to procreate. The most commonly asserted reasons for limiting coital reproduction are overpopulation, unfitness of parents, harm to offspring, and costs to the state or others. Technologies that treat infertility raise additional concerns that are discussed below.

The moral right to reproduce is respected because of the centrality of reproduction to personal identity, meaning, and dignity. This importance makes the liberty to procreate an important moral right, both for an ethic of individual autonomy and for ethics of community or family that view the purpose of marriage and sexual union as the reproduction and rearing of offspring. Because of this importance, the right to reproduce is widely recognized as a prima facie moral right that cannot be limited except for very good reason.

Recognition of the primacy of procreation does not mean that all reproduction is morally blameless, much less that reproduction is always responsible and praiseworthy and can never be limited. However, the presumptive primacy of procreative liberty sets a very high standard for limiting those rights, tilting the balance in favor of reproducing but not totally determining its acceptability. A two-step process of analysis is envisaged here. The first question is whether a distinctively procreative interest is involved. If so, the question then is whether the harm threatened by reproduction satisfies the strict standard for overriding this liberty interest....

An entirely different set of concerns arises with noncoital reproductive techniques. Charges that noncoital reproduction is unethical or irresponsible arise because of its expense, its highly technological character, its decomposition of parenthood into genetic, gestational, and social components, and its potential effects on women and offspring. To assess whether these effects justify moral condemnation or public limitation, we must first determine whether noncoital reproduction implicates important aspects of procreative liberty.

The Right to Reproduce and Noncoital Technology

If the moral right to reproduce presumptively protects coital reproduction, then it should protect noncoital reproduction as well. The moral right of the coitally infertile to reproduce is based on the same desire for offspring that the coitally fertile have. They too wish to replicate themselves, transmit genes, gestate, and rear children biologically related to them. Their infertility should no more disqualify them from reproductive experiences than physical disability should disqualify persons from walking with mechanical assistance. The unique risks posed by noncoital reproduction may provide independent justifications for limiting its use, but neither the noncoital nature of the means used nor the infertility of their beneficiaries mean that the presumptively protected moral interest in reproduction is not present.

A major question about this position, however, is whether the noncoital or collaborative nature of the means used truly implicates reproductive interests. For example, what if only one aspect of reproduction—genetic transfer, gestation, or rearing—occurs, as happens with gamete donors or surrogates who play no rearing role? Is a person's procreative liberty substantially implicated in such partial reproductive roles? The answer will depend on the value attributed to the particular collaborative contribution and on whether the collaborative enterprise is viewed from the donor's or recipient's perspective.

Gamete donors and surrogates are clearly reproducing even though they have no intention to rear. Because reproduction *tout court* may seem less important than reproduction with intent to rear, the donor's reproductive interest may appear less important. However, more experience with these practices is needed to determine the inherent value of "partial" reproductive experiences to donors and surrogates. Experience may show that it is independently meaningful, regardless of their contact with offspring. If not, then countervailing interests would more easily override their right to enter these roles.

Viewed from the recipient's perspective, however, the donor or surrogate's reproduction *tout court* does not lessen the reproductive importance of her contribution. A woman who receives an egg or embryo donation has no genetic connection with offspring but has a gestational relation of great personal significance. In addition, gamete donors and surrogates enable one or both rearing partners to have a biological relation with offspring. If one of them has no biological connection at all, they will still have a strong interest in rearing their partner's biologic offspring. Whether viewed singly through the eyes of the partner who is reproducing, or jointly as an endeavor of a couple seeking to rear children who are biologically related to at least one of the two, a significant reproductive interest is at stake. If so, noncoital, collaborative treatments for infertility should be respected to the same extent as coital reproduction is.

Questions about the core meaning of reproduction will also arise in the temporal dislocations that cryopreservation of sperm and embryos make possible. For example, embryo freezing allows siblings to be conceived at the same time, but born years apart and to different gestational mothers. Twins could be created by splitting one embryo into two. If one half is frozen for later use, identical twins could be born at widely different times. Sperm, egg, and embryo freezing also make posthumous reproduction possible.

Such temporally dislocative practices clearly implicate core reproductive interests when the ultimate recipient has no alternative means of re-production. However, if the procreative interests of the recipient couple are not directly implicated, we must ask whether those whose gametes are used have an independent procreative interest, as might occur if they directed that gametes or embryos be thawed after their death for purposes of posthumous reproduction.

In that case the question is whether the expectancy of posthumous reproduction is so central to an individual's procreative identity or life-plan that it should receive the same respect that one's reproduction when alive receives. The answer to such a question will be important in devising policy for storing and posthumously disposing of gametes and embryos. The answer will also affect inheritance questions and have implications for management of pregnant women who are irreversibly comatose or brain dead.

The problem of determining whether technology implicates a major reproductive interest also arises with technologies that select offspring characteristics. Some degree of quality control would seem logically to fall within the realm of procreative liberty. For many couples the decision whether to procreate depends on the ability to have healthy children. Without some guarantee or protection against the risk of handicapped children, they might not reproduce at all.

Thus viewed, quality control devices become part of the liberty interest in procreating or in avoiding procreation, and arguably should receive the same degree of protection. If so, genetic screening and selective abortion, as well as the right to select a mate or a source for donated eggs, sperm, or embryos should be protected as part of procreative liberty. The same arguments would apply to positive interventions to cure disease at the fetal or embryo stage. However, futuristic practices such as nontherapeutic enhancement, cloning, or intentional diminishment of offspring characteristics may so deviate from the core interests that make reproduction meaningful as to fall outside the protective canopy of procreative liberty.

Finally, technology will present questions of whether one may use one's reproductive capacity to produce gametes, embryos, and fetuses for nonreproductive uses in research or therapy. Here the purpose is not to have children to rear, but to get material for research or transplant. Are such uses of reproductive capacity tied closely enough to the values and interests that underlie procreative freedom to warrant similar respect? Even if procreative choice is not directly involved, other liberties may protect the activity.

Are Noncoital Technologies Unethical?

If this analysis is accepted, then procreative liberty would include the right to use noncoital and other technologies to form a family and shape the characteristics of offspring. Neither infertility nor the fact that one will only partially reproduce eliminates the existence of a prima facie reproductive experience for someone. However, judgments about the proximity of these partial reproductive experiences to the core meanings of reproduction will be required in balancing those claims against competing moral concerns.

Judgment about the reproductive importance of noncoital technologies is crucial because many people have serious ethical reservations about them, and are more than willing to restrict their use. The concerns here are not the fears of overpopulation, parental unfitness, and societal costs that arise with allegedly irresponsible coital reproduction. Instead, they include reduction of demand for hard-to-adopt children, the coercive or exploitive bargains that will be offered to poor women, the commodification of both children and reproductive collaborators, the objectification of women as reproductive vessels, and the undermining of the nuclear family.

However, often the harms feared are deontological in character. In some cases they stem from a religious or moral conception of the unity of sex and reproduction or the definition of family. Such a view characterizes the Vatican's strong opposition to IVF, donor sperm, and other noncoital and collaborative techniques. Other deontological concerns derive from a particular conception of the proper reproductive role of women. Many persons, for example, oppose paid surrogate motherhood because of a judgment about the wrongness of a woman's willingness to sever the mother-child bond for the sake of money. They also insist that the gestational mother is always morally entitled to rear, despite her preconception promise to the contrary. Closely related are dignitary objections to allowing any reproductive factors to be purchased, or to having offspring selected on the basis of their genes.

Finally, there is a broader concern that noncoital reproduction will undermine the deeper community interest in having a clear social framework to define boundaries of families, sexuality, and reproduction. The traditional family provides a container for the narcissism and irrationality that often drives human reproduction. This container assures commitments to the identifications and taboos that protect children from various types of abuse. The technical ability to disaggregate and recombine genetic, gestational, and rearing connections and to control the genes of offspring may thus undermine essential protections for offspring, couples, families, and society.

These criticisms are powerful ones that explain much of the ambivalence that surrounds the use of certain reproductive technologies. They call into question the wisdom of individual decisions to use them, and the willingness of society to promote or facilitate their use. Unless one is operating out of a specific religious or deontological ethic, however, they do not show that all individual uses of these techniques are immoral, much less that public policy should restrict or discourage their use....

Resolving Disputes Over Procreative Liberty

As this brief survey shows, new reproductive technologies will generate ethical and legal disputes about the meaning and scope of procreative liberty. Because procreative liberty has never been fully elaborated, the importance of procreative choice in many novel settings will be a question of first impression. The ultimate decision reached will reflect the value assigned to the procreative interest at stake in light of the effects causing concern. In an important sense, the meaning of procreative liberty will be created or constituted for society in the process of resolving such disputes.

If procreative liberty is taken seriously, a strong presumption in favor of using technologies that centrally implicate reproductive interests should be recognized. Although procreative rights are not absolute, those who would limit procreative choice should have the burden of establishing substantial harm. This is the standard used in ethical and legal analyses of restrictions on traditional reproductive decisions. Because the same procreative goals are involved, the same standard of scrutiny should be used for assessing moral or governmental restrictions on novel reproductive techniques.

In arbitrating these disputes, one has to come to terms with the importance of procreative interests relative to other concerns. The precise procreative interest at stake must be identified and weighed against the core values of reproduction. As noted, this will raise novel and unique questions when the technology deviates from the model of two-person coital reproduction, or otherwise disaggregates or alters ordinary reproductive practices. However, if an important reproductive interest exists, then use of the technology should be presumptively permitted. Only substantial harm to tangible interests of others should then justify restriction.

In determining whether such harm exists, it will be necessary to distinguish between harms to individuals and harms to personal conceptions of morality, right order, or offense, discounted by their probability of occurrence. As previously noted, many objections to reproductive technology rest on differing views of what "proper" or "right" reproduction is aside from tangible effects on others. For example, concerns about the decomposition of parenthood through the use of donors and surrogates, about the temporal alteration of conception, gestation and birth, about the alienation or commercialization of gestational capacity, and about selection and control of offspring characteristics do not directly affect persons so much as they affect notions of right behavior. Disputes over early abortion and discard or manipulation of IVF-created embryos also exemplify this distinction, if we grant that the embryo/previable fetus is not a person or entity with rights in itself.

At issue in these cases is the symbolic or constitutive meaning of actions regarding prenatal life, family, maternal gestation, and respect for persons over which people in a secular, pluralistic society often differ. A majoritarian view of "right" reproduction or "right" valuation of prenatal life, family, or the role of women should not suffice to restrict actions based on differing individual views of such preeminently personal issues. At a certain point, however, a practice such as cloning, enhancement, or intentional diminishment of offspring may be so far removed from even pluralistic notions of reproductive meaning that they leave the realm of protected reproductive choice. People may differ over where that point is, but it will not easily exclude most reproductive technologies of current interest.

To take procreative liberty seriously, then, is to allow it to have presumptive priority in an individual's life. This will give persons directly involved the final say about use of a particular technology, unless tangible harm to the interests of others can be shown. Of course, people may differ over whether an important procreative interest is at stake or over how serious the harm posed from use of the reproductive technology is. Such a focused debate, however, is legitimate and ultimately essential in developing ethical standards and public policy for use of new reproductive technologies.

The Limits of Procreative Liberty

The emphasis on procreative liberty that informs this book provides a useful but by no means complete or final perspective on the technologies in question. Theological, social, psychological, economic, and feminist perspectives would emphasize different aspects of reproductive technology, and might be much less sanguine about potential benefits and risks. Such perspectives might also offer better guidance in how to use these technologies to protect offspring, respect women, and maintain other important values.

A strong rights perspective has other limitations as well. Recognition of procreative liberty, whether in traditional or in new technological settings, does not guarantee that people will achieve their reproductive goals, much less that they will be happy with what they do achieve. Nature may be recalcitrant to the latest technology. Individuals may lack the will, the perseverance, or the resources to use effective technologies. Even if they do succeed, the results may be less satisfying than envisaged. In addition, many individual instances of procreative choice may cumulate into larger social changes that from our current vantage point seem highly undesirable. But these are the hazards and limitations of any scheme of individual rights.

Recognition of procreative liberty will protect the right of persons to use technology in pursuing their reproductive goals, but it will not eliminate the ambivalence that such technologies engender. Societal ambivalence about reproductive technology is recapitulated at the individual level, as individuals and couples struggle with whether to use the technologies in question. Thus recognition of procreative liberty will not eliminate the dilemmas of personal choice and responsibility that reproductive choice entails. The freedom to act does not mean that we will act wisely, yet denying that freedom may be even more unwise, for it denies individuals' respect in the most fundamental choices of their lives.

Surrogate Mothering: Exploitation or Empowerment?

LAURA M. PURDY

Taking a consequentialist approach, Purdy asserts that in some cases the benefits of surrogate mothering may outweigh its costs and thus be morally permissible. Some feminists argue that the practice is necessarily wrong because it transfers the burden and risks of pregnancy from one woman to another, because it separates sex from reproduction, or because it separates reproduction from child-rearing. But Purdy finds these arguments unconvincing. She examines the claim that surrogacy is baby-selling and concludes that "selling babies" is not an accurate description of what happens in surrogacy. A better characterization is that the birth mother is "giving up her parental right to have a relationship with the child." Certainly in some circumstances, surrogate mothering can be rendered immoral by coercion of the surrogate or by unjust surrogacy contracts. "Fair and reasonable regulations," she says, "are essential to prevent exploitation of women."

Introduction

"Pregnacy is barbaric"[1] proclaimed Shulamith Firestone in the first heady days of the new women's movement; she looked forward to the time when technology would free women from the oppression of biological reproduction. Yet as reproductive options multiply, some feminists are making common cause with conservatives for a ban on innovations. What is going on?

Firestone argued that nature oppresses women by leaving them holding the reproductive bag, while men are free of such burden; so long as this biological inequality holds, women will never be free (pp. 198–200). It is now commonplace to point out the naivety of her claim: it is not the biological difference per se that oppresses women, but its social significance. So we need not change biology, only attitudes and institutions.

This insight has helped us to see how to achieve a better life for women, but I wonder if it is the whole story. Has Firestone's brave claim no lesson at all for us?

Her point was that being with child is uncomfortable and dangerous, and it can limit women's lives. We have become more sensitive to the ways in which social arrangements can determine how much these difficulties affect us. However, even in feminist utopias, where sex or gender are considered morally irrelevant except where they may entail special needs, a few difficulties would remain. Infertility, for instance, would exist, as would the desire for a child in circumstances where pregnancy is impossible or undesirable.

At present, the problem of infertility is generating a whole series of responses and solutions. Among them are high-tech procedures like IVF, and social arrangements like surrogate motherhood. Both these techniques are also provoking a storm of concern and protest. As each raises a distinctive set

From *Bioethics*, vol. 3, no. 1 (1989), pp. 18–34. Copyright © Basil Blackwell Ltd. Reprinted with permission.

of issues, they need to be dealt with separately, and I shall here consider only surrogate motherhood.

One might argue that no feminist paradise would need any practice such as this. As Susan Sherwin argues, it could not countenance "the capitalism, racism, sexism, and elitism of our culture [that] have combined to create a set of attitudes which views children as commodities whose value is derived from their possession of parental chromosomes."[2] Nor will society define women's fulfilment as only in terms of their relationship to genetically-related children. No longer will children be needed as men's heirs or women's livelihood.

We will, on the contrary, desire relationships with children for the right reasons: the urge to nurture, teach and be close to them. No longer will we be driven by narcissistic wishes for clones or immortality to seek genetic offspring no matter what the cost. Indeed, we will have recognized that children are the promise and responsibility of the whole human community. And child-rearing practices will reflect these facts, including at least a more diffuse family life that allows children to have significant relationships with others. Perhaps child-rearing will be communal.

This radically different world is hard to picture realistically, even by those like myself who—I think—most ardently wish for it. The doubts I feel are fanned by the visions of so-called cultural feminists who glorify traditionally feminine values. Family life can be suffocating, distorting, even deadly.[3] Yet there is a special closeness that arises from being a child's primary caretaker, just as there can be a special thrill in witnessing the unfolding of biologically-driven traits in that child. These pleasures justify risking neither the health of the child[4] nor that of the mother; nobody's general well-being should be sacrificed to them, nor do they warrant high social investment. However, they are things that, other things being equal, it would be desirable to preserve so long as people continue to have anything like their current values. If this is so, then evaluating the morality of practices that open up new ways of creating children is worthwhile.[5]

Moral or Immoral?

What is surrogate mothering exactly? Physically, its essential features are as follows: a woman is inseminated with the sperm of a man to whom she is not married. When the baby is born she relinquishes her claim to it in favour of another, usually the man from whom the sperm was obtained. As currently practiced, she provides the egg, so her biological input is at least equal to that of the man.[6] Surrogate mothering may not therefore be the best term for what she is doing.

By doing these things she also acts socially—to take on the burden and risk of pregnancy for another, and to separate sex and reproduction, reproduction and child-rearing, and reproduction and marriage. If she takes money for the transaction (apart from payment of medical bills), she may even be considered to be selling a baby.

The bare physical facts would not warrant the welter of accusation and counter-accusation that surrounds the practice.[7] It is the social aspects that have engendered the acrimony about exploitation, destruction of the family, and baby-selling. So far we have reached no consensus about the practice's effect on women or its overall morality.

I believe that the appropriate moral framework for addressing questions about the social aspects of contracted pregnancy is consequentialist.[8] This framework requires us to attempt to separate those consequences that invariably accompany a given act from those that accompany it only in particular circumstances. Doing this compels us to consider whether a practice's necessary features lead to unavoidable overridingly bad consequences. It also demands that we look at how different circumstances are likely to affect the outcome. Thus a practice which is moral in a feminist society may well be immoral in a sexist one. This distinction allows us to tailor morality to different conditions for optimum results without thereby incurring the charge of malignant relativism.

Before examining arguments against the practice of contracted pregnancy, let us take note of why people might favour it. First, as noted before, alleviating infertility can create much happiness. Secondly, there are often good reasons to consider transferring burden and risk from one individual to another. Pregnancy may be a serious burden or risk for one woman, whereas it is much less so for another. Some women love being pregnant, others hate it; pregnancy interferes with work for some, not for others; pregnancy also poses much higher levels of risk to health (or even life) for some than for others. Reducing burden and risk is a benefit not only for the woman involved, but also for the resulting child. High-risk pregnancies create, among other things, serious risk of prematurity, one of the major sources of handicap in babies. Furthermore, we could prevent serious genetic diseases by allowing carriers to avoid pregnancy. A third benefit of "surrogate mothering" is that it makes possible the creation of non-traditional families. This can be a significant source of happiness to single women and gay couples.

All of the above presuppose that there is some advantage in making possible at least partially genetically-based relationships between parents and offspring. Although, as I have argued above, we might be better off without this desire, I doubt that we will soon be free of it. Therefore, if we can satisfy it at little cost, we should try to do so.

Is Surrogate Mothering Always Wrong?

Despite the foregoing advantages, some feminists argue that the practice is *necessarily* wrong: it is wrong because it must betray women's and society's basic interests.[9]

What, if anything is wrong with the practice? Let us consider the first three acts I described earlier: transferring burden and risk, separating sex and reproduction, and separating reproduction and child-rearing. Separation of reproduction and marriage will not be dealt with here.

Is it wrong to take on the burden of pregnancy for another? Doing this is certainly supererogatory, for pregnancy can threaten comfort, health, even life. One might argue that women should not be allowed to take these risks, but that would be paternalistic. We do not forbid mountain-climbing or riding a motorcycle on these grounds. How could we then forbid a woman to undertake this particular risk?

Perhaps the central issue is the transfer of burden from one woman to another. However, we frequently do just that—much more often than we recognize. Anyone who has her house cleaned, her hair done, or her clothes dry-cleaned is engaging in this procedure;[10] so is anyone who depends on agriculture or public works such as bridges.[11] To the objection that in this case the bargain includes the risk to

life and limb, as well as use of time and skills, the answer is that the other activities just cited entail surprisingly elevated risk rates from exposure to toxic chemicals or dangerous machinery.[12]

Furthermore, it is not even true that contracted pregnancy merely shifts the health burden and risks associated with pregnancy from one woman to another. In some cases (infertility, for example) it makes the impossible possible; in others (for women with potentially high-risk pregnancies) the net risk is lowered.[13] As we saw, babies benefit, too, from better health and fewer handicaps. Better health and fewer handicaps in both babies and women also means that scarce resources can be made available for other needs, thus benefiting society in general.

I do think that there is, in addition, something suspect about all this new emphasis on risk. Awareness of risks inherent in even normal pregnancy constitutes progress: women have always been expected to forge ahead with child-bearing oblivious to risk. Furthermore, child-bearing has been thought to be something women owed to men or to society at large, regardless of their own feelings about a given—or any—pregnancy. When women had little say about these matters, we never heard about risk.[14] Why are we hearing about risk only now, now that women finally have some choices, some prospect of remuneration?[15] For that matter, why is our attention not drawn to the fact that surrogacy is one of the least risky approaches to non-traditional reproduction?[16]

Perhaps what is wrong about this kind of transfer is that it necessarily involves exploitation. Such exploitation may take the form of exploitation of women by men and exploitation of the rich by the poor. This possibility deserves serious consideration, and will be dealt with shortly.

Is there anything wrong with the proposed separation of sex and reproduction? Historically, this separation—in the form of contraception—has been beneficial to women and to society as a whole. Although there are those who judge the practice immoral, I do not think we need belabour the issue here.

It may be argued that not all types of separation are morally on a par. Contraception is permissible, because it spares women's health, promotes autonomy, strengthens family life, and helps make population growth manageable. But separation of sex and reproduction apart from contraception is quite another kettle of fish: it exploits women, weakens family life, and may increase population. Are these claims true and relevant?

Starting with the last first, if we face a population problem, it would make sense to rethink overall population policy, not exploit the problems of the infertile.[17] If family strengthing is a major justification for contraception, we might point out that contracted pregnancy will in some cases do the same. Whether or not having children can save a failing marriage, it will certainly prevent a man who wants children from leaving a woman incapable of providing them. We may bewail his priorities, but if his wife is sufficiently eager for the relationship to continue it would again be paternalistic for us to forbid "surrogacy" in such circumstances. That "surrogacy" reduces rather than promotes women's autonomy may be true under some circumstances, but there are good grounds for thinking that it can also enhance autonomy. It also remains to be shown that the practice systematically burdens women, or one class of women. In principle, the availability of new choices can be expected to nourish rather than stunt women's lives, so long as they retain control over their bodies and lives. The claim that contracted pregnancy destroys women's individuality and constitutes alienated labour, as Christine Overall argues, depends not only on a problematic Marxist analysis, but on the assumption that other jobs available to women are seriously less alienating.[18]

Perhaps what is wrong here is that contracted pregnancy seems to be the other side of the coin of prostitution. Prostitution is sex without reproduction; "surrogacy" is reproduction without sex. But it is difficult to form a persuasive argument that goes beyond mere guilt by association. Strictly speaking, contracted pregnancy is not prostitution; a broad-based Marxist definition would include it, but also traditional marriage. I think that in the absence of further argument, the force of this accusation is primarily emotional.

Perhaps the dreaded feature contracted pregnancy shares with prostitution is that it is a lazy person's way of exploiting their own "natural resources." But I suspect that this idea reveals a touchingly naive view of what it takes to be a successful prostitute, not to mention the effort involved in running an optimum pregnancy. Overall takes up this point by asserting that it

> is not and cannot be merely one career choice among others. It is not a real alternative. It is implausible to suppose that fond parents would want it for their daughters. We are unlikely to set up training courses for surrogate mothers. Schools holding "career days" for their future graduates will surely not invite surrogate mothers to address the class on advantages of "vocation." And surrogate motherhood does not seem to be the kind of thing one would put on one's curriculum vitae. (p. 126)

But this seems to me to be a blatant *ad populum* argument.

Such an objection ought, in any case, to entail general condemnation of apparently effortless ways of life that involved any utilization of our distinctive characteristics.

We surely exploit our personal "natural resources" whenever we work. Ditchdiggers use their bodies, professors use their minds. Overall seems particularly to object to some types of "work": contracted pregnancy "is no more a real job option than selling one's blood or one's gametes or one's bodily organs can be real job options" (p. 126). But her discussion makes clear that her denial that such enterprises are "real" jobs is not based on any social arrangements that preclude earning a living wage doing these things, but rather on the moral judgement that they are wrong. They are wrong because they constitute serious "personal and bodily alienation." Yet her arguments for such alienation are weak. She contends that women who work as "surrogates" are deprived of any expression of individuality (p. 126), are interchangeable (p. 127), and that they have no choice about whose sperm to harbour (p. 128). It is true that, given a reasonable environment (partly provided by the woman herself), bodies create babies without conscious effort. This fact, it seems to me, has no particular moral significance: many tasks can be accomplished in similar ways yet are not thought valueless.[19]

It is also usually true that women involved in contracted pregnancy are, in some sense, interchangeable. But the same is true, quite possibly necessarily so, of most jobs. No one who has graded mounds of logic exams or introductory ethics essays could reasonably withhold their assent to this claim, even though college teaching is one of the most autonomous careers available. Even those of us lucky enough to teach upper-level courses that involve more expression of individual expertise and choice can be slotted into standardized job descriptions. Finally, it is just false that a woman can have no say about whose sperm she accepts: this could be guaranteed by proper regulation.

I wonder whether there is not some subtle devaluing of the physical by Overall. If so, then we are falling into the trap set by years of elitist equations of women, nature and inferiority.

What I think is really at issue here is the disposition of the fruit of contracted pregnancy: babies. However, it seems to be generally permissible to dispose of or barter what we produce with both our minds and our bodies—except for that which is created by our reproductive organs. So the position we are considering may just be a version of the claim that it is wrong to separate reproduction and child-rearing.

Why? It is true that women normally expect to become especially attached to the product of this particular kind of labour, and we generally regard such attachment as desirable. It seems to be essential for successfully rearing babies the usual way. But if they are to be reared by others who are able to form the appropriate attachment, then what is wrong if a surrogate mother fails to form it? It seems to me that the central question here is whether this "maternal instinct" really exists, and, if it does, whether suppressing it is always harmful.

Underlying these questions is the assumption that bonding with babies is "natural" and therefore "good." Perhaps so: the evolutionary advantage of such a tendency would be clear. It would be simple-minded, however, to assume that our habits are biologically determined: our culture is permeated with pronatalist bias.[20] "Natural" or not, whether a tendency to such attachment is desirable could reasonably be judged to depend on circumstance. When infant mortality is high[21] or responsibility for child-rearing is shared by the community, it could do more harm than good. Beware the naturalistic fallacy![22]

But surely there is something special about gestating a baby. That is, after all, the assumption behind the judgement that Mary Beth Whitehead, not William Stern, had a stronger claim to Baby M. The moral scoreboard seems clear: they both had the same genetic input, but she gestated the baby, and therefore has a better case for social parenthood.[23]

We need to be very careful here. Special rights have a way of being accompanied by special responsibilities: women's unique gestational relationship with babies may be taken as reason to confine them once more to the nursery. Furthermore, positing special rights entailed directly by biology flirts again with the naturalistic fallacy and undermines our capacity to adapt to changing situations and forge our destiny.[24]

Furthermore, we already except many varieties of such separation. We routinely engage in sending children to boarding school, foster parenting, daycare, and so forth; in the appropriate circumstances, these practices are clearly beneficial. Hence, any blanket condemnation of separating reproduction and child-rearing will not wash; additional argument is needed for particular classes of cases.

John Robertson points out that the arguments against separating reproduction and child-rearing used against contracted pregnancy are equally valid—but unused—with respect to adoption.[25] Others, such as Herbert Krimmel, reject this view by arguing that there is a big moral difference between giving away an already existing baby and deliberately creating one to give away. This remains to be shown, I think. It is also argued that as adoption outcomes are rather negative, we should be wary of extending any practice that shares its essential features. In fact, there seems to be amazingly little hard information about adoption outcomes. I wonder if the idea that they are bad results from media reports of offspring seeking their biological forebears. There is, in any case, reason to think that there are differences between the two practices such that the latter is likely to be more successful than the former.[26]

None of the social descriptions of surrogacy thus seem to clearly justify the outcry against the practice. I suspect that the remaining central issue is the crucial one: surrogacy is baby-selling and participating in this practice exploits and taints women.

Is Surrogacy Baby-Selling?

In the foregoing, I deliberately left vague the question of payment in contracted pregnancy. It is clear that there is a recognizable form of the practice that does not include payment; however, it also seems clear that controversy is focusing on the commercial form. The charge is that it is baby-selling and that this is wrong.

Is paid "surrogacy" baby-selling? Proponents deny that it is, arguing that women are merely making available their biological services. Opponents retort that as women are paid little or nothing if they fail to hand over a live, healthy child, they are indeed selling a baby. If they are merely selling their services they would get full pay, even if the child were born dead.

It is true women who agree to contracts relieving clients of responsibility in this case are being exploited. They, after all, have done their part, risked their risks, and should be paid—just like the physicians involved. Normal child-bearing provides no guarantee of a live, healthy child—why should contracted pregnancy?

There are further reasons for believing that women are selling their services, not babies. Firstly, we do not consider children property. Therefore, as we cannot sell what we do not own, we cannot be selling babies. What creates confusion here is that we do think we own sperm and ova. (Otherwise, how could men sell their sperm?) Yet we do not own what they become, persons. At what point, then, does the relationship cease to be describable as "ownership"?

Resolution of this question is not necessary to the current discussion. If we can own babies, there seems to be nothing problematic about selling them. If ownership ceases at some time before birth (and could thus be argued to be unconnected with personhood), then it is not selling of babies that is going on.

Although this response deals with the letter of the objection about baby-selling, it fails to heed its spirit, which is that we are trafficking in persons, and that such trafficking is wrong. Even if we are not "selling," something nasty is happening.

The most common analogy, with slavery, is weak. Slavery is wrong according to any decent moral theory: the institution allows people to be treated badly. Their desires and interests, whose satisfaction is held to be essential for a good life, are held in contempt. Particularly egregious is the callous disregard of emotional ties to family and self-determination generally. But the institution of surrogate mothering deprives babies of neither.[27] In short, as Robertson contends, "the purchasers do not buy the right to treat the child . . . as a commodity or property. Child abuse and neglect laws still apply" (p. 655).

If "selling babies" is not the right description of what is occurring, then how are we to explain what happens when the birth mother hands the child over to others? One plausible suggestion is that she is giving up her parental right to have a relationship with the child.[28] That it is wrong to do this for pay remains to be shown. Although it would be egoistic and immoral to "sell" an ongoing, friendly relationship (doing so would raise questions about whether it was friendship at all), the immorality of selling a relationship with an organism your body has created but with which you do not yet have a unique social bond, is a great deal less clear.[29]

People seem to feel much less strongly about the wrongness of such acts when motivated by altruism; refusing compensation is the only acceptable proof of such altruism. The act is, in any case, socially valuable. Why then must it be motivated by altruistic considerations? We do not frown upon those who provide other socially valuable services even when they do not have the "right" motive. Nor do we require them to be unpaid. For instance, no one expects physicians, no matter what their motivation, to work for beans. They provide an important service; their motivation is important only to the extent that it affects quality.

In general, workers are required to have appropriate skills, not particular motivations.[30] Once again, it seems that there is a different standard for women and for men.

One worry is that women cannot be involved in contracted pregnancy without harming themselves, as it is difficult to let go of a child without lingering concern. So far, despite the heavily-publicized Baby M case, this appears not to be necessarily true.[31]

Another worry is that the practice will harm children. Children's welfare is, of course, important.

Children deserve the same consideration as other persons, and no society that fails to meet their basic needs is morally satisfactory. Yet I am suspicious of the objections raised on their behalf in these discussions: recourse to children's alleged well-being is once again being used as a trump card against women's autonomy.

First, we hear only about possible risks, never possible benefits, which, as I have been arguing, could be substantial.[32] Second, the main objection raised is the worry about how children will take the knowledge that their genetic mother conceived on behalf of another. We do not know how children will feel about having had such "surrogate" mothers. But as it is not a completely new phenomenon we might start our inquiry about this topic with historical evidence, not pessimistic speculation. In any case, if the practice is dealt with in an honest and common-sense way, particularly if it becomes quite common (and therefore "normal"), there is likely to be no problem. We are also hearing about the worries of existing children of women who are involved in the practice: there are reports that they fear their mother will give them away, too. But surely we can make clear to children the kinds of distinctions that distinguish the practice from slavery or baby-selling in the first place.

Although we must try to foresee what might harm children, I cannot help but wonder about the double standards implied by this speculation. The first double standard occurs when those who oppose surrogacy (and reproductive technologies generally) also oppose attempts to reduce the number of handicapped babies born.[33] In the latter context, it is argued that despite their problems handicapped persons are often glad to be alive. Hence it would be paternalistic to attempt to prevent their birth.

Why then do we not hear the same argument here? Instead, the possible disturbance of children born of surrogacy is taken as a reason to prevent their birth. Yet this potential problem is both more remote and most likely involves less suffering than such ailments as spina bifida, Huntington's Disease or cystic fibrosis, which some do not take to be reasons to refrain from child-bearing.[34]

Considering the sorts of reasons why parents have children, it is hard to see why the idea that one

was conceived in order to provide a desperately-wanted child to another is thought to be problematic. One might well prefer that to the idea that one was an "accident," adopted, born because contraception or abortion were not available, conceived to cement a failing marriage, to continue a family line, to qualify for welfare aid, to sex-balance a family, or as an experiment in child-rearing. Surely what matters for a child's well-being in the end is whether it is being raised in a loving, intelligent environment.

The second double standard involves a disparity between the interests of women and children. Arguing that surrogacy is wrong because it may upset children suggests a disturbing conception of the moral order. Women should receive consideration at least equal to that accorded children. Conflicts of interest between the two should be resolved according to the same rules we use for any other moral subjects. Those rules should never prescribe sacrificing one individual's basic interest at the mere hint of harm to another.

In sum, there seems to be no reason to think that there is anything necessarily wrong with "surrogate mothering," even the paid variety. Furthermore, some objections to it depend on values and assumptions that have been the chief building blocks of women's inequality. Why are some feminists asserting them? Is it because "surrogacy" as currently practiced often exploits women?

Is "Surrogate Mothering" Wrong in Certain Situations?

Even if "surrogate mothering" is not necessarily immoral, circumstances can render it so. For instance, it is obviously wrong to coerce women to engage in the practice. Also, certain conditions are unacceptable. Among them are clauses in a contract that subordinate a woman's reasonable desires and judgements to the will of another contracting party,[35] clauses legitimating inadequate pay for the risks and discomforts involved, and clauses that penalize her for the birth of a handicapped or dead baby through no fault of her own. Such contracts are now common.[36]

One popular solution to the problem of such immoral contracts is a law forbidding all surrogacy agreements; their terms would then be unenforceable. But I believe that women will continue to engage in surrogate mothering, even if it is unregulated, and this approach leaves them vulnerable to those who change their mind, or will not pay. Fair and reasonable regulations are essential to prevent exploitation of women. Although surrogate mothering may seem risky and uncomfortable to middle-class persons safely ensconced in healthy, interesting, relatively well-paid jobs, with adequate regulation it becomes an attractive option for some women. That these women are more likely than not to be poor is no reason to prohibit the activity.

As I suggested earlier, poor women now face substantial risks in the workplace. Even a superficial survey of hazards in occupations available to poor women would give pause to those who would prohibit surrogacy on the grounds of risk.[37]

Particularly shocking is the list of harmful substances and conditions to which working women are routinely exposed. For instance, cosmeticians and hairdressers, dry-cleaners and dental technicians are all exposed to carcinogens in their daily work (Stellman, Appendixes 1 and 2). Most low-level jobs also have high rates of exposure to toxic chemicals and dangerous machinery, and women take such jobs in disproportionate numbers. It is therefore unsurprising that poor women sicken and die more often than other members of society.[38]

This is not an argument in favour of adding yet another dangerous option to those already facing such women. Nor does it follow that the burdens they already bear justify the new ones. On the contrary, it is imperative to clean up dangerous workplaces. However, it would be utopian to think that this will occur in the near future. We must therefore attempt to improve women's lot under existing conditions. Under these circumstances it would be irrational to prohibit surrogacy on the grounds of risk when women would instead have to engage in still riskier pursuits.

Overall's emphatic assertion that contracted pregnancy is not a "real choice" for women is unconvincing. Her major argument, as I suggested earlier, is that it is an immoral, alienating option. But she also believes that such apparently expanded choices simply mask an underlying contraction of choice (p. 124). She also fears that by "endorsing an uncritical freedom of reproductive choice, we may also be implicitly endorsing all conceivable alternatives that an individual might adopt; we thereby abandon the responsibility for evaluating substantive actions in favour of advocating merely formal freedom of choice" (p. 125). Both worries are, as they stand, unpersuasive.

As I argued before, there is something troubling here about the new and one-sided emphasis on risk. If nothing else, we need to remember that contracted pregnancy constitutes a low-tech approach to a social problem, one which would slow the impetus toward expensive and dangerous high-tech solutions.[39]

A desire for children on the part of those who normally could not have them is not likely to disappear anytime soon. We could discount it, as many participants in debate about new reproductive technologies do. After all, nobody promised a rose garden to infertile couples, much less to homosexuals or to single women. Nor is it desirable to propagate the idea that having children is essential for human fulfilment.

But appealing to the sacrosanctity of traditional marriage or of blood ties to prohibit otherwise acceptable practices that would satisfy people's desires hardly makes sense, especially when those practices may provide other benefits. Not only might contracted pregnancy be less risky and more enjoyable than other jobs women are forced to take, but there are other advantages as well. Since being pregnant is not usually a full-time occupation, "surrogate mothering" could buy time for women to significantly improve their lot: students, aspiring writers, and social activists could make real progress toward their goals.

Women have until now done this reproductive labour for free.[40] Paying women to bear children should force us all to recognize this process as the socially useful enterprise that it is, and children as socially valuable creatures whose upbringing and welfare are critically important.

In short, "surrogate mothering" has the potential to empower women and increase their status in society. The darker side of the story is that it also has frightening potential for deepening their exploitation.

The outcome of the current warfare over control of new reproductive possibilities will determine which of these alternatives comes to pass.

NOTES

1. Shulamith Firestone, *The Dialectic of Sex* (New York: Bantam Books, 1970), p. 198. A version of this paper was given at the Eastern SWIP meeting, 26 March 1988. I would like especially to thank Helen B. Holmes and Sara Ann Ketchum for their useful comments on this paper; they are, of course, in no way responsible for its perverse position! Thanks also to the editors and referees of *Bioethics* for their helpful criticisms.

2. Susan Sherwin, "Feminist Ethics and *In Vitro* Fertilization," *Science, Morality and Feminist Theory*, ed. Marsha Hanen and Kai Nielsen, *Canadian Journal of Philosophy*, supplementary volume 13 (1987), p. 277.

3. Consider the many accounts of the devastating things parents have done to children, in particular.

4. See L. M. Purdy. "Genetic Diseases: Can Having Children be Immoral?" *Moral Problems in Medicine*, ed. Samuel Gorovitz (Englewood Cliffs, NJ: Prentice-Hall, 1983), pp. 377–84.

5. Another critical issue is that no feminist utopia will have a supply of "problem" children whom no one wants. Thus the proposal often heard nowadays that people should just adopt all those handicapped, non-white kids will not do. (Nor does it "do" now.)

6. I share with Sara Ann Ketchum the sense that this term is not adequate, although I am not altogether happy with her suggestion that we call it "contracted motherhood" ("New Reproductive Technologies and the Definition of Parenthood: A Feminist Perspective," paper given at the 1987 *Feminism and Legal Theory Conference*, at the University of Wisconsin at Madison, summer 1987, pp. 44ff.). It would be better, I think, to reserve terms like "mother" for the social act of nurturing. I shall therefore substitute the terms "contracted pregnancy" and "surrogacy" (in quotes).

7. This is not to say that no one would take the same view as I: the Catholic Church, for instance, objects to the masturbatory act required for surrogacy to proceed.

8. The difficulty in choosing the "right" moral theory to back up judgments in applied ethics, given that none are fully satisfactory, continues to be vexing. I would like to reassure those who lose interest at the mere sight of consequentialist—let alone utilitarian—judgement, that there are good reasons for considering justice an integral part of moral reasoning, as it quite obviously has utility.

   A different issue is raised by the burgeoning literature on feminist ethics. I strongly suspect that utilitarianism could serve feminists well, if properly applied. (For a defence of this position, see my paper "Do Feminists Need a New Moral Theory," given at the University of Minnesota, Duluth, at the conference *Explorations in Feminist Ethics: Theory and Practice*, 8–9 October 1988.)

9. See for example Gena Corea, *The Mother Machine*, and Christine Overall, *Ethics and Human Reproduction* (Winchester, MA: Allen & Unwin, 1987).

10. These are just a couple of examples in the sort of risky service that we tend to take for granted.

11. Modern agricultural products are brought to us as some risk by farm workers. Any large construction project will also result in some morbidity and mortality.

12. Even something so mundane as postal service involves serious risk on the part of workers.

13. The benefit to both high-risk women, and to society is clear. Women need not risk serious deterioration of health or abnormally high death rates.

14. See Laura Purdy, "The Morality of New Reproductive Technologies," *Journal of Social Philosophy* (Winter 1987), 38–48.

15. For elaboration of this view, consider Jane Ollenburger and John Hamlin, "'All Birthing Should Be Paid Labor'"—a Marxist Analysis of the Commodification of Motherhood," in *On the Problem of Surrogate Parenthood: Analyzing the Baby M Case*, ed. Herbert Richardson, (Lewiston, NY: Edwin Mellen Press, 1987).

16. Compare the physical risk with that of certain contraceptive technologies, and high-tech fertility treatments like IVF.

17. Infertility is often a result of social arrangements. This process would therefore be especially unfair to those who have already been exposed to more than their share of toxic chemicals or other harmful conditions.

18. Christine Overall, *Ethics and Human Reproduction*, (Winchester, MA: Allen & Unwin, 1987), ch. 6. Particularly problematic are her comments about women's loss of individuality, as I will be arguing shortly.

19. Men have been getting handsome pay for sperm donation for years; by comparison with child-bearing, such donation is a lark. Yet there has been no outcry about its immorality. Another double standard?

20. See Ellen Peck and Judith Senderowitz, *Pronatalism: The Myth of Mom and Apple Pie* (New York: Thomas Y. Crowell, 1974).

21. As it has been at some periods in the past: see for example information about family relationships in Philippe Ariès, *Centuries of Childhood: A Social History of Family Life*, trans. Robert Baldick (New York, 1982), and Lloyd DeMause's work.

22. Consider the arguments in ch. 8 of *Women's Work*, by Ann Oakley (New York: Vintage Books, 1974).

23. One of the interesting things about the practice of contracted pregnancy is that it can be argued to both strengthen and weaken the social recognition of biological relationships. On the one hand, the pregnant woman's biological relationship is judged irrelevant beyond a certain point; on the other, the reason for not valuing it is to

enhance that of the sperm donor. This might be interpreted as yet another case where men's interests are allowed to overrule women's. But it might also be interpreted as a salutary step toward awareness that biological ties can and sometimes should be subordinated to social ones. Deciding which interpretation is correct will depend on the facts of particular cases, and the arguments taken to justify the practice in the first place.

24. Science fiction, most notably John Wyndham's *The Midwich Cuckoos*, provides us with thought-provoking material.

25. John Robertson, "Surrogate Mothers: Not so Novel After All," *Hastings Center Report*, vol. 13, no. 5 (October 1983). This article is reprinted in *Bioethics*, ed. Rem B. Edwards and Glen C. Graber (San Diego, CA: Harcourt, Brace Jovanovich, 1988). Krimmel's article ("The Case Against Surrogate Parenting") was also originally published in the *Hastings Center Report* and is reprinted in *Bioethics*. References here are to the latter.

26. One major difference between adoption and contracted pregnancy is that the baby is handed over virtually at birth, thus ensuring that the trauma sometimes experienced by older adoptees is not experienced. Although children of contracted pregnancy might well be curious to know about their biological mother, I do not see this as a serious obstacle to the practice, since we could change our policy about this. There is also reason to believe that carefully-screened women undertaking a properly-regulated contracted pregnancy are less likely to experience lingering pain of separation. First, they have deliberately chosen to go through pregnancy, knowing that they will give the baby up. The resulting sense of control is probably critical to their short- and long-term well-being. Second, their pregnancy is not the result of trauma. See also Monica B. Morris, "Reproductive Technology and Restraints," *Transaction/SOCIETY* (March/April 1988), 16–22, esp. p. 18.

27. There may be a problem for the woman who gives birth, as the Baby M case has demonstrated. There is probably a case for a waiting period after the birth during which the woman can change her mind.

28. Heidi Malm suggested this position in her comment on Sara Ann Ketchum's paper "Selling Babies and Selling Bodies: Surrogate Motherhood and the Problem of Commodificaton," at the Eastern Division *APA* meetings, 30 December 1987.

29. Mary Anne Warren suggests, alternately, that this objection could be obviated by women and children retaining some

rights and responsibilities toward each other in contracted pregnancy. Maintaining a relationship of sorts might also, she suggests, help forestall and alleviate whatever negative feelings children might have about such transfers. I agree that such openness is probably a good idea in any case. (Referee's comment.)

30. Perhaps lurking behind the objections of surrogacy is some feeling that it is wrong to earn money by letting your body work, without active effort on your part. But this would rule out sperm selling, as well as using women's beauty to sell products and services.

31. See, for example, James Rachels, "A Report from America: The Baby M Case," *Bioethics*, vol. 1, no. 4 (October 1987), 365. He reports that there have been over 600 successful cases; see also the above note on adoption.

32. Among them the above-mentioned one of being born healthier.

33. To avoid the difficulties about abortion added by the assumption that we are talking about existing fetuses, let us consider here only the issue of whether certain couples should risk pregnancy.

34. There is an interesting link here between these two aspects of reproduction, as the promise of healthier children is, I think, one of the strongest arguments for contracted pregnancy.

35. What this may consist of naturally requires much additional elucidation.

36. See Susan Ince, "Inside the Surrogate Industry," *Test-Tube Women*, ed. Rita Arditti, Renate Duelli Klein, and Shelley Minden (London: Pandora Press, 1984).

37. See, for example, Jeanne Mager Stellman, *Women's Work, Women's Health* (New York: Pantheon, 1977).

38. See George L. Waldbott, *Health Effects of Environmental Pollutants* (St Louis: C.V. Mosby, 1973); Nicholas Ashford, *Crisis in the Workplace: Occupational Disease and Injury* (Cambridge: MIT Press, 1976); *Cancer and the Worker* (New York Academy of Science, 1977); *Environmental Problems in Medicine*, ed. William D. McKee (Springfield, IL: Charles C. Thomas, 1977).

39. These are the ones most likely to put women in the clutches of the paternalistic medical establishment. Exploitation by commercial operations such as that of Noel Keane could be avoided by tight regulation or prohibition altogether of for-profit enterprises.

40. The implications of this fact remain to be fully understood; I suspect that they are detrimental to women and children, but that this is a topic for another paper.

Is Women's Labor a Commodity?

ELIZABETH S. ANDERSON

Anderson opposes commercial surrogacy on the grounds that it reduces both surrogate mothers and babies to market commodities. This "commodification," she says, entails a type of evaluation that regards women and children as property, as things to be used—which is a far cry from seeing them as they should be seen: beings worthy of respect.

In the past few years the practice of commercial surrogate motherhood has gained notoriety as a method for acquiring children. A commercial surrogate mother is anyone who is paid money to bear a child for other people and terminate her parental rights, so that the others may raise the child as exclusively their own. The growth of commercial surrogacy has raised with new urgency a class of concerns regarding the proper scope of the market. Some critics have objected to commercial surrogacy on the ground that it improperly treats children and women's reproductive capacities as commodities.[1] The prospect of reducing children to consumer durables and women to baby factories surely inspires revulsion. But are there good reasons behind the revulsion? And is this an accurate description of what commercial surrogacy implies? This article offers a theory about what things are properly regarded as commodities which supports the claim that commercial surrogacy constitutes an unconscionable commodification of children and of women's reproductive capacities.

What Is a Commodity?

The modern market can be characterized in terms of the legal and social norms by which it governs the production, exchange, and enjoyment of commodities. To say that something is properly regarded as a commodity is to claim that the norms of the market are appropriate for regulating its production, exchange, and enjoyment. To the extent that moral principles or ethical ideals preclude the application of market norms to a good, we may say that the good is not a (proper) commodity.

Why should we object to the application of a market norm to the production or distribution of a good? One reason may be that to produce or distribute the good in accordance with the norm is to *fail to value it in an appropriate way.* Consider, for example, a standard Kantian argument against slavery, or the commodification of persons. Slaves are treated in accordance with the market norm that owners may use commodities to satisfy their own interests without regard for the interests of the commodities themselves. To treat a person without regard for her interests is to fail to respect her. But slaves are persons who may not be merely used in this fashion, since as rational beings they possess a dignity which commands respect. In Kantian theory, the problem with slavery is that it treats beings worthy of *respect* as if they were worthy merely of *use.* "Respect" and "use" in this context denote what we may call different *modes of valuation.* We value things and persons in other ways than by respecting and using them. For example, love, admiration, honor, and appreciation constitute distinct modes of valuation. To value a thing or person in a distinctive way involves treating it in accordance with a particular set of norms. For example, courtesy expresses a mode of valuation we may call "civil respect," which differs from Kantian respect in that it calls for obedience to the rules of etiquette rather than to the categorical imperative.

Any ideal of human life includes a conception of how different things and persons should be valued.

From Elizabeth S. Anderson, "Is Women's Labor a Commodity?" *Philosophy and Public Affairs*, vol. 19, no. 1 (Winter 1990), 71–92.

Let us reserve the term "use" to refer to the mode of valuation proper to commodities, which follows the market norm of treating things solely in accordance with the owner's nonmoral preferences. Then the Kantian argument against commodifying persons can be generalized to apply to many other cases. It can be argued that many objects which are worthy of a higher mode of valuation than use are not properly regarded as mere commodities.[2] Some current arguments against the colorization of classic black-and-white films take this form. Such films have been colorized by their owners in an attempt to enhance their market value by attracting audiences unused to black-and-white cinematography. But some opponents of the practice object that such treatment of the film classics fails to appreciate their aesthetic and historical value. True appreciation of these films would preclude this kind of crass commercial exploitation, which debases their aesthetic qualities in the name of profits. Here the argument rests on the claim that the goods in question are worthy of appreciation, not merely of use.

The ideals which specify how one should value certain things are supported by a conception of human flourishing. Our lives are enriched and elevated by cultivating and exercising the capacity to appreciate art. To fail to do so reflects poorly on ourselves. To fail to value things appropriately is to embody in one's life an inferior conception of human flourishing.[3]

These considerations support a general account of the sorts of things which are appropriately regarded as commodities. Commodities are those things which are properly treated in accordance with the norms of the modern market. We can question the application of market norms to the production, distribution, and enjoyment of a good by appealing to ethical ideals which support arguments that the good should be valued in some other way than use. Arguments of the latter sort claim that to allow certain market norms to govern our treatment of a thing expresses a mode of valuation not worthy of it. If the thing is to be valued appropriately, its production, exchange, and enjoyment must be removed from market norms and embedded in a different set of social relationships.

The Case of Commercial Surrogacy

Let us now consider the practice of commercial surrogate motherhood in the light of this theory of commodities. Surrogate motherhood as a commercial enterprise is based upon contracts involving three parties: the intended father, the broker, and the surrogate mother. The intended father agrees to pay a lawyer to find a suitable surrogate mother and make the requisite medical and legal arrangements for the conception and birth of the child, and for the transfer of legal custody to himself.[4] The surrogate mother agrees to become impregnated with the intended father's sperm, to carry the resulting child to term, and to relinquish her parental rights to it, transferring custody to the father in return for a fee and medical expenses. Both she and her husband (if she has one) agree not to form a parent-child bond with her child and to do everything necessary to effect the transfer of the child to the intended father. At current market prices, the lawyer arranging the contract can expect to gross $15,000 from the contract, while the surrogate mother can expect a $10,000 fee.[5]

The practice of commercial surrogacy has been defended on four main grounds. First, given the shortage of children available for adoption and the difficulty of qualifying as adoptive parents, it may represent the only hope for some people to be able to raise a family. Commercial surrogacy should be accepted as an effective means for realizing this highly significant good. Second, two fundamental human rights support commercial surrogacy: the right to procreate and freedom of contract. Fully informed autonomous adults should have the right to make whatever arrangements they wish for the use of their bodies and the reproduction of children, so long as the children themselves are not harmed. Third, the labor of the surrogate mother is said to be a labor of love. Her altruistic acts should be permitted and encouraged.[6] Finally, it is argued that commercial surrogacy is no different in its ethical implications from many already accepted practices which separate genetic, gestational, and social parenting, such as artificial insemination by donor, adoption, wet-nursing, and day care. Consistency demands that society accept this new practice as well.[7]

In opposition to these claims, I shall argue that commercial surrogacy does raise new ethical issues, since it represents an invasion of the market into a new sphere of conduct, that of specifically women's labor—that is, the labor of carrying children to term in pregnancy. When women's labor is treated as a commodity, the women who perform it are degraded. Furthermore, commercial surrogacy degrades children by reducing their status to that of commodities. Let us consider each of the goods of concern in surrogate motherhood—the child, and women's reproductive labor—to see how the commercialization of parenthood affects people's regard for them.

Children as Commodities

The most fundamental calling of parents to their children is to love them. Children are to be loved and cherished by their parents, not to be used or manipulated by them for merely personal advantage. Parental love can be understood as a passionate, unconditional commitment to nurture one's child, providing it with the care, affection, and guidance it needs to develop its capacities to maturity. This understanding of the way parents should value their children informs our interpretation of parental rights over their children. Parents' rights over their children are trusts, which they must always exercise for the sake of the child. This is not to deny that parents have their own aspirations in raising children. But the child's interests beyond subsistence are not definable independently of the flourishing of the family, which is the object of specifically parental aspirations. The proper exercise of parental rights includes those acts which promote their shared life as a family, which realize the shared interests of the parents and the child.

The norms of parental love carry implications for the ways other people should treat the relationship between parents and their children. If children are to be loved by their parents, then others should not attempt to compromise the integrity of parental love or work to suppress the emotions supporting the bond between parents and their children. If the rights to children should be understood as trusts, then if those rights are lost or relinquished, the duty of those in charge of transferring custody to others is to consult the best interests of the child.

Commercial surrogacy substitutes market norms for some of the norms of parental love. Most importantly, it requires us to understand parental rights no longer as trusts but as things more like property rights—that is, rights of use and disposal over the things owned. For in this practice the natural mother deliberately conceives a child with the intention of giving it up for material advantage. Her renunciation of parental responsibilities is not done for the child's sake, nor for the sake of fulfilling an interest she shares with the child, but typically for her own sake (and possibly, if "altruism" is a motive, for the intended parents' sakes). She and the couple who pay her to give up her parental rights over her child thus treat her rights as a kind of property right. They thereby treat the child itself as a kind of commodity, which may be properly bought and sold.

Commercial surrogacy insinuates the norms of commerce into the parental relationship in other ways. Whereas parental love is not supposed to be conditioned upon the child having particular characteristics, consumer demand is properly responsive to the characteristics of commodities. So the surrogate industry provides opportunities to adoptive couples to specify the height, I.Q., race, and other attributes of the surrogate mother, in the expectation that these traits will be passed on to the child.[8] Since no industry assigns agents to look after the "interests" of its commodities, no one represents the child's interests in the surrogate industry. The surrogate agency promotes the adoptive parents' interests and not the child's interests where matters of custody are concerned. Finally, as the agent of the adoptive parents, the broker has the task of policing the surrogate (natural) mother's relationship to her child, using persuasion, money, and the threat of a lawsuit to weaken and destroy whatever parental love she may develop for her child.[9]

All of these substitutions of market norms for parental norms represent ways of treating children as commodities which are degrading to them. Degradation occurs when something is treated in accordance with a lower mode of valuation than is proper to it. We value things not just "more" or "less," but in qualitatively higher and lower ways. To love or respect someone is to value her in a higher way than one would if one merely used her. Children are properly loved by their parents and respected by others. Since children are valued as mere use-objects by the mother and the surrogate agency when they are sold to others, and by the adoptive parents when they seek to conform the child's genetic makeup to their own wishes, commercial surrogacy degrades children insofar as it treats them as commodities.[10]

One might argue that since the child is most likely to enter a loving home, no harm comes to it from permitting the natural mother to treat it as property. So the purchase and sale of infants is unobjectionable, at least from the point of view of children's interests.[11] But the sale of an infant has an expressive significance which this argument fails to recognize. By engaging in the transfer of children by sale, all of the parties to the surrogate contract express a set of attitudes toward children which undermine the norms of parental love. They all agree in treating the ties between a natural mother and her children as properly loosened by a monetary incentive. Would it be any wonder if a child born of a surrogacy agreement feared resale by parents who have such an attitude? And a child who knew how anxious her parents were that she have the "right" genetic makeup might fear that her parent's love was contingent upon her expression of these characteristics.[12]

The unsold children of surrogate mothers are also harmed by commercial surrogacy. The children of some surrogate mothers have reported their fears that they may be sold like their half-brother or half-sister, and express a sense of loss at being deprived of a sibling.[13] Furthermore, the widespread acceptance of commercial surrogacy would psychologically threaten all children. For it would change the way children are valued by people (parents and surrogate brokers)—from being loved by their parents and respected by others, to being sometimes used as objects of commercial profit-making.[14]

Proponents of commercial surrogacy have denied that the surrogate industry engages in the sale of children. For it is impossible to sell to someone what is already his own, and the child is already the father's own natural offspring. The payment to the surrogate mother is not for her child, but for her services in carrying it to term.[15] The claim that the parties to the surrogate contract treat children as commodities, however, is based on the way they treat the *mother's* rights over her child. It is irrelevant that the natural father also has some rights over the child; what he pays for is exclusive rights to it. He would not pay her for the "service" of carrying the child to term if she refused to relinquish her parental rights to it. That the mother regards only her labor and not her child as requiring compensation is also irrelevant. No one would argue that the baker does not treat his bread as property just because he sees the income from its sale as compensation for his labor and expenses and not for the bread itself, which he doesn't care to keep.[16]

Defenders of commercial surrogacy have also claimed that it does not differ substantially from other already accepted parental practices. In the institutions of adoption and artificial insemination by donor (AID), it is claimed, we already grant parents the right to dispose of their children.[17] But these practices differ in significant respects from commercial surrogacy. The purpose of adoption is to provide a means for placing children in families when their parents cannot or will not discharge their parental responsibilities. It is not a sphere for the existence of a supposed parental right to dispose of one's children for profit. Even AID does not sanction the sale of fully formed human beings. The semen donor sells only a product of his body, not his child, and does not initiate the act of conception.

Two developments might seem to undermine the claim that commercial surrogacy constitutes a degrading commerce in children. The first is technological: the prospect of transplanting a human embryo into the womb of a genetically unrelated woman. If commercial surrogacy used women only as gestational mothers and not as genetic mothers, and if it was thought that only genetic and not gestational parents could properly claim that a child was "theirs," then the child born of a surrogate mother would not be hers to sell in the first place. The second is a legal development: the establishment of the proposed "consent-intent" definition of parenthood.[18] This would declare the legal parents of a child to be whoever consented to a procedure which leads to its birth, with the intent of assuming parental responsibilities for it. This rule would define away the problem of commerce in children by depriving the surrogate mother of any legal claim to her child at all, even if it was hers both genetically and gestationally.[19]

There are good reasons, however, not to undermine the place of genetic and gestational ties in these ways. Consider first the place of genetic ties. By upholding a system of involuntary (genetic) ties of obligation among people, even when the adults among them prefer to divide their rights and obligations in other ways, we help to secure children's interests in having an assured place in the world, which is more firm than the wills of their parents. Unlike the consent-intent rule, the principle of respecting genetic ties does not make the obligation to care for those whom one has created (intentionally or not) contingent upon an arbitrary desire to do so. It thus provides children with a set of preexisting social sanctions which give them a more secure place in the world. The genetic principle also places children in a far wider network of associations and obligations than the consent-intent rule sanctions. It supports the roles of grandparents and other relatives in the nurturing of children, and provides children with a possible focus of stability and an additional source of claims to care if their parents cannot sustain a well-functioning household.

In the next section I will defend the claims of gestational ties to children. To deny these claims, as commercial surrogacy does, is to deny the significance of reproductive labor to the mother who undergoes it and thereby to dehumanize and degrade the mother herself. Commercial surrogacy would be a corrupt practice even if it did not involve commerce in children.

Women's Labor as a Commodity

Commercial surrogacy attempts to transform what is specifically women's labor—the work of bringing forth children into the world—into a commodity. It does so by replacing the parental norms which usually govern the practice of gestating children with the economic norms which govern ordinary production processes. The application of commercial norms to women's labor reduces the surrogate mothers from persons worthy of respect and consideration to objects of mere use.

Respect and consideration are two distinct modes of valuation whose norms are violated by the practices of the surrogate industry. To respect a person is to treat her in accordance with principles she rationally accepts—principles consistent with the protection of her autonomy and her rational interests. To treat a person with consideration is to respond with sensitivity to her and to her emotional relations with others, refraining from manipulating or denigrating these for one's own purposes. Given the understanding of respect as a dispassionate, impersonal regard for people's interests, a different ethical concept—consideration—is needed to capture the engaged and sensitive regard we should have for people's emotional relationships. The failure of consideration on the part of the other parties to the surrogacy contract explains the judgment that the contract is not simply disrespectful of the surrogate mother, but callous as well.[20]

The application of economic norms to the sphere of women's labor violates women's claims to respect and consideration in three ways. First, by requiring the surrogate mother to repress whatever parental love she feels for the child, these norms convert women's labor into a form of alienated labor. Second, by manipulating and denying legitimacy to the surrogate mother's evolving perspective on her own pregnancy, the norms of the market degrade her. Third, by taking advantage of the surrogate mother's noncommercial motivations without offering anything but what the norms of commerce demand in return, these norms leave her open to exploitation. The fact that these problems arise in the attempt to commercialize the labor of bearing children shows that women's labor is not properly regarded as a commodity.

The key to understanding these problems is the normal role of the emotions in noncommercialized pregnancies. Pregnancy is not simply a biological process but also a social practice. Many social expectations and considerations surround women's gestational labor, marking it off as an occasion for the parents to prepare themselves to welcome a new life into their family. For example, obstetricians use ultrasound not simply for diagnostic purposes but also to encourage maternal bonding with the fetus.[21] We can all recognize that it is good, although by no means inevitable, for loving bonds to be established between the mother and her child during this period.

In contrast with these practices, the surrogate industry follows the putting-out system of manufacturing. It provides some of the raw materials of production (the father's sperm) to the surrogate mother, who then engages in production of the child. Although her labor is subject to periodic supervision by her doctors and by the surrogate agency, the agency does not have physical control over the product of her labor as firms using the factory system do. Hence, as in all putting-out systems, the surrogate industry faces the problem of extracting the final product from the mother. This problem is exacerbated by the fact that the social norms surrounding pregnancy are designed to encourage parental love for the child. The surrogate industry addresses this problem by requiring the mother to engage in a form of emotional labor.[22] In the surrogate contract, she agrees not to form or to attempt to form a parent-child relationship with her offspring.[23] Her labor is alienated, because she must divert it from the end which the social practices of pregnancy rightly promote—an emotional bond with her child. The surrogate contract thus replaces a norm of parenthood, that during pregnancy one create a loving attachment to one's child, with a norm of commercial production, that the producer shall not form any special emotional ties to her product.

The demand to deliberately alienate oneself from one's love for one's own child is a demand which can reasonably and decently be made of no one. Unless we were to remake pregnancy into a form of drudgery which is only performed for a wage, there is every reason to expect that many women who do sign a surrogate contract will, despite this fact, form a loving attachment to the child they bear. For this is what the social practices surrounding pregnancy encourage. Treating women's labor as just another kind of commercial production process violates the precious emotional ties which the mother may rightly and properly establish with her "product," the child, and thereby violates her claims to consideration.[24]

Commercial surrogacy is also a degrading practice. The surrogate mother, like all persons, has an independent evaluative perspective on her activities and relationships. The realization of her dignity demands that the other parties to the contract acknowledge rather than evade the claims which her independent perspective makes upon them. But the surrogate industry has an interest in suppressing, manipulating, and trivializing her perspective, for there is an ever-present danger that she will see her involvement in her pregnancy from the perspective of a parent rather than from the perspective of a contract laborer.

How does this suppression and trivialization take place? The commercial promoters of surrogacy commonly describe the surrogate mothers as inanimate objects: mere "hatcheries," "plumbing," or "rented property"—things without emotions which could make claims on others.[25] They also refuse to acknowledge any responsibility for the consequences of the mother's emotional labor. Should she suffer psychologically from being forced to give up her child, the father is not liable to pay for therapy after her pregnancy, although he is liable for all other medical expenses following her pregnancy.[26]

The treatment and interpretation of surrogate mothers' grief raises the deepest problems of degradation. Most surrogate mothers experience grief upon giving up their children—in 10 percent of cases, seriously enough to require therapy.[27] Their grief is not compensated by the $10,000 fee they receive. Grief is not an intelligible response to a successful deal, but rather reflects the subject's judgment that she has suffered a grave and personal loss. Since not all cases of grief resolve themselves into cases of regret, it may be that some surrogate mothers do not regard their grief, in retrospect, as reflecting an authentic judgment on their part. But in the circumstances of emotional manipulation which pervade the surrogate industry, it is difficult to determine which interpretation of her grief more truly reflects the perspective of the surrogate mother. By insinuating a trivializing interpretation of her emotional responses to the prospect of losing her child, the surrogate agency may be able to manipulate her into accepting her fate without too much fuss, and may even succeed in substituting its interpretation of her emotions for her own. Since she has already signed a contract to perform emotional labor—to express or repress emotions which are dictated by the interests of the surrogate industry—his might not be a difficult task.[28] A considerate treatment of the mothers' grief, on the other hand, would take the evaluative basis of their grief seriously.

Some defenders of commercial surrogacy demand that the provision for terminating the surrogate mother's parental rights in her child be legally enforceable, so that peace of mind for the adoptive parents can be secured.[29] But the surrogate industry makes no corresponding provision for securing the peace of mind of the surrogate. She is expected to assume the risk of a transformation of her ethical and emotional perspective on herself and her child with the same impersonal detachment with which a futures trader assumes the risk of a fluctuation in the price of pork bellies. By applying the market norms of enforcing contracts to the surrogate mother's case, commercial surrogacy treats a moral transformation as if it were merely an economic change.[30]

The manipulation of the surrogate mother's emotions which is inherent in the surrogate parenting contract also leaves women open to grave forms of exploitation. A kind of exploitation occurs when one party to a transaction is oriented toward the exchange of "gift" values, while the other party operates in accordance with the norms of the market exchange of commodities. Gift values, which include love, gratitude, and appreciation of others, cannot be bought or obtained through piecemeal calculations of individual advantage. Their exchange requires a repudiation of a self-interested attitude, a willingness to give gifts to others without demanding some specific equivalent good in return each time one gives. The surrogate mother often operates according to the norms of gift relationships. The surrogate agency, on the other hand, follows market norms. Its job is to get the best deal for its clients and itself, while leaving the surrogate mother to look after her own interests as best as she can. This situation puts the surrogate agencies in a position to manipulate the surrogate mothers' emotions to gain favorable terms for themselves. For example, agencies screen prospective surrogate mothers for submissiveness, and emphasize to them the importance of the motives of generosity and love. When applicants question some of the terms of the contract,

the broker sometimes intimidates them by questioning their character and morality: if they were really generous and loving they would not be so solicitous about their own interests.[31]

Some evidence supports the claim that most surrogate mothers are motivated by emotional needs and vulnerabilities which lead them to view their labor as a form of gift and not a purely commercial exchange. Only 1 percent of applicants to surrogate agencies would become surrogate mothers for money alone; the others have emotional as well as financial reasons for applying. One psychiatrist believes that most, if not all, of the 35 percent of applicants who had had a previous abortion or given up a child for adoption wanted to become surrogate mothers in order to resolve their guilty feelings or deal with their unresolved loss by going through a process of losing a child again.[32] Women who feel that giving up another child is an effective way to punish themselves for past abortions, or a form of therapy for their emotional problems, are not likely to resist manipulation by surrogate brokers.

Many surrogate mothers see pregnancy as a way to feel "adequate," "appreciated," or "special." In other words, these women feel inadequate, unappreciated, or unadmired when they are not pregnant.[33] Lacking the power to achieve some worthwhile status in their own right, they must subordinate themselves to others' definitions of their proper place (as baby factories) in order to get from them the appreciation they need to attain a sense of self-worth. But the sense of self-worth one can attain under such circumstances is precarious and ultimately self-defeating. For example, those who seek gratitude on the part of the adoptive parents and some opportunity to share the joys of seeing their children grow discover all too often that the adoptive parents want nothing to do with them.[34] For while the surrogate mother sees in the arrangement some basis for establishing the personal ties she needs to sustain her emotionally, the adoptive couple sees it as an impersonal commercial contract, one of whose main advantages to them is that all ties between them and the surrogate are ended once the terms of the contract are fulfilled.[35] To them, her presence is a threat to marital unity and a competing object for the child's affections.

These considerations should lead us to question the model of altruism which is held up to women by the surrogacy industry. It is a strange form of altruism which demands such radical self-effacement, alienation from those whom one benefits, and the subordination of one's body, health, and emotional life to the independently defined interests of others.[36] Why should this model of "altruism" be held up to *women?* True altruism does not involve such subordination, but rather the autonomous and self-confident exercise of skill, talent, and judgment. (Consider the dedicated doctor.) The kind of altruism we see admired in surrogate mothers involves a lack of self-confidence, a feeling that one can be truly worthy only through self-effacement. This model of altruism, far from affirming the freedom and dignity of women, seems all too conveniently designed to keep their sense of self-worth hostage to the interests of a more privileged class.[37]

The primary distortions which arise from treating women's labor as a commodity—the surrogate mother's alienation from loved ones, her degradation, and her exploitation—stem from a common source. This is the failure to acknowledge and treat appropriately the surrogate mother's emotional engagement with her labor. Her labor is alienated, because she must suppress her emotional ties with her own child, and may be manipulated into reinterpreting these ties in a trivializing way. She is degraded, because her independent ethical perspective is denied, or demoted to the status of a cash sum. She is exploited, because her emotional needs and vulnerabilities are not treated as characteristics which call for consideration, but as factors which may be manipulated to encourage her to make a grave self-sacrifice to the broker's and adoptive couple's advantage. These considerations provide strong grounds for sustaining the claims of women's labor to its "product," the child. The attempt to redefine parenthood so as to strip women of parental claims to the children they bear does violence to their emotional engagement with the project of bringing children into the world.

Commercial Surrogacy, Freedom, and the Law

In the light of these ethical objections to commercial surrogacy, what position should the law take on the practice? At the very least, surrogate contracts should not be enforceable. Surrogate mothers should not be forced to relinquish their children if they have formed emotional bonds with them. Any other treatment of women's ties to the children they bear is degrading.

But I think these arguments support the stronger conclusion that commercial surrogate contracts should be illegal, and that surrogate agencies who arrange such contracts should be subject to criminal penalties.[38] Commercial surrogacy constitutes a degrading and harmful traffic in children, violates the dignity of women, and subjects both children and women to a serious risk of exploitation. But are these problems inherent in the practice of commercial surrogacy? Defenders of the practice have suggested three reforms intended to eliminate these problems:

(1) give the surrogate mother the option of keeping her child after birth; (2) impose stringent regulations on private surrogate agencies; (3) replace private surrogate agencies with a state-run monopoly on surrogate arrangements. Let us consider each of these options in turn.

Some defenders of commercial surrogacy suggest that the problem of respecting the surrogate mother's potential attachment to her child can be solved by granting the surrogate mother the option to reserve her parental rights after birth.[39] But such an option would not significantly change the conditions of the surrogate mother's labor. Indeed, such a provision would pressure the agency to demean the mother's self-regard more than ever. Since it could not rely on the law to enforce the adoptive parents' wishes regardless of the surrogate's feelings, it would have to make sure that she assumed the perspective which it and its clients have of her: as "rented plumbing."

Could such dangers be avoided by careful regulation of the surrogate industry? Some have suggested that exploitation of women could be avoided by such measures as properly screening surrogates, setting low fixed fees (to avoid tempting women in financial duress), and requiring independent counsel for the surrogate mother.[40] But no one knows how to predict who will suffer grave psychological damage from surrogacy, and the main forms of duress encountered in the industry are emotional rather than financial. Furthermore, there is little hope that regulation would check the exploitation of surrogate mothers. The most significant encounters between the mothers and the surrogate agencies take place behind closed doors. It is impossible to regulate the multifarious ways in which brokers can subtly manipulate the emotions of the vulnerable to their own advantage. Advocates of commercial surrogacy claim that their failure rate is extremely low, since only five out of the first five hundred cases were legally contested by surrogate mothers. But we do not know how many surrogate mothers were browbeaten into relinquishing their children, feel violated by their treatment, or would feel violated had their perspectives not been manipulated by the other parties to the contract. The dangers of exploiting women through commercial surrogacy are too great to ignore, and too deep to effectively regulate.

Could a state-run monopoly on surrogate arrangements eliminate the risk of degrading and exploiting surrogate mothers?[41] A nonprofit state agency would arguably have no incentive to exploit surrogates, and it would screen the adoptive parents for the sake of the best interests of the child. Nevertheless, as long as the surrogate mother is paid money to bear a child and terminate her parental rights, the commercial norms leading to her degradation still apply. For these norms are constitutive of our understanding of what the surrogate contract is for. Once such an arrangement becomes socially legitimized, these norms will govern the understandings of participants in the practice and of society at large, or at least compete powerfully with the rival parental norms. And what judgment do these norms make of a mother who, out of love for her child, decides that she cannot relinquish it? They blame her for commercial irresponsibility and flighty emotions. Her transformation of moral and emotional perspective, which she experiences as real but painful growth, looks like a capricious and selfish exercise of will from the standpoint of the market, which does not distinguish the deep commitments of love from arbitrary matters of taste.[42]

The fundamental problem with commercial surrogacy is that commercial norms are inherently manipulative when they are applied to the sphere of parental love. Manipulation occurs whenever norms are deployed to psychologically coerce others into a position where they cannot defend their own interests or articulate their own perspective without being charged with irresponsibility or immorality for doing so. A surrogate contract is inherently manipulative, since the very form of the contract invokes commercial norms which, whether upheld by the law or by social custom only, imply that the mother should feel guilty and irresponsible for loving her own child.

But hasn't the surrogate mother decided in advance that she is not interested in viewing her relationship to her child in this way? Regardless of her initial state of mind, once she enters the contract, she is not free to develop an autonomous perspective on her relationship with her child. She is contractually bound to manipulate her emotions to agree with the interests of the adoptive parents. Few things reach deeper into the self than a parent's evolving relationship with her own child. To lay claim to the course of this relationship in virtue of a cash payment constitutes a severe violation of the mother's personhood and a denial of the mother's autonomy.

Two final objections stand in the way of criminalizing commercial surrogacy. Prohibiting the practice might be thought to infringe two rights: the right of procreation, and the right to freedom of contract. Judge Harvey Sorkow, in upholding the legality and enforceability of commercial surrogate parenting contracts, based much of his argument on an interpretation of the freedom to procreate. He argued that the protection of the right to procreate requires the protection of noncoital means of procreation, including commercial surrogacy. The interests upheld by the creation of the family are the same, regardless of the means used to bring the family into existence.[43]

Sorkow asserts a blanket right to procreate, without carefully examining the specific human interests protected by such a right. The interest protected by the right to procreate is that of being able to create and sustain a family life with some integrity. But the enforcement of surrogate contracts against the will of the mother destroys one family just as surely as it creates another. And the same interest which generates the right to procreate also generates an obligation to uphold the integrity of family life which constrains the exercise of this right.[44]

To recognize the legality of commercial surrogate contracts would undermine the integrity of families by giving public sanction to a practice which expresses contempt for the moral and emotional ties which bind a mother to her children, legitimates the view that these ties are merely the product of arbitrary will, properly loosened by the offering of a monetary incentive, and fails to respect the claims of genetic and gestational ties to children which provide children with a more secure place in the world than commerce can supply.

The freedom of contract provides weaker grounds for supporting commercial surrogacy. This freedom is already constrained, notably in preventing the purchase and sale of human beings. Yet one might object that prohibiting surrogate contracts could undermine the status of women by implying that they do not have the competence to enter into and rationally discharge the obligations of commercial contracts. Insofar as the justification for prohibiting commercial surrogacy depends upon giving special regard to women's emotional ties to their children, it might be thought to suggest that women as a group are too emotional to subject themselves to the dispassionate discipline of the market. Then prohibiting surrogate contracts would be seen as an offensive, paternalistic interference with the autonomy of the surrogate mothers.

We have seen, however, that the content of the surrogate contract itself compromises the autonomy of surrogate mothers. It uses the norms of commerce in a manipulative way and commands the surrogate mothers to conform their emotions to the interests of the other parties to the contract. The surrogate industry fails to acknowledge the surrogate mothers as possessing an independent perspective worthy of consideration. And it takes advantage of motivations—such as self-effacing "altruism"—which women have formed under social conditions inconsistent with genuine autonomy. Hence the surrogate industry itself, far from expanding the realm of autonomy for women, actually undermines the external and internal conditions required for fully autonomous choice by women.

If commercial surrogate contracts were prohibited, this would be no cause for infertile couples to lose hope for raising a family. The option of adoption is still available, and every attempt should be made to open up opportunities for adoption to couples who do not meet standard requirements—for example, because of age. While there is a shortage of healthy white infants available for adoption, there is no shortage of children of other races, mixed-race children, and older and handicapped children who desperately need to be adopted. Leaders of the surrogate industry have proclaimed that commercial surrogacy may replace adoption as the method of choice for infertile couples who wish to raise families. But we should be wary of the racist and eugenic motivations which make some people rally to the surrogate industry at the expense of children who already exist and need homes.

The case of commercial surrogacy raises deep questions about the proper scope of the market in modern industrial societies. I have argued that there are principled grounds for rejecting the substitution of market norms for parental norms to govern the ways women bring children into the world. Such substitutions express ways of valuing mothers and children which reflect an inferior conception of human flourishing. When market norms are applied to the ways we allocate and understand parental rights and responsibilities, children are reduced from subjects of love to objects of use. When market norms are applied to the ways we treat and understand women's reproductive labor, women are reduced from subjects of respect and consideration to objects of use. If we are to retain the capacity to value children and women in ways consistent with a rich conception of human flourishing, we must resist the encroachment of the market upon the sphere of reproductive labor. Women's labor is *not* a commodity.

NOTES
The author thanks David Anderson, Steven Darwall, Ezekiel Emanuel, Daniel Hausman, Don Herzog, Robert Nozick, Richard Pildes, John Rawls, Michael Sandel, Thomas Scanlon, and Howard Wial for helpful comments and criticisms.
1. See, for example, Gena Corea, *The Mother Machine* (New York: Harper and Row, 1985), pp. 216, 219; Angela Holder, "Surrogate Motherhood: Babies for Fun and Profit," *Case and Comment* 90 (1985): 3–11; and Margaret Jane Radin,

"Market Inalienability," *Harvard Law Review* 100 (June 1987): 1849–1937.

2. The notion of valuing something more highly than another can be understood as follows. Some preferences are neither obligatory nor admirable. To value a thing as a mere use-object is to treat it solely in accordance with such non-ethical preferences. To value a thing or person more highly than as a mere use-object is to recognize it as having some special intrinsic worth, in virtue of which we form preferences about how to treat the thing which we regard as obligatory or admirable. The person who truly appreciates art does not conceive of art merely as a thing which she can use as she pleases, but as something which commands appreciation. It would be contemptible to willfully destroy the aesthetic qualities of a work of art simply to satisfy some of one's nonethical preferences, and it is a mark of a cultivated and hence admirable person that she has preferences for appreciating art. This account of higher and lower modes of valuation is indebted to Charles Taylor's account of higher and lower values. See Charles Taylor, "The Diversity of Goods," in *Utilitarianism and Beyond*, ed. Amartya Sen and Bernard Williams (Cambridge: Cambridge University Press, 1982), pp. 129–44.

3. This kind of argument shows why treating something as a commodity may be deplorable. Of course, more has to be said to justify prohibiting the commodification of a thing. I shall argue below that the considerations against the commodification of children and of women's labor are strong enough to justify prohibiting the practice of commercial surrogacy.

4. State laws against selling babies prevent the intended father's wife (if he has one) from being a party to the contract.

5. See Katie Marie Brophy, "A Surrogate Mother Contract to Bear a Child," *Journal of Family Law* 20 (1981–82): 263–91, and Noel Keane, "The Surrogate Parenting Contract," *Adelphia Law Journal* 2 (1983): 45–53, for examples and explanations of surrogate parenting contracts.

6. Mary Warnock, *A Question of Life* (Oxford: Blackwell, 1985), p. 45. This book reprints the Warnock Report on Human Fertilization and Embryology, which was commissioned by the British government for the purpose of recommending legislation concerning surrogacy and other issues. Although the Warnock Report mentions the promotion of altruism as one defense of surrogacy, it strongly condemns the practice overall.

7. John Robertson, "Surrogate Mothers: Not So Novel after All," *Hastings Center Report,* October 1983, pp. 28–34; John Harris, *The Value of Life* (Boston: Routledge and Kegan Paul, 1985).

8. See "No Other Hope for Having a Child," *Time*, 19 January 1987, pp. 50–51. Radin argues that women's traits are also commodified in this practice. See "Market Inalienability," pp. 1932–35.

9. Here I discuss the surrogate industry as it actually exists today. I will consider possible modifications of commercial surrogacy in the final section below.

10. Robert Nozick has objected that my claims about parental love appear to be culture-bound. Do not parents in the Third World, who rely on children to provide for the family subsistence, regard their children as economic goods? In promoting the livelihood of their families, however, such children need not be treated in accordance with market norms—that is, as commodities. In particular, such children usually remain a part of their families, and hence can still be loved by their parents. But insofar as children are treated according to the norms of modern capitalist markets, this treatment is deplorable wherever it takes place.

11. See Elizabeth Landes and Richard Posner, "The Economics of the Baby Shortage," *Journal of Legal Studies* 7 (1978): 323–48, and Richard Posner, "The Regulation of the Market in Adoptions," *Boston University Law Review* 67 (1987): 59–72.

12. Of course, where children are concerned, it is irrelevant whether these fears are reasonable. One of the greatest fears of children is separation from their parents. Adopted children are already known to suffer from separation anxiety more acutely than children who remain with their natural mothers, for they feel that their original mothers did not love them. In adoption, the fact that the child would be even worse off if the mother did not give it up justifies her severing of ties and can help to rationalize this event to the child. But in the case of commercial surrogacy, the severing of ties is done not for the child's sake, but for the parents' sakes. In the adoption case there are explanations for the mother's action which may quell the child's doubts about being loved which are unavailable in the case of surrogacy.

13. Kay Longcope, "Surrogacy: Two Professionals on Each Side of Issue Give Their Arguments for Prohibition and Regulation," *Boston Globe*, 23 March 1987, pp. 18–19; and Iver Peterson, "Baby M Case: Surrogate Mothers Vent Feelings," *New York Times*, 2 March 1987, pp. B1, B4.

14. Herbert Krimmel, "The Case against Surrogate Parenting," *Hastings Center Report*, October 1983, pp. 35–37.

15. Judge Sorkow made this argument in ruling on the famous case of Baby M. See *In Re Baby* M, 217 N.J. Super 313. Reprinted in *Family Law Reporter* 13 (1987): 2001–30. Chief Justice Wilentz of the New Jersey Supreme Court overruled Sorkow's judgment. See In the Matter of Baby M, 109 N.J. 396, 537 A.2d 1227 (1988).

16. Sallyann Payton has observed that the law does not permit the sale of parental rights, only their relinquishment or forced termination by the state, and these acts are subject to Court review for the sake of the child's best interests. But this legal technically does not change the moral implications of the analogy with baby-selling. The mother is still paid to do what she can to relinquish her

parental rights and to transfer custody of the child to the father. Whether or not the courts occasionally prevent this from happening, the actions of the parties express a commercial orientation to children which is degrading and harmful to them. The New Jersey Supreme Court ruled that surrogacy contracts are void precisely because they assign custody without regard to the child's best interests. See *In the Matter of Baby M*, p. 1246

17. Robertson, "Surrogate Mothers: Not So Novel after All," p. 32; Harris, *The Value of Life*, pp. 144–45.

18. See Philip Parker, "Surrogate Motherhood: The Interaction of Litigation, Legislation and Psychiatry," *International Journal of Law and Psychiatry* 5 (1982): 341–54.

19. The consent-intent rule would not, however, change the fact that commercial surrogacy replaces parental norms with market norms. For the rule itself embodies the market norm which acknowledges only voluntary, contractual relations among people as having moral force. Whereas familial love invites children into a network of unwilled relationships broader than those they have with their parents, the willed contract creates an exclusive relationship between the parents and the child only.

20. I thank Steven Darwall and David Anderson for clarifying my thoughts on this point.

21. I am indebted to Dr. Ezekiel Emanuel for this point.

22. One engages in emotional labor when one is paid to express or repress certain emotions. On the concept of emotional labor and its consequences for workers, see Arlie Hochschild, *The Managed Heart* (Berkeley and Los Angeles: University of California Press, 1983).

23. Noel Keane and Dennis Breo, *The Surrogate Mother* (New York: Everest House, 1981), p. 291; Brophy, "A Surrogate Mother Contract," p. 267. The surrogate's husband is also required to agree to this clause of the contract.

24. One might ask why this argument does not extend to all cases in which one might form an emotional attachment to an object one has contracted to sell. If I sign a contract with you to sell my car to you, can I back out if I decide I am too emotionally attached to it? My argument is based upon the distinctive characteristics of parental love—a mode of valuation which should not be confused with less profound modes of valuation which generate sentimental attachments to things. The degree to which other modes of valuation generate claims to consideration which tell against market norms remains an open question.

25. Corea, *The Mother Machine*, p. 222.

26. Keane and Breo, *The Surrogate Mother*, p. 292.

27. Kay Longcope, "Standing Up for Mary Beth," *Boston Globe*, 5 March 1987, p. 83; Daniel Goleman, "Motivations of Surrogate Mothers," *New York Times*, 20 January 1987, p. C1; Robertson, "Surrogate Mothers: Not So Novel after All," pp. 30, 34 n. 8. Neither the surrogate mothers themselves nor psychiatrists have been able to predict which women will experience such grief.

28. See Hochschild, *The Managed Heart,* for an important empirical study of the dynamics of commercialized emotional labor.

29. Keane and Breo, *The Surrogate Mother,* pp. 236–37.

30. For one account of how a surrogate mother who came to regret her decision viewed her own moral transformation, see Elizabeth Kane: *Birth Mother: The Story of America's First Legal Surrogate Mother* (San Diego: Harcourt Brace Jovanovich, 1988). I argue below that the implications of commodifying women's labor are not significantly changed even if the contract is unenforceable.

31. Susan Ince, "Inside the Surrogate Industry," in *Test-Tube Women,* ed. Rita Arditti, Ranate Duelli Klein, and Shelley Minden (Boston: Pandora Press, 1984), p. 110.

32. Philip Parker, "Motivation of Surrogate Mothers: Initial Findings," *American Journal of Psychiatry* 140(1983): 117–18.

33. The surrogate broker Noel Keane is remarkably open about reporting the desperate emotional insecurities which shape the lives of so many surrogate mothers, while displaying little sensitivity to the implications of his taking advantage of these motivations to make his business a financial success. See especially Keane and Breo, *The Surrogate Mother,* pp. 247ff.

34. See, for example, the story of the surrogate mother Nancy Barrass in Anne Fleming, "Our Fascination with Baby M," *New York Times Magazine,* 29 March 1987, p. 38.

35. For evidence of these disparate perspectives, see Peterson, "Baby M Case: Surrogate Mothers Vent Feelings," p. B4.

36. The surrogate mother is required to obey all doctor's orders made in the interests of the child's health. (See Brophy, "A Surrogate Mother Contract"; Keane, "The Surrogate Parenting Contract"; and Ince, "Inside the Surrogate Industry.") These orders could include forcing her to give up her job, travel plans, and recreational activities. The doctor could confine her to bed, and order her to submit to surgery and take drugs. One can hardly exercise an autonomous choice over one's health if one could be held in breach of contract and liable for $35,000 damages for making a decision contrary to the wishes of one's doctor.

37. See Corea, *The Mother Machine,* pp. 227–33, and Christine Overall, *Ethics and Human Reproduction* (Boston: Allen and Unwin, 1987), pp. 122–28. Both emphasize the social conditions which undermine the claim that women choose to be surrogate mothers under conditions of autonomy.

38. Both of these conclusions follow the Warnock commission's recommendations. See Warnock, *A Question of life,* pp. 43–44, 46–47. Since the surrogate mother is a victim of commercial surrogacy arrangements, she should not be prosecuted for entering into them. And my arguments are directed only against surrogacy as a commercial enterprise.

39. Barbara Cohen, "Surrogate Mothers: Whose Baby Is It?" *American Journal of Law and Medicine* 10 (1984): 282; Peter Singer and Deane Wells, *Making Babies* (New York: Scribner, 1985), pp. 106–7, 111.

40. Harris, *The Value of Life,* pp. 143–44, 156.

41. Singer and Wells support this recommendation in *Making Babies,* pp. 110–11. See also the dissenting opinion of the Warnock commission, *A Question of Life,* pp. 87–89.

42. See Fleming, "Our Fascination with Baby M," for a sensitive discussion of Americans' conflicting attitudes toward surrogate mothers who find they cannot give up their children.

43. *In Re Baby M,* p. 2022. See also Robertson, "Surrogate Mothers: Not So Novel after All," p. 32.

44. The Catholic Church makes this principle the fundamental basis for its own criticism of surrogate motherhood. See Congregation for the Doctrine of the Faith, "Instruction on Respect for Human Life In Its Origin and on the Dignity of Procreation: Replies to Certain Questions of the Day," reproduced in *New York Times,* 11 March 1987, pp. A14–A17.

Egg Donation and Commodification

BONNIE STEINBOCK

Bonnie Steinbock is a professor of philosophy at the State University of New York, Albany. In this essay she addresses the ethical issues raised by egg donation and its commodification. She argues that payment to donors is morally permissible provided the payment is not for the eggs but for the burdens of egg retrieval. She suggests that this distinction will help limit payment and ensure that payment is not made based on the donor's traits or on the number or quality of eggs retrieved.

Both payment for egg donation and payment for surrogacy raise ethical issues. I will address only egg donation, for two reasons. First, more has been written about surrogacy than about egg donation. Second, and more important, the two practices raise very different ethical issues. Surrogacy, or contract pregnancy as some prefer to call it, involves giving birth to a child and then waiving one's rights to custody of that child. In a few well-publicized cases, surrogates have changed their minds and attempted to keep the children. This has never, to my knowledge, occurred with egg donation. This is because there is a huge psychological and emotional difference between giving someone else your egg to gestate and deliver a baby, and gestating and delivering a baby yourself and then giving that baby to someone else. Indeed, in most cases, the egg donor does not even know if a child resulted from her donation. While a donor certainly should think about how she will feel about the possibility that there will be a child, or children, genetically linked to her out there in the world, she does not have to contemplate surrendering a child to whom she has given birth. Additionally, a child born from a surrogate arrangement may feel abandoned by the biological mother, just as an adopted child often does. The feelings of rejection by such children are likely to be compounded by the recognition that the birth mothers conceived them and relinquished them for money. It is implausible that a child conceived through egg donation would feel the same way. Finally, whatever may be wrong with commercial egg donation, it cannot plausibly be characterized as "baby selling." . . .

Noncommercial Gamete Donation

The Roman Catholic Church opposes gamete (ovum or sperm) donation because of its views on the unity of sexual intercourse and procreation. Sexual intercourse without openness to procreation is wrong, the Church claims (hence its opposition to birth control), but equally so is procreation without sexual intercourse (hence its opposition to most forms of

Presented at the Issues in Medical Ethics 2001 Conference on "Medicine, Money, and Morals" at the Mount Sinai School of Medicine, New York, NY, on November 2, 2001, and updated as of February 2004.

assisted reproduction). Even the "simple case" of *in vitro* fertilization (IVF), where the husband and wife provide the gametes and the resulting embryos are implanted in the wife's uterus, is impermissible, according to Catholic teaching. The wrong is compounded in gamete donation, as the introduction of "a third party" violates the unity of marriage. In addition, according to the Rev. Albert Moraczewski, egg donation is demeaning to women. "A donor woman is not really being treated as a person," he said. "Whether she is paid or acts out of kindness, her egg is being used, so she is not fully treated as a person whose reproductive capacity should be expressed as a result of the love of her husband." (6)

But why is egg donation demeaning? Presumably blood donation is not demeaning, and does not fail to treat the donor as a person. What is the difference? The answer, according to the Vatican, is that egg donation involves a wrongful use of reproductive capacity. But then to characterize egg donation as demeaning is not to give a reason why it is wrong; rather, egg donation is demeaning because it is wrong. To see egg donation as demeaning, one must accept the principle that reproductive capacity should be exercised only through a sexual act in the context of a loving marriage. And that principle is justified by the supposedly indissolvable unity of sex, love and procreation. There is nothing inconsistent or incoherent in this view, but it is unlikely to be persuasive to non-Catholics who accept contraception or assisted reproduction.

A different objection to gamete, specifically sperm, donation comes from Daniel Callahan. AID is "fundamentally wrong," according to Callahan, because a sperm donor is a father, who has all the duties of any other biological father, including rearing responsibilities. Sperm donation, according to Callahan, is as irresponsible as abandoning a woman when she becomes pregnant. He writes: (7)

> The only difference between the male who impregnates a woman in the course of sexual liaison and then disappears, and the man who is asked to disappear voluntarily after providing sperm, is that the latter kind of irresponsibility is, so to speak, licensed and legitimated. Indeed, it is treated as a kindly, beneficent action. The effect on the child is of course absolutely identical—an unknown, absent father.

Certainly, it is true that the child born from sperm donation does not know his or her genetic father. But it is not true that these children are fatherless, as is true of most children whose fathers abandon their mothers. They do have fathers—the men who are raising them. Why, one may ask, is it irresponsible to enable an infertile man, who wants very much to parent a child, to become a father? Sperm donors, it may be said, do not evade or abandon their obligations, as do men who abandon women they have impregnated, but rather transfer their rearing rights and duties to others. These others may be men or they may be single women or lesbian couples, who are increasingly using sperm donation. Is it wrong to donate sperm if the resulting child will grow up in a fatherless home? Is this an abandonment of one's responsibility as a father? In my view, this depends on whether the child can be expected to have a reasonably good life. There is evidence that children in single-parent households are at a disadvantage (since it is usually more stressful to raise a child on one's own), but growing up in a lesbian family does not appear to have a negative impact on quality of parenting or children's psychological development. (8) Many lesbian mothers attempt to mitigate the disadvantages of not having a father by making sure that there are other men in their child's life.

David Benatar (9) acknowledges that "gamete donation is not a unilateral abandonment of responsibility," but rather a transference of responsibility. Nevertheless, Benatar thinks that the responsibility of child rearing is one that should not be transferred, that doing so shows a lack of moral seriousness. Certainly, transferring child-rearing responsibilities without much thought is reprehensible; one thinks of Rousseau, who took five illegitimate children he had with his mistress to an orphanage. But is that what gamete donors do? Sperm and ova are not, after all, children. In my opinion, gamete donors do not give others their children to raise. Rather, they enable people who very much want to have children of their own to do so by providing them with genetic material. A woman who does not have eggs can still experience gestation, birth, and lactation, giving her a biological, if not genetic, connection to her child. In addition, if her husband's sperm is used, he will also have a biological connection to the child....

Why Do Women Want to Donate?

Given the rigors of egg donation, why would a woman who was not undergoing IVF or tubal ligation be willing to undergo egg donation for strangers? Some donors are curious about their own bodies and fertility. They want to know if their eggs are "good." (10) Some have a personal reason for helping, such as having friends or relatives who have struggled with infertility or have undergone miscarriages. Others are attracted by the idea of giving "the gift of life," as the advertisements for egg donors put it. One donor explained it as follows, on a donor website: "I can't even describe how it felt to know that in some small way I helped this couple achieve a huge dream in their life." But while most egg donors are motivated in part by altruistic considerations, most women would not be egg donors for strangers without financial compensation. Many say that egg donation would be impossible if they were not compensated for lost work time, transportation, daycare costs, and the like. However, most donors think that reimbursement for pecuniary expenses alone is not enough. They think that it is only fair that they should receive reasonable compensation for what they go through in order to provide eggs: the inconvenience, burden, and medical risk they have endured.

How Much Payment?

Compensation has been increasing rapidly over the years. In the mid-1980s, egg donors were paid only about $250 per cycle. Today, the payment is usually between $1,500 and $3,000—depending on the location of the clinic. In an effort to attract donors, some clinics offer substantially more. In 1998, Brooklyn IVF raised its donor compensation from $2,500 to $5,000 per cycle to keep pace with St. Barnabas Medical Center in nearby Livingston, New Jersey. "It's obvious why we had to do it," says Susan Lobel, Brooklyn IVF's assistant director. "Most New York area IVF programs have followed suit." (13)

Donors with particular attributes, such as enrollment in an Ivy League college, high SAT scores, physical attractiveness, or athletic or musical ability, have allegedly been offered far larger sums. "The International Fertility Center in Indianapolis, Indiana, for instance, places ads in the *Daily Princetonian* offering Princeton women as much as $35,000 per cycle. The National Fertility Registry, which, like many egg brokerages, features an online catalogue for couples to browse in, advertises $35,000 to $50,000 for Ivy League eggs." (13) In March 2000, an ad appeared in *The Daily Californian* (the campus newspaper for the University of California, Berkeley), which read, "Special Egg Donor Needed," and listed the following criteria for a "preferred donor": "height approximately 5'6", Caucasian, S.A.T. score around 1250 or high A.C.T., college student or graduate under 30, no genetic medical issues." The compensation was listed as $80,000 "paid to you and/or the charity of your choice." In addition, all related expenses would be paid. Extra compensation was available for someone especially gifted in athletics, science/mathematics or music.

Perhaps the most well-known instance of commercial egg donation is Ron Harris's website, www.ronsangels.com, which offered models as egg donors, "auctioning their ova via the Internet to would-be parents willing to pay up to $150,000 in hopes of having a beautiful child." (14) A subsequent story suggested that the "egg auction" might just be a publicity stunt to attract people to an erotic website, a claim that a spokesman for Mr. Harris denied. (15) Some infertility experts maintain that the ads offering large sums of money for special donors are not genuine offers, but rather a "bait and switch" tactic to recruit donors. Donors who respond are told that the ad has been filled, but that there are other recipients (offering substantially less money) seeking donors. *The Daily Californian* ad mentioned above specifically stated, "This ad is being placed for a particular client and is not soliciting eggs for a donor bank." I recently e-mailed the International Infertility Center in Indianapolis, asking them if the fee of $35,000 mentioned in the news report was actually paid to anyone. They responded that the "high-profile client" on whose behalf they had advertised did not find an ovum donor meeting the requirements, and so no ovum donor was compensated $35,000 for a cycle. I have not been able to discover if any "special donors" have received the sums in the ads.

Most people would distinguish between reasonable compensation and offering $30,000 or more to special donors. What explains the negative reaction most people experience when learning of these huge offers? Perhaps we think that people who are so intent on getting superior eggs (or "designer genes") will be incompetent parents. Instead of anticipating having a child to love, it seems that the couple is focusing on the traits their child will have. They are not satisfied with having a healthy child, which is the reason for genetic screening of donors. Nor is their aim simply to have children who resemble them, something that adoptive parents also usually want. These are reasonable requests, whereas seeking donors from Ivy League schools, with high SATs and athletic ability, indicates something else. The placers of these ads want, and are willing to pay huge sums to get, a "superior" child, and this seems inconsistent with an ideal of unconditional parental love and acceptance.

Moreover, anyone who thinks that it is possible to guarantee that a child will be brilliant, athletic, musically talented, or even blond haired and blue eyed, is likely to be disappointed. According to several prominent geneticists writing in *The New Republic*, "despite what your high school biology teacher told you, Mendelian rules do not apply even to eye color or hair color." (16) Even genetic diseases widely considered to follow Mendelian rules, like sickle-cell anemia, may be more or less severe, due to the interaction with other genes in the genome. Predicting or determining non-disease-related traits like intelligence, athletic ability, or musical talent is even less likely, as there are probably thousands of genes that play a role. Finally, the interaction of genes and the environment makes it very difficult to know in advance what phenotypic traits an individual will have. This is not to deny that traits like intelligence or athletic ability have a genetic component, but only to say that they cannot be guaranteed by the choice of an egg donor (who, after all, only provides half the genes). We may well worry about the welfare of a child who fails to live up to parental expectations, after the parents have spent all that money.

The welfare of offspring is a legitimate concern, despite philosophical worries over how to conceptualize it. (17) If commercial egg donation led to poor parenting or had adverse effects on the parent-child relationship, that would be an important moral objection. Yet such an objection might not justify the conclusion that the buying and selling of eggs is morally impermissible, still less that it should be legally banned. For we do not think that procreation is morally permissible only for ideal parents. Nevertheless, concern about effects on parenting and the parent-child relationship fall under the heading of "thick" moral assessments, and may be legitimate.

On the other hand, it is possible that couples who place the ads understand that they cannot determine their children's traits and that they do not have false expectations. Nevertheless, they might say, they want to give their child an advantage, a better chance at traits likely to help the child in life. It is not that they can only love a tall, brilliant, athletic child, they might say, but rather than they are well aware how advantageous such traits can be. Why, they might ask, if they have the money to spend, should they not use it to give their child the best chance in life? Indeed, some have argued that prospective parents are morally required to have the best child they can. (18)

The Human Fertilization and Embryology Authority (HFEA) in the U.K. cited "the physical and psychological well-being of children born from egg donation" as a reason to ban all payments, not just large ones, to egg donors. According to one member of HFEA, (19) "Children produced by egg donation could be adversely affected psychologically if they knew that payment had been made as part of their creation." This seems not only speculative, but implausible. Children may be psychologically harmed if they sense that their parents' love is contingent on their having certain traits, but why would a child be psychologically harmed by learning that the woman who provided the egg from which he or she was conceived received payment? It seems to me that this concern stems from an inappropriate analogy with commercial surrogacy. Children might well be upset to learn that their biological mothers gave them away for money, but it seems implausible that any child would have similar feelings about an egg donor. This being the case, it is hard to see why children would be affected by whether donors were paid or not.

Another moral objection to these ads is that they are elitist and violate a principle of equality. There is something offensive in the idea that the eggs of Princeton women are worth $50,000, while the eggs of women at Brooklyn College are worth only $5,000. (John Arras has jokingly suggested that perhaps *US News & World Report* should include how much their coeds can get for their eggs in their rankings of colleges [personal communication].) Yet it is not clear why we should be offended at the difference in the price put on eggs if we are not offended by differences in employment opportunities or salary.

Some people are disturbed not only by the payment of large sums to egg donors, but by any payment at all. Commercial egg donation is criticized on the grounds that this "commodifies" the human body or "commodifies" reproduction.

Commodification

To commodify something is to give it a market price. That in itself is not a bad thing. We could not buy our groceries or clothes or the morning paper if they did not have a market price. If some things should not be commodified, we need a rationale for this. This is not always forthcoming. As the guest editors of a recent special issue on commodification in the *Kennedy Institute of Ethics Journal* say, (20) "Unfortunately, a great deal of the talk about 'commodification' has been clumsy and sloppy. The term has been used as a magic bullet, as if saying, 'But that's commodification!' is the same as having made an argument."

The challenge is to distinguish legitimate activities in which the human body or its abilities are used, from those thought to be illegitimate. As Ruth Macklin has put it, (21) "Every service in our economy is sold: academics sell their minds; athletes sell their bodies. . . . If a pretty actress can sell her appearance and skill for television, why should a fecund woman be denied the ability to sell her eggs? Why is one more demeaning than the other?"

Those who tend to oppose commodification typically portray those who are skeptical about its moral wrongness as being enamored of the market, of thinking that freedom of choice is the only or the most important moral value. They say, ". . .there are some categories of human activities that should not be for sale." (22) But this, even if true, is unhelpful. We want to know *what* things and activities should not be for sale and *why*? Michael Walzer gives voting

as an example of a market exchange that should be blocked. Citizens may not sell their votes or vote a certain way for a price. (23) This is so even if the exchange is fully voluntary and even if it makes both parties better off. The reason why votes may not be sold is that this conflicts with the rationale for having the institution of voting in the first place. Voting is intended to express the will of the people in a democracy. Democracy is subverted if votes can be bought.

What we want, then, is a similarly persuasive rationale for the wrongness of selling human body parts. Suzanne Holland attempts to give one. She writes: (24)

> For many of us, our sense of the dignity of humanity is fundamentally disturbed by the suggestion that that which bears the marks of personhood can somehow be equated with property. We do not wish to have certain aspects of that which we associate with our personhood sold off on the market for whatever the market will bear.

Eggs should not be seen as property, according to Holland, because the human body is "inalienable." But what does this mean? To call rights "inalienable" is to say that they cannot be taken away from us, though Joel Feinberg has argued that we can waive them. (25) If calling the human body "inalienable" means that others cannot use my body or body parts without my permission, that is undeniable. But why does this imply that I may not sell my gametes? If "inalienable" just means "may not be treated like property," then Holland has not given a reason why eggs are not property, but rather a tautology.

The fact that something is a human body part does not make it obviously wrong to sell it. In the novel *Little Women*, Jo sells her hair to raise money for her father, who is serving as a chaplain in the Union Army. Surely that was not morally wrong of Jo, nor demeaning to her. Indeed, her willingness to part with "her one beauty" is an unselfish and noble gesture. If selling one's hair is morally permissible, but selling one's gametes is not, what is the moral difference?

It might be thought that I am missing an obvious point. Selling one's hair is not wrong because hair is unrelated to sex and reproduction. Selling one's eggs is akin to selling one's body in prostitution, and "we all know" that prostitution is wrong. Actually, prostitutes do not literally sell their bodies, since they do not relinquish control. It is more accurate to say that they rent them out, or rather that they perform sexual acts in exchange for money. Most of us believe that this is wrong, but this belief may be due in part to sexual puritanism. Perhaps the distaste we feel for prostitution stems (at least in part) from the way prostitutes have typically been regarded in patriarchal societies—as women of no value, undeserving of respect. Imagine a world in which those who provided sexual services were treated with as much respect as psychotherapists, trainers, and masseurs are in our society. It might be that, under such conditions, prostitution would not be as degrading. But even if this argument is invalid, there is a vast personal difference between these two types of "selling," and there is no obvious reason why paying egg donors is incompatible with treating them with respect.

There are two more reasons why selling eggs might be wrong. Providing eggs is both painful and risky. Perhaps offering money to women will lead them to take undue risks, opening up the potential for coercion or exploitation. In addition, some argue that payment for eggs inserts the values of the market into the family. I will consider these objections in turn.

The Potential for Coercion or Exploitation

In its report on *Assisted Reproductive Technologies*, the New York State Task Force made the following recommendation: (2)

> Gametes and embryos should not be bought and sold, but gamete and embryo donors should be offered compensation for the time and inconvenience associated with donation. Payments to egg donors should not be so high as to become coercive or so low that they provide inadequate reimbursement for time and inconvenience.

Can offering large sums of money for eggs be seen as coercive? That depends on the theory of coercion that one adopts. (26) In one theory, to coerce is to make a threat: do this or I will make you worse off. The classic example is the highwayman who says,

"Your money or your life." Clearly, potential egg donors are not coerced in this sense, no matter how much money is offered to them. They can turn down the offer and be no worse off than they were.

Perhaps this is too narrow a view of coercion. Perhaps there can be "coercive offers" as well as threats. Consider the following example:

The Lecherous Millionaire: Betty's child will die without expensive surgery, which is not covered by her insurance. Alan, a millionaire, offers to pay for the surgery if Betty will have sex with him.

Alan is not threatening Betty. He will not harm her if she refuses. Yet there is a very real sense in which she has "no choice," and for this reason we might see the offer as coercive. But even if this is true, and there can be "coercive offers," does this apply to egg donation? It might, if the money were offered to terribly poor women whose lives, or the lives of their children, depended on their donating eggs. A woman whose only choice was to give away her eggs or see her child die of starvation might well be seen as the victim of coercion. However, poor women are not usually sought out as egg donors. Typical egg donors are middle-class, often professional, young women. It is simply not true to say that they have no choice but to sell their eggs.

Very large offers of money could be quite tempting to any woman, not just those in desperate need of money. But, as Alan Wertheimer points out, offers are not coercive just because they are tempting. And they are not coercive because they are so good that it would be irrational to refuse. It is not coercive to offer someone a great job at double the salary she is currently earning. (27)

However, if offers of large sums of money are not coercive, they may still be criticized as being "undue inducements." Offering "too much" money may be an attempt to manipulate women into becoming donors. The lure of financial gain may lead them to discount the risks to themselves and to make decisions they will later regret. To take advantage of this is a form of exploitation.

It might be argued that we should not attempt to protect adults from irrational assessments or choices they will later regret, because this is paternalistic. However, paternalism involves preventing people from doing what they want on the grounds that this is in their best interest. It is not paternalistic to refrain from taking advantage of someone's susceptibility to temptation.

Some people have tried to meet the charge of commodification by distinguishing between compensating egg donors for their time, risk, and inconvenience, and payment for their eggs. This distinction has been challenged by several commentators, including Ruth Macklin, who writes, (21) "If there is something suspect about commodifying human reproductive products, it is similarly suspect to commodify human reproductive services." However, I think there are two reasons to distinguish between payment for time, risk, and inconvenience, and payment for eggs. First, if payment is viewed as compensation for the burdens of egg retrieval, then large payments based on the donor's college, height, or SAT scores would be unjustified. It is as burdensome for a SUNY-Albany student as it is for a Princeton student to go through the egg retrieval process. Additionally, if payment is compensation for the donor's time, risk, and burden, then donors would be compensated regardless of the number or quality of eggs retrieved, whereas this makes no sense if payment is for the product (eggs). Despite Macklin's rejection of the product/service distinction, she makes precisely this recommendation.

If excessive payments exploit donors, so do payments that are too low. Justice would seem to require that the women who go through the rigors of egg retrieval be fairly compensated. Why are only egg donors expected to act altruistically, when everyone else involved in egg donation receives payment? In light of the sacrifices of time, risk, and burden that egg donors make, it seems only fair that they receive enough money to make the sacrifice worthwhile.

Other Worries About Exploitation

Concerns about the exploitation of egg donors are not limited to payment issues. When the New York State Task Force on Life and the Law completed its report on assisted reproductive technologies, (2) one of its findings was that there were serious omissions in the process of gaining informed consent of egg donors. Donors did not always know how strenuous donation would be, or how much time it would take. They often had only the vaguest idea about who would pay their expenses, should there be medical complications stemming from donation. In one study, researchers were told by a number of women that all of their follow-up care was provided free of charge, but two women were billed for medical expenses for follow-up care and medical complications even though both were promised that the clinic would cover these costs:

> One woman was promised follow-up care prior to donating, but after the donation, that care was denied. She sought out her own personal physician for a sonogram and had to pay hundreds of dollars out of pocket because she was uninsured at the time. (28)

Another woman fainted at work while taking hormonal injections. She had muscle spasms and started to convulse, and had to stay overnight in the hospital. "The clinic denied that her condition was related to the donation and refused to pay for her hospitalization. She is currently fighting with her own health insurance and worker's compensation over the $3500 bill." (28)

One of the most significant sources of conflict in egg donation is the pressure on health care providers to hyperstimulate the donor to produce the maximum number of oocytes. The more eggs, the better the recipient's chances at implantation, but the greater the danger to the donor of suffering from hyperstimulation syndrome. (28) One donor who testified before the advisory committee to the New York State Task Force on Life and the Law revealed that one of her cycles had been stopped, but she had no idea that this was due to excessive stimulation, which had posed health risks to her. She thought that the reason so many eggs had been retrieved was that she was "super-fertile." One of the fertility doctors on the committee said that it was not uncommon for clinics to "flatter" donors in this way, to get them to be repeat donors. Such deceptive treatment of donors is, in my view, a greater source of exploitation, and an area of greater moral concern, than offering payment.

Altruistic egg donation would not necessarily be immune from exploitation. In fact, the true risks and burdens of egg donation might be less likely to be revealed in a voluntary system than in a carefully regulated commercial market, if only because the counseling and screening of donors costs money. Yet altruism can be an appropriate factor. When egg donation imposes little or no extra burden, as in the case of women who are undergoing IVF themselves or women having tubal ligations, there is less reason to compensate women for donating. Altruism in such cases is morally appropriate, as is the case with blood donation, which also involves minimal time and risk. The greater the burdens and risks, the less appropriate is the expectation of altruistic donation.

For some critics, it is not concerns about vulnerable donors that lie at the heart of their objections to commercial egg donation, but rather the effects on the families that are created, and ultimately on society at large.

Threats to Families
Tom Murray writes: (1)

> New reproductive technologies are a challenge to our notions of family because they expose what has been at the core of the family to the vicissitudes of the market. At the heart of our often vague concerns about the impact of new reproductive technologies, such as those about the purchase of human eggs, is our sense that they threaten somehow what is valuable about families.

While Murray acknowledges that even noncommercial gamete donation raises "morally relevant difficulties" (presumably those raised by Callahan [7] and Benatar [9], as well as the issue of the introduction of "a third party" into the marital relationship), he thinks it likely that these difficulties are outweighed by the good of creating new parent-child relationships. It is payment that Murray finds morally objectionable. He writes: (1)

> If you believe that markets, the values markets exemplify, and the relationships that typify market interactions, celebrate human freedom, and that such freedom is the preeminent good, then none of this should bother you. If, however, you regard families as a sphere distinct from the marketplace, a sphere whose place in human flourishing requires that it be kept free of destructive incursions by the values of the market, paying gamete providers should trouble you.

I think we would all agree that families should be protected from destructive incursions by the values of the market—but which incursions are destructive? Presumably it is okay to pay the people who care for our children: daycare workers, nannies, and babysitters. These transactions, supposedly, do not commercialize families. Also, presumably, there is nothing wrong with paying those who provide fertility treatment: doctors, nurses, receptionists, lawyers, and genetics counselors. So what is it about paying gamete providers that is threatening to families? Murray does not say. One can agree with his view (1) that "thinking of children as property, and of family life as essentially a series of commercial transactions, is a grievous distortion," but it is unclear what this has to do with paying gamete donors. Eggs are not children, and buying eggs (or even embryos) is not buying children. Still less is it clear why reasonable compensation to egg providers should turn family life into a series of commercial transactions.

Incomplete Commodification: A Reasonable Compromise
Is there room for compromise between those who prefer an altruistic system of egg donation and those who think that egg donors should be paid? Suzanne Holland suggests we take an approach she calls "incomplete commodification": (24)

> With respect to gamete donors, an incompletely commodified approach could recognize that donors are contributing to something that can be seen as a social and personal good (remedying infertility), even as they deserve a degree of compensation that constitutes neither a financial burden ([if they are paid] too little) nor a [temptation to undergo] health risk ([if paid] too much). I see no reason not to follow the suggestion of [the] ASRM [American Society for Reproductive Medicine] and cap egg donor compensation at $5000. . . . Allowing some compensation, but capping it at $5000, would reduce the competition for eggs and perhaps curb the lure of advertising that is targeted to college students in need of "easy money."

Not everyone agrees that $5,000 is appropriate compensation. Mark V. Sauer, a reproductive endocrinologist at Columbia-Presbyterian Medical Center, was "shocked" by the decision of St. Barnabas to double compensation from the community standard of $2,500 to $5,000 per cycle: "Even if one considers the time spent in traveling to the local office and waiting for an ultrasound exam to be 'work,' donors now will be earning in excess of $300 per hour. I find it hard to believe that anyone thinks this 'reasonable compensation' according to the recommendations of the Ethics Committee of the American Society for Reproductive Medicine." (29) However, Sauer's figure apparently takes into consideration only the number of hours spent traveling to and waiting at the clinic, together with the time required for the procedure. It does not consider compensation for risk or discomfort, or the time that some donors will have to take off from work or classes due to side effects from the drugs they must take. When these factors are considered, reimbursement of $5,000 may not be an "indecent proposal." Perhaps if, like Sauer, doctors are worried that (29) "most importantly, and most unfortunately, these expenses will have to be passed on directly to our patients, who are already spending considerable sums of money to seek this procedure," they might consider reducing their fees.

If compensation were completely banned, few women would agree to be egg donors. Very little egg donation would occur, and this would be unfortunate for those women who cannot have babies any other way. This is part of the justification for paying egg donors; the other part has to do with treating donors fairly. At the same time, legitimate concerns about the psychological welfare of the offspring created, and the potential for exploitation of donors, speaks to the need to limit payments to amounts that are reasonable and fair.

REFERENCES

1. Murray TH. New reproductive technologies and the family. In: Cohen CB, editor. *New ways of making babies: the case of egg donation.* Bloomington (IN) and Indianapolis (IN): Indiana University Press; 1996. pp. 51–69.
2. *Assisted reproductive technologies: analysis and recommendations for public policy.* New York: The New York State Task Force on Life and the Law; 1998. p. 237.
3. Bonnicksen AL. Private and public policy alternatives in oocyte donation. In: Cohen CB, editor, *New ways of making babies: the case of egg donation.* Bloomington (IN)
and Indianapolis (IN): Indiana University Press; 1996. pp. 156–174.
4. Executive summary. *New reproductive and genetic technologies: setting boundaries, enhancing health.* Jun 1996. p. 7; Health Canada (last updated 2002-02-07)
5. Little MO. The morality of abortion. In; Wellman C, Frey R. editors. *Companion to applied ethics.* Oxford (UK): Black-well; 2003.
6. Brozan N. Babies from donated eggs: growing use stirs questions, *New York Times* 1988 Jan 18; Sect. A:I.
7. Callahan D. Bioethics and fatherhood. *Utah Law Rev* 1992; 3:735–746.
8. Golombok S, Tasker F, Murray C. Children raised in fatherless families from infancy: family relationships and the socioemotional development of children of lesbian and single heterosexual mothers. *J Child Psychol Psychiatry* 1997; 38(7):783–791.
9. Brozan N. Babies from donated eggs: growing use stirs questions. *New York Times* 1988 Jan 18: Sect. A:1.
10. Callahan D. Bioethics and fatherhood. *Utah Law Rev* 1992; 3:735–746.
11. Golombok S. Tasker F. Murray C. Children raised in fatherless families from infancy: family relationships and the socioemotional development of children of lesbian and single heterosexual mothers. *J Child Psychol Psychiatry* 1997; 38(7):783–791.
12. Benatar D. The unbearable lightness of bringing into being. *J Applied Phil* 1999; 16(2):173–180.
13. Jones M. Donating your eggs. *Glamour* 1996 Jul. p. 169.
14. Lopez KJ. Egg heads: young women in need of cash are increasingly deciding to sell their bodies. *National Review* 1998 Sept 1; 50(16):26.
15. Goldberg C. On web, models auction their eggs to bidders for beautiful children, *New York Times* 1999 Oct 23; Sect. A:11.
16. Goldberg C. Egg auction on internet is drawing high scrutiny. *New York Times* 1999 Oct 26; Sect. A:26.
17. Collins F. Weiss L, Hudson K. Heredity and humanity. *The New Republic* 2001 Jun 25, p. 27.
18. Buchanan A. Brock DW, Daniels N, Wikler D. *From chance to choice: genetics and justice.* Cambridge (UK): Cambridge University Press; 2000.
19. Savulescu J. Procreative beneficence: why we should select the best children. *Bioethics* 2001; 15(5–6):413–426.
20. Johnson MH. The culture of unpaid and voluntary egg donation should be strengthened. *BMJ* 1997; 314:1401–1402.
21. Davis DS. Holland S. Introduction. *Kennedy Inst Ethics J* 2001; 11(3):219.
22. Macklin R. What is wrong with commodification? In: Cohen CB. editor. *New ways of making babies: the case of egg donation.* Bloomington (IN) and Indianapolis (IN): Indiana University Press; 1996. pp. 106–121.
23. Ketchum SA. Selling babies and selling bodies. *Hypatia* 1989; 4(3):116–127.

24. Walzer M. *Spheres of justice.* New York: Basic Books; 1983.

25. Holland S. Contested commodities at both ends of life: buying and selling gametes, embryos, and body tissues. *Kennedy Inst Ethics J* 2001; 11(3):263–284.

26. Feinberg J. Voluntary euthanasia and the inalienable right to life. *Phil and Pub Aff* 1978; 7(2):93–123.

27. *Assisted reproductive technologies: analysis and recommendations for public policy.* New York: The New York State Task Force on Life and the Law; 1998. p. 237.

28. Wertheimer A. *Coercion.* Princeton (NJ): Princeton University Press; 1987.

29. Wertheimer A. *Exploitation.* Princeton (NJ): Princeton University Press; 1996.

30. Kalfoglou AL, Geller G. Navigating conflict of interest in oocyte donation: an analysis of donors' experiences. *Womens Health Issues* 2000; 10(5):226–239.

31. Murray TH. New reproductive technologies and the family. In: Cohen CB, editor. *New ways of making babies: the case of egg donation.* Bloomington (IN) and Indianapolis (IN): Indiana University Press; 1996. pp. 51–69.

32. Sauer MV. Indecent proposal: $5,000 is not "reasonable compensation" for oocyte donors [editorial]. *Fertil Steril* 1999; 71(1):7–8.

The Wisdom of Repugnance

LEON R. KASS

Kass contends that human cloning is both unethical and dangerous in its consequences. People are repelled by many aspects of human cloning, and although this revulsion is not an argument, it is "the emotional expression of deep wisdom, beyond reason's power fully to articulate it." Kass argues that human cloning should also be rejected because it is a major violation of our "given nature" and the social relations based in this nature, it creates serious issues of identity and individuality for the cloned person, it turns begetting into dehumanizing manufacture, and it is "inherently despotic" because it seeks to make children according to their parents' will and in their own image.

Our habit of delighting in news of scientific and technological breakthroughs has been sorely challenged by the birth announcement of a sheep named Dolly. Though Dolly shares with previous sheep the "softest clothing, woolly, bright," William Blake's question, "Little Lamb, who made thee?" has for her a radically different answer: Dolly was, quite literally, made. She is the work not of nature or nature's God but of man, an Englishman, Ian Wilmut, and his fellow scientists. What's more, Dolly came into being not only sexually—ironically, just like "He [who] calls Himself a Lamb"—but also as the genetically identical copy (and the perfect incarnation of the form or blueprint) of a mature ewe, of whom she is a clone. This long-awaited yet not quite expected success in cloning a mammal raised immediately the prospect—and the specter—of cloning human beings: "I a child and Thou a lamb," despite our differences, have always been equal candidates for creative making, only now, by means of cloning, we may both spring from the hand of man playing at being God.

After an initial flurry of expert comment and public consternation, with opinion polls showing overwhelming opposition to cloning human beings, President Clinton ordered a ban on all federal support for human cloning research (even though none was being supported) and charged the National Bioethics Advisory Commission to report in ninety days on the ethics of human cloning research. The commission (an eighteen-member panel, evenly balanced between scientists and nonscientists, appointed by the president and reporting to the National Science and Technology Council) invited testimony from

From the *New Republic* 216 (June 2, 1997), pp. 17–26.

scientists, religious thinkers and bioethicists, as well as from the general public. It is now deliberating about what it should recommend, both as a matter of ethics and as a matter of public policy.

Congress is awaiting the commission's report, and is poised to act. Bills to prohibit the use of federal funds for human cloning research have been introduced in the House of Representatives and the Senate; and another bill, in the House, would make it illegal "for any person to use a human somatic cell for the process of producing a human clone." A fateful decision is at hand. To clone or not to clone a human being is no longer an academic question.

Taking Cloning Seriously, Then and Now

Cloning first came to public attention roughly thirty years ago, following the successful asexual production, in England, of a clutch of tadpole clones by the technique of nuclear transplantation. The individual largely responsible for bringing the prospect and promise of human cloning to public notice was Joshua Lederberg, a Nobel Laureate geneticist and a man of large vision. In 1966, Lederberg wrote a remarkable article in *The American Naturalist* detailing the eugenic advantages of human cloning and other forms of genetic engineering, and the following year he devoted a column in *The Washington Post*, where he wrote regularly on science and society, to the prospect of human cloning. He suggested that cloning could help us overcome the unpredictable variety that still rules human reproduction, and allow us to benefit from perpetuating superior genetic endowments. These writings sparked a small public debate in which I became a participant. At the time a young researcher in molecular biology at the National Institutes of Health (NIH), I wrote a reply to the *Post*, arguing against Lederberg's amoral treatment of this morally weighty subject and insisting on the urgency of confronting a series of questions and objections, culminating in the suggestion that "the programmed reproduction of man will, in fact, dehumanize him."

Much has happened in the intervening years. It has become harder, not easier, to discern the true meaning of human cloning. We have in some sense been softened up to the idea—through movies, cartoons, jokes and intermittent commentary in the mass media, some serious, most lighthearted. We have become accustomed to new practices in human reproduction: not just in vitro fertilization, but also embryo manipulation, embryo donation and surrogate pregnancy. Animal biotechnology has yielded transgenic animals and a burgeoning science of genetic engineering, easily and soon to be transferable to humans.

Even more important, changes in the broader culture make it now vastly more difficult to express a common and respectful understanding of sexuality, procreation, nascent life, family, and the meaning of motherhood, fatherhood and the links between the generations. Twenty-five years ago, abortion was still largely illegal and thought to be immoral, the sexual revolution (made possible by the extramarital use of the pill) was still in its infancy, and few had yet heard about the reproductive rights of single women, homosexual men and lesbians (Never mind shameless memoirs about one's own incest!) Then one could argue, without embarrassment, that the new technologies of human reproduction—babies without sex—and their confounding of normal kin relations—who's the mother: the egg donor, the surrogate who carries and delivers, or the one who rears?—would "undermine the justification and support that biological parenthood gives to the monogamous marriage." Today, defenders of stable, monogamous marriage risk charges of giving offense to those adults who are living in "new family forms" or to those children who, even without the benefit of assisted reproduction, have acquired either three or four parents or one or none at all. Today, one must even apologize for voicing opinions that twenty-five years ago were nearly universally regarded as the core of our culture's wisdom on these matters. In a world whose once-given natural boundaries are blurred by technological change and whose moral boundaries are seemingly up for grabs, it is much more difficult to make persuasive the still compelling case against cloning human beings. As Raskolnikov put it, "man gets used to everything—the beast!"

———

Indeed, perhaps the most depressing feature of the discussions that immediately followed the news about Dolly was their ironical tone, their genial cynicism, their moral fatigue: "AN UDDER WAY OF MAKING LAMBS" (*Nature*), "WHO WILL CASH IN ON BREAKTHROUGH IN CLONING?" (*The Wall Street Journal*), "IS CLONING BAAAAAAAAD?" (*The Chicago Tribune*). Gone from the scene are the wise and courageous voices of Theodosius Dobzhansky (genetics), Hans Jonas (philosophy) and Paul Ramsey (theology) who, only twenty-five years ago, all made powerful moral arguments against ever cloning a human being. We are now too sophisticated for such argumentation; we wouldn't be caught in public with a strong moral stance, never mind an absolutist one. We are all, or almost all, postmodernists now.

Cloning turns out to be the perfect embodiment of the ruling opinions of our new age. Thanks to the sexual revolution, we are able to deny in practice, and increasingly in thought, the inherent procreative teleology of sexuality itself. But, if sex has no intrinsic connection to generating babies, babies need have no necessary connection to sex. Thanks to feminism and the gay rights movement, we are increasingly encouraged to treat the natural heterosexual difference and its preeminence as a matter of "cultural construction." But if male and female are not normatively complementary and generatively significant, babies need not come from male and female complementarity. Thanks to the prominence and the acceptability of divorce and out-of-wedlock births, stable, monogamous marriage as the ideal home for procreation is no longer the agreed-upon cultural norm. For this new dispensation, the clone is the ideal emblem: the ultimate "single-parent child."

Thanks to our belief that all children should be *wanted* children (the more high-minded principle we use to justify contraception and abortion), sooner or later only those children who fulfill our wants will be fully acceptable. Through cloning, we can work our wants and wills on the very identity of our children, exercising control as never before. Thanks to modern notions of individualism and the rate of cultural change, we see ourselves not as linked to ancestors and defined by traditions, but as projects for our own self-creation, not only as self-made men but also man-made selves; and self-cloning is simply an extension of such rootless and narcissistic self-recreation.

Unwilling to acknowledge our debt to the past and unwilling to embrace the uncertainties and the limitations of the future, we have a false relation to both: cloning personifies our desire fully to control the future, while being subject to no controls ourselves. Enchanted and enslaved by the glamour of technology, we have lost our awe and wonder before the deep mysteries of nature and of life. We cheerfully take our own beginnings in our hands and, like the last man, we blink.

––––––––––

Part of the blame for our complacency lies, sadly, with the field of bioethics itself, and its claim to expertise in these moral matters. Bioethics was founded by people who understood that the new biology touched and threatened the deepest matters of our humanity: bodily integrity, identity and individuality, lineage and kinship, freedom and self-command, eros and aspiration, and the relations and strivings of body and soul. With its capture by analytic philosophy, however, and its inevitable routinization and professionalization, the field has by and large come to content itself with analyzing moral arguments, reacting to new technological developments and taking on emerging issues of public policy, all performed with a naïve faith that the evils we fear can all be avoided by compassion, regulation and a respect for autonomy. Bioethics has made some major contributions in the protection of human subjects and in other areas where personal freedom is threatened; but its practitioners, with few exceptions, have turned the big human questions into pretty thin gruel.

One reason for this is that the piecemeal formation of public policy tends to grind down large questions of morals into small questions of procedure. Many of the country's leading bioethicists have served on national commissions or state task forces and advisory boards, where understandably, they have found utilitarianism to be the only ethical vocabulary acceptable to all participants in discussing issues of law, regulation and public policy. As many of these commissions have been either officially under the aegis of NIH or the Health and Human Services Department, or otherwise dominated by powerful voices for scientific progress, the ethicists have for the most part been content, after some "values clarification" and wringing of hands, to pronounce their blessings upon the inevitable. Indeed, it is the bioethicists, not the scientists, who are now the most articulate defenders of human cloning: the two witnesses testifying before the National Bioethics Advisory Commission in favor of cloning human beings were bioethicists, eager to rebut what they regard as the irrational concerns of those of us in opposition. One wonders whether this commission, constituted like the previous commissions, can tear itself sufficiently free from the accommodationist pattern of rubber-stamping all technical innovation, in the mistaken belief that all other goods must bow down before the gods of better health and scientific advance.

If it is to do so, the commission must first persuade itself, as we all should persuade ourselves, not to be complacent about what is at issue here. Human cloning, though it is in some respects continuous with previous reproductive technologies, also represents something radically new, in itself and in its easily foreseeable consequences. The stakes are very high indeed. I exaggerate, but in the direction of the truth, when I insist that we are faced with having to decide nothing less than whether human procreation is going to remain human, whether children are going to be made rather than begotten, whether it is a good thing, humanly speaking, to say yes in principle to the road which leads (at best) to the dehumanized rationality *of Brave New World*. This is not business as usual, to be fretted about for a while but finally to be given our seal of approval. We must rise to the occasion and make our judgments as if the future of our humanity hangs in the balance. For so it does.

The State of the Art

If we should not underestimate the significance of human cloning, neither should we exaggerate its imminence or misunderstand just what is involved. The procedure is conceptually simple. The nucleus of a mature but unfertilized egg is removed and replaced with a nucleus obtained from a specialized cell of an adult (or fetal) organism (in Dolly's case, the donor nucleus came from mammary gland epithelium). Since almost all the hereditary material of a cell is contained within its nucleus, the renucleated egg and the individual into which this egg develops are genetically identical to the organism that was the source of the transferred nucleus. An unlimited number of genetically identical individuals—clones—could be produced by nuclear transfer. In principle, any person, male or female, newborn or adult, could be cloned, and in any quantity. With laboratory cultivation and storage of tissues, cells outliving their sources make it possible even to clone the dead.

The technical stumbling block, overcome by Wilmut and his colleagues, was to find a means of reprogramming the state of the DNA in the donor cells, reversing its differentiated expression and restoring its full totipotency, so that it could again direct the entire process of producing a mature organism. Now that this problem has been solved, we should expect a rush to develop cloning for other animals, especially livestock, in order to propagate in perpetuity the champion meat or milk producers. Though exactly how soon someone will succeed in cloning a human being is anybody's guess. Wilmut's technique, almost certainly applicable to humans, makes *attempting* the feat an imminent possibility.

Yet some cautions are in order and some possible misconceptions need correcting. For a start, cloning is not Xeroxing. As has been reassuringly reiterated, the clone of Mel Gibson, though his genetic double, would enter the world hairless, toothless and peeing in his diapers, just like any other human infant. Moreover, the success rate, at least at first, will probably not be very high: the British transferred 277 adult nuclei into enucleated sheep eggs, and implanted twenty-nine clonal embryos, but they achieved the birth of only one live lamb clone. For this reason, among others, it is unlikely that, at least for now, the practice would be very popular, and there is no immediate worry of mass-scale production of multicopies. The need of repeated surgery to obtain eggs and, more crucially, of numerous borrowed wombs for implantation will surely limit use, as will the expense; besides, almost everyone who is able will doubtless prefer nature's sexier way of conceiving.

Still, for the tens of thousands of people already sustaining over 200 assisted reproduction clinics in the United States and already availing themselves of in vitro fertilization, intracytoplasmic sperm injection and other techniques of assisted reproduction, cloning would be an option with virtually no added fuss (especially when the success rate improves). Should commercial interests develop in "nucleus-banking," as they have in sperm-banking; should famous athletes or other celebrities decide to market their DNA the way they now market their auto-graphs and just about everything else; should techniques of embryo and germline genetic testing and manipulation arrive as anticipated, increasing the use of laboratory assistance in order to obtain "better" babies—should all this come to pass, then cloning, if it is permitted, could become more than a marginal practice simply on the basis of free reproductive choice, even without any social encouragement to upgrade the gene pool or to replicate superior types. Moreover, if laboratory research on human cloning proceeds, even without any intention to produce cloned humans, the existence of cloned human embryos in the laboratory, created to begin with only for research purposes, would surely pave the way for later baby-making implantations.

In anticipation of human cloning, apologists and proponents have already made clear possible uses of the perfected technology, ranging from the sentimental and compassionate to the grandiose. They include: providing a child for an infertile couple; "replacing" a beloved spouse or child who is dying or has died; avoiding the risk of genetic disease; permitting reproduction for homosexual men and lesbians who want nothing sexual to do with the opposite sex; securing a genetically identical source of organs or tissues perfectly suitable for transplantation; getting a child with a genotype of one's own choosing, not excluding oneself; replicating individuals of great genius, talent or beauty—having a child who really could "be like Mike"; and creating large sets of genetically identical humans suitable for research on, for instance, the question of nature versus nurture, or for special missions in peace and war (not excluding espionage), in which using identical humans would be an advantage. Most people who envision the cloning of human beings, of course, want none of these scenarios. That they cannot say why is not surprising. What is surprising, and welcome, is that, in our cynical age, they are saying anything at all.

The Wisdom of Repugnance

"Offensive." "Grotesque." "Revolting." "Repugnant." "Repulsive." These are the words most commonly heard regarding the prospect of human cloning. Such reactions come both from the man or woman in the street and from the intellectuals, from

believers and atheists, from humanists and scientists. Even Dolly's creator has said he "would find it offensive" to clone a human being.

People are repelled by many aspects of human cloning. They recoil from the prospect of mass production of human beings, with large clones of look-alikes, compromised in their individuality; the idea of father-son or mother-daughter twins; the bizarre prospects of a woman giving birth to and rearing a genetic copy of herself, her spouse or even her deceased father or mother; the grotesqueness of conceiving a child as an exact replacement for another who has died; the utilitarian creation of embryonic genetic duplicates of oneself, to be frozen away or created when necessary, in case of need for homologous tissues or organs for transplantation; the narcissism of those who would clone themselves and the arrogance of others who think they know who deserves to be cloned or which genotype any child-to-be should be thrilled to receive; the Frankensteinian hubris to create human life and increasingly to control its destiny; man playing God. Almost no one finds any of the suggested reasons for human cloning compelling; almost everyone anticipates its possible misuses and abuses. Moreover, many people feel oppressed by the sense that there is probably nothing we can do to prevent it from happening. This makes the prospect all the more revolting.

———

Revulsion is not an argument; and some of yesterday's repugnances are today calmly accepted—though, one must add, not always for the better. In crucial cases, however, repugnance is the emotional expression of deep wisdom, beyond reason's power fully to articulate it. Can anyone really give an argument fully adequate to the horror which is father-daughter incest (even with consent), or having sex with animals, or mutilating a corpse, or eating human flesh, or even just (just!) raping or murdering another human being? Would anybody's failure to give full rational justification for his or her revulsion at these practices make that revulsion ethically suspect? Not at all. On the contrary, we are suspicious of those who think that they can rationalize away our horror, say, by trying to explain the enormity of incest with arguments only about the genetic risks of inbreeding.

The repugnance at human cloning belongs in this category. We are repelled by the prospect of cloning human beings not because of the strangeness or novelty of the undertaking, but because we intuit and feel, immediately and without argument, the violation of things that we rightfully hold dear. Repugnance, here as elsewhere, revolts against the excesses of human willfulness, warning us not to transgress what is unspeakably profound. Indeed, in this age in which everything is held to be permissible so long as it is freely done, in which our given human nature no longer commands respect, in which our bodies are regarded as mere instruments of our autonomous rational wills, repugnance may be the only voice left that speaks up to defend the central core of our humanity. Shallow are the souls that have forgotten how to shudder.

The goods protected by repugnance are generally overlooked by our customary ways of approaching all new biomedical technologies. The way we evaluate cloning ethically will in fact be shaped by how we characterize it descriptively, by the context into which we place it, and by the perspective from which we view it. The first task for ethics is proper description. And here is where our failure begins.

————

Typically, cloning is discussed in one or more of three familiar contexts, which one might call the technological, the liberal and the meliorist. Under the first, cloning will be seen as an extension of existing techniques for assisting reproduction and determining the genetic makeup of children. Like them, cloning is to be regarded as a neutral technique, with no inherent meaning or goodness, but subject to multiple uses, some good, some bad. The morality of cloning thus depends absolutely on the goodness or badness of the motives and intentions of the cloners: as one bioethicist defender of cloning puts it, "the ethics must be judged [only] by the way the parents nurture and rear their resulting child and whether they bestow the same love and affection on a child brought into existence by a technique of assisted reproduction as they would on a child born in the usual way."

The liberal (or libertarian or liberationist) perspective sets cloning in the context of rights, freedoms and personal empowerment. Cloning is just a new option for exercising an individual's right to reproduce or to have the kind of child that he or she wants. Alternatively, cloning enhances our liberation (especially women's liberation) from the confines of nature, the vagaries of chance, or the necessity for sexual mating. Indeed, it liberates women from the need for men altogether, for the process requires only eggs, nuclei and (for the time being) uteri—plus, of course, a healthy dose of our (allegedly "masculine") manipulative science that likes to do all these things to mother nature and nature's mothers. For those who hold this outlook, the only moral restraints on cloning are adequately informed consent and the avoidance of bodily harm. If no one is cloned without her consent, and if the clonant is not physically damaged, then the liberal conditions for licit, hence moral, conduct are met. Worries that go beyond violating the will or maiming the body are dismissed as "symbolic"—which is to say, unreal.

The meliorist perspective embraces valetudinarians and also eugenicists. The latter were formerly more vocal in these discussions, but they are now generally happy to see their goals advanced under the less threatening banners of freedom and technological growth. These people see in cloning a new prospect for improving human beings—minimally, by ensuring the perpetuation of healthy individuals by avoiding the risks of genetic disease inherent in the lottery of sex, and maximally, by producing "optimum babies," preserving outstanding genetic material, and (with the help of soon-to-come techniques for precise genetic engineering) enhancing inborn human capacities on many fronts. Here the morality of cloning as a means is justified solely by the excellence of the end, that is, by the outstanding traits or individuals cloned—beauty, or brawn, or brains.

————

These three approaches, all quintessentially American and all perfectly fine in their places, are sorely wanting as approaches to human procreation. It is, to say the least, grossly distorting to view the wondrous mysteries of birth, renewal and individuality, and the deep meaning of parent-child relations, largely through the lens of our reductive science and its potent technologies. Similarly, considering reproduction (and the intimate relations of family life!) primarily under the political-legal, adversarial and individualistic notion of rights can only under-mine the private yet fundamentally social, coop-erative and duty-laden character of child-bearing, child-rearing and their bond to the covenant of marriage. Seeking to escape entirely from nature (in order to satisfy a natural desire or a natural right to reproduce!) is self-contradictory in theory and self-alienating in practice. For we are erotic beings only because we are embodied beings, and not merely intellects and wills unfortunately imprisoned in our bodies. And, though health and fitness are clearly great goods, there is something deeply disquieting in looking on our prospective children as artful products perfectible by genetic engineering, increasingly held to our willfully imposed designs, specifications and margins of tolerable error.

The technical, liberal and meliorist approaches all ignore the deeper anthropological, social and, indeed, ontological meanings of bringing forth new life. To this more fitting and profound point of view, cloning shows itself to be a major alteration, indeed, a major violation, of our given nature as embodied, gendered and engendering beings—and of the social relations built on this natural ground. Once this perspective is recognized, the ethical judgment on cloning can no longer be reduced to a matter of mo-tives and intentions, rights and freedoms, benefits and harms, or even means and ends. It must be re-garded primarily as a matter of meaning: Is cloning a fulfillment of human begetting and belonging? Or is cloning rather, as I contend, their pollution and perversion? To pollution and perversion, the fitting response can only be horror and revulsion; and con-versely, generalized horror and revulsion are prima facie evidence of foulness and violation. The burden of moral argument must fall entirely on those who want to declare the widespread repugnances of hu-mankind to be mere timidity or superstition.

Yet repugnance need not stand naked before the bar of reason. The wisdom of our horror at human cloning can be partially articulated, even if this is finally one of those instances about which the heart has its reasons that reason cannot entirely know.

The Profundity of Sex

To see cloning in its proper context, we must begin not, as I did before, with laboratory technique, but with the anthropology—natural and social—of sexual reproduction.

Sexual reproduction—by which I mean the gen-eration of new life from (exactly) two complementary elements, one female, one male, (usually) through coitus—is established (if that is the right term) not by human decision, culture or tradition, but by nature; it is the natural way of all mammalian reproduction. By nature, each child has two complementary bio-logical progenitors. Each child thus stems from and unites exactly two lineages. In natural generation, moreover, the precise genetic constitution of the resulting offspring is determined by a combination of nature and chance, not by human design: each human child shares the common natural human species genotype, each child is genetically (equally) kin to each (both) parent(s), yet each child is also genetically unique.

These biological truths about our origins fore-tell deep truths about our identity and about our human condition altogether. Every one of us is at once equally human, equally enmeshed in a partic-ular familial nexus of origin, and equally individu-ated in our trajectory from birth to death—and, if all goes well, equally capable (despite our morality) of participating, with a complementary other, in the very same renewal of such human possibility through procreation. Though less momentous than our common humanity, our genetic individuality is not humanly trivial. It shows itself forth in our dis-tinctive appearance through which we are every-where recognized; it is revealed in our "signature" marks of fingerprints and our self-recognizing immune system; it symbolizes and foreshadows ex-actly the unique, never-to-be-repeated character of each human life.

Human societies virtually everywhere have struc-tured child-rearing responsibilities and systems of identity and relationship on the bases of these deep natural facts of begetting. The mysterious yet ubiq-uitous "love of one's own" is everywhere culturally exploited, to make sure that children are not just produced but well cared for and to create for every-one clear ties of meaning, belonging and obligation. But it is wrong to treat such naturally rooted social practices as mere cultural constructs (like left- or right-driving, or like burying or cremating the dead) that we can alter with little human cost. What would kinship be without its clear natural grounding? And what would identity be without kinship? We must resist those who have begun to refer to sexual reproduction as the "traditional method of reproduction," who would have us regard as merely traditional, and by implication arbitrary, what is in truth not only natural but most certainly profound.

Asexual reproduction, which produces "single-parent" offspring, is a radical departure from the natural human way, confounding all normal understandings of father, mother, sibling, grandparent, etc., and all moral relations tied thereto. It becomes even more of a radical departure when the resulting offspring is a clone derived not from an embryo, but from a mature adult to whom the clone would be an identical twin; and when the process occurs not by natural accident (as in natural twinning), but by deliberate human design and manipulation; and when the child's (or children's) genetic constitution is preselected by the parent(s) (or scientists). Accordingly, as we will see, cloning is vulnerable to three kinds of concerns and objections, related to these three points: cloning threatens confusion of identity and individuality, even in small-scale cloning; cloning represents a giant step (though not the first one) toward transforming procreation into manufacture, that is, toward the increasing depersonalization of the process of generation and, increasingly, toward the "production" of human children as artifacts, products of human will and design (what others have called the problem of "commodification" of new life); and cloning—like other forms of eugenic engineering of the next generation—represents a form of despotism of the cloners over the cloned, and thus (even in benevolent cases) represents a blatant violation of the inner meaning of parent-child relations, of what it means to have a child, of what it means to say "yes" to our own demise and "replacement."

Before turning to these specific ethical objections, let me test my claim of the profundity of the natural way by taking up a challenge recently posed by a friend. What if the given natural human way of reproduction were asexual, and we now had to deal with a new technological innovation—artificially induced sexual dimorphism and the fusing of complementary gametes—whose inventors argued that sexual reproduction promised all sorts of advantages, including hybrid vigor and the creation of greatly increased individuality? Would one then be forced to defend natural asexuality because it was natural? Could one claim that it carried deep human meaning?

The response to this challenge broaches the ontological meaning of sexual reproduction. For it is impossible, I submit, for there to have been human life—or even higher forms of animal life—in the absence of sexuality and sexual reproduction. We find asexual reproduction only in the lowest forms of life: bacteria, algae, fungi, some lower invertebrates. Sexuality brings with it a new and enriched relationship to the world. Only sexual animals can seek and find complementary others with whom to pursue a goal that transcends their own existence. For a sexual being, the world is no longer an indifferent and largely homogeneous *otherness*, in part edible, in part dangerous. It also contains some very special and related and complementary beings, of the same kind but of opposite sex, toward whom one reaches out with special interest and intensity. In higher birds and mammals, the outward gaze keeps a lookout not only for food and predators, but also for prospective mates; the beholding of the many splendored world is suffused with desire for union, the animal antecedent of human eros and the germ of sociality. Not by accident is the human animal both the sexiest animal—whose females do not go into heat but are receptive throughout the estrous cycle and whose males must therefore have greater sexual appetite and energy in order to reproduce successfully—and also the most aspiring, the most social, the most open and the most intelligent animal.

———

The soul-elevating power of sexuality is, at bottom, rooted in its strange connection to mortality, which it simultaneously accepts and tries to overcome. Asexual reproduction may be seen as a continuation of the activity of self-preservation. When one organism buds or divides to become two, the original being is (doubly) preserved, and nothing dies. Sexuality, by contrast, means perishability and serves replacement; the two that come together to generate one soon will die. Sexual desire, in human beings as in animals, thus serves an end that is partly hidden from, and finally at odds with, the self-serving individual. Whether we know it or not, when we are sexually active we are voting with our genitalia for our own demise. The salmon swimming upstream to spawn and die tell the universal story: sex is bound up with death, to which it holds a partial answer in procreation.

The salmon and the other animals evince this truth blindly. Only the human being can understand what it means. As we learn so powerfully from the story of the Garden of Eden, our humanization is coincident with sexual self-consciousness, with the recognition of our sexual nakedness and all that it implies: shame at our needy incompleteness, unruly self-division and finitude; awe before the eternal; hope in the self-transcending possibilities of children and a relationship to the divine. In the sexually self-conscious animal, sexual desire can become eros, lust can become love. Sexual desire humanly regarded is thus sublimated into erotic longing for wholeness, completion and immortality which drives us knowingly into the embrace and its generative fruit—as well as into all the higher human possibilities of deed, speech and song.

Through children, a good common to both husband and wife, male and female achieve some genuine unification (beyond the mere sexual "union," which fails to do so). The two become one through sharing generous (not needy) love for this third being as good. Flesh of their flesh, the child is the parents' own commingled being externalized, and given a separate and persisting existence. Unification is enhanced also by their commingled work of rearing. Providing an opening to the future beyond the grave, carrying not only our seed but also our names, our ways and our hopes that they will surpass us in goodness and happiness, children are a testament to the possibility of transcendence. Gender duality and sexual desire, which first draws our love upward and outside of ourselves, finally provide for the partial overcoming of the confinement and limitation of perishable embodiment altogether.

Human procreation, in sum, is not simply an activity of our rational wills. It is a more complete activity precisely because it engages us bodily, erotically and spiritually, as well as rationally. There is

wisdom in the mystery of nature that has joined the pleasure of sex, the inarticulate longing for union, the communication of the loving embrace and the deep-seated and only partly articulate desire for children in the very activity by which we continue the chain of human existence and participate in the renewal of human possibility. Whether or not we know it, the severing of procreation from sex, love and intimacy is inherently dehumanizing, no matter how good the product.

We are now ready for the more specific objections to cloning.

The Perversities of Cloning

First, an important if formal objection: any attempt to clone a human being would constitute an unethical experiment upon the resulting child-to-be. As the animal experiments (frog and sheep) indicate, there are grave risks of mishaps and deformities. Moreover, because of what cloning means, one cannot presume a future cloned child's consent to be a clone, even a healthy one. Thus, ethically speaking, we cannot even get to know whether or not human cloning is feasible.

I understand, of course, the philosophical difficulty of trying to compare a life with defects against nonexistence. Several bioethicists, proud of their philosophical cleverness, use this conundrum to embarrass claims that one can injure a child in its conception, precisely because it is only thanks to that complained-of conception that the child is alive to complain. But common sense tells us that we have no reason to fear such philosophisms. For we surely know that people can harm and even maim children in the very act of conceiving them, say, by paternal transmission of the AIDS virus, maternal transmission of heroin dependence or, arguably, even by bringing them into being as bastards or with no capacity or willingness to look after them properly. And we believe that to do this intentionally, or even negligently, is inexcusable and clearly unethical.

The objection about the impossibility of presuming consent may even go beyond the obvious and sufficient point that a clonant, were he subsequently to be asked, could rightly resent having been made a clone. At issue are not just benefits and harms, but doubts about the very independence needed to give proper (even retroactive) consent, that is, not just the capacity to choose but the disposition and ability to choose freely and well. It is not at all clear to what extent a clone will truly be a moral agent. For, as we shall see, in the very fact of cloning, and of rearing him as a clone, his makers subvert the cloned child's independence, beginning with that aspect that comes from knowing that one was an unbidden surprise, a gift, to the world, rather than the designed result of someone's artful project.

————

Cloning creates serious issues of identity and individuality. The cloned person may experience concerns about his distinctive identity not only because he will be in genotype and appearance identical to another human being, but, in this case, because he may also be twin to the person who is his "father" or "mother"—if one can still call them that. What would be the psychic burdens of being the "child" or "parent" of your twin? The cloned individual, moreover, will be saddled with a genotype that has already lived. He will not be fully a surprise to the world. People are likely always to compare his performances in life with that of his alter ego. True, his nurture and his circumstance in life will be different; genotype is not exactly destiny. Still, one must also expect parental and other efforts to shape this new life after the original—or at least to view the child with the original version always firmly in mind. Why else did they clone from the star basketball player, mathematician and beauty queen—or even dear old dad—in the first place?

Since the birth of Dolly, there has been a fair amount of doublespeak on this matter of genetic identity. Experts have rushed in to reassure the public that the clone would in no way be the same person, or have any confusions about his or her identity: as previously noted, they are pleased to point out that the clone of Mel Gibson would not be Mel Gibson. Fair enough. But one is shortchanging the truth by emphasizing the additional importance of the intrauterine environment, rearing and social setting: genotype obviously matters plenty. That, after all, is the only reason to clone, whether human beings or sheep. The odds that clones of Wilt Chamberlain will play in the NBA are, I submit, infinitely greater than they are for clones of Robert Reich.

Curiously, this conclusion is supported, inadvertently, by the one ethical sticking point insisted on by friends of cloning: no cloning without the donor's consent. Though an orthodox liberal objection, it is in fact quite puzzling when it comes from people (such as Ruth Macklin) who also insist that genotype is not identity or individuality, and who deny that a child could reasonably complain about being made a genetic copy. If the clone of Mel Gibson would not be Mel Gibson, why should Mel Gibson have grounds to object that someone had been made his clone? We already allow researchers to use blood and tissue samples for research purposes of no benefit to their sources: my falling hair, my expectorations, my urine and even my biopsied tissues are "not me" and not mine. Courts have held that the profit gained from uses to which scientists put my discarded tissues do not legally belong to me. Why, then, no cloning without consent—including, I assume, no cloning from the body of someone who just died? What harm is done the donor, if genotype is "not me"? Truth to tell, the only powerful justification for objecting is that genotype really does have something to do with identity, and everybody knows it. If not, on what basis could Michael Jordan object that someone cloned "him," say, from cells taken from a "lost" scraped-off piece of his skin? The insistence on donor consent unwittingly reveals the problem of identity in all cloning.

Genetic distinctiveness not only symbolizes the uniqueness of each human life and the independence of its parents that each human child rightfully attains. It can also be an important support for living a worthy and dignified life. Such arguments apply with great force to any large-scale replication of human individuals. But they are sufficient, in my view, to rebut even the first attempts to clone a human being. One must never forget that these are human beings upon whom our eugenic or merely playful fantasies are to be enacted.

Troubled psychic identity (distinctiveness), based on all-too-evident genetic identity (sameness), will be made much worse by the utter confusion of social identity and kinship ties. For, as already noted, cloning radically confounds lineage and social relations, for "offspring" as for "parents." As bioethicist James Nelson has pointed out, a female child cloned from her "mother" might develop a desire for a relationship to her "father," and might understandably seek out the father of her "mother," who is after all also her biological twin sister. Would "grandpa," who thought his paternal duties concluded, be pleased to discover that the clonant looked to him for paternal attention and support?

Social identity and social ties of relationship and responsibility are widely connected to, and supported by, biological kinship. Social taboos on incest (and adultery) everywhere serve to keep clear who is related to whom (and especially which child belongs to which parents), as well as to avoid confounding the social identity of parent-and-child or brother-and-sister) with the social identity of lovers, spouses and co-parents. True, social identity is altered by adoption (but as a matter of the best interest of already living children: we do not deliberately produce children for adoption). True, artificial insemination and in vitro fertilization with donor sperm, or whole embryo donation, are in some way forms of "prenatal adoption"—a not altogether unproblematic practice. Even here, though, there is in each case (as in all sexual reproduction) a known male source of sperm and a known single female source of egg—a genetic father and a genetic mother—should anyone care to know (as adopted children often do) who is genetically related to whom.

In the case of cloning, however, there is but one "parent." The usually sad situation of the "single-parent child" is here deliberately planned, and with a vengeance. In the case of self-cloning, the "offspring" is, in addition, one's twin; and so the dreaded result of incest—to be parent to one's sibling—is here brought about deliberately, albeit without any act of coitus. Moreover, all other relationships will be confounded. What will father, grandfather, aunt, cousin, sister mean? Who will bear what ties and what burdens? What sort of social identity will someone have with one whole side—"father's" or "mother's"—necessarily excluded? It is no answer to say that our society, with its high incidence of divorce, remarriage, adoption, extramarital childbearing and the rest, already confounds lineage and confuses kinship and responsibility for children (and everyone else), unless one also wants to argue that this is, for children, a preferable state of affairs.

Human cloning would also represent a giant step toward turning begetting into making, procreation into manufacture (literally, something "handmade"), a process already begun with in vitro fertilization and genetic testing of embryos. With cloning, not only is the process in hand, but the total genetic blueprint of the cloned individual is selected and determined by the human artisans. To be sure, subsequent development will take place according to natural processes; and the resulting children will still be recognizably human. But we here would be taking a major step into making man himself simply another one of the man-made things. Human nature becomes merely the last part of nature to succumb to the technological project, which turns all of nature into raw material at human disposal, to be homogenized by our rationalized technique according to the subjective prejudices of the day.

How does begetting differ from making? In natural procreation, human beings come together, complementarily male and female, to give existence to another being who is formed, exactly as we were, *by what we are*: living, hence perishable, hence aspiringly erotic, human beings. In clonal reproduction, by contrast, and in the more advanced forms of manufacture to which it leads, we give existence to a being not by what we are but by what we intend and design. As with any product of our making, no matter how excellent, the artificer stands above it, not as an equal but as a superior, transcending it by his will and creative prowess. Scientists who clone animals make it perfectly clear that they are engaged in instrumental making; the animals are, from the start, designed as means to serve rational human purposes. In human cloning, scientists and prospective "parents" would be adopting the same technocratic mentality to human children: human children would be their artifacts.

Such an arrangement is profoundly dehumanizing, no matter how good the product. Mass-scale cloning of the same individual makes the point vividly; but the violation of human equality, freedom and dignity are present even in a single planned clone. And procreation dehumanized into manufacture is further degraded by commodification, a virtually inescapable result of allowing baby-making to proceed under the banner of commerce. Genetic and reproductive biotechnology companies are already growth industries, but they will go into commercial orbit once the Human Genome Project nears completion. Supply will create enormous demand. Even before the capacity for human cloning arrives, established companies will have invested in the harvesting of eggs from ovaries obtained at autopsy or through ovarian surgery, practiced embryonic genetic alteration, and initiated the stockpiling of prospective donor tissues. Through the rental of surrogate-womb services, and through the buying and selling of tissues and embryos, priced according to the merit of the donor, the commodification of nascent human life will be unstoppable.

———

Finally, and perhaps most important, the practice of human cloning by nuclear transfer—like other anticipated forms of genetic engineering of the next generation—would enshrine and aggravate a profound and mischievous misunderstanding of the meaning of having children and of the parent-child relationship. When a couple now chooses to procreate, the partners are saying yes to the emergence of new life in its novelty, saying yes not only to having a child but also, tacitly, to having whatever child this child turns out to be. In accepting our finitude and opening ourselves to our replacement, we are tacitly confessing the limits of our control. In this ubiquitous way of nature, embracing the future by procreating means precisely that we are relinquishing our grip, in the very activity of taking up our own share in what we hope will be the immortality of human life and the human species. This means that our children are not *our* children: they are not our property, not our possessions. Neither are they supposed to live our lives for us, or anyone else's life but their own. To be sure, we seek to guide them on their way, imparting to them not just life but nurturing, love, and a way of life; to be sure, they bear our hopes that they will live fine and flourishing lives, enabling us in small measure to transcend our own limitations. Still, their genetic distinctiveness and independence are the natural foreshadowing of the deep truth that they have their own and never-before-enacted

life to live. They are sprung from a past, but they take an uncharted course into the future.

Much harm is already done by parents who try to live vicariously through their children. Children are sometimes compelled to fulfill the broken dreams of unhappy parents; John Doe Jr. or the III is under the burden of having to live up to his forebear's name. Still, if most parents have hopes for their children, cloning parents will have expectations. In cloning, such overbearing parents take at the start a decisive step which contradicts the entire meaning of the open and forward-looking nature of parent-child relations. The child is given a genotype that has already lived, with full expectation that this blueprint of a past life ought to be controlling of the life that is to come. Cloning is inherently despotic, for it seeks to make one's children (or someone else's children) after one's own image (or an image of one's choosing) and their future according to one's will. In some cases, the despotism may be mild and benevolent. In other cases, it will be mischievous and downright tyrannical. But despotism—the control of another through one's will—it inevitably will be.

Meeting Some Objections

The defenders of cloning, of course, are not wittingly friends of despotism. Indeed, they regard themselves mainly as friends of freedom: the freedom of individuals to reproduce, the freedom of scientists and inventors to discover and devise and to foster "progress" in genetic knowledge and technique. They want large-scale cloning only for animals, but they wish to preserve cloning as a human option for exercising our "right to reproduce"—our right to have children, and children with "desirable genes." As law professor John Robertson points out, under our "right to reproduce" we already practice early forms of unnatural, artificial and extramarital reproduction, and we already practice early forms of eugenic choice. For this reason, he argues, cloning is no big deal.

We have here a perfect example of the logic of the slippery slope, and the slippery way in which it already works in this area. Only a few years ago, slippery slope arguments were used to oppose artificial insemination and in vitro fertilization using unrelated sperm donors. Principles used to justify these practices, it was said, will be used to justify more artificial and more eugenic practices, including cloning. Not so, the defender's retorted, since we can make the necessary distinctions. And now, without even a gesture at making the necessary distinctions, the continuity of practice is held by itself to be justificatory.

The principle of reproductive freedom as currently enunciated by the proponents of cloning logically embraces the ethical acceptability of sliding down the entire rest of the slope—to producing children ectogenetically from sperm to term (should it become feasible) and to producing children whose entire genetic makeup will be the product of parental eugenic planning and choice. If reproductive freedom means the right to have a child of one's own choosing, by whatever means, it knows and accepts no limits.

But, far from being legitimated by a "right to reproduce," the emergence of techniques of assisted reproduction and genetic engineering should compel us to reconsider the meaning and limits of such a putative right. In truth, a "right to reproduce" has always been a peculiar and problematic notion. Rights generally belong to individuals, but this is a right which (before cloning) no one can exercise alone. Does the right then inhere only in couples? Only in married couples? Is it a (woman's) right to carry or deliver or a right (of one or more parents) to nurture and rear? Is it a right to have your own biological child? Is it a right only to attempt reproduction, or a right also to succeed? Is it a right to acquire the baby of one's choice?

The assertion of a negative "right to reproduce" certainly makes sense when it claims protection against state interference with procreative liberty, say, through a program of compulsory sterilization. But surely it cannot be the basis of a tort claim against nature, to be made good by technology, should free efforts at natural procreation fail. Some insist that the right to reproduce embraces also the right against state interference with the free use of all technological means to obtain a child. Yet such a position cannot be sustained: for reasons having to do with the means employed, any community may rightfully prohibit surrogate pregnancy, or polygamy, or the sale of babies to infertile couples, without violating anyone's basic human "right to reproduce." When the exercise of a previously innocuous freedom now involves or impinges on troublesome practices that the original freedom never was intended to reach, the general presumption of liberty needs to be reconsidered.

———

We do indeed already practice negative eugenic selection, through genetic screening and prenatal diagnosis. Yet our practices are governed by a norm of health. We seek to prevent the birth of children who suffer from known (serious) genetic diseases. When and if gene therapy becomes possible, such diseases could then be treated, in utero or even before implantation—I have no ethical objection in principle to such a practice (though I have some practical worries), precisely because it serves the medical goal of healing existing individuals. But therapy, to be therapy, implies not only an existing "patient." It also implies a norm of health. In this respect, even germ-line gene "therapy," though practiced not on a human being but on egg and sperm, is less radical than cloning, which is in no way therapeutic. But once one blurs the distinction between health promotion and genetic enhancement, between so-called negative and positive eugenics, one opens the door to all future eugenic designs. "To make sure that a child will be healthy and have good chances in life": this is Robertson's principle, and owing to its latter clause it is an utterly elastic principle, with no boundaries. Being over eight feet tall will likely produce some very good chances in life, and so will having the looks of Marilyn Monroe, and so will a genius-level intelligence.

Proponents want us to believe that there are legitimate uses of cloning that can be distinguished from illegitimate uses, but by their own principles no such limits can be found. (Nor could any such limits be enforced in practice.) Reproductive freedom, as they understand it, is governed solely by the subjective wishes of the parents-to-be (plus the avoidance of bodily harm to the child). The sentimentally appealing case of the childless married couple is, on these grounds, indistinguishable from the case of an individual (married or not) who would like to clone someone famous or talented, living or dead. Further, the principle here endorsed justifies not only cloning but, indeed, all future artificial attempts to create (manufacture) "perfect" babies.

A concrete example will show how, in practice no less than in principle, the so-called innocent case will merge with, or even turn into, the more troubling ones. In practice, the eager parents-to-be will necessarily be subject to the tyranny of expertise. Consider an infertile married couple, she lacking eggs or he lacking sperm, that wants a child of their (genetic) own, and propose to clone either husband or wife. The scientist-physician (who is also co-owner of the cloning company) points out the likely difficulties—a cloned child is not really their (genetic) child, but the child of only *one* of them; this imbalance may produce strains on the marriage; the child might suffer identity confusion; there is a risk of perpetuating the cause of sterility; and so on—and he also points out the advantages of choosing a donor nucleus. Far better than a child of their own would be a child of their own choosing. Touting his own expertise in selecting healthy and talented donors, the doctor presents the couple with his latest catalog containing the pictures, the health records and the accomplishments of his stable of cloning donors, samples of whose tissues are in his deep freeze. Why not, dearly beloved, a more perfect baby?

The "perfect baby," of course, is the project not of the infertility doctors, but of the eugenic scientists and their supporters. For them, the paramount right is not the so-called right to reproduce but what biologist Bentley Glass called, a quarter of a century ago, "the right of every child to be born with a sound physical and mental constitution, based on a sound genotype . . . the inalienable right to a sound heritage." But to secure this right, and to achieve the requisite quality control over new human life, human conception and gestation will need to be brought fully into the bright light of the laboratory, beneath which it can be fertilized, nourished, pruned, weeded, watched, inspected, prodded, pinched, cajoled, injected, tested, rated, graded, approved, stamped, wrapped, sealed and delivered. There is no other way to produce the perfect baby.

Yet we are urged by proponents of cloning to forget about the science fiction scenarios of laboratory manufacture and multiple-copied clones,

and to focus only on the homely cases of infertile couples exercising their reproductive rights. But why, if the single cases are so innocent, should multiplying their performance be so off-putting? (Similarly, why do others object to people making money off this practice, if the practice itself is perfectly acceptable?) When we follow the sound ethical principle of universalizing our choice—"would it be right if everyone cloned a Wilt Chamberlain (with his consent, of course)? Would it be right if everyone decided to practice asexual reproduction?"—we discover what is wrong with these seemingly innocent cases. The so-called science fiction cases make vivid the meaning of what looks to us, mistakenly, to be benign.

Though I recognize certain continuities between cloning and, say, in vitro fertilization, I believe that cloning differs in essential and important ways. Yet those who disagree should be reminded that the "continuity" argument cuts both ways. Sometimes we establish bad precedents, and discover that they were bad only when we follow their inexorable logic to places we never meant to go. Can the defenders of cloning show us today how, on their principles, we will be able to see producing babies ("perfect babies") entirely in the laboratory or exercising full control over their genotypes (including so-called enhancement) as ethically different, in any essential way, from present forms of assisted reproduction? Or are they willing to admit, despite their attachment to the principle of continuity, that the complete obliteration of "mother" or "father," the complete depersonalization of procreation, the complete manufacture of human beings and the complete genetic control of one generation over the next would be ethically problematic and essentially different from current forms of assisted reproduction? If so, where and how will they draw the line, and why? I draw it at cloning, for all the reasons given.

Ban the Cloning of Humans

What, then, should we do? We should declare that human cloning is unethical in itself and dangerous in its likely consequences. In so doing, we shall have the backing of the overwhelming majority of our fellow Americans, and of the human race, and (I believe) of most practicing scientists. Next, we should do all that we can to prevent the cloning of human beings. We should do this by means of an international legal ban if possible, and by a unilateral national ban, at a minimum. Scientists may secretly undertake to violate such a law, but they will be deterred by not being able to stand up proudly to claim the credit for their technological bravado and success. Such a ban on clonal baby-making, moreover, will not harm the progress of basic genetic science and technology. On the contrary, it will reassure the public that scientists are happy to proceed without violating the deep ethical norms and intuitions of the human community.

This still leaves the vexed question about laboratory research using early embryonic human clones, specially created only for such research purposes, with no intention to implant them into a uterus. There is no question that such research holds great promise for gaining fundamental knowledge about normal (and abnormal) differentiation, and for developing tissue lines for transplantation that might be used, say, in treating leukemia or in repairing brain or spinal cord injuries—to mention just a few of the conceivable benefits. Still, unrestricted clonal embryo research will surely make the production of living human clones much more likely. Once the genies put the cloned embryos into the bottles, who can strictly control where they go (especially in the absence of legal prohibitions against implanting them to produce a child)?

I appreciate the potentially great gains in scientific knowledge and medical treatment available from embryo research, especially with cloned embryos. At the same time, I have serious reservations about creating human embryos for the sole purpose of experimentation. There is something deeply repugnant and fundamentally transgressive about such a utilitarian treatment of prospective human life. This total, shameless exploitation is worse, in my opinion, than the "mere" destruction of nascent life. But I see no added objections, as a matter of principle, to creating and using *cloned* early embryos for research purposes, beyond the objections that I might raise to doing so with embryos produced sexually.

And yet, as a matter of policy and prudence, any opponent of the manufacture of cloned humans must, I think, in the end oppose also the creating of cloned human embryos. Frozen embryonic clones (belonging to whom?) can be shuttled around without detection. Commercial ventures in human cloning will be developed without adequate oversight. In order to build a fence around the law, prudence dictates that one oppose—for this reason alone—all production of cloned human embryos, even for research purposes. We should allow for all cloning research on animals to go forward, but the only safe trench that we can dig across the slippery slope, I suspect, is to insist on the inviolable distinction between animal and human cloning.

Some readers, and certainly most scientists, will not accept such prudent restraints, since they desire the benefits of research. They will prefer, even in fear and trembling, to allow human embryo cloning research to go forward.

Very well. Let us test them. If the scientists want to be taken seriously on ethical grounds, they must at the very least agree that embryonic research may proceed if and only if it is preceded by an absolute and effective ban on all attempts to implant into a uterus a cloned human embryo (cloned from an adult) to produce a living child. Absolutely no permission for the former without the latter.

The National Bioethics Advisory Commission's recommendations regarding this matter should be watched with the greatest care. Yielding to the wishes of the scientists, the commission will almost surely recommend that cloning human embryos for research be permitted. To allay public concern, it will likely also call for a temporary moratorium—not a legislative ban—on implanting cloned embryos to make a child, at least until such time as cloning techniques will have been perfected and rendered "safe" (precisely through the permitted research with cloned embryos). But the call for a moratorium rather than a legal ban would be a moral and a practical failure. Morally, this ethics commission would (at best) be waffling on the main ethical question, by refusing to declare the production of human clones unethical (or ethical). Practically, a moratorium on implantation cannot provide even the minimum protection needed to prevent the production of cloned humans.

Opponents of cloning need therefore to be vigilant. Indeed, no one should be willing even to consider a recommendation to allow the embryo research to proceed unless it is accompanied by a call for *prohibiting* implantation and until steps are taken to make such a prohibition effective.

———

Technically, the National Bioethics Advisory Commission can advise the president only on federal policy, especially federal funding policy. But given the seriousness of the matter at hand, and the grave public concern that goes beyond federal funding, the commission should take a broader view. (If it doesn't, Congress surely will.) Given that most assisted reproduction occurs in the private sector, it would be cowardly and insufficient for the commission to say, simply, "no federal funding" for such practices. It would be disingenuous to argue that we should allow federal funding so that we would then be able to regulate the practice; the private sector will not be bound by such regulations. Far better, for virtually everyone concerned, would be to distinguish between research on embryos and baby-making, and to call for a complete national and international ban (effected by legislation and treaty) of the latter, while allowing the former to proceed (at least in private laboratories).

The proposal for such a legislative ban is without American precedent, at least in technological matters, though the British and others have banned cloning of human beings, and we ourselves ban incest, polygamy and other forms of "reproductive freedom." Needless to say, working out the details of such a ban, especially a global one, would be tricky, what with the need to develop appropriate sanctions for violators. Perhaps such a ban will prove ineffective; perhaps it will eventually be shown to have been a mistake. But it would at least place the burden of practical proof where it belongs: on the proponents of this horror, requiring them to show very clearly what great social or medical good can be had only by the cloning of human beings.

We Americans have lived by, and prospered under, a rosy optimism about scientific and technological progress. The technological imperative—if it can be done, it must be done—has probably served

us well, though we should admit that there is no accurate method for weighing benefits and harms. Even when, as in the cases of environmental pollution, urban decay or the lingering deaths that are the unintended by-products of medical success, we recognize the unwelcome outcomes of technological advance, we remain confident in our ability to fix all the "bad" consequences—usually by means of still newer and better technologies. How successful we can continue to be in such post hoc repairing is at least an open question. But there is very good reason for shifting the paradigm around, at least regarding those technological interventions into the human body and mind that will surely effect fundamental and likely irreversible) changes in human nature, basic human relationships, and what it means to be a human being. Here we surely should not be willing to risk everything in the naïve hope that, should things go wrong, we can later set them right.

The president's call for a moratorium on human cloning has given us an important opportunity. In a truly unprecedented way, we can strike a blow for the human control of the technological project, for wisdom, prudence and human dignity. The prospect of human cloning, so repulsive to contemplate, is the occasion for deciding whether we shall be slaves of unregulated progress, and ultimately its artifacts, or whether we shall remain free human beings who guide our technique toward the enhancement of human dignity. If we are to seize the occasion, we must, as the late Paul Ramsey wrote,

> raise the ethical questions with a serious and not a frivolous conscience. A man of frivolous conscience announces that there are ethical quandaries ahead that we must urgently consider before the future catches up with us. By this he often means that we need to devise a new ethics that will provide the rationalization for doing in the future what men are bound to do because of new actions and interventions science will have made possible. In contrast a man of serious conscience means to say in raising urgent ethical questions that there may be some things that men should never do. The good things that men do can be made complete only by the things they refuse to do.

Cloning Human Beings: An Assessment of the Ethical Issues Pro and Con

DAN W. BROCK

In this essay Brock reviews the arguments for and against human reproductive cloning. He maintains that there is probably a right to reproductive freedom that covers human cloning, but there could be other rights in conflict with this right, or serious enough harms involved to override it. The possible benefits of human cloning include the ability to relieve infertility, to avoid transmitting serious genetic disease to offspring, and to clone someone (such as a child who died) who had special meaning to individuals. Arguments against the practice include that it violates a right to unique identity or to an open future, that it would cause psychological harm to the later twin, that it would carry unacceptable risks for the clone, and that it would lessen the worth of individuals and diminish respect for human life. Brock finds little merit in the identity and open-future arguments but thinks that human cloning does carry risk of significant harms, although most of the harms that people fear are based on common misconceptions.

The world of science and the public at large were both shocked and fascinated by the announcement in the journal *Nature* by Ian Wilmut and his colleagues that they had successfully cloned a sheep from a single cell of an adult sheep (Wilmut, 1997). But many were troubled or apparently even horrified at the prospect that cloning of adult humans by the same process might be possible as well. The response of most scientific and political leaders to the prospect of human cloning, indeed of Dr. Wilmut as well, was of immediate and strong condemnation.

A few more cautious voices were heard both suggesting some possible benefits from the use of human cloning in limited circumstances and questioning its too quick prohibition, but they were a clear minority. A striking feature of these early responses was that their strength and intensity seemed far to outrun the arguments and reasons offered in support of them—they seemed often to be "gut level" emotional reactions rather than considered

reflections on the issues. Such reactions should not be simply dismissed, both because they may point us to important considerations otherwise missed and not easily articulated, and because they often have a major impact on public policy. But the formation of public policy should not ignore the moral reasons and arguments that bear on the practice of human cloning—these must be articulated in order to understand and inform people's more immediate emotional responses. This essay is an effort to articulate, and to evaluate critically, the main moral considerations and arguments for and against human cloning. Though many people's religious beliefs inform their views on human cloning, and it is often difficult to separate religious from secular positions, I shall restrict myself to arguments and reasons that can be given a clear secular formulation.

On each side of the issue there are no distinct kinds of moral arguments brought forward. On the one hand, some opponents claim that human cloning would violate fundamental moral or human rights, while some proponents argue that its prohibition would violate such rights. While moral and even human rights need not be understood as absolute, they do place moral restrictions on permissible actions that an appeal to a mere balance of benefits over harms cannot justify overriding; for example, the rights of human subjects in research must be respected even if the result is that some potentially beneficial research is more difficult or cannot be done. On the other hand, both opponents and proponents also cite the likely harms and benefits, both to individuals and to society, of the practice. I shall begin with the arguments in support of permitting human cloning, although with no implication that it is the stronger or weaker position.

Moral Arguments in Support of Human Cloning

Is There a Moral Right to Use Human Cloning?

What moral right might protect at least some access to the use of human cloning? A commitment to individual liberty, such as defended by J. S. Mill, requires that individuals be left free to use human cloning if they so choose and if their doing so does not cause significant harms to others, but liberty is too broad in scope to be an uncontroversial moral right (Mill, 1859; Rhodes, 1995). Human cloning is a means of reproduction (in the most literal sense) and so the most plausible moral right at stake in its use is a right to reproductive freedom or procreative liberty (Robertson, 1994a; Brock, 1994), understood to include both the choice not to reproduce, for example, by means of contraception or abortion, and also the right to reproduce.

The right to reproductive freedom is properly understood to include the right to use various assisted reproductive technologies (ARTs), such as in vitro fertilization (IVF), oocyte donation, and so forth. The reproductive right relevant to human cloning is a negative right, that is, a right to use ARTs without interference by the government or others when made available by a willing provider. The choice of an assisted means of reproduction should be protected by reproductive freedom even when it is not the only means for individuals to reproduce, just as the choice among different means of preventing conception is protected by reproductive freedom. However, the case for permitting the use of a particular means of reproduction is strongest when it is necessary for particular individuals to be able to procreate at all, or to do so without great burdens or harms to themselves or others. In some cases human cloning could be the only means for individuals to procreate while retaining a biological tie to their child, but in other cases different means of procreating might also be possible.

It could be argued that human cloning is not covered by the right to reproductive freedom because whereas current ARTs and practices covered by that right are remedies for inabilities to reproduce sexually, human cloning is an entirely new means of reproduction; indeed, its critics see it as more a means of manufacturing humans than of reproduction. Human cloning is a different means of reproduction than sexual reproduction, but it is a means that can serve individuals' interest in reproducing. If it is not protected by the moral right to reproductive freedom, I believe that must be not because it is a new means of reproducing, but instead because it has other objectionable or harmful features; I shall evaluate these other ethical objections to it later.

When individuals have alternative means of procreating, human cloning typically would be chosen because it replicates a particular individual's genome. The reproductive interest in question then is not simply reproduction itself, but a more specific interest in choosing what kind of children to have. The right to reproductive freedom is usually understood to cover at least some choice about the kind of children one will have. Some individuals choose reproductive partners in the hope of producing offspring with desirable traits. Genetic testing of fetuses or preimplantation embryos for genetic disease or abnormality is done to avoid having a child with those diseases or abnormalities. Respect for individual self-determination, which is one of the grounds of a moral right to reproductive freedom, includes respecting individuals' choices about whether to have a child with a condition that will place severe burdens on them, and cause severe burdens to the child itself.

The less a reproductive choice is primarily the determination of one's own life, but primarily the determination of the nature of another, as in the case of human cloning, the more moral weight the interests of that other person, that is the cloned child, should have in decisions that determine its nature (Annas, 1994). But even then parents are typically accorded substantial, but not unlimited, discretion in shaping the persons their children will become, for example, through education and other child-rearing decisions. Even if not part of reproductive freedom, the right to raise one's children as one sees fit, within limits mostly determined by the interests of the children, is also a right to determine within limits what kinds of persons one's children will become. This right includes not just preventing certain diseases or harms to children, but selecting and shaping desirable features and traits in one's children. The use of human cloning is one way to exercise that right.

Public policy and the law now permit prospective parents to conceive, or to carry a conception to term, when there is a significant risk or even certainty that the child will suffer from a serious genetic disease. Even when others think the risk or certainty of genetic disease makes it morally wrong to conceive, or to carry a fetus to term, the parents' right to reproductive freedom permits them to do so. Most possible harms to a cloned child are less serious than the genetic harms with which parents can now permit their offspring to be conceived or born.

I conclude that there is good reason to accept that a right to reproductive freedom presumptively includes both a right to select the means of reproduction, as well as a right to determine what kind of children to have, by use of human cloning. However, the specific reproductive interest of determining what kind of children to have is less weighty than are other reproductive interests and choices whose impact falls more directly and exclusively on the parents rather than the child. Even if a moral right to reproductive freedom protects the use of human cloning, that does not settle the moral issue about human cloning, since there may be other moral rights in conflict with this right, or serious enough harms from human cloning to override the right to use it; this right can be thought of as establishing a serious moral presumption supporting access to human cloning.

What Individual or Social Benefits Might Human Cloning Produce?

Largely Individual Benefits

The literature on human cloning by nuclear transfer or by embryo splitting contains a few examples of circumstances in which individuals might have good reasons to want to use human cloning. However, human cloning seems not to be the unique answer to any great or pressing human need and its benefits appear to be limited at most. What are the principal possible benefits of human cloning that might give individuals good reasons to want to use it?

1. *Human cloning would be a new means to relieve the infertility some persons now experience.* Human cloning would allow women who have no ova or men who have no sperm to produce an offspring that is biologically related to them (Eisenberg, 1976; Robertson, 1994b, 1997; LaBar, 1984). Embryos might also be cloned, by either nuclear transfer or embryo splitting, in order to increase the number of embryos for implantation and improve the chances of successful conception (NABER, 1994). The benefits from human cloning to relieve infertility are greater the more persons there are who cannot overcome their infertility by any other means acceptable to them. I do not know of data on this point, but the numbers who would use cloning for this reason are probably not large.

The large number of children throughout the world possibly available for adoption represents an alternative solution to infertility only if we are prepared to discount as illegitimate the strong desire of many persons, fertile and infertile, for the experience of pregnancy and for having and raising a child biologically related to them. While not important to all infertile (or fertile) individuals, it is important to many and is respected and met through other forms of assisted reproduction that maintain a biological connection when that is possible; that desire does not become illegitimate simply because human cloning would be the best or only means of overcoming an individual's infertility.

2. *Human cloning would enable couples in which one party risks transmitting a serious hereditary disease to an offspring to reproduce without doing so* (Robertson, 1994b). By using donor sperm or egg donation, such hereditary risks can generally be avoided now without the use of human cloning. These procedures may be unacceptable to some couples, however, or at least considered less desirable than human cloning because they introduce a third party's genes into their reproduction instead

of giving their offspring only the genes of one of them. Thus, in some cases human cloning could be a reasonable means of preventing genetically transmitted harms to offspring. Here too, we do not know how many persons would want to use human cloning instead of other means of avoiding the risk of genetic transmission of a disease or of accepting the risk of transmitting the disease, but the numbers again are probably not large.

3. *Human cloning to make a later twin would enable a person to obtain needed organs or tissues for transplantation* (Robertson, 1994b, 1997; Kahn, 1989; Harris, 1992). Human cloning would solve the problem of finding a transplant donor whose organ or tissue is an acceptable match and would eliminate, or drastically reduce, the risk of transplant rejection by the host. The availability of human cloning for this purpose would amount to a form of insurance to enable treatment of certain kinds of medical conditions. Of course, sometimes the medical need would be too urgent to permit waiting for the cloning, gestation, and development that is necessary before tissues or organs can be obtained for transplantation. In other cases, taking an organ also needed by the later twin, such as a heart or a liver, would be impermissible because it would violate the later twin's rights.

Such a practice can be criticized on the ground that it treats the later twin not as a person valued and loved for his or her own sake, as an end in itself in Kantian terms, but simply as a means for benefiting another. This criticism assumes, however, that only this one motive defines the reproduction and the relation of the person to his or her later twin. The well-known case some years ago in California of the Ayalas, who conceived in the hopes of obtaining a source for a bone marrow transplant for their teenage daughter suffering from leukemia, illustrates the mistake in this assumption. They argued that whether or not the child they conceived turned out to be a possible donor for their daughter, they would value and love the child for itself, and treat it as they would treat any other member of their family. That one reason they wanted it, as a possible means to saving their daughter's life, did not preclude their also loving and valuing it for its own sake; in Kantian terms, it was treated as a possible means to saving their daughter, but not *solely as a means*, which is what the Kantian view proscribes.

Indeed, when people have children, whether by sexual means or with the aid of ARTs, their motives and reasons for doing so are typically many and complex, and include reasons less laudable than obtaining lifesaving medical treatment, such as having someone who needs them, enabling them to live on their own, qualifying for government benefit programs, and so forth. While these are not admirable motives for having children and may not bode well for the child's upbringing and future, public policy does not assess prospective parents' motives and reasons for procreating as a condition of their doing so.

4. *Human cloning would enable individuals to clone someone who had special meaning to them, such as a child who had died* (Robertson, 1994b). There is no denying that if human cloning were available, some individuals would want to use it for this purpose, but their desire usually would be based on a deep confusion. Cloning such a child would not replace the child the parents had loved and lost, but would only create a different child with the same genes. The child they loved and lost was a unique individual who had been shaped by his or her environment and choices, not just his or her genes, and more importantly who had experienced a particular relationship with them. Even if the later cloned child could not only have the same genes but also be subjected to the same environment, which of course is impossible, it would remain a different child than the one they had loved and lost because it would share a different history with them (Thomas, 1974). Cloning the lost child might help the parents accept and move on from their loss, but another already existing sibling or a new child that was not a clone might do this equally well; indeed, it might do so better since the appearance of the cloned later twin would be a constant reminder of the child they had lost. Nevertheless, if human cloning enabled some individuals to clone a person who had special meaning to them and doing so gave them deep satisfaction, that would be a benefit to them even if their reasons for wanting to do so, and the satisfaction they in turn received, were based on a confusion.

Largely Social Benefits

5. *Human cloning would enable the duplication of individuals of great talent, genius, character, or other exemplary qualities.* Unlike the first four reasons for human cloning which appeal to benefits to specific individuals, this reason looks to benefits to the broader society from being able to replicate extraordinary individuals—a Mozart, Einstein, Gandhi, or Schweitzer (Lederberg, 1966; McKinnell, 1979). Much of the appeal of this reason, like much support and opposition to human cloning, rests largely on a confused and false assumption of genetic determinism, that is, that one's genes fully determine what one will become, do, and accomplish. What made Mozart, Einstein, Gandhi, and Schweitzer the extraordinary individuals they were was the confluence of their particular genetic endowments with the environments in which they were raised and lived and the particular historical moments they in different ways seized. Cloning them would produce individuals with the same genetic inheritances (nuclear transfer does not even produce 100 percent genetic identity, although for the sake of exploring the moral issues I have followed the common assumption that it does), but it is not possible to replicate their environments or the historical contexts in which they lived and their greatness flourished. We do not know the degree or specific respects in which any individual's greatness depended on "nature" or "nurture," but we do know that it always depends on an interaction of them both. Cloning could not even replicate individuals' extraordinary capabilities, much less their accomplishments, because these too are the product of their inherited genes and their environments, not of their genes alone.

None of this is to deny that Mozart's and Einstein's extraordinary musical and intellectual capabilities, nor even Gandhi's and Schweitzer's extraordinary moral greatness, were produced in part by their unique genetic inheritances. Cloning them might well produce individuals with exceptional capacities, but we simply do not know how close their clones would be in capacities or accomplishments to the great individuals from whom they were cloned. Even so, the hope for exceptional, even if less and different, accomplishment from cloning such extraordinary individuals might be a reasonable ground for doing so.

Worries here about abuse, however, surface quickly. Whose standards of greatness would be used to select individuals to be cloned? Who would control use of human cloning technology for the benefit of society or mankind at large? Particular groups, segments of society, or governments might use the technology for their own benefit, under the cover of benefiting society or even mankind at large.

6. *Human cloning and research on human cloning might make possible important advances in scientific knowledge, for example, about human development* (Walters, 1982; Smith, 1983). While important potential advances in scientific or medical knowledge from human cloning or human cloning research have frequently been cited, there are at least three reasons for caution about such claims. First, there is always considerable uncertainty about the nature and importance of the new scientific or medical knowledge to which a dramatic new technology like human cloning will lead; the road to new knowledge is never mapped in advance and takes many unexpected turns. Second, we do not know what new knowledge from human cloning or human cloning research could also be gained by other means that do not have the problematic moral features to which its opponents object. Third, what human cloning research would be compatible with ethical and legal requirements for the use of human subjects in research is complex, controversial, and largely unexplored. Creating human clones solely for the purpose of research would be to use them solely for the benefit of others without their consent, and so unethical. But if and when human cloning was established to be safe and effective, then new scientific knowledge might be obtained from its use for legitimate, nonresearch reasons.

Although there is considerable uncertainty concerning most of human cloning's possible individual and social benefits that I have discussed, and although no doubt it could have other benefits or uses that we cannot yet envisage, I believe it is reasonable to conclude at this time that human cloning does not seem to promise great benefits or uniquely to meet great human needs. Nevertheless, despite these limited benefits, a moral case can be made that freedom to use human cloning is protected by the important moral right to reproductive freedom. I shall turn now to what moral rights might be violated, or harms produced, by research on or use of human cloning.

Moral Arguments Against Human Cloning

Would the Use of Human Cloning Violate Important Moral Rights?

Many of the immediate condemnations of any possible human cloning following Wilmut's cloning of Dolly claimed that it would violate moral or human rights, but it was usually not specified precisely, or often even at all, what rights would be violated (WHO, 1997). I shall consider two possible candidates for such a right: a right to have a unique identity and a right to ignorance about one's future or to an open future. Claims that cloning denies individuals a unique identity are common, but I shall argue that even if there is a right to a unique identity, it could not be violated by human cloning. The right to ignorance or to an open future has only been explicitly defended, to my knowledge, by two commentators, and in the context of human cloning, only by Hans Jonas; it supports a more promising, but in my view ultimately unsuccessful, argument that human cloning would violate an important moral or human right.

Is there a moral or human right to a unique identity, and if so would it be violated by human cloning? For human cloning to violate a right to a unique identity, the relevant sense of identity would have to be genetic identity, that is, a right to a unique unrepeated genome. This would be violated by human cloning, but is there any such right? It might be thought that cases of identical twins show there is no such right because no one claims that the moral or human rights of the twins have been violated. However, this consideration is not conclusive (Kass, 1985; NABER, 1994). Only human actions can violate others' rights; outcomes that would constitute a rights violation if deliberately caused by human action are not a rights violation if a result of natural causes. If Arthur deliberately strikes Barry on the head so hard as to cause his death, he violates Barry's right not to be killed; if lightning strikes Cheryl, causing her death, her right not to be killed has not been violated. Thus, the case of twins does not show that there could not be a right to a unique genetic identity.

What is the sense of identity that might plausibly be what each person has a right to have uniquely, that constitutes the special uniqueness of each individual (Macklin 1994; Chadwick 1982)? Even with the same genes, homozygous twins are numerically distinct and not identical, so what is intended must be the various properties and characteristics that make each individual qualitatively unique and different from others. Does having the same genome as another person undermine that unique qualitative identity? Only on the crudest genetic determinism, according to which an individual's genes completely and decisively determine everything else about the individual, all his or her other nongenetic features and properties, together with the entire history or biography that constitutes his or her life. But there is no reason whatever to believe that kind of genetic determinism. Even with the same genes, differences in genetically identical twins' psychological and personal characteristics develop over time together with differences in their life histories, personal relationships, and life choices; sharing an identical genome does not prevent twins from developing distinct and unique personal identities of their own.

We need not pursue whether there is a moral or human right to a unique identity—no such right is found among typical accounts and enumerations of moral or human rights—because even if there is such a right, sharing a genome with another individual as a result of human cloning would not violate it. The idea of the uniqueness, or unique identity, of each person historically predates the development of modern genetics. A unique genome thus could not be the ground of this long-standing belief in the unique human identity of each person.

I turn now to whether human cloning would violate what Hans Jonas called a right to ignorance, or what Joel Feinberg called a right to an open future (Jonas, 1974; Feinberg, 1980). Jonas argued that human cloning in which there is a substantial time gap between the beginning of the lives of the earlier and later twin is fundamentally different from the simultaneous beginning of the lives of homozygous twins that occur in nature. Although contemporaneous twins begin their lives with the same genetic inheritance, they do so at the same time, and so in ignorance of what the other who shares the same genome will by his or her choices make of his or her life.

A later twin created by human cloning, Jonas argues, knows, or at least believes she knows, too much about herself. For there is already in the world another person, her earlier twin, who from the same genetic starting point has made the life choices that are still in the later twin's future. It will seem that her life has already been lived and played out by another, that her fate is already determined; she will lose the sense of human possibility in freely and spontaneously creating her own future and authentic self. It is tyrannical, Jonas claims, for the earlier twin to try to determine another's fate in this way.

Jonas's objection can be interpreted so as not to assume either a false genetic determinism, or a belief in it. A later twin might grant that he is not determined to follow in his earlier twin's footsteps, but nevertheless the earlier twin's life might always haunt him, standing as an undue influence on his life, and shaping it in ways to which others' lives are not vulnerable. But the force of the objection still seems to rest on the false assumption that having the same genome as his earlier twin unduly restricts his freedom to create a different life and self than the earlier twin's. Moreover, a family environment also importantly shapes children's development, but there is no force to the claim of a younger sibling that the existence of an older sibling raised in that same family is an undue influence on the younger sibling's freedom to make his own life for himself in that environment. Indeed, the younger twin or sibling might gain the benefit of being able to learn from the older twin's or sibling's mistakes.

A closely related argument can be derived from what Joel Feinberg has called a child's right to an open future. This requires that others raising a child not so close off the future possibilities that the child would otherwise have as to eliminate a reasonable range of opportunities for the child autonomously to construct his or her own life. One way this right might be violated is to create a later twin who will believe her future has already been set for her by the choices made and the life lived by her earlier twin.

The central difficulty in these appeals to a right either to ignorance or to an open future is that the right is not violated merely because the later twin is likely to *believe* that his future is already determined, when that belief is clearly false and supported only by the crudest genetic determinism. If we know the later twin will falsely believe that his open future has been taken from him as a result of being cloned, even though in reality it has not, then we know that cloning will cause the twin psychological distress, but not that it will violate his right. Jonas's right to ignorance, and Feinberg's right of a child to an open future, are not violated by human cloning, though they do point to psychological harms that a later twin may be likely to experience and that I will take up later.

Neither a moral or human right to a unique identity, nor one to ignorance and an open future, would be violated by human cloning. There may be other moral or human rights that human cloning would violate, but I do not know what they might be. I turn now to consideration of the harms that human cloning might produce.

What Individual or Social Harms Might Human Cloning Produce?

There are many possible individual or social harms that have been posited by one or another commentator and I shall only try to cover the more plausible and significant of them.

Largely Individual Harms

1. *Human cloning would produce psychological distress and harm in the later twin.* No doubt knowing the path in life taken by one's earlier twin might often have several bad psychological effects (Callahan, 1993; LaBar, 1984; Macklin, 1994; McCormick, 1993; Studdard, 1978; Rainer, 1978; Verhey, 1994). The later twin might feel, even if mistakenly, that her fate has already been substantially laid out, and so have difficulty freely and spontaneously taking responsibility for and making her own fate and life. The later twin's experience or sense of autonomy and freedom might be substantially diminished, even if in actual fact they are diminished much less than it seems to her. She might have a diminished sense of her own uniqueness and individuality, even if once again these are in fact diminished little or not at all

by having an earlier twin with the same genome. If the later twin is the clone of a particularly exemplary individual, perhaps with some special capabilities and accomplishments, she might experience excessive pressure to reach the very high standards of ability and accomplishment of the earlier twin (Rainer, 1978). These various psychological effects might take a heavy toll on the later twin and be serious burdens to her.

While psychological harms of these kinds from human cloning are certainly possible, and perhaps even likely in some cases, they remain at this point only speculative since we have no experience with human cloning and the creation of earlier and later twins. Nevertheless, if experience with human cloning confirmed that serious and unavoidable psychological harms typically occurred to the later twin, that would be a serious moral reason to avoid the practice. Intuitively at least, psychological burdens and harms seem more likely and more serious for a person who is only one of many identical later twins cloned from one original source, so that the clone might run into another identical twin around every street corner. This prospect could be a good reason to place sharp limits on the number of twins that could be cloned from any one source.

One argument has been used by several commentators to undermine the apparent significance of potential psychological harms to a later twin (Chadwick, 1982; Robertson, 1994b, 1997; Macklin, 1994). The point derives from a general problem, called the nonidentity problem, posed by the philosopher Derek Parfit, although not originally directed to human cloning (Parfit, 1984). Here is the argument. Even if all these psychological burdens from human cloning could not be avoided for any later twin, they are not harms to the twin, and so not reasons not to clone the twin. That is because the only way for the twin to avoid the harms is never to be cloned, and so never to exist at all. But these psychological burdens, hard though they might be, are not so bad as to make the twin's life, all things considered, not worth living. So the later twin is not harmed by being given a life even with these psychological burdens, since the alternative of never existing at all is arguably worse—he or she never has a worthwhile life—but certainly not better for the twin.

And if the later twin is not harmed by having been created with these unavoidable burdens, then how could he or she be wronged by having been created with them? And if the later twin is not wronged, then why is any wrong being done by human cloning? This argument has considerable potential import, for if it is sound it will undermine the apparent moral importance of any bad consequence of human cloning to the later twin that is not so serious as to make the twin's life, all things considered, not worth living.

I defended elsewhere the position regarding the general case of genetically transmitted handicaps, that if one could have a *different* child without comparable burdens (for the case of cloning, by using a different method of reproduction which did not result in a later twin), there is as strong a moral reason to do so as there would be not to cause similar burdens to an already existing child (Brock, 1995). Choosing to create the later twin with serious psychological burdens instead of a different person who would be free of them, without weighty overriding reasons for choosing the former, would be morally irresponsible or wrong, even if doing so does not harm or wrong the later twin who could only exist with the burdens. These issues are too detailed and complex to pursue here and the nonidentity problem remains controversial and not fully resolved, but at the least, the argument for disregarding the psychological burdens to the later twin because he or she could not exist without them is controversial, and in my view mistaken. Such psychological harms, as I shall continue to call them, are speculative, but they should not be disregarded because of the nonidentity problem.

2. Human cloning procedures would carry unacceptable risks to the clone. There is no doubt that attempts to clone a human being at the present time would carry unacceptable risks to the clone. Further research on the procedure with animals, as well as research to establish its safety and effectiveness for humans, is clearly necessary before it would be ethical to use the procedure on humans. One risk to the clone is the failure to implant, grow, and develop successfully, but this would involve the embryo's death or destruction long before most people or the law consider it to be a person with moral or legal protections of its life.

Other risks to the clone are that the procedure in some way goes wrong, or unanticipated harms come to the clone; for example, Harold Varmus, director of the National Institutes of Health, raised the concern that a cell many years old from which a person is cloned could have accumulated genetic mutations during its years in another adult that could give the resulting clone a predisposition to cancer or other diseases of aging (Weiss, 1997). Risks to an ovum donor (if any), a nucleus donor, and a woman who receives the embryo for implantation would likely be ethically acceptable with the informed consent of the involved parties.

I believe it is too soon to say whether unavoidable risks to the clone would make human cloning forever unethical. At a minimum, further research is needed to better define the potential risks to humans. But we should not insist on a standard that requires risks to be lower than those we accept in sexual reproduction, or in other forms of ART.

Largely Social Harms

3. *Human cloning would lessen the worth of individuals and diminish respect for human life.* Unelaborated claims to this effect were common in the media after the announcement of the cloning of Dolly. Ruth Macklin explored and criticized the claim that human cloning would diminish the value we place on, and our respect for, human life because it would lead to persons being viewed as replaceable (Macklin, 1994). As I have argued concerning a right to a unique identity, only on a confused and indefensible notion of human identity is a person's identity determined solely by his or her genes, and so no individual could be fully replaced by a later clone possessing the same genes. Ordinary people recognize this clearly. For example, parents of a child dying of a fatal disease would find it insensitive and ludicrous to be told they should not grieve for their coming loss because it is possible to replace him by cloning him; it is *their child who is dying* whom they love and value, and that child and his importance to them is not replaceable by a cloned later twin. Even if they would also come to love and value a later twin as much as they now love and value their child who is dying, that would be to love and value that *different child* for its own sake,

not as a replacement for the child they lost. Our relations of love and friendship are with distinct, historically situated individuals with whom over time we have shared experience and our lives, and whose loss to us can never be replaced.

A different version of this worry is that human cloning would result in persons' worth or value seeming diminished because we would come to see persons as able to be manufactured or "handmade." This demystification of the creation of human life would reduce our appreciation and awe of human life and of its natural creation. It would be a mistake, however, to conclude that a person created by human cloning is of less value or is less worthy of respect than one created by sexual reproduction. At least outside of some religious contexts, it is the nature of a being, not how it is created, that is the source of its value and makes it worthy of respect. For many people, gaining a scientific understanding of the truly extraordinary complexity of human reproduction and development increases, instead of decreases, their awe of the process and its product.

A more subtle route by which the value we place on each individual human life might be diminished could come from the use of human cloning with the aim of creating a child with a particular genome, either the genome of another individual especially meaningful to those doing the cloning or an individual with exceptional talents, abilities, and accomplishments. The child then comes to be objectified, valued only as an object and for its genome, or at least for its genome's expected phenotypic expression, and no longer recognized as having the intrinsic equal moral value of all persons, simply as persons. For the moral value and respect due all persons to come to be seen as resting only on the instrumental value of individuals and of their particular qualities to others would be to fundamentally change the moral status properly accorded to persons. Individuals would lose their moral standing as full and equal members of the moral community, replaced by the different instrumental value each has to others.

Such a change in the equal moral value and worth accorded to persons should be avoided at all costs, but it is far from clear that such a change would result from permitting human cloning. Parents, for example, are quite capable of distinguishing their children's intrinsic value, just as individual persons, from their instrumental value based on their particular qualities or properties. The equal moral value and respect due all persons simply as persons is not incompatible with the different instrumental value of different individuals; Einstein and an untalented physics graduate student have vastly different value as scientists, but share and are entitled to equal moral value and respect as persons. It is a confused mistake to conflate these two kinds of value and respect. If making a large number of clones from one original person would be more likely to foster it, that would be a further reason to limit the number of clones that could be made from one individual.

4. *Human cloning might be used by commercial interests for financial gain.* Both opponents and proponents of human cloning agree that cloned embryos should not be able to be bought and sold. In a science fiction frame of mind, one can imagine commercial interests offering genetically certified and guaranteed embryos for sale, perhaps offering a catalogue of different embryos cloned from individuals with a variety of talents, capacities, and other desirable properties. This would be a fundamental violation of the equal moral respect and dignity owed to all persons, treating them instead as objects to be differentially valued, bought, and sold in the marketplace. Even if embryos are not yet persons at the time they would be purchased or sold, they would be being valued, bought, and sold for the persons they will become. The moral consensus against any commercial market in embryos, cloned or otherwise, should be enforced by law whatever the public policy ultimately is on human cloning.

5. *Human cloning might be used by governments or other groups for immoral and exploitative purposes.* In *Brave New World*, Aldous Huxley imagined cloning individuals who have been engineered with limited abilities and conditioned to do, and to be happy doing, the menial work that society needed done (Huxley, 1932). Selection and control in the creation of people was exercised not in the interests of the persons created, but in the interests of the society and at the expense of the persons created; nor did it serve individuals' interests in

reproduction and parenting. Any use of human cloning for such purposes would exploit the clones solely as means for the benefit of others, and would violate the equal moral respect and dignity they are owed as full moral persons. If human cloning is permitted to go forward, it should be with regulations that would clearly prohibit such immoral exploitation.

Fiction contains even more disturbing or bizarre uses of human cloning, such as Mengele's creation of many clones of Hitler in Ira Levin's *The Boys from Brazil* (Levin, 1976), Woody Allen's science fiction cinematic spoof *Sleeper* in which a dictator's only remaining part, his nose, must be destroyed to keep it from being cloned, and the contemporary science fiction film *Blade Runner*. These nightmare scenarios may be quite improbable, but their impact should not be underestimated on public concern with technologies like human cloning. Regulation of human cloning must assure the public that even such farfetched abuses will not take place.

Conclusion

Human cloning has until now received little serious and careful ethical attention because it was typically dismissed as science fiction, and it stirs deep, but difficult to articulate, uneasiness and even revulsion in many people. Any ethical assessment of human cloning at this point must be tentative and provisional. Fortunately, the science and technology of human cloning are not yet in hand, and so a public and professional debate is possible without the need for a hasty, precipitate policy response.

The ethical pros and cons of human cloning, as I see them at this time, are sufficiently balanced and uncertain that there is not an ethically decisive case either for or against permitting it or doing it. Access to human cloning can plausibly be brought within a moral right to reproductive freedom, but its potential legitimate uses appear few and do not promise substantial benefits. It is not a central component of the moral right to reproductive freedom and it does not uniquely serve any major or pressing individual or social needs. On the other hand, contrary to the pronouncements of many of its opponents, human cloning seems not to be a violation of moral or human rights. But it does risk some significant individual or social harms, although most are based on common public confusions about genetic determinism, human identity, and the effects of human cloning. Because most potential harms feared from human cloning remain speculative, they seem insufficient to warrant at this time a complete legal prohibition of either research on or later use of human cloning, if and when its safety and efficacy are established. Legitimate moral concerns about the use and effects of human cloning, however, underline the need for careful public oversight of research on its development, together with a wider public and professional debate and review before cloning is used on human beings.

REFERENCES

Annas, G. J. (1994). "Regulatory Models for Human Embryo Cloning: The Free Market, Professional Guidelines, and Government Restrictions." *Kennedy Institute of Ethics Journal* 4, 3:235–249.

Brock, D. W. (1994). "Reproductive Freedom: Its Nature, Bases and Limits," in *Health Care Ethics: Critical Issues for Health Professionals*, eds. D. Thomasma and J. Monagle. Gaithersburg, MD: Aspen Publishers.

Brock, D. W. (1995). "The Non-Identity Problem and Genetic Harm." *Bioethics* 9:269–275.

Callahan, D. (1993). "Perspective on Cloning: A Threat to Individual Uniqueness." *Los Angeles Times*, November 12, 1993:B7.

Chadwick, R. F. (1982). "Cloning." *Philosophy* 57:201–209.

Eisenberg. L. (1976). "The Outcome as Cause: Predestination and Human Cloning." *Journal of Medicine and Philosophy* 1:318–331.

Feinberg, J. (1980). "The Child's Right to an Open Future," in *Whose Child? Children's Rights, Patental Authority, and State Power*, eds. W. Aiken and H. LaFollette. Totowa, NJ: Rowman and Littlefield.

Harris, J. (1992). *Wonderwoman and Superman: The Ethics of Biotechnology*. Oxford: Oxford University Press.

Huxley, A. (1932). *Brave New World*. London: Chalto and Winders.

Jonas, H. (1974). *Philosophical Essays: From Ancient Creed to Technological Man*. Englewood Cliffs, NJ: Prentice-Hall.

Kahn, C. (1989). "Can We Achieve Immortality?" *Free Inquiry* 9:14–18.

Kass, L. (1985). *Toward a More Natural Science*. New York: The Free Press.

LaBar, M. (1984). "The Pros and Cons of Human Cloning." *Thought* 57:318–333.

Lederberg, J. (1966). "Experimental Genetics and Human Evolution." *American Naturalist* 100:519–531.

Levin, I. (1976). *The Boys from Brazil*. New York: Random House.

Macklin, R. (1994). "Splitting Embryos on the Slippery Slope: Ethics and Public Policy." *Kennedy Institute of Ethics Journal* 4:209–226.

McCormick, R. (1993). "Should We Clone Humans?" *Christian Century* 110:1148–1149.

McKinnell, R. (1979). *Cloning: A Biologist Reports*. Minneapolis, MN: University of Minnesota Press.

Mill, J. S. (1859). *On Liberty*. Indianapolis, IN: Bobbs-Merrill Publishing.

NABER (National Advisory Board on Ethics in Reproduction) (1994). "Report on Human Cloning Through Embryo Splitting: An Amber Light." *Kennedy Institute of Ethics Journal* 4:251–282.

Parfit, D. (1984). *Reasons and Persons*. Oxford: Oxford University Press.

Rainer, J. D. (1978). "Commentary." *Man and Medicine: The Journal of Values and Ethics in Health Care* 3:115–117.

Rhodes, R. (1995). "Clones, Harms, and Rights." *Cambridge Quarterly of Healthcare Ethics* 4:285–290.

Robertson, J. A. (1994a). *Children of Choice: Freedom and the New Reproductive Technologies*. Princeton, NJ: Princeton University Press.

Robertson, J. A. (1994b). "The Question of Human Cloning." *Hastings Center Report* 24:6–14.

Robertson, J. A. (1997). "A Ban on Cloning and Cloning Research is Unjustified." Testimony Presented to the National Bioethics Advisory Commission, March 1997.

Smith, G. P. (1983). "Intimations of Immortality: Clones, Cyrons and the Law." *University of New South Wales Law Journal* 6:119–132.

Studdard, A. (1978). "The Lone Clone." *Man and Medicine: The Journal of Values and Ethics in Health Care* 3:109–114.

Thomas, L. (1974). "Notes of a Biology Watcher: On Cloning a Human Being." *New England Journal of Medicine* 291:1296–1297.

Verhey, A. D. (1994). "Cloning: Revisiting an Old Debate." *Kennedy Institute of Ethics Journal* 4:227–234.

Walters, W. A. W. (1982). "Cloning, Ectogenesis, and Hybrids: Things to Come?" in *Test-Tube Babies,* eds. W. A. W. Walters and P. Singer. Melbourne: Oxford University Press.

Weiss, R. (1997). "Cloning Suddenly Has Government's Attention." *International Herald Tribune*, March 7, 1997.

WHO (World Health Organization Press Office) (March 11, 1997). "WHO Director General Condemns Human Cloning." World Health Organization, Geneva, Switzerland.

Wilmut, I., et al. (1997). "Viable Offspring Derived from Fetal and Adult Mammalian Cells." *Nature* 385:810–813.

Opinion in the Matter of Baby M

NEW JERSEY SUPREME COURT

This case concerned the legal custody of "Baby M," an infant born to Mary Beth Whitehead in accordance with her agreement to become a surrogate mother for William and Elizabeth Stern. Whitehead consented to be artificially inseminated with Mr. Stern's sperm, to carry the child to term, and to hand it over to the Sterns after birth. But she refused to give up the baby and left the state with it. Eventually the dispute between Whitehead and the Sterns wound up in the New Jersey Supreme Court, which found that the surrogacy contract was invalid and that Whitehead was the legal mother. It also held that Baby M should live with the Sterns and that Whitehead should have visitation rights.

In this matter the Court is asked to determine the validity of a contract that purports to provide a new way of bringing children into a family. For a fee of $10,000, a woman agrees to be artificially inseminated with the semen of another woman's husband; she is to conceive a child, carry it to term, and after its birth surrender it to the natural father and his wife. The intent of the contract is that the child's natural mother will thereafter be forever separated from her child. The wife is to adopt the child, and she and the natural father are to be regarded as its parents for all purposes. The contract providing for this is called a "surrogacy contract," the natural mother inappropriately called the "surrogate mother."

We invalidate the surrogacy contract because it conflicts with the law and public policy of this State. While we recognize the depth of the yearning of infertile couples to have their own children, we find the payment of money to a "surrogate" mother illegal, perhaps criminal, and potentially degrading to women. Although in this case we grant custody to the natural father, the evidence having clearly proved such custody to be in the best interests of the infant, we void both the termination of the surrogate mother's parental rights and the adoption of the child by the wife/stepparent. We thus restore the "surrogate" as the mother of the child. We remand the issue of the natural mother's visitation rights to

the trial court, since that issue was not reached below and the record before us is not sufficient to permit us to decide it *de novo*.

We find no offense to our present laws where a woman voluntarily and without payment agrees to act as a "surrogate" mother, provided that she is not subject to a binding agreement to surrender her child. Moreover, our holding today does not preclude the Legislature from altering the current statutory scheme, within constitutional limits, so as to permit surrogacy contracts. Under current law, however, the surrogacy agreement before us is illegal and invalid.

Facts

In February 1985, William Stern and Mary Beth Whitehead entered into a surrogacy contract. It recited that Stern's wife, Elizabeth, was infertile, that they wanted a child, and that Mrs. Whitehead was willing to provide that child as the mother with Mr. Stern as the father.

The contract provided that through artificial insemination using Mr. Stern's sperm, Mrs. Whitehead would become pregnant, carry the child to term, bear it, deliver it to the Sterns, and thereafter do whatever was necessary to terminate her maternal rights so that Mrs. Stern could thereafter adopt the child. Mrs. Whitehead's husband, Richard, was also a party to the contract; Mrs. Stern was not. Mr. Whitehead promised to do all acts necessary to rebut the presumption of paternity under the Parentage Act.

From New Jersey Supreme Court (1988) 109 N.J. 396, 537 A.2d 1227 (1988).

Although Mrs. Stern was not a party to the surrogacy agreement, the contract gave her sole custody of the child in the event of Mr. Stern's death. Mrs. Stern's status as a nonparty to the surrogate parenting agreement presumably was to avoid the application of the baby-selling statute to this arrangement.

Mr. Stern, on his part, agreed to attempt the artificial insemination and to pay Mrs. Whitehead $10,000 after the child's birth, on its delivery to him. In a separate contract, Mr. Stern agreed to pay $7,500 to the Infertility Center of New York ("ICNY"). The Center's advertising campaigns solicit surrogate mothers and encourage infertile couples to consider surrogacy. ICNY arranged for the surrogacy contract by bringing the parties together, explaining the process to them, furnishing the contractual form, and providing legal counsel.

The history of the parties' involvement in this arrangement suggests their good faith. William and Elizabeth Stern were married in July 1974, having met at the University of Michigan, where both were Ph.D. candidates. Due to financial considerations and Mrs. Stern's pursuit of a medical degree and residency, they decided to defer starting a family until 1981. Before then, however, Mrs. Stern learned that she might have multiple sclerosis and that the disease in some cases renders pregnancy a serious health risk. Her anxiety appears to have exceeded the actual risk, which current medical authorities assess as minimal. Nonetheless that anxiety was evidently quite real, Mrs. Stern fearing that pregnancy might precipitate blindness, paraplegia, or other forms of debilitation. Based on the perceived risk, the Sterns decided to forgo having their own children. The decision had special significance for Mr. Stern. Most of his family had been destroyed in the Holocaust. As the family's only survivor, he very much wanted to continue his bloodline.

Initially the Sterns considered adoption, but were discouraged by the substantial delay apparently involved and by the potential problem they saw arising from their age and their differing religious backgrounds. They were most eager for some other means to start a family.

The paths of Mrs. Whitehead and the Sterns to surrogacy were similar. Both responded to advertising by ICNY. The Sterns' response, following their inquiries into adoption, was the result of their long-standing decision to have a child. Mrs. Whitehead's response apparently resulted from her sympathy with family members and others who could have no children (she stated that she wanted to give another couple the "gift of life"); she also wanted the $10,000 to help her family. . . .

. . . The two couples met to discuss the surrogacy arrangement and decided to go forward. On February 6, 1985, Mr. Stern and Mr. and Mrs. Whitehead executed the surrogate parenting agreement. After several artificial inseminations over a period of months, Mrs. Whitehead became pregnant. The pregnancy was uneventful and on March 27, 1986, Baby M was born.

Not wishing anyone at the hospital to be aware of the surrogacy arrangement, Mr. and Mrs. Whitehead appeared to all as the proud parents of a healthy female child. Her birth certificate indicated her name to be Sara Elizabeth Whitehead and her father to be Richard Whitehead. In accordance with Mrs. Whitehead's request, the Sterns visited the hospital unobtrusively to see the newborn child.

Mrs. Whitehead realized, almost from the moment of birth, that she could not part with this child. She had felt a bond with it even during pregnancy. Some indication of the attachment was conveyed to the Sterns at the hospital when they told Mrs. Whitehead what they were going to name the baby. She apparently broke into tears and indicated that she did not know if she could give up the child. She talked about how the baby looked like her other daughter, and made it clear that she was experiencing great difficulty with the decision.

Nonetheless, Mrs. Whitehead was, for the moment, true to her word. Despite powerful inclinations to the contrary, she turned her child over to the Sterns on March 30 at the Whiteheads' home.

The Sterns were thrilled with their new child. They had planned extensively for its arrival, far beyond the practical furnishing of a room for her. It was a time of joyful celebration—not just for them but for their friends as well. The Sterns looked forward to raising their daughter, whom they named Melissa. While aware by then that Mrs. Whitehead was undergoing an emotional crisis, they were as yet not

Chapter 8: Reproductive Technology

cognizant of the depth of that crisis and its implications for their newly enlarged family.

Later in the evening of March 30, Mrs. Whitehead became deeply disturbed, disconsolate, stricken with unbearable sadness. She had to have her child. She could not eat, sleep, or concentrate on anything other than her need for her baby. The next day she went to the Sterns' home and told them how much she was suffering.

The depth of Mrs. Whitehead's despair surprised and frightened the Sterns. She told them that she could not live without her baby, that she must have her, even if only for one week, that thereafter she would surrender her child. The Sterns, concerned that Mrs. Whitehead might indeed commit suicide, not wanting under any circumstances to risk that, and in any event believing that Mrs. Whitehead would keep her word, turned the child over to her. It was not until four months later, after a series of attempts to regain possession of the child, that Melissa was returned to the Sterns, having been forcibly removed from the home where she was then living with Mr. and Mrs. Whitehead, the home in Florida owned by Mary Beth Whitehead's parents.

The struggle over Baby M began when it became apparent that Mrs. Whitehead could not return the child to Mr. Stern. Due to Mrs. Whitehead's refusal to relinquish the baby, Mr. Stern filed a complaint seeking enforcement of the surrogacy contract. He alleged, accurately, that Mrs. Whitehead had not only refused to comply with the surrogacy contract but had threatened to flee from New Jersey with the child in order to avoid even the possibility of his obtaining custody. The court papers asserted that if Mrs. Whitehead were to be given notice of the application for an order requiring her to relinquish custody, she would, prior to the hearing, leave the state with the baby. And that is precisely what she did. After the order was entered, *ex parte*, the process server, aided by the police, in the presence of the Sterns, entered Mrs. Whitehead's home to execute the order. Mr. Whitehead fled with the child, who had been handed to him through a window while those who came to enforce the order were thrown off balance by a dispute over the child's current name.

The Whiteheads immediately fled to Florida with Baby M. They stayed initially with Mrs. Whitehead's

parents, where one of Mrs. Whitehead's children had been living. For the next three months, the Whiteheads and Melissa lived at roughly twenty different hotels, motels, and homes in order to avoid apprehension. From time to time Mrs. Whitehead would call Mr. Stern to discuss the matter; the conversations, recorded by Mr. Stern on advice of counsel, show an escalating dispute about rights, morality, and power, accompanied by threats of Mrs. Whitehead to kill herself, to kill the child, and falsely to accuse Mr. Stern of sexually molesting Mrs. Whitehead's other daughter.

Eventually, the Sterns discovered where the Whiteheads were staying, commenced supplementary proceedings in Florida, and obtained an order requiring the Whiteheads to turn over the child. Police in Florida enforced the order, forcibly removing the child from her grandparents' home. She was soon thereafter brought to New Jersey and turned over to the Sterns. The prior order of the court, issued *ex parte*, awarding custody of the child to the Sterns *pendente lite*, was reaffirmed by the trial court after consideration of the certified representations of the parties (both represented by counsel) concerning the unusual sequence of events that had unfolded. Pending final judgment, Mrs. Whitehead was awarded limited visitation with Baby M.

The Sterns' complaint, in addition to seeking possession and ultimately custody of the child, sought enforcement of the surrogacy contract. Pursuant to the contract, it asked that the child be permanently placed in their custody, that Mrs. Whitehead's parental rights be terminated, and that Mrs. Stern be allowed to adopt the child, i.e., that, for all purposes, Melissa become the Sterns' child.

The trial took thirty-two days over a period of more than two months. . . . Soon after the conclusion of the trial, the trial court announced its opinion from the bench. It held that the surrogacy contract was valid; ordered that Mrs. Whitehead's parental rights be terminated and that sole custody of the child be granted to Mr. Stern; and, after hearing brief testimony from Mrs. Stern, immediately entered an order allowing the adoption of Melissa by Mrs. Stern, all in accordance with the surrogacy contract. Pending the outcome of the appeal, we granted a continuation of visitation to Mrs. Whitehead, although slightly more limited than the visitation allowed during the trial.

Although clearly expressing its view that the surrogacy contract was valid, the trial court devoted the major portion of its opinion to the question of the baby's best interests. . . .

On the question of best interests—and we agree, but for different reasons, that custody was the critical issue—the court's analysis of the testimony was perceptive, demonstrating both its understanding of the case and its considerable experience in these matters. We agree substantially with both its analysis and conclusions on the matter of custody. . . .

Invalidity and Unenforceability of Surrogacy Contract

We have concluded that this surrogacy contract is invalid. Our conclusion has two bases: direct conflict with existing statutes and conflict with the public policies of this State, as expressed in its statutory and decisional law.

One of the surrogacy contract's basic purposes, to achieve the adoption of a child through private placement, though permitted in New Jersey "is very much disfavored." Its use of money for this purpose—and we have no doubt whatsoever that the money is being paid to obtain an adoption and not, as the Sterns argue, for the personal services of Mary Beth Whitehead—is illegal and perhaps criminal. In addition to the inducement of money, there is the coercion of contract: the natural mother's irrevocable agreement, prior to birth, even prior to conception, to surrender the child to the adoptive couple. Such an agreement is totally unenforceable in private placement adoption. Even where the adoption is through an approved agency, the formal agreement to surrender occurs only after birth, and then, by regulation, only *after* the birth mother has been offered counseling. Integral to these invalid provisions of the surrogacy contract is the related agreement, equally invalid, on the part of the natural mother to cooperate with, and not to contest, proceedings to terminate her parental rights, as well as her contractual concession, in aid of the adoption, that the child's best interests would be served by awarding custody to the natural father and his wife—all of this before she has even conceived,

and, in some cases, before she has the slightest idea of what the natural father and adoptive mother are like.

The foregoing provisions not only directly conflict with New Jersey statutes, but also offend long-established State policies. These critical terms, which are at the heart of the contract, are invalid and unenforceable, the conclusion therefore follows, without more, that the entire contract is unenforceable.

A. Conflict with Statutory Provisions

The surrogacy contract conflicts with: (1) laws prohibiting the use of money in connection with adoptions; (2) laws requiring proof of parental unfitness or abandonment before termination of parental rights is ordered or an adoption is granted; and (3) laws that make surrender of custody and consent to adoption revocable in private placement adoptions.

Our law prohibits paying or accepting money in connection with any placement of a child for adoption. Violation is a high misdemeanor. Excepted are fees of an approved agency (which must be a nonprofit entity) and certain expenses in connection with childbirth. . . .

B. Public Policy Considerations

The surrogacy contract's invalidity, resulting from its direct conflict with the above statutory provisions, is further underlined when its goals and means are measured against New Jersey's public policy. The contract's basic premise, that the natural parents can decide in advance of birth which one is to have custody of the child, bears no relationship to the settled law that the child's best interests shall determine custody. . . .

The surrogacy contract guarantees permanent separation of the child from one of its natural parents. Our policy, however, has long been that to the extent possible, children should remain with and be brought up by both of their natural parents. . . . This is not simply some theoretical ideal that in practice has no meaning. The impact of failure to follow that policy is nowhere better shown than in the results of this surrogacy contract. A child, instead of starting off its life with as much peace and security as possible, finds itself immediately in a tug-of-war between contending mother and father.

The surrogacy contract violates the policy of this State that the rights of natural parents are equal concerning their child, the father's right no greater than the mother's. . . . The whole purpose and effect of the surrogacy contract was to give the father the exclusive right to the child by destroying the rights of the mother.

The policies expressed in our comprehensive laws governing consent to the surrender of a child stand in stark contrast to the surrogacy contract and what it implies. Here there is no counseling, independent or otherwise, of the natural mother, no evaluation, no warning. . . .

Under the contract, the natural mother is irrevocably committed before she knows the strength of her bond with her child. She never makes a totally voluntary, informed decision, for quite clearly any decision prior to the baby's birth is, in the most important sense, uninformed, and any decision after that, compelled by a pre-existing contractual commitment, the threat of a lawsuit, and the inducement of a $10,000 payment, is less than totally voluntary. Her interests are of little concern to those who controlled this transaction. . . .

Worst of all, however, is the contract's total disregard of the best interests of the child. There is not the slightest suggestion that any inquiry will be made at any time to determine the fitness of the Sterns as custodial parents, of Mrs. Stern as an adoptive parent, their superiority to Mrs. Whitehead, or the effect on the child of not living with her natural mother.

This is the sale of a child, or, at the very least, the sale of a mother's right to her child, the only mitigating factor being that one of the purchasers is the father. Almost every evil that prompted the prohibition on the payment of money in connection with adoptions exists here. . . .

In the scheme contemplated by the surrogacy contract in this case, a middleman, propelled by profit, promotes the sale. Whatever idealism may have motivated any of the participants, the profit motive predominates, permeates, and ultimately governs the transaction. The demand for children is great and the supply small. The availability of contraception, abortion, and the greater willingness of single mothers to bring up their children has led to a shortage of babies offered for adoption. The situation is ripe for

the entry of the middleman who will bring some equilibrium into the market by increasing the supply through the use of money.

Intimated, but disputed, is the assertion that surrogacy will be used for the benefit of the rich at the expense of the poor. In response it is noted that the Sterns are not rich and the Whiteheads not poor. Nevertheless, it is clear to us that it is unlikely that surrogate mothers will be as proportionately numerous among those women in the top twenty percent income bracket as among those in the bottom twenty percent. Put differently, we doubt that infertile couples in the low-income bracket will find upper income surrogates.

In any event, even in this case one should not pretend that disparate wealth does not play a part simply because the contrast is not the dramatic "rich versus poor." At the time of trial, the Whiteheads' net assets were probably negative—Mrs. Whitehead's own sister was foreclosing on a second mortgage. Their income derived from Mr. Whitehead's labors. Mrs. Whitehead is a homemaker, having previously held part-time jobs. The Sterns are both professionals, she a medical doctor, he a biochemist. Their combined income when both were working was about $89,500 a year and their assets sufficient to pay for the surrogacy contract arrangements.

The point is made that Mrs. Whitehead *agreed* to the surrogacy arrangement, supposedly fully understanding the consequences. Putting aside the issue of how compelling her need for money may have been, and how significant her understanding of the consequences, we suggest that her consent is irrelevant. There are, in a civilized society, some things that money cannot buy. In America, we decided long ago that merely because conduct purchased by money was "voluntary" did not mean that it was good or beyond regulation and prohibition. Employers can no longer buy labor at the lowest price they can bargain for, even though that labor is "voluntary," or buy women's labor for less money than paid to men for the same job, or purchase the agreement of children to perform oppressive labor, or purchase the agreement of workers to subject themselves to unsafe or unhealthful working conditions. There are, in short, values that society deems more important than granting to wealth whatever it can buy, be it labor, love, or life. Whether this principle recommends prohibition of surrogacy, which presumably sometimes results in great satisfaction to all of the parties, is not for us to say. We note here only that, under existing law, the fact that Mrs. Whitehead "agreed" to the arrangement is not dispositive.

The long-term effects of surrogacy contracts are not known, but feared—the impact on the child who learns her life was bought, that she is the offspring of someone who gave birth to her only to obtain money; the impact on the natural mother as the full weight of her isolation is felt along with the full reality of the sale of her body and her child; the impact on the natural father and adoptive mother once they realize the consequences of their conduct. Literature in related areas suggests these are substantial considerations, although, given the newness of surrogacy, there is little information.

The surrogacy contract is based on principles that are directly contrary to the objectives of our laws. It guarantees the separation of a child from its mother; it looks to adoption regardless of suitability; it totally ignores the child; it takes the child from the mother regardless of her wishes and her maternal fitness; and it does all of this, it accomplishes all of its goals, through the use of money.

Beyond that is the potential degradation of some women that may result from this arrangement. In many cases, of course, surrogacy may bring satisfaction, not only to the infertile couple, but to the surrogate mother herself. The fact, however, that many women may not perceive surrogacy negatively but rather see it as an opportunity does not diminish its potential for devastation to other women.

In sum, the harmful consequences of this surrogacy arrangement appear to us all too palpable. In New Jersey the surrogate mother's agreement to sell her child is void. Its irrevocability infects the entire contract, as does the money that purports to buy it.

Termination

We have already noted that under our laws termination of parental rights cannot be based on contract, but may be granted only on proof of the statutory requirements. That conclusion was one of the bases for invalidating the surrogacy contract. Although excluding the contract as a basis for parental termination, we did not explicitly deal with the question of whether the statutory bases for termination existed. We do so here.

As noted before, if termination of Mrs. Whitehead's parental rights is justified, Mrs. Whitehead will have no further claim either to custody or to visitation, and adoption by Mrs. Stern may proceed pursuant to the private placement adoption statute. If termination is not justified. Mrs. Whitehead remains the legal mother, and even if not entitled to custody, she would ordinarily be expected to have some rights of visitation. . . .

Nothing in this record justifies a finding that would allow a court to terminate Mary Beth Whitehead's parental rights under the statutory standard. It is not simply that obviously there was no "intentional abandonment or very substantial neglect of parental duties without a reasonable expectation of reversal of that conduct in the future," quite the contrary, but furthermore that the trial court never found Mrs. Whitehead an unfit mother and indeed affirmatively stated that Mary Beth Whitehead had been a good mother to her other children. . . .

Custody

. . . [T]he question of custody in this case, as in practically all cases, assumes the fitness of both parents, and no serious contention is made in this case that either is unfit. The issue here is which life would be *better* for Baby M, one with primary custody in the Whiteheads or one with primary custody in the Sterns.

The circumstances of this custody dispute are unusual and they have provoked some unusual contentions. The Whiteheads claim that even if the child's best interests would be served by our awarding custody to the Sterns, we should not do so, since that will encourage surrogacy contracts—contracts claimed by the Whiteheads, and we agree, to be violative of important legislatively stated public policies. Their position is that in order that surrogacy contracts be deterred, custody should remain in the surrogate mother unless she is unfit, regardless of the best interests of the child. We disagree. Our declaration that this surrogacy contract is unenforceable and illegal is sufficient to deter similar agreements. We need not sacrifice the child's interests in order to make that point sharper. . . .

Our custody conclusion is based on strongly persuasive testimony contrasting both the family life of the Whiteheads and the Sterns and the personalities and characters of the individuals. The stability of the Whitehead family life was doubtful at the time of trial. Their finances were in serious trouble (foreclosure by Mrs. Whitehead's sister on a second mortgage was in process). Mr. Whitehead's employment, though relatively steady, was always at risk because of his alcoholism, a condition that he seems not to have been able to confront effectively. Mrs. Whitehead had not worked for quite some time, her last two employments having been part-time. One of the Whiteheads' positive attributes was their ability to bring up two children, and apparently well, even in so vulnerable a household. Yet substantial question was raised even about that aspect of their home life. The expert testimony contained criticism of Mrs. Whitehead's handling of her son's educational difficulties. Certain of the experts noted that Mrs. Whitehead perceived herself as omnipotent and omniscient concerning her children. She knew what they were thinking, what they wanted, and she spoke for them. As to Melissa, Mrs. Whitehead expressed the view that she alone knew what that child's cries and sounds meant. Her inconsistent stories about various things engendered grave doubts about her ability to explain honestly and sensitively to Baby M—and at the right time—the nature of her origin. Although faith in professional counseling is not a *sine qua non* of parenting, several experts believed that Mrs. Whitehead's contempt for professional help, especially professional psychological help, coincided with her feelings of omnipotence in a way that could be devastating to a child who most likely will need such help. In short, while love and affection there would be, Baby M's life with the Whiteheads promised to be too closely controlled by Mrs. Whitehead. The prospects for wholesome, independent psychological growth and development would be at serious risk.

The Sterns have no other children, but all indications are that their household and their personalities promise a much more likely foundation for Melissa to grow and thrive. There *is* a track record of sorts—during the one-and-a-half-years of custody Baby M has done very well, and the relationship between both Mr. and Mrs. Stern and the baby has become very strong. The household is stable, and likely to remain so. Their finances are more than adequate, their circle of friends supportive, and their marriage happy. Most important, they are loving, giving, nurturing, and open-minded people. They have demonstrated the wish and ability to nurture and protect Melissa, yet at the same time to encourage her independence. Their lack of experience is more than made up for by a willingness to learn and to listen, a willingness that is enhanced by their professional training, especially Mrs. Stern's experience as a pediatrician They are honest; they can recognize error, deal with it, and learn from it. They will try to determine rationally the best way to cope with problems in their relationship with Melissa. When the time comes to tell her about her origins, they will probably have found a means of doing so that accords with the best interests of Baby M. All in all, Melissa's future appear's solid, happy, and promising with them.

Based on all of this we have concluded, independent of the trial court's identical conclusion, that Melissa's best interests call for custody in the Sterns. Our above-mentioned disagreements with the trial court do not, as we have noted, in any way diminish our concurrence with its conclusions. . . .

Visitation

The trial court's decision to terminate Mrs. Whitehead's parental rights precluded it from making any determination on visitation. Our reversal of the trial court's order, however, requires delineation of Mrs. Whitehead's rights to visitation. It is apparent to us that this factually sensitive issue, which was never addressed below, should not be determined *de novo* by this Court. We therefore remand the visitation issue to the trial court for an abbreviated hearing and determination. . . .

The fact that the trial court did not address visitation is only one reason for remand. The ultimate question is whether, despite the absence of the trial court's guidance, the record before us is sufficient to allow an appellate court to make this essentially factual determination. We can think of no issue that is more dependent on a trial court's factual findings and evaluation than visitation.

We have decided that Mrs. Whitehead is entitled to visitation at some point, and that question is not open to the trial court on this remand. The trial court will determine what kind of visitation shall be granted to her, with or without conditions, and when and under what circumstances it should commence. . . .

Conclusion

This case affords some insight into a new reproductive arrangement: the artificial insemination of a surrogate mother. The unfortunate events that have unfolded illustrate that its unregulated use can bring suffering to all involved. Potential victims include the surrogate mother and her family, the natural father and his wife, and most importantly, the child. Although surrogacy has apparently provided positive results for some infertile couples, it can also, as this case demonstrates, cause suffering to participants, here essentially innocent and well-intended.

We have found that our present laws do not permit the surrogacy contract used in this case. Nowhere, however, do we find any legal prohibition against surrogacy when the surrogate mother volunteers, without any payment, to act as a surrogate and is given the right to change her mind and to assert her parental rights. Moreover, the Legislature remains free to deal with this most sensitive issue as it sees fit, subject only to constitutional constraints. . . .

CHAPTER 9

Genetic Choices

We are now in the Genetic Era, a time when the century-old trickle of scientific facts about our genetic selves has given way to a torrent. The rivulet widened suddenly in 1953 when Francis Crick and James Watson discovered that the double helix was the shape of DNA—the chemical compound that encodes the encyclopedic set of instructions for producing and maintaining all living things. It broadened into a flood in 2003 when scientists finally were able to chart the length and breadth of the human genome, determining the exact sequence of a human being's 3 billion letters of DNA code, all grouped into 20,000–25,000 genes. Now scientists are rapidly pinpointing genetic factors that cause or contribute to diseases, developing tests to identify and predict (even before conception) specific human conditions, researching ways to alter genes to effect cures or devise treatments, enabling parents to have control over the genetic makeup of their children, and peering into the future at the power to change profoundly the human genome itself.

At each step, moral questions press in, and they intersect with almost every major ethical concern in this text—paternalism, autonomy, beneficence, rights, confidentiality, abortion, killing, personhood, reproductive technology, justice in providing health care, research ethics, and more. Science has once again outpaced conventional moral understanding as genetics inserts a host of raw, hard questions into our lives: Should genetic testing be used to identify or predict diseases even when no treatment is available? Do carriers of a deadly genetic disease that is likely to be passed on to their children have a duty to warn those children of the risk? Who should control genetic information about a person, and what is a physician's duty regarding truth-telling and confidentiality? Is it "playing God" to alter someone's genes to treat diseases or prevent them in future generations? Is it wrong for parents to use preconception genetic testing and embryo selection to avoid having a disabled baby? Do these practices discriminate against disabled people? Should genetic technology be used to select a child's gender or other attributes such as eye and hair color and musical or athletic ability? Should eugenics be employed? That is, should genetic knowledge be applied to whole populations in an attempt to improve the human genome?

Such questions could continue for several pages, but let us try to grapple with some of the main ones.

GENES AND GENOMES

Cells are the fundamental components of every living thing, and DNA (deoxyribonucleic acid) makes up the chemical coding that directs their construction, development, and operation. For nearly all organisms, DNA is the language of the genetic software that runs the cells and ensures the inheritance of traits from one generation to the next. Whether in ants, worms, gazelles, or humans, DNA consists of the same chemical ingredients and has the same molecular architecture: double, parallel strands linked together by chemical crossbars and twisted like a spiral staircase—the classic double helix. Each crossbar is formed by a matching pair of chemical bases, called a base pair. There are only four bases—adenine (A), guanine (G), cytosine (C), and thymine (T)—yet they constitute the entire "alphabet" of the genetic code. Their order (the DNA sequence) along the strands (ATTCCGGA, for example) encodes all the instructions required for making and maintaining an organism. As it "reads" the code, a cell constructs, according to the precise specifications, various proteins, which carry out most biological processes and provide almost all of the material for building cells.

An organism's entire complement of DNA is known as its **genome**. The human genome consists of about 3 billion base pairs, and there is a complete genome in nearly every human cell. (A mouse genome has 2.6 billion base pairs; a fruit fly, 137 million; and an *E. coli* bacterium, 4.6 million.) In a typical human cell, the DNA strands total about six feet, coiled and crammed efficiently into an incredibly small space.

A cell does not "read" the 3 billion base pairs as one long stream of letters but as separate segments, or "words," of the stream, each segment providing instructions to the cell for manufacturing a customized protein or small group of proteins. These words of genetic code are **genes**, the fundamental units of biological inheritance. The human genome contains 20,000–25,000 genes, which vary in the length of their instructions from hundreds of DNA bases up to 2 million. Each gene has a duplicate, with one copy inherited from the male parent and one from the female parent.

In the cell's nucleus, the genes are neatly organized—bundled into 46 stringlike molecules known as **chromosomes**. These bundles are arranged into 23 pairs, with 22 of the pairs appearing the same for both males and females, and the twenty-third pair—the sex chromosomes—differing for males and females. Males have both an X and Y chromosome, while females have two X chromosomes.

Through the workings of all this genetic machinery, a human organism is produced and sustained, and a vast share of its characteristics is determined. (Genes have their say, but not necessarily the final say, on how a person turns out, for he or she is also affected by the incredibly complex interactions between genetic systems and environmental factors.) When the machinery operates properly, the organism thrives. But flaws in the system—mistakes in the genes' coded instructions—can sometimes lead to devastating disease or disability. Mistakes (mutations or alterations) can arise when the order of bases in a DNA sequence is wrong or when bases have been added, deleted, or duplicated. Occasionally extra genes or chromosomes are added, or essential ones are left out.

Some genetic mutations are acquired—they happen in people randomly or because of exposure to noxious agents such as radiation, chemicals, or cigarette smoke. The exposure disorders can "run in families" not because they are hereditary but because family members are exposed to the same harmful environmental factors. But many mutations are indeed hereditary and are transmitted through families, triggering the same genetic disease in subsequent generations. The genetic errors are responsible for more than 4,000 hereditary diseases.

Unfortunately, the relation between genetic flaws and genetic disease is usually anything but simple. In most cases, genetic diseases arise not from a single gene defect but from many mutations in one or more genes, coupled with a person's lifestyle habits and environmental influences. Researchers believe that many common disorders such as heart disease, cancer, and diabetes are in this category.

GENETIC TESTING

Thanks to scientific advances in genetics (most notably the tracing of the human genome sequence by the Human Genome Project), it is now possible to check for genetic disorders by looking for changes in a person's DNA. This is the power of **genetic testing**, which now includes over two thousand tests designed to detect disease. With a small blood or tissue sample from a patient, clinicians can test for a host of genetic mutations that can unmask a variety of disorders. The testing is done for several reasons, including:

- *Newborn screening* to uncover genetic diseases for early treatment. Every state mandates some kind of genetic testing for newborns, with some states screening for as many as 30 disorders. The first mandatory genetic testing was for phenylketonuria (PKU), a disorder resulting in profound mental retardation when not treated early with a special diet.
- *Carrier testing* to determine whether someone is a carrier of a type of genetic disease known as an autosomal recessive disorder. A carrier possesses just one copy of a mutated gene and will not get the disease, but if two carriers together have a child, that child could inherit two copies of the mutated gene (one from each parent) and therefore greatly increase its chances of having the disease. PKU is such a disorder, and so is cystic fibrosis (a life-shortening illness affecting respiratory and gastrointestinal systems), sickle cell disease (a painful, debilitating blood cell disorder), and Tay-Sachs (a devastating metabolic disease usually causing death by age 5).
- *Predictive testing* to find out before any symptoms appear if someone is likely to develop a genetic disease later in life. This kind of testing is often recommended to people who have a family history of a genetic disorder. In a few cases, the testing can predict with high probability that a person will develop a disorder, but usually its implications are much more uncertain. For example, if testing shows that someone has the gene defect responsible for Huntington's disease (a life-shortening disorder causing dementia and physical deterioration), the chances that she will develop the disease are nearly 100 percent. But someone found to have a single copy of the gene mutation linked to venous thrombosis (a blot-clotting disorder) has only a slightly higher risk of getting the disease than the general population.
- *Diagnostic testing* to confirm or rule out a genetic disorder in someone with symptoms.
- *Prenatal testing* to determine if a fetus has genetic abnormalities likely to cause physical or mental impairments. It is performed when there is reason to suspect genetic risk—for example, when the mother is age 35 or older (Down syndrome babies are more likely in this age group), when inherited disorders are evident in family history, or when ancestry or ethnicity suggests a greater chance of particular genetic disorders such as sickle cell and Tay-Sachs. Several prenatal genetic testing procedures are now used, the most common being amniocentesis, which analyzes a sample of amniotic fluid, and chorionic villus sampling (CVS), which tests a few cells from the placenta. Fetuses can now be tested for a long list of genetic disorders causing physical deformities, developmental defects, mental retardation, deafness, blindness, and death. Often if the news derived from prenatal testing is bad, parents must decide whether to terminate the pregnancy.
- *Preimplantation genetic diagnosis (PGD)* to test embryos produced through in vitro fertilization (IVF) for genetic abnormalities. Typically several embryos are produced in each cycle of IVF. Through PGD, those with genetic defects are screened out and only the mutation-free embryos are transferred to the woman's uterus for implantation. A typical procedure is to remove only one or two cells from a five- to eight-cell embryo for testing. PGD is costly and is usually reserved for cases in which there is a high probability of giving birth to a baby with serious disorders such as Down syndrome or Tay-Sachs disease.

Because genetics is bewilderingly complex, genetic testing itself is laden with complications that erode its usefulness and provoke medical and moral questions. For one thing, genetic tests almost never yield conclusive answers. In most cases, they can give only probabilities of developing a disease. Tests can identify a genetic mutation with certainty but usually can convey only in probabilities what ills that mutation might cause. For example, we can accurately determine that a woman has a mutation in the BRCA1 or BRCA2 gene, and this will tell us not that she will surely develop breast cancer but that she has a greater than 80 percent chance of doing so by age 70. So a positive test result (one identifying a mutation) does not guarantee the development of a genetic disorder. Moreover, though some disorders like Huntington's and Tay-Sachs are caused by mutations in a single gene (and thus are easier to predict), most genetic disorders result from abnormalities in several genes or in interactions between multiple genes and environmental factors. Scientists may not know about all the mutations responsible for a disorder, so available tests may identify only some of them. Or environmental influences later in life may cause mutations that earlier tests miss. So a negative test result (no mutation) does not guarantee a disease-free future.

Even when tests correctly predict a genetic disorder, they usually cannot foretell how severe its symptoms will be or when they will appear. Two people with mutations in the cystic fibrosis gene may differ dramatically in the severity of their respiratory and intestinal problems, and symptoms of Huntington's disease may arise in one person a decade before they appear in another.

Perhaps the most painful fact about genetic testing is that the power to identify and predict genetic disorders has outpaced our ability to do anything about them. We can now test for many diseases—and treat only some of them. We can ascertain that someone has a terrible disorder that has no treatment. Some argue that in such a situation, knowledge is not a blessing but curse. A 2002 Harris poll found that 81 percent of adults would likely want a genetic test for a disease that was treatable or otherwise responsive to

risk reduction. But only 49 percent would be likely to have the test if there was no known treatment or any other ways to cut risks.[1]

Genetic testing can also take an emotional toll. Though some people find it reassuring or empowering, others do not. After getting their test results, some feel depressed, angry, or frightened. If the testing shows they are at no or low risk of having a disorder, they may be tormented by survivor's guilt. If the news is bad, they may become fatalistic; if the news is good, they may develop a feeling of invulnerability. Either way, they may ignore opportunities to lower their risk (when that's possible), or they may make things worse by behaving recklessly. Though some people who test positive for being carriers take steps to avoid passing on the genetic defect, some also feel ashamed, guilty, or socially stigmatized for being carriers. Along with all these scenarios comes the possibility of family conflicts, for testing can divulge facts not just about the person tested but also about her relatives.

From all these complexities a multitude of ethical issues arise, including the following.

Personal Knowledge. Many moral quandaries begin when people suspect they might have a genetic disorder for which testing is available. Should a person choose to be tested when an incurable genetic disease is suspected (and no one else is affected)? This is a question about personal values and worldviews. If a young man suspects he might have a devastating disease like Huntington's (which has no cure and does not affect people until middle age), and he understands that testing could confirm or disconfirm his suspicions, he must decide whether to know or not know his status. In accordance with his values, he may choose to know because he wants to confront life's hazards with his eyes wide open and to exert as much control over his fortunes as he can. Or he may forgo the chance to learn his fate, seeking instead to live in hope as long as possible without the weight of a terrible diagnosis pressing down on him. This kind of choice is not merely hypothetical: Many

DIRECT-TO-CONSUMER GENETIC TESTS

Many genetic tests are ordered for patients not by their physicians but by the patients themselves. The physician-ordered tests are widely used and trusted by medical professionals; the patient-ordered direct-to-consumer (DTC) tests often are not. Here's what the National Institutes of Health and other agencies have to say about DTC tests:

If a consumer chooses to purchase a genetic test directly, the test kit is mailed to the consumer instead of being ordered through a doctor's office. The test typically involves collecting a DNA sample at home, often by swabbing the inside of the cheek, and mailing the sample back to the laboratory. . . .

The growing market for direct-to-consumer genetic testing may promote awareness of genetic diseases, allow consumers to take a more proactive role in their health care, and offer a means for people to learn about their ancestral origins. At-home genetic tests, however, have

significant risks and limitations. Consumers are vulnerable to being misled by the results of unproven or invalid tests. Without guidance from a healthcare provider, they may make important decisions about treatment or prevention based on inaccurate, incomplete, or misunderstood information about their health. Consumers may also experience an invasion of genetic privacy if testing companies use their genetic information in an unauthorized way.

Genetic testing provides only one piece of information about a person's health—other genetic and environmental factors, lifestyle choices, and family medical history also affect a person's risk of developing many disorders. These factors are discussed during a consultation with a doctor or genetic counselor, but in many cases are not addressed by at-home genetic tests. More research is needed to fully understand the benefits and limitations of direct-to-consumer genetic testing.

From Lister Hill National Center for Biomedical Communications; U.S. National Library of Medicine, National Institutes of Health, et al., "What Is Direct-to-Consumer Genetic Testing?," October 2015, http://ghr.nlm.nih.gov/handbook/testing/directtoconsumer (31 October 2015).

symptomless people at risk for Huntington's disease decide not to be tested.

The moral equation changes when others are involved besides the one deciding whether to be tested. Imagine that a 45-year-old woman with grown children comes to believe that she probably has Huntington's disease because she has a family history and is beginning to experience some mild symptoms characteristic of the disease's early stages. If she has the gene mutation responsible for Huntington's, then each of her children has a 50 percent chance of inheriting it and thus having the disease. The average onset of the disorder is 35 to 44 years of age, with death usually occurring 13 to 15 years after that. Symptoms progress to extreme cognitive impairment and motor disability. The question is:

Assuming she knows these facts, does she have a moral duty to be tested and, if the test is positive, to tell her children? Or, more generally, do we sometimes have a moral *obligation to know* and then a *duty to warn*?

Some might contend that she has no such obligation since the disease is untreatable. But others would disagree, arguing from the principle that we have a duty to prevent harm to others (especially those with whom we have a special relationship) if we are in a position to do so. Dutifully warned by their mother, the children could choose to be tested themselves and perhaps avoid transmitting the disorder to another generation by not having children or by using reproductive technology. In any case, the children could better arrange their lives to take the genetic facts into account, avoiding the harm of decisions made in ignorance.[2]

Often in genetic testing cases, people view the main ethical issue as a conflict between the duty to prevent harm to others and the principle of autonomy (typically construed as involving a right to privacy). Consider the case of three 20-something siblings, one of whom, Maria, has been diagnosed with Wilson's disease, an inherited metabolic disorder causing liver dysfunction and serious psychiatric problems. Wilson's is an autosomal recessive disorder, and since Maria definitely has it, her siblings each possess a one in four chance of also having it. Effective treatment is possible if it is started before symptoms appear. So far the siblings show no symptoms, and they are unaware that Wilson's has affected their family. Maria understands that her siblings could possibly be spared a dreadful disease if they are tested and treated early. But she is ashamed of her condition, especially the psychiatric symptoms, and insists that her privacy be respected and that her diagnosis not be disclosed to any of her relatives.

According to any plausible view of the principle of autonomy, Maria should be permitted to make choices affecting her own life, and her privacy should be respected. But many would assume that she also has an obligation to prevent harm—specifically, a duty to warn her siblings of the danger posed by Wilson's disease. Assuming this description of the ethical parameters is correct, which duty makes a stronger demand on Maria? Many would argue that the duty to prevent harm is stronger. Respect for autonomy is not absolute; we may—and often should—violate someone's autonomy to prevent harm to others. But some would say that autonomy is supreme or that we have no obligation at all to prevent harm, arguing that we do have a duty not to directly *harm* others but not a duty to *save* others.

Paternalism, Autonomy, and Confidentiality. Dilemmas of genetic knowledge also afflict clinicians—most sharply when the duty to maintain patient confidentiality clashes with a duty to warn family members of serious genetic peril. In Maria's case, a physician is caught in the middle, duty-bound to respect her privacy yet seeing clearly the harm that could befall her siblings if they are not told the very thing that Maria wants to keep secret. The law has been equivocal about disclosure of medical information against the patient's will, though some legal cases suggest that physicians may have a duty to warn people who are likely to be seriously harmed. A few physicians have been sued for their failure to inform relatives about genetic risks. Some physicians argue that breeching confidentiality may be morally permissible if the harm done by keeping silent outweighs the harm done by revealing private information about the patient. Others insist on strict adherence to a policy of nondisclosure. (Professional codes of ethics also differ on this issue.) But whatever view physicians take, they are likely to try to get around the dilemma by urging patients to warn their own family members.

In genetic testing, as in so many other areas of medicine, the principles of beneficence and autonomy collide, and the extent of physician paternalism is a live issue. For example, physicians have debated whether they should reveal to a patient the results of a genetic test showing that he or she is at high risk for an unpreventable, untreatable disease. They wonder if doing so is really in the patient's best interests. The question is especially keen when genetic testing targeted at one disorder incidentally uncovers a danger of falling prey to another—as when the APOE gene test for coronary heart disease shows a very high risk of eventually having Alzheimer's disease. The main argument against revealing this additional (and possibly unwanted) information is that it will not benefit the patient (because there is no way to prevent or treat Alzheimer's) and will cause the patient psychological harm. But many reject this view as strongly paternalistic and argue that the principle of autonomy gives patients the right to know their medical condition, including the results of genetic tests—even if the news is upsetting.

The same sorts of arguments are offered on the question of whether the public availability of genetic tests should be restricted. Most people can probably see the wisdom in restricting access to genetic tests that yield misleading, confusing, or otherwise unhelpful information. (Many genetic tests are like this and are useful only when combined with family history.) But some physicians favor restricting access to genetic tests for more paternalistic reasons, arguing that genetic self-knowledge causes psychological harms such as depression, anxiety, and panic or that patients cannot understand the complexities and implications of genetic information. Those who disagree with this view maintain that there is no reason to think that most patients will be psychologically wrecked by learning the truth about their genetic risks, that patient autonomy trumps any such concerns, and that the complexity of medical information is usually not considered an adequate justification for overriding patient autonomy.

Many people welcome the chance to discover the facts about their genetic predispositions, but others think they have good reasons to conceal such information or to decline testing altogether. Their wariness is prompted by the possibility of **genetic discrimination**, the use of genetic information by employers, insurance companies, and others to discriminate against or stigmatize people. Many fear that employers may use genetic information to decide whether to hire or fire them, weeding out those who may be healthy now but at risk for future diseases that could reduce productivity. They are also afraid that to cut costs, insurance companies will deny them health coverage or cancel it because genetic tests suggest a likelihood of eventual illness. These possibilities have left some people reluctant to undergo genetic testing because the results could be used as evidence against them, and this reluctance has been reinforced by some documented cases of genetic discrimination. Until recently, no comprehensive federal law addressed genetic discrimination, while state laws were inconsistent and limited in their approach to the issue. In 2008 the Genetic

Information Nondiscrimination Act was signed into law, prohibiting genetic discrimination by either insurance companies or employers and barring them from requesting genetic tests.

The main ethical concern here is justice, whether people are being treated fairly. Employers and insurers have a plausible interest in controlling the costs of doing business, but can this interest legitimately include granting economic benefits to some people and not to others merely because of a difference in genes? Is it morally permissible to discriminate against people in this way because of factors over which they have no control? Can it be right to discriminate against people who are now healthy but may someday be unhealthy? If this type of discrimination is legitimate, for what genetic mutations and conditions would it be appropriate? In most cases, the chances that specific mutations will result in a particular disease are difficult or impossible to gauge. Is it acceptable to discriminate against people when the basis for that discrimination is so dubious?

Reproductive Decisions. The possibility of detecting genetic mutations in a fetus or in an embryo inspires both hope and anguish—the hope of avoiding birth impairments, the anguish of moral conflict. The moral issues arise primarily because prenatal testing is coupled with the option of abortion (called *selective* when done to avoid impairments), and PGD entails embryo selection. In nearly every case, selective abortion and embryo selection are the only options for avoiding the birth of a severely impaired baby. Once a genetic mutation is discovered, there is little or nothing that can be done to correct the mutation or the disorder. Those opposed to all abortions and the screening or destruction of embryos will judge these procedures morally impermissible, and they may see no wrong in permitting the birth of children with serious abnormalities. But many think that abortion and embryo selection may be justified when used to avoid having babies with such terrible defects.

A typical statement of the latter view is that it would be wrong not to prevent devastating diseases or disabilities in a child. Explaining exactly why a failure to prevent defects would be wrong, however, is not as easy as it might seem. We could say that failing to prevent an impairment is wrong because the child would be better off if the impairment were prevented, but philosophers have thought this notion incoherent. Bioethicist Dan W. Brock explains:

> The difficulty is that it would *not* be better for the person with the handicap to have had it prevented since that can only be done by preventing him from ever having existed at all; preventing the handicap would deny the individual a worthwhile, although handicapped, life. . . . But if [a mother's] failing to prevent the handicap has not made her child worse off, then failing to prevent the handicap does not harm her child. And if she does not harm her child by not preventing its handicap, then why does she wrong her child morally by failing to do so?[3]

Philosophers have responded to this incoherence problem by arguing that even if failing to prevent a serious disability does not wrong the child, the failure is still morally wrong for other reasons—for example, because it contributes to overall suffering in the world or because it treats children unfairly by disregarding their legitimate interests in having a decent chance at a good life.

A common charge against genetic testing to prevent birth impairments is that it amounts to disrespect or discrimination against people with disabilities. Some critics are adamantly opposed to testing, claiming that its purpose is to eliminate an entire class of people (the disabled), which puts genetic testing in the same moral category as heinous attempts to eradicate whole races of people. Even if not discriminatory, others say, genetic testing is meant to prevent the existence of the disabled and make possible the existence of the normal, and that fact sends a message of disrespect to people now living with disabilities. The message is that it would be better if disabled people did not exist.

Genetic testing is discriminatory if it involves violating people's rights, and it is disrespectful if it entails an attitude of contempt or condescension. But some bioethicists have insisted that discrimination or disrespect for persons is not entailed by genetic testing. For example:

> Much of what is involved in equality of respect is compatible with screening. Aiming for the conception and birth of normal people, for instance, is perfectly compatible with insisting that the rights of disabled people are fully respected and with seeing them as equals. Medical treatment presupposes that health is better than sickness, but those who believe in it treat sick people as their equals.[4]

It has also been argued that anti-testing attitudes themselves have unsavory moral implications. Jeff McMahan points out that the critics of testing believe that "it is wrong for people to try to avoid having a disabled child and to have a non-disabled child instead." But this seems to imply that an action that most think is wrong must be permissible:

> [I]f it is morally *mandatory* to *allow* oneself to have a disabled child rather than to try, through screening, to have a child who would not be disabled, then it must be at least *permissible* to *cause* oneself to have a disabled rather than a non-disabled child.[5]

Yet most of us think it wrong deliberately to cause a disabled child to exist instead of a healthy child.

Even if we grant that embryo or prenatal testing is permissible, its use still raises a range of moral concerns. If a fetus has the gene for Huntington's disease, it is almost certain to suffer from the disease as an adult. The probability of being affected is extremely high, so we might conclude that testing (and possibly a selective abortion) is justified. But what if the chances of being affected are lower or uncertain (as is the case with the BRCA1 or BRCA2 gene)? Would abortion or embryo selection be justified? Would it be permissible if the odds of having the disease were low but the suffering it could cause was horrendous? Some diseases predicted by testing are late-onset (Huntington's and Alzheimer's, for instance); a person could live a satisfying life for decades before having symptoms. Is selective abortion permissible in such cases? Would it be permissible if the suffering at the end of life was likely to overshadow whatever happiness occurs earlier? Some predicted disorders are mild or treatable. Would parents have an obligation to screen out embryos with such disorders? Would it at least be permissible for parents to do so?

GENE THERAPY

After deciphering the vast codex of the human genome and peering into the rich patterning of genes, humans have taken the next, seemingly inevitable, step: to try to repair the genetic flaws they see. This incredible repair work is known as **gene therapy** (also referred to as genetic engineering), the manipulation of someone's genetic material to prevent or treat disease. It is an attempt to alter the workings of cells by, among other things, (1) replacing a missing or defective gene with a normal one, (2) repairing a faulty gene so it will function properly, or (3) activating or deactivating a gene (switching it on or off).

To date, most uses of gene therapy have been of the first kind, the insertion of a normal copy of a gene into cells to do the job that defective or absent genes should be doing. But delivering a gene to a cell is tricky and usually must be done with a carrier, or vector, such as a virus. Viruses can seek out particular cells and transfer pieces of DNA into them. Scientists put this natural talent of viruses to work by inactivating their harmful characteristics and modifying them to carry particular genes into designated cells. The genes can then induce the production of the proteins needed for normal functioning. A good example of this approach is the treatment of hemophilia (hemophilia A and B), a disorder that puts people at risk of bleeding to death because of impaired blood-clotting. The problem is caused by mutations in the genes that manufacture the proteins necessary for clotting (called blood-clotting factors), resulting in deficiencies of the proteins. In both animals and humans, scientists have used viruses to transfer normal copies of these genes into cells, enabling the genes to start producing the blood-clotting factors. The therapy has worked in animals and has shown promise in humans.

Gene therapy is of two types: somatic cell and germ-line cell. The former involves altering genes in a person's somatic (body) cells, such as liver or muscle cells, to treat an existing disorder. The alterations can help the person suffering from the disease but are not inheritable—they cannot be passed on to the person's offspring. They affect the person's genome but not the genomes of subsequent generations. The other type of gene therapy entails modifying genes in germ-line cells (egg and sperm cells) and zygotes—and these alterations are inheritable. Currently the scientific focus is on somatic-cell gene therapy, with most research evaluating treatments for cancer, heart disease, and infectious diseases. Gene therapy in germ-line cells is not yet feasible. But the ability to manipulate germ-line cells evokes both the dream of eradicating mutations from future generations (and thus permanently banishing particular disorders) and the nightmare of fabricating "designer" babies or introducing horrible errors into the human genome.

For scientists, physicians, and policymakers, the potential of gene therapy to effect cures is too great to ignore, so research will likely continue (and expand) indefinitely. But devising effective gene therapies is extremely difficult, and they can pose risks to patients. To develop any kind of effective gene therapy, scientists have to solve several technical problems. Chief among them are the difficulty of controlling viruses to accurately deliver genes to cells, the risk of virus carriers causing disease or provoking a harmful immune system response, and the complexity of treating disorders generated by multiple genes (such as diabetes, arthritis, heart diseases, and Alzheimer's). For these and other reasons, the

Fact File **Available Genetic Tests for Cancer Risk**

Scientists have uncovered more than fifty hereditary cancer syndromes. Here's a list of some of the more common ones, the genetic tests available for them, the genes involved, and the cancer types most often linked with the syndromes.

Hereditary Breast Cancer and Ovarian Cancer Syndrome
- Genes: *BRCA1, BRCA2*
- Related cancer types: Female breast, ovarian, and other cancers, including prostate, pancreatic, and male breast cancer

Li-Fraumeni Syndrome
- Gene: *TP53*
- Related cancer types: Breast cancer, soft tissue sarcoma, osteosarcoma (bone cancer), leukemia, brain tumors, adrenocortical carcinoma (cancer of the adrenal glands), and other cancers

Cowden Syndrome (PTEN Hamartoma Tumor Syndrome)
- Gene: *PTEN*
- Related cancer types: Breast, thyroid, endometrial (uterine lining), and other cancers

Lynch Syndrome (Hereditary Nonpolyposis Colorectal Cancer)
- Genes: *MSH2, MLH1, MSH6, PMS2, EPCAM*
- Related cancer types: Colorectal, endometrial, ovarian, renal pelvis, pancreatic, small intestine, liver and biliary tract, stomach, brain, and breast cancers

Familial Adenomatous Polyposis
- Gene: *APC*
- Related cancer types: Colorectal cancer, multiple non-malignant colon polyps, and both non-cancerous (benign) and cancerous tumors in the small intestine, brain, stomach, bone, skin, and other tissues

Retinoblastoma
- Gene: *RB1*
- Related cancer types: Eye cancer (cancer of the retina), pinealoma (cancer of the pineal gland), osteosarcoma, melanoma, and soft tissue sarcoma

Multiple Endocrine Neoplasia Type 1 (Wermer Syndrome)
- Gene: *MEN1*
- Related cancer types: Pancreatic endocrine tumors and (usually benign) parathyroid and pituitary gland tumors

Multiple Endocrine Neoplasia Type 2
- Gene: *RET*
- Related cancer types: Medullary thyroid cancer and pheochromocytoma (benign adrenal gland tumor)

Von Hippel-Lindau Syndrome
- Gene: *VHL*
- Related cancer types: Kidney cancer and multiple noncancerous tumors, including pheochromocytoma

From National Cancer Institute, "Genetic Testing for Hereditary Cancer Syndromes," 11 April, 2013, http://www.cancer.gov/about-cancer/causes-prevention/genetics/genetic-testing-fact-sheet#q3 (31 October 2015).

field is still experimental, with hundreds of gene therapy studies in progress all over the world but few or no therapies approved for routine use. So far, scientific studies demonstrating success in using gene therapy have been intriguing and encouraging but preliminary. But there is little doubt among experts that safe and effective gene therapies (at least the somatic-cell kind) will be devised in the next few years.

In 1990 researchers conducted the first federally approved study of gene therapy, treating a 4-year-old girl suffering from adenosine deaminase (ADA) deficiency, a life-shortening disorder of severely weakened immunity. A normal gene generates ADA, an enzyme crucial to a healthy immune system, but in the girl the gene was missing, leaving her without any defense against life-threatening infections. Using a virus carrier, the researchers delivered the normal ADA gene to the girl's immune cells, hoping that it would produce the needed enzyme. The treatment worked. Her immune system soon began to function normally and did so for years.

Since that promising experiment, there have also been disappointments—and lessons to learn about the risks involved in gene therapy. In 1999 18-year-old Jesse Gelsinger experienced multiple organ failures and died during gene therapy to treat ornithine transcarboxylase deficiency (OTCD). The ultimate cause of death was traced back to his immune system's devastating reaction to the virus carrier. A few years later scientists used gene therapy to treat children with severe combined immunodeficiency (SCID), an intractable disorder that usually results in death by the age of 1. Amazingly, most of the children

were cured. But two of these developed a condition like leukemia, so in 2003 the Food and Drug Administration (FDA) temporarily suspended clinical trials using these procedures. Later the trials resumed with closer FDA oversight and a greater appreciation among scientists generally of the inherent risks and the curative possibilities of gene therapy.

As you might suspect, many moral questions about gene therapy center on its potential for harm and help. In somatic-cell gene therapy, the risks and benefits of using the technology have become the primary moral concern, spurred on by much soul-searching after the early clinical mistakes. Regulatory agencies and review boards have sprung up to oversee clinical trials and to ensure an acceptable balance of risks and benefits for study subjects. The prevailing view is that if such steps are taken to minimize harm, and if the potential benefits are substantial, somatic-cell therapy is morally permissible.

Germ-line therapy is a different matter. The safety concerns surrounding the technology are so worrisome that, at least in its current immature stage, it is generally thought to be morally unacceptable. The main problem is that scientists do not yet fully understand the likely ramifications of refashioning the genetic machinery of germ-line cells. The addition or modification of genes might make a condition worse or prevent one disease but cause others that are more severe. The result could be catastrophic or fatal to a child born of such engineering, and the calamities could happen at birth or years later. Worse, the resulting disorders could be passed on to future children. The nightmare scenario is that the genetic changes are inherited by many people, and the human genome itself is altered for the worse. These unknowns have compelled scientists not to renounce this research but to proceed with extreme caution and to forgo clinical trials until the genetics of germ-line cells is better understood.

Many moral arguments for and against gene therapy—perhaps the most controversial ones—do not appeal to the possibility of harm from the procedure itself, or they work from the assumption that the safety and effectiveness of gene therapy will eventually be established. Those arguments in favor of applying gene therapy (in either form) mirror many of those made for reproductive technology and genetic testing: If it is within our power to correct genetic flaws and thereby prevent or cure diseases, aren't we obligated to do so? If gene therapy offers us the chance to prevent harm to future people, don't we have a duty to try? If the principle of autonomy (or reproductive liberty) grants us the freedom to reproduce or not reproduce, doesn't it also give us the right to decide whether our offspring will have a disability or disease?

The responses to these views should also sound familiar: Reproductive freedom has limits, and germ-line therapy crosses the line; the manipulation or destruction of embryos that may occur in germ-line therapy shows disrespect for human life; and gene therapy (especially germ-line) disrespects or discriminates against people with disabilities.

Some argue that gene therapy should not be permitted because it amounts to **eugenics**, the deliberate attempt to improve the genetic makeup of humans by manipulating reproduction. The word calls up images of the Nazi drive to racial purity through mandatory sterilization of undesirables as well as the early twentieth-century programs in the United States to forcibly sterilize criminals, "imbeciles," and other "defective persons." Such misdeeds are morally objectionable for several reasons, most notably because they violate people's autonomy, the central feature of state-sponsored coercion. But the term *eugenics* is broad, covering a range of practices that are not necessarily coercive and that have been called eugenics of either a *negative* or *positive* kind. Negative eugenics is thought to involve the prevention or treatment of diseases, typically through genetic testing, embryo selection, selective abortion, or germ-line therapy. By this definition, prenatal screening—which is a matter of public policy and generally considered morally permissible—is a type of negative eugenics. Positive eugenics is said to include attempts to improve on normal functions. It seeks not repair, but enhancement. Theoretically through germ-line therapy, parents could produce children who are smarter, taller, or more resistant to certain diseases than normal children are. Such enhancements are controversial, even though they may not be technically possible for many years.

The idea of a distinction between repair and enhancement is prominent in moral debates because some argue that the former is morally obligatory while the latter is not. That is, we may have a duty to use gene therapy to treat Tay-Sachs disease or cystic fibrosis, but not to give a child an abnormally long life or a super immune system. Several bioethicists reject this view. For example, John Harris:

> [S]uppose genes coding for repair enzymes which would not only repair radiation damage or damage by other environmental pollutants but would also prolong healthy life expectancy could be inserted into humans. Again, would it be permissible to let people continue suffering such damage when they could be protected against it? Would it in short be OK to let them suffer?
>
> It is not normal for the human organism to be self-repairing in this way; this must be eugenic if anything is. But if available, its use would surely, like penicillin before it, be more than merely [permissible].
>
> . . . There is in short no moral difference between attempts to cure dysfunction and attempts to enhance function where the enhancement protects life or health.[6]

Others insist that there is indeed a clear difference between the two, asserting that gene therapy is moral if it is intended to ensure or restore

Fact File **Recent Research in Gene Therapy**

According to the National Institutes of Health, "Gene therapy is currently available only in a research setting. The U.S. Food and Drug Administration (FDA) has not yet approved any gene therapy products for sale in the United States." But hundreds of gene therapy clinical trials are now testing the safety and effectiveness of treatments for a wide range of conditions. Here are a few of the more impressive recent developments highlighted by *Gene Therapy Net*:

- **July 2015. Gene therapy for hearing loss.** A study in mice published in the journal *Science Translational Medicine* "demonstrated gene therapy as an effective way to improve hearing in patients with two genes linked to genetic prelingual deafness, or hearing loss that occurs before a child learns to speak."
- **October 2015. Increasing glioblastoma survival rate.** "An experimental gene therapy drug doubled the survival rate for glioblastoma [patients], an aggressive brain cancer that kills two-thirds of patients within five years. . . . Typically, glioblastoma patients whose cancer comes back are expected to survive for weeks or months."
- **September 2015. Promising results with gene therapy for congestive heart failure.** "[A] gene therapy treatment for patients with reduced left-ventricular ejection fraction congestive heart failure (CHF) is proving safe and effective. The treatment involves delivering a therapeutic gene encoding adenylyl clyclase type 6 (AC6) directly into the heart via a modified adenovirus."
- **March 2015. Possible treatment for HIV.** "Experimental stem cell gene therapy that could act as functional cure for HIV infection has been approved by the Food and Drug Administration to move into early human test trials. Unlike other treatments that use healthy stem cells from uninfected donors, this form of therapy uses cells harvested from a positive person's own body. The stem cells are genetically manipulated to develop into white blood cells that are missing the key cellular receptors that the HIV virus uses to insert its genetic code into healthy cells. The modification effectively models an HIV-positive person's white blood cells after the cells of people who have a natural resistance to HIV."
- **February 2015. Curing brain cancer in mice.** "Despite decades of surgery, chemotherapy and radiation therapy treatments for glioma, a cure for this life-threatening brain cancer has remained elusive. . . . [Researchers] have successfully used compound-filled biodegradable nanoparticles to effectively kill brain cancer cells—and extend survival in rats."
- **August 2014. Gene therapy possibly replacing pacemakers.** "A new technology that allows genes to be injected into hearts with damaged electrical systems may replace the need for pacemaker implants in humans in the future. In the United States alone, there are more than 500,000 patients that get pacemaker implants annually. When the batteries on the Pacemakers run out in seven to 10 years, another surgery is required to implant a new device."
- **January 2014. Nanotech robots deliver gene therapy through blood.** "U.S. researchers [using research animals] have developed tiny nanoparticle robots that can travel through a patient's blood and into tumors where they deliver a therapy that turns off an important cancer gene. The finding, reported in the journal *Nature* . . . offers early proof that a new treatment approach called RNA interference or RNAi might work in people."

(continued)

• **January 2014. Gene therapy for Parkinson's.** "Patients in a clinical trial to treat Parkinson's disease with a form of gene therapy have showed signs of significant improvements in their motor-function, according to a report published in the *Lancet*. Fifteen advanced-stage Parkinson's patients (three from the UK and 12 from France) were followed up a year after being injected with low, mid and high doses of a modified virus containing genes required for brain cells to produce dopamine. . . . A lack of dopamine causes patients with Parkinson's to experience tremors and difficulty in coordinating their movement. The researchers observed that after receiving the treatment the patients' scores on movement tests improved on average by 30 percent. The patients also reported having a better quality of life. Although the patients showed some side effects, overall the treatment was found to be safe and no serious side effects were observed."

From Lister Hill National Center for Biomedical Communications; U.S National Library of Medicine, National Institutes of Health, et al., "What Is Direct-to-Consumer Genetic Testing?" October 2015, http://ghr.nlm.nih.gov/handbook/testing/directtoconsumer (31 October 2015); *Gene Therapy Net*, "Gene Therapy News," 2014–2015, http://www.genetherapynet.com/gene-therapy-news.html (31 October 2015).

normal functions, but immoral if it is aimed at enhancing functions beyond normal. Their strongest objection to genetic enhancement is that it would lead to the most flagrant kind of social injustice. As Walter Glannon argues,

> The main moral concern about genetic enhancement of physical and mental traits is that it would give some people an unfair advantage over others with respect to competitive goods like beauty, sociability, and intelligence. . . . Enhancement would be unfair because only those who could afford the technology would have access to it, and many people are financially worse off than others through no fault of their own. Insofar as the possession of these goods gives some people an advantage over others in careers, income, and social status, the competitive nature of these goods suggests that there would be no limit to the benefits that improvements to physical and mental capacities would yield to those fortunate enough to avail themselves of the technology.[7]

STEM CELLS

There are over 200 different kinds of cells in the human body—muscle cells, blood cells, skin cells,

nerve cells, and more. Yet all these cell types arise from just one sort of cell present in the early embryo, or blastocyst, five days after fertilization and before implantation in the uterus. These early cells are undifferentiated, having no specialized function as the other kinds of cells do; but they are also *pluripotent*, which means they are able to *become* differentiated, to turn into any of the body's specialty cells. They number only 30 or so inside the blastocyst, which is no larger than the dot on this letter *i*. Under normal conditions, they quickly differentiate into the various cell types. But when they are extracted from the blastocyst and nurtured in culture dishes, they can remain undifferentiated and retain their power to transform into any kind of cell, while replicating themselves continuously without limit. At this point they are *embryonic stem cells*. Because they can reproduce indefinitely, creating replicating cell lines, just a few of them are needed to generate a large supply.

Other stem cells in the developed human—*adult stem cells*—stand ever ready to differentiate themselves to replace worn out or damaged cells, constantly renewing and repairing the body's parts. Adult stem cells generate new bone, cartilage, skin, muscle, blood, and many other tissues. But their potential to produce diverse kinds of cells is constrained—unlike the nearly unbounded powers of differentiation found in embryonic stem cells.

It is this regenerative potential of stem cells (especially the embryonic kind) that has excited so much scientific and medical interest. Researchers have found that by getting stem cells to differentiate into particular kinds of cells, new cells and tissues can be generated to treat diseases and injuries characterized by a lack of functioning cell types. The therapeutic possibilities include Parkinson's disease, diabetes, heart disease, Alzheimer's, stroke, spinal cord injuries, burns, and arthritis. For example, type I diabetes occurs for lack of the cells that produce insulin, but scientists think it may be possible to prod embryonic stem cells into becoming insulin-producing cells and then to transplant those cells into patients with diabetes. On another front, researchers are now investigating the possibility of using stem cells to generate new heart muscle tissue to transplant to damaged hearts. These and many other stem-cell investigations are preliminary and may not yield effective treatments for years, and so far the established stem-cell therapies are few (only blood and skin cell transplants). But the amazing potential for treatments and cures of seemingly unstoppable diseases spurs on the research, raises the stakes, and makes debates about halting stem-cell research all the more volatile.

Most of the moral controversy over embryonic stem cells has focused on their source. The main source is, of course, embryos (blastocysts), which are inevitably destroyed in the process of retrieving the cells. The majority of the embryos are produced through IVF used in the treatment of infertility. IVF involves the production of multiple blastocysts, only some of which are eventually implanted in the uterus. The leftover blastocysts are frozen, and some that are neither implanted nor discarded may be used to extract stem cells. Another possibility is the use of IVF to create blastocysts specifically for stem-cell extraction in research—an option that is much more controversial than using the surplus blastocysts. Beyond the blastocyst stage there is one more stem-cell source: Researchers have been able to derive embryonic stem cells from fetuses obtained after elective abortions.

It is possible—but not yet technically feasible—to derive embryonic stem cells from blastocysts produced through what has been called *research* (or *therapeutic*) *cloning.* Many distinguish this kind of cloning-for-research-purposes from *reproductive cloning*, which aims at the live birth of a baby. In both forms, the underlying method is the same: Replace the nucleus of an egg cell with the nucleus of an ordinary somatic cell (a skin cell, for example) from an adult, then stimulate this reconstructed cell to start cell division and growth into a blastocyst. In research cloning, stem cells would be derived from the blastocyst; in reproductive cloning, the blastocyst would be implanted in the uterus to continue the reproductive process to birth. An advantage of research cloning is that body tissues derived from the stem cells would be genetically matched to the nucleus donor, so the new tissues could be used to treat the donor with less risk of tissue rejection by the donor's body. To date, no one has extracted human embryonic stem cells from cloned embryos successfully, but judging from research in animals, the feat eventually will be accomplished.

In the United States the availability of embryonic stem cells for research has been influenced heavily by existing laws and policies. A law enacted in 1995 bans the use of federal funds for any research involving the destruction of human embryos—a significant restriction since federal money drives an enormous portion of biomedical research. In 2001 President George W. Bush declared that no federal funding may support research that obtains stem cells by destroying embryos, although research may continue on the few existing stem-cell lines previously derived.

In March 2009 President Barack Obama issued an executive order that revoked the Bush restrictions and made way for a new policy allowing the National Institutes of Health to "support and conduct responsible, scientifically worthy human stem cell research, including human embryonic stem cell research."

In 2007 a scientific breakthrough looked like it might solve the stem-cell source problem. Scientists announced that they were able to genetically reprogram ordinary human skin cells to take on the characteristics of embryonic stem cells. The findings seemed to promise an abundant future supply of embryonic stem cells for research without destroying embryos or using embryos already deceased. Many commentators immediately declared that science had finally ended the stem-cell debates that it began. Scientists everywhere welcomed the news of the breakthrough, but many also thought it premature to proclaim embryo research superfluous. They pointed out that it is not yet known whether the new engineered stem cells are as versatile, safe, or hearty as stem cells derived from embryos. They therefore favored pursuing, at least for now, both paths simultaneously.

Whether or not public disputes about embryonic stem cells subside, the underlying moral issues remain. The core question is this: Is it morally permissible to destroy human embryos in a search for cures? For those who believe that embryos have the moral status of persons, the answer must be no (just as it would be on the issue of abortion). The same goes for those who think using embryos as a source of stem cells shows disrespect for human life by reducing it to a mere commodity. In either case, people who grant embryos this special moral status are likely to argue that destroying them cannot be justified by any potential medical and scientific benefits. Some who take this view insist that just using or benefiting from stem cells previously derived from embryos or aborted fetuses is also impermissible. But to be involved in this way is to participate, however indirectly, in the immoral act of destroying innocent human life.

At the other end of the moral spectrum are those who maintain that blastocysts have no moral status at all and should be treated like any other human cell. They therefore contend that the use of embryos in stem-cell research is permissible, especially since it promises to help alleviate much human suffering. Their main concerns are the safety, integrity, and usefulness of the research and the resulting therapies.

For many who adopt intermediate positions, early embryos have less than full moral status but are still deserving of some respect. Stem-cell research using embryos is therefore morally acceptable—within limits. Bonnie Steinbock, for example, takes this view:

> Lacking the kinds of ends that persons have, embryos cannot be given the respect that is due to persons. Nevertheless, they have a significance and moral value that other bodily tissues do not have because they are "potent symbols of human life.". . . We show respect for human embryos by not using them in unimportant or frivolous ways, say, to teach high school biology or to make cosmetics or jewelry. However, respect for embryos does not require refraining from research likely to have significant benefits, such as treating disease and prolonging life.[8]

Some stake out some middle ground in the stem-cell debate in other ways. They may argue that mining stem cells from embryos is objectionable but that manipulating already available stem-cell lines is not. Or that taking stem cells from aborted fetuses or from embryos left over after reproductive IVF is permissible but that using embryos created for research through IVF or therapeutic cloning is wrong. Or that using IVF embryos, created originally for whatever reason, is moral but that generating embryos for stem-cell extraction through any kind of cloning is immoral.

APPLYING MAJOR THEORIES

The moral theories that have been applied to familiar ethical problems for generations also do work in the epoch of genetic testing and intervention. A utilitarian perspective is likely to favor genetic testing and gene therapy if they tend to promote the general welfare. A utilitarian might say that tests providing useful information about people's genetic risks are probably beneficial

The Kingsburys

Increasing numbers of prospective parents are choosing to use PGD to screen their embryos for genetic diseases. In the past, many would-be parents who requested PGD knew this: They had a particular gene mutation, there was a good chance of passing it to their offspring, any child with the mutation is almost certain to develop the disease, and the disease is devastating and untreatable. The horrors in this category include cystic fibrosis, Huntington's disease, and Tay-Sachs. Now some couples in similar situations are taking PGD a step further: They are using it to screen for disorders that have much less than 100 percent probability of arising and that in many cases respond to treatment. The Kingsburys were among the first to face such a choice.

In their quest to have children, Chad and Colby Kingsbury were up against some dire genetic facts. Chad had inherited a genetic defect that causes a form of colon cancer—a disease that had already taken his mother and her two brothers, afflicted his cousin, and could very well soon affect him. For anyone with the mutation, the chances of having colon cancer are 20 times greater than normal. The disease generally appears in middle age, and most people can survive it if it's treated early. There is a 50 percent probability that any child of Chad's will inherit the mutation.

The Kingsburys understood these risks and knew that PGD could eliminate them. But there were other factors to weigh. PGD involves culling defective embryos (which are likely to be destroyed) and deliberating selecting those that are genetically acceptable. Is such a procedure morally permissible when the disorder to be avoided is not invariably lethal, not guaranteed to arise, and not likely to develop, if at all, until middle age?

As reported in the *New York Times*, to opt for PGD,

[The Kingsburys] had to overcome their own misgivings about meddling with nature. They had to listen to the religious concerns of Mr. Kingsbury's family and to the insistence of Ms. Kingsbury's that the expense and physical demands of in vitro fertilization were not worth it, given that the couple could probably get pregnant without it. They had to stop asking themselves the unanswerable question of whether a cure would be found by the time their child grew up. . . . It took them two months to make the decision.[9]

In the end they chose PGD, and a healthy baby girl, Chloe, was the result. She will not get—and her children will not inherit from her—the kind of colon cancer that has ravaged Chad Kingsbury's family.

He says that he and his wife made the right decision: "I couldn't imagine them telling me my daughter has cancer when I could have stopped it."

Many people object to PGD and the embryo selection that it entails, arguing that it is morally equivalent to abortion, that it amounts to arrogant interference in natural processes, that it is eugenics run amok to create "designer babies," and that it demonstrates disrespect for people with disabilities. Nevertheless, the use of PGD is likely to increase—and to be applied to an ever-widening range of diseases with varying degrees of severity.

---

overall, though benefits must be weighed against the harm that can result from misleading test results, genetic discrimination, and breeches of doctor-patient confidentiality. She almost certainly would argue that prenatal testing and PGD (combined with selective abortion and embryo selection) are morally acceptable because they can prevent devastating diseases and disabilities in children as well as emotional or economic suffering in families. Gene therapy (both somatic and germ-line cell) is likely to be viewed in the same way—morally permissible if its benefits outweigh its risks. The utilitarian also would not hesitate to employ positive eugenics if altering the human genome would, on balance, increase human happiness and ease suffering. She would probably sanction the therapeutic use of embryonic stem cells (derived from any source) as long as there was a net benefit to society.

A natural law theorist might view some forms of genetic testing (newborn screening and predictive testing, for example) as morally acceptable ways to gain knowledge about health risks and to guide treatment. But a theorist in the Roman Catholic tradition would in most instances object to pre-natal testing and PGD because they usually lead directly to selective abortion and embryo selection—clear violations of the unborn's right to life. Natural law theory would seem to countenance somatic-cell gene therapy because the aims are therapeutic, like conventional medical treatment. But germ-line gene therapy as a tool of positive eugenics would probably be condemned as contrary to nature. Research using stem cells derived from embryos would be considered immoral because it involves destroying innocent human life.

The Kantian notions of autonomy and of persons as ends-in-themselves support the right of patients to know (or not to know) the results of genetic tests, to have those results guarded according to rules of privacy and confidentiality, and to be treated fairly without fear of genetic discrimination. If by Kantian lights an embryo is a person, then destroying it after genetic testing may be impermissible. It's possible, however, to construe Kant as allowing the destruction of this person-embryo on the grounds that preventing its future suffering could actually be an act of respect for its personhood. Likewise, positive eugenics could be seen through Kantian eyes as a way to improve human life while leaving personhood untouched.

KEY TERMS
chromosome
eugenics
gene
gene therapy
genetic discrimination
genetic testing
genome

SUMMARY
DNA makes up the chemical coding that directs the development and operation of cells, the fundamental components of every organism. Genes, the basic units of biological inheritance, are discrete segments of DNA strands. Genes in turn are organized into 46 chromosomes, arranged in 23 pairs. According to the instructions written in genes, a human organism is produced and sustained, and a large portion of its characteristics is determined. Mistakes, or mutations, in the DNA coding can lead to a variety of diseases and conditions, some of them grave.

Genetic testing involves procedures to check for genetic disorders by looking for changes in a person's DNA. Common forms of testing include newborn screening; carrier, predictive, diagnostic, and prenatal testing; and preimplantation genetic diagnosis (PGD). Genetic tests rarely yield certain predictions. For several reasons, a positive test result does not guarantee the presence of a disorder, and a negative test result does not ensure its absence. Unfortunately, our ability to detect diseases through genetic testing has outstripped our power to treat many of them. Many moral questions that arise from genetic testing are about duties to warn family members when an inherited disorder is discovered, the obligation of physicians regarding patient autonomy and confidentiality, the permissibility of genetic discrimination, and the morality of using testing to avoid causing seriously disabled persons to exist.

Gene therapy is the manipulation of someone's genetic material to prevent or treat disease. The somatic-cell type involves altering genes in a person's body cells; the germ-line type entails modifying genes in egg and sperms cells and zygotes. Ethical issues concern the medical risks and benefits of the therapy, duties to use the procedures to prevent suffering, reproductive freedom, and the morality of practicing positive genetics.

Embryonic stem cells can be derived from blastocysts, aborted fetuses, research cloning, and—apparently—genetically engineered somatic cells. The core issue regarding them is whether it is morally permissible to destroy them in a search for cures. Those who assign personhood status to embryos say no. Those who reject that view may grant embryos no special status at all, or they may say that embryos are not persons but are still worthy of some respect. In either case, embryonic stem-cell research is thought to be permissible.

Cases for Evaluation

CASE I

Selecting Babies

(*TimesOnline*)—A British couple have won the right to test embryos for a gene that leads to high cholesterol levels and an increased risk of heart attacks, *The Times* has learnt.

The decision by the fertility watchdog will reopen controversy over the ethics of designer babies, as it allows doctors to screen embryos for a condition that is treatable with drugs and can be influenced by lifestyle as well as genes.

While the procedure is designed to detect a rare version of a disease called familial hypercholesterolaemia (FH), which often kills children before puberty, it will also identify a milder form that can be controlled by drugs and diet.

Critics argue that the test will allow couples to destroy embryos that would have had a good chance of becoming children with fulfilling and reasonably healthy lives.

The test will also create an unprecedented moral dilemma for some couples, as it could show that they have produced no embryos completely unaffected by the disease. This would force them to decide whether to implant embryos that they know have a genetic risk of premature heart disease and death, or to throw them away and deny them a chance of life.

Britain's first licence to test embryos for FH will be awarded next week to Paul Serhal, of University College Hospital in London, by the Human Fertilisation and Embryology Authority (HFEA).

Its decision breaks new ground because it permits Mr. Serhal to screen out not only the severe form of the condition but also the milder type, which is usually treatable.

Embryo screening has previously been approved only for disorders in which a gene invariably causes a serious disease, or for conditions such as breast cancer in which mutations carry an 80 per cent lifetime risk.

FH occurs in two forms. The more common version, heterozygous FH, affects 1 in 500 people. It is caused by a single mutated gene, which raises cholesterol and thus the risk of hardened arteries, heart disease, and stroke. It can usually be managed with statin drugs and diet.

One in 250,000 people inherits two defective copies of the gene and develops homozygous FH, which is much more serious. Sufferers show severely elevated cholesterol from the age of 5, and can suffer angina by 6 or 7. Many die in childhood, and most have suffered at least one heart attack by the end of their twenties.

Mr. Serhal's patients, who are in their thirties, both have the milder heterozygous FH. They discovered their status only when they had a daughter, now 5, with the homozygous form, and they also have an unaffected son.

They said yesterday that they were delighted. "We had no idea that we both carried a gene for high cholesterol until the double gene was expressed in our first child. We are very lucky that our child has responded so well to the very high-dose drug regime. We have been led to understand that other children with the same double gene may not be so lucky." . . .

Mr. Serhal said: "This obnoxious disease can cause cardiovascular accidents at a very young age. Ideally, we will find embryos with no FH genes, but it is possible we will not and it will be up to the patients to choose. Some people would think twice about using embryos that they know have a risky gene, and others would say you shouldn't screen out a condition that can be managed so people can live with it. It will be an awkward choice."*

Is it wrong for parents to screen out embryos with disorders that are treatable? What about embryos that will probably—not certainly—develop a serious disease? Or those that will develop a fatal disease only in middle age? Is it morally permissible to cause to exist persons who are severely disabled and likely to suffer horribly throughout their lives? Give reasons for your answer.

---

*Mark Henderson, "Designer Baby Fear over Heart Gene Test," TimesOnline, 15 December 2007, http://www.timesonline.co.uk/tol/news/uk/science/article3054249.ece? (15 January 2008).

CASE 2

Causing Deaf Children

(*New Scientist*)—A few years ago, a lesbian couple in the U.S. sparked controversy when they chose a deaf sperm donor to ensure their children, like them, would be deaf. Now it appears that some would-be parents are resorting to pre-implantation genetic diagnosis (PGD) to achieve the same thing, by selecting and implanting embryos that will develop into deaf children.

This comes from a survey by the Genetics and Public Policy Center in Washington DC on how PGD is being used in the U.S.

Deep inside the report is this paragraph: "Some prospective parents have sought PGD to select an embryo for the presence of a particular disease or disability, such as deafness, in order that the child would share that characteristic with the parents. Three per cent of IVF-PGD clinics report having provided PGD to couples who seek to use PGD in this manner."

It is not clear how many, if any, children have been born after embryo selection for a disability, or which disabilities have been selected for. I asked Susannah Baruch, the lead author of the GPPC report, who told me that the team does not have any more details.

So let's do the sums: Since the survey included 137 IVF-PGD clinics, 3% means 4 couples at least, more if you assume some of the 200 clinics who did not respond to the survey have also provided this service. And since the success rate of IVF is roughly 30%, even if each couple made only one attempt at least one child must have been born with a designer disability, most likely deafness, with the help of PGD.*

Is it right to deliberately cause a child to be deaf and thereby limit her opportunities in life? If so, why? If not, why not? Should medical authorities or the government restrict the use of IVF and PGD to selecting only healthy embryos? If both prospective parents have inherited deafness, there is a high probability that their child will be deaf. So their failing to use IVF/PGD to select healthy embryos would almost guarantee a deaf baby. Is such a failure morally wrong? If so, is deliberately selecting impaired embryos equally wrong? Explain.

---

*Michael Le Page, "Designer Deafness," *New Scientist*, 29 September 2006.

CASE 3

Cosmetic Embryo Selection

(*London Telegraph*)—Embryos are to be screened for a cosmetic defect for the first time in a British clinic.

Doctors have been given permission to create a baby free from a genetic disorder which would have caused the child to have a severe squint.

The Bridge Centre family clinic, in London, has been licensed to treat a businessman and his wife to create the baby. Both the businessman and his father suffer from the condition, which causes the eyes only to look downwards or sideways.

Critics have said that the permission is another step on the road to creating only perfect-looking babies in the laboratory.

The licence was granted by the Human Fertilisation and Embryology Authority (HFEA) to Prof. Gedis Grudzinskas, who believes the landmark ruling marks a shift away from granting licences only for life-threatening conditions.

He said: "We will increasingly see the use of embryo screening for severe cosmetic conditions."

He added that he would seek to screen for any genetic factor at all that would cause a family severe distress.

When asked if he would screen embryos for factors like hair colour, he said: "If there is a cosmetic aspect to an individual case I would assess it on its merits. [Hair colour] can be a cause of bullying which can lead to suicide. With the agreement of the HFEA, I would do it. If a parent suffered from asthma, and it was possible to detect the genetic factor for this, I would do it. It all depends on the family's distress."

He argued that a baby born with the squint condition, congenital fibrosis of the extramacular muscles, would have to undergo several potentially dangerous operations from a young age. . . .

If successful, the screening could be the first case in the world where doctors have been able to select embryos without the condition. . . .

Until last year screening was restricted to life-threatening conditions such as cystic fibrosis or fatal blood disorders.*

Should prospective parents be permitted to screen their embryos for cosmetic reasons? Is there a moral difference between embryo selection against severe disabilities and embryo selection against cosmetic imperfections that cause the child to suffer psychological distress or social discrimination? Is embryo selection for cosmetic reasons a form of discrimination or disrespect for people with disabilities or imperfections? Explain your answers.

---

*Roland Hancock, "Clinic to Weed Out Embryos with a Squint," Telegraph.co.uk, 5 July 2007, http://www.telegraph.co.uk/news/main.jhtml?xml=/news/2007/05/07/nbaby07.xml (15 January 2008).

FURTHER READING

American Society for Reproductive Medicine, "Assisted Reproductive Technologies: A Guide for Patients," undated, 2007, http://www.asrm.org/ (27 November 2007).

Adrienne Asch, "Real Moral Dilemmas," *Christianity and Crisis* 46.10 (1986).

Dan W. Brock, "Genetic Engineering," in *A Companion to Applied Ethics*, ed. R. G. Frey and Christopher Heath Wellman (Oxford: Blackwell Publishing, 2003), 356–57, 361–67.

Ruth Chadwick, "Gene Therapy," in *A Companion to Bioethics*, ed. Helga Kuhse and Peter Singer (Oxford: Blackwell Publishing, 2001), 189–97.

Angus Clarke, "Genetic Screening and Counselling," in *A Companion to Bioethics*, ed. Helga Kuhse and Peter Singer (Oxford: Blackwell Publishing, 2001), 215–28.

Cold Spring Harbor Laboratory, "DNA from the Beginning: An Animated Primer on the Basics of DNA, Genes, and Heredity," undated, 2002, http://www.dnaftb.org/dnaftb/ (05 December 2007).

Department of Health and Human Services, *Regenerative Medicine*, August 2006, http://stemcells.nih.gov/info/scireport/2006report.htm (1 January 2008).

Gene Therapy Net, http://www.genetherapynet.com/gene-therapy-news.html?start=30 (31 October 2015).

Genetic Home Reference, "Gene Therapy," National Institutes of Health, 26 October, 2015, http://ghr.nlm.nih.gov/handbook/therapy?show=all (31 October 2015).

Walter Glannon, *Genes and Future People: Philosophical Issues in Human Genetics* (Boulder, CO: Westview Press, 2001).

Jonathan Glover, "Future People, Disability, and Screening," in *Justice Between Age Groups and Generations*, ed. J. Fishkin and P. Laslett (New Haven, CT: Yale University Press, 1992).

Human Genome Program, U.S. Department of Energy, *Genomics and Its Impact on Science and Society: A 2003 Primer* (Washington, DC: U.S. Department of Energy, 2003).

National Academy of Sciences, *Understanding Stem Cells* (Washington, DC: National Academies Press, 2006).

National Bioethics Advisory Commission (NBAC), *Ethical Issues in Human Stem Cell Research: Executive Summary*, September 1999, http://bioethics.georgetown.edu/nbac (1 January 2008).

President's Council on Bioethics, *Human Cloning and Human Dignity: An Ethical Inquiry*, July 2002, http://www.bioethics.gov/reports/cloningreport (9 January 2008).

John A. Robertson, "Extending Preimplantation Genetic Diagnosis: Medical and Non-Medical Uses," *Journal of Medical Ethics* 29 (August 2003), 213–16.

Bonnie Steinbock and Ron McClamrock, "When Is Birth Unfair to the Child?," *Hastings Center Report* 24.6 (November 1994), 15–21.

U.S. National Library of Medicine, *Handbook: Help Me Understand Genetics, Genetics Home Reference*, 26 November 2007, http:ghr.nlm.nih.gov (3 December 2007).

U.S. National Library of Medicine, *MedlinePlus*, 23 October, 2015, https://www.nlm.nih.gov/medlineplus/genetictesting.html (31 October 2015).

LeRoy Walters and Julie Gage Palmer, *The Ethics of Human Gene Therapy* (New York: Oxford University Press, 1997).

NOTES

1. The Harris Poll, Harris Interactive, 5 June 2002, www.harrisinteractive.com (18 December 2007).

2. This example and its analysis are inspired by Walter Glannon, in *Biomedical Ethics* (New York: Oxford University Press, 2005), 98–99.

3. Dan W. Brock, "The Non-Identity Problem and Genetic Harms—The Case of Wrongful Handicaps," *Bioethics* 9.3/4 (1995), 275–89.

4. Jonathan Glover, "Future People, Disability, and Screening," in *Justice Between Age Groups and Generations,* ed. J. Fishkin and P. Laslett (New Haven, CT: Yale University Press, 1992), 127–143.

5. Jeff McMahan, "The Morality of Screening for Disability," *Ethics, Law and Moral Philosophy of Reproductive Biomedicine* 1.1 (March 2005), 129–32.

6. John Harris, "Is Gene Therapy a Form of Eugenics?" in *Bioethics: An Anthology,* ed. Helga Kuhse and Peter Singer (Oxford: Blackwell Publishers, 1999), 165–70.

7. Walter Glannon, *Genes and Future People: Philosophical Issues in Human Genetics* (Boulder, CO: Westview Press, 2001), 94–101.

8. Bonnie Steinbock, "What Does 'Respect for Embryos' Mean in the Context of Stem Cell Research?" *Women's Health Issues* 10.3 (May/June 2000), 127–30.

9. Amy Harmon, "Couples Cull Embryos to Halt Heritage of Cancer," *New York Times,* 3 September 2006.

READINGS

Implications of Prenatal Diagnosis for the Human Right to Life

LEON R. KASS

In this article Kass explores the morality of aborting fetuses known through genetic testing to be defective. He condemns the practice, arguing that it could lead us to take a less sympathetic view toward people who are genetic "abnormals" and to embrace the insidious principle that "defectives should not be born." He concludes that "we should indeed be cautious and move slowly as we give serious consideration to the question 'What price the perfect baby?'"

It is especially fitting on this occasion to begin by acknowledging how privileged I feel and how pleased I am to be a participant in this symposium. I suspect that I am not alone among the assembled in considering myself fortunate to be here. For I was conceived after antibiotics yet before amniocentesis, late enough to have benefited from medicine's ability to prevent and control fatal infectious diseases, yet early enough to have escaped from medicine's ability to prevent me from living to suffer from

From *Ethical Issues in Human Genetics*, edited by Bruce Hilton et al., 1973. Copyright © Plenum Publishing Corporation.

my genetic diseases. To be sure, my genetic vices are, as far as I know them, rather modest, taken individually—myopia, asthma and other allergies, bilateral forefoot adduction, bowleggedness, loquaciousness, and pessimism, plus some four to eight as yet undiagnosed recessive lethal genes in the heterozygous condition—but, taken together, and if diagnosable prenatally, I might never have made it.

Just as I am happy to be here, so am I unhappy with what I shall have to say. Little did I realize when I first conceived the topic, "Implications of Prenatal Diagnosis for the Human Right to Life," what a painful and difficult labor it would lead to. More than once while this paper was gestating, I considered obtaining permission to abort it, on the grounds that, by prenatal diagnosis, I knew it to be defective. My lawyer told me that I was legally in the clear, but my conscience reminded me that I had made a commitment to deliver myself of this paper, flawed or not. Next time, I shall practice better contraception.

Any discussion of the ethical issues of genetic counseling and prenatal diagnosis is unavoidably haunted by a ghost called the morality of abortion. This ghost I shall not vex. More precisely, I shall not vex the reader by telling ghost stories. However, I would be neither surprised nor disappointed if my discussion of an admittedly related matter, the ethics of aborting the genetically defective, summons that hovering spirit to the reader's mind. For the morality of abortion is a matter not easily laid to rest, recent efforts to do so notwithstanding. A vote by the legislature of the State of New York can indeed legitimatize the disposal of fetuses, but not of the moral questions. But though the questions remain, there is likely to be little new that can be said about them, and certainly not by me.

Yet before leaving the general question of abortion, let me pause to drop some anchors for the discussion that follows. Despite great differences of opinion both as to what to think and how to reason about abortion, nearly everyone agrees that abortion is a moral issue.[1] What does this mean? Formally, it means that a woman seeking or refusing an abortion can expect to be asked to justify her action. And we can expect that she should be able to give reasons for her choice other than "I like it" or "I don't like it." Substantively, it means that, in the absence of good reasons for intervention, there is some presumption in favor of allowing the pregnancy to continue once it has begun. A common way of expressing this presumption is to say that "the fetus has a right to continued life."[2] In this context, disagreement concerning the moral permissibility of abortion concerns what rights (or interests or needs), and whose, override (take precedence over, or outweigh) this fetal "right." Even most of the "opponents" of abortion agree that the mother's right to live takes precedence, and that abortion to save her life is permissible, perhaps obligatory. Some believe that a woman's right to determine the number and spacing of her children takes precedence, while yet others argue that the need to curb population growth is, at least at this time, overriding.

Hopefully, this brief analysis of what it means to say that abortion is a moral issue is sufficient to establish two points. First, that the fetus is a living thing with some moral claim on us not to do it violence, and therefore, second, that justification must be given for destroying it.

Turning now from the general questions of the ethics of abortion, I wish to focus on the special ethical issues raised by the abortion of "defective" fetuses (so-called "abortion for fetal indications"). I shall consider only the cleanest cases, those cases where well-characterized genetic diseases are diagnosed with a high degree of certainty by means of amniocentesis, in order to side-step the added moral dilemmas posed when the diagnosis is suspected or possible, but unconfirmed. However, many of the questions I shall discuss could also be raised about cases where genetic analysis gives only a statistical prediction about the genotype of the fetus, and also about cases where the defect has an infectious or chemical rather than a genetic cause (e.g., rubella, thalidomide).

My first and possibly most difficult task is to show that there is anything left to discuss once we have agreed not to discuss the morality of abortion in general. There is a sense in which abortion for genetic defect is, after abortion to save the life of the mother, perhaps the most defensible kind of abortion. Certainly, it is a serious and not a frivolous reason for abortion, defended by its proponents in sober and rational speech—unlike justifications based upon the false notion that a fetus is a mere part of a woman's body, to be used and abused at her pleasure. Standing behind genetic abortion are serious and well-intentioned people, with reasonable ends in view: the prevention of genetic diseases, the elimination of suffering in families, the preservation of precious financial and medical resources, the protection of our genetic heritage. No profiteers, no sex-ploiters, no racists. No arguments about the connection of abortion with promiscuity and licentiousness, no perjured testimony about the mental health of the mother, no arguments about the seriousness of the population problem. In short, clear objective data, a worthy cause, decent men and women. If abortion, what better reason for it?

Yet if genetic abortion is but a happily wagging tail on the dog of abortion, it is simultaneously the nose of a camel protruding under a rather different tent.

Precisely because the quality of the fetus is central to the decision to abort, the practice of genetic abortion has implications which go beyond those raised by abortion in general. What may be at stake here is the belief in the radical moral equality of all human beings, the belief that all human beings possess equally and independent of merit certain fundamental rights, one among which is, of course, the right to life.

To be sure, the belief that fundamental human rights belong equally to all human beings has been but an ideal, never realized, often ignored, sometimes shamelessly. Yet it has been perhaps the most powerful moral idea at work in the world for at least two centuries. It is this idea and ideal that animates most of the current political and social criticism around the globe. It is ironic that we should acquire the power to detect and eliminate the genetically unequal at a time when we have finally succeeded in removing much of the stigma and disgrace previously attached to victims of congenital illness, in providing them with improved care and support, and in preventing, by means of education, feelings of guilt on the part of their parents. One might even wonder whether the development of amniocentesis and prenatal diagnosis may represent a backlash against these same humanitarian and egalitarian tendencies in the practice of medicine, which, by helping to sustain to the age of reproduction persons with genetic disease has itself contributed to the increasing incidence of genetic disease, and with it, to increased pressures for genetic screening, genetic counseling, and genetic abortion. . . .

Genetic Abortion and the Living Defective

The practice of abortion of the genetically defective will no doubt affect our view of and our behavior toward those abnormals who escape the net of detection and abortion. A child with Down syndrome or with hemophilia or with muscular dystrophy born at a time when most of his (potential) fellow sufferers were destroyed prenatally is liable to be looked upon by the community as one unfit to be alive, as a second-class (or even lower) human type. He may be seen as a person who need not have been, and who would not have been, if only someone had gotten to him in time.

The parents of such children are also likely to treat them differently, especially if the mother would have wished but failed to get an amniocentesis because of ignorance, poverty, or distance from the testing station, or if the prenatal diagnosis was in error. In such cases, parents are especially likely to resent the child. They may be disinclined to give it the kind of care they might have before the advent of amniocentesis and genetic abortion, rationalizing that a second-class specimen is not entitled to first-class treatment. If pressed to do so, say by physicians, the parents might refuse, and the courts may become involved. This has already begun to happen.

In Maryland, parents of a child with Down syndrome refused permission to have the child operated on for an intestinal obstruction present at birth. The physicians and the hospital sought an injunction to require the parents to allow surgery. The judge ruled in favor of the parents, despite what I understand to be the weight of precedent to the contrary, on the grounds that the child was Mongoloid, that is, had the child been "normal," the decision would have gone the other way. Although the decision was not appealed to and hence not affirmed by a higher court, we can see through the prism of this case the possibility that the new powers of human genetics will strip the blindfold from the lady of justice and will make official the dangerous doctrine that some men are more equal than others.

The abnormal child may also feel resentful. A child with Down syndrome or Tay-Sachs disease will probably never know or care, but what about a child with hemophilia or with Turner's syndrome? In the past decade, with medical knowledge and power over the prenatal child increasing and with parental authority over the postnatal child decreasing, we have seen the appearance of a new type of legal action, suits for wrongful life. Children have brought suit against their parents (and others) seeking to recover damages for physical and social handicaps inextricably tied to their birth (e.g., congenital deformities, congenital syphilis, illegitimacy). In some of the American cases, the courts have recognized the justice of the child's claim (that he was injured due to parental negligence), although they have so far refused to award damages, due to policy considerations. In other countries, e.g., in Germany, judgments with compensation have gone for the plaintiffs. With the spread of amniocentesis and genetic abortion, we can only expect such cases to increase. And here it will be the soft-hearted rather than the hard-hearted judges who will establish the doctrine of second-class human beings, out of compassion for the mutants who escaped the traps set out for them.

It may be argued that I am dealing with a problem which, even if it is real, will affect very few people. It may be suggested that very few will escape the traps once we have set them properly and widely, once people are informed about amniocentesis, once the power to detect prenatally grows to its full capacity, and once our "superstitious" opposition to abortion dies out or is extirpated. But in order even to come close to this vision of success, amniocentesis will have to become part of every pregnancy—either by making it mandatory, like the test for syphilis, or by making it "routine medical practice," like the Pap smear. Leaving aside the other problems with universal amniocentesis, we could expect that the problem for the few who escape is likely to be even worse precisely because they will be few.

The point, however, should be generalized. How will we come to view and act toward the many "abnormals" that will remain among us—the retarded, the crippled, the senile, the deformed, and the true mutants—once we embark on a program to root out genetic abnormality? For it must be remembered that we shall always have abnormls—some who escape detection or whose disease is undetectable *in utero*, others as a result of new mutations, birth injuries, accidents, maltreatment, or disease—who will require our care and protection. The existence of "defectives" cannot be fully prevented, not even by totalitarian breeding and weeding programs. Is it not likely that our principle with respect to these people will change from "We try harder" to "Why accept second best?" The idea of "the unwanted because abnormal child" may become a self-fulfilling prophecy, whose consequences may be worse than those of the abnormality itself.

Genetic and Other Defectives

The mention of other abnormals points to a second danger of the practice of genetic abortion. Genetic abortion may come to be seen not so much as the prevention of genetic disease, but as the prevention of birth of defective or abnormal children—and, in a way, understandably so. For in the case of what other diseases does preventive medicine consist in the elimination of the patient-at-risk? Moreover,

the very language used to discuss genetic disease leads us to the easy but wrong conclusion that the afflicted fetus or person is rather than has a disease. True, one is partly defined by his genotype, but only partly. A person is more than his disease. And yet we slide easily from the language of possession to the language of identity, from "He has hemophilia" to "He is a hemophiliac," from "She has diabetes" through "She is diabetic" to "She is a diabetic," from "The fetus has Down syndrome" to "The fetus is a Down's." This way of speaking supports the belief that it is defective persons (or potential persons) that are being eliminated, rather than diseases.

If this is so, then it becomes simply accidental that the defect has a genetic cause. Surely, it is only because of the high regard for medicine and science, and for the accuracy of genetic diagnosis, that genotypic defectives are likely to be the first to go. But once the principle, "Defectives should not be born," is established, grounds other than cytological and biochemical may very well be sought. Even ignoring racialists and others equally misguided—of course, they cannot be ignored—we should know that there are social scientists, for example, who believe that one can predict with a high degree of accuracy how a child will turn out from a careful, systematic study of the socio-economic and psycho-dynamic environment into which he is born and in which he grows up. They might press for the prevention of sociopsychological disease, even of "criminality," by means of prenatal environmental diagnosis and abortion. I have heard rumor that a crude, unscientific form of eliminating potential "phenotypic defectives" is already being practiced in some cities, in that submission to abortion is allegedly being made a condition for the receipt of welfare payments. "Defectives should not be born" is a principle without limits. We can ill afford to have it established.

Up to this point, I have been discussing the possible implications of the practice of genetic abortion for our belief in and adherence to the idea that, at least in fundamental human matters such as life and liberty, all men are to be considered as equals, that for these matters we should ignore as irrelevant the real qualitative differences amongst men, however important these differences may be for other purposes. Those who are concerned about abortion fear that the permissible time of eliminating the unwanted will be moved forward along the time continuum, against newborns, infants, and children. Similarly, I suggest that we should be concerned lest the attack on gross genetic inequality in fetuses be advanced along the continuum of quality and into the later stages of life.

I am not engaged in predicting the future; I am not saying that amniocentesis and genetic abortion will lead down the road to Nazi Germany. Rather, I am suggesting that the principles underlying genetic abortion simultaneously justify many further steps down that road. The point was very well made by Abraham Lincoln:

> If A can prove, however conclusively, that he may, of right, enslave B—Why may not B snatch the same argument and prove equality, that he may enslave A?
>
> You say A is white, and B is black. It is color, then; the lighter having the right to enslave the darker? Take care. By this rule, you are to be slave to the first man you meet with a fairer skin than your own.
>
> You do not mean color exactly? You mean the whites are intellectually the superiors of the blacks, and, therefore have the right to enslave them? Take care again. By this rule, you are to be slave to the first man you meet with an intellect superior to your own.
>
> But, say you, it is a question of interest; and, if you can make it your interest, you have the right to enslave another. Very well. And if he can make it his interest, he has the right to enslave you.

Perhaps I have exaggerated the dangers; perhaps we will not abandon our inexplicable preference for generous humanitarianism over consistency. But we should indeed be cautious and move slowly as we give serious consideration to the question "What price the perfect baby?"[3]

NOTES

1. This strikes me as by far the most important inference to be drawn from the fact that men in different times and cultures have answered the abortion question differently. Seen in this light, the differing and changing answers themselves suggest that it is a question not easily put under, at least not for very long.

2. Other ways include: one should not do violence to living or growing things; life is sacred; respect nature; fetal life has value; refrain from taking innocent life; protect and preserve life. As some have pointed out, the terms chosen are of different weight, and would require reasons of different weight to tip the balance in favor of abortion. My choice of the "rights" terminology is not meant to beg the questions of whether such rights really exist, or of where they come from. However, the notion of a "fetal right to life" presents only a little more difficulty in this regard than does the notion of a "human right to life," since the former does not depend on a claim that the human fetus is already "human." In my sense of terms "right" and "life," we might even say that a dog or fetal dog has a "right to life," and that it would be cruel and immoral for a man to go around performing abortions even on dogs for no good reason.

3. For a discussion of the possible biological rather than moral price of attempts to prevent the birth of defective children see Motulsky, A. G., G. R. Fraser, and J. Felsenstein (1971).

Genetics and Reproductive Risk: Can Having Children Be Immoral?

LAURA M. PURDY

Purdy contends that it is morally wrong to "reproduce when we know there is a high risk of transmitting a serious disease or defect." This conclusion is based on the judgment that we have an obligation to provide each child with "something like a minimally satisfying life."

Is it morally permissible for me to have children?[1] A decision to procreate is surely one of the most significant decisions a person can make. So it would

seem that it ought not to be made without some moral soul-searching.

There are many reasons why one might hesitate to bring children into this world if one is concerned about their welfare. Some are rather general, like the deteriorating environment or the prospect of poverty. Others have a narrower focus, like continuing civil war in Ireland, or the lack of essential social support for child rearing persons in the United States. Still others may be relevant only to individuals at risk of passing harmful diseases to their offspring.

There are many causes of misery in this world, and most of them are unrelated to genetic disease. In the general scheme of things, human misery is most efficiently reduced by concentrating on noxious social and political arrangements. Nonetheless, we shouldn't ignore preventable harm just because it is confined to a relatively small corner of life. So the question arises: can it be wrong to have a child because of genetic risk factors?[2]

Unsurprisingly, most of the debate about this issue has focused on prenatal screening and abortion: much useful information about a given fetus can be made available by recourse to prenatal testing. This fact has meant that moral questions about reproduction have become entwined with abortion politics, to the detriment of both. The abortion connection has made it especially difficult to think about whether it is wrong to prevent a child from coming into being since doing so might involve what many people see as wrongful killing; yet there is no necessary link between the two. Clearly, the existence of genetically compromised children can be prevented not only by aborting already existing fetuses but also by preventing conception in the first place.

Worse yet, many discussions simply assume a particular view of abortion, without any recognition of other possible positions and the difference they make in how people understand the issues. For example, those who object to aborting fetuses with genetic problems often argue that doing so would undermine our conviction that all humans are in some important sense equal.[3] However, this position rests on the assumption that conception marks the point at which humans are endowed with a right to life. So aborting fetuses with genetic problems looks morally the same as killing "imperfect" people without their consent.

This position raises two separate issues. One pertains to the legitimacy of different views on abortion. Despite the conviction of many abortion activists to the contrary, I believe that ethically respectable views

can be found on different sides of the debate, including one that sees fetuses as developing humans without any serious moral claim on continued life. There is no space here to address the details, and doing so would be once again to fall into the trap of letting the abortion question swallow up all others. Fortunately, this issue need not be resolved here. However, opponents of abortion need to face the fact that many thoughtful individuals do not *see* fetuses as moral persons. It follows that their reasoning process and hence the implications of their decisions are radically different from those envisioned by opponents of prenatal screening and abortion. So where the latter see genetic abortion as murdering people who just don't measure up, the former see it as a way to prevent the development of persons who are more likely to live miserable lives. This is consistent with a world view that values persons equally and holds that each deserves high quality life. Some of those who object to genetic abortion appear to be oblivious to these psychological and logical facts. It follows that the nightmare scenarios they paint for us are beside the point: many people simply do not share the assumptions that make them plausible.

How are these points relevant to my discussion? My primary concern here is to argue that conception can sometimes be morally wrong on grounds of genetic risk, although this judgment will not apply to those who accept the moral legitimacy of abortion and are willing to employ prenatal screening and selective abortion. If my case is solid, then those who oppose abortion must be especially careful not to conceive in certain cases, as they are, of course, free to follow their conscience about abortion. Those like myself who do not see abortion as murder have more ways to prevent birth.

Huntington's Disease
There is always some possibility that reproduction will result in a child with a serious disease or handicap. Genetic counselors can help individuals determine whether they are at unusual risk, and, as the Human Genome Project rolls on, their knowledge will increase by quantum leaps. As this knowledge becomes available, I believe we ought to use it to determine whether possible children are at risk *before* they are conceived.

I want in this paper to defend the thesis that it is morally wrong to reproduce when we know there is a high risk of transmitting a serious disease or defect. This thesis holds that some reproductive acts are wrong, and my argument puts the burden of proof on those who disagree with it to show why its conclusions can be overridden. Hence it denies that people should be free to reproduce mindless of the consequences.[4] However, as moral argument, it should be taken as a proposal for further debate and discussion. It is not, by itself, an argument in favor of legal prohibitions of reproduction.[5]

There is a huge range of genetic diseases. Some are quickly lethal; others kill more slowly, if at all. Some are mainly physical, some mainly mental; others impair both kinds of function. Some interfere tremendously with normal functioning, others less. Some are painful, some are not. There seems to be considerable agreement that rapidly lethal diseases, especially those, like Tay-Sachs, accompanied by painful deterioration, should be prevented even at the cost of abortion. Conversely, there seems to be substantial agreement that relatively trivial problems, especially cosmetic ones, would not be legitimate grounds for abortion.[6] In short, there are cases ranging from low risk of mild disease or disability to high risk of serious disease or disability. Although it is difficult to decide where the duty to refrain from procreation becomes compelling, I believe that there are some clear cases. I have chosen to focus on Huntington's Disease to illustrate the kinds of concrete issues such decisions entail. However, the arguments presented here are also relevant to many other genetic diseases.[7]

The symptoms of Huntington's Disease usually begin between the ages of thirty and fifty. It happens this way:

> Onset is insidious. Personality changes (obstinacy, moodiness, lack of initiative) frequently antedate or accompany the involuntary choreic movements. These usually appear first in the face, neck, and arms, and are jerky, irregular, and stretching in character. Contractions of the facial muscles result in grimaces; those of the respiratory muscles, lips, and tongue lead to hesitating, explosive speech. Irregular movements of the trunk are present; the gait is shuffling and dancing. Tendon reflexes are increased. . . .

> Some patients display a fatuous euphoria; others are spiteful, irascible, destructive, and violent. Paranoid reactions are common. Poverty of thought and impairment of attention, memory, and judgment occur. As the disease progresses, walking becomes impossible, swallowing difficult, and dementia profound. Suicide is not uncommon.[8]

The illness lasts about fifteen years, terminating in death.

Huntington's Disease is an autosomal dominant disease, meaning that it is caused by a single defective gene located on a non-sex chromosome. It is passed from one generation to the next via affected individuals. Each child of such an affected person has a fifty percent risk of inheriting the gene and thus of eventually developing the disease, even if he or she was born before the parent's disease was evident.[9]

Until recently, Huntington's Disease was especially problematic because most affected individuals did not know whether they had the gene for the disease until well into their childbearing years. So they had to decide about childbearing before knowing whether they could transmit the disease or not. If, in time, they did not develop symptoms of the disease, then their children could know they were not at risk for the disease. If unfortunately they did develop symptoms, then each of their children could know there was a fifty percent chance that they, too, had inherited the gene. In both cases, the children faced a period of prolonged anxiety as to whether they would develop the disease. Then, in the 1980s, thanks in part to an energetic campaign by Nancy Wexler, a genetic marker was found that, in certain circumstances, could tell people with a relatively high degree of probability whether or not they had the gene for the disease.[10] Finally, in March 1993, the defective gene itself was discovered.[11] Now individuals can find out whether they carry the gene for the disease, and prenatal screening can tell us whether a given fetus has inherited it. These technological developments change the moral scene substantially.

How serious are the risks involved in Huntington's Disease? Geneticists often think a ten percent risk is high.[12] But risk assessment also depends on what is at stake: the worse the possible outcome the more undesirable an otherwise small risk seems. In medicine, as elsewhere, people may regard the same result quite differently. But for devastating diseases like Huntington's this part of the judgment should be unproblematic: no one wants a loved one to suffer in this way.[13]

There may still be considerable disagreement about the acceptability of a given risk. So it would be difficult in many circumstances to say how we should respond to a particular risk. Nevertheless, there are good grounds for a conservative approach, for it is reasonable to take special precautions to avoid very bad consequences, even if the risk is small. But the possible consequences here *are* very bad: a child who may inherit Huntington's Disease has a much greater than average chance of being subjected to severe and prolonged suffering. And it is one thing to risk one's own welfare, but quite another to do so for others and without their consent.

Is this judgment about Huntington's Disease really defensible? People appear to have quite different opinions. Optimists argue that a child born into a family afflicted with Huntington's Disease has a reasonable chance of living a satisfactory life. After all, even children born of an afflicted parent still have a fifty percent chance of escaping the disease. And even if afflicted themselves, such people will probably enjoy some thirty years of healthy life before symptoms appear. It is also possible, although not at all likely, that some might not mind the symptoms caused by the disease. Optimists can point to diseased persons who have lived fruitful lives, as well as those who seem genuinely glad to be alive. One is Rick Donohue, a sufferer from the Joseph family disease: "You know, if my mom hadn't had me, I wouldn't be here for the life I have had. So there is a good possibility I will have children."[14] Optimists therefore conclude that it would be a shame if these persons had not lived.

Pessimists concede some of these facts, but take a less sanguine view of them. They think a fifty percent risk of serious disease like Huntington's appallingly high. They suspect that many children born into afflicted families are liable to spend their youth in dreadful anticipation and fear of the disease. They expect that the disease, if it appears, will be perceived as a tragic and painful end to a blighted life. They point out that Rick Donohue is still young, and has not experienced the full horror of his

sickness. It is also well-known that some young persons have such a dilated sense of time that they can hardly envision themselves at thirty or forty, so the prospect of pain at that age is unreal to them.[15]

More empirical research on the psychology and life history of sufferers and potential sufferers is clearly needed to decide whether optimists or pessimists have a more accurate picture of the experiences of individuals at risk. But given that some will surely realize pessimists' worst fears, it seems unfair to conclude that the pleasures of these who deal best with the situation simply cancel out the suffering of those others when that suffering could be avoided altogether.

I think that these points indicate that the morality of procreation in situations like this demands further investigation. I propose to do this by looking first at the position of the possible child, then at that of the potential parent.

Possible Children and Potential Parents

The first task in treating the problem from the child's point of view is to find a way of referring to possible future offspring without seeming to confer some sort of morally significant existence upon them. I will follow the convention of calling children who might be born in the future but who are not now conceived "possible" children, offspring, individuals, or persons.

Now, what claims about children or possible children are relevant to the morality of childbearing in the circumstances being considered? Of primary importance is the judgment that we ought to try to provide every child with something like a minimally satisfying life. I am not altogether sure how best to formulate this standard but I want clearly to reject the view that it is morally permissible to conceive individuals so long as we do not expect them to be so miserable that they wish they were dead.[16] I believe that this kind of moral minimalism is thoroughly unsatisfactory and that not many people would really want to live in a world where it was the prevailing standard. Its lure is that it puts few demands on us, but its price is the scant attention it pays to human well-being.

How might the judgment that we have a duty to try to provide a minimally satisfying life for our children be justified? It could, I think, be derived fairly straightforwardly from either utilitarian or contractarian theories of justice, although there is no space here for discussion of the details. The net result of such analysis would be the conclusion that neglecting this duty would create unnecessary unhappiness or unfair disadvantage for some persons.

Of course, this line of reasoning confronts us with the need to spell out what is meant by "minimally satisfying" and what a standard based on this concept would require of us. Conceptions of a minimally satisfying life vary tremendously among societies and also within them. De rigueur in some circles are private music lessons and trips to Europe, while in others providing eight years of schooling is a major accomplishment. But there is no need to consider this complication at length here since we are concerned only with health as a prerequisite for a minimally satisfying life. Thus, as we draw out what such a standard might require of us, it seems reasonable to retreat to the more limited claim that parents should try to ensure something like normal health for their children. It might be thought that even this moderate claim is unsatisfactory since in some places debilitating conditions are the norm, but one could circumvent this objection by saying that parents ought to try to provide for their children health normal for that culture, even though it may be inadequate if measured by some outside standard.[17] This conservative position would still justify efforts to avoid the birth of children at risk for Huntington's Disease and other serious genetic diseases in virtually all societies.[18]

This view is reinforced by the following considerations. Given that possible children do not presently exist as actual individuals, they do not have a right to be brought into existence, and hence no one is maltreated by measures to avoid the conception of a possible person. Therefore, the conservative course that avoids the conception of those who would not be expected to enjoy a minimally satisfying life is at present the only fair course of action. The alternative is a laissez-faire approach which brings into existence the lucky, but only at the expense of the unlucky. Notice that attempting to avoid the creation of the unlucky does not necessarily lead to *fewer* people being brought into being; the question boils down to taking steps to bring those with better prospects into existence, instead of those with worse ones.

I have so far argued that if people with Huntington's Disease are unlikely to live minimally satisfying lives, then those who might pass it on should not have genetically related children. This is consonant with the principle that the greater the danger of serious problems, the stronger the duty to avoid them. But this principle is in conflict with what people think of as the right to reproduce. How might one decide which should take precedence?

Expecting people to forego having genetically related children might seem to demand too great a sacrifice of them. But before reaching that conclusion we need to ask what is really at stake. One reason for wanting children is to experience family life, including love, companionship, watching kids grow, sharing their pains and triumphs, and helping to form members of the next generation. Other reasons emphasize the validation of parents as individuals within a continuous family line, children as a source of immortality, or perhaps even the gratification of producing partial replicas of oneself. Children may also be desired in an effort to prove that one is an adult, to try to cement a marriage or to benefit parents economically.

Are there alternative ways of satisfying these desires? Adoption or new reproductive technologies can fulfil many of them without passing on known genetic defects. Replacements for sperm have been available for many years via artificial insemination by donor. More recently, egg donation, sometimes in combination with contract pregnancy,[19] has been used to provide eggs for women who prefer not to use their own. Eventually it may be possible to clone individual humans, although that now seems a long way off. All of these approaches to avoiding the use of particular genetic material are controversial and have generated much debate. I believe that tenable moral versions of each do exist.[20]

None of these methods permits people to extend both genetic lines, or realize the desire for immortality or for children who resemble both parents; nor is it clear that such alternatives will necessarily succeed in proving that one is an adult, cementing a marriage, or providing economic benefits. Yet, many people feel these desires strongly. Now, I am sympathetic to William James's dictum regarding desires: "Take any demand, however slight, which any creature, however weak, may make. Ought it not, for its own sole sake be satisfied? If not, prove why not."[21] Thus a world where more desires are satisfied is generally better than one where fewer are. However, not all desires can be legitimately satisfied since, as James suggests, there may be good reasons—such as the conflict of duty and desire—why some should be overruled.

Fortunately, further scrutiny of the situation reveals that there are good reasons why people should attempt—with appropriate social support—to talk themselves out of the desires in question or to consider novel ways of fulfilling them. Wanting to see the genetic line continued is not particularly rational when it brings a sinister legacy of illness and death. The desire for immortality cannot really be satisfied anyway, and people need to face the fact that what really matters is how they behave in their own lifetime. And finally, the desire for children who physically resemble one is understandable, but basically narcissistic, and its fulfillment cannot be guaranteed even by normal reproduction. There are other ways of proving one is an adult, and other ways of cementing marriages—and children don't necessarily do either. Children, especially prematurely ill children, may not provide the expected economic benefits anyway. Nongenetically related children may also provide benefits similar to those that would have been provided by genetically related ones, and expected economic benefit is, in many cases, a morally questionable reason for having children.

Before the advent of reliable genetic testing, the options of people in Huntington's families were cruelly limited. On the one hand, they could have children, but at the risk of eventual crippling illness and death for them. On the other, they could refrain from childbearing, sparing their possible children from significant risk of inheriting this disease, perhaps frustrating intense desires to procreate—only to discover, in some cases that their sacrifice was unnecessary because they did not develop the disease. Or they could attempt to adopt or try new reproductive approaches.

Reliable genetic testing has opened up new possibilities. Those at risk who wish to have children can get tested. If they test positive, they know their possible children are at risk. Those who are opposed to abortion must be especially careful to avoid conception if they are to behave responsibly. Those not opposed to abortion can responsibly conceive children, but only if they are willing to test each fetus and abort those who carry the gene. If individuals at risk test negative, they are home free.

What about those who cannot face the test for themselves? They can do prenatal testing and abort fetuses who carry the defective gene. A clearly positive test also implies that the parent is affected, although negative tests do not rule out that possibility. Prenatal testing can thus bring knowledge that enables one to avoid passing the disease to others, but only, in some cases, at the cost of coming to know with certainty that one will indeed develop the disease. This situation raises with peculiar force the question of whether parental responsibility requires people to get tested.

Some people think that we should recognize a right "not to know." It seems to me that such a right could be defended only where ignorance does not put others at serious risk. So if people are prepared to forego genetically related children, they need not get tested. But if they want genetically related children then they must do whatever is necessary to ensure that affected babies are not the result. There is, after all, something inconsistent about the claim that one has a right to be shielded from the truth, even if the price is to risk inflicting on one's children the same dread disease one cannot even face in oneself.

In sum, until we can be assured that Huntington's Disease does not prevent people from living a minimally satisfying life, individuals at risk for the disease have a moral duty to try not to bring affected babies into this world. There are now enough options available so that this duty needn't frustrate their reasonable desires. Society has a corresponding duty to facilitate moral behavior on the part of individuals. Such support ranges from the narrow and concrete (like making sure that medical testing and counseling is available to all) to the more general social environment that guarantees that all pregnancies are voluntary, that pronatalism is eradicated, and that women are treated with respect regardless of the reproductive options they choose.

NOTES

1. This paper is loosely based on "Genetic Diseases: Can Having Children Be Immoral?" originally published in *Genetics Now*, ed. John L. Buckley (Washington, DC:

University Press of America, 1978) and subsequently anthologized in a number of medical ethics texts. Thanks to Thomas Mappes and David DeGrazia for their helpful suggestions about updating the paper.

2. I focus on genetic considerations, although with the advent of AIDS the scope of the general question here could be expanded. There are two reasons for sticking to this relatively narrow formulation. One is that dealing with a smaller chunk of the problem may help us think more clearly, while realizing that some conclusions may nonetheless be relevant to the larger problem. The other is the peculiar capacity of some genetic problems to affect ever more individuals in the future.

3. For example, see Leon Kass, "Implications of Prenatal Diagnosis for the Human Right to Life," *Ethical Issues in Human Genetics*, eds. Bruce Hilton et al. (New York: Plenum Press, 1973).

4. This is, of course, a very broad thesis. I defend an even broader version in "Loving Future People," *Reproduction, Ethics and the Law*, ed. Joan Callahan (Bloomington: Indiana University Press, forthcoming).

5. Why would we want to resist legal enforcement of every moral conclusion? First, legal action has many costs, costs not necessarily worth paying in particular cases. Second, legal enforcement would tend to take the matter in question out of the realm of debate and treat it as settled. But in many cases, especially where mores or technology is rapidly evolving, we don't want that to happen. Third, legal enforcement would undermine individual freedom and decision-making capacity. In some cases, the ends envisioned are important enough to warrant putting up with these disadvantages, but that remains to be shown in each case.

6. Those who do not see fetuses as moral persons with a right to life may nonetheless hold that abortion is justifiable in these cases. I argue at some length elsewhere that lesser defects can cause great suffering. Once we are clear that there is nothing discriminatory about failing to conceive particular possible individuals, it makes sense, other things being equal, to avoid the prospect of such pain if we can. Naturally, other things rarely are equal. In the first place, many problems go undiscovered until a baby is born. Secondly, there are often substantial costs associated with screening programs. Thirdly, although women should be encouraged to consider the moral dimensions of routine pregnancy, we do not want it to be so fraught with tension that it becomes a miserable experience. (See "Loving Future People.")

7. It should be noted that failing to conceive a single individual can affect many lives: in 1916, nine hundred and sixty-two cases could be traced from six seventeenth-century arrivals in America. See Gordon Rattray Taylor, *The Biological Time Bomb* (New York, 1968), p. 176.

8. *The Merck Manual* (Rahway, NJ: Merck, 1972), pp. 1363, 1346. We now know that the age of onset and severity of the disease is related to the number of abnormal replications of the glutamine code on the abnormal gene.

See Andrew Revkin, "Hunting Down Huntington's," *Discover*, December 1993, p. 108.

9. Hymie Gordon, "Genetic Counseling," *JAMA*, Vol. 217, n. 9 (August 30, 1971), p. 1346.

10. See Revkin, "Hunting Down Huntington's," pp. 99–108.

11. "Gene for Huntington's Disease Discovered," *Human Genome News*, Vol. 5, n. 1 (May 1993), p. 5.

12. Charles Smith, Susan Holloway, and Alan E. H. Emery, "Individuals at Risk in Families—Genetic Disease," *Journal of Medical Genetics*, Vol. 8 (1971), p. 453.

13. To try to separate the issue of the gravity of the disease from the existence of a given individual, compare this situation with how we would assess a parent who neglected to vaccinate an existing child against a hypothetical viral version of Huntington's.

14. *The New York Times*, September 30, 1975, p. 1, col. 6. The Joseph family disease is similar to Huntington's Disease except that symptoms start appearing in the twenties. Rick Donohue was in his early twenties at the time he made this statement.

15. I have talked to college students who believe that they will have lived fully and be ready to die at those ages. It is astonishing how one's perspective changes over time, and how ages that one once associated with senility and physical collapse come to seem the prime of human life.

16. The view I am rejecting has been forcefully articulated by Derek Parfit, *Reasons and Persons* (Oxford: Oxford University Press, 1984). For more discussion, see "Loving Future People."

17. I have some qualms about this response since I fear that some human groups are so badly off that it might still be wrong for them to procreate, even if that would mean great changes in their cultures. But this is a complicated issue that needs its own investigation.

18. Again, a troubling exception might be the isolated Venezuelan group Nancy Wexler found where, because of in-breeding, a large proportion of the population is affected by Huntington's. See Revkin, "Hunting Down Huntington's."

19. Or surrogacy, as it has been popularly known. I think that "contract pregnancy" is more accurate and more respectful of women. Eggs can be provided either by a woman who also gestates the fetus or by a third party.

20. The most powerful objections to new reproductive technologies and arrangements concern possible bad consequences for women. However, I do not think that the arguments against them on these grounds have yet shown the dangers to be as great as some believe. So although it is perhaps true that new reproductive technologies and arrangements shouldn't be used lightly, avoiding the conceptions discussed here is well worth the risk. For a series of viewpoints on this issue, including my own "Another Look at Contract Pregnancy," see Helen B. Holmes, *Issues in Reproductive Technology I: An Anthology* (New York: Garland Press, 1992).

21. *Essays in Pragmatism*, ed. A. Castell (New York, 1948), p. 73.

The Morality of Screening for Disability

JEFF MCMAHAN

McMahan examines arguments against using screening technologies such as PGD to avoid giving birth to a disabled child. The most common objections are that screening and selection are discriminatory, diminish human diversity, cause disabled people social harms, and express a hurtful view toward them. McMahan says these objections imply that "it is wrong for people to try to avoid having a disabled child and to have a non-disabled child instead." This view in turn implies that it must be at least permissible to cause oneself to have a disabled rather than a non-disabled child. But, he argues, it is wrong to deliberately cause a disabled child to exist instead of a healthy child; therefore we must reject some or all of the objections against testing.

My topic is the morality of using screening technologies to enable potential parents to avoid having a disabled child. The relevant techniques include preconception genetic and non-genetic testing of potential parents, preimplantation genetic diagnosis (PGD), and prenatal screening with the option of abortion. Many people use these techniques and are grateful to have them. Others, however, object to their use, even when abortion is not an issue. The most common objections can be grouped into four basic types.

First, the opponents of screening and selection urge that these practices are perniciously discriminatory, in that their aim is to rid the world of people of a certain type, people who have increasingly come to share a sense of collective identity and solidarity. Some might even argue that for society to endorse and support screening for disability is analogous to promoting efforts to prevent the births of people of a particular racial group.

Second, the practices of screening and selection are not just detrimental to the disabled as a group but may also be harmful to individual disabled people in various ways. They may, for example, reinforce or seem to legitimize forms of discrimination against existing disabled people. And, if effective, they also reduce the *number* of disabled people, thereby making each disabled person a bit more

From *Ethics, Law and Moral Philosophy of Reproductive Biomedicine*, vol. 10, supp. 1, March 2005, pp. 129–32. Copyright © 2005 and published by Reproductive Healthcare Limited. Reprinted with permission.

unusual and a bit more isolated. The reduction in numbers may, in addition, diminish the visibility and political power of disabled people generally.

Third, it is often held that a reduction in the number of disabled people would have an adverse effect on human diversity. To eliminate the disabled would be to eliminate a type of human being who makes a unique contribution to the world. For the disabled themselves, and indeed their mere presence among the rest of us, teach valuable lessons about respect for difference, about the nobility of achievement in the face of grave obstacles, and even about the value of life and what makes a life worth living.

Fourth, it is often held that practices of screening and selection express a view of disabled people that is hurtful to existing disabled people. Efforts to prevent disabled people from existing are said to express such views as that disabled people ought not to exist, that it is bad if disabled people exist, or at least worse than if normal people exist, that disabled people are not worth the burdens they impose on their parents and on the wider society, and so on. Screening and selection, in other words, seem to say to existing disabled people: The rest of us are trying to prevent the existence of other people like you.

One can respond to these objections to screening and selection, as some of the speakers at this conference have done, by appealing to rights of individual liberty. One could grant that the practices are objectionable for the reasons given but argue that those reasons are overridden by rights to reproductive freedom and by the benefits to those who are able to exercise those rights. But I want to advance a reason for scepticism about the force of the objections themselves.

The objections do of course express serious and legitimate concerns, concerns that must be addressed in appropriate ways. But I will argue that they're insufficiently strong to show that screening and selection are wrong or should be prohibited. For if they were taken to show that, they would also have implications beyond the practices of screening and selection. They would also imply the permissibility of certain types of action that most people believe are impermissible.

Consider this hypothetical example: Suppose there is a drug that has a complex set of effects. It is an aphrodisiac that enhances a woman's pleasure during sexual intercourse. But it also increases fertility by inducing ovulation. If ovulation has recently occurred naturally, this drug causes destruction of the egg that is present in one of the fallopian tubes but also causes a new and different egg to be released from the ovaries. In addition, however, it has a very high probability of damaging the new egg in a way that will cause any child conceived through the fertilization of that egg to be disabled. The disability caused by the drug is, let us suppose, one that many potential parents seek to avoid through screening. But it is also, like virtually all disabilities, not so bad as to make life not worth living. Suppose that a woman takes this drug primarily to increase her pleasure but also with the thought that it may increase the probability of conception—for she wants to have a child. She is aware that the drug is likely to cause her to have a disabled child but she is eager for pleasure and reflects that it might be rather nice to have a child who might be more dependent than children usually are. Although she does not know it, she has in fact just ovulated naturally so the drug destroys and replaces the egg that was already present but also damages the new egg, thereby causing the child she conceives to be disabled.

Note that because the drug causes the woman's ovaries to release a new egg, the disabled child she conceives is a different individual from the child she would have had if she hadn't taken the drug.

Many people think that this woman's action is morally wrong. It is wrong to cause the existence of a disabled child rather than a child without a disability, just for the sake of one's own sexual pleasure. There

are, of course, some who think that rights to reproductive freedom make it permissible to choose to have a disabled child just as they also make it permissible to try to avoid having a disabled child. But most of us do not share that view. Most of us think that if it would be wrong to cause an already born child to become disabled, and if it would be wrong to cause a future child to be disabled through the infliction of prenatal injury, it should also be wrong to cause a disabled child to exist rather than a child without a disability.

There are of course differences. Whether they are morally significant and if so to what extent, are matters to which I will return shortly. For the moment, the important point to notice is that if the arguments I cited earlier show that screening and selection are wrong, they should also show that the action of the woman who takes the aphrodisiac is permissible. This is because if it is morally *mandatory* to *allow* oneself to have a disabled child rather than to try, through screening, to have a child who would not be disabled, than it must be at least *permissible* to *cause* oneself to have a disabled rather than a non-disabled child.

Let me try to explain this in greater detail. If it is wrong for the woman to take the aphrodisiac, that must be because there is a moral objection to voluntarily having a disabled child—an objection that's strong enough to make it wrong to cause oneself, by otherwise permissible means, to have a disabled rather than a non-disabled child. But if there is such an objection, it must surely be strong enough to make it at least permissible for people to try, by morally acceptable means, to avoid having a disabled child and to have a non-disabled child instead, and to make it impermissible for others to prevent them from making this attempt.

Yet the critics of screening believe not only that it is wrong for people to try to avoid having a disabled child and to have a non-disabled child instead, but even that it is permissible for others to prevent them from having a non-disabled rather than a disabled child. It would be inconsistent for these critics to condemn the woman in this example for causing herself to have a disabled rather than a non-disabled child and to condemn those who try to cause themselves *not* to have a disabled rather than a non-disabled child.

The crucial premise here is that if it would be morally objectionable to try to *prevent* a certain outcome, and permissible to deprive people of the means of preventing that outcome, then it ought to be permissible to *cause* that outcome, provided one does so by otherwise permissible means.

Note also that if we were to assert publicly that it would be wrong for this woman to do what would cause her to have a disabled child rather than a non-disabled child, or if we were to attempt to prevent her from taking the drug—for example, by making the drug illegal on the ground that it causes "birth defects"—our action would be vulnerable to the same objections that opponents of screening and selection urge against those practices.

If, for example, we were publicly to state the reasons why it would be objectionable for the woman to take the drug—that the disabled child's life might be likely to contain more hardship and less good than the life of a non-disabled child, that provision for the disabled child's special needs would involve greater social costs, and so on—the evaluations of disability and of disabled people that might be thought to be implicit in these claims could be deeply hurtful to existing disabled people, and if we were to prevent this woman and others from being able to take the drug, this would reduce the number of disabled people relative to the number there would otherwise have been, thereby threatening the collective identity and political power of existing disabled people.

In short, the arguments of the opponents of screening seem to imply not only that it would be permissible for the woman to take the aphrodisiac, thereby causing herself to have a disabled child, but also that it would be wrong even to voice objections to her action.

Some opponents of screening and selection may be willing to accept these implications. They might argue that there are relevant differences between causing oneself to have a disabled child rather than a different non-disabled child and causing an existing individual to be disabled. For example, in the latter case but not the former, there is a victim, someone for whom one's act is worse. So there are objections to causing an existing individual to be disabled that do not apply to merely causing a disabled person to exist, and to assert these objections merely expresses the view that it can be worse to be disabled than not to be, which seems unobjectionable, since it does

not imply any view of disabled people themselves. Screening and selection, by contrast, are held to express a pernicious and degrading view of disabled people.

Thus, opponents of screening and selection typically think that they can draw the line between action by a woman that may cause her to conceive a child who will be disabled and, for example, action taken by a pregnant woman that injures her fetus, causing it to be disabled when it otherwise would not have been. But in fact many people, especially among the disabled themselves, contend that it is no worse to be disabled than not to be. They claim that disabilities are "neutral" traits. So, for example, Harriet McBryde Johnson (2003), a disabled lawyer, emphatically repudiates the "unexamined assumption that disabled people are inherently 'worse off,' that we 'suffer,' that we have lesser 'prospects of a happy life.'"

The view that it is not bad to be disabled, apart from any ill effects caused by social discrimination, would be very difficult to sustain if it implied that to cause a person to become disabled would not harm that person, or that it is irrational to be averse to becoming disabled. But in fact those who claim that it is not bad in itself to *be* disabled can accept without inconsistency that it can be bad to *become* disabled. They can appeal to the *transition costs*. It is bad to become disabled because this can involve loss and discontinuity, requiring that one abandon certain goals and projects and adapt to the pursuit of different ones instead. It is these effects that make it rational to fear becoming disabled and they are a major part of the explanation of why it is wrong to cause someone to become disabled. The other major part is that the causation of disability involves a violation of the victim's autonomy.

But notice that these considerations do not count against causing disability through prenatal injury. For congenital disability does not have transition costs, and fetuses are not autonomous.

It seems, therefore, that opponents of screening and selection who also claim that it is not worse to be disabled have no basis for objecting to the infliction of prenatal injury that causes congenital disability. Moreover, to object to the infliction of disabling prenatal injury or to enact measures to prevent it would seem to express a negative view of disability and perhaps of the disabled themselves. At a minimum, it expresses the view that it is bad to be disabled, or at least worse than not to be disabled. And, if effective, efforts to prevent disabling prenatal injury would have other effects comparable to those of prohibiting or restricting screening for disability and selection, such as reducing the number of disabled people who would be born, thereby also threatening the sense of collective identity and solidarity among the disabled as well as diminishing their visibility and political power. Finally, prevention of prenatal injury would also threaten human diversity. It would deprive those who would have had contact with the person if he had been disabled of the unique benefits that disabled people offer to others.

So for those opponents of selection who also hold that it is not a harm or misfortune to be disabled, it seems that there are not only no reasons to object to the infliction of disabling prenatal injury but even positive reasons not to object to it and not to try to prevent it.

Suppose there were an aphrodisiac that would greatly enhance a woman's pleasure during sex but would, if taken during pregnancy, injure the fetus in a way that would cause it to be congenitally severely disabled. Those who oppose screening and selection for the reasons I cited earlier and who also hold that it is not bad in itself to be disabled are logically committed by their own arguments to accept that it would be permissible for a pregnant woman to take this aphrodisiac just to increase her own pleasure, and they are further committed to accept that it would be wrong to try to prevent the woman from taking the aphrodisiac or even to criticize her for doing so.

If we think that these conclusions are mistaken, which they surely are, we must reject some part of the case against screening and selection.

I will conclude by briefly suggesting a more positive way of addressing the concerns of those who oppose screening and selection. My sense is that the chief worry of those opposed to screening and selection has to do with the expressive effects of these practices. The worry is, as I noted earlier, that these practices give social expression to a negative view of disabled people, thereby reinforcing other forms of discrimination against them.

But notice that it is usually only people who have not had a disabled child who are averse to doing so.

Those people who actually have a disabled child tend overwhelmingly to be glad that they had the particular child they had. If any child they might have had would have been disabled, they tend to prefer having had their actual disabled child to having had no child at all. If they could have had a non-disabled child but it would have been a different child, they tend to prefer their actual disabled child. Of course, what they would usually most prefer is that their actual child had not been disabled. But it is almost invariably the case that any action that would have enabled them to avoid having a disabled child would have caused them to have a different child. When the parents appreciate this fact, they cease to wish that anything had been different in the past, and focus their hopes on the possibility of a cure.

In short, most people who currently have or have had a disabled child in the past do not regret having done so. They are, instead, glad to have had their actual child and frequently testify to the special joy and illumination afforded by being bound to a disabled child. This very different evaluation of having a disabled child by those who actually have experience of it is no less rational and no less authoritative than the evaluation that many people make prospectively that it would be bad or worse to have a disabled child.

We could therefore try to offset any negative expressive effects of screening and selection by giving public expression to these different and equally valid evaluations. I do not have any suggestions for how we might do this. That's a matter for specialists in public policy, not philosophers. But the crucial point is that it would be morally and strategically better for disabled people and their advocates to focus their efforts on positive proposals of this sort rather than to stigmatize and to seek to restrict or suppress practices such as screening and selection. By crusading against screening and selection, they risk making themselves appear to the wider public as fanatics bent on imposing harmful restrictions on others. That would certainly not serve the cause of obtaining justice for the disabled.

REFERENCE

Johnson HM. 2003. Unspeakable conversations. *New York Times Magazine*, 16 February 2003, p. 79.

Genetic Dilemmas and the Child's Right to an Open Future

DENA S. DAVIS

Davis explores whether genetic counselors—who are fiercely committed to respecting the autonomy of their patients—are duty bound to respect the requests of parents who want help in deliberately producing children with disabilities. She focuses on the example of deaf parents who would like their children to be deaf. She concludes that counselors should not participate in purposely creating deaf children, for such a result would violate a child's right to an open future.

The profession of genetic counseling is strongly characterized by a respect for patient autonomy that is greater than in almost any other area of medicine. When moral challenges arise in the clinical practice of genetics, they tend to be understood as conflicts between the obligation to respect patient autonomy and other ethical norms, such as doing good and avoiding harm. Thus, a typical counseling dilemma exists when a person who has been tested and found to be carrying the gene for Tay-Sachs disease refuses to share that information with siblings and other relatives despite the clear benefits to them of having that knowledge, or when a family member declines to participate in a testing protocol necessary to help another member discover his or her genetic status.

This way of looking at moral issues in genetic counseling often leaves both the counselors and commentators frustrated, for two reasons. First, by elevating respect for patient autonomy above all other values, it may be difficult to give proper weight to other factors, such as human suffering. Second, by privileging patient autonomy and by defining the patient as the person or couple who has come for counseling, there seems no "space" in which to give proper attention to the moral claims of the future child who is the endpoint of many counseling interactions.

These difficulties have been highlighted of late by the surfacing of a new kind of genetic counseling request: parents with certain disabilities who seek help in trying to assure that they will have a child who shares their disability. The two reported instances are in families affected by achondroplasia (dwarfism) and by hereditary deafness. This essay will focus on deafness.

Such requests are understandably troubling to genetic counselors. Deeply committed to the principle of giving clients value-free information with which to make their own choices, most counselors nonetheless make certain assumptions about health and disability—for example, that it is preferable to be a hearing person rather than a deaf person. Thus, counselors typically talk of the "risk" of having a child with a particular genetic condition. Counselors may have learned (sometimes with great difficulty) to respect clients' decisions not to find out if their fetus has a certain condition or not to abort a fetus which carries a genetic disability. But to respect a parental value system that not only favors what most of us consider to be a disability, but actively expresses that preference by attempting to have a child with the condition, is "the ultimate test of nondirective counseling."[1]

To describe the challenge primarily as one that pits beneficence (concern for the child's quality of life) against autonomy (concern for the parents' right to decide about these matters) makes for obvious difficulties. These are two very different values, and comparing and weighing them invites the proverbial analogy of "apples and oranges." After all,

From Dena S. Davis, "Genetic Dilemmas and the Child's Right to an Open Future," *Hastings Center Report*, vol. 27, no. 2 (1997): 7–15.

the perennial critique of a principle-based ethics is that it offers few suggestions for ranking principles when duties conflict. Further, beneficence and respect for autonomy are values that will always exist in some tension within genetic counseling. For all the reasons I list below, counselors are committed to the primacy of patient autonomy and therefore to nondirective counseling. But surely, most or all of them are drawn to the field because they want to help people avoid or at least mitigate suffering.

Faced with the ethical challenge of parents who wish to ensure children who have a disability, I suggest a different way to look at this problem. Thinking this problem through in the way I suggest will shed light on some related topics in genetics as well, such as sex selection. I propose that, rather than conceiving this as a conflict between autonomy and beneficence, we recast it as a conflict between parental autonomy and the child's future autonomy: what Joel Feinberg has called "the child's right to an open future."

New Challenges

The Code of Ethics of the National Society of Genetic Counselors states that its members strive to:

- Respect their clients' beliefs, cultural traditions, inclinations, circumstances, and feelings.
- Enable their clients to make informed independent decisions, free of coercion, by providing or illuminating the necessary facts and clarifying the alternatives and anticipated consequences.[2]

Considering the uncertain and stochastic nature of genetic counseling, and especially in light of the difficulty physicians experience in sharing uncertainty with patients, it is remarkable that medical geneticists have hewed so strongly to an ethic of patient autonomy. This phenomenon can be explained by at least five factors: the desire to disassociate themselves as strongly as possible from the discredited eugenics movement;[3] an equally strong desire to avoid the label of "abortionist," a realistic fear if counselors are perceived as advocates for abortion of genetically damaged fetuses;[4] the fact that few treatments are available for genetic diseases (p. 29);

an awareness of the intensely private nature of reproductive decisions; and the fact that genetic decisions can have major consequences for entire families.[5] As one counselor was quoted, "I am not going to be taking that baby home—they will."[6]

The commitment to patient autonomy faces new challenges with the advances arising from the Human Genome Project. The example of hereditary deafness is reported by Walter E. Nance, who writes:

> It turns out that some deaf couples feel threatened by the prospect of having a hearing child and would actually prefer to have a deaf child. The knowledge that we will soon acquire [due to the Human Genome Project] will, of course, provide us with the technology that could be used to assist such couples in achieving their goals. This, in turn, could lead to the ultimate test of nondirective counseling. Does adherence to the concept of nondirective counseling actually require that we assist such a couple in terminating a pregnancy with a hearing child or is this nonsense?[7]

Several issues must be unpacked here. First, I question Nance's depiction of deaf parents as feeling "threatened" by the prospect of a hearing child. From Nance's own depiction of the deaf people he encounters, it is at least as likely that deaf parents feel that a deaf child would fit into their family better, especially if the parents themselves are "deaf of deaf" or if they already have one or more deaf children. Or perhaps the parents feel that Deafness (I use the capital "D," as Deaf people do, to signify Deafness as a culture) is an asset—tough at times but worthwhile in the end— like belonging to a racial or religious minority.

Second, I want to avoid the issue of abortion by discussing the issue of "deliberately producing a deaf child" as distinct from the question of achieving that end by aborting a hearing fetus. The latter topic is important, but it falls outside the purview of this paper. I will focus on the scenario where a deaf child is produced without recourse to abortion. We can imagine a situation in the near future where eggs or sperm can be scrutinized for the relevant trait before fertilization, or the present situation in which preimplantation genetic diagnosis after in vitro fertilization allows specialists to examine the genetic makeup of the very early embryo before it is implanted.

Imagine a Deaf couple approaching a genetic counselor. The couple's goals are to learn more about the cause(s) of their own deafness, and, if possible, to maximize the chance that any pregnancy they embark upon will result in a Deaf child. Let us suppose that the couple falls into the 50 percent of clients whose Deafness has a genetic origin.[8] The genetic counselor who adheres strictly to the tenets of client autonomy will respond by helping the couple to explore the ways in which they can achieve their goal: a Deaf baby. But as Nance's depiction of this scenario suggests, the counselor may well feel extremely uneasy about her role here. It is one thing to support a couple's decision to take their chances and "let Nature take its course," but to treat as a goal what is commonly considered to be a risk may be more pressure than the value-neutral ethos can bear. What is needed is a principled argument against such assistance. This refusal need not rise to a legal prohibition, but could become part of the ethical norms and standard of care for the counseling profession.[9]

The path I see out of this dilemma relies on two steps. First, we remind ourselves why client autonomy is such a powerful norm in genetic counseling. Clients come to genetic counselors with questions that are simultaneously of the greatest magnitude and of the greatest intimacy. Clients not only have the right to bring their own values to bear on these questions, but in the end they must do so because they—and their children—will live with the consequences. As the President's Commission said in its 1983 report on Screening and Counseling for Genetic Conditions:

> The silence of the law on many areas of individual choice reflects the value this country places on pluralism. Nowhere is the need for freedom to pursue divergent conceptions of the good more deeply felt than in decisions concerning reproduction. It would be a cruel irony, therefore, if technological advances undertaken in the name of providing information to expand the range of individual choices resulted in unanticipated social pressures to pursue a particular course of action. Someone who feels compelled to undergo screening or to make particular reproductive choices at the urging of health care professionals or others or as a result of implicit social pressure is deprived of the choice-enhancing benefits of the new advances. The Commission recommends that those who counsel patients and

those who educate the public about genetics should not only emphasize the importance of preserving choice but also do their utmost to safeguard the choices of those they serve.[10]

Now let us take this value of respect for autonomy and put it on both sides of the dilemma. Why is it morally problematic to seek to produce a child who is deaf? Being deaf does not cause one physical pain or shorten one's life span, two obvious conditions which it would be prima facie immoral to produce in another person. Deaf people might (or might not) be less happy on average than hearing people, but that is arguably a function of societal prejudice. The primary argument against deliberately seeking to produce deaf children is that it violates the child's own autonomy and narrows the scope of her choices when she grows up; in other words, it violates her right to an "open future."

The Child's Right to an Open Future

Joel Feinberg begins his discussion of children's rights by noticing that rights can ordinarily be divided into four kinds. First, there are rights that adults and children have in common (the right not to be killed, for example). Then, there are rights that are generally possessed only by children (or by "childlike" adults). These "dependency-rights," as Feinberg calls them, derive from the child's dependence on others for such basics as food, shelter, and protection. Third, there are rights that can only be exercised by adults (or at least by children approaching adulthood), for example, the free exercise of religion. Finally, there are rights that Feinberg calls "rights-in-trust," rights which are to be "saved for the child until he is an adult." These rights can be violated by adults now, in ways that cut off the possibility that the child, when it achieves adulthood, can exercise them. A striking example is the right to reproduce. A young child cannot physically exercise that right, and a teenager might lack the legal and moral grounds on which to assert such a right. But clearly the child, when he or she attains adulthood, will have that right, and therefore the child now has the right not to be sterilized, so that the child may exercise that right in the future. Rights in this category include a long list: virtually all the important rights we believe adults have, but which must be protected now to be exercised later. Grouped together, they constitute what Feinberg calls "the child's right to an open future."[11]

Feinberg illustrates this concept with two examples. The first is that of the Jehovah's Witness child who needs a blood transfusion to save his life but whose parents object on religious grounds. In this case, the parents' right to act upon their religious beliefs and to raise their family within the religion of their choice conflicts with the child's right to live to adulthood and to make his own life-or-death decisions. As the Supreme Court said in another (and less defensible) case involving Jehovah's Witnesses:

> Parents may be free to become martyrs themselves. But it does not follow that they are free in identical circumstances to make martyrs of their children before they have reached the age of full and legal discretion when they can make that decision for themselves.[12]

The second example is more controversial. In 1972, in a famous Supreme Court case, a group of Old Order Amish argued that they should be exempt from Wisconsin's requirement that all children attend school until they are either sixteen years old or graduate from high school.[13] The Amish didn't have to send their children to public school, of course; they were free to create a private school of their own liking. But they framed the issue in the starkest manner: to send their children to any school, past eighth grade, would be antithetical to their religion and their way of life, and might even result in the death of their culture.

The case was framed as a freedom of religion claim on the one hand, and the state's right to insist on an educated citizenry on the other. And within that frame, the Amish won. First, they were able to persuade the Court that sending their children to school after eighth grade would potentially destroy their community, because it

> takes them away from their community, physically and emotionally, during the crucial and formative adolescent period. During this period, the children must acquire Amish attitudes favoring manual work and self-reliance and the specific skills needed to perform the adult role of an Amish farmer or housewife. In the Amish belief higher learning tends to develop values they reject as influences that alienate man from God. (p. 211)

Second, the Amish argued that the state's concerns—that children be prepared to participate in the political and economic life of the state—did not apply in this case. The Court listened favorably to expert witnesses who explained that the Amish system of home-based vocational training—learning from your parent—worked well for that community, that the community itself was prosperous, and that few Amish were likely to end up unemployed. The Court said:

> the value of all education must be assessed in terms of its capacity to prepare the child for life.... It is one thing to say that compulsory education for a year or two beyond the eighth grade may be necessary when its goal is the preparation of the child for life in modern society as the majority live, but it is quite another if the goal of education can be viewed as the preparation of the child for life in the separated agrarian community that is the keystone of the Amish faith. (p. 222)

What only a few justices saw was that the children themselves were largely ignored in this argument. The Amish wanted to preserve their way of life. The state of Wisconsin wanted to make sure that its citizens could vote wisely and make a living. No justice squarely faced the question of whether the liberal democratic state owes all its citizens, especially children, a right to a basic education that can serve as a building block if the child decides later in life that she wishes to become an astronaut, a playwright, or perhaps to join the army As we constantly hear from politicians and educators, without a high school diploma one's future is virtually closed. By denying them a high school education or its equivalent, parents are virtually ensuring that their children will remain housewives and agricultural laborers. Even if the children agree, is that a choice parents ought to be allowed to make for them?

From my perspective, the case was decided wrongly. If Wisconsin had good reasons for settling on high school graduation or age sixteen as the legal minimum to which children are entitled then I think that the Amish children were entitled to that minimum as well, despite their parents' objections. In deciding the issue primarily on grounds that the Amish were not likely to create problems for the state if allowed to keep their children out of school, the Court reflected a rather minimalist form of liberalism. In fact, the abiding interest of this case for many political philosophers lies in the deep conflict it highlights between two different concepts of liberalism: commitment to autonomy and commitment to diversity. William Galston, for example, argues that:

> A standard liberal view (or hope) is that these two principles go together and complement one another: the exercise of autonomy yields diversity, while the fact of diversity protects and nourishes autonomy. By contrast, my ... view is that these principles do not always, perhaps even do not usually, cohere; that in practice, they point in quite different directions in currently disputed areas such as education.... Specifically: the decision to throw state power behind the promotion of individual autonomy can weaken or undermine individuals and groups that do not and cannot organize their affairs in accordance with that principle without undermining the deepest sources of their identity.[14]

Galston claims that "properly understood, liberalism is about the protection of diversity, not the valorization of choice To place an ideal of autonomous choice ... at the core of liberalism is in fact to narrow the range of possibilities available within liberal societies" (p. 523).

One can see this conflict quite sharply if one returns to the work of John Stuart Mill. On the one hand, there is probably no philosopher who gives more weight to the value of individual choice than does Mill. In *On Liberty,* he claims that the very measure of a human being is the extent to which he makes life choices for himself, free of societal pressure:

> The human faculties of perception, judgment, discriminative feeling, mental activity, and even moral preference, are exercised only in making a choice. He who does anything because it is the custom makes no choice.[15]

Mill would abhor a situation like that of the Amish communities in *Yoder,* which unabashedly want to give their children as few choices as possible. But, on the other hand, it is clear from both common sense and from Mill's own statements that in order for people to have choices about the pattern of their lives (and to be inspired to create new patterns) there must be more than one type of community available to them. To quote Mill again, "There is no reason that all human existence should be constructed on some one or some small number of patterns" (p. 64). As we look at the last three centuries of American history, we see what an important role different community "patterns" have played, from the Shakers to the Mormons to Bronson Alcott's Fruitlands to the communal experiments of the 1960s. If those patterns are to exhibit the full range of human endeavor and experiment, they must include communities that are distinctly anti-liberal. Not only does the panoply of widely different communities enrich our culture, but it also provides a welcome for those who do not fit into the mainstream. As Mill says, "A man cannot get a coat or pair of shoes to fit him unless they are either made to his measure, or he has a whole warehouseful to choose from: and is it easier to fit him with a life than with a coat[?]" (p. 64). Some of us are geniuses who make our lives to "fit our measure," others are happy enough to fit into the mainstream, but for others, the availability of a "warehouseful" of choices increases the possibility of finding a good fit. And for some, a good fit means an authoritarian community based on tradition, where one is freed from the necessity of choice. Thus Galston is correct in pointing to the paradox: if the goal of a liberal democracy is to actively promote something like the greatest number of choices for the greatest number of individuals, this seems to entail hostility toward narrow-choice communities like the Amish. But if the Amish, because of that hostility, fail to flourish, there will be fewer choices available to all.

The compromise I promote is that a liberal state must tolerate even those communities most unsympathetic to the liberal value of individual choice. However, this tolerance must exist within a limiting context, which is the right of individuals to choose which communities they wish to join and to leave if they have a mind to. Even Galston begins with the presumption that society must "defend ... the liberty not to be coerced into, or trapped within, ways of life. Accordingly, the state must safeguard the ability of individuals to shift allegiances and cross boundaries."[16] Thus, I argue that the autonomy of the individual is ethically prior to the autonomy of the group. Both ideals have powerful claims on us, but when group rights would extinguish the abilities of the individuals within them to make their own life choices, then the liberal state must support the individual against the group. This is especially crucial when the individual at issue is a child, who is particularly vulnerable to adult coercion and therefore has particular claims on our protection.

Unfortunately, it is precisely where children are concerned that groups are understandably most jealous of their prerogatives to guide and make decisions. The Amish are an example of a group guarding its ability to shape the lives of its children; Deaf parents wishing to ensure Deaf children are an example of families pursuing the same goals. Of course, groups and families ought to—in fact, they must—strive to shape the values and lives of the children in their care, not to do so leads to social and individual pathology. But when that shaping takes the form of a radically narrow range of choices available to the child when she grows up, when it impinges substantially on the child's right to an open future, then liberalism requires us to intervene to support the child's future ability to make her own choices about which of the many diverse visions of life she wishes to embrace.

But I concede one problem with this point of view. As a liberal who believes that the state should not dictate notions of "the good life," Feinberg believes that the state must be neutral about the goals of education, skewing the question neither in favor of the Amish lifestyle nor in favor of the "modern," technological life most Americans accept. The goal of education is to allow the child to make up its own mind from the widest array of options; the best education is the one which gives the child the most open future. A neutral decision would assume only that education should equip the child with the knowledge and skills that will help him choose whichever sort of life best fits his native endowment and matured disposition. It should send him out into the adult world with as many open opportunities as possible, thus maximizing his chances for self-fulfillment.[17]

The problem here is that an education which gave a child this array of choices would quite possibly make it impossible for her to choose to remain Old Order Amish. Her "native endowment and matured disposition" might now have taken her away from the kind of personality and habits that would make Amish life pleasant. Even if she envies the peace, warmth, and security that a life of tradition offers, she may find it impossible to turn her back on "the world," and return to her lost innocence. To quote the Amish, she may have failed irreversibly to "acquire" Amish attitudes" during "the crucial and formative adolescent period." This problem raises two issues. First, those of us who would make arguments based on the child's right to an open future need to be clear and appropriately humble about what we are offering. Insisting on a child's right to a high school education may open a future wider than she otherwise could have dreamed, but it also may foreclose one possible future: as a contented member of the Amish community. Second, if the Amish are correct in saying that taking their children out of school at grade eight is crucial for the child's development into a member of the Amish community, then there is no "impartial" stance for the state to take. The state may well be impartial about whether the "better life" is to be found within or without the Amish community, but it cannot act in an impartial fashion. Both forcing the parents to send their children to school or exempting them from the requirement has likely consequences for the child's continued existence within the community when she grows up and is able to make a choice. Feinberg seeks to avoid this second problem by claiming that the neutral state would act to

> let all influences…work equally on the child, to open up all possibilities to him, without itself influencing him toward one or another of these. In that way, it can be hoped that the chief determining factor in the grown child's choice of a vocation and life-style will be his own governing values, talents, and propensities. (pp. 134–35)

The problem with this is that, as I understand the Amish way of life, being Amish is precisely not to make one's life choices on the basis of one's own "talents and propensities," but to subordinate those individual leanings to the traditions of the group. If one discovers within oneself a strong passion and talent for jazz dancing, one ought to suppress it, not nurture it.

Is Creating a Deaf Child a Moral Harm?

Now, as we return to the example of the couple who wish to ensure that they bear only deaf children, we have to confront two distinctly different issues. The first is, in what sense is it ever possible to do harm by giving birth to a child who would otherwise not have been born at all? The second is whether being deaf rather than hearing is in fact a harm.

The first issue has been well rehearsed elsewhere.[18] The problem is, how can it be said that one has harmed a child by bringing it into the world with a disability, when the only other choice was for the child not to have existed at all? In the case of a child whose life is arguably not worth living, one can say that life itself is a cruelty to the child. But when a child is born in less than ideal circumstances, or is partially disabled in ways that do not entail tremendous suffering, there seems no way to argue that the child herself has been harmed. This may appear to entail the conclusion, counter to our common moral sense, that therefore no harm has been done. "A wrong action must be bad for someone, but [a] choice to create [a] child with its handicap is bad for no one."[19]

All commentators agree that there is no purely logical way out of what Dan Brock calls the "wrongful handicap" conundrum (p. 272). However, most commentators also agree that one can still support a moral critique of the parents' decision. Bonnie Steinbock and Ron McClamrock argue for a principle of "parental responsibility" by which being a good parent entails refraining from bringing a child into the world when one cannot give it "even a decent chance at a good life."[20] Brock, following Parfit, distinguishes same person from same number choices In same person choices, the same person exists in each of the alternative courses of action the agent chooses, but the person may exist more or less harmed. In same number choices, "the choice affects who, which child, will exist."[21] Brock claims that moral harms can exist in both instances, despite the fact that in same number choices the moral harm cannot be tied to a specific person. Brock generates the following principle:

> Individuals are morally required not to let any possible child … for whose welfare they are responsible experience serious suffering or limited opportunity if they can act so that, without imposing substantial burdens or costs on themselves or others, any alternative possible child…for whose welfare they would be responsible will not experience serious suffering or limited opportunity. (pp. 272–73)

While agreeing with Brock, Steinbock, and others, I locate the moral harm differently, at least with respect to disabled persons wishing to reproduce themselves in the form of a disabled child. Deliberately creating a child who will be forced irreversibly into the parents' notion of "the good life" violates the Kantian principle of treating each person as an end in herself and never as a means only. All parenthood exists as a balance between fulfillment of parental hopes and values and the individual flowering of the actual child in his or her own direction. The decision to have a child is never made for the sake of the child—for no child then exists. We choose to have children for myriad reasons, but before the child is conceived those reasons can only be self-regarding. The child is a means to our ends: a certain kind of joy and pride, continuing the family name, fulfilling religious or societal expectations, and so on. But morally the child is first and foremost an end in herself. Good parenthood requires a balance between having a child for our own sakes and being open to the moral reality that the child will exist for her own sake, with her own talents and weaknesses, propensities and interests, and with her own life to make. Parental practices that close exits virtually forever are insufficiently attentive to the child as end in herself. By closing off the child's right to an open future, they define the child as an entity who exists to fulfill parental hopes and dreams, not her own.

Having evaded the snares of the wrongful handicap conundrum, we must tackle the second problem: is being deaf a harm? At first glance, this might appear as a silly question. Ethically, we would certainly include destroying someone's hearing under the rubric of "harm"; legally, one could undoubtedly receive compensation if one were rendered deaf through someone else's negligence. Many Deaf people, however, have recently been claiming that Deafness is better understood as a cultural identity than as a disability. Particularly in the wake of the Deaf President Now revolution at Gallaudet University in 1988, Deaf people have been asserting their claims not merely to equal access (through increased technology) but also to equal respect as a cultural minority. As one (hearing) reporter noted:

> So strong is the feeling of cultural solidarity that many deaf parents cheer on discovering that their baby is deaf. Pondering such a scene, a hearing person can experience a kind of vertigo. The surprise is not simply the unfamiliarity of the views; it is that, as in a surrealist painting, jarring notions are presented as if they were commonplace.[22]

From this perspective, the use of cochlear implants to enable deaf children to hear, or the abortion of deaf fetuses, is characterized as "genocide."[23] Deaf pride advocates point out that as Deaf people they lack the ability to hear, but they also have many positive gains: a cohesive community, a rich cultural heritage built around the various residential schools, a growing body of drama, poetry, and other artistic traditions, and, of course, what makes all this possible, American Sign Language.[24] Roslyn Rosen, the president of the National Association of the Deaf, is Deaf, the daughter of Deaf parents, and the mother of Deaf children. "I'm happy with who I am," she says, "and I don't want to be 'fixed.' Would an Italian-American rather be a WASP? In our society everyone agrees that whites have an easier time than blacks. But do you think a black person would undergo operations to become white?"[25]

On the other side of the argument is evidence that deafness is a very serious disability. Deaf people have incomes thirty to forty percent below the national average.[26] The state of education for the deaf is unacceptable by anyone's standards; the typical deaf student graduates from high school unable to read a newspaper.[27]

However, one could also point to the lower incomes and inadequate state of education among some racial and ethnic minorities in our country, a situation we do not (or at least ought not) try to ameliorate by eradicating minorities. Deaf advocates often cite the work of Nora Ellen Groce, whose oral history of Martha's Vineyard, *Everyone Here Spoke Sign Language,* tells a fascinating story. For over two hundred years, ending in the middle of the twentieth century, the Vineyard experienced a degree of hereditary deafness exponentially higher than that of the mainland. Although the number of deaf people was low in non-comparative terms (one in 155), the result was a

community in which deaf people participated fully in the political and social life of the island, had an economic prosperity on par with their neighbors, and communicated easily with the hearing population, for "everyone here spoke sign language." So endemic was sign language for the general population of the island that hearing islanders often exploited its unique properties even in the absence of deaf people. Old-timers told Groce stories of spouses communicating through sign language when they were outdoors and did not want to raise their voices against the wind. Or men might turn away and finish a "dirty" joke in sign when a woman walked into the general store. At church, deaf parishioners gave their testimony in sign.

As one Deaf activist said, in a comment that could have been directly related to the Vineyard experience, "When Gorbachev visited the U.S., he used an interpreter to talk to the President. Was Gorbachev disabled?"[28] Further, one might argue that, since it is impossible to eradicate deafness completely even if that were a worthy goal, the cause of deaf equality is better served when parents who are proud to be Deaf deliberately have Deaf children who augment and strengthen the existing population. Many of the problems that deaf people experience are the result of being born, without advance warning, to hearing parents. When there is no reason to anticipate the birth of a deaf child, it is often months or years before the child is correctly diagnosed. Meanwhile, she is growing up in a world devoid of language, unable even to communicate with her parents. When the diagnosis is made, her parents first must deal with the emotional shock, and then sort through the plethora of conflicting advice on how best to raise and educate their child. Most probably, they have never met anyone who is deaf. If they choose the route recommended by most Deaf activists and raise their child with sign language, it will take the parents years to learn the language. Meanwhile, their child has missed out on the crucial development of language at the developmentally appropriate time, a lack that is associated with poor reading skills and other problems later (p. 43).

Further, even the most accepting of hearing parents often feel locked in conflict with the Deaf community over who knows what is best for their child. If Deafness truly is a culture rather than a disability, then raising a deaf child is somewhat like white parents trying to raise a black child in contemporary America (with a background chorus of black activists telling them that they can't possibly make a good job of it!). Residential schools, for example, which can be part of the family culture for a Deaf couple, can be seen by hearing parents as Dickensian nightmares or, worse, as a "cultlike" experience in which their children will be lost to them forever.

By contrast, deaf children born to Deaf parents learn language (sign) at the same age as hearing children. They are welcomed into their families and inculcated into Deaf culture in the same way as any other children. Perhaps for these reasons, by all accounts the Deaf of Deaf are the acknowledged leaders of the Deaf Pride movement, and the academic crème de la crème. In evaluating the choice parents make who deliberately ensure that they have Deaf children, we must remember that the statistics and descriptions of deaf life in America are largely reflective of the experience of deaf children born to hearing parents, who make up the vast majority of deaf people today.

But if Deafness is a culture rather than a disability, it is an exceedingly narrow one. One factor that does not seem clear is the extent to which children raised with American Sign Language as their first language ever will be completely comfortable with the written word. (Sign language itself has no written analogue and has a completely different grammatical structure from English.) At present, the conflicted and politicized state of education for the deaf, along with the many hours spent (some would say "wasted") on attempting to teach deaf children oral skills, makes it impossible to know what is to blame for the dismal reading and writing skills of the average deaf person. Some deaf children who are raised with sign language from birth do become skilled readers. But there is reason to question whether a deaf child may have very limited access to the wealth of literature, drama, and poetry that liberals would like to consider every child's birthright.

Although Deaf activists rightly show how many occupations are open to them with only minor technological adjustments, the range of occupations will always be inherently limited. It is not

likely that the world will become as Martha's Vineyard, where everyone knew sign. A prelingually deafened person not only cannot hear, but in most instances cannot speak well enough to be understood. This narrow choice of vocation is not only a harm in its own sake but also is likely to continue to lead to lower standards of living. (Certainly one reason why the Vineyard deaf were as prosperous as their neighbors was that farming and fishing were just about the only occupations available.)

Either Way, A Moral Harm

If deafness is considered a disability, one that substantially narrows a child's career, marriage, and cultural options in the future, then deliberately creating a deaf child counts as a moral harm. If Deafness is considered a culture, as Deaf activists would have us agree, then deliberately creating a Deaf child who will have only very limited options to move outside of that culture, also counts as a moral harm. A decision, made before a child is even born, that confines her forever to a narrow group of people and a limited choice of careers, so violates the child's right to an open future that no genetic counseling team should acquiesce in it. The very value of autonomy that grounds the ethics of genetic counseling should preclude assisting parents in a project that so dramatically narrows the autonomy of the child to be.

Coda

Although I rest my case at this point, I want to sketch out some further ramifications of my argument. Are there other, less obvious, ways in which genetic knowledge and manipulation can interfere with the child's right to an open future?

The notion of the child's right to an open future can help in confronting the question of whether to test children for adult-onset genetic diseases, for example Huntington disease.[29] It is well known that the vast majority of adults at risk for Huntington disease choose not to be tested. However, it is not uncommon for parents to request that their children be tested; their goals may be to set their minds at rest, to plan for the future, and so on. On one account, parental authority to make medical decisions suggests that clinicians should accede to these requests (after proper counseling about possible risks). A better account, in my opinion, protects the child's right to an open future by preserving into adulthood his own choice to decide whether his life is better lived with that knowledge or without.[30]

Finally, a provocative argument can be made that sex selection can be deleterious to the child's right to an open future. I am ignoring here all the more obvious arguments against sex selection, even when accomplished without abortion. Rather, I suspect that parents who choose the sex of their offspring are more likely to have gender-specific expectations for those children, expectations that subtly limit the child's own individual flowering. The more we are able to control our children's characteristics (and the more time, energy, and money we invest in the outcome), the more invested we will become in our hopes and dreams for them. It is easy to sympathize with some of the reasons why parents might want to ensure a girl or boy. People who already have one or two children of one sex can hardly be faulted for wanting to "balance" their families by having one of each. And yet, this ought to be discouraged. If I spent a great deal of time and energy to get a boy in the hope of having a football player in the family, I think I would be less likely to accept it with good grace if the boy hated sports and spent all his spare time at the piano. If I insisted on having a girl because I believed that as a grandparent I would be more likely to have close contact with the children of a daughter than of a son, I think I would find it much harder to raise a girl who saw motherhood as a choice rather than as a foregone conclusion. Parents whose preferences are compelling enough for them to take active steps to control the outcome, must, logically, be committed to certain strong gender role expectations. If they want a girl that badly, whether they are hoping for a Miss America or the next Catherine McKinnon, they are likely to make it difficult for the actual child to resist their expectations and to follow her own bent.

NOTES

1. Walter E. Nance, "Parables," in *Prescribing Our Future: Ethical Challenges in Genetic Counseling,* ed. Dianne M. Bartels, Bonnie S. LeRoy, and Arthur L. Caplan (New York: Aldine De Gruyter, 1993), p. 92.
2. National Society of Genetic Counselors, Code of Ethics, reprinted in *Prescribing Our Future,* pp. 169–71.
3. James R. Sorenson, "Genetic Counseling: Values that have Mattered," *Prescribing Our Future,* p. 11; Arthur L. Caplan, "The Ethics of Genetic Counseling," *Prescribing Our Future,* p. 161.
4. Charles Bosk, "Workplace Ideology," *Prescribing Our Future,* pp. 27–28.
5. Dianne M. Bartels, "Preface," *Prescribing Our Future,* pp. ix–xiii.
6. Barbara Katz Rothman, *The Tentative Pregnancy: Prenatal Diagnosis and the Future of Motherhood* (New York: Viking Press, 1986), p. 41.
7. Nance, "Parables," p. 92.
8. D. Lindhout, P. G. Frets, and M. C. Niermeijer, "Approaches to Genetic Counseling," *Annals of the New York Academy of Sciences* 630 (1991): 223–29, at 224.
9. Jeffrey R. Botkin, "Fetal Privacy and Confidentiality," *Hastings Center Report* 25, no. 3 (1995): 32–39.
10. President's Commission for the Study of Ethical Problems in Biomedical and Behavioral Research, *Screening and Counseling for Genetic Conditions: A Report on the Ethical, Social, and Legal Implications of Genetic Screening, Counseling, and Education Programs* (Washington, DC: Government Printing Office, 1983), p. 56.
11. Joel Feinberg, "The Child's Right to an Open Future," in *Whose Child? Children's Rights, Parental Authority, and State Power,* ed. William Aiken and Hugh LaFollette (Totowa, N.J.: Littlefield, Adams & Co., 1980), pp. 124–53.
12. Prince v. Massachusetts, 321 U.S. 158 (1944), at 170.
13. Wisconsin v. Yoder, 406 U.S. 205 (1972).
14. William Galston, "Two Concepts of Liberalism," *Ethics* 105, no. 3 (1995): 516–34, at 521.
15. John Stuart Mill, *On Liberty* (New York: W.W. Norton, 1975), p. 55.
16. Galston, "Two Concepts of Liberalism," p. 522.
17. Feinberg, *The Child's Right,* pp. 134–35.
18. Cynthia Cohen, "'Give Me Children or I Shall Die!' New Reproductive Technologies and Harm to Children," *Hastings Center Report* 26, no. 2 (1996): 19–29.
19. Dan Brock, "The Non-Identity Problem and Genetic Harms," Bioethics 9, no. 3/4 (1995): 269–75, at 271.
20. Bonnie Steinbock and Ron McClamrock, "When Is Birth Unfair to the Child?" *Hastings Center Report* 24, no. 6 (1994): 15–21, at p. 17.
21. Brock, "The Non-Identity Problem," p. 272.
22. Edward Dolnick, "Deafness as Culture," *The Atlantic Monthly* 272/3 (1993): 37–53.
23. Amy Elizabeth Brusky, "Making Decisions for Deaf Children Regarding Cochlear Implants: The Legal Ramifications of Recognizing Deafness as a Culture Rather than a Disability," *Wisconsin Law Review* (1995): 235–70.
24. John B. Christiansen, "Sociological Implications of Hearing Loss," *Annals of the New York Academy of Science* 630 (1991): 230–35.
25. Dolnick, "Deafness as Culture," p. 38.

26. Nora Ellen Groce, *Everyone Here Spoke Sign Language: Hereditary Deafness on Martha's Vineyard* (Cambridge: Harvard University Press, 1985), p. 85.

27. Andrew Solomon; "Defiantly Deaf," *New York Times Magazine,* 28 August 1994: 40–45 et passim.

28. Dolnick, "Deafness as Culture," p. 43.

29. I am grateful to Thomas H. Murray and Ronald M. Green for bringing this topic to my attention.

30. "The Genetic Testing of Children," *Journal of Medical Genetics* 31 (1994): 785–97.

Disowning Knowledge: Issues in Genetic Testing

ROBERT WACHBROIT

Wachbroit considers whether physicians are justified in limiting patients' access to certain kinds of genetic tests or test results. He argues that sometimes such restrictions can be justified on scientific grounds, but too often they represent a "resurgent paternalism" in which physicians make nonmedical judgments out of concern that genetic information might cause social or psychological harm to patients. We should respect people's decisions to know—as well as their decisions not to know.

Last fall in Chicago, at a conference sponsored by the Alzheimer's Association and the National Institute on Aging, doctors and researchers met to discuss an ethical dilemma that has grown increasingly familiar as advances in diagnostic techniques outstrip the therapeutic abilities of the medical profession. The meeting focused on the use of a medical test for a particular heart condition—a test that can also, in some cases, predict with 90 percent accuracy whether someone will develop Alzheimer's disease by the age of 80. Should patients tested for the heart condition be told of their risk of contracting Alzheimer's disease, when there is little if anything medicine at present can do to prevent or ameliorate the condition?

Some people, including many of those attending the meeting, believe that the answer to this question is no: if the information is of little therapeutic value, it's of little value to the patient as well. It is wrong to burden the patient with troubling news when there is little or nothing that the physician can do about it.

At this stage in the history of medical practice, we may well be surprised to encounter such a response. Over the past few decades there has been an intense

effort to articulate and defend a person's right to be informed of his or her medical condition. Not so long ago, this right was not widely acknowledged. Health professionals generally assumed that, in the case of certain diseases, patients didn't really want to know. Moreover, even if they did want to, they wouldn't really understand the diagnosis; and even if they did want to know and could understand, they would be so psychologically harmed by the information that the result would likely be, if not suicide, then a clinical depression that would interfere with any sort of available care. Over the years the arguments attempting to defend this medical paternalism have been carefully examined and successfully undermined. The very idea of health professionals deciding whether a patient should know his or her medical condition is now routinely criticized in bioethics courses. Nonetheless, the advent of genetic testing appears to have provoked a resurgence of paternalistic thinking, especially in those cases where doctors can detect the genetic condition associated with a particular disease but are as yet unable to prevent or treat that disease.

The association between a genetic condition and a disease, and so the type of information a genetic test reveals, is subject to considerable variation. With results from the test for a specific mutation at the tip of chromosome 4, we can predict with near certainty whether an individual will suffer from

From "Disowning Knowledge: Issues in Genetic Testing," *Report from the Institute for Philosophy and Public Policy,* vol. 16, no. 3/4 (1996), pp. 14–18. Reprinted with permission.

Huntington's disease, a severe late-onset neurological disorder, but we can't yet tell when the disease will occur. With information from the test for mutations of the BRCA1 gene, we can, in particular situations, conclude that an individual has a susceptibility to a specific type of breast cancer, but we don't yet know what other conditions must be in place to trigger this susceptibility. With information from the test discussed in Chicago—a test that detects the presence of the apolipoprotein E genotype—we can, in particular situations, conclude that an individual is at an increased risk of contracting Alzheimer's disease, but there is still some controversy about the relative importance of this risk factor.

Recent concern has largely focused on these last two tests. At the Chicago meeting, the issue was the disclosure of certain additional information from a test already administered. In other cases, professional oganizations, as well as some advocacy groups, have proposed limits on the very availability of certain genetic tests. It is argued that tests for certain conditions should be restricted to research settings for the time being and not offered routinely or to all.

Are these proposals based on medical paternalism? Or can restrictions on genetic testing be defended on other grounds? I wish to examine possible justifications for limiting testing, distinguishing between those that are paternalistic and those that are not. I shall then consider the reasons and responsibilities that might influence patients in deciding whether to be tested or to receive genetic information.

Grounds for Restrictions

A discussion of reasons for restricting genetic testing should begin by acknowledging that there is no *right* to genetic testing. A right to be informed of test results (assuming that such a right exists) would not entail a right to *be* tested. And a "right to health care" (in the usual ways that phrase is understood) is not taken to include a right to have every diagnostic test, including genetic tests, performed. But though there is no right to genetic testing, a decision to withhold or restrict certain tests should be based on good public reasons (as opposed to private, economic reasons). This is especially true in the case of genetic tests, since in many cases genetic testing facilities, e.g., those connected with teaching hospitals, are supported, directly or indirectly, with public funds.

Reasons for restricting certain kinds of genetic tests can be divided into two broad categories. One set of reasons focuses on the *time and resources* that would be lost by the inappropriate use of genetic testing. Given the current state of knowledge, the results obtained from certain tests may include such a high number of false-positives or false-negatives, or be so difficult to interpret, that performing these tests would be a waste of the health professional's or laboratory's time, diverting resources from tests that are diagnostically more useful. For example, research has revealed a large number of possible mutations in BRCA1. Unless a woman's family history implicates a particular mutation in the occurrence of breast cancer, there is no point in testing her for that mutation; whatever the test result may be, it will not be interpretable. Thus, a decision not to offer BRCA1 testing to all women would be defensible on the grounds that widespread testing would needlessly draw upon society's limited resources of expertise and technology. Where the best available evidence shows that a given procedure would yield no meaningful information, it is entirely appropriate, so the argument goes, to restrict that procedure.

The second set of grounds for restricting the availability of genetic tests focuses on claims about the *social or psychological harms* that individuals might suffer from knowing their test results, where these harms are not offset by any corresponding medical benefit. Indeed, in many cases these harms are considered to be so palpable and the medical benefits so clearly nonexistent that it is assumed people would not want to know their genetic condition even if they had the opportunity.

One widely cited harm of knowing one's genetic condition arises from the prospect of discrimination in employment or insurance coverage. Someone with a known genetic condition indicating a susceptibility to breast cancer might be denied a job or a promotion, or denied health or life insurance, because she is regarded as a health risk and therefore as too great an economic risk. This concern about discrimination chiefly provides a reason why *third parties* should not be given access to an individual's genetic information. Yet an individual may well decide to forgo this information in order to maintain deniability. For example, suppose an insurance contract requires the individual to tell all she knows about her genetic condition, so that discovering that any information was withheld would constitute grounds for dismissing later claims. A person in this situation might well decide to remain ignorant, since she can't be penalized for withholding information she doesn't have.

However, a person can maintain ignorance of her genetic condition only up to a point, since genetic tests are not the only source of information about that condition. Standard family medical histories can sometimes tell a good deal, and claiming ignorance of this history may not be possible. If an individual suffers from Huntington's disease, then his or her children have a 50 percent probability of contracting it as well. If a woman's sister, mother, and aunt suffer from breast cancer, then it is likely that the woman is at greater risk than the general population of contracting breast cancer herself. Futhermore, genetic information is not always bad news. Someone who appears to be at risk for a certain disease because of her family history could discover, and so presumably assure an employer or insurer, that she is in fact not at risk because her test result was negative. Nevertheless, we should acknowledge that there can be perverse incentives to be ignorant, especially in the absence of appropriate laws regarding "genetic discrimination" or regulations regarding insurance and preexisting conditions.

A completely different harm that is associated with genetic information has to do with the psychological burden of knowing. Indeed, one writer refers to such infomation as "toxic knowledge." Unlike concerns about employment discrimination or insurance, fears about the burden of knowing speak directly to the question of the desirability of self-knowledge. For some people, the discovery that they have a genetic condition that places them at an especially high risk of suffering certain diseases could so depress them that the quality, joy, and purpose of their lives would evaporate. Moreover, even if the results of a genetic test were negative, some people might experience the reaction commonly known as "survivor's guilt," as they contemplate the prospects of their less fortunate siblings or other relatives.

The applicabilitiy of this reason will vary from person to person. Some people might be able to handle bad news calmly and move on, while others might become irrevocably incapacitated. We are individuals in how we each deal with the disappointments and tragedies in our lives. Genetic knowledge might be extremely toxic for one individual but less so for another. Presumably however, if a person does raise this issue in his own case, it probably applies.

Deciding for the Patient

It is this last set of reasons, when invoked to justify limits on the availability of genetic testing, that suggests a resurgent paternalism with respect to medical information. They involve explicit judgments by medical professionals about what would be good for the patient, where the "good" (i.e., the avoidance of certain social and psychological harms) extends beyond matters of medical expertise. Whatever force they may have as reasons an *individual* might give for not wanting to know genetic information, their persuasiveness weakens considerably when they are offered by third parties as reasons for restrictions on genetic testing. While certain people might be psychologically devastated by their test results, there is no evidence to support the assumption that most people will be so devastated; indeed, such an assumption flies in the face of our commonsense knowledge of people's differences. Similarly, the likelihood that people will confront employment discrimination or insurance problems, and the seriousness with which they regard such a prospect, will vary with circumstances. It is therefore paternalistic to cite these concerns as grounds for restricting genetic testing.

The same can be said of arguments that the results of genetic tests are too complex or ambiguous for patients to understand. Test results may identify risk factors rather than yield predictions; the information may consist of probabilities rather than certainties. In other medical contexts, however, the complexity of information is not accepted as an excuse for taking decisions out of the patient's hands. For example, we require physicians to obtain informed consent before they engage in an intervention. However complex the relevant information might be, usefully communicating it to the patient is a challenge to which the professional must rise.

A rejection of the paternalistic arguments does not yield the conclusion that all genetic tests should be available to the public. As we have seen, restrictions on the availability of certain genetic tests, or of any medical procedure, need not be based on paternalism. For example, none of these comments affects the legitimacy or persuasiveness of the scientific reasons for restricting certain tests.

Unfortunately, some of the professional organizations and advocacy groups seeking to restrict genetic testing have allowed an admixture of paternalism to enter into what would otherwise be sound scientific arguments. Instead of simply pointing out that a test for BRCA1 mutations can yield no useful information about most women, they express worries about the "fear" and "panic" that widespread testing might provoke. The first objection to indiscriminate testing is valid; the second is not. By including arguments that would in other contexts be rejected as unwarranted medical paternalism, these organizations have inadvertently ceded the moral high ground to the for-profit laboratories that have rushed in to perform these tests. Whether the labs can provide testing with the appropriate care and counseling is an open question. But efforts to regulate or even comment upon their services are likely to be ineffectual so long as the laboratories can self-righteously affirm the patient's "right to know" against the paternalism of their critics.

Similarly, when the researchers in Chicago tried to formulate a policy regarding the disclosure of test results, paternalistic assumptions clouded the issue. It was agreed that a cardiac test yielding information about the risk of Alzheimer's disease poses an ethical problem for the physician, who must either inform patients of their condition or withhold that information. But there is another alternative: the physician can tell patients, before testing for one condition, that information about another condition will be available. Whether or not to be informed becomes the patient's decision. Indeed, this option is standard in communicating the results of various medical tests, including results where disease is not at issue. The obstetrician performing amniocentesis doesn't typically agonize over whether to inform the couple of the fetus's sex. The couple are simply asked whether they want to know. And in our society at this time, the patient's desire to know or not to know is taken to settle the matter.

A Responsibility to Know

It is mainly those who wish to know their genetic condition who are likely to object to paternalistic restrictions on genetic testing. We cannot assume, however, that most people would fall into this category. In one recent study, only 43 percent of research subjects who were offered the BRCA1 test agreed to have it performed. Many who refused the test cited the concerns about employment and insurance that I have already described, while others pointed to the psychological distress that knowledge might bring.

If the challenge to medical paternalism is based on the notion that people should be free to make their own choices with respect to information, then in general the decision not to know should be as fully respected as the decision *to* know. No one would be in favor of frog-marching people to a genetics lab, having them tested, and then compelling them to listen to the results. The widely acknowledged right people have to refuse treatment surely includes a right to refuse diagnostic tests. If some people simply don't want their decisions about how they live their lives to depend upon genetic information, it would seem that they have no reason, and certainly no obligation, to know.

Nevertheless, there are many circumstances in which people might have a moral responsibility to know—a responsibility that grows out of their professional or personal obligations. The case for professional obligations, though limited, is fairly clear. The same reasoning that supports drug testing of individuals in particular professions—air traffic controller, train conductor, airline pilot—also supports claiming that these individuals have an obligation to know their genetic information. If an individual might have a condition that, if manifested, would interfere with his job performance in such a way as to endanger other people, that person has an obligation to know and monitor that condition, whether he wants to or not.

Since most of us are not employed in such professions, however, this obligation attaches to relatively few people. Moreover, most genetic conditions are unlikely to have an impact on the safety of other people. It is difficult to argue that an airline pilot's refusal to know whether she is at special risk of contracting breast cancer would endanger the lives of the passengers.

The ways in which personal obligations may generate a responsibility to know one's genetic condition have not been given comparable attention, even though they are more widely applicable. Most of us are enmeshed in a network of personal obligations and commitments—to families, dependents, loved ones. In many cases, with information about our medical condition, we can more effectively discharge our obligations, or at least avoid measures that, under the circumstances, may be futile. Consider the case of a 50-year-old parent of minor children who refuses to know whether he is at high risk of contracting Alzheimer's disease within the next ten years. His refusal to know might be irresponsible; it might amount to a failure to engage fully in the (not just financial) planning that is part of a parent's commitment to his children. Whether one has a moral responsibility to know one's genetic condition, and the strength of that responsibility, will depend upon the particulars of the situation. In all likelihood, however, a person's *responsibility* to know will not depend upon the strength of his or her *desire* to know or not to know.

The idea of having a responsibility to know can seem jarring at first. We are drawn to a picture of an individual, faced with the prospect of knowing, weighing how that knowledge would affect her personally. The thought that someone ought to know seems to go against our cultural assumptions, as if such an obligation were an unwelcome interference in the private relationship a person has with her own life. The problem with this picture of solitary individuals contemplating whether to know about their future is that it fits so few of us.

How should the responsibility of knowing be balanced against the possible burden and cost of knowing? There is probably little of use that can be said at this level of generality, since much will depend on the circumstances. The 50-year-old who has minor children, by birth or adoption, is in a different situation from the footloose 20-year-old. In any event it should be clear that if we are to make responsible decisions about accepting or refusing medical information, we must begin by acknowledging that these decisions affect others as well as ourselves.

The Non-Identity Problem and Genetic Harms—
The Case of Wrongful Handicaps

DAN W. BROCK

In this essay Brock scrutinizes the claim that it would be wrong not to prevent devastating genetic diseases or disabilities in a child. Some have held that failing to prevent an impairment is wrong because the child would be better off if the impairment were prevented. But Brock finds this view incoherent, arguing on logical grounds that a failure to prevent a serious disability cannot in fact *wrong the child*. He maintains instead that although failing to prevent a serious disability does not wrong the child, it is nevertheless wrong for "non-person-affecting" reasons.

The world-wide Human Genome Project (HGP) will produce information permitting genetic screening for an increasing number of genetic diseases and genetically based increased susceptibilities to diseases and other harmful conditions. In the foreseeable future, the capacities for preconception and prenatal

From *Bioethics*, vol. 9, no. 3, pp. 269–75, 1995. Reprinted with permission of Blackwell Publishing, Ltd. and the author.

screening for these diseases and conditions will almost certainly far outstrip our capacities for genetic therapy to correct for the harmful genes and their effects. The vast majority of decisions faced by prospective parents, consequently, will be whether to screen for particular genetic risks and/or conditions and when they are found to be present, whether to avoid conception or to terminate a pregnancy. Moreover, the vast majority of genetic risks that will be subject to screening will not be for diseases or conditions incompatible with life worth living—wrongful life cases—but rather for diseases and conditions sufficiently less severe or grave as to be compatible with having a life worth living. These genetic conditions and diseases will take different forms and many factors will affect the moral case for preventing them. But there is a systematic objection to all preconception wrongful handicap cases which must be resolved to clear the way for judgment about specific cases.

To fix attention on the general sort of case and problem in question, which is not restricted to the context of genetic disease, let us alter slightly a case of Derek Parfit's, call it case P1, in which a woman is told by her physician that she should not attempt to become pregnant now because she has a condition that would be highly likely to result in mild retardation in her child.[1] Her condition is easily and fully treatable by taking a quite safe medication for one month. If she takes the medication and delays becoming pregnant for two months there is every reason to expect that she will have a normal child. Because she is impatient to begin a family she refuses to wait, gets pregnant now, and gives birth to a child who is mildly retarded. In common sense moral views, the woman in case P1 acts wrongly, and in particular wrongs her child, by not preventing its handicap for such a morally trivial reason. Most people would likely say that her action in P1 is no different morally than if she failed to take the medicine in a case, P2, identical to P1 except that the condition is discovered, and so the medicine must be taken, after conception and when she is already pregnant, or if, in a case, P3, she failed to provide a similar medication to her born child, in each case necessary to prevent a comparable degree of mental retardation to her child. On what Derek Parfit has called the "no difference" view, the view of common sense morality that he endorses, her failure to employ the medication to prevent her child's mental retardation would be equally and seriously wrong in each of the three cases. But her action in P1, which is analogous in relevant respects to genetic screening to prevent handicaps, has a special feature that makes it not so easily shown to be wrong as common sense morality might suppose.

In wrongful handicap cases such as this, the person's handicap leaves him with a worthwhile life, a life that is better than no life at all. The philosophical problem, as noted earlier, is how this judgment is compatible with the common view that it would be wrong not to prevent the handicap. The difficulty is that it would *not* be better for the person with the handicap to have had it prevented since that can only be done by preventing him from ever having existed at all; preventing the handicap would deny the individual a worthwhile, although handicapped, life. The handicap could be prevented either by conceiving at a different time and/or under different circumstances, in which case a different child would be conceived, or by terminating the pregnancy, in which case this child never comes into existence and a different child may or may not be conceived instead. None of those possible means of preventing the handicap would be better for the child with the handicap—all would deny him or her a worthwhile life. But if the mother's failing to prevent the handicap has not made her child worse off, then failing to prevent the handicap does not harm her child. And if she does not harm her child by not preventing its handicap, then why does she wrong her child morally by failing to do so? How could making her child better off by giving it a life worth living, albeit a life with a significant handicap, wrong it? A wrong action must be bad for someone, but her choice to create her child with its handicap is bad for no one. So actions with effects for a child that would constitute seriously wrongful child abuse if done to an existing child are no harm, and so no wrong, if done to a child when they are inextricable from the choice to bring that child into existence with a worthwhile life. This argument threatens to undermine common and firmly held moral judgments, as well as public policy measures, concerning prevention of such handicaps to children.

Some philosophers accept the implications of this argument and hold that in choices of whether a particular individual will be brought into existence, only the interests of actual persons, not the interests of possible persons, which here means the individual whose existence is in question, are relevant to the choice.[2] So in case P1 above, the effects on the parents and the broader society, such as the greater childrearing costs and difficulties of having the mildly retarded child instead of taking the medication and having a normal child two months later are relevant to the decision; but the effects on and interests of the child itself who would be mildly retarded are not relevant. In P2 and P3, on the other hand, the fundamental reason the woman's action would be wrong is the easily preventable harm that she causes her child, or allows it to suffer.

I share with Parfit the no difference view that the woman's action would be equally wrong in P1, P2, and P3. As Parfit notes, the difficulty is identifying and formulating the moral principle on the basis of which the woman's actions in all three cases are equally wrong, and which therefore remedies the limits of traditional ethical theories and their principles of beneficence—doing good—and non-maleficence—not causing or preventing harm. Perhaps the most natural way of trying to account for the moral wrong in wrongful handicap cases is to abandon the feature of the moral principles we appealed to above that generates the difficulty when we move from standard cases of prevention of harm to already existing persons, as in P3 above, to harm prevention in what David Heyd has called genesis cases like P1. That feature is what philosophers have called the person-affecting property of principles of beneficence and non-maleficence, such as principle M:

> M: Those individuals responsible for a child's, or other dependent person's, welfare are morally required not to let it suffer a serious harm or handicap that they could have prevented without imposing substantial burdens or costs on themselves or others.

Since harms to persons must always be harms to some person, it may seem that there is no alternative to principles that are person-affecting, but that is not so. The alternative is clearest if we follow Derek Parfit by distinguishing "same person" from "same number" choices. In same person choices, the same persons exist in each of the different alternative courses of action from which an agent chooses. Cases P2 and P3 above were same person choices; the harm of mild retardation prevented is to the woman's fetus or born child. In same number choices, the same number of persons exist in each of the alternative courses of action from which an agent chooses, but the identities of some of the persons who exist in those alternatives are affected by the choice. P1 is a same number, but not same person choice—the choice affects *who*, which child, will exist. If the woman does not take the medication nor wait to conceive, her child is born mildly retarded, whereas if she takes the medication and waits to conceive she gives birth to a different child who is not mildly retarded. Arguably, the concept of "harm" is necessarily comparative, and so the concept of "harm prevention" may seem necessarily person-affecting, which is why harm prevention principles seem not to apply to different person choices like P1. But it is a mistake to believe that non person-affecting principles, even harm prevention principles, are not possible. Suppose for simplicity that the harm in question in P1 from the mild retardation is suffering and limited opportunity. Then there would be suffering and limited opportunity in P1 if the woman were to choose to have the mildly retarded child which will not exist and so would be prevented if she made the other choice and took the medication while waiting to conceive a different normal child. An example of a non person-affecting principle that applies to P1 is:

> N: Individuals are morally required not to let any possible child or other dependent person for whose welfare they are responsible experience serious suffering or limited opportunity if they can act so that, without imposing substantial burdens or costs on themselves or others, any alternative possible child or other dependent person for whose welfare they would be responsible will not experience serious suffering or limited opportunity.

Although, of course, suffering and limited opportunity must be experienced by some person—they cannot exist in disembodied form so in that sense N remains person-affecting, N does not require that the individuals who experience suffering and limited opportunity in one alternative exist without those effects in the other alternative; it is a same number, not same person principle. The non person-affecting nature of a moral principle concerning the evils of suffering and limited opportunity is clearer still in the following principle:

> N′: It is morally good to act in a way that results in less suffering and less limited opportunity in the world.

On N′, the woman in P1 acts in a morally good way by taking the medication and waiting to conceive a normal child. In the genetic screening analog, a couple acts in a morally good way by taking steps not to have a child whom they learn from genetic screening will experience suffering and limited opportunity that another child they could have instead would not experience. On N′, it is morally good to act in a way that makes the suffering and limited opportunity "avoidable by substitution," as Philip G. Peters, Jr. has put it.[3]

There is time to mention only one apparent difficulty with this way of avoiding the non-identity problem. It is that it does not account for the apparent aspect of the common sense moral judgment about P1 that the woman specifically wrongs her child by not preventing its handicap, that is, that her child is the victim of her wrong and so has a moral grievance against her. Her child is the person with the handicap which should have been prevented, but applying N or N′ the handicap should not have been prevented for the sake of that child since doing so would have made that child worse off (it would never have had its worthwhile life). Rather, applying N or N′, it should have been done only for the sake of less overall suffering and loss of opportunity.

This apparent difficulty with N and N′ is that they fail to identify a victim of the harm done who as victim has a special moral complaint against its mother. But when we appeal to non person-affecting principles to criticize the failure of the mother to prevent harm in P1, her child who suffers the harm is not a victim who is worse-off and so does not have a special moral complaint against her for her failure which must be accounted for. Unlike the typical cases of harm and rights violations, her child *cannot* claim that *he* has a special complaint against her because he is better, not worse, off as a result of her not meeting her obligation. It is therefore unclear that our moral principles must account for any special wrong done the woman's child, as opposed to a non person-affecting wrong done. This suggests that non person-affecting principles like N or N′ may not only be adequate for cases like P1, but that they are indeed preferable to person-affecting principles like M precisely because they do not direct us to the special standpoint and complaint of a victim who has been made worse-off; principles for P1 and other wrongful handicap cases should not direct us to a victim in that way because there is no victim who has been made worse-off and so has a special complaint.

Abandoning person-affecting principles of beneficence and non-maleficence to account for wrongful handicap cases may thus be a promising approach to those cases, especially if reflection on them leaves us confident of our judgment that the woman in P1 acts wrongly, but weakens our earlier confidence that she wrongs her child in letting it be born handicapped. The latter confidence that she wrongs her child may be further weakened by reflection on wrongful life, not wrongful handicap, cases. Wrongful life cases arise only when the child has a life that is overall not worth living, a life that is worse than no life at all. That is the correct threshold for the claim that the mother acted wrongly in conceiving and/or carrying the child to term knowing how bad its quality of life would be. But since her child's handicap in P1 could also be prevented only by not conceiving it, or by terminating her pregnancy after it had been conceived, she would not wrong it by allowing it to be born unless its life is not worth living, which by definition in wrongful handicap cases like P1 it is not. If she does act wrongly, then perhaps it is correct to insist that she nevertheless wrongs no one, as N and N′ imply, and that there is no wrong to her handicapped child for which our principles must account.

What principally explains resistance to this view, I believe, is the handicap that her child suffers, but if her child suffered a similar handicap as a result of an accident for which no one was at fault and which no one could have prevented, there would be no temptation to insist that it had been wronged. The difference, of course, is that she could, and I believe should, have prevented the handicap, but she could not have prevented this child from having the handicap except by never having conceived it, and so we should resist saying that she wrongs this child. In same number, but not same person, cases such as this, if anyone is wronged it is the class—her children—whom she permits without adequate reason or justification to be worse off than her children could have been.[4] But if this class—her children—has been wronged, it is in a sense from which it does not follow that any member of that class—that is, any one child—has been wronged. This is exactly the implication that N and N′ have. I conclude that the apparent difficulty with abandoning person-affecting principles—that they fail to identify a victim of the wrong who has a special moral complaint in favor of impersonal principles like N and N′ in wrongful handicap cases—is no difficulty after all.

It is worth pointing out one implication of my argument that any moral principle which best fits the features of wrongful handicap cases will be a non person-affecting principle. Others have attempted to solve Parfit's non-identity problem by seeking to show that person-affecting principles, such as appeal to moral rights, can be successfully applied to it.[5] But my argument has been that appeal to any person-affecting moral principles in cases of wrongful handicap like P1 will mischaracterize the wrong done. The very features of any appeal to person-affecting principles that are typically their advantage—that they make the wrong

a wrong done *to the child* and the loss from the wrong a loss suffered *by the child*—mischaracterize wrongful handicap cases. Non person-affecting principles are correct for wrongful handicap cases because the non-identity problem at the heart of those cases makes the wrong that is done *not* done to the child and the handicap *not a loss* that is suffered by anyone. No person-affecting account of wrongful handicap cases will be correct. The general philosophical non-identity problem is not an obstacle to the position that a woman in cases like P1 is guilty of causing a wrongful handicap.

NOTES

1. Derek Parfit, *Reasons and Persons*, Oxford University Press, 1984, ch. 16.
2. David Heyd, *Genethics: Moral Issues in the Creation of People*, Berkeley, CA: University of California Press. 1992.
3. Philip G. Peters, "Protecting the Unconceived: Nonexistence, Avoidability, and Reproductive Technology," *Arizona Law Review* 31, 1989, 487–548.
4. Peters, *op cit.*; Michael D. Bayles, "Harm to the Unconceived." *Philosophy & Public Affairs* 5, 1976, 292–304.
5. James Woodward, "The Non-Identity Problem," *Ethics* 96, July 1986, 804–31; see also, Derek Parfit, "Comments," *Ethics* 96, July 1986, 854–62.

Is Gene Therapy a Form of Eugenics?

JOHN HARRIS

Harris addresses a common claim in debates about genetic therapy—that while we have a duty to cure disease (to restore normal functioning), we do not have a duty to enhance or improve upon a normal healthy life. He rejects this distinction, arguing that "[t]here is in short no moral difference between attempts to cure dysfunction and attempts to enhance function where the enhancement protects life or health."

Eugenic A. *adj.* Pertaining or adapted to the production of fine offspring. B. *sb.* in *pl.* The science which treats of this. (*The Shorter Oxford English Dictionary*, 3rd edn., 1965.)

It has now become a serious necessity to better the breed of the human race. The average citizen is too base for the everyday work of modern civilization.

Civilized man has become possessed of vaster powers than in old times for good or ill but has made no corresponding advance in wits and goodness to enable him to conduct his conduct rightly. (Sir Francis Galton)

If, as I believe, gene therapy is in principle ethically sound except for its possible connection with eugenics, then there are two obvious ways of giving a simple and straightforward answer to a question such as this. The first is to say "yes it is, and so

From *Bioethics*, vol. 7, no. 2/3 (1993), pp. 178–187. Copyright © Basil Blackwell Ltd. 1993. Reprinted with permission.

what?" The second is to say "no it isn't, so we shouldn't worry." If we accept the first of the above definitions we might well be inclined to give the first of our two answers. If, on the other hand, we accept the sort of gloss that Ruth Chadwick gives on Galton's account, "those who are genetically weak should simply be discouraged from reproducing," either by incentives or compulsory measures, we get a somewhat different flavour, and one which might incline a decent person who favours gene therapy towards the second answer.

The nub of the problem turns on how we are to understand the objective of producing "fine children." Does "fine" mean "as fine as children normally are," or does it mean "as fine as a child can be"? Sorting out the ethics of the connection between gene therapy and eugenics seems to involve the resolution of two morally significant issues. The first is whether or not there is a relevant moral distinction between attempts to remove or repair dysfunction on the one hand and measures designed to enhance function on the other, such that it would be coherent to be in favour of curing dysfunction but against enhancing function? The second involves the question of whether gene therapy as a technique involves something specially morally problematic.

The Moral Continuum

Is it morally wrong to wish and hope for a fine baby girl or boy? Is it wrong to wish and hope that one's child will not be born disabled? I assume that my feeling that such hopes and wishes are not wrong is shared by every sane decent person. Now consider whether it would be wrong to wish and hope for the reverse? What would we think of someone who hoped and wished that their child would be born with disability? Again I need not spell out the answer to these questions.

But now let's bridge the gap between thought and action, between hopes and wishes and their fulfilment. What would we think of someone who, hoping and wishing for a fine healthy child, declined to take the steps necessary to secure this outcome when such steps were open to them?

Again I assume that unless those steps could be shown to be morally unacceptable our conclusions would be the same.

Consider the normal practice at IVF clinics where a woman who has had say, five eggs fertilized *in vitro*, wishes to use some of these embryos to become pregnant. Normal practice would be to insert two embryos or at most three. If pre-implantation screening had revealed two of the embryos to possess disabilities of one sort or another, would it be right to implant the two embryos with disability rather than the others? Would it be right to choose the implantation embryos randomly? Could it be defensible for a doctor to override the wishes of the mother and implant the disabled embryos rather than the healthy ones—would we applaud her for so doing?[1]

The answer that I expect to all these rhetorical questions will be obvious. It depends, however, on accepting that disability is somehow disabling and therefore undesirable. If it were not, there would be no motive to try to cure or obviate disability in health care more generally. If we believe that medical science should try to cure disability where possible, and that parents would be wrong to withhold from their disabled children cures as they become available, then we will be likely to agree on our answers to the rhetorical questions posed.

What Is Disability?

It is notoriously hard to give a satisfactory definition of disability although I believe we all know pretty clearly what we mean by it. A disability is surely a physical or mental condition we have a strong rational preference not to be in; it is, more importantly, a condition which is in some sense a "harmed condition."[2] I have in mind the sort of condition in which if a patient presented with it unconscious in the casualty department of a hospital and the condition could be easily and immediately reversed, but not reversed unless the doctor acts without delay, a doctor would be negligent were she not to attempt reversal. Or, one which, if a pregnant mother knew that it affected her fetus and knew also she could remove the condition by simple dietary adjustment, then to fail to do so would be to knowingly harm her child.[3]

To make clearer what's at issue here let's imagine that as a result of industrial effluent someone had contracted a condition that she felt had disabled or harmed her in some sense. How might she convince a court say, that she had suffered disability or injury?

The answer is obvious but necessarily vague. Whatever it would be plausible to say in answer to such a question is what I mean (and what is clearly meant) by disability and injury. It is not possible to stipulate exhaustively what would strike us as plausible here, but we know what injury is and we know what disability or incapacity is. If the condition in question was one which set premature limits on their lifespan—made their life shorter than it would be with treatment—or was one which rendered her specially vulnerable to infection, more vulnerable than others, we would surely recognize that she had been harmed and perhaps to some extent disabled. At the very least such events would be plausible candidates for the description ''injuries'' or "disabilities."

Against a background in which many people are standardly protected from birth or before against pollution hazards and infections and have their healthy life expectancy extended, it would surely be plausible to claim that failure to protect in this way constituted an injury and left them disabled. Because of their vulnerability to infection and to environmental pollutants, there would be places it was unsafe for them to go and people with whom they could not freely consort. These restrictions on liberty are surely at least prima facie disabling as is the increased relative vulnerability.

These points are crucial because it is sometimes said that while we have an obligation to cure disease—to restore normal functioning—we do not have an obligation to enhance or improve upon a normal healthy life, that enhancing function is permissive but could not be regarded as obligatory. But, what constitutes a normal healthy life is determined in part by technological and medical and other advances (hygiene, sanitation, etc.). It is normal now, for example, to be protected against tetanus; the continued provision of such protection is not merely permissive. If the AIDS pandemic continues unabated and the only prospect, or the best prospect, for stemming its advance is the use of gene therapy to insert genes coding for antibodies to AIDS, I cannot think that it would be coherent to regard making available such therapy as permissive rather than mandatory.[4]

If this seems still too like normal therapy to be convincing, suppose genes coding for repair enzymes which would not only repair radiation damage or damage by other environmental pollutants but would also prolong healthy life expectancy could be inserted into humans. Again, would it be permissible to let people continue suffering such damage when they could be protected against it? Would it in short be OK to let them suffer?

It is not normal for the human organism to be self-repairing in this way, this must be eugenic if anything is. But if available, its use would surely, like penicillin before it, be more than merely permissive.

Of course, there will be unclarity at the margins, but at least this conception of disability captures and emphasizes the central notion that a disability is disabling in some sense, that it is a harm to those who suffer it, and that to knowingly disable another individual or leave them disabled when we could remove the disability is to harm that individual.[5]

This is not an exhaustive definition of disability but it is a way of thinking about it which avoids certain obvious pitfalls. First it does not define disability in terms of any conception of normalcy. Secondly it does not depend on *post hoc* ratification by the subject of the condition—it is not a prediction about how the subject of the condition will feel. This is important because we need an account of disability we can use for the potentially self-conscious gametes, embryos, fetuses and neonates, and for the temporarily unconscious, which does not wait upon subsequent ratification by the person concerned.

With this account in mind we can extract the sting from at least one dimension of the charge that attempts to produce fine healthy children might be wrongful. Two related sorts of wrongfulness are often alleged here. One comes from some people and groups of people with disability or from their advocates. The second comes from those who are inclined to label such measures as attempts at eugenic control.

It is often said by those with disability or by their supporters[6] that abortion for disability, or failure to keep disabled infants alive as long as possible, or even positive infanticide for disabled neonates, constitutes discrimination against the disabled as a group, that it is tantamount to devaluing them as persons, to devaluing them in some existential sense. Alison Davis identifies this view with utilitarianism and comments further that "(i)t would also justify using me as a donor bank for someone more physically perfect (I am confined to a wheelchair due to spina bifida) and, depending on our view of relative worth, it would justify using any of us as a donor if someone of the status of Einstein or Beethoven, or even Bob Geldof, needed one of our organs to survive."[7] This is a possible version of utilitarianism, of course, but not I believe one espoused by anyone today. On the view assumed here and which I have defended in detail elsewhere,[8] all persons share the same moral status whether disabled or not. To decide not to keep a disabled neonate alive no more constitutes an attack on the disabled than does curing disability. To set the badly broken legs of an unconscious casualty who cannot consent does not constitute an attack on those confined to wheelchairs. To prefer to remove disability where we can is not to prefer non-disabled individuals as persons. To reiterate, if a pregnant mother can take steps to cure a disability affecting her fetus she should certainly do so, for to fail to do so is to deliberately handicap her child. She is not saying that she prefers those without disability as persons when she says she would prefer not to have a disabled child.

The same is analogously true of charges of eugenics in related circumstances. The wrong of practising eugenics is that it involves the assumption that "those who are genetically weak should be discouraged from reproducing" or are less morally important than other persons and that compulsory measures to prevent them reproducing might be defensible.

It is not that the genetically weak should be discouraged from reproducing but that everyone should be discouraged from reproducing children who will be significantly harmed by their genetic constitution.[9]

Indeed, gene therapy offers the prospect of enabling the genetically weak to reproduce and give birth to the genetically strong. It is to this prospect and to possible objections to it that we must now turn.

In so far as gene therapy might be used to delete specific genetic disorders in individuals or repair damage that had occurred genetically or in any other way, it seems straightforwardly analogous to any other sort of therapy and to fail to use it would

be deliberately to harm those individuals whom its use would protect.

It might thus, as we have just noted, enable individuals with genetic defects to be sure of having healthy rather than harmed children and thus liberate them from the terrible dilemma of whether or not to risk having children with genetic defects.

Suppose now that it becomes possible to use gene therapy to introduce into the human genome genes coding for antibodies to major infections like AIDS, hepatitis B, malaria and others, or coding for repair enzymes which could correct the most frequently occurring defects caused by radiation damage, or which could retard the ageing process and so lead to greater health longevity, or which might remove predispositions to heart disease, or which would destroy carcinogens or maybe permit human beings to tolerate other environmental pollutants?[10]

I have called individuals who might have these protections built into their germ line a "new breed."[11] It might be possible to use somatic cell therapy to make the same changes. I am not here interested in the alleged moral differences between germ line and somatic line therapy, though elsewhere I have argued strongly that there is no morally relevant difference.[12] The question we must address is whether it would be wrong to fail to protect individuals in ways like these which would effectively enhance their function rather than cure dysfunction, which would constitute improvements in human individuals or indeed to the human genome, rather than simple (though complex in another sense and sophisticated) repairs? I am assuming of course that the technique is tried, tested and safe.

To answer this question we need to know whether to fail to protect individuals whom we could protect in this way would constitute a harm to them.[13] The answer seems to be clearly that it would. If the gene therapy could enhance prospects for healthy longevity then just as today, someone who had a life expectancy of fifty years rather than one of seventy would be regarded as at a substantial disadvantage, so having one of only seventy when others were able to enjoy ninety or so would be analogously disadvantageous. However, even if we concentrate on increased resistance, or reduced susceptibility to disease, there would still be palpable harm involved. True, to be vulnerable is not necessaily to suffer the harm to which one is vulnerable, although even this may constitute some degree of psychological damage. However, the right analogy here seems to be drawn from aviation.

Suppose aircraft manufacturers could easily build in safety features which would render an aircraft immune to, or at least much less susceptible to, a wide range of aviation hazards. If they failed to do so we would regard them as culpable whether or not a particular aircraft did in fact succumb to any of these hazards in the course of its life. They would in short be like a parent who failed to protect her children from dangerous diseases via immunization or our imagined parent who fails to protect through gene therapy.

I hope enough has been said to make clear that where gene therapy will effect improvements to human beings or to human nature that provide protections from harm or the protection of life itself in the form of increases in life expectancy ("death postponing" is after all just "life saving" redescribed) then call it what you will, eugenics or not, we ought to be in favour of it. There is in short no moral difference between attempts to cure dysfunction and attempts to enhance function where the enhancement protects life or health.

What Sorts of Enhancement Protect Health?

I have drawn a distinction between attempts to protect life and health and other uses of gene therapy. I have done so mostly for the sake of brevity and to avoid the more contentious area of so-called cosmetic or frivolous uses of gene therapy. Equally and for analogous reasons I have here failed to distinguish between gene therapy on the germ line and gene therapy on the somatic line. I avoid contention here not out of distaste for combat but simply because to deploy the arguments necessary to defend cosmetic uses of gene therapy would take up more space than I have available now. Elsewhere I have deployed these arguments.[14] However, the distinction between preservation of life and health or normal medical uses and other uses of gene therapy is difficult to draw and it is worth here just illustrating this difficulty.

The British Government's "Committee on the Ethics of Gene Therapy" in its report to Parliament attempted to draw this distinction. The report, known by the surname of its chairman as *The Clothier Report*, suggested "in the current state of knowledge it would not be acceptable to attempt to change traits not associated with disease."[15] This was an attempt to rule out so called cosmetic uses of gene therapy which would include attempts to manipulate intelligence.[16]

Imagine two groups of mentally handicapped or educationally impaired children. In one the disability is traceable to a specific disease state or injury, in the other it has no obvious cause. Suppose now that gene therapy offered the chance of improving the intelligence of children generally and those in both these groups in particular. Those who think that using gene therapy to improve intelligence is wrong because it is not a dimension of health care would have to think that neither group of children should be helped, and those, like Clothier, who are marginally more enlightened would have to think that it might be ethical to help children in the first group but not those in the second.[17]

I must now turn to the question of whether or not gene therapy as a technique is specially morally problematic.

What's Wrong with Gene Therapy?

Gene therapy may of course be scientifically problematic in a number of ways and in so far as these might make the procedure unsafe we would have some reason to be suspicious of it. However, these problems are ethically uninteresting and I shall continue to assume that gene therapy is tried and tested from a scientific perspective. What else might be wrong with it?

One other ethical problem for gene therapy has been suggested and it deserves the small space left. Ruth Chadwick has given massive importance to the avoidance of doubt over one's genetic origins. Chadwick suggests that someone

> who discovers that her parents had an extra gene or genes added . . . may suffer from what today in the "problem pages" is called an "identity crisis" . . . Part of this may be an uncertainty about her genetic history. We have stressed the importance of this knowledge, and pointed out that when one does not know where 50 per cent of one's genes come from, it can cause unhappiness.[18]

Chadwick then asks whether this problem can be avoided if only a small amount of genetic makeup is involved. Her answer is equivocal but on balance she seems to feel that "we must be cautious about producing a situation where children feel they do not really belong anywhere, because their genetic history is confused."[19] This sounds mild enough until we examine the cash value of phrases like "can cause unhappiness" or "be cautious" as Chadwick uses them.

In discussing the alleged unhappiness caused by ignorance of 50 per cent of one's genetic origin, Chadwick argued strongly that such unhappiness was so serious that "it seems wise to restrict artificial reproduction to methods that do not involve donation of genetic material. This rules out AID, egg donation, embryo donation and partial surrogacy."[20]

In elevating doubt about one's genetic origin to a cause of unhappiness so poignant that it would be better that a child who might experience it had never been born, Chadwick ignores entirely the (in fact false) truism that, while motherhood is a fact, paternity is always merely a hypothesis. It is a wise child indeed that knows her father and since such doubt might reasonably cloud the lives of a high proportion of the population of the world, we have reason to be sceptical that its effects are so terrible that people should be prevented from reproducing except where such doubt can be ruled out.

The effect of Chadwick's conclusion is to deny gay couples and single people the possibility of reproducing. Chadwick denies this, suggesting "they are not being denied the opportunity to have children. If they are prepared to take the necessary steps ('the primitive sign of wanting is trying to get') their desire to beget can be satisfied." What are we to make of this? It seems almost self-consciously mischievous. In the first place, gay couples and single women resorting to what must, *ex hypothesi*, be distasteful sex with third parties merely for procreational purposes, are unlikely to preserve the identity of their sexual partners for the benefit of their offspring's alleged future peace of mind. If this is right then doubt over genetic origin will not be removed. Since Chadwick is explicitly addressing public policy issues she should in consistency advocate legislation against such a course of action rather than recommend it.

But surely, if we are to comtemplate legislating against practices which give rise to doubt about genetic origins we would need hard evidence not only that such practices harm the resulting children but that the harm is of such a high order that not only would it have been better that such children had never been born but also better that those who want such children should suffer the unhappiness consequent on a denial of their chance to have children using donated genetic material?

Where such harm is not only unavoidable but is an inherent part of sexual reproduction and must affect to some degree or other a high percentage of all births, it is surely at best unkind to use the fear of it as an excuse for discriminating against already persecuted minorities in the provision of reproductive services.

Where, as in the case of gene therapy, such donated[21] material also protects life and health or improves the human condition, we have an added reason to welcome it.

NOTES

This paper was presented at the Inaugural Congress of the International Association of Bioethics, Amsterdam, The Netherlands, 5–7 October 1992. I am grateful to the audience at that meeting and particularly to Dan Brock, Norman Daniels, Raanan Gillon, Douglas Maclean and Maurice de Wachter for helpful comments.

1. The argument here follows that of my paper "Should We Attempt to Eradicate Disability," published in the Proceedings of the Fifteenth International Wittgenstein Symposium.

2. See my discussion of the difference between harming and wronging in my *Wonderwoman & Superman: The Ethics of Human Biotechnology* (Oxford, 1992), ch. 4.

3. This goes for relatively minor conditions like the loss of a finger or deafness and also for disfiguring conditions right through to major disability like paraplegia.

4. In this sense the definition of disability is like that of "poverty."

5. See my more detailed account of the relationship between harming and wronging in my *Wonderwoman & Superman* (Oxford: Oxford University Press, 1992), ch. 4.

6. Who should of course include us all.

7. Davis, "The Status of Anencephalic Babies: should their bodies be used as donor banks?" *Journal of Medical Ethics*, 14 (1988), p. 150.

8. See my *The Value of Life* (London: Routledge, 1985 and 1990), ch. 1 and my "Not all babies should be kept alive as long as possible" in Raanan Gillon and Anne Lloyd (eds.), *Principles of Health Care Ethics* (Chichester: John Wiley, 1993).

9. I use the term "weak" here to echo Chadwick's use of the term. I take "genetically weak" to refer to those possessing a debilitating genetic condition or those who will inevitably pass on such a condition. All of us almost certainly carry some genetic abnormalities and are not thereby rendered "weak."

10. Here I borrow freely from my *Wonderwoman & Superman: The Ethics of Human Biotechnology* (Oxford University Press, 1992), ch. 9, where I discuss all these issues in greater depth than is possible here.

11. *Ibid.*

12. *Ibid.*, ch. 8.

13. For an elaboration on the importance of this distinction see my discussion of "the wrong of wrongful life" in *Wonderwoman & Superman*, ch. 4.

14. *Ibid.*, ch. 7.

15. *Report of the Committee on the Ethics of Gene Therapy*, presented to Parliament by Command of Her Majesty, January 1992. London HMSO para. 4. 22.

16. In fact intelligence is unlikely to prove responsive to such manipulation because of its multifactorial nature.

17. There would be analogous problems about attempts to block the use of gene therapy to change things like physical stature and height since it might be used in the treatment of achondroplasia or other forms of dwarfism.

18. Ruth Chadwick, *Ethics, Reproduction and Genetic Control* (London: Routledge, 1987), p. 126.

19. *Ibid.*, p. 127.

20. *Ibid.*, p. 39.

21. I use the term "donated" here, but I do not mean to rule out commerce in such genetic material. See my *Wonderwoman & Superman*, ch. 6.

Genetic Enhancement

WALTER GLANNON

On the question of genetic enhancement, Glannon argues that a line of demarcation can be drawn between treatment and enhancement. Gene therapy is permissible if it is intended to ensure or restore normal functions, but it is morally illegitimate if it is aimed at enhancing functions beyond normal. He thinks there are several moral problems with enhancement, but his main moral concern is "that it would give some people an unfair advantage over others with respect to competitive goods like beauty, sociability, and intelligence."

Gene therapy must be distinguished from genetic enhancement. The first is an intervention aimed at treating disease and restoring physical and mental functions and capacities to an adequate baseline. The second is an intervention aimed at improving functions and capacities that already are adequate. Genetic enhancement augments functions and capacities "that without intervention would be considered entirely normal."[1] Its goal is to "amplify 'normal' genes in order to make them better."[2] In chapter 1 [of *Genes and Future People*], I cited Norman Daniels's definitions of health and disease as well as what the notion of just health care entailed. This involved maintaining or restoring mental and physical functions at or to

normal levels, which was necessary to ensure fair equality of opportunity for all citizens. Insofar as this aim defines the goal of medicine, genetic enhancement falls outside this goal. Furthermore, insofar as this type of intervention is not part of the goal of medicine and has no place in a just health care system, there are no medical or moral reasons for genetically enhancing normal human functions and capacities.

Some have argued that it is mistaken to think that a clear line of demarcation can be drawn between treatment and enhancement, since certain forms of enhancement are employed to prevent disease. LeRoy Walters and Julie Gage Palmer refer to the immune system as an example to make this point:

> In current medical practice, the best example of a widely accepted health-related physical enhancement is immunization against infectious disease.

With immunization against diseases like polio and hepatitis B, what we are saying is in effect, "The immune system that we inherited from our parents may not be adequate to ward off certain viruses if we are exposed to them." Therefore, we will enhance the capabilities of our immune system by priming it to fight against these viruses.

From the current practice of immunizations against particular diseases, it would seem to be only a small step to try to enhance the general function of the immune system by genetic means. . . . In our view, the genetic enhancement of the immune system would be morally justifiable if this kind of enhancement assisted in preventing disease and did not cause offsetting harms to the people treated by the technique.[3]

Nevertheless, because the goal of the technique would be to prevent disease, it would not, strictly speaking, be enhancement, at least not in terms of the definitions given at the outset of this section. Genetically intervening in the immune system as described by Walters and Palmer is a means of maintaining it in proper working order so that it will be better able to ward off pathogens posing a threat to the organism as a whole. Thus, it is misleading to call this intervention "enhancement." When we consider what is normal human functioning, we refer to the whole human organism consisting of immune, endocrine, nervous, cardiovascular, and other systems, not to these systems understood as isolated parts. The normal functioning in question here pertains to the ability of the immune system to protect the organism from infectious agents and thus ensure its survival. Any preventive genetic intervention in this system would be designed to maintain the normal functions of the organism, not to restore them or raise them above the norm. It would be neither therapy nor enhancement but instead a form of maintenance. Therefore, the alleged ambiguity surrounding what Walters and Palmer call "enhancing" the immune system does not impugn the distinction between treatment and enhancement.

If enhancement could make adequately functioning bodily systems function even better, then presumably there would be no limit to the extent to which bodily functions can be enhanced. Yet, beyond a certain point, heightened immune sensitivity to infectious agents can lead to an overly aggressive response, resulting in autoimmune disease that can damage healthy cells, tissues, and organs. In fact, there would be a limit to the beneficial effects of genetic intervention in the immune system, a limit beyond which the equilibrium between humoral and cellular response mechanisms would be disturbed.[4] If any intervention ensured that the equilibrium of the immune system was maintained in proper working order, then it would be inappropriate to consider it as a form of enhancement.

To further support the treatment-enhancement distinction, consider a nongenetic intervention, the use of a bisphosphonate such as alendronate sodium. Its purpose is to prevent postmenopausal women from developing osteoporosis, or to rebuild bone in women or men who already have osteoporosis. Some might claim that, because it can increase bone density, it is a form of enhancement. But its more general purpose is to prevent bone fractures and thus maintain proper bone function so that one can have normal mobility and avoid the morbidity resulting from fractures. In terms of the functioning of the entire organism, therefore, it would be more accurate to consider the use of bisphosphonates as prevention, treatment, or maintenance rather than enhancement.

Some might raise a different question. Suppose that the parents of a child much shorter than the norm for his age persuaded a physician to give him growth hormone injections in order to increase his height. Suppose further that the child's shortness was not due to an iatrogenic cause, such as radiation to treat a brain tumor. Would this be treatment or enhancement? The question that should be asked regarding this issue is not whether the child's height is normal for his age group. Rather, the question should be whether his condition implies something less than normal physical functioning, such that he would have fewer opportunities for achievement and a decent minimum level of well-being over his lifetime. Diminutive stature alone does not necessarily imply that one's functioning is or will be so limited as to restrict one's opportunities for achievement. Of course, being short might limit one's opportunities if one wanted to become a professional basketball player. But most of us are quite flexible when it comes to formulating and carrying out life plans. Robert

Reich, the treasury secretary in President Clinton's first administration, is just one example of how one can achieve very much in life despite diminutive stature. If a child's stature significantly limited his functioning and opportunities, then growth-hormone injections should be considered therapeutic treatment. If his stature were not so limiting, then the injections should be considered enhancement.

Admittedly, there is gray area near the baseline of adequate functioning where it may be difficult to distinguish between treatment and enhancement. Accordingly, we should construe the baseline loosely or thickly enough to allow for some minor deviation above or below what would be considered normal functioning. An intervention for a condition near the baseline that would raise one's functioning clearly above the critical level should be considered an enhancement. An intervention for a condition making one's functioning fall clearly below the baseline, with the aim of raising one's functioning to the critical level, should be considered a treatment. For example, an athlete with a hemoglobin level slightly below the norm for people his age and mildly anemic may want to raise that level significantly in order to be more competitive in his sport. To the extent that his actual hemoglobin level does not interfere with his ordinary physical functioning, an intervention to significantly raise that level would be an instance of enhancement. In contrast, for a child who has severe thalassemia and severe anemia, with the risk of bone abnormalities and heart failure, an intervention to correct the disorder would be an instance of treatment.

The main moral concern about genetic enhancement of physical and mental traits is that it would give some people an unfair advantage over others with respect to competitive goods like beauty, sociability, and intelligence. . . . Enhancement would be unfair because only those who could afford the technology would have access to it, and many people are financially worse off than others through no fault of their own. Insofar as the possession of these goods gives some people an advantage over others in careers, income, and social status, the competitive nature of these goods suggests that there would be no limit to the benefits that improvements to physical and mental capacities would yield to those fortunate enough to avail themselves of the technology. This is altogether different from the example of immune-system enhancement. There would be no diminishing marginal value in the degree of competitive advantage that one could have over others for the social goods in question and presumably no limit to the value of enhancing the physical and mental capacities that would give one this advantage. Not having access to the technology that could manipulate genetic traits in such a way as to enhance these capacities would put one at a competitive disadvantage relative to others who would have access to it.

Advancing an argument similar to the one used by those who reject the treatment-enhancement distinction, one might hold that competitive goods collapse the categorical distinction between correcting deficient capacities and improving normal ones. This is because competitive goods are continuous, coming in degrees, and therefore the capacities that enable one to achieve these goods cannot be thought of as either normal or deficient.[5] Nevertheless, to the extent that any form of genetic intervention is motivated by the medical and moral aim to enable people to have adequate mental and physical functioning and fair equality of opportunity for a decent minimum level of well-being, the goods in question are not *competitive* but *basic*. In other words, the aim of any medical intervention by genetic means is to make people better off than they were before by raising or restoring them to an absolute baseline of normal physical and mental functioning, not to make them comparatively better off than others. Competitive goods above the baseline may be continuous; but the basic goods that enable someone to reach or remain at the baseline are not. Given that these two types of goods are distinct, and that they result from the distinct aims and practices of enhancement and treatment, we can affirm that enhancement and treatment can and should be treated separately. We can uphold the claim that the purpose of any genetic intervention should be to treat people's abnormal functions and restore them to a normal level, not to enhance those functions that already are normal.

As I have mentioned, genetic enhancement that gave some people an advantage over others in possessing competitive goods would entail considerable unfairness. A likely scenario would be one in which parents paid to use expensive genetic technology to raise the cognitive ability or improve the physical beauty of their children. This would give them an advantage over other children with whom they would compete for education, careers, and income. Children of parents who could not afford to pay for the technology would be at a comparative disadvantage. Even if the goods in question fell above the normal functional baseline, one still could maintain that such an advantage would be unfair. It would depend on people's ability to pay, and inequalities in income are unfair to the extent that they result from some factors beyond people's control.

We could not appeal to the notion of a genetic lottery to resolve the problem of fairness regarding genetic enhancement. For, as I argued in the last section [of *Genes and Future People*], such a lottery is better suited to meeting people's needs than their preferences, and enhancements correspond to people's preferences. Moreover, a lottery might only exacerbate the problem by reinforcing the perception of unfairness, depending on how losers in the lottery interpreted the fact that others won merely as a result of a random selection. One suggestion for resolving the fairness problem (short of banning the use of the technology altogether) would be to make genetic enhancement available to all. Of course, how this system could be financed is a question that admits of no easy answer. But the more important substantive point is that universal access to genetic enhancement would not be a solution. Indeed, the upshot of such access would provide a reason for prohibiting it.

Universal availability of genetic enhancement would mean that many competitive goods some people had over others would be canceled out collectively. The idea of a competitive advantage gradually would erode, and there would be more equality among people in their possession of goods. There would not be complete equality, however. Differing parental attitudes toward such goods as education could mean differences in the extent to which cognitive enhancement was utilized. Some parents would be more selective than others in sending their children to better schools or arranging for private tutors. So, there still would be some inequality in the general outcome of the enhancement. But quite apart from this, the process of neutralizing competitive goods

could end up being self-defeating on a collective level.[6] More specifically, one probable side-effect of boosting children's mental capacity on a broad scale would be some brain damage resulting in cognitive and affective impairment in some of the children who received the genetic enhancement. The net social cost of using the technology would outweigh any social advantage of everyone using it. If no one is made better off than others in their possession of social goods, but some people are made worse off than they were before in terms of their mental functioning, then the net social disadvantage would provide a reason for prohibiting collective genetic enhancement.

There is another moral aspect of enhancement that should be considered. I have maintained that inequalities above the baseline of normal physical and mental functioning are of no great moral importance and may be neutral on the question of fairness. Although equality and fairness are closely related, one does not necessarily imply the other. Again, fairness pertains to meeting people's needs. Once these needs have been met, inequalities in the possession of goods relating to preferences are not so morally significant. Thus, if the idea of an absolute baseline implies that people's basic physical and mental needs have been met, and if people who are comparatively better or worse off than others all have functioning at or above the baseline, then any inequalities in functioning above this level should not matter very much morally. If this is plausible, then it seems to follow that there would be nothing unfair and hence nothing morally objectionable about enhancements that made some people better off than others above the baseline. Nevertheless, this could undermine our belief in the importance of the fundamental equality of all people, regardless of how well off they are in absolute terms. Equality is one of the social bases of self-respect, which is essential for social harmony and stability.[7] Allowing inequalities in access to and possession of competitive goods at any level of functioning or welfare might erode this basis and the ideas of harmony and stability that rest on it. Although it would be difficult to measure, this type of social cost resulting from genetic enhancement could constitute another reason for prohibiting it.

Yet, suppose that we could manipulate certain genes to enhance our noncompetitive virtuous traits, such as altruism, generosity, and compassion.[8] Surely, these would contribute to a stable, well-ordered society and preserve the principle of fair equality of opportunity. Nothing in this program would be incompatible with the goal of medicine as the prevention and treatment of disease. But it would threaten the individual autonomy essential to us as moral agents who can be candidates for praise and blame, punishment and reward. What confers moral worth on our actions, and indeed on ourselves as agents, is our capacity to cultivate certain dispositions leading to actions. This cultivation involves the exercise of practical reason and a process of critical self-reflection, whereby we modify, eliminate, or reinforce dispositions and thereby come to identify with them as our own. Autonomy consists precisely in this process of reflection and identification. It is the capacity for reflective self-control that enables us to take responsibility for our mental states and the actions that issue from them. Given the importance of autonomy, it would be preferable to have fewer virtuous dispositions that we can identify with as our own than to have more virtuous dispositions implanted in us through genetic enhancement. These would threaten to undermine our moral agency because they would derive from an external source.[9] Even if our genes could be manipulated in such a way that our behavior always conformed to an algorithm for the morally correct course of action in every situation, it is unlikely that we would want it. Most of us would rather make autonomous choices that turned out not to lead to the best courses of action. This is because of the intrinsic importance of autonomy and the moral growth and maturity that come with making our own choices under uncertainty. The dispositions with which we come to identify, imperfect as they may be, are what make us autonomous and responsible moral agents. Enhancing these mental states through artificial means external to our own exercise of practical reason and our own process of identification would undermine our autonomy by making them alien to us.

In sum, there are four reasons why genetic enhancement would be morally objectionable. First, it would give an unfair advantage to some people over others because some would be able to pay for expensive enhancement procedures while others would not. Second, if we tried to remedy the first problem by making genetic enhancement universally accessible, then it would be collectively self-defeating. Although much competitive unfairness at the individual level would be canceled out at the collective level, there would be the unacceptable social cost of some people suffering from adverse cognitive or emotional effects of the enhancement. Third, inequalities resulting from enhancements above the baseline of normal physical and mental functioning could threaten to undermine the conviction in the fundamental importance of equality as one of the bases of self-respect, and in turn social solidarity and stability. Fourth, enhancement of noncompetitive dispositions would threaten to undermine the autonomy and moral agency essential to us as persons.

NOTES

1. Jon Gordon, "Genetic Enhancement in Humans," *Science* 283 (March 26, 1999): 2023–2024.

2. Eric Juengst, "Can Enhancement Be Distinguished from Prevention in Genetic Medicine?" *Journal of Medicine and Philosophy* 22 (1997): 125–142, and "What Does Enhancement Mean?" in Erik Parens, ed., *Enhancing Human Traits: Ethical and Social Implications* (Washington, DC: Georgetown University Press, 1998): 27–47, at 27. Also, Dan Brock, "Enhancements of Human Function: Some Distinctions for Policymakers," *Ibid.*, 48–69.

3. *The Ethics of Human Gene Therapy* (New York: Oxford University Press, 1997), 110. Instead of distinguishing between treatments and enhancements, Walters and Palmer distinguish between health-related and non-health-related enhancements. But I do not find this distinction to be very helpful.

4. Brock points this out in "Enhancements of Human Function," 59. Marc Lappe makes a more compelling case for the same point in *The Tao of Immunology* (New York: Plenum Press, 1997).

5. Kavka develops and defends the idea that competitive goods are continuous in "Upside Risks: Social Consequences of Beneficial Biotechnology," in Carl Cranor, ed., *Are Genes Us? The Social Consequences of the New Genetics* (New Brunswick, NJ: Rutgers University Press, 1994): 155–179, at 164–165.

6. Kavka, "Upside Risks," 167. Also, Brock, "Enhancements of Human Function," 60; and Buchanan et al., *From Chance to Choice* (New York: Cambridge University Press, 2000), chap. 8.

7. Rawls makes this point in *A Theory of Justice* (Cambridge, MA: Harvard Belknap Press, 1971), 7–11,

and in "Social Unity and Primary Goods," in A. Sen and B. Williams, eds., *Utilitarianism and Beyond* (Cambridge: Cambridge University Press, 1982), 162. See also Daniels, *Just Health Care* (New York: Cambridge University Press, 1985).

8. Walters and Palmer present this thought-experiment in *The Ethics of Human Gene Therapy*, 123–128. As they note, Jonathan Glover introduced this idea in *What Sort of People Should There Be?* (Harmondsworth: Penguin, 1984).

9. Drawing on the work of Lionel Trilling and Charles Taylor, Carl Elliott discusses cognitive and affective enhancements that undermine what he calls the "ethics of authenticity" in "The Tyranny of Happiness: Ethics and Cosmetic Psychopharmacology," in Parens, *Enhancing Human Traits*, 177–188. Also relevant to this issue is Harry Frankfurt, "Identification and Externality," in Frankfurt, *The Importance of What We Care About* (New York: Cambridge University Press, 1989): 58–68.

Genetic Interventions and the Ethics of Enhancement of Human Beings

JULIAN SAVULESCU

Julian Savulescu is an Australian philosopher and bioethicist and the Uehiro Professor of Practical Ethics at the University of Oxford. Savulescu explores the morality of genetic enhancement, presenting three arguments in favor of the ethical use of enhancement while critiquing the main objections to it. He asserts that not only is enhancement permissible; it is a moral obligation.

Should we use science and medical technology not just to prevent or treat disease, but to intervene at the most basic biological levels to improve biology and enhance people's lives? By enhance, I mean help them to live a longer and/or better life than normal. There are various ways in which we can enhance people but I want to focus on biological enhancement, especially genetic enhancement.

There has been considerable recent debate on the ethics of human enhancement. A number of prominent authors have been concerned about or critical of the use of technology to alter or enhance human beings, citing threats to human nature and dignity as one basis for these concerns. The President's Council Report entitled *Beyond Therapy* was strongly critical of human enhancement. Michael Sandel, in a widely discussed article, has suggested that the problem with genetic enhancement "is in the hubris of the designing parents, in their drive to master the mystery of birth. . . . [I]t would disfigure the relation between

parent and child, and deprive the parent of the humility and enlarged human sympathies that an openness to the unbidden can cultivate. . . . [T]he promise of mastery is flawed. It threatens to banish our appreciation of life as a gift, and to leave us with nothing to affirm or behold outside our own will."

Frances Kamm has given a detailed rebuttal of Sandel's arguments, arguing that human enhancement is permissible. Nicholas Agar, in his book, *Liberal Eugenics*, argues that enhancement should be permissible but not obligatory. He argues that what distinguishes liberal eugenics from the objectionable eugenic practices of the Nazis is that it is not based on a single conception of a desirable genome and that it is voluntary and not obligatory.

. . . I want to argue that far from being merely permissible, we have a moral obligation or moral reason to enhance ourselves and our children. Indeed, we have the same kind of obligation as we have to treat and prevent disease. Not only *can* we enhance, we *should* enhance. . . .

From Julian Savulescu, "Genetic Interventions and the Ethics of Enhancement of Human Beings," in *The Oxford Handbook of Bioethics*, ed. Bonnie Steinbock (Oxford: Oxford University Press, 2007), pp. 516–35 (http://www. practicalethics.ox.ac.uk/).

The Ethics of Enhancement

I will now give three arguments in favor of enhancement and then consider several objections.

First Argument for Enhancement: Choosing Not to Enhance Is Wrong

Consider the case of the Neglectful Parents. The Neglectful parents give birth to a child with a special condition. The child has a stunning intellect but requires a simple, readily available, cheap dietary supplement to sustain his intellect. But they neglect the diet of this child and this results in a child with a stunning intellect becoming normal. This is clearly wrong.

But now consider the case of the Lazy Parents. They have a child who has a normal intellect but if they introduced the same dietary supplement, the child's intellect would rise to the same level as the child of the Neglectful Parent. They can't be bothered with improving the child's diet so the child remains with a normal intellect. Failure to institute dietary supplementation means a normal child fails to achieve a stunning intellect. The inaction of the Lazy Parents is as wrong as the inaction of the Neglectful Parents. It has exactly the same consequence: a child exists who could have had a stunning intellect but is instead normal.

Some argue that it is not wrong to fail to bring about the best state of affairs. This may or may not be the case. But in these kinds of case, when there are no other relevant moral considerations, the failure to introduce a diet which sustains a more desirable state is as wrong as the failure to introduce a diet which brings about a more desirable state. The costs of inaction are the same, as are the parental obligations.

If we substitute "biological intervention" for "diet," we see that in order not to wrong our children, we should enhance them. Unless there is something special and optimal about our children's physical, psychological or cognitive abilities, or something different about other biological interventions, it would be wrong not to enhance them.

Second Argument: Consistency

Some will object that, while we do have an obligation to institute better diets, biological interventions like genetic interventions are different [from] dietary supplementation. I will argue that there is no difference between these interventions.

In general, we accept environmental interventions to improve our children. Education, diet and training are all used to make our children better people and increase their opportunities in life. We train children to be well behaved, co-operative and intelligent. Indeed, researchers are looking at ways to make the environment more stimulating for young children to maximize their intellectual development. But in the study of the rat model of Huntington's Disease, the stimulating environment acted to change the brain structure of the rats. The drug Prozac acted in just the same way. These environmental manipulations do not act mysteriously. They alter our biology.

The most striking example of this is a study of rats which were extensively mothered and rats who were not mothered. The mothered rats showed genetic changes (changes in the methylation of the DNA) which were passed on to the next generation. As Michael Meaney has observed, "Early experience can actually modify protein-DNA interactions that regulate gene expression." More generally, environmental manipulations can profoundly affect biology. Maternal care and stress have been associated with abnormal brain (hippocampal) development, involving altered nerve growth factors and cognitive, psychological and immune deficits later in life.

Some argue that genetic manipulations are different because they are irreversible. But environmental interventions can equally be irreversible. Child neglect or abuse can scar a person for life. It may be impossible to unlearn the skill of playing the piano or riding a bike, once learned. One may be wobbly, but one is a novice only once. Just as the example of mothering of rats shows that environmental interventions can cause biological changes which are passed onto the next generation, so too can environmental interventions be irreversible, or very difficult to reverse, within one generation.

Why should we allow environmental manipulations which alter our biology but not direct biological manipulations? What is the moral difference between producing a smarter child by immersing that child in a stimulating environment, giving the child a drug or directly altering the child's brain or genes?

One example of a drug which alters brain chemistry is Prozac. It is a serotonin reuptake inhibitor. Early in life it acts as a nerve growth factor. But it may alter the brain early in life to make it more prone to stress and anxiety later in life, by altering receptor development (*Science*, 29 October 2004). People with a polymorphism that reduced their serotonin activity were more likely than others to become depressed in response to stressful experiences (*Science*, 18 July 2003). Both drugs like Prozac and maternal deprivation may have the same biological effects.

If the outcome is the same, why treat biological manipulation differently from environmental manipulation? Not only may a favorable environment improve a child's biology and increase a child's opportunities, so too may direct biological interventions. Couples should maximize the genetic opportunity of their children to lead a good life and a productive, cooperative social existence. There is no relevant moral difference between environmental and genetic intervention.

Third Argument: No Difference to Treating Disease

If we accept the treatment and prevention of disease, we should accept enhancement. The goodness of health is what drives a moral obligation to treat or prevent disease. But health is not what ultimately matters—health enables us to live well; disease prevents us from doing what we want and what is good. Health is instrumentally valuable—valuable as a resource that allows us to do what really matters, that is, lead a good life.

What constitutes a good life is a deep philosophical question. According to hedonistic theories, what is good is having pleasant experiences and being happy. According to desire fulfillment theories, and economics, what matters is having our preferences satisfied. According to objective theories, certain activities are good for people—developing deep personal relationships, developing talents, understanding oneself and the world, gaining knowledge, being a part of a family, and so on. We need not decide on which of these theories is correct to understand what is bad about ill health. Disease is important because it causes pain, is not what we want and stops us engaging in those activities that giving meaning to life. Sometimes people trade health for well-being—mountain climbers take on risk to achieve, smokers sometimes believe that

the pleasures outweigh the risks of smoking, and so on. Life is about managing risk to health and life to promote well-being.

Beneficence—the moral obligation to benefit people—provides a strong reason to enhance people insofar as the biological enhancement increases their chance of having a better life. But can biological enhancements increase people's opportunities for well-being? There are reasons to believe they might.

Many of our biological and psychological characteristics profoundly affect how well our lives go. In the 1960s Walter Mischel conducted impulse control experiments where 4-year-old children were left in a room with one marshmallow, after being told that if they did not eat the marshmallow, they could later have two. Some children would eat it as soon as the researcher left, others would use a variety of strategies to help control their behavior and ignore the temptation of the single marshmallow. A decade later, they reinterviewed the children and found that those who were better at delaying gratification had more friends, better academic performance and more motivation to succeed. Whether the child had grabbed for the marshmallow had a much stronger bearing on their SAT scores than did their IQ.

Impulse control has also been linked to socioeconomic control and avoiding conflict with the law. The problems of a hot and uncontrollable temper can be profound.

Shyness too can greatly restrict a life. I remember one newspaper story about a woman who blushed violet every time she went into a social situation. This led her to a hermitic, miserable existence. She eventually had the autonomic nerves to her face surgically cut. This revolutionized her life and had a greater effect on her well-being than the treatment of many diseases.

Buchanan and colleagues have discussed the value of "all purpose goods." These are traits which are valuable regardless of which kind of life a person choose to live. They give us greater all-around capacities to live a vast array of lives. Examples include intelligence, memory, self-discipline, patience, empathy, a sense of humor, optimism and just having a sunny temperament. All of these characteristics—sometimes may include virtues—may have some biological and psychological basis capable of manipulation with technology.

Technology might even be used to improve our *moral character*. We certainly seek through good instruction and example, discipline and other methods to make better children. It may be possible to alter biology to make people predisposed to be more moral by promoting empathy, imagination, sympathy, fairness, honesty, etc.

Insofar as these characteristics have some genetic basis, genetic manipulation could benefit us. There is reason to believe that complex virtues like fairmindedness may have a biological basis. In one famous experiment, a monkey was trained to perform a task and rewarded either a grape or piece of cucumber. He preferred the grape. On one occasion, he performed the task successfully and was given a piece of cucumber. He watched as another monkey who had not performed the task was given a grape. He became very angry. This shows that even monkeys have a sense of fairness and desert—or at least self-interest!

At the other end, there are characteristics which we believe do not make for a good and happy life. One Dutch family illustrates the extreme end of the spectrum. For over 30 years this family recognized that there were a disproportionate number of male family members who exhibited aggressive and criminal behavior. This was characterized by aggressive outbursts resulting in arson, attempted rape and exhibitionism. The behavior has been documented for almost forty years ago by an unaffected maternal grandfather who could not understand why some of the men in his family appeared to be prone to this type of behavior. Male relatives who did not display this aggressive behavior did not express *any* type of abnormal behavior. Unaffected males reported difficulty in understanding the behavior of their brothers and cousins. Sisters of the males who demonstrated these extremely aggressive outbursts reported intense fear of their brothers. The behavior did not appear to be related to environment and appeared consistently in different parts of the family, regardless of social context and degree of social contact. All affected males were also found to be mildly mentally retarded with a

typical IQ of about 85 (females had normal intelligence). When a family tree was constructed, the pattern of inheritance was clearly X-linked recessive. This means, roughly, that women can carry the gene without being affected; 50 percent of men at risk of inheriting the gene get the gene and are affected by the disease.

Genetic analysis suggested that the likely defective gene was a part of the X chromosome known as the Monoamine Oxidase (MAO) region. The MAO region codes for two enzymes which assist in the breakdown of neurotransmitters. Neurotransmitters are substances that play a key role in the conduction of nerve impulses in our brain. Enzymes like the monoamine oxidases are required to degrade the neurotransmitters after they have performed their desired task. It was suggested that the monoamine oxidase activity might be disturbed in the affected individuals. Urine analysis showed a higher than normal amount of neurotransmitters being excreted in the urine of affected males. These results found were consistent with a reduction in the functioning of one of the enzymes (monoamine oxidase A).

How could such a mutation result in violent and antisocial behavior? A deficiency of the enzyme results in a buildup of neurotransmitters. These abnormal levels of neurotransmitters result in excessive, and even violent, reactions to stress. This hypothesis was further supported by the finding that genetically modified mice which lack this enzyme are more aggressive.

This family is an extreme example of how genes can influence behavior. This mutation has only been isolated in this family. Most genetic contributions to behavior will be weaker predispositions. Yet there may be some association between genes and behavior which results in criminal prosecution and other antisocial behavior.

How could such information be used? Some criminals have attempted a "genetic defense" in the U.S. which stated that their genes caused them to commit the crime. This has never succeeded. However, it is clear that a couple should be allowed to use this test to select offspring who do not have the mutation which predisposes them to act in this way. And if interventions were available, it might be rational to correct it. Children without this mutation have a better chance of a better life.

"Genes, Not Men, May Hold the Key to Female Pleasure" ran the title of one recent newspaper article. It reported the results of a large study of female identical twins in Britain and Australia. It found that "genes accounted for 31 percent of the chance of having an orgasm during intercourse and 51 percent during masturbation." It concluded that the "ability to gain sexual satisfaction is largely inherited" and went on to speculate that "[t]he genes involved could be linked to physical differences is sex organs and hormone levels or factors such as mood and anxiety."

Our biology profoundly affects how our lives go. If we can increase sexual satisfaction by modifying biology, we should. Indeed, vast numbers of men attempt to do this already through the use of Viagra.

Summary: The Case in Favor of Enhancement

What matters is human well-being, not only treatment and prevention of disease. Our biology affects our opportunities to live well. The biological route to improvement is no different [from] the environmental. Biological manipulation to increase opportunity is ethical. If we have an obligation to treat and prevent disease, we have an obligation to try to manipulate these characteristics to give an individual the best opportunity [for] the best life.

How Do We Decide?

If we are to enhance certain qualities, how should we decide which to choose? Eugenics was the movement early last century which aimed to use selective breeding to prevent degeneration of the gene pool by weeding out criminals, those with mental illness and the poor, on the false belief that these conditions were simple genetic disorders. The eugenics movement had its inglorious peak when the Nazis moved beyond sterilization to extermination of the genetically unfit.

What was objectionable about the eugenics movement, besides its shoddy scientific basis, was that it involved the imposition of a State vision for a healthy population and aimed to achieve this through coercion. The eugenics movement was not aimed at what was good for individuals, but rather what benefited society. Modern eugenics in the form of testing for disorders, such as Down syndrome, occurs very commonly but is acceptable because it is voluntary, gives couples a choice over what kind of child to have and enables them to have a child with the greatest opportunity for a good life.

There are four possible ways in which our genes and biology will be decided.

1. Nature or God
2. "Experts"—philosophers, bioethicists, psychologists, scientists
3. "Authorities"—government, doctors
4. By people themselves—liberty and autonomy

It is a basic principle of liberal states like the UK that the State be "neutral" to different conceptions of the good life. This means that we allow individuals to lead the life that they believe is best for themselves—respect for their personal autonomy or capacity for self-rule. The sole ground for interference is when that individual choice may harm others. Advice, persuasion, information, dialogue are permissible. But coercion and infringement of liberty are impermissible.

There are limits to what a liberal state should provide:

1. Safety—the intervention should be reasonably safe.
2. Harm to others—the intervention (like some manipulation that increases uncontrollable aggressiveness) should not result in harm. Such harm should not be direct or indirect, for example, by causing some unfair competitive advantage.
3. Distributive justice—the interventions should be distributed according to principles of justice.

The situation is more complex with young children, embryos and fetuses who are incompetent. These human beings are not autonomous and cannot make choices themselves about whether a putative enhancement is a benefit or harm. If a proposed intervention can be delayed until that human reaches maturity and can decide for himself or herself, then the intervention should be delayed. However, many genetic interventions will have to be performed very early in life if they are to have an effect. Decisions about such interventions should be left to parents, according to a principle of procreative liberty and autonomy. This states that parents have the freedom to choose when to have children, how many children to have, and arguably what kind of children to have.

Just as parents have wide scope to decide on the conditions of the upbringing of their child, including schooling and religious education, they should have similar freedom over their children's genes. Procreative autonomy or liberty should be extended to enhancement for two reasons. Firstly, reproduction, bearing and raising children is a very private matter. Parents must bear much of the burden of having children and they have a legitimate stake in the nature of the child they must invest so much of their lives raising.

But there is a second reason. John Stuart Mill argued that when our actions only affect ourselves, we should be free to construct and act on our own conception of what is the best life for us. Mill was not a libertarian. He did not believe that such freedom was solely valuable for its own sake. He believed freedom was important for people to discover for themselves what kind of life is best for themselves. It is only through "experiments in living" that people discover what works for them. And do others see the richness and variety of lives that can be good. Mill strongly praised "originality" and variety in choice as being essential to discovering which lives are best for human beings.

Importantly, Mill believed that some lives are worse than others. Famously, he said it is better to be Socrates dissatisfied than a fool satisfied. He distinguished between "higher pleasures" of "feelings and imagination" and "lower pleasures" of "mere sensation." Mill criticized "ape-like imitation," subjugation of oneself to custom and fashion, indifference to individuality and lack of originality. Nonetheless, he was the champion of people's right to live their lives as they choose.

> "I have said that it is important to give the freest scope possible to uncustomary things, in order that it may appear in time which of these are fit to be converted into customs. But independence of action, and disregard of custom, are not solely deserving of

encouragement for the chance they afford that better modes of action, and customs more worthy of general adoption, may be struck out; nor is it only persons of decided mental superiority who have a just claim to carry on their lives in their own way. There is no reason that all human existence should be constructed on some one or small number of patterns. If a person possesses any tolerable amount of common sense and experience, his own mode of laying out his existence is the best, not because it is the best in itself, but because it is his own mode."

I believe that reproduction should be about having children with the best prospects. But to discover what are the best prospects, we must give individual couples the freedom to act on their own value judgement of what constitutes a life of good prospect. "Experiments in reproduction" are as important as "experiments in living" (as long as they don't harm the children who are produced.) For this reason, procreative freedom is important.

There is one important limit to procreative autonomy that is different [from] the limits to personal autonomy. The limits to procreative autonomy should be:

1. Safety
2. Harm to others
3. Distributive justice
4. *The parent's choices are based on a plausible conception of well-being and a better life for the child*
5. *Consistent with development of autonomy in child and a reasonable range of future life plans*

These last two limits are important. It makes for a higher standard of "proof" that an intervention will be an enhancement because the parents are making choices for their child, not themselves. The critical question to ask in considering whether to alter some gene related to complex behavior is: would the change be better for the individual? Is it better for the individual to have a tendency to be lazy or hardworking; monogamous or polygamous? These questions are difficult to answer. While we might let adults choose to be monogamous or polygamous, we would not let parents decide on their child's predispositions unless we were reasonably clear that some trait was better for the child.

There will be cases where some intervention is plausibly in a child's interests: increased empathy with other people, better capacity to understand oneself and the world around, or improved memory. One quality is especially associated with socioeconomic success and staying out of prison: impulse control. If it were possible to correct poor impulse control, we should correct it. Whether we should remove impulsiveness altogether is another question.

Joel Feinberg has described a child's right to an open future. An open future is one in which a child has a reasonable range of possible lives to choose from and an opportunity to choose what kind of person to be. That is, to develop autonomy. Some critics of enhancement have argued that genetic interventions are inconsistent with a child's right to an open future. Far from restricting a child's future, however, some biological interventions may increase the possible futures or at least their quality. It is hard to see how improved memory or empathy would restrict a child's future. Many worthwhile possibilities would be open. But is true that parental choices should not restrict the development of autonomy or [the] reasonable range of possible futures open to a child. In general, fewer enhancements will be permitted in children than in adult[s]. Some interventions, however, may still be clearly enhancements for our children and so just like vaccinations or other preventative health care.

Objections
I. Playing God or Against Nature
This objection has various forms. Some people in society believe that children are a gift, of God or of Nature, and that we should not interfere in human nature. Most people implicitly reject this view—we screen embryos and fetuses for diseases, even mild correctible diseases. We interfere in Nature or God's will when we vaccinate, provide pain relief to women in labor (despite objections of some earlier Christians that these practices thwarted God's will) and treat cancer. No one would object to the treatment of disability in a child, if it were possible. Why then, not treat the embryo with genetic therapy if that intervention is safe? This is no more thwarting God's will than giving antibiotics.

Another variant of this objection is that we are arrogant to assume we can have sufficient knowledge to meddle with human nature. Some people object that we cannot know the complexity of the human system, which is like an unknowable magnificent symphony. To attempt to enhance one characteristic may have other unknown, unforeseen effects elsewhere in the system. We should not play God—we should be humble and recognize the limitations of our knowledge. Unlike God, we are not omnipotent or omniscient.

A related objection is that genes are pleiotropic—which means they have different effects in different environments. The gene or genes which predispose to manic depression may also be responsible for heightened creativity and productivity.

One response to both of these objections is to limit our interventions, until our knowledge grows, to selections between different embryos and not intervene to enhance particular embryos or people. Since we would be choosing between complete systems on the basis of their type, we would not be interfering with the internal machinery. In this way, selection is less risky than enhancement.

But such precaution can be also misplaced when considering biological interventions. When benefits are on offer, such objections remind us to refrain from hubris and overconfidence. We must do adequate research before intervening. And because the benefits may be less than when we treat or prevent disease, we may require the standards of safety to be higher than for medical interventions. But we must weigh the risks against the benefit. If confidence is justifiably high, and benefits outweigh harms, we should enhance.

Once technology affords us with the power to enhance our and our children's lives, to fail to do so will be to be responsible for the consequences. To fail to treat our children's disease, is to wrong them. To fail to prevent them getting depression, is to wrong them. To fail to improve their physical, musical, psychological and other capacities is to wrong them, just as it would be to harm them if we gave them a toxic substance that stunted or reduced these capacities.

Another variant of the "Playing God" objection is that there is a special value in the balance and diversity that natural variation affords, and enhancement will reduce this. But insofar as we are products of evolution, we are merely random chance variations of genetic traits selected for our capacity to survive long enough to reproduce. There is no design to evolution. Evolution selects genes according to environment which confer the greatest chance of survival and reproduction. Evolution would select a tribe which was highly fertile but suffered great pain the whole of their lives over another tribe which was less fertile but suffered less pain. Medicine has changed evolution—we can now select individuals who experience less pain and disease. The next stage of human evolution will be rational evolution, where we select children who not only have the greatest chance of surviving, reproducing and being free of disease, but who have the greatest opportunities to have the best lives in their likely environment. Evolution was indifferent to how well our lives went. We are not. We want to retire, play golf, read and watch our grandchildren have children.

Enhancement is a misnomer. It suggests luxury. But enhancement is no luxury. Insofar as it promotes well-being, it is the very essence of what is necessary for a good human life.

There is no moral reason to preserve some traits—such as uncontrollable aggressiveness, a sociopathic personality or extreme deviousness. Tell the victim of rape and murder that we must preserve the natural balance and diversity.

2. Genetic Discrimination

Some people fear the creation of a two-class society of the enhanced and the unenhanced, where the inferior unenhanced are discriminated against and disadvantaged all through life.

We must remember that nature allots advantage and disadvantage with no gesture to fairness. Some are born horribly disadvantaged, destined to die after short and miserable lives. Some suffer great genetic disadvantage while others are born gifted, physically, musically or intellectually. There is no secret that there are "gifted" children naturally. Allowing choice to change our biology will, if anything, be more egalitarian—allowing the ungifted to approach the gifted. There is nothing fair about

the natural lottery—allowing enhancement may be more fair.

But more importantly, how well the lives of those who are disadvantaged go depends not on whether enhancement is permitted, but on the social institutions we have in place to protect the least well off and provide everyone with a fair go. People have disease and disability—egalitarian social institutions and laws against discrimination are designed to make sure everyone, regardless of natural inequality, has a decent chance of a decent life. This would be no different if enhancement were permitted. There is no necessary connection between enhancement and discrimination, just as there is no necessary connection between curing disability and discrimination against people with disability.

3. The Perfect Child, Sterility and Loss of the Mystery of Life

If we engineered perfect children, this objection goes, the world would be a sterile, monotonous place where everyone is the same, and the mystery and surprise of life is gone.

It is impossible to create perfect children. We can only attempt to create children with better opportunities [for] a better life. There will necessarily be difference. Even in the case of screening for disability, like Down syndrome, 10 percent of people choose not to abort a pregnancy known to have Down syndrome. People value different things. There will never be complete convergence. Moreover, there will remain massive challenges for individuals to meet in their personal relationships and in the hurdles our unpredictable environment presents. There will remain much mystery and challenge—we will just be better able to deal with these. We will still have to work to achieve, but our achievements may have greater value.

4. Against Human Nature

One of the major objections to enhancement is that it is against human nature. Common alternative phrasings are that enhancement is tampering with our nature or an affront to human dignity. I believe that what separates us from other animals is our rationality, our capacity to make normative judgements and act on the basis of reasons. When we make decisions to improve our lives by biological and other manipulations, we express our rationality and express what is fundamentally important about our nature. And if those manipulations improve our capacity to make rational and normative judgements, they further improve what is fundamentally human. Far from being against the human spirit, such improvements express the human spirit. To be human is to be better.

5. Enhancements Are Self-Defeating

Another familiar objection to enhancement is that enhancements will have self-defeating or other adverse social effects. A typical example is increase in height. If height is socially desired, then everyone will try to enhance the height of their children at great cost to themselves and the environment (as taller people consume more resources), with no advantage in the end since there will be no relative gain.

If a purported manipulation does not improve well-being or opportunity, there is no argument in favor of it. In this case, the manipulation is not an enhancement. In other cases, such as enhancement of intelligence, the enhancement of one individual may increase that individual's opportunities only at the expense of another. So-called positional goods are goods only in relative sense.

But many enhancements will have both positional and non-positional qualities. Intelligence is good not just because it allows an individual to be more competitive for complex jobs, but because it allows an individual to more rapidly process information in her own life, and to develop greater understanding of herself and others. These nonpositional effects should not be ignored. Moreover, even in the case of so-called purely positional goods, such as height, there may be important non-positional values. It is better to be taller to be a basketball player, but being tall is a disadvantage in balance sports such as gymnastics, skiing and surfing.

Nonetheless, if there are significant social consequences of enhancement, this is of course a valid objection. But it is not particular to enhancement—there is an old question about how far individuals in society can pursue their own self-interest at cost to others. It applies to education, health care, and virtually all areas of life.

Not all enhancements will be ethical. The critical issue is that the intervention is expected to bring about more benefits than harms to the individual. It must be safe and there must be a reasonable expectation of improvement. Some of the other features of ethical enhancements are summarized next.

What is an ethical enhancement?
1. It is in the person's interests
2. Reasonably safe
3. Increases the opportunity to have the best life
4. Promotes or does not unreasonably restrict the range of possible lives open to that person
5. Does not harm others directly through excessive costs by making it freely available (but balance against the costs of prohibition)
6. Does not place that individual at an unfair competitive advantage with respect to others, e.g., mind reading
7. The person retains significant control or responsibility for her achievements and self which cannot be wholly or directly attributed to the enhancement
8. Does not reinforce or increase unjust inequality and discrimination—economic inequality, racism (but balance the costs of social/environmental manipulations against biological manipulations)

What is an ethical enhancement for a child or incompetent human being?
All of the above plus:

1. The intervention cannot be delayed until the child can make its own decision
2. The intervention is plausibly in [the] child's interests
3. The intervention is compatible with the development of autonomy.

Conclusion

Enhancement is already occurring. In sport, human erythropoietin boosts red blood cells. Steroids and growth hormone improve muscle strength. Many people seek cognitive enhancement—nicotine, ritalin, modavigil, caffeine. Prozac, recreational drugs and alcohol all enhance mood. Viagra is used to improve sexual performance.

And of course mobile phones and airplanes are examples of external enhancing technologies. In the future, genetic technology, nanotechnology, and artificial intelligence may profoundly affect our capacities.

Will the future be better or just disease-free? We need to shift our frame of reference from health to life enhancement. What matters is how we live. Technology can now improve that. We have two options:

1. Intervention
   - Treating disease
   - Preventing disease
   - Supraprevention of disease—preventing disease in a radically unprecedented way
   - Protection of well-being
   - Enhancement of well-being
2. No intervention, and to remain in a state of nature—no treatment or prevention of disease, no technological enhancement.

I believe to be human is to be better. Or, at least, to strive to be better. We should be here for a *good* time, not just a *long* time. Enhancement, far from being merely permissible, is something we should aspire to achieve.

Germ-Line Gene Therapy

LEROY WALTERS AND JULIE GAGE PALMER

In this essay Walters and Palmer examine arguments for and against germ-line gene therapy. Major moral arguments in its favor include that it may be the only way to prevent damage to some people, that it may enable parents to avoid passing on a genetic disorder to children or grandchildren, and that this kind of therapy "best accords with the health professions' healing role and with the concern to protect rather than penalize individuals who have disabilities." Among the arguments against germ-line therapy are that any unanticipated negative effects will hurt not only the patient but also his descendants and that the intervention fails to show proper respect for preimplantation embryos and implanted fetuses. Walters and Palmer conclude that some of the pro arguments are strong and all of the con arguments are weak.

. . . Standard medical therapies, like somatic cell gene therapy, are somatic treatments and do not correct genetic defects in a patient's germ line. They may allow patients to live and to reproduce, passing on genetic mistakes which, without treatment, would not be perpetuated. Preimplantation and prenatal selection, like somatic medicine, may also result in a higher incidence of germ-line genetic defects because, unless they employ selective discard and selective abortion of unaffected carriers, both strategies increase the number of carriers of genetic defects that are born.

Successful germ-line gene replacement, on the other hand, will not perpetuate genetic mistakes. It will not only cure the patient at hand; it will also prevent the disease in question from arising in that patient's descendants. Applied to heterozygous carriers on a large scale, it could theoretically eliminate chosen disease-causing genes from the human gene pool.

As long as germ-line gene therapy must be performed on human zygotes or embryos one at a time after in vitro fertilization, it is likely to remain an expensive technology with limited use. Only if a technique is developed for performing gene

From *The Ethics of Human Gene Therapy* by LeRoy Walters and Julie Gage Palmer, pp. 78, 76–86. Copyright © 1997 by Oxford University Press. Reprinted with permission.

replacement or gene repair within the reproductive cells of human adults—perhaps through the injection of highly refined vectors that "home in" only on those cells (or their precursors in males)—are we likely to see the widespread diffusion of germ-line genetic intervention for disease prevention. . . .

For What Clinical Situations Will Germ-Line Gene Therapy Be Proposed?

It is difficult to predict the precise context in which germ-line gene therapy will first be considered. Tables 1 through 4 show four scenarios where the issue of germ-line intervention may at least be discussed at some point in the future.

TABLE I MODE OF INHERITANCE I

Both the wife and the husband are afflicted with a recessive genetic disorder. That is, both have two copies of the same malfunctioning gene at a particular site in their chromosomes. Therefore, all of their offspring are likely to be affected with the same genetic disorder.

TABLE 2 MODE OF INHERITANCE 2

Both the wife and the husband are carriers of a recessive genetic disorder. That is, each has one copy of a properly functioning and one copy of a malfunctioning gene at a particular site in their chromosomes. Following Mendel's laws, 25% of the couple's offspring are likely to be "normal," 50% are likely to be carriers like their parents, and 25% are likely to be afflicted with the genetic disorder.

TABLE 3 DISEASE CONDITION I

A diagnosable genetic disorder results in major irreversible damage to the brains of affected fetuses during the first trimester of pregnancy. There is no known method for making genetic repairs in the uterus during pregnancy. If any genetic repair is to be made, it must be completed before the embryo begins its intrauterine development.

TABLE 4 DISEASE CONDITION 2

A diagnosable genetic disorder affects many different cell types in many different parts of the bodies of patients affected by the disorder. Somatic cell gene therapy that targets a particular cell type is therefore unlikely to be successful in combating the disorder. Therefore, germ-line gene therapy delivered early enough to affect *all* cell types may be the only feasible way to prevent disease in a particular future person.

The kind of situation described in Table 1 is likely to arise as medical care succeeds in prolonging the lives of people with genetic disorders such as sickle cell disease or cystic fibrosis. If somatic cell gene therapy is employed in significant numbers of people afflicted with recessive genetic diseases, some of those people's somatic cells will be able to function normally, but their reproductive cells will remain unchanged, thus assuring that they will be carriers of genetic disease to the next generation. If two such phenotypically cured people marry and have children, all or almost all of their children will be afflicted with the disease which their parents had. Each succeeding generation of these children will need somatic cell gene therapy for the treatment of their disease.

Table 2 sketches a scenario frequently encountered by genetic counselors. In this case, germ-line genetic intervention could be viewed as an alternative to prenatal diagnosis and selective abortion of affected fetuses or to preimplantation diagnosis and the selective discard of affected early embryos. A couple might also elect germ-line genetic intervention in order to avoid producing children who are *carriers* of genetic defects, even if the children are not themselves afflicted with genetic disease. The parents would know that children who are carriers may one day face precisely the kind of difficult reproductive decisions that they as parents are facing.

In the type of case outlined in Table 3, somatic cell gene therapy might be effective if one could deliver it to the developing embryo and fetus during the earliest stages of pregnancy, that is, shortly after the embryo has implanted in the uterus. However, there is no known method of administering intrauterine therapy to an early first-trimester embryo, and a deferral of treatment until the second or third trimester would probably allow irreversible damage to occur. Preimplantation treatment, which would almost certainly affect the future germ-line cells as well as the future somatic cells, could be the only feasible approach to producing children who are not brain damaged, especially for couples who reject the alternative of selectively discarding early embryos.[1]

The scenario presented in Table 4 may be especially relevant to the development of particular kinds of cancers as a result of inborn genetic factors and subsequent mutations. For example, about 40% of people with a cancer of the retina called *retinoblastoma* transmit a dominant gene for this disorder to their children. In patients with this germ-line type of retinoblastoma, somatic mutational events that occur after birth seem to activate the cancer-causing gene and can result in multiple types of cancer developing in different cell types within the patient's body. For example, a kind of cancer called *osteogenic sarcoma* frequently develops later in life in patients who have been successfully treated for retinoblastoma.[2] With germ-line retinoblastoma, the only effective antidote to the development of multiple types of cancers may be early germ-line gene therapy that effectively repairs *all* of the cells in a developing embryo.[3]

The Needed Technological Breakthough: Gene Replacement or Gene Repair

As we noted earlier in this chapter [of *The Ethics of Human Gene Therapy*], the current technique for somatic-cell gene therapy relies on rather imprecise methods of gene addition. For safe and effective germ-line gene therapy, it seems likely that a more precisely targeted method of gene replacement or gene repair will be necessary. The most obvious reason for preferring gene replacement is that gene addition in embryos would result in their (later-developing) sperm or egg cells containing *both* the malfunctioning and the properly functioning genes. Thus, one undesirable effect of researchers' treating present or future reproductive cells by gene addition is that the researchers would be directly contributing to an increase in the number of malfunctioning

genes in future generations. In addition, if any of the germ-line disorders are dominant, as retinoblastoma seems to be, then only gene replacement is likely to eradicate the deleterious effects of the malfunctioning gene.

Major Ethical Arguments in Favor of Germ-Line Gene Therapy

In this and the following section we will analyze the major ethical arguments[4] for and against germ-line gene therapy.[5] For this analysis we will make the optimistic assumption that germ-line intervention methods will gradually be refined until they reach the point where gene replacement or gene repair is technically feasible and able to be accomplished in more than 95% of attempted gene transfer procedures. Thus, the following analysis presents the arguments for and against germ-line intervention under the most favorable conditions for such intervention.

A first argument in favor of germ-line intervention is that it may be the only way to prevent damage to particular biological individuals when that damage is caused by certain kinds of genetic defects. This argument is most closely related to the last two scenarios presented above. That is, only genetic modifications introduced into preimplantation embryos are likely to be early enough to affect all of the important cell types (as in retinoblastoma), or to reach a large enough fraction of brain cells, or to be in time to prevent irreversible damage to the developing embryo. In these circumstances the primary intent of gene therapy would, or at least could, be to provide gene therapy for the early embryo. A side effect of the intervention would be that all of the embryonic cells, including the reproductive cells that would later develop, would be genetically modified.[6]

A second moral argument for germ-line genetic intervention might be advanced by parents. It is that they wish to spare their children and grandchildren from either (1) having to undergo somatic cell gene therapy if they are born affected with a genetic defect or (2) having to face difficult decisions regarding possibly transmitting a disease-related gene to their own children and grandchildren. In our first scenario, admittedly a rare case, two homozygous parents who have a genetic disease know in advance that all of their offspring are likely to be affected with the same genetic disease. In the second scenario, there is a certain probability that the parents' offspring will be affected or carriers. An assumption lying behind this second argument is that parents should enjoy a realm of moral and legal protection when they are making good-faith decisions about the health of their children. Only if their decisions are clearly adverse to the health interests of the children should moral criticism or legal intervention be considered.

A third moral argument for germ-line intervention is more likely to be made by health professionals, public-health officials, and legislators casting a wary eye toward the expenditures for health care. This argument is that, from a social and economic point of view, germ-line intervention is more efficient than repeating somatic cell gene therapy generation after generation. From a medical and public health point of view, germ-line intervention fits better with the increasingly preferred model of disease prevention and health promotion. In the very long run, germ-line intervention, if applied to both affected individuals and asymptomatic carriers of serious genetic defects, could have a beneficial effect on the human gene pool and the frequency of genetic disease.[7]

A fourth argument refers to the roles of researchers and health professionals. As a general rule, researchers deserve to have the freedom to explore new modes of treating and/or preventing human disease.[8] To be sure, moral rules set limits on how this research is conducted. For example, animals involved in the preclinical stages of the research should be treated humanely. In addition, the human subjects involved in the clinical trials should be treated with respect. When and if germ-line gene therapy is some day validated as a safe and effective intervention, health care providers should be free to, and may have a moral obligation to, offer it to their patients as a possible treatment. This freedom is based on the professional's general obligation to seek out and offer the best possible therapeutic alternatives to patients and society's recognition of a sphere in which health professionals are at liberty to exercise their best judgment on behalf of their patients.

A fifth and final argument in favor of germ-line gene therapy is that this kind of intervention best accords with the health professions' healing role and with the concern to protect rather than penalize individuals who have disabilities. This argument is not simply a plea for protecting all embryos and fetuses from the time of fertilization forward. Both authors of this book [*The Ethics of Human Gene Therapy*] think that abortion is morally justifiable in certain circumstances. However, prenatal diagnosis followed by selective abortion and preimplantation diagnosis followed by selective discard seem to us to be uncomfortable and probably discriminatory halfway technologies that should eventually be replaced by effective modes of treatment. The options of selective abortion and selective discard essentially say to prospective parents, "There is nothing effective that the health care system has to offer. You may want to give up on this fetus or embryo and try again." To people with disabilities that are diagnosable at the prenatal or preimplantation stages of development the message of selective abortion and selective discard may seem more threatening. That message may be read as, "If we health professionals and prospective parents had known you were coming, we would have terminated your development and attempted to find or create a nondisabled replacement."

This argument is not intended to limit the legal access of couples to selective abortion in the case of serious health problems for the fetus. We support such access. Rather, it is an argument about what the long-term goal of medicine and society should be. In our view, that long-term goal should be to prevent disability and disease wherever possible. Where prevention is not possible, the second-best alternative is a cure or other definitive remedy. In cases where neither prevention nor cure is possible, our goal should be to help people cope with disability and disease while simultaneously seeking to find a cure.

Major Arguments Against Germ-Line Gene Therapy

First, if the technique has unanticipated negative effects, those effects will be visited not only on the recipient of the intervention himself or herself but also on all of the descendants of that recipient. This argument seems to assume that a mistake, once made, could not be corrected, or at least that the mistake might not become apparent until the recipient became the biological parent of at least one child. For that first child, at least, the negative effects could be serious, as well as uncorrectable.

Second, some critics of germ-line genetic intervention argue that this technique will never be necessary because of available alternative strategies for preventing the transmission of diagnosable genetic diseases. Specifically, critics of germ-line gene therapy have sometimes suggested that preimplantation diagnosis and the selective discard of affected embryos might be a reasonable alternative to the high-technology, potentially risky attempt to repair genetic defects in early human embryos. Even without in vitro fertilization and preimplantation diagnosis, the option of prenatal diagnosis and selective abortion is available for many disorders. According to this view, these two types of selection, before embryos or fetuses have reached the stage of viability, are effective means for achieving the same goal.

The third argument is closely related to the second: this technique will always be an expensive option that cannot be made available to most couples, certainly not by any publicly funded health care system. Therefore, like in vitro fertilization for couples attempting to overcome the problem of infertility, germ-line gene therapy will be available only to wealthy people who can afford to pay its considerable expense on their own.

The fourth argument builds on the preceding two: precisely because germ-line intervention will be of such limited utility in preventing disease, there will be strong pressures to use this technique for genetic enhancement at the embryonic stage, when it could reasonably be expected to make a difference in the future life prospects of the embryo. Again in this case, only the affluent would be able to afford the intervention. However, if enhancement interventions were safe and efficacious, the long-term effect of such germ-line intervention would probably be to exacerbate existing differences between the most-well-off and the least-well-off segments of society.

Fifth, even though germ-line genetic intervention aims in the long run to treat rather than to abort or discard, the issue of appropriate respect for preimplantation embryos and implanted fetuses will nonetheless arise in several ways. After thoroughgoing studies of germ-line intervention have been conducted in nonhuman embryos, there will

undoubtedly be a stage at which parallel studies in human embryos will be proposed. The question of human embryo research was recently studied by a committee appointed by the director of the National Institutes of Health.[9] Although the committee specifically avoided commenting on germ-line intervention, its recommendation that certain kinds of human embryo research should be continued and that such research should be funded by NIH provoked considerable controversy. Critics of the committee's position would presumably also oppose the embryo research that would be proposed to prepare the way for germ-line gene therapy in humans.[10] Their principal argument would be that the destruction or other harming of preimplantation embryos in research is incompatible with the kind of respect that should be shown to human embryos.

Even after the research phase of germ-line genetic intervention is concluded, difficult questions about the treatment of embryos will remain. For example, preimplantation diagnosis may continue to involve the removal of one or two totipotential cells from a four- to eight-cell embryo. While the moral status of totipotential human embryonic cells has received scant attention in bioethical debates, there is at least a plausible argument that a totipotential cell, once separated from the remainder of a preimplantation embryo, is virtually equivalent to a zygote; that is, under favorable conditions it could develop into an embryo, a fetus, a newborn, and an adult. This objection to the destruction of totipotential embryonic cells will only be overcome if a noninvasive genetic diagnostic test for early embryos (like an x-ray or a CT scan) can be developed. Further, even if a noninvasive diagnostic test is available, as we have noted above, a postintervention diagnostic test will probably be undertaken with each embryo to verify that the intervention has been successful. Health professionals and prospective parents will probably be at least open to the possibility of selective discard or selective abortion if something has gone radically wrong in the intervention procedure. Thus, germ-line genetic intervention may remain foreclosed as a moral option to those who are conscientiously opposed to any action that would directly terminate the life of a preimplantation embryo or a fetus.

The sixth argument points to potential perils of concentrating great power in the hands of human beings. According to this view, the technique of germ-line intervention would give human beings, or a small group of human beings, too much control over the future evolution of the human race. This argument does not necessarily attribute malevolent intentions to those who have the training that would allow them to employ the technique. It implies that there are built-in limits that humans ought not to exceed, perhaps for theological or metaphysical reasons, and at least hints that corruptibility is an ever-present possibility for the very powerful.

The seventh argument explicitly raises the issue of malevolent use. If one extrapolates from Nazi racial hygiene programs, this argument asserts, it is likely the germ-line intervention will be used by unscrupulous dictators to produce a class of superior human beings. The same techniques could be also used in precisely the opposite way, to produce humanlike creatures who would willingly perform the least-attractive and the most-dangerous work for a society. According to this view, Aldous Huxley's *Brave New World* should be updated, for modern molecular biology provides tyrants with tools for modifying human beings that Huxley could not have imagined in 1932.

The eighth and final argument against germline genetic intervention is raised chiefly by several European authors who place this argument in the context of human rights.[11] According to these commentators, human beings have a moral right to receive from their parents a genetic patrimony that has not been subjected to artificial tampering. Although the term "tampering" is not usually defined, it seems to mean any intentional effort to introduce genetic changes into the germ line, even if the goal is to reduce the likelihood that a genetic disease will be passed on to the children and grandchildren of a particular couple. The asserted right to be protected against such tampering may be a slightly different formulation of the sixth argument noted above—namely, that there are built-in limits, embedded in the nature of things, beyond which not even the most benevolent human beings should attempt to go.

A Brief Evaluation of the Arguments

In our view, the effort to cure and prevent serious disease and premature death is one of the noblest of all human undertakings. For this reason the first pro argument—that germ-line intervention may be the only way to treat or prevent certain diseases—seems to us to be of overriding importance. We also find the third pro argument to be quite strong, that a germ-line correction, if demonstrated to be safe and effective, would be more efficient than repeated applications of somatic cell gene therapy. In addition, the final pro argument about the overall mission of the health professions and about society's approach to disabilities seems to us to provide a convincing justification for the germline approach, when gene replacement is available.

Our replies to the objections raised by critics of germ-line intervention are as follows:

1. *Irreversible mistakes.* While we acknowledge that mistakes may be made in germ-line gene therapy, we think that the same sophisticated techniques that were employed to introduce the new genes will be able to be used to remove those genes or to compensate for their presence in some other way. Further, in any sphere of innovative therapy, a first step into human beings must be taken at some point.

2. *Alternative strategies.* Some couples, perhaps even most couples, will choose the alternative strategies of selective abortion or selective discard. In our view, a strategy of attempting to prevent or treat potential disease or disability in the particular biological individual accords more closely with the mission of the health sciences and shows greater respect for children and adults who are afflicted with disease or disability.

3. *High cost, limited availability.* It is too early to know what the relative cost of germ-line intervention will be when the technique is fully developed. In addition, the financial costs and other personal and social harms of preventable diseases will need to be compared with the financial costs of germ-line gene therapy. It is at least possible that this new technology could become widely diffused and available to many members of society.

4. *Use for enhancement.* Prudent social policy should be able to set limits on the use of germ-line genetic intervention. Further, some enhancements of human capabilities may be morally justifiable, especially when those enhancements are health related. We acknowledge that the distribution of genetic enhancement is an important question for policy makers.

5. *Human embryos.* In our view, research with early human embryos that is directed toward the development of germ-line gene therapy is morally justifiable in principle. Further, we acknowledge the potential of a totipotential cell but think that the value of a genetic diagnosis outweighs the value of such a cell. We also accept that, if a serious error is made in germ-line gene therapy, terminating the life of the resulting embryo or fetus may be morally justifiable. In short, there is a presumption in favor of fostering the continued development of human embryos and fetuses, but that presumption can in our view be overridden by other considerations like serious harm to the developing individual or others and the needs of preclinical research.

6. *Concentration of power.* We acknowledge that those who are able to use germ-line intervention will have unprecedented ability to introduce precise changes into the germ lines of particular individuals and families. However, in our view, it is better for human beings to possess this ability and to use it for constructive purposes like preventing disease in families than not to possess the ability. The central ethical question is public accountability by the scientists, health providers, and companies that will be involved with germ-line intervention. Such accountability presupposes transparency about the use of the technology and an ongoing monitoring process aimed at preventing its misuse.

7. *Misuse by dictators.* This objection focuses too much attention on technology and too little on politics. There is no doubt that bona fide tyrants have existed in the 20th century and that they have made use of all manner of technologies—whether the low-tech methods of surgical sterilization or the annihilation of concentration camp inmates with poison gas or high-tech weapons like nuclear warheads and long-range missiles—to terrify and to dominate. However, the best approach to preventing the misuse of genetic technologies may not be to discourage the development of the technologies but rather to preserve and encourage democratic institutions that can serve as an antidote to tyranny. A second possible reply to the tyrannical misuse objection is that germ-line intervention requires a long lead time, in order to allow the offspring produced to grow to adulthood. Tyrants are often impatient people and are likely to prefer the more instantaneous methods of propaganda, intimidation, and annihilation of enemies to the relatively slow pace of germ-line modification.

8. *Human rights and tampering.* It is a daunting task to imagine what the unborn and as-yet-unconceived generations of people coming after us will want.[12] Even more difficult is the effort to ascribe rights to [future] human beings. Insofar as we can anticipate the needs and wants of future generations, we think that any reasonable future person would prefer health to serious disease and would therefore welcome a germ-line intervention in his or her family line that effectively prevented cystic fibrosis from being transmitted to him or her. In our view, such a person would not regard this intervention as tampering and would regard as odd the claim that his or her genetic patrimony has been artificially tampered with. Cystic fibrosis was not a part of his or her family's heritage that the future person was eager to receive or to claim. . . .

NOTES

1. It is perhaps worth noting that researchers performing somatic-cell gene therapy have carefully avoided diseases and subtypes of diseases that affect mental functioning. One thinks, for example, of Lesch-Nyhan syndrome, of certain subtypes of Gaucher disease and Hunter syndrome, of Tay-Sachs disease, and of metachromatic leukodystrophy.
2. We owe the suggestion of retinoblastoma as a candidate disorder to Kevin FitzGerald, S. J. We are also indebted to

Nelson A. Wivel for information on the genetics of retino-blastoma. See Nelson A. Wivel and LeRoy Walters, "Germ-Line Gene Modification and Disease Prevention: Some Medical and Ethical Perspectives," *Science* 262(5133): 533–538; 22 October 1993. See also Stephen H. Friend et al., "A Human DNA Segment with Properties of the Gene That Predisposes to Retinoblastoma and Osteosarcoma," *Nature* 323(6089): 643–646; 16 October 1986; and Ei Matsunaga, "Hereditary Retinoblastoma: Host Resistance and Second Primary Tumors," *Journal of the National Cancer Institute* 65(1): 47–51; July 1980.

3. Although the genetics of the germ-line p53 gene mutation are more complex than the genetics of the germ-line muta-tion that causes retinoblastoma, p53 may turn out to be another important tumor suppressor gene to which the same comments apply. On the germ-line p53 mutation, see Frederick P. Li et al., "Recommendations on Predictive Testing for Germ Line p53 Mutations Among Cancer-Prone Individuals," *Journal of the National Cancer Institute* 84(15): 1156–1160; 5 August 1992; and Curtis C. Harris and Monica Hollstein, "Clinical Implications of the *p53* Tumor-Suppressor Gene," *New England Journal of Medicine* 329(18): 1318–1327; 28 October 1993.

4. Eric T. Juengst, "Germ-Line Gene Therapy: Back to Basics," *Journal of Medicine and Philosophy* 16(6): 589–590; December 1991.

5. Burke K. Zimmerman, "Human Germ-Line Therapy: The Case for Its Development and Use," *Journal of Medicine and Philosophy* 16(6): 596–598; December 1991.

6. For a detailed discussion of and justification for germ-line intervention in this setting, see Marc Lappé, "Ethical Issues in Manipulating the Human Germ Line," *Journal of Medicine and Philosophy* 16(6): 621–639; December 1991.

7. As noted above, already in 1962 Joshua Lederberg was arguing against H. J. Muller's proposals for improving the human gene pool through programs of "voluntary germinal choice" by appealing to the prospect of rapid, global genetic intervention by means of germ-line gene therapy. See Joshua Lederberg, "Biological Future of Man," in Gordon Wolstenholme, ed., *Man and His Future* (London: J. & A. Churchill, 1963), pp. 265 and 269.

8. On the general issue of the freedom of scientific inquiry, see Loren R. Graham, "Concerns About Science and Attempts to Regulate Inquiry," *Daedalus* 107(2): 1–21; Spring 1978.

9. National Institutes of Health, Human Embryo Research Panel, *Report* (Bethesda, MD: NIH, 27 September 1994).

10. See, for example, the following critiques of human embryo research: "The Inhuman Use of Human Beings," *First Things* 49: 17–21; January 1995; Dianne N. Irving, "Testimony Before the NIH Human Embryo Research Panel," *Linacre Quarterly* 61(4): 82–89; November 1994; and Kevin O'Rourke, "Embryo Research: Ethical Issues," *Health Care Ethics USA* 2(4): 2–3; Fall 1994.

11. Alex Mauron and Jean-Marie Thévoz, "Germ-Line Engineering: A Few European Voices," *Journal of Medicine and Philosophy* 16(6): 654–655; December 1991.

12. There is a rather substantial literature on this topic. See, for example, Ruth Faden, Gail Geller, and Madison Powers, eds., *AIDS, Women and the Next Generation* (New York: Oxford University Press, 1991); LeRoy Walters, "Ethical Issues in Maternal Serum Alpha-Fetoprotein Testing and Screening: A Reappraisal," in Mark I. Evans et al., eds., *Fetal Diagnosis and Therapy: Science, Ethics and the Law* (Philadelphia: J.B. Lippincott, 1989), pp. 54–60; and Lori B. Andrews et al., eds., *Assessing Genetic Risks: Implications for Health and Social Policy: Report* (Washington, DC: National Academy Press, 1994).

What Does "Respect for Embryos" Mean in the Context of Stem Cell Research?

BONNIE STEINBOCK

Steinbock examines the question of whether embryonic stem-cell research is con-sistent with proper respect for embryos. She argues that early embryos have less than full moral status—they are not due the same respect that we give persons—but they still have a "significance and moral value that other bodily tissues do not have." We must not use embryos in frivolous ways, she says, but "respect for em-bryos does not require refraining from research likely to have significant benefits, such as treating disease and prolonging life."

Like abortion, embryo research polarizes those who believe that embryos have as much of a right to life as any born human being, and those who maintain that embryos are not the kinds of entities that can have rights, because rights are restricted either to persons or to sentient beings.[1] However, those who deny that embryos can be possessors of rights need not strip them of moral significance altogether. There is a "third alternative," which is that although human embryos do not have full moral status, or human moral status, they are a form of human life and, as such, deserving of respect. This is the view that virtually every commission considering the issue has taken, including the Human Embryo Research Panel of the National Institutes of Health (NIH)[2] and the Warnock Committee[3] in Great Britain. But what does "respect for embryos" mean? Is this simply an empty phrase, solemnly invoked by national commissions to soften or conceal the fact that they are endorsing killing embryos?

This was charged by Daniel Callahan,[4] who took the NIH Human Embryo Research Panel to task for failing to demonstrate (as opposed to merely asserting) that progress in scientific research depends on using human embryos. Callahan's point is not that respect for embryos entails that they never be destroyed or used in research. Rather, it is that the interests or goals to be accomplished by using human embryos in research must be shown to be compelling, and unreachable by other means. If less than compelling purposes can justify the destruction of embryos, or if compelling goals could be reached without destroying embryos, the idea that embryos are due profound respect rings hollow.

A similar view regarding embryonic stem (ES) cell research was expressed by Richard M. Doerflinger.[5] He cited advances in isolating and culturing adult stem (AS) cells and suggested that AS cells might be more clinically useful than embryonic cells because treatments based on a patient's own cells would avoid problems of tissue rejection[5]:

No one can say with certainty at this time whether embryonic stem cells will have any clinical use

From *Women's Health Issues*, vol. 10, no. 3 (May/June 2000), pp. 127–30. Copyright © 2000 The Jacobs Institute of Women's Health. Reprinted with permission.

that cannot equally well be addressed by other means. . . . At a minimum, an ethic that demands serious respect for human embryonic life will also demand that other, morally accepted alternatives be explored first. (p. 144)

The suggestion that other alternatives should be explored first makes sense only if there is some reason to believe that these alternatives are likely to yield comparable results. As a nonscientist, I cannot evaluate the research cited by Doerflinger. A recent article in *Science*[6] says, "Scientists are now speeding ahead with work on adult stem cells, hoping to discover whether their promise will rival that of embryonic stem (ES) cells." If that is so, it is possible that it will not be necessary to use ES cells for therapeutic purposes. At the same time, no one can accuse the National Bioethics Advisory Commission of simply assuming that there will be scientific benefits from embryonic stem cell research, or ignoring the possibility that AS could be used instead of ES cells. Its report, *Ethical Issues in Human Stem Cell Research*,[7] examines at great length the scientific evidence, and the possibility that AS cells can replace embryonic cells. It concludes that this is unlikely because ES cells have a property that AS cells do not: the ability to differentiate into all cell types. The report states[7]:

. . . although much promising research currently is being conducted with stem cells obtained from adult organisms, studies in animals suggest that this approach will be scientifically and technically limited. . . . Moreover, because important biological differences exist between embryonic and adult stem cells, this source of stem cells should not be considered an alternative to ES and EG [embryonic germ] cell research. (p. ii)

This raises the intriguing question of how promising evidence for the utility of AS cells must be to pursue that line of research while delaying research using ES cells, out of respect for embryos. Certainly, if current research indicated that significant medical benefit was just as likely from research using AS, as opposed to ES, cells, respect for embryos would require us to use AS cells. However, no one is making this claim. Although no one can say for sure, the likelihood is that stopping research using

ES cells and exploring instead the therapeutic possibilities of AS cells will result in the loss of significant medical benefits for people. A better alternative would be to conduct both kinds of research simultaneously. In any event, Doerflinger's reference to doing research with AS cells appears to be a red herring because it is clear from what he says in his Abstract that he rejects absolutely stem cell research that involves the destruction of human embryos. If such research is never morally acceptable, why go on about doing other research "first"? Doerflinger's views about embryo research derive from the right-to-life position on the moral status of the human embryo. They are unrelated to the "third alternative" which accords respect, but not full moral status, to the human embryo.

What, then, does respect for embryos require? It is important, first, to differentiate respect for embryos from respect for persons. Respect for persons means, as Kant instructs us, never treating persons as mere means to our ends, but always treating them as ends in themselves. This obscure phrase means that we must take seriously the ends—the projects, the goals—that other people have (at least if they are morally permissible ends). We cannot do this with embryos as they do not have ends of their own. Lacking the kinds of ends that persons have, embryos cannot be given the respect that is due to persons. Nevertheless, they have a significance and moral value that other bodily tissues do not have because they are "potent symbols of human life."[8] In this respect, embryos are like dead bodies, which also do not have interests.[9] Unlike dead bodies, embryos are potential human beings in the sense that, under certain conditions, embryos can develop into human persons. This potential gives them a significance and importance that does not belong to other cells of the body, and imposes restrictions on what it is permissible to do to embryos. We show respect for human embryos by not using them in unimportant or frivolous ways, say, to teach high school biology or to make cosmetics or jewelry. However, respect for embryos does not require refraining from research likely to have significant benefits, such as treating disease and prolonging life.

Embryonic stem cells can be derived from embryos remaining after infertility treatment (sometimes called "spare" embryos), or they can be derived from embryos made solely for research purposes using in vitro fertilization (IVF). Both involve the destruction of embryos. However, the NBAC report distinguished morally between the two. It recommended that an exception should be made to the present ban on federal funding of embryo research to permit funding of research using spare embryos, but it recommended that federal agencies should not fund research involving the derivation of human ES cells from embryos made solely for research purposes[7]:

> The primary objection to creating embryos specifically for research is that there is a morally relevant difference between generating an embryo for the sole purpose of creating a child and producing an embryo with no such goal. Those who object to creating embryos for research often appeal to arguments about respecting human dignity by avoiding instrumental use of human embryos (i.e., using embryos merely as a means to some other goal does not treat them with appropriate respect or concern as a form of human life). (p. v)

Certainly, if one takes the right-to-life view of human embryos, it is morally wrong to create embryos and then destroy them, regardless of the purpose. However, according to the right-to-life view, it is also wrong to create more embryos than will be transferred for implantation; that is, it is wrong to create spare embryos and also wrong to use them in research. Because NBAC does not reject using spare embryos in research, but only creating embryos for the purpose of research, the question is, what justifies this distinction? Here is NBAC's argument[7]:

> Embryos that are discarded following the completion of IVF treatment were presumably created by individuals who had the primary intention of implanting them for reproductive purposes. . . . By contrast, research embryos are created for use in research and, in the case of stem cell research, their destruction in the process of research. Hence, one motivation that encourages serious consideration of the "discarded-created" distinction is a concern about instrumentalization—treating the embryo as a mere object—a practice that may increasingly lead us to think of embryos generally as means to our ends rather than as ends in themselves. (p. 56)

The first part of this paragraph simply reiterates the difference between spare and created embryos; it does not explain why there is a moral difference between the two. The last part attempts to provide a justification for a moral difference, but it relies on the view I have argued is conceptually confused: namely, that embryos should be treated as ends in themselves.

If we reject the view that embryos are ends in themselves, what follows? In my view, it makes no moral difference whether one creates an embryo for reproductive purposes but ends up using it in research, or whether one creates an embryo for the explicit purpose of research. Respect for embryos is demonstrated by restricting their use to important ends. Research that promises to cure disease and save lives clearly qualifies.

The acceptability of this view depends, of course, on one's view of the moral status of the embryo. If embryos are people, there is a moral difference between creating embryos for reproductive purposes and creating them for research purposes. Creating embryos for birth benefits the embryo, whereas creating them for research purposes harms (kills) the embryos to benefit others. But if you reject the idea that preimplantation embryos are the kinds of beings who can be benefited or harmed,[1] creating embryos for research purposes is just as acceptable as creating them for reproductive purposes. Both are valid; neither is frivolous. Therefore, neither contravenes the principle of respect for embryos as a form of human life.

REFERENCES

1. Steinbock B. Life before birth: The moral and legal status of embryos and fetuses. New York: Oxford University Press, 1992.
2. National Institutes of Health. Report of the human embryo research panel. Bethesda (MD): National Institutes of Health, 1994.
3. Warnock M. A question of life: The Warnock report on human fertilisation and embryology. New York: Basil Blackwell. 1985:63–4.
4. Callahan D. The puzzle of profound respect. Hastings Center Rep 1995;25:39–40.
5. Doerflinger R. The ethics of funding embryonic stem cell research: A Catholic viewpoint. Kennedy Inst Ethics J 1999; 9:137–50.
6. Vogel G. Capturing the promise of youth. Science 1999; 286:2238–9.
7. National Bioethics Advisory Commission. Ethical issues in human stem cell research, Vol 1. Rockville (MD), 1999.
8. Robertson J. A. Symbolic issues in embryo research. Hastings Center Rep 1995; 2 5:37–8.
9. Feinberg J. The mistreatment of dead bodies. Hastings Center Rep 1985; 15:31–7.

Declaration on the Production and the Scientific and Therapeutic Use of Human Embryonic Stem Cells

PONTIFICAL ACADEMY FOR LIFE

In this official position statement on embryonic stem cells, the Roman Catholic Church declares that it is morally impermissible to produce or use living human embryos to obtain embryonic stem (ES) cells, to produce and then destroy cloned human embryos to acquire ES cells, or to use ES cells that others have already derived.

Ethical Problems

. . . Given the nature of this article, the key ethical problems implied by these new technologies are presented briefly, with an indication of the

From Pontifical Academy for Life, Vatican City, August 25, 2000.

responses which emerge from a careful consideration of the human subject from the moment of conception. It is this consideration which underlies the position affirmed and put forth by the Magisterium of the Church.

The *first ethical problem*, which is fundamental, can be formulated thus: *Is it morally licit to produce and/or use living human embryos for the preparation of ES cells?*

The answer is negative, for the following reasons:

1. On the basis of a complete biological analysis, the living human embryo is—from the moment of the union of the gametes—a *human subject* with a well defined identity, which from that point begins its own *coordinated, continuous and gradual development,* such that at no later stage can it be considered as a simple mass of cells.

2. From this it follows that as a *"human individual"* it has the *right* to its own life; and therefore every intervention which is not in favour of the embryo is an act which violates that right. Moral theology has always taught that in the case of *"jus certum tertii"* the system of probabilism does not apply.

3. Therefore, the ablation of the inner cell mass (ICM) of the blastocyst, which critically and irremediably damages the human embryo, curtailing its development, is a *gravely immoral* act and consequently is *gravely illicit.*

4. *No end believed to be good,* such as the use of stem cells for the preparation of other differentiated cells to be used in what look to be promising therapeutic procedures, *can justify an intervention of this kind.* A good end does not make right an action which in itself is wrong.

5. For Catholics, this position is explicitly confirmed by the Magisterium of the Church which, in the Encyclical *Evangelium Vitae,* with reference to the Instruction *Donum Vitae* of the Congregation for the Doctrine of the Faith, affirms: "The Church has always taught and continues to teach that the result of human procreation, from the first moment of its existence, must be guaranteed that unconditional respect which is morally due to the human being in his or her totality and unity in body and spirit: The human being is to be respected and treated as a person from the moment of conception; and therefore from that same moment his right as a person must be recognized, among which in the first place is the inviolable right of every innocent human being to life."

The **second ethical problem** can be formulated thus: *Is it morally licit to engage in so-called "therapeutic cloning" by producing cloned human embryos and then destroying them in order to produce ES cells?*

The answer is negative, for the following reason: Every type of therapeutic cloning, which implies producing human embryos and then destroying them in order to obtain stem cells, is illicit; for there is present the ethical problem examined above, which can only be answered in the negative.

The **third ethical problem** can be formulated thus: *Is it morally licit to use ES cells, and the differentiated cells obtained from them, which are supplied by other researchers or are commercially obtainable?*

The answer is negative, since: prescinding from the participation—formal or otherwise—in the morally illicit intention of the principal agent, the case in question entails a proximate material cooperation in the production and manipulation of human embryos on the part of those producing or supplying them.

In conclusion, it is not hard to see the seriousness and gravity of the ethical problem posed by the desire to extend to the field of human research the production and/or use of human embryos, even from an humanitarian perspective.

The possibility, now confirmed, of using **adult stem cells** to attain the same goals as would be sought with embryonic stem cells—even if many further steps in both areas are necessary before clear and conclusive results are obtained—indicates that adult stem cells represent a more reasonable and human method for making correct and sound progress in this new field of research and in the therapeutic applications which it promises. These applications are undoubtedly a source of great hope for a significant number of suffering people.

CHAPTER 10

Euthanasia and Physician-Assisted Suicide

No one escapes death—or the ethical issues that come with it. Advances in medicine now raise the old life-and-death questions anew, force new ones more unsettling, and provoke answers that are disturbing even when plausible. In euthanasia and physician-assisted suicide, the bioethical heart of the matter is the moral rightness of killing or letting die for the good of the patient. The countless disputes on this terrain are often fierce and elemental, for they are the visible signs of deep conflicts among fundamental moral principles and perspectives. Doctors and nurses have sworn to preserve life and relieve suffering—but how to do this when the only way to end suffering is to end life? They understand the need to respect patient autonomy, the right of self-determination—but what should they do when the patient freely chooses to forgo all their best efforts and to embrace extinction? Or if the terminal patient, inching in agony toward destruction, asks them to cut short her torment by killing her with a lethal injection? Or if she begs only for some help in dying by her own hand? Or if she has never expressed a choice about such matters and has slipped into permanent unconsciousness, withering in pain to the inevitable? In such cases, what does beneficence or mercy or respect for autonomy or regard for the sanctity of life demand?

More so than most other issues in bioethics, the morality of euthanasia and physician-assisted suicide is tangled with legal and policy debates. The ethical questions are, of course, logically distinct from these concerns. You are not necessarily guilty of inconsistency if you think some instances of physician-assisted suicide are morally permissible but believe the practice should never be legalized because legalization might lead to abuses. Or you may, without contradicting yourself, favor legalization to protect patient autonomy but argue that suicide in any form is almost never morally acceptable. In the heat of controversy, these distinctions often get blurred, and a major task of good moral reasoning is to keep the focus sharp.

Nowhere was moral reasoning and conceptual clarity needed more and used less than in the recent case of Terri Schiavo. In 1990, when she was 26, Schiavo's heart stopped suddenly for reasons that are still unclear; by the time she was resuscitated, she had suffered catastrophic and irreversible brain damage. She was left in what doctors call a persistent vegetative state—wakeful but without consciousness or intentional behavior and almost no chance of significant improvement. In this condition she was sustained for years by food and water injected into her body through tubes. The question arose: Would Terri have wanted to be kept alive like this? Would she have chosen death over this perpetual darkness? She could not answer and had left no written record of her preferences. Her husband, Michael Schiavo, became her legal guardian and claimed that Terri had once told him that she would rather die than be artificially sustained as she eventually was. He said he wanted to have Terri's feeding tube removed so she could die with dignity. Terri's parents would have none of this and insisted that efforts to keep her alive should continue because she could eventually regain consciousness. Across the country people debated the moral questions. Would removing Terri's feeding tube be murder? Would allowing her to die be a permissible act of mercy?

All the while, the legal war between Michael Schiavo and Terri's parents dragged on, with the former seeking permission to disconnect the feeding tube and the latter trying to thwart him. The essential legal issue was who had the legal right to decide Terri Schiavo's fate. The list of people who weighed in on both the legal and moral questions is long and diverse—President George W. Bush, state legislators, members of the U.S. Congress, bioethicists, religious leaders, pro-life groups, the governor of Florida, disability rights organizations, and a vast assortment of media commentators. Time after time, state and federal courts sided with Michael Schiavo, and in the end a judge gave permission to remove Terri's feeding tube. Thirteen days after its removal, on March 31, 2005, Terri Schiavo was dead.

In some ways the Schiavo case is unique, but several of its more disturbing features are not. Many compelling end-of-life dramas are being played out right now behind closed hospital doors, away from news cameras, the posturing of politicians, and the gaze of unaffected people. The need for informed moral reasoning to come to terms with the heart-breaking realities is acute—and likely to grow.

DECIDING LIFE AND DEATH

Almost all of the terms used to discuss the morality of killing and letting die are controversial to some degree. Even the meaning of *death*—a seemingly straightforward concept to most people—has been a point of dispute. Nevertheless, some helpful distinctions are possible. For the sake of clarity (and neutrality), **euthanasia** can be characterized as directly or indirectly bringing about the death of another person for that person's sake.[1] The term derives from the Greek words meaning "good death" and evokes the idea that causing or contributing to someone's end may bestow on that person a good. Death is usually considered an evil, perhaps the greatest evil, but many think it can be a blessing if it spares someone from a slow, horrific dying or a hopeless, vegetative sleep.

Many philosophers maintain that there are two forms of euthanasia. **Active euthanasia** is said to involve performing an action that directly causes someone to die—what most people think of as "mercy killing." Giving a patient a lethal injection to end his suffering, then, is a case of active euthanasia. **Passive euthanasia** is allowing someone to die by *not* doing something that would prolong life. It includes removing a patient's feeding tube or ventilator, failing to perform necessary surgery, and refraining from giving life-saving antibiotics. The distinction between the two is thought to be essentially this: Active euthanasia is *killing*, but passive euthanasia is *letting die*.

To some people, this conceptual border between active and passive euthanasia is crucial for assessing the morality of euthanasia. They point out that whereas letting a patient die is sometimes morally permissible, deliberately and directly killing a patient is always wrong. The former practice is legal and officially endorsed by the medical profession; the latter is illegal and officially condemned. The American Medical Association sanctioned this dichotomy in a 1973 policy statement:

> The intentional termination of the life of one human being by another—mercy killing—is contrary to that for which the medical profession stands and is contrary to the policy of the American Medical Association.
>
> . . . The cessation of the employment of extraordinary means to prolong the life of the body when there is irrefutable evidence that biological death is imminent is the decision of the patient and/or immediate family.[2]

For many (including most physicians), passive euthanasia may be moral, but active euthanasia is not.

But not everyone thinks this active-passive distinction makes sense. Some argue that there is no morally significant difference between mercifully killing a patient and mercifully letting the patient die. In both situations the doctor causes the patient's death—by either intentionally doing something in the one instance or intentionally refraining from doing something in the other. Thus an act of euthanasia may be morally right or wrong, but the rightness or wrongness does not depend purely on this active-passive divide. Moreover in practice, distinguishing examples of active and passive euthanasia may not be as easy as some think. The usual view is that passive euthanasia can sometimes be performed by disconnecting a dying patient's feeding tube and ventilator. But this event can also be seen as an instance of performing an action that directly causes someone to die—that is, active euthanasia.

If euthanasia in some form is morally permissible, its permissibility must be linked to the patient's consent. Thus bioethicists talk about euthanasia that is voluntary, nonvoluntary, or involuntary. **Voluntary euthanasia** refers to situations in which competent patients voluntarily request or agree to euthanasia, communicating their wishes either while competent or through instructions to be followed if they become incompetent (if they fall into a persistent vegetative state, for example). Patients can indicate what is to be done in incompetence by formulating an advance directive—usually a living will or a document designating a surrogate, or proxy, to act on their behalf. **Nonvoluntary euthanasia** is performed when patients are not competent to chose death for themselves and have not previously disclosed their preferences. (Incompetent patients include not only incapacitated adults but infants and small children as well.) In these circumstances, the patient's family, physician, or other officially designated persons decide for the patient. **Involuntary euthanasia** is bringing about someone's death against her will or without asking for her consent while she is competent to decide. It is illegal and considered morally impermissible by both those who approve and disapprove of euthanasia. It is therefore generally left out of moral debates, except perhaps in slippery-slope arguments warning that voluntary or nonvoluntary euthanasia will inevitably become involuntary.

Combining the terms *active, passive, voluntary,* and *nonvoluntary,* we can identify four kinds of

euthanasia that have been the main focus in bioethics:

1. **Active voluntary**—Directly causing death (mercy killing) with the consent of the patient
2. **Active nonvoluntary**—Directly causing death (mercy killing) without the consent of the patient
3. **Passive voluntary**—Withholding or withdrawing life-sustaining measures with the consent of the patient
4. **Passive nonvoluntary**—Withholding or withdrawing life-sustaining measures without the consent of the patient

Legally and ethically, the starkest contrast among these is between active and passive euthanasia. Active euthanasia (whether voluntary or nonvoluntary) is unlawful, while passive euthanasia (both voluntary and nonvoluntary) is legal provided certain conditions are met. Judicial rulings have firmly established a right of patients to refuse treatment—and thus to have life-sustaining treatment withheld or withdrawn—even though the patient dies as a result. Withdrawing or withholding treatment from an incompetent patient is generally legal if the patient has left instructions or if an appropriate person can be chosen to make the necessary decisions. Contemporary moral debate centers more on active than on passive euthanasia. There is considerable agreement about the moral rightness of allowing a patient to die but intense controversy about the permissibility of deliberately causing a patient's death (by administering a lethal injection, for example), whether the act is considered voluntary or nonvoluntary.

Recently, disputes over euthanasia have raged alongside arguments about **physician-assisted suicide**, in which a patient takes his own life with the aid of a physician. In a typical scenario, a patient asks the physician for help in committing suicide, the physician assists the patient by prescribing lethal doses of drugs or explaining a method of suicide, and the patient—not the physician—performs the final act that causes

Euthanasia and Assisted Suicide: Major Developments

1990 In *Cruzan v. Director, Missouri Department of Health,* the U.S. Supreme Court recognizes the right of patients to refuse treatment (essentially a "right to die") and finds constitutional justification for living wills and surrogates who make medical decisions for incompetent patients.

1994 Oregon passes the Death With Dignity Act, legalizing the use of physician-assisted suicide under specific conditions. It permits doctors to prescribe drugs that terminally ill patients can use to commit suicide.

1997 In separate cases—*Washington v. Glucksberg* and *Vacco v. Quill*—the Supreme Court rules that there is no constitutional right to physician-assisted suicide but notes that each state may establish its own policy on the issue. It explicitly acknowledges a distinction between assisted suicide and the withdrawal of life-sustaining treatment.

2001 U.S. Attorney General John Ashcroft tries to thwart the Oregon right-to-die law by authorizing the Drug Enforcement Agency to act against physicians prescribing drugs for assisted suicide.

2006 The Supreme Court rules that the Justice Department (headed by Ashcroft and later Alberto Gonzales) had no authority to interfere with physicians acting under the Oregon law.

2008 Through a referendum vote, Washington becomes the second state to legalize physician-assisted suicide.

2008 A district court ruling in the case of *Baxter v. State of Montana* asserts that Montana residents have a right to physician-assisted suicide, thereby legalizing the practice in a third state. In 2009 the Montana Supreme Court affirmed the earlier court ruling.

2013 Vermont becomes the fourth state to legalize physician-assisted suicide. The Vermont legislature passed the "End of Life Choices" bill, and the governor signed it into law.

2015 The New Mexico Court of Appeals invalidates a lower-court ruling that had legalized physician-assisted suicide. The Court asserted that "aid in dying is not a fundamental liberty interest under the New Mexico Constitution."

2015 California becomes the fifth state to legalize physician-assisted suicide. Governor Jerry Brown signed into law a bill permitting physicians to prescribe fatal doses of drugs to help terminally ill patients end their lives.

death. In contrast, in active euthanasia the physician performs the final act. Many argue that this difference in the ultimate cause of death implies a difference in moral responsibility. In physician-assisted suicide, the patient is thought to bear ultimate moral responsibility for the taking of life. Others doubt that any distinction in ultimate causes can amount to a moral difference. Thus they contend that physician-assisted suicide and active voluntary euthanasia are morally equivalent. What is the moral difference, they ask, between a physician helping a patient die by (1) administering a lethal injection upon request or (2) prescribing a lethal dose of medications upon request?

The American Medical Association has denounced physician-assisted suicide as unethical and inconsistent with physicians' duty to promote healing and preserve life. Surveys suggest, however, that many doctors support the use of physician-assisted suicide, and up to half of adults believe it should be legal in cases of terminal illness or incurable disease with severe pain. To date, it is legal only in Oregon, Washington, Montana, Vermont, and California. The U.S. Supreme Court has ruled that states may legalize or prohibit it as they see fit.

IN DEPTH

EUTHANASIA AND PHYSICIAN-ASSISTED SUICIDE: WHAT DO DOCTORS THINK?

In 2008 a survey of 2,000 practicing physicians (members of the American Medical Association) revealed that:

PHYSICIAN-ASSISTED SUICIDE

- **69%** objected to physician-assisted suicide
- **42%** had both a "religious and nonreligious objection" to physician-assisted suicide
- **31%** had no objection to physician-assisted suicide
- **21%** had a "nonreligious objection" to physician-assisted suicide
- **5%** had a "religious objection" to physician-assisted suicide

TERMINAL SEDATION

- **18%** objected to terminal sedation
- **82%** had no objection to terminal sedation
- **9%** had both a "religious and nonreligious objection" to terminal sedation
- **7%** had a "nonreligious objection" to terminal sedation
- **2%** had a "religious objection" to terminal sedation

WITHDRAWAL OF LIFE SUPPORT

- **5%** objected to withdrawal of life support
- **95%** had "no objection" to withdrawal of life support
- **3%** had both a "religious and nonreligious objection" to withdrawal of life support
- **1%** had a "nonreligious objection" to withdrawal of life support
- **1%** had a "religious objection" to withdrawal of life support

From Farr A. Curlin, Chinyere Nwodin, et al., "To Die, to Sleep: US Physicians' Religious and Other Objections to Physician-Assisted Suicide, Terminal Sedation, and Withdrawal of Life Support," *American Journal of Hospice and Palliative Medicine*, Apr./May 2008.

Part of the difficulty of making everyday moral decisions about end-of-life situations is that death itself is not so easy to define. Traditionally death was understood to occur when breathing and heartbeat ceased. A person who wasn't breathing and had no heartbeat was dead. But thanks to modern medicine, machines can maintain someone's breathing and heartbeat indefinitely—even though there is permanent loss of all brain function. Heart and lungs keep going, but the individual is irreversibly brain-dead and can remain that way for decades. By the traditional standard, the individual is alive, but this seems counterintuitive.

We seem to need a new concept of death—an important consideration since any notion we adopt would dramatically influence our judgments about morally permissible behavior toward the living and the dead. If we judge an individual to be dead, then we would presumably think her no longer a person. If she is no longer a person, then it would seem to be permissible to disconnect all life support, harvest organs from the body for transplant, or prepare the body for burial. But if, despite appearances, she is still a person, wouldn't doing any of these things be murder? If so, those who perform these acts would be morally and legally culpable.

In 1968 a committee at Harvard Medical School formulated a new way of conceiving death, a perspective that has since become the standard in legal and medical matters. According to this *whole brain* view of death, an individual should be judged dead when all brain functions permanently cease. Brain death means genuine death. But several experts take issue with this view. They point out that some physiological processes such as respiration are partly independent of brain functions, and individuals that many would regard as dead (those in persistent vegetative states, for example) may have some residual brain activity. By the whole brain standard, Terri Schiavo, being wakeful but lacking consciousness, was alive until all brain activity stopped. To some, this consequence makes sense; to others, it seems odd. A better notion of death, some argue, is the *higher brain* view, which says that an individual should be considered dead when the higher brain operations responsible for consciousness permanently shut down. The thought behind this standard is that individuals are dead when they are no longer persons, regardless of what physiological activity persists, and individuals are no longer persons when consciousness permanently terminates. By the higher brain criterion, Terri Schiavo died when her higher brain functions permanently stopped, even though other brain activity continued for years. Again, some would find this judgment plausible; others, bizarre.

AUTONOMY, MERCY, AND HARM

Let us examine the two main flashpoints in end-of-life bioethics: active voluntary euthanasia and physician-assisted suicide. We can focus mostly on the former since arguments for and against it are largely relevant to the latter.

What arguments might be offered to support active voluntary euthanasia? The strongest one derives from the principle of autonomy—a person's inherent right of self-determination. Proponents say that respecting autonomous persons means respecting their autonomous choices, including the choice to end their lives in their own way. Their right is preeminent, its only limit marking the point where their choices bring harm to others. As one philosopher explains it,

> People have an interest in making important decisions about their lives in accordance with

their own conception of how they want their lives to go. In exercising autonomy or self-determination, people take responsibility for their lives; since dying is a part of life, choices about the manner of their dying and the timing of their death are, for many people, part of what is involved in taking responsibility for their lives. Many people are concerned about what the last phase of their lives will be like, not merely because of fears that their dying might involve them in great suffering, but also because of the desire to retain dignity and as much control over their lives as possible during this phase. . . . There is no single, objectively correct answer as to when, if at all, life becomes a burden and unwanted. But that simply points up the importance of individuals being able to decide autonomously for themselves whether their own lives retain sufficient quality and dignity to make life worth living.[3]

Proponents believe that this right to die, though strong, does not necessarily compel others. Almost no one who seriously urges the autonomy argument thinks that having a right to die forces a duty on others (physicians, for example) to help in the dying.

Another major argument for active euthanasia appeals to the principle of beneficence, or mercy: If we are in a position to relieve the severe suffering of another without excessive cost to ourselves, we have a duty to do so. To refuse would be cruel, inhumane, and wrong. The argument would run something like this: If a competent, hopelessly ill patient in unrelieved agony requests help to be put out of his misery, we may have a duty to bring about his death. As bioethicist Dan W. Brock says,

> When there is a life-sustaining treatment that, if forgone, will lead relatively quickly to death [passive euthanasia], then doing so can bring an end to these patients' suffering without recourse to [active] euthanasia. For patients receiving no such treatment, however, [active] euthanasia may be the only release from their otherwise prolonged suffering and agony. This argument from mercy has always been the strongest argument for euthanasia in those cases to which it applies.[4]

By these lights, active euthanasia is sometimes better than passive, for withholding or withdrawing treatment from a dying patient in unspeakable pain may only draw out his agony.

The argument from beneficence taps into very deep intuitions about the point of mercy killing. Consider this variation of a twice-told tale in bioethics: A truck overturns on the highway, pinning the screaming driver under the cabin as the wreckage bursts into flames. He is burning alive, and there is no hope of pulling him out of the fire. To avoid slow incineration, he begs the lone onlooker to smash him in the head with a rock to kill him immediately. Should the onlooker oblige him?

A common response to such horrific suffering, at least in cases of medical euthanasia, is to insist that the torment can almost always be relieved without resort to lethal means. It is likely that most patients who request euthanasia because of unrelenting pain and deep depression can get relief through improved pain treatment and enlightened psychiatric care. Therefore euthanasia or physician-assisted suicide is unnecessary. But many bioethicists are not convinced. They argue that there will always be some patients whose pain cannot be eased by any means short of death, or who have no access to adequate palliative care, or whose suffering is neither physical nor psychiatric but social, philosophical, or spiritual. The main cause of the suffering may be loss of dignity or independence or concern for loved ones who will be left behind.

Those who oppose active voluntary euthanasia give moral weight to autonomy and beneficence but argue that other considerations undermine the pro-euthanasia arguments. One such matter is the supposed moral difference between killing and letting die, or between active and passive euthanasia. The thought is that killing a person is morally worse than letting that person die. Killing is wrong; letting die is permissible. Thus giving a patient a lethal injection is wrong, but unplugging his feeding tube or ventilator may be morally acceptable. Some think that killing is morally worse because it involves a person causing the death of another person (murder), while

letting die is a matter of allowing nature to do its work. In the first, a person kills; in the second, a disease kills.

But critics deny that there is a morally significant difference between killing and letting die. If there is no difference, they can argue that since passive euthanasia is permissible, and it is morally equivalent to active euthanasia, active euthanasia must be permissible as well. James Rachels tries to demonstrate this no-difference thesis in a famous thought experiment about parallel cases:

> In the first case, Smith stands to gain a large inheritance if anything should happen to his six-year-old cousin. One evening while the child is taking his bath, Smith sneaks into the bathroom, drowns the child, and arranges things so that it will look like an accident.
>
> In the second, Jones also stands to gain if anything should happen to his six-year-old cousin. Like Smith, Jones sneaks in, planning to drown the child in his bath. However, as he enters the bathroom Jones sees the child slip, hit his head and fall face down in the water. Jones is delighted; he stands by, ready to push the child's head back under if it is necessary, but it is not necessary. With only a little thrashing about, the child drowns all by himself, "accidentally," as Jones watches and does nothing.
>
> Now Smith killed the child, while Jones merely let the child die. That is the only difference between them. Did either man behave better, from a moral point of view?[5]

Rachels concludes that any dissimilarity between killing and letting die does not make a moral difference.

Winston Nesbitt rejects Rachels' no-difference view, arguing that the real reason Smith and Jones seem equally reprehensible is that they are both *prepared to kill*. If we assumed that Jones is ready to let his cousin die but is not prepared to kill him, we would judge Jones less harshly than Smith. If this is correct, Nesbitt says, then Rachels fails to make his case.[6]

Some argue against active voluntary euthanasia by advancing another kind of distinction—between *intending* someone's death and *not*

IN DEPTH
OREGON'S DEATH WITH DIGNITY ACT

Under Oregon's Death With Dignity Act (DWDA), terminally ill adults may get prescriptions from their physicians for lethal drugs and self-administer them. In 2006, Oregon doctors wrote 65 such prescriptions, and 35 patients used the medications. From 1997 to 2006, 292 patients died under the law. The law specifies requirements for both doctor and patient.

To request a prescription for lethal medications, the DWDA requires that a patient must be:

- An adult (18 years of age or older)
- A resident of Oregon
- Capable (defined as able to make and communicate health care decisions)
- Diagnosed with a terminal illness that will lead to death within six months

Patients meeting these requirements are eligible to request a prescription for lethal medication from a licensed Oregon physician. To receive a prescription for lethal medication, the following steps must be fulfilled:

- The patient must make two oral requests to his physician, separated by at least 15 days.
- The patient must provide a written request to his or her physician, signed in the presence of two witnesses.
- The prescribing physician and a consulting physician must confirm the diagnosis and prognosis.
- The prescribing physician and a consulting physician must determine whether the patient is capable.
- If either physician believes the patient's judgment is impaired by a psychiatric or psychological disorder, the patient must be referred for a psychological examination.
- The prescribing physician must inform the patient of feasible alternatives to DWDA, including comfort care, hospice care, and pain control.
- The prescribing physician must request, but may not require, the patient to notify his or her next-of-kin of the prescription request.

From Oregon Department of Human Services, "Death With Dignity Act," *Oregon.gov*, March 2007, http://www.oregon.gov/DHS/ph/pas (2 February 2008).

intending but foreseeing it. This difference is emphasized in the doctrine of double effect, an essential feature of Roman Catholic ethics (see Chapter 2). Applying the distinction to euthanasia, we get this principle: It is wrong to intentionally harm someone (cause her death) to produce a good result (release from suffering, for example), but it is permissible to do something intended to produce a good result (release from suffering), even if the action leads to unintended but foreseen harm (her death). The difference is that in the former, a bad thing is directly intended; in the latter, a bad thing is not intended, only foreseen. By this formula, it would be wrong for a physician to try to relieve the chronic misery of a terminally ill patient by deliberately giving her high doses of morphine to hasten her death. But it would be morally acceptable for that physician to give the patient the same amount of morphine with the sole intention of easing her pain, even though the physician foresees that she will die as a result. (Giving a dying, suffering patient extremely high does of analgesics to the point of unconsciousness and accelerated death is known as terminal sedation; provided the patient consents, it is legal and generally considered morally permissible in medical practice.)

Many question whether in practice this intended/unintended distinction can always be drawn as clearly as proponents assume. For example:

In the case of euthanasia, just as in pain and symptom control, critics maintain, the physician's end may be the good one of relieving the patient's suffering. In neither case would death be wanted by the patient or the physician if the suffering could be avoided without it, but both patient and physician may be prepared to accept the patient's earlier death in order to relieve his or her suffering. Although the patient's death in the case of euthanasia may be the necessary means taken in the causal path to relief of suffering, it is the unavoidable side-effect following upon the relief of the patient's suffering in the causal path taken to achieve pain and symptom control.[7]

Others are skeptical of the intended/unintended principle itself. Their view is that even if it is wrong to intentionally do harm to bring about good, directly intending a patient's death may still be permissible because to her, *death may not be a harm*. If her pain is unbearable and untreatable, and she makes an autonomous request to die, then active euthanasia may be a blessing—and therefore within ethical bounds.

Probably the most straightforward arguments against active euthanasia and physician-assisted suicide are appeals to bad consequences. They make their case at the policy level, asking us to consider the ramifications of legalizing or widely accepting these practices. Often their logical shape is the slippery slope: Allowing active euthanasia or physician-assisted suicide will inevitably lead to heinous extensions or perversions of the original practices. The usual worries are that legalization will lead quickly from active voluntary euthanasia to active nonvoluntary euthanasia to outright involuntary forms of killing. Or that physicians or families will start pushing unwilling or unsure patients toward assisted suicide or voluntary euthanasia. Or that physicians and nurses will become increasingly willing to give lethal injections to people who are elderly, mentally ill, chronically ill, uninsured, and disabled. As one philosopher explains it,

[E]uthanasia as a policy is a slippery slope. A person apparently hopelessly ill may be allowed to take his own life. Then he may be permitted to deputize others to do it for him

should he no longer be able to act. The judgment of others then becomes the ruling factor. Already at this point euthanasia is not personal and voluntary, for others are acting "on behalf of" the patient as they see fit. This may well incline them to act on behalf of other patients who have not authorized them to exercise their judgment. It is only a short step, then, from voluntary euthanasia (self-inflicted or authorized), to directed euthanasia administered to a patient who has given no authorization, to involuntary euthanasia conducted as part of a social policy.[8]

The key premise in most slippery-slope arguments, then, is an empirical claim that a policy permitting active voluntary euthanasia or assisted-suicide will lead to unjustified killing (involuntary euthanasia, for example). Much of the debate therefore has centered on whether any good empirical evidence supports such a premise. Unfortunately, scientific research on the issue has been scant, with most of it focused on the Netherlands, where physician-assisted suicide and active voluntary euthanasia have been legal since 2002. (There is even less data on Oregon, where a law permitting physician-assisted suicide was passed by Oregon voters in 1994 but not green-lighted until the Supreme Court decision of 2006.) Thus both those who favor and those who oppose euthanasia and assisted suicide have tried to make their case with data from the Dutch experience. One question they want the research to answer is whether legalization of voluntary euthanasia has expanded the use of nonvoluntary euthanasia, for a significant expansion would seem to support slippery-slope arguments. Opponents of legalization point to all the instances of Dutch physicians performing active euthanasia without the patient's consent (approximately 1000 per year, or about 0.8 percent of all deaths nationwide). Proponents reply that most of those patients were already near death or had become incompetent after initially asking for euthanasia or that the euthanasia was passive, consisting of withholding or withdrawing treatment. Most of all, they emphasize that the few studies done so far do not demonstrate that legalization has significantly multiplied the cases of nonvoluntary euthanasia. Dutch authorities have reported that data gathered so far indicate that physician misconduct in euthanasia cases is extremely rare, despite rumors in the United States about rampant involuntary euthanasia committed by Dutch doctors.

The best minds on all sides of these debates recognize the need for better evidence to assess the slipperiness of the slippery slope. But they also know that the *mere possibility* of abuses arising from allowing euthanasia or assisted suicide is not in itself a good reason to ban the practices. If merely possible dangers or abuses justified prohibiting a practice, then we would have good reason to disallow advance directives, surrogate decision-making, and any kind of voluntary passive euthanasia. For a slippery-slope argument to work, there must be good evidence that the bad consequences of taking the first step are probable and serious.

APPLYING MAJOR THEORIES

Utilitarians can consistently adopt different views on active euthanasia and assisted suicide depending on how they define the good to be maximized, whether their moral focus is acts or rules, and how much importance they give to self-determination. Classic utilitarianism defines the good as happiness and would therefore judge the issues by how much happiness various actions might produce for everyone involved. From this perspective, euthanasia or assisted suicide for someone suffering horrible, inescapable pain might be permissible because ending life would bring about the most net happiness. Of course, the calculations would have to include other factors such as the psychological, social, and financial impact on the patient's family, friends, and caregivers. With everything factored in, the utilitarian answer could easily come out against euthanasia.

On the other hand, many utilitarians (following John Stuart Mill) think that there's more to

consider in making moral judgments than just net happiness. As utilitarian philosopher Peter Singer says,

> Many people prefer to live a life with less happiness or pleasure in it, and perhaps even more pain and suffering, if they can thereby fulfill other important preferences. For example, they may choose to strive for excellence in art, or literature, or sport, even though they know that they are unlikely to achieve it, and may experience pain and suffering in the attempt.[9]

Those in utilitarianism's camp who take this view are known as *preference utilitarians*, holding that right actions are those that satisfy more of a person's preferences overall. To them, killing is bad when it prevents someone from satisfying his own preferences; it can be good (as in euthanasia) when more of the person's future preferences will be frustrated than satisfied. According to Singer,

> [I]f the goods that life holds are, in general, reasons against killing, those reasons lose all their force when it is clear that those killed will not have such goods, or that the goods they have will be outweighed by bad things that will happen to them. When we apply this reasoning to the case of someone who is capable of judging the matter, and we add Mill's view that individuals are the best judges of their own interests, we can conclude that this reason against killing does not apply to a person who, with unimpaired capacities for judgment, comes to the conclusion that his or her future is so clouded that it would be better to die than to continue to live. Indeed, the reason against killing is turned into its opposite, a reason for acceding to that person's request.[10]

Rule-utilitarian approaches can lead to positions both favoring and opposing euthanasia and assisted suicide. Most slippery-slope arguments are essentially rule-utilitarian, asserting that a general policy of authorized killing will, step by step, take society down a path to awful consequences. The outcomes to be avoided are many, including increases in nonvoluntary or

PHYSICIAN-ASSISTED SUICIDE AND PUBLIC OPINION

When a person has a disease that cannot be cured and is living in severe pain, do you think doctors should or should not be allowed by law to assist the patient to commit suicide if the patient requests it?

Should	Should Not
68%	28%

Regardless of whether or not you think it should be legal, please tell me whether you personally believe that in general doctor-assisted suicide is morally acceptable or morally wrong.

Morally Acceptable	Morally Wrong
56%	37%

Gallup Poll, May 6–10, 2015; 1,024 adults nationwide; margin of error ±4.

Do you think a person has a moral right to suicide in any of the following circumstances?

When this person is suffering great pain and has no hope of improvement?

Yes 62%

When this person has an incurable disease?

Yes 56%

When this person is ready to die because living has become a burden?

Yes 38%

When this person is an extremely heavy burden on his or her family?

Yes 32%

Pew Research Center nationwide survey of 1,944 adults, March 21–April 8, 2013; margin of error ±2.9.

involuntary euthanasia, erosion of respect for the medical profession, and a weakening of society's abhorrence of homicide. Some also argue on rule-utilitarian grounds *for* a general policy, citing relief of suffering as the most obvious benefit.

The natural law view in Roman Catholicism condemns active and passive euthanasia, though the condemnation comes with qualifications. Directly intending to bring about a person's death to end suffering is prohibited, but the doctrine of double effect permits actions that have unintended but fatal results. As discussed earlier, the doctrine would not allow doctors to give high-dose analgesics to put patients out of their misery, but it would sanction their doing the same thing with the intention of easing pain though death is foreseen. In addition, under Catholic principles there is no obligation to use every means possible to prolong a person's life in every case. The Vatican declares:

When inevitable death is imminent in spite of the means used, it is permitted in conscience to take the decision to refuse forms of treatment that would only secure a precarious and burdensome prolongation of life, so long as the normal care due to the sick person in similar cases is not interrupted.[11]

What is clear in Kant's theory is that suicide is prohibited because it treats persons as mere things and obliterates personhood. Kant asserts that "the rule of morality does not admit of [suicide] under any condition because it degrades human nature below the level of animal nature and so destroys it." It is also apparent on Kant's view that competent persons must not be killed or permitted to die. But it is not obvious what Kant's opinion would be of individuals no longer regarded as persons because they have lapsed into a persistent vegetative state. Would

Nancy Cruzan

In the 1990 case of *Cruzan v. Director, Missouri Department of Health*, the U.S. Supreme Court issued its first momentous ruling involving an individual's "right to die." The question was whether a feeding tube could be removed from a young woman named Nancy Cruzan, who had been left in a persistent vegetative state after a terrible car crash.

On January 11, 1983, Nancy Cruzan's car overturned on an icy road in Missouri, flinging her into a ditch and stopping her heart. By the time paramedics restarted it, her brain had been oxygen-deprived for at least 15 minutes. The resulting brain damage was profound and permanent. So at age 25 she fell into a persistent vegetative state, a benighted condition of minimal brain activity without consciousness or purposeful behavior. "The vegetative state," says an expert panel, "is a clinical condition of complete unawareness of the self and the environment. . . . Recovery from a nontraumatic persistent vegetative state after three months is exceedingly rare."[12] Nancy lingered in that state for years, her body coiled into a rigid fetal position, nourished only by a surgically implanted feeding tube.

After three years of hoping that Nancy would somehow recover, her parents finally asked that the feeding tube be removed so she could die in peace. "You try your damnedest as long as there's hope," said Nancy's father, "and then when there is none anymore, you must let her go."

But authorities in the state of Missouri saw things differently. They sought to block the removal of Nancy's feeding tube. The Missouri Supreme Court said that the state has an extremely strong interest in preserving life and that the Cruzans may not disconnect their daughter's feeding tube without "clear and convincing evidence" of what Nancy would have wanted. At one time she had mentioned to a friend that she would not want to be kept alive like a "vegetable," but she had left no living will or other explicit instructions.

The Cruzans appealed to the U.S. Supreme Court, and in June 1990 the Court delivered its far-reaching decision in its first right-to-die case. The Court held that Missouri had a legitimate interest in demanding "clear and convincing evidence" of an incompetent individual's preferences. By sanctioning this strict standard of evidence, the Court effectively ruled against the Cruzans. But in making its decision, it also laid out some weighty principles pertaining to a person's end-of-life choices.

The Court found that competent individuals have a constitutionally guaranteed "liberty interest" in refusing medical treatment, even when refusing could bring about their death. And for the first time, it acknowledged that if a person became incompetent, this right could be exercised through a living will or by a designated surrogate. States could still restrict this liberty interest, however, if a person's refusal of treatment was not stated clearly or strongly enough.

As part of its case, the state argued that there was a difference between withdrawing medical treatment and withdrawing food and fluids. But the Supreme Court recognized no such distinction.

A few months after the Court's ruling, Missouri said it would stop opposing the Cruzans' efforts, and a Missouri judge declared that the evidence of Nancy's intent was sufficiently convincing. In December 1990 he ordered her feeding tube removed.

On December 26, 1990, at the age of 33 and nearly eight years after her accident, Nancy Cruzan died peacefully.

respect for persons demand that they be kept alive at all costs—or that we perform nonvoluntary euthanasia to allow them to die with dignity?

KEY TERMS
active euthanasia
euthanasia
involuntary euthanasia
nonvoluntary euthanasia
passive euthanasia
physician-assisted suicide
voluntary euthanasia

SUMMARY
Euthanasia is directly or indirectly bringing about the death of another person for that person's sake. A common distinction is that active euthanasia involves performing an action that directly causes someone's death, while passive euthanasia is allowing someone to die by not doing something to prolong life. Voluntary euthanasia is performed when competent patients request or agree to it; nonvoluntary euthanasia, when patients are not competent to chose for themselves and have not previously disclosed their preferences. Involuntary euthanasia, both illegal and morally impermissible, is bringing about someone's death against her will or without asking for her consent. In physician-assisted suicide a patient takes his own life with the help of a physician.

Death traditionally has been understood as the cessation of breathing and heartbeat, but medical advances have rendered this notion problematic. The whole brain view is now the standard in legal and medical matters. It says that an individual should be judged dead when all brain functions permanently stop. Many experts object to this definition because some physiological processes such as respiration are partly independent of brain functions, a fact that would suggest on the whole brain view that individuals in persistent vegetative states with some brain activity must be considered alive. An alternative notion is the higher brain standard, which asserts that individuals are dead when the higher brain functions responsible for consciousness permanently close down. This view implies that those in persistent vegetative states whose higher brain functions have irreversibly ceased are dead.

The main argument for the moral permissibility of active voluntary euthanasia is an appeal to autonomy. It contends that respecting people's inherent right of self-determination means respecting their autonomous choices about ending their lives. Another major argument appeals to the principle of beneficence, or mercy: If we are in a position to relieve the severe suffering of another without excessive cost to ourselves, we have an obligation to do so.

An important argument against active voluntary euthanasia appeals to the supposed moral difference between killing and letting die. Killing is thought to be worse than letting die, so giving a patient a lethal injection to effect an easy death is wrong, but disconnecting his feeding tube may be permissible. Critics argue that there is no morally significant difference between these two. Those opposed to voluntary euthanasia make a related distinction between intending someone's death and not intending but foreseeing it. The former is said to be wrong; the latter, permissible. Many are skeptical of this distinction as well.

Very often cases against active euthanasia and physician-assisted suicide are built on slippery-slope arguments, which contend that allowing these practices would inevitably lead to abuses, most notably unjustified killing. Typically, both those who make these arguments and those who criticize them appeal to empirical data on the legalized use of euthanasia or physician-assisted suicide in Oregon or the Netherlands. But the data are sparse and subject to much debate, leaving the key premise in most slippery-slope arguments weak.

Cases for Evaluation

CASE I

Doctor-Aided Suicide and "Vulnerable Groups"

(*ScienceDaily*)—Contrary to arguments by critics, a University of Utah–led study found that legalizing physician-assisted suicide in Oregon and the Netherlands did not result in a disproportionate number of deaths among the elderly, poor, women, minorities, uninsured, minors, chronically ill, less educated, or psychiatric patients.

Of 10 "vulnerable groups" examined in the study, only AIDS patients used doctor-assisted suicide at elevated rates.

"Fears about the impact on vulnerable people have dominated debate about physician-assisted suicide. We find no evidence to support those fears where this practice already is legal," says the study's lead author, bioethicist Margaret Battin, a University of Utah distinguished professor of philosophy and adjunct professor of internal medicine.

The study will be published in the October 2007 issue of the *Journal of Medical Ethics*. Battin conducted the research with public health physician Agnes van der Heide, of Erasmus Medical Center, Rotterdam; psychiatrist Linda Ganzini at Oregon Health & Science University, Portland; and physician Gerrit van der Wal and health scientist Bregje Onwuteaka-Philipsen, of the VU University Medical Center, Amsterdam. Van der Wal currently is inspector general of the Netherlands Health Care Inspectorate, which advises that nation's health minister.

The research deals with the so-called "slippery-slope" argument that has been made by critics of doctor-assisted suicide and has raised concern even among proponents. The argument is that by making it legal for medical doctors to help certain patients end their lives, vulnerable people will die in disproportionately large numbers.

"Would these patients be pressured, manipulated or forced to request or accept physician-assisted dying by overburdened family members, callous physicians, or institutions or insurers concerned about their own profits," the researchers asked.

The American College of Physicians said in 2005 that it was "concerned with the risks that legalization [of physician-assisted suicide] posed to vulnerable populations, including poor persons, patients with dementia, disabled persons, those from minority groups that have experienced discrimination, those confronting costly chronic illnesses, or very young children." . . .

Battin's team analyzed data on assisted suicide and voluntary active euthanasia in the Netherlands during 1985–2005—data taken from four government studies and several smaller ones. They analyzed Oregon Department of Human Services annual reports for 1998–2006, and surveys of physicians and hospice professionals.

The findings fell into three categories, based on the strength of the data. The researchers found:

- Direct evidence that elderly people, women, and uninsured people do not die in disproportionate numbers where physician-assisted death is legal, but AIDS patients do. (The insurance data is from Oregon only; everyone is insured in the Netherlands.)
- Evidence that is partly direct and partly inferred showing that physician-assisted death does not kill disproportionate numbers of people who are poor, uneducated, racial and ethnic minorities, minors, or people with chronic physical or mental disabilities or chronic but not terminal illnesses.
- Evidence that is based on inference or that is partly contested showing that people with psychiatric illness—including depression and Alzheimer's disease—are not likely to die in lopsided numbers.

"Those who received physician-assisted dying . . . appeared to enjoy comparative social, economic, educational, professional and other privileges," the researchers write.

The researchers noted that in both Oregon and the Netherlands, people who received a doctor's help in dying averaged 70 years old, and 80 percent were cancer patients.*

Suppose the data of this study are accurate. Would they show that all slippery-slope arguments against physician-assisted suicide are unsuccessful? Suppose the study proved that legalization did harm vulnerable populations. Would that finding support the conclusion that physician-assisted suicide should not be legalized under any circumstances? What might someone who is opposed to legalization say about this study? Or someone who favors legalization? How does the news of this study affect your own views on legalization? Give reasons for your answer.

*"Doctor-Aided Suicide: No Slippery Slope, Study Finds," Science Daily, 29 September 2007, http://www.sciencedaily.com/releases/2007/09/070926191348.htm (10 February 2008).

CASE 2

Suicide Pacts Among Friends

(*London Telegraph*)—Jenni Murray, the presenter of BBC Radio 4's *Woman's Hour*, has made plans to end her life if she becomes a burden to her family.

She said: "When my time comes I want to be able to decide about my destiny."

The last thing she wanted, she said, was for her children to suffer from her being desperately ill.

She is sealing a pact with two friends that they will assist each other to die if any of them is diagnosed with a debilitating and incurable illness. Methods they might use include injections or smothering with a pillow.

This is despite a law outlawing assisted suicide, which Murray says is sustained by a religious minority.

She speaks of the pact tomorrow night on a Channel 5 documentary, *Don't Get Me Started!*, that produces statistics to back the theory that many people in the country share her views on euthanasia.

Her appearance is part of a "personal rant" series in which noted people are given the chance to sound off about a subject they feel strongly about.

Publicity material for the show says that Murray "does not want to look after her sick and aging mother, and plans to end her own life when she becomes a burden to those around her."

The network said: "Jenni is angry that, having fought so hard to become liberated and independent, women are now being trapped into caring for dependent parents."

Murray, 56, from Barnsley, South Yorks, has been presenting *Woman's Hour* since 1987. In 1999 she was awarded an OBE for radio broadcasting.

Her pact is with Sally Feldman, a former editor of *Woman's Hour*, and Jane Wilton, another friend. They plan to sign a written agreement.

Murray is the vice-president of a society that concerns itself with Parkinson's disease, which her mother suffers from. Her father is a carer.

In the programme she emphasises that, while she supports her friends helping her to die, she would find it hard to do the same if her mother told her "Let me go."*

Do you agree with Murray's decision? Does she have a right to take her life for any reason? Is not wanting to be a burden to one's family a good reason? Should assisted-suicide pacts be legalized? Is it just as moral (or immoral) to assist in a friend's suicide as it is to directly kill her? Explain your answers.

*Hugh Davies, "Jenni Murray Makes a Suicide Pact," Telegraph.co.uk, 14 August 2006, http://www.telegraph.co.uk/news/main.jhtml?xml;eq/news/2006/08/14/nmurray14.xml (10 February 2008).

CASE 3

"Baby Euthanasia"

(*TimesOnline*)—When Frank and Anita's daughter Chanou was born with an extremely rare, incurable illness in August 2000, they knew that her life would be short and battled against the odds to make it happy.

They struggled around the clock against their baby's pain. "We tried all sorts of things," said Anita, a 37-year-old local government worker. "She cried all the time. Every time I touched her it hurt."

Chanou was suffering from a metabolic disorder that had resulted in abnormal bone development. Doctors gave her no more than 30 months to live.

"We felt terrible watching her suffer," said Anita at their home near Amsterdam. "We felt we were letting her down."

Frank and Anita began to believe that their daughter would be better off dead. "She kept throwing up milk that was fed through a tube in her nose," said Anita. "She seemed to be saying, 'Mummy, I don't want to live any more. Let me go.'"

Eventually, doctors agreed to help the baby die at seven months. The feeding was stopped. Chanou was given morphine. "We were with her at that last moment," said Anita. "She was exhausted. She took a very deep last breath. It was so peaceful. It made me feel at peace inside to know that she wasn't suffering any more."

Even so, they felt that the suffering had gone on too long. Child euthanasia is illegal in Holland and doctors were afraid of being prosecuted. "It was a long road to find the humane solution that we reluctantly decided we wanted," said Frank, a bank worker.

Each year in Holland at least 15 seriously ill babies, most of them with severe spina bifida or chromosomal abnormalities, are helped to die by doctors acting with the parents' consent. But only a fraction of those cases are reported to the authorities because of the doctors' fears of being charged with murder.

Things are about to change, however, making it much easier for parents and doctors to end the suffering of an infant.

A committee set up to regulate the practice will begin operating in the next few weeks, effectively making Holland, where adult euthanasia is legal, the first country in the world to allow "baby euthanasia" as well.

The development has angered opponents of euthanasia who warn of a "slippery slope" leading to abuses by doctors and parents, who will be making decisions for individuals incapable of expressing a will.

Others welcome more openness about a practice that, according to doctors, goes on secretly anyway—even in Britain—regardless of the law. "It is a giant step forward and we are very happy about it," said Eduard Verhagen, clinical director of paediatrics at the University Medical Centre in Groningen, northern Holland.

Anti-euthanasia campaigners have been addressing hate mail to "Dr. Death," as they call him, ever since he admitted having personally overseen four "assisted neo-natal terminations." He then began drawing up guidelines for doctors carrying out euthanasia on babies.

It forced the government to confront the issue and Verhagen's so-called "Groningen protocol" has been adopted as the standard to be upheld by the regulatory committee.

It emphasises that life can be ended only in cases involving "unbearable suffering," with parental consent and after consultation with other physicians.

"If a child is untreatably ill," Verhagen explained, "there can be horrendous suffering that makes the last few days or weeks of this child's life unbearable. Now the question is: Are you going to leave the child like that or are you going to prevent that suffering?" He went on: "Does the child have to sit it out until the end? We think that the answer is no. There can be circumstances where, under very strict conditions, if all the requirements are fulfilled, active ending of life can be an option—but only in cases of untreatable disease and unbearable suffering."*

How would you respond to Verhagen's questions in the last paragraph? Do you believe that neonatal euthanasia performed under the strict conditions described by Verhagen is morally permissible? Why or why not? Should it be legalized?

---

*"Holland to Allow 'Baby Euthanasia,'" *TimesOnline*, 5 March 2006, http://www.timesonline.co.uk/article/0,2089-2069963,00.html (10 February 2008).

FURTHER READING

Margaret Pabst Battin, *Ending Life: Ethics and the Way We Die* (New York: Oxford University Press, 2005).

Tom L. Beauchamp, ed., *Intending Death: The Ethics of Assisted Suicide and Euthanasia* (Upper Saddle River, NJ: Prentice-Hall, 1996).

R. B. Brandt, "The Morality and Rationality of Suicide," in *A Handbook for the Study of Suicide*, ed. Seymour Perlin (New York: Oxford University Press, 1975), 61–75.

Lonnie R. Bristow, President of the American Medical Association, "Statement on Physician-Assisted Suicide

Before the United States House of Representatives Committee on the Judiciary, Subcommittee on the Constitution," *Congressional Record*, April 29, 1996.

Dan W. Brock, "Medical Decisions at the End of Life," in *A Companion to Bioethics*, ed. Helga Kuhse and Peter Singer (Malden, MA: Blackwell, 2001), 231–41.

Rebecca Dresser, "Schiavo's Legacy: The Need for an Objective Standard," *Hastings Center Report*, vol. 35, no. 3 (May–June 2005), pp. 20–22.

Death with Dignity National Center, "Death with Dignity Around the U.S.," 14 October 2015, http://www.deathwithdignity.org/advocates/national (2 November 2015).

Gerald Dworkin, "Physician-Assisted Death: The State of the Debate," in *The Oxford Handbook of Bioethics*, ed. Bonnie Steinbock (Oxford: Oxford University Press, 2007), 375–92.

Gerald Dworkin, R. Frey, and S. Bok, *Euthanasia and Physician-Assisted Suicide* (Cambridge, UK: Cambridge University Press, 1998).

Ezekiel J. Emanuel, "Whose Right to Die?" *The Atlantic*, March 1997, http://www.theatlantic.com/magazine/archive/1997/03/whose-right-to-die/304641/ (2 November 2015).

Philippa Foot, "Euthanasia," *Philosophy & Public Affairs* 6.2 (1977), 85–112.

Walter Glannon, "Medical Decisions at the End of Life," in *Biomedical Ethics* (New York: Oxford University Press, 2005), 119–42.

Jonathan Glover, "The Sanctity of Life," in *Bioethics: An Anthology*, ed. Helga Kuhse and Peter Singer (Oxford: Blackwell, 1999), 193–202.

Leon Kass, "Is There a Right to Die?" *Hastings Center Report* 23.1 (1993), 34–43.

Mark Murphy, "The Natural Law Tradition in Ethics," in *Stanford Encyclopedia of Philosophy*, 11 March 2008, http://plato.stanford.edu/entries/natural-law-ethics (9 June 2008).

New York State Task Force on Life and the Law, *When Death Is Sought: Assisted Suicide and Euthanasia in the Medical Context* (Albany: New York State Department of Health, April 1997).

Louis P. Pojman, "Euthanasia," in *Life and Death* (Belmont, CA: Wadsworth, 2000), 85–94.

The President's Commission for the Study of Ethical Problems in Medicine and Biomedical and Behavioral Research, *Defining Death* (Washington, DC: Government Printing Office, 1981).

ProCon.org, "Should Euthanasia or Physician-Assisted Suicide Be Legal?" 6 October 2015, http://euthanasia.procon.org/view.answers.php?questionID=001320 (2 November 2015).

Peter Singer, "Voluntary Euthanasia: A Utilitarian Perspective," *Bioethics* 17.5–6 (2003), 526–41.

Bonnie Steinbock and Alastair Norcross, ed., *Killing and Letting Die*, 2nd ed. (New York: Fordham University Press, 1994).

R. M. Veatch, "Terri Schiavo, Son Hudson and 'Nonbeneficial' Medical Treatments," *Health Affairs*, vol. 24, no. 4 (July–August 2005), pp. 976–9.

Robert Young, "Voluntary Euthanasia," in *The Stanford Encyclopedia of Philosophy* (Winter 2007 ed.), ed. Edward N. Zalta, http://plato.stanford.edu/archives/win2007/entries/euthanasia-voluntary/ (2008).

NOTES

1. A definition suggested by Philippa Foot (in "Euthanasia," *Philosophy & Public Affairs* 6.2 [1977], 85–112) and by Helga Kuhse (in "Euthanasia," in *A Companion to Ethics*, ed. Peter Singer [Oxford: Blackwell, 1933], 294–302.)

2. American Medical Association, *Opinions of the Judicial Council* (Chicago: American Medical Association, 1973).

3. Robert Young, "Voluntary Euthanasia," in *The Stanford Encyclopedia of Philosophy* (Winter 2007 ed.), ed. Edward N. Zalta, http://plato.stanford.edu/archives/win2007/entries/euthanasia-voluntary (28 January 2008).

4. Dan W. Brock, "Voluntary Active Euthanasia," *Hastings Center Report* 22.2 (March/April 1992), 11–12, 14–17, 19–21.

5. James Rachels, "Active and Passive Euthanasia," *New England Journal of Medicine* 292.2 (9 January 1975), 79.

6. Winston Nesbitt, "Is Killing No Worse Than Letting Die?" *Journal of Applied Philosophy* 12.1 (1995), 101–5.

7. Dan W. Brock, "Medical Decisions at the End of Life," in *A Companion to Bioethics*, ed. Helga Kuhse and Peter Singer (Malden, MA: Blackwell, 2001), 240.

8. J. Gay-Williams, "The Wrongfulness of Euthanasia," in *Intervention and Reflection: Basic Issues in Medical Ethics*, 7th ed., ed. Ronald Munson (Belmont, CA: Wadsworth, 2004), 710–11.

9. Peter Singer, "Voluntary Euthanasia: A Utilitarian Perspective," *Bioethics* 17.5–6 (2003), 526–41.

10. Sacred Congregation for the Doctrine of the Faith, *Declaration on Euthanasia* (Vatican City: The Vatican, 1980).

11. The Multi-Society Task Force on PVS, "Medical Aspects of the Persistent Vegetative State," *New England Journal of Medicine* 330.21 (26 May 1994), 1499–1508.

READINGS

Death and Dignity: A Case of Individualized Decision Making

TIMOTHY E. QUILL

Quill recounts the story of Diane, a patient of his with terminal cancer who wanted to face death with dignity and on her own terms. He admits that although he did not directly assist her in committing suicide, he "helped indirectly to make it possible, successful, and relatively painless." Quill says that from this experience he learned about, among other things, "the range of help I can provide if I know people well and if I allow them to say what they really want."

Diane was feeling tired and had a rash. A common scenario, though there was something subliminally worrisome that prompted me to check her blood count. Her hematocrit was 22, and the white-cell count was 4.3 with some metamyelocytes and unusual white cells. I wanted it to be viral, trying to deny what was staring me in the face. Perhaps in a repeated count it would disappear. I called Diane and told her it might be more serious than I had initially thought—that the test needed to be repeated and that if she felt worse, we might have to move quickly. When she pressed for the possibilities, I reluctantly opened the door to leukemia. Hearing the word seemed to make it exist. "Oh, shit!" she said. "Don't tell me that." Oh, shit! I thought, I wish I didn't have to.

Diane was no ordinary person (although no one I have ever come to know has been really ordinary). She was raised in an alcoholic family and had felt alone for much of her life. She had vaginal cancer as a young woman. Through much of her adult life, she had struggled with depression and her own alcoholism. I had come to know, respect, and admire her over the previous eight years as she confronted these problems and gradually overcame them. She was an incredibly clear, at times brutally honest, thinker and communicator. As she took control of her life, she developed a strong sense of independence and confidence. In the previous 3½ years, her hard work had paid off. She was completely abstinent from alcohol, she had established much deeper connections with her husband, college-age son, and several friends, and her business and her artistic work were blossoming. She felt she was really living fully for the first time.

Not surprisingly, the repeated blood count was abnormal, and detailed examination of the peripheral-blood smear showed myelocytes. I advised her to come into the hospital, explaining that we needed to do a bone marrow biopsy and make some decisions relatively rapidly. She came to the hospital knowing what we would find. She was terrified, angry, and sad. Although we knew the odds, we both clung to the thread of possibility that it might be something else.

The bone marrow confirmed the worst: acute myelomonocytic leukemia. In the face of this tragedy, we looked for signs of hope. This is an area of medicine in which technological intervention has been successful, with cures 25 percent of the time—long-term cures. As I probed the costs of these cures, I heard about induction chemotherapy (three weeks in the hospital, prolonged neutropenia, probable infectious complications, and hair loss; 75 percent of patients respond, 25 percent do not). For the survivors, this is followed by consolidation chemotherapy (with similar side effects; another 25 percent die, for a

From Timothy E. Quill, "Death and Dignity: A Case of Individualized Decision Making," *New England Journal of Medicine*, 324, no. 10 (March 7, 1991): 691–694.

net survival of 50 percent). Those still alive, to have a reasonable chance of long-term survival, then need bone marrow transplantation (hospitalization for two months and whole-body irradiation, with complete killing of the bone marrow, infectious complications, and the possibility for graft-versus-host disease—with a survival of approximately 50 percent, or 25 percent of the original group). Though hematologists may argue over the exact percentages, they don't argue about the outcome of no treatment—certain death in days, weeks, or at most a few months.

Believing that delay was dangerous, our oncologist broke the news to Diane and began making plans to insert a Hickman catheter and begin induction chemotherapy that afternoon. When I saw her shortly thereafter, she was enraged at his presumption that she would want treatment, and devastated by the finality of the diagnosis. All she wanted to do was go home and be with her family. She had no further questions about treatment and in fact had decided that she wanted none. Together we lamented her tragedy and the unfairness of life. Before she left, I felt the need to be sure that she and her husband understood that there was some risk in delay, that the problem was not going to go away, and that we needed to keep considering the options over the next several days. We agreed to meet in two days.

She returned in two days with her husband and son. They had talked extensively about the problem and the options. She remained very clear about her wish not to undergo chemotherapy and to live whatever time she had left outside the hospital. As we explored her thinking further, it became clear that she was convinced she would die during the period of treatment and would suffer unspeakably in the process (from hospitalization, from lack of control over her body, from the side effects of chemotherapy, and from pain and anguish). Although I could offer support and my best effort to minimize her suffering if she chose treatment, there was no way I could say any of this would not occur. In fact, the last four patients with acute leukemia at our hospital had died very painful deaths in the hospital during various stages of treatment (a fact I did not share with her). Her family wished

she would choose treatment but sadly accepted her decision. She articulated very clearly that it was she who would be experiencing all the side effects of treatment and that odds of 25 percent were not good enough for her to undergo so toxic a course of therapy, given her expectations of chemotherapy and hospitalization and the absence of a closely matched bone marrow donor. I had her repeat her understanding of the treatment, the odds, and what to expect if there were no treatment. I clarified a few misunderstandings, but she had a remarkable grasp of the options and implications.

I have been a longtime advocate of active, informed patient choice of treatment or nontreatment, and of a patient's right to die with as much control and dignity as possible. Yet there was something about her giving up a 25 percent chance of long-term survival in favor of almost certain death that disturbed me. I had seen Diane fight and use her considerable inner resources to overcome alcoholism and depression, and I half expected her to change her mind over the next week. Since the window of time in which effective treatment can be initiated is rather narrow, we met several times that week. We obtained a second hematology consultation and talked at length about the meaning and implications of treatment and nontreatment. She talked to a psychologist she had seen in the past. I gradually understood the decision from her perspective and became convinced that it was the right decision for her. We arranged for home hospice care (although at that time Diane felt reasonably well, was active, and looked healthy), left the door open for her to change her mind, and tried to anticipate how to keep her comfortable in the time she had left.

Just as I was adjusting to her decision, she opened up another area that would stretch me profoundly. It was extraordinarily important to Diane to maintain control of herself and her own dignity during the time remaining to her. When this was no longer possible, she clearly wanted to die. As a former director of a hospice program, I know how to use pain medicines to keep patients comfortable and lessen suffering. I explained the philosophy of comfort care, which I strongly believe in. Although Diane understood and appreciated this, she had known of people lingering in what was called relative comfort, and she wanted no part of it. When the time came, she wanted to take her life in the least painful way possible. Knowing of her desire for independence and her decision to stay in control, I thought this request made perfect sense. I acknowledged and explored this wish but also thought that it was out of the realm of currently accepted medical practice and that it was more than I could offer or promise. In our discussion, it became clear that preoccupation with her fear of a lingering death would interfere with Diane's getting the most out of the time she had left until she found a safe way to ensure her death. I feared the effects of a violent death on her family, the consequences of an ineffective suicide that would leave her lingering in precisely the state she dreaded so much, and the possibility that a family member would be forced to assist her, with all the legal and personal repercussions that would follow. She discussed this at length with her family. They believed that they should respect her choice. With this in mind, I told Diane that information was available from the Hemlock Society that might be helpful to her.

A week later she phoned me with a request for barbiturates for sleep. Since I knew that this was an essential ingredient in a Hemlock Society suicide, I asked her to come to the office to talk things over. She was more than willing to protect me by participating in a superficial conversation about her insomnia, but it was important to me to know how she planned to use the drugs and to be sure that she was not in despair or overwhelmed in a way that might color her judgment. In our discussion, it was apparent that she was having trouble sleeping, but it was also evident that the security of having enough barbiturates available to commit suicide when and if the time came would leave her secure enough to live fully and concentrate on the present. It was clear that she was not despondent and that in fact she was making deep, personal connections with her family and close friends. I made sure that she knew how to use the barbiturates for sleep, and also that she knew the amount needed to commit suicide. We agreed to meet regularly, and she promised to meet with me before taking her life, to ensure that all other avenues had been exhausted. I wrote the prescription with an uneasy feeling about the boundaries

I was exploring—spiritual, legal, professional, and personal. Yet I also felt strongly that I was setting her free to get the most out of the time she had left, and to maintain dignity and control on her own terms until her death.

The next several months were very intense and important for Diane. Her son stayed home from college, and they were able to be with one another and say much that had not been said earlier. Her husband did his work at home so that he and Diane could spend more time together. She spent time with her closest friends. I had her come into the hospital for a conference with our residents, at which she illustrated in a most profound and personal way the importance of informed decision making, the right to refuse treatment, and the extraordinarily personal effects of illness and interaction with the medical system. There were emotional and physical hardships as well. She had periods of intense sadness and anger. Several times she became very weak, but she received transfusions as an outpatient and responded with marked improvement of symptoms. She had two serious infections that responded surprisingly well to empirical courses of oral antibiotics. After three tumultuous months, there were two weeks of relative calm and well-being, and fantasies of a miracle began to surface.

Unfortunately, we had no miracle. Bone pain, weakness, fatigue, and fevers began to dominate her life. Although the hospice workers, family members, and I tried our best to minimize the suffering and promote comfort, it was clear that the end was approaching. Diane's immediate future held what she feared the most—increasing discomfort, dependence, and hard choices between pain and sedation. She called up her closest friends and asked them to come over to say goodbye, telling them that she would be leaving soon. As we had agreed, she let me know as well. When we met, it was clear that she knew what she was doing, that she was sad and frightened to be leaving, but that she would be even more terrified to stay and suffer. In our tearful goodbye, she promised a reunion in the future at her favorite spot on the edge of Lake Geneva, with dragons swimming in the sunset.

Two days later her husband called to say that Diane had died. She had said her final goodbyes to her husband and son that morning, and asked them to leave her alone for an hour. After an hour, which must have seemed an eternity, they found her on the couch, lying very still and covered by her favorite shawl. There was no sign of struggle. She seemed to be at peace. They called me for advice about how to proceed. When I arrived at their house, Diane indeed seemed peaceful. Her husband and son were quiet. We talked about what a remarkable person she had been. They seemed to have no doubts about the course she had chosen or about their cooperation, although the unfairness of her illness and the finality of her death were overwhelming to us all.

I called the medical examiner to inform him that a hospice patient had died. When asked about the cause of death, I said, "acute leukemia." He said that was fine and that we should call a funeral director. Although acute leukemia was the truth, it was not the whole story. Yet any mention of suicide would have given rise to a police investigation and probably brought the arrival of an ambulance crew for resuscitation. Diane would have become a "coroner's case," and the decision to perform an autopsy would have been made at the discretion of the medical examiner. The family or I could have been subject to criminal prosecution, and I to professional review, for our roles in support of Diane's choices. Although I truly believe that the family and I gave her the best care possible, allowing her to define her limits and directions as much as possible, I am not sure the law, society, or the medical profession would agree. So I said "acute leukemia" to protect all of us, to protect Diane from an invasion into her past and her body, and to continue to shield society from the knowledge of the degree of suffering that people often undergo in the process of dying. Suffering can be lessened to some extent, but in no way eliminated or made benign, by the careful intervention of a competent, caring physician, given current social constraints.

Diane taught me about the range of help I can provide if I know people well and if I allow them to say what they really want. She taught me about life, death, and honesty and about taking charge and facing tragedy squarely when it strikes. She taught me that I can take small risks for people that I really know and care about. Although I did not assist in her suicide directly, I helped indirectly to make it possible, successful, and relatively painless. Although I know we have measures to help control pain and lessen suffering, to think that people do not suffer in the process of dying is an illusion. Prolonged dying can occasionally be peaceful, but more often the role of the physician and family is limited to lessening but not eliminating severe suffering.

I wonder how many families and physicians secretly help patients over the edge into death in the face of such severe suffering. I wonder how many severely ill or dying patients secretly take their lives, dying alone in despair. I wonder whether the image of Diane's final aloneness will persist in the minds of her family, or if they will remember more the intense, meaningful months they had together before she died. I wonder whether Diane struggled in that last hour, and whether the Hemlock Society's way of death by suicide is the most benign. I wonder why Diane, who gave so much to so many of us, had to be alone for the last hour of her life. I wonder whether I will see Diane again, on the shore of Lake Geneva at sunset, with dragons swimming on the horizon.

Voluntary Active Euthanasia

DAN W. BROCK

Brock argues that the same two basic moral principles that support a patient's right to make choices about life-sustaining treatment also support the permissibility of voluntary active euthanasia. The first principle is individual self-determination; the second is individual well-being. Individual self-determination applies to the manner, circumstances, and timing of one's death and dying. A concern for individual well-being may justify euthanasia when a suffering patient determines that life is no longer a benefit.

. . . The central ethical argument for euthanasia is familiar. It is that the very same two fundamental ethical values supporting the consensus on patient's rights to decide about life-sustaining treatment also support the ethical permissibility of euthanasia. These values are individual self-determination or autonomy and individual well-being. By self-determination as it bears on euthanasia, I mean people's interest in making important decisions about their lives for themselves according to their own values or conceptions of a good life, and in being left free to act on those decisions. Self-determination is valuable because it permits people to form and live in accordance with their own conception of a good life, at least within the bounds of justice and consistent with others doing so as well. In exercising self-determination people take responsibility for their lives and for the kinds of persons they become. A central aspect of human dignity lies in people's capacity to direct their lives in this way. The value of exercising self-determination presupposes some minimum of decision making capacities or competence, which thus limits the scope of euthanasia supported by self-determination; it cannot justifiably be administered, for example, in cases of serious dementia or treatable clinical depression.

Does the value of individual self-determination extend to the time and manner of one's death? Most people are very concerned about the nature of the last stage of their lives. This reflects not just a fear of

experiencing substantial suffering when dying, but also a desire to retain dignity and control during this last period of life. Death is today increasingly preceded by a long period of significant physical and mental decline, due in part to the technological interventions of modern medicine. Many people adjust to these disabilities and find meaning and value in new activities and ways. Others find the impairments and burdens in the last stage of their lives at some point sufficiently great to make life no longer worth living. For many patients near death, maintaining the quality of one's life, avoiding great suffering, maintaining one's dignity, and insuring that others remember us as we wish them to become of paramount importance and outweigh merely extending one's life. But there is no single, objectively correct answer for everyone as to when, if at all, one's life becomes all things considered a burden and unwanted. If self-determination is a fundamental value, then the great variability among people on this question makes it especially important that individuals control the manner, circumstances, and timing of their dying and death.

The other main value that supports euthanasia is individual well-being. It might seem that individual well-being conflicts with a person's self-determination when the person requests euthanasia. Life itself is commonly taken to be a central good for persons, often valued for its own sake, as well as necessary for pursuit of all other goods within a life. But when a competent patient decides to forgo all further life-sustaining treatment then the patient, either explicitly or implicitly, commonly decides that the best life possible for him or her with treatment is of sufficiently poor quality that it is worse than no further life at all. Life is no longer considered a benefit by the patient, but has now become a burden. The same judgment underlies a request for euthanasia: continued life is seen by the patient as no longer a benefit, but now a burden. Especially in the often severely compromised and debilitated states of many critically ill or dying patients, there is no objective standard, but only the competent patient's judgment of whether continued life is no longer a benefit.

Of course, sometimes there are conditions, such as clinical depression, that call into question whether the patient has made a competent choice, either to forgo life-sustaining treatment or to seek euthanasia, and then the patient's choice need not be evidence that continued life is no longer a benefit for him or her. Just as with decisions about treatment, a determination of incompetence can warrant not honoring the patient's choice; in the case of treatment, we then transfer decisional authority to a surrogate, though in the case of voluntary active euthanasia a determination that the patient is incompetent means that choice is not possible.

The value or right of self-determination does not entitle patients to compel physicians to act contrary to their own moral or professional values. Physicians are moral and professional agents whose own self-determination or integrity should be respected as well. If performing euthanasia became legally permissible, but conflicted with a particular physician's reasonable understanding of his or her moral or professional responsibilities, the care of a patient who requested euthanasia should be transferred to another.

Most opponents do not deny that there are some cases in which the values of patient self-determination and well-being support euthanasia. Instead, they commonly offer two kinds of arguments against it that on their view outweigh or override this support. The first kind of argument is that in any individual case where considerations of the patient's self-determination and well-being do support euthanasia, it is nevertheless always ethically wrong or impermissible. The second kind of argument grants that in some individual cases euthanasia may not be ethically wrong, but maintains nonetheless that public and legal policy should never permit it.

The first kind of argument focuses on features of any individual case of euthanasia, while the second kind focuses on social or legal policy. In the next section I consider the first kind of argument.

Euthanasia Is the Deliberate Killing of an Innocent Person

The claim that any individual instance of euthanasia is a case of deliberate killing of an innocent person is, with only minor qualifications, correct. Unlike forgoing life-sustaining treatment, commonly understood as allowing to die, euthanasia is clearly killing, defined as depriving of life or causing the death of a living being. While providing morphine for pain relief at doses where the risk of respiratory depression and an earlier death may be a foreseen but unintended side effect of treating the patient's pain, in a case of euthanasia the patient's death is deliberate or intended even if in both the physician's ultimate end may be respecting the patient's wishes. If the deliberate killing of an innocent person is wrong, euthanasia would be nearly always impermissible.

In the context of medicine, the ethical prohibition against deliberately killing the innocent derives some of its plausibility from the belief that nothing in the currently accepted practice of medicine is deliberate killing. Thus, in commenting on the "It's Over, Debbie" case, four prominent physicians and bioethicists could entitle their paper "Doctors Must Not Kill."[1] The belief that doctors do not in fact kill requires the corollary belief that forgoing life-sustaining treatment, whether by not starting or by stopping treatment, is allowing to die, not killing. Common though this view is, I shall argue that it is confused and mistaken.

Why is the common view mistaken? Consider the case of a patient terminally ill with ALS disease. She is completely respirator dependent with no hope of ever being weaned. She is unquestionably competent but finds her condition intolerable and persistently requests to be removed from the respirator and allowed to die. Most people and physicians would agree that the patient's physician should respect the patient's wishes and remove her from the respirator, though this will certainly cause the patient's death. The common understanding is that the physician thereby allows the patient to die. But is that correct?

Suppose the patient has a greedy and hostile son who mistakenly believes that his mother will never decide to stop her life-sustaining treatment and that even if she did her physician would not remove her from the respirator. Afraid that his inheritance will be dissipated by a long and expensive hospitalization, he enters his mother's room while she is sedated, extubates her, and she dies. Shortly thereafter the medical staff discovers what he has done and confronts the son. He replies, "I didn't kill her, I merely allowed her to die. It was her ALS disease that caused her death." I think this would rightly be dismissed as transparent sophistry—the son went into his mother's room and deliberately killed her. But, of course, the son performed just the same physical actions, did just the same thing, that the physician would have done. If that is so, then doesn't the physician also kill the patient when he extubates her?

I underline immediately that there are important ethical differences between what the physician and the greedy son do. First, the physician acts with the patient's consent whereas the son does not. Second, the physician acts with a good motive—to respect the patient's wishes and self-determination—whereas the son acts with a bad motive—to protect his own inheritance. Third, the physician acts in a social role through which he is legally authorized to carry out the patient's wishes regarding treatment whereas the son has no such authorization. These and perhaps other ethically important differences show that what the physician did was morally justified whereas what the son did was morally wrong. What they do not show, however, is that the son killed while the physician allowed to die. One can either kill or allow to die with or without consent, with a good or bad motive, within or outside of a social role that authorizes one to do so.

The difference between killing and allowing to die that I have been implicitly appealing to here is roughly that between acts and omissions resulting in death.[2] Both the physician and the greedy son act in a manner intended to cause death, do cause death, and so both kill. One reason this conclusion is resisted is that on a different understanding of the distinction between killing and allowing to die, what the physician does is allow to die. In this account, the mother's ALS is a lethal disease whose normal progression is being held back or blocked by the life-sustaining respirator treatment. Removing this artificial intervention is then viewed as standing aside and allowing the patient to die of her underlying disease. I have argued elsewhere that this alternative account is deeply problematic, in part because it commits us to accepting that what the greedy son does is to allow to die, not kill.[3] Here, I want to note two other reasons why the conclusion that stopping life support is killing is resisted.

The first reason is that killing is often understood, especially within medicine, as unjustified causing of death; in medicine it is thought to be done only accidentally or negligently. It is also increasingly widely accepted that a physician is ethically justified in stopping life support in a case like that of the ALS patient. But if these two beliefs are correct, then what the physician does cannot be killing, and so must be allowing to die. Killing patients is not, to put it flippantly, understood to be part of physicians' job description. What is mistaken in this line of reasoning is the assumption that all killings are unjustified causings of death. Instead, some killings are ethically justified, including many instances of stopping life support.

Another reason for resisting the conclusion that stopping life support is often killing is that it is psychologically uncomfortable. Suppose the physician had stopped the ALS patient's respirator and had made the son's claim, "I didn't kill her, I merely allowed her to die. It was her ALS disease that caused her death." The clue to the psychological role here is how naturally the "merely" modifies "allowed her to die." The characterization as allowing to die is meant to shift felt responsibility away from the agent—the physician—and to the lethal disease process. Other language common in death and dying contexts plays a similar role; "letting nature take its course" or "stopping prolonging the dying process" both seem to shift responsibility from the physician who stops life support to the fatal disease process. However psychologically helpful these conceptualizations may be in making the difficult responsibility of a physician's role in the patient's death bearable, they nevertheless are confusions. Both physicians and family members can instead be helped to understand that it is the patient's decision and consent to stopping treatment that limits their responsibility for the patient's death and that shifts that responsibility to the patient.

Many who accept the difference between killing and allowing to die as the distinction between acts and omissions resulting in death have gone on to argue that killing is not in itself morally different from allowing to die.[4] In this account, very roughly, one kills when one performs an action that causes the death of a person (we are in a boat, you cannot swim, I push you overboard, and you drown), and one allows to die when one has the ability and opportunity to prevent the death of another, knows this, and omits doing so, with the result that the person dies (we are in a boat, you cannot swim, you fall overboard, I don't throw you an available life ring, and you drown). Those who see no moral difference between killing and allowing to die typically employ the strategy of comparing cases that differ in these and no other potentially morally important respects. This will allow people to consider whether the mere difference that one is a case of killing and the other of allowing to die matters morally, or whether instead it is other features that make most cases of killing worse than most instances of allowing to die. Here is such a pair of cases:

Case 1

A very gravely ill patient is brought to a hospital emergency room and sent up to the ICU. The patient begins to develop respiratory failure that is likely to require intubation very soon. At that point the patient's family members and long-standing physician arrive at the ICU and inform the ICU staff that there had been extensive discussion about future care with the patient when he was unquestionably competent. Given his grave and terminal illness, as well as his state of debilitation, the patient had firmly rejected being placed on a respirator under any circumstances, and the family and physician produce the patient's advance directive to that effect. The ICU staff do not intubate the patient, who dies of respiratory failure.

Case 2

The same as Case 1 except that the family and physician are slightly delayed in traffic and arrive shortly after the patient has been intubated and placed on the respirator. The ICU staff extubate the patient, who dies of respiratory failure.

In Case 1 the patient is allowed to die, in Case 2 he is killed, but it is hard to see why what is done in Case 2 is significantly different morally than what is done in Case 1. It must be other factors that make most killings worse than most allowings to die, and if so, euthanasia cannot be wrong simply because it is killing instead of allowing to die.

Suppose both my arguments are mistaken. Suppose that killing is worse than allowing to die and that withdrawing life support is not killing, although euthanasia is. Euthanasia still need not for that reason be morally wrong. To see this, we need to determine the basic principle for the moral evaluation of killing persons. What is it that makes paradigm cases of wrongful killing wrongful? One very plausible answer is that killing denies the victim something that he or she values greatly—continued life or a future. Moreover, since continued life is necessary for pursuing any of a person's plans and purposes, killing brings the frustration of all of these plans and desires as well. In a nutshell, wrongful killing deprives a person of a valued future, and of all the person wanted and planned to do in that future.

A natural expression of this account of the wrongness of killing is that people have a moral right not to be killed.[5] But in this account of the wrongness of killing, the right not to be killed, like other rights, should be waivable when the person makes a competent decision that continued life is no longer wanted or a good, but is instead worse than no further life at all. In this view, euthanasia is properly understood as a case of a person having waived his or her right not to be killed.

This rights view of the wrongness of killing is not, of course, universally shared. Many people's moral views about killing have their origins in religious views that human life comes from God and cannot be justifiably destroyed or taken away, either by the person whose life it is or by another. But in a pluralistic society like our own with a strong commitment to freedom of religion, public policy should not be grounded in religious beliefs which many in that society reject. I turn now to the general evaluation of public policy on euthanasia.

Would the Bad Consequences of Euthanasia Outweigh the Good?

The argument against euthanasia at the policy level is stronger than at the level of individual cases, though even here I believe the case is ultimately unpersuasive, or at best indecisive. The policy level is the place where the main issues lie, however, and where moral considerations that might override arguments in favor of euthanasia will be found, if they are found anywhere. It is important to note two kinds of disagreement about the consequences for public policy of permitting euthanasia. First, there is empirical or factual disagreement about what the consequences would be. This disagreement is greatly exacerbated by the lack of firm data on the issue. Second, since on any reasonable assessment there would be both good and bad consequences, there are moral disagreements about the relative importance of different effects. In addition to these two sources of disagreement, there is also no single, well-specified policy proposal for legalizing euthanasia on which policy assessments can focus. But without such specification, and especially without explicit procedures for protecting against well-intentioned misuse and ill-intentioned abuse, the consequences for policy are largely speculative. Despite these difficulties, a preliminary account of the main likely good and bad consequences is possible. This should help clarify where better data or more moral analysis and argument are needed, as well as where policy safeguards must be developed.

Potential Good Consequences of Permitting Euthanasia

What are the likely good consequences? First, if euthanasia were permitted it would be possible to respect the self-determination of competent patients who want it, but now cannot get it because of its illegality. We simply do not know how many such patients and people there are. In the Netherlands, with a population of about 14.5 million (in 1987), estimates in a recent study were that about 1,900 cases of voluntary active euthanasia or physician-assisted suicide occur annually. No straightforward extrapolation to the United States is possible for many reasons, among them, that we do not know how many people here who want euthanasia now get it, despite its illegality. Even with better data on the number of persons who want euthanasia but cannot get it, significant moral disagreement would remain about how much weight should be given to any instance of failure to respect a person's self-determination in this way.

One important factor substantially affecting the number of persons who would seek euthanasia is the extent to which an alternative is available. The widespread acceptance in the law, social policy, and medical practice of the right of a competent patient to forgo life-sustaining treatment suggests that the number of competent persons in the United States who would want euthanasia if it were permitted is probably relatively small.

A second good consequence of making euthanasia legally permissible benefits a much larger group. Polls have shown that a majority of the American public believes that people should have a right to obtain euthanasia if they want it.[6] No doubt the vast majority of those who support this right to euthanasia will never in fact come to want euthanasia for themselves. Nevertheless, making it legally permissible would reassure many people that if they ever do want euthanasia they would be able to obtain it. This reassurance would supplement the broader control over the process of dying given by the right to decide about life-sustaining treatment. Having fire insurance on one's house benefits all who have it, not just those whose houses actually burn down, by reassuring them that in the unlikely event of their house burning down, they will receive the money needed to rebuild it. Likewise, the legalization of euthanasia can be thought of as a kind of insurance policy against being forced to endure a protracted dying process that one has come to find burdensome and unwanted, especially when there is no life-sustaining treatment to forgo. The strong concern about losing control of their care expressed by many people who face serious illness likely to end in death suggests that they give substantial importance to the legalization of euthanasia as a means of maintaining this control.

A third good consequence of the legalization of euthanasia concerns patients whose dying is filled with severe and unrelievable pain or suffering. When there is a life-sustaining treatment that, if forgone, will lead relatively quickly to death, then doing so can bring an end to these patients' suffering without recourse to euthanasia. For patients receiving no such treatment, however, euthanasia may be the only release from their otherwise prolonged suffering and agony. This argument from mercy has always been the strongest argument for euthanasia in those cases to which it applies.[7]

The importance of relieving pain and suffering is less controversial than is the frequency with which patients are forced to undergo untreatable agony that only euthanasia could relieve. If we focus first on suffering caused by physical pain, it is crucial to distinguish pain that could be adequately relieved with modern methods of pain control, though it in fact is not, from pain that is relievable only by death.[8] For a variety of reasons, including some physicians' fear of hastening the patient's death, as well as the lack of a publicly accessible means for assessing the amount of the patient's pain, many patients suffer pain that could be, but is not, relieved.

Specialists in pain control, as for example the pain of terminally ill cancer patients, argue that there are very few patients whose pain could not be adequately controlled, though sometimes at the cost of so sedating them that they are effectively unable to interact with other people or their environment. Thus, the argument from mercy in cases of physical pain can probably be met in a large majority of cases by providing adequate measures of pain relief. This should be a high priority, whatever our legal policy on euthanasia—the relief of pain and suffering has long been, quite properly, one of the central goals of medicine. Those cases in which pain could be effectively relieved, but in fact is not, should only count significantly in favor of legalizing euthanasia if all reasonable efforts to change pain management techniques have been tried and have failed.

Dying patients often undergo substantial psychological suffering that is not fully or even principally the result of physical pain.[9] The knowledge about how to relieve this suffering is much more limited than in the case of relieving pain, and efforts to do so are probably more often unsuccessful. If the argument from mercy is extended to patients experiencing great and unrelievable psychological suffering, the numbers of patients to which it applies are much greater.

One last good consequence of legalizing euthanasia is that once death has been accepted, it is often more humane to end life quickly and peacefully, when that is what the patient wants. Such a death will often be seen as better than a more prolonged one. People who suffer a sudden and unexpected death, for example by dying quickly or in their sleep from a heart attack or stroke, are often considered lucky to have died in this way. We care about how we die in part because we care about how others remember us, and we hope they will remember us as we were in "good times" with them and not as we might be when disease has robbed us of our dignity as human beings. As with much in the treatment and care of the dying, people's concerns differ in this respect, but for at least some people, euthanasia will be a more humane death than what they have often experienced with other loved ones and might otherwise expect for themselves.

Some opponents of euthanasia challenge how much importance should be given to any of these good consequences of permitting it, or even whether some would be good consequences at all. But more frequently, opponents cite a number of bad consequences that permitting euthanasia would or could produce, and it is to their assessment that I now turn.

Potential Bad Consequences of Permitting Euthanasia

Some of the arguments against permitting euthanasia are aimed specifically against physicians, while others are aimed against anyone being permitted to perform it. I shall first consider one argument of the former sort. Permitting physicians to perform euthanasia, it is said, would be incompatible with their fundamental moral and professional commitment as healers to care for patients and to protect life. Moreover, if euthanasia by physicians became common, patients would come to fear that a medication was intended not to treat or care, but instead to kill, and would thus lose trust in their physicians.

This position was forcefully stated in a paper by Willard Gaylin and his colleagues:

> The very soul of medicine is on trial. . . . This issue touches medicine at its moral center; if this moral center collapses, if physicians become killers or are even licensed to kill, the profession—and, therewith, each physician—will never again be worthy of trust and respect as healer and comforter and protector of life in all its frailty.

These authors go on to make clear that, while they oppose permitting anyone to perform euthanasia, their special concern is with physicians doing so:

> We call on fellow physicians to say that they will not deliberately kill. We must also say to each of our fellow physicians that we will not tolerate killing of patients and that we shall take disciplinary action against doctors who kill. And we must say to the broader community that if it insists on tolerating or legalizing active euthanasia, it will have to find nonphysicians to do its killing.[10]

If permitting physicians to kill would undermine the very "moral center" of medicine, then almost certainly physicians should not be permitted to perform euthanasia. But how persuasive is this claim? Patients should not fear, as a consequence of permitting voluntary active euthanasia, that their physicians will substitute a lethal injection for what patients want and believe is part of their care. If active euthanasia is restricted to cases in which it is truly voluntary, then no patient should fear getting it unless she or he has voluntarily requested it. (The fear that we might in time also come to accept nonvoluntary, or even involuntary, active euthanasia is a slippery slope worry I address below.) Patients' trust of their physicians could be increased, not eroded, by knowledge that physicians will provide aid in dying when patients seek it.

Might Gaylin and his colleagues nevertheless be correct in their claim that the moral center of medicine would collapse if physicians were to become killers? This question raises what at the deepest level should be the guiding aims of medicine, a question that obviously cannot be fully explored here. But I do want to say enough to indicate the direction that I believe an appropriate response to this challenge should take. In spelling out above what I called the positive argument for voluntary active euthanasia, I suggested that two principal values—respecting patients' self-determination and promoting their well-being—underlie the consensus that competent patients, or the surrogates of incompetent patients, are entitled to refuse any life-sustaining treatment and to choose from among available alternative treatments. It is the commitment to these two values in guiding physicians' actions as healers, comforters, and protectors of their patients' lives that should be at the "moral center" of medicine, and these two values support physicians' administering euthanasia when their patients make competent requests for it. . . .

A second bad consequence that some foresee is that permitting euthanasia would weaken society's commitment to provide optimal care for dying patients. We live at a time in which the control of health care costs has become, and is likely to continue to be, the dominant focus of health care policy. If euthanasia is seen as a cheaper alternative to adequate care and treatment, then we might become less scrupulous about providing sometimes costly support and other services to dying patients. Particularly if our society comes to embrace deeper and more explicit rationing of health care, frail, elderly, and dying patients will need to be strong and effective advocates for their own health care and other needs, although they are hardly in a position to do this. We should do nothing to weaken their ability to obtain adequate care and services.

This second worry is difficult to assess because there is little firm evidence about the likelihood of the feared erosion in the care of dying patients. There are at least two reasons, however, for skepticism about this argument. The first is that the same worry could have been directed at recognizing patients' or surrogates' rights to forgo life-sustaining treatment, yet there is no persuasive evidence that recognizing the right to refuse treatment has caused a serious erosion in the quality of care of dying patients. The second reason for skepticism about this worry is that only a very small proportion of deaths would occur from euthanasia if it were permitted. In the Netherlands, where euthanasia under specified circumstances is permitted by the courts, though not authorized by statute, the best estimate of the proportion of overall deaths that result from it is about 2 percent.[11] Thus, the vast majority of critically ill and dying patients will not request it, and so will still have to be cared for by physicians, families, and others. Permitting euthanasia should not diminish people's commitment and concern to maintain and improve the care of these patients.

A third possible bad consequence of permitting euthanasia (or even a public discourse in which strong support for euthanasia is evident) is to threaten the progress made in securing the rights of patients or their surrogates to decide about and to refuse life-sustaining treatment.[12] This progress has been made against the backdrop of a clear and firm legal prohibition of euthanasia, which has provided a relatively bright line limiting the dominion of others over patients' lives. It has therefore been an important reassurance to concerns about how the authority to take steps ending life might be misused, abused, or wrongly extended.

Many supporters of the right of patients or their surrogates to refuse treatment strongly oppose euthanasia, and if forced to choose might well withdraw their support of the right to refuse treatment rather than accept euthanasia. Public policy in the last fifteen years has generally let life-sustaining treatment decisions be made in health care settings between physicians and patients or their surrogates, and without the involvement of the courts. However, if euthanasia is made legally permissible greater involvement of the courts is likely, which could in turn extend to a greater court involvement in life-sustaining treatment decisions. Most agree, however, that increased involvement of the courts in these decisions would be undesirable, as it would make sound decisionmaking more cumbersome and difficult without sufficient compensating benefits.

As with the second potential bad consequence of permitting euthanasia, this third consideration too is speculative and difficult to assess. The feared erosion of patients' or surrogates' rights to decide about life-sustaining treatment, together with greater court involvement in those decisions, are both possible. However, I believe there is reason to discount this general worry. The legal rights of competent patients and, to a lesser degree, surrogates of incompetent patients to decide about treatment are very firmly embedded in a long line of informed consent and life-sustaining treatment cases, and are not likely to be eroded by a debate over, or even acceptance of, euthanasia. It will not be accepted without safeguards that reassure the public about abuse, and if that debate shows the need for similar safeguards for some life-sustaining treatment decisions they should be adopted there as well. In neither case are the only possible safeguards greater court involvement, as the recent growth of institutional ethics committees shows.

The fourth potential bad consequence of permitting euthanasia has been developed by David Velleman and turns on the subtle point that making a new option or choice available to people can sometimes make them worse off, even if once they have the choice they go on to choose what is best for them.[13] Ordinarily, people's continued existence is viewed by them as given, a fixed condition with which they must cope. Making euthanasia available to people as an option denies them the alternative of staying alive by default. If people are offered the option of euthanasia, their continued existence is now a choice for which they can be held responsible and which they can be asked by others to justify. We care, and are right to care, about being able to justify ourselves to others. To the extent that our society is unsympathetic to justifying a severely dependent or impaired existence, a heavy psychological burden of proof may be placed on patients who think their terminal illness or chronic infirmity is not a sufficient reason for dying. Even if they otherwise view their life as worth living, the opinion of others around them that it is not can threaten their reason for living and make euthanasia a rational choice. Thus the existence of the option becomes a subtle pressure to request it.

This argument correctly identifies the reason why offering some patients the option of euthanasia would not benefit them. Velleman takes it not as a reason for opposing all euthanasia, but for restricting it to circumstances where there are "unmistakable and overpowering reasons for persons to want the option of euthanasia," and for denying the option in all other cases. But there are at least three reasons why such restriction may not be warranted. First, polls and other evidence support that most Americans believe euthanasia should be permitted (though the recent defeat of the referendum to permit it in the state of Washington raises some doubt about this support). Thus, many more people seem to want the choice than would be made worse off by getting it. Second, if giving people the option of ending their life really makes them worse off, then we should not only prohibit euthanasia, but also take back from people the right they now have to decide about life-sustaining treatment. The feared harmful effect should already have occurred from securing people's right to refuse life-sustaining treatment, yet there is no evidence of any such widespread harm or any broad public desire to rescind that right. Third, since there is a wide range of conditions in which reasonable people can and do disagree about whether they would want continued life, it is not possible to restrict the permissibility of euthanasia as narrowly as Velleman suggests without thereby denying it to most persons who would want it; to permit it only in cases in which virtually everyone would want it would be to deny it to most who would want it.

A fifth potential bad consequence of making euthanasia legally permissible is that it might weaken the general legal prohibition of homicide. This prohibition is so fundamental to civilized society, it is argued, that we should do nothing that erodes it. If most cases of stopping life support are killing, as I have already argued, then the court cases permitting such killing have already in effect weakened this prohibition. However, neither the courts nor most people have seen these cases as killing and so as challenging the prohibition of homicide. The courts have usually grounded patients' or their surrogates' rights to refuse life-sustaining treatment in rights to privacy, liberty, self-determination, or bodily integrity, not in exceptions to homicide laws.

Legal permission for physicians or others to perform euthanasia could not be grounded in patients' rights to decide about medical treatment. Permitting euthanasia would require qualifying, at least in effect, the legal prohibition against homicide, a prohibition that in general does not allow the consent of the victim to justify or excuse the act. Nevertheless, the very same fundamental basis of the right to decide about life-sustaining treatment—respecting a person's self-determination—does support euthanasia

as well. Individual self-determination has long been a well-entrenched and fundamental value in the law, and so extending it to euthanasia would not require appeal to novel legal values or principles. That suicide or attempted suicide is no longer a criminal offense in virtually all states indicates an acceptance of individual self-determination in the taking of one's own life analogous to that required for voluntary active euthanasia. The legal prohibition (in most states) of assisting in suicide and the refusal in the law to accept the consent of the victim as a possible justification of homicide are both arguably a result of difficulties in the legal process of establishing the consent of the victim after the fact. If procedures can be designed that clearly establish the voluntariness of the person's request for euthanasia it would under those procedures represent a carefully circumscribed qualification on the legal prohibition of homicide. Nevertheless, some remaining worries about this weakening can be captured in the final potential bad consequence, to which I will now turn.

This final potential bad consequence is the central concern of many opponents of euthanasia and, I believe, is the most serious objection to a legal policy permitting it. According to this "slippery slope" worry, although active euthanasia may be morally permissible in cases in which it is unequivocally voluntary and the patient finds his or her condition unbearable, a legal policy permitting euthanasia would inevitably lead to active euthanasia being performed in many other cases in which it would be morally wrong. To prevent those other wrongful cases of euthanasia we should not permit even morally justified performance of it.

Slippery slope arguments of this form are problematic and difficult to evaluate.[14] From one perspective, they are the last refuge of conservative defenders of the status quo. When all the opponent's objections to the wrongness of euthanasia itself have been met, the opponent then shifts ground and acknowledges both that it is not in itself wrong and that a legal policy which resulted only in its being performed would not be bad. Nevertheless, the opponent maintains, it should still not be permitted because doing so would result in its being performed in other cases in which it is not voluntary and would be wrong. In this argument's most extreme form, permitting euthanasia is the first and fateful step down the slippery slope to Nazism. Once on the slope we will be unable to get off.

Now it cannot be denied that it is possible that permitting euthanasia could have these fateful consequences, but that cannot be enough to warrant prohibiting it if it is otherwise justified. A similar possible slippery slope worry could have been raised to securing competent patients' rights to decide about life support, but recent history shows such a worry would have been unfounded. It must be relevant how likely it is that we will end with horrendous consequences and an unjustified practice of euthanasia. How likely and widespread would the abuses and unwarranted extensions of permitting it be? By abuses, I mean the performance of euthanasia that fails to satisfy the conditions required for voluntary active euthanasia, for example, if the patient has been subtly pressured to accept it. By unwarranted extensions of policy, I mean later changes in legal policy to permit not just voluntary euthanasia, but also euthanasia in cases in which, for example, it need not be fully voluntary. Opponents of voluntary euthanasia on slippery slope grounds have not provided the data or evidence necessary to turn their speculative concerns into well-grounded likelihoods.

It is at least clear, however, that both the character and likelihood of abuses of a legal policy permitting euthanasia depend in significant part on the procedures put in place to protect against them. I will not try to detail fully what such procedures might be, but will just give some examples of what they might include:

1. The patient should be provided with all relevant information about his or her medical condition, current prognosis, available alternative treatments, and the prognosis of each.
2. Procedures should ensure that the patient's request for euthanasia is stable or enduring (a brief waiting period could be required) and fully voluntary (an advocate for the patient might be appointed to ensure this).
3. All reasonable alternatives must have been explored for improving the patient's quality of life and relieving any pain or suffering.

4. A psychiatric evaluation should ensure that the patient's request is not the result of a treatable psychological impairment such as depression.[15]

These examples of procedural safeguards are all designed to ensure that the patient's choice is fully informed, voluntary, and competent, and so a true exercise of self-determination. Other proposals for euthanasia would restrict its permissibility further—for example, to the terminally ill—a restriction that cannot be supported by self-determination. Such additional restrictions might, however, be justified by concern for limiting potential harms from abuse. At the same time, it is important not to impose procedural or substantive safeguards so restrictive as to make euthanasia impermissible or practically infeasible in a wide range of justified cases.

These examples of procedural safeguards make clear that it is possible to substantially reduce, though not to eliminate, the potential for abuse of a policy permitting voluntary active euthanasia. Any legalization of the practice should be accompanied by a well-considered set of procedural safeguards together with an ongoing evaluation of its use. Introducing euthanasia into only a few states could be a form of carefully limited and controlled social experiment that would give us evidence about the benefits and harms of the practice. Even then firm and uncontroversial data may remain elusive, as the continuing controversy over what has taken place in the Netherlands in recent years indicates.[16]

The Slip into Nonvoluntary Active Euthanasia

While I believe slippery slope worries can largely be limited by making necessary distinctions both in principle and in practice, one slippery slope concern is legitimate. There is reason to expect that legalization of voluntary active euthanasia might soon be followed by strong pressure to legalize some nonvoluntary euthanasia of incompetent patients unable to express their own wishes. Respecting a person's self-determination and recognizing that continued life is not always of value to a person can support not only voluntary active euthanasia, but some nonvoluntary euthanasia as well. These are the same values that ground competent patients' right to refuse life-sustaining treatment. Recent history here is instructive. In the medical ethics literature, in the courts since Quinlan, and in norms of medical practice, that right has been extended to incompetent patients and exercised by a surrogate who is to decide as the patient would have decided in the circumstances if competent.[17] It has been held unreasonable to continue life-sustaining treatment that the patient would not have wanted just because the patient now lacks the capacity to tell us that. Life-sustaining treatment for incompetent patients is today frequently forgone on the basis of a surrogate's decision, or less frequently on the basis of an advance directive executed by the patient while still competent. The very same logic that has extended the right to refuse life-sustaining treatment from a competent patient to the surrogate of an incompetent patient (acting with or without a formal advance directive from the patient) may well extend the scope of active euthanasia. The argument will be, Why continue to force unwanted life on patients just because they have now lost the capacity to request euthanasia from us?

A related phenomenon may reinforce this slippery slope concern. In the Netherlands, what the courts have sanctioned has been clearly restricted to voluntary euthanasia. In itself, this serves as some evidence that permitting it need not lead to permitting the nonvoluntary variety. There is some indication, however, that for many Dutch physicians euthanasia is no longer viewed as a special action, set apart from their usual practice and restricted only to competent persons.[18] Instead, it is seen as one end of a spectrum of caring for dying patients. When viewed in this way it will be difficult to deny euthanasia to a patient for whom it is seen as the best or most appropriate form of care simply because that patient is now incompetent and cannot request it.

Even if voluntary active euthanasia should slip into nonvoluntary active euthanasia, with surrogates acting for incompetent patients, the ethical evaluation is more complex than many opponents of euthanasia allow. Just as in the case of surrogates' decisions to forgo life-sustaining treatment for incompetent patients, so also surrogates' decisions to request euthanasia for incompetent persons would often accurately reflect what the incompetent person would have wanted and would deny the person nothing that he or she would have considered worth having. Making nonvoluntary active euthanasia legally permissible, however, would greatly enlarge the number of patients on whom it might be performed and substantially enlarge the potential for misuse and abuse. As noted above, frail and debilitated elderly people, often demented or otherwise incompetent and thereby unable to defend and assert their own interests, may be especially vulnerable to unwanted euthanasia.

For some people, this risk is more than sufficient reason to oppose the legalization of voluntary euthanasia. But while we should in general be cautious about inferring much from the experience in the Netherlands to what our own experience in the United States might be, there may be one important lesson that we can learn from them. One commentator has noted that in the Netherlands families of incompetent patients have less authority than do families in the United States to act as surrogates for incompetent patients in making decisions to forgo life-sustaining treatment.[19] From the Dutch perspective, it may be we in the United States who are already on the slippery slope in having given surrogates broad authority to forgo life-sustaining treatment for incompetent persons. In this view, the more important moral divide, and the more important with regard to potential for abuse, is not between forgoing life-sustaining treatment and euthanasia, but instead between voluntary and nonvoluntary performance of either. If this is correct, then the more important issue is ensuring the appropriate principles and procedural safeguards for the exercise of decisionmaking authority by surrogates for incompetent persons in all decisions at the end of life. This may be the correct response to slippery slope worries about euthanasia.

I have cited both good and bad consequences that have been thought likely from a policy change permitting voluntary active euthanasia, and have tried to evaluate their likelihood and relative importance. Nevertheless, as I noted earlier, reasonable disagreement remains both about the consequences of permitting euthanasia and about which of these consequences are more important. The depth and strength of public and professional debate about whether, all things considered, permitting euthanasia would be desirable or undesirable reflects these disagreements. While my own view is that the balance of considerations supports permitting the practice, my principal purpose here has been to clarify the main issues.

NOTES

1. Willard Gaylin, Leon R. Kass, Edmund D. Pellegrino, and Mark Siegler, "Doctors Must Not Kill," *JAMA* 259 (1988): 2139–40.
2. Bonnie Steinbock, ed., *Killing and Allowing to Die* (Englewood Cliffs, N.J.: Prentice-Hall, 1980).
3. Dan W. Brock, "Forgoing Food and Water: Is It Killing?" in *By No Extraordinary Means: The Choice to Forgo Life-Sustaining Food and Water*, ed. Joanne Lynn (Bloomington: Indiana University Press, 1986), pp. 117–31.
4. James Rachels, "Active and Passive Euthanasia," *NEJM* 292 (1975): 78–80; Michael Tooley, *Abortion and Infanticide* (Oxford: Oxford University Press, 1983). In my paper, "Taking Human Life," *Ethics* 95 (1985): 851–65, I argue in more detail that killing in itself is not morally different from allowing to die and defend the strategy of argument employed in this and the succeeding two paragraphs in the text.
5. Dan W. Brock, "Moral Rights and Permissible Killing," in *Ethical Issues Relating to Life and Death*, ed. John Ladd (New York: Oxford University Press, 1979), pp. 94–117.
6. P. Painton and E. Taylor, "Love or Let Die," *Time*, 19 March 1990, pp. 62–71; *Boston Globe*/Harvard University Poll, *Boston Globe*, 3 November 1991.
7. James Rachels, *The End of Life* (Oxford: Oxford University Press, 1986).
8. Marcia Angell, "The Quality of Mercy," *NEJM* 306 (1982): 98–99; M. Donovan, P. Dillon, and L. Mcguire, Incidence and Characteristics of Pain in a Sample of Medical-Surgical Inpatients," *Pain* 30 (1987): 69–78.
9. Eric Cassell, *The Nature of Suffering and the Goals of Medicine* (New York: Oxford University Press, 1991).
10. Gaylin et al., "Doctors Must Not Kill."
11. Paul J. Van der Maas et al., "Euthanasia and Other Medical Decisions Concerning the End of Life," *Lancet* 338 (1991): 669–74.
12. Susan M. Wolf, "Holding the Line on Euthanasia," Special Supplement, *Hastings Center Report* 19, no. 1 (1989): 13–15.
13. My formulation of this argument derives from David Velleman's statement of it in his commentary on an earlier version of this paper delivered at the American Philosophical Association Central Division meetings; a similar point was made to me by Elisha Milgram in discussion on another occasion. For more general development of the point see Thomas Schelling, *The Strategy of Conflict* (Cambridge, Mass.: Harvard University Press, 1960); and Gerald Dworkin, "Is More Choice Better Than Less?" in *The Theory and Practice of Autonomy* (Cambridge: Cambridge University Press, 1988).
14. Frederick Schauer, "Slippery Slopes," *Harvard Law Review* 99 (1985): 361–83; Wibren van der Burg, "The Slippery Slope Argument," *Ethics* 102 (October 1991): 42–65.
15. There is evidence that physicians commonly fail to diagnose depression. See Robert I. Misbin, "Physicians Aid in Dying." *NEJM* 325 (1991): 1304–7.
16. Richard Fenigsen, "A Case against Dutch Euthanasia," Special Supplement, *Hastings Center Report* 19, no. 1 (1989): 22–30.
17. Allen E. Buchanan and Dan W. Brock, *Deciding for Others: The Ethics of Surrogate Decisionmaking* (Cambridge: Cambridge University Press, 1989).
18. Van der Maas et al., "Euthanasia and Other Medical Decisions."
19. Margaret P. Battin, "Seven Caveats Concerning the Discussion of Euthanasia in Holland," *American Philosophical Association Newsletter on Philosoply and Medicine* 89, no. 2 (1990).

When Self-Determination Runs Amok

DANIEL CALLAHAN

Callahan is opposed to the use of voluntary euthanasia and assisted suicide. He argues that a person's right of self-determination does not morally justify someone else killing that person, even for mercy's sake. He contends that, contrary to common opinion, there is indeed a moral difference between killing and letting die. A policy that lets physicians practice euthanasia will lead to dire consequences and pervert the profession of medicine.

The euthanasia debate is not just another moral debate, one in a long list of arguments in our pluralistic society. It is profoundly emblematic of three important turning points in Western thought. The first is that of the legitimate conditions under which one person can kill another. The acceptance of voluntary active euthanasia would morally sanction what can only be called "consenting adult killing." By the term I mean the killing of one person by another in the name of their mutual right to be killer and killed if they freely agree to play those roles. This turn flies in the face of a long-standing effort to limit the circumstances under which one person can take the life of another, from efforts to control the free flow of guns and arms, to abolish capital punishment, and to more tightly control warfare. Euthanasia would add a whole new category of killing to a society that already has too many excuses to indulge itself in that way.

The second turning point lies in the meaning and limits of self-determination. The acceptance of euthanasia would sanction a view of autonomy holding that individuals may, in the name of their own private, idiosyncratic view of the good life, call upon others, including such institutions as medicine, to help them pursue that life, even at the risk of harm to the common good. This works against the idea that the meaning and scope of our own right to lead our own lives must be conditioned by, and be compatible with, the good of the community, which is more than an aggregate of self-directing individuals.

The third turning point is to be found in the claim being made upon medicine: it should be prepared to make its skills available to individuals to help them achieve their private vision of the good life. This puts medicine in the business of promoting the individualistic pursuit of general human happiness and well-being. It would overturn the traditional belief that medicine should limit its domain to promoting and preserving human health, redirecting it instead to the relief of that suffering which stems from life itself, not merely from a sick body.

I believe that, at each of these three turning points, proponents of euthanasia push us in the wrong direction. Arguments in favor of euthanasia fall into four general categories, which I will take up in turn: (1) the moral claim of individual self-determination and well-being; (2) the moral irrelevance of the difference between killing and allowing to die; (3) the supposed paucity of evidence to show likely harmful consequences of legalized euthanasia; and (4) the compatibility of euthanasia and medical practice.

Self-Determination

Central to most arguments for euthanasia is the principle of self-determination. People are presumed to have an interest in deciding for themselves, according to their own beliefs about what makes life good, how they will conduct their lives. That is an important value, but the question in the euthanasia context is, What does it mean and how far should it extend? If it were a question of suicide, where a person takes their own life without assistance from another, that principle might be pertinent, at least for debate. But euthanasia is not that limited a matter. The self-determination in that case can only be effected by the moral and physical assistance of another. Euthanasia is thus no longer a matter only of self-determination, but of a mutual, social decision between two people, the one to be killed and the other to do the killing.

How are we to make the moral move from my right of self-determination to some doctor's right to kill me—from *my* right to *his* right? Where does the doctor's moral warrant to kill come from? Ought doctors to be able to kill anyone they want as long as permission is given by competent persons? Is our right to life just like a piece of property, to be given away or alienated if the price (happiness, relief of suffering) is right? And then to be destroyed with our permission once alienated?

In answer to all those questions, I will say this: I have yet to hear a plausible argument why it should be permissible for us to put this kind of power in the hands of another, whether a doctor or anyone else. The idea that we can waive our right to life, and then give to another the power to take that life, requires a justification yet to be provided by anyone.

Slavery was long ego outlawed on the ground that one person should not have the right to own another, even with the other's permission. Why? Because it is a fundamental moral wrong for one person to give over his life and fate to another, whatever the good consequences, and no less a wrong for another person to have that kind of total, final power. Like slavery, dueling was long ago banned on similar grounds: even free, competent individuals should not have the power to kill each other, whatever their motives, whatever the circumstances. Consenting adult killing, like consenting adult slavery or degradation, is a strange route to human dignity.

There is another problem as well. If doctors, once sanctioned to carry out euthanasia, are to be themselves responsible moral agents—not simply hired hands with lethal injections at the ready—then they must have their own *independent* moral grounds to kill those who request such services. What do I mean?

As those who favor euthanasia are quick to point out, some people want it because their life has become so burdensome it no longer seems worth living.

The doctor will have a difficulty at this point. The degree and intensity to which people suffer from their diseases and their dying, and whether they find life more of a burden than a benefit, has very little directly to do with the nature or extent of their actual physical condition. Three people can have the same condition, but only one will find the suffering unbearable. People suffer, but suffering is as much a function of the values of individuals as it is of the physical causes of that suffering. Inevitably in that circumstance, the doctor will in effect be treating the patient's values. To be responsible, the doctor would have to share those values. The doctor would have to decide, on her own, whether the patient's life was "no longer worth living."

But how could a doctor possibly know that or make such a judgment? Just because the patient said so? I raise this question because, while in Holland at the euthanasia conference reported by Maurice de Wachter . . . , the doctors present agreed that there is no objective way of measuring or judging the claims of patients that their suffering is unbearable. And if it is difficult to measure suffering, how much more difficult to determine the value of a patient's statement that her life is not worth living?

However one might want to answer such questions, the very need to ask them, to inquire into the physician's responsibility and grounds for medical and moral judgment, points out the social nature of the decision. Euthanasia is not a private matter of self-determination. It is an act that requires two people to make it possible, and a complicit society to make it acceptable.

Killing and Allowing to Die

Against common opinion, the argument is sometimes made that there is no moral difference between stopping life-sustaining treatment and more active forms of killing, such as lethal injection. Instead I would contend that the notion that there is no morally significant difference between omission and commission is just wrong. Consider in its broad implications what the eradication of the distinction implies: that death from disease has been banished, leaving only the actions of physicians in terminating treatment as the cause of death. Biology, which used to bring about death, has apparently been displaced by human agency. Doctors have finally, I suppose, thus genuinely become gods, now doing what nature and the deities once did.

What is the mistake here? It lies in confusing causality and culpability, and in failing to note the way in which human societies have overlaid natural causes with moral rules and interpretations. Causality (by which I mean the direct physical causes of death) and culpability (by which I mean our attribution of moral responsibility to human actions) are confused under three circumstances.

They are confused, first, when the action of a physician in stopping treatment of a patient with an underlying lethal disease is construed as *causing* death. On the contrary, the physician's omission can only bring about death on the condition that the patient's disease will kill him in the absence of treatment. We may hold the physician morally responsible for the death, if we have morally judged such actions wrongful omissions. But it confuses reality and moral judgment to see an omitted action as having the same causal status as one that directly kills. A lethal injection will kill both a healthy person and a sick person. A physician's omitted treatment will have no effect on a healthy person. Turn off the machine on me, a healthy person, and nothing will happen. It will only, in contrast, bring the life of a sick person to an end because of an underlying fatal disease.

Causality and culpability are confused, second, when we fail to note that judgments of moral responsibility and culpability are human constructs. By that I mean that we human beings, after moral reflection, have decided to call some actions right or wrong, and to devise moral rules to deal with them. When physicians could do nothing to stop death, they were not held responsible for it. When, with medical progress, they began to have some power over death—but only its timing and circumstances, not its ultimate inevitability—moral rules were devised to set forth their obligations. Natural causes of death were not thereby banished. They were, instead, overlaid with a medical ethics designed to determine moral culpability in deploying medical power.

To confuse the judgments of this ethics with the physical causes of death—which is the connotation of the word *kill*—is to confuse nature and human action. People will, one way or another, die of some disease; death will have dominion over all of us. To say that a doctor "kills" a patient by allowing this to happen should only be understood as a moral judgment about the licitness of his omission, nothing more. We can, as a fashion of speech only, talk about a doctor *killing* a patient by omitting treatment he should have provided. It is a fashion of speech precisely because it is the underlying disease that brings death when treatment is omitted; that is its cause, not the physician's omission. It is a misuse of the word *killing* to use it when a doctor stops a treatment he believes will no longer benefit the patient—when, that is, he steps aside to allow an eventually inevitable death to occur now rather than later. The only deaths that human beings invented are those that come from direct killing—when, with a lethal injection, we both cause death and are morally responsible for it. In the case of omissions, we do not cause death even if we may be judged morally responsible for it.

This difference between causality and culpability also helps us see why a doctor who has omitted a treatment he should have provided has "killed" that patient while another doctor—performing precisely the same act of omission on another patient in different circumstances—does not kill her, but only allows her to die. The difference is that we have come, by moral convention and conviction, to classify unauthorized or illegitimate omissions as acts of "killing." We call them "killing" in the expanded sense of the term: a culpable action that permits the real cause of death, the underlying disease, to proceed to its lethal conclusion. By contrast, the doctor who, at the patient's request, omits or terminates unwanted treatment does not kill at all. Her underlying disease, not his action, is the physical cause of death; and we have agreed to consider actions of that kind to be morally licit. He thus can truly be said to have "allowed" her to die.

If we fail to maintain the distinction between killing and allowing to die, moreover, there are some disturbing possibilities. The first would be to confirm many physicians in their already too-powerful belief that, when patients die or when physicians stop treatment because of the futility of continuing it, they are somehow both morally and physically responsible for the deaths that follow. That notion needs to be abolished, not strengthened. It needlessly and wrongly burdens the physician, to whom should not be attributed the powers of the gods. The second possibility would be that, in every case where a doctor judges medical treatment no longer effective in prolonging life, a quick and direct killing of the patient would be seen as the next, most reasonable step, on grounds of both humaneness and economics. I do not see how that logic could easily be rejected.

Calculating the Consequences

When concerns about the adverse social consequences of permitting euthanasia are raised, its advocates tend to dismiss them as unfounded and overly speculative. On the contrary, recent data about the Dutch experience suggests that such concerns are right on target. From my own discussions in Holland, and from the articles on that subject in this issue and elsewhere, I believe we can now fully see most of the *likely* consequences of legal euthanasia.

Three consequences seem almost certain, in this or any other country: the inevitability of some abuse of the law; the difficulty of precisely writing, and then enforcing, the law; and the inherent slipperiness of the moral reasons for legalizing euthanasia in the first place.

Why is abuse inevitable? One reason is that almost all laws on delicate, controversial matters are to some extent abused. This happens because not everyone will agree with the law as written and will bend it, or ignore it, if they can get away with it. From explicit admissions to me by Dutch proponents of euthanasia, and from the corroborating information provided by the Remmelink Report and the outside studies of Carlos Gomez and John Keown, I am convinced that in the Netherlands there are a substantial number of cases of nonvoluntary euthanasia, that is, euthanasia undertaken without the explicit permission of the person being killed. The other reason abuse is inevitable is that the law is likely to have a low enforcement priority in the criminal justice system. Like other laws of similar status, unless there is an unrelenting and harsh

willingness to pursue abuse, violations will ordinarily be tolerated. The worst thing to me about my experience in Holland was the casual, seemingly indifferent attitude toward abuse. I think that would happen everywhere.

Why would it be hard to precisely write, and then enforce, the law? The Dutch speak about the requirement of "unbearable" suffering, but admit that such a term is just about indefinable, a highly subjective matter admitting of no objective standards. A requirement for outside opinion is nice, but it is easy to find complaisant colleagues. A requirement that a medical condition be "terminal" will run aground on the notorious difficulties of knowing when an illness is actually terminal.

Apart from those technical problems there is a more profound worry. I see no way, even in principle, to write or enforce a meaningful law that can guarantee effective procedural safeguards. The reason is obvious yet almost always overlooked. The euthanasia transaction will ordinarily take place within the boundaries of the private and confidential doctor-patient relationship. No one can possibly know what takes place in that context unless the doctor chooses to reveal it. In Holland, less than 10 percent of the physicians report their acts of euthanasia and do so with almost complete legal impunity. There is no reason why the situation should be any better elsewhere. Doctors will have their own reasons for keeping euthanasia secret, and some patients will have no less a motive for wanting it concealed.

I would mention, finally, that the moral logic of the motives for euthanasia contain within them the ingredients of abuse. The two standard motives for euthanasia and assisted suicide are said to be our right of self-determination, and our claim upon the mercy of others, especially doctors, to relieve our suffering. These two motives are typically spliced together and presented as a single justification. Yet if they are considered independently—and there is no inherent reason why they must be linked—they reveal serious problems. It is said that a competent, adult person should have a right to euthanasia for the relief of suffering. But why must the person be suffering? Does not that stipulation already compromise the principle of self-determination? How can self-determination have any limits? Whatever the person's motives may be, why are they not sufficient?

Consider next the person who is suffering but not competent, who is perhaps demented or mentally retarded. The standard argument would deny euthanasia to that person. But why? If a person is suffering but not competent, then it would seem grossly unfair to deny relief solely on the grounds of incompetence. Are the incompetent less entitled to relief from suffering than the competent? Will it only be affluent, middle-class people, mentally fit and savvy about working the medical system, who can qualify? Do the incompetent suffer less because of their incompetence?

Considered from these angles, there are no good moral reasons to limit euthanasia once the principle of taking life for that purpose has been legitimated. If we really believe in self-determination, then any competent person should have a right to be killed by a doctor for any reason that suits him. If we believe in the relief of suffering, then it seems cruel and capricious to deny it to the incompetent. There is, in short, no reasonable or logical stopping point once the turn has been made down the road to euthanasia, which could soon turn into a convenient and commodious expressway.

Euthanasia and Medical Practice

A fourth kind of argument one often hears both in the Netherlands and in this country is that euthanasia and assisted suicide are perfectly compatible with the aims of medicine. I would note at the very outset that a physician who participates in another person's suicide already abuses medicine. Apart from depression (the main statistical cause of suicide), people commit suicide because they find life empty, oppressive, or meaningless. Their judgment is a judgment about the value of continued life, not only about health (even if they are sick). Are doctors now to be given the right to make judgments about the kinds of life worth living and to give their blessing to suicide for those they judge wanting? What conceivable competence, technical or moral, could doctors claim to play such a role? Are we to medicalize suicide, turning judgments about its worth and value into one more clinical issue? Yes, those are rhetorical questions.

Yet they bring us to the core of the problem of euthanasia and medicine. The great temptation of modern medicine, not always resisted, is to move

beyond the promotion and preservation of health into the boundless realm of general human happiness and well-being. The root problem of illness and mortality is both medical and philosophical or religious. "Why must I die?" can be asked as a technical, biological question or as a question about the meaning of life. When medicine tries to respond to the latter, which it is always under pressure to do, it moves beyond its proper role.

It is not medicine's place to lift from us the burden of that suffering which turns on the meaning we assign to the decay of the body and its eventual death. It is not medicine's place to determine when lives are not worth living or when the burden of life is too great to be borne. Doctors have no conceivable way of evaluating such claims on the part of patients, and they should have no right to act in response to them. Medicine should try to relieve human suffering, but only that suffering which is brought on by illness and dying as biological phenomena, not that suffering which comes from anguish or despair at the human condition.

Doctors ought to relieve those forms of suffering that medically accompany serious illness and the threat of death. They should relieve pain, do what they can to allay anxiety and uncertainty, and be a comforting presence. As sensitive human beings, doctors should be prepared to respond to patients who ask why they must die, or die in pain. But here the doctor and the patient are at the same level. The doctor may have no better an answer to those old questions than anyone else; and certainly no special insight from his training as a physician. It would be terrible for physicians to forget this, and to think that in a swift, lethal injection, medicine has found its own answer to the riddle of life. It would be a false answer, given by the wrong people. It would be no less a false answer for patients. They should neither ask medicine to put its own vocation at risk to serve their private interests, nor think that the answer to suffering is to be killed by another. The problem is precisely that, too often in human history, killing has seemed the quick, efficient way to put aside that which burdens us. It rarely helps, and too often simply adds to one evil still another. That is what I believe euthanasia would accomplish. It is self-determination run amok.

Physician-Assisted Suicide: A Tragic View

JOHN D. ARRAS

Arras is a firm believer in autonomy and finds himself "deeply sympathetic to the central values motivating the case for [physician-assisted suicide] and euthanasia." Nevertheless, he argues that legalizing the practices poses "too great a threat to the rights and welfare of too many people."

For many decades now, the calls for PAS and euthanasia have been perennial lost causes in American society. Each generation has thrown up an assortment of earnest reformers and cranks who, after attracting their fifteen minutes of fame, inevitably have been defeated by the combined weight of traditional law and morality. Incredibly, two recent federal appellate court decisions suddenly changed the legal landscape in this area, making the various states within their respective jurisdictions the first governments in world history, excepting perhaps the Nazi regime in Germany, to officially sanction PAS. Within the space of a month, both an eight-to-three majority of the United States Court of Appeals for the Ninth Circuit[1] on the West Coast, and a three-judge panel in the United States Court of Appeals for the Second Circuit,[2] in the Northeast, struck down long-standing state laws forbidding physicians to aid or abet their patients in acts of suicide. Within a virtual blink of an eye, the unthinkable had come to pass: PAS and euthanasia had emerged from their exile beyond the pale of law to occupy center stage in a dramatic public debate that eventually culminated in the United States Supreme Court's unanimous reversal of both lower court decisions in June 1997.[3]

Judge Reinhardt, writing for a majority of an *en banc* decision of the Ninth Circuit,[4] held that competent, terminally ill patients have a powerful "liberty interest," what used to be called a Constitutional right, to enlist the aid of their physicians in hastening death via prescriptions for lethal drugs.[5]

From *Physician Assisted Suicide: Expanding the Debate* by Margaret P. Battin, Rosamond Rhodes, and Anita Silvers. New York and London: Routledge 1998, pp. 279–300. Reprinted with permission.

He argued that, just as the right to privacy guarantees women the right to choose an abortion, this liberty interest protects a right to choose the time and manner of one's death.[6]

In response to warnings against the expansion of this right to broader categories of patients (e.g., to the mentally incapacitated) and against the great likelihood of mistake and abuse, Judge Reinhardt permitted the regulation of PAS in order to avoid such evils; however, he pointedly ruled out any and all blanket prohibitions.[7] In response to the traditional objections that allowing PAS would subvert the state's interests in preventing suicide and maintaining the integrity of the medical profession, Judge Reinhardt contended that our society already has effectively erased the distinction between merely allowing patients to die and killing them.[8] Reinhardt claimed that by allowing patients or their surrogates to forgo life-sustaining medical treatments, including artificially administered nutrition and hydration, and by sanctioning the administration of pain-killing drugs that might also hasten death, our society already permits a variety of "death inducing" practices. Thus, the social risks of allowing PAS are only different in degree, not in kind, from risks that we already countenance.

Writing for the Second Circuit in striking down a similar New York statute, Judge Miner explicitly rejected the claim of the Second Circuit majority that a "substantive due process" right of PAS exists in the Constitution. While presciently conceding that the Supreme Court was unlikely to extend the boundaries of the so-called right to privacy, Judge Miner found nevertheless that the statute violated the equal protection clause of the Constitution.[9] Echoing Judge Reinhardt's assertion that only a difference of degree separates PAS from the foregoing of life-sustaining treatments—claiming in effect that the administration of potentially death hastening analgesics constitutes a kind of suicide—Judge Miner observed that New York's law allowed some people relief from the ravages of terminal illness (i.e., those connected to some form of removable life-support) while denying relief to those not so connected, for whom PAS was the only remaining exit.[10] Concurring with Judge Reinhardt that the social risks of PAS are identical to those of our more socially approved "death inducing" practices, Judge Miner concluded that this kind of differential treatment serves no legitimate state purpose. Thus, he held that the law was unconstitutional even in the absence of a new fundamental right to PAS.[11]

What to think of these startling decisions? Were they harbingers of a new world brave enough to overcome centuries of religious censure and fear-mongering, a world that will no longer permit human beings to suffer unwillingly the torments of terminal illness? Or were they dangerous aberrations, decisions that simultaneously affirmed the autonomy of some, while endangering the lives of society's most vulnerable citizens?

The Supreme Court has finally left little doubt about where it stands on these questions. In a set of majority and concurring opinions remarkable for their ideological restraint, compassion, and thoughtfulness, the various Justices have concluded that extant state laws barring PAS and euthanasia violate neither the Fourteenth Amendment protection of liberty nor the Fifth Amendment's due process provision.[12] While thus issuing a painful rebuke to the partisans of liberalization, each of the Justices tempered his or her final judgment with the recognition that their collective decision would by no means end public debate, but would rather displace it onto the agendas of the fifty state legislatures.

As a firm believer in patient autonomy, I find myself to be deeply sympathetic to the central values motivating the case for PAS and euthanasia; I have concluded, however, that these practices pose too great a threat to the rights and welfare of too many people to be legalized in this country at the present time. Central to my argument in this essay will be the claim that the recently overturned decisions of the circuit courts employ a form of case-based reasoning that is ill-suited to the development of sound social policy in this area. I shall argue that in order to do justice to the very real threats posed by the widespread social practices of PAS and euthanasia, we need to adopt precisely the kind of policy perspective that the circuit courts rejected on principle. Thus, this essay presents the case for a forward-looking, legislative approach to PAS and euthanasia, as opposed to an essentially backward-looking, judicial or constitutional approach.[13] Although I suggest below that the soundest legislative policy at the present time would be to extend the legal prohibition of PAS into the near future, I remain open to the possibility that a given legislature, presented with sufficient evidence of the reliability of various safeguards, might come to a different conclusion.

Arguments and Motivations in Favor of PAS/Euthanasia

Let us begin, then, with the philosophical case for PAS and euthanasia, which consists of two distinct prongs, both of which speak simply, directly, and powerfully to our commonsensical intuitions. First, there is the claim of autonomy, that all of us possess a right to self-determination in matters profoundly touching on such religious themes as life, death, and the meaning of suffering. Just as we should each be free to make important choices bearing on how we shall live our own lives, so we should be equally free in choosing the time and manner of our deaths. For some, more life will always be welcome as a gift or perhaps even as a test of faith, but for others, continued life signifies only disfiguring suffering and the unrelenting loss of everything that invested their lives with meaning and dignity. As philosopher Ronald Dworkin has eloquently argued, it is a form of *tyranny* to force someone to endure terrible suffering at the end-of-life merely for the sake of someone else's values.[14] Each of us should be free to live or die as we see fit according to our own conceptions of the meaning of life and death.

Second, PAS and/or euthanasia are merciful acts that deliver terminally ill patients from a painful and protracted death. According to the utilitarian, acts are morally right insofar as they promote happiness and alleviate unhappiness, and wrong insofar as they cause or allow others to suffer needlessly. Even according to the traditional ethic of the medical profession, physicians have a solemn duty not merely to extend life whenever possible (and desirable), but also to alleviate pain and suffering whenever possible. For patients suffering from the final ravages of end-stage AIDS or cancer, a doctor's lethal prescription or injection can be, and often is, welcomed as a blessed relief. Accordingly, we should treat human beings at least as well as we treat grievously ill or injured animals by putting them, at their own request, out of their misery.

These philosophical reflections can be supplemented with a more clinical perspective addressed to the motivational factors lying behind many requests to die. Many people advocate legalization because they fear a loss of control at the end-of-life. They fear falling victim to the technological imperative; they fear dying in chronic and uncontrolled pain; they fear the psychological suffering attendant upon the relentless disintegration of the self; they fear, in short, a bad death. All of these fears, it so happens, are eminently justified. Physicians routinely ignore the documented wishes of patients and all too often allow patients to die with uncontrolled pain.[15] Studies of cancer patients have shown that over 50 percent suffer from unrelieved pain,[16] and many researchers have found that uncontrolled pain, particularly when accompanied by feelings of hopelessness and untreated depression, is a significant contributing factor for suicide and suicidal ideation.[17]

Clinical depression is another major factor influencing patients' choice of suicide.[18] Depression, accompanied by feelings of hopelessness, is the strongest predictor of suicide for both individuals who are terminally ill and those who are not.[19] Yet most doctors are not trained to notice depression, especially in complex cases such as the elderly suffering from terminal illnesses. Even when doctors succeed in diagnosing depression, they often do not successfully treat it with sufficient amounts of readily available medications.[20]

Significantly, the New York State Task Force on Life and Law found that the vast majority of patients who request PAS or euthanasia can be treated successfully both for their depression and their pain, and that when they receive adequate psychiatric and palliative care, their requests to die usually are withdrawn.[21] In other words, patients given the requisite control over their lives and relief from depression and pain usually lose interest in PAS and euthanasia.[22]

With all due respect for the power of modern methods of pain control, it must be acknowledged that a small percentage of patients suffer from conditions, both physical and psychological, that currently lie beyond the reach of the best medical and humane care. Some pain cannot be alleviated short of inducing a permanent state of unconsciousness in the patient, and some depression is unconquerable. For such unfortunate patients, the present law on PAS/euthanasia can represent an insuperable barrier to a dignified and decent death.[23]

Objections to PAS/Euthanasia

Opponents of PAS and euthanasia can be grouped into three main factions. One strongly condemns both practices as inherently immoral, as violations of the moral rule against killing the innocent. Most members of this group tend to harbor distinctly religious objections to suicide and euthanasia, viewing them as violations of God's dominion over human life.[24] They argue that killing is simply wrong in itself, whether or not it is done out of respect for the patient's autonomy or out of concern for her suffering. Whether or not this position ultimately is justifiable from a theological point of view, its imposition on believers and nonbelievers alike is incompatible with the basic premises of a secular, pluralistic political order.[25]

A second faction primarily objects to the fact that physicians are being called upon to do the killing. While conceding that killing the terminally ill or assisting in their suicides might not always be morally wrong for others to do, this group maintains that the participation of physicians in such practices undermines their role as healers and fatally compromises the physician-patient relationship.[26]

Finally, a third faction[27] readily grants that neither PAS nor active euthanasia, practiced by ordinary citizens or by physicians, are always morally wrong. On the contrary, this faction believes that in certain rare instances early release from a painful or intolerably degrading existence might constitute both a positive good and an important exercise of personal autonomy for the individual. Indeed, many members of this faction concede that should such a terrible fate befall them, they would hope to find a thoughtful, compassionate, and courageous physician to release them from their misery. But in spite of these important concessions, the members of this faction shrink from endorsing or regulating PAS and active euthanasia due to fears bearing on the social consequences of liberalization. This view is based on two distinct kinds of so-called "slippery slope" arguments. One bears on the inability to cabin PAS/euthanasia within the confines envisioned by its proponents; the other focuses on the likelihood of abuse, neglect, and mistake.

An Option Without Limits

The first version of the slippery slope argument contends that a socially sanctioned practice of PAS would in all likelihood prove difficult, if not impossible, to cabin within its originally anticipated boundaries. Proponents of legalization usually begin with a wholesomely modest policy agenda, limiting their suggested reforms to a narrow and highly specified range of potential candidates and practices.[28] "Give us PAS," they ask, "not the more controversial practice of active euthanasia, for presently competent patients who are terminally ill and suffering unbearable pain." But the logic of the case for PAS, based as it is upon the twin pillars of patient autonomy and mercy, makes it highly unlikely that society could stop with this modest proposal once it had ventured out on the slope. As numerous other critics have pointed out, if autonomy is the prime consideration, then additional constraints based upon terminal illness or unbearable pain, or both, would appear hard to justify.[29] Indeed, if autonomy is crucial, the requirement of unbearable suffering would appear to be entirely subjective. Who is to say, other than the patient herself, how much suffering is too much? Likewise, the requirement of terminal illness seems an arbitrary standard against which to judge patients' own subjective evaluation of their quality of life. If my life is no longer worth living, why should a terminally ill cancer patient be granted PAS but not me, merely because my

suffering is due to my "nonterminal" arterio-lateral sclerosis ("ALS") or intractable psychiatric disorder?[30]

Alternatively, if pain and suffering are deemed crucial to the justification of legalization, it is hard to see how the proposed barrier of contemporaneous consent of competent patients could withstand serious erosion. If the logic of PAS is at all similar to that of forgoing life-sustaining treatments, and we have every reason to think it so, then it would seem almost inevitable that a case soon would be made to permit PAS for incompetent patients who had left advance directives. That would then be followed by a "substituted judgment" test for patients who "would have wanted" PAS, and finally an "objective" test would be developed for patients (including newborns) whose best interests would be served by PAS or active euthanasia even in the absence of any subjective intent.[31]

In the same way, the joint justifications of autonomy and mercy combine to undermine the plausibility of a line drawn between PAS and active euthanasia. As the authors of one highly publicized proposal have come to see, the logic of justification for active euthanasia is identical to that of PAS.[32] Legalizing PAS, while continuing to ban active euthanasia, would serve only to discriminate unfairly against patients who are suffering and wish to end their lives, but cannot do so because of some physical impairment. Surely these patients, it will be said, are "the worst off group," and therefore they are the most in need of the assistance of others who will do for them what they can no longer accomplish on their own.

None of these initial slippery slope considerations amount to knock-down objections to further liberalization of our laws and practices. After all, it is not obvious that each of these highly predictable shifts (e.g., from terminal to "merely" incurable, from contemporaneous consent to best interests, and from PAS to active euthanasia), are patently immoral and unjustifiable. Still, in pointing out this likely slippage, the consequentialist opponents of PAS/euthanasia are calling on society to think about the likely consequences of taking the first tentative step onto the slope. If all of the extended practices predicted above pose substantially greater risks for vulnerable patients than the more highly circumscribed initial liberalization proposals, then we need to factor in these additional risks even as we ponder the more modest proposals.[33]

The Likelihood of Abuse

The second prong of the slippery slope argument argues that whatever criteria for justifiable PAS and active euthanasia ultimately are chosen, abuse of the system is highly likely to follow. In other words, patients who fall outside the ambit of our justifiable criteria will soon be candidates for death. This prong resembles what I have elsewhere called an "empirical slope" argument, as it is based not on the close logical resemblance of concepts or justifications, but rather on an empirical prediction of what is likely to happen when we insert a particular social practice into our existing social system.[34]

In order to reassure skeptics, the proponents of PAS/euthanasia concur that any potentially justifiable social policy in this area must meet at least the following three requirements.[35] The policy would have to insist: first, that all requests for death be truly voluntary; second, that all reasonable alternatives to PAS and active euthanasia must be explored before acceding to a patient's wishes; and, third, that a reliable system of reporting all cases must be established in order to effectively monitor these practices and respond to abuses. As a social pessimist on these matters, I believe, given social reality as we know it, that all three assumptions are problematic.

With regard to the voluntariness requirement, we pessimists contend that many requests would not be sufficiently voluntary. In addition to the subtly coercive influences of physicians and family members, perhaps the most slippery aspect of this slope is the highly predictable failure of most physicians to diagnose reliably and treat reversible clinical depression, particularly in the elderly population. As one geriatric psychiatrist testified before the New York Task Force, we now live in the "golden age" of treating depression, but the "lead age" of diagnosing it.[36] We have the tools, but physicians are not adequately trained and motivated to use them. Unless dramatic changes are effected in the practice of medicine, we can predict with confidence that many instances of PAS and active euthanasia will fail the test of voluntariness.

Second, there is the lingering fear that any legislative proposal or judicial mandate would have to be implemented within the present social system, one marked by deep and pervasive discrimination against the poor and members of minority groups.[37] We have every reason to expect that a policy that worked tolerably well in an affluent community like Scarsdale or Beverly Hills might not work so well in a community like Bedford-Stuyvesant or Watts, where your average citizen has little or no access to basic primary care, let alone sophisticated care for chronic pain at home or in the hospital. There is also reason to worry about any policy of PAS initiated within our growing system of managed care, capitation, and physician incentives for delivering less care.[38] Expert palliative care no doubt is an expensive and time-consuming proposition, requiring more, rather than less, time spent just talking with patients and providing them with humane comfort. It is highly doubtful that the context of physician-patient conversation within this new dispensation of "turnstile medicine" will be at all conducive to humane decisions untainted by subtle economic coercion.

In addition, given the abysmal and shameful track record of physicians in responding adequately to pain and suffering, we also can confidently predict that in many cases all reasonable alternatives will *not* have been exhausted.[39] Instead of vigorously addressing the pharmacological and psychosocial needs of such patients, physicians no doubt will continue to ignore, undertreat, or treat many of their patients in an impersonal manner. The result is likely to be more depression, desperation, and requests for physician-assisted death from patients who could have been successfully treated.[40] The root causes of this predictable failure are manifold, but high on the list is the inaccessibility of decent primary care to over thirty-seven million Americans. Other notable causes include an appalling lack of training in palliative care among primary care physicians and cancer specialists alike;[41] discrimination in the delivery of pain control and other medical treatments on the basis of race and economic status; various myths shared by both physicians and patients about the supposed ill effects of pain medications; and restrictive state laws on access to opioids.[42]

Finally, with regard to the third requirement, pessimists doubt that any reporting system would adequately monitor these practices. A great deal depends here on the extent to which patients and practitioners will regard these practices as essentially *private* matters to be discussed and acted upon within the privacy of the doctor-patient relationship. As the Dutch experience has conclusively demonstrated, physicians will be extremely loath to report instances of PAS and active euthanasia to public authorities, largely for fear of bringing the harsh glare of publicity upon the patients' families at a time when privacy is most needed.[43] The likely result of this predictable lack of oversight will be society's inability to respond appropriately to disturbing incidents and long-term trends. In other words, the practice most likely will not be as amenable to regulation as the proponents contend.

The moral of this story is that deeply seated inadequacies in physicians' training, combined with structural flaws in our healthcare system, can be reliably predicted to secure the premature deaths of many people who would in theory be excluded by the criteria of most leading proposals to legalize PAS. If this characterization of the status quo is at all accurate, then the problem will not be solved by well-meaning assurances that abuses will not be tolerated, or that patients will, of course, be offered the full range of palliative care options before any decision for PAS is ratified.[44] While such regulatory solutions are possible in theory, and may well justly prevail in the future, we should be wary of legally sanctioning any negative right to be let alone by the state when the just and humane exercise of that right will depend upon the provision of currently nonexistent services. The operative analogy here, I fear, is our failed and shameful policy of "deinstitutionalization," which left thousands of vulnerable and defenseless former residents of state psychiatric hospitals to fend for themselves on the streets, literally "rotting with their rights on."[45] It is now generally agreed that the crucial flaw in this well-intended but catastrophic policy was our society's willingness to honor such patients' negative right to be free of institutional fetters without having first made available reliable local alternatives to institutionalization. The operative lesson for us here is that judges and courts are much better at enunciating negative rights than they are at providing the services required for their successful implementation.

Two Approaches to Social Policy

We come now to the difficult task of assessing the capacity of various social policy approaches to address adequately all of the conflicting values implicated in this debate. This section shall contrast a forward-looking, policy-oriented legislative approach to the backward-looking, case-oriented judicial approach taken in the *Compassion in Dying* and *Vacco* cases. Before coming to that comparison, however, a crucial preliminary point must be noted. Central to any serious evaluation of competing policy approaches to PAS and euthanasia is the distinction between the morality of individual acts and the wisdom of social policy. Much of the debate in the popular media is driven by the depiction of especially dramatic and poignant instances of suffering humanity, desperate for release from the painful thrall of terminal illness.[46] Understandably, many of us are prompted to respond: "Should such a terrible fate ever befall me, I certainly would not want to suffer interminably; I would want the option of an early exit and the help of my trusted physician in securing it." The problem, however, lies in getting from such compelling individual cases to social policy. The issue is not simply, "What would I want?" but rather, what is the best social policy, all things considered. Social pessimists warn that we cannot make this jump from individual case to policy without endangering the autonomy and the very lives of others, many of whom are numbered among our most vulnerable citizens.

A Judge-Made Policy Based on Constitutional Law

Appellate judges in the Ninth and Second Circuits authored powerful opinions giving constitutional protection to PAS for competent patients facing terminal illness. While these opinions fully vindicated patients' important stake in having a freely chosen and pain-free death, they seriously and fatally discounted the states' important interests in preventing the kinds of slippage and abuse catalogued above.

Dismissal of Social Consequences The opinion of the Ninth Circuit, *Compassion in Dying*, authored by Judge Reinhardt, is particularly troubling with regard to the dismissal of social consequences.[47] In response to the objection that legalizing PAS inevitably will prove "infinitely expansive," the court acknowledged the difficulty that it may be hard to distinguish the moral logic of PAS from that animating the call for direct physician-administered euthanasia. He further conceded that in some cases, patients will need the help of a physician in carrying out their choice of an autonomous and painless death.[48] Instead of carefully weighing this sobering possibility in the balance, or asking whether this likelihood of slippage should make us hesitate in taking the first step onto the slope, the court immediately dismissed it as a problem for future cases, not this one, noting that, "here we decide only the issue before us."[49] For those who worry that direct euthanasia carried out by physicians might impose too great a risk in the current social climate,[50] the dictum will prove less than comforting, especially in view of the judge's confession that "it [is] less important who administers the medication than who determines whether the terminally ill person's life shall end."[51]

Thus, although we have argued that this kind of forward-looking, policy-oriented perspective is crucial for adequately assessing the individual benefits and social risks involved in the proposal to legalize PAS, the judicial approach to the problem operates fully equipped with social blinders, and willfully dismisses the very real dangers lurking further down the slope, all in the name of individual rights. Indeed, at one point Judge Reinhardt implied that a refusal to contemplate such dangers is demanded by the judicial role itself.[52] To put it mildly and most charitably, this rights-orientated mind-set does not put us in a learning mode. When life and death are at stake, we need to base our social policy on a more comprehensive picture of the likely benefits and risks.

Judge Reinhardt's grasp of the clinical realities of depression and the ubiquitous absence of adequate pain control was no more impressive than the scope of his social vision. In response to the objection that the legalization of PAS eventually would lead physicians to treat requests to die in a routine and impersonal manner, Judge Reinhardt reassured us, in the face of massive evidence to the contrary, that "doctors would not assist a terminally ill patient to hasten his death as long as there were any reasonable chance of alleviating the patient's suffering or enabling him to live under tolerable conditions."[53] Judge Reinhardt's faith in professional and governmental regulations to ensure that all requests truly are voluntary (i.e., not due to depression), and free from the taint of untreated pain and suffering, is perhaps refreshing in the age of governmental regulation-bashing, but it is a naive and dangerous faith all the same.

Equal Protection and the Fate of Responsible Regulation
The ability of a constitutional right to assisted suicide to provide adequately for safeguards against abuse, neglect, and mistake is especially problematic within the context of the Second Circuit's equal protection analysis in *Vacco*. That court's assertion of the moral and legal equivalence of withholding life-sustaining treatments, the provision of potentially death-hastening analgesics, and assisted suicide raised extremely troubling questions about the constitutionality of a wide variety of possibly effective regulations.[54] The basic question is: If we have a constitutionally protected liberty interest in determining the time and manner of our deaths, then to what extent will various regulatory schemes cut too deeply into our personal choices?

We actually have seen this script played out before in the context of abortion law. Prior to *Roe* v. *Wade*, many states already had begun liberalizing their statutes to allow women to opt for abortion under specified conditions.[55] One regulatory constraint that had been placed on women's choice in some jurisdictions was mandatory review by a hospital-based committee.[56] Now, whether or not we think that such committee review was a good idea in the context of abortion—I do not think it was—it is still interesting to note that this regulatory mechanism, along with a host of others, was discarded unceremoniously by the Supreme Court in *Doe* v. *Bolton*,[57] the companion case to *Roe* v. *Wade*.[58] In sum, the Court held that such mechanisms only serve to encumber the woman's choice, which really belongs to her (and perhaps also her doctor) alone.[59]

Now, if the Second Circuit's equal protection analysis had prevailed, and had the Supreme Court come to see no cognizable legal or moral differences between "allowing to die" and assisted suicide, then presumably the regulatory mechanisms surrounding the two sets of practices would have been subjected to identical standards of moral analysis and judicial review.[60] This kind of legally mandated parity would have had two likely consequences. First, all the paraphernalia of surrogate decision-making that currently surrounds decisions to forgo treatment would have been extended to PAS.[61] Just as most states presently allow family or close friends to make life-and-death decisions for loved ones on the basis of so-called "substituted judgment" ("What would the patient have wanted?") or best-interests or reasonable-person determinations, so we would have to allow family members the same role in those cases in which suicide "would have been chosen" by the patient or "would have been" in his best interest.[62] Obviously, this implication of the equal protection approach would have required proponents of PAS to bite a very large bullet indeed regarding the charge of indefinite expansion.

The second implication of the equal protection analysis is that a broad range of possibly helpful regulatory mechanisms, including waiting periods, committee review, second opinions, mandatory reporting, and perhaps even the requirement of terminal illness, might well have been swept aside in the name of individual liberty.[63] Currently, we do not require these kinds of substantive and procedural constraints for most decisions to forgo life-sustaining treatments by competent, terminally ill patients.[64] If, however, there is really no moral or legal difference between "allowing to die" and "assisting suicide"— if, as Judge Miner opines, adding PAS to our repertoire of choices would not add one iota of additional risk to individuals or society over and above those we already countenance—then encumbering the choice for PAS with all sorts of extra protective devices would seemingly lack constitutional validity.[65] In sum, then, the equal protection analysis championed in the Second Circuit threatened precisely those braking mechanisms that arguably might make the slippery slope a far safer place on which to practice physician-assisted death.

The Conflation of Killing and Allowing to Die Proceeding directly to the fulcrum of Judge Miner's analysis, we now consider the denial of a significant moral or legal difference between allowing a patient to die by means of forgoing life-sustaining treatments and assisting a patient in committing suicide. According to both circuit court opinions, there is no significant difference between withdrawing a ventilator, discontinuing a feeding tube, administering pain-killing but (potentially) life-shortening opioids, and prescribing a lethal dose of barbiturates.[66] In all these cases, the judges alleged, the intention is the same (i.e., to hasten death), the cause of death is the same (an *act* attributable to human agency), and the social risks of mistake and abuse are the same (e.g., misdiagnosis, undue pressure, etc.). Consequently, Judge Reinhardt concluded that PAS poses no greater threat to the state's interests in preventing suicide and in safeguarding the integrity of the medical profession than the already accepted practice of forgoing life-sustaining treatment.[67] For identical reasons Judge Miner saw no point in a more restrictive public policy towards PAS and based his entire Constitutional argument upon the purported identity of the intentions and effects of these two social practices.[68]

Along with a majority of the Supreme Court, I wish to uphold, for purposes of social policy analysis, the distinction between forgoing treatment and assisting suicide. Although the boundaries between these two practices at times are admittedly quite fuzzy, overlooking relevant differences between them leads proponents of legalization to ignore the very real social risks inherent in the judicial approach to policy.[69]

Whatever the outcome of our long-standing conceptual skirmishes bearing on the "intrinsic" distinctions between PAS, direct euthanasia, and forgoing life-sustaining treatments, the crucial question remains whether any of the purported distinctions between these activities constitute important differences for purposes of social policy.[70] As a slippery slope opponent of PAS and euthanasia, I have already conceded that individual acts involving either PAS or active euthanasia can be morally justified under certain circumstances. Having thus conceded that certain individual actions can be morally appropriate even when the intent is simply and unambiguously to end the patient's life, and even when "the cause" of death is simply and unambiguously attributable to the action of the physician, the crucial question is whether there are any remaining distinctions between allowing to die and actively killing (or assisting in a suicide) that might illuminate the negative policy implications of PAS and euthanasia.

Two points can be made in this connection. First, as the New York Task Force pointed out, the social consequences of not honoring requests to forgo treatment are very different from the consequences of failing to honor requests for PAS and euthanasia.[71] When society fails to honor requests to prescribe or deliver a lethal dose, the results can admittedly be very onerous for individual patients. The patient may face a prolonged period of deterioration before death, with increased pain and decreased dignity, contrary to what they otherwise would have wished. It is important to note, however, that in many such cases there are alternatives to prolonged and painful deaths. Under the present legal regime it is still permissible for a patient to seek out effective and compassionate hospice care, to refuse further administration of life-sustaining treatments, to request "terminal sedation" (inducing a loss of consciousness until death), and even to starve to death with the aid of a physician.[72] It is also legal for an individual truly to take matters into his own hands and to kill himself, perhaps with the guidance of a popular "self-help" book.[73] Finally, it is possible for many patients with good and trusting relationships with compassionate physicians to achieve their objectives within the bounds of private and discreet relationships, but without the cover and consolations of law.[74]

By contrast, were society, systematically and as a matter of policy, to refuse to honor requests to forgo life-sustaining treatments in order to curb possible abuses, then everyone would have to submit to the imposition of unwanted and often invasive measures. Whereas the refusal to honor a request for PAS or direct euthanasia amounts to a refusal of a positive benefit or assistance, the imposition of medical treatment against one's will represents a violation of personal autonomy and physical integrity totally incompatible with the deepest meaning of our traditional respect for liberty. Such a refusal would entail the virtual imprisonment of the entire population of terminally ill and dying patients. While the failure to offer a deadly drug to a dying patient represents a failure of mercy requiring moral justification, the forced imposition of medical treatment against a patient's will arguably constitutes a trespass, or technically a legal battery, so profound that it simply cannot be justified, especially at the level of broad gauged social policy.[75]

Without trying to sound especially hyperbolical, we can say that the practice of forgoing treatment is by now so deeply embedded in our social and medical practices that a reversal of policy on this point would throw most of our major medical institutions into a state approaching chaos. The same cannot be said of a refusal to honor requests for PAS and euthanasia. Thus, while there may well be many overlapping similarities between withholding treatment and participating in PAS or euthanasia, their respective denial at the level of social policy would entail vastly different individual and social consequences. If our goal is to reduce the level of social risk surrounding all practices involving the treatment of incurable and/or dying patients, a blanket prohibition of PAS can arguably advance this goal without totally unacceptable moral, legal, and social consequences. The same cannot be said of a blanket prohibition of forgoing life-sustaining treatments.

The second point in this connection is that the practice of PAS and/or active euthanasia would be bound to implicate many more persons than the practice of forgoing treatment.[76] While we should definitely worry about the possibility of error, neglect, and abuse in the context of allowing patients to die, it is at least somewhat comforting to realize that just about every patient in this category must be very badly off indeed. By the time that physicians discuss forgoing treatment with a patient or family, the patient is usually well into the process of dying.

With regard to PAS and euthanasia, however, we can expect that many candidates will be perfectly ambulatory and far from the dreaded scene of painful terminal illness depicted by advocates.

Depending on how great the social slippage, this category may well come to encompass those with an incurable condition but who are not presently "terminal," such as persons in the early stages of HIV infection or Alzheimer's disease.[77] It also may come to encompass patients suffering from prolonged and intractable depression who exhibit no other symptoms of physical illness. Although one important legislative proposal specifically excludes patients whose only symptoms are psychiatric in nature, this reluctance was likely motivated in no small measure by political considerations.[78] Once PAS or active euthanasia, or both, are firmly in place, however, it will be extremely difficult to withhold them from persons whose suffering is every bit as real but whose source is entirely psychological rather than physical. That, Judge Miner and many others would surely object, would constitute an invidious distinction and thus a form of unconstitutional discrimination against the mentally ill.

If the States Are the Laboratory, What's the Experiment?

Although the Ninth Circuit was prepared to grant that states have a legitimate interest in avoiding the possibly adverse social consequences of PAS, the court insisted that regulation, rather than prohibition, is the only constitutionally permissible means of so doing.[79] Toward that end, it would have assigned the challenging task of crafting appropriate regulations to the "laboratory of the states." In view of the very real possibility that the social and individual harms attendant upon the legalization of PAS eventually would prove disproportionate to their benefits, this division of labor between the judiciary and the state legislatures is highly problematic. Had the Supreme Court affirmed the Ninth Circuit's reasoning in granting constitutional protection to the liberty interest in choosing death, states would have been deprived of their ability to put a stop to the widespread practice of PAS even if credible studies were to demonstrate that abuses were rampant and highly resistant to procedural safeguards. Short of a Constitutional amendment, there would have been no turning back had the right to PAS been guaranteed by either the due process or equal protection clauses.

Instead of putting ourselves into this precarious position, we should assign a different and more fundamental task to the laboratory of the states. Given the very real possibilities for extension and abuse of this liberty interest, state legislatures should be entrusted with the basic questions of whether, when, and under what circumstances such a risky social experiment should be attempted in the first place. State legislatures are in a better position than federal judges to study the social and clinical facts and come to a reasonable conclusion on the likely balance of individual benefit and social risks.[80] Given the social and medical realities of this country, I would hope that most states would follow the lead of the New York Task Force in refusing to countenance the legalization and routinization of PAS at this time. However, even if some states do decide to run these risks as a social experiment, i.e., to determine for themselves on the basis of empirical evidence and moral judgment whether more good than harm will come from legalizing PAS, they would have the flexibility, absent rigidly defined constitutional mandates, both to impose very strict regulations and, if necessary, to stop the experiment cold in the face of disconcerting evidence of serious moral slippage. Such an approach is, I believe, much better suited to asking the relevant policy questions and taking appropriate and prudent action.[81]

In addition to being safer, the legislative approach is also, at least potentially, much more democratic than the judicial, rights-based orientation. The legislature is the traditional site in this country for the resolution of most difficult and divisive questions of social policy, especially those marked by deep moral questions and highly troubling empirical uncertainties involving the lives and welfare of many citizens. A court-mandated solution to the question of PAS would, I believe, have secured a decisive and irrevocable victory for one side of this controversy before a thorough and robust public debate had taken place. One significant merit of a legislative approach is that, while it would not guarantee such a debate, it would at least be compatible with large-scale efforts at the state and local levels to foster a more democratically deliberative public dialogue on this matter. Such efforts could give citizens a chance to weigh the nature and value of the liberties at stake against the extent and probability of the social dangers posed by PAS. They could thus serve as a valuable *via media* between the judicial approach, which can often short circuit public debate, and decision-making by public referendum, which is more democratic in theory but often lacks an explicitly deliberative dimension that would allow citizens a deeper understanding of the issues involved before their legislatures took action.[82]

Toward a Policy of Prudent (Legal) Restraint and Aggressive (Medical) Intervention

In contrast to the judicial approach, which totally vindicates the value of patient autonomy at the expense of protecting the vulnerable, my own preferred approach to a social policy of PAS and euthanasia conceives of this debate as posing essentially a "tragic choice."[83] It frankly acknowledges that whatever choice we make, whether we opt for a reaffirmation of the current legal restraints or for a policy of legitimation and regulation, there are bound to be victims. The victims of the current policy are easy to identify: They are on the news, the talk shows, the documentaries, and often on Dr. Kevorkian's roster of so-called "patients." The victims of legalization, by contrast, will be largely hidden from view; they will include the clinically depressed eighty-year-old man who could have lived for another year of good quality if only he had been adequately treated, and the fifty-year-old woman who asks for death because doctors in her financially stretched HMO cannot, or will not, effectively treat her unrelenting, but mysterious, pelvic pain. Perhaps eventually, if we slide far enough down the slope, the uncommunicative stroke victim, whose distant children deem an earlier death to be a better death, will fall victim. There will be others besides these, many coming from the ranks of the uninsured and the poor. To the extent that minorities and the poor already suffer from the effects of discrimination in our healthcare system, it is reasonable to expect that any system of PAS and euthanasia will exhibit similar effects, such as failure to access adequate primary care, pain management, and psychiatric diagnosis and treatment. Unlike Dr. Kevorkian's "patients," these victims will not get their pictures in the papers, but they all will have faces and they will all be cheated of good months or perhaps even years.

This "tragic choice" approach to social policy on PAS/euthanasia takes the form of the following argument formulated at the legislative level. First, the number of "genuine cases" justifying PAS, active euthanasia, or both, will be relatively small. Patients who receive good personal care, good pain relief, treatment for depression, and adequate psychosocial supports tend not to persist in their desire to die.

Second, the social risks of legalization are serious and highly predictable. They include the expansion of these practices to nonvoluntary cases, the advent of active euthanasia, and the widespread failure to pursue readily available alternatives to suicide motivated by pain, depression, hopelessness, and lack of access to good primary medical care.

Third, rather than propose a momentous and dangerous policy shift for a relatively small number of "genuine cases"—a shift that would surely involve a great deal of persistent social division and strife analogous to that involved in the abortion controversy—we should instead attempt to redirect the public debate toward a goal on which we can and should all agree, namely the manifest and urgent need to reform the way we die in America. Instead of pursuing a highly divisive and dangerous campaign for PAS, we should attack the problem at its root with an ambitious program of reform in the areas of access to primary care and the education of physicians in palliative care. At least as far as the "slippery slope" opponents of PAS are concerned, we should thus first see to it that the vast majority of people in this country have access to adequate, affordable, and nondiscriminatory primary and palliative care. At the end of this long and arduous process, when we finally have an equitable, effective, and compassionate healthcare system in place, one that might be compared favorably with that in the Netherlands, then we might well want to reopen the discussion of PAS and active euthanasia.

Finally, there are those few unfortunate patients who truly are beyond the pale of good palliative, hospice, and psychiatric care. The opponents of legalization must face up to this suffering remnant and attempt to offer creative and humane solutions.

One possibility is for such patients to be rendered permanently unconscious by drugs until such time, presumably not a long time, as death finally claims them. Although some will find such an option to be aesthetically unappealing, many would find it a welcome relief.[84] Other patients beyond the reach of the best palliative and hospice care could take their own lives, either by well-known traditional means, or with the help of a physician who could sedate them while they refused further food and (life-extending) fluids. Those who find the latter option to be unacceptable might still be able to find a compassionate physician who, like Dr. Timothy Quill, will ultimately be willing, albeit in fear and trembling, to "take small risks for people [they] really know and care about."[85] Such actions will continue to take place within the privacy of the patient-physician relationship, however, and thus will not threaten vulnerable patients and the social fabric to the same extent as would result from full legalization and regulation.[86] As the partisans of legalized PAS correctly point out, the covert practice of PAS will not be subject to regulatory oversight, and is thus capable of generating its own abuses and slippery slope. Still, I believe that the ever-present threat of possible criminal sanctions and revocation of licensure will continue to serve, for the vast majority of physicians, as powerful disincentives to abuse the system. Moreover, as suggested earlier, it is highly unlikely that the proposals for legalization would result in truly effective oversight.

Conclusion

Instead of conceiving this momentous debate as a choice between, on the one hand, legalization and regulation with all of their attendant risks, and on the other hand, the callous abandonment of patients to their pain and suffering,[87] enlightened opponents must recommend a positive program of clinical and social reforms. On the clinical level, physicians must learn how to really listen to their patients, to unflinchingly engage them in sensitive discussions of their needs and the meaning of their requests for assisted death, to deliver appropriate palliative care, to distinguish fact from fiction in the ethics and law of pain relief, to diagnose and treat clinical depression, and finally, to ascertain and respect their patients' wishes for control regarding the forgoing of life-sustaining treatments. On the social level, opponents of PAS must aggressively promote major initiatives in medical and public education regarding pain control, in the sensitization of insurance companies and licensing agencies to issues of the quality of dying, and in the reform of state laws that currently hinder access to pain relieving medications.[88]

In the absence of an ambitious effort in the direction of aggressive medical and social reform, I fear that the medical and nursing professions will have lost whatever moral warrant and credibility they might still have in continuing to oppose physician-assisted suicide and active euthanasia. As soon as these reforms are in place, however, we might then wish to proceed slowly and cautiously with experiments in various states to test the overall benefits of a policy of legalization. Until that time, however, we are not well served as a society by court decisions allowing for legalization of PAS. The Supreme Court has thus reached a sound decision in ruling out a constitutional right to PAS. As the justices acknowledged, however, this momentous decision will not end the moral debate over PAS and euthanasia. Indeed, it should and hopefully will intensify it.

NOTES

The author would like to thank Carl Coleman, David DeGrazia, Yale Kamisar, Tom Murray, David Orentlicher, and Bonnie Steinbock for helpful discussions and exchanges on the issues dealt with in this paper. Longer versions of this article, published before the Supreme Court's decisions, appeared in *Biolaw* (July/August 1996), Special Section: 171–88 and *The Journal of Contemporary Health Law and Policy* 13 (1997): 361–89.

1. *Compassion in Dying* v. *Washington*, 79 F. 3d 790, 838 (9th Cir. 1996).

2. *Quill* v. *Vacco*, 80 F. 3d 716, 731 (2nd Cir. 1996).

3. *Vacco, Attorney General of New York, et al.* v. *Quill et al.*, certiorari to the United States Court of Appeals for the second circuit, No. 95–1858. Argued January 8, 1997—Decided June 26, 1997. *Washington et al.* v. *Glucksberg et al.*, certiorari to the United States Court of Appeals for the ninth circuit, No. 96–110. Argued January 8, 1997—Decided June 26, 1997.

4. See *Compassion in Dying*, 79 F. 3d at 790.

5. Ibid., 816.

6. Ibid., 813–14.

7. Ibid., 816–32, 836–37 (reviewing state interests and illustrating the application of the balancing test and holding).

8. Ibid., 822–23.

9. *Vacco* v. *Quill*, 80 F. 3d 716, 724–25 (2nd Cir. 1996).

10. Ibid., 727–29.

11. Ibid., 727.

12. *Washington* v. *Glucksberg*, 117 Sup. Ct. 2258 (1997). *Vacco* v. *Quill*, 117 Sup. Ct. 2293 (1997).

13. My stance on these issues has been profoundly influenced by my recent work with the New York State Task Force on Life and the Law (hereinafter "the Task Force") to come to grips with this issue. Following a thorough review of the moral, legal, and social arguments, this highly pluralistic advisory committee unanimously concluded against the legalization of either PAS or direct killing by physicians. A reading of the Supreme Court opinions in these cases suggests that the Task Force's analysis of the social policy of PAS was accepted by most, if not all, of the Justices. See Task Force, *When Death Is Sought: Assisted Suicide and Euthanasia in the Medical Context* (May 1994).

14. Ronald Dworkin, *Life's Dominion: An Argument About Abortion, Euthanasia, and Individual Freedom* (New York: Knopf, 1993), 217. While I agree with Professor Dworkin on the inadmissibility of religious rationales for the legal prohibition of PAS, we disagree on the availability of convincing secular justifications.

15. "A Controlled Trial to Improve Care for Seriously Ill Hospitalized Patients; The Study to Understand Prognoses and Preferences for Outcomes and Risks of Treatments (SUPPORT)," *Journal of the American Medical Association* 274 (Nov. 22, 1995): 1591–92.

16. Task Force, *When Death Is Sought*, x–xi.

17. Ibid., xiv.

18. Ezekiel J. Emanuel et al., "Euthanasia and Physician-Assisted Suicide: Attitudes and Experiences of Oncology Patients, Oncologists, and the Public," *Lancet* 347 (1996): 1805. See also D. Saltzburg et al., "The Relationship of Pain and Depression to Suicidal Ideation in Cancer Patients," *Proc. ASCO* 8 (1989): 312 (abstract).

19. W. Breitbart, "Cancer Pain and Suicide," in K. M. Foley, ed., *Advances in Pain Research and Therapy* 16 (1990): 399–412 (showing that studies indicate that depression "is present in 50 percent of all suicides, and those suffering from depression are at 25 times greater risk for suicide than the general population").

20. New York State Task Force, *When Death Is Sought*, 127–28 (documenting the claim that doctors fail to diagnose and treat depression). See also Y. Conwell and E. D. Caine, "Rational Suicide and the Right to Die," *New England Journal of Medicine* 325 (1991): 1101.

21. New York State Task Force, *When Death Is Sought*, xiv.

22. As we shall see later, this fact is of enormous importance for our evaluation of PAS and euthanasia as social policies, for if the root causes or motivations for assisted death can be addressed successfully for most patients through the delivery of technically competent and compassionate medicine, the case for changing the law loses much of its urgency.

23. The above section thus signals two important points of agreement with the so-called Philosophers' Brief submitted to the Supreme Court in *Compassion in Dying* and *Vacco* by Ronald Dworkin, Thomas Nagel, Robert Nozick, John Rawls, Thomas Scanlon, and Judith Jarvis Thomson. I agree that individuals in the throes of a painful or degrading terminal illness may well have a very strong moral and even legal interest in securing PAS. I also agree that the pain and suffering of a small percentage of dying patients cannot be adequately controlled by currently available medical interventions. (*New York Review of Books* 44 (5) [March 27, 1997]: 41–47. See also appendix B of this volume.) As we shall see, however, I disagree with the philosophers' conclusion that this interest is sufficiently strong in the face of current medical and social inadequacies as to justify a legal right that would void the reasonably cautious prohibitions of PAS and euthanasia in effect in every State.

24. For religious objections to suicide and euthanasia, see St. Thomas Aquinas, "Whether It Is Lawful to Kill Oneself," in Tom L. Beauchamp and Robert Veatch, eds., *Ethical Issues in Death and Dying*, 2nd. ed. (1996), pp. 119–21. See also Dworkin, *Life's Dominion*, 193. See also Richard John Neuhaus, "The Return of Eugenics," *Commentary* 22 (1988) (arguing that life is a good of the person, not simply for the person).

25. Here too I agree with the Philosophers' Brief.

26. Willard Gaylin et al., "Doctors Must Not Kill," *Journal of the American Medical Association* 259 (1988): 2139–40. See also David Orentlicher, "Physician Participation in Assisted Suicide," *Journal of the American Medical Association* 262 (1989): 1844–45.

27. The author was a part of this faction during his tenure with the New York State Task Force.

28. See Christine Cassel et al., "Care of the Hopelessly Ill: Proposed Clinical Criteria for Physician-Assisted Suicide," *New England Journal of Medicine* 327 (1992): 1380–84 (approving of PAS but not of active euthanasia because it poses excessive social risks).

29. See Daniel Callahan, *The Troubled Dream of Life: Living With Mortality* (New York: Simon and Schuster, 1993). See also Yale Kamisar, "Against Assisted Suicide—Even a Very Limited Form," *University of Detroit-Mercy Law Review* 72 (1995): 735.

30. ALS also is known as Lou Gehrig's disease.

31. *In re Conroy*, 486 A. 2d 1209 (1985) (summarizing the logic of foregoing life-sustaining treatments).

32. Cassel et al., "Care of the Hopelessly Ill," 1380–84. See also Franklin G. Miller et al., "Regulating Physician-Assisted Death," *New England Journal of Medicine* 331

(1994): 199–23 (conceding the untenability of the previous distinction).

33. Professors Dworkin, et al. consistently fail to mention the possibility, let alone the high likelihood, of this first sort of slippage; I take this to be a serious omission both in their joint brief and in Professor Dworkin's individually authored articles on this subject. These authors simply assume (with the plaintiffs and circuit court majority opinions) that this right will be restricted by means of procedural safeguards to presently competent, incurably ill individuals manifesting great pain and suffering due to physical illness. (For evidence of Professor Dworkin's continuing failure to acknowledge this problem, see his assessment of the Supreme Court opinions in "Assisted Suicide: What the Court Really Said," *New York Review of Books* 44 (14) (Sept. 25, 1997): 40–44.) Failure to notice this sort of dynamic might be due either to the philosophers' lack of familiarity with the recent history of bioethics or to their belief that the social risks of PAS are equivalent to the risks inherent in the widely accepted practice of forgoing life-sustaining treatments, and thus that such slippage would not present any additional risk. The latter assumption is, of course, vigorously contested by the opponents of PAS and euthanasia.

34. John Arras, "The Right to Die on the Slippery Slope," *Social Theory and Practice* 8 (1982): 285 (describing the "slippery slope" argument in favor of PAS).

35. See, e.g., Cassel et al., "Care of the Hopelessly Ill"; Miller et al., "Regulating Physician-Assisted Death"; Charles H. Baron et al., "Statute: A Model State Act to Authorize and Regulate Physician-Assisted Suicide," *Harvard Journal of Legislation* 33 (1996): 1.

36. Dr. Gary Kennedy, Division of Geriatrics, Montefiore Medical Center, Albert Einstein College of Medicine, Testimony before the New York Task Force on Life and the Law.

37. Task Force, *When Death Is Sought*, 143 (illustrating discrimination against minority groups). See also C. S. Cleeland et al., "Pain and Its Treatment in Outpatients with Metastic Cancer," *New England Journal of Medicine* 320 (1994): 592–96 (illustrating a study that found that patients treated for cancer at centers that care predominantly for minority individuals were three times more likely to receive inadequate therapy to relieve pain).

38. Susan M. Wolf, "Physician-Assisted Suicide in the Context of Managed Care," *Duquesne Law Review* 35 (1996): 455.

39. Task Force, *When Death Is Sought*, 43–47. "Despite dramatic advances in pain management, the delivery of pain relief is grossly inadequate in clinical practice.... Studies have shown that only 2 to 60 percent of cancer pain, is treated adequately." Ibid., 43.

40. Wolf, "Physician-Assisted Suicide in the Context of Managed Care."

41. Task Force, *When Death Is Sought*, 44: "In general, researchers report that many doctors and nurses are poorly informed about, and have limited experience with, pain and symptom management. Health care professionals appear to have a limited understanding of the physiology of pain and the pharmacology of narcotic analgesics. Accordingly, many lack the understanding, skills, and confidence necessary for effective pain and symptom management." See also K. M. Foley, "The Relationship of Pain and Symptom Management to Patient Requests for Physician-Assisted Suicide," *Journal of Pain and Symptom Management* 6 (1991): 290.

42. Task Force, *When Death Is Sought*, 17.

43. One source estimates that in the early 1990s, no more than 30 percent of cases of PAS were reported. During 1994, the rate of reporting increased to roughly 50 percent of cases. See John Keown, "Further Reflections on Euthanasia in the Netherlands in the Light of the Remmelink Report and the Van Der Maas Survey," in Luke Gormally, ed., *Euthanasia: Clinical Practice and the Law* (1994) 219. See also Daniel Callahan and Margot White, "The Legalization of Physician-Assisted Suicide: Creating a Regulatory Potemkin Village," *University of Richmond Law Review* 30 (1996): 17.

44. See, e.g., Ronald Dworkin, "Introduction to the Philosophers' Brief," *New York Review of Books*, 41–42; and Dworkin, "Assisted Suicide: What the Court Really Said," 44.

45. Nancy Rhoden, "The Limits of Liberty: Deinstitutionalization, Homelessness, and Libertarian Theory," *Emory Law Journal* 32 (2) (Spring 1982): 375–440.

46. Tom Kuntz, "Helping a Man Kill Himself, As Shown on Dutch TV," *New York Times* (Nov. 13, 1994), at E–7 (describing the first national broadcast of an actual mercy killing in the Netherlands).

47. *Compassion in Dying* v. *Washington*, 79 F. 3d 790, 830–32 (9th Cir. 1996).

48. Ibid., 831.

49. Ibid., 832.

50. This group once included such distinguished physicians and advocates of PAS as Dr. Timothy Quill, Christine Cassel, and Diane Meier. See Cassel et al., "Care of the Hopelessly Ill."

51. *Compassion in Dying*, 79 F. 3d at 832.

52. Ibid., 831 ("In fact, the Court has never refused to recognize a substantive due process liberty right or interest merely because there were difficulties in determining when and how to limit its exercise or because others might someday attempt to use it improperly.").

53. Ibid., 827. Judge Reinhardt's optimism is contradicted by evidence amassed in the SUPPORT study. See note 15 above.

54. *Quill* v. *Vacco*, 80 F. 3d 716, 729 (2nd Cir. 1996).

55. 410 U.S. 113 (1973).

56. *Doe* v. *Bolton*, 410 U.S. 179, 184 (1973).

57. 410 U.S. 179 (1973).

58. Ibid., 198.

59. Ibid.

60. See Frank G. Miller, "Legalizing Physician-Assisted Suicide by Judicial Decision: A Critical Appraisal," *Biolaw* (Jul.–Aug. 1996).

61. Ibid., S–143.

62. For a comprehensive account of practices and laws governing the forgoing of life-sustaining treatment and surrogate decision making, see Alan Meisel, *The Right to Die*, 2d ed. (New York: Wiley Law Publications, 1995).

63. Miller, "Legalizing Physician-Assisted Suicide by Judicial Decision."

64. Meisel, *The Right to Die*.

65. Miller, "Legalizing Physician-Assisted Suicide by Judicial Decision."

66. *Quill v. Vacco*, 80 F. 3d 716, 729 (2nd Cir. 1996); see also *Compassion in Dying v. Washington*, 79 F. 3d 790, 822–24 (9th Cir. 1996).

67. Miller, "Legalizing Physician-Assisted Suicide by Judicial Decision," S-139.

68. *Quill v. Vacco*, 80 F. 3d 716, 729 (2nd Cir. 1996).

69. Dan Brock, "Voluntary Active Euthanasia," *Hastings Center Report* 22 (1992): 10. See also Brock, "Borderline Cases of Morally Justified Taking Life in Medicine," in Tom Beauchamp, ed., *Intending Death: The Ethics of Assisted Suicide and Euthanasia* (Upper Saddle River, NJ: Prentice Hall, 1996): 131–49.

70. For a helpful review of the arguments surrounding the distinction between "letting die" and PAS/euthanasia, see Kamisar, "Against Assisted Suicide—Even a Very Limited Form," 753–60. For those wishing to go deeper into these troubled waters, see B. Steinbock & Alastair Norcross, eds., *Killing and Letting Die* (New York: Fordham University Press, 1995). See also Beauchamp, ed., *Intending Death: The Ethics of Assisted Suicide and Euthanasia*.

71. Task Force, *When Death Is Sought*, 146–47.

72. David M. Eddy, "A Conversation with My Mother," *Journal of the American Medical Association* 272 (1994): 179 (illustrating the possibility of death by starvation).

73. Derek Humphrey, *Final Exit: The Practicalities of Self-deliverance and Assisted Suicide for the Dying*, 2nd ed., (New York: Bantam Doubleday, 1997).

74. Dick Lehr, "Death and the Doctor's Hand: Increasingly, Secretly, Doctors Are Helping the Incurably Ill to Die," *Boston Globe* (Apr. 25, 1993), p. 1 (featuring the experience of physicians who have helped patients to commit suicide).

75. *Restatement (second) of Torts*, sec. 13 (1965) (defining battery).

76. See also Seth Kreimer, "Does Pro-Choice Mean Pro-Kevorkian?: An Essay on Roe, Casey, and the Right to Die," *American University Law Review* 44 (1995): 803, 841.

77. The prospects for slippage here are excellent. The step from a requirement of terminal illness, viewed by these courts as canonical, to one of merely "untreatable" or "incurable" illness, already has been recommended by a panel of distinguished proponents of PAS. See Miller et al., "Regulating Physician-Assisted Death." It is interesting to note in this connection that one of Jack Kevorkian's earliest "patients," Janet Atkins, reportedly was playing tennis a week or two before her assisted suicide.

78. Baron et al., "A Model State Act to Authorize and Regulate Physician-Assisted Suicide," 11. At an American Philosophical Association symposium on PAS in December, 1995, Professor Brock conceded that political-strategic considerations played a significant role in his group's decision not to sanction PAS for the chronically mentally ill.

79. *Compassion in Dying v. Washington*, 79 F. 3d 790, 832–33, 836–37 (9th Cir. 1996).

80. Carl E. Schneider, "Making Sausage: The Ninth Circuit's Opinion," *Hastings Center Report* 27 (1997): 27–28 (reviewing the shortcomings of judges in coming to terms with the complexities of highly contextualized social problems such as PAS).

81. For similar reasons, I am highly skeptical of state ballot initiatives, such as the 1994 initiative in Oregon, which do not make use of the legislatures' superior fact-finding capabilities or, for that matter, of the citizens' capacity for more deliberative approaches to democratic problem solving.

82. It does not speak well for the level of public understanding of this issue, as gauged by polls and referenda, that I, a middling public speaker at best, am unfailingly able to convert (or at least shake the confidence of) largely pro-PAS audiences by the end of a half-hour exploration of the social risks and available alternatives. For an excellent discussion of the promise of a more deliberative mode of democracy, see Amy Gutmann and Dennis Thompson, *Democracy and Disagreement* (Cambridge: Harvard University Press, 1996).

83. For an explication of the notion of a "tragic choice" in the sense that I employ here, see Guido Calabresi & Philip Bobbit, *Tragic Choices* (New York: W.W. Norton, 1978).

84. For a good example of how such "terminal sedation" can fit into an overall plan of palliative care, bringing relief to patients and families alike, see Ira Byock's compassionate and instructive account in *Dying Well: The Prospect for Growth at the End of Life* (New York: Riverhead Books, 1997), ch. 10.

85. Timothy Quill, "Death and Dignity: A Case of Individualized Decision Making," *New England Journal of Medicine* 324 (1991): 694.

86. Allowing for the occasional covert practice of PAS would, it is true, favor well-educated, middle-class individuals with access to willing physicians and would thus perpetuate an undesirable double standard that excludes the poor and unconnected from the benefit of a better death. (For a powerful formulation of this criticism, see Dworkin, "Introduction: The Philosophers' Brief," 41.) I take this double standard to be a definite liability of

my approach, but one required by the moral necessity of avoiding other harms to other people. Describing my approach as informed by a "tragic" vision acknowledges the unhappy fact that no solution to the problem of dying in our society will be acceptable, fair, or humane to all. The most we can hope for here is "the least worst" policy.

87. In framing the question in just this way, Ronald Dworkin is guilty of posing a false dilemma in his otherwise admirable book. See Dworkin, *Life's Dominion*, p. 198.
88. This brief sketch of suggested reforms merely summarizes the careful work of the New York State Task Force. See *When Death Is Sought*, pp. 153–184.

Active and Passive Euthanasia

JAMES RACHELS

In this famous essay, Rachels argues that the traditional distinction between killing and letting die is untenable, that "killing is not in itself any worse than letting die." If so, then active euthanasia is no worse than passive euthanasia. Thus doctors may have to distinguish between active and passive euthanasia for legal reasons, but "they should not give the distinction any added authority and weight by writing it into official statements of medical ethics."

The distinction between active and passive euthanasia is thought to be crucial for medical ethics. The idea is that it is permissible, at least in some cases, to withhold treatment and allow a patient to die, but it is never permissible to take any direct action designed to kill the patient. This doctrine seems to be accepted by most doctors, and it is endorsed in a statement adopted by the House of Delegates of the American Medical Association on December 4, 1973:

> The intentional termination of the life of one human being by another—mercy killing—is contrary to that for which the medical profession stands and is contrary to the policy of the American Medical Association.
>
> The cessation of the employment of extraordinary means to prolong the life of the body when there is irrefutable evidence that biological death is imminent is the decision of the patient and/or his immediate family. The advice and judgment of the physician should be freely available to the patient and/or his immediate family.

However, a strong case can be made against this doctrine. In what follows I will set out some of the

From *The New England Journal of Medicine*, vol. 292, no. 2. Copyright © 1975 by the Massachusetts Medical Society. All rights reserved. Reprinted with permission.

relevant arguments, and urge doctors to reconsider their views on this matter.

To begin with a familiar type of situation, a patient who is dying of incurable cancer of the throat is in terrible pain, which can no longer be satisfactorily alleviated. He is certain to die within a few days, even if present treatment is continued, but he does not want to go on living for those days since the pain is unbearable. So he asks the doctor for an end to it, and his family joins in the request.

Suppose the doctor agrees to withhold treatment, as the conventional doctrine says he may. The justification for his doing so is that the patient is in terrible agony, and since he is going to die anyway, it would be wrong to prolong his suffering needlessly. But now notice this. If one simply withholds treatment, it may take the patient longer to die, and so he may suffer more than he would if more direct action were taken and a lethal injection given. This fact provides strong reason for thinking that, once the initial decision not to prolong his agony has been made, active euthanasia is actually preferable to passive euthanasia, rather than the reverse. To say otherwise is to endorse the option that leads to more suffering rather than less, and is contrary to the humanitarian impulse that prompts the decision not to prolong his life in the first place.

Part of my point is that the process of being "allowed to die" can be relatively slow and painful, whereas being given a lethal injection is relatively quick and painless. Let me give a different sort of example. In the United States about one in 600 babies is born with Down's syndrome. Most of these babies are otherwise healthy—that is, with only the usual pediatric care, they will proceed to an otherwise normal infancy. Some, however, are born with congenital defects such as intestinal obstructions that require operations if they are to live. Sometimes, the parents and the doctor will decide not to operate, and let the infant die. Anthony Shaw describes what happens then:

> . . . When surgery is denied [the doctor] must try to keep the infant from suffering while natural forces sap the baby's life away. As a surgeon whose natural inclination is to use the scalpel to fight off death, standing by and watching a salvageable baby die is the most emotionally exhausting experience I know. It is easy at a conference, in a theoretical discussion, to decide that such infants should be allowed to die. It is altogether different to stand by in the nursery and watch as dehydration and infection wither a tiny being over hours and days. This is a terrible ordeal for me and the hospital staff—much more so than for the parents who never set foot in the nursery.*

I can understand why some people are opposed to all euthanasia, and insist that such infants must be allowed to live. I think I can also understand why other people favor destroying these babies quickly and painlessly. But why should anyone favor letting "dehydration and infection wither a tiny being over hours and days"? The doctrine that says that a baby may be allowed to dehydrate and wither, but may not be given an injection that would end its life without suffering, seems so patently cruel as to require no further refutation. The strong language is not intended to offend, but only to put the point in the clearest possible way.

My second argument is that the conventional doctrine leads to decisions concerning life and death made on irrelevant grounds.

---

*Shaw A: Doctor, Do we have a choice? *The New York Times Magazine*, January 30, 1972, p. 54.

Consider again the case of the infants with Down's syndrome who need operations for congenital defects unrelated to the syndrome to live. Sometimes, there is no operation, and the baby dies, but when there is no such defect, the baby lives on. Now, an operation such as that to remove an intestinal obstruction is not prohibitively difficult. The reason why such operations are not performed in these cases is, clearly, that the child has Down's syndrome and the parents and doctor judge that because of that fact it is better for the child to die.

But notice that this situation is absurd, no matter what view one takes of the lives and potentials of such babies. If the life of such an infant is worth preserving, what does it matter if it needs a simple operation? Or, if one thinks it better that such a baby should not live on, what difference does it make that it happens to have an unobstructed intestinal tract? In either case, the matter of life and death is being decided on irrelevant grounds. It is the Down's syndrome, and not the intestines, that is the issue. The matter should be decided, if at all, on that basis, and not be allowed to depend on the essentially irrelevant question of whether the intestinal tract is blocked.

What makes this situation possible, of course, is the idea that when there is an intestinal blockage, one can "let the baby die," but when there is no such defect there is nothing that can be done, for one must not "kill" it. The fact that this idea leads to such results as deciding life or death on irrelevant grounds is another good reason why the doctrine should be rejected.

One reason why so many people think that there is an important moral difference between active and passive euthanasia is that they think killing someone is morally worse than letting someone die. But is it? Is killing, in itself, worse than letting die? To investigate this issue, two cases may be considered that are exactly alike except that one involves killing whereas the other involves letting someone die. Then, it can be asked whether this difference makes any difference to the moral assessments. It is important that the cases be exactly alike, except for this one difference, since otherwise one cannot be confident that it is this difference and not some other that accounts for any variation in the assessments of the two cases. So, let us consider this pair of cases:

In the first, Smith stands to gain a large inheritance if anything should happen to his six-year-old cousin. One evening while the child is taking his bath, Smith sneaks into the bathroom and drowns the child, and then arranges things so that it will look like an accident.

In the second, Jones also stands to gain if anything should happen to his six-year-old cousin. Like Smith, Jones sneaks in planning to drown the child in his bath. However, just as he enters the bathroom Jones sees the child slip and hit his head, and fall face down in the water. Jones is delighted; he stands by, ready to push the child's head back under if it is necessary, but it is not necessary. With only a little thrashing about, the child drowns all by himself, "accidentally," as Jones watches and does nothing.

Now Smith killed the child, whereas Jones "merely" let the child die. That is the only difference between them. Did either man behave better, from a moral point of view? If the difference between killing and letting die were in itself a morally important matter, one should say that Jones's behavior was less reprehensible than Smith's. But does one really want to say that? I think not. In the first place, both men acted from the same motive, personal gain, and both had exactly the same end in view when they acted. It may be inferred from Smith's conduct that he is a bad man, although that judgment may be withdrawn or modified if certain further facts are learned about him—for example, that he is mentally deranged. But would not the very same thing be inferred about Jones from his conduct? And would not the same further considerations also be relevant to any modification of this judgment? Moreover, suppose Jones pleaded, in his own defense, After all, I didn't do anything except just stand there and watch the child drown. I didn't kill him; I only let him die." Again, if letting die were in itself less bad than killing, this defense should have at least some weight. But it does not. Such a "defense" can only be regarded as a grotesque perversion of moral reasoning. Morally speaking, it is no defense at all.

Now, it may be pointed out, quite properly, that the cases of euthanasia with which doctors are concerned are not like this at all. They do not involve personal gain or the destruction of normal healthy children. Doctors are concerned only with cases in which the patient's life is of no further use to him, or in which the patient's life has become or will soon become a terrible burden. However, the point is the same in these cases: the bare difference between killing and letting die does not, in itself, make a moral difference. If a doctor lets a patient die, for humane reasons, he is in the same moral position as if he had given the patient a lethal injection for humane reasons. If his decision was wrong—if, for example, the patient's illness was in fact curable—the decision would be equally regrettable no matter which method was used to carry it out. And if the doctor's decision was the right one, the method used is not in itself important.

The AMA policy statement isolates the crucial issue very well; the crucial issue is "the intentional termination of the life of one human being by another." But after identifying this issue, and forbidding "mercy killing," the statement goes on to deny that the cessation of treatment is the intentional termination of a life. This is where the mistake comes in, for what is the cessation of treatment, in these circumstances, if it is not "the intentional termination of the life of one human being by another"? Of course it is exactly that, and if it were not, there would be no point to it.

Many people will find this judgment hard to accept. One reason, I think, is that it is very easy to conflate the question of whether killing is, in itself, worse than letting die, with the very different question of whether most actual cases of killing are more reprehensible than most actual cases of letting die. Most actual cases of killing are clearly terrible (think, for example, of all the murders reported in the newspapers), and one hears of such cases every day. On the other hand, one hardly ever hears of a case of letting die, except for the actions of doctors who are motivated by humanitarian reasons. So one learns to think of killing in a much worse light than of letting die. But this does not mean that there is something about killing that makes it in itself worse than letting die, for it is not the bare difference between killing and letting die that makes the difference in these cases. Rather, the other factors—the murderer's motive of personal gain, for example, contrasted with the doctor's humanitarian motivation—account for different reactions to the different cases.

I have argued that killing is not in itself any worse than letting die: if my contention is right, it follows that active euthanasia is not any worse than passive euthanasia. What arguments can be given on the other side? The most common, I believe, is the following:

"The important difference between active and passive euthanasia is that, in passive euthanasia, the doctor does not do anything to bring about the patient's death. The doctor does nothing, and the patient dies of whatever ills already afflict him. In active euthanasia, however, the doctor does something to bring about the patient's death: he kills him. The doctor who gives the patient with cancer a lethal injection has himself caused his patient's death: whereas if he merely ceases treatment, the cancer is the cause of the death."

A number of points need to be made here. The first is that it is not exactly correct to say that in passive euthanasia the doctor does nothing, for he does do one thing that is very important: he lets the patient die. "Letting someone die" is certainly different, in some respects, from other types of action—mainly in that it is a kind of action that one may perform by way of not performing certain other actions. For example, one may let a patient die by way of not giving medication, just as one may insult someone by way of not shaking his hand. But for any purpose of moral assessment, it is a type of action nonetheless. The decision to let a patient die is subject to moral appraisal in the same way that a decision to kill him would be subject to moral appraisal: it may be assessed as wise or unwise, compassionate or sadistic, right or wrong. If a doctor deliberately let a patient die who was suffering from a routinely curable illness, the doctor would certainly be to blame for what he had done, just as he would be to blame if he had needlessly killed the patient. Charges against him would then be appropriate. If so, it would be no defense at all for him to insist that he didn't "do anything." He would have done something very serious indeed, for he let his patient die.

Fixing the cause of death may be very important from a legal point of view, for it may determine whether criminal charges are brought against the doctor. But I do not think that this notion can be used to show a moral difference between active and passive euthanasia. The reason why it is considered bad to be the cause of someone's death is that death is regarded as a great evil—and so it is. However, if it has been decided that euthanasia—even passive euthanasia—is desirable in a given case, it has also been decided that in this instance death is no greater an evil than the patient's continued existence. And if this is true, the usual reason for not wanting to be the cause of someone's death simply does not apply.

Finally, doctors may think that all of this is only of academic interest—the sort of thing that philosophers may worry about but that has no practical bearing on their own work. After all, doctors must be concerned about the legal consequences of what they do, and active euthanasia is clearly forbidden by the law. But even so, doctors should also be concerned with the fact that the law is forcing upon them a moral doctrine that may well be indefensible, and has a considerable effect on their practices. Of course, most doctors are not now in the position of being coerced in this matter, for they do not regard themselves as merely going along with what the law requires. Rather, in statements such as the AMA policy statement that I have quoted, they are endorsing this doctrine as a central point of medical ethics. In that statement, active euthanasia is condemned not merely as illegal but as "contrary to that for which the medical profession stands," whereas passive euthanasia is approved. However, the preceding considerations suggest that there is really no moral difference between the two, considered in themselves (there may be important moral differences in some cases in their *consequences*, but, as I pointed out, these differences may make active euthanasia, and not passive euthanasia, the morally preferable option). So, whereas doctors may have to discriminate between active and passive euthanasia to satisfy the law, they should not do any more than that. In particular, they should not give the distinction any added authority and weight by writing it into official statements of medical ethics.

Dying at the Right Time: Reflections on (Un)Assisted Suicide

JOHN HARDWIG

John Hardwig is a professor emeritus of the Department of Philosophy at the University of Tennessee. In this essay he argues that when "death comes too late," we may have a duty to die or a duty to help someone else die. Severe, unrelieved pain is just one of several problems that could justify ending a life. Sometimes preserving a life can devastate the lives of those who care about the person. In particularly dire situations, there may be moral justification for unassisted suicide, family-assisted suicide, or physician-assisted suicide.

Let us begin with two observations about chronic illness and death:

1. Death does not always come at the right time. We are all aware of the tragedies involved when death comes too soon. We are afraid that it might come too soon for us. By contrast, we may sometimes be tempted to deny that death can come too late—wouldn't everyone want to live longer? But in our more sober moments, most of us know perfectly well that death can come too late.

2. Discussions of death and dying usually proceed as if death came only to hermits—or others who are all alone. But most of the time, death is a death in the family. We are connected to family and loved ones. We are sustained by these connections. They are a major part of what makes life worth living for most of us.

Because of these connections, when death comes too soon, the tragedy is often two-fold: a tragedy both for the person who is now dead and for those of us to whom she was connected. We grieve both for our loved one who is gone and for ourselves who have lost her. On one hand, there is the unrealized good that life would have been for the dead person herself—what she could have become, what she could

have experienced, what she wanted for herself. On the other, there is the contribution she would have made to others and the ways *their* lives would have been enriched by her.

We are less familiar with the idea that death can come too late. But here, too, the tragedy can be two-fold. Death can come too late because of what living on means to the person herself. There are times when someone does not (or would not) want to live like this, times when she believes she would be better off dead. At times like these, suicide or assisted suicide becomes a perfectly rational choice, perhaps even the best available option for her. We are then forced to ask, "Does someone have a right to die?" Assisted suicide may then be an act of compassion, no more than relieving her misery.

There are also, sadly, times when death comes too late because *others*—family and loved ones—would be better off if someone were dead. (Better off overall, despite the loss of a loved one.) Since lives are deeply intertwined, the lives of the rest of the family can be dragged down, impoverished, compromised, perhaps even ruined because of what they must go through if she lives on. When death comes too late because of the effect of someone's life on her loved ones, we are, I think, forced to ask, "Can someone have a duty to die?" Suicide may then be an attempt to do what is right; it may be the only loving thing to do. Assisted suicide would then be helping someone do the right thing.

Most professional ethicists—philosophers, theologians, and bioethicists—react with horror at the

John Hardwig, "Dying at the Right Time: Reflections on (Un)Assisted Suicide," in *Ethics in Practice*, ed. Hugh LoFollette (Oxford: Blackwell, 2007), 91–102.

very idea of a duty to die. Many of them even argue that euthanasia and physician-assisted suicide should not be legalized because then some people might somehow get the idea that they have a duty to die. To this way of thinking, someone who got that idea could only be the victim of vicious social pressure or perverse moral reasoning. But when I ask my classes for examples of times when death would come too late, one of the first conditions students always mention is: "when I become a burden to my family." I think there is more moral wisdom here than in the dismay of these ethicists.

Death does not always come at the right time. I believe there are conditions under which I would prefer not to live, situations in which I would be better off dead. But I am also absolutely convinced that I may one day face a duty or responsibility to die. In fact, as I will explain later, I think many of us will one day have this duty.

To my way of thinking, the really serious questions relating to euthanasia and assisted suicide are: Who would be better off dead? Who has a duty to die? *When* is the right time to die? And if my life should be over, who should kill me?[1] However, I know that others find much of what I have said here surprising, shocking, even morally offensive. So before turning to these questions that I want us to think about, I need to explain why I think someone can be better off dead and why someone can have a duty to die. (The explanation of the latter will have to be longer, since it is by far the less familiar and more controversial idea.)

When Someone Would Be Better Off Dead

Others have discussed euthanasia or physician-assisted suicide when the patient would be better off dead.[2] Here I wish to emphasize two points often omitted from discussion: (1) Unrelieved pain is not the only reason someone would be better off dead. (2) Someone can be better off dead even if she has no terminal illness.

(1) If we think about it for even a little while, most of us can come up with a list of conditions under which we believe we would rather be dead than continue to live. Severe and unrelieved pain is one item on that list. Permanent unconsciousness may

be another. Dementia so severe that we no longer recognize ourselves or our loved ones is yet another. There are some people who prefer not to live with quadriplegia. A future shaped by severe deterioration (such as that which accompanies MS, ALS, AIDS, or Huntington's chorea) is a future that some people prefer not to live out.

(Our lists would be different because our lives and values are different. The fact that some people would not or do not want to live with quadriplegia or AIDS, for example, does not mean that others should not want to live like that, much less that their lives are not worth living. That is very important. The point here is that almost all of us can make a list of conditions under which we would rather not live, and that uncontrolled pain is not the only item on most of our lists.)

Focusing the discussion of euthanasia and assisted suicide on pain ignores the many other varieties of suffering that often accompany chronic illness and dying: dehumanization, loss of independence, loss of control, a sense of meaninglessness or purposelessness, loss of mental capabilities, loss of mobility, disorientation and confusion, sorrow over the impact of one's illness and death on one's family, loss of ability even to recognize loved ones, and more. Often, these causes of suffering are compounded by the awareness that the future will be even bleaker. Unrelieved pain is simply not the only condition under which death is preferable to life, nor the, only legitimate reason for a desire to end one's life.

(2) In cases of terminal illness, death eventually offers the dying person, relief from all her suffering. Consequently, things can be even worse when there is *NO* terminal illness, for then there is no end in sight. Both pain and suffering are often much worse when they are *not* accompanied by a terminal illness. People with progressive dementia, for example, often suffer much more if they are otherwise quite healthy. I personally know several old people who would be delighted to learn that they have a terminal illness. They feel they have lived long enough— long enough to have outlived all their loved ones and all sense of a purpose for living. For them, even daily existence is much worse because there is no end in sight.

Discussions of euthanasia and physician-assisted suicide cannot, then, be restricted to those with unrelieved pain and terminal illness. We must also consider requests made by those who have no untreatable pain and no terminal illness. Often, their case for relief is even more compelling.

Sometimes, a refusal of medical treatment will be enough to bring relief. Competent adults who are suffering from an illness have a well-established moral and legal right to decline any form of medical treatment, including life-prolonging medical treatment. Family members who must make medical decisions for incompetent people also have the right to refuse any form of medical treatment on their behalf, so long as they are acting in accordance with the known wishes or best interests of their loved one. No form of medical treatment is compulsory when someone would be better off dead.[3]

But those who would be better off dead do not always have terminal illnesses; they will not always need any form of medical treatment, not even medically supplied food and water. The right to refuse medical treatment will not help these people. Moreover, death due to untreated illness can be agonizingly slow, dehumanizing, painful, and very costly, both in financial and emotional terms. It is often very hard. Refusing medical treatment simply will not always ensure a dignified, peaceful, timely death. We would not be having a national debate about physician-assisted suicide and euthanasia if refusal of medical treatment were always enough to lead to a reasonably good death. When death comes too late, we may need to do more than refuse medical treatment.

Religion and Ending a Life

Some people can easily see that there are people who would be better off dead. But they still cannot accept suicide or physician-assisted suicide because they believe we have a duty to God not to take our own lives. For them, human life is a gift from God and it remains a gift no matter how much pain and suffering it may bring. It is a sin or an offense against God, the giver of life, to take your own life or to help someone else end theirs. Such believers may also feel that no one should be allowed to end their lives—every life is a gift from God, even the lives of those who do not believe that this is so.

I do not understand this position for two reasons. First, it involves the assumption that it is possible to take a human life (our own or someone else's) *before* God wants it ended, but we cannot possibly preserve it *after* God wants it ended. For if we do not make that assumption, we face *two dangers*—the danger that we are prolonging human life beyond its divine purpose, as well as the danger that we are ending it too soon. If we can extend life longer than God intends, suicide and physician-assisted suicide may be more in accord with God's wishes than attempts to preserve that life.

I can understand the view that everyone dies at precisely the right time, the moment God intends. If that is so, people who commit suicide or who are intentionally killed by physicians also die at precisely the moment God wants them to die. I can also understand the view that we can take life before God wants it ended but we can also extend life longer than God wants it prolonged. But I cannot make sense of the view that we can end a human life too soon but not preserve it too long. Surely, God has given us both abilities or neither one.

I also have a second difficulty with this religious objection to suicide, assisted suicide and euthanasia. Suppose there is a right time to die, a divinely ordained moment when God wants each life to end. Even so, we have no right to assume that God will "take my life" when it's the right time for me to die. In fact, we cannot even assume that God will send a terminal illness that will kill me at the right time. There could be a religious test—God may want me to take my own life and the question is whether I will meet this final challenge. Or a God who loves me might see that I would benefit spiritually from the process of coming to the conclusion that I should end my own life and then preparing to take it. That might be a fitting ending for me, the culminating step in my spiritual growth or development.

In short, a God not totally obsessed with the sheer quantity of our lives may well have purposes for us that are incompatible with longer life—even if we want to live longer. So, I think we should not believe that we always have a duty to God not to take our lives or to assist others in ending theirs. God may want me to step up and assume the responsibility for ending my own life or for seeing that someone else's suffering is ended. This observation leads to our next question: Can there be a responsibility or duty to die?

The Duty to Die

I may well one day have a duty to die, a duty most likely to arise out of my connections with my family and loved ones.[4] Sometimes preserving my life can only devastate the lives of those who care about me. I do not believe I am idiosyncratic, morbid or morally perverse in believing this. I am trying to take steps to prepare myself mentally and spiritually to make sure that I will be able to take my life if I should one day have such a duty. I need to prepare myself; it might be a very difficult thing for me to do.

Our individualistic fantasy about ourselves sometimes leads us to imagine that lives are separate and unconnected, or that they could be so if we chose. If lives were unconnected, then things that happen in my life would not or need not affect others. And if others were not (much) affected by my life, I would have no duty to consider the impact of my life on others. I would then be morally free to choose whatever life and death I prefer for myself. I certainly would have no duty to die when I would prefer to live.

Most discussions of assisted suicide and euthanasia implicitly share this individualistic fantasy: they just ignore the fact that people are connected and lives intertwined. As a result, they approach issues of life or death as if the only person affected is the one who lives or dies. They mistakenly assume the pivotal issue is simply whether the person *herself* prefers not to live like this and whether *she herself* would be better off dead.[5]

But this is morally obtuse. The fact is we are not a race of hermits—most of us are connected to family and loved ones. We prefer it that way. We would not want to be all alone, especially when we are seriously ill, as we age, and when we are dying. But being with others is not all benefits and pleasures; it brings responsibilities, as well. For then what happens to us and the choices we make can dramatically affect the lives of our loved ones. It is these connections that can, tragically, generate obligations to die, as continuing to live takes too much of a toll on the lives of those connected to us.[6]

The lives of our loved ones can, we know, be seriously compromised by caring for us. The burdens of providing care or even just supervision 24 hours a day, 7 days a week, are often overwhelming.[7] But it can also be emotionally devastating simply to be married to a spouse who is increasingly distant, uncommunicative, unresponsive, foreign and unreachable. A local newspaper tells the story of a woman with Alzheimer's who came running into her den screaming: "That man's trying to have sex with me! He's trying to have sex with me! Who *IS* that man?!" That man was her loving husband of more than 40 years who had devoted the past 10 years of his life to caring for her (Smith, 1995). How terrible that experience must have been for her. But how terrible those years must be for him, too.

We must also acknowledge that the lives of our loved ones can also be devastated just by having to *pay* for health care for us. A recent study documented the financial aspects of caring for a dying member of a family. Only those who had illnesses severe enough to give them less than a 50 percent chance to live six more months were included in this study. When these patients survived their initial hospitalization and were discharged, about one-third required considerable caregiving from their families; in 20 percent of cases a family member had to quit work or make some other major lifestyle change; almost one-third of these families lost all of their savings, and just under 30 percent lost a major source of income (Covinsky et al., 1994).

A chronic illness or debilitating injury in a family is a misfortune. It is, most often, nobody's fault; no one is responsible for this illness or injury. But then we face choices about how we will respond to this misfortune. That is where the responsibility comes in and fault can arise. Those of us with families and loved ones always have a responsibility not to make selfish or self-centered decisions about our lives. We should not do just what we want or just what is best for *us*. Often, we should choose in light of what is best for all concerned.

Our families and loved ones have obligations to stand by us and to support us through debilitating illness and death. They must be prepared to make sacrifices to respond to an illness in the family. We are well aware of this responsibility and most families meet it rather well. In fact, families deliver more than 80 percent of the long-term care in the US, almost always at great personal cost.

But responsibility in a family is not a one-way street. When we become seriously ill or debilitated, we too may have to make sacrifices. There are limits to what we can ask our loved ones to do to support us, even in sickness. There are limits to what they should be prepared to do for us—only rarely and for a limited period of time should they do all they can for us.

Somehow we forget that sick, infirm, and dying adults also have obligations to their families and loved ones: a responsibility, for example, to try to protect the lives of loved ones from serious threats or greatly impoverished quality, or an obligation to avoid making choices that will jeopardize or seriously compromise their futures. Our obligations to our loved ones must be taken into consideration in making decisions about the end of life. It is out of these responsibilities that a duty to die can develop.

Tragically, sometimes the best thing you can do for your loved ones is to remove yourself from their lives. And the only way you can do that may be to remove yourself from existence. This is not a happy thought. Yet we must recognize that suicides and requests for assisted suicide may be motivated by love. Sometimes, it's simply the only loving thing to do.

Who Has a Duty to Die?

Sometimes it is clear when someone has a duty to die. But more often, not. *WHO* has a duty to die? And *WHEN*—under what conditions? To my mind, these are the right questions, the questions we should be asking. Many of us may one day badly need answers to just these questions.

But I cannot supply answers here, for two reasons. In the first place, answers will have to be very particular and individualized . . . to the person, to the situation of her family, to the relationships within the family, etc. There will not be simple answers that apply to everyone.

Secondly and perhaps even more importantly, those of us with family and loved ones should not define our duties unilaterally. Especially not a decision about a duty to die. It would be isolating and distance-creating for me to decide without consulting them what is too much of a burden for my loved ones to bear. That way of deciding about my moral duties is not only atomistic, it also treats my family and loved ones paternalistically—*THEY* must be allowed to speak for themselves about the burdens my life imposes on them and how they feel about bearing those burdens.

I believe in family decision making. Important decisions for those whose lives are interwoven should be made *together,* in a family discussion. Granted, a conversation about whether I have a duty to die would often be a tremendously difficult conversation. The temptations to be dishonest in such conversations could be enormous. Nevertheless, if we can, we should have just such an agonizing discussion—partly because it will act as a check on the information, perceptions and reasoning of all of us; but perhaps even more importantly, because it affirms our connectedness at a critical juncture in our lives. Honest talk about difficult matters almost always strengthens relationships.

But many families seem to be unable to talk about death at all, much less a duty to die. Certainly most families could not have this discussion all at once, in one sitting. It might well take a number of discussions to be able to approach this topic. But even if talking about death is impossible, there are always behavioral clues—about your caregiver's tiredness, physical condition, health, prevailing mood, anxiety, outlook, overall well-being, etc. And families unable to talk about death can often talk about those clues. There can be conversations about how the caregiver is feeling, about finances, about tensions within the family resulting from the illness, about concerns for the future. Deciding whether you have a duty to die based on these behavioral clues and conversation about them is more relational than deciding on your own about how burdensome this relationship and care must be.[8]

For these two reasons, I cannot say when someone has a duty to die. But I can suggest a few ideas for discussion of this question. I present them here without much elaboration or explanation.

1. There is more duty to die when prolonging your life will impose greater burdens—emotional burdens, caregiving, disruption

of life plans, and, yes, financial hardship—on your family and loved ones. This is the fundamental insight underlying a duty to die.

2. There is greater duty to die if your loved ones' lives have already been difficult or impoverished (not just financially)—if they have had only a small share of the good things that life has to offer.

3. There is more duty to die to the extent that your loved ones have already made great contributions—perhaps even sacrifices—to make your life a good one. Especially if you have not made similar sacrifices for their well-being.

4. There is more duty to die to the extent that you have *already* lived a full and rich life. You have already had a full share of the good things life offers.

5. Even if you have not lived a full and rich life, there is more duty to die as you grow older. As we become older, there is a diminishing chance that we will be able to make the changes that would now be required to turn our lives around. As we age, we will also be giving up less by giving up our lives, if only because we will sacrifice fewer years of life.

6. There is less duty to die to the extent that you can make a good adjustment to your illness or handicapping condition, for a good adjustment means that smaller sacrifice will be required of loved ones and there is more compensating interaction for them. (However, we must also recognize that some diseases—Alzheimer's or Huntington's chorea—will eventually take their toll on your loved ones no matter how courageously, resolutely, even cheerfully you manage to face that illness.)

7. There is more duty to die to the extent that the part of you that is loved will soon be gone or seriously compromised. There is also more duty to die when you are no longer capable of giving love. Part of the horror of Alzheimer's or Huntington's, again, is that it destroys the person we loved, leaving a stranger and eventually only a shell behind. By contrast, someone can be seriously debilitated and yet clearly still the person we love.

In an old person, "I am not ready to die yet" does not excuse one from a duty to die. To have reached the age of, say, 80 years without being ready to die is itself a moral failing, the sign of a life out of touch with life's basic realities.

A duty to die seems very harsh, and sometimes it is. But if I really do care for my family, a duty to protect their lives will often be accompanied by a deep desire to do so. I will normally *want* to protect those I love. This is not only my duty, it is also my desire. In fact, I can easily imagine wanting to spare my loved ones the burden of my existence more than I want anything else.

If I Should Be Dead, Who Should Kill Me?

We need to reframe our discussions of euthanasia and physician-assisted suicide. For we must recognize that pleas for assisted suicide are sometimes requests for relief from pain and suffering, sometimes requests for help in fulfilling one's obligations, and sometimes both. If I should be dead for either of these reasons, who should kill me?

Like a responsible life, a responsible death requires that we think about our choices in the context of the web of relationships of love and care that surround us. We must be sensitive to the suffering as well as the joys we cause others, to the hardships as well as the benefits we create for them. So, when we ask, "Who should kill me?" we must remember that we are asking for a death that will reduce the suffering of *both* me and my family as much as possible. We are searching for the best ending, not only for me, but for *everyone concerned*—in the preparation for death, the moment of death, and afterwards, in the memory and on-going lives of loved ones and family.

Although we could perhaps define a new profession to assist in suicides—euthanasians??—there are now really only three answers to the question, "Who should kill me?" (1) I should kill myself. (2) A loved one or family member should kill me. (3) A physician should kill me. I will consider these three possibilities. I will call these *unassisted* suicide, *family*-assisted suicide, and *physician*-assisted suicide.

I Unassisted Suicide: I Should Kill Myself

The basic intuition here is that each of us should take responsibility for herself. I am primarily the one who wants relief from my pain and suffering, or it is fundamentally my own duty to die and *I* should be the one to do my duty. Moreover, intentionally ending a life is a very messy business—a heavy, difficult thing for anyone to have to do. If possible, I should not drag others into it. Often, I think, this is the right idea—I should be the one to kill myself.

But not always. We must remember that some people are physically unable to do so—they are too weak or incapacitated to commit suicide without assistance. Less persuasive perhaps are those who just can't bring themselves to do it. Without the assistance of someone, many lack the know-how or means to end their lives in a peaceful, dignified fashion. Finally, many attempted suicides—even serious attempts at suicide—fail or result in terrible deaths. Those who have worked in hospitals are familiar with suicide attempts that leave people with permanent brain damage or their faces shot off. There are also fairly common stories of people eating their own vomit after throwing up the medicine they hoped would end their lives.

Even more importantly, if I must be the one to kill myself, that may force me to take my life earlier than would otherwise be necessary. I cannot wait until I become physically debilitated or mentally incompetent, for then it will be too late for me to kill myself. I might be able to live quite comfortably for a couple more years, if I could count on someone else to take my life later. But if I cannot count on help from anyone, I will feel pressure to kill myself when unavoidable suffering for myself or my loved ones appears on the horizon, instead of waiting until it actually arrives.

Finally, many suicides are isolating—I can't die with my loved ones around me if I am planning to use carbon monoxide from automobile exhaust to end my life. For most of us, a meaningful end of life requires an affirmation of our connection with loved ones and so we do not want to die alone.

The social taboo against ending your own life promotes another type of isolation. The secrecy preceding many suicides creates conditions for misunderstanding or lack of understanding on the part of loved ones—Why did she do it? Why didn't I see that she was going to kill herself? Why didn't I do something to help? Secrecy and lack of understanding often compound the suffering family and loved ones go through when someone ends their life.

Unassisted suicide—I should kill myself—is not always the answer. Perhaps, then, my loved ones should participate in ending my life.

2 Family-Assisted Suicide: A Member of My Family Should Kill Me

At times, we may have a moral obligation to help others end their lives, especially those close to us, those we love. I can easily imagine myself having an obligation to help a loved one end her life and I hope my family will come to my assistance if my death does not come at the right time. What should be the role of family and loved ones in ending a life?

They might help me get information about reliable and peaceful methods for ending my life. They might also be able to help me get the drugs I need, if that is the method I choose. Like most people, I would also very much want my loved ones to participate, at least to the extent of being there with me when I die.

For reasons already mentioned, I would hope I could talk over my plans with my loved ones, both to reassure myself and check on my reasoning, and also to help them work through some of the emotional reaction to my death. Some people believe that families should not be involved in decisions about the end of life because they are in the grips of powerful emotions that lead to wildly inappropriate decisions. (A familiar example is the difficulty many families have in deciding to withdraw medical treatment even when their loved one is clearly dying.) Families will always be gripped by powerful emotions over a death in the family. But appropriate decisions are not necessarily unemotional or uninvolved decisions. And I think inappropriate reactions or decisions stem largely from lack of the discussions I advocate or from an attempt to compress them into one, brief, pressure-packed conversation, often in the uncomfortable setting of a hospital.

So, a good death for all concerned would usually involve my family—the preparation for taking my life, at least, would be family-assisted. My loved ones should know; they should, if possible, understand. They should not be surprised. Hopefully my loved ones could come to agree with my decision.

They should have had time to come to terms with the fact that I plan to end my life. Indeed, I should have helped them begin to deal emotionally with my death. All that would help to ease their suffering and also my concern about how my death will affect them. It would reaffirm our connectedness. It would also comfort me greatly to feel that I am understood and known by my loved ones as I take this important step.

More than this I cannot ask of them, for two related reasons. The first is that actually killing a loved one would usually be extremely difficult. It would be a searing and unforgettable experience that could well prove very hard to live with afterwards. Killing a loved one at her request *might* leave you feeling relieved—it could give you the satisfaction of feeling you had done what needed to be done. In cases of extreme debility or great suffering, family-assisted suicide might be experienced as a loving act of kindness, compassion and mercy. It would still be very hard. Much harder would be killing me because I have a duty to die, a duty to die because my life is too great a burden *for the one who now must kill me*. I cannot ask that of someone I love. I fear that they would suffer too much from taking my life.

I might be wrong about this, however. It might be that, though difficult indeed, being killed lovingly and with your consent by your spouse or your child would be a final testimonial to a solid, trusting, and caring relationship. There might be no more powerful reaffirmation of the strength of your relationship, even in the face of death. The traumatic experience for the family members who assist in the suicide might be a healing experience for them, as well. We know so little about family-assisted suicide.

But in any case, there is also a second reason: I cannot ask for family-assisted suicide because it is not legally protected—a loved one who killed me might well be charged with murder. I could not ask my family to subject themselves to such a risk. Moreover, unlike physician-assisted suicide, we would not want to legalize family-assisted suicide. The lives of families are just too complex and too often laced with strong negative emotions—guilt, resentment, hatred, anger, desire for revenge. Family members also often have multiple motives stemming from deeply conflicting interests. As a result, there would be just too many cases in which family-assisted suicide would be indistinguishable from murder.[9]

Finally, family members may also fail. They also may lack know-how or bungle the job. Caught in the compelling emotions of grief and/or guilt, they may be unable to end a life that should be ended.

All this notwithstanding, family-assisted suicide may be the right choice, especially if physician-assisted suicide is unavailable. But should it be unavailable?

3 Physician-Assisted Suicide: My Doctor Should Kill Me

There are, then, important difficulties with both unassisted suicide and family-assisted suicide. These difficulties are arguments for physician-assisted suicide and euthanasia. If my death comes too late, a physician is often the best candidate to kill me . . . or at the very least, to help me kill myself.

Perhaps the main argument for physician-assisted suicide grows out of the physician's extensive knowledge of disease and of dying. If it is a medical condition that leads me to contemplate ending my life, a key question for determining *when* or even *whether* I should end my life is: What is the prognosis? To what extent can my illness be treated or at least alleviated? How long do I have to live with my condition? How much worse will it get and how soon? What will life with that condition be like for me and my family? Few besides physicians possess all this critical information. I will be more likely to reach the right decision at the right time if a trusted physician is in on my plans to end my life.

A related point is physicians' knowledge of and access to drugs. Few of us know what drugs to take and in what amounts without the advice of a physician. Often, only a physician will know what to do to ensure that I do not vomit up the "suicide pill" or what to do if it fails. Physicians also have a monopoly on access to drugs. If my physician were more closely involved in the process, I could be more certain—and thus reassured—that my death will be peaceful and dignified, a death that permits reaffirmation of my connections with family and close friends.

A second argument for physician-assisted suicide grows out of physicians' greater experience with death and dying. Physicians know what to expect; those of us outside the health professions often do not. Granted, few physicians nowadays will know *me* and *my* family. For this reason, physicians should seldom make unilateral decisions about assisted suicide. Still, most physicians could provide a rich source of information about death and about strategies to minimize the trauma, suffering, and agony of a death, both for the dying person and for the family.

Thirdly, physician-assisted suicide does not carry the same social stigma that unassisted suicide carries and physicians are not exposed to the legal risks involved in family-assisted suicide. Although many physicians are unwilling to take *any* risks to help someone end her life, there is really very little legal risk in physician-assisted suicide, especially if the family is in agreement. Physicians are also not morally censored the way family members would be for ending a life.

Finally, physicians ought not to abandon their patients, certainly not at the moment of death. Much has been made of the possibility that Americans would lose their trust in physicians if they knew that physicians sometimes kill. But many of us would trust our physicians *more* if we knew that we could count on them when death is needed or required (Quill and Cassell, 1995).

We have come, then, by a very round-about route to another argument for *physician*-assisted suicide. Often it is simply better—safer, more secure, more peaceful, less emotionally-damaging for others—than unassisted suicide or family-assisted suicide. If physicians refuse to assist or are not permitted to do so, families and seriously ill people will be forced back on their own resources. And many deaths will be much worse than they need to be. When death comes too late, a physician will often be the best candidate to kill me.

And yet, physician-assisted suicide is not always the answer, either. Many physicians take themselves to be sworn to preserve human life in all its forms. Also, many people want doctors who are sworn not to kill, for fear that physicians might start making presumptuous, single-handed decisions about when death comes too late. Moreover, in a time when most people lack a significant personal relationship with their physicians, physician-assisted suicide is often a death that is remote, isolated, disconnected from the relationships that gave meaning to life. It is not always the best death. At times, then, family-assisted suicide and unassisted suicide remain the best answers.

Conclusion

We have a long cultural tradition of attempts to deal with the problems of death that comes too soon. Modern medicine, with its dramatic high-tech rescue attempts in the emergency room and the intensive care unit, is our society's attempt to prevent death from coming too soon. On a more personal level, we are bombarded with advice about ways to avoid a death that would be too soon—sooner than we wished, before we were ready for it.

We have much less cultural wisdom about the problems of a death that comes too late. It is almost as if we had spent all our cultural resources trying to avoid deaths that come too soon, only to find that we then had no resources left to help us when death comes too late.

Deaths that come too soon usually raise no difficult moral problems, however difficult they may be in other ways. Such deaths normally occur despite our best attempts to prevent them. "There's nothing more we can do," we say to the dying person, her family, and ourselves. And there is ethical solace in this, despite the tragedy of the death itself. We admit our failure. But our failure is not a moral failure—we did what we could.

Deaths that come too late are ethically much more troubling. They call on us to assume responsibility—to make difficult decisions and to do difficult things. We can try to hide from this responsibility by claiming that we should always try to prolong life, no matter what. Or by not deciding anything. But we know that not to decide is to decide. And it is very often just not clear what we should do. The weight of life-or-death decision pushes down upon us.

The recognition that the lives of members of families are intertwined makes the moral problems of a death that comes too late even more difficult. For they deprive us of our easiest and most comfortable answers—"it's up to the individual," "whatever the patient wants." But we do know that measures to improve or lengthen one life often compromise the quality of the lives of those to whom that person is connected.

So, we are morally troubled by deaths that come too late. We don't know what to do. Beyond that, the whole idea is unfamiliar to us. But in other societies—primarily technologically primitive and especially nomadic societies—almost everyone knew that death could come too late. People in those cultures knew that if they managed to live long enough, death would come too late and they would have to do something about it. They were prepared by their cultural traditions to find meaning in death and to do what needed to be done.

We have largely lost those traditions. Perhaps we have supposed that our wealth and technological sophistication have purchased exemption for us from any need to worry about living too long, from any need to live less than every minute we enjoy living. For a while it looked that way. But we must now face the fact: deaths that come too late are only the other side of our miraculous life-prolonging modern medicine.

We have so far avoided looking at this dark side of our medical triumphs. Our modern medicine saves many lives and enables us to live longer. That is wonderful, indeed. But it thereby also enables more of us to survive longer than we are able to care for ourselves, longer than we know what to do with ourselves, longer than we even *are* ourselves. Moreover, if further medical advances wipe out many of today's "killer diseases"—cancers, AIDS, heart attacks, etc.—then most of us will one day find that death is coming too late. And there will be a very common duty to die.

Our political system and health-care reform (in the USA) are also moving in a direction that will put many more of us in the position of having a duty to die. Measures designed to control costs (for the government, and for employers who pay for retirement benefits and health insurance) often switch the burdens of care onto families. We are dismantling our welfare system and attempting to shift the costs of long-term health care onto families. One important consequence of these measures is that more of us will one day find ourselves a burden to our families and loved ones.[10]

Finally, we ourselves make choices that increase the odds that death will come too late. Patient autonomy gives us the right to make choices about our own medical treatment. We use that right to opt again and again for life-prolonging treatment—even when we have chronic illnesses, when we are debilitated, and as we begin to die. Despite this autonomy, we may feel we really have no choice, perhaps because we are unable to find meaning in death or to bring our lives to a meaningful close. But if we repeatedly opt for life-prolonging treatment, we thereby also increase the chances that death will come too late. This is the cost of patient autonomy, combined with powerful life-prolonging medical technology and inability to give meaning to death or even to accept it.

Death is very difficult for us. I have tried here to speak about it in plain language; I have used hard words and harsh tones to try to make us attend to troubling realities. We may question the arguments and conclusions of this paper. We should do so. But this questioning must not be fueled by denial or lead to evasion. For one thing seems very clear: We had better start learning how to deal with the problems of a death that comes too late. Some day, many of us will find that we should be dead or that one of our loved ones should be dead. What should we do then? We had better prepare ourselves—mentally, morally, culturally, spiritually, and socially. For many of us, if we are to die at the right time, it will be up to us.

NOTES

I get by with a little help from my friends. I wish to thank Hilde and Jim Nelson, Mary English, Tom Townsend, and Hugh LaFollette for helpful comments on earlier versions of this essay. And more: these friends have been my companions and guides throughout my attempt to think through the meaning of love and family in our lives.
1. A note about language: I will be using "responsibility," "obligation," and "duty" interchangeably, despite significant differences in meaning. I generally use the word "duty" because it strikes me as a hard word for what can be a hard reality. (It also echoes Richard Lamm's famous statement: "Old people have a duty to die and get out of the way to give the next generation a chance.") Similarly, I use "kill" despite its connotations of destruction because I think we should not attempt to soften what we are doing. War and capital

punishment have already taught us too much about how to talk in sweet and attractive ways about what we do. So I have resisted talking about "bringing my life to a close" and similar expressions. I have tried to use the plain, hard words.

2. There are many articles on this topic. Perhaps the classic article is Rachels (1975). It has been widely reprinted. A good collection of articles can be found in the *Journal of Medicine and Philosophy* (June 1993), which was devoted to the topic, "Legal Euthanasia: Ethical Issues in an Era of Legalized Aid in Dying." Recent anthologies include Beauchamp (1996) and Moreno (1995).

3. A few states in the US—currently (January 1996) New York, Missouri, Delaware, and Michigan—do require that family members be able to supply "clear and convincing evidence" that withdrawal of treatment is what their loved one would have wanted. This can be hard to prove. So it is especially important for those who live in these states to put their wishes about the kind of treatment they would want (if they become unable to decide for themselves) in writing. For information about the laws that apply in your state, write to Choice in Dying, 200 Varick Street, New York, NY 10014, or call them at 212-366-5540.

4. I believe we may also have a duty to ourselves to die, or a duty to the environment or a duty to the next generation to die. But I think for most of us, the strongest duty to die comes from our connections to family and loved ones, and this is the only source of a duty to die that I will consider here.

5. Most bioethicists advocate a "patient-centered ethics"—an ethics which claims only the patient's interests should be considered in making medical treatment decisions. Most health-care professionals have been trained to accept this ethic and to see themselves as patient advocates. I have argued elsewhere that a patient-centered ethic is deeply mistaken. See Hardwig (1989, 1993).

6. I am considering only mentally competent adults. I do not think those who have never been competent—young children and those with severe retardation—can have moral duties. I do not know whether formerly competent people—e.g., those who have become severely demented—can still have moral duties. But if they cannot, I think some of us may face a duty to die even sooner—before we lose our moral agency.

7. A good account of the burdens of caregiving can be found in Brody (1990). To a large extent, care of the elderly is a women's issue. Most people who live to be 75 or older are women. But care for the elderly is almost always provided by women, as well—even when the person who needs care is the husband's parent.

8. Ultimately, in cases of deep and unresolvable disagreement between yourself and your loved ones, you may

have to act on *your own* conception of your duty and your own conception of the burdens on them. But that is a fallback position to resort to when the better, more relational ways of arriving at a belief in a duty to die fail or are unavailable.

9. Although this is true, we also need to rethink our reactions to the motives of the family. Because lives are intertwined, if someone "wants Dad to be dead" and is relieved when he dies, this does not necessarily mean that she did not genuinely love him. Or that she is greedy, selfish, or self-centered. Her relief may stem from awareness of his suffering. It could also grow out of recognition of the sad fact that his life was destroying the lives of other family members whom she also loved.

10. Perhaps a more generous political system and a more equitable health-care system could counteract the trend toward a more and more common duty to die. For now, at least, we could pay for the care of those who would otherwise be a burden on their families. If we were prepared to do so, far fewer would face a duty to die. But we (in the US, at least) are not prepared to pay. Moreover, as medical advances enable more people to live longer (though also in various states of disability), it may be that the costs would overwhelm any society. Even if we could afford it, we should not continue to try to buy our way out of the problems of deaths that come too late. We would be foolish to devote all our resources to creating a society dedicated solely to helping all of us live just as long as we want.

REFERENCES

Beauchamp, T. L. (ed.) (1996) *Intending Death: The Ethics of Assisted Suicide and Euthanasia.* Englewood Cliffs, NJ: Prentice-Hall.

Brody, Elaine M. (1990) *Women in the Middle: Their Parent-Care Years.* New York: Springer.

Covinsky, Kenneth E., Goldman, Less et al. (1994) "The Impact of Serious Illness on Patients' Families," *Journal of the American Medical Association* 272: 1839–44.

Hardwig, John (1989) "What about the Family?," *Hastings Center Report* 20 (March/April): 5–10.

——— (1993) "The Problem of Proxies with Interests of Their Own: Toward a Better Theory of Proxy Decisions," *Journal of Clinical Ethics* 4 (Spring): 20–7.

Moreno, Jonathan (ed.) (1995) *Arguing Euthanasia.* New York: Simon & Schuster.

Quill, Timothy E. and Cassell, Christine K. (1995) "Non-abandonment: A Central Obligation for Physicians," *Annals of Internal Medicine* 122: 368–74.

Rachels, James (1975) "Active and Passive Euthanasia," *New England Journal of Medicine* 292 (1995): 78–80.

Smith, V. P. [pen name of Val Prendergrast] (1995) "At Home with Alzheimer's" *Knoxville Metro Pulse* 5/30: 7, 27.

The Philosophers' Brief

RONALD DWORKIN, THOMAS NAGEL, ROBERT NOZICK, JOHN RAWLS,
THOMAS SCANLON, AND JUDITH JARVIS THOMSON

In the 1997 Supreme Court cases *Vacco v. Quill* and *Washington v. Glucksberg*,
six prominent philosophers presented this amicus brief, urging that states should
recognize a right to assisted suicide. They argued that "individuals have a constitutionally protected interest in making those grave decisions [about their own deaths]
for themselves, free from the imposition of any religious or philosophical orthodoxy
by court or legislature." They conceded that states have a legitimate interest in
protecting people from irrational or unstable decisions about their dying but
asserted that states cannot deny people wishing to die a chance to demonstrate
that their decisions are informed, stable, and free. They maintained that there is no
morally significant difference between a physician deliberately withdrawing medical
treatment to let a patient die from a natural process and a physician hastening the
patient's death by more active means.

Amici are six moral and political philosophers who differ on many issues of public morality and policy. They are united, however, in their conviction that respect for fundamental principles of liberty and justice, as well as for the American constitutional tradition, requires that the decisions of the Courts of Appeals be affirmed.

Introduction and Summary of Argument

These cases do not invite or require the Court to make moral, ethical, or religious judgments about how people should approach or confront their death or about when it is ethically appropriate to hasten one's own death or to ask others for help in doing so. On the contrary, they ask the Court to recognize that individuals have a constitutionally protected interest in making those grave judgments for themselves, free from the imposition of any religious or philosophical orthodoxy by court or legislature. States have a constitutionally legitimate interest in protecting individuals from irrational, ill-informed, pressured, or unstable decisions to hasten their own

Brief for Ronald Dworkin, Thomas Nagel, Robert Nozick, John Rawls, Thomas Scanlon, and Judith Jarvis Thomson as *Amici Curiae* in Support of Respondents at 2, *Washington v. Glucksberg*, 117 S. Ct. 2258 (1997) (No. 96–110), and *Vacco v. Quill*, 117 S. Ct. 2293 (1997) (No. 95–1858).

death. To that end, states may regulate and limit the assistance that doctors may give individuals who express a wish to die. But states may not deny people in the position of the patient-plaintiffs in these cases the opportunity to demonstrate, through whatever reasonable procedures the state might institute—even procedures that err on the side of caution—that their decision to die is indeed informed, stable, and fully free. Denying that opportunity to terminally ill patients who are in agonizing pain or otherwise doomed to an existence they regard as intolerable could only be justified on the basis of a religious or ethical conviction about the value or meaning of life itself. Our Constitution forbids government to impose such convictions on its citizens.

Petitioners [i. e., the state authorities of Washington and New York] and the amici who support them offer two contradictory arguments. Some deny that the patient-plaintiffs have any constitutionally protected liberty interest in hastening their own deaths. But that liberty interest flows directly from this Court's previous decisions. It flows from the right of people to make their own decisions about matters "involving the most intimate and personal choices a person may make in a lifetime, choices central to personal dignity and autonomy," *Planned Parenthood* v. *Casey*, 505 U.S. 833, 851(1992).

The Solicitor General, urging reversal in support of Petitioners, recognizes that the patient-plaintiffs do have a constitutional liberty interest at stake in these cases. *See* Brief for the United States as Amicus Curiae Supporting Petitioners at 12, *Washington* v. *Vacco* (hereinafter Brief for the United States) ("The term 'liberty' in the Due Process Clause . . . is broad enough to encompass an interest on the part of terminally ill, mentally competent adults in obtaining relief from the kind of suffering experienced by the plaintiffs in this case, which includes not only severe physical pain, but also the despair and distress that comes from physical deterioration and the inability to control basic bodily functions."); *see also id.* at 13 ("*Cruzan* . . . supports the conclusion that a liberty interest is at stake in this case.")

The Solicitor General nevertheless argues that Washington and New York properly ignored this profound interest when they required the patient-plaintiffs to live on in circumstances they found intolerable. He argues that a state may simply declare that it is unable to devise a regulatory scheme that would adequately protect patients whose desire to die might be ill informed or unstable or foolish or not fully free, and that a state may therefore fall back on a blanket prohibition. This Court has never accepted that patently dangerous rationale for denying protection altogether to a conceded fundamental constitutional interest. It would be a serious mistake to do so now. If that rationale were accepted, an interest acknowledged to be constitutionally protected would be rendered empty.

Argument

**I. The Liberty Interest Asserted Here
Is Protected by the Due Process Clause**

The Due Process Clause of the Fourteenth Amendment protects the liberty interest asserted by the patient-plaintiffs here.

Certain decisions are momentous in their impact on the character of a person's life decisions about religious faith, political and moral allegiance, marriage, procreation, and death, for example. Such deeply personal decisions pose controversial questions about how and why human life has value. In a free society, individuals must be allowed to make those decisions for themselves, out of their own faith, conscience, and convictions. This Court has insisted, in a variety of contexts and circumstances, that this great freedom is among those protected by the Due Process Clause as essential to a community of "ordered liberty." *Palko v. Connecticut*, 302 U.S. 319, 325 (1937). In its recent decision in *Planned Parenthood v. Casey*, 505 U.S. 833, 851(1992), the Court offered a paradigmatic statement of that principle:

> matters involving the most intimate and personal choices a person may make in a lifetime, choices central to a person's dignity and autonomy, are central to the liberty protected by the Fourteenth Amendment.

That declaration reflects an idea underlying many of our basic constitutional protections. As the Court explained in *West Virginia State Board of Education v. Barnette,* 319 U.S. 624, 642 (1943):

> If there is any fixed star in our constitutional constellation, it is that no official . . . can prescribe what shall be orthodox in politics, nationalism, religion, or other matters of opinion or force citizens to confess by word or act their faith therein.

A person's interest in following his own convictions at the end of life is so central a part of the more general right to make "intimate and personal choices" for himself that a failure to protect that particular interest would undermine the general right altogether. Death is, for each of us, among the most significant events of life. As the Chief Justice said in *Cruzan v. Missouri*, 497 U.S. 261, 281 (1990), "[t]he choice between life and death is a deeply personal decision of obvious and overwhelming finality." Most of us see death—whatever we think will follow it—as the final act of life's drama, and we want that last act to reflect our own convictions, those we have tried to live by, not the convictions of others forced on us in our most vulnerable moment.

Different people, of different religious and ethical beliefs, embrace very different convictions about which way of dying confirms and which contradicts the value of their lives. Some fight against death with every weapon their doctors can devise. Others will do nothing to hasten death even if they pray it will come soon. Still others, including the patient-plaintiffs in these cases, want to end their lives when they think that living on, in the only way they can, would disfigure rather than enhance the lives they had created. Some people make the latter choice not just to escape pain. Even if it were possible to eliminate all pain for a dying patient—and frequently that is not possible—that would not end or even much alleviate the anguish some would feel at remaining alive, but intubated, helpless, and often sedated near oblivion.

None of these dramatically different attitudes about the meaning of death can be dismissed as irrational. None should be imposed, either by the pressure of doctors or relatives or by the fiat of government, on people who reject it. Just as it would be intolerable for government to dictate that doctors never be permitted to try to keep someone alive as long as possible, when that is what the patient wishes, so it is intolerable for government to dictate that doctors may never, under any circumstances, help someone to die who believes that further life means only degradation. The Constitution insists that people must be free to make these deeply personal decisions for themselves and must not be forced to end their lives in a way that appalls them, just because that is what some majority thinks proper.

II. This Court's Decisions in *Casey* and *Cruzan* Compel Recognition of a Liberty Interest Here
A. *Casey* Supports the Liberty Interest Asserted Here
In Casey, this Court, in holding that a state cannot constitutionally proscribe abortion in all cases, reiterated that the Constitution protects a sphere of autonomy in which individuals must be permitted to make certain decisions for themselves. The Court began its analysis by pointing out that "[a]t the heart of liberty is the right to define one's own concept of existence, of meaning, of the universe, and of the mystery of human life." 505 U.S. at 851. Choices flowing out of these conceptions, on matters "involving the most intimate and personal choices a person may make in a lifetime, choices central to personal dignity and autonomy, are central to the liberty protected by the Fourteenth Amendment." *Id.* "Beliefs about these matters," the Court continued, "could not define the attributes of personhood were they formed under compulsion of the State." *Id.*

In language pertinent to the liberty interest asserted here, the Court explained why decisions about abortion fall within this category of "personal and intimate" decisions. A decision whether or not to have an abortion, "originat[ing] within the zone of conscience and belief," involves conduct in which "the liberty of the woman is at stake in a sense unique to the human condition and so unique to the law." *Id.* at 852. As such, the decision necessarily involves the very "destiny of the woman" and is inevitably "shaped to a large extent on her own conception of her spiritual imperatives and her place in society." *Id.* Precisely because of these characteristics of the decision, "the State is [not] entitled to proscribe [abortion] in all instances." *Id.* Rather, to allow a total prohibition on abortion would be to permit a state to impose one conception of the meaning and value of human existence on all individuals. This the Constitution forbids.

The Solicitor General nevertheless argues that the right to abortion could be supported on grounds other than this autonomy principle, grounds that would not apply here. He argues, for example, that the abortion right might flow from the great burden an unwanted child imposes on its mother's life. Brief for the United States at 14–15. But whether or not abortion rights could be defended on such grounds, they were not the grounds on which this Court in fact relied. To the contrary, the Court explained at length that the right flows from the constitutional protection accorded all individuals to "define one's own concept of existence, of meaning, of the universe, and of the mystery of human life." *Casey*, 505 U.S. at 851.

The analysis in *Casey* compels the conclusion that the patient-plaintiffs have a liberty interest in this case that a state cannot burden with a blanket prohibition. Like a woman's decision whether to have an abortion, a decision to die involves one's very "destiny" and inevitably will be "shaped to a large extent on (one's) own conception of [one's] spiritual imperatives and [one's] place in society" *Id.* at 852. Just as a blanket prohibition on abortion would involve the improper imposition of one conception of the meaning and value of human existence on all individuals, so too would a blanket prohibition on assisted suicide. The liberty interest asserted here cannot be rejected without undermining the rationale of *Casey*. Indeed, the lower court opinions in the Washington case expressly recognized the parallel between the liberty interest in *Casey* and the interest asserted here. *See Compassion in Dying* v. *Washington*, 79 F.3d 790, 801 (9th Cir. 1996) (en banc) ("In deciding right-to-die cases, we are guided by the Court's approach to the abortion cases. *Casey* in particular provides a powerful precedent, for in that case the Court had the opportunity to evaluate its past decisions and to determine whether to adhere to its original judgment."), *aff'g.* 850 F. Supp. 1454, 1459 (W. D. Wash. 1994) ("[T]he reasoning in *Casey* [is] highly instructive and almost prescriptive . . ."). This Court should do the same.

B. Cruzan *Supports the Liberty Interest Asserted Here*

We agree with the Solicitor General that this Court's decision in "*Cruzan* . . . supports the conclusion that a liberty interest is at stake in this case." Brief for the United States at 8. Petitioners, however, insist that the present cases can be distinguished because the right at issue in Cruzan was limited to a right to reject an unwanted invasion of one's body.[1] But this Court repeatedly has held that in appropriate circumstances a state may require individuals to accept unwanted invasions of the body. See, e.g., *Schmerber v. California*, 384 U.S. 757 (1966) (extraction of blood sample from individual suspected of driving while intoxicated, notwithstanding defendant's objection, does not violate privilege against self-incrimination or other constitutional rights); *Jacobson v. Massachusetts*, 197 U.S. 11(1905) (upholding compulsory vaccination for smallpox as reasonable regulation for protection of public health).

The liberty interest at stake in *Cruzan* was a more profound one. If a competent patient has a constitutional right to refuse life-sustaining treatment, then, the Court implied, the state could not override that right. The regulations upheld in *Cruzan* were designed only to ensure that the individual's wishes were ascertained correctly. Thus, if *Cruzan* implies a right of competent patients to refuse life-sustaining treatment, that implication must be understood as resting not simply on a right to refuse bodily invasions but on the more profound right to refuse medical intervention when what is at stake is a momentous personal decision, such as the timing and manner of one's death. In her concurrence, Justice O'Connor expressly recognized that the right at issue involved a "deeply personal decision" that is "inextricably intertwined" with our notion of "self-determination." 497 U.S. at 287–89.

Cruzan also supports the proposition that a state may not burden a terminally ill patient's liberty interest in determining the time and manner of his death by prohibiting doctors from terminating life support. Seeking to distinguish *Cruzan*, Petitioners insist that a state may nevertheless burden that right in a different way by forbidding doctors to assist in the suicide of patients who are not on life-support machinery. They argue that doctors who remove life support are only allowing a natural process to end in death whereas doctors who prescribe lethal drugs are intervening to cause death. So, according to this argument, a state has an independent justification for forbidding doctors to assist in suicide that it does not have for forbidding them to remove life support. In the former case though not the latter, it is said, the state forbids an act of killing that is morally much more problematic than merely letting a patient die.

This argument is based on a misunderstanding of the pertinent moral principles. It is certainly true that when a patient does not wish to die, different acts, each of which foreseeably results in his death, nevertheless have very different moral status. When several patients need organ transplants and organs are scarce, for example, it is morally permissible for a doctor to deny an organ to one patient, even though he will die without it, in order to give it to another. But it is certainly not permissible for a doctor to kill one patient in order to use his organs to save another. The morally significant difference between those two acts is not, however, that killing is a positive act and not providing an organ is a mere omission, or that killing someone is worse than merely allowing a "natural" process to result in death. It would be equally impermissible for a doctor to let an injured patient bleed to death, or to refuse antibiotics to a patient with pneumonia—in each case the doctor would have allowed death to result from a "natural" process—in order to make his organs available for transplant to others. A doctor violates his patient's rights whether the doctor acts or refrains from acting, against the patient's wishes, in a way that is designed to cause death.

When a competent patient does want to die, the moral situation is obviously different, because then it makes no sense to appeal to the patient's right not to be killed as a reason why an act designed to cause his death is impermissible. From the patient's point of view, there is no morally pertinent difference between a doctor's terminating treatment that keeps him alive, if that is what he wishes, and a doctor's helping him to end his own life by providing lethal pills he may take himself, when ready, if that is what he wishes—except that the latter may be quicker and more humane. Nor is that a pertinent difference from the doctor's point of view. If and when it is permissible for him to act with death in view, it does not matter which of those two means he and his patient choose. If it is permissible for a doctor deliberately to withdraw medical treatment in order to allow death to result from a natural process, then it is equally permissible for him to help his patient hasten his own death more actively, if that is the patient's express wish.

It is true that some doctors asked to terminate life support are reluctant and do so only in deference to a patient's right to compel them to remove unwanted invasions of his body. But other doctors, who believe that their most fundamental professional duty is to act in the patient's interests and that, in certain circumstances, it is in their patient's best interests to die, participate willingly in such decisions: they terminate life support to cause death because they know that is what their patient wants. *Cruzan* implied that a state may not absolutely prohibit a doctor from deliberately causing death, at the patient's request, in that way and for that reason. If so, then a state may not prohibit doctors from deliberately using more direct and often more humane means to the same end when that is what a patient prefers. The fact that failing to provide life-sustaining treatment may be regarded as "only letting nature take its course" is no more morally significant in this context, when the patient wishes to die, than in the other, when he wishes to live. Whether a doctor turns off a respirator in accordance with the patient's request or prescribes pills

that a patient may take when he is ready to kill himself, the doctor acts with the same intention: to help the patient die.

The two situations do differ in one important respect. Since patients have a right not to have life-support machinery attached to their bodies, they have, in principle, a right to compel its removal. But that is not true in the case of assisted suicide: patients in certain circumstances have a right that the state not forbid doctors to assist in their deaths, but they have no right to compel a doctor to assist them. The right in question, that is, is only a right to the help of a willing doctor.

III. State Interests Do Not Justify a Categorical Prohibition on All Assisted Suicide

The Solicitor General concedes that "a competent, terminally ill adult has a constitutionally cognizable liberty interest in avoiding the kind of suffering experienced by the plaintiffs in this case." Brief for the United States at 8. He agrees that this interest extends not only to avoiding pain, but to avoiding an existence the patient believes to be one of intolerable indignity or incapacity as well. *Id.* at 12. The Solicitor General argues, however, that states nevertheless have the right to "override" this liberty interest altogether, because a state could reasonably conclude that allowing doctors to assist in suicide, even under the most stringent regulations and procedures that could be devised, would unreasonably endanger the lives of a number of patients who might ask for death in circumstances when it is plainly not in their interests to die or when their consent has been improperly obtained.

This argument is unpersuasive, however, for at least three reasons. *First*, in *Cruzan*, this Court noted that its various decisions supported the recognition of a general liberty interest in refusing medical treatment, even when such refusal could result in death. 497 U.S. at 278–79. The various risks described by the Solicitor General apply equally to those situations. For instance, a patient kept alive only by an elaborate and disabling life-support system might well become depressed, and doctors might be equally uncertain whether the depression is curable: such a patient might decide for death only because he has been advised that he will die soon anyway or that he will never live free of the burdensome apparatus, and either diagnosis might conceivably be mistaken. Relatives or doctors might subtly or crudely influence that decision, and state provision for the decision may (to the same degree in this case as if it allowed assisted suicide) be thought to encourage it.

Yet there has been no suggestion that states are incapable of addressing such dangers through regulation. In fact, quite the opposite is true. In *McKay* v. *Bergstedt*, 106 Nev. 808, 801 P.2d 617 (1990), for example, the Nevada Supreme Court held that "competent adult patients desiring to refuse or discontinue medical treatment" must be examined by two nonattending physicians to determine whether the patient is mentally competent, understands his prognosis and treatment options, and appears free of coercion or pressure in making his decision. *Id.* at 827–28, 801 P.2d at 630. See also: *id.* (in the case of terminally ill patients with natural life expectancy of less than six months, [a] patient's right of self-determination shall be deemed to prevail over state interests, whereas [a] non-terminal patient's decision to terminate life-support systems must first be weighed against relevant state interests by trial judge); [and] *In re Farrell*, 108 N.J. 335, 354, 529 A.2d 404, 413 (1987) ([which held that a] terminally-ill patient requesting termination of life-support must be determined to be competent and properly informed about [his] prognosis, available treatment options and risks, and to have made decision voluntarily and without coercion). Those protocols served to guard against precisely the dangers that the Solicitor General raises. The case law contains no suggestion that such protocols are inevitably insufficient to prevent deaths that should have been prevented.

Indeed, the risks of mistake are overall greater in the case of terminating life support. *Cruzan* implied that a state must allow individuals to make such decisions through an advance directive stipulating either that life support be terminated (or not initiated) in described circumstances when the individual was no longer competent to make such a decision himself, or that a designated proxy be allowed to make that decision. All the risks just described are present when the decision is made through or pursuant to such an advance directive,

and a grave further risk is added: that the directive, though still in force, no longer represents the wishes of the patient. The patient might have changed his mind before he became incompetent, though he did not change the directive, or his proxy may make a decision that the patient would not have made himself if still competent. In *Cruzan*, this Court held that a state may limit these risks through reasonable regulation. It did not hold—or even suggest—that a state may avoid them through a blanket prohibition that, in effect, denies the liberty interest altogether.

Second, nothing in the record supports the [Solicitor General's] conclusion that no system of rules and regulations could adequately reduce the risk of mistake. As discussed above, the experience of states in adjudicating requests to have life-sustaining treatment removed indicates the opposite. The Solicitor General has provided no persuasive reason why the same sort of procedures could not be applied effectively in the case of a competent individual's request for physician-assisted suicide.

Indeed, several very detailed schemes for regulating physician-assisted suicide have been submitted to the voters of some states and one has been enacted. In addition, concerned groups, including a group of distinguished professors of law and other professionals, have drafted and defended such schemes. *See, e.g.*, Charles H. Baron, *et. al, A Model State Act to Authorize and Regulate Physician-Assisted Suicide*, 33 Harv. J. Legis. 1 (1996). Such draft statutes propose a variety of protections and review procedures designed to insure against mistakes, and neither Washington nor New York attempted to show that such schemes would be porous or ineffective. Nor does the Solicitor General's brief: it relies instead mainly on flat and conclusory statements. It cites a New York Task Force report, written before the proposals just described were drafted, whose findings have been widely disputed and were implicitly rejected in the opinion of the Second Circuit below. *See generally Quill* v. *Vacco*, 80 F.3d 716 (2d Cir. 1996). The weakness of the Solicitor General's argument is signaled by his strong reliance on the experience in the Netherlands which, in effect, allows assisted suicide pursuant to published guidelines. Brief for the United States at 23–24. The

Dutch guidelines are more permissive than the proposed and model American statutes, however. The Solicitor General deems the Dutch practice of ending the lives of people like neonates who cannot consent particularly noteworthy, for example, but that practice could easily and effectively be made illegal by any state regulatory scheme without violating the Constitution.

The Solicitor General's argument would perhaps have more force if the question before the Court were simply whether a state has any rational basis for an absolute prohibition; if that were the question, then it might be enough to call attention to risks a state might well deem not worth running. But as the Solicitor General concedes, the question here is a very different one: whether a state has interests sufficiently compelling to allow it to take the extraordinary step of altogether refusing the exercise of a liberty interest of constitutional dimension. In those circumstances, the burden is plainly on the state to demonstrate that the risk of mistakes is very high, and that no alternative to complete prohibition would adequately and effectively reduce those risks. Neither of the Petitioners has made such a showing.

Nor could they. The burden of proof on any state attempting to show this would be very high. Consider, for example, the burden a state would have to meet to show that it was entitled altogether to ban public speeches in favor of unpopular causes because it could not guarantee, either by regulations short of an outright ban or by increased police protection, that such speeches would not provoke a riot that would result in serious injury or death to an innocent party. Or that it was entitled to deny those accused of crime the procedural rights that the Constitution guarantees, such as the right to a jury trial, because the security risk those rights would impose on the community would be too great. One can posit extreme circumstances in which some such argument would succeed. *See, e.g., Korematsu* v. *United States*, 323 U.S., 214 (1944) (permitting United States to detain individuals of Japanese ancestry during wartime). But these circumstances would be extreme indeed, and the *Korematsu* ruling has been widely and severely criticized.

Third, it is doubtful whether the risks the Solicitor General cites are even of the right character to serve as justification for an absolute prohibition on the exercise of an important liberty interest. The risks fall into two groups. The first is the risk of medical mistake, including a misdiagnosis of competence or terminal illness. To be sure, no scheme of regulation, no matter how rigorous, can altogether guarantee that medical mistakes will not be made. But the Constitution does not allow a state to deny patients a great variety of important choices, for which informed consent is properly deemed necessary, just because the information on which the consent is given may, in spite of the most strenuous efforts to avoid mistake, be wrong. Again, these identical risks are present in decisions to terminate life support, yet they do not justify an absolute prohibition on the exercise of the right.

The second group consists of risks that a patient will be unduly influenced by considerations that the state might deem it not in his best interests to be swayed by, for example, the feelings and views of close family members. Brief for the United States at 20. But what a patient regards as proper grounds for such a decision normally reflects exactly the judgments of personal ethics—of why his life is important and what affects its value—that patients have a crucial liberty interest in deciding for themselves. Even people who are dying have a right to hear and, if they wish, act on what others might wish to tell or suggest or even hint to them, and it would be dangerous to suppose that a state may prevent this on the ground that it knows better than its citizens when they should be moved by or yield to particular advice or suggestion in the exercise of their right to make fateful personal decisions for themselves. It is not a good reply that some people may not decide as they really wish—as they would decide, for example, if free from the "pressure" of others. That possibility could hardly justify the most serious pressure of all—the criminal law which tells them that they may not decide for death if they need the help of a doctor in dying, no matter how firmly they wish it.

There is a fundamental infirmity in the Solicitor General's argument. He asserts that a state may reasonably judge that the risk of "mistake" to some persons justifies a prohibition that not only risks but insures and even aims at what would undoubtedly be a vastly greater number of "mistakes" of the opposite kind—preventing many thousands of competent people who think that it disfigures their lives to continue living, in the only way left to them, from escaping that—to them—terrible injury. A state grievously and irreversibly harms such people when it prohibits that escape. The Solicitor General's argument may seem plausible to those who do not agree that individuals are harmed by being forced to live on in pain and what they regard as indignity. But many other people plainly do think that such individuals are harmed, and a state may not take one side in that essentially ethical or religious controversy as its justification for denying a crucial liberty.

Of course, a state has important interests that justify regulating physician-assisted suicide. It may be legitimate for a state to deny an opportunity for assisted suicide when it acts in what it reasonably judges to be the best interests of the potential suicide, and when its judgment on that issue does not rest on contested judgments about "matters involving the most intimate and personal choices a person may make in a lifetime, choices central to personal dignity and autonomy." *Casey*, 505 U.S. at 851. A state might assert, for example, that people who are not terminally ill, but who have formed a desire to die, are, as a group, very likely later to be grateful if they are prevented from taking their own lives. It might then claim that it is legitimate, out of concern for such people, to deny any of them a doctor's assistance [in taking their own lives].

This Court need not decide now the extent to which such paternalistic interests might override an individual's liberty interest. No one can plausibly claim, however—and it is noteworthy that neither Petitioners nor the Solicitor General does claim—that any such prohibition could serve the interests of any significant number of terminally ill patients. On the contrary, any paternalistic justification for an absolute prohibition of assistance to such patients would of necessity appeal to a widely contested religious or ethical conviction many of them, including the patient-plaintiffs, reject. Allowing *that* justification to prevail would vitiate the liberty interest.

Even in the case of terminally ill patients, a state has a right to take all reasonable measures to insure that a patient requesting such assistance has made an informed, competent, stable and uncoerced decision. It is plainly legitimate for a state to establish procedures through which professional and administrative judgments can be made about these matters, and to forbid doctors to assist in suicide when its reasonable procedures have not been satisfied. States may be permitted considerable leeway in designing such procedures. They may be permitted, within reason, to err on what they take to be the side of caution. But they may not use the bare possibility of error as justification for refusing to establish any procedures at all and relying instead on a flat prohibition.

Conclusion

Each individual has a right to make the "most intimate and personal choices central to personal dignity and autonomy." That right encompasses the right to exercise some control over the time and manner of one's death.

The patient-plaintiffs in these cases were all mentally competent individuals in the final phase of terminal illness and died within months of filing their claims.

Jane Doe described how her advanced cancer made even the most basic bodily functions such as swallowing, coughing, and yawning extremely painful and that it was "not possible for [her] to reduce [her] pain to an acceptable level of comfort and to retain an alert state." Faced with such circumstances, she sought to be able to "discuss freely with [her] treating physician [her] intention of hastening [her] death through the consumption of drugs prescribed for that purpose." *Quill* v. *Vacco*, 80 F.2d 716, 720 (2d Cir. 1996) (quoting declaration of Jane Doe).

George A. Kingsley, in advanced stages of AIDS which included, among other hardships, the attachment of a tube to an artery in his chest which made even routine functions burdensome and the development of lesions on his brain, sought advice from his doctors regarding prescriptions which could hasten his impending death. *Id.*

Jane Roe, suffering from cancer since 1988, had been almost completely bedridden since 1993 and experienced constant pain which could not be alleviated by medication. After undergoing counseling for herself and her family, she desired to hasten her death by taking prescription drugs. *Compassion in Dying* v. *Washington*, 850 F. Supp. 1454, 1456 (1994).

John Doe, who had experienced numerous AIDS-related ailments since 1991, was "especially cognizant of the suffering imposed by a lingering terminal illness because he was the primary caregiver for his long-term companion who died of AIDS" and sought prescription drugs from his physician to hasten his own death after entering the terminal phase of AIDS. *Id.* at 1456–57.

James Poe suffered from emphysema which caused him "a constant sensation of suffocating" as well as a cardiac condition which caused severe leg pain. Connected to an oxygen tank at all times but unable to calm the panic reaction associated with his feeling of suffocation even with regular doses of morphine, Mr. Poe sought physician-assisted suicide. *Id.* at 1457.

A state may not deny the liberty claimed by the patient-plaintiffs in these cases without providing them an opportunity to demonstrate, in whatever way the state might reasonably think wise and necessary, that the conviction they expressed for an early death is competent, rational, informed, stable, and uncoerced.

Affirming the decisions by the Courts of Appeals would establish nothing more than that there is such a constitutionally protected right in principle. It would establish only that some individuals, whose decisions for suicide plainly cannot be dismissed as irrational or foolish or premature, must be accorded a reasonable opportunity to show that their decision for death is informed and free. It is not necessary to decide precisely which patients are entitled to that opportunity. If, on the other hand, this Court reverses the decisions below, its decision could only be justified by the momentous proposition—a proposition flatly in conflict with the spirit and letter of the Court's past decisions—that an American citizen does not, after all, have the right, even in principle, to live and die in the light of his own religious and ethical beliefs, his own convictions about why his life is valuable and where its value lies.

NOTE

1. In that case, the parents of Nancy Cruzan, a woman who was in a persistent vegetative state following an automobile accident, asked the Missouri courts to authorize doctors to end life support and therefore her life. The Supreme Court held that Missouri was entitled to demand explicit evidence that Ms. Cruzan had made a decision that she would not wish to be kept alive in those circumstances, and to reject the evidence the family had offered as inadequate. But a majority of justices assumed, for the sake of the argument, that a competent patient has a right to reject life-preserving treatment, and it is now widely assumed that the Court would so rule in an appropriate case.

An Alternative to Brain Death

JEFF McMAHAN

Jeff McMahan is a professor of philosophy at Rutgers University and the author of *The Ethics of Killing: Problems at the Margins of Life* (Oxford University Press, 2002). In this selection he argues that many of our assumptions about the nature of death are unfounded and that the whole-brain criterion for death is inadequate. He distinguishes between the human organism and the human person and arrives at the view that irreversible loss of consciousness is the one necessary condition for a person's death.

Some Common but Mistaken Assumptions about Death

Most contributors to the debate about brain death, including Dr. James Bernat, share certain assumptions. They believe that the concept of death is univocal, that death is a biological phenomenon, that it is necessarily irreversible, that it is paradigmatically something that happens to *organisms*, that we are human organisms, and therefore that our deaths will be deaths of organisms. These claims are supposed to have moral significance. It is, for example, only when a person dies that it is permissible to extract her organs for transplantation.

It is also commonly held that our univocal notion of death is the permanent cessation of integrated functioning in an organism and that the criterion for determining when this has occurred in animals with brains is the death of the brain as a whole—that is, brain death. The reason most commonly given for this is that the brain is the irreplaceable master control of the organism's integration.

Before presenting my own view, let me say something about a couple of these assumptions and about the case for brain death. It is, perhaps, a measure of the heretical cast of my mind that I reject *all* of these widely shared assumptions.

I do not think the concept of death is univocal. When Jesus says that "whosoever liveth and believeth in me shall never die," he does not mean that some human organisms will remain functionally integrated forever. He means that believers will never cease to exist. (Admittedly, Jesus did not use the English word "die." But this seemed an intelligible use of the word to the translators.)

But "death" also has a biological meaning. It makes sense to say that when a unicellular organism, such as an ameba, undergoes binary fission, it ceases to exist; but in the biological sense it does not *die*. There is no cessation of functioning that turns this once-living organism into a corpse. So death as a biological phenomenon is different from the ceasing to exist of a living being and may or may not involve an entity's ceasing to exist. It is intelligible, for example, to say that when an animal organism dies, it does not cease to exist. Rather, it simply becomes a corpse. The living animal becomes a dead animal—but nothing ceases to exist until the animal organism disintegrates.

I also do not think our concept of death makes it a necessary truth that death is irreversible. If that were true, the claim that Lazarus was raised from the dead, or that Jesus was resurrected, would be incoherent. I think these claims are false; but if it

From Jeff McMahan, "An Alternative to Brain Death," *Journal of Law, Medicine, and Ethics*, Spring 2006, 44–48.

were a conceptual truth that death is irreversible, they would not be false, but nonsensical.

I do think, however, that there is something true and important in the idea that death as a biological phenomenon is irreversible. It may well be a conceptual truth that an organism can be revived from death only by a violation of the laws of nature—that is, only by a literal miracle of the sort that Jesus is thought by some to have performed. For in cases not involving miracles, if an organism that was thought to be dead is restored to integrated functioning, our tendency is to conclude that we were mistaken in assuming that it was dead. (Subsequent references to irreversibility should be understood as having the implicit qualification "except by miracle.")

Some people, of course, will say that the organism was dead but was non-miraculously restored to life. To make this claim acceptable, they will need to offer good reasons for thinking the organism was dead, given that it is now alive. For reasons that I will give later, I think that nothing of importance depends on this. It is just a question of how we use certain words. But for those who believe that we are organisms and that we always have special value or sanctity while we are alive, this is a very important issue indeed.

While we are considering whether death is necessarily irreversible, I should mention that I am puzzled that Bernat and others define death as the permanent cessation of functioning—or of the critical functions—of an organism as a whole.[1] Surely what they should say is that it is the irreversible cessation of functioning. (By "irreversible" I mean irreversible in principle, not in practice.) If an organism stops functioning but its functioning could be recovered by means of a device that we do not in fact possess, it is not dead. There are, however, metaphysically determined constraints on what kind of device this could be. It would, for example, have to restore the same life, not create a new one.

Let me explain why the notion of irreversibility is preferable to that of permanence. Suppose there is an organism in which integrated functioning has ceased but could be revived. If it is up to you whether to revive the functioning, your decision now will determine whether the organism was dead a moment ago. For if you decide to revive the functioning, the cessation will not have been permanent and the organism will have been alive a moment ago. But if you decide not to revive it, you thereby make permanent the cessation of functioning that occurred in the past. But whether the organism was dead a moment ago is a matter of its intrinsic state at the time; it cannot be determined retroactively by what you do now. (Bernat, I should note, urges a similar point in his cogent objections to the proposal for non-heart-beating organ donation.[2])

Brain Death and the Cessation of Integrated Functioning

Turn now to the central contention of the defenders of brain death, which is that at least certain critical functions of the brain are necessary for integrated functioning in the organism. (I put aside the interesting question whether they are also sufficient.) This claim raises two related questions. First, what counts as the right sort of integration? Second, is the claim empirical or conceptual?

There are several ways in which the functions of the various organs and subsystems of an organism might be integrated so as to maintain homeostasis and resist entropy. It might be, for example, that integration occurs via a central integrator, a master control that receives signals from the various organs and subsystems, processes them, and then sends return signals that coordinate the functions of the organism's many parts. The defenders of brain death typically claim that the only possible central integrator is the brain. They say that the brain is irreplaceable, that nothing else could possibly carry out its regulative functions.

Critics of brain death, by contrast, often speculate that a mechanical brain—or to be more precise, a mechanical substitute for the brain stem—could adequately replicate the regulative functions of the brain and hence could be the central integrator of a living human organism. Some, indeed, have claimed that the resources of the modern intensive care unit (ICU) already constitute an external and multifaceted substitute for the regulatory functions of the brain stem.[3]

In defending the irreplaceability of the brain, Bernat writes that, "although some of the brain's regulatory functions may be replaced mechanically, the brain's functions of awareness, sentience, sapience, and its capacities, to experience and communicate cannot be reproduced or simulated by any machine."[4] Let us grant that this is true. The problem is that these are not somatic regulatory functions.[5]

A second way in which the functions of an organism's various organs and subsystems might be integrated is through decentralized interaction, in which these parts achieve coordination by sending, receiving, and processing signals among themselves. In a series of papers, Alan Shewmon has argued that this sort of decentralized integration of functioning can and sometimes does occur among the parts of an organism without any input from the brain at all.[6] He cites numerous actual cases involving high cervical transection, functional isolation of the brain in Guillain-Barré Syndrome, or even brain death with artificially induced respiration in which there is a high degree of functional integration in the absence of regulation by the brain—and, indeed, without any central integrator at all. He notes, for example, that some brain dead organisms have the same range of functions as certain uncontroversially living patients in an ICU, and yet maintain these functions with *fewer* sources of external support.

If the familiar claims about the necessary role of the brain in integrating the functions of an organism are empirical claims, I think that Shewmon's cases and arguments force the defender of brain death to admit defeat. But it is possible for the defender of brain death to respond to Shewmon's challenge by interpreting the claim that the brain is necessary for integrated functioning as a conceptual rather than empirical claim.

The defender of brain death can, in other words, retreat to the claim that while certain forms of integrated functioning can be sustained via an artificial central regulator or via decentralized interaction, these forms of integration are not the kind of integration that is necessary for life in a human organism. Only the brain as central regulator can provide that.

This may be a reasonable interpretation of Bernat's claim that "the brain is the critical system of the organism without which the remaining organs may continue to function independently but cannot together comprise an organism as a whole."[7]

He might be saying that, even if all the organs are alive and doing their job, they cannot together constitute a living organism without the mediation of the brain.

There are various responses to such a view. One is to ask how much the brain must contribute to the integration of functioning among the parts of the organism in order for the organism to be alive. Clearly it need not regulate *every* aspect of functioning. Indeed, it seems that those who would defend the idea that somatic regulation by the brain is a conceptually necessary condition for life in a human organism must accept something like the following. First we have to identify a range of "critical" regulatory functions. As long as the brain continues to carry out any single one of these functions, that is sufficient for life in the organism. For if we were to insist on the necessity of the brain's carrying out more than one, then an organism in which the brain carried out only one critical regulatory function would be dead—but it would not be brain dead.

But now imagine a case in which only one critical regulatory function is being carried out by the brain. All others are being carried out by external life support. Suppose that right at the moment the brain is about to lose the capacity to carry out this one remaining critical function, a mechanical replacement takes over for it with perfect efficiency. Could *this* be the difference between life and death? Note that, because the mechanical replacement would carry out the regulatory functions in exactly the same way the brain did, the state of the organism would be unchanged apart from this one small change in the brain itself. It is very hard to believe that such a change could make the difference between life and death in an organism, either as a matter of fact or, especially, as a matter of conceptual necessity.

If presented only with information about the loss of supposed critical functions in the brain and information about the unchanged but externally supported functioning of the various organs and subsystems within the organism, most people, I suspect, would not know what to say about whether such an organism was alive or dead. Our concept of death simply fails to deliver an immediately intuitive verdict that the organism is dead. This strongly suggests that the loss by the brain of critical regulatory functions is no part of our *concept* of death.

Another response is simply to point to the case of human embryos, which seem to be living human organisms whose somatic functions are not regulated or integrated by the brain. If this is a correct description, it cannot be a necessary truth that the kind of integrated functioning necessary for life must be regulated to some degree by the brain.

There are a great many other problems with the notion of brain death but I will not rehearse them here.[8] Instead I will conclude by sketching an alternative view.

An Alternative Understanding of Death

I accept that it is largely correct to say that a human organism dies when it irreversibly loses the capacity for integrated functioning among its various major organs and subsystems. But the death of a human organism will necessarily be *my* death only if I am an organism. The view that we are organisms is the most important of the widely shared assumptions that I noted at the outset. But, as I mentioned, I think it is mistaken.

The question whether we are organisms is not a biological question, or even a scientific question—just as it is not a scientific question whether a statue and the lump of bronze of which it is composed are one and the same thing or distinct substances. Whether we are organisms is also, and more obviously, not an ethical question. It is a metaphysical question.

There are two arguments that convince me that the answer to this question is "no." One appeals to the hypothetical case of brain transplantation—or, better yet, cerebrum transplantation. If my cerebrum were successfully grafted onto the brain stem of my identical twin brother (whose own cerebrum had been excised), I would then exist in association with what was once his organism. What was formerly my organism would have an intact brain stem and might, therefore, be idling nicely in a persistent vegetative state without even mechanical ventilation. Since I can thus in principle exist separately from the organism that is now mine, I cannot be identical with it.

The second argument appeals not to a science fiction scenario but to an actual phenomenon: dicephalus. Certain instances of dicephalic twinning, in which two heads sprout from a single torso, seem to be clear cases in which a single organism supports the existence of two distinct people. The transitivity of identity prevents us from saying that *both* these people *are* that organism; for that implies that the people are identical, that is, that there are not really two people but only one. And because each twin's relation to the organism is the same as the other's, it cannot be that one twin but not the other is the organism. The best thing to say, therefore, is that neither of them is identical to the organism. Since we are essentially the same kind of thing they are, we cannot be organisms either.

If I am right that we are not organisms, what are we? The most widely held alternative view is that each of us is essentially a cartesian soul—that is, a nonmaterial conscious entity that in life is linked with a particular brain and body but at death continues to exist and indeed remains conscious and is psychologically continuous with the person prior to death. Because the soul, so conceived, is nonphysical, it can be individuated only by reference to a single field of consciousness. Thus, any conscious state that is not accessible in my field of consciousness must belong to a different person, or soul. This conception of the soul is, however, undermined by what we know about the results of hemispheric commissurotomy—a procedure in which the tissues connecting a patient's cerebral hemispheres are surgically severed. This procedure gives rise, at least in certain experimental settings, to two separate centers of consciousness in a single human organism. If persons were cartesian souls, we would have to conclude that the procedure creates two persons where formerly there was only one. Since this is clearly not what happens, we cannot be cartesian souls.[9]

How should we think about the problem of determining what kind of thing we essentially are? Here is a quick thought-experiment. Imagine that you were facing the prospect of progressive dementia. At what point would you cease to exist? To most of us it seems clear that you would persist at least as

long as the brain in your body retained the capacity for consciousness. For there would be somebody there, and who might it be, if not you? But would you still survive if your brain irreversibly lost the capacity for consciousness? It seems that the only thing there that might qualify as you would be a living human organism. But if I am right that you are not a human organism and there would be nothing else there for you to be, it seems that you must have ceased to exist when your brain lost the capacity for consciousness. I infer from this that you are in fact a mind, a mind that is necessarily embodied.

Recall now my earlier claim that the concept of death is not univocal. The term "death" can refer to our ceasing to exist (as in the earlier quotation from Jesus) or it can refer to a biological event in the history of an organism. This makes things easy; for we already have the two concepts of death that we require if I am right that we are not organisms.

An organism dies in the biological sense when it loses the capacity for integrated functioning. The best criterion for when this happens is probably a circulatory-respiratory criterion. There is bound to be considerable indeterminacy about how much functional integration is required for life in an organism. But if we are not organisms, this is of little consequence.

What it is important to be able to determine is when we die in the nonbiological sense—that is, when we cease to exist. If we are embodied minds, we die or cease to exist when we irreversibly lose the capacity for consciousness—or, to be more precise, when there is irreversible loss of function in those areas of the brain in which consciousness is realized. The best criterion for when this happens is a higher-brain criterion—for example, what is called "cerebral death." But I do not pretend to any expertise here.

Note that when I say the right criterion of our death is a higher-brain criterion, I am not claiming that a human organism in a persistent vegetative state is dead. If persistent vegetative state involves the loss of the capacity for consciousness, then neither you nor I could ever exist in a persistent vegetative state. But you could be survived by your organism, which could remain biologically alive in a persistent vegetative state even though you were dead (that is, had ceased to exist). My view thus avoids the embarrassing implication of most proposals for a higher-brain criterion of death that an organism with spontaneous respiration and heartbeat might be dead.

From an ethical point of view, what matters is not whether an organism remains alive, but whether one of us continues to exist. Of course, we cannot survive unless our organisms remain alive (though this might change if brain transplantation were to become possible). Indeed, although brain death is not sufficient for the biological death of a human organism, it is sufficient for the death or ceasing to exist of a person.

The problematic cases are those in which a person has ceased to exist but her organism remains alive. Might it be permissible to remove the organs from such an organism for transplantation? I believe that it would be, provided that this would not be against the expressed will of the person whose organism it was. But if the person had consented in advance, there would be no moral objection to killing the unoccupied organism in order to use its organs to save the lives of others.

The organism itself cannot be harmed in the relevant sense, it has no rights, and it is not an appropriate object of respect in the Kantian sense. I believe that the treatment of a living but unoccupied human organism is governed morally by principles similar to those that govern the treatment of a corpse. The latter also cannot be harmed or possess rights. But respect for the person who once animated a corpse dictates that there are certain things that must not be done to it. Taking its organs for transplantation with the person's prior consent is not one of these.

REFERENCES
1. J. L. Bernat, "A Defense of the Whole-Brain Concept of Death," *Hastings Center Report* 28, no. 2 (1998): 14–23, at 17.
2. See J. L. Bernat, "Defending Challenges to the Concept of 'Brain Death,'" *at* <http://www.lahey.org/NewsPubs/Publications/Ethics/JournalFall1998/Journal_Fall1998_Feature.asp> (last visited December 5, 2005); and M. A. DeVita and R. M. Arnold, "The Concept of Brain Death," *at* <http://www.lahey.org/NewsPubs/Publications/Ethics/JournalWinter1999/Journal_Winter1999_Dialogue.asp> (last visited December 5, 2005).
3. For an early suggestion of this sort, see M. B. Green and D. Wikler, "Brain Death and Personal Identity," *Philosophy and Public Affairs* 9 (1980): 105–33, at 113.
4. Bernat, *supra* note 1, at 19.
5. Bernat also claims that "consciousness, which is required for the organism to respond to requirements for hydration, nutrition, and protection, among other needs," is therefore among the "critical functions of the organism as a whole." *Ibid.,* at 17. But this still does not make it a somatic regulatory function of the brain.
6. See, for example, A. Shewmon, "Recovery from 'Brain Death': A Neurologist's Apologia," *Linacre Quarterly* 64 (1997): 30–96; A. Shewmon, "Chronic 'Brain Death,'" *Neurology* 51 (1998): 1538–45; and A. Shewmon, "The Disintegration of Somatic Integrative Unity: Demise of the Orthodox but Physiologically Untenable Physiological Rationale for 'Brain Death,'" manuscript on file with the author.
7. Bernat, *supra* note 2.
8. See J. McMahan, *The Ethics of Killing: Problems at the Margins of Life* (New York: Oxford University Press: 2002): chapter 5, section 1.2.
9. For further argument, see McMahan, *supra* note 8, at 7–24.

Vacco v. Quill

UNITED STATES SUPREME COURT

At issue in this case is whether a ban on assisted suicide enacted in New York state is constitutional—specifically whether the prohibition violates the Equal Protection Clause of the Fourteenth Amendment. The Court finds that it does not, that in fact there is no constitutional right to a physician's help in dying. But each state may establish its own policy on the issue.

In New York, as in most States, it is a crime to aid another to commit or attempt suicide, but patients may refuse even lifesaving medical treatment. The question presented by this case is whether New York's prohibition on assisting suicide therefore violates the Equal Protection Clause of the Fourteenth Amendment. We hold that it does not.

Petitioners are various New Yolk public officials. Respondents Timothy E. Quill, Samuel C. Klagsbrun, and Howard A. Grossman are physicians who practice in New York. They assert that although it would be "consistent with the standards of [their] medical practice[s]" to prescribe lethal medication for "mentally competent, terminally ill patients" who are suffering great pain and desire a doctor's help in taking their own lives, they are deterred from doing so by New York's ban on assisting suicide. Respondents, and three gravely ill patients who have since died, sued the State's Attorney General in the United States District Court. They urged that because New York permits a competent person to refuse life-sustaining medical treatment, and because the refusal of such treatment is "essentially the same thing" as physician-assisted suicide, New York's assisted-suicide ban violates the Equal Protection Clause.

The District Court disagreed: "[I]t is hardly unreasonable or irrational for the State to recognize a difference between allowing nature to take it course, even in the most severe situations, and intentionally using an artificial death-producing device." The court noted New York's "obvious legitimate interests in preserving life, and in protecting vulnerable persons," and concluded that "[u]nder the United

States Constitution and the federal system it establishes, the resolution of this issue is left to the normal democratic processes within the State."

The Court of Appeals for the Second Circuit reversed. The court determined that, despite the assisted-suicide ban's apparent general applicability, "New York law does not treat equally all competent persons who are in the final stages of fatal illness and wish to hasten their deaths," because "those in the final stages of terminal illness who are on life-support systems are allowed to hasten their deaths by directing the removal of such systems; but those similarly situated except for the previous attachment of life-sustaining equipment, are not allowed to hasten death by self-administering prescribed drugs." In the court's view, "[t]he ending of life by [the withdrawal of life-support systems] is *nothing more nor less than assisted suicide*" (emphasis added). The Court of Appeals then examined whether this supposed unequal treatment was rationally related to any legitimate state interest, and concluded that "to the extent that [New York's statutes] prohibit a physician from prescribing medications to be self-administered by a mentally competent, terminally-ill person in the final stages of his terminal illness, they are not rationally related to any legitimate state interest." We granted certiorari and now reverse.

The Equal Protection Clause commands that no State shall "deny to any person within its jurisdiction the equal protection of the laws." This provision creates no substantive rights. Instead, it embodies a general rule that States must treat like cases alike but may treat unlike cases accordingly. If a legislative classification or distinction "neither burdens a fundamental right nor targets a suspect class, we

United States Supreme Court. 521 U.S. 793 (1997).

will uphold [it] so long as it bears a rational relation to some legitimate end."

New York's statutes outlawing assisting suicide affect and address matters of profound significance to all New Yorkers alike. They neither infringe fundamental rights nor involve suspect classifications. These laws are therefore entitled to a "strong presumption of validity."

On their faces, neither New York's ban on assisting suicide nor its statutes permitting patients to refuse medical treatment treat anyone differently than anyone else or draw any distinctions between persons. *Everyone*, regardless of physical condition, is entitled, if competent, to refuse unwanted lifesaving medical treatment; *no one* is permitted to assist a suicide. Generally speaking, laws that apply even-handedly to all "unquestionably comply" with the Equal Protection Clause.

The Court of Appeals, however, concluded that some terminally ill people—those who are on life-support systems—are treated differently than those who are not, in that the former may "hasten death" by ending treatment, but the latter may not "hasten death" through physician-assisted suicide. This conclusion depends on the submission that ending or refusing lifesaving medical treatment "is nothing more nor less than assisted suicide." Unlike the Court of Appeals, we think the distinction between assisting suicide and withdrawing life-sustaining treatment, a distinction widely recognized and endorsed in the medical profession and in our legal traditions, is both important and logical: it is certainly rational. ("When the basic classification is rationally based, uneven effects upon particular groups within a class are ordinarily of no constitutional concern.")

The distinction comports with fundamental legal principles of causation and intent. First, when a patient refuses life-sustaining medical treatment, he dies from an underlying fatal disease or pathology, but if a patient ingests lethal medication prescribed by a physician, he is killed by that medication.

Furthermore, a physician who withdraws, or honors a patient's refusal to begin, life-sustaining medical treatment purposefully intends, or may so intend, only to respect his patient's wishes and "to cease doing useless and futile or degrading things to the patient when [the patient] no longer stands to

benefit from them." Assisted Suicide in the United States, Hearing before the Subcommittee on the Constitution of the House Committee on the Judiciary, 104th Cong., 2d Sess., 368 (1996) (testimony of Dr. Leon R. Kass). The same is true when a doctor provides aggressive palliative care; in some cases, painkilling drugs may hasten a patient's death, but the physician's purpose and intent is, or may be, only to ease his patient's pain. A doctor who assists a suicide, however, "must, necessarily and indubitably, intend primarily that the patient be made dead." *Id.*, at 367. Similarly, a patient who commits suicide with a doctor's aid necessarily has the specific intent to end his or her own life, while a patient who refuses or discontinues treatment might not.

The law has long used actors' intent or purpose to distinguish between two acts that may have the same result. Put differently, the law distinguishes actions taken "because of" a given end from actions taken "in spite of" their unintended but foreseen consequences. ("When General Eisenhower ordered American soldiers onto the beaches of Normandy, he knew that he was sending many American soldiers to certain death. . . . His purpose, though, was to . . . liberate Europe from the Nazis.")

Given these general principles, it is not surprising that many courts, including New York courts, have carefully distinguished refusing life-sustaining treatment from suicide. In fact, the first state court decision explicitly to authorize withdrawing lifesaving treatment noted the "real distinction between the self-infliction of deadly harm and a self-determination against artificial life support." . . .

Similarly, the overwhelming majority of state legislatures have drawn a clear line between assisting suicide and withdrawing or permitting the refusal of unwanted lifesaving medical treatment by prohibiting the former and permitting the latter. And "nearly all states expressly disapprove of suicide and assisted suicide either in statutes dealing with durable powers of attorney in health-care situations, or in 'living will' statutes." Thus, even as the States move to protect and promote patients' dignity at the end of life, they remain opposed to physician-assisted suicide.

New York is a case in point. The State enacted its current assisted-suicide statutes in 1965.[1] Since then, New York has acted several times to protect patients common-law right to refuse treatment. In so doing, however, the State has neither endorsed a general right to "hasten death" not approved physician-assisted suicide. Quite the opposite: The State has reaffirmed the line between "killing" and "letting die." More recently the New York State Task Force on Life and the Law studied assisted suicide and euthanasia and, in 1994, unanimously recommended against legalization. When Death is Sought: Assisted Suicide and Euthanasia in the Medical Context vii (1994). In the Task Force's view, "allowing decisions to forego life-sustaining treatment and allowing assisted suicide or euthanasia have radically different consequences and meanings for public policy." *Id.*, at 146.

This Court has also recognized, at least implicitly, the distinction between letting a patient die and making that patient die. In *Cruzan v. Director, Mo. Dept. of Health* (1990), we concluded that "[t]he principle that a competent person has a constitutionally protected liberty interest in refusing unwanted medical treatment may be inferred from our prior decisions," and we assumed the existence of such a right for purposes of that case. But our assumption of a right to refuse treatment was grounded not, as the Court of Appeals supposed, on the proposition that patients have a general and abstract "right to hasten death," but on well established, traditional rights to bodily integrity and freedom from unwanted touching. In fact, we observed that "the majority of States in this country have laws imposing criminal penalties on one who assists another to commit suicide." *Cruzan* therefore provides no support for the notion that refusing life-sustaining medical treatment is "nothing more nor less than suicide."

For all these reasons we disagree with respondents' claim that the distinction between refusing lifesaving medical treatment and assisted suicide is "arbitrary" and "irrational."[2] Granted, in some cases, the line between the two may not be clear, but certainty is not required, even were it possible. Logic and contemporary practice support New York's judgment that the two acts are different, and New York may therefore, consistent with the Constitution, treat them differently. By permitting everyone to refuse unwanted medical treatment while prohibiting anyone from assisting a suicide, New York law follows a longstanding and rational distinction.

New York's reasons for recognizing and acting on this distinction—including prohibiting intentional killing and preserving life; preventing suicide; maintaining physicians' role as their patients' healers; protecting vulnerable people from indifference, prejudice, and psychological and financial pressure to end their lives; and avoiding a possible slide towards euthanasia—are discussed in greater detail in our opinion in *Glucksberg, ante.* These valid and important public interests easily satisfy the constitutional requirement that a legislative classification bear a rational relation to some legitimate end.

The judgment of the Court of Appeals is reversed.

NOTES

1. It has always been a crime, either by statute or under the common law, to assist a suicide in New York.

2. Respondents also argue that the State irrationally distinguishes between physician-assisted suicide and "terminal sedation," a process respondents characterize as "induc[ing] barbiturate coma and then starv[ing] the person to death." Petitioners insist, however, that "'[a]lthough proponents of physician-assisted suicide and euthanasia contend that terminal sedation is covert physician-assisted suicide or euthanasia, the concept of sedating pharmacotherapy is based on informed consent and the principle of double effect.'" Reply Brief for Petitioners 12 (quoting P. Rousseau, Terminal Sedation in the Care of Dying Patients, 156 Archives Internal Med. 1785, 1785–1786 ([1996]). Just as a State may prohibit assisting suicide while permitting patients to refuse unwanted lifesaving treatment, it may permit palliative care related to that refusal, which may have the foreseen but unintended "double effect" of hastening the patient's death. See New York Task Force, "When Death is Sought," at 163 ("It is widely recognized that the provision of pain medication is ethically and professionally acceptable even when the treatment may hasten the patient's death, if the medication is intended to alleviate pain and severe discomfort, not to cause death").

Washington v. Glucksberg

UNITED STATES SUPREME COURT

In this companion case to *Vacco v. Quill*, the question is whether Washington state's prohibition against causing or aiding a suicide offends the Due Process Clause of the Fourteenth Amendment. The Court determines that it does not and upholds Washington's law forbidding assisted suicide.

The question presented in this case is whether Washington's prohibition against "caus[ing]" or "aid[ing]" a suicide offends the Fourteenth Amendment to the United States Constitution. We hold that it does not.

It has always been a crime to assist a suicide in the State of Washington. In 1854, Washington's first Territorial Legislature outlawed "assisting another in the commission of self-murder." Today, Washington law provides: "A person is guilty of promoting a suicide attempt when he knowingly causes or aids another person to attempt suicide." Wash. Rev. Code 9A.36.060(l) (1994). "Promoting a suicide attempt" is a felony, punishable by up to five years' imprisonment and up to a $10,000 fine. At the same time, Washington's Natural Death Act, enacted in 1979, states that the "withholding or withdrawal of life-sustaining treatment" at a patient's direction "shall not, for any purpose, constitute a suicide."

Petitioners in this case are the State of Washington and its Attorney General. Respondents Harold Glucksberg, M.D., Abigail Halperin, M.D., Thomas A. Preston, M.D., and Peter Shalit, M.D., are physicians who practice in Washington. These doctors occasionally treat terminally ill, suffering patients, and declare that they would assist these patients in ending their lives if not for Washington's assisted-suicide ban. In January 1994, respondents, along with three gravely ill, pseudonymous plaintiffs who have since died and Compassion in Dying, a non-profit organization that counsels people considering physician-assisted suicide, sued in the United States District Court, seeking a declaration that

United States Supreme Court. 521 U.S. 702 (1997).

Wash Rev. Code 9A.36.060(1) (1994) is, on its face, unconstitutional. *Compassion in Dying v. Washington* (WD Wash. 1994).

The plaintiffs asserted "the existence of a liberty interest protected by the Fourteenth Amendment which extends to a personal choice by a mentally competent, terminally ill adult to commit physician-assisted suicide." Relying primarily on *Planned Parenthood v. Casey* (1992) and *Cruzan v. Director, Missouri Dept. of Health* (1990), the District Court agreed and concluded that Washington's assisted-suicide ban is unconstitutional because it "places an undue burden on the exercise of [that] constitutionally protected liberty interest." The District Court also decided that the Washington statute violated the Equal Protection Clause's requirement that "'all persons similarly situated . . . be treated alike.'"

A panel of the Court of Appeals for the Ninth Circuit reversed, emphasizing that "[i]n the two hundred and five years of our existence no constitutional right to aid in killing oneself has ever been asserted and upheld by a court of final jurisdiction." *Compassion in Dying v. Washington* (1995). The Ninth Circuit reheard the case en banc, reversed the panel's decision, and affirmed the District Court. *Compassion in Dying v. Washington* (1996). Like the District Court, the en banc Court of Appeals emphasized our *Casey* and *Cruzan* decisions. The court also discussed what is described as "historical" and "current societal attitudes" toward suicide and assisted suicide, and concluded that "the Constitution encompasses a due process liberty interest in controlling the time and manner of one's death—that there is, in short, a constitutionally-recognized 'right to die.'" After "[w]eighing and then balancing" this interest against Washington's various interests, the court held that the State's assisted-suicide ban was unconstitutional "as applied to terminally ill competent adults who wish to hasten their deaths with medication prescribed by their physicians." The court did not reach the District Court's equal-protection holding. We granted certiorari and now reverse.

I

We begin, as we do in all due-process cases, by examining our Nation's history, legal traditions, and practices. In almost every State—indeed, in almost every western democracy—it is a crime to assist a suicide. The States' assisted-suicide bans are not innovations. Rather, they are longstanding expressions of the States' commitment to the protection and preservation of all human life. Indeed, opposition to and condemnation of suicide—and, therefore, of assisting suicide—are consistent and enduring themes of our philosophical, legal, and cultural heritages.

More specifically, for over 700 years, the Anglo-American common-law tradition has punished or otherwise disapproved of both suicide and assisting suicide. . . .

Over time, however, the American colonies abolished these harsh common-law penalties. . . . [But] the movement away from the common law's harsh sanctions did not represent an acceptance of suicide; rather, as Chief Justice Swift observed this change reflected the growing consensus that it was unfair to punish the suicide's family for his wrongdoing. . . .

That suicide remained a grievous, though nonfelonious, wrong is confirmed by the fact that colonial and early state legislatures and courts did not retreat from prohibiting assisting suicide. . . . And the prohibitions against assisting suicide never contained exceptions for those who were near death. . . .

The earliest American statute explicitly to outlaw assisting suicide was enacted in New York in 1828, and many of the new States and Territories followed New York's example. Between 1857 and 1865, a New York commission led by Dudley Field drafted a criminal code that prohibited "aiding" a suicide and, specifically, "furnish[ing] another person with any deadly weapon or poisonous drug, knowing that such person intends to use such weapon or drug in taking his own life." By the time the Fourteenth Amendment was ratified, it was a crime in most States to assist a suicide. . . .

Though deeply rooted, the States' assisted-suicide bans have in recent years been reexamined and, generally, reaffirmed. Because of advances in medicine and technology, Americans today are increasingly likely to die in institutions, from chronic illnesses. Public concern and democratic action are therefore sharply focused on how best to protect dignity and independence at the end of life, with the result that there have been many significant changes in state laws and in the attitudes these laws reflect. Many States, for example, now permit "living wills," surrogate health-care decisionmaking, and the withdrawal or refusal of life-sustaining medical treatment. At the same time, however, voters and legislators continue for the most part to reaffirm their States' prohibitions on assisting suicide. . . .

Attitudes toward suicide itself have changed since Bracton, but our laws have consistently condemned, and continue to prohibit, assisting suicide. Despite changes in medical technology and notwithstanding an increased emphasis on the importance of end-of-life decisionmaking, we have not retreated from this prohibition. Against this backdrop of history, tradition, and practice, we now turn to respondents' constitutional claim.

II

The Due Process Clause guarantees more than fair process, and the "liberty" it protects includes more than the absence of physical restraint. The Clause also provides heightened protection against government interference with certain fundamental rights and liberty interests. In a long line of cases, we have held that, in addition to the specific freedoms protected by the Bill of Rights, the "liberty" specially protected by the Due Process Clause includes the rights to marry, to have children, to direct the education and upbringing of one's children, to marital privacy, to use contraception, to bodily integrity, and to abortion. We have also assumed, and strongly suggested, that the Due Process Clause protects the traditional right to refuse unwanted lifesaving medical treatment.

But we "ha[ve] always been reluctant to expand the concept of substantive due process because guideposts for responsible decisionmaking in this unchartered area are scarce and open-ended." By extending constitutional protection to an asserted right or liberty interest, we, to a great extent, place the matter outside the arena of public debate and legislative action. We must therefore "exercise the utmost care whenever we are asked to break new ground in this field," lest the liberty protected by the Due Process Clause be subtly transformed into the policy preferences of the members of this Court.

Our established method of substantive-due-process analysis has two primary features: First, we have regularly observed that the Due Process Clause specially protects those fundamental rights and liberties which are, objectively, "deeply rooted in this Nation's history and tradition" and "implicit in the concept of ordered liberty," such that "neither, liberty nor justice would exist if they were sacrificed." Second, we have required in substantive-due-process cases a "careful description" of the asserted fundamental liberty interest. Our Nation's history, legal traditions, and practices thus provide the crucial "guideposts for responsible decision-making" that direct and restrain our exposition of the Due Process Clause. As we stated recently . . . the Fourteenth Amendment "forbids the government to infringe . . . 'fundamental' liberty interests *at all*, no matter what process is provided, unless the infringement is narrowly tailored to serve a compelling state interest." . . .

Turning to the claim at issue here, the Court of Appeals stated that "[p]roperly analyzed, the first issue to be resolved is whether there is a liberty interest in determining the time and manner of one's death," or, in other words, "[i]s there a right to die?" Similarly, respondents assert a "liberty to choose how to die" and a right to "control of one's final days," and describe the asserted liberty as "the right to choose a humane, dignified death" and "the liberty to shape death." As noted above, we have a tradition of carefully formulating the interest at stake in substantive-due-process cases. For example, although *Cruzan* is often described as a "right to die" case, we were, in fact, more precise: we assumed that the Constitution granted competent persons a "constitutionally protected right to refuse lifesaving hydration and nutrition." The Washington statute at issue in this case prohibits "aid[ing] another person to attempt

suicide," Wash. Rev. Code §9A.36.060 . . . (1) (1994), and, thus, the question before us is whether the "liberty" specially protected by the Due Process Clause includes a right to commit suicide which itself includes a right to assistance in doing so.

We now inquire whether this asserted right has any place in our Nation's traditions. Here, as discussed above, we are confronted with a consistent and almost universal tradition that has long rejected the asserted right, and continues explicitly to reject it today, even for terminally ill, mentally competent adults. To hold for respondents, we would have to reverse centuries of legal doctrine and practice, and strike down the considered policy choice of almost every State.

Respondents contend, however, that the liberty interest they assert is consistent with this Court's substantive-due-process line of cases, if not with this Nation's history and practice. Pointing to *Casey* and *Cruzan*, respondents read our jurisprudence in this area as reflecting a general tradition of "self-sovereignty" and as teaching that the "liberty" protected by the Due Process Clause includes "basic and intimate exercises of personal autonomy." According to respondents, our liberty jurisprudence, and the broad, individualistic principles it reflects, protects the "liberty of competent, terminally ill adults to make end-of-life decisions free of undue government interference." The question presented in this case, however, is whether the protections of the Due Process Clause include a right to commit suicide with another's assistance. With this "careful description" of respondents' claim in mind, we turn to *Casey* and *Cruzan*.

In *Cruzan*, we considered whether Nancy Beth Cruzan, who had been severely injured in an automobile accident and was in a persistive vegetative state, "ha[d] a right under the United States Constitution which would require the hospital to withdraw life-sustaining treatment" at her parents' request. We began with the observation that "[a]t common law, even the touching of one person by another without consent and without legal justification was a battery." We then discussed the related rule that "informed consent is generally required for medical treatment." After reviewing a long line of relevant state cases, we concluded that "the common-law doctrine of informed consent is viewed as generally encompassing the right of a competent individual to refuse medical treatment." Next, we reviewed our own cases on the subject, and stated that "[t]he principle that a competent person base constitutionally protected liberty interest in refusing unwanted medical treatment may be inferred from our prior decisions." Therefore, "for purposes, of [that] case, we assume[d] that the United States Constitution would grant a competent person a constitutionally protected right to refuse lifesaving hydration and nutrition." We concluded that, notwithstanding this right, the Constitution permitted Missouri to require clear and convincing evidence of an incompetent patient's wishes concerning the withdrawal of life-sustaining treatment.

Respondents contend that in *Cruzan* we "acknowledged that competent, dying persons have the right to direct the removal of life-sustaining medical treatment and thus hasten death," and that "the constitutional principle behind recognizing the patient's liberty to direct the withdrawal of artificial life support applies at least as strongly to the choice to hasten impending death by consuming lethal medication." Similarly, the Court of Appeals concluded that "*Cruzan*, by recognizing a liberty interest that includes the refusal of artificial provision of life-sustaining food and water, necessarily recognize[d] a liberty interest in hastening one's own death."

The right assumed in *Cruzan*, however, was not simply deduced from abstract concepts of personal autonomy. Given the common-law rule that forced medication was a battery, and the long legal tradition protecting the decision to refuse unwanted medical treatment, our assumption was entirely consistent with this Nation's history and constitutional traditions. The decision to commit suicide with the assistance of another may be just as personal and profound as the decision to refuse unwanted medical treatment, but it has never enjoyed similar legal protection. Indeed, the two acts are widely and reasonably regarded as quite distinct. See *Quill v. Vacco* (1997). In *Cruzan* itself, we recognized that most States outlawed assisted suicide—and even more do today—and we certainly gave no intimation that the right to refuse unwanted medical treatment could be

somehow transmuted into a right to assistance in committing suicide.

Respondents also rely on *Casey*. There, the Court's opinion concluded that "the essential holding of *Roe v. Wade* should be retained and once again reaffirmed." We held, first, that a woman has a right, before her fetus is viable, to an abortion "without undue interference from the State"; second, that States may restrict post-viability abortions, so long as exceptions are made to protect a woman's life and health; and third, that the State has legitimate interests throughout a pregnancy in protecting the health of the woman and the life of the unborn child. In reaching this conclusion, the opinion discussed in some detail this Court's substantive-due-process tradition of interpreting the Due Process Clause to protect certain fundamental rights and "personal decisions relating to marriage, procreation, contraception, family relationships, child rearing, and education," and noted that many of those rights and liberties "involv[e] the most intimate and personal choices a person may make in a lifetime."

The Court of Appeals, like the District Court, found *Casey* "'highly instructive'" and "'almost prescriptive'" for determining "'what liberty interest may inhere in a terminally ill person's choice to commit suicide'":

> Like the decision of whether or not to have an abortion, the decision how and when to die is one of "the most intimate and personal choices a person may make in a lifetime," a choice "central to personal dignity and autonomy."

. . . That many of the rights and liberties protected by the Due Process Clause sound in personal autonomy does not warrant the sweeping conclusion that any and all important, intimate, and personal decisions are so protected, and *Casey* did not suggest otherwise.

The history of the law's treatment of assisted suicide in this country has been and continues to be one of the rejection of nearly all efforts to permit it. That being the case, our decisions lead us to conclude that the asserted "right" to assistance in committing suicide is not a fundamental liberty interest protected by the Due Process Clause. The Constitution also requires, however, that Washington's assisted-suicide ban be rationally related to legitimate government interests. This requirement is unquestionably met here. As the court below recognized, Washington's assisted-suicide ban implicates a number of state interests.

First, Washington has an "unqualified interest in the preservation of human life." The State's prohibition on assisted suicide, like all homicide laws, both reflects and advances its commitment to this interest. This interest is symbolic and aspirational as well as practical:

> While suicide is no longer prohibited or penalized, the ban against assisted suicide and euthanasia shores up the notion of limits in human relationships. It reflects the gravity with which we view the decision to take one's own life or the life of another, and our reluctance to encourage or promote these decisions. New York State Task Force on Life and the Law, When Death is Sought: Assisted Suicide and Euthanasia in the Medical Context 131–132 (May 1994) (hereinafter New York Task Force).

Respondents admit that "[t]he State has a real interest in preserving the lives of those who can still contribute to society and enjoy life." The Court of Appeals also recognized Washington's interest in protecting life, but held that the "weight" of this interest depends on the "medical condition and the wishes of the person whose life is at stake." Washington, however, has rejected this sliding-scale approach and, through its assisted-suicide ban, insists that all persons' lives, from beginning to end, regardless of physical or mental condition, are under the full protection of the law. As we have previously affirmed, the States "may properly decline to make judgments about the 'quality' of life that a particular individual may enjoy." This remains true, as *Cruzan* makes clear, even for those who are near death.

Relatedly, all admit that suicide is a serious public-health problem, especially among persons in otherwise vulnerable groups. The State has an interest in preventing suicide, and in studying, identifying, and treating its causes.

Those who attempt suicide—terminally ill or not—often suffer from depression or other mental disorders. See New York Task Force 13–22, 126–128 (more than 95% of those who commit suicide had a major psychiatric illness at the time of death;

among the terminally ill, uncontrolled pain is a "risk factor" because it contributes to depression). Research indicates . . . that many people who request physician-assisted suicide withdraw that request if their depression and pain are treated. The New York Task Force, however, expressed its concern that, because depression is difficult to diagnose, physicians and medical professionals often fail to respond adequately to seriously ill patients' needs. Thus, legal physician-assisted suicide could make it more difficult for the State to protect depressed or mentally ill persons, or those who are suffering from untreated pain, from suicidal impulses.

The State also has an interest in protecting the integrity and ethics of the medical profession. In contrast to the Court of Appeals' conclusion that "the integrity of the medical profession would [not] be threatened in any way by [physician-assisted suicide]," the American Medical Association, like many other medical and physicians' groups, has concluded that "[p]hysician-assisted suicide is fundamentally incompatible with the physician's role as healer." American Medical Association, Code of Ethics §2.211(1994). And physician-assisted suicide could, it is argued, undermine the trust that is essential to the doctor-patient relationship by blurring the time-honored line between healing and harming.

Next, the State has an interest in protecting vulnerable groups—including the poor, the elderly, and disabled persons—from abuse, neglect, and mistakes. The Court of Appeals dismissed the State's concern that disadvantaged persons might be pressured into physician-assisted suicide as "ludicrous on its face." We have recognized, however, the real risk of subtle coercion and undue influence in end-of-life situations. Similarly, the New York Task Force warned that "[l]egalizing physician-assisted suicide would pose profound risks to many individuals who are ill and vulnerable. . . . The risk of harm is greatest for the many individuals in our society whose autonomy and well-being are already compromised by poverty, lack of access to good medical care, advanced age, or membership in a stigmatized social group." New York Task Force 120. If physician-assisted suicide were permitted, many might resort to it to spare their families the substantial financial burden of end-of-life health-care costs.

The State's interest here goes beyond protecting the vulnerable from coercion; it extends to protecting disabled and terminally ill people from prejudice, negative and inaccurate stereotypes, and "societal indifference." The State's assisted-suicide ban reflects and reinforces its policy that the lives of terminally ill, disabled, and elderly people must be no less valued than the lives of the young and healthy, and that a seriously disabled person's suicidal impulses should be interpreted and treated the same way as anyone else's.

Finally, the State may fear that permitting assisted suicide will start it down the path to voluntary and perhaps even involuntary euthanasia. The Court of Appeals struck down Washington's assisted-suicide ban only "as applied to competent, terminally ill adults who wish to hasten their deaths by obtaining medication prescribed by their doctors." Washington insists, however, that the impact of the court's decision will not and cannot be so limited. If suicide is protected as a matter of constitutional right, it is argued, "every man and woman in the United States must enjoy it." The Court of Appeals' decision, and its expansive reasoning, provide ample support for the State's concerns. The court noted, for example, that the "decision of a duly appointed surrogate decision maker is for all legal purposes the decision of the patient himself," that "in some instances, the patient may be unable to self-administer the drugs and . . . administration by the physician . . . may be the only way the patient may be able to receive them," and that not only physicians, but also family members and loved ones, will inevitably participate in assisting suicide. Thus, it turns out that what is couched as a limited right to "physician-assisted suicide" is likely, in effect, a much broader license, which could prove extremely difficult to police and contain. Washington's ban on assisting suicide prevents such erosion. . . .

We need not weigh exactly the relative strengths of these various interests. They are unquestionably important and legitimate, and Washington's ban on assisted suicide is at least reasonably related to their promotion and protection. We therefore hold that Wash. Rev. Code §9A.36.060(1) (1994) does not violate the Fourteenth Amendment, either on its face or "as applied to competent, terminally ill adults who wish to hasten their deaths by obtaining medication prescribed by their doctors."

Throughout the Nation, Americans are engaged in an earnest and profound debate about the morality, legality, and practicality of physician-assisted suicide. Our holding permits this debate to continue, as it should in a democratic society. The decision of the en banc Court of Appeals is reversed, and the case is remanded for further proceedings consistent with this opinion.

4

Justice and Health Care

CHAPTER II

Dividing Up Health Care Resources

In this land of plenty, many are rich; many are poor. Many are healthy; many are not. Many who are afflicted by disease, disability, or injury can get the health care they need; many cannot—and they suffer and die for its lack. For any sensitive observer (and any decent society), these cold inequalities are surely cause for concern, dismay, even alarm. They also raise ethical questions of the most basic kind. To what are the less fortunate entitled, and what is society obligated to give? Are the needy due only the health care they can afford to buy for themselves, even if they can afford nothing? Or is society obligated to provide more? Is society obliged to provide everyone with access to health care regardless of ability to pay? Or is the claim on society's resources even stronger: Do people have a *right* to health care? If so, to what exactly are they entitled? To a guarantee of a state of well-being equal to that of everyone else? To an equal share of health care resources? To the best health care available? Or to something more modest—a decent minimum amount of health care? And what, exactly, is a decent minimum?

These are moral concerns on a larger scale than most of those we have grappled with in previous chapters. Here we ask not what is right or good in the person-to-person dramas of moral conflict; rather, we ask what is good or right in the policies and actions of society or government. The central issue is: Who should get health care, who should provide it, and who should pay for it? In other words, *what is just*? In the painful, complicated task of dividing up society's health care resources (including medical treatment, disease prevention, emergency care, and public health measures), what does justice demand?

Whatever answer is devised, it must take into account some hard realities. No system can provide maximum health care for everyone; there are limits—sometimes severe—to what any system can provide. Costs restrict how much health care can be delivered and how much can be obtained, and they can rise rapidly enough to destroy the best laid plans for fair access. Moreover, a society's finite resources must be allocated to satisfy many needs besides health care—education, defense, transportation, law enforcement, and others. Some kinds of health care can increase the well-being of more people to a greater degree than others, so considerations of efficiency will have to shape the allocation of resources. And somehow these quantitative factors must be reconciled with freedom of choice. In a free society, this value is paramount and cannot be entirely discarded for the sake of a more rational distribution of health care.

Most careful thinkers on the subject believe that a just apportioning of health care is possible. But how?

HEALTH CARE IN TROUBLE

The question is both grave and urgent because the current system for allocating health care is widely believed to be not only unjust but also ineffective and unsustainable. Many claim that, by several measures, it has failed or is failing.

Regardless of their political views, most tend to think that in this free and prosperous nation, all citizens should somehow have access to health care. But many people go without. Health care is so expensive that few can afford it unless they have some type of health insurance, which is itself expensive—so expensive in fact that the high cost is the main reason for lack of coverage. In 2010, almost 49 million people under the age of 65 were uninsured, and almost 8 million of those were children. Nearly a third of the under-65 population—almost 90 million people—had no health insurance for at least part of 2006 or 2007.[1] From 2010 to 2014, as the economy improved and the main provisions of the Affordable Care Act (the ACA, or "Obamacare") took effect, the number of uninsured among people under 65 dropped to 32 million. But the reasons for lack of coverage remain the same: high cost of insurance, the absence of coverage acquired through employment, and ineligibility for public coverage.[2]

The consequences of going without health coverage are just what you might expect. The uninsured are less likely than the insured to get needed medical treatment, prescription drugs, preventive tests (pap smears and prostate exams, for example), and follow-up care when they do manage to see a doctor. Not surprisingly, researchers have estimated that the risk of death is 25 percent higher for the uninsured than the insured, resulting in about 18,000 more deaths in 2000 among those aged 25 to 64.[3]

Traditionally most people under age 65 got health coverage as a benefit of employment, but a smaller percentage of them are now obtaining insurance this way—69 percent in 2000 down to 56 percent in 2011. Fewer employers are offering this benefit, and even when they do, many employees are either not eligible for it or cannot afford to pay their portion of the insurance premium. Over 75 percent of the uninsured are members of families with full-time workers.[4]

People who are age 65 and older and some adults under 65 with permanent disabilities are covered by the public health insurance program known as Medicare. It collects payroll taxes from workers during their employment years and provides coverage when they turn 65, paying many health care expenses including physician and hospital services and prescription drugs. Medicaid, another publicly supported program, covers some under-65 low-income

people including children and the disabled. But coverage varies from state to state and, because of eligibility rules, does not extend to millions of people below the federal poverty level.

Critics of the U.S. health care system point to discrepancies between the huge expenditures for health care and surprisingly low grades on standard measures of national health. According to 2007 data, the country's per capita spending on health care was $6,102—more than twice as much as the average amount spent by the richest nations in the world. (The list of the richest comprises 30 democracies in the Organization for Economic Cooperation and Development [OECD], including France, Germany, Switzerland, Denmark, Canada, the United Kingdom, Norway, and Japan.) The country coming closest to that level of spending was Luxembourg at $5,352; Canada spent $3,326; the United Kingdom, $2,724; and Japan, $2,358. Yet in the United States, life expectancy at birth (77.8 years) was lower than the average for the OECD countries (78.6 years) and lower than that of other economically advanced nations such as Canada, France, Japan, the United Kingdom, Switzerland, Iceland, Australia, and Spain. The infant mortality rate in the United States was also higher than the OECD average—6.8 deaths per 1000 live births compared to 5.4. In fact, it was higher than the rate of any of the other developed countries.[5]

Though the United States spends more on health care than any other country, the quality of the care is not obviously better overall than that of other countries. The U.S. system outshines them in some ways, but lags behind in others. For example, it excels in the development and use of medical technologies and has lower wait times for non-emergency surgeries. But it also has higher death rates from medical errors and fewer physicians per capita, and Americans have more trouble getting treated on nights and weekends and obtaining same-day appointments with doctors.[6] Research shows that for almost half of people who do receive care, that care is inadequate—that is, it does not meet established standards of recommended care.[7]

IN DEPTH
UNEQUAL HEALTH CARE FOR MINORITIES

Research has established that many minorities have much poorer health and higher mortality than the rest of the population.

At the same time, they are also likely to receive lower-quality health care. According to the Institute of Medicine, "Racial and ethnic minorities tend to receive lower-quality health care than whites do, even when insurance status, income, age, and severity of conditions are comparable." The CDC's Office of Minority Health and Health Disparities has detailed many of the differences between the health of minorities and that of others:

> Current information about the biologic and genetic characteristics of minority populations does not explain the health disparities experienced by these groups compared with the white, non-Hispanic population in the United States....

- Even though the nation's infant mortality rate is down, the infant death rate among African Americans is still more than double that of whites. Heart disease death rates are more than 40 percent higher for African Americans than for whites. The death rate for all cancers is 30 percent higher for African Americans than for whites; for prostate cancer, it is more than double that for whites. African-American women have a higher death rate from breast cancer despite having a mammography screening rate that is nearly the same as the rate for white women. The death rate from HIV/AIDS for African Americans is more than seven times that for whites; the rate of homicide is six times that for whites.

- Hispanics living in the United States are almost twice as likely to die from diabetes as are non-Hispanic whites. Although constituting only 11 percent of the total population in 1996, Hispanics accounted for 20 percent of the new cases of tuberculosis. Hispanics also have higher rates of high blood pressure and obesity than non-Hispanic whites. There are differences among Hispanic populations as well. For example, whereas the rate of low birth weight infants is lower for the total Hispanic population compared with that of whites, Puerto Ricans have a low birth weight rate that is 50 percent higher than the rate for whites.

- American Indians and Alaska Natives have an infant death rate almost double that for whites. The rate of diabetes for this population group is more than twice that for whites. The Pima of Arizona have one of the highest rates of diabetes in the world. American Indians and Alaska Natives also have disproportionately high death rates from unintentional injuries and suicide.

- Asians and Pacific Islanders, on average, have indicators of being one of the healthiest population groups in the United States. However, there is great diversity within this population group, and health disparities for some specific segments are quite marked. Women of Vietnamese origin, for example, suffer from cervical cancer at nearly five times the rate for white women. New cases of hepatitis and tuberculosis also are higher in Asians and Pacific Islanders living in the United States than in whites.

From The National Academies, "Minorities More Likely to Receive Lower-Quality Health Care, Regardless of Income and Insurance Coverage," 20 March 2002, http://www8.nationalacademies.org/onpinews/newsitem.aspx?RecordID 10260 (14 June 2008); CDC, Office of Minority Health & Health Disparities, "About Minority Health," 6 June 2007, http://www.cdc.gov/omhd/amh/amh.htm (14 June 2008).

Fact File U.S. Health Care

- In 2014, 32 million Americans under age 65 had no health insurance; in 2013, the uninsured rate for this group was 16.7%.
- In 2014, 48% of uninsured adults said the main reason they were uninsured was because the cost was too high.
- Enrollment in ACA (Affordable Care Act) coverage corresponds with large declines in the uninsured rate. Between 2013 and 2014, the uninsured rate dropped significantly, from 16.2% in the last quarter of 2013 to 12.1% in the last quarter of 2014. Declines have continued into 2015, with preliminary data indicating an uninsured rate of 10.7% in the first quarter of 2015.
- Many people do not have access to coverage through a job, and some people, particularly poor adults in states that did not expand Medicaid under ACA, remain ineligible for public coverage.
- In 2014, over 80% of uninsured people were in a family with a worker.
- In 2010, there were almost 8 million uninsured children—over 10 percent of all children.
- According to data published in 2007, per capita spending on health care in the United States was $6,102; in Canada, $3,326; and in the United Kingdom, $2,724.
- Infant mortality in the United States was 6.8 deaths per 1,000 live births, higher than that of all other developed countries.
- Almost half of the health care that people receive in the United States does not meet established standards of recommended care.

From Kaiser Family Foundation, "Key Facts about the Uninsured Population," 5 October 2015, http://kff.org /uninsured/fact-sheet/key-facts-about-the-uninsured-population/ (3 November 2015); the Kaiser Commission on Medicaid and the Uninsured, "The Uninsured: A Primer," Kaiser Family Foundation, October 2010, http:// www.kff.org/uninsured/7451.cfm (21 March 2008); the National Coalition on Health Care, "Health Insurance Coverage," the National Coalition on Health Care, undated, 2008, http://www.nchc.org/facts/coverage.shtml (21 March 2008); Organization for Economic Cooperation and Development, OECD Health Data 2007, July 2007, http:// www.oecd.org (27 March 2008); E. A. McGlynn et al., "The Quality of Health Care Delivered in the United States," *New England Journal of Medicine*, vol. 348, no. 26 (2003), pp. 2635–45; S. Asch et al., "Who Is at Greatest Risk for Receiving Poor-Quality Health Care?" *New England Journal of Medicine*, vol. 354, no. 11 (2006), pp. 1147–56.

In the United States most health care is allocated through **managed care**, a system for providing care to a particular group of patients (members of the system) using regulatory restraints to control costs and increase efficiency. People who enroll in a managed care plan—such as a health maintenance organization (HMO) or a preferred provider organization (PPO)—get health care at discounted prices from the plan's network of providers (physicians, hospitals, etc.). Managed care plans try to control costs by influencing the kind and amount of care that providers offer and by restricting the choices that members have. Though cost control and efficiency are laudable goals, many critics worry that they are at odds with patient welfare. The concern is that for the sake of economical medicine, providers may cut corners, decide not to order necessary tests, pay less attention to patients' needs, or refuse to treat certain serious health problems. Some charge that managed care as it is currently practiced forces physicians to try to serve both the patient and organizational efficiency, an impossible task that weakens the patient's trust in the physician.

In 2010 this troubling picture of American health care began to change with President

Barack Obama's signing into law of the Patient Protection and Affordable Care Act (ACA). It was an attempt to provide health coverage to many more Americans and to contain the insidious rise of health care costs. Getting the law through Congress was a wrenching ordeal of high-stakes partisan brawling that seemed to arise largely from diverging answers to fundamental philosophical questions: What duties does the state have towards its citizens? How much should the state do to ensure the well-being of its people? What benefits do citizens have a right to expect from a government that's supposed to "promote the general welfare"?

Here's a rundown of the legislation's major provisions summarized by a nonpartisan foundation:

- Most individuals will be required to have health insurance beginning in 2014.
- Individuals who do not have access to affordable employer coverage will be able to purchase coverage through a health insurance exchange with premium and cost-sharing credits available to some people to make coverage more affordable. Small businesses will be able to purchase coverage through a separate exchange.
- Employers will be required to pay penalties for employees who receive tax credits for health insurance through the exchange, with exceptions for small employers.
- New regulations will be imposed on all health plans that will prevent health insurers from denying coverage to people for any reason, including health status, and from charging higher premiums based on health status and gender.
- Medicaid will be expanded to 133 percent of the federal poverty level ($14,404 for an individual and $29,327 for a family of four in 2009) for all individuals under age 65.

The Congressional Budget Office estimates that the legislation will reduce the number of uninsured by 32 million in 2019 at a net cost of $938 billion over ten years, while reducing the deficit by $124 billion during this time period.[8]

The provisions of the law are to be implemented over the next few years. In the meantime it has been repeatedly challenged in the federal courts, and the partisan divide over it remains as wide as ever.

In 2012, in the case of *National Federation of Independent Business v. Sebelius*, the Supreme Court held that the ACA was constitutional but that states could opt out of the law's requirement to expand Medicaid. In 2014 the Court ruled that under the law, employers with religious objections are not required to cover contraceptives. In 2015, the Court upheld the legality of the ACA's mandate to provide health insurance subsidies to all qualifying Americans.

THEORIES OF JUSTICE

All these difficulties bring us around again to the question of what is just. Justice in the most general sense refers to people getting what is fair or what is their due (see Chapter 1). At the heart of every plausible notion of justice is the principle that equals should be treated equally—that people should be treated the same unless there is a morally relevant reason for treating them differently. When we ask what justice demands in society's allocation of health care, we are dealing with matters of **distributive justice**—justice regarding the fair distribution of society's advantages and disadvantages, or benefits and burdens, including income, property, employment, rights, taxes, and public service.

Debates about ethical allocations of health care resources rely heavily on general theories of justice. To justify a particular scheme of allocation, philosophers, politicians, and others may appeal to a theory of justice, and those who criticize the scheme may do so by arguing against that underlying theory of justice or by offering an alternative theory they believe to be superior. Three types of theories have had—and continue to have—an enormous impact on the discussions: libertarian, utilitarian, and egalitarian.

According to **libertarian theories of justice**, the benefits and burdens of society should be

IN DEPTH
PUBLIC OPINION: OBTAINING ADEQUATE HEALTH CARE

Overall, how would you rate the quality of health care you receive—as excellent, good, only fair, or poor?

Excellent	Good	Only Fair	Poor
35%	44%	15%	5%

Gallup Poll, November 6–9, 2014; adults nationwide.

Most urgent U.S. health problem:

Access	Costs	Government Involvement	Obesity	Cancer
24%	19%	10%	14%	12%

Gallup Poll, November 6–9, 2014; adults nationwide.

Do you think it is the responsibility of the federal government to make sure all Americans have health coverage, or is that not the responsibility of the federal government?

Is	Is Not
45%	52%

Gallup Poll, November 6–9, 2014; adults nationwide.

Do you approve or disapprove of the health care law called the Affordable Care Act?

Approve	Disapprove
47%	44%

CBS News/*New York Times* Poll, June 10–14, 2015, adults nationwide.

distributed through the fair workings of a free market and the exercise of liberty rights of noninterference. The role of government is to protect the rights of individuals to freely pursue their own interests in the economic marketplace without violations of their liberty through coercion, manipulation, or fraud. Government may use coercion, but only to preserve liberty. Beyond these protections, the government has no obligation to adjust the distribution of benefits and burdens among people; the distribution is the responsibility of free and autonomous individuals. People may have equal rights or equal worth, but that does not entitle them to an equal distribution of society's benefits. The government acts unjustly if it coercively redistributes those benefits.

On this view, no one has a right to health care, and a government program using tax dollars to provide universal health care or even health care only for low-income families would be unjust. Such a program would be a coercive violation of people's right to use their resources as they see

fit. The libertarian would accept a system of health care only if it is freely endorsed and financed by those who participate in it. So health insurance acquired through free choice by a group of private citizens to meet their own health care needs is acceptable. State-supported health insurance financed by taxes is not. But none of this would rule out voluntary charity by well-off citizens to provide health care for the poor.

In **utilitarian theories of justice**, a just distribution of benefits and burdens is one that maximizes the net good (utility) for society. Some allocations (or principles of allocation) of society's resources are more beneficial overall than others, and these are what utilitarian justice demands. A utilitarian may grant some principles of allocation the status of rights—rules that can be enforced by society and that can override considerations of utility in specific situations. But the ultimate justification of the rules is utilitarian (actually, rule-utilitarian): Consistently following the rules may maximize utility generally, although rule adherence in some instances may not produce a net good.

On a utilitarian view, a just allocation of health care can take several forms depending on the facts about society's resources and needs and the likely effects of various allocation policies and programs. Thus, depending on calculations of net benefits, a utilitarian might endorse a system of universal health care insurance, or a qualified right to health care, or a two-tiered plan (like the U.S. arrangement) in which government-supported health insurance is combined with the option of privately purchased health coverage for those who can afford it.

Egalitarian theories of justice affirm that important benefits and burdens of society should be distributed equally. To achieve greater equality, the egalitarian (unlike the libertarian) would not be averse to mandating changes to the distribution of society's goods or to interfering in the workings of a free market. And the egalitarian (unlike the utilitarian) would not allow utility to be the ultimate overriding consideration in a system of distribution. From egalitarian premises, theorists have derived several schemes for allocating health care, including systems that give equal access to all legitimate forms of health care, that offer a guaranteed minimal level of health care for everyone, or that provide care only to those most in need.

Besides these familiar theories of justice, there is another entirely different perspective on justice and health care: the *human rights approach*. The idea is that we can best achieve just distributions of health and health care by ensuring that human rights in general are respected. Respecting human rights (which encompass fair treatment, freedom from coercion, nondiscrimination, protection from abuse, equality, and other entitlements) contributes to well-being and health (including access to health care), and these positive contributions to health depend on respect for human rights. According to proponents of this view,

> Health and human rights are not distinct but intertwined. Viewed as a universal aspiration,

the notion of health as the attainment of physical, mental, and social well-being implies its dependency on and contribution to the realization of human rights. From the same perspective, the enjoyment by everyone of the highest attainable standard of physical and mental health is in itself a recognized human right. From a global normative perspective, health and human rights are closely intertwined in many international treaties and declarations supported by mechanisms of monitoring and accountability (even as their effectiveness can be questioned) that draw from both fields.[9]

A RIGHT TO HEALTH CARE

No matter what theory of justice people accept, they are likely to agree that it would be good for everyone to have adequate health care, or that beneficence may justify society's providing health care to the neediest, or that making particular kinds of health care available to certain groups may produce a net benefit for society. But some assert a much stronger claim: People have a moral *right* to health care. A right is an entitlement, a bona fide claim, to something. A person's rights impose duties on others—either (1) duties not to interfere with that person's obtaining something or (2) duties to help that person in her efforts to get something. Rights entailing the former obligations are called *negative rights*; those entailing the latter are called *positive rights*. Those who insist that an individual has a right to health care are referring to a positive right and are claiming that society has an obligation to provide that benefit in some way.

Libertarians are likely to deny that there is a right to health care, for generally they accept negative rights and disallow positive rights. Utilitarians can admit a right to health care, though it would be what some have called a *derivative right,* a rule ultimately justified by assessments of utility. Others, including egalitarians, can accommodate a right to health care and interpret it in the strong sense of being an entitlement that ultimately outweighs calculations of maximized utility.

But what reasons are there for believing that there is such a strong right to health care? Norman Daniels believes that such a right can be derived from one of the principles of justice articulated by John Rawls, specifically the right to "fair equality of opportunity."[10] Rawls maintains that everyone is entitled to an equal chance to obtain the basic goods of society, though there is no guarantee of an equal share of them (see the discussion of Rawls' theory in Chapter 2). A just society would ensure equal opportunities to its citizens. Daniels argues that disease and disability diminish people's "normal species functioning" and thus restrict the range of opportunities open to them. But "health care in all its forms, whether public health or medical, preventive or acute or chronic, aims to keep people functioning as close to normally as possible....Health care thus preserves for us the range of opportunities we would have, were we not ill or disabled, given our talents and skills."[11] Since people are entitled to fair equality of opportunity, and adequate health care can protect or restore their normal range of opportunities, they have a positive right to adequate health care.

A pivotal question that confronts every serious advocate of a moral right to health care is what health care resources it includes. Some have thought the right encompasses universal equal access to all available health care resources. But this arrangement is not technically or economically feasible; a right to health care, it seems, must have limits. Recognizing this, many have argued for a weaker right to a "decent minimum" level of health care. On this view, everyone would have access to a minimal, basic array of health care resources. This tier of care would be universally available, publicly supported, and guaranteed for all in need. A second tier of additional health care services (elective or nonessential therapies, for example) would be available in the free marketplace for those who can afford them.

Allen Buchanan rejects the idea of a right to a decent minimum of care, but he understands its attractions:

> First, the notion that people have a right to a decent minimum or adequate level, rather than to *all* health care that produces any net benefit, clearly acknowledges that, because not all health care is of equal importance, allocational priorities must be set within health care and that resources must also be allocated to goods other than health care. Second, this [decent minimum] position is also consonant with the intuitively plausible conviction that our obligations to the less fortunate, although fundamental enough to be expressed in the language of rights, are nonetheless *not unlimited*. Third, the decent minimum is a floor beneath which no one should be allowed to fall, not a ceiling above which the better-off are prohibited from purchasing services if they wish.[12]

But the implications of the decent-minimum standard have been extremely difficult to specify in a plausible way. What is, after all, a *decent minimum* of health care? We may assume it includes such things as immunizations, annual physical exams, and "routine" medical care. Should it also include heart transplants, treatments for rare or orphan diseases, cosmetic surgery, expensive but marginally effective care for very elderly or dying patients, and costly lifelong therapies for mentally impaired persons who will never reach "normal" functioning?

Buchanan believes that although there is no right to a decent minimum of health care, there are good reasons for supposing that society should nevertheless provide the kind and amount of health care that a decent-minimum right would demand. That is, there is no individual right, but there may be a societal duty. Among these reasons are arguments that people have special rights (as opposed to universal rights) to health care—rights of restitution to certain groups for past wrongs, rights of compensation for "those who have suffered unjust harm or who have been unjustly

IN DEPTH
PUBLIC HEALTH
AND BIOETHICS

Public health is bioethics on a large scale. Most of the time bioethics concerns ethics as it applies to individuals and personal morality, but it also encompasses morality as it pertains to the health of whole populations. This is *public health*. It focuses on communities, from neighborhoods to countries to the world, working to prevent disease and disabilities, promoting health and well-being, tracking the incidence of illness, and intervening when the health of a community is imperiled.

Public health involves agencies of the government but also many professionals and nonprofessionals in the community. It can function locally, nationally, or globally. Public health programs provide vaccinations, promote healthful habits such as handwashing and not smoking, guide the treatment of wastewater, distribute condoms to prevent the spread of sexually transmitted diseases, help insure the safety of food and water, investigate pandemics and other disease outbreaks, provide early warning of emerging public health hazards, prevent epidemics after natural disasters, and much more.

Public health ethics, like any other area of applied ethics, deals with the application and reconciliation of moral norms. The same moral principles and concepts that inform the whole field of bioethics also do work in the subfield of public health. In public health, we still must strive to respect autonomy, avoid harming others, act with beneficence, maximize utility, behave justly, protect privacy and confidentiality, deal honestly with others, and keep promises. The proper balancing of these demands—a job that falls to both professionals and ordinary citizens—is often difficult and controversial. Implementing these ideas is a separate job that is frequently even more challenging.

Moral norms can conflict in public health ethics just as they do in personal ethics. Suppose public health officials quarantine or treat a man against his will because he has contracted a deadly communicable disease. Here respect for the man's autonomy clashes with the need to protect the public from harm. In other cases the need to protect the public might conflict with people's right to privacy or with fairness or with confidentiality. Suppose the state mandates that all adults must be vaccinated against a lethal, spreading infection. A key issue is whether the government is wrongfully infringing on the population's personal liberty. Disputes like these can (and do) happen in nearly every public health endeavor, and disagreement is frequently widespread.

exposed to health risks by the assignable actions of private individuals or corporations," and rights to health care for honorable service to society (for wounded soldiers, for instance). There are also prudential arguments, Buchanan says, such as that "the availability of certain basic forms of health care make for a more productive labor force or improve the fitness of the citizenry for national defense." Arguments for what he calls "enforced beneficence" can also be made out. To maximize the practical effect of our moral obligations of charity or beneficence regarding health care for those in need, "an enforced decent minimum principle is needed to achieve coordinated

joint effort."[13] Thus, for example, the government could levy taxes to provide health care to the poor—not in the name of egalitarian justice, but for the sake of beneficence.

THE ETHICS OF RATIONING

Rationing has been a dirty word in debates about health care, laden as it is with images of extreme measures of last resort for managing a dearth of resources. But in health care, rationing—in the broad sense of parceling out important limited goods—has always been with us and probably always will be. People's health care needs are virtually boundless, yet the supply of health care resources is ever limited. So we ration: Medicare and Medicaid allot health care to the elderly and the poor; HMOs limit medical procedures, tests, and access to doctors to control costs; hospitals restrict the use of intensive care units (ICUs), cardiac surgical teams, emergency departments, hospital beds, and expensive drugs; organ transplants are doled out to the few because of shortages of usable organs; and the health care system as a whole rations a great deal of care by people's ability to pay for it.

Thus the tough choices of rationing fall hard upon us, and we are forced to ask: Who should get what share of limited health care goods and services? In countless troubling instances, the question reduces to this: Who should live and who must die? In nearly the same breath we have to ask: On what ethical grounds do we make these choices? The fundamental issue of the proper allocation of insufficient resources troubles on several levels at once. It arises both on the scale of the total health care system (concerning what portion of society's resources should go to health care and how this allotment should be used—so-called *macroallocation*) and on the scale of individual patients and providers (regarding who should receive specific resources—known as *microallocation*).

Let's consider just a few of the smaller scale (microallocation) questions raised by one of our scarcest life-saving resources—organ transplants. Transplant operations are incredibly expensive, organs are in very short supply, and transplants are desperately needed by far more people than can be accommodated. The waiting list for transplants is long, and thousands die every year for their lack. Screening committees at transplant centers decide whether someone should be placed on the waiting list and what ranking they should receive. They use various criteria to make these decisions, some explicit, some informal or unspoken, some plausible (such as the patient's need and likelihood of benefit), and some controversial (such as ability to pay, social worthiness, and health habits).

But what criteria *should* be used? What rationing policy for transplants is morally justified? Many proposed criteria are utilitarian, concerned with maximizing benefits to the patient and society. Many are egalitarian, focusing on justice and the moral equality of persons. Some philosophers propose rationing policies that emphasize one or the other, while some try systematically to accommodate both.[13] No policy is completely satisfactory, but some seem to capture our moral intuitions better than others.

One utilitarian approach to rationing care to patients is to measure objectively the benefits that a treatment is likely to give each patient, then selectively treat particular patients or conditions to maximize total benefits. The objective measure of benefits that has often been used in such calculations is known as QALY, or quality-adjusted life year. One QALY is equivalent to one year of life in good health, and a year of life in poor health is equal to less than 1 QALY. The lower the quality of life for a person in poor health, the lower the QALY value. A transplant operation that allows a patient to live seven years without disability or suffering is worth 7 QALYs; if it results in the patient's living seven years burdened by severe pain, it is worth less than 7 QALYs. Thus QALYs gauge a treatment's impact by, plausibly, trying to take into account both the length of life and its quality. Intuitively this seems right because both quality of life and length of life matter to people. Most would probably rather enjoy a few years of good health than suffer through many years of terrible illness or disability. Suppose, then, that three people are awaiting heart transplants, without which they will die within six months, and only two transplants are possible. Two of the potential recipients are young, so a transplant for either one of them would yield 10 QALYs. The third person is much older; a transplant for her would yield only 5 QALYs. So a transplant selection committee using the QALY standard alone would likely allocate the available transplants to the two younger patients, maximizing total benefits.

The utilitarian purpose behind using QALYs is to do the most good with the resources available. But critics have charged that relying on QALYs to allocate or ration health care can lead to morally unacceptable decisions. John Harris argues, for example, that QALYs discriminate against older people:

> Maximizing QALYs involves an implicit and comprehensive ageist bias. For saving the lives of younger people is, other things being equal, always likely to be productive of more QALYs than saving older people. Thus on the QALY arithmetic we always have a reason to prefer, for example, neonatal or paediatric care to all "later" branches of medicine. This is because any calculation of the life-years generated for a particular patient by a particular therapy, must be based on the life expectancy of that patient. The older a patient is when treated, the fewer the life-years that can be achieved by the therapy.[14]

QALYs, he says, are also unfair to the disabled:

> Suppose for example that if an accident victim were treated, he would survive, but with paraplegia. This might always cash out at fewer QALYs than a condition which with treatment would give a patient perfect remission for about five years after which the patient would die. Suppose that both candidates wanted to go on living as long as they could and so both wanted, equally fervently, to be given the treatment that would save their lives. Is it clear that the candidate with most QALYs on offer should always and inevitably be the one to have priority? To judge so would be to count the paraplegic's desire to live the life that was available to him as of less value than his rival's.[15]

Harris and others contend that a crucial failing of QALYs is that these objective measurements cannot accommodate the subjective nature of people's assessments of the value of their own lives. A paraplegic may value his life and think its quality extremely high despite his disability. A perfectly healthy person may think her life miserable despite a lack of physical ailments. The subjective valuation seems to be the important one; the objective measurement seems to be beside the point.

Policies for rationing transplants to a particular group of patients generally try to take into account the probability of transplant success or the urgency of the patients' needs. Both factors can be morally relevant. Regarding the former, because transplants are a scarce resource, fairness seems to demand that they be given to those who are likely to benefit from them—otherwise the resource will be wasted, and people will be deprived of a treatment that could have saved them. Regarding the latter, giving transplants to those who cannot survive for much longer without them fulfills a duty to preserve lives.

Nevertheless, some maintain that allocating resources in light of one of these considerations while disregarding the other is a mistake:

> For example, although heart-transplant surgeons sometimes list their patients as urgent priority candidates for an available heart because the patients will soon die if they do not receive a transplant, some of these patients are virtually certain to die even if they do receive the heart. High quality candidates are passed over in the process. A classification and queuing system that permits urgent need to determine priority exclusively is as unjust as it is inefficient.[16]

Neither probability of success nor urgent need seems to be as controversial as another kind of criterion: the *social value* of people's lives. Here the question is which potential recipients—if given the chance to live—are expected to contribute most to the good of society. To state the issue concretely: All things being equal, should the medical student get the transplant instead of the poet or prostitute? Nicholas Rescher thinks this question of social utility important and morally relevant:

> In "choosing to save" one life rather than another, "the society," through the mediation of the particular medical institution in question—which should certainly look upon itself as a

Christine deMeurers

The era of managed care has changed health care in the United States radically—for the worse, many say. Whatever the case, it has surely set off a host of conflicts that were previously unimagined: clashes between patients and their insurance companies, between physicians and their cost-conscious managed care employers, and between the physicians' duty to put the patient's welfare first and the economic incentives to put it last. Out of this maelstrom many unsettling stories have come, including this one.

In 1992 Christine deMeurers—a 32-year-old wife, mother of two, and schoolteacher—found out that she had breast cancer. She fought back promptly and aggressively, enduring a radical mastectomy, radiation therapy, and chemotherapy. But in May 1993, a bone scan revealed that the cancer had spread and now rated the ominous label of Stage IV metastatic breast cancer. Every standard therapy available had been used against her disease with no apparent effect. She was running out of time.

Christine and her husband, Alan, were subscribers in an HMO, Health Net of Woodland Hills,

California. They got the insurance through their employer (they both were teachers at the same school) and had opted for the least expensive coverage.

After the standard treatments failed, the deMeurers thought they had no options left, but Christine's oncologist, Dr. Mahesh Gupta, was hopeful. He held out the possibility that she could benefit from a promising new treatment, a bone marrow transplant. Its effectiveness against Christine's type of cancer was unproven, but it had been used successfully on other kinds of malignancies. In violation of Health Net rules on referrals, Dr. Gupta referred Christine directly to an expert he knew, an oncologist at the Scripps Clinic in La Jolla.

According to the deMeurers, the Scripps doctor was reluctant to help them or even to provide them with information about the bone marrow transplant. So they flew to Denver, where Christine was examined by Dr. Roy B. Jones at the University of Colorado. He told them that the bone marrow procedure might be beneficial to Christine. But about the time that the deMeurers consulted with Dr. Jones, Health Net

---

trustee for the social interest—is clearly warranted in considering the likely pattern of future *services to be rendered* by the patient (adequate recovery assumed), considering his age, talent, training, and past record of performance. In its allocations of [exotic life-saving therapy], society "invests" a scarce resource in one person as against another and is thus entitled to look to the probable prospective "return" on its investment.[16]

Others reject this line altogether, arguing from an egalitarian or Kantian perspective that all persons have equal worth. Morally, the medical student is not worth more than the poet or prostitute, and vice versa. Education,

achievement, occupation, and the like are not morally relevant.

Nevertheless, while generally taking this view, some philosophers maintain that in very rare cases, social worth can outweigh egalitarian concerns. It seems reasonable that in a natural disaster involving mass casualties, injured physicians or nurses should be treated first if they can aid the other survivors. We can imagine analogous situations involving organ transplants, says Walter Glannon:

> Suppose that Nelson Mandela needed a liver transplant in 1992. This was the time when he was leading the transition from apartheid to democracy in South Africa. The transition turned out to be peaceful; but the political situation was potentially

resolved that the company would not pay for the transplant because it was disallowed under the investigational clause in Christine's contract.

Increasingly desperate, the deMeurers started trying to raise the thousands of dollars needed to pay for the procedure, and they hired a lawyer to appeal Health Net's ruling. They also got permission to see another oncologist. He too encouraged Christine to consider the bone marrow transplant and referred her to the UCLA Medical Center, where Dr. John Glaspy presented the operation as an option and agreed to perform it.

This encounter between the deMeurers and Dr. Glaspy was strained by mutual ignorance of some significant facts. Wary of possible interference from Health Net, they did not tell Dr. Glaspy that they were Health Net subscribers and told him instead that they would pay for the transplant out of pocket. At the same time the deMeurers did not know that Dr. Glaspy was on the Health Net committee that had voted recently not to cover bone marrow transplants for Stage IV breast cancer patients.

Later, news came that Health Net had rejected the appeal filed by the deMeurers' lawyer.

Dr. Glaspy found himself caught between conflicting loyalties. As the deMeurers' physician, he felt a responsibility to help Christine get the transplant. But as a Health Net physician, he was required to uphold the regulations of the HMO, some of which he had helped make. Discussions ensued between Health Net administrators and UCLA physicians and officials. Finally, a way out of the conflict appeared when UCLA agreed that it would pay for Christine's operation.

Christine began the treatment on September 22, 1993, at UCLA Medical Center. She died March 10, 1995. Health Net officials expressed doubt that the treatment helped much. Alan deMeurers said that it gave Christine four disease-free months.

Eventually an arbitration panel ruled that Health Net should have paid for Christine's transplant and that the company had improperly interfered in the doctor-patient relationship.

---

volatile. Mandela was essential to maintaining social stability. Suppose further that a younger individual also needed a liver and would have at least as good an outcome with a transplant. In the light of the political and social circumstances, Mandela should have been given priority over the younger patient in receiving a liver. His survival would have ensured the social stability of the country. It would have ensured that many people would not suffer a loss of welfare or life from the social instability that might have resulted otherwise. Mandela's social worth was a function of the dependence of many people's welfare and lives on his survival. That worth would have been a decisive factor in giving the organ to him rather than to another person with the same need.[17]

KEY TERMS

distributive justice
egalitarian theories of justice
libertarian theories of justice
managed care
utilitarian theories of justice

SUMMARY

The U.S. system of health care has been ailing—or failing, as some would say—for years. Its most obvious symptoms are 47 million uninsured people under age 65, soaring costs, and low grades on some measures of national health, such as infant mortality rates.

Debates about ethical allocations of health care resources often reduce to clashes between theories of distributive justice—that is, theories regarding the fair distribution of society's benefits and burdens. Libertarian theories of justice say that the benefits and burdens of society should be distributed through the fair workings of a free market and the exercise of liberty rights of noninterference. The role of government is to protect the rights of individuals to freely pursue their own interests in the economic marketplace without violations of their liberty through coercion, manipulation, or fraud. On this view, no one has a right to health care. In utilitarian theories of justice, a just distribution of benefits and burdens is one that maximizes the net utility for society. Depending on calculations of net benefits, a utilitarian might endorse a system of universal health care insurance, or a qualified right to health care, or a two-tiered plan. Egalitarian theories of justice say that important benefits and burdens of society should be distributed equally. To achieve greater equality, the egalitarian would not be averse to mandating changes to the distribution of society's goods or to interfering in the workings of a free market. Egalitarian theorists could consistently endorse several schemes for allocating health care, including systems that give equal access to all legitimate forms of health care, that offer a guaranteed minimal level of health care for everyone, or that provide care only to those most in need.

Some theorists assert the strong claim that people have a positive moral right to health care. Libertarians would reject this view, utilitarians could endorse a derivative right to health care, and egalitarians could favor a bona fide entitlement to a share of society's health care resources. Some of the latter argue for a right to a decent minimum of health care.

Because people's health care needs are virtually limitless and the supply of resources is always bounded, rationing of health care in some form is ever with us. The dilemmas of rationing arise most visibly and acutely on the level of individual patients and providers who must contend with scarce life-saving resources such as organ transplants. The central moral issue in these cases is what criteria should be used to decide which patients get transplants and who should make the decisions.

Cases for Evaluation

CASE 1

Black Market in Organ Transplants

(*San Francisco Chronicle*)—Tears well up in P. Guna's eyes as he stares at a long scar running down his side. A year ago, he attempted to stave off mounting debt by swapping one of his healthy kidneys for quick cash.

"Humans don't need two kidneys, I was made to believe," he said. "I can sell my extra kidney and become rich, I thought."

At the time, an organ trader promised Guna, 38, a motorized-rickshaw driver with a fourth-grade education, $2,500 for the kidney, of which he eventually received only half. Since then, he has experienced excruciating pain in his hip that has kept him from working full time and pushed him deeper in debt.

In recent years, many Indian cities—like Chennai in southern India—have become hubs of a murky business in kidney transplants, despite a 1994 nationwide ban on human organ sales (the Transplant of Human Organ Act states only relatives of patients can donate kidneys).

An influx of patients, mainly foreigners, seeking the transplants has made the illicit market a lucrative business. Some analysts say the business thrives for the same reasons that have made India a top destination for medical tourism: low cost and qualified doctors. In fact, medical tourism is expected to reach $2.2 billion by 2012, according to government estimates.

Not surprisingly, an organized group of organ traders in cahoots with unscrupulous doctors is constantly on the prowl for donors like Guna.

In Gurgaon, a posh New Delhi suburb, police last month busted an illegal organ racket, which included doctors, nurses, pathology clinics, and hospitals. In the past 14 years, the participants allegedly removed kidneys from about 500 day laborers, the majority of them abducted or conned, before selling the organs to wealthy clients.

Police say the doctor believed to be the mastermind behind the operation, Amit Kumar, searched for donors by cruising in luxury cars outfitted with medical testing machines, and kept sophisticated surgical equipment in a residential apartment. In his office, police found letters and e-mail messages from 48 people from nine countries inquiring about transplants.

On Thursday, police arrested Kumar in Chitwan, a Nepalese jungle resort. Local news reports said he was identified by a hotel employee who recognized him from Indian television broadcasts seen in Nepal. "I have not duped anybody," Kumar later told reporters in Kathmandu, according to the Associated Press.

Nepalese authorities say they won't extradite Kumar until they finish an investigation on whether he violated currency laws by not declaring $230,000 in cash and a check for $24,000 that he was carrying when arrested. He is scheduled to appear in a Nepalese court Sunday.

In another high-profile arrest, a renowned Chennai surgeon, Palani Ravichandran, was arrested in October in Mumbai for involvement in a kidney racket. He admitted to arranging organ transplants for wealthy foreigners—mainly from Persian Gulf states and Malaysia, whom he charged up to $25,000. Mumbai police say Ravichandran had performed between 40 and 100 illegal transplants since 2002.

Police say kidney donors can earn between $1,250 and $2,500, while recipients pay as much as $25,000, according to ActionAid India, an antipoverty organization that has worked with kidney trade victims in the southern state of Tamil Nadu.

The same procedure can cost as much as $70,000 in China and $85,000 in the United States.

"These middlemen act more like cut-and-grab men whose only interest is to hack out the organ," said Annie Thomas, a field co-coordinator for ActionAid in Chennai, formerly known as Madras. "This is a reprehensible abuse of the poor, and this practice needs to be curbed."

Thomas says many middlemen typically masquerade the donors as relatives to circumvent the law while many foreigners in need of a kidney arrive on tourist visas rather than the required medical visas; some resort to false documents.*

Is it morally permissible to sell your own organs? Is it morally permissible to buy organs from consenting adult donors? Should organ selling be illegal in all cases? Are the Indian organ donors described in this article being exploited? How? Give reasons for your answers.

---

*Anuj Chopra, "Organ-Transplant Black Market Thrives in India," *SFGate*, 9 February 2008, http://www.sfgate.com (11 April 2008).

CASE 2

Expensive Health Care for a Killer

(*Statesman Journal*)—Oregon taxpayers are shelling out more than $120,000 a year to provide lifesaving dialysis for a condemned killer.

Horacio Alberto Reyes-Camarena was sent to death row six years ago for stabbing to death an 18-year-old girl and dumping her body near the Oregon Coast.

At the Two Rivers Correctional Institution in Eastern Oregon, Reyes-Camarena, 47, gets hooked up to a dialysis machine for four hours three times a week to remove toxins from his blood.

Without dialysis, he would die because his kidneys are failing.

Each dialysis session costs $775.80 for treatment and medication, according to Corrections Department figures. At that rate, his dialysis costs $121,025 a year.

As the state keeps Reyes-Camarena alive, thousands of older, poor, sick and disabled Oregonians are trying to survive without medications and care that vanished amid state budget cuts.

Some Oregon hospitals are considering closing dialysis units because of Medicaid-related reductions.

Reyes-Camarena said he wants to sever his ties to the dialysis machine. The convicted killer wants to be the first Oregon inmate to receive a taxpayer-financed organ transplant.

"It's much better for me, and them, too," Reyes-Camarena said, referring to his desire for a kidney transplant, a procedure sought by nearly 57,000 Americans.

The prisoner cited medical reports indicating that transplant costs prove to be cheaper than dialysis in the long run.

Even so, transplant surgery is costly: $80,000 to $120,000. It also requires $500 to $1,200 a month in lifelong drugs to keep the recipient from rejecting the new organ.

Studies have found that the death rate for dialysis patients is about 23 percent a year. A successful transplant reduces that risk to about 3 percent a year.

But the number of transplants is severely limited by a national scarcity of available organs. As of this month, 56,895 Americans, including 192 Oregonians, were waiting for kidney transplants, according to the Virginia-based United Network for Organ Sharing, which maintains the nation's waiting list for organs.

Because the waiting list is long and there aren't enough organs to go around, some people die before a transplant becomes available.

Overall, 86,157 Americans are waiting for organ transplants—mostly kidneys, livers, pancreases and lungs. Officials estimate that about 700 will die this year while waiting.

Lifesaving care for Reyes-Camarena raises questions about the bounds of medical treatment for prisoners.*

Is society obligated to prolong the life of felons like Reyes-Camarena? As thousands of dollars are spent each year by the state to provide him with health care, many lawful citizens cannot afford critical care and die as a result. Is this arrangement just? Do prisoners have a right to health care? Does anyone have a right to health care? Explain your answers.

---

*Alan Gustafson, "Death Row Inmate Seeks Organ Transplant," *Statesman Journal*, 28 April 2003, http://news. statesmanjournal.com/article.cfm?i=59756 (11 April 2008).

CASE 3

Should We Have Universal Health Care?

(*TCU360*)—Since the dawn of the twentieth century, a debate over health care has raged in America.

The debate centers around the argument over whether the federal government is obligated to ensure that its citizens have health care, thus preventing them from economic headaches associated with rising costs of basic medical care.

Historian and sociologist Paul Starr wrote in his book, *Remedy and Reaction: The Peculiar American Struggle over Health Care Reform*, that efforts to "provide all Americans access to medical care and protect them from economic ruin" have long been a "liberal inspiration."

Beginning in the early decades of the twentieth century, reform from the Progressive Era gave Americans antitrust laws, labor legislation, the Federal Reserve and workers' compensation, but reforming health care proved to be more challenging.

Reform has come slowly. After the New Deal, Social Security was passed to give seniors a fiscal safety net in their later years. Along with Social Security came the GI Bill and the minimum wage.

For decades liberals sought a system of universal health care that would protect all Americans from the pain of illness and burdensome medical bills.

With the establishment of Medicare and Medicaid, progressives hoped they had broken through—not so.

Starr wrote that "if Americans came to know one thing about the history of battles over health insurance, it was that a government program to make health care a right of citizenship had always been defeated."

Early ideas for government-led health insurance programs came from Europe.

British national health care and German sickness funds were unpopular and never gained traction in America. Workers compensation shows similarities to German sickness funds, but the idea of national health care similar to Britain was, to the chagrin of progressives, politely frowned upon in the States.

In 1912, progressives within the Republican Party established the Progressive Party that included in its platform support for social health insurance.

Canada boasts a single payer system with striking similarities to the United States' Medicare system. Progressives had hoped that the Medicare system would serve as a precursor to a more wide-reaching program to establish a system for all Americans, offering insurance akin to the coverage offered to seniors by Medicare....

In reality, none of the proposals in the United States even closely resembles true government health care like Britain's universal health care system.

Reality shows that Democrats largely played on Republican turf.

Coupling reform with deficit reduction, championing the originally Republican idea of the individual mandate and dropping advocacy for a government-run "public option" meant that Democrats sought compromise on the bill.

They sought agreement on one of the most divisive issues in America's history. Agreement may have been sought, but discord was found.

Perhaps the fact that the debate requires Americans to draw upon deep-seated ethical principles precludes agreement.

Or perhaps the problem is deeper.

Perhaps Americans are truly divided over the role government should play in people's lives.*

Should the United States establish a system of universal health care? Why or why not? What moral principle seems to underpin opposition to such a system? What moral principle seems to favor it? What would be the negative effects of having universal health care? What would be the positive effects?

---

*Alex Apple, "Universal Health Care Debate a Controversial Topic for the United States," *TCU360* (Texas Christian University), 22 November 2012, https://www.tcu360.com/ (21 January 2016).

FURTHER READING

Michael Boylan, "The Universal Right to Health Care," in *Medical Ethics*, ed. Michael Boylan (Upper Saddle River, NJ: Prentice-Hall, 2000), 391–402.

Tom L. Beauchamp and James F. Childress, "Justice," in *Principles of Biomedical Ethics*, 5th ed. (New York: Oxford University Press, 2001), 225–82.

Allen Buchanan, "Justice: A Philosophical Review," in *Justice and Health Care*, ed. Earl Shelp (Dordrecht: D. Reidel Publishing, 1981), 3–21.

Allen Buchanan, "Health-Care Delivery and Resource Allocation," in *Medical Ethics*, ed. Robert M. Veatch (Sudbury, MA: Jones and Bartlett, 1997), 321–61.

Norman Daniels, "Health-Care Needs and Distributive Justice," in *Justice and Justification* (Cambridge, UK: Cambridge University Press, 1996), 179–207.

Norman Daniels, *Just Health Care* (Cambridge, UK: Cambridge University Press, 1985).

Walter Glannon, "Allotting Scarce Medical Resources," in *Biomedical Ethics* (Oxford: Oxford University Press, 2005), 143–66.

Kaiser Commission on Medicaid and the Uninsured, "The Uninsured: A Primer," October 2007, http://www.kff.org/uninsured/7451.cfm (21 March 2008).

Rosamond Rhodes, Margaret P. Battin, and Anita Silvers, eds., *Medicine and Social Justice* (New York: Oxford University Press, 2002).

NOTES

1. Kaiser Commission on Medicaid and the Uninsured, "The Uninsured: A Primer," October 2007 and 2011, http://www.kff.org/uninsured/7451.cfm (10 November 2011); National Coalition on Health Care, "Health Insurance Coverage," undated, 2008, http://www.nchc.org/facts/coverage.shtml (21 March 2008).

2. Kaiser Family Foundation, "Key Facts about the Uninsured Population," 5 October 2015, http://kff.org/uninsured/fact-sheet/key-facts-about-the-uninsured-population/ (3 November 2015).

3. Institute of Medicine, "Insuring America's Health: Principles and Recommendations," National Academy Press, undated, 2004, http://www.nap.edu/catalog.php?record_id 10874#toc (21 March 2008).

4. Kaiser Commission, "The Uninsured."

5. Organization for Economic Cooperation and Development, *OECD Health Data 2007,* July 2007, http://www.oecd.org (27 March 2008).

6. Congressional Research Service, *CRS Report for Congress: U.S. Health Care Spending: Comparison with Other OECD Countries* (Washington, DC: Congressional Research Service, 17 September 2007).

7. E. A. McGlynn et al., "The Quality of Health Care Delivered in the United States," *New England Journal of Medicine* 348.26 (2003), 2635–45; S. Asch et al., "Who Is at Greatest Risk for Receiving Poor-Quality Health

Care?" *New England Journal of Medicine* 354.11 (2006), 1147–56.

8. Henry J. Kaiser Family Foundation, "Summary of Coverage Provisions in the Patient Protection and Affordable Care Act," 14 April 2011, www.kff.org, (11 November 2011).

9. D. Tarantola and S. Gruskin, "Human Rights Approach to Public Health Policy," *International Encyclopedia of Public Health*, 2008, vol. 3, 477–486.

10. John Rawls, *A Theory of Justice,* rev. ed. (Cambridge, MA: Harvard University Press, 1999).

11. Norman Daniels, "Is There a Right to Health Care and, if So, What Does It Encompass?" in *A Companion to Bioethics,* ed. Helga Kuhse and Peter Singer (Oxford: Blackwell Publishing, 1998), 316–25.

12. Allen Buchanan, "Health-Care Delivery and Resource Allocation," in *Medical Ethics,* ed. Robert M. Veatch (Boston: Jones and Bartlett Publishers, 1997), 351.

13. *Ibid.*

14. I owe this distinction to Tom L. Beauchamp and James F. Childress, *Principles of Biomedical Ethics,* 5th ed. (New York: Oxford University Press, 2001), 264–65.

15. John Harris, "QALYfying the Value of Life," *Journal of Medical Ethics* 13 (1987), 117–22.

16. *Ibid.* Beauchamp and Childress, *Principles of Biomedical Ethics,* 266.

17. Nicholas Rescher, "The Allocation of Exotic Medical Lifesaving Therapy," *Ethics* 79 (April 1969), 173–86.

18. Walter Glannon, *Biomedical Ethics* (New York: Oxford University Press, 2005), 158–59.

READINGS

Is There a Right to Health Care and, if So, What Does It Encompass?

NORMAN DANIELS

Daniels argues for a strong right to health care, deriving it from John Rawls' justice principle of "fair equality of opportunity." He reasons that disease and disability diminish people's "normal species functioning" and thus restrict the range of opportunities open to them. Since people are entitled to fair equality of opportunity, and adequate health care can protect or restore their normal range of opportunities, they have a positive right to adequate health care.

Is There a Right to Health Care?

Legal Versus Moral Rights to Health Care

One way to answer this question is to adopt the stance of legal positivists, who claim that there are no rights except those that are embodied in actual institutions through law. We would then be able to reply that in nearly every advanced industrial democracy in the world, there is a right to health care, since institutions exist in them that assure everyone

access to needed services regardless of ability to pay. The notable exception is the United States, where many poor and near poor people have no insurance coverage for, and thus no assured access to, medically necessary services, although by law they cannot be denied emergency services.

The legal right to health care is embodied in a wide variety of types of health-care systems. These range from national health services, where the government is the provider of services, as in Great Britain, to public insurance schemes, where the government finances services, as in Canada, to mixed public and private insurance schemes, as in Germany and the Netherlands. Despite these differences in the design of systems, there is a broad overlap in the scope or content of the legal right to health care in these countries. Most cover "medically necessary" services, including a broad range of preventive, curative, rehabilitative and long-term care for physical and mental diseases, disorders and disabilities. Most exclude uses of medical technologies that enhance otherwise normal functioning or appearance, such as purely cosmetic surgery. The legal rights vary in significant ways, however, for example, in the degree to which they cover new reproductive technologies, or in the types of mental health and long-term care services that are offered.

In the context of rising costs and the rapid dissemination of new technologies there is growing debate in many countries about how to set limits on the scope of a right to health care. This debate about the scope of rights to health care pushes moral deliberation about such a right into the forefront, even where a legal right is recognized. Legal entitlements, most people believe, should reflect what society is morally obliged to provide by way of medical services. What, then, is the basis and scope of a moral right to health care?

Positive Versus Negative Rights

A right to health care is a *positive* as opposed to a *negative* right. Put quite simply, a positive right requires others to do something beneficial or enabling for right-bearers, whereas a negative right requires others to refrain from doing something, usually harmful or restrictive, to right-bearers. To say that others are required to do something or to refrain from doing something is to say they must so act or refrain even if they could produce more good or improve the world by not doing so (Thomson, 1990). For example, a negative right to free expression requires others to refrain from censuring the expression of the right-bearer even if censuring this speech would make a better world. Some public-health measures that protect people against interference with their health, such as environmental protections that protect people against polluters of air, water and food sources, might be construed as requirements of a negative right. More generally, however, a right to health care imposes an obligation on others to assist the right-bearers in obtaining needed and appropriate services. Specifically, claiming a right to health care includes these other claims; society has the duty to its members to allocate an adequate share of its total resources to health-related needs; society has the duty to provide a just allocation of different types of health care services, taking into account the competing claims of different types of health-care needs; each person is entitled to a fair share of such services, where a "fair share" includes an answer to the question, who should pay for the services? (Daniels, 1985). Health-care rights thus form a part of a broader family of positive "welfare" rights that includes rights to education and to income support. Because positive rights require other people to contribute their resources or skills to benefit right-bearers, rather than merely refraining from interfering with them, they have often been thought more difficult to justify than negative rights, and their scope and limits have been harder to characterize.

Theories of Justice and Rights to Health Care

If we are to think of a right to health care as a requirement of justice, then we should look to more general theories of justice as a way to specify the scope and limits of that right. On some theories of justice, however, there is little basis for requiring people to assist others by meeting their health care or other needs. Libertarians, for example, believe that fundamental rights to property, including rights to personal assets, such as talents and skills, are violated if society coerces individuals into providing "needed" resources or skills (Nozick, 1974). Libertarians generally recognize an "imperfect" duty to act beneficently or charitably, but this duty involves discretion. It can be discharged in different ways that are matters of choice. People denied charity have no right to it and have no complaint against people who act charitably in other ways. Though some have argued that the difficulty of coordinating the delivery of charitable assistance might justify coercive measures (Buchanan, 1984), and others have tried to show that even libertarians must recognize some forms of welfare rights (Sterba, 1985), most libertarians resist any weakening of the property rights at the core of their view (Brennan and Friedman, 1981).

A spectre sometimes raised by libertarians against the idea of a right to health care is that such a right is a "bottomless pit." Since new technologies continuously expand the scope of "medical needs," a right to health care would give rise to unlimited claims on the resources of others (Fried, 1969; Engelhardt, 1986). Protecting such an expansive right to health care would thus not be compatible with the function of a libertarian "minimal state" to assure the non-violation of rights to liberty and property.

Though there remains controversy about whether utilitarians can provide a basis for recognizing true moral rights, there are strong utilitarian arguments in favour of governments assuring access to at least some broad range of effective medical services. Preventing or curing disease or disability reduces suffering and enables people to function in ways that contribute to aggregate welfare. In addition, knowing that health-care services are available increases personal security and strengthens the ties of community. Utilitarians can also justify redistributing the burden of delivering these benefits to society as a whole, citing the decreasing marginal utility of money to support progressive financing of health-care services (Brandt, 1979).

Beneath these quite general arguments, however, there lies a more specific controversy about the scope of utilitarian entitlements to health care. There seems to be little utilitarian justification for investing resources in health care if those resources would produce more net welfare when invested in other things, yet many people believe they have moral obligations to assist others with their health-care needs even at a net cost in utility. For example, some highly expensive and effective medical treatments that most people believe should be offered to people might not be "cost beneficial" and thus not defensible on utilitarian grounds. Similarly, many forms of long-term care, especially for those who cannot be restored to productive social activity, are also difficult to defend on utilitarian grounds, yet we insist our health-care systems are obliged to provide such services.

Lack of moral acceptance of the distributive implications of utilitarianism makes many uncomfortable with the use of methods, such as cost-effectiveness analysis, that are intended to guide decisions about resource allocation in health care. For example, an assumption of cost-effectiveness analysis is that a unit of health benefit, such as a quality-adjusted life year (QALY), is of equal value or importance regardless of where it is distributed. But this assumption does not capture the concerns many people have about how much priority to give to the sickest patients, or when aggregating modest benefits to large numbers of people it outweighs the moral importance of delivering more significant benefits to fewer people (Nord, 1993; Daniels, 1993).

Two points about a utilitarian framework for a right to health care are worth noting. Recognizing a right to health care is compatible with recognizing limits on entitlements that result from resource scarcity and the fact that there are competing uses of those resources. Consequently, recognizing a right to health care need not open a bottomless pit. Second, just what entitlements to services follow from a right to health care cannot be specified outside the context of a *system* properly designed to deliver health care in a way that promotes aggregate utility. For the utilitarian, entitlements are *system-relative*. The same two points apply to other accounts of the foundations and limits of a right to health care.

Because many people reject the utilitarian rationales for health care (and other welfare) rights, theorists have explored other ways to ground such rights. Some claim that these rights are presupposed as enabling conditions for the exercise of other rights or liberties, or as practical presuppositions of all views of justice (Braybrooke, 1987) or as a way of avoiding vulnerability and exploitation (Goodin, 1988). One approach that has been developed in some detail views a right to health care as a special case of a right to equality of opportunity (Daniels, 1985). This approach shows how the most important contractarian theory of justice, Rawls' (1971) account of justice as fairness, can be extended to the problem of health care, since that theory gives prominence to a principle protecting equality of opportunity (Rawls, 1993). Without endorsing that account here, we shall use it to illustrate further the complexity surrounding the concept of a right to health care.

Equal Opportunity and a Right to Health Care

The central observation underlying this account of a right to health care is that disease and disability restrict the range of opportunities that would otherwise be open to individuals. This is true whether they shorten our lives or impair our ability to function, including through pain and suffering. Health care in all its forms, whether public health or medical, preventive or acute or chronic, aims to keep people functioning as close to normally as possible. Since we are complex social creatures, our normal functional capabilities include our capabilities for emotional and cognitive functioning and not just physical capabilities. Health care thus preserves for us the range of opportunities we would have, were we not ill or disabled, given our talents and skills.

The significant contribution health care makes to protecting the range of opportunities open to individuals is nevertheless *limited* in two important ways. It is limited because other things, such as the distribution of wealth and income and education, also profoundly affect equality of opportunity. It is also limited because health care, by restricting its aim to protecting normal functioning, leaves the normal distribution of talents and skills unmodified. It aims to help us function as "normal" competitors, not strictly equal ones.

Some argue that an equal opportunity account of health care should abandon the limit set by a focus on normal functioning (see Arneson, 1988; G. A. Cohen, 1989; Sen, 1992). They claim our concerns about equality, including equality of opportunity, require us to use health-care technologies whenever doing so would equalize opportunity for welfare or equalizes capabilities. For example, if through medical intervention we can "enhance" the otherwise normal capabilities of those who are at a competitive disadvantage, then our commitment to equality of opportunity requires us to do so. Obviously, this version of an equal opportunity account would vastly expand the moral requirements on medicine, yielding a right to health care much more expansive than any now embodied in actual systems and, arguably, one that would make administration of a health-care system unwieldy (Sabin and Daniels, 1994).

This expansive version of the appeal to equal opportunity ignores an important fact about justice: our concern for equality must be reconciled with considerations of liberty and efficiency in arriving at the overall requirements of justice (see Sen, 1992; Cohen, 1995; Daniels, 1996). Such a reconciliation seems to underlie the limits we commonly accept when we appeal to equality of opportunity. We generally believe that rights to equal opportunity are violated only if unfair social practices or preventable or curable diseases or disabilities interfere with the pursuit of reasonable plans of life within our society by making us lose competitive advantage. We accept, however, the fact that the natural distribution of talents and skills, working in an efficient market for them, will both enhance the social product and lead to inequalities in social outcomes. A just society will try to mitigate the effects of these inequalities in competitive advantage in other ways than by eliminating all eliminable differences in capabilities. For example, on Rawls' account, transfers that make the worst off as well off as they can be mitigate the effects on equality of allowing the natural distribution of talents and skills to enhance productivity. In what follows, the account of a right to health care rests on a more limited appeal to equal opportunity, one that takes the maintenance of normal functioning as a reasonable limit.

What Does a Right to Health Care Include?
System-Relative Entitlements

By making the right to health care a special case of rights to equality of opportunity, we arrive at a reasonable, albeit incomplete and imperfect, way of restricting its scope while still recognizing its importance. The account does not give individuals a basic right to have all of their health-care needs met. At the same time, there are social obligations to design a health-care system that protects opportunity through an appropriate set of health-care services. If social obligations to provide appropriate health care are not met, then individuals are definitely wronged. For example, if people are denied access—because of discrimination or inability to pay—to a basic tier of services adequate to protect normal functioning, injustice is done to them. If the basic tier available to people omits important categories of services without consideration of their effects on normal functioning, for example, whole categories of mental health or long-term care or preventive services, their rights are violated.

Still, not every medical need gives rise to an entitlement to services. The scope and limits of rights to health care, that is, the entitlements they actually carry with them, will be relative to certain facts about a given system. For example, a health-care system can protect opportunity only within the limits imposed by resource scarcity and technological development within a society. We cannot make a direct inference from the fact that an individual has a right to health care to the conclusion that this person is entitled to some specific health-care service, even if the service would meet a health-care need. Rather the individual is entitled to a specific service only if, in the light of facts about a society's technological capabilities and resource limitations, it should be a part of a system that appropriately protects fair equality of opportunity. The equal opportunity account of a right to health care, like the utilitarian account, makes entitlements to health care system-relative.

Effective Treatment of Disease and Disability

The health care we have strongest claim to is care that effectively promotes normal functioning by reducing the impact of disease and disability, thus protecting the range of opportunities that would otherwise be open to us. Just what counts as "effective," however? And what should we do about hard cases on the boundary between treatment of disease or disability and enhancement of capabilities?

It is a common feature of public and private insurance systems to limit care to treatments that are not "experimental" and have some "proven effectiveness." Unfortunately, many services that count as standard treatment have little direct evidence about outcomes to support their use (Hadorn, 1992). They are often just customary treatment. Furthermore, it is often controversial just when new treatments or technologies should count as "safe and efficacious." What counts as "reasonably effective" is then a matter of judgement and depends on the kind of condition and the consequences of not correcting it. We might, for example, want to lower our

standards for effectiveness when we face a treatment of last resort, or raise them if resource scarcity is very great. On the other hand, we do not owe people a chance to obtain miracles through whatever unproven procedures they prefer to try.

By focusing a right to health care on the maintenance of normal functioning, a line is drawn between uses of medical technologies that count as legitimate "treatments" and those that we may want but which do not meet our "health-care needs." Although we may want medical services that can enhance our appearance, like cosmetic (as opposed to reconstructive) plastic surgery, or that can optimize our otherwise normal functioning, like some forms of counselling or some uses of Prozac, we do not truly need these services to maintain normal functioning. We are obliged to help others achieve normal functioning, but we do not "owe" each other whatever it takes to make us more beautiful or strong or completely happy (Daniels, 1985).

Though this line is widely used in both public and private insurance practices, it leaves us with hard cases. Some of the hardest issues involve reproductive technologies. Abortion, where there is no preventive or therapeutic need, does not count as "treatment" because an unwanted pregnancy is not a disease or disability. Some nevertheless insist that requirements of justice, including a right to control one's body, means that non-therapeutic abortion should be included as an entitlement in a health-care system. Some national health-insurance schemes do not cover infertility services. Yet infertility is a departure from normal functioning, even if some people never want to bear children. Controversy may remain about how much social obligation we have to correct this form of impaired opportunity, especially where the costs of some interventions, such as in vitro fertilization, are high and their effectiveness is modest. Different societies will judge this question differently, in part because they may place different values on the rearing of biologically related children or on the experience of child-bearing.

Hard cases involve non-reproductive technologies as well. In the United States, for example, many insurers will cover growth hormone treatment only for children deficient in growth hormone, not for those who are equally short but without any pathology. Yet the children denied therapy will suffer just as much as those who are eligible. Similar difficulties are involved in drawing a line between covered and non-covered uses of mental health services (Sabin and Daniels, 1994). As in the cases of reproductive technologies, there is room for different societies to "construct" the concept of mental disorder somewhat differently, with resulting variation in decisions about insurance coverage.

Rights and Limits on Effective Treatments

Even when some health-care service is reasonably effective at meeting a medical need, not all such needs are equally important. When a disease or disability has little impact on the range of opportunities open to someone, it is not as morally important to treat as other conditions that more seriously impair opportunity. The effect on opportunity thus gives us some guidance in thinking about resource allocation priorities.

Unfortunately, the impact on our range of opportunities gives only a crude and incomplete measure of the importance or priority we should give to a need or service. In making decisions about priorities for purposes of resource allocation in health care, we face difficult questions about distributive fairness that are not answered by this measure of importance. For example, we must sometimes make a choice between investing in a technology that delivers a significant benefit to few people or one that delivers a more modest benefit to a larger number of people. Sometimes we must make a choice between investing in a service that helps the sickest, most impaired patients or one that helps those whose functioning is less impaired. Sometimes we must decide between the fairness of giving a scarce resource to those who derive the largest benefit or giving a broader range of people some chance at getting a benefit. In all of these cases, we lack clear principles for deciding how to make our choices, and the account of a right to health care we are discussing does not provide those principles either (Daniels, 1993). Some methodologies, like cost-effectiveness analysis, are intended to help us make appropriate resource allocation decisions in these kinds of cases. But these methodologies may themselves embody controversial moral assumptions about distributive

fairness. This means they cannot serve as decision procedures for making these choices and can at best serve as aids to decision-makers who must be explicit about the moral reasoning that determines the distributive choices they make (Gold et al., 1996).

In any health-care system, then, some choices will have to be made by a fair, publicly accountable, decision-making process. Just what constitutes a fair decision-making procedure for resolving moral disputes about health care entitlements is itself a matter of controversy. It is a problem that has been addressed little in the literature. Our rights are not violated, however, if the choices that are made through fair decision-making procedures turn out to be ones that do not happen to meet our personal needs, but instead meet needs of others that are judged more important (Daniels and Sabin, 1997).

How Equal Must Our Rights to Health Care Be?

How equal must our rights to health care be? Specifically, must everyone receive exactly the same kinds of health-care services and coverage, or is fairness in health care compatible with a "tiered" system? Around the world, even countries that offer universal health insurance differ in their answers to this question. In Canada and Norway, for example, no supplementary insurance is permitted. Everyone is served solely by the national health-insurance schemes, though people who seek additional services or more rapid service may go elsewhere, as some Canadians do by crossing the border. In Britain, supplementary private insurance allows about 10 per cent of the population to gain quicker access to services for which there is extensive queuing in the public system. Basing a right to health care on an obligation to protect equality of opportunity is compatible with the sort of tiering the British have, but it does not require it, and it imposes some constraints on the kind of tiering allowed.

The primary social obligation is to assure everyone access to a tier of services that effectively promotes normal functioning and thus protects equality of opportunity. Since health care is not the only important good, resources to be invested in the basic tier are appropriately and reasonably limited, for example, by democratic decisions about how much to invest in education or job training as opposed to health care. Because of their very high "opportunity costs," there will be some beneficial medical services that it will be reasonable not to provide in the basic tier, or to provide only on a limited basis, for example, with queuing. To say that these services have "high opportunity costs" means that providing them consumes resources that would produce greater health benefits and protect opportunity more if used in other ways.

In a society that permits significant income and wealth inequalities, some people will want to buy coverage for these additional services. Why not let them? After all, we allow people to use their after-tax income and wealth as they see fit to pursue the "quality of life" and opportunities they prefer. The rich can buy special security systems for their homes. They can buy safer cars. They can buy private schooling for their children. Why not allow them to buy supplementary health care for their families?

One objection to allowing a supplementary tier is that its existence might undermine the basic tier either economically or politically. It might attract better-quality providers away from the basic tier, or raise costs in the basic tier, reducing the ability of society to meet its social obligations. The supplementary tier might undermine political support for the basic tier, for example, by undercutting the social solidarity needed if people are to remain committed to protecting opportunity for all. These objections are serious, and where a supplementary tier undermines the basic tier in either way, economically or politically, priority must be given to protecting the basic tier. In principle, however, it seems possible to design a system in which the supplementary tier does not undermine the basic one. If that can be done, then a system that permits tiering avoids restricting liberty in ways that some find seriously objectionable.

A second objection is not to tiering itself but to the structure of inequality that results. Compare two scenarios. In one, most people are adequately served by the basic tier and only the best-off groups in society have the means and see the need to purchase supplementary insurance. That is the case in Great Britain. In the other, the basic tier serves only the poorest groups in society and most other people buy supplementary insurance. The Oregon plan to expand Medicaid eligibility partly through rationing the services it covers has aspects of this structure of inequality, since most people are covered by plans that avoid these restrictions (Daniels, 1991). The first scenario seems preferable to the second on grounds of fairness. In the second, the poorest groups can complain that they are left behind by others in society even in the protection of their health. In the first, the majority has less grounds for reasonable resentment or regret.

If the basic tier is not undermined by higher tiers, and if the structure of the inequality that results is not objectionable, then it is difficult to see why some tiering should not be allowed. There is a basic conflict here between concerns about equality and concerns about liberty, between wanting to make sure everyone is treated properly with regard to health care and wanting to give people the liberty to use their resources (after tax) to improve their lives as they see fit. In practice, the crucial constraint on the liberty we allow people seems to depend on the magnitude of the benefit available in the supplementary tier and unavailable in the basic tier. Highly visible forms of saving lives and improving function would be difficult to exclude from the basic tier while we make them available in a supplementary tier. In principle, however, some forms of tiering will not be unfair even when they involve medical benefits not available to everyone.

REFERENCES

Arneson, Richard (1988). Equality and equal opportunity for welfare. *Philosophical Studies*, 54, 79–95.

Brandt, Richard (1979). *A Theory of the Good and the Right*, Oxford: Oxford University Press.

Braybrooke, David (1987). *Meeting Needs*. Princeton, NJ: Princeton University Press.

Brennan, Geoffrey and Friedman, David (1981). A libertarian perspective on welfare. In Peter G. Brown, Conrad Johnson and Paul Vernier (eds), *Income Support: Conceptual and policy issues*. Totowa, NJ: Rowman and Littlefield.

Buchanan, Allen (1984). The right to a decent minimum of health care. *Philosophy and Public Affairs*, 13, 55–78.

Cohen, G. A. (1989). On the currency of egalitarian justice. *Ethics*, 99, 906–44.

Cohen, Joshua (1995). Amartya Sen: *Inequality Reexamined*. *Journal of Philosophy*, 92/5, 275–88.

Daniel, N. (1985). *Just Health Care*. Cambridge: Cambridge University Press.

——(1991). Is the Oregon rationing plan fair? *Journal of the American Medical Association*, 265, 2232–5.

——(1993). Rationing fairly: programmatic considerations. *Bioethics*, 7, 224–33.

——(1996). *Justice and Justification: reflective equilibrium in theory and practice*. Cambridge: Cambridge University Press.

Daniels, N. and Sabin, J. (1997). Limits to health care: fair procedures, democratic deliberation, and the legitimacy problem for insurers. *Philosophy and Public Affairs*. 26/4, 303–50.

Engelhardt, H. Tristram (1986). *The Foundations of Bioethics*. Oxford: Oxford University Press.

Fried, Charles (1969). *An Anatomy of Value*. Cambridge, MA: Harvard University Press.

Gold, Marthe, Siegel, Joanna, Russell, Louise and Weinstein, Milton (eds) (1996). *Cost-Effectiveness in Health and Medicine: recommendations of the Panel on Cost-Effectiveness in Health and Medicine*. New York: Oxford University Press.

Goodin, Robert (1988). *Reasons for Welfare*. Princeton, NJ: Princeton University Press.

Hadorn, David (ed.) (1992). *Basic Benefits and Clinical Guidelines*. Boulder, CO: Westview Press.

Nord, Eric (1993). The relevance of health state after treatment in prioritizing between different patients. *Journal of Medical Ethics*, 19, 37–42.

Nozick, R. (1974). *Anarchy, State, and Utopia*. New York: Basic Books.

Rawls, J. (1971). *A Theory of Justice*. Cambridge, MA: Harvard University Press.

——(1993). *Political Liberalism*. New York: Columbia University Press.

Sabin, James and Daniels, Norman (1994). Determining "medical necessity" in mental health practice. *Hastings Center Report*, 24/6, 5–13.

Sen, Amartya (1992). *Inequality Reexamined*. Cambridge, MA: Harvard University Press.

Sterba, James (1985). From liberty to welfare, *Social Theory and Practice*, 11, 285–305.

Thomson, Judith (1990). *The Realm of Rights*. Cambridge, MA: Harvard University Press.

The Right to a Decent Minimum of Health Care
ALLEN E. BUCHANAN

In this article Buchanan argues that the notion of a universal right to a decent minimum of health care cannot justify a mandatory decent minimum policy. But the combined weight of other arguments, he says, can establish that the state should provide certain individuals or groups with a decent minimum. The necessary arguments are from special rights, from the prevention of harm, from prudential considerations, and from enforced beneficence.

The Assumption That There Is a Right to a Decent Minimum

A consensus that there is (at least) a right to a decent minimum of health care pervades recent policy debates and much of the philosophical literature on health care. Disagreement centers on two issues. Is there a more extensive right than the right to a decent minimum of health care? What is included in the decent minimum to which there is a right?

From the President's Commission, *Securing Access to Health Care* , Vol. II. Washington, D.C., U.S. Government Printing Office, 1983.

Preliminary Clarification of the Concept

Different theories of distributive justice may yield different answers both to the question "Is there a right to a decent minimum?" and to the question "What comprises the decent minimum?" The justification a particular theory provides for the claim that there is a right to a decent minimum must at least cohere with the justifications it provides for other right-claims. Moreover, the character of this justification will determine, at least in part, the way in which the decent minimum is specified, since it will include an account of the nature and significance of health-care needs. To the extent that the concept of a decent minimum is theory-dependent, then, it would be naive to assume that a mere analysis of the concept of a decent minimum would tell us whether there is such a right and what its content is. Nonetheless, before we proceed to an examination of various theoretical attempts to ground and specify a right to a decent minimum, a preliminary analysis will be helpful.

Sometimes the notion of a decent minimum is applied not to health care but to health itself, the claim being that everyone is entitled to some minimal level, or welfare floor, of health. I shall not explore this variant of the decent minimum idea because I think its implausibility is obvious. The main difficulty is that assuring any significant level of health for all is simply not within the domain of social control. If the alleged right is understood instead as the right to everything which can be done to achieve some significant level of health for all, then the claim that there is such a right becomes implausible simply because it ignores the fact that in circumstances of scarcity the total social expenditure on health must be constrained by the need to allocate resources for other goods.

Though the concept of a right is complex and controversial, for our purposes a partial sketch will do. To say that person A has a right to something, X, is first of all to say that A is entitled to X, that X is due to him or her. This is not equivalent to saying that if A were granted X it would be a good thing, even a morally good thing, or that X is desired by or desirable for A. Second, it is usually held that valid right-claims, at least in the case of basic rights, may be backed by sanctions, including coercion if necessary (unless doing so would produce extremely great disutility or grave moral evil), and that (except in such highly exceptional circumstances) failure of an appropriate authority to apply the needed sanctions is itself an injustice. Recent right-theorists have also emphasized a third feature of rights, or at least of basic rights or rights in the strict sense: valid right-claims "trump" appeals to what would maximize utility, whether it be the utility of the right-holder, or social utility. In other words, if A has a right to X, then the mere fact that infringing A's right would maximize overall utility or even A's utility is not itself a sufficient reason for infringing it.[1] Finally, a universal (or general) right is one which applies to all persons, not just to certain individuals or classes because of their involvement in special actions, relationships, or agreements.

The second feature—enforceability—is of crucial importance for those who assume or argue that there is a universal right to a decent minimum of health care. For, once it is granted that there is such a right and that such a right may be enforced (absent any extremely weighty reason against enforcement), the claim that there is a universal right provides the moral basis for using the coercive power of the state to assure a decent minimum for all. Indeed, the surprising absence of attempts to justify a coercively backed decent minimum policy by arguments that do *not* aim at establishing a universal right suggests the following hypothesis: advocates of a coercively based decent minimum have operated on the assumption that such a policy must be based on a universal right to a decent minimum. The chief aim of this article is to show that this assumption is false.

I think it is fair to say that many who confidently assume there is a (universal) right to a decent minimum of health care have failed to appreciate the significance of the first feature of our sketch of the concept of a right. It is crucial to observe that the claim that there is a right to a decent minimum is much stronger than the claim that everyone *ought* to have access to such a minimum, or that if they did it would be a good thing, or that any society which is capable, without great sacrifice, of providing a decent minimum but fails to do so is deeply morally defective. None of the latter assertions implies the existence of a right, if this is understood as a moral entitlement which ought to be established by the coercive power of the state if necessary....

The Attractions of the Idea of a Decent Minimum

There are at least three features widely associated with the idea of a right to a decent minimum which, together with the facile consensus that vagueness promotes, help explain its popularity over competing conceptions of the right to health care. First, it is usually, and quite reasonably, assumed that the idea of a decent minimum is to be understood in a society-relative sense. Surely it is plausible to assume that, as with other rights to goods or services, the content of the right must depend upon the resources available in a given society and perhaps also upon a certain consensus of expectations among its members. So the first advantage of the idea of a decent minimum, as it is usually understood, is that it allows us to adjust the level of services to be provided as a matter of right to relevant social conditions and also allows for the possibility that as a society becomes more affluent the floor provided by the decent minimum should be raised.

Second, the idea of a decent minimum avoids the excesses of what has been called the strong equal access principle, while still acknowledging a substantive universal right. According to the strong equal access principle, everyone has an equal right to the best health-care services available. Aside from the weakness of the justifications offered in support of it, the most implausible feature of the strong equal access principle is that it forces us to choose between two unpalatable alternatives. We can either set the publicly guaranteed level of health care lower than the level that is technically possible or we can set it as high as is technically possible. In the former case, we shall be committed to the uncomfortable conclusion that no matter how many resources have been expended to guarantee equal access to that level, individuals are forbidden to spend any of their resources for services not available to all. Granted that individuals are allowed to spend their after-tax incomes on more frivolous items, why shouldn't they be allowed to spend it on health? If the answer is that they should be so allowed, as long as this does not interfere with the provision of an adequate package of health-care services for everyone, then we have retreated from the strong equal access principle to something very like the principle of a decent minimum. If, on the other hand, we set the level of services guaranteed for all so high as to eliminate the problem of persons seeking extra care beyond this level, this would produce a huge drain on total resources, foreclosing opportunities for producing important goods other than health care.

So both the recognition that health care must compete with other goods and the conviction that beyond some less than maximal level of publicly guaranteed services individuals should be free to purchase additional services point toward a more

limited right than the strong access principle asserts. Thus, the endorsement of a right to a decent minimum may be more of a recognition of the implausibility of the stronger right to equal access than a sign of any definite position on the content of the right to health care.

A third attraction of the idea of a decent minimum is that since the right to health care must be limited in scope (to avoid the consequences of a strong equal access right), it should be limited to the "most basic" services, those normally "adequate" for health, or for a "decent" or "tolerable" life. However, although this aspect of the idea of a decent minimum is useful because it calls attention to the fact that health-care needs are heterogeneous and must be assigned some order of priority, it does not itself provide any basis for determining which are most important.

The Need for a Supporting Theory

In spite of these attractions, the concept of a right to a decent minimum of health care is inadequate as a moral basis for a coercively backed decent minimum policy in the absence of a coherent and defensible theory of justice. Indeed, when taken together they do not even imply that there is a right to a decent minimum. Rather, they only support the weaker conditional claim that if there is a right to health care, then it is one that is more limited than a right of strong equal access, and is one whose content depends upon available resources and some scheme of priorities which shows certain health services to be more basic than others....

My suggestion is that the combined weight of arguments from special (as opposed to universal) rights to health care, harm-prevention, prudential arguments of the sort used to justify public health measures, and two arguments that show that effective charity shares features of public goods (in the technical sense) is sufficient to do the work of an alleged universal right to a decent minimum of health care.

Arguments from Special Rights

The right-claim we have been examining (and find unsupported) has been a *universal* right-claim: one that attributes the same right to all persons. *Special* right-claims, in contrast, restrict the right in question to certain individuals or groups.

There are at least three types of arguments that can be given for special rights to health care. First, there are arguments from the requirements of rectifying past or present institutional injustices. It can be argued, for example, that American blacks and native Americans are entitled to a certain core set of health-care services owing to their history of unjust treatment by government or other social institutions, on the grounds that these injustices have directly or indirectly had detrimental effects on the health of the groups in question. Second, there are arguments from the requirements of compensation to those who have suffered unjust harm or who have been unjustly exposed to health risks by the assignable actions of private individuals or corporations—for instance, those who have suffered neurological damage from the effects of chemical pollutants.

Third, a strong moral case can be made for special rights to health care for those who have undergone exceptional sacrifices for the good of society as a whole—in particular those whose health has been adversely affected through military service. The most obvious candidates for such compensatory special rights are soldiers wounded in combat.

Arguments from the Prevention of Harm

The content of the right to a decent minimum is typically understood as being more extensive than those traditional public health services that are usually justified on the grounds that they are required to protect the citizenry from certain harms arising from the interactions of persons living together in large numbers. Yet such services have been a major factor—if not *the* major factor—in reducing morbidity and mortality rates. Examples include sanitation and immunization. The moral justification of such measures, which constitute an important element in a decent minimum of health care, rests upon the widely accepted Harm (Prevention) Principle, not upon a right to health care.

The Harm Prevention argument for traditional public health services, however, may be elaborated in a way that brings them closer to arguments for a universal right to health care. With some plausibility one might contend that once the case has been made

for expending public resources on public health measures, there is a moral (and perhaps Constitutional) obligation to achieve some standard of *equal protection* from the harms these measures are designed to prevent. Such an argument, if it could be made out, would imply that the availability of basic public health services should not vary greatly across different racial, ethnic, or geographic groups within the country.

Prudential Arguments

Prudent arguments for health-care services typically emphasize benefits rather than the prevention of harm. It has often been argued, in particular, that the availability of certain basic forms of health care make for a more productive labor force or improve the fitness of the citizenry for national defense. This type of argument, too, does not assume that individuals have moral rights (whether special or universal) to the services in question.

It seems very likely that the combined scope of the various special health-care rights discussed above, when taken together with harm prevention and prudential arguments for basic health services and an argument from equal protection through public health measures, would do a great deal toward satisfying the health-care needs which those who advocate a universal right to a decent minimum are most concerned about. In other words, once the strength of a more pluralistic approach is appreciated, we may come to question the popular dogma that policy initiatives designed to achieve a decent minimum of health care for all must be grounded in a universal moral right to a decent minimum. This suggestion is worth considering because it again brings home the importance of the methodological difficulty encountered earlier. Even if, for instance, there is wide consensus on the considered judgment that the lower health prospects of inner city blacks are not only morally unacceptable but an injustice, it does not follow that this injustice consists of the infringement of a universal right to a decent minimum of health care. Instead, the injustice might lie in the failure to rectify past injustices or in the failure to achieve public health arrangements that meet a reasonable standard of equal protection for all.

Two Arguments for Enforced Beneficence

The pluralistic moral case for a legal entitlement to a decent minimum of health care (in the absence of a universal moral right) may be strengthened further by non-rights-based arguments from the principle of beneficence.[2] The possibility of making out such arguments depends upon the assumption that some principles may be justifiably enforced even if they are not principles specifying valid right-claims. There is at least one widely recognized class of such principles requiring contribution to the production of "public goods" in the technical sense (for example, tax laws requiring contribution to national defense). It is characteristic of public goods that each individual has an incentive to withhold his contribution to the collective goal even though the net result is that the goal will not be achieved. Enforcement of a principle requiring all individuals to contribute to the goal is necessary to overcome the individual's incentive to withhold contribution by imposing penalties for his own failure to contribute and by assuring him that others will contribute. There is a special subclass of principles whose enforcement is justified not only by the need to overcome the individual's incentive to withhold compliance with the principle but also to ensure that individuals' efforts are appropriately *coordinated*. For example, enforcing the rule of the road to drive only on the right not only ensures a joint effort toward the goal of safe driving but also coordinates individuals' efforts so as to make the attainment of that goal possible. Indeed, in the case of the "rule of the road" a certain kind of coordinated joint effort is the public good whose attainment justifies enforcement. But regardless of whether the production of a public good requires the solution of a coordination problem or not, there may be no *right* that is the correlative of the coercively backed obligation specified by the principle. There are two arguments for enforced beneficence, and they each depend upon both the idea of coordination and on certain aspects of the concept of a public good.

Both arguments begin with an assumption reasonable libertarians accept: there is a basic moral obligation of charity or beneficence to those in need. In a society that has the resources and technical knowledge to improve health or at least to ameliorate important health defects, the application of this requirement of beneficence includes the provision of resources for at least certain forms of health care. If we are sincere, we will be concerned with the efficacy of our charitable or beneficent impulses. It is all well and good for the libertarian to say that voluntary giving *can* replace the existing array of government entitlement programs, but this *possibility* will be cold comfort to the needy if, for any of several reasons, voluntary giving falters.

Social critics on the left often argue that in a highly competitive acquisitive society such as ours it is naive to think that the sense of beneficence will win out over the urgent promptings of self-interest. One need not argue, however, that voluntary giving fails from weakness of the will. Instead one can argue that even if each individual recognizes a moral duty to contribute to the aid of others and is motivationally capable of acting on that duty, some important forms of beneficence will not be forthcoming because each individual will rationally conclude that he should not contribute.

Many important forms of health care, especially those involving large-scale capital investment for technology, cannot be provided except through the contibutions of large numbers of persons. This is also true of the most important forms of medical research. But if so, then the beneficent individual will not be able to act effectively, in isolation. What is needed is a coordinated joint effort.

First argument. There are many ways in which I might help others in need. Granted the importance of health, providing a decent minimum of health care for all, through large-scale collective efforts, will be a more important form of beneficence than the various charitable acts A, B, and C, which I might perform *independently*, that is, whose success does not depend upon the contributions of others. Nonetheless, if I am rationally beneficent I will reason as follows: either enough others will contribute to the decent minimum project to achieve this goal, even if I do not contribute to it; or not enough others will contribute to achieve a decent minimum, even if I do contribute. In either case, my contribution will be wasted. In other words, granted the scale of the investment required and the virtually negligible size of my own contribution, I can disregard the minute possibility that my contribution might make the difference between success and failure. But if so, then the rationally beneficent thing for me to do is not to waste my contribution on the project of ensuring a decent minimum but instead to undertake an independent act of beneficence; A, B, or C—where I know my efforts will be needed and efficacious. But if everyone, or even many people, reason in this way, then what we each recognize as the most effective form of beneficence will not come about. Enforcement of a principle requiring contributions to ensuring a decent minimum is needed

The first argument is of the same form as standard public goods arguments for enforced contributions to national defense, energy conservation, and many other goods, with this exception. In standard public goods arguments, it is usually assumed that the individual's incentive for not contributing is self-interest and that it is in his interest not to contribute because he will be able to partake of the good, if it is produced, even if he does not contribute. In the case at hand, however, the individual's incentive for not contributing to the joint effort is not self-interest, but rather his desire to maximize the good he can do for others with a given amount of his resources. Thus if he contributes but the goal of achieving a decent minimum for all would have been achieved without his contribution, then he has still failed to use his resources in a maximally beneficent way relative to the options of either contributing or not to the joint project, even though the goal of achieving a decent minimum is attained. The rationally beneficent thing to do, then, is not to contribute, even though the result of everyone's acting in a rationally beneficent way will be a relatively ineffective patchwork of small-scale individual acts of beneficence rather than a large-scale, coordinated effort.

Second argument. I believe that ensuring a decent minimum of health care for all is more important than projects A, B, or C, and I am willing to contribute to the decent minimum project, but only if I have assurance that enough others will contribute to achieve the threshold of investment necessary for success. Unless I have this assurance, I will conclude that it is less than rational—and perhaps even morally irresponsible—to contribute my resources to the decent minimum project. For my contribution will be wasted if not enough others contribute. If I lack assurance of sufficient contributions by others, the rationally beneficent thing for me to do is to expend my "beneficence budget" on some less-than-optimal project A, B, or C, whose success does not depend on the contribution of others. But without enforcement, I cannot be assured that enough others will contribute, and if others reason as I do, then what we all believe to be the most effective form of beneficence will not be forthcoming. Others may fail to contribute either because the promptings of self-interest overpower their sense of beneficence, or because they reason as I did in the First Argument, or for some other reason.

Both arguments conclude that an enforced decent minimum principle is needed to achieve coordinated joint effort. However, there is this difference. The Second Argument focuses on the *assurance problem*, while the first does not. In the Second Argument all that is needed is the assumption that rational beneficence requires assurance that enough others will contribute. In the First Argument the individual's reason for not contributing is not that he lacks assurance that enough others will contribute, but rather that it is better for him not to contribute regardless of whether others do or not.

Neither argument depends on an assumption of conflict between the individual's moral motivation of beneficence and his inclination of self-interest. Instead the difficulty is that in the absence of enforcement, individuals who strive to make their beneficence most effective will thereby fail to benefit the needy as much as they might.

A standard response to those paradoxes of rationality known as public goods problems is to introduce a coercive mechanism which attaches penalties to non-contribution and thereby provides each individual with the assurance that enough others will reciprocate so that his contribution will not be wasted and an effective incentive for him to contribute even if he has reason to believe that enough others will contribute to achieve the goal without his contribution. My suggestion is that the same type of argument that is widely accepted as a justification for enforced principles requiring contributions toward familiar public goods provides support for a coercively backed principle specifying a certain list of health programs for the needy and requiring those who possess the needed resources to contribute to the establishment of such programs, even if the needy have no *right* to the services those programs provide. Such an arrangement would serve a dual function: it would coordinate charitable efforts by focusing them on one set of services among the indefinitely large constellation of possible expressions of beneficence,

and it would ensure that the decision to allocate resources to these services will become effective.

NOTES

1. Ronald Dworkin, *Taking Rights Seriously* (Cambridge, MA: Harvard University Press, 1977), pp. 184–205.
2. For an exploration of various arguments for a duty of beneficence and an examination of the relationship between justice and beneficence, in general and in health care, see Allen E. Buchanan, "Philosophical Foundations of Beneficence," *Beneficence and Health Care*, ed. Earl E. Shelp (Dordrecht, Holland: Reidel Publishing Co., 1982).

Rights to Health Care, Social Justice, and Fairness in Health Care Allocations: Frustrations in the Face of Finitude

H. TRISTRAM ENGELHARDT, JR.

Engelhardt asserts that "a basic human secular moral right to health care does not exist—not even to a 'decent minimum of health care.'" He distinguishes between losses that people suffer because of bad fortune and those due to unfairness. The former do not establish a duty of aid to the unfortunate (there is no moral right to such aid), but the latter may constitute claims on others. Out of compassion or benevolence, society may freely consent to help those in need, but there is no forced obligation to do so.

The imposition of a single-tier, all-encompassing health care system is morally unjustifiable. It is a coercive act of totalitarian ideological zeal, which fails to recognize the diversity of moral visions that frame interests in health care, the secular moral limits of state authority, and the authority of individuals over themselves and their own property. It is an act of secular immorality.

A basic human secular moral right to health care does not exist—not even to a "decent minimum of health care." Such rights must be created.

The difficulty with supposed right to health care, as well as with many claims regarding justice or fairness in access to health care, should be apparent.

From *Foundations of Bioethics*, 2d ed., by H. Tristram Engelhardt, Jr., (1996). Reprinted by permission of Oxford University Press.

Since the secular moral authority for common action is derived from permission or consent, it is difficult (indeed, for a large-scale society, materially impossible) to gain moral legitimacy for the thoroughgoing imposition on health care of one among the many views of beneficence and justice. There are, after all, as many accounts of beneficence, justice, and fairness as there are major religions.

Most significantly, there is a tension between the foundations of general secular morality and the various particular positive claims founded in particular visions of beneficence and justice. It is materially impossible both to respect the freedom of all and to achieve their long-range best interests. Loose talk about justice and fairness in health care is therefore morally misleading, because it suggests that there is a particular canonical vision of justice or fairness that all have grounds to endorse....

Rights to health care constitute claims on services and goods. Unlike rights to forbearance, which require others to refrain from interfering, which show the unity of the authority to use others, rights to beneficence are rights grounded in particular theories or accounts of the good. For general authority, they require others to participate actively in a particular understanding of the good life or justice. Without an appeal to the principle of permission, to advance such rights is to claim that one may press others into labor or confiscate their property. Rights to health care, unless they are derived from special contractual agreements, depend on particular understandings of beneficence rather than on authorizing permission. They may therefore conflict with the decisions of individuals who may not wish to participate in, and may indeed be morally opposed to, realizing a particular system of health care. Individuals always have the secular moral authority to use their own resources in ways that collide with fashionable understandings of justice or the prevailing consensus regarding fairness.

Health Care Policy: The Ideology of Equal, Optimal Care

It is fashionable to affirm an impossible commitment in health care delivery, as, for example, in the following four widely embraced health care policy goals, which are at loggerheads:

1. The best possible care is to be provided for all.
2. Equal care should be guaranteed.
3. Freedom of choice on the part of health care provider and consumer should be maintained.
4. Health care costs are to be contained.

One cannot provide the best possible health care for all and contain health care costs. One cannot provide equal health care for all and respect the freedom of individuals peaceably to pursue with others their own visions of health care or to use their own resources and energies as they decide. For that matter, one cannot maintain freedom in the choice of health care services while containing the costs of health care. One may also not be able to provide all with equal health care that is at the same time the very best care because of limits on the resources themselves.

That few openly address these foundational moral tensions at the roots of contemporary health care policy suggests that the problems are shrouded in a collective illusion, a false consciousness, an established ideology within which certain facts are politically unacceptable.

These difficulties spring not only from a conflict between freedom and beneficence, but from a tension among competing views of what it means to pursue and achieve the good in health care (e.g., is it more important to provide equal care to all or the best possible health care to the least-well-off class?). The pursuit of incompatible or incoherent health care is rooted in the failure to face the finitude of secular moral authority, the finitude of secular moral vision, the finitude of human powers in the face of death and suffering, the finitude of human life, and the finitude of human financial resources. A health care system that acknowledges the moral and financial limitations on the provision of health care would need to

1. endorse inequality in access to health care as morally unavoidable because of private resources and human freedom;
2. endorse setting a price on saving human life as a part of establishing a cost-effective health care system established through communal resources.

Even though all health care systems de facto enjoy inequalities and must to some extent ration the health care they provide through communal resources, this is not usually forthrightly acknowledged. There is an ideological bar to recognizing and coming to terms with the obvious.

Only a prevailing collective illusion can account for the assumption in U.S. policy that health care may be provided (1) while containing costs (2) without setting a price on saving lives and preventing suffering when using communal funds and at the same time (3) ignoring the morally unavoidable inequalities due to private resources and human freedom. This false consciousness shaped the deceptions central to the Clinton health care proposal, as it was introduced in 1994. It was advanced to support a health care system purportedly able to provide all with (1) the best of care and (2) equal care, while achieving (3) cost containment, and still (4) allowing those who wish the liberty to purchase fee-for-service health care.[1] While not acknowledging the presence of rationing, the proposal required silent rationing in order to contain costs by limiting access to high-cost, low-yield treatments that a National Health Board would exclude from the "guaranteed benefit package."[2] In addition, it advanced mechanisms to slow technological innovation so as further to reduce the visibility of rationing choices.[3] One does not have to ration that which is not available. There has been a failure to acknowledge the moral inevitability of inequalities in health care due to the limits of secular governmental authority, human freedom, and the existence of private property, however little that may be. There was also the failure to acknowledge the need to ration health care within communal programs if costs are to be contained. It has been ideologically unacceptable to recognize these circumstances....

Justice, Freedom, and Inequality

Interests in justice as beneficence are motivated in part by inequalities and in part by needs. That some have so little while others have so much properly evokes moral concerns of beneficence. Still,... the moral authority to use force to set such inequalities aside is limited. These limitations are in part due to the circumstance that the resources one could use to aid those in need are already owned by other people. One must establish whether and when inequalities and needs generate rights or claims against others.

The Natural and Social Lotteries

"Natural lottery" is used to identify changes in fortune that result from natural forces, not directly from the actions of persons. The natural lottery shapes the distribution of both naturally and socially conditioned assets. The natural lottery contrasts with the social lottery, which is used to identify changes in fortune that are not the result of natural forces but the actions of persons. The social lottery shapes the distribution of social and natural assets. The natural and social lotteries, along with one's own free decisions, determine the distribution of natural and social assets. The social lottery is termed a lottery, though it is the outcome of personal actions, because of the complex and unpredictable interplay of personal choices and because of the unpredictable character of the outcomes, which do not conform to an ideal pattern and because the outcomes are the results of social forces, not the immediate choices of those subject to them.

All individuals are exposed to the vicissitudes of nature. Some are born healthy and by luck remain so for a long life, free of disease and major suffering. Others are born with serious congenital or genetic diseases, others contract serious crippling fatal illnesses early in life, and yet others are injured and maimed. Those who win the natural lottery will for most of their lives not be in need of medical care. They will live full lives and die painless and peaceful deaths. Those who lost the natural lottery will be in need of health care to blunt their sufferings and, where possible, to cure their diseases and to restore function. There will be a spectrum of losses, ranging from minor problems such as having teeth with cavities to major tragedies such as developing childhood leukemia, inheriting Huntington's chorea, or developing amyelotrophic lateral sclerosis.

These tragic outcomes are the deliverances of nature, for which no one, without some special view of accountability or responsibility, is responsible (unless, that is, one recognizes them as the results of the Fall or as divine chastisements). The circumstance that individuals are injured by hurricanes, storms, and earthquakes is often simply no one's fault. When no one is to blame, no one may be charged with the responsibility of making whole those who lose the natural lottery on the ground of accountability for the harm. One will need an argument dependent on a particular sense of fairness to show that the readers of this volume should submit to the forcible redistribution of their resources to provide health care for those injured by nature. It may very well be unfeeling, unsympathetic, or uncharitable not to provide such help. One may face eternal hellfires for failing to provide aid.[4] But it is another thing to show in general secular moral terms that individuals owe others such help in a way that would morally authorize state force to redistribute their private resources and energies or to constrain their free choices with others. To be in dire need does not by itself create a secular moral right to be rescued from that need. The natural lottery creates inequalities and places individuals at disadvantage without creating a straightforward secular moral obligation on the part of others to aid those in need.

Individuals differ in their resources not simply because of outcomes of the natural lottery, but also due to the actions of others. Some deny themselves immediate pleasures in order to accumulate wealth or to leave inheritances; through a complex web of love, affection, and mutual interest, individuals convey resources, one to another, so that those who are favored prosper and those who are ignored languish. Some as a consequence grow wealthy and others grow poor, not through anyone's malevolent actions or omissions, but simply because they were not favored by the love, friendship, collegiality, and associations through which fortunes develop and individuals prosper. In such cases there will be neither fairness nor unfairness, but simply good and bad fortune.

In addition, some will be advantaged or disadvantaged, made rich, poor, ill, diseased, deformed, or disabled because of the malevolent and blameworthy actions and omissions of others. Such will be unfair circumstances, which just and beneficent states should try to prevent and to rectify through legitimate police protection, forced restitution, and charitable programs. Insofar as an injured party has a claim against an injurer to be made whole, not against society, the outcome is unfortunate from the perspective of society's obligations and obligations of innocent citizens to make restitution. Restitution is owed by the injurer, not society or others. There will be outcomes of the social lottery that are on the one hand blameworthy in the sense of resulting from the culpable actions of others, though on the other hand a society has no obligation to rectify them. The social lottery includes the exposure to the immoral and unjust actions of others. Again, one will need an argument dependent on a particular sense of fairness to show that the readers of this volume should submit to the forcible redistribution of their resources to provide health care to those injured by others.

When individuals come to purchase health care, some who lose the natural lottery will be able at least in part to compensate for those losses through their winnings at the social lottery. They will be able to afford expensive health care needed to restore health and to regain function. On the other hand, those who lose in both the natural and the social lottery will be in need of health care, but without the resources to acquire it.

The Rich and the Poor: Differences in Entitlements

If one owns property by virtue of just acquisition or just transfer, then one's title to that property will not be undercut by the tragedies and needs of others. One will simply own one's property. On the other hand, if one owns property because such ownership is justified within a system that ensures a beneficent distribution of goods (e.g., the achievement of the greatest balance of benefits over harms for the greatest number or the greatest advantage for the least-well-off class), one's ownership will be affected by the needs of others.... Property is in part privately owned in a strong sense that cannot be undercut by the needs of others. In addition, all have a general right to the fruits of the earth, which constitutes the basis for a form of taxation as rent to provide fungible payments to individuals, whether or not they are in need. Finally, there are likely to be resources held in common by groups that may establish bases for their distribution to meet health care concerns. The first two forms of entitlement or ownership exist unconstrained by medical or other needs. The last form of entitlement or ownership, through the decision of a community, may be conditioned by need.

The existence of any amount of private resources can be the basis for inequalities that secular moral authority may not set aside. Insofar as people own things, they will have a right to them, even if others need them. Because the presence of permission is cardinal, the test of whether one must transfer one's goods to others will not be whether such a redistribution will not prove onerous or excessive for the person subjected to the distribution, but whether the resources belong to that individual. Consider that you may be reading this book next to a person in great need. The test of whether a third person may take resources from you to help that individual in need will not be whether you will suffer from the transfer, but rather whether you have consented—at least this is the case if the principle of permission functions in general secular morality.... The principle of permission is the source of authority when moral strangers collaborate, because they do not share a common understanding of fairness or of the good. As a consequence, goal-oriented approaches to the just distribution of resources must be restricted to commonly owned goods, where there is authority to create programs for their use.

Therefore, one must qualify the conclusions of the 1983 American President's Commission for the Study of Ethical Problems that suggest that excessive burdens should determine the amount of tax persons should pay to sustain an adequate level of health care for those in need.[5] Further, one will have strong grounds for morally condemning systems that attempt to impose an all-encompassing health care plan that would require "equality of care [in the sense of avoiding] the creation of a tiered system [by] providing care based only on differences of need, not individual or group characteristics."[6] Those who are rich are always at secular moral liberty to purchase more and better health care.

Drawing the Line Between the Unfortunate and the Unfair

How one regards the moral significance of the natural and social lotteries and the moral force of private ownership will determine how one draws the line between circumstances that are simply unfortunate and those that are unfortunate and in addition unfair in the sense of constituting a claim on the resources of others.

Life in general, and health care in particular, reveal circumstances of enormous tragedy, suffering, and deprivation. The pains and sufferings of illness, disability, and disease, as well as the limitations of deformity, call on the sympathy of all to provide aid and give comfort. Injuries, disabilities, and diseases due to the forces of nature are unfortunate. Injuries, disabilities, and diseases due to the unconsented-to actions of others are unfair. Still, outcomes of the unfair actions of others are not necessarily society's fault and are in this sense unfortunate. The horrible injuries that come every night to the emergency rooms of major hospitals may be someone's fault, even if they are not the fault of society, much less that of uninvolved citizens. Such outcomes, though unfair with regard to the relationship of the injured with the injurer, may be simply unfortunate with respect to society and other citizens (and may licitly be financially exploited). One is thus faced with distinguishing the difficult line between acts of God, as well as immoral acts of individuals that do not constitute a basis for societal retribution on the one hand, and injuries that provide such a basis on the other.

A line must be created between those losses that will be made whole through public funds and those that will not. Such a line was drawn in 1980 by Patricia Harris, the then secretary of the Department of Health, Education, and Welfare, when she ruled that heart transplantations should be considered experimental and therefore not reimbursable through Medicare.[7] To be in need of a heart transplant and not have the funds available would be an unfortunate circumstance but not unfair. One was not eligible for a heart transplant even if another person had intentionally damaged one's heart. From a moral point of view, things would have been different if the federal government had in some culpable fashion injured one's heart. So, too, if promises of treatment had been made. For example, to suffer from appendicitis or pneumonia and not as a qualifying patient receive treatment guaranteed through a particular governmental or private insurance system would be unfair, not simply unfortunate.

Drawing the line between the unfair and the unfortunate is unavoidable because it is impossible in general secular moral terms to translate all needs into rights, into claims against the resources of others. One must with care decide where the line is to be drawn. To distinguish needs from mere desires, one must endorse one among the many competing visions of morality and human flourishing. One is forced to draw a line between those needs (or desires) that constitute claims on the aid of others and those that do not. The line distinguishing unfortunate from unfair circumstances justifies by default certain social and economic inequalities in the sense of determining who, if anyone, is obliged in general secular immorality to remedy such circumstances or achieve equality. Is the request of an individual to have life extended through a heart transplant at great cost, and perhaps only for a few years, a desire for an inordinate extension of life? Or is it a need to be secure against a premature death?...Outside a particular view of the good life, needs do not create rights to the services or goods of others.[8] Indeed, outside of a particular moral vision there is no canonical means for distinguishing desires from needs.

There is a practical difficulty in regarding major losses at the natural and social lotteries as generating claims to health care: attempts to restore health indefinitely can deplete societal resources in the pursuit of ever-more incremental extensions of life of marginal quality. A relatively limited amount of food and shelter is required to preserve the lives of individuals. But an indefinite amount of resources can in medicine be committed to the further preservation of human life, the marginal postponement of death, and the marginal alleviation of human suffering and disability. Losses at the natural lottery with regard to health can consume major resources with little return. Often one can only purchase a little relief, and that only at great costs. Still, more decisive than the problem of avoiding the possibly overwhelming costs involved in satisfying certain health care desires (e.g., postponing death for a while through the use of critical care) is the problem of selecting the correct content-full account of justice in order canonically to distinguish between needs and desires and to translate needs into rights.

Beyond Equality: An Egalitarianism of Altruism Versus an Egalitarianism of Envy

The equal distribution of health care is itself problematic, a circumstance recognized in *Securing Access to Health Care*, the 1983 report of the President's Commission.[9] The difficulties are multiple:

1. Although in theory, at least, one can envisage providing all with equal levels of decent shelter, one cannot restore all to or preserve all in an equal state of health. Many health needs cannot be satisfied in the same way one can address most needs for food and shelter.
2. If one provided all with the same amount of funds to purchase health care or the same amount of services, the amount provided would be far too much for some and much too little for others who could have benefited from more investment in treatment and research.
3. If one attempts to provide equal health care in the sense of allowing individuals to select health care only from a predetermined list of available therapies, or through some managed health care plan such as accountable (to the government) health care plans or regional health alliances, which would be provided to all so as to prevent the rich from having access to better health care than the poor, one would have immorally confiscated private property and have restricted the freedom of individuals to join in voluntary relationships and associations.

That some are fortunate in having more resources is neither more nor less arbitrary or unfair than some having better health, better looks, or more talents. In any event, the translation of unfortunate circumstances into unfair circumstances, other than with regard to violations of the principle of permission, requires the imposition of a particular vision of beneficence or justice....

Conflicting Models of Justice: From Content to Procedure

John Rawls's *A Theory of Justice* and Robert Nozick's *Anarchy, State, and Utopia* offer contrasting understandings of what should count as justice or fairness. They sustain differing suggestions regarding the nature of justice in health care. They provide a contrast between justice as primarily structural, a pattern of distributions that is amenable to rational disclosure, versus justice as primarily procedural, a matter of fair negotiation.[10] In *A Theory of Justice* Rawls forwards an expository device of an ahistorical perspective from which to discover the proper pattern for the distribution of resources, and therefore presumably for the distribution of health care resources. In this understanding, it is assumed that societally based entitlements have moral priority. Nozick, in contrast, advances a historical account of just distributions within which justice depends on what individuals have agreed to do with and for each other. Nozick holds that individually based entitlements are morally prior to societally based entitlements. In contrast with Rawls, who argues that one can discover a proper pattern for the allocation of resources, Nozick argues that such a pattern cannot be discovered and that instead one can only identify the characteristics of a just process for fashioning rights to health care....

The differences between Nozick of *Anarchy, State, and Utopia* and Rawls of *A Theory of Justice* express themselves in different accounts of entitlements and ownership, and in different understandings of nonprincipled fortune and misfortune. For Rawls, one has justifiable title to goods if such a title is part of a system that ensures the greatest benefit to the least advantaged, consistent with a just-savings principle, and with offices and positions open to all under conditions of fair equality and opportunity, and where each person has an equal right to the most extensive total system of equal basic liberties compatible with a similar system of liberty for all. In contrast, for Nozick, one simply owns things: "Things come into the world already attached to people having entitlements over them."[11] If one really owns things, there will be freedom-based limitations on principles of distributive justice. One may not use people or their property without their permission or authorization. The needs of others will not erase one's property rights. The readers of this book should consider that they may be wearing wedding rings or other jewelry not essential to their lives, which could be sold to buy antibiotics to save identifiable lives in the third world. Those who keep such baubles may in part be acting in agreement with Nozick's account and claiming that "it is my right to keep my wedding ring for myself, even though the proceeds from its sale could save the lives of individuals in dire need."

Nozick's account requires a distinction between someone's secular moral rights and what is right, good, or proper to do. At times, selling some (perhaps all) of one's property to support the health care of those in need will be the right thing to do, even though one has a secular moral right to refuse to sell. This contrast derives from the distinction Nozick makes between *freedom as a side constraint*, as the very condition for the possibility of a secular moral

community, and *freedom as one value among others*. This contrast can be understood as a distinction between those claims of justice based on the very possibility of a moral community, versus those claims of justice that turn on interests in particular goods and values, albeit interests recognized in the original position. For Nozick, one may not use innocent free persons without their consent, even if that use will save lives by providing needed health care or securing equality of opportunity. Even if such would be a good thing to do (e.g., in this sense of saving lives), no one has a right to do it. Because for Nozick one needs the *actual* consent of *actual* persons in order to respect them as free persons, their rights can morally foreclose the pursuit of many morally worthy goals. In contrast, Rawls treats freedom or liberty as a value. As a consequence, in developing just institutions, Rawls does not require actual consent of those involved. As a result, Rawls would allow rights to self-determination to be limited in order to achieve important social goals....

This contrast between Rawls and Nozick can be appreciated more generally as a contrast between two quite different principles of justice, each of which has strikingly different implications for the allocation of health care resources.

1. Freedom- or permission-based justice is concerned with distributions of goods made in accord with the notion of the secular moral community as a peaceable social structure binding moral strangers, members of diverse concrete moral communities. Such justice will therefore require the consent of the individuals involved in a historical nexus of justice-regarding institutions understood in conformity with the principle of permission. The principle of beneficence may be pursued only within constraints set by the principle of permission.

2. Goals-based justice is concerned with the achievement of the good of individuals in society, where the pursuit of beneficence is not constrained by a strong principle of permission, but driven by some particular understanding of morality, justice, or fairness. Such justice will vary in substance as one

attempts, for example, to (a) give each person an equal share; (b) give each person what that person needs; (c) give each person a distribution as a part of a system designed to achieve the greatest balance of benefits over harms for the greatest number of persons; (d) give each person a distribution as a part of a system designed to maximize the advantage of the least-well-off class with conditions of equal liberty for all and of fair opportunity.

Allocations of health care in accord with freedom- or permission-based justice must occur within the constraint to respect the free choices of persons, including their exercise of their property rights. Allocations of health care in accord with goals-based justice will need to establish what it means to provide a just pattern of health care, and what constitutes true needs, not mere desires, and how to rank the various health goals among themselves and in comparison with nonhealth goals. Such approaches to justice in health care will require a way of ahistorically discovering the proper pattern for the distribution of resources.

Permission-based and goals-based approaches to justice in health care contrast because they offer competing interpretations of the maxim, "Justitia est constans et perpetua voluntas jus suum cuique tribuens" (Justice is the constant and perpetual will to render everyone his due).[12] A permission-based approach holds that justice is first and foremost giving to each the right to be respected as a free individual as the source of secular moral authority, in the disposition of personal services and private goods: that which is due (*ius*) to individuals is respect of their authority over themselves and their possessions. In contrast, a goals-based approach holds that justice is receiving a share of the goods, which is fair by an appeal to a set of ahistorical criteria specifying what a fair share should be, that is, what share is due to each individual. Since there are various senses of a fair share (e g., an equal share, a share in accordance with the system that maximizes the balance of benefits over harms, etc.), there will be various competing senses of justice in health care under the rubric of goals-based justice....

The Moral Inevitability of a Multitier Health Care System

. . . In the face of unavoidable tragedies and contrary moral intuitions, a multitiered system of health care is in many respects a compromise. On the one hand, it provides some amount of health care for all, while on the other hand allowing those with resources to purchase additional or better services. It can endorse the use of communal resources for the provision of a decent minimal or basic amount of health care for all, while acknowledging the existence of private resources at the disposal of some individuals to purchase better basic as well as luxury care. While the propensity to seek more than equal treatment for oneself or loved ones is made into a vicious disposition in an egalitarian system, a multitier system allows for the expression of individual love and the pursuit of private advantage, though still supporting a general social sympathy for those in need. Whereas an egalitarian system must suppress the widespread human inclination to devote private resources to the purchase of the best care for those whom one loves, a multitier system can recognize a legitimate place for the expression of such inclinations. A multitier system (1) should support individual providers and consumers against attempts to interfere in their free association and their use of their own resources, though (2) it may allow positive rights to health care to be created for individuals who have not been advantaged by the social lottery.

The serious task is to decide how to define and provide a decent minimum or basic level of care as a floor of support for all members of society, while allowing money and free choice to fashion special tiers of services for the affluent. In addressing this general issue of defining what is to be meant by a decent minimum basic level or a minimum adequate amount of health care, the American President's Commission in 1983 suggested that in great measure content is to be created rather than discovered by democratic processes, as well as by the forces of the market. "In a democracy, the appropriate values to be assigned to the consequences of policies must ultimately be determined by people expressing their values through social and political processes as well as in the marketplace."[13]

The Commission, however, also suggested that the concept of adequacy could in part be discovered by an appeal to that amount of care that would meet the standards of sound medical practice. "Adequacy does require that everyone receive care that meets standards of sound medical practice."[14] But what one means by "sound medical practice" is itself dependent on particular understandings within particular cultures. Criteria for sound medical practice are as much created as discovered. The moral inevitability of multiple tiers of care brings with it multiple standards of proper or sound medical practice and undermines the moral plausibility of various obiter dicta concerning the centralized allocation of medical resources....

NOTES

1. The White House Domestic Policy Council, *The President's Health Security Plan* (New York: Times Books, 1993).
2. The White House Domestic Policy Council, *The President's Health Security Plan*, p. 43.
3. Innovation would be discouraged as drug prices are subject to review as reasonable. The White House Domestic Policy Council, *The President's Health Security Plan*, p. 45.
4. In considering how to respond to the plight of the impecunious, one might consider the story Jesus tells of the rich man who fails to give alms to "a certain beggar named Lazarus, full of sores, who was laid at his gate, desiring to be fed with the crumbs which fell from the rich man's table" (Luke 16:20–21). The rich man, who was not forthcoming with alms, was condemned to a hell of excruciating torment.
5. President's Commission for the Study of Ethical Problems in Medicine and Biomedical and Behavioral Research, *Securing Access to Health Care* (Washington, DC.: U.S. Government Printing Office, 1983), vol. 1, pp. 43–46.
6. The White House Domestic Policy Council. "Ethical Foundations of Health Reform," in *The President's Health Security Plan*, p. 11.
7. H. Newman, "Exclusion of Heart Transplantation Procedures from Medicare Coverage," *Federal Register* 45 (Aug. 6, 1980): 52296. See also H. Newman, "Medicare Program: Solicitation of Hospitals and Medical Centers to Participate in a Study of Heart Transplants," *Federal Register* 46 (Jan. 22. 1981): 7072–75.
8. The reader should understand that the author holds that almsgiving is one of the proper responses to human suffering (in addition to being an appropriate expression of repentance, an act of repentance to which surely the author is obligated). It is just that the author acknowledges the limited secular moral authority of the state to compel charity coercively.
9. President's Commission, *Securing Access to Health Care*, vol. 1, pp. 18–19.
10. John Rawls, *A Theory of Justice* (Cambridge, Mass.: Harvard University Press, 1971), and Robert Nozick, *Anarchy, State, and Utopia* (New York: Basic Books, 1974).
11. Nozick, *Anarchy, State, and Utopia*, p. 160.
12. Flavius Petrus Sabbatius Justinianus, *The Institutes of Justinian*, trans. Thomas C. Sandars (1922; repr. Westport, Conn.: Greenwood Press, 1970), 1.1 p. 5.
13. President's Commission, *Securing Access to Health Care*, vol. 1, p. 37.
14. Ibid.

Health Care Reform: Lessons from Canada

RAISA BERLIN DEBER

Deber examines the workings of the Canadian health care system and highlights its advantages and disadvantages in relation to that in the United States. She points out that the Canadian system provides health care that is universal, low cost, and well regarded by Canadians. Lessons for the United States include: (1) universal health

From Raisa Berlin Deber, "Health Care Reform: Lessons from Canada," *American Journal of Public Health*, vol. 93, no. 1, January 2003.

insurance does not require a cumbersome bureaucracy, (2) a single-payer system has cost advantages, and (3) a federalist form of government causes problems for health care systems.

To Americans, Canada resembles the girl next door—familiar but often taken for granted. Despite flurries of interest in the Canadian health care system whenever the United States contemplates implementing universal health insurance, misunderstandings about its nature abound. Indeed, there is no Canadian system; instead, there are a set of publicly financed, provincially run insurance plans covering all legal residents for specified service categories, primarily "medically necessary" physician and hospital care. Neither does Canada have socialized medicine; these services are delivered by private providers. In all industrialized nations, health care seems to be perennially in crisis; however, access and quality in Canada are relatively high, spending relatively well controlled, and satisfaction high, although declining. Canadians remain devoted to their system, but they are increasingly worried that it may not survive.

Recently, several provincial commissions investigated health care and weighed in with their recommendations,[1-3] while the Kirby Senate Committee[4] and the national Romanow Royal Commission[5] are completing extensive research and consultation activities and readying their final reports. What will emerge is unclear, but Canadians have loudly indicated their hopes and fears for the future. Although the Canadian model per se is unlikely to be adopted in the United States, it can provide clear lessons for its neighbor—both positive and negative.

Health Systems and the Limits to Markets

Most markets distribute goods on the basis of supply and demand, with price signals used to affect production and consumption decisions. When price drops, demand should increase, with a near-infinite demand for free goods. Conversely, with fixed supply and high demand, price should rise until enough people get priced out of the market to balance supply against this new (lower) level of demand at the new equilibrium price. Yet health care markets stubbornly refuse to follow these economic laws. Economists have debated why this is so and whether they can force health care to behave in accordance with theory. If the discrepancies result only from "asymmetry of information" (because the person who provides services also determines which services must be purchased), providing better information can produce better-informed consumers and allow market forces to prevail. Yet most health economists, particularly outside the United States, recognize that the key problem instead rests with "need." Consider the following scenarios[6]:

1. You want a taxi to take you to a destination across the city but have no money. Should you be taken there anyhow?
2. You win an all-expenses-paid week for two to a destination of your choice, which must be taken within the next 12 months. Do you accept?
3. You enter a hospital emergency room with a ruptured appendix but no money. Should you be treated anyhow?
4. You win free open-heart surgery in the hospital of your choice, which must be performed within the next 12 months, Do you accept?

Although the first 2 scenarios fit the predictions of economic models, the next two do not. Most people agree that the taxi driver need not take you, thus pricing you out of the taxicab market. Yet most also agree that the hospital must treat your appendix, and they would be horrified were you turned away for financial reasons. In economic terms, however, this means that you cannot be priced out of the market for appendix care; attempting to incorporate market forces means that we have set up an economic model in which there is a "floor price" (whatever charity or government will pay) but no ceiling price, because anyone priced out falls back into the publicly funded tier.

Although this model is attractive for providers, who are ensured that they will get at least the floor price, with any additional private charges as a bonus,

2 disquieting consequences follow. First, market forces are less able to achieve cost control. Second, deterioration of publicly funded services is likely because there would be no reason for consumers to pay extra for care unless the publicly funded tier is inadequate (or perceived to be inadequate). Accordingly, Canadian health policy analysts have vehemently defended the principle of "single-tier" publicly funded medicine for "medically necessary" services, not only on the usual grounds of equity but on the grounds of economic efficiency. Multiple payers are seen not only as diminishing equity but also as increasing the burden on business and the economy to pay those extra costs.

Similarly, although most people would be eager to take free trips, few wish open-heart surgery unless they need it. Canadian health policy has rejected the language of consumer sovereignty in favor of the language of need. However, balancing consumerism against need is an ongoing tension. Most recent reform documents—in Canada and abroad—pay deference to both the language of patient rights and the language of evidence-based medicine, with little attention to how these potentially conflicting concepts are to be reconciled.

All health systems must perform similar functions. Mechanisms must be in place to determine how care will be *financed*. Policymakers must determine which costs will remain the responsibility of individuals and which will be *socialized* across many potential recipients. This risk spreading can occur on a voluntary basis or can be mandatory. However, the distribution of risks is not uniform—a very small number of individuals will account for a very large proportion of health expenditures.[7] Accordingly, almost all nations except the United States have recognized that voluntary risk pooling within a competitive market for financing is unlikely to work, precisely because insurers need only avoid a small number of potential clients to avoid a large proportion of health expenditures, often making high risks uninsurable. Canada retains a widespread consensus that a single payer should be retained for core services; the debates are over what counts as core services and how much financing is required.

Systems also vary according to how care is organized and *delivered*. What is the role of the hospital?

How will different sectors be coordinated? How much authority rests with physicians?

Finally, systems must pay attention to how resources will flow from those paying for care to those delivering it. This dimension, which we have termed *allocation*, incorporates the incentives guiding the behavior of providers and care recipients.

Federalism and Health Care

Because Canada's 1867 constitution assigned most health care responsibilities to provincial jurisdiction,[8] Canadian health policy is inextricably intertwined with federal–provincial relationships. Canada is a federation of 10 provinces plus 3 sparsely populated northern territories. These provinces vary enormously in both size and fiscal capacity, ranging from the Atlantic province of Prince Edward Island, with a 2001 population of 135 000, to the industrial heartland of Ontario, with 11.4 million. The history of the often contentious evolution of the system (and the reactions by physicians) has been told else-where.[9-12] From the outset, it represented an attempt to balance the desire of Canadians for national standards of service against the differing fiscal capacities of the various provinces and provincial insistence that their jurisdiction be respected.

Financing the Canadian health care system accordingly evolved incrementally within individual provinces, as they responded to market failure, with national government involvement through a series of programs to share costs with the provinces. Initially, Ottawa provided funding for particular programs, such as public health, hospital construction, and training health personnel. In 1957, the Hospital Insurance and Diagnostic Services Act (HIDS)[13] was passed with all-party approval; it paid approximately half the cost of provincial insurance plans for hospital-based care, as long as the plans complied with specified national conditions. The 1966 Medical Care Act[14] cost-shared provincial insurance plans for physician services under similar provisions. By 1971, all provinces had complying plans insuring their populations for hospital and physician services. Because provinces have jurisdiction, one size does not fit all; there are considerable variations within Canada. In addition, although the financing arrangements were changed in 1977 to a mixture of cash and tax points (reducing the federal tax rates to allow the provinces to take up the resulting "tax room"), the same national terms and conditions initially introduced in HIDS were reinforced in the 1984 Canada Health Act.[15] The system accordingly reflects a hospital/doctor-centered view of health care as practiced in 1957, which is becoming increasingly inadequate.

In order to receive federal money, the provincial insurance plans had only to comply with the following national terms and conditions:

1. Public administration. This frequently misunderstood condition does not mandate public delivery of health services; most care is privately delivered. It represents a reaction to the high overheads associated with private insurance when the system was introduced,[16] and it requires that the health care insurance plan of a province "be administered and operated on a non-profit basis by a public authority appointed or designated by the government of the province"[15] and its activities subject to audit. This administration can be delegated, as long as accountability arrangements are in place.

2. Comprehensiveness. Coverage must include "all insured health services provided by hospitals, medical practitioners or dentists, and where the law of the province so permits, similar or additional services rendered by other health care practitioners."[15] (Insured dental services are defined as those that must be performed within hospitals; practically, less than 1% of dental services so qualify.)

3. Universality. The plan must entitle "one hundred per cent of the insured persons of the province to the insured health services provided for by the plan on uniform terms and conditions."[15]

4. Portability. Provisions must be in place to cover insured people when they move between provinces, and to ensure orderly (and uniform) provisions as to when coverage is deemed to have switched. The details are worked out by interprovincial agreements. Although there are some irritants, in general,

out-of-province care incurred during short visits (less than 3 months) remains the responsibility of the home province, which can set limitations (e.g., refuse to cover elective procedures). Out-of-country care is reimbursed at the rates payable in the home province. Since these rates are considerably less than what would be charged in the United States, Canadians leaving the country are strongly advised to have supplementary travel health insurance.

5. Accessibility. Provincial plans must "provide for insured health services on uniform terms and conditions and on a basis that does not impede or preclude, either directly or indirectly, whether by charges made to insured persons or otherwise, reasonable access to those services by insured persons."[15] Other provisions require that hospitals and health providers (usually physicians) receive "reasonable compensation," although the mechanisms are not defined.

In practice, this balancing act means that the federal government cannot act as decisionmaker, although it may occasionally attempt to influence policy directions through providing money or attempting to suggest guidelines. However, the comprehensiveness definition gives Ottawa a major influence on what services must be insured by provincial governments. The Canadian Institute for Health Information estimates that approximately 99% of expenditures for physician services, and 90% of expenditures for hospital care, come from public sector sources. Insurance coverage for such services is not tied to employment. However, other sectors (especially pharmaceuticals, chronic care, and dental care) are much more heavily funded from the private sector, including reliance on employment-based benefits.[17] Overall, about 70% of Canadian health expenditures comes from public sources, putting it among the least publicly financed of industrialized countries.[18]

For decades, delivery was largely unaffected by public financing. Most hospitals were private, not-for-profit organizations with independent boards. Recently, all provinces except Ontario subsumed hospitals into independent (or quasi-independent) regional health authorities, which were given responsibility for delivering an assortment of services.[19,20] (Ontario retains private not-for-profit hospitals, although the provincial government has become increasingly obtrusive, especially for those hospitals running deficits.) Physicians are private small businessmen, largely working fee-for-service, and moving only slowly (and voluntarily) from solo practice into various forms of groups. In some provinces, provincial governments have been attempting to encourage the move toward rostered group practice paid on a capitated basis, with remarkably little success to date.[21] Individual patients have free choice of physicians. Bills are usually submitted directly to the single payer, which means a decided lack of paperwork for either patient or provider. Indeed, in 1991, the US General Accounting Office estimated that, if the United States could get its administrative costs to the Canadian level, it could afford to cover the entire uninsured population.[22]

Issues Arising
Financing the System
In the mid-1980s, Canada faced a deficit trap. To avoid it, they squeezed supply. The federal government unilaterally changed the formula for transfers to the provincial governments, which led to a significant reduction in the cash portion of the transfer. In turn, provincial governments chopped budgets to hospitals, which in turn led to considerable growth in day surgery, reduction in hospital bed numbers, and instability in the nursing employment market.[23] They also attempted to squeeze physician fees. The result was that provincial expenditures per capita for health care, inflation adjusted, were lower in 1997 than they had been in 1989.[6] The search for efficiency proceeded apace, to the point where most hospitals were running at 95% occupancy or greater, and most providers felt that they were overworked and underpaid.[24]

Under the rubric of "sustainability," the pent-up demand for restoring funding (and incomes) to previous levels has dominated recent health policy discussions. Advocates of privatization claim that this increased spending cannot be met from public sources, while health reformers argue that if the issue is the ability to meet total costs (rather than the more political question of who will bear them),

a single payer should be retained. Some business leaders, recognizing that the search for alternative sources of revenue may represent a greater burden on payroll, support a single payer. Others retain an ideological objection to government involvement. Providers voice support in theory for public payment, but only if it guarantees that they will receive the resources they require to provide the level of services they feel is necessary. The public agrees; they are highly supportive of a single payer, but not if this means they would be denied care. Although it is not clear the extent to which waiting lists are an actual problem (this varying considerably by procedure and geographic area), they remain a highly potent and symbolic issue.

Another key dilemma is comprehensiveness, spoken of in terms of "defining the basket of services." Although provinces are free to go beyond the federal conditions—which establish a floor rather than a ceiling—in practice, many prefer to cut taxes. As care shifts from hospitals, it can shift beyond the boundaries of public insurance. Patients being treated in a hospital have full coverage for such necessities as pharmaceuticals, physiotherapy, and nursing. Once they are discharged, these costs need no longer be paid for from public funds.[25] Some provinces still pay for such care; others do not. The ongoing debate as to what should be "in" or "out" of the publicly financed services, and the role (if any) for user charges, has focused largely but not exclusively on "pharmacare" (coverage for outpatient prescription drugs) and home care.

The "first law of cost containment" states that the easiest way to control costs is to shift them to someone else. These issues have flowed over to massive disputes between levels of government (particularly the federal and provincial governments) and between provincial governments and providers, including some work stoppages by physicians and nurses in certain provinces. These disputes in turn are often resolved by sizeable reimbursement increases, which in turn increases pressure on other provinces to match the enriched contracts.

Delivery
There has been strong pressure to modernize delivery and eliminate "silos," which are seen as

impeding smooth delivery and efficient use of resources. The US experience with managed care and the UK experience with general practitioner fundholders are frequently cited examples of what should or should not be achieved, depending on the political and managerial preferences of the observer. The push for integration has been expressed in many ways, including establishing regional health authorities and the ongoing attempt to achieve primary care reform. Physicians within the Canadian clinical workforce are unusual in the degree of autonomy they have enjoyed with respect to where they will work and in the volume and mix of services they choose to deliver.[12] Most other clinicians must be hired by a provider organization and are accordingly subject to labor market forces in determining whether (and where) employment is available. The question of whether this state of affairs should be continued or not is an ongoing source of dispute.

Allocation

Two opposing trends have been evident. Some provinces, for some sectors, have moved toward the planned end of the allocation continuum, usually accompanied by rhetoric about the need for integrated services, better planning, and more efficiency.[19] For other sectors, there has been a movement toward more market-oriented approaches to allocation, usually linked to attempts to encourage competition. For example, Ontario assigned budgets for home care services to a series of regionally based Community Care Access Centres, which in turn are expected to contract out publicly funded services on the basis of "best quality, best price." The competing providers (both for profit and not-for-profit) respond to each request for proposals; the expectation is that competition will lead to efficiencies (which usually translate into a downward pressure on the wages, skill mix, and working conditions of the nurses, rehabilitation workers, and homemakers employed by these agencies).[26,27] Alberta wants to use competition and for-profit delivery to encourage similar efficiencies in the delivery of clinic services. Some academics suggest setting up competing integrated delivery models.[28]

Considerable attention has been paid to benchmarking, quality assurance, "report cards," and other mechanisms of improving accountability. Those seeking major reform tend to point with glee to any international evidence that Canada is no longer the best system. In that connection, the fact that the World Health Organization, using a controversial methodology that adjusted health system performance for the educational attainment of the population, ranked Canada 30th received considerably more attention than Canada's preadjustment ranking of 7th in the same document.[29] Similarly, considerable attention was paid to Canada's high level of health spending as a proportion of gross domestic product (GDP) (10.1% in 1992), but less to the fact that this reflected the relatively poorer performance of the economy, with actual spending in US dollars per capita being much lower.[30] (Indeed, as the economy did better, the ratio of spending to GDP dropped considerably, reaching 9.2% by 2000.)

Lessons for the United States
Size

A common fear about universal health insurance is that it requires a large and cumbersome bureaucracy. In that connection, it is important to recognize both that single-payer systems yield administrative efficiencies and that Canada's model is organized at the provincial (state) level. Canada's 2001 population was 30 million (vs 284.8 million in the United States); the largest provincial plan (Ontario's) served 11.4 million. In contrast, the largest US insurance plan, Aetna, served 17.2 million health care members, 13.5 million dental members, and 11.5 million group insurance customers. A US model organized at the state (or even substate) level would allow for flexibility to account for local circumstances and would probably result in a less bureaucratic system than at present.

Another feature of size is the recognition that most Canadian communities are not large enough to support competition (particularly for specialized services), even should this be considered desirable.[31] Small size also leads to problems in risk pooling, since one expensive case may place the entire plan at fiscal risk. Single-payer models encouraging cooperation are likely to be particularly applicable to the more rural portions of the United States.

Universal Coverage

A major advantage of a single-payer system is that one can attain universal coverage at a lower cost than is attained by pluralistic funding approaches. Canada has universal coverage, excellent health outcomes, minimal paperwork, and high public satisfaction, although coverage or reimbursement decisions do tend to become political. One key advantage is the avoidance of risk selection; no one is uninsurable. In a pluralistic system, government often ends up with the worst risks, and the high costs associated with them. A single payer allows these costs to be spread more equitably. Canadian health policy largely accepts the limitations of markets in health care, at least for the portions deemed medically necessary.

It is striking that there are more people in the United States without health insurance than the entire population of Canada, with many more in the United States underinsured. Even in 1998, the United States was spending more per capita from public funds for health care than was Canada, in addition to the considerable spending from private sources.[18] Hospitals, physicians, and patients are faced with considerably less administrative costs than in the United States, although this savings may also translate into considerably less administrative data. The one component in Canada that does use a US mix of public and private financing—outpatient pharmaceuticals—is the one part of the system where costs have been rising most quickly, and access is seen as most problematic.

Jurisdiction

Another lesson is that federalism imposes difficulties. Health policy has been damaged by the pitched battles between the national and provincial governments, which have also undermined public confidence in the system. The balance between imposing national standards (and accountability for money spent) and respecting provincial jurisdiction and allowing flexibility is a tricky one, and it would be hard to argue that the present mix is optimal.

Conclusion

Despite the angst, the objective evidence suggests that the Canadian model has much to recommend it. Ironically, it is most threatened by proximity to the United States, and the concerted attacks from those favoring for-profit, market-oriented care on both sides of the border.[32, 33] The success of earlier reforms may also have produced an excess of "efficiency" at the expense of health care workers and clients alike.[34] Nonetheless, the Romanow Commission has elicited a national, and heartfelt, public reaction. Canadians prize their system of universal coverage. Various changes at the margin are likely. The shape of the overall system, however, will probably remain relatively stable. The major lesson of the Canadian model is precisely the reluctance of Canadians to lose it.

REFERENCES

1. *Report and Recommendations: Emerging Solutions.* Québec, Québec: Commission d'étude sur les services de santé et les services sociaux (CESSSS); December 18, 2000. Available at: http://www.cessss.gouv.qc.ca/pdf/en/ 01–109-01a.pdf. Accessed October 11, 2002.
2. *Report of the Premier's Advisory Council on Health. A Framework for Reform.* Edmonton, Alberta: Premier's Advisory Council on Health for Alberta; December 2001. Available at: http://www.gov.ab.ca/home/health_first/ documents_maz_report.cfm. Accessed October 11, 2002.
3. *Caring for Medicare: Sustaining a Quality System.* Regina, Saskatchewan: Saskatchewan Commission on Medicare; April 6, 2001. Available at: http:// www. health.gov.sk.ca/info_center_pub_ commission_on_ medicare_bw.pdf. Accessed October 11, 2002.
4. *The Health of Canadians: The Federal Role.* 6 vol. Ottawa, Ontario: Standing Senate Committee on Social Affairs Science and Technology; 2001–2002. Available at: http://www.parl.gc.ca/37/ 2/parlbus/commbus/ sentate/com-e/ soci-e/rep-e/repocto2vol6-e.htm. Accessed November 22, 2002.
5. Commission on the Future of Health Care in Canada. Shape the future of health care: interim report. Available at: http://www.healthcarecommission.ca. gov. Accessed October 11, 2002.
6. Deber RB. Getting what we pay for: myths and realities about financing Canada's health care system. *Health Law Can.* 2000;21(2):9–56. Available at: http://www. utoronto.ca/hpme/dhr/pdf/ atrevised3.pdf. Accessed November 22, 2002.
7. Forget EL, Deber RB, Roos LL. Medical savings accounts: will they reduce costs? *Can Med Assoc J.* 2002; 167:143–147.
8. *The Constitution Acts,* 1867 to 1982. Ottawa, Ontario: Government of Canada; 1982.

9. Taylor MG. *Health Insurance and Canadian Public Policy. The Seven Decisions That Created the Canadian Health Insurance System and Their Outcomes.* 2nd ed. Kingston, Ontario; McGill-Queen's University Press; 1987.

10. Maioni A. Parting at the crossroads: the development of health insurance in Canada and the United States. *CompPolit.* 1997;29:411–432.

11. Naylor CD. *Private Practice, Public Payment: Canadian Medicine and the Politics of Health Insurance* 1911–1966. Kingston, Ontario: McGill-Queen's University Press; 1986.

12. Tuohy CH. *Accidental Logics: The Dynamics of Change in the Health Care Arena in the United States, Britain, and Canada.* New York, NY: Oxford University Press; 1999.

13. Government of Canada. *Hospital Insurance and Diagnostic Services Act.* Statutes of Canada, 5–6 Elizabeth II (c 28, S1 1957), 1957.

14. Government of Canada. *Medical Care Act.* Statutes of Canada (c 64, s 1), 1966–1967.

15. Government of Canada. *Canada Health Act, Bill* C-3. Statutes of Canada, 32–33 Elizabeth II (RSC 1985, c 6; RSC 1989, c C-6), 1984.

16. *Canada Royal Commission on Health Services.* Vol 1. Ottawa, Ontario: Canada Royal Commission on Health Services; 1964.

17. *Preliminary Provincial and Territorial Government Health Expenditure Estimates 1974/1975 to 2001/2002.* Ottawa, Ontario: Canadian Institute for Health Information; October 2001.

18. *OECD Health Data 2001: A Comparative Analysis of 30 OECD Countries* [CD-ROM], Paris, France: Organization for Economic Cooperation and Development.

19. Church J, Barker P. Regionalization of health services in Canada: a critical perspective, *Int J Health Serv.* 1998;28: 467–486.

20. Lomas J, Woods J, Veenstra G. Devolving authority for health care in Canada's provinces, I: an introduction to the issues. *Can Med Assoc J.* 1997;156: 371–377.

21. Hutchison B, Abelson J, Lavis J. Primary care in Canada: so much innovation, so little change. *Health Aff (Millwood).* 2001;20(3):116–131.

22. *Canadian Health Insurance: Lessons for the United States. Report to the Chairman, Committee on Government Operations, House of Representatives.* Washington, DC: US General Accounting Office; 1991.

23. Naylor CD. Health care in Canada: incrementalism under fiscal duress. *Health Aff (Millwood).* 1999;18(3):9–26.

24. Armstrong P, Armstrong H, Coburn D, eds. *Unhealthy Times: Political Economy Perspectives on Health and Care in Canada.* Don Mills, Ontario: Oxford University Press; 2001.

25. Williams AP, Deber RB, Baranek P, Gildiner A. From Medicare to home care: globalization, state retrenchment and the profitization of Canada's health care system. In: Armstrong P, Armstrong H, Coburn D, eds. *Unhealthy Times: Political Economy Perspectives on Health and Care in Canada.* Don Mills, Ontario: Oxford University Press; 2001: 7–30.

26. Baranek P. Deber RB, Williams AP. Policy trade-offs in "home care": the Ontario example. *Can Public Adm.* 1999; 42(l):69–92.

27. Williams AP, Barnsley J, Leggat S, Deber RB, Baranek P. Long term care goes to market: managed competition and Ontario's reform of community based services. *Can J Aging.* 1999; 18(2):125–151.

28. Leatt P, Pink GH. Towards a Canadian model of integrated healthcare. *HealthcarePapers.* 2000;1(2):13–36.

29. *The World Health Report 2000: Health Systems: Improving Performance.* Geneva, Switzerland: World Health Organization; 2000.

30. Deber RB, Swan B. Canadian health expenditures: where do we really stand internationally? *Can Med Assoc J.* 1999;160:1730–1734.

31. Griffin P, Cockerill R, Deber RB. Potential impact of population-based funding on delivery of pediatric services. *Ann R Coll Physicians Surg Can.* 2001;34:272–279.

32. Evans RG. Going for the gold: the redistributive agenda behind market-based health care reform. *J Health Polit Policy Law.* 1997;22:427–466.

33. Evans RG, Roos NP. What is right about the Canadian health care system? *Milbank Q.* 1999;77:393–399.

34. Stein JG. *The Cult of Efficiency.* Toronto, Ontario: House of Anansi Press Ltd; 2001.

The Allocation of Exotic Medical Lifesaving Therapy

NICHOLAS RESCHER

Rescher addresses the problem of fairly allocating scarce medical resources when the critical question is: Whose life should be saved? He distinguishes between (1) criteria for selecting candidates to be seriously considered for a therapy and (2) criteria for choosing final recipients from the list of candidates. He maintains that five plausible criteria should be used to select the final recipients: (1) the relative likelihood of success of the therapy, (2) the life expectancy of the patient, (3) the nature of the patient's relationships with his immediate family, (4) the patient's likely pattern of future services to be rendered to society, and (5) the patient's past services and contributions.

I. The Problem

Technological progress has in recent years transformed the limits of the possible in medical therapy. However, the elevated state of sophistication of modern medical technology has brought the economists' classic problem of scarcity in its wake as an unfortunate side product. The enormously sophisticated and complex equipment and the highly trained teams of experts requisite for its utilization are scarce resources in relation to potential demand. The administrators of the great medical institutions that preside over these scarce resources thus come to be faced increasingly with the awesome choice: *Whose life to save?*

A (somewhat hypothetical) paradigm example of this problem may be sketched within the following set of definitive assumptions: We suppose that persons in some particular medically morbid condition are "mortally afflicted": It is virtually certain that they will die within a short time period (say ninety days). We assume that some very complex course of treatment (e.g., a heart transplant) represents a substantial probability of life prolongation for persons in this mortally afflicted condition. We assume that the facilities available in terms of human resources, mechanical instrumentalities, and requisite materials (e.g., hearts in the case of

heart transplant) make it possible to give a certain treatment—this "exotic (medical) lifesaving therapy," or ELT for short—to a certain, relatively small number of people. And finally we assume that a substantially greater pool of people in the mortally afflicted condition is at hand. The problem then may be formulated as follows: How is one to select within the pool of afflicted patients the ones to be given the ELT treatment in question; how to select those "whose lives are to be saved"? Faced with many candidates for an ELT process that can be made available to only a few, doctors and medical administrators confront the decision of who is to be given a chance at survival and who is, in effect, to be condemned to die.

As has already been implied, the "heroic" variety of spare-part surgery can pretty well be assimilated to this paradigm. One can foresee the time when heart transplantation, for example, will have become pretty much a routine medical procedure, albeit on a very limited basis, since a cardiac surgeon with the technical competence to transplant hearts can operate at best a rather small number of times each week and the elaborate facilities for such operations will most probably exist on a modest scale. Moreover, in "sparepart" surgery there is always the problem of availability of the "spare parts" themselves. A report in one British newspaper gives the following picture: "Of the 150,000 who die of heart disease each year [in the U.K.], Mr. Donald Longmore, research surgeon at the National Heart Hospital [in London] estimated that 22,000 might be eligible for heart surgery. Another 30,000 would need heart and lung transplants. But there are probably only between 7,000 and 14,000 potential donors a year." Envisaging this situation in which at the very most something like one in four heart-malfunction victims can be saved, we clearly confront a problem in ELT allocation.

A perhaps even more drastic case in point is afforded by long-term haemodialysis, an ongoing process by which a complex device—an "artificial kidney machine"—is used periodically in cases of chronic renal failure to substitute for a nonfunctional kidney in "cleaning" potential poisons from the blood. Only a few major institutions have chronic haemodialysis units, whose complex operation is an extremely expensive proposition. For the present and foreseeable future the situation is that "the number of places available for chronic haemodialysis is hopelessly inadequate."

The traditional medical ethos has insulated the physician against facing the very existence of this problem. When swearing the Hippocratic Oath, he commits himself to work for the benefit of the sick in "whatsoever house I enter." In taking this stance, the physician substantially renounces the explicit choice of saving certain lives rather than others. Of course, doctors have always in fact had to face such choices on the battlefield or in times of disaster, but there the issue had to be resolved hurriedly, under pressure and in circumstances in which the very nature of the case effectively precluded calm deliberation by the decision maker as well as criticism by others. In sharp contrast, however, cases of the type we have postulated in the present discussion arise predictably, and represent choices to be made deliberately and "in cold blood."

It is, to begin with, appropriate to remark that this problem is not fundamentally a medical problem. For when there are sufficiently many afflicted candidates for ELT then—so we may assume—there will also be more than enough for whom the purely medical grounds for ELT allocation are decisively strong in any individual case, and just about equally strong throughout the group. But in this circumstance a selection of some afflicted patients over and against others cannot *ex hypothesi* be made on the basis of purely medical considerations.

The selection problem, as we have said, is in substantial measure not a medical one. It is a problem *for* medical men, which must somehow be solved by them, but that does not make it a medical issue—any more than the problem of hospital building is a medical issue. As a problem it belongs to the category of philosophical problems—specifically a problem of moral philosophy or ethics. Structurally, it bear's a substantial kinship with those issues in this field that revolve about the notorious whom-to-save-on-the-lifeboat and whom-to-throw-to the wolves-pursuing-the-sled questions. But whereas questions of this just-indicated sort are artificial, hypothetical, and farfetched, the ELT issue poses a genuine policy question for the responsible administrators in medical institutions, indeed a question that threatens to become commonplace in the foreseeable future.

Now what the medical administrator needs to have, and what the philosopher is presumably *ex officio* in a position to help in providing, is a body of *rational guidelines* for making choices in these literally life-or-death situations. This is an issue in which many interested parties have a substantial stake, including the responsible decision maker who wants to satisfy his conscience that he is acting in a reasonable way. Moreover; the family and associates of the man who is turned away—to say nothing of the man himself—have the right to an acceptable explanation. And indeed even the general public wants to know that what is being done is fitting and proper. All of these interested parties are entitled to insist that a reasonable code of operating principles provides a defensible rationale for making the life-and-death choices involved in ELT.

II. The Two Types of Criteria

Two distinguishable types of criteria are bound up in the issue of making ELT choices. We shall call these *Criteria of Inclusion* and *Crieria* of *Comparison*, respectively. The distinction at issue here requires some explanation. We can think of the selection as being made by a two-stage process: (1) the selection from among all possible candidates (by a suitable screening process) of a group to be taken under serious consideration as candidates for therapy, and then (2) the actual singling out, within this group, of the particular individuals to whom therapy is to be given. Thus the first process narrows down the range of comparative choices by eliminating en bloc whole categories of potential candidates. The second process calls for a more refined case-by-case comparison of those candidates that remain. By means of the first set of criteria one forms a selection group; by means of the second set, an actual selection is made within this group.

Thus what we shall call a "selection system" for the choice of patients to receive therapy of the ELT type will consist of criteria of these two kinds. Such a system will be acceptable only when the reasonableness of its component criteria can be established.

III. Essential Features of an Acceptable ELT Selection System

To qualify as reasonable, an ELT selection must meet two important "regulative" requirements: it must be *simple* enough to be readily intelligible, and it must be *plausible*, that is, patently reasonable in a way that can be apprehended easily and without involving ramified subtleties. Those medical administrators responsible for ELT choices must follow a modus operandi that virtually all the people involved can readily understand to be acceptable (at a reasonable level of generality, at any rate). Appearances are critically important here. It is not enough that the choice he made in a *justifiable* way; it must be possible for people—plain people to "see" (i.e., understand without elaborate teaching or indoctrination) that *it is justified*, insofar as any mode of procedure can be justified in cases of this sort.

One "constitutive" requirement is obviously an essential feature of a reasonable selection system: all of its component criteria—those of inclusion and those of comparison alike—must be reasonable: in the sense of being *rationally defensible*. The ramifications of this requirement call for detailed consideration. But one of its aspects should be noted without further ado: it must be *fair*—it must treat relevantly like cases alike, leaving no room for "influence" or favoritism, etc.

IV. The Basic Screening Stage: Criteria of Inclusion (and Exclusion)

Three sorts of considerations are prominent among the plausible criteria of inclusion/exclusion at the basic screening stage: the constituency factor; the progress-of-science factor, and the prospect-of-success factor.

A. The Constituency Factor

It is a "fact of life" that ELT, can be available only in the institutional setting of a hospital or medical institute or the like. Such institutions generally have normal clientele boundaries. A veterans' hospital will not concern itself primarily with treating non-veterans, a children's hospital cannot he expected to accommodate the "senior citizen," an army hospital can regard college professors as outside its sphere. Sometimes the boundaries are geographic—a state hospital may admit only residents of a certain state. There are, of course, indefensible constituency principles—say race or religion, party membership, or ability to pay; and there are cases of borderline legitimacy e.g., sex. A medical institution is justified in considering for ELT only persons within its own constituency, provided this constituency is constituted upon a defensible basis. Thus the haemodialysis selection committee in Seattle "agreed to consider only those applications who were residents of the state of Washington.... They justified this stand on the grounds that since the basic: research...had been done at...a state-supported institution—the people whose taxes had paid for the research should be its first beneficiaries." While thus insisting that constituency considerations represent a valid and legitimate factor in ELT selection, I do feel there is much to be said for minimizing their role in life-or-death cases. Indeed a refusal to recognize them at all is a significant part of medical tradition, going back to the very oath of Hippocrates. They represent a departure from the ideal arising with the institutionalization of medicine, moving it away from its original status as an art practiced by an individual practitioner.

B. The Progress-of-Science Factor

The needs of medical research can provide a second valid principle of inclusion. The research interests of the medical staff in relation to the specific nature of the cases at issue is a significant consideration. It may be important for the progress of medical science—and thus of potential benefit to many persons in the future—to determine how effective the ELT at issue is with diabetics or persons over sixty or with a negative Rh factor. Considerations of this sort represent another type of legitimate factor in ELT selection.

A very definitely *borderline* case under this head would revolve around the question of a patient's willingness to pay, not in monetary terms, but in offering himself as an experimental subject, say by contracting to return at designated times for a series of tests substantially unrelated to his own health, but yielding data of importance to medical knowledge in general.

C. The Prospect-of-Success Factor

It may be that while the ELT at issue is not without *some* effectiveness in general, it has been established to be highly effective only with patients in certain specific categories (e.g., females under forty of a specific blood type). This difference in effectiveness—in the absolute or in the probability of success—is (we assume) so marked as to constitute virtually a difference in kind rather than in degree. In this case, it would be perfectly legitimate to adopt the general rule of making the ELT at issue available only or primarily to persons in this substantial-promise-of-success category. (It is on grounds of this sort that young children and persons over fifty are generally ruled out as candidates for haemodialysis.)

We have maintained that the three factors of constituency, progress of science, and prospect of success represent legitimate criteria of inclusion for ELT selection. But it remains to examine the considerations which legitimate them. The legitimating factors are in the final analysis practical or pragmatic in nature. From the practical angle it is advantageous—indeed to some extent necessary—that the arrangements governing medical institutions should embody certain constituency principles. It makes good pragmatic and utilitarian sense that progress-of-science considerations should be operative here. And, finally, the practical aspect is reinforced by a whole host of other considerations—including moral ones—in supporting the prospect-of-success criterion. The workings of each of these factors are of course conditioned by the ever-present element of limited availability. They are operative only in this context, that is, prospect of success is a legitimate

consideration at all only because we are dealing with a situation of scarcity.

V. The Final Selection Stage: Criteria of Selection

Five sorts of elements must, as we see it, figure primarily among the plausible criteria of selection that are to be brought to bear in further screening the group constituted after application of the criteria of inclusion: the relative-likelihood-of-success factor, the life expectancy factor, the family role factor, the potential contributions factor, and the services-rendered factor. The first two represent the *biomedical* aspect, the second three the *social* aspect.

A. The Relative-Likelihood-of-Success Factor

It is clear that the relative likelihood of success is a legitimate and appropriate factor in making a selection within the group of qualified patients that are to receive ELT. This is obviously one of the considerations that must count very significantly in a reasonable selection procedure.

The present criterion is of course closely related to item C of the preceding section. There we were concerned with prospect-of-success considerations categorically and en bloc. Here at present they come into play in a particularized case-by-case comparison among individuals. If the therapy at issue is not a once-and-for-all proposition and requires ongoing treatment, cognate considerations must be brought in. Thus, for example, in the case of a chronic ELT procedure such as haemodialysis it would clearly make sense to give priority to patients with a potentially reversible condition (who would thus need treatment for only a fraction of their remaining lives).

B. The Life-Expectancy Factor

Even if the ELT is "successful" in the patient's case he may, considering his age and/or other aspects of his general medical condition, look forward to only a very short probable future life. This is obviously, another factor that must be taken into account.

C. The Family Role Factor

A person's life is a thing of importance not only to himself but to others—friends, associates, neighbors, colleagues, etc. But his (or her) relationship to his immediate family is a thing of unique intimacy and significance. The nature of his relationship to his wife, children, and parents, and the issue of their financial and psychological dependence upon him, are obviously matters that deserve to be given weight in the ELT selection. Other things being anything like equal, the mother of minor children must take priority over the middle-aged bachelor.

D. The Potential-Future-Contributions Factor(Prospective Service)

In "choosing to save" one life rather than another, "the society," through the mediation of the particular medical institution in question—which should certainly look upon itself as a trustee for the social interest—is clearly warranted in considering the likely pattern of future *services to be rendered* by the patient (adequate recovery assumed), considering his age, talent, training, and past record of performance. In its allocations of ELT, society "invests" a scarce resource in one person as against another and is thus entitled to look to the probable prospective "return" on its investment.

It may well be that a thoroughly egalitarian society is reluctant to put someone's social contribution into the scale in situations of the sort at issue. One popular article states that "the most difficult standard would be the candidate's value to society," and goes on to quote someone who said: "You can't just pick a brilliant painter over a laborer. The average citizen would be quickly eliminated." But what if it were not a brilliant painter but a brilliant surgeon or medical researcher that was at issue? One wonders if the author of the *obiter dictum* that one "can't just pick" would still feel equally sure of his ground. In any case, the fact that the standard is difficult to apply is certainly no reason for not attempting to apply it. The problem of ELT selection is inevitably burdened with difficult standards.

Some might feel that in assessing a patient's value to society one should ask not only who if permitted to continue living can make the greatest contribution to society in some creative or constructive way, but also who by dying would leave behind the greatest burden on society in assuming

the discharge of their residual responsibilities. Certainly the philosophical utilitarian would give equal weight to both these considerations. Just here is where I would part ways with orthodox utilitarianism. For—though this is not the place to do so—I should be prepared to argue that a civilized society has an obligation to promote the furtherance of positive achievements in cultural and related areas even if this means the assumption of certain added burdens.

E. The Past-Services-Rendered Factor (Retrospective Service)

A person's services to another person or group have always been taken to constitute a valid basis for a claim upon this person or group—of course a moral and not necessarily a legal claim. Society's obligation for the recognition and reward of services rendered—an obligation whose discharge is also very possibly conducive to self-interest in the long run—is thus another factor to be taken into account. This should be viewed as a morally necessary correlative of the previously considered factor of *prospective* service. It would be morally indefensible of society in effect to say: "Never mind about services you rendered yesterday—it is only the services to be rendered tomorrow that will count with us today." We live in very future- oriented times, constantly preoccupied in a distinctly utilitarian way with future satisfactions. And this disinclines us to give much recognition to past services. But parity considerations of the sort just adduced indicate that such recognition should be given *on grounds of equity*. No doubt a justification for giving weight to services rendered can also be attempted along utilitarian lines. ("The reward of past services rendered spurs people on to greater future efforts and is thus socially advantageous in the long-run future.") In saying that past services should be counted "on grounds of equity"—rather than "on grounds of utility"—I take the view that even if this utilitarian defense could somehow be shown to be fallacious, I should still be prepared to maintain the propriety of taking services rendered into account. The position does not rest on a utilitarian basis and so would not collapse with the removal of such a basis.

As we have said, these five factors fall into three groups: the biomedical factors A and B, the familial factor C, and the social factors D and E. With items A and B the need for a detailed analysis of the medical considerations comes to the fore. The age of the patient, his medical history, his physical and psychological condition, his specific disease, etc., will all need to be taken into exact account. These biomedical factors represent technical issues: they call for the physicians' expert judgment and the medical statisticians' hard data. And they are ethically uncontroversial factors—their legitimacy and appropriateness are evident from the very nature of the case.

Greater problems arise with the familial and social factors. They involve intangibles that are difficult to judge. How is one to develop subcriteria for weighing the relative social contributions of (say) an architect or a librarian or a mother of young children? And they involve highly problematic issues. (For example, should good moral character be rated a plus and bad a minus in judging services rendered?) And there is something strikingly unpleasant in grappling with issues of this sort for people brought up in times greatly inclined towards maxims of the type "Judge not!" and "Live and let live!" All the same, in the situation that concerns us here such distasteful problems must be faced, since a failure to choose to save some is tantamount to sentencing all. Unpleasant choices are intrinsic to the problem of ELT selection; they are of the very essence of the matter.

But is reference to all these factors indeed inevitable? The justification for taking account of the medical factors is pretty obvious. But why should the social aspect of services rendered and to be rendered be taken into account at all? The answer is that they must be taken into account not from the *medical* but from the *ethical* point of view. Despite disagreement on many fundamental issues, moral philosophers of the present day are pretty well in consensus that the justification of human actions is to be sought largely and primarily—if not exclusively—in the principles of utility and of justice. But utility requires reference of services to be rendered and justice calls for a recognition of services that have been rendered. Moral considerations would thus demand recognition of these two factors. (This, of course, still leaves open the question of whether the point of view provides a valid basis of action: Why base one's actions upon moral principles—or, to put it bluntly—Why be moral? The present paper is, however, hardly the place to grapple with so fundamental an issue, which has been canvassed in the literature of philosophical ethics since Plato.)

VI. More Than Medical Issues Are Involved

An active controversy has of late sprung up in medical circles over the question of whether non-physician laymen should be given a role in ELT selection (in the specific context of chronic haemodialysis). One physician writes: "I think that the assessment of the candidates should be made by a senior doctor on the [dialysis] unit but I am sure that it would be helpful to him—both in sharing responsibility and in avoiding personal pressure—if a small unnamed group of people [presumably including laymen] officially made the final decision. I visualize the doctor bringing the data to the group, explaining the points in relation to each case, and obtaining their approval of his order of priority."

Essentially this procedure of a selection committee of laymen has for some years been in use in one of the most publicized chronic dialysis units, that of the Swedish Hospital of Seattle, Washington. Many physicians are apparently reluctant to see the choice of allocation of medical therapy pass out of strictly medical hands. Thus in a recent symposium on the "Selection of Patients for Haemodialysis," Dr. Ralph Shakman writes: "Who is to implement the selection? In my opinion it must ultimately be the responsibility of the consultants in charge of the renal units....I can see no reason for delegating this responsibility to lay persons. Surely the latter would be better employed if they could be persuaded to devote their time and energy to raise more and more money for us to spend on our patients." Other contributors to this symposium strike much the same note. Dr F. M. Parsons writes: In an attempt to overcome...difficulties in selection some have advocated introducing certain specified lay people into the discussions. Is it wise? I doubt whether a committee of this type can adjudicate as satisfactorily as two medical colleagues, particularly as successful therapy involves close cooperation between doctor and patient." And Dr. M. A. Wilson writes in the same symposium, "The suggestion has been made that lay panels should select individuals for dialysis from among a group who are medically suitable. Though this would relieve the doctor-in-charge of a heavy load of responsibility, it would place the burden on those who have no personal knowledge and have to base their judgments on medical or social reports. I do not believe this would result in better decisions for the group or improve the doctor–patient relationship in individual cases."

But no amount of flag waving about the doctor's facing up to his responsibility—or prostrations before the idol of the doctor-patient relationship and reluctance to admit laymen into the sacred precincts of the conference chambers of medical consultations—can obscure the essential fact that ELT selection is not a wholly medical problem. When there are more than enough places in an ELT program to accommodate all who need it, then it will clearly be a medical question to decide who does have the need and which among these would successfully respond. But when an admitted gross insufficiency of places exists, when there are ten or fifty or one hundred highly eligible candidates for each place in the program, then it is unrealistic to take the view that purely medical criteria can furnish a sufficient basis for selection. The question of ELT selection becomes serious as a phenomenon of scale—because, as more candidates present themselves, strictly medical factors are increasingly less adequate as a selection criterion precisely because by numerical category-crowding there will be more and more cases whose "status is much the same" so far as purely medical considerations go.

The ELT selection problem clearly poses issues that transcend the medical sphere because—in the nature of the case—many residual issues remain to be dealt with once *all* of the medical questions have been faced. Because of this there is good reason why laymen as well as physicians should be involved in the selection process. Once the medical considerations have been brought to bear, fundamental social issues remain to be resolved. The instrumentalities of ELT have been created through the social investment of scarce resources, and the interests of the society deserve to play a role in their utilization. As representatives of their social interests, lay opinions should function to complement and supplement medical views once the proper arena of medical considerations is left behind. Those physicians who have urged the presence of lay members on selection panels can, from this point of view, be recognized as having seen the issue in proper perspective.

One physician has argued against lay representation on selection panels for haemodialysis as follows:

"If the doctor advises dialysis and the lay panel refuses, the patient will regard this as a death sentence passed by an anonymous court from which he has no right of appeal." But this drawback is not specific to the use of a lay panel. Rather, it is a feature inherent in every *selection* procedure, regardless of whether the selection is done by the head doctor of the unit, by a panel of physicians, etc. No matter who does the selecting among patients recommended for dialysis, the feelings of the patient who has been rejected (and knows it) can be expected to be much the same, provided that he recognizes the actual nature of the choice (and is not deceived by the possibly convenient but ultimately poisonous fiction that because the selection was made by physicians it was made entirely on medical grounds).

In summary, then, the question of ELT selection would appear to be one that is in its very nature heavily laden with issues of medical research, practice, and administration. But it will not be a question that can be resolved on solely medical grounds. Strictly social issues of justice and utility will invariably arise in this area—questions going outside the medical area in whose resolution medical laymen can and should play a substantial role.

VII. The Inherent Imperfection (Non-Optimality) of Any Selection System

Our discussion to this point of the design of a selection system for ELT has left a gap that is a very fundamental and serious omission. We have argued that five factors must be taken into substantial and explicit account:

A. *Relative likelihood of success.* Is the chance of the treatment's being "successful" to be rated as high, good, average, etc.?

B. *Expectancy of future life.* Assuming the "success" of the treatment, how much longer does the patient stand a good chance (75 per cent or better) of living—considering his age and general condition?

C. *Family role.* To what extent does the patient have responsibilities to others in his immediate family?

D. *Social contributions rendered.* Are the patient's past services to his society outstanding, substantial, average, etc.?

E. *Social contributions to be rendered.* Considering his age, talents, training, and past record of performance, is there a substantial probability that the patient will—*adequate recovery being assured*—render in the future services to his society that can be characterized as outstanding, substantial, average, etc.?

This list is clearly insufficient for the construction of a reasonable selection system, since that would require not only *that these factors be taken into account* (somehow or other), but—going beyond this—would *specify a specific set of procedures for taking account of them.* The specific procedures that would constitute such a system would have to take account of the interrelationship of these factors (e.g., B and E), and to set out exact guidelines as to the relevant weight that is to be given to each of them. This is something our discussion has not as yet considered.

In fact, I should want to maintain that there is no such thing here as a single rationally superior selection system. The position of affairs seems to me to be something like this: (1) It is necessary (for reasons already canvassed) to have a system, and to have a system that is rationally defensible, and (2) to be rationally defensible, this system must take the factors *A–E* into substantial and explicit account. But (3) the exact manner in which a rationally defensible system takes account of these factors cannot be fixed in any one specific way on the basis of general considerations. Any of the variety of ways that give *A–E* "their due" will be acceptable and viable. One cannot hope to find within this range of workable systems some one that is optimal in relation to the alternatives. There is no one system that does "the (uniquely) best"—only a variety of systems that do "as well as one can expect to do" in cases of this sort.

The situation is structurally very much akin to that of rules of partition of an estate among the relations of a decedent. It is important that there be such rules. And it is reasonable that spouse, children, parents, siblings, etc., be taken account of in these rules. But the question of the exact method of division—say that when the decedent has neither living spouse nor living children then his estate is to be divided, dividing 60 per cent between parents, 40 per cent between siblings versus dividing 90 per cent between parents, 10 per cent between siblings—cannot be settled on the basis of any general abstract considerations of reasonableness. Within broad limits, a variety of resolutions are all perfectly acceptable—so that no one procedure can justifiably be regarded as "the (uniquely) best" because it is superior to all others.

VIII. A Possible Basis for a Reasonable Selection System

Having said that there is no such thing as *the optimal* selection system for ELT, I want now to sketch out the broad features of what I would regard as *one acceptable* system.

The basis for the system would be a point rating. The scoring here at issue would give roughly equal weight to the medical considerations *A* and *B*) in comparison with the extramedical considerations (*C* = family role, *D* = services rendered, and *E* = services to be rendered), also giving roughly equal weight to the three items involved here (*C, D,* and *E*). The result of such a scoring procedure would provide the essential starting point of our ELT selection mechanism. I deliberately say "starting point" because it seems to me that one should not follow the results of this scoring in an *automatic* way. I would propose that the actual selection should only be guided but not actually be dictated by this scoring procedure, along lines now to be explained.

IX. The Desirability of Introducing an Element of Chance

The detailed procedure I would propose—not of course as optimal (for reasons we have seen), but as eminently acceptable—would combine the scoring procedure just discussed with an element of chance. The resulting selection system would function as follows:

1. First the criteria of inclusion of Section IV above would be applied to constitute a *first phase selection group*—which (we shall suppose) is substantially larger than the number *n* of persons who can actually be accommodated with ELT.

2. Next the criteria of selection of Section V are brought to bear via a scoring procedure of the type described in Section VIII. On this basis a *second phase selection group* is constituted which is only *somewhat* larger—say by a third or a half—than the critical number *n* at issue.

3. If this second phase selection group is relatively homogeneous as regards rating by the scoring procedure—that is, if there are no really major disparities within this group (as would be likely if the initial group was significantly larger than *n*)—then the final selection is made by *random* selection of *n* persons from within this group.

This introduction of the element of chance—in what could be dramatized as a "lottery of life and death"—must be justified. The fact is that such a procedure would bring with it three substantial advantages.

First, as we have argued above (in Section VII), any acceptable selection system is inherently nonoptimal. The introduction of the element of chance prevents the results that life-and-death choices are made by the automatic allocation of an admittedly imperfect selection method.

Second, a recourse to chance would doubtless make matters easier for the rejected patient and those who have a specific interest in him. It would surely be quite hard for them to accept his exclusion by relatively mechanical application of objective criteria in whose implementation subjective judgment is involved. But the circumstances of life have conditioned us to accept the workings of chance and to tolerate the element of luck (good or bad): human life is an inherently contingent process. Nobody, after all, has an absolute right to ELT—but most of us would feel that we have "every bit as much right" to it as anyone else in significantly similar circumstances. The introduction of the element of chance assures a like handling of like cases over the widest possible area that seems reasonable in the circumstances.

Third (and perhaps least), such a recourse to random selection does much to relieve the administrators of the selection system of the awesome burden of ultimate and absolute responsibility.

These three considerations would seem to build up a substantial case for introducing the element of chance into the mechanism of the system for ELT selection in a way limited and circumscribed by other weightier considerations, along some such lines as those set forth above.

It should be recognized that this injection of *man-made* chance supplements the element of *natural* chance that is present inevitably and in any case (apart from the role of chance in singling out certain persons as victims for the affliction at issue). As F. M. Parsons has observed: "any vacancies [in an ELT program—specifically haemodialysis] will be filled immediately by the first suitable patients, even though their claims for therapy may subsequently prove less than those of other patients refused later." Life is a chancy business and even the most rational of human arrangements can cover this over to a very limited extent at best.

QALYfying the Value of Life

JOHN HARRIS

One utilitarian approach to rationing is to measure objectively the benefits that a treatment is likely to give each patient, then selectively treat particular patients or conditions to maximize total benefits. An often-used objective measure of benefits is known as QALY, or quality-adjusted life year. Harris argues that QALYs discriminate against older people because "saving the lives of younger people is, other things being equal, always likely to be productive of more QALYs than saving older people." QALYs, he says, are also unfair to the disabled for similar reasons. Harris maintains that a crucial failing of QALYs is that these objective measurements cannot accommodate the subjective nature of people's assessments of the value of their own lives.

Against a background of permanently scarce resources it is clearly crucial that such health care resources as are available be not used wastefully. This point is often made in terms of "efficiency" and it is argued, not implausibly, that to talk of efficiency implies that we are able to distinguish between efficient and inefficient use of health care resources, and hence that we are in some sense able to measure the results of treatment. To do so of course we need a standard of measurement. Traditionally, in life-endangering conditions, that standard has been easy to find. Successful treatment removes the danger to life, or at least postpones it, and so the survival rates of treatment have been regarded as a good indicator of success.[1] However, equally clearly, it is also of crucial importance to those treated that the help offered them not only removes the threat to life, but leaves them able to enjoy the remission granted. In short, gives them reasonable quality, as well as extended quantity of life.

A new measure of quality of life which combines length of survival with an attempt to measure the quality of that survival has recently[2] been suggested and is becoming influential. The need for such a measure has been thus described by one of its chief architects: We need a simple, versatile, measure of success which incorporates both life expectancy and quality of life, and which reflects the values and ethics of the community served. The 'Quality Adjusted Life Year' (QALY) measure fulfills such a role.[3] This is a large claim and an important one; if it can be sustained its consequences for health care will be profound indeed.

There are, however, substantial theoretical problems in the development of such a measure, and more important by far, grave dangers of its misuse. I shall argue that the dangers of misuse, which partly derive from inadequacies in the theory which generates them, make this measure itself a life-threatening device. In showing why this is so I shall attempt to say something positive about just what is involved in making scrupulous choices between people in situations of scarce resources, and I will end by saying something about the entitlement to claim in particular circumstances, that resources are indeed scarce.

We must first turn to the task of examining the QALY and the possible consequences of its use in resource allocation. A task incidentally which, because it aims at the identification and eradication of a life-threatening condition, itself (surprisingly perhaps for a philosophical paper) counts also as a piece of medical research,[4] which if successful will prove genuinely therapeutic.

The QALY

I. What Are QALYs?

It is important to be as clear as possible as to just what a QALY is and what it might be used for. I cannot do better than let Alan Williams, the

From *Journal of Medical Ethics*, vol. 13, no. 3 (September 1987), pp. 117–23. Reprinted with permission from the BMJ Publishing Group.

architect of QALYs referred to above, tell you in his own words:

> The essence of a QALY is that it takes a year of healthy life expectancy to be worth one, but regards a year of unhealthy life expectancy as worth less than 1. Its precise value is lower the worse the quality of life of the unhealthy person (which is what the "quality adjusted" bit is all about). If being dead is worth zero, it is, in principle, possible for a QALY to be negative, ie for the quality of someone's life to be judged worse than being dead.
>
> The general idea is that a beneficial health care activity is one that generates a positive amount of QALYs, and that an efficient health care activity is one where the cost-per-QALY is as low as it can be. A high priority health care activity is one where the cost-per-QALY is low, and a low priority activity is one where cost-per-QALY is high.[5]

The plausibility of the QALY derives from the idea that "given the choice, a person would prefer a shorter healthier life to a longer period of survival in a state of severe discomfort and disability."[6] The idea that any rational person would endorse this preference provides the moral and political force behind the QALY. Its acceptability as a measurement of health then depends upon its doing all the theoretical tasks assigned to it, and on its being what people want, or would want, for themselves.

II. How Will QALY Be Used?

There are two ways in which QALYs might be used. One is unexceptionable and useful, and fully in line with the assumptions which give QALYs their plausibility. The other is none of these.

QALYS might be used to determine which of rival therapies to give to a particular patient or which procedure to use to treat a particular condition. Clearly the one generating the most QALYs will be the better bet, both for the patient and for a society with scarce resources. However, QALYs might also be used to determine not what treatment to give *these* patients, but which group of patients to treat, or which conditions to give priority in the allocation of health care resources. It is clear that it is this latter use which Williams has in mind, for he specifically cites as one of the rewards of the development of QALYs, their use in

"priority setting in the health care system in general."[7] It is this use which is likely to be of greatest interest to all those concerned with efficiency in the health service. And it is for this reason that it is likely to be both the most influential and to have the most far-reaching effects. It is this use which is I believe positively dangerous and morally indefensible. Why?

III. What's Wrong with QALYs?

It is crucial to realize that the whole plausibility of QALYS depends upon our accepting that they simply involve the generalization of the "truth"[8] that "given the choice a person would prefer a shorter healthier life to a longer period of survival in a state of severe discomfort." On this view giving priority to treatments which produce more QALYs or for which the cost-per-QALY is low, is both efficient and is also what the community as a whole, and those at risk in particular, actually want. But whereas it follows from the fact that given the choice a person would prefer a shorter healthier life to a longer one of severe discomfort, that the best treatment *for that person* is the one yielding the most QALYs, it does not follow that treatments yielding more QALYs are preferable to treatments yielding fewer where *different people* are to receive the treatments. That is to say, while it follows from the fact (if it is a fact) that I and everyone else would prefer to have, say one year of healthy life rather than three years of severe discomfort, that we value healthy existence more than uncomfortable existence for ourselves, it does not follow that where the choice is between three years of discomfort for *me* or immediate death on the one hand, and one year of health for you, or immediate death on the other, that I am somehow committed to the judgement that you ought to be saved rather than me.

Suppose that Andrew, Brian, Charles, Dorothy, Elizabeth, Fiona and George all have zero life-expectancy without treatment, but with medical care, all but George will get one year's complete remission and George will get seven years' remission. The costs of treating each of the six are equal but George's operation costs five times as much as the cost of the other operations. It does not follow that even if each person, if asked, would prefer seven years' remission to one for themselves, that they are all committed to the view that George should be treated rather than that they should. Nor does it follow that this is a preference that society should endorse. But it is the preference that QALYs dictate.

Such a policy does not value life or lives at all, for it is individuals who are alive, and individuals who lose their lives. And when they do the loss is principally their loss. The value of someone's life is, primarily and overwhelmingly, its value to him or her; the wrong done when an individual's life is cut short is a wrong to that individual. The victim of a murder or a fatal accident is the person who loses his life. A disaster is the greater the more victims there are, the more lives that are lost. A society which values the lives of its citizens is one which tries to ensure that as few of them die prematurely (that is when their lives could continue) as possible. Giving value to life-years or QALYs, has the effect in this case of sacrificing six lives for one. If each of the seven *wants* to go on living for as long as he or she can, if each values the prospective term of remission available, then to choose between them on the basis of life-years (quality adjusted or not), is in this case to give no value to the lives of six people.

IV. The Ethics of QALYs

Although we might be right to claim that people are not committed to QALYs as a measurement of health simply in virtue of their acceptance of the idea that each would prefer to have more QALYs rather than fewer for themselves, are there good moral reasons why QALYs should none the less be accepted?

The idea, which is at the root of both democratic theory and of most conceptions of justice, that each person is as morally important as any other and hence, that the life and interests of each is to be given equal weight, while apparently referred to and employed by Williams plays no part at all in the theory of QALYs. That which is to be given equal weight is not persons and their interests and preferences, but quality-adjusted life-years. And giving priority to the manufacture of QALYs can mean them all going to a few at the expense of the interests and wishes of the many. It will also mean that

all available resources will tend to be deployed to assist those who will thereby gain the maximum QALYs—the young.

V. The Fallacy of Valuing Time

There is a general problem for any position which holds that time-spans are of equal value no matter who gets them, and it stems from the practice of valuing life-units (life-years) rather than people's lives.

If what matters most is the number of life-years the world contains, then the best thing we can do is devote our resources to increasing the population. Birth control, abortion and sex education come out very badly on the QALY scale of priorities.

In the face of a problem like this, the QALY advocate must insist that what he wants is to select the therapy that generates the most QALYs for those people who already exist, and not simply to create the maximum number of QALYs. But if it is people and not units of life-span that matter, if the QALY is advocated because it is seen as a moral and efficient way to fulfill our obligation to provide care for our fellows, then it does matter who gets the QALYs—because it matters how people are treated. And this is where the ageism of QALYs and their other discriminatory features become important.

VI. QALYs Are Ageist

Maximizing QALYs involves an implicit and comprehensive ageist bias. For saving the lives of younger people is, other things being equal, always likely to be productive of more QALYs than saving older people. Thus on the QALY arithmetic we always have a reason to prefer, for example, neonatal or pediatric care to all "later" branches of medicine. This is because any calculation of the life-years generated for a particular patient by a particular therapy, must be based on the life expectancy of that patient. The older a patient is when treated, the fewer the life-years that can be achieved by the therapy.

It is true that QALYs dictate that we prefer people, not simply who have *more life expectancy*, but rather people who have *more life expectancy to be gained from treatment*. But wherever treatment saves a life, and this will be frequently, for quite simple treatments, like a timely antibiotic, can be life-saving, it will, other things being equal, be the case that younger people have more life expectancy to gain from the treatment than do older people.

VII. Ageism and Aid

Another problem with such a view is that it seems to imply, for example, that when looking at societies from the outside, those with a lower average age have somehow a greater claim on our aid. This might have important consequences in looking at questions concerning aid policy on a global scale. Of course it is true that a society's having a low average age might be a good indicator of its need for help, in that it would imply that people were dying prematurely. However, we can imagine a society suffering a disaster which killed off many of its young people (war perhaps) and which was consequently left with a high average age but was equally deserving of aid despite the fact that such aid would inevitably benefit the old. If QALYs were applied to the decision as to whether to provide aid to this society or another much less populous and perhaps with less pressing problems, but with a more normal age distribution, the "older" society might well be judged "not worth" helping.

VIII. QALYs Can Be Racist and Sexist

If a "high priority health care activity is one where the cost-per-QALY is low, and a low priority activity is one where cost-per-QALY is high" then people who just happen to have conditions which are relatively cheap to treat are always going to be given priority over those who happen to have conditions which are relatively expensive to treat. This will inevitably involve not only a systematic pattern of disadvantage to particular groups of patients, or to people afflicted with particular diseases or conditions, but perhaps also a systematic preference for the survival of some kinds of patients at the expense of others. We usually think that justice requires that we do not allow certain sections of the community or certain types of individual to become the victims of systematic disadvantage and that there are good moral reasons for doing justice, not just when it costs us nothing or when it is convenient or efficient, but also and particularly, when there is a price to be paid. We'll return shortly to this crucial issue of justice, but it is important to be clear about the possible social consequences of adopting QALYs.

Adoption of QALYs as the rationale for the distribution of health care resources may, for the above reasons, involve the creation of a systematic pattern of preference for certain racial groups or for a particular gender or, what is the same thing, a certain pattern of discrimination against such groups. Suppose that medical statistics reveal that say women, or Asian males, do better than others after a particular operation or course of treatment, or, that a particular condition that has a very poor prognosis in terms of QALYs afflicts only Jews, or gay men. Such statistics abound and the adoption of QALYs may well dictate very severe and systematic discrimination against groups identified primarily by race, gender or colour, in the allocation of health resources, where it turns out that such groups are vulnerable to conditions that are not QALY-efficient.[9]

Of course it is just a fact of life and far from sinister that different races and genders are subject to different conditions, but the problem is that QALYs may tend to reinforce and perpetuate these "structural" disadvantages.

IX. Double Jeopardy

Relatedly, suppose a particular terminal condition was treatable, and would, with treatment, give indefinite remission but with a very poor quality of life. Suppose for example that if an accident victim were treated, he would survive, but with paraplegia. This might always cash out at fewer QALYs than a condition which with treatment would give a patient perfect remission for about five years after which the patient would die. Suppose that both candidates wanted to go on living as long as they could and so both wanted, equally fervently, to be given the treatment that would save their lives. Is it clear that the candidate with most QALYs on offer should always and inevitably be the one to have priority? To judge so would be to count the paraplegic's desire to live the life that was available to him as of less value than his rival's—what price equal weight to the preferences of each individual?

This feature of QALYs involves a sort of double jeopardy. QALYs dictate that because an individual is unfortunate, because she has once become a victim of disaster, we are required to visit upon her a second and perhaps graver misfortune. The first disaster leaves her with a poor quality of life, and QALYs then require that in virtue of this she be ruled out as a candidate for life-saving treatment, or at best, that she be given little or no chance of benefiting from what little amelioration her condition admits of. Her first disaster leaves her with a poor quality of life and when she presents herself for help, along come QALYs and finish her off!

X. Life-Saving and Life-Enhancing

A distinction, consideration of which is long overdue, is that between treatments which are life-saving (or death-postponing) and those which are simply life-enhancing, in the sense that they improve the quality of life without improving life-expectancy. Most people think, and for good as well as for prudential reasons, that life-saving has priority over life-enhancement and that we should first allocate resources to those areas where they are immediately needed to save life and only when this has been done should the remainder be allocated to alleviating non-fatal conditions. Of course there are exceptions even here and some conditions, while not life-threatening, are so painful that to leave someone in a state of suffering while we attend even to the saving of life, would constitute unjustifiable cruelty. But these situations are rare and for the vast majority of cases we judge that life-saving should have priority.

It is important to notice that QALYs make no such distinction between types of treatment. Defenders of QALYs often cite with pride the example of hip-replacement operations which are more QALY-efficient than say kidney dialysis.[10] While the difficulty of choosing between treating very different groups of patients, some of whom need treatment simply to stay alive, while others need it to relieve pain and distress, is clearly very acute, and while it may be that life-saving should not *always* have priority over life-enhancement, the dangers of adopting QALYs which regard only one dimension of the rival claims, and a dubious one at that, as morally relevant, should be clear enough.

There is surely something fishy about QALYs. They can hardly form "an appropriate basis for health service policy." Can we give an account of just where they are deficient from the point of view of morality? We

can, and indeed we have already started to do so. In addition to their other problems, QALYs and their use for priority setting in health care or for choosing not which treatment to give these patients, but for selecting which patients or conditions to treat, involve profound injustice, and if implemented would constitute a denial of the most basic civil rights. Why is this?

Moral Constraints

One general constraint that is widely accepted and that I think most people would judge should govern life and death decisions, is the idea that many people believe expresses the values animating the health service as a whole. These are the belief that the life and health of each person matters, and matters as much as that of any other and that each person is entitled to be treated with equal concern and respect both in the way health resources are distributed and in the way they are treated generally by health care professionals, however much their personal circumstances may differ from that of others.

This popular belief about the values which animate the health service depends on a more abstract view about the source and structure of such values and it is worth saying just a bit about this now.

I. The Value of Life

One such value is the value of life itself. Our own continued existence as individuals is the *sine qua non* of almost everything. So long as we want to go on living, practically everything we value or want depends upon our continued existence. This is one reason why we generally give priority to life-saving over life-enhancing.

To think that *life is valuable*, that in most circumstances, the worst thing that can happen to an individual is that she lose her life when this need not happen, and that the worst thing we can do is make decisions, a consequence of which, is that others die prematurely, we must think that *each life is valuable*. Each life counts for one and that is why more count for more. For this reason we should give priority to saving as many lives as we can, not as many life-years.[11]

One important point must be emphasized at this stage. We talk of "life-saving" but of course this must always be understood as "death-postponing." Normally we want to have our death postponed for as long as possible but where what's possible is the gaining of only very short periods of remission, hours or days, these may not be worth having. Even those who are moribund in this sense can usually recognize this fact, particularly if they are aware that the cost at postponing their death for a few hours or days at the most will mean suffering or death for others. However, even brief remission can be valuable in enabling the individual to put her affairs in order, make farewells and so on, and this can be important. It is for the individual to decide whether the remission that she can be granted is worth having. This is a delicate point that needs more discussion than I can give it here. However, inasmuch as QALYs do not help us to understand the features of a short and painful remission that might none the less make that period of vital importance to the individual, perhaps in terms of making something worthwhile out of her life as a whole, the difficulties of these sorts of circumstances, while real enough, do not undermine the case against QALYs.[12]

II. Treating People as Equals

If each life counts for one, then the life of each has the same value as that of any. This is why accepting the value of life generates a principle of equality. This principle does not of course entail that we treat each person equally in the sense of treating each person *the same*. This would be absurd and self-defeating. What it does involve is the idea that we treat each person with the same concern and respect. An illustration provided by Ronald Dworkin, whose work on equality informs this entire discussion, best illustrates this point: "If I have two children, and one is dying from a disease that is making the other uncomfortable, I do not show equal concern if I flip a coin to decide which should have the remaining dose of a drug."[13]

It is not surprising then that the pattern of protections for individuals that we think of in terms of civil rights[14] centres on the physical protection of the individual and of her most fundamental interests. One of the prime functions of the State is to protect the lives and fundamental interests of its citizens and to treat each citizen as the equal of any other. This is why the State has a basic obligation, *inter alia*, to treat all citizens as equals in the distribution of benefits and

opportunities which affect their civil rights. The State must, in short, treat each citizen with equal concern and respect. The civil rights generated by this principle will of course include rights to the allocation of such things as legal protections and educational and health care resources. And this requirement that the State uphold the civil rights of citizens and deal justly between them, means that it must not choose between individuals, or permit choices to be made between individuals, that abridge their civil rights or in ways that attack their right to treatment as equals.

Whatever else this means, it certainly means that a society, through its public institutions, is not entitled to discriminate between individuals in ways that mean life or death for them on grounds which count the lives or fundamental interests of some as worth less than those of others. If for example some people were given life-saving treatment in preference to others because they had a better quality of life than those others, or more dependents and friends, or because they were considered more useful, this would amount to regarding such people as more valuable than others on that account. Indeed it would be tantamount, literally, to sacrificing the lives of others so that they might continue to live.[15]

Because my own life would be better and even of more value to me if I were healthier, fitter, had more money, more friends, more lovers, more children, more life expectancy, more everything I want, it does not follow that others are entitled to decide that because I lack some or all of these things I am less entitled to health care resources, or less worthy to receive those resources, than are others, or that those resources would somehow be wasted on me.

III. Civil Rights

I have spoken in terms of civil rights advisedly. If we think of the parallel with our attitude to the system of criminal justice the reasons will be obvious. We think that the liberty of the subject is of fundamental importance and that no one should be wrongfully detained. This is why there are no financial constraints on society's obligation to attempt to ensure equality before the law. An individual is entitled to a fair trial no matter what the financial costs to society (and the can be substantial). We don't adopt rubrics for the allocation of justice which dictate that only those for whom justice can be cheaply provided will receive it. And the reason is that something of fundamental importance is at stake—the liberty of the individual.

In health care something of arguably greater importance is often at stake—the very life of the individual. Indeed, since the abolition of capital punishment [in the United Kingdom], the importance of seeing that individuals' civil rights are respected in health care is pre-eminent.

IV. Discrimination

The only way to deal between individuals in a way which treats them as equals when resources are scarce, is to allocate those resources in a way which exhibits no preference. To discriminate between people on the grounds of quality of life, or QALY, or life-expectancy, is as unwarranted as it would be to discriminate on grounds of race or gender.

So, the problem of choosing how to allocate scarce resources is simple. And by that of course I mean "theoretically simple," not that the decisions will be easy to make or that it will be anything but agonisingly difficult actually to determine, however justly, who should live and who should die. Life-saving resources should simply be allocated in ways which do not violate the individual's entitlement to be treated as the equal of any other individual in the society: and that means the individual's entitlement to have his interests and desires weighed at the same value as those of anyone else. The QALY and the other bases of preference we have considered are irrelevant.

If health professionals are forced by the scarcity of resources, to choose, they should avoid unjust discrimination. But how are they to do this?

Just Distribution

If there were a satisfactory principle or theory of just distribution now would be the time to recommend its use. Unfortunately there is not a satisfactory principle available. The task is to allocate resources between competing claimants in a way that does not violate the individual's entitlement to be treated as the equal of any other individual—and that means her

entitlement to have her fundamental interests and desires weighed at the same value as those of anyone else. The QALY and other quality-of-life criteria are, as I we have seen, both dangerous and irrelevant as are considerations based on life-expectancy or on "life-years" generated by the proposed treatment. If health professionals are forced by the scarcity of resources to choose, not *whether* to treat but *who* to treat, they must avoid any method that amounts to unjust discrimination.

I do not pretend that the task of achieving this will be an easy one, nor that I have any satisfactory solution. I do have views on how to approach a solution, but the development of those ideas is a task for another occasion. I will be content for the moment if I have shown that QALYs are not the answer and that efforts to find one will have to take a different direction.

I. Defensive Medicine

While it is true that resources will always be limited it is far from clear that resources for health care are justifiably as limited as they are sometimes made to appear. People within health care are too often forced to consider simply the question of the best way of allocating the *health care budget*,* and consequently are forced to compete with each other for resources. Where lives are at stake however, the issue is a moral issue which faces the whole community, and in such circumstances, is one which calls for a fundamental reappraisal of priorities. The question should therefore be posed in terms, not of the health care budget alone, but of the *national budget*.[16] If this is done it will be clearer that it is simply not true that the resources necessary to save the lives of citizens are not available. Since the citizens in question are in real and present danger of death, the issue of the allocation of resources to life-saving is naturally one of, among other things, national defense. Clearly then health professionals who require additional resources simply to save the lives of citizens, have a prior and priority claim on the defense budget.

QALYs encourage the idea that the task for health economics is to find more efficient ways of doing the wrong thing—in this case sacrificing the

---

*In the United Kingdom, most people receive health care through the publicly financed National Health Service.

lives of patients who could be saved. All people concerned with health care should have as their priority defensive medicine: defending their patients against unjust and lethal policies, and guarding themselves against devices that tend to disguise the immorality of what they are asked to do.

II. Priority in Life-Saving

It is implausible to suppose that we cannot deploy vastly greater resources than we do at present to save the lives of all those in immediate mortal danger. It should be only in exceptional circumstances—unforeseen and massive disasters for example—that we cannot achieve this. However, in such circumstances our first duty is to try to save the maximum number of lives possible. This is because, since each person's life is valuable, and since we are committed to treating each person with the same concern and respect that we show to any, we must preserve the lives of as many individuals as we can. To fail to do so would be to value at zero the lives and fundamental interests of those extra people we could, but do not, save. Where we cannot save all, we should select those who are not to be saved in a way that shows no unjust preference.

We should be very clear that the obligation to save as many lives as possible is *not the obligation to save as many lives as we can cheaply or economically save*. Among the sorts of disasters that force us to choose between lives, is not the disaster of overspending a limited health care budget!

There are multifarious examples of what I have in mind here and just a couple must suffice to illustrate the point. Suppose, as is often the case, providing health care in one region of a country[17] is more expensive than doing so in another, or where saving the lives of people with particular conditions, is radically more expensive than other life-saving procedures, and a given health care budget won't run to the saving of all. Then any formula employed to choose priorities should do just that. Instead of attempting to measure the value of people's lives and select which are worth saving, any rubric for resource allocation should *examine the national budget afresh* to see whether there are any headings of expenditure that are more important to the community than rescuing citizens in mortal danger. For only if all other claims on funding are plausibly

more important than that, is it true that resources for life-saving are limited.

III. Conclusion

The principle of equal access to health core is sustained by the very, same reasons that sustain both the principle of equality before the law and the civil rights required to defend the freedom of the individual. These are rightly considered so important that no limit is set on the cost of sustaining them. Equal access to health care is of equal importance and should be accorded the same priority for analogous reasons. Indeed, since the abolition of capital punishment, due process of law is arguably of less vital importance than is access to health care. We have seen that QALYs involve denying that the life and health of each citizen is as important as that of any. If, for example, we applied the QALY principle to the administration of criminal justice we might find that those with little life expectancy would have less to gain from securing their freedom and therefore should not be defended at all, or perhaps given a jury trial only if not in competition for such things with younger or fitter fellow citizens.

A recent BBC television programme calculated[18] that if a health authority had £200,000 to spend it would get 10 QALYs from dialysis of kidney patients, 266 QALYs from hip-replacement operations or 1197 QALYs from anti-smoking propaganda. While this information is undoubtedly useful and while advice to stop smoking is an important part of health care, we should be wary of a formula which seems to dictate that such a health authority would use its resources most efficiently if it abandoned hip replacements and dialysis in favor of advice to stop smoking.

NOTES

1. See the excellent discussion of the recent history of this line of thought in the Office of Health Economics publication *The measurement of health* London, 1985.
2. Williams A. Economics of coronary artery bypass grafting. *British medical journal* 1985; 291; and his contribution to the article, Centre eight—in search of efficiency. *Health and social service journal* 1985. These are by no means the first such attempts.
3. Williams A. The value of QALYs. *Health and social services journal* 1985.

4. I mention this in case anyone should think that it is only medical scientists who do medical research.

5. See reference (3): 3.

6. See reference (l): 16.

7. See reference (3): 5, and reference (3).

8. I'll assume this can be described as "true" for the sake of argument.

9. I am indebted to Dr S G Potts for pointing out to me some of these statistics and for other helpful comments.

10. For examples see reference (1) and reference (2).

11. See Parfit D. Innumerate ethics. *Philosophy and public affairs* 1978; 7, 4 Parfit's arguments provide a detailed defense of the principle that each is to count for one.

12. I consider these problems in more detail in my: eQALYty. In: Byrne P, ed. *King's College studies*. London: King's Fund Press, 1987/8. Forthcoming.

13. Dworkin R. *Taking rights seriously*. London: Duckworth, 1977: 227.

14. I do not of course mean to imply that there are such things as rights, merely that our use of the language of rights captures the special importance we attach to certain freedoms and protections. The term "civil rights" is used here as a "term of art" referring to those freedoms and protections that are customarily classed as "civil rights."

15. For an interesting attempt to fill this gap see Dworkin R. What is equality? *Philosophy and public affairs* 1981; 4 and 5.

16. And of course the international budget; see my *The value of life*. London: Routledge & Kegan Paul 1985: chapter 3.

17. See Townsend P, Davidson N, eds. *Inequalities in health: the Black Report*. Harmondsworth, Penguin: 1982.

18. BBC 1. *The heart of the matter* 1986, Oct.

Public Health Ethics: Mapping the Terrain

JAMES F. CHILDRESS, RUTH R. FADEN, RUTH D. GAARE, LAWRENCE O. GOSTIN, JEFFREY KAHN, RICHARD J. BONNIE, NANCY E. KASS, ANNA C. MASTROIANNI, JONATHAN D. MORENO, AND PHILLIP NIEBURG

Childress et al. discuss the main concepts and issues in public health ethics, providing a working definition of the public health sphere, identifying the considerations that dominate moral deliberations, and outlining how moral conflicts arise. They also examine a central question in public health ethics: "When can paternalistic interventions [by the state or other authorities] . . . be ethically justified if they infringe general moral considerations such as respect for autonomy, including liberty of action?"

Public health ethics, like the field of public health it addresses, traditionally has focused more on practice and particular cases than on theory, with the result that some concepts, methods, and boundaries remain largely undefined. This paper attempts to provide a rough conceptual map of the terrain of public health ethics. We begin by briefly defining public health and identifying general features of the field that are particularly relevant for a discussion of public health ethics.

Public health is primarily concerned with the health of the entire population, rather than the health of individuals. Its features include an emphasis on the promotion of health and the prevention of disease and disability; the collection and use of epidemiological data, population surveillance, and other forms of empirical quantitative assessment; a recognition of the multidimensional nature of the determinants of health; and a focus on the complex interactions of many factors—biological, behavioral, social, and environmental—in developing effective interventions.

How can we distinguish public health from medicine? While medicine focuses on the treatment and cure of individual patients, public health aims to understand and ameliorate the causes of disease and disability in a population. In addition, whereas the physician-patient relationship is at the center of medicine, public health involves interactions and relationships among many professionals and members of the community as well as agencies of government

Journal of Law, Medicine & Ethics, 30 (2002): 170–78.

in the development, implementation, and assessment of interventions. From this starting point, we can suggest that public health systems consist of all the people and actions, including laws, policies, practices, and activities, that have the primary purpose of protecting and improving the health of the public.[1] While we need not assume that public health systems are tightly structured or centrally directed, we recognize that they include a wide range of governmental, private and non-profit organizations, as well as professionals from many disciplines, all of which (alone and together) have a stake in and an effect on a community's health. Government has a unique role in public health because of its responsibility, grounded in its police powers, to protect the public's health and welfare, because it alone can undertake certain interventions, such as regulation, taxation, and the expenditure of public funds, and because many, perhaps most, public health programs are public goods that cannot be optimally provided if left to individuals or small groups.

The Institute of Medicine's landmark 1988 definition of public health provides additional insight: "Public health is what we, as a society, do collectively to assure the conditions in which people can be healthy."[2] The words "what we, as a society, do collectively" suggest the need for cooperative behavior and relationships built on overlapping values and trust. The words "to assure the conditions in which people can be healthy" suggest a far-reaching agenda for public health that focuses attention not only on the medical needs of individuals, but on fundamental social conditions that affect population levels of morbidity and mortality. From an ethical standpoint, public health activities are generally understood to be teleological (end-oriented) and consequentialist—the health of the public is the primary end that is sought and the primary outcome for measuring success.[3] Defining and measuring "health" is not easy, as we will emphasize below, but, in addition, "public" is a complex concept with at least three dimensions that are important for our discussion of ethics.

First, public can be used to mean the "numerical public," i.e., the target population. In view of public health's goal of producing net health benefits for the population, this meaning of public is very

important. In measurement and analysis, the "numerical public" reflects the utilitarian view that each individual counts as one and only one. In this context, ethical analysis focuses on issues in measurement, many of which raise considerations of justice. For example, how should we define a population, how should we compare gains in life expectancy with gains in health-related quality of life, and whose values should be used in making those judgments?

Second, public is what we collectively do through government and public agency—we can call this "political public." Government provides much of the funding for a vast array of public health functions, and public health professionals in governmental roles are the focal point of much collective activity. In the United States, as Lawrence Gostin notes, government "is compelled by its role as the elected representative of the community to act affirmatively to promote the health of the people," even though it "cannot unduly invade individuals' rights in the name of the communal good."[4] The government is a central player in public health because of the collective responsibility it must assume and implement. The state's use of its police powers for public health raises important ethical questions, particularly about the justification and limits of governmental coercion and about its duty to treat all citizens equally in exercising these powers. In a liberal, pluralistic democracy, the justification of coercive policies, as well as other policies, must rest on moral reasons that the public in whose name the policies are carried out could reasonably be expected to accept.[5]

Third, public, defined as what we do collectively in a broad sense, includes all forms of social and community action affecting public health—we can call this "communal public." Ethical analysis on this level extends beyond the political public. People collectively, outside of government and with private funds, often have greater freedom to undertake public health interventions since they do not have to justify their actions to the political public. However, their actions are still subject to various moral requirements, including, for instance, respect for individual autonomy, liberty, privacy and confidentiality, and transparency in disclosure of conflicts of interest.

General Moral Considerations

In providing a map of the terrain of public health ethics, we do not suggest that there is a consensus about the methods and content of public health ethics.[6] Controversies persist about theory and method in other areas of applied or practical ethics, and it should not be surprising that variety also prevails in public health ethics.[7] The terrain of public health ethics includes a loose set of general moral considerations—clusters of moral concepts and norms that are variously called values, principles, or rules—that are arguably relevant to public health. Public health ethics, in part, involves ongoing efforts to specify and to assign weights to these general moral considerations in the context of particular policies, practices, and actions, in order to provide concrete moral guidance.

Recognizing general moral considerations in public health ethics does not entail a commitment to any particular theory or method. What we describe and propose is compatible with several approaches. To take one major example, casuistical reasoning (examining the relevant similarities and differences between cases) is not only compatible with but indispensable to our conception of public health ethics. Not only do—or should—public health agents examine new situations they confront in light of general moral considerations, but they should also focus on a new situation's relevant similarities to and differences from paradigm or precedent cases—cases that have gained a relatively settled moral consensus. Whether a relatively settled moral consensus is articulated first in a general moral consideration or in precedent cases does not constitute a fundamental issue—both are relevant. Furthermore, some of the precedents may concern how general moral considerations are interpreted, specified, and balanced in some public health activity, especially where conflicts emerge.

Conceptions of morality usually recognize a formal requirement of universalizability in addition to a substantive requirement of attention to human welfare. Whatever language is used, this formal feature requires that we treat similar cases in a similar way. This requirement undergirds casuistical reasoning in morality as well as in law. In public health ethics, for example, any recommendations for an HIV screening policy must take into account both past precedents in screening for other infectious diseases and the precedents the new policy will create for, say, screening for genetic conditions. Much of the moral argument will hinge on which similarities and differences between cases are morally relevant, and that argument will often, though not always, appeal to general moral considerations.[8] We can establish the relevance of a set of these considerations in part by looking at the kinds of moral appeals that public health agents make in deliberating about and justifying their actions as well as at debates about moral issues in public health. The relevant general moral considerations include:

- producing benefits;
- avoiding, preventing, and removing harms;
- producing the maximal balance of benefits over harms and other costs (often called utility);
- distributing benefits and burdens fairly (distributive justice) and ensuring public participation, including the participation of affected parties (procedural justice);
- respecting autonomous choices and actions, including liberty of action;
- protecting privacy and confidentiality;
- keeping promises and commitments;
- disclosing information as well as speaking honestly and truthfully (often grouped under transparency); and
- building and maintaining trust.

Several of these general moral considerations—especially benefiting others, preventing and removing harms, and utility—provide a *prima facie* warrant for many activities in pursuit of the goal of public health. It is sufficient for our purposes to note that public health activities have their grounding in general moral considerations, and that public health identifies one major broad benefit that societies and governments ought to pursue. The relation of public health to the whole set of general moral considerations is complex. Some general moral considerations support this pursuit; institutionalizing several others may be a condition for or means to public health (we address this point later when we discuss human rights and public health); and yet, in particular cases, some of the same general moral considerations may limit or constrain what may be done in pursuit of public health. Hence, conflicts may occur among these general moral considerations.

The content of these various general moral considerations can be divided and arranged in several ways—for instance, some theories may locate one or more of these concepts under others. But, whatever theory one embraces, the whole set of general moral considerations roughly captures the moral content of public health ethics. It then becomes necessary to address several practical questions. First, how can we make these general moral considerations more specific and concrete in order to guide action? Second, how can we resolve conflicts among them? Some of the conflicts will concern how much weight and significance to assign to the ends and effects of protecting and promoting public health relative to the other considerations that limit and constrain ways to pursue such outcomes. While each general moral consideration may limit and constrain public health activities in some circumstances, for our purposes, justice or fairness, respect for autonomy and liberty, and privacy and confidentiality are particularly noteworthy in this regard.

Specifying and Weighting General Moral Considerations

We do not present a universal public health ethic. Although arguably these general moral considerations find support in various societies and cultures, an analysis of the role of cultural context in public health ethics is beyond the scope of this paper. Instead, we focus here on public health ethics in the particular setting of the United States, with its traditions, practices, and legal and constitutional requirements, all of which set directions for and circumscribe public health ethics. (Below we will indicate how this conception of public health ethics relates to human rights.)

General moral considerations have two major dimensions. One is their meaning and range or scope; the other is their weight or strength. The first determines the extent of conflict among them—if their range or scope is interpreted in certain ways, conflicts may be increased or reduced. The second

dimension determines when different considerations yield to others in cases of conflict.

Specifying the meaning and range or scope of general moral considerations—the first dimension—provides increasingly concrete guidance in public health ethics. A common example is specifying respect for autonomy by rules of voluntary, informed consent. However, it would be a mistake to suppose that respect for autonomy requires consent in all contexts of public health or to assume that consent alone sufficiently specifies the duty to respect autonomy in public health settings. Indeed, specifying the meaning and scope of general moral considerations entails difficult moral work. Nowhere is this more evident in public health ethics than with regard to considerations of justice. Explicating the demands of justice in allocating public health resources and in setting priorities for public health policies, or in determining whom they should target, remains among the most daunting challenges in public health ethics.

The various general moral considerations are not absolute. Each may conflict with another and each may have to yield in some circumstances. At most, then, these general moral considerations identify features of actions, practices, and policies that make them *prima facie* or presumptively right or wrong, i.e., right or wrong, all other things being equal. But since any particular action, practice, or policy for the public's health may also have features that infringe one or more of these general moral considerations, it will be necessary to determine which of them has priority. Some argue for a lexical or serial ordering, in which one general moral consideration, while not generally absolute, has priority over another. For instance, one theory might hold that protecting or promoting public health always has priority over privacy, while another might hold that individual liberty always has priority over protecting or promoting public health. Neither of these priority rules is plausible, and any priority rule that is plausible will probably involve tight or narrow specifications of the relevant general moral considerations to reduce conflicts. From our standpoint, it is better to recognize the need to balance general moral considerations in particular circumstances when conflicts arise. We cannot determine their weights in advance, only in particular contexts that may affect their weights—for instance, promises may not have the same moral weights in different contexts.

Resolving Conflicts Among General Moral Considerations

We do not believe it is possible to develop an algorithm to resolve all conflicts among general moral considerations. Such conflicts can arise in multiple ways. For example, it is common in public health practice and policy for conflicts to emerge between privacy and justice (for instance, the state collects and records private information in disease registries about individuals in order to allocate and provide access to resources for appropriate prevention and treatment services), or between different conceptions of justice (for instance, a government with a finite public health budget must decide whether to dedicate resources to vaccination or to treatment of conditions when they arise). In this paper, however, we focus on one particular permutation of conflicts among general moral considerations that has received the most attention in commentary and in law. This is the conflict between the general moral considerations that are generally taken to instantiate the goal of public health—producing benefits, preventing harms, and maximizing utility—and those that express other moral commitments. For conflicts that assume this structure, we propose five "justificatory conditions": effectiveness, proportionality, necessity, least infringement, and public justification. These conditions are intended to help determine whether promoting public health warrants overriding such values as individual liberty or justice in particular cases.

Effectiveness. It is essential to show that infringing one or more general moral considerations will probably protect public health. For instance, a policy that infringes one or more general moral considerations in the name of public health but has little chance of realizing its goal is ethically unjustified.

Proportionality. It is essential to show that the probable public health benefits outweigh the infringed general moral considerations—this condition is sometimes called proportionality. For instance, the

policy may breach autonomy or privacy and have undesirable consequences. All of the positive features and benefits must be balanced against the negative features and effects.

Necessity. Not all effective and proportionate policies are necessary to realize the public health goal that is sought. The fact that a policy will infringe a general moral consideration provides a strong moral reason to seek an alternative strategy that is less morally troubling. This is the logic of a *prima facie* or presumptive general moral consideration. For instance, all other things being equal, a policy that provides incentives for persons with tuberculosis to complete their treatment until cured will have priority over a policy that forcibly detains such persons in order to ensure the completion of treatment. Proponents of the forcible strategy have the burden of moral proof. This means that the proponents must have a good faith belief, for which they can give supportable reasons, that a coercive approach is necessary. In many contexts, this condition does not require that proponents provide empirical evidence by actually trying the alternative measures and demonstrating their failure.[9]

Least Infringement. Even when a proposed policy satisfies the first three justificatory conditions—that is, it is effective, proportionate, and essential in realizing the goal of public health—public health agents should seek to minimize the infringement of general moral considerations. For instance, when a policy infringes autonomy, public health agents should seek the least restrictive alternative; when it infringes privacy, they should seek the least intrusive alternative; and when it infringes confidentiality, they should disclose only the amount and kind of information needed, and only to those necessary, to realize the goal.[10] The justificatory condition of least infringement could plausibly be interpreted as a corollary of necessity—for instance, a proposed coercive measure must be necessary in degree as well as in kind.

Public Justification. When public health agents believe that one of their actions, practices, or policies infringes one or more general moral considerations, they also have a responsibility, in our judgment, to explain and justify that infringement, whenever possible, to the relevant parties, including those affected by the infringement. In the context of what we called "political public," public health agents should offer public justification for policies in terms that fit the overall social contract in a liberal, pluralistic democracy. This transparency stems in part from the requirement to treat citizens as equals and with respect by offering moral reasons, which in principle they could find acceptable, for policies that infringe general moral considerations. Transparency is also essential to creating and maintaining public trust; and it is crucial to establishing accountability. (Below we elaborate a process-oriented approach to public accountability that goes beyond public justification to include, as an expression of justice and fairness, input from the relevant affected parties in the formulation of policy.)

Screening Program Example

An extended example may illustrate how these moral justificatory conditions function in public health ethics. Let us suppose that public health agents are considering whether to implement a screening program for HIV infection, tuberculosis, another infectious or contagious disease, or a genetic condition (see Figure 1 for some morally relevant features of screening programs).

The relevant justificatory conditions will require public health agents to consider whether any proposed program will be likely to realize the public health goal that is sought (effectiveness), whether its probable benefits will outweigh the infringed general moral considerations (proportionality), whether the policy is essential to realize the end (necessity), whether it involves the least infringement possible

consistent with realizing the goal that is sought (least infringement), and whether it can be publicly justified. These conditions will give priority to selective programs over universal ones if the selective programs will realize the goal (as we note below, questions may arise about universality within selected categories, such as pregnant women), and to voluntary programs over mandatory ones if the voluntary programs will realize the goal.[11]

Different screening programs may fail close scrutiny in light of one or more of these conditions. For instance, neither mandatory nor voluntary universal screening for HIV infection can meet these conditions in the society as a whole. Some voluntary and some mandatory selective screening programs for HIV infection can be justified, while others cannot. Mandatory screening of donated blood, organs, sperm, and ova is easily justified, and screening of individuals may also be justified in some settings where they can expose others to bodily fluids and potential victims cannot protect themselves. The question of whether and under what conditions screening of pregnant women for HIV infection should be instituted has been particularly controversial. Even before the advent of effective treatment for HIV infection and the identification of zidovudine (AZT) as effective in reducing the rate of perinatal transmission, there were calls for mandatory screening of pregnant women, especially in "high risk" communities. These calls were defeated by sound arguments that such policies entailed unjustifiable violations of autonomy, privacy, and justice.[12] In effect, the recommended policies failed to satisfy any of the justificatory conditions we have proposed here.

However, once it was established that zidovudine could interrupt maternal-fetal transmission of

Extent of Screening		Degree of Voluntariness	
		Voluntary	Mandatory
	Universal		
	Selective		

FIGURE 1   Features of Public Health Screening Programs

HIV, the weight of the argument shifted in the direction of instituting screening programs of some type. The focus of the debate became the tensions between the public health interests in utility and efficiency, which argued for mandatory, selective screening in high-risk communities, and considerations of liberty, privacy, and justice, which argued for voluntary, universal screening.[13]

In many situations, the most defensible public health policy for screening and testing *expresses* community rather than *imposes* it. Imposing community involves mandating or compelling testing through coercive measures. By contrast, expressing community involves taking steps to express solidarity with individuals, to protect their interests, and to gain their trust. Expressing community may include, for example, providing communal support, disclosing adequate information, protecting privacy and confidentiality, and encouraging certain choices. This approach seeks to make testing a reasonable, and perhaps moral, choice for individuals, especially by engendering public trust, rather than making it compulsory. Several diseases that might be subjected to screening for public health reasons involve stigma, and breaches of privacy and confidentiality may put individuals' employment and insurance at risk. Expressing community is often an appropriate strategy for public health, and, *ceteris paribus*, it has priority over imposing community through coercive policies.

Processes of Public Accountability

Our discussion of the fifth justificatory condition—public justification—focused on providing public reasons for policies that infringe general moral considerations; this condition is particularly applicable in the political context. While public accountability includes public justification, it is broader—it is prospective as well as retrospective. It involves soliciting input from the relevant publics (the numerical, political, and communal publics) in the process of formulating public health policies, practices, and actions, as well as justifying to the relevant publics what is being undertaken. This is especially, but not only, important when one of the other *prima facie* general moral considerations is infringed, as with coercive protective measures to prevent epidemics. At a minimum, public accountability involves transparency in openly seeking information from those affected and in honestly disclosing relevant information to the public; it is indispensable for engendering and sustaining public trust, as well as for expressing justice.[14]

Public accountability regarding health promotion or priority-setting for public health funding additionally might involve a more developed fair process. Noting that in a pluralistic society we are likely to find disagreement about which principles should govern issues such as priority-setting in health care, Norman Daniels calls for a fair process that includes the following elements: transparency and publicity about the reasons for a decision; appeals to rationales and evidence that fair-minded parties would agree are relevant; and procedures for appealing and revising decisions in light of challenges by various stakeholders. He explains why this process can facilitate social learning: "Since we may not be able to construct principles that yield fair decisions ahead of time, we need a process that allows us to develop those reasons over time as we face real cases."[15]

Public accountability also involves acknowledging the more complex relationship between public health and the public, one that addresses fundamental issues such as those involving characterization of risk and scientific uncertainty. Because public health depends for its success on the satisfaction of deeply personal health goals of individuals and groups in the population, concepts such as "health" and "risk" cannot be understood or acted upon on the basis of *a priori*, formal definitions or scientific analysis. Public accountability recognizes that the fundamental conceptualization of these terms is a critical part of the basic formulation of public health goals and problems to be addressed. This means that the public, along with scientific experts, plays an important role in the *analysis* of public health issues, as well as in the development and assessment of appropriate *strategies* for addressing them.

Risk characterization provides a helpful example. A National Research Council report, *Understanding Risk: Informing Decisions in a Democratic Society,* concluded that risk characterization is not properly understood if defined only as a summary of scientific information; rather, it is the outcome of a complex analytic-deliberative process—"a decision-driven activity, directed toward informing choices and solving problems."[16] The report explains that scientific analysis, which uses rigorous, replicable methods, brings new information into the process, and that deliberation helps to frame analysis by posing new questions and new ways of formulating problems, with the result that risk characterization is the output of a recursive process, not a linear one, and is a decision-driven activity.

Assessment of the health risks of dioxin illustrates this process. While scientific analysis provides information about the dose-response relationship between dioxin exposure and possible human health effects, public health focuses on the placement of waste incinerators and community issues in which dioxin is only one of many hazardous chemicals involved and cancer only one of many outcomes of concern. The critical point is that good risk characterization results from a process that "not only gets the science right," but also "gets the right science."[17]

Public health accountability addresses the responsibility of public health agents to work with the public and scientific experts to identify, define, and understand at a fundamental level the threats to public health, and the risks and benefits of ways to address them. The appropriate level of public involvement in the analytic-deliberative process depends on the particular public health problem.

Public accountability requires an openness to public deliberation and imposes an obligation on decision-makers to provide honest information and justifications for their decisions. No ethical principle can eliminate the fact that individual interests must sometimes yield to collective needs. Public accountability, however, ensures that such trade-offs will be made openly, with an explicit acknowledgment that individuals' fundamental well-being and values are at stake and that reasons, grounded in ethics, will be provided to those affected by the decisions.[18] It provides a basis for public trust, even when policies infringe or appear to infringe some general moral considerations.

Public Health Interventions vs. Paternalistic Interventions

An important empirical, conceptual, and normative issue in public health ethics is the relationship between protecting and promoting the health of individuals and protecting and promoting public health. Although public health is directed to the health of populations, the indices of population health, of course, include an aggregation of the health of individuals. But suppose the primary reason for some restrictions on the liberties of individuals is to prevent harm to those whose actions are substantially voluntary and do not affect others adversely. The ethical question then is, when can paternalistic interventions (defined as interventions designed to protect or benefit individuals themselves against their express wishes) be ethically justified if they infringe general moral considerations such as respect for autonomy, including liberty of action?

Consider the chart in Figure 2: An individual's actions may be substantially voluntary (competent, adequately in formed, and free of controlling influences) or non-voluntary (incompetent, inadequately informed, or subject to controlling influences). In addition, those actions may be self-regarding (the adverse effects of the actions fall primarily on the individual himself or herself) or other-regarding (the adverse effects of the actions fall primarily on others).

Paternalism in a morally interesting and problematic sense arises in the first quadrant (marked by the number "1" in Figure 2)—where the individual's actions are both voluntary and self-regarding. According to John Stuart Mill, whose *On Liberty* has inspired this chart, other-regarding conduct not only affects others adversely, but also affects them directly and without "their free, voluntary, and undeceived consent and participation."[19] If others, in the maturity of their faculties, consent to an agent's imposition of risk, then the agent's actions are not other-regarding in Mill's sense.

Whether an agent's other-regarding conduct is voluntary or non-voluntary, the society may justifiably intervene in various ways, including the use of coercion, to reduce or prevent the imposition of serious risk on others. Societal intervention in non-voluntary self-regarding conduct is considered weak (or soft) paternalism, if it is paternalistic at all, and it is easily justified. By contrast, societal interference in voluntary self-regarding conduct would be strong (or hard) paternalism. Coercive intervention in the name of strong paternalism would be

		Adverse Effects of Individuals' Actions	
Voluntariness of Individuals' Actions		Self-reagarding	Other-regarding
	Voluntary	1	2
	Non-voluntary	3	4

FIGURE 2   Types of Individual Action

insulting and disrespectful to individuals because it would override their voluntary actions for their own benefit, even though their actions do not harm others. Such interventions are thus very difficult to justify in a liberal, pluralistic democracy.

Because of this difficulty, proponents of public health sometimes contend that the first quadrant is really a small class of cases because individuals' risky actions are, in most cases, other-regarding or non-voluntary, or both. Thus, they insist, even if we assume that strong or hard paternalism cannot be ethically justified, the real question is whether most public health interventions in personal life plans and risk budgets are paternalistic at all, at least in the morally problematic sense.

To a great extent, the question is where we draw the boundaries of the self and its actions; that is, whether various influences on agents so determine their actions that they are not voluntary, and whether the adverse effects of those actions extend beyond the agents themselves. Such boundary drawing involves empirical, conceptual, and normative questions that demand attention in public health ethics. On the one hand, it is not sufficient to show that social-cultural factors influence an individual's actions; it is necessary to show that those influences render that individual's actions substantially non-voluntary and warrant societal interventions to protect him or her. Controversies about the strong influence of food marketing on diet and weight (and, as a result, on the risk of disease and death) illustrate the debates about this condition.

On the other hand, it is not sufficient to show that an individual's actions have some adverse effects on others; it is necessary to show that those adverse effects on others are significant enough to warrant overriding the individual's liberty. Controversies about whether the state should require motorcyclists to wear helmets illustrate the debates about this condition. These controversies also show how the inclusion of the financial costs to society and the emotional costs to, say, observers and rescue squads can appear to make virtually any intervention non-paternalistic. But even if these adverse financial and emotional effects on others are morally relevant as a matter of social utility, it would still be necessary to show that they are significant enough to justify the intervention.

Either kind of attempt to reduce the sphere of autonomous, self-regarding actions, in order to warrant interventions in the name of public health, or, more broadly, social utility, can sometimes be justified, but either attempt must be subjected to careful scrutiny. Sometimes both may represent rationalization and bad faith as public health agents seek to evade the stringent demands of the general moral consideration of respect for autonomy. Requiring consistency across an array of cases may provide a safeguard against rationalization and bad faith, particularly when motives for intervention may be mixed.

Much of this debate reflects different views about whether and when strong paternalistic interventions can be ethically justified. In view of the justificatory conditions identified earlier, relevant factors will include the nature of the intervention, the degree to which it infringes an individual's fundamental values, the magnitude of the risk to the individual apart from the intervention (either in terms of harm or lost benefit), and so forth. For example, even though the authors of this paper would disagree about some cases, we agree that strong paternalistic interventions that do not threaten individuals' core values and that will probably protect them against serious risks are more easily justifiable than strong paternalistic interventions that threaten individuals' core values and that will reduce only minor risks. Of course, evaluating actual and proposed policies that infringe general moral considerations becomes very complicated when both paternalistic and public health reasons exist for, and are intertwined in, those policies.

Social Justice, Human Rights, and Health

We have noted potential and actual conflicts between promoting the good of public health and other general moral considerations. But it is important not to exaggerate these conflicts. Indeed, the societal institutionalization of other general moral considerations in legal rights and social-cultural practices generally contributes to public health. Social injustices expressed in poverty, racism, and sexism have long been implicated in conditions of poor health. In recent years, some evidence suggests that societies that embody more egalitarian conceptions of socioeconomic justice have higher levels of health than ones that do not.[20] Public health activity has traditionally encompassed much more than medicine and health care. Indeed, historically much of the focus of public health has been on the poor and on the impact of squalor and sanitation on health. The focus today on the social determinants of health is in keeping with this tradition. The data about social determinants are impressive even though not wholly uncontroversial. At any rate, they are strong enough to warrant close attention to the ways conditions of social justice contribute to the public's health.

Apart from social justice, some in public health argue that embodying several other general moral considerations, especially as articulated in human rights, is consistent with and may even contribute to public health. For example, Jonathan Mann contended that public health officials now have two fundamental responsibilities—protecting and promoting public health and protecting and promoting human rights. Sometimes public health programs burden human rights, but human rights violations "have adverse effects on physical, mental,

and social well-being" and "promoting and protecting human rights is inextricably linked with promoting and protecting health."[21] Mann noted, and we concur, that, ultimately, "ethics and human rights derive from a set of quite similar, if not identical, core values," several of which we believe are captured in our loose set of general moral considerations.[22] Often, as we have suggested, the most effective ways to protect public health respect general moral considerations rather than violate them, employ voluntary measures rather than coercive ones, protect privacy and confidentiality, and, more generally, express rather than impose community. Recognizing that promoting health and respecting other general moral considerations or human rights may be mutually supportive can enable us to create policies that avoid or at least reduce conflicts.

While more often than not public health and human rights—or general moral considerations not expressed in human rights—do not conflict and may even be synergistic, conflicts do sometimes arise and require resolution.[23] Sometimes, in particular cases, a society cannot simultaneously realize its commitments to public health and to certain other general moral considerations, such as liberty, privacy, and confidentiality. We have tried to provide elements of a framework for thinking through and resolving such conflicts. This process needs to be transparent in order to engender and sustain public trust.

REFERENCES

1. Our definition builds on the definition of health systems offered by the World Health Organization: Health systems include "all the activities whose primary purpose is to promote, restore, or maintain health." See *World Health Report 2000 Health Systems: Improving Performance* (Geneva: World Health Organization, 2000): at 5.
2. Committee for the Study of the Future of Public Health, Division of Health Care Services, Institute of Medicine, *The Future of Public Health* (Washington, D.C.: National Academy Press, 1988): at 1.
3. We recognize that there are different views about the ultimate moral justification for the social institution of public health. For example, some communitarians appear to support public health as an instrumental goal to achieve community. Others may take the view that the state has a duty to ensure the public's health as a

matter of social justice. Although these different interpretations and others are very important for some purposes, they do not seriously affect the conception of public health ethics that we are developing, as long as public health agents identify and inform others of their various goals.

4. L. O. Gostin, *Public Health Law: Power, Duty, Restraint* (Berkeley: University of California Press; New York: The Milbank Memorial Fund, 2000): at 20.

5. T. Nagel, "Moral Epistemology," in R. E. Bulger, E. M. Bobby, and H. V. Fineberg, eds., Committee on the Social and Ethical Impacts of Developments in Biomedicine, Division of Health Sciences Policy, Institute of Medicine, *Society's Choices: Social and Ethical Decision Making in Biomedicine* (Washington, D.C.: National Academy Press, 1995): 201–14.

6. For some other approaches, see P. Nieburg, R. Gaare-Bernheim, and R. Bonnie, "Ethics and the Practice of Public Health," in R. A. Goodman et al., eds., *Law in Public Health Practice* (New York: Oxford University Press, in press), and N. E. Kass, "An Ethics Framework for Public Health," *American Journal of Public Health,* 91 (2001): 1776–82.

7. We do not explore here the overlaps among public health ethics, medical ethics, research ethics, and public policy ethics, although some areas of overlap and difference will be evident throughout the discussion. Further work is needed to address some public health activities that fall within overlapping areas—for instance, surveillance, outbreak investigations, and community-based interventions may sometimes raise issues in the ethics of research involving human subjects.

8. Recognizing universalizability by attending to past precedents and possible future precedents does not preclude a variety of experiments, for instance, to determine the best ways to protect the public's health. Thus, it is not inappropriate for different states, in our federalist system, to try different approaches, as long as each of them is morally acceptable.

9. This justificatory condition is probably the most controversial. Some of the authors of this paper believe that the language of "necessity" is too strong. Whatever language is used, the point is to avoid a purely utilitarian strategy that accepts only the first two conditions of effectiveness and proportionality and to ensure that the non-utilitarian general moral considerations set some *prima facie* limits and constraints and establish moral priorities, *ceteris paribus.*

10. For another version of these justificatory conditions, see T. L. Beauchamp and J. F. Childress, *Principles of Biomedical Ethics,* 5th ed. (New York: Oxford University Press, 2001): at 19–21. We observe that some of these justificatory conditions are quite similar to the justificatory conditions that must be met in U.S. constitutional law when there is strict scrutiny because, for instance, a fundamental liberty is at stake. In such cases, the government must demonstrate that it has a "compelling interest," that its methods are strictly necessary to achieve its objectives, and that it has adopted the "least restrictive alternative." See Gostin, *supra* note 4, at 80–81.

11. Of course, this chart is oversimplified, particularly in identifying only voluntary and mandatory options. For a fuller discussion, see R. Faden, M. Powers, and N. Kass, "Warrants for Screening Programs: Public Health, Legal and Ethical Frameworks," in R. Faden, G. Geller, and M. Powers, eds., *AIDS, Women and the Next Generation* (New York: Oxford University Press, 1991): 3–26.

12. Working Group on HIV Testing of Pregnant Women and Newborns, "HIV Infection, Pregnant Women, and Newborns," *Journal of the American Medical Association,* 264, no. 18 (1990): 2416–20.

13. See Faden, Geller, and Powers, *supra* note 11; Gostin, *supra* note 4, at 199–201.

14. In rare cases, it may be ethically justifiable to limit the disclosure of some information for a period of time (for example, when there are serious concerns about national security; about the interpretation, certainty, or reliability of public health data; or about the potential negative effects of disclosing the information, such as with suicide clusters).

15. N. Daniels, "Accountability for Reasonableness," *British Medical Journal,* 321 (2000): 1300–01, at 1301.

16. P. C. Stern and H. V. Fineberg, eds., Committee on Risk Characterization, Commission on Behavioral and Social Sciences and Education, National Research Council, *Understanding Risk: Informing Decisions in a Democratic Society* (Washington, D.C.: National Academy Press, 1996): at 155.

17. *Id.* at 16–17, 156.

18. See, for example, N. Daniels and J. Sabin, "Limits to Health Care: Fair Procedures, Democratic Deliberation, and the Legitimacy Problem for Insurers," *Philosophy and Public Affairs,* 26 (Fall 1997): 303–50, at 350.

19. J. S. Mill, *On Liberty,* ed. G. Himmelfarb (Harmondsworth, England: Penguin Books, 1976): at 71. For this chart, see J. F. Childress, *Who Should Decide? Paternalism in Health Care* (New York: Oxford University Press, 1982): at 193.

20. See, for example, the discussion in I. Kawachi, B. P. Kennedy, and R. G. Wilkinson, eds., *Income Inequality and Health,* vol. 1 of *The Society and Population Health Reader* (New York: The New Press, 2000).

21. J. M. Mann, "Medicine and Public Health, Ethics and Human Rights," *The Hastings Center Report,* 27 (May–June 1997): 6–13, at 11–12. Contrast Gostin,

supra note 4, at 21. For a fuller analysis and assessment of Mann's work, see L. O. Gostin, "Public Health, Ethics, and Human Rights: A Tribute to the Late Jonathan Mann," S. P. Marks, "Jonathan Mann's Legacy to the 21st Century: The Human Rights Imperative for Public Health," and L. O. Gostin, "A Vision of Health and Human Rights for the 21st Century: A Continuing Discussion with Stephen P. Marks," *Journal of Law, Medicine, and Ethics*, 29, no. 2 (2001): 121–40.

22. Mann, *supra* note 21, at 10. Mann thought that the language of ethics could guide individual behavior, while the language of human rights could best guide societal-level analysis and response. See Mann, *supra* note 21, at 8; Marks, *supra* note 21, at 131–38. We disagree with this separation and instead note the overlap of ethics and human rights, but we endorse the essence of Mann's position on human rights.

23. See Gostin, *supra* note 4, at 21.

Human Rights Approach to Public Health Policy

D. TARANTOLA AND S. GRUSKIN

Tarantola and Gruskin, both scholars in public health issues, argue for a human rights approach in public health. They contend that we can produce just distributions of health and health care by ensuring that human rights in general are respected. Respecting human rights contributes to well-being and health, and these contributions to health depend on respect for human rights.

Introduction

The origin and justification for human rights, whether anchored in natural law, positive law, or other theories and approaches laid out by various authors, as well as their cultural specificity and actual value as international legal commitments, remains subject to ongoing lively debate. Theoretical and rhetorical discourses continue to challenge and enrich current understanding of the relevance of human rights for policy and governance. Nonetheless, human rights have found their way into public health and play today an increasing role in the shaping of health policies, programs, and practice.

Health and human rights are not distinct but intertwined aspirations. Viewed as a universal aspiration, the notion of health as the attainment of physical, mental, and social well-being implies its dependency on and contribution to the realization of all human rights. From the same perspective, the enjoyment by everyone of the highest attainable standard of physical and mental health is in itself a recognized human right. From a global normative perspective, health and human rights are closely intertwined in many international treaties and declarations supported by mechanisms of monitoring and accountability (even as their effectiveness can be questioned) that draw from both fields.

With respect to health specifically, it is arguably viewed as an important prerequisite for and desirable outcome of human development and progress. Health is

... directly constitutive of the person's well-being and it enables a person to function as an agent—that is, to pursue the various goals and projects in life that she has reason to value. (Anand, 2004: 17–18)

Health is also the most extensively measured component of well-being; it benefits from dedicated services and is commonly seen as a *sine-qua-non* for the fulfillment of all other aspirations. It may also be..."a marker, a way of keeping score of how well the society is doing in delivering well-being" (Marmot, 2004: 37).

Health and human rights individually occupy privileged places in the public discourse, political debates, public policy, and the media, and both are at the top of human aspirations. There is hardly a proposed political agenda that does not refer to health in

International Encyclopedia of Public Health, First Edition (2008), vol. 3, pp. 477–486.

its own right, as well as justice, security, housing, education, and employment opportunities—all with relevance to health. These aspirations are often not framed as human rights but the fact that they are contained in human rights treaties and often translated into national constitutions and legislations provides legal support for efforts in these areas.

Incorporating human rights in public health policy therefore responds to the demands of people, policy makers, and political leaders for outcomes that meet public aspirations. It also creates opportunities for helping decipher how all human rights and other determinants of well-being and social progress interact. It allows progress toward these goals to be measured and shapes policy directions and agendas for action.

This article highlights the evolution that has brought human rights and health together in mutually reinforcing ways. It draws from the experience gained in the global response to HIV/AIDS, summarizes key dimensions of public health and of human rights and suggests a manner in which these dimensions intersect that may be used as a framework for health policy analysis, development, and evaluation.

Human Rights as Governmental Obligations

Human rights constitute a set of normative principles and standards which as a philosophical concept can be traced back to antiquity, with mounting interest among intellectuals and political leaders since the seventeenth century (Tomushat, 2003). The atrocities perpetrated during World War II gave rise, in 1948, to the Universal Declaration of Human Rights (United Nations, 1948) and later to a series of treaties and conventions that extended the aspirational nature of the UDHR into instruments that would be binding on states under international human rights law. Among these are the International Covenant on Civil and Political Rights (ICCPR) and the International Covenant on Economic, Social, and Cultural Rights (ICESCR), both of which came into force in 1976.

Human rights are legal claims that persons have on governments simply on the basis of their being human. They are "what governments can do to you, cannot do to you and should do for you" (Gruskin, 2004). Even though people hold their human rights throughout their lives, they are nonetheless often constrained in their ability to fully realize them. Those who are most vulnerable to violations or neglect of their rights are also often those who lack sufficient power to claim the impact of the lack of enjoyment of their rights on their well-being, including their state of personal health. Human rights are intended to be inalienable (individuals cannot lose these rights any more than they can cease being human beings); they are indivisible (individuals cannot be denied a right because it is deemed less important or nonessential); they are interdependent (all human rights are part of a complementary framework, one right impacting on and being impacted by all others) (United Nations, 1993). They bring into focus the relationship between the State—the first-line provider and protector of human rights—and individuals who hold their human rights simply for being human. In this regard, governments have three sets of obligations toward their people (Eide, 1995):

- They have the obligation to respect human rights, which requires governments to refrain from interfering directly or indirectly with the enjoyment of human rights. In practice, no health policy, practice, program, or legal measure should violate human rights. Policies should ensure the provision of health services to all population groups on the basis of equality and freedom from discrimination, paying particular attention to vulnerable and marginalized groups.
- They have the obligation to protect human rights, which requires governments to take measures that prevent non-state actors from interfering with human rights, and to provide legal means of redress that people know about and can access. This relates to such important non-state actors as private health-care providers, pharmaceutical companies, health insurance companies and, more generally, the health-related industry, but also national and multinational enterprises whose actions can impact significantly on lifestyle, labor, and the

environment such as oil and other energy-producing companies, car manufacturers, agriculture, food industry, and labor-intensive garment factories.

- They have the obligation to fulfill human rights, which requires States to adopt appropriate legislative, administrative, budgetary, judicial, promotional, and other measures toward the full realization of human rights, including putting into place appropriate health and health-related policies that ensure human rights promotion and protection. In practice, governments should be supported in their efforts to develop and apply these measures and monitor their impact, with an immediate focus on vulnerable and marginalized groups.

Government responsibility for health exists in several ways. The right to the highest attainable standard of health appears in one form or another in most international and regional human rights documents, and equally importantly, nearly every article of every document can be understood to have clear implications for health.

The Right to Health

The right to the highest attainable standard of health builds on, but is by no means limited to, Article 12 of the ICESCR (**Table 1**). Rights relating to autonomy, information, education, food and nutrition, association, equality, participation, and nondiscrimination are integral and indivisible parts of the achievement of the highest attainable standard of health, just as the enjoyment of the right to health is inseparable from all other rights, whether they are categorized as civil and political, economic, social, or cultural. This recognition is based on empirical observation and on a growing body of evidence that establishes the impact that lack of fulfillment of any and all of these rights has on people's health status: Education, nondiscrimination, food and nutrition epitomizing this relationship (Gruskin and Tarantola, 2001). Conversely, ill-health constrains the fulfillment of all rights as the capacity of individuals to claim and enjoy all their human rights depends on their physical, mental, and social well-being.

TABLE 1 The right to highest attainable standard of health, Article 12 of the International Covenant on Economic, Social and Cultural Rights

1. The States Parties to the present Covenant recognize the right of everyone to the enjoyment of the highest attainable standard of physical and mental health
2. The steps to be taken by the States Parties to the present Covenant to achieve the full realization of this right shall include those necessary for:
   a. The provision for the reduction of the still-birth rate and of infant mortality and for the healthy development of the child
   b. The improvement of all aspects of environmental and industrial hygiene
   c. The prevention, treatment, and control of epidemic, endemic, occupational and other diseases
   d. The creation of conditions which would assure to all medical service and medical attention in the event of sickness

From United Nations (1966a) *Article 2, International Covenant on Economic, Social and Cultural Rights.* United Nations General Assembly Resolution 2200A [XX1], 16/12/1966, entered into force 03/01/1976 in accordance with Art 17. New York: United Nations.

The right to health does not mean the right to be healthy as such, but the obligation on the part of the government to create the conditions necessary for individuals to achieve their optimal health status. In addition to the ICESCR, the right to health is further elaborated in CERD (Convention on the Elimination of all forms of Racial Discrimination, 1965); in CEDAW (Convention on the Elimination of all forms of Discrimination against Women, 1979), and CRC (Convention on the Rights of the Child art 24 1989) and in a range of regional human rights documents.

In May 2000, the United Nations Committee on Economic, Social, and Cultural Rights adopted a General Comment further clarifying the substance of government obligations relating to the right to health (UN Committee on Economic,

Social and Cultural Rights, 2000). In addition to clarifying governmental responsibility for policies, programs and practices impacting the underlying conditions necessary for health, it sets out requirements related to the delivery of health services including their availability, acceptability, accessibility, and quality. It lays out directions for the practical application of Article 12 and proposes a monitoring framework. Reflecting the mounting interest in determining international policy focused on the right to health, the UN Commission on Human Rights appointed in 2002 a Special Rapporteur whose mandate concerns the right of everyone to the enjoyment of the highest attainable standard of physical and mental health. The Special Rapporteur's role is to undertake country visits, transmit communications to states on alleged violations of the right to health, and submit annual reports to the Commission and the UN General Assembly. Accordingly, through publication review and country visits, the Special Rapporteur has explored policies and programs related to such issues as maternal mortality, neglected medicines, and reproductive health as they connect to human rights (Hunt, 2007).

All international human rights treaties and conventions contain provisions relevant to health as defined in the preamble of the Constitution of the World Health Organization (WHO), repeated in many subsequent documents and currently adopted by the 191 WHO Member States: Health is a "state of complete physical, mental, and social well-being, and not merely the absence of disease or infirmity." The Constitution further stipulates that "The enjoyment of the highest attainable standard of health is one of the fundamental rights of every human being without distinction of race, political belief, economic or social condition." The Constitution was adopted by the International Health Conference held in New York from 19 June to 22 July 1946, signed on 22 July 1946 by the representatives of 61 States (World Health Organization, 1946), and entered into force on 7 April 1948. Amendments adopted by the Twenty-sixth, Twenty-ninth, Thirty-ninth and Fifty-first World Health Assemblies (resolutions WHA26.37, WHA29.38, WHA39.6 and WHA51.23) came into force on 3 February 1977, 20 January 1984,

11 July 1994 and 15 September 2005, respectively, and are incorporated in the present text....

HIV and Genesis of the Integration of Human Rights into Health Practice

Cognizant of the need to engage HIV-affected communities in the response to the fast-spreading epidemics in order to achieve their public health goals, human rights were understood as valuable by policy makers not for their moral or legal value but to open access to prevention and care for those who needed these services most, away from fear, discrimination and other forms of human rights violations, and as a way to ensure communities that needed to be reached did not go underground. The deprivation of such entitlements as access to health and social services, employment, or housing imposed on people living with HIV was understood to constrain their capacity to become active subjects rather than the objects of HIV programs, and this was recognized as unsound from a public health perspective.

The evolution of thinking about HIV/AIDS moved from the initial recognition of negative effects of human rights violations among people living with HIV to principles that guided the formulation of a global strategy on HIV/AIDS and, beyond, to the application of these principles to other health issues. In the decade that followed the emergence of AIDS, tremendous efforts were made to induce behavior change through policies that supported intensified, targeted prevention efforts. Everywhere, the initial approaches to HIV had been focused on the reduction of risk of acquiring HIV infection through policies that supported the creation of protective barriers: The use of condoms, early diagnosis and treatment of sexually transmitted infections, and reduction in the number of sexual partners. Some of these efforts were successful on a small scale, in particular where communities were educated and cohesive, as was the case for communities of gay men on the East and West Coasts of the United States, Western Europe, and Australia. Less immediately successful were interventions in communities under immediate social or economic stress and those hampered in their ability to confront HIV/AIDS as a result of strong cultural and other barriers. In sub-Saharan African countries, for example, early interventions related to condoms and other prevention methods, even when supported by national-level policy, were confronted with denial and rejection. Gender-related discrimination was often at the core of resistance to change. Stigma and discrimination directed toward people living with HIV or people whose behaviors were associated with a risk of acquiring and transmitting infection (sex workers, injecting drug users, as well as people defined by their racial or ethnic characteristics) also created obstacles to reaching those who, even perhaps more than others, needed open access to prevention and care. For these reasons, the protection of human rights and combating discrimination became important underlying principles of the first Global Strategy on HIV/AIDS formulated by WHO in 1987 (World Health Organization, 1987).

The risk-reduction strategies of the late 1980s confronted several obstacles in implementation. One was the practical difficulty of scaling up successful approaches to national or international levels. Another was the poor results achieved from applying models proven successful in some settings to different social and cultural environments: Clearly, one size did not fit all. Empirical evidence showed that even as the capacity of individuals to minimize or modulate their risk of exposure to HIV was closely related to specific behaviors or situations, these were in turn influenced by a variety of other factors. In 1992, a risk-vulnerability analysis and reduction model was put forward, positing that in order to successfully impact on risk-taking behaviors, it was necessary to recognize and act on factors that determined the likelihood of individuals engaging in such behaviors (Mann and Tarantola, 1992). A broader perspective suggesting the need for an expanded response to HIV began to emerge, bridging risk, as measured by the occurrence of HIV infection, to risk-taking behaviors, and to their vulnerability determinants. Vulnerability factors could be categorized for simpler analysis as individual (linked to personal history and status, agency, knowledge, or skills); societal (linked to social, economic, and cultural characteristics of the community within which people lived or had lived, including the policy and legal environment); and program-related (dependent on the capacity and approach of programs—health and social in particular) and the extent to which they

responded appropriately to people's needs and expectations and assured their participation (Mann and Tarantola, 1996).

While the linkages between health outcomes and health determinants were already very present in the public health discourse, the mounting HIV epidemic made clear the need for policy to simultaneously address a wide and complex assembly of health outcome and determinants touching many facets of society. Simply listing these determinants born out of the established and empirical evidence was overwhelming. There was a need to categorize these determinants in a logical fashion and in a way that would allow them to be taken up by different sectors engaged in human development. The human rights framework was very well suited to this purpose in that it allowed vulnerability factors to be categorized as civil, political, social, economic, or cultural, and each of these factors, recognized through research or empirical evidence, could be easily linked to one or more specific human rights. This expanded approach helped clarify the related responsibilities of different sectors, thereby expanding the scope of public policy change and possible interventions. Importantly, these interventions could build on commitments already expressed, and obligations subscribed to, by governments under international human rights law. From an initial focus on nondiscrimination toward people known or assumed to live with HIV/AIDS, human rights was now helping guide the analysis of the roots, manifestations, and impacts of the HIV epidemics. Stemming from an instrumental approach rather than moral or legal principles, the response to HIV had exposed the congruence between sound public health policy and the upholding of human rights norms and standards (Mann et al., 1994).

The analytical and action-oriented risk and vulnerability framework that linked HIV to the neglect or violations of human rights and the call for needed structural and societal changes grounded in solid policy were important features of the 1994 Paris Summit Declaration on HIV/AIDS (UNAIDS, 1999) and later served as one of the founding principles of the 1996 UNAIDS global strategy and its subsequent revisions (UNAIDS, 1996). These ideas are also apparent in the Declaration of Commitment which emerged from the 2001 United Nations General Assembly.

International activism and a series of international political conferences that took place in this period facilitated similar changes in the approach taken to a wide range of diseases and health conditions, in particular with respect to reproductive and sexual health issues (Freedman, 1997). The 1994 Cairo International Conference on Population and Development was a watershed in recognizing the responsibility of governments worldwide to translate their international-level commitments into national laws, policies, programs, and practices that promote and do not hinder sexual and reproductive health among their populations. National laws and policies were thus open to scrutiny to determine both the positive and negative influences they could have on sexual and reproductive health programming, information, services, and choices. Human rights concerns, including legal, policy, and practice barriers that impact on the delivery and use of sexual and reproductive health services thereafter became a valid target for international attention.

Human Rights and Health Policy in the New Millennium: Key Concepts

As, from a theoretical perspective, the interaction between health and human rights was drawing increased attention from policy makers in an expanding array of health-related domains, two issues were and continue to be cited as creating obstacles to the translation of theory into practice. The first is that the realization of the right to health cannot be made real in view of the structures, services, and resources it requires. The second, often cited by those concerned with communicable disease control, is that the protection of human rights should not be the prime concern of policy makers when and where such public health threats as emerging epidemics call for the restriction of certain individual rights. As these two obstacles are often used and misused to question the validity of the health and human rights framework, they are discussed briefly below.

Progressive Realization of Health-Related Human Rights

In all countries, resource and other constraints can make it impossible for a government to fulfill all rights immediately and completely. The principle of progressive realization is fundamental to the achievement of human rights as they apply to health (United Nations, 1966a), and applies equally to resource-poor countries as to wealthier countries whose responsibilities extend not only to what they do within their own borders, but also their engagement in international assistance and cooperation (United Nations, 1966b).

Given that progress in health necessitates infrastructure and human and financial resources that may not match existing or future needs in any country, the principle of progressive realization takes into account the inability of governments to meet their obligations overnight. Yet, it creates an obligation on governments to set their own benchmarks, within the maximum of the resources available to them, and to show how and to what extent, through their policies and practices, they are achieving progress toward the health goals they have agreed to in international forums such as the World Health Assembly, as well as those they have set for themselves. In theory, States account for progress in health (or lack thereof) through a variety of mechanisms that include global monitoring mechanisms, as well as national State of the Health of the Nation reports or similar forms of domestic public reporting.

Human Rights Limitations in the Interest of Public Health

There remains a deeply rooted concern of many in the health community that application of a health and human rights approach to health policy will deprive the State from applying such measures as isolation or quarantine or travel restrictions when public health is at stake. Public health and care practitioners alike, acting on behalf of the State, are used to applying restrictions to individual freedom in cases where the enjoyment of these rights creates a real or perceived threat to the population at large. Recently, the SARS and Avian flu epidemics have demonstrated that such restrictions can also be applied globally under the revised International Health Regulations (IHR), the only binding agreement thus far under the auspices of WHO (World Health Organization, 2005). They stipulate that WHO can make recommendations on an *ad hoc,* time-limited, risk-specific basis, as a result of a public health emergency of international concern, and that implementation of these Regulations "shall be with full respect for the dignity, human rights and fundamental freedoms of persons." The human rights framework recognizes that these are situations where there can be legitimate and valid restriction of rights, and this under several circumstances relevant to the creation of health policies: Public emergencies and public health imperatives. Public emergencies stipulate that in time of a public emergency that threatens the life of the nation and the existence of which is officially proclaimed, the States Parties to the present Covenant may take measures derogating from their obligations under the present Covenant to the extent strictly required by the exigencies of the situation, provided that such measures are not inconsistent with their other obligations under international law and do not involve discrimination solely on the ground of race, color, sex, language, religion, or social origin (Art 49, ICCPR). Public health imperatives give governments the right to take the steps they deem necessary for the prevention, treatment, and control of epidemic, endemic, occupational, and other diseases (Art 16, ICCPR).

Public health may therefore justify the limitation of certain rights under certain circumstances. Policies that interfere with freedom of movement when instituting quarantine or isolation for a serious communicable disease—for example, Ebola fever, syphilis, typhoid, or untreated tuberculosis, more recently SARS and pandemic influenza—are examples of limitation of rights that may be necessary for the public good and therefore may be considered legitimate under international human rights law. Yet arbitrary restrictive measures taken or planned by public health authorities that fail to consider other valid alternatives may be found to be both abusive of human rights principles and in contradiction with public health best practice. The limitation of most rights in the interest of public health remains an option under both international human rights law and public health laws, but the decision to impose such limitations must be achieved through a structured and accountable process. Increasingly, such consultative processes are put in place by national authorities to debate over the approach taken to public health issues as they arise, such as in the case of immunization, disability, mental health, HIV, smoking, and more recently pandemic influenza preparedness.

Limitations on rights are considered a serious issue under international human rights law—as noted in specific provisions within international human treaties—regardless of the apparent importance of the public good involved. When a government limits the exercise or enjoyment of a right, this action must be taken only as a last resort and will only be considered legitimate if the following criteria are met:

1. The restriction is provided for and carried out in accordance with the law.
2. The restriction is in the interest of a legitimate objective of general interest.
3. The restriction is strictly necessary in a democratic society to achieve the objective.
4. There are no less intrusive and restrictive means available to reach the same goal.
5. The restriction is not imposed arbitrarily, i.e., in an unreasonable or otherwise discriminatory manner (United Nations, 1984).

The restriction of rights, if legitimate, is therefore consistent with human rights principles. Both principles of progressive realization and legitimate limitations of rights are directly relevant to public health policy as they can inform decisions on how to achieve the optimal balance between protecting the rights of the individual and the best interest of the community. Examples of the impact of human rights violations and protection on public health are set out below. Discrimination—a frequent, severe, and persistent issue confronted both in society and in the health-care setting—has been chosen to illustrate how public health can be hampered by the neglect of human rights and enhanced by their incorporation in public health policy.

Public Health Policy and Nondiscrimination

Discrimination can impact directly on the ways that morbidity, mortality, and disability—the burden of disease—are both measured and acted upon. In fact, the burden of disease itself discriminates: Disease, disability, and death are not distributed randomly or equally within populations, nor are their devastating effects within communities. Tuberculosis, for example, is exploding in disenfranchised communities, in particular among prison inmates and people already affected by HIV and subjected to dual discrimination both in their communities and in the health-care setting.

Far from uncommon, discrimination in health systems, including health centers, hospitals, or mental institutions, may further contribute to exacerbating disparities in health. A few examples of myriads that could be cited are named here. Undocumented migrant workers receive poor or no treatment for fear of having to justify their civil status. Documented migrant workers, refugees, and asylum seekers and their families may not avail themselves of services that have not been designed to suit their culture and respond to their specific needs. People with hemophilia have been given unsafe blood products on the premise that this adds only a marginal risk to their lives. People with physical or mental disabilities receive substandard care; they are unable to complain or if they do, they fare poorly in legal action (Moss et al., 2007). Discrimination in health systems concerns not only diseases that are already stigmatized, such as AIDS, hepatitis B and C, tuberculosis, and cancer, but also others, such as diabetes and cardiovascular diseases, which could be alleviated if equal treatment within societies and within health-care settings became the norm. A health and human rights approach to policy development concerning health systems requires that state authorities refrain from enacting discriminatory policies and provide information, education, training, and support to their staff toward eliminating discrimination in public health practice and within the workforce.

Discrimination can also be at the root of unsound human development policies and programs that may impact directly or indirectly on health. For example, an infrastructure development project may require the displacement of entire populations and fail to pay sufficient attention to the new environment to which these populations will have to adjust. In the developing world, when the health impact of large-scale development programs at the local level is considered, it is often from the perspective of the possible further spread of such infectious diseases as malaria and other waterborne diseases. The psychological capacity of displaced communities to relocate and rebuild new lives or the long-term physical and social consequences of such displacement are seldom factored into the equation.

The ongoing international movement toward poverty alleviation has emphasized the critical importance of health in the fight against poverty. The eight Millennium Development Goals (MDGs)—which set targets for 2015 to halve extreme poverty, halt the spread of HIV/AIDS, and improve health and education—have been agreed to by all the world's countries and all the world's leading development institutions (United Nations, 2005). Arguably, all MDGs have a linkage to health either by their direct bearing on health outcomes and the needed services (e.g., through efforts to reduce child and maternal mortality, HIV, malaria, and other diseases) or by underscoring principles central to public health policy (e.g., gender equality) or else by calling for the creation of policies addressing the underlying conditions for progress in health (e.g., education, environmental sustainability, and global partnerships).

Public Health Policy and the Value of Health and Human Rights

Human rights and public health policy intersect in a number of ways, which, for practical purposes, can be regrouped into three broad categories: The national and international context within which policy is developed; the outcome of public policy; and the process through which it is developed, applied, and monitored.

Context

A distinction exists between public policy affecting health (most of them do) and public health policy (often emerging from public health governmental authorities or on their initiative). Policies affecting health—for example, those related to gender, trade, intellectual property, the environment, migration, education, housing, or labor—are contingent upon national laws and international treaties or agreements which often overlook—by omission or commission—their potential health consequences. As the Health Impact Assessment of development and social policies gained credence in the 1990s, the development of a human rights assessment for the formulation and evaluation of public health policies emerged (Gostin and Mann, 1999). Health Impact Assessment (HIA), applying different methods, has become more frequently practiced to guide policy options both nationally and internationally. While the aim of such exercises is to forecast the health impact of a single or alternative policies or programs (including those related to infrastructure, financing, service delivery, transportation, or production and many others), the impact of such policies and programs on both health and human rights remains to be adequately tested. Much work is currently ongoing toward the development of a Health and Human Rights Impact Assessment for which assessment methods and health and human rights indicators are required.

An example where such an impact assessment might have been useful was when a number of countries—industrialized and developing alike—applied for membership of the World Trade Organization when such a membership implied for the signatory country to become party to the Agreement on Trade Related Aspects of Intellectual Property Rights (TRIPS). The constraints imposed by TRIPS on developing countries with regards to intellectual protection of pharmaceuticals in particular only became evident in the late 1990s as new, proven therapies for HIV-AIDS were reaching the international market. Civil society movements and some international organizations embarked on an active campaign to overcome the constraints set by TRIPS to the production or importation of generic medicines by developing countries needing them most. It was not until 2002, however, that WHO and WTO jointly produced a document on WTO agreements and public health (World Health Organization and World Trade Organization, 2002). In most developing countries, Ministries of Health had not been consulted, been equipped to assess, or had underestimated, the possible health impacts of the new trade and intellectual property agreement they were signing on to as new members of the WTO. This was and continues to be a painful reminder of the oversight

or deliberate neglect of the possible health consequences of public policy guided by other agendas, international trade in this case.

Public health policy should seek the optimal synergy between health and human rights, building on the premise that the optimal quality of a public health policy is attained when the highest possible health outcome and the fullest realization of human rights are both attained. This requires a close interaction between public health professionals, human rights practitioners and representatives of affected communities. The response to HIV has been shaped by such an interaction with significant positive impact—at least in the short term—in such countries as Australia, Sweden, Thailand, Brazil, or Uganda. Where misconceptions about either sound public health or human rights have distorted HIV policies and programs, the epidemic has continued to strive, as illustrated by the situation in South Africa or China.

As it is generally formulated and monitored by the State, public health policy should operate in the context of the obligations the State has subscribed to under international human rights treaties and national law. Central to these obligations are those to respect, protect, and fulfill all human rights, including the rights to participate in public affairs and policy making, equality, nondiscrimination, and dignity.

Outcome and Impact

Both public health policy and human rights emphasize the importance of outcome and impact, crudely measured in public health terms by the reduction of mortality, morbidity and disability, and the improvement of quality of life, along with economic measurement enabling an assessment of the value for money of particular policies or programs that can guide priority setting. The extent to which outcome includes the fulfillment of human rights is seldom factored in. For example, one would like to see the value of policies that promote sex education in school measured not only in terms of reduction of teenage pregnancy or the incidence of sexually transmitted diseases, but how the right of the child to information is fulfilled in this way and how it impacts on further demands for other health-related, life-saving information. Likewise, when assessing the outcome and impact of policies that prioritize childhood immunization programs, one would want to know not only how immunization makes people healthier, both early and later in their childhood, but also how such public health policies will advance the right of the child to growth and development and her right to education by improving her attendance to and performance at school.

Measuring the outcome and impact of health and health-related policies from a combined health and human rights perspective implies measurement indicators that are neither fully developed nor tested. One of the constraints is that measuring health and human rights on the national, aggregate level is not sensitive to disparities that may exist within the nation, for example, as a result of discrimination.

Process

The human rights to information, assembly, and participation in public affairs—including policy making—imply, among other practical steps, the engagement of communities in decisions affecting their health. As highlighted earlier, the history of health and human rights has amply established that community representation in decision-making bodies increases the quality and impact of public health measures. An important issue is to determine who can legitimately speak on behalf of concerned communities. In the last two decades, stimulated by the response to HIV in particular, nongovernmental organizations, and more broadly civil society, have played key roles in drawing attention to policies that were or could be detrimental to health (e.g., restrictions in access to medicines, denial of sex education of young people, access to harm reduction methods among substance users, promotion of tobacco products in young people, marginalized communities and low-income countries, environmental degradation, marketing of unhealthy foods). While state machineries are increasingly cognizant of the growing need for transparency in policy development, civil society is likely to sustain its contribution to such a process, and this through active monitoring by national-level NGOs and such international groups as Amnesty International, Human Rights Watch, or Physicians for Social Responsibility.

In Conclusion

This article has attempted to lay out the principles underlying the application of health and human rights principles to public health policy, and it has done so by recalling the historical emergence of these concepts and the opportunities they provide for new approaches to policy development.

Health and human rights, together and independently from each other, have achieved today a degree of prominence in the political and public discourse never witnessed before. The fields of health and rights are illuminated today by their commonalties, no longer by their differences. Both are obligations of governments toward their people; and each supports and requires the fulfillment of the other.

Overall, health and human rights provide a framework for all aspects of policy and program development. In practice, human rights considerations are often built into public health policy through the application of what are today called rights-based approaches. The practical application of these principles is a subject of active and rich debates. Rights-based approaches to health are but some of the attempts currently being made to offer practical guidance to health policy makers and other stakeholders in health and human rights toward translating these principles into health policies, programs, and interventions. Through further reflection, practice and research, public health and human rights practitioners can further establish how and to what extent the promotion and protection of health and human rights interact. In the search for a world where the attainment of the highest standard of physical, mental, and social well-being necessitates, and reinforces, the dignity, autonomy, and progress of every human being, the broad goals of health and human rights are universal and eternal. They give us direction for our understanding of humanity and practical tools for use in our daily work.

REFERENCES

Anand S (2004) The concerns for equity in health. In: Anand S, Peter F, and Sen A (eds.) *Public Health and Ethics*, pp. 17–18. Oxford, UK: Oxford University Press.

Freedman L (1997) Human rights and the politics of risk and blame: Lessons from the international reproductive health movement. *Journal of the American Medical Women's Association* 52(4): 165–168.

Gostin L and Mann J (1999) Toward the development of a human rights impact assessment for the formulation and evaluation of public health policies. In: Mann J, Gruskin S, Grodin M, and Annas G (eds.) *Health and Human Rights: A Reader*, pp. 54–71. New York: Routledge.

Hunt P (2007) *Report of the Special Rapporteur on the Right of Everyone to the Enjoyment of the Highest Attainable Standard of Physical and Mental Health*. Human Rights Council 4th session, A/HRC/28, 17 January 2007. pp. 15–21.

Mann J and Tarantola D (1992) Assessing the Vulnerability to HIV infection and AIDS. In: Mann J, Tarantola D, and Netter T (eds.) *AIDS in the World*, pp. 557–602. Cambridge, MA: Harvard University Press.

Mann J and Tarantola D (1996) Societal vulnerability: Contextual analysis. In: Mann J and Tarantola D (eds.) *AIDS in the World II*, pp. 444–462. London: Oxford University Press.

Mann JM, Gostin L, Gruskin S. Brennan T, Lazzarini Z, and Fineberg H (1994) Health and human rights. *Health and Human Rights* 1(1): 58–80.

Marmot M (2004) Social causes of inequity in health. In: Anand S, Peter F, and Sen A (eds.) *Public Health and Ethics*, p. 37. Oxford, UK: Oxford University Press.

Tomuschat C (2003) *Human Rights, Between Idealism and Realism*. New York: Oxford University Press.

UNAIDS (1996) *Global Strategy, 1996/2001*. Geneva, Switzerland: United Nations Joint Programme on HIV AIDS.

UNAIDS (1999) *From Principle to Practice: Greater Involvement of People Living with or Affected by HIV/AIDS (GIPA) UNAIDS/99.43E*. http://data.unaids.org/Publications/IRC-pub01/JC252-GIPA-i_en.pdf (accessed December 2007).

United Nations (1948) *Universal Declaration of Human Rights. G.A. Res. 217A (III) UN GAOP, Res 71, UN Doc.A/810*. New York: United Nations.

United Nations (1966a) *Article 2, International Covenant on Economic, Social and Cultural Rights. United Nations General Assembly Resolution 2200A [XX1], 16/12/1966*, entered into force 03/01/1976 in accordance with Art 17. New York: United Nations.

United Nations (1966b) *Article 2, International Covenant on Civil and Political Rights. United Nations General Assembly Resolution 2200A [XX1], 16/12/1966*, entered into force 23/03/1976 in accordance with Article 49. New York: United Nations.

United Nations (1984) The Siracusa principles on the limitation and derogation provisions. In: *The International Covenant on Civil and Political Rights*. Annex to UN Document E/CN.4/1985/4 of 28/09/1984. New York: United Nations.

United Nations (1993) *Vienna Declaration and Programme of Action (A/CONF. 157/23)*. http://www.unhchr.ch/huridocda/huridoca.nsf/(Symbol)/A.CONF.157.23.En (accessed December 2007).

United Nations Committee on Economic, Social and Cultural Rights (2000) *General Comment 14 on the Right to the Highest Attainable Standard of Health*. New York: United Nations.

World Health Organization (1946) *Constitution of the World Health Organization*. Off. Rec. Wld Hlth Org., 2, 100. Geneva, Switzerland: World Health Organization. http://www.who.int/governance/eb/who_constitution_en.pdf (accessed December 2007).

World Health Organization (1987) *The Global Strategy for AIDS Prevention and Control*. Geneva, Switzerland: World Health Organization; unpublished document SPA/INF/87.1.

World Health Organization (2005) *Revisions of the International Health Regulations, endorsed by the Fifty-eighth World Health Assembly in Resolution 58.3*. Geneva, Switzerland: World Health Assembly 23/05/2005.

World Health Organization and World Trade Organization (2002) *WTO Agreements and Public Health, a joint study by the WHO and the WTO Secretariat, World Health Organization and World Trade Organization*. Geneva, Switzerland: World Health Organization. http://www.wto.org/english/news_e/pres02_e/pr310_e.htm (accessed December 2007).

Answers to Chapter 1 Exercises

EXERCISE 1.1

1. People should keep their promises. Noah promised to drive Thelma to Los Angeles, so he should stop bellyaching and do it.

2. The authorities have a moral obligation to intervene when refugees are being shot at and lied to. The refugees were shot at and lied to, and the authorities did nothing to stop any of this. The authorities should have intervened.

3. The United States is justified in invading another country only when that country poses an imminent threat. There was never any imminent threat from the Iraqi government, so the United States should not have invaded Iraq.

4. The Indian government posed an imminent threat to Pakistan and the world. When a foreign government poses an imminent threat to Pakistan and the world, Pakistanis are justified in attacking that government. So the Pakistanis were justified in attacking Indian troops.

5. Anyone who uses a gun in the commission of a crime deserves to receive a long prison sentence. Burton used a gun in the commission of a crime; therefore he should get a long prison term.

6. Anyone who knows that murder is going to take place has a moral obligation to try to stop it. Ellen knew that a murder was going to take place. It was her duty to try to stop it. (Often people who put forth an argument like this also assume that a person is obligated to intervene only if it's physically *possible* for him or her to intervene.)

7. Any procedure that is unnatural should not be permitted for use on people. In vitro fertilization is unnatural. Ahmed should never have allowed his daughter to receive in vitro fertilization.

8. Doctors should never experiment on people without their consent. The doctors performed the experiment on twenty patients without their consent. Obviously, that was wrong.

9. Hacking into a database containing personal information on thousands of people and invading their privacy is immoral. You hacked into a database containing personal information on thousands of people and invaded their privacy. Therefore, what you did was immoral.

10. If someone does another person a favor (performs a service for no pay), that other person is obligated to return the favor by doing a minimum service ("the least you can do"). Ling spent all day weeding Mrs. Black's garden for no pay. The least Mrs. Black should do is let Ling borrow some gardening tools.

EXERCISE 1.2

1. *Conclusion*: Janet should be arrested. *Premises*: (1) Anyone who runs away from an automobile accident should be arrested. (2) Janet ran away from an automobile accident. [If premise 1 is true (and we assume that premise 2 is a reliable report of Janet's behavior), the argument is *sound*.]

2. *Conclusion*: Fears [about a group home] are very much unfounded. *Premises*: (1) The [group] home in which my sister resides is large, lovely, brand new, well staffed, and well maintained. (2) It does nothing but enhance the community, bring neighbors together, and create a wonderfully diverse neighborhood.

[Since it can be difficult to generalize from one particular group home to all group homes, we are not justified in regarding this inductive argument as *cogent*.]

3. *Conclusion*: Ms. Leet's characterization of offensive graffiti as protected by the First Amendment and "not a hate crime" is outrageous. *Premises*: (1) Such graffiti can cause tremendous hurt and damage, especially when a professor defends it. (2) Words can be just as destructive as physical violence.

4. *Conclusion*: Yolanda shouldn't have taken that money. *Premises*: (1) People shouldn't steal unless they are destitute. (2) Yolanda took the money from petty cash even though she had plenty of money in her pocket.

5. *Conclusion*: Stem cell research is immoral. *Premises*: (1) We should never do anything to disrespect human life. (2) The artificial use of human cells—as scientists are now doing in stem cell research—shows a complete disregard for human life.

EXERCISE 1.3

1. Any form of expression or speech that offends people of faith should not be tolerated. *Penthouse* magazine definitely offends people of faith. Ban it! *Evaluation: The first premise is dubious, for it would have us violate the autonomy of persons—by, for example, dramatically curtailing freedom of speech.*

2. Anyone who disagrees with the basic moral dictums of the prevailing culture should be censured. Dr. Tilden's graduation speech clearly was inconsistent with the prevailing moral opinions on campus. She should be reprimanded. *Evaluation: The first premise runs counter to several plausible moral principles, including respect for autonomy, freedom of speech and conscience, and tolerance.*

EXERCISE 1.4

1. It is immoral to do harm to others. The movie *Lorenzo's Oil* does harm to others by giving people false hope about a deadly disease and by misleading people about the medical facts. The movie is therefore immoral (or, those who produced and promoted the movie have acted immorally).

2. Regardless of whether the victims are Muslim or not, the vicious murder of innocent human beings is reprehensible and repugnant, an affront to everything Islam stands for. Al Qaeda has viciously murdered innocent human beings—both Muslim and non-Muslim. Therefore, these acts committed by Al Qaeda are reprehensible and repugnant. No one should have any sympathy for an organization that murders innocent human beings. Therefore, the Saudis should have had no sympathy for Al Qaeda after the May bombings.

GLOSSARY

abortion The ending of a pregnancy.

act-utilitarianism The view that the rightness of actions depends solely on the relative good produced by individual actions.

active euthanasia Performing an action that directly causes someone to die; "mercy killing."

applied ethics The use of moral norms and concepts to resolve practical moral issues.

autonomy A person's rational capacity for self-governance or self-determination.

bioethics Applied ethics focused on health care, medical science, and medical technology.

blinding A procedure for ensuring that subjects and researchers do not know which interventions the subjects receive (standard treatment, new treatment, or placebo).

chromosome A stringlike, gene-containing molecule in the nucleus of a cell.

clinical trial A scientific study designed to test systematically a medical intervention in humans.

cloning The asexual production of a genetically identical entity from an existing one.

cloning, reproductive Cloning aimed at the live birth of an individual.

cloning, therapeutic or research Cloning done for purposes other than producing a live individual.

competence The ability to render decisions about medical interventions.

confidentiality An obligation or pledge of physicians, nurses, and others to keep secret the personal health information of patients unless they consent to disclosure.

consequentialist theory A moral theory asserting that the rightness of actions depends solely on their consequences or results.

contractarianism Moral or political theories based on the idea of a social contract or agreement among individuals for mutual advantage.

cultural relativism The view that right actions are those sanctioned by one's culture.

cycle (in assisted reproductive technology) A sequence of steps involved in trying to achieve pregnancy through ART (assisted reproductive technology), typically extending from egg retrieval to embryo transfer.

deductive argument An argument intended to give logically conclusive support to its conclusion.

deontological (or nonconsequentialist) theory A moral theory asserting that the rightness of actions is determined partly or entirely by their intrinsic nature.

descriptive ethics The study of morality using the methodology of science.

distributive justice Justice regarding the fair distribution of society's advantages and disadvantages.

divine command theory The view that right actions are those commanded by God and wrong actions are those forbidden by God.

doctrine of double effect The principle that performing a bad action to bring about a good effect is never morally acceptable, but performing a good action may sometimes be acceptable even if it produces a bad effect.

egalitarian theories of justice Doctrines affirming that important benefits and burdens of society should be distributed equally.

ethical relativism The view that moral standards are not objective but are relative to what individuals or cultures believe.

ethics The study of morality using the tools and methods of philosophy.

eugenics The deliberate attempt to improve the genetic makeup of humans by manipulating reproduction.

euthanasia Directly or indirectly bringing about the death of another person for that person's sake.

gene The fundamental unit of biological inheritance.

gene therapy The manipulation of someone's genetic material to prevent or treat disease.

genetic discrimination The use of genetic information by employers, insurance companies, and others to discriminate against or stigmatize people.

genetic testing Procedures used to check for genetic disorders by looking for changes in a person's DNA.

genome An organism's entire complement of DNA.

in vitro fertilization The uniting of sperm and egg in a laboratory dish.

induced abortion The intentional termination of a pregnancy through drugs or surgery.

inductive argument An argument intended to give probable support to its conclusion.

infertility The inability to get pregnant after one year of unprotected sex.

informed consent The action of an autonomous, informed person agreeing to submit to medical treatment or experimentation.

in vitro fertilization The uniting of sperm and egg in a laboratory dish.

involuntary euthanasia Bringing about someone's death against her will or without asking for her consent while she is competent to decide.

libertarian theories of justice Doctrines holding that the benefits and burdens of society should be distributed through the fair workings of a free market and the exercise of liberty rights of noninterference.

managed care A system for providing health care to a particular group of patients (members of the system) using restraints to control costs and increase efficiency.

medical futility The alleged pointlessness or ineffectiveness of administering particular treatments.

metaethics The study of the meaning and justification of basic moral beliefs.

moral absolutism The belief that objective moral principles allow no exceptions or must be applied the same way in all cases and cultures.

moral argument An argument whose conclusion is a moral statement.

moral objectivism The view that there are moral norms or principles that are valid or true for everyone.

moral theory An explanation of why an action is right or wrong or why a person or a person's character is good or bad.

morality Beliefs regarding morally right and wrong actions and morally good and bad persons or character.

natural law theory The view that right actions are those that conform to moral standards discerned in nature through human reason.

nonmaleficence The moral principle that says we should not cause unnecessary injury or harm to others.

nonvoluntary euthanasia Euthanasia performed when patients are not competent to choose it for themselves and have not previously disclosed their preferences.

normative ethics The search for, and justification of, moral standards, or norms.

passive euthanasia Allowing someone to die by not doing something that would prolong life.

paternalism The overriding of a person's actions or decision-making for his own good.

physician-assisted suicide A patient's taking her own life with the aid of a physician.

placebo An inactive or sham treatment.

quickening At about 16 to 20 weeks of pregnancy, a pregnant woman's experience of fetal movement inside her.

randomization The assigning of subjects randomly to both experimental and control groups.

right to privacy The authority of persons to control who may possess and use information about themselves.

rule-utilitarianism The view that a right action is one that conforms to a rule that, if followed consistently, would create for everyone involved the most beneficial balance of good over bad.

spontaneous abortion (miscarriage) An abortion due to natural causes such as a birth defect or maternal injury.

strong paternalism The overriding of a person's actions or choices even though he is substantially autonomous.

subjective relativism The view that right actions are those sanctioned by a person.

surrogate A woman who gestates a fetus for others, usually for a couple or another woman.

therapeutic abortion Abortion performed to preserve the life or health of the mother.

therapeutic privilege The withholding of relevant information from a patient when the physician believes disclosure would likely do harm.

utilitarian theories of justice Doctrines asserting that a just distribution of benefits and burdens is one that maximizes the net good (utility) for society.

utilitarianism The view that right actions are those that result in the most beneficial balance of good over bad consequences for everyone involved.

viability The development stage when the fetus can survive outside the uterus.

virtue ethics A moral theory that focuses on the development of virtuous character.

waiver The patient's voluntary and deliberate giving up of the right to informed consent.

weak paternalism Paternalism directed at persons who cannot act autonomously or whose autonomy is greatly diminished.

voluntary euthanasia Euthanasia performed when competent patients voluntarily request or agree to it.